The Concise Mrs Beeton's
Book of Cookery

D1382038

The Concise Mrs Beeton's Book of Cookery

Consultant Editor
Bridget Jones

CASSELL&CO

L121,994/640

First published in 1861 by S. O. Beeton
This revised edition published in the UK 1996
Cassell
Wellington House
125 Strand
London WC2R 0BB

First paperback edition 1998
Reprinted 2002

Copyright © Ward Lock 1996
All rights reserved. No part of this book
may be reproduced or transmitted in any form
or by any means, electronic or mechanical,
including photocopying, recording or any
information storage and retrieval system,
without prior permission in writing
from the copyright holder and Publisher.

**Mrs Beeton's is a registered trademark of
Ward Lock Ltd**

ISBN 0-304-36475-4

Typeset by MS Filmsetting Limited
Frome, Somerset
Printed and bound in Finland
WS Bookwell Ltd

Contents

Acknowledgements

Edited by Jenni Fleetwood

Compiled and Revised by Bridget Jones

Wine Consultant Steven Spurrier

Editorial
Alison Leach ·Barbara Croxford · Dulcie Andrews (Household Management)

Index
Hilary Bird

Designers
Ronald Clark · Peter Holroyd · Chris Warner

Photographers
Sue Atkinson · John Kevern · Clive Streeter

Food Prepared for Photographs by
Jacqui Hine · Stella Joyce · Sarah Maxwell · Lynn Rutherford

Cake Decorating Information by
Jacqui Hine

Stylists
Marie Kelly · Valerie Kevern · Alison Meldrum

Illustrations
Tony Randell · John Woodcock (game chapter)

The publishers would like to thank the following for their assistance
in the preparation of this book:
British Bankers' Association · British Sugar plc
Butter Information Council · Council of Mortgage Lenders
Eye Care Information Bureau · Law Centres Federation · Milk Marketing Board
Sea Fish Industry Authority · The British Egg Information Service
The Building Societies Association · The Law Society · The Prestige Group plc

Foreword

When *Beeton's Book of Household Management* was first published in 1861, it paved the way for generations of future cookery books. Isabella Beeton had taken four long years to research and write her book, and she said of her labours, 'I must frankly own, that had I known, beforehand, that this book would have cost me the labour which it has, I should never have been courageous enough to commence it'.

As the wife of a young publisher, Isabella Beeton was aware of the difficulties which faced many women who were confronted with the task of running their own homes for the first time, and as a woman working in publishing she recognised that there was a frustrating lack of practical advice for those who were less experienced with family life than herself. She set out to write a book which would, in one volume, pass on the knowledge of previous generations: this book would offer a source of recipes for dishes to suit every occasion; it would also provide thoroughly practical advice on all aspects of running a home, from dealing with tradesmen and organising staff to consulting a doctor, understanding legal matters and coping with emergencies. However, it was not merely the content that concerned Isabella Beeton, it was also the arrangement of the information – she wanted to ensure that the facts were accurate and easy to follow and that the text was interesting and a pleasure to read.

Mrs Beeton's work was the first cookery book to provide 'an intelligible arrangement to every recipe, a list of the *ingredients*, a plain statement of the *mode* of preparing each dish, a careful estimate of its *cost*, the *number of people* for whom it is *sufficient*, and the time when it is *seasonable*'. Her approach was unmatched and her work was soon recognised for all the qualities she had hoped to achieve: it was an outstanding success which was not short-lived.

It was Mrs Beeton's intention that her work should remain up-to-date. Her husband undertook to complete the first revision of the book, and he also went on to publish short editions and extracts on specific food topics according to the requirements of the day. In keeping with the original intention of making the work invaluable and practical for everyday use, this concise version concentrates on food, providing recipes and information on basic cooking. Extracts on nutrition, first aid and health are included along with advice on social customs.

Through its many editions, *Mrs Beeton's Book of Cookery and Household Management* has established an unrivalled reputation as an indispensable source of home reference, and this, *The Concise Mrs Beeton's Book of Cookery*, presented in an easy-to-use format, is the reliable and practical kitchen bible for today's cook.

Useful Weights and Measures

USING METRIC OR IMPERIAL MEASURES

Throughout the book, all weights and measures are given first in metric, then in Imperial. For example 100 g/4 oz, 150 ml/¼ pint or 15 ml/1 tbsp.

When following any of the recipes use either metric or Imperial – do not combine the two sets of measures as they are not interchangeable.

EQUIVALENT METRIC/IMPERIAL MEASURES

Weights The following chart lists some of the metric/Imperial weights that are used in the recipes.

METRIC	IMPERIAL	METRIC	IMPERIAL
15 g	½ oz	375 g	13 oz
25 g	1 oz	400 g	14 oz
50 g	2 oz	425 g	15 oz
75 g	3 oz	450 g	1 lb
100 g	4 oz	575 g	1¼ lb
150 g	5 oz	675 g	1½ lb
175 g	6 oz	800 g	1¾ lb
200 g	7 oz	900 g	2 lb
225 g	8 oz	1 kg	2¼ lb
250 g	9 oz	1.4 kg	3 lb
275 g	10 oz	1.6 kg	3½ lb
300 g	11 oz	1.8 kg	4 lb
350 g	12 oz	2.25 kg	5 lb

Liquid Measures The following chart lists some metric/Imperial equivalents for liquids. Millilitres (ml), litres and fluid ounces (fl oz) or pints are used throughout.

METRIC	IMPERIAL
50 ml	2 fl oz
125 ml	4 fl oz
150 ml	¼ pint
300 ml	½ pint
450 ml	¾ pint
600 ml	1 pint

Spoon Measures Both metric and Imperial equivalents are given for all spoon measures, expressed as millilitres and teaspoons (tsp) or tablespoons (tbsp).

All spoon measures refer to British standard measuring spoons and the quantities given are always for level spoons.

Do not use ordinary kitchen cutlery instead of proper measuring spoons as they will hold quite different quantities.

METRIC	IMPERIAL
1.25 ml	¼ tsp
2.5 ml	½ tsp
5 ml	1 tsp
15 ml	1 tbsp

Length All linear measures are expressed in millimetres (mm), centimetres (cm) or metres (m) and inches or feet. The following list gives examples of typical conversions.

METRIC	IMPERIAL
5 mm	¼ inch
1 cm	½ inch
2.5 cm	1 inch
5 cm	2 inches
15 cm	6 inches
30 cm	12 inches (1 foot)

MICROWAVE INFORMATION

Occasional microwave hints and instructions are included for certain recipes, as appropriate. The information given is for microwave ovens rated at 650–700 watts.

The following terms have been used for the microwave settings: High, Medium, Defrost and Low. For each setting, the power input is as follows: High = 100% power, Medium = 50% power, Defrost = 30% power and Low = 20% power.

All microwave notes and timings are for guidance only: always read and follow the manufacturer's instructions for your particular appliance. Remember to avoid putting any metal in the microwave and never operate the microwave empty.

OVEN TEMPERATURES

Whenever the oven is used, the required setting is given as three alternatives: degrees Celsius (°C), degrees Fahrenheit (°F) and gas.

The temperature settings given are for conventional ovens. If you have a fan oven, adjust the temperature according to the manufacturer's instructions.

°C	°F	GAS
110	225	¼
120	250	½
140	275	1
150	300	2
160	325	3
180	350	4
190	375	5
200	400	6
220	425	7
230	450	8
240	475	9

Flavourings, Herbs and Spices

Used with skill and care, these ingredients bring cooking to life, adding zest and colour to bland foods and complementing stronger flavours.

Seasonings are usually added to food at the start of cooking, and are adjusted afterwards. A seasoning should not give its own flavour to the food, but merely heighten or temper the flavour of the food to which it is added.

Flavourings are generally added during or after cooking. A flavouring agent is used in food to give it added or improved flavour.

The general title 'flavourings' includes herbs, spices, purées, natural and synthetic essences, meat and yeast extracts, wines and spirits. Any of these can be mixed with other ingredients in making a dish, added to them temporarily, as in the case of a bay leaf infused in milk, or added to a marinade in which the food is soaked before cooking. Some can be rubbed on the surface of the food before cooking, or used to baste it while it is cooking, eg garlic can be rubbed over meat and poultry before grilling or frying, and a barbecue sauce containing different flavourings can be used to baste the meat while cooking.

Herbs can be used fresh or dried; generally, fresh herbs give a better, cleaner flavour. Dried herbs tend to be more aromatic, so must be used more sparingly; as a general rule, half to two-thirds of the quantity given for fresh herbs is sufficient. If dried herbs are left unused for any length of time they become flavourless or musty. Once opened, store in a dry jar for up to six months, and replace them when they are past their best. Most fresh herbs can be frozen,

and if well sealed in airtight containers, or chopped and frozen in cubes of ice, will keep their aroma for up to six months.

Many spices are derived from herbs and other plants. They are used in various forms: whole leaves (eg bay leaves), husks or seeds (eg blades of mace, whole peppercorns), stems, flowers or leaves. Some are available both whole and ground in powder form: ginger, nutmeg, and cloves are common examples. Whole spices are generally infused in one of the ingredients for a dish, or are cooked with the dish and removed before serving. Powdered spices are mixed in direct, or sprinkled over the finished dish. Most spices are strongly flavoured, and should therefore be used sparingly; it is best to add them to a dish gradually, tasting between each addition. Curry powder, being a mixture of spices, must be cooked long and slowly to let the flavours develop and blend. Highly spiced mixtures can develop unpleasant flavours when frozen, so spices are best added to frozen dishes after thawing, if possible. Since spices, like herbs, deteriorate with long keeping, they should be bought in small quantities, and stored in airtight containers.

Essences include concentrated extracts and purées, and natural and synthetic bottled concentrates. Most of these are strong, and should be used very sparingly. Bottled colourings are equally potent, and unless used with care will make foods look unnatural. Gravy browning, which is made from caramelized sugar, is a common and useful colouring not only for savoury dishes, but also to darken the colour of fruit cakes. Some spices, such as saffron and turmeric, colour the food as well as flavour it, as do coffee, cocoa and powdered drinking chocolate.

COMMON HERBS, SPICES AND ESSENCES

Allspice (Jamaica pepper, Myrtle pepper) Dried berries (like large peppercorns), whole or ground. Tastes like a mixture of cloves, juniper and cinnamon. Used in a variety of savoury and sweet dishes, especially as an ingredient in pickling spice and in fruit cakes.

Almond *Sweet almonds* have a very subtle, bland flavour, and are widely used, especially in sweet foods, such as cakes and desserts, and as a garnish or decoration. Ground sweet almonds are used for sweetmeats, to add body to flours, and for flavouring. *Bitter almonds* have a quite different, stronger flavour, and are used sparingly in sweet dishes and biscuits. They should not be used raw, as the nut contains the substance used as a basis for prussic acid. *Almond essence* is a commercial preparation of varying strength, made from bitter almonds. *Ratafia* is, strictly speaking, a liqueur made by infusing various substances in spirit, but the term is now generally used of an almond-flavoured infusion, ie a subtler form of almond essence. Ratafia biscuits are flavoured with ratafia essence, made from oil of bitter almonds.

Angelica Candied angelica (stem) is used to decorate cakes, biscuits and desserts, but in Scandinavia the plant is eaten as a vegetable, and the leaves can be used in salads, or to flavour rhubarb or marmalade.

Anise (Aniseed) Used for fish and shellfish, and in curries, but mainly for flavouring sweets, cakes and breads; also in liqueurs such as Anis and Pastis.

Asafoetida Dried resinous juice from plant stem, usually ground. A powerful, rank flavour, used in curry powder and South Indian vegetable dishes.

Basil Leaf, fresh or dried, crushed. The flavour varies slightly according to variety. Popular in Southern European cookery, and used with well-flavoured savoury foods, especially tomatoes, eggs and cheese. A traditional flavouring for turtle soup.

Bay Essential ingredient of bouquet garni, and used as an infused flavouring for many savoury and sweet dishes, especially casseroles and milk puddings. Also used in chutneys, pickles and marinades.

Bergamot Little used in cooking, but leaves or flowers can be used to flavour drinks, or in salads.

Borage Fresh leaves or flowers are mainly used to impart a flavour of cucumber to drinks, but can also be used in salads or as fritters.

Bouquet garni Sprigs of fresh herbs and whole spice berries tied together, often in a square of muslin or cheesecloth, and dropped into stocks, soups, stews and other dishes. The bouquet garni is removed before serving. The classic herb bundle consists of 3 parsley stalks to 1 sprig of thyme and 1 bay leaf. Other ingredients, eg sprigs of marjoram, basil, chervil, tarragon or rosemary, can vary to suit the dish. Black peppercorns, juniper berries, whole cloves, nutmeg fragments or orange peel may also be included if the herbs are tied in a cloth bag.

Burnet There are several varieties which, when crushed, have an aroma similar to cucumber. An important ingredient in certain classic butters and sauces; also used in salads and for flavouring drinks.

Caper A pickled bud which is used as a garnish for hors d'oeuvres and fish, and in salads and stuffings, but especially important in sauces, such as Caper Sauce for mutton.

Capsicum See Peppers.

Caraway Fresh caraway seeds have a dominant flavour, used extensively in German and Austrian dishes and in cakes, bread, cheeses, cabbage, and sauerkraut. Kümmel liqueur is flavoured with caraway.

Cardamom Ground cardamom is an ingredient of curry powder, and is widely used in Indian and Middle Eastern cookery. It is also used to flavour drinks. In the UK it is used in pickling spice, and sometimes in cakes. Green, white and black pods are used. Whole pods should be lightly crushed before use.

Cassia See Cinnamon.

Cayenne pepper See Peppers.

Celery Dried celery seed is sometimes substituted for salt. It is also used in pickles, sauces, and soups (especially those containing tomato), and with shellfish.

Chervil When fresh, the flavour is similar to parsley, but more delicate; dried chervil has little flavour. Used in seasonings of chopped, mixed herbs to flavour sauces and butters, and with soups, fish and white meats.

Chicory Leaves are eaten raw in salads, or cooked as a vegetable. Roots are eaten raw, as a vegetable, or dried, ground and added to coffee.

Chilli See Peppers.

Chive Chopped chives can be used in any dish, especially salads, when a delicate onion flavour is needed; chives are also an important garnish. Some varieties have a garlic flavour.

Cinnamon Dried, whole or ground bark, this is a flavouring for spice or fruit puddings, gingerbread, cakes and apple dishes, also some savoury stews and curries. It is also delicious sprinkled on hot buttered toast. *Cassia* has a similar but less subtle flavour.

Citron Peel, candied, dried, or as essence. The fruit is like a large lemon, but the peel has a peculiar aromatic taste unlike other citrus fruits. Used in candied peel mixtures, and for making flavouring essences. Candied citron peel is a familiar decoration for Madeira cake.

Clove Bud, dried whole or ground. A strong, intrusive flavour, used sparingly in dishes containing apples and pears, and infused in milk for Bread Sauce. Also inserted in onions to flavour stews and casseroles. Whole cloves are used to garnish ham, and as a pickling spice or in a marinade.

Cocoa Seeds of the cacao tree are dried, partially fermented, roasted and processed in various ways to make cocoa, chocolate, and drinking chocolate powder. Used in numerous sweet recipes, and to flavour certain savoury ones. Cocoa is also used for flavoured drinks, and in a liqueur, Crème de Caçao.

Coffee Used as whole, roasted and ground beans or as essence. Ground, or processed 'instant' coffee is used not only as a drink, but to flavour cakes, confectionery, puddings and desserts. Commercial coffee essences are inferior in flavour to the strained liquid from a strong infusion of ground coffee, or instant coffee powder. To obtain a particularly delicate coffee flavour for a dish containing cream, infuse whole or cracked beans in the cream before cooking.

Coriander Leaves are used in curries, chutney and some casseroles and salads. Seeds have a different flavour, and are used in curries, chutney, cheese and vegetable dishes, and some spiced fruit recipes. Also made into a flavoured vinegar.

Cumin Dried, whole or ground cumin seed is widely used in curries and Eastern and Mexican dishes.

Curry Leaves The fresh or dried leaves give the characteristic smell to curry powder, though imparting less flavour than the other ingredients.

Dill Fresh or dried leaves or seeds are an essential flavouring in many Scandinavian and Northern European recipes, especially fish dishes. Can be used in salads, soups and sauces, and as a flavouring for pickles, particularly those containing cucumber.

Fennel A subtle, aniseed-like flavour especially effective with fish. Fish can be flamed over dried fennel stalks or cooked with the chopped leaves or seeds. Also used with pork or veal, and in salads. The bulb can be eaten cooked as a vegetable or raw as a salad, and the leaves used as a garnish.

Fenugreek Ground fenugreek seed is an ingredient in curry powder, and can be used in other spiced Eastern dishes. The fresh leaf can be curried, or used when young as a salad.

Fines Herbes A mixture of finely chopped fresh herbs – usually chervil, chives, parsley and tarragon – used extensively in French cookery.

Garlic A bulb composed of sections (cloves). Used for almost any type of savoury dish when a fairly strong flavour is needed; raw garlic is more pungent than cooked, and is used for salads, garlic mayonnaise, and butters. Also available dried, as granules or powder.

Geranium Scented leaf varieties can be used to line the baking tin for sponge cakes, and to flavour custards, jellies, and preserves.

Ginger One of the most widely used flavourings for jams, chutneys, gingerbread and cakes, also in many Eastern savoury recipes. Fresh ginger root is generally bruised with a rolling-pin to release its flavour for use in jams and preserves. It can also be grated for salads and curries, and preserved in syrup ('stem' ginger), and candied as a sweetmeat or for use in cakes, etc. The root, when dried with the skin on, is called 'green' or 'black' ginger. Ground ginger is used in cakes, biscuits, puddings, fruit dishes, and for sprinkling on melon or grapefruit.

Horseradish The grated fresh root has a very strong flavour and must be used sparingly. Use in horseradish sauces, savoury butters, and some stuffings.

Hyssop A Biblical 'bitter herb'; the fresh or dried leaf is used to flavour liqueurs, and sparingly in salads.

Juniper Fresh or dried berries, used whole or crushed as a flavouring for game dishes, but also for pork, poultry stuffings, pâtés and marinades. Principal flavouring agent for gin.

Ketchup Name given to a salty, pungent and well-reduced extract for flavouring savoury dishes. Anchovy and oyster ketchup are the most common fish extracts, mushroom and walnut the best-known vegetable ketchups. 'Tomato ketchup' is in fact a sauce.

Lemon Lemon juice is a widely used souring and tenderizing agent, also used to prevent the discoloration of fruit and vegetables after peeling. It is particularly important for accentuating the flavour of fish, and some fruit and vegetables. Lemon rind, grated or in strips, is infused in both sweet and savoury dishes.

Lemon balm The fresh or dried leaves may be used with fish, mushrooms, salads, for drinks and with strawberries.

Lime The juice and rind of the fruit are used in the same way as lemon, when a sourer flavour is needed, especially in West Indian cookery. Limes make an excellent marmalade and are used in flavouring drinks. The dried flower of the lime tree is made into herbal teas, and used in sweet creams and desserts.

Liquorice Extract of liquorice root is used in flavouring stout and other drinks; the prepared root is eaten as a sweetmeat.

Lovage Fresh or dried stems, leaves and seeds are used. Lovage has a warm, aromatic flavour, reminiscent of both celery and angelica; the stems can be candied, like angelica. The leaves are used fresh in salads, and fresh or dried in soups and casseroles. The seeds are baked in biscuits for cheese.

Mace Dried outer husk of nutmeg. Whole 'blades' of mace are used as an infused flavouring; ground mace is used like nutmeg, especially in fish dishes and for pâtés and sausages.

Marigold The flower can be used as a substitute for saffron in colouring butter and cheese; also as a flavouring in fish soups, salads and some cakes.

Marjoram Fresh or dried leaves are very widely used for savoury dishes, particularly lamb, veal, sausages, some fish dishes, mushrooms and tomatoes.

Mint The flavour varies according to variety, but mint is always best used fresh. *Spearmint* is the type most commonly grown, but some prefer *apple mints*, which have larger, rounded leaves. Both are used for the traditional Mint Sauce, in vegetable dishes and salads, and for flavouring drinks. *Cologne mint* has a slightly orange flavour and is used for drinks; *Pennyroyal* is used in black puddings and in peppermint essence, of which the principal ingredient is *peppermint*. Peppermint, in the form of oils, essences, certain cordials or liqueurs, is the type of mint flavouring most often used in sweet dishes and confectionery.

Mustard Whole black, brown or white mustard seeds are used in chutneys and pickles, and the ground seeds for seasoning meat, fish, salad dressings, vegetable dishes and particularly cheese dishes. English and French mustards, in which the mustard seeds are mixed to a paste with herbs and spices, are widely used as condiments, especially with beef.

Myrtle Fresh leaves and berries are used as a substitute for bay leaves, especially with lamb and pork, and in marinades.

Nasturtium Fresh leaves and seeds can be used as an alternative to capers, and in salads, salad dressings, and to flavour vinegar. The flowers are also sometimes added to salads.

Nutmeg Nutmeg seeds, either whole, grated or ground are used in a variety of sweet and savoury dishes. Nutmeg is a traditional flavouring for spinach and is also used in fruit cakes, mincemeat and for drinks.

Onion Onions, including shallots and spring onions, are by far the most common vegetable flavouring used raw or cooked.

Orange The juice and rind are used for flavouring in the same way as lemon. Orange is also used for orange flower water and in many liqueurs.

Oregano Leaves of milder variety grown in the UK are generally used fresh in the same way as marjoram, while the stronger Southern European varieties are usually used dried. Oregano is widely used for cheese dishes and pizzas, and in Greek and Mexican cooking.

Paprika See Peppers.

Parsley The leaves and stalks of fresh parsley are an essential ingredient of a bouquet garni, and are also used in sauces, salads and many other savoury dishes. Dried parsley has little flavour or aroma.

Peppers or Capsicum

CHILLI PEPPERS Green when unripe, yellow or red when ripe, have a very pungent flavour. Used for hot, spicy dishes, in pickles and chutneys, and in a variety of Eastern, Mexican and West Indian recipes. Fresh green chillies have an interesting capsicum flavour, but red chillies should be used sparingly, and are usually added in the form of Tabasco sauce. Handle chillies with care. Wear gloves or wash hands thoroughly after handling to avoid irritating delicate skin on lips or eyes.

Chilli powder is usually sold with other spices added. *Cayenne pepper* is finer ground, and used more often as a seasoning in European cooking. The yellow *Nepal pepper* is less pungent.

SWEET OR BELL PEPPERS These are used as a vegetable and in salads.

Paprika or *Hungarian pepper* is a powder ground from a pointed variety of capsicum, and is fairly mild; much used in Spanish and Hungarian cooking. It should be bought in small quantities as it deteriorates very rapidly with keeping.

VINE PEPPERS (PEPPERCORNS) The most important seasoning spice after salt, used with almost all savoury dishes, and in some rich fruit cakes and puddings. Whole peppercorns can be included in a bouquet garni, and in many marinades, chutneys, and pickles. Whole peppercorns should be freshly ground for use in cooking and at the table; the flavour of ground pepper deteriorates rapidly. *Mignonette pepper* is a mixture of black and white peppercorns ground together.

Pickling Spice A mixture of spices such as black peppercorns, red chillies, allspice berries, mustard seed, cardamom, coriander, and mace. Used for pickling, brining and in marinades.

Poppy Fresh poppy seed has a nutty flavour when baked. It is often sprinkled on bread and cakes. £121,993/640

Purslane Fresh leaves can be cooked as a vegetable, or used in salads and pickled in vinegar.

Rocket Fresh leaves can be cooked as a vegetable or used in salads; much used in Italian and other Mediterranean cookery.

Rose Fresh petals are used for candied sweetmeats and decorating sweet dishes, and rose water is used as an alternative to vanilla in old recipes for desserts, cakes and biscuits, and in Eastern cookery. Rose-hips are used for preserves, jellies, syrups and drinks.

Rosemary Used especially with lamb, either sprinkled over the meat or inserted in it, and with oily fish, pork, veal or game. Rosemary is also included in stuffings, apple jams and jellies, and with drinks.

Rue Fresh leaves have a strong, bitter flavour; large quantities can be poisonous. Rue is used in Southern European cookery, and to make the liqueur Grappa.

Safflower Fresh seeds and flowers are used: the seeds to make cooking oil with a high polyunsaturated fat content; the flowers to make yellow food colouring.

Saffron Stamens of the saffron crocus are used whole or in the powdered form. The cost of saffron prevents its extensive use; it is essential for a classic Bouillabaisse, and can be used as an infusion to flavour breads, cakes and rice dishes, and in Middle Eastern meat dishes and Spanish paellas.

Sage Sage and onion stuffing is traditional with pork, duck and goose, and fresh or dried sage can also flavour lamb, veal and sausages. Some cheeses, such as Sage Derby, are flavoured with sage.

Salad burnet With a flavour similar to borage, salad burnet is used in salads, cream soups and omelettes, and for flavouring drinks.

Salt The most common of all seasonings, used in virtually all savoury and many sweet dishes. *Rock salt* is obtained from underground deposits, and *sea salt* is evaporated from sea water. Both these have large granules, and must be ground in a mill for use at the table, but their flavour is better than *table salt*, which is finely ground and has magnesium carbonate added to prevent caking. Sea salt and table salt are the salts most commonly used in cookery. *Kitchen salt* or *common salt* is mined by a process slightly different from rock salt, and has finer granules. *Flavoured salt*, with added spices or herb flavourings such as garlic, onion or celery, is used for some dishes.

Savory *Summer* and *winter savory* are two different plants with a similar flavour; summer savory has the stronger taste. In Mediterranean cooking the fresh or dried leaves are traditionally used with beans and peas. Savory is also used with trout and liver, and in sausages and stuffings.

Sesame The seeds are an important source of vegetable oil, and are used extensively in Greek and Middle Eastern cookery. In the UK they are used in breads, cakes and biscuits.

Sorrel There are many varieties of sorrel. The leaves can be cooked as a vegetable, or used in a salad, or used with fish, eggs and veal. The flavour is sour but pleasant, and makes excellent soups and sauces.

Soy Soy beans can be eaten fresh or dried, and are made into *soy sauce* by fermentation with salt, water and barley or wheat flour. There are many varieties of soy sauce. It has a strong, slightly meaty flavour, and is essential in Far Eastern cookery. It is also an ingredient of Worcestershire sauce and Harvey's sauce, and is used in marinades, barbecue sauces, and with meat and vegetable dishes.

Star anise The dried fruit has a flavour similar to that of anise; star anise is used in some Chinese dishes, and for making drinks.

Sunflower Fresh or dried seeds are an important source of vegetable oil, and are also eaten alone, raw or toasted.

Sweet cicely The whole herb can be boiled and used as a vegetable, or the cooked root dressed as a salad. Fresh or dried leaves are used to flavour soups, sauces, salad dressings, herb butters and stewed fruit.

Tamarind An infusion made from the partly-dried pod is an essential souring agent for authentic Indian curries.

Tansy Fresh tansy leaves have a strong, bitter flavour. At one time tansy was used for cakes, puddings, custards and herb teas, but the herb is little used today.

Tarragon *French tarragon* is an essential ingredient in fines herbes mixtures, some bouquets garnis, and as a flavouring for vinegar. It is used in numerous dishes, particularly with chicken and fish, and in many classic French sauces. It does not dry well; *Russian tarragon,* often used as a substitute, has an inferior flavour.

Thyme *Garden thyme* is used in a bouquet garni, and with almost every kind of savoury dish. It has a strong but delicate flavour. *Lemon thyme* is similar, but with a taste of lemon. It is used especially with eggs and in cream sauces, and with drinks.

Turmeric Ground turmeric root has a powerful yellow colour, but not a very strong flavour. It can be used as an inferior substitute for saffron, to colour rice, curries and mustard pickles, and in some Indian sweet dishes, but should not be used where a saffron flavour is required.

Vanilla Vanilla has a subtle and distinctive flavour, suitable for almost all sweet dishes, particularly those containing chocolate. Whole pods can be used to infuse the flavour, or *vanilla essence* can be added. Vanilla pods are also used to flavour sugar.

Cookery Terms and Techniques

Modern cookery owes an enormous debt to the French. Many of their culinary terms have entered our language along with the recipes and techniques they describe. Other countries have contributed words and phrases to this linguistic casserole.

KEY

(Am) American	(Pol) Polish
(Aus) Austrian	(Port) Portuguese
(Bel) Belgian	(Mex) Mexican
(Can) Canadian	(N Afr) North African
(Fr) French	(Rus) Russian
(Ger) German	(S Afr) South African
(Gr) Greek	(Scot) Scottish
(Hun) Hungarian	(Sp) Spanish
(It) Italian	(Sw) Swedish
(Indon) Indonesian	(Tur) Turkish

COOKERY TERMS

Absorption method Method of cooking rice in a lidded saucepan with twice its volume of liquid, until the liquid has been absorbed.

Acidulated water Cold water mixed with lemon juice or vinegar, and used to soak certain fruits and vegetables, eg apples and potatoes, to prevent them from discolouring. Also used in the base of an aluminium pressure cooker for recipes to be cooked in a container.

Agar agar Setting agent obtained from certain seaweed; often used in vegetarian cooking as an alternative to a meat-based jelly. See also page 32.

Aiguillettes, en (Fr) Manner in which fish, meat or poultry is cut into long or small thin strips.

Aïle (Fr) Wing of poultry or game bird.

Aïoli, aïlloli (Fr) Garlic mayonnaise.

À la, au, aux (Fr) **Alla** (It) In the style of, or made with.

Albumen White of egg.

Al dente (It) Term meaning tender, but still firm to the bite. Used to describe cooked pasta, rice, and blanched vegetables.

Allemande, à l' (Fr) In the German style, eg with smoked sausages, or garnished with buttered noodles and mashed potatoes.

All-in-one Method of preparing sauces and cakes using all the basic ingredients simultaneously. Also known as the 'One-stage method'.

Allumettes (Fr) 1. Small strips of vegetables cut like matchsticks, eg potato straws. 2. Puff pastry cut into strips and baked. Can be sweet or savoury.

Américaine, à l' (Fr) 1. Lobster dissected (usually while live) and baked with lobster coral over herbs and tomatoes, then served with a fish Velouté sauce or mayonnaise. 2. Braised chicken in a cream sauce with port, button onions, and mushrooms. 3. Poached fish in white wine sauce with parsley, butter, onions, and mushrooms.

Andalouse (Fr) 1. Cold mayonnaise sauce mixed with tomato purée and garnished with red peppers. 2. Garnish for meat and poultry consisting of halved peppers stuffed with rice à la Grecque and slices of cooked tomato and aubergine.

Anglaise, à l' (Fr) 1. In the English style; usually plainly boiled or steamed. 2. Food dipped in egg, coated with breadcrumbs and fried or grilled.

Aperitifs (Fr) **Aperitivi** (It) Pre-meal drinks.

Arrowroot Thickening agent used in clear sauces and soups; gives a translucent appearance. See also page 32.

Artois, d' (Fr) 1. Garnish of potato croquettes and peas for meat, or vegetables and artichoke hearts for poultry; both served with a Madeira wine sauce. 2. Savoury pastry made from a mixture of cheeses and flour.

Aspic Jelly made from meat, fish or poultry stock and either gelatine or calf's foot. Used as a setting agent, for coating food, or chopped, as a garnish.

Aurore, à l' (Fr) Sauce for chicken, fish and eggs made from a Béchamel, Velouté or Hollandaise sauce with either tomato sauce, tomato purée or tomato juice added to give it a pink colour.

Avgolemono (Gr) Egg and lemon soup or sauce.

Baba (Fr) **Babka** (Pol) Small or large round cake made from a basic savarin mixture with sultanas, raisins or currants. Usually soaked in a rum or kirsch syrup.

Bacalao (Sp) **Bacalhau** (Port) Dried salt cod.

Bagna cauda (It) Warm garlic and anchovy sauce into which raw vegetables are dipped.

Bain-marie (Fr) Large shallow pan filled with hot water into which smaller pans, etc can be placed allowing their contents to keep warm, or to cook without boiling or reducing. Also called Water-bath.

Baking powder Raising agent made from bicarbonate of soda and cream of tartar. See also page 33.

Baklava (East Med) Dessert made from filo pastry, walnuts or almonds, and a honeyed syrup.

Ballottine, de (Fr) 1. Meat or poultry boned and shaped into a bundle or roll. Served hot or cold. 2. Boned, stuffed duck or turkey rolled like a galantine, but served hot or cold.

Barbecue To grill over charcoal. Coals must be lit well in advance so that flames have subsided and the charcoal is very hot, but grey in appearance, when cooking begins. The rate of cooking is controlled by adjusting the height of the cooking rack over the coals. Covered barbecues are useful for larger food items as they retain heat and cook more quickly and evenly; the domed type is known as a kettle barbecue. Safety precautions must be observed when cooking on a barbecue, particularly when lighting the coals and when cooking fatty foods which cause flaming. Children and pets should be supervised to avoid accidents when barbecuing.

Baron Large joint of beef including both sirloins with the backbone intact. Can also include the saddle and hind legs of mutton or lamb, or the hindquarters of lamb. Baron of hare is the body section without head, neck or limbs.

Bâton (Fr) Pastry, biscuit or bread loaf made in the form of a stick.

Bavarois, à la crème (Fr) Bavarian cream. Rich cold dessert made with custard and cream, and set with gelatine. Can have many flavours.

Béarnaise, à la (Fr) Thick sauce made with vinegar or wine, herbs, eggs, shallots or onions, and butter. Traditionally served with grilled steak, poached eggs and poached fish.

Béchamel (Fr) Classic foundation French white sauce, more flavoured than British white sauce.

Beef Wellington Fillet of beef in pastry.

Beignet (Fr) Fritters both sweet and savoury.

Bercy, au (Fr) Sauce of white wine, shallots, Velouté sauce made with fish or chicken stock, butter and parsley. Served with fish or meat.

Beurre, au (Fr) Cooked or dressed with butter.

Beurre à la Meunière (Fr) Browned butter with seasonings, parsley and lemon juice, usually poured over fish which has been fried in butter.

Beurre manié (Fr) Butter and flour kneaded into a paste; added to soups and sauces as a thickening agent. An alternative to a roux.

Beurre noir, au (Fr) Butter heated until rich brown in colour, then mixed with vinegar. Parsley and capers are often included. Generally served over skate or brains.

Bigarade (Fr) Brown sauce made with Seville oranges.

Biscuit glacé (Fr) Different kinds of ice cream or water ice layered together in a box-shaped mould.

Bisque (Fr) Thick, creamy soup made with shellfish.

Bitok (Rus) Small meat patty made from raw minced beef and breadcrumbs, and bound with an egg.

Bivalve mollusc Shellfish enclosed by two shells, eg mussel, cockle, oyster, scallop.

Blaeberry Another name for bilberry or whortleberry.

Blanquette (Fr) White stew, usually of veal or chicken in a white sauce enriched with cream and sometimes egg yolks.

Blatjang (S Afr) Chutney usually made from dried apricots.

Bleu, au (Fr) 1. Term applied to freshly caught fish, usually trout, cooked in boiling water, vinegar and seasonings, giving the skin a blue tinge. 2. Very rare steak.

Blini, bliny (Rus) Pancakes, generally yeasted, traditionally made with a mixture of plain and buckwheat flour. Served with caviar and soured cream.

Blintz (Rus) Pancake stuffed with a cheese or other filling, and fried until crisp.

Bombay duck (Indian, S Asian) Dried and salted small fish. Served with curry.

Bombe glacé (Fr) Moulded ice cream dessert usually round or cone shaped, and of two or more different flavours, or an outer layer of ice cream around a mousse or parfait centre.

Bonne femme (Fr) Fillets of fish, generally sole, in a white wine sauce with mushrooms, shallots, and parsley.

Bordelaise, à la (Fr) Applies to a variety of dishes, but most commonly to a sauce for grilled meats consisting of red wine, shallots, seasoning, and herbs, often finished with a meat glaze.

Borsch (Rus) Beetroot soup served hot or chilled and garnished with soured cream.

Bouchée (Fr) Mouthful. Small, filled puff pastry patty or vol-au-vent case.

Bouillabaisse (Fr) Mixed fish soup/stew from the French Mediterranean.

Boulangère, à la (Fr) Baker's style. Sliced potatoes and onions cooked in stock. Often served with a roast joint such as lamb.

Bourguignonne à la (Fr) Cooked with red wine, onions, and mushrooms. This is a speciality of Burgundy. Boeuf Bourguignonne is the best known example.

Bran Flaked outer husks of grain separated from flour during the milling process. Supplies fibre in the diet.

Brandade (Fr) Pounded fish pâté; *Brandade de Morue* made from salt cod is the most common example.

Brawn Meat from a pig or boar's head, encased in jelly made from the broth in which it has simmered.

Bretonne, à la (Fr) Brittany style. 1. Garnished with haricot beans. 2. White wine sauce for eggs or fish garnished with shredded leeks, carrots, and celery.

Brine Salt water solution used for pickling and preserving.

Brioche (Fr) Rich yeasted dough baked in a variety of shapes and sizes; the most common is a rounded loaf with a knob on top.

Brisling Small sprats.

Brochette (Fr) Method of grilling small chunks of meat or fish on skewers.

Broiled-on topping (Am) Grilled topping of nuts, shredded coconut, brown sugar, etc on plain and light fruit cakes.

Brulé (Fr) Burnt. Glaze formed by grilling sugar until caramelized on top of a custard base dessert.

Brun, au (Fr) Cooked in brown sauce.

Brunoise, à la (Fr) Garnish for soup and other dishes of finely chopped spring vegetables, eg carrots, onions, leeks, celery, turnips, etc.

Brut (Fr) Dry wine.

Burghul, bulgur (Mid East) Cracked wheat.

Butter muslin Thin, open-weave cotton cloth. Used for straining dairy products, jellies, stocks, etc; should be scalded before use.

Caille (Fr) Quail.

Calabrese (It) Variety of broccoli.

Campden tablets Sodium metabisulphite. In solution this produces sulphur dioxide.

Canard (Fr) Duck.

Caneton (Fr) Duckling.

Caper Pickled flower bud of the caper bush. Used in sauces and as a garnish.

Capon Castrated cockerel.

Caquelon (Fr) Open ceramic or earthenware pan. Used for cheese fondues.

Caramel Sugar dissolved in water and then boiled until brown. Used for lining moulds, colouring sauces, and confectionery, etc.

Carbonnade 1. (Bel) Beef stew made with beer. 2. Method of grilling meat so that the outside is well done and the inside very rare. 3. (Fr) Braised lamb or mutton dish.

Cardinal, à la (Fr) 1. Red-tinted sauce of fish stock, Béchamel sauce, lobster butter, and Cayenne pepper. 2. Fish dishes garnished with lobster.

Carob Ground pod of an evergreen tree; used as an alternative to chocolate.

Carolines (Fr) Small savoury éclairs.

Carré d'Agneau (Fr) Loin of lamb.

Casein Protein in milk which is coagulated by rennet. Used in making cheeses.

Cassata alla Siciliana (It) 1. Mould of two or more different coloured layers of ice cream with fruits, nuts or small macaroons as a filling. 2. Rich gâteau surrounded by green almond paste.

Casserole 1. Deep lidded cooking pot made of flameproof or ovenproof materials for cooking stews or meat, poultry or vegetables. 2. Name for dishes cooked in a casserole pot.

Cassolette (Fr) 1. Special flameproof dish used for serving various hot or cold hors d'oeuvres, entrées or sweets. 2. A fried case used as a container for a savoury filling.

Cassoulet (Fr) Stew of haricot beans, pork, sausages, vegetables and herbs. Lamb and goose or duck are also used.

Caul Animal membrane often used as a casing for minced offal.

Cèpe Edible fungus with sponge-like gills.

Cereal Farinaceous food such as wheat, oats, barley, rye, millet, rice, Indian corn and buckwheat.

Cervelas (Fr) Smoked sausage made with pork meat and fat, garlic and seasonings.

Cervelat (Ger) Smoked, highly spiced sausage made from minced pork and beef.

Chafing-dish Metal dish or frying pan placed on a trivet over a spirit lamp which allows food to be either cooked at the table or kept warm. A chafing dish is also used for flambé recipes, such as Crêpes suzette.

Chambord, à la (Fr) Fish, often carp or trout, cooked in wine, and garnished with fish quenelles, mushrooms, soft roes, shrimps, crayfish tails, and truffles.

Chantilly (Fr) Sweetened whipped cream flavoured with vanilla essence; often lightened with a whisked egg white.

Chapatti (Indian) Unleavened round Indian bread.

Charlotte (Fr) 1. Cold moulded dessert lined with biscuits and filled with a cream or custard, eg Charlotte Russe. 2. Hot pudding lined with bread and filled with fruit, eg Apple Charlotte. 3. A similar savoury dish.

Charlotte mould (Fr) A deep, round,

straight-sided mould that tapers in slightly at the base. Used for moulded desserts.

Chasseur, à la (Fr)   Hunter's style, ie game, poultry or meat which is cooked in white wine with shallots.

Châteaux [pommes de terre] (Fr)   Potatoes cut into olive shapes, blanched and roasted.

Chaudfroid (Fr)   Classic French sauce, cooked but served cold. Prepared from a foundation sauce, into which gelatine dissolved in aspic is blended. It is poured over cold joints, poultry cutlets, fish, eggs, etc and allowed to set.

Cheesecloth   Butter muslin.

Chiffonade, Chiffonnade (Fr)   1. Salad dressing of hard-boiled eggs, red pepper, parsley, shallots and French dressing. 2. Shredded sorrel or lettuce leaves sautéed in butter.

Chinois, à la (Fr)   Chinese style.

Chipolata (It)   1. Small sausage. 2. Garnish of spicy sausages, chestnuts and various vegetables.

Chorizo (Sp)   Spicy, smoked sausage flavoured with paprika.

Choron (Fr)   1. Béarnaise sauce, without tarragon and chervil, blended with tomato purée. 2. Type of mustard made with tomato purée.

Choucroute (Fr)   Sauerkraut. The basis of several dishes from Alsace.

Chourico (Port)   Sausage spiced with paprika.

Choux pastry   Rich cooked mixture, piped or spooned on to trays for baking. The cooked pastry is light and aerated and is frequently filled. Used in sweet and savoury dishes.

Chowder   Thick soup made with fish or shellfish; vegetables are often added.

Chrane (Jewish)   Bitter-sweet preserve made with beetroot, horseradish, vinegar and sugar.

Citric acid   Acid which occurs naturally in citrus fruits. Bottled commercially, it is used as a preservative or alternative to freshly squeezed lemon juice.

Civet (Fr)   Game casserole using a marinade and generally the blood of the animal.

Clafouti (Fr)   Pastry or thick pancake baked with a topping of fruit, usually black cherries.

Clamart, à la (Fr)   Garnished with peas.

Clarified butter/fat   Butter or fat cleared of water and impurities through slow heating and straining. See also **Ghee**.

Cochineal   Natural red food colouring of insect origin. Carmine is also a cochineal extract, but of a deeper colour. Cochineal gives a pink-red colour, not a 'Christmas' red.

Cocotte (Fr)   Small ramekin dish of porcelain or earthenware in which eggs, mousses, soufflés, etc are baked.

Coeur à la crème (Fr)   Light cream or curd cheese from which the whey has been drained; usually set in heart-shaped moulds and served with fresh fruit or cream.

Colbert, à la (Fr)   1. Food, generally fish and especially sole, dipped in egg and breadcrumbs, then fried. 2. Classic French sauce made from butter, meat stock and glaze, lemon juice, and chopped parsley or tarragon. 3. Clear soup.

Collop   Sliced or minced meat or offal; similar to French escalope.

Compôte (Fr)   1. Dish of stewed fruit served cold. 2. Pigeon or partridge stew.

Concasse, concasser (Fr)   To pound, grind or chop roughly.

Condé (Fr)   1. Dish with a rice base, usually sweet, but can be savoury. 2. Cake with almond icing. 3. Red haricot bean soup or garnish.

Condiment   Seasonings added to dishes at the table, eg mustard, salt, pepper, various relishes.

Conservation method   Method of cooking carrots and similar root vegetables to retain flavour, colour and vitamins.

Conserve   1. Whole fruit preserve with a thick syrup. 2. Meat preserved in its own fat so that air cannot penetrate, eg *confit d'oie* – preserved goose, *confit de porc* – preserved pork.

Consistency   Term describing the texture of a cake, pudding or similar mixture.

Consommé (Fr)   Clear soup based on stock.

Coquille St. Jacques (Fr)　Scallops. Also describes a recipe for scallops served in their shells with a sauce.

Coral　Ovaries of a hen lobster used in various sauces and as a garnish.

Cornflour　Finely ground kernel of Indian corn or maize. Used in puddings and cakes, or as a thickening agent in sauces. See also page 33.

Corn syrup　Obtained from maize and mainly sold in the U.S.A. Used to make various biscuits and sweets.

Côtelette (Fr)　Chop, cutlet.

Cotriade (Fr)　Fish soup or stew.

Coulibiac, kulebyaka (Rus)　Fish pie (originally sturgeon) with other ingredients; usually encased in a brioche paste.

Coupe (Fr)　1. Stemmed, round goblet used for serving ice cream, fruit or shellfish cocktails. 2. Ice cream sundae.

Coupe Jacques (Fr)　Fresh fruits soaked in liqueur and served with ice cream in a coupe (goblet).

Couronne, en (Fr)　Meat or pastry preparations shaped in a ring or piled like a crown, eg crown roast of lamb.

Court bouillon (Fr)　Liquid flavoured with herbs, vinegar or lemon juice and vegetables in which fish, meat or vegetables can be cooked or poached.

Couscous (N Afr)　1. Ground wheat meal, usually semolina, mixed with salted water and formed into pellets; cooked in a special steaming pan called a couscousier. 2. A meat stew served with couscous.

Couverture (Fr)　Cooking chocolate containing a high proportion of cocoa butter; has excellent flavour and glossy finish.

Crécy, à la (Fr)　With carrots.

Crème, à la (Fr)　With a creamy or cream-based sauce.

Crème Anglaise (Fr)　Basic egg custard used either as a sauce or as a dessert.

Crème brûlée (Fr)　Baked egg custard made with cream and a crisp caramel topping.

Crème fraîche (Fr)　Cream which has ripened and thickened naturally, but not soured.

Crème renversée (Fr)　1. Moulded custard inverted on to a dish when cold. 2. Moulded custard flavoured with vanilla, fruit, etc, and served cold.

Créole (Fr)　Of southern U.S.A. or Caribbean origin. Refers to dishes with a spicy sauce, red and green peppers, tomatoes, okra, rice, etc.

Crêpe (Fr)　Thin pancake.

Crêpe Suzette (Fr)　Thin pancake heated in an orange sauce and flamed with orange liqueur or brandy.

Crépinette (Fr)　Small flat pork sausage.

Crevette (Fr)　Shrimp; **crevette rouge**, prawn.

Croissant (Fr)　Crescent shaped roll made with a light butter- and egg-enriched dough.

Croquembouche (Fr)　1. Madeira cake topped with custard-filled profiteroles mounted on a paper cone and glazed with caramelized sugar. 2. Oranges or other fruits dipped in caramel and mounted on a cone.

Croque Monsieur (Fr)　Fried, grilled, toasted or baked sandwich with a ham and cheese filling.

Croquette (Fr)　Minced or chopped food bound together, formed into various shapes, coated and fried.

Croustades (Fr)　Cases of fried baked bread, rice, noodles, potatoes or pastry which are filled with savoury mixtures.

Croûte (Fr)　1. Pastry case for savoury fillings. 2. Shapes of fried or toasted bread. Used as a base for either small, whole or portioned game birds or poultry, or for spreads such as canapés. 3. Dice of fried or toasted bread served with soup or egg dishes (now usually called croûtons). 4. Small round or triangular shapes of fried or toasted bread used to garnish fricassées and other sauced dishes as an alternative to fleurons of puff pastry.

Croûton (Fr)　Small dice of fried or toasted bread used as a garnish.

Crudités (Fr) Small raw or blanched vegetables, eg carrots, tomatoes, courgettes, fennel, cucumber, etc, cut up or grated, and served with an oil and vinegar dressing. French dressing or dip.

Crustacea Shellfish. Crustacean (sing).

Curd 1. Solids remaining after coagulated milk separated from whey. 2. Fruit custard made with citrus fruit, and used in the same way as jam.

Cushion Topside of veal.

Dal, Dhal (Indian) Lentils and tomatoes spiced with chillies, garlic and various herb and spice seasonings.

Dariole mould (Fr) Small, smooth sided cylindrical mould used for making puddings, sweet and savoury jellies and creams.

Darne (Fr) Thick slice cut from the middle of a fish, eg salmon, and cooked on the bone.

Daube (Fr) Meat, vegetables and herbs cooked very slowly.

Déglacer (Fr) To add wine, stock, cream or other liquid to juices left in the pan after roasting or sautéeing. Referred to as deglazing in English.

Délice (Fr) Fillet of fish, poultry or meat.

Demi-glace (Fr) Well reduced Espagnole sauce with the juices from roasted meat added. Also the basis for a Madeira sauce.

Dieppoise, à la (Fr) Garnished with shrimps, mussels and mushrooms.

Digestifs (Fr) **Digestivi** (It) Drinks including some liqueurs served either before or, more often, after a meal to aid digestion.

Dobos torte (Hun) Layered cake with thick layers of sweet or savoury filling. Sweet cakes are topped with crisp caramel.

Dolma, dolmades, dolmas, dolmadakia (Gr, Tur, Rus) Stuffed vine leaves. Can also be cabbage leaves.

Doner Kebab (Gr and Tur) Pounded minced lamb or mutton, formed into a roll and grilled. Slices are put into a piece of pitta, together with chopped cabbage, onion, lettuce, tomato, etc.

Duchesse [pommes de terre] (Fr) Purée of potatoes blended with eggs and butter, and piped into whorled shapes or into a border, and then baked. Used as a garnish.

Duxelles (Fr) Basic preparation of chopped mushrooms, spring onions, seasonings, and sometimes Madeira. Used as a flavouring.

Eclair (Fr) Choux pastry oblong in shape, filled with flavoured cream, and topped with chocolate or coffee fondant icing. Can also be savoury.

Ecrevisse (Fr) Crayfish.

Egg wash Mixture of beaten egg and water used for glazing pastries, breads and buns to give them a shiny surface.

Elver Young eel about 5 cm (2 inches) long; cooked whole.

Emincé (Fr) 1. Finely sliced or shredded meat. 2. Dish using cooked meat.

Emulsion 1. Liquid of milky appearance containing minute drops of fat or oil. 2. Butter or oil mixed with egg yolks.

Enchilada (Mex) Pancake softened in hot oil, then rolled up with grated cheese and chilli sauce.

Epigramme, Epigram (Fr) Small slice of poultry, game or breast of lamb dipped in egg, rolled in breadcrumbs, and deep fried.

Escalope (Fr) Small thin slice of lean meat, generally veal, but may be pork, turkey, etc.

Espagnole Classic French foundation brown sauce.

Essence 1. Concentrate of natural juices from meat, poultry and fish. 2. Extraction from the distillation of herbs, spices and flowers, eg essence of anise, cinnamon, orange, rose, etc.

Faggot 1. Dish of minced pork offal shaped into squares or balls, and baked until brown. 2. Bunch of herbs used for flavouring.

Farce (Fr) Stuffing.

Farci (Fr) Stuffed.

Farmed Animal or vegetable bred or grown for the table.

Fermière, à la (Fr) Farmer's style, ie garnished with vegetables, usually carrots, onions, celery and turnips.

Fibre   Roughage; fibrous products which are not digestible, but essential for a healthy digestive and alimentary system.

Fillet   1. Underside of a sirloin of beef; the same cut of lamb, pork or beef. 2. Small, thin slice of poultry or game. 3. Side, whole or halved, of fish taken off the bone.

Filo (Gr)   Flour and water dough worked until paper-thin. Used for pastries such as baklava; also savoury dishes.

Financière (Fr)   Rich garnish consisting of some or all of the following: cock's combs, veal or poultry quenelles, olives, truffles, mushrooms, etc.

Flambé (Fr)   Flamed; sprinkled with warm alcohol and set alight.

Flameproof   Cookery utensils which can withstand direct heat as on a gas flame or electric ring.

Flan   Open flat tart.

Flapjack   1. Bar- or square-shaped oat biscuit. 2. (Am) Griddle scone.

Fleurons (Fr)   Small, half-moon shapes of puff pastry. Used as a garnish.

Florentine, à la (Fr)   1. Made or garnished with spinach. 2. Flat thin biscuit containing dried fruits, nuts, and candied peel, and coated on one side with dark chocolate.

Flummery   Pudding based on oatmeal or custard with regional variations of dried or stewed fruit, wine, etc added.

Foie d'agneau, de veau (Fr)   Lamb's or calf's liver.

Foie gras (Fr)   Goose liver from specially fattened geese.

Fondant (Fr)   Solution of sugar, glucose and water boiled to soft ball stage and worked until pliable. Diluted with a stock syrup, it is used as an icing, or flavoured, as a sweetmeat.

Fonds d' (Fr)   1. Round fleshy bases beneath the choke of an artichoke. 2. Broths and stocks made from veal, fowl or beef. Used as the basis for a variety of sauces. 3. Any basic cooking preparation, eg flavoured vinegar, pastry or roux.

Fondue (Swiss)   1. Cheese melted with white wine and kirsch, and served at the table in the dish in which it is cooked. Cubes of bread are dipped into it. 2. Puréed vegetables cooked in butter.

Fondue Bourguignonne (Fr)   Cubed steak, speared on forks, cooked briefly at the table in hot oil, then dipped in various seasonings before being eaten.

Fool   Cold dessert consisting of fruit purée, whipped cream and/or custard.

Forcemeat   Stuffing.

Forestière, à la (Fr)   Garnish for small cuts of meat and poulty consisting of mushrooms, diced lean bacon and diced potatoes, fried until browned.

Four, au (Fr)   Cooked in the oven.

Frappé (Fr)   Iced or chilled.

Fricadelles (Bel)   Meat balls made from finely minced pork or veal, herbs, spices, breadcrumbs, milk or cream, and eggs, then poached in stock and fried.

Fricassée (Fr)   Velouté or white stew, usually of chicken, rabbit, lamb or veal.

Frit (Fr)   Fried in shallow or deep fat.

Frites [pommes de terre] (Fr)   Chipped potatoes.

Fritot (Fr)   Fritter made with pieces of poultry, lamb or veal sweetbreads, brains or calves' heads.

Frittata (It)   Flat omelette.

Fritter   Variety of foods coated in batter, or chopped and mixed with batter, and fried.

Fritto misto (It)   Small mixed pieces of coated and deep-fried food.

Friture (Fr)   Fried food.

Fromage à la crème (Fr)   Sweet cheese dessert made with fromage blanc.

Fromage blanc (Fr)   Light, soft curd cheese, usually home-made.

Fromage frais   Soft, light curd cheese, fermented for a short time only. Used in cooking and desserts. Low fat. See also page 37.

Frosting (Am)   Icing.

Fruits de mer (Fr)   Seafood, usually shellfish.

Fry 1. Tiny fish, very young. 2. Pig's and lamb's offal.

Fumé (Fr) Smoked.

Fumet (Fr) Fish or vegetable stock reduced by heating uncovered, until thick and shiny.

Galantine (Fr) Boned poultry or meat cooked and pressed or moulded with aspic.

Galette (Fr) 1. Flat cake of sliced or mashed potato. 2. Traditional, flat, round puff or choux pastry cake.

Game chips Thin slices of potato fried until crisp.

Ganache paste (Fr) Melted chocolate and warm cream well mixed and cooled until firm. Used for decorations, fillings, and to make truffles.

Garam masala (Indian) Mixture of various ground spices used as a base for curries.

Garbure (Fr) Thick vegetable broth.

Garni, -e (Fr) Garnished with.

Gâteau (Fr) 1. Rich, elaborate sweet cake. 2. Round, square or oval shape of pâté, sliced meat, etc.

Gâteau Saint-Honoré (Fr) Cake made with short crust and choux pastry, filled with a pastry cream mixed with whisked egg whites.

Gelatine Setting agent made from animal bones, skin and tissues. See also page 37.

Genoese sponge Light, rich cake made with melted butter and eggs. Used as a base for desserts, for petits fours, etc.

Ghee (Indian) A form of clarified butter made from the milk of the water buffalo or goat.

Gherkin Small fruit from a plant of the cucumber family; gathered green, pickled and used as a condiment or garnish.

Giblets Neck, gizzard, liver and heart of poultry or game. Can also include head, pinions, feet and kidney.

Gigot (Fr, Scot) Whole leg of lamb.

Gizzard Small second stomach in birds and poultry. Part of the giblets.

Glacé (Fr) 1. Glazed. 2. Frozen or iced.

Glucose Sugar found in its natural form in honey, grapes and a few other fruits. Not very sweet. Available also as liquid and powder.

Gluten Substance in flour which gives it elasticity and strength.

Glycerine A syrup used as a sugar substitute in diabetic foods and in confectionery.

Gnocchi (It) Small dumplings made from semolina, maize, flour, choux pastry or potatoes.

Goujon, en (Fr) Small strips of deep-fried fish, eg plaice or sole.

Goulash (Hun) Thick soup or meat casserole often containing tomatoes and paprika.

Gram flour Flour made from chick-peas.

Granité (Fr) **Granita** (It) Water ice with a crystalline texture.

Gras, au (Fr) Served with a rich gravy or sauce.

Gratin, au (Fr) Dishes prepared with a sauce; usually sprinkled with breadcrumbs and/or grated cheese, baked in the oven or put under the grill until browned.

Grecque, à la (Fr) Greek style, ie vegetables such as courgettes and aubergines cooked in stock, olive oil and herbs.

Green bacon Unsmoked bacon.

Grenadins (Fr) Small fillets of veal or fowl, larded and braised.

Griddle, girdle Flat iron pan used for making scones, soda bread, etc.

Griskin 1. Backbone, spine or chine of pig cut away when preparing a side for bacon. 2. Shoulder of pork stripped of fat; top of the spare rib.

Grissini (It) Long sticks of hard-baked bread dough.

Groats Crushed hulled oat grains. Used generally to make porridge or gruel or for thickening broths, etc.

Guglhupf, Gugelhopf (Ger) Sweetened yeast cake with raisins, almonds and lemon rind, traditionally baked in a fluted dish of pottery or metal known as a guglhupf mould.

Gumbo (West Indian, Am) Okra; also okra soup or various dishes made with okra.

Halva (East Med) Sweet paste used as a sweetmeat, dessert or cake; made with almonds or sesame seeds, and sweetened with honey or syrup. Pale gold in colour.

Hard sauce Whipped butter sauce such as brandy or rum butter.

Haricot (Fr) 1. Bean. 2. Different dried white beans.

Haricot de mouton (Fr) Mutton stew. Often served with potatoes and turnips.

Haricots verts (Fr) Green or French beans.

Heatproof Surface or material which can withstand a minimum amount of indirect heat, but not a direct flame or a high temperature.

Homard (Fr) Lobster.

Hongroise, à la (Fr) Hungarian style, ie prepared with paprika and fresh or soured cream.

Horse mushroom Common edible fungus, larger and coarser than a field mushroom and with a stronger flavour.

Hough (Scot) Shin of beef boiled in stock.

Hummus (Mid East) Paste or dip consisting of pounded, cooked chick-peas flavoured with tahina, oil, garlic and lemon juice.

Impératrice, à la (Fr) Desserts with a rice base.

Impériale, à la (Fr) Dishes garnished with foie gras, truffles, kidneys, etc.

Indienne, à la (Fr) Indian style, ie usually curry flavoured.

Infusion Liquid in which herbs or other flavouring agents have been boiled, heated or steeped until their flavour has been absorbed.

Italienne, à la (Fr) Italian style, ie garnished with pasta, cooked or garnished with mushrooms and artichoke bases.

Jalopeño pepper (West Indian) Hot red chilli.

Jambalaya (West Indian) Rice dish made with pork, chicken or shellfish, vegetables, garlic and herbs.

Japonaise, à la (Fr) 1. Japanese style, ie garnished with croustades containing Japanese artichokes and croquette potatoes.

2. Bombe of peach ice cream and a mousse.

Jardinière, à la (Fr) 1. Garnished with mixed spring vegetables cut into small shapes or bâtons. 2. Vegetables stewed in their own juice.

Jugged dishes 1. Game cooked in a covered earthenware pot. The sauce or gravy can be thickened with the blood of the animal. 2. Kippers placed in a jug and covered with boiling water.

Julienne, à la (Fr) Vegetables cut into fine strips. Used as a garnish or added to consommé, etc.

Junket Milk with enough rennet added to set the milk to a soft curd. Flavouring and sweetening can be added.

Jus (Fr) Meat or fruit juice.

Jus, au (Fr) In its own juice, broth or gravy, seasoned, but without thickening.

Kale Type of cabbage with green curled leaves.

Kascha, kasha (Rus) Cooked buckwheat, semolina or rice.

Kebab, kebob, shish kebab (East Med) Cubes of meat or fish cooked on skewers.

Keffedes, Kephtethakia, keftethes (Gr) Meat balls.

Knödel (Ger, Aus) Light dumplings either sweet or savoury.

Köfta (Tur) Meat balls.

Kosher (Jewish) Food prepared according to Orthodox Jewish Law.

Kromeski, Cromesqui (Pol, Fr) Savoury croquette often wrapped in a pancake, bacon rasher, etc before being coated and deep fried.

Kulich (Rus, Eastern European) Easter cake made of yeasted dough, usually tall and cylindrical in shape.

Lait, au (Fr) With milk, or cooked in milk.

Laitance (Fr) Soft fish roe used for garnishing or as a savoury.

Langouste (Fr) Crawfish.

Langoustine (Fr) Dublin Bay prawn.

Larding bacon Fat bacon or pork cut from the belly or flank of the pig.

Lardoons Strips of larding fat or bacon threaded through lean meat, poultry and game with a larding needle.

Lasagne al forno (It) Flat broad sheets of pasta layered with a savoury mixture and sauce, and then baked.

Laver Edible seaweed.

Leaven Rising agent.

Légumes (Fr) 1. Vegetables. 2. Podded vegetables, eg peas, beans.

Leveret (Fr) A hare, up to 1 year old.

Liaison (Fr) Any thickening or binding agent for soups, sauces and stews, eg roux, batter, beurre manié, arrowroot, tapioca, egg or blood.

Liègoise, à la (Fr) Cooked with gin or juniper berries or garnished with juniper.

Lights, lites Lungs of certain animals.

Lockshen (Jewish) Vermicelli.

Lumpfish Large seafish. Its roe, either red or black, is an inexpensive alternative to caviar.

Lyonnaise, à la (Fr) Lyons style, ie fried, shredded onion usually added to the preparation.

Macédoine (Fr) Mixture of various kinds of vegetables or fruits cut into even-sized dice.

Mâche (Fr) Lamb's lettuce or corn salad.

Madère, au (Fr) Cooked or flavoured with Madeira wine.

Madrilène, à la (Fr) Madrid style, ie with tomato juice added.

Maison, à la (Fr) Cooked to a recipe of the house or restaurant.

Maître d'Hôtel, à la (Fr) Dishes usually plainly cooked and garnished with parsley, or accompanied with Maître d'Hôtel butter, or Maître d'Hôtel sauce.

Maltaise, à la (Fr) Maltese style. Usually indicates oranges have been used.

Mange tout Immature peas eaten with their pods. Sugar snaps are more substantial but similar vegetables.

Maple syrup (Am, Can) Natural syrup tapped from the trunks of maple trees. Used as a sweet flavouring for desserts, cakes, sweetmeats, etc, or as a syrup poured over pancakes.

Maraichère, à la (Fr) Large joints of roasted or braised meat garnished with salsify, Brussels sprouts and potatoes.

Marbling Flecks of fat in the best quality cuts of meat.

Maréchale, à la (Fr) Small cuts of meat and poultry dipped in egg and breadcrumbs, fried in butter, and garnished with truffles and asparagus tips.

Marinière, à la (Fr) Fisherman's style, ie with mussels.

Marmite (Fr) Large, deep, metal or earthenware casserole with close-fitting lid. Dishes cooked à la Marmite are usually slow cooking casseroles.

Marsala, au (Fr) Cooked in or with Marsala wine.

Masséna, à la (Fr) Tournedos, fillets and noisettes of lamb garnished with artichokes, filled with Béarnaise sauce and strips of poached beef marrow.

Matelote (Fr) Sailor's style, ie fish stew made with wine or cider.

Matzo (Jewish) Flat cake or biscuit made of unleavened wheat flour and water. Traditionally eaten at Passover festival.

Médaillons (Fr) Fillets, meat mixtures, etc, cut or shaped into a round form.

Melts Animal's spleen.

Meunière, à la (Fr) Fish lightly dusted with flour, fried in butter and sprinkled with parsley and lemon juice.

Mignon (Fr) 1. Thin end of the fillet of beef. 2. Small oval steak.

Milanaise, à la (Fr) 1. Milanese style, ie escalope or poultry traditionally garnished with strips of tongue, mushrooms and ham in a tomato sauce with spaghetti or macaroni. 2. Food dipped in egg and crumbs mixed with Parmesan cheese, then fried. 3. Sweet soufflé flavoured with lemon.

Mille feuille (Fr) Puff pastry cake, or small pastry made of layers of cooked puff pastry, whipped cream, raspberry or strawberry jam, and a glacé icing on the top.

Mimosa (Fr)   Garnish of sieved, hard-boiled egg yolks sprinkled over salads.

Minute, à la (Fr)   Quickly prepared dishes, usually meat, eg fillet steak, escalopes, which can be served with a variety of sauces.

Miroton (Fr)   Stew made from small thin slices of cooked meat, flavoured with onions.

Mocha (Fr)   Mixture of coffee and chocolate flavours in desserts, cakes, beverages, etc.

Mode, à la (Fr)   1. In the style of. 2. Basic braised large joint, eg beef, strictly cooked with calves' feet and onions. 3. (Am) Any sweet dish with ice cream.

Mollusc   Edible shellfish, both univalve and bivalve. The snail, too, is a mollusc.

Montmorency (Fr)   1. Type of cherry. 2. Flavoured with cherries. 3. Vegetable garnish for noisettes or tournados.

Mornay (Fr)   With a cheese sauce.

Moussaka (Gr)   Minced meat, tomatoes, aubergines (sometimes potatoes) layered with a cheese sauce or savoury egg custard.

Mousse (Fr)   Light sweet or savoury cold dish with a base of whipped cream and, sometimes, egg whites.

Must   The name given to any liquid about to be converted into wine.

Nantua, à la (Fr)   Sauce or garnish using crayfish tails.

Napolitaine, à la (Fr)   1. Neapolitan style. 2. Spaghetti bound with tomato sauce, butter, cheese, and roughly chopped tomatoes. 3. Ice cream and sweet cake layered in 3 different colours and flavours; pink, green and white.

Naturel, au (Fr)   Uncooked or plainly cooked food which is served simply.

Navarin (Fr)   Mutton or lamb stew.

Nibbed   Finely chopped nuts, especially almonds.

Niçoise (Fr)   1. In the style of Nice, ie cooked with tomatoes, garlic and oil. 2. Salad of beans, tomatoes, tuna, lettuce, hard-boiled eggs, black olives and anchovy fillets.

Noisettes (Fr)   1. Pommes noisettes. Potatoes scooped out with a melon scoop and browned in butter. 2. Neatly trimmed round or oval shapes of boneless lamb or beef.

Noix (Fr)   1. Nut. 2. Walnut. 3. Cushion of veal.

Normande, à la (Fr)   1. With apples or apple flavour. Refers to dishes often cooked with cider or Calvados. 2. Cooked with cream. 3. Shellfish garnish.

Norway lobster   Dublin Bay prawn.

Nougatines (Fr)   Small cakes of Genoese sponge layered with praline cream and iced with chocolate fondant.

Noyau (Fr)   1. Nut or kernel. 2. Liqueur made from the stones of fruits, also Noyeau.

One-stage method   see *All-in-one*.

Orange flower water   Liquid flavouring distilled from the oil of orange flowers.

Oven brick   Terracotta container of various sizes and shapes that completely encases fish, game or poultry to seal in flavours and juices while baking.

Ovenproof   Cooking utensils which can withstand oven heat but not direct heat as on a hob.

Paella (Sp)   Dish of saffron or plain rice with chicken and shellfish; named after the flat dish with handles in which it is cooked.

Pailles (Fr)   Fried potato or cheese straws.

Pain d'épice (Fr)   Spiced gingerbread made with honey and rye flour.

Palmiers (Fr)   Small or large pastries made from a sheet of puff pastry sprinkled with sugar; each side is rolled up towards the centre and then the whole is cut into slices and baked.

Panada   Thick mixture made of flour, butter, seasonings and milk, stock or water. Used for binding meat, poultry or fish.

Pannequet (Fr)   Sweet or savoury pancake folded into a 'packet' round a filling.

Papillote, en (Fr)   Food wrapped, cooked and served in greased paper or foil.

Parfait (Fr)   Chilled or frozen dessert made with egg white and fruit purée or other flavourings.

Parma ham   see *Prosciutto*.

Parmentier, à la (Fr) With potatoes.

Parson's Nose Extreme end portion of the carcass of a bird.

Pasty Boat-shaped filled pastry case, or a double crust patty.

Pâté (Fr) 1. Cold meat pie or pasty. 2. A cooked meat paste generally made of pork, chicken, game or offal coarsely or finely ground.

Pâte (Fr) General term for sweet and savoury pastry, eg pâte sucrée.

Pâtisserie (Fr) **Pasticceria** (It) 1. Fancy cakes and pastries. 2. Shop selling these items.

Patty 1. Small, double crust pie. 2. Puff or flaky pastry case with a recessed centre for savoury or sweet fillings. 3. Small shaped cake of food, eg hamburger.

Paupiettes (Fr) Thin slices of meat rolled around a savoury filling and served with a sauce.

Paysanne, à la (Fr) Garnish of bacon and buttered vegetables.

Pectin Gum-like substance in certain fruits and vegetables which acts as a natural setting agent. Also available commercially in bottles.

Peperonata (It) Cooked vegetable dish of peppers, onions, tomatoes and seasoning. Served as a garnish, on its own as a starter or as a filling.

Pérsillade, à la (Fr) Garnished with chopped parsley to which a little crushed garlic is sometimes added.

Pesto (It) Cold sauce made with basil, garlic, pine kernels and Parmesan cheese.

Petits pois (Fr) Small, tender, young peas.

Phyllo pastry see *Filo*.

Pikelet Yeasted variation of a crumpet or pancake cooked without rings on a griddle.

Pilaff, pilau (East Med, Indian) Rice cooked in the Eastern manner, usually a savoury dish to which meat, fish or vegetables are added.

Pinion 1.Tip of a bird's wing. 2. Bone in the fin of a fish.

Pissaladière (Fr) Flan containing anchovies, olives and onion; a speciality of Nice.

Pistou (Fr) 1. Soup of vegetables, vermicelli, garlic, tomatoes, olive oil and basil. 2. A variation of pesto, served with soup.

Pita, Pitta (Mid East and Yugoslavia) Flat disc-shaped bread which rises when baked to create a pocket in the centre.

Pith White lining in the rind of citrus fruits.

Pizza (It) Round of yeast dough on which a variety of fillings may be spread and baked.

Pizzaiola, alla (It) Meat or chicken cooked in a tomato and red wine sauce flavoured with garlic.

Plombière (Fr) Rich ice cream mixture with almonds or chestnuts and cream, either frozen in a single mould or formed into a pyramid and topped with a sweet sauce. It may also be flavoured with fruit.

Pluck Lungs, heart, liver and sometimes entrails, of a slaughtered animal.

Poivrade, au poivre (Fr) 1. With pepper, generally either freshly ground black pepper or green peppercorns. 2. Meat or game served with a Poivrade sauce, eg foundation brown or Espagnole sauce with added shallots, herbs, red wine, vinegar and pepper.

Pommes de terre (Fr) Potatoes.

Portugaise, à la (Fr) Portuguese style; usually indicates that tomatoes, onions and olive oil are included.

Poussin (Fr) Baby chicken.

Praline (Fr) Nut and sugar mixture, usually crushed and used as a flavouring or decoration. Can also be a caramel covered almond sweatmeat.

Presunto (Port) Cooked ham which is highly cured.

Printanière, à la (Fr) Spring style, ie with a garnish of spring vegetables.

Profiteroles (Fr) Small balls of choux pastry filled with various sweet creams, Chantilly, confectioners' custard, or savoury fillings. If sweet, can be glazed and covered with a chocolate sauce.

Prosciutto (It) Parma ham, ie raw smoked ham served thinly sliced.

Provençale, à la (Fr) Provençal style, ie generally garlic, onions, tomatoes, olive oil, red and green peppers, etc.

Ptarmigan Game bird of the grouse family which has white feathers in the winter and brown feathers in the spring.

Pudding cloth Scalded cloth, which is floured and used for wrapping suet pudding before boiling or steaming.

Pulled sugar Boiled sugar mixture which has been manipulated with oiled hands and palette knives.

Pumpernickel (Ger) Dark yeasted rye bread.

Purée (Fr) Smooth pulp of fruit or vegetables; occasionally of meat or fish.

Puris (Indian) Deep-fried unleavened wholemeal bread.

Putu, mealie meal (Central Afr) Type of cornmeal porridge.

Quark (Ger) Bland low-fat soft cheese resembling *fromage frais*.

Quenelles (Fr) Smooth light oval-shaped dumplings of fish, poultry, game, meat or vegetables. Served as a garnish or as a main course.

Quiche (Fr) Open pastry flan filled with a savoury egg custard and other solid additions, eg vegetables, meats.

Ragoût (Fr) Well-seasoned, slowly cooked stew of meat and vegetables.

Raised pie Moulded hot water crust pastry enclosing a meat or game filling.

Raita (Indian) Vegetables, especially cucumber, in yogurt.

Ramekin Small, round ovenproof dish.

Rascasse Fish found in Mediterranean waters; essential part of authentic bouillabaisse.

Raspings Bread or crusts dried and browned in a moderate oven, and crushed or rolled to make fine breadcrumbs for coating purposes.

Ratafia 1. Small biscuit made with almond flavouring. Used as a base for trifle. 2. Almond extract flavouring. 3. Liqueur made by infusing fruit kernels, eg peach, almond, in spirit.

Ratatouille (Fr) Vegetable stew made with aubergines, onions, tomatoes, peppers, courgettes. Can be eaten hot or cold.

Reform Sauce based on Poivrade sauce, with port, gherkins, tongue, mushrooms and hard-boiled egg white.

Relish Vinegar-based pickle or sauce.

Rennet Enzyme from the stomach of a calf. Used as a coagulant for junket and cheese.

Rice paper Made from pith of Chinese tree. Used for macaroon and other similar bases.

Ricotta (It) Soft whey cheese.

Rillettes (Fr) Pounded pork, rabbit, etc, sealed with pork fat; similar to pâté.

Rind Thin layer of skin of some fruits, vegetables and pork. Also outer layer on cheeses.

Risotto (It) Savoury rice dish in which the rice is fried, then cooked in stock; meat, poultry or fish is sometimes added.

Romaine, à la (Fr) 1. Garnish of gnocchi browned with Parmesan cheese. 2. Mould of chicken or spinach.

Rossini, à la (Fr) Garnished strictly with foie gras and truffles.

Rôtisserie (Fr) Rotating spit used for grilling or roasting meat, poultry or game.

Roulade (Fr) 1. Rolled meat, veal or pork. 2. Galantine of veal or pork. 3. Baked soufflé mixture rolled up like a Swiss roll.

Roux (Fr) Equal quantities of fat and flour cooked together. There are 3 kinds – white, blond and brown, depending upon the length of time of the preliminary cooking. A roux is used to thicken soups and sauces, and as an alternative to beurre manié.

Rubané (Fr) Ribbon-like or layered.

Ryjsttavel, rijsstafel (Dutch-Indon) 30–40 side dishes consisting of meat, fish and vegetables, sometimes curried. Served with a large bowl of rice and a variety of sweet and sour relishes and sauces.

Sabayon (Fr) 1. Hot or cold sweet egg sauce with alcohol flavouring; served with desserts. 2. French version of Italian zabaglione dessert made with white wine.

Saccharometer Sugar boiling thermometer.

Sago Thickening agent derived from the sago palm tree. Also made into a hot pudding.

Saignant (Fr) Very rare or underdone meat, especially steak.

Saint-Germain (Fr) 1. Thick pea soup. 2. Garnished with peas.

Salamander Metal utensil which, when heated until red-hot, is used to brown the tops of puddings.

Salame, salami (It) Beef and pork sausage which is spiced, salted, and smoked or air dried.

Salmi, salmis (Fr) Casserole made from game or poultry in which the birds have usually been partially roasted.

Salpicon (Fr) Vegetables, poultry or game finely cubed or diced, and bound together with a white or brown sauce.

Saltpetre Potassium nitrate. Used for curing and preserving meats.

Sanieh (Mid East) A large shallow pan used for cooking.

Saté, sates, sateh (Dutch-Indon) Highly seasoned, small pieces of meat, poultry or fish marinated and roasted on a skewer. Served hot with a sweet-sour sauce containing peanuts or peanut oil.

Sauerkraut (Ger) Pickled shredded white cabbage.

Savarin (Fr) Light yeasted cake made in a ring mould. It is usually soaked in a rum syrup, or the centre is filled with fruit, fruit purée or a flavoured whipped cream.

Savoy cake or finger Small, bar-shaped sponge cake.

Scallop Bivalve mollusc with white flesh and orange coral or roe.

Scallopine (It) Small escalopes of meat, generally served with a sauce.

Schnitzel (Ger) A thin slice of veal. See also *Escalope*.

Scone Quick bread made from a variety of flours, a small proportion of fat to flour, and fresh milk, soured milk or buttermilk. Cheese,

nuts, currants, potatoes, treacle, etc can be added. Usually round or wedge shaped.

Seasoned flour Flour flavoured with salt and pepper, and occasionally other spices.

Sediment Solid residue left in the bottom of the pan after roasting meat or poultry.

Shashlik, Shashlek, Shashlyk (Rus) Marinated lamb or mutton grilled on skewers.

Sippets Pieces of toast cut into 'fingers', triangles and other shapes. Used as a garnish.

Skillet Frying pan, especially in the U.S.A.

Slack consistency Mixture which falls off the spoon almost of its own accord.

Smetana (Rus) Soured cream.

Smörgasbord (Swed) Literally means sandwich table, but is actually a large display of small hot and cold dishes.

Smørrebrød (Danish) Open sandwiches.

Sodium metabisulphite Campden tablet. Used to make sterilizing solution.

Soubise (Fr) 1. With onions. 2. Sauce based on a Béchamel sauce made with onions, butter and nutmeg.

Spätzli (Ger) Small noodles.

Spring chicken Young chicken, 2–4 months old.

Springform mould Baking tin with hinged sides held together by a metal clamp or pin. Has a loose base.

Sprue Thin stalks of asparagus.

Spurtle (Scot) Wooden stick used for stirring porridge.

Squab Young pigeon.

Stollen (Ger) Traditional Christmas and holiday yeasted bread with dried fruits.

Strudel (Aus) Thin leaves of pastry dough rolled around a sweet or savoury mixture.

Sugar nibs Small pointed crystals of sugar.

Sugar snap see *Mange tout*.

Sulphur dioxide see *Campden tablet*.

Sundae (Am) Ice cream combined with fruit or other flavourings, nuts, crumbs, etc.

Suprême (Fr) 1. Boned wing and breast of a bird; or choicest pieces of fish, veal, etc. 2. Sauce or liaison of cream and egg.

Syllabub Cold dessert of sweetened thick cream with alcohol and other flavourings.

Szechwan (Chinese) 1. Method of cookery practised in the province of Szechwan. 2. Very hot peppercorn.

Tahina (Mid East) Sesame seeds pounded to a paste.

Tamarind (Asian, West Indian) Leaves, flowers and fruit pods of the tamarind tree. Pod used for making curries, relishes, chutney, etc.

Tarte (Fr) see *Tourte*.

Terrine (Fr) 1. Earthenware dish in which pâtés are cooked. 2. Strictly a cold pâté, but now generally interchangeable with all types of pâtés.

Timbale (Fr) 1. Rounded cup-shaped, plain or fluted mould in earthenware or metal. 2. Any of the many dishes prepared in such a mould. Can be sweet or savoury.

Tisane (Fr) Medicinal drink prepared by soaking or infusing herbs or flowers.

Torte (Ger, Am) A flan or an elaborate gâteau.

Tortilla (Mex) 1. Thin pancake made from cornmeal. 2. (Sp) Flat omelette which can have a variety of meats or vegetables mixed in with the eggs.

Tourte (Fr) Round savoury or sweet tart. A sweet tourte is also called a tarte.

Trail Intestines of small game birds.

Trivet 1. Metal tripod, bracket or rack used for supporting utensils or food above the heat. 2. Raised, perforated plate fitted into the base of a pressure cooker.

Tronçon (Fr) Slice of flat fish, with the bone.

Truffle 1. Edible fungus. 2. Chocolate sweetmeat.

Turban (Fr) 1. Food arranged on a dish in a circle. 2. Forcemeats of poultry, game, etc cooked in a border mould.

Tutti frutti (It) 1. Mixture of fruits, generally candied or crystallized. 2. Vanilla ice cream mixed with such fruits.

TVP (Textured Vegetable Protein, TSP) Commercially prepared protein substance made of soya beans (soybean) or wheat. Can be flavoured to taste like various meats or fish.

Univalves Shellfish which live in a single shell, eg whelks, winkles.

Unleavened bread Bread made without a raising agent.

Vacherin (Fr, Swiss) 1. Full flavoured soft cheese. 2. Layered cake made with circles of meringue, cream, fresh fruit or chestnut purée.

Vanilla sugar Sugar flavoured by being stored with a vanilla pod.

Vegetable extract Product obtained by evaporating vegetable juice. Commercial preparations may have yeast added.

Vegetable parchment Product similar to greaseproof paper but with non-stick properties. Used for lining baking tins, etc.

Velouté (Fr) Basic French sauce, with a rich fawn colour, usually made with fish or chicken stock.

Venison Deer or buck meat.

Véronique, à la (Fr) Garnished with white grapes.

Viennoise, à la (Fr) Viennese style, ie garnished with anchovy fillets, olives, capers and chopped hard-boiled eggs.

Vinaigrette, à la (Fr) Oil and vinegar based dressing, generally used for vegetables.

Vol-au-vent (Fr) Round or oval puff pastry case. Usually filled with small pieces of meat, game, fish or vegetables in a creamy sauce.

Waterbath see *Bain-marie*.

Whey Liquid left after draining coagulated milk.

Whey butter Butter manufactured from the fat solids in whey.

Wishbone A 'Y' shaped bone between the neck and breast of a chicken or turkey.

Wok (Chinese) Round-bottomed pan with gently sloping sides. Used over a spirit lamp or burner with a trivet. Excellent for stir frying finely sliced food.

Yeast In cookery, a raising agent, and an agent of fermentation in brewery and wine making. See also page 41.

Yeast extract Derived from fresh brewer's yeast through a process in which the soluble and insoluble materials are separated and the liquid is reduced to a sticky brown substance which is rich in B group vitamins.

Zabaglione, Zabaione (It) Dessert made from whipped egg yolks, sugar and Marsala wine. Usually served warm.

Zéphire (Fr) Light preparation.

Zest Outer rind of citrus fruits which contains the flavoured oils from the skin. Obtained by rubbing a sugar lump against the rind, or by using an implement known as a zester.

Zucchini (It, Am) Courgette.

Zuppe Inglese (It) Sweet dish similar to an English trifle.

THE MENU

GENERAL

A la carte (Fr) **Alla carta** (It) List of the available dishes on the menu; each dish is individually priced.

Carte du jour (Fr) **Carta del giorno** (It) Menu of the day. This may change daily or periodically.

Menu à prix fixe (Fr) Fixed-price set meal.

Plat du jour (Fr) **Piatti del giorno** (It) Dish or dishes of the day.

Table d'hôte (Fr) **Menu del giorno** (It) 1. Set meal of two or more courses offered at a fixed price. 2. Selection of dishes from the à la carte menu offered at a slightly cheaper price.

Diners fixes au choix (Fr) **Menu a prezzo fisso** (It) When a choice of alternative dishes is offered for one or more courses in a table d'hôte menu, this term may replace or follow the heading: table d'hôte.

Carte du vin (It) **Lista dei vini** (It) List of all wines available at the restaurant.

COURSES

Hors d'oeuvre (Fr) **Zakuski** (Rus) **Antipasti** (It) Light hot or cold dishes, served as a starter.

Mezze (It) 2. Assorted small hot or cold dishes. Sometimes chosen as an alternative to the above or to soup. Normally referred to as *hors d'oeuvre variés*.

Potage (Fr) **Minestre** (It) Soup. 1. May be alternative choice to the above. 2. In a formal dinner, the second course, ie coming after the hors d'oeuvre.

Farineuses (Fr) **Farinacei** (It) Pasta dishes. 1. An alternative to hors d'oeuvre. 2. Main course.

Oeufs (Fr) **Uova** (It) Egg dishes. Offered in some restaurants as a light main-course dish.

Poissons (Fr) **Pesci** (It) Fish dishes. 1. Main course alternative to meat. 2. Course before the meat. 3. In a formal dinner, the third course, ie coming after the soup.

Entrée (Fr) **Pietanze** (It) 1. Main course. 2. In a formal dinner, light dishes served after the fish and before the solid meat course. May consist of eggs, pasta, or very light meat or fish dishes such as quenelles.

Relevé (Fr) In a formal dinner, the main meat or poultry dish, served after the entrée; almost obsolete.

Rôti (Fr) **Arrosti** (It) Roasts. 1. Often used as a heading to distinguish from grillades and other meat courses. 2. When occasionally two meat courses are served in a formal dinner, the relevé consists of butcher's meat, the rôti of poultry or game.

Grillades (Fr) **Grigliati** (It) Steaks and any other items from the grill.

Buffet froid (Fr) **Piatti Freddi** (It) Choice of cold cooked meat and fish, usually served with salads.

Légumes (Fr) **Legumi** (It) Vegetables served with an entrée, rôti, grillade or relevé.

Salades (Fr) **Insalata** (It) Salad. 1. Main course. 2. An alternative or addition to hot vegetables. 3. In a formal dinner, part of the buffet or eaten after the roast or other main course.

Sorbet (Fr) **Sorbetto** (It)   Half-frozen water ice often with liqueur. 1. Served in the middle of a formal dinner to refresh the palate. 2. Served as a dessert on an à la carte menu.

Entremets (Fr)   French term originally used to indicate sweet and savoury dishes; now generally refers to all sweet dishes, hot or cold.

Tramessi (It)   Italian term equating to original French term, entremets. *Dolci* generally used nowadays.

Desserts (Fr)   Last course of a meal; can consist either of sweet desserts, cheese and/or fruit.

Glacés (Fr) **Gelati** (It)   Iced and frozen desserts.

Fromages (Fr) **Fromaggi** (It)   Cheese(s) available.

Café (Fr) **Caffé** (It)   Coffee.

Friandises (Fr) **Frivolezze** (It)   Sometimes called Petits Fours (Fr) or Lecornie (It). Very small sweetmeats, biscuits, etc, served with coffee.

COOKERY TECHNIQUES

Many of the cookery techniques listed here are explored in greater detail in the appropriate chapters of the book.

Bake   To cook by dry heat in the oven.

Bake blind   To bake pastry cases either partially or completely before a particular filling or preparation is added. The dough is rolled out, placed in a tin, pressed well into the sides, and trimmed. The base is pricked with a fork and lined with greaseproof paper, cut slightly larger than the pastry case. The case is filled with ceramic 'beans', dried beans, bread crusts or rice to prevent the pastry rising. For both partially and fully cooked cases the paper and weights are removed at the end of the cooking time, and the case returned to the oven for 5-7 minutes to dry out the inside.

Bard   To cover delicate parts of lean meat, poultry or game with thin rashers of bacon, held in place with string, and removed before serving. When cooking birds, barding keeps the breast moist, and protects it while other parts of the bird, such as the legs, require further cooking.

Baste   To pour, spoon or brush melted fat, pan juices, milk or other liquids over meat, poultry or game while cooking to keep in moisture.

Bat   To beat out a thick slice of meat into a larger, thinner slice, tenderizing the meat in the process. The slice is usually placed between two thicknesses of greaseproof or waxed paper, and beaten from the centre outwards on both sides with a cutlet bat or rolling-pin.

Beat   To turn over a cake mixture, egg or batter with firm, quick strokes of a spoon, fork or wooden spoon, lifting the mixture a little with each stroke to incorporate air in order to make the food lighter or more liquid. An electric mixer or food processor can also be used.

Bind   To add moist ingredients, eg cream, egg, melted fat, a sauce or panada, to dry, eg breadcrumbs, stuffings, forcemeats, etc, in such proportions that the dry ingredients are held together.

Blanch   1. To place food in a saucepan of cold water, bring to the boil, then strain off the water. 2. To pour boiling water over the food. Both methods are used to preserve the colour of certain foods, to remove strong, undesirable flavours, or to loosen the skin of nuts before skinning. Blanching also halts enzyme activity prior to freezing.

Blend   To mix evenly one ingredient with another, using a spoon or electric blender.

Braise   To cook vegetables alone or with meat, poultry, fish or game, by first browning the vegetables and meat in hot fat. The vegetables are then put in a heavy-bottomed saucepan or ovenproof casserole and the meat placed on top. A little stock or water is added, the pan covered, and the food simmered over low heat or in a warm oven until tender.

Brand To burn the surface of a finished dish, such as a steak or omelette, with a hot skewer, or to place on a red-hot grill so that the food is seared at points of contact.

Broil (Am) To grill or spit roast.

Brown 1. To seal in the juices of meat or fish by searing the surface. 2. To finish cooking a dish by letting its outer surface cook uncovered under a grill or in a hot oven, until it becomes brown.

Bruise To beat with a weight or heavy object in order to release flavour, as when using root ginger.

Caramelize 1. To heat sugar and water until the mixture turns a rich golden colour. 2. To coat a mould with sugar and water heated to caramel point.

Carve To cut up meat, poultry or other food for serving.

Casserole To cook meat, game, poultry, fish and/or vegetables slowly, generally with stock or other liquid added, in a covered pan, either over heat or in the oven.

Chill To cool food, preferably in a refrigerator, until it is thoroughly cold, but not frozen.

Chine To sever the backbone from the ribs of joints such as loin or best end of neck of lamb, before cooking, so that the joint can be divided easily into chops or cutlets when carving.

Chip To cut potatoes or root vegetables into sticks.

Chop To divide food into very small pieces. On a board, slice or cut the food up roughly. Use a heavy knife with a very sharp blade and keep one hand on the top of the knife blade, near the point, and the other hand on the handle. Cut the food into small pieces with sharp up and down movements.

Clarify 1. To remove the impurities from fat used for frying or roasting. Heat an equal quantity of fat and cold water in a large pan until the water begins to boil. Simmer for about 5 minutes, then strain into a bowl and leave the fat to solidify. Remove in one piece, dry, and scrape any sediment off the bottom. Heat the fat gently until bubbling ceases to drive off any water. 2. Butter and margarine can be clarified to remove any milk solids, salt and water by heating gently until melted. The water is expelled when the fat ceases to bubble. Remove from the heat and strain the fat into a bowl through a fine sieve or muslin, which catches the salt; or skim off any scum that has risen to the top. Leave for a few minutes, then pour off the clear or clarified fat into a clean container, leaving the sediment behind.

Clear 1. To remove impurities and opaque matter from stocks, consommés or jellies. Add beaten egg white and crushed shell to the liquid, and bring it to the boil without stirring. When cooked, the egg white rises to the top of the liquid, taking with it the unwanted particles, which are then strained off. 2. Jelly preserves are cleared by pouring the fruit juice through a jelly bag, felt or flannel cloth which has been scalded first with boiling water. The juice is allowed to drip for 45 minutes–1 hour.

Coat 1. To cover fish fillets, slices of liver, cubes of meat, slices of fruit, etc, completely in flour, egg and breadcrumbs or batter. This is most frequently done before frying. The coating protects the food, and keeps in all the juices and flavour during cooking. 2. To cover food with a sauce or icing before serving.

Core 1. To remove the core from fruit such as apples, pears, pineapples, etc, usually leaving the fruit in one piece. Use an apple corer, or a long, narrow, sharp knife. Place the fruit upright on a board, and push the corer or knife through the fruit, then twist, and remove the core. 2. To snip out the cores in kidneys.

Cream 1. To beat to a creamy consistency. 2. To mix fat and sugar by beating until the mixture is light, fluffy and pale in colour.

Crimp To decorate the edge of a tart or pie by pressing the layers of pastry together and pinching with the thumb and first finger of both hands, then twisting in opposite directions.

Crumb To crumble bread for fresh or soft breadcrumbs. Remove the crusts from white bread which is at least 1 day old, and either grate the bread on a grater, rub it through a wire sieve or between the palms of the hand, or process in a blender or food processor. Soft crumbs can be stored in a sealed container for 2–3 days in a refrigerator or up to 3 months in a freezer.

Cube To cut food into evenly sized, cube-shaped pieces. Small cubes, up to 1 cm ($\frac{1}{2}$ inch) across, are referred to as dice.

Deep fry To fry food, generally coated with batter or egg and breadcrumbs, by immersing in deep hot fat or oil.

De-seed To remove the seeds or pips from food such as peppers, tomatoes or marrows. Cut the tomatoes and marrows in half, and scoop out the seeds with a spoon. If the vegetable is required whole, eg stuffed peppers, cut around the stem end only, and lift this out, then scoop out any remaining membranes and seeds.

Devil To spread food, usually fish or meat, either with hot, dry seasonings, or with a strongly flavoured sauce, before grilling or frying.

Dice see *Cube*.

Dot To place small pieces or knobs of butter or fat over the surface of food before cooking, to prevent it from drying up.

Drain To remove surplus liquid or fat from food by pouring the food into a colander or sieve placed over a bowl, or by lifting small quantities of food out of the liquid on a perforated spoon and placing it on absorbent kitchen paper.

Draw To remove the head, neck, feet and viscera from poultry and game.

Dredge To sprinkle food with flour or sugar so that it is evenly coated.

Dress 1. To pluck, draw and truss poultry or game. 2. To arrange cooked shellfish in the shell. 3. To add an oil-based dressing to a salad. 4. To decorate food with a garnish. 5. To blanch tripe.

Dust To distribute flour, sugar or other finely ground ingredients very sparingly, eg sifting icing sugar lightly over a cake, or flour over a greased tin.

Fillet To remove whole pieces of flesh from the main carcass of meat, poultry or fish.

Flake 1. To break up cooked fish or shellfish into pieces with a fork. 2. To cut fat into thin silvers. 3. To mark pastry edges with horizontal lines, using a knife blade.

Flame 1. To ignite alcohol poured over food during or after cooking. This burns off some of the excess fat and drives off the alcohol content, leaving only the essential flavour of the spirit or liqueur used. Dishes prepared in this way are described as *flambéed*. 2. To singe poultry or game before cooking, to burn off small hairs.

Flute To decorate the edges of a pastry pie by pressing the thumb on the top outer edge, and drawing the pastry about 1 cm ($\frac{1}{2}$ inch) towards the centre of the pie with the back of a knife, repeating the process of intervals of 2 cm ($\frac{3}{4}$ inch) for savoury pies and 5 mm ($\frac{1}{4}$ inch) for sweet pies.

Fold in To combine an aerated ingredient with other ingredients, so that the entrapped air is retained, as when combining sifted flour with other ingredients, or combining two whisked mixtures. Gently sift or pile the ingredient to be folded in on top of the other ingredient. If folding in whisked egg whites, first stir up to a quarter of the foam into the main mixture to lighten it. Cut down through the centre of the mixture with a metal spoon, and round half the bowl, then spoon up half the mixture and lay it lightly on the other half, thus trapping the added ingredient between two layers of the main mixture. Turn the bowl and repeat until the ingredient has been folded in.

Frick To spread glacé icing or an icing sugar glaze over another icing of contrasting colour or flavour so that the top coating trickles down over the edges of a cake revealing the base icing underneath.

Frothing To dredge meat or poultry with flour and baste it with cooking juices or fat shortly before the end of cooking time, before returning it to the oven at a high heat until it appears brown and glazed.

Fry To cook in hot fat or oil.

Glaze To brush or coat food with beaten egg, egg white, milk, sugar syrup, sweet or aspic jellies, or meat glaze, to give it a glossy surface.

Grate To reduce food to coarse or fine shreds, crumbs or powder, by rubbing them against a grater, or by using a food processor fitted with a grating plate. The food to be grated should be firm, and the correct sized grater or grating plate used. Apples and onions should be grated coarsely, otherwise they produce more liquid than pulp. Hard cheese can be grated coarsely for cooking, or finely for a garnish. Nutmegs are grated finely on a small grater kept for the purpose.

Grill To cook food over or under direct, dry heat.

Grind 1. To reduce hard foods to granules or powder by working in a mortar with a pestle, or by processing in an electric blender, food processor, mill or grinder. 2. (Am) To mince.

Gut To remove the entrails from a fish and clean it before cooking.

Hang To suspend meat, poultry and game in a cool, airy place, which tenderizes the meat and gives it the characteristic gamey flavour.

Hull To pluck or twist off the calyx and stalk from soft berry fruits.

Ignite To set fire to brandy, sherry or liqueur, previously warmed in a chafing-dish, saucepan or ladle, before or after pouring it over crêpes, Christmas pudding, etc. (See also *Flame*.)

Infuse To pour boiling liquid over herbs, spices, vegetables, tea or coffee, allowing the liquid to draw off and absorb the flavour. Alternatively, the ingredients can be brought to the boil with a liquid, eg water, milk, sugar syrup, alcohol or fruit juices, then removed from the heat and allowed to stand in a warm place.

Joint To divide poultry, game, or small animals such as rabbit, into suitable pieces for serving by severing the cartilage between the joints.

Knead To press and stretch dough with the heel of the hand or an electric dough hook, until it is smooth and elastic.

Knock back To knead yeast dough after the first rising, in order to knock out the air bubbles and ensure an even texture. (See also *Prove*.)

Knock up To make a raised edge to double crust pastry pies or tarts by lifting up the sealed pastry edges with the back of a knife blade, before baking.

Lard To thread long, thin strips of pork fat or lardoons into game or very lean meat, to prevent them drying up during roasting.

Liquidize To reduce moist foods to a smooth liquid in an electric blender.

Macerate To soften food by soaking it in a liquid. Lentils and other dried pulses are macerated in water or stock to soften before cooking. Dried fruits are macerated in water, fruit juice, wine or liqueur, then cooked if required.

Marinate To steep meat or fish in a mixture usually containing oil, acid in the form of vinegar, lemon juice or wine, and herbs and spices, to tenderize and improve the flavour of the food, before or instead of cooking.

Mash To reduce food to a smooth consistency with a fork or an instrument called a masher.

Mask 1. To cover food with a thin layer of jelly, glaze, sauce or icing. 2. To coat the inside of a mould with jelly.

Mince To reduce foods to pieces by passing them through a mincing machine. Both electric and hand-operated machines have different sized blades to mince food finely or coarsely.

Parboil To cook food partially by boiling for only part of the usual time. The cooking is then often completed by another method, eg frying.

Pare To remove the thin outer layer of skin from vegetables or fruit with a sharp knife.

Peel To remove the outer layer of shell or skin (and sometimes pith) from shrimps, vegetables, fruit, etc.

Pick over To discard any damaged fruit.

Pipe To force soft foods through a forcing bag and nozzle to make a particular shape.

Pit To remove stones from fruits and vegetables.

Pluck To remove the feathers from poultry and game birds.

Poach To cook food gently in liquid which is kept just below boiling point. The liquid should be moving gently, but not bubbling.

Polish To give a shine to food, such as apples for dessert, by rubbing gently with a soft cloth.

Pot roast To cook a smaller, less tender joint of meat by first browning it in hot fat, then placing it on a wire rack or a bed of root vegetables in a heavy-bottomed pan. Cover with a tight-fitting lid and slowly cook either over low heat or in a warm oven.

Prove To leave a yeast dough to rise for a second time after it has been knocked back and shaped ready for baking. (See also *Knock Back*.)

Purée To reduce raw or cooked food to a smooth pulp by pounding, sieving, or processing in an electric blender or food processor.

Reduce To evaporate surplus liquid, usually from soups, sauces and syrups, by fast boiling in an uncovered pan, to obtain a concentrated, well-flavoured, final mixture.

Refresh To rinse vegetables in cold water after blanching, to preserve their colour.

Render To extract fat from bacon rinds or small fatty meat trimmings, by heating gently either in the oven or over low heat, until the fat runs and the pieces of skin, etc are crisp. Strain through a fine metal strainer into a clean basin, pressing the crisp pieces against the strainer to extract all the fat.

Roast To cook food by dry heat, either in an oven or over or under dry heat, generally using a small amount of fat and usually with frequent basting.

Roll out To flatten pastry or dough smoothly with a cylindrical object. The process prepares the dough for cutting into shapes, for lining a mould or baking tin, or for covering a pie.

Roll up To turn in one end of a strip or other piece of food, and continue rolling to make a cylindrical shape, as for a Swiss Roll.

Rub in To combine fat and flour for short crust pastry, plain cakes, etc. First cut the fat into small pieces with a knife, then, using the tips of the fingers, rub the fat into the flour, lifting the hands up from the bowl so that as the flour falls back into the bowl the mixture becomes aerated. When all the lumps of fat have been worked in, the mixture should resemble breadcrumbs.

Sauter (Sauté) To fry food rapidly in shallow fat, turning or shaking it all the time to prevent burning.

Scald 1. To dip vegetables or fruit into boiling water, usually to make it easier to remove the skins. 2. To heat milk or cream to near boiling point. 3. To clean a pan or other utensil thoroughly with boiling water.

Scallop see *Flute*.

Score To make cuts in the surface of food, eg the skin on pork joints before roasting, to facilitate carving, and to make the outside skin crisper.

Scrape To shave away the top layer of a vegetable, eg carrot, without actually peeling it, using a sharp knife drawn quickly across the surface.

Seal or Sear To brown the surface of meat, poultry, game or fish in hot fat or in a hot oven to keep in the juices during cooking.

Season To add salt, pepper and other flavourings to food, if recipe requires, to bring out the flavour.

Shallow fry To fry food in a small amount of fat or in no fat at all.

Shield To protect sensitive areas of food from cooking too quickly, usually by wrapping or covering them. Largely used in microwave cookery, when small strips of foil are used, provided that this is permitted for the appliance.

Shred To reduce vegetables, fruit or fruit peel to fine pieces or shavings, either with a sharp knife or a grater or mandoline. The shredding plate of a food processor may also be used. Shredding produces a coarser texture than grating.

Sieve To rub or pass food through a sieve to reduce it to very fine crumbs, pulp or purée, or to separate the pips and skin from fruit and vegetables. The process is also used to separate unwanted solid matter.

Sift To shake a dry ingredient through a sieve, sifter or dredger to remove lumps and to incorporate air.

Simmer To heat liquid until boiling point, then reduce the heat to keep the liquid just below boiling point, over a gentle heat. The surface of the liquid should be moving gently with only occasional slow bubbles.

Singe see *Flame* (2).

Skewer To pass a metal or wooden spike through meat to hold it in a neat shape while cooking, or to thread small pieces of food on metal skewers for cooking under the grill.

Skim To remove surface fat, scum or cream from a liquid. To remove fat, lay a piece of soft absorbent kitchen paper on the surface, and lift off when saturated. For scum, pass a shallow or perforated metal spoon slowly across the surface. To remove cream from the top of milk, use a shallow metal spoon.

Skin To remove the outer layer of peel or membrane from vegetables, fruit, meat or fish.

Slake To mix a starchy material with liquid before adding it to a hot liquid for thickening.

Slash To make shallow cuts across raw foods, such as herrings and sausage rolls, to allow heat to penetrate and steam to escape during cooking. Slashing can also be decorative.

Snip 1. To cut into the edge of the fat round cuts of meat such as gammon rashers, to prevent the meat curling while cooking. 2. To cut up food, using kitchen scissors.

Souse To immerse and cook food, usually fish or pork, in a vinegar and spiced pickling solution. The food should be allowed to cool in the liquid.

Spit roast To cook meat, uncovered, by rotating it on a metal skewer, over or in front of direct heat, or under a grill. Some cookers are equipped with a 'rôtisserie', which revolves so that the food is roasted evenly on all sides.

Stand To rest. Used in microwave cookery for a period of time when a dish is set aside – usually at the end of a cooking cycle – allowing residual heat to spread evenly. See also *Tent.*

Steam To cook food in the steam rising from boiling liquid.

Steam fry To cook moist food in a very little fat in a covered pan, so that the food gives off its own liquid and is actually steamed rather than fried.

Steep To soak food in liquid, either to soften it or to extract the flavour.

Stew To cook food, eg tougher cuts of meat or vegetables, fish, fruit, etc, with a liquid by simmering it in a covered pan, either over heat or in the oven.

Stir fry To fry finely chopped food quickly in a very little fat, stirring to prevent burning. Use a wok, or large frying pan with curved base and sides.

Stone To remove the stone from fruit such as plums, olives, etc.

Strain To separate liquids from solids by pouring the mixture through a colander, sieve or muslin.

Stud To stick cloves into onions, the skin of bacon, or other meat and vegetables, to impart flavour.

Sweat To release the juices from vegetables to be used in soups or as a base for casseroled or stewed meat. Melt a little fat in a pan, add the vegetables, cover, and leave over low heat until the juices run.

Tammy To force soups or sauces through a fine woollen cloth, to produce a smooth, glossy finish. Nowadays, nylon or fine-meshed metal sieves are generally used instead of a tammy.

Tent To cover cooked meat or poultry with a tented sheet of foil so that the heat is retained. The term is generally used for microwave cookery, during the standing time.

Thicken To give a thick consistency to sauces, gravies and soups usually by adding cream, egg and cream or farinaceous substances blended with fat or cold liquid.

Top and Tail To remove the stubs and stems at both ends of gooseberries, currants and green beans before cooking.

Toss To turn meat in flour or breadcrumbs, or salad in a dressing, so as to coat the food evenly.

Truss To tie poultry, meat or game into a neat shape before cooking, either with string or with string and a skewer.

Weight or Press To place a weight over a piece of meat, tongue, pâté or home made cheese, to expel excess moisture and condense the texture of the food before serving. Cover the food with greaseproof paper, and place a plate or piece of cardboard on top. Put a weight or heavy object on the plate, and leave for several hours or overnight.

Whip To beat with a whisk, rotary beater or mixer to incorporate air and so make the ingredient(s) thick, stiff or light-textured.

Whisk To beat with light, rapid strokes, using a balloon or rotary whisk, to incorporate air into an ingredient.

Stocks and Soups

The secret of a good soup lies in the stock, which should marry the various components without in itself dominating the flavour. This chapter therefore begins with recipes and suggestions for essential stocks, which are then used to advantage in a selection of classic recipes.

RICH STRONG STOCK

This recipe makes a large quantity of stock which freezes well for future use. Although the quantities may be reduced, a large volume of liquid is required to cover marrow bones. It is more practical to invest in a large stockpot or saucepan and to boil a large quantity occasionally than to reduce the weight of ingredients in proportion to water to make a weaker meat stock.

675 g/1½ lb shin of beef on the bone
675 g/1½ lb knuckle of veal on the bone, or
    other stewing veal
450 g/1 lb beef marrow bones
1 chicken drumstick or poultry trimmings
1 onion, sliced
1 carrot, quartered
100 g/4 oz gammon or bacon, diced
1 small turnip, roughly chopped
2 celery sticks, quartered
2 open cup mushrooms, quartered
1 tomato, quartered
1 bouquet garni
4 white peppercorns
2 cloves
1 blade of mace

Set the oven at 200°C/400°F/gas 6. Put the bones in a roasting tin and roast for about 2 hours until browned. Transfer the bones to a large saucepan. Pour off the fat from the tin, add some boiling water and stir to scrape all the sediment off the tin. Then add to the bones in the pan. Add the onion and carrot.

Add about 5.6 litres/10 pints water to cover the bones generously. Bring to the boil, skim the surface, then lower the heat and add the remaining ingredients. Simmer for about 5 hours. Cool, then strain. Skim off surface fat. Season and use as required.

MAKES ABOUT 5.6 LITRES/10 PINTS

CLARIFYING STOCK

Scald a saucepan (not aluminium), a piece of muslin, a metal sieve and a whisk. Pour the strained stock into the pan. Lightly whisk 2 egg whites and crush the shells from 2 eggs; add to the stock. Heat slowly to simmering point, whisking to form a thick white crust. Stop whisking, allow the stock to rise in the pan, then turn the heat off just before it boils. Repeat twice more. Line the sieve with the muslin and place it over a clean bowl. Strain the stock through the muslin. Try not to break the crust which acts as a filter.

 PRESSURE COOKER TIP

Meat and poultry stocks, made with raw or cooked meat and bones, can be prepared in the pressure cooker in approximately 40 minutes at 15 lb pressure. Follow the manufacturer's recommendations regarding the maximum quantity of ingredients and liquid for the pan; failing this, make a concentrated stock by reducing the volume of water to ensure that the pan is no more than half to two-thirds full. Add extra water and simmer briefly in the open pan after the pressure has been reduced.

CHICKEN STOCK

**4 chicken drumsticks or 1 meaty chicken
   carcass
1 small onion, sliced
1 carrot, roughly chopped
1 celery stick, sliced
1 bouquet garni
5 ml/1 tsp white peppercorns**

Break or chop the carcass into manageable pieces. Put it in a large saucepan with 1.75 litres/3 pints cold water. Bring to the boil; skim the surface. Add the remaining ingredients, lower the heat and simmer for 3–4 hours. Cool quickly, then strain. Skim off surface fat. Season and use as required.

MAKES ABOUT 1.4 LITRES/2½ PINTS

VARIATION

Rich Chicken Stock Use drumsticks and roast them at 200°C/400°F/gas 6 for 40 minutes. Drain off the fat. Continue as above, adding 225 g/8 oz cubed belly pork with the chicken.

Game Stock Use the carcasses of 1 or 2 game birds such as pheasant or grouse, with the giblets, instead of the chicken.

WHITE STOCK

**1.4 kg/3 lb knuckle of veal on the bone, or
   other stewing veal
2 chicken drumsticks or poultry trimmings
1 onion, sliced
1 carrot, quartered
2 celery sticks, quartered
2 open cup mushrooms, quartered
1 bouquet garni
4 white peppercorns
1 blade of mace**

Put the bones in a large saucepan. Add 900 ml/1½ pints water. Bring to the boil, skim the surface, then add the remaining ingredients. Lower the heat and simmer for 30 minutes. Add a further 900 ml/1½ pints water and simmer for about 3 hours more. Cool quickly, then strain. Skim off surface fat. Season and use as required.

MAKES ABOUT 1.5 LITRES/2¾ PINTS

VEGETABLE STOCK

Vary the vegetables according to the market selection and your personal taste.

**2 onions, sliced
2 leeks, trimmed, sliced and washed
1 small turnip, chopped
4 celery sticks, sliced
2 tomatoes, chopped
1 bouquet garni
6 black peppercorns
2 cloves
a few lettuce leaves
a few spinach leaves
a few watercress sprigs
2.5 ml/½ tsp yeast extract (optional)
salt**

Put the root vegetables, celery, tomatoes, herbs and spices in a large saucepan. Add 2 litres/3½ pints water. Bring to the boil, lower the heat and simmer for 1 hour.

Add the lettuce, spinach and watercress and simmer for 1 hour more. Stir in the yeast extract, if using, and add salt to taste.

MAKES ABOUT 1.75 LITRES/3 PINTS

BOUILLABAISSE

This famous French dish had its origins in Marseilles where it depends for its success on the use of fresh Mediterranean fish and shellfish, good olive oil, sun-warmed local tomatoes and other vegetables and fresh herbs. The fish content varies but always includes the rascasse or scorpion fish. Angler fish, John Dory, red mullet and crawfish are invariably present and other fish include weever, gurnard, whiting and mussels or baby crabs in shells.

The stew is boiled fast for 12–20 minutes. This process of boiling serves to thicken the soup as well as extract full flavour from the seafood. The fish should be cooked through but should not be allowed to disintegrate.

1 small French bread stick, thickly sliced
1 red mullet, cleaned, scaled and trimmed
1 red gurnard, cleaned, scaled and trimmed
350g/12oz whiting fillet, skinned
350g/12oz monkfish fillet, skinned
60ml/4tbsp olive oil (or more, see method)
2 onions, chopped
2 garlic cloves, crushed
2 celery sticks, sliced
1kg/2¼lb tomatoes, peeled and roughly
  chopped
salt and pepper
600ml/1 pint dry white wine
1 bouquet garni
1 whole uncooked lobster, killed by
  freezing (page 116)
6 uncooked Mediterranean prawns, in
  shells if possible or 12 cooked prawns in
  shells
2.5ml/½tsp saffron threads or 1.25ml/¼tsp
  saffron powder
plenty of chopped parsley
Rouille and Aïoli to serve (page 468)

Set the oven at 160°C/325°F/gas 3. Lay the bread slices on a baking sheet and bake them for about 30 minutes until dry and crisp but not toasted.

Rinse the whole fish and dry on absorbent kitchen paper. Cut the fish fillets into large chunks. Set aside on a plate. Heat the olive oil in a very large saucepan – more oil may be added if liked.

Add the onions, garlic and celery and cook, stirring frequently over low heat for 15 minutes, until the onion is soft. Stir in the tomatoes with plenty of salt and pepper, then stir over high heat until the tomatoes are soft. Pour in the wine and add 1.1 litres/2 pints water. Add the bouquet garni and bring the soup to the boil.

When the soup is boiling add the lobster. Put a lid on the pan and regulate the heat so that the liquid boils without spilling over. Cook for 15 minutes.

Next add the gurnard and boil for 3 minutes with the lid off. Add the mullet and boil for 2 minutes more. Lastly add the chunks of fish fillet and the uncooked prawns (if used). Boil for a final 3 minutes, or until all the fish is cooked but not breaking up. If cooked prawns in shells are used they should be added last – their contribution to flavour will be small.

Pound the saffron threads to a powder with a pestle in a mortar. Stir in a little of the hot soup to dissolve the saffron, then add the liquid to the pan. Saffron powder may be sprinkled directly into the soup. Add plenty of parsley and taste the liquid. Add more salt and pepper if required. Ladle the fish into a large warmed serving bowl. Arrange some of the slices of bread in soup plates and ladle the soup over them. Offer the remaining bread separately, with Rouille and Aïoli.

SERVES SIX

FISH STOCK

**fish bones and trimmings without gills,
which cause bitterness**
5 ml/1 tsp salt
1 small onion, sliced
2 celery sticks, sliced
4 white peppercorns
1 bouquet garni

Break up any bones and wash the fish trimmings, if used. Put the bones, trimmings or
heads in a saucepan and cover with 1 litre/1¾
pints cold water. Add the salt.

Bring the liquid to the boil and add the vegetables, peppercorns and bouquet garni. Lower
the heat, cover and simmer gently for 30–40
minutes. Do not cook the stock for longer than
40 minutes or it may develop a bitter taste.
Strain, cool quickly and use as required.

MAKES ABOUT 1 LITRE/1¾ PINTS

VARIATION

White Wine Fish Stock   Add 100 ml/3½ fl oz
dry white wine, 4–5 mushroom stalks and 1
sliced carrot. Simmer for 30 minutes only.

CHANNEL CHOWDER

25 g/1 oz butter
450 g/1 lb onions, chopped
¼ green pepper, seeded and chopped
**75 g/3 oz rindless streaky bacon rashers,
chopped**
**450 g/1 lb huss fillets, skinned and cut into
bite-sized pieces**
**450 g/1 lb tomatoes, peeled, seeded and
roughly chopped**
1 bay leaf
salt and pepper
125 ml/4 fl oz Fish Stock (above)
chopped parsley to garnish

Set the oven at 180°C/350°F/gas 4. Melt the
butter in a flameproof casserole. Add the
onions, pepper and bacon and fry gently for
4–5 minutes.

Add the fish to the casserole with the chopped
tomatoes. Place the bay leaf on top and add
plenty of salt and pepper.

Pour in the fish stock, cover and bake for 45
minutes. Remove the bay leaf. Serve hot, garnished with the parsley.

SERVES FOUR

FISH BALL SOUP

**50 g/2 oz fresh root ginger, peeled and finely
chopped**
1 spring onion, finely chopped
15 ml/1 tbsp dry sherry
1 egg white
**225 g/8 oz firm white fish fillet, skinned and
cut into pieces**
25 ml/5 tsp cornflour
salt
25 g/1 oz lard, softened
snipped chives to garnish

CHINESE CHICKEN STOCK
2 chicken quarters
½ onion, thickly sliced
1 large carrot, thickly sliced
¼ celery stick, thickly sliced
1 thin slice of fresh root ginger
5 ml/1 tsp dry sherry

Make the stock. Put the chicken quarters in a
heavy-bottomed saucepan. Add 2 litres/3½
pints water and bring to the boil. Skim, lower
the heat, cover and simmer for 1½ hours.
Remove the chicken from the stock and set
aside for use in another recipe.

Add the vegetables to the stock, cover and
simmer for 20 minutes. Stir in the root ginger

and sherry, with salt to taste. Remove the lid and simmer for 10 minutes more. Strain the stock into a clean saucepan, making it up to 1.25 litres/2¼ pints with water if necessary. Skim off any fat on the surface and set aside.

To make the fish balls, sieve the root ginger and spring onion into a bowl containing 75 ml/5 tbsp water. Stir briskly. Alternatively, process the root ginger, spring onion and water in a blender or food processor. Strain the liquid into a clean bowl, discarding any solids. Add a further 75 ml/5 tbsp water to the liquid, with the sherry and the egg white. Whisk until smooth.

Place the fish in a basin or large mortar and pound it to a paste. Alternatively, purée the fish in a food processor. Transfer 15 ml/1 tbsp of the sherry mixture to a shallow bowl and add the fish. Stir in the cornflour, salt and lard, and mix thoroughly so that the ingredients bind together. The mixture should be soft and malleable; add more of the sherry mixture as necessary.

Form the fish mixture into balls about 4 cm/1½ inches in diameter and drop them into a large pan of cold water. Bring the water to the boil, lower the heat and simmer until the fish balls float. Remove with a slotted spoon.

Bring the pan of Chinese chicken stock to the boil. Drop in the fish balls and heat through for 1–2 minutes. Serve immediately, garnished with the chives.

SERVES SIX

 ✳ FREEZER TIP

The shaped fish balls may be frozen before cooking. Open freeze them on a baking sheet lined with freezer film, then pack in polythene bags when firm. Cook from frozen in soup. Alternatively, the fish balls may be deep fried or stir fried.

SPANISH FISH SOUP

225 g/8 oz monkfish fillet
225 g/8 oz sea bass fillet, skinned
225 g/8 oz hake steak, skinned and boned
15 ml/1 tbsp olive oil
3 onions, finely chopped
2 garlic cloves, crushed
30 ml/2 tbsp plain flour
5 ml/1 tsp chopped parsley
15 ml/1 tbsp white wine vinegar
1 bay leaf
450 g/1 lb mussels
salt and pepper
croûtons to garnish

Cut the monkfish, sea bass and hake into small pieces and put into a large saucepan with the oil, onions, garlic, flour, parsley, vinegar and bay leaf. Cover and marinate for 30 minutes at room temperature.

Meanwhile, wash, scrape and beard the mussels, following the instructions on page 117.

Add 1 litre/1¾ pints water to the fish in the pan, with salt and pepper to taste. Bring to the boil, lower the heat and simmer for 15 minutes.

Add the mussels and simmer for 5 minutes or until open. Remove any mussels that remain shut, together with the bay leaf.

Using a slotted spoon, ladle a few pieces of fish and several mussels into each individual soup bowl, top with fish broth and garnish with croûtons. Serve at once.

SERVES FOUR

SOUTHWOLD COD SOUP

25 g/1 oz butter
20 ml/4 tsp olive oil
2 large onions, thinly sliced
1 large carrot, thinly sliced
2 celery sticks, thinly sliced
225 g/8 oz potatoes, peeled and diced
5 ml/1 tsp curry powder
1 bouquet garni
salt and pepper
575 g/1¼ lb cod fillet, skinned and cut into
    small pieces
45 ml/3 tbsp white wine (optional)
25 g/1 oz cornflour
125 ml/4 fl oz milk
75 ml/5 tbsp single cream

Melt the butter in the oil in a deep saucepan.
Add the vegetables and fry for 10 minutes.

Stir in the curry powder and cook for 3
minutes. Stir in 750 ml/1¼ pints boiling water.
Add the bouquet garni, with salt and pepper to
taste. Add the fish and bring the soup back to
simmering point. Cover and simmer for 3–5
minutes until the fish is tender.

Using a slotted spoon, transfer the best pieces
of fish to a bowl. Ladle in a little of the soup
stock and keep hot.

Reduce the remaining soup by simmering,
uncovered, for 15 minutes. Remove the bouquet garni. Rub the soup through a sieve into a
clean pan, or process in a blender or food
processor. Add the wine, if used, and reheat.

Meanwhile, blend the cornflour with a little of
the milk in a bowl. Stir in the rest of the milk.
Add the mixture to the soup, stirring constantly. Bring to the boil and cook for 2–3
minutes, stirring constantly. Add the fish,
remove the pan from the heat and stir in the
cream. Serve at once.

SERVES SIX

EEL SOUP

25 g/1 oz butter
450 g/1 lb eel, skinned and cut into chunks
1 large onion, sliced
1 bouquet garni
1 blade of mace
1 strip of lemon rind
5 ml/1 tsp lemon juice
salt and pepper
25 g/1 oz cornflour
30 ml/2 tbsp milk
100 ml/3½ fl oz single cream

Melt the butter in a saucepan, add the eel and
onion and fry gently for 10 minutes until the
onion is soft and pale gold. Add 1.25 litres/2¼
pints water and boil.

Add the bouquet garni, mace, lemon rind and
juice, with salt and pepper to taste. Lower the
heat, cover and simmer very gently for 30
minutes or until the eel fillets start to come
away from the bones.

Strain the soup into a clean pan. Discard the
bones. Cut the fillets into pieces and place in a
heated dish. Keep warm.

In a cup, blend the cornflour to a paste with the
milk. Stir the mixture into the soup, bring to
the boil, and cook for 2–3 minutes, stirring
constantly, until thick and smooth. Check the
seasoning.

Off the heat, add the cream and the pieces of
eel. Return the pan to the heat and warm
through gently. Do not boil.

SERVES SIX

 MRS BEETON'S TIP

If conger eel is used, increase the cooking
time by about 15 minutes or until tender.

SMOKED HADDOCK CHOWDER

450 g/1 lb smoked haddock fillet, skinned
750 ml/1¼ pints milk
50 g/2 oz butter
1 small onion, finely chopped
100 g/4 oz mushrooms, finely chopped
40 g/1½ oz plain flour
250 ml/8 fl oz single cream
freshly ground black pepper

Put the haddock fillets into a saucepan with the milk and heat to simmering point. Simmer for about 10 minutes until just tender. Drain the fish, reserving the cooking liquid, remove the skin and shred lightly.

Melt the butter in a clean pan, add the onion and mushrooms and fry gently for about 10 minutes until soft. Do not allow the onion to colour.

Stir in the flour and cook for 1 minute, stirring constantly. Gradually add the fish-flavoured milk, stirring until smooth. Bring to the boil, lower the heat and simmer until thickened.

Off the heat, add the cream and the shredded haddock. Return the pan to the heat and warm through gently. Do not allow the soup to boil after adding the cream. Top with a generous grinding of black pepper and serve at once.

SERVES FOUR TO SIX

 MRS BEETON'S TIP

Reserve a few perfect mushrooms for a garnish if liked. Slice them thinly and sprinkle a few slices on top of each portion of soup. It is not necessary to cook the mushrooms.

CREAM OF SCALLOP SOUP

100 g/4 oz butter
3 large onions, finely chopped
225 g/8 oz carrots, finely chopped
12–16 large scallops
1 thyme sprig
½ bay leaf
45 ml/3 tbsp chopped parsley
salt and pepper
150 ml/¼ pint dry white wine
1.25 litres/2¼ pints Fish Stock (page 48)
800 g/1¾ lb potatoes, diced
250 ml/8 fl oz single cream
pinch of cayenne pepper

Melt 75 g/3 oz of the butter in a large heavy-bottomed saucepan. Cut the remaining butter into small cubes and chill until required. Add the onions and carrots to the melted butter and fry gently for 15 minutes.

Add the scallops and herbs to the pan, with salt and pepper to taste. Pour in the wine and fish stock, bring to the boil, lower the heat and simmer for 10 minutes.

Using a slotted spoon, transfer the scallops to a heated dish and keep warm. Add the potatoes to the soup and cook for about 15 minutes or until soft. Rub the soup through a sieve or remove the thyme sprig and bay leaf, then process in a blender or food processor.

Transfer the soup to a clean saucepan and stir in the cream. Chop the reserved scallops into 2 or 3 pieces each and add them to the pan. Heat gently to just below boiling point, stir in the chilled butter, sprinkle with cayenne and serve.

SERVES SIX

LOBSTER BISQUE

shell, trimmings and a little of the flesh of
  1 small or medium cooked lobster
1 onion, thinly sliced
1 carrot, thinly sliced
1 garlic clove, thinly sliced
1 bay leaf
1 blade of mace
5 ml/1 tsp lemon juice
5 ml/1 tsp anchovy essence
125 ml/4 fl oz white wine
750 ml/1¼ pints Fish Stock (page 48)
salt and pepper
15 ml/1 tbsp cooked lobster coral (optional)
50 g/2 oz butter
25 g/1 oz plain flour
125 ml/4 fl oz single cream

Crush the lobster shell and put it in a heavy-
bottomed saucepan with the trimmings. Flake
the flesh finely, setting a few neat pieces aside
for the garnish. Add the flesh to the pan with
the onion, carrot and garlic. Put in the bay leaf,
mace, lemon juice, anchovy essence and wine
and bring to the boil. Cook briskly for 3–5
minutes (see Mrs Beeton's Tip). Add the fish
stock and a little salt. Bring the boil, lower the
heat and simmer for 1 hour.

Strain the soup through a metal sieve into a
large jug or bowl, rubbing through any pieces of
firm lobster. Pound the lobster coral (if used)
with half the butter in a small bowl, then rub
through a clean sieve into a bowl. Set the coral
butter aside.

 MRS BEETON'S TIP

It is important to boil the lobster trimmings
and flesh in the wine for at least 3 minutes.
The alcohol in the wine extracts much of
the flavour from the lobster, vegetables
and herbs.

Melt the remaining butter in a saucepan and
stir in the flour. Cook for 1 minute, stirring,
then gradually add the strained soup. Bring to
the boil, stirring constantly. Add the reserved
lobster coral butter or plain butter, stirring all
the time.

Off the heat, add the cream and the reserved
lobster pieces, with salt and pepper, if required.
Return the pan to the heat and warm through
gently. Do not allow the soup to boil after
adding the cream. Serve at once.

SERVES FOUR TO SIX

LOBSTER SOUP

shell trimmings and flesh of 1 small or
  medium cooked lobster
soft middle from 1 crusty breakfast roll
1 (50 g/2 oz) can anchovy fillets, drained
1 onion, chopped
1 bouquet garni
1 strip of lemon peel
5 ml/1 tsp plain flour
25 g/1 oz butter
grated nutmeg
salt and pepper
150 ml/¼ pint milk
150 ml/¼ pint single cream

FORCEMEAT BALLS
75 g/3 oz fresh breadcrumbs
1.25 ml/¼ tsp ground mace
1 small egg, beaten

Crush the lobster shell as for Lobster Bisque
(left). Reserve the main piece of tail meat but
flake any other flesh and add it to the saucepan.
Add the bread, anchovy fillets, onion, bouquet
garni and lemon peel. Pour in 750 ml/1¼ pints
water and cook as for the bisque.

Meanwhile, cream the flour and butter to a smooth paste, add a little nutmeg and salt and pepper. Any lobster coral may be pounded into the butter, then set aside. Next make the forcemeat balls. Chop the reserved lobster meat and mix it with the breadcrumbs, salt and pepper, and mace. Mix in enough egg to bind the mixture, then shape it into small balls and set aside.

Strain the soup as for the bisque and return it to a clean pan. Bring to simmering point, add the forcemeat balls and cook gently for 5 minutes. Remove with a slotted spoon. Whisk the butter mixture into the soup and simmer for 3 minutes. Stir in the milk and cream, replace the forcemeat balls and heat without boiling. Serve at once.

SERVES SIX

SHRIMP AND CIDER BISQUE

Cooked whole prawns, thawed if frozen, may be used instead of the shrimps in this bisque.

750 ml/1¼ pints Fish Stock (page 48)
225 g/8 oz cooked whole shrimps
45 ml/3 tbsp fresh white breadcrumbs
50 g/2 oz butter
pinch of grated nutmeg
5 ml/1 tsp lemon juice
100 ml/3½ fl oz cider
salt and pepper
1 egg yolk
125 ml/4 fl oz single cream

Pour the fish stock into a large saucepan. Peel the shrimps and add the shells to the pan. Set the shrimps aside. Bring the stock and shrimp shells to the boil, cover and cook for 10 minutes. Strain into a large measuring jug or heatproof bowl.

Put the breadcrumbs in a small bowl with 250 ml/8 fl oz of the strained stock. Set aside to soak for 10 minutes.

Meanwhile, melt 25 g/1 oz of the butter in a pan. Add the shrimps and toss over gentle heat for 5 minutes. Add the nutmeg, lemon juice and breadcrumb mixture and heat gently for 5 minutes. Beat in the rest of the butter.

Purée the mixture in a blender or food processor or rub through a sieve into a clean pan. Gradually add the cider and the remaining stock. Bring to the boil, remove from the heat and add salt and pepper to taste.

In a small bowl, mix the egg yolk with the cream. Stir a little of the hot soup into the egg mixture, mix well, then add the contents of the bowl to the soup, stirring the bisque over low heat until it thickens. Serve at once.

SERVES FOUR TO SIX

✳ FREEZER TIP

The unused egg white may be frozen. It is a good idea to freeze several egg whites together in usable quantities of 2, 3 or 4. Whisk lightly before freezing in lidded containers. Thaw for 2–3 hours before use. 1 egg white is equal to about 30 ml/2 tbsp.

NORWEGIAN FISH SOUP

1 small onion, roughly chopped
¼ celeriac, roughly chopped
1 leek, trimmed, sliced and washed
2 carrots, roughly chopped
1.5 litres/2½ pints Fish Stock (page 48)
1 rindless bacon rasher, roughly chopped
30 ml/2 tbsp tomato purée
25 g/1 oz butter
15 ml/1 tbsp plain flour
salt
100 ml/3½ fl oz dry sherry
dill sprigs to garnish

FISH BALLS
225 g/8 oz firm white fish fillet, skinned and
    cut into pieces
25 ml/5 tsp cornflour
1 egg white
15 ml/1 tbsp chopped dill

Combine all the vegetables in a large saucepan.
Add the stock and bacon, bring to the boil and
cook for about 20 minutes. Strain the stock,
add the tomato purée and mix well.

To make the fish balls, pound the fish to a
coarse paste or process it briefly in a food
processor. Thoroughly mix in the cornflour, a
good pinch of salt, the egg white and dill. With
wet hands shape mixture into balls.

Melt the butter in a large pan, add the flour and
cook until nut brown but not burnt. Gradually
add the stock, stirring constantly. Bring to the
boil, lower the heat and add the fish balls.
Simmer for 5 minutes, stirring, until the fish
balls rise. Stir in salt to taste and the sherry.
Garnish with dill.

SERVES SIX

CULLEN SKINK

1 large finnan haddock on the bone
1 onion, finely chopped
450 g/1 lb potatoes, halved
salt and pepper
25 g/1 oz butter
150 ml/¼ pint single cream
250 ml/8 fl oz milk
chopped parsley to garnish

Put the haddock in a large saucepan with the
onion. Add 1 litre/1¾ pints water. Bring to the
boil, lower the heat and simmer for 20
minutes. Lift out the fish and remove the skin
and bones, returning these to the stock. Flake
the fish roughly and set it aside in a clean
saucepan. Simmer the stock for a further 45
minutes until flavoursome.

Meanwhile cook the potatoes in a saucepan of
lightly salted water for about 30 minutes or
until tender. Drain thoroughly and mash with
the butter.

Strain the fish stock into the pan containing the
flaked fish. Set aside 60 ml/4 tbsp of the cream
in a small jug. Add the remaining cream to the
pan with the milk. Stir in the mashed potato
and heat through, stirring to make a thick soup.
If a thinner soup is preferred, add more milk.

Check the seasoning. The soup is unlikely to
need salt, but pepper may be added, if liked.
Ladle into individual bowls, drizzling a little of
the reserved cream on to the surface of each
portion. Sprinkle with chopped parsley and
serve at once.

SERVES FOUR

CONSOMME

**100 g/4 oz lean shin of beef, trimmed of all
fat, finely shredded**
1 small onion, sliced
1 small carrot, sliced
1 small celery stick, sliced
**1.25 litres/2¼ pints cold Rich Strong Stock
(page 45)**
1 bouquet garni
1.25 ml/¼ tsp salt
4 white peppercorns
white and crushed shell of 1 egg

Before you begin, scald a large enamel or
stainless steel (not aluminium) saucepan, a
piece of clean muslin or thin white cotton, a
metal sieve and a whisk in boiling water. Put
the meat in a large bowl, add 125 ml/4 fl oz
water and set aside to soak for 15 minutes.

Transfer the meat and soaking liquid to the
pan. Add the vegetables, stock, bouquet garni,
salt and peppercorns. Finally add the egg white
and shell. Heat slowly to simmering point,
whisking constantly. A thick white crust of
foam will develop on the top.

Remove the whisk, cover the pan and simmer
the stock very gently for 1½–2 hours. Do not
allow the stock to boil or the froth will break up
and cloud the consommé.

Line the sieve with the muslin and place it over
a perfectly clean bowl. Strain the crust and
liquid very gently through the muslin into the
bowl. Try not to break the crust. The consommé
should be sparkling clear.

Transfer to a clean saucepan, reheat and add
more salt and pepper if required.

SERVES FOUR

VARIATIONS

Consommé Brunoise Add 2.5 ml/½ tsp
lemon juice and 15 ml/1 tbsp sherry when
reheating the consommé. The traditional garnish consists of 15 ml/1 tbsp each of finely
diced carrot, turnip, green leek and celery,
lightly cooked in salted boiling water, drained
and placed in the soup tureen before the consommé is added.

Consommé Madrilene Add 450 g/1 lb
chopped fresh or canned tomatoes and 1 sliced
green pepper to the vegetables when making
the consommé. Substitute 1 litre/1¾ pints
Chicken Stock (page 46) for the Rich Strong
Stock and simmer very gently for 1 hour. Serve
hot or iced, with a garnish of 2 peeled and diced
tomatoes.

Consommé Dubarry To the basic consommé add a custard garnish: Mix 1 egg yolk,
15 ml/1 tbsp milk or cream and salt and pepper
to taste in a bowl. Strain into a small greased
basin and cover with buttered greaseproof
paper or foil. Stand the basin in a pan of
simmering water and steam the custard for
about 8 minutes or until firm. Leave until cold,
then turn out. Cut into thin slices and then into
fancy shapes. Add to the boiling consommé
just before serving.

Iced Consommé Make the basic consommé
with veal bones to give a firmer jelly when iced.
Add salt and pepper before cooling the consommé. When cool, add 15 ml/1 tbsp dry
sherry. Chill for 1–2 hours or until the consommé forms a soft jelly. Whip lightly with a
fork before serving with a garnish of chopped
herbs, diced raw cucumber, finely chopped
hard-boiled egg or small squares of peeled
firm tomato.

PRINCE OF WALES'S SOUP

This soup was invented in 1859, in honour of the 18th birthday of Albert Edward, Prince of Wales. Use the smaller cup of a double-ended melon baller to shape the turnips.

4 slices of day-old white bread
1 litre/1¾ pints Consommé (page 55)
12 young turnips, cut into balls
salt and white pepper
1.25 ml/¼ tsp sugar

Set the oven at 150°C/300°F/gas 2. Cut the bread into small discs, using a small round cutter or the rounded end of a piping tube. Spread out the discs on a baking sheet and bake until golden and very crisp.

Bring the consommé to the boil in a large saucepan. Add the turnip balls, with salt, pepper and sugar to taste. Lower the heat and simmer the soup for 10–20 minutes until the turnips are tender. Serve the soup very hot, with the rounds of baked bread.

SERVES FOUR

HODGE-PODGE

450g/1lb shin of beef, diced
300 ml/½ pint bitter beer or mild ale
2 onions, chopped
2 carrots, diced
2 turnips, diced
1 head of celery, sliced
salt and pepper
40g/1½ oz butter
25g/1oz plain flour

Place the beef, beer and 1.25 litres/2¼ pints water in a large saucepan and bring to the boil. Skim the surface, then add the vegetables and plenty of seasoning. Reduce the heat and cover

the pan. Simmer gently for 3 hours, until the meat is thoroughly tender.

Cream the butter and flour to a paste. Stir into the soup and bring to the boil. Simmer for 3 minutes, check the seasoning and serve.

SERVES SIX

BORSCH

30 ml/2 tbsp oil
1 onion, roughly chopped
1 garlic clove, sliced
1 carrot, sliced
1 turnip, sliced
1 swede, sliced
2 tomatoes, peeled and chopped
350g/12oz raw beetroot, grated
1 bay leaf
2 litres/3½ pints Rich Strong Stock (page 45)
30 ml/2 tbsp tomato purée
salt and pepper
225 g/8 oz cabbage, sliced
225 g/8 oz potatoes, cubed
5 ml/1 tsp cider vinegar
150 ml/¼ pint soured cream
chopped dill to garnish

Heat the oil in a large saucepan. Add the onion, garlic, carrot, turnip and swede and cook for 10 minutes, stirring frequently to prevent the vegetables from sticking to the base of the pan. Stir in the tomatoes and beetroot, with the bay leaf. Add the stock and tomato purée, with salt and pepper to taste. Bring to the boil, lower the heat, cover and simmer for 1 hour.

Add the sliced cabbage and cubed potato. Stir in the vinegar and simmer for 15 minutes more or until the potato cubes are tender. Taste the soup and add more salt and pepper, if required.

Leave to stand for 5 minutes. Serve topped with soured cream and garnished with dill.

SERVES SIX

COCK-A-LEEKIE

100 g/4 oz prunes
450 g/1 lb leeks, trimmed, sliced and washed
1 (1.4 kg/3 lb) chicken
3 rindless streaky bacon rashers, chopped
2.5 ml/½ tsp salt
1 bouquet garni
1.25 ml/¼ tsp pepper

Soak the prunes overnight in a small bowl of water, then drain them and remove the stones. Set aside, with about one-third of the drained leek slices.

Put the chicken, with its giblets if available, and bacon in a deep saucepan. Add cold water to cover (about 2 litres/3½ pints). Stir in the salt and bring slowly to simmering point.

Add the remaining leeks to the pan, with the bouquet garni and pepper. Cover, then simmer gently for about 3 hours or until the chicken is cooked through and tender.

Carefully remove the chicken, discard the skin, then carve off the meat and cut it into fairly large serving pieces. Return the chicken meat to the soup and add the reserved prunes and leeks. Simmer gently for about 30 minutes, until the prunes are cooked but not broken. Skim off surface fat and check seasoning before serving.

SERVES SIX TO EIGHT

 MRS BEETON'S TIP

Ready-to-eat dried prunes may be used. There is no need to presoak them.

SCOTCH BROTH

This economical soup was originally intended to furnish two meals: the meat was removed after cooking and served separately. Today it is more usual to cut up the meat and add it to the soup.

25 g/1 oz pearl barley
450/1 lb middle neck of lamb, trimmed of excess fat
1.4 litres/2½ pints White Stock or Chicken Stock (page 46)
1 onion, chopped
1 leek, trimmed, sliced and washed
2 carrots, sliced
1 swede, cubed
salt and pepper

Put the barley in a small saucepan with water to cover. Bring to the boil, then drain off the water and transfer the barley to a large pan with the meat and stock. Bring the mixture to the boil, skim off any scum on the surface, then lower the heat and simmer gently for 2 hours.

Add the vegetables with plenty of salt and pepper. Simmer for a further 45-60 minutes. Lift out the meat, remove it from the bones, and roughly chop it. Skim off any fat from the broth, add more salt and pepper if required, then replace the chopped meat. Serve very hot.

SERVES FOUR

 PRESSURE COOKER TIP

It is not necessary to blanch the barley. Simply combine the ingredients in the cooker, reducing the amount of stock to 900 ml/1½ pints. The cooker should not be more than half full. Put the lid on, bring to 15 lb pressure and cook for 10 minutes. Reduce the pressure slowly. Continue as above, reheating the soup in the open pan, and adding more stock if liked.

OXTAIL SOUP

Prepare this soup a day ahead and refrigerate it overnight. This will not only allow the full flavour to develop, but will also permit the removal of the fat that solidifies on the surface.

1.4 kg/3 lb oxtail, jointed
25 g/1 oz beef dripping or 30 ml/2 tbsp oil
1 onion, sliced
2 large carrots, sliced
1 small turnip, diced
2 celery sticks, sliced
2 litres/3½ pints Rich Strong Stock (page 45),
    Vegetable Stock (page 46), or water
5 ml/1 tsp salt
6 black peppercorns
1 bouquet garni
15 g/½ oz butter
15 ml/1 tbsp plain flour
chopped parsley to garnish

Wash the oxtail, dry it thoroughly and trim off any excess fat. Cut into joints, if not already jointed by the butcher, and divide the thick parts in half. Heat the fat in a large saucepan, add the oxtail and fry until the meat is browned.

Remove the oxtail pieces and set them aside. Add the vegetables to the fat remaining in the pan and fry, stirring occasionally, for about 10 minutes until lightly browned. Drain off excess fat from the pan.

Return the oxtail pieces to the pan. Add the stock, salt, peppercorns and bouquet garni. Bring to the boil, skim the surface, then lower the heat and simmer the soup for 3–4 hours. Strain into a clean pan, discarding the bouquet garni and flavouring vegetables. Return the meat and bones to the pan. Cool quickly, then refrigerate overnight.

Next day, lift off the fat from the surface of the soup. Remove the oxtail meat from the bones, chop it finely and return it to the pan. Heat the soup to simmering point, taste and add more salt and pepper if required.

In a cup, blend the butter with the flour. Gradually add small pieces of the mixture to the soup, stirring thoroughly after each addition and for about 5 minutes after all the butter mixture has been added. Serve in individual bowls, garnished with chopped parsley.

SERVES SIX TO EIGHT

VARIATION

Mrs Beeton's Rich Oxtail Soup   Dice 225 g/8 oz raw gammon and add with the vegetables. Add 3 cloves with the peppercorns. Finally, stir in 30 ml/2 tbsp mushroom ketchup and 60–90 ml/4–6 tbsp port before serving the soup.

BAKED SOUP

It isn't always convenient to make soup on top of the cooker. This simple solution – a soup baked in the oven – dates from Victorian times.

450 g/1 lb lean boneless stewing beef or
    lamb, cubed
2 onions, finely sliced
2 carrots, finely sliced
25 g/1 oz long-grain rice
225 g/8 oz split peas
salt and pepper

Preheat the oven to 150°C/300°F/gas 2. Combine all the ingredients in a large flameproof casserole. Add 1.25 litres/2¼ pints water.

Bring to the boil, cover tightly and transfer to the oven. Bake for 3½–4 hours. Taste the soup and add more salt and pepper if necessary. Skim off surface fat and serve.

SERVES SIX TO EIGHT

MRS BEETON'S MULLIGATAWNY

25 g/1 oz butter
30 ml/2 tbsp oil
1 chicken, skinned and jointed or 900 g/2 lb
    chicken portions
4 rindless back bacon rashers, chopped
3 onions, sliced
1 garlic clove, crushed
15 ml/1 tbsp mild curry powder
25 g/1 oz ground almonds
2 litres/3½ pints Chicken Stock (page 46)
175 g/6 oz red lentils
salt and pepper
hot boiled rice to serve

Heat the butter and oil in a large, heavy-bottomed saucepan. Add the chicken and brown the joints all over, then remove them from the pan and set aside. Add the bacon, onions and garlic to the fat remaining in the pan and cook over gentle heat for 5 minutes, then stir in the curry powder and cook for 2 minutes more.

In a small bowl, mix the ground almonds to a paste with a little of the stock. Set aside. Add the remaining stock to the pan and return the chicken joints. Bring to the boil, lower the heat and simmer for 1 hour or until the chicken is tender.

Remove the chicken and cut the meat off the bones, then set aside. Skim any fat off the soup. Add the lentils and bring back to the boil. Reduce the heat, cover and simmer the soup for 30 minutes.

Stir the almond paste into the pan and replace the chicken meat. Simmer for a further 5-10 minutes. Taste for seasoning before serving very hot, with boiled rice.

SERVES EIGHT

SOUP A LA CANTATRICE

According to Mrs Beeton, this soup is 'very beneficial for the voice'. Rumour has it that it was favoured by the famous 'Swedish Nightingale', Jenny Lind. Good stock is the essential basic ingredient as the soup is delicately flavoured and lightly thickened with sago.

45 g/1½ oz sago
1.1 litres/2 pints Chicken Stock (page 46)
1 bay leaf
salt and pepper
2 egg yolks
5 fl oz/¼ pint single cream

Soak the sago in cold water to cover for 1 hour. Drain thoroughly.

Put the stock into a large saucepan with the bay leaf. Bring to just below boiling point. Add the sago, heat until just simmering, then cover and simmer, stirring, for 30 minutes. The sago should be well cooked and the soup slightly thickened. Stir in salt and pepper to taste.

In a small bowl, mix the egg yolks with the cream. Stir a little of the hot soup into the egg mixture, mix well, then add the contents of the bowl to the soup, stirring over low heat until it thickens. Do not allow the soup to boil or the eggs will curdle. Remove the bay leaf and serve at once.

SERVES FOUR

MINESTRONE

**75 g/3 oz small haricot beans, soaked
  overnight in water to cover**
15 ml/1 tbsp oil
2 rindless streaky bacon rashers, chopped
1 leek, trimmed, thinly sliced and washed
1 onion, chopped
1 garlic clove, crushed
2 carrots, thinly sliced
50 g/2 oz French beans, sliced
3 celery sticks, sliced
2 potatoes, diced
150 g/5 oz white cabbage, shredded
1 bay leaf
30 ml/2 tbsp tomato purée
1.25 litres/2¼ pints White Stock (page 46)
salt and pepper
50 g/2 oz small pasta shells or rings
grated Parmesan cheese to serve

Drain the beans. Put them in a saucepan with
fresh water to cover. Bring to the boil, boil
vigorously for 10 minutes, then drain
thoroughly.

Heat the oil in a large saucepan, add the bacon,
leek, onion and garlic and fry gently for about
10 minutes.

 PRESSURE COOKER TIP

Minestrone can be made very successfully
in the pressure cooker. Make the soup as
suggested above, but do not add the cabbage with the other vegetables. Reduce the
quantity of stock to 900 ml/1½ pints. Put
the lid on and bring to 15 lb pressure. Cook
for 10 minutes; reduce the pressure slowly.
Add the cabbage and pasta, stirring well.
Close the lid again, bring the soup back to
15 lb pressure and cook for 5 minutes
more. Reduce the pressure slowly, remove
the bay leaf and add salt to taste. Serve as
suggested above.

Add the remaining vegetables and cook, stirring frequently, for 2–3 minutes. Stir in the
drained beans, with the bay leaf, tomato purée,
stock and pepper. Do not add salt at this stage.
Bring the soup to the boil, lower the heat, cover
the pan and simmer for 45–60 minutes or until
the haricot beans are tender. Add salt to taste.

Stir in the pasta and cook for 8–12 minutes or
until tender but still firm to the bite. Remove
the bay leaf. Serve the soup at once, sprinkled
with Parmesan cheese.

SERVES SIX

CREAMY ONION SOUP

50 g/2 oz butter
4 large onions, finely chopped
50 g/2 oz plain flour
1.1 litres/2 pints White Stock (page 46)
salt and white pepper
1.25 ml/¼ tsp ground mace
2 egg yolks
150 ml/¼ pint double cream

Melt the butter in the top of a double saucepan.
Add the onions and cook over gentle heat for
10 minutes until soft but not coloured.

Stir in the flour and cook for 1 minute, then
gradually add the stock. Cook over moderate
heat until the mixture boils and thickens.
Season to taste with salt, pepper and mace.

Set the pan over simmering water and cook the
soup, stirring occasionally, for about 30
minutes or until the onions are very tender and
the soup is creamy.

In a small bowl, mix the egg yolks with the
cream. Stir a little of the hot soup into the egg
mixture, mix well, then add the contents of the
bowl to the soup, stirring over the simmering
water until it thickens. Serve at once.

SERVES FOUR TO SIX

MIXED VEGETABLE SOUP

For extra flavour, add a small piece of beef shin, smoked ham or chicken to the soup. Increase the cooking time if necessary so that the meat or poultry is very tender.

30 ml/2 tbsp oil
1 onion, chopped
2 leeks, trimmed, sliced and washed
3 celery sticks, sliced
2 potatoes, diced
2 carrots, diced
1 swede, diced
1 parsnip, diced
1.75 litres/3 pints beef, chicken or vegetable
stock (pages 45–46)
salt and pepper

Heat the oil in a large, heavy-bottomed saucepan. Add the onion and leeks, and cook gently for 10 minutes, stirring occasionally. Add the remaining vegetables, pour in the stock and add salt and pepper to taste. Bring to the boil, lower the heat and cover the pan. Simmer for about 1 hour or until all the vegetables are tender and the soup is well flavoured.

If a clear soup with identifiable vegetables is preferred, serve at once. To thicken the soup, purée it in a blender or food processor, and return to the pan.

SERVES SIX

 PRESSURE COOKER TIP

Put the vegetables in the cooker with only 1 litre/1¾ pints of stock; the cooker should not be more than half full. Put the lid on the cooker and bring to 15 lb pressure. Cook for 5 minutes. Reduce pressure quickly. Add more stock if liked.

FRENCH ONION SOUP

75 g/3 oz butter, plus extra for toast
6 onions, about 575 g/1¼ lb, thinly sliced
1 litre/1¾ pints Consommé (page 55)
30 ml/2 tbsp dry white wine
salt and pepper
6 slices of French bread
50 g/2 oz Gruyère, grated

Melt the butter in a large heavy-bottomed saucepan. Add the onions and cook slowly, turning occasionally, for at least 30 minutes, or until golden brown.

Stir in the consommé and white wine. Bring to the boil, lower the heat and cover the pan, then simmer for about 1 hour, or until the onions are quite soft. Add salt and pepper to taste.

Toast the French bread, spread it with butter and top with grated cheese. Pour the soup into individual bowls, float a slice of toast on each, and brown the cheese under a preheated hot grill or in a very hot oven.

SERVES FOUR

 MRS BEETON'S TIP

Sprinkle 2.5 ml/½ tsp sugar over the onions while browning them in the butter. This will encourage the browning process. The wine may be omitted from the soup, and a little brandy added just before floating the toast on top.

SOUP A LA FLAMANDE

45g/1½oz butter
2 large onions, chopped
1 leek, trimmed, sliced and washed
8 celery sticks, thinly sliced
450g/1lb potatoes, diced
1.1 litres/2 pints Chicken Stock (page 46) or
  Vegetable Stock (page 46)
salt and pepper
300ml/½ pint single cream

Melt the butter in a large saucepan. Add the onions, leek and celery and fry over gentle heat for about 10 minutes or until the onions and leeks are soft.

Stir in the potatoes and stock, bring to the boil, then lower the heat and simmer the soup for about 30 minutes or until the potatoes and celery are tender.

Purée the soup in a blender or food processor, or rub through a sieve into a clean pan. Add plenty of salt and pepper.

Stir in the cream and heat through gently. Do not allow the soup to boil.

SERVES SIX

BREAD SOUP

Originally intended for times when extreme economy was the object, this version with vegetables is satisfying and tasty.

40g/1½oz butter
2 onions, chopped
100g/4oz fresh white breadcrumbs
2 carrots, diced
1 bay leaf
1.1 litres/2 pints Chicken Stock (page 46)
60ml/4 tbsp chopped parsley
salt and pepper
grated nutmeg

Melt the butter in a large saucepan. Add the onions and fry for 10 minutes without browning. Add the breadcrumbs and cook, stirring, for 5 minutes, then add all the remaining ingredients.

Bring to the boil, reduce the heat and cover the pan. Simmer for 45 minutes. Taste for seasoning, then serve piping hot.

SERVES FOUR

SOUP A LA CRECY

This soup is extremely tasty and quite filling if served with the addition of rice.

salt and pepper
100g/4oz long-grain rice (optional)
50g/2oz butter
4 carrots, sliced
2 onions, thinly sliced
100g/4oz red lentils
1.75 litres/3 pints Chicken Stock (page 46)
1 lettuce, shredded
50g/2oz fresh white breadcrumbs

If using the rice, bring a saucepan of salted water to the boil. Add the rice and cook for 12 minutes. Drain thoroughly, rinse under cold water and drain again. Set aside.

Melt the butter in a large saucepan, add the carrots and onions and fry over gentle heat for about 10 minutes until soft. Stir in the lentils, turning them in the butter, then add the stock. Bring to the boil, lower the heat and simmer for 20 minutes, stirring occasionally.

Stir in the lettuce and breadcrumbs, with plenty of salt and pepper. Simmer for 10 minutes more. Purée the soup in a blender or food processor, or rub through a sieve into a clean pan. Reheat with the rice if using and serve.

SERVES EIGHT

JERUSALEM ARTICHOKE SOUP

Unlike the globe artichoke, which grows above the ground, the Jerusalem artichoke is a tuber. It makes a delicious winter soup.

45 g/1½ oz butter
3 rindless back bacon slices, chopped
4 celery sticks, thinly sliced
1 small turnip, cubed
1 onion, chopped
1 kg/2¼ lb Jerusalem artichokes, see Mrs
   Beeton's Tip
1.5 litres/2½ pints White Stock (page 46)
salt and pepper
cayenne pepper
300 ml/½ pint double cream

Melt the butter in a large saucepan. Add the bacon, celery, turnip and onion and fry over gentle heat for about 10 minutes until the vegetables are soft but not coloured.

Peel and cube the artichokes. Add them to the pan with the stock. Bring to the boil, lower the heat and simmer for about 15 minutes or until all the vegetables are tender.

Purée the soup in a blender or food processor, or rub through a sieve into a clean pan. Add salt, pepper and cayenne to taste. Stir in the cream and reheat gently. Do not allow the soup to boil after adding the cream.

SERVES SIX

 MRS BEETON'S TIP

The flesh of Jerusalem artichokes discolours very rapidly, so prepare the vegetables only when required or put the cubes into water to which a little lemon juice or wine vinegar has been added.

PARSNIP SOUP

25 g/1 oz butter
1 onion, chopped
450 g/1 lb parsnips, sliced
1 litre/1¾ pints Chicken Stock (page 46) or
   Vegetable Stock (page 46)
salt and cayenne pepper
150 ml/¼ pint single cream
30 ml/2 tbsp pine nuts (optional)

Melt the butter in a large saucepan, add the onion and parsnips, and cook over gentle heat for 10 minutes, turning frequently to coat them in the butter.

Add the stock, with salt and cayenne pepper to taste. Bring to the boil, lower the heat and simmer for 20 minutes until the parsnips are very soft.

Purée the soup in a blender or food processor, or rub through a sieve into a clean pan. Reheat it to just below boiling point, then stir in most of the cream, reserving about 30 ml/2 tbsp for the garnish.

Meanwhile spread out the pine nuts (if used) in a grill pan and toast them under a hot grill until golden. Ladle the soup into individual bowls and top each portion with a swirl of cream and a sprinkling of toasted pine nuts.

SERVES FOUR

VARIATION

Spiced Parsnip Soup   Add 5 ml/1 tsp good-quality curry powder to the onion and parsnips when cooking in the butter. Substitute plain yogurt for the cream and use roughly chopped cashew nuts instead of the pine nuts. Sprinkle with a little chopped fresh coriander leaves, if liked.

GREEN PEA SOUP

675 g/1¼ lb peas in the pod
15 ml/1 tbsp butter
1 onion, chopped
1 litre/1¾ pints White Stock (page 46)
salt and pepper
3–4 fresh young spinach leaves, roughly
   chopped
1 mint sprig
2–3 parsley sprigs
pinch of sugar (optional)
60 ml/4 tbsp single cream

GARNISH
60 ml/4 tbsp young fresh or frozen peas
4 small mint sprigs

Shell the peas, reserving about half the pods (the youngest and most tender). Melt the butter in a large saucepan. Add the onion and cook over gentle heat for 3–4 minutes. Add the pea pods, turning them over until coated in the butter, and cook gently for 10 minutes.

Stir in the stock, with salt and pepper to taste. Bring to the boil, then lower the heat and add the peas, spinach leaves, mint and parsley. Simmer for 10–20 minutes or until the peas are just tender.

Purée the soup in a blender or food processor, or rub through a sieve into a clean pan. Check the seasoning and add more salt and pepper if required. A pinch of sugar may also be added to bring out the flavour of the peas.

Reheat the soup to just below boiling point. In a separate pan, cook the peas for the garnish in salted boiling water until tender. Remove the soup from the heat, swirl in the cream and serve in individual bowls. Using a slotted spoon, ladle 15 ml/1 tbsp freshly cooked peas into each bowl. Complete the garnish by adding the mint.

SERVES FOUR

CHANTILLY SOUP

Use fresh young peas to make this simple soup. The best pods are plump and well filled without being too tightly packed.

30 ml/2 tbsp butter
2 onions, finely chopped
1.4 kg/3 lb peas in the pod (about 675 g/1½ lb
   when shelled)
1 small bunch of parsley, chopped
1.5 litres/2½ pints Chicken Stock (page 46)
salt and pepper

Melt the butter in a large saucepan. Add the onions and cook over gentle heat for 10 minutes until soft but not coloured.

Meanwhile shell the peas, reserving about 6 of the best pods. Stir the peas and parsley into the pan and add the stock, with salt and pepper to taste. Wash the pods and add them to the pan.

Bring the stock to simmering point (see Mrs Beeton's Tip) and cook for about 20 minutes, or until the peas are very soft. Remove the pods.

Purée the soup in a blender or food processor, or rub through a sieve into a clean pan. Bring to just below boiling point and serve at once.

SERVES SIX

 MRS BEETON'S TIP

Do not allow the soup to boil after the peas have been added, or you will spoil the colour.

CABBAGE SOUP

Cabbage and bacon go wonderfully well together, a fact that is celebrated in this hearty soup.

15 ml/1 tbsp oil
175 g/6 oz rindless streaky bacon rashers
2 carrots, thinly sliced
1 large onion, thinly sliced
1 large cabbage, shredded
1.1 litres/2 pints White Stock (page 46)
pepper to taste
croûtons to serve (optional)

Heat the oil in a large heavy-bottomed saucepan or flameproof casserole. Add the bacon and cook, stirring, for 5 minutes. Add the carrots and onion, then cook gently for 10 minutes. Stir in the cabbage and add the stock. Bring to the boil, lower the heat and cover the pan. Simmer for 45 minutes, until the vegetables are tender and the soup well flavoured.

Taste the soup for seasoning and add pepper. The bacon usually makes the soup sufficiently salty, depending on the stock. Skim off any excess surface fat, then serve the soup very hot, with croûtons, if liked.

SERVES EIGHT

 MRS BEETON'S TIP

If the soup is slightly too salty when cooked, then add 2 peeled and diced potatoes, and simmer for 20–30 minutes, keeping the pan closely covered.

CARROT SOUP

Grating the vegetables speeds up the cooking time considerably, making this an ideal soup for those occasions when time is short.

600 ml/1 pint Chicken Stock (page 46) or
   Vegetable Stock (page 46)
3 carrots, grated
1 onion, finely chopped
1 potato, grated
25 g/1 oz butter
25 g/1 oz plain flour
300 ml/½ pint milk
salt and pepper
grated nutmeg

Combine the stock, carrots, onion and potato in a saucepan. Bring to the boil, lower the heat and simmer for about 15 minutes or until the vegetables are tender.

Meanwhile melt the butter in a separate saucepan, add the flour and cook for 1 minute. Gradually stir in the milk, then add the stock and vegetables. Heat, stirring constantly, until the mixture boils and thickens. Add salt, pepper and nutmeg to taste. Serve at once, with triangles of hot toast, if liked.

SERVES FOUR

VARIATION

Carrot and Orange Soup Cut the carrot into matchstick strips and use 1 parsnip, cut into similar strips, instead of the potato. Use 900 ml/1½ pints stock and add 60 ml/4 tbsp fresh orange juice. Omit the milk and do not thicken the soup.

CREAM OF TOMATO SOUP

25 g/1 oz butter
2 rindless back bacon rashers, chopped
1 small onion, chopped
1 carrot, chopped
900 g/2 lb tomatoes, chopped
600 ml/1 pint Chicken Stock or White Stock
(page 46)
1 bouquet garni
salt and pepper
10 ml/2 tsp sugar
300 ml/½ pint double cream
chopped parsley or snipped chives to
garnish

Melt the butter in a large saucepan, add the bacon and fry for 2-3 minutes. Stir in the onion and carrot and fry over gentle heat for 5 minutes, then add the tomatoes and cook for 5 minutes more.

Add the stock and bouquet garni, with salt and pepper to taste. Bring to the boil, lower the heat and simmer for about 20 minutes, until the vegetables are soft.

Remove the bouquet garni. Purée the soup in a blender or food processor, then rub through a sieve to remove traces of skin and seeds.

Return the soup to the rinsed-out pan. Stir in the sugar and reheat to just below boiling point. Stir in the cream, heat briefly but do not allow to simmer or the soup will curdle. Taste and adjust the seasoning, then serve at once, topped with chopped parsley or snipped chives.

SERVES SIX

FENNEL AND TOMATO SOUP

30 ml/2 tbsp oil
1 small onion, finely chopped
2 Florence fennel bulbs
4 tomatoes, peeled and chopped
1.5 litres/2½ pints Chicken Stock (page 46)
salt and pepper

Heat the oil in a large heavy-bottomed saucepan, add the onion and fry over gentle heat for 5 minutes.

Cut off any feathery fronds from the fennel and set them aside for the garnish. Slice the fennel bulbs into quarters, cut away the core, and roughly chop the flesh. Add the chopped fennel to the pan and fry over gentle heat for 10 minutes, turning frequently, until soft.

Add the tomatoes and chicken stock, with salt and pepper to taste. Bring stock to the boil, lower the heat and simmer for 15-20 minutes until the fennel is tender. Serve at once, garnished with chopped fennel fronds.

SERVES SIX

VARIATION

Creamed Fennel Soup Omit the tomato. When the fennel is tender, purée the soup in a blender or food processor. Return it to the clean pan and stir in 150 ml/¼ pint single cream. Reheat without boiling.

PUMPKIN SOUP

25 g/1 oz butter
1 onion, finely chopped
1 garlic clove, crushed
1 kg/2¼ lb pumpkin, peeled, seeded and
    cubed
1.5 litres/2½ pints Chicken Stock (page 46)
    or Vegetable Stock (page 46)
5 ml/1 tsp ground coriander seeds
5 ml/1 tsp ground cinnamon
2.5 ml/½ tsp ground cumin
salt and pepper
150 ml/¼ pint whipping cream or fromage
    frais

Melt the butter in a large saucepan, add the
onion and garlic and cook over gentle heat for
10 minutes until soft but not coloured.

Add the pumpkin cubes, stock and spices, with
salt and pepper to taste. Bring to the boil, lower
the heat and simmer for about 30 minutes or
until the pumpkin is tender.

Purée the soup in a blender or food processor,
or rub through a sieve into a clean pan. Taste
and add more salt and pepper if required. The
soup should be quite spicy. Reheat without
boiling.

Whip the cream, if using. Ladle the soup into
individual bowls and top each portion with a
spoonful of whipped cream or fromage frais.

SERVES SIX

VARIATION

Pumpkin and Apple Soup Omit the coriander and cumin. Add 2 peeled, cored and
sliced cooking apples with the pumpkin. Continue as above, then stir in a little sugar to taste
when reheated. The sweetness should just
balance the tang of the apples. Serve as above.

CAULIFLOWER SOUP

1 large cauliflower
25 g/1 oz butter
1 onion, finely chopped
900 ml/1½ pints milk
salt and pepper
2 egg yolks
150 ml/¼ pint single cream
50 g/2 oz flaked almonds, toasted

Steam the cauliflower whole for 20–30 minutes
until tender. Cut it into florets, reserving any
leaves or tender stem.

Melt the butter in a small frying pan. Add the
onion and cook over gentle heat for about 10
minutes, until soft but not coloured. Purée the
cauliflower and the onion mixture with
250 ml/8 fl oz of the milk in a blender or food
processor, then rub through a fine sieve into a
clean pan.

Stir the remaining milk into the pan, with salt
and pepper to taste. Heat the soup to just below
boiling point, then lower the heat so that it
barely simmers. In a small bowl, mix the egg
yolks with the cream. Stir a little of the hot soup
into the egg mixture, mix well, then add the
contents of the bowl to the soup, stirring over
low heat until it thickens. Serve at once, topping each portion with toasted almonds.

SERVES FOUR

 MRS BEETON'S TIP

To make a quick cauliflower soup, break
the vegetable into florets and place in a
saucepan with 1 diced potato and 1
chopped onion. Add 600 ml/1 pint chicken
stock and bring to the boil. Simmer,
covered for 30 minutes, then purée. Add
300 ml/½ pint milk and seasoning to taste.
Heat without boiling.

YELLOW SPLIT PEA SOUP

30 ml/2 tbsp oil
6 rindless streaky bacon rashers, chopped
1 large onion, finely chopped
100 g/4 oz yellow split peas, soaked
    overnight in water to cover
2 litres/3½ pints Chicken Stock (page 46) or
    Vegetable Stock (page 46)
60 ml/4 tbsp chopped celery leaves
2 parsley sprigs
2 bay leaves
5 ml/1 tsp chopped summer savory or
    2.5 ml/½ tsp dried savory
salt and pepper

Heat the oil in a large saucepan. Add the bacon
and onion. Fry for 10 minutes over gentle heat,
until the onion is soft but not coloured.

Drain the split peas and add them to the pan
with the stock, celery leaves, parsley, bay
leaves and savory. Add salt and pepper to taste.
Bring to the boil, lower the heat and simmer for
about 2 hours, or until the peas are very tender.
If the soup becomes too thick, add water or
extra stock.

Remove the parsley sprigs and bay leaves.
Serve the soup as it is, or purée in a blender or
food processor. Alternatively, rub through a
sieve into a clean pan. Reheat, stirring frequently to prevent the soup from sticking to the
pan, and serve at once.

SERVES FOUR TO SIX

VARIATION

Pea and Ham Soup Save the stock when
boiling a joint of ham or bacon as it makes
delicious split pea soup. Omit the streaky
bacon and do not add seasoning until the soup
is cooked.

LEEK AND OAT BROTH

1 litre/1¾ pints White Stock (page 86)
3 leeks, trimmed, sliced and washed
1 bay leaf
salt and pepper
60 ml/4 tbsp fine or medium oatmeal
150 ml/¼ pint single cream

Bring the stock and leeks to the boil in a large
saucepan. Add the bay leaf and salt and pepper
to taste. Lower the heat and simmer for 20
minutes.

Sprinkle the oatmeal into the simmering soup,
whisking all the time and simmer for 5
minutes more. Then cover and simmer gently
for a further 15–20 minutes, until thickened.

Stir in the cream, reheat without boiling and
serve at once.

SERVES FOUR

 PRESSURE COOKER TIP

It is not necessary to soak the split peas if
the soup is to be made in a pressure cooker.
Fry the bacon and onion in the oil in the
open cooker. Add the split peas and herbs
as in the recipe above, but reduce the
amount of stock to 1 litre/1¾ pints. Put the
lid on the cooker and bring to 15 lb pressure. Cook for 12 minutes. Reduce pressure
slowly, then continue as described above,
adding more stock to adjust the consistency as desired.

 MRS BEETON'S TIP

Quick-cook porridge oats may be substituted for oatmeal and the soup simmered
for just 5 minutes before adding the cream.

BEAN SOUP

The perfect warmer for a chilly winter's night, this soup is a meal in itself.

450 g/1 lb haricot beans, soaked overnight in
  water to cover
100 g/4 oz fat bacon, diced
2 onions, sliced
10 ml/2 tsp dried thyme
salt and pepper
15 ml/1 tbsp chopped parsley

Drain the beans. Put them in a large heavy-bottomed saucepan. Add 2.25 litres/4 pints water and bring to the boil. Boil vigorously for 10 minutes, then lower the heat and simmer for 45 minutes or until the beans are almost tender. Drain, reserving the bean stock.

Put the bacon in the clean pan and heat gently until the fat runs. Add the onions and fry over moderate heat for 3–4 minutes. Stir in the beans with the thyme. Add the reserved bean stock, with salt and pepper to taste. Simmer for 1 hour, stirring occasionally to prevent the soup from sticking to the pan.

Check the seasoning and add more salt and pepper if required. Stir in the parsley and serve at once, with chunks of wholemeal bread.

SERVES SIX TO EIGHT

VARIATIONS

Two-bean Soup Use half red kidney beans instead of haricot beans alone. Add 1 diced green pepper with the onions.

Vegetarian Bean Soup Omit the bacon and fry the onion in 25 g/1 oz butter with 1 crushed garlic clove. Stir in 45 ml/3 tbsp tahini with the parsley.

LENTIL AND PARSLEY SOUP

25 g/1 oz butter or margarine
2 carrots, diced
1 large leek, trimmed, finely sliced and
  washed
100 g/4 oz red lentils
300 ml/½ pint milk
1 bay leaf
salt and pepper
30 ml/2 tbsp chopped parsley

Melt the butter or margarine in a saucepan, add the carrots and leek and fry gently for about 5 minutes, stirring frequently, until the leek slices are soft but not coloured.

Add the lentils, milk, bay leaf and 600 ml/1 pint water. Heat gently to simmering point, cover and simmer for about 20 minutes or until the lentils are soft. Remove the bay leaf. Add salt and pepper to taste, stir in the chopped parsley and serve.

SERVES FOUR

 PRESSURE COOKER TIP

Having added the liquid, put the lid on the cooker and bring to 15 lb pressure. Cook for 15 minutes. Reduce pressure slowly, then remove the bay leaf and add the seasoning and parsley.

FRESH ASPARAGUS SOUP

450 g/1 lb fresh asparagus
salt and white pepper
1.4 litres/2½ pints Chicken Stock (page 46)
50 g/2 oz butter
1 small onion, chopped
50 g/2 oz plain flour
1 egg yolk
150 ml/¼ pint double cream

Cut off the asparagus tips and put them in a saucepan. Add salted water to cover, bring to the boil, then simmer for about 5 minutes or until tender. Drain and set aside.

Slice the asparagus stalks and cook them in 600 ml/1 pint of the stock for about 15 minutes or until tender. Purée in a blender or food processor, or rub through a sieve into a bowl or large jug.

Melt the butter in a large saucepan, add the onion and fry over gentle heat for about 10 minutes until soft but not coloured. Stir in the flour and cook for 1 minute, stirring constantly.

Gradually add the remaining stock, stirring until the mixture boils and thickens. Stir in the asparagus purée, with salt and pepper to taste. Reheat.

In a small bowl, mix the egg yolk with the cream. Stir a little of the hot soup into the egg mixture, mix well, then add the contents of the bowl to the soup, stirring over low heat until the mixture thickens slightly. Add the reserved asparagus tips and heat through without boiling. Serve at once.

SERVES SIX

SPINACH SOUP

25 g/1 oz butter
1 large onion, finely chopped
1.1 litres/2 pints Chicken Stock (page 46)
2 potatoes, diced
900 g/2 lb spinach, washed, trimmed and
    roughly chopped
2.5 ml/½ tsp grated nutmeg
salt and pepper
150 ml/¼ pint single cream
2 rindless back bacon rashers, grilled and
    crumbled, to garnish (optional)

Melt the butter, add the onion and cook over gentle heat for 10 minutes until soft but not coloured. Add the stock and potatoes and cook for 15 minutes.

Add the spinach and cook for 10 minutes more or until both potatoes and spinach are tender. Purée the soup in a blender or food processor, or rub through a sieve into a clean pan. Add the nutmeg, with salt and pepper to taste.

Stir in the cream and reheat without boiling. Serve the soup in individual bowls, topping each portion with crumbled bacon, if liked.

SERVES FOUR

VARIATION

Green and Gold Fry the onion in the butter as described above. Meanwhile cook the spinach with just the water that clings to the leaves after washing. Drain thoroughly, pressing the spinach against the sides of the colander with a wooden spoon to extract as much liquid as possible, then mix the spinach with the onion mixture. Form into egg-sized balls. Bring the stock to the boil. Spoon a few spinach balls into each soup bowl, add the boiling stock and serve at once.

CREAM OF LETTUCE SOUP

400 g/14 oz lettuce, shredded
600 ml/1 pint White Stock (page 46)
30 ml/2 tbsp butter
1 onion, finely chopped
1 garlic clove, crushed
225 g/8 oz potatoes, cubed
1 bouquet garni
salt and pepper
150 ml/¼ pint single cream
1 egg yolk

Put the lettuce in a large heatproof bowl. Bring the stock to the boil in a deep saucepan, pour over the lettuce and set aside.

Melt the butter in the clean pan, add the onion, garlic and potato and fry over gentle heat, turning the vegetables frequently, for 10 minutes. Add the lettuce and stock with the bouquet garni. Stir in salt and pepper to taste. Bring to the boil, then lower the heat and simmer for 2 minutes or until the lettuce is tender.

Remove the bouquet garni. Purée the soup in a blender or food processor, or rub through a sieve into a clean pan. Reheat to simmering point, then remove the pan from the heat.

Mix the cream and egg yolk together in a small bowl, stir in a little of the hot soup and mix well. Whisk the mixture into the remaining soup, return it to the heat and reheat without boiling, stirring all the time. Taste and adjust the seasoning, if necessary. Serve hot.

SERVES FOUR

 MRS BEETON'S TIP

For a cheaper and less rich soup, substitute 125 ml/4 fl oz milk for the egg and cream mixture. Add the milk to the lettuce purée when reheating.

SOUP MAIGRE

Originally, the soup was not sieved or puréed but enriched by adding an egg yolk with the vinegar. The puréed soup is refreshing and pleasing on the palate.

50 g/2 oz butter
2 onions, thinly sliced
4 celery sticks, sliced
1 lettuce, shredded
3–4 tender spinach leaves, shredded
30 ml/2 tbsp chopped parsley
1 litre/1¾ pints Vegetable Stock (page 46) or
  Chicken Stock (page 46)
1 blade of mace
salt and pepper
5 ml/1 tsp cider vinegar

Melt the butter in a large saucepan, add the onions and fry over moderate heat for 5 minutes until slightly softened. Stir in the celery, lettuce and spinach. Cook for 10 minutes over gentle heat, stirring frequently to coat the vegetables in butter and prevent them from sticking to the base of the pan.

Stir in the parsley, stock and mace, with salt and pepper to taste. Simmer for 30 minutes.

Remove the blade of mace, then purée the soup in a blender or food processor. Reheat and sharpen with the vinegar. Taste for seasoning before serving.

SERVES FOUR

 FREEZER TIP

The puréed soup freezes very well and is an excellent recipe for using a glut of home-grown lettuce. Add the vinegar after thawing and reheating. The frozen soup will keep for up to 6 months.

CELERY SOUP

45 g/1½ oz butter
1 head of celery, finely sliced
2 leeks, trimmed, sliced and washed
1 litre/1¾ pints White Stock (page 46)
salt and pepper
grated nutmeg
2 egg yolks
150 ml/¼ pint single cream

Melt the butter in a large saucepan. Add the celery and leeks and cook over gentle heat for 10 minutes until soft.

Add the stock. Bring to the boil, then lower the heat and simmer for 15–20 minutes or until the vegetables are tender. Purée the soup in a blender or food processor, or rub through a sieve into a clean pan. Add salt, pepper and nutmeg to taste. Return the soup to the heat and simmer for 10 minutes.

In a small bowl, mix the egg yolks with the cream. Stir a little of the hot soup into the egg mixture, mix well, then add the contents of the bowl to the soup, stirring over low heat until heated but do not allow to boil. Serve at once.

SERVES FOUR

VARIATION

Celery and Stilton Soup Omit the nutmeg. When mixing the egg yolks with the cream, add 75 g/3 oz crumbled Stilton.

 MRS BEETON'S TIP

Celery seeds may be used to flavour soup. They are very small and pale green-beige in colour. Pound them to a powder in a mortar, using a pestle, then add to potato soup or other plain vegetable soups.

CUCUMBER SOUP

For extra piquancy, a little chopped sorrel may be added with the chervil. Home-grown cucumbers sometimes have large, unpleasant seeds which must be removed before cooking. However, if the centre of the vegetable is fine-textured there is no need to scoop it out.

1 large cucumber
salt
15 g/½ oz butter
1.1 litres/2 pints well-flavoured Chicken
  Stock (page 46)
30 ml/2 tbsp chopped chervil
2 egg yolks
150 ml/¼ pint single cream

Peel the cucumber and cut it into quarters. Spoon out the seeds. Slice the cucumber thickly, put the slices in a colander and sprinkle with a little salt to draw out the excess liquid. Set aside for 20 minutes, then rinse the cucumber slices thoroughly and pat them dry with absorbent kitchen paper.

Melt the butter in a large saucepan. Add the cucumber slices and heat them through, turning frequently until well coated in butter. Stir in the stock and chervil. Simmer for 30 minutes or until the cucumber is tender.

In a small bowl, mix the egg yolks with the cream. Stir a little of the hot soup into the egg mixture, mix well, then add the contents of the bowl to the soup, stirring over low heat until heated but do not allow to boil. Serve at once.

SERVES FOUR

VARIATION

Smooth Cucumber Soup For a smooth soup, purée the cooked cucumber with the stock before adding the yolks and cream.

AVGOLEMONO SOUP

This classic Greek soup, smooth and tangy, may also be made with fish or lamb stock.

1.5 litres/2½ pints Chicken Stock (page 46)
75 g/3 oz short-grain rice or pasta shapes
4 eggs, separated
salt and pepper
50 ml/2 fl oz lemon juice

Bring the stock to the boil in a large saucepan. Add the rice or pasta and cook over moderate heat until tender.

In a clean, grease-free bowl, whisk the egg whites with 1.25 ml/¼ tsp salt until stiff. Continue to whisk while adding the egg yolks. Finally whisk in the lemon juice and about 250 ml/8 fl oz of the hot stock.

Stir the stock and rice or pasta vigorously over very low heat, at the same time adding the egg and lemon mixture. Continue to stir for 2 minutes more. Serve at once.

SERVES EIGHT TO TEN

 MRS BEETON'S TIP

Do not allow the stock to approach boiling point after the egg mixture has been added, or the soup will curdle.

SOUP A LA SOLFERINO

1.7 litres/3 pints Chicken Stock (page 46),
   Consommé (page 55) or clear soup
225 g/8 oz plain flour
2.5 ml/½ tsp salt
25 g/1 oz butter, softened, plus extra for
   shallow frying
2 eggs, lightly beaten
150 ml/¼ pint single cream
oil for shallow frying

Heat the chicken stock or soup in a large saucepan to just below boiling point.

Put the flour and salt into a mixing bowl. Make a well in the centre and add the softened butter, eggs and cream. Mix to a soft, sticky dough.

Melt the butter for shallow frying with a little oil in a large heavy-bottomed frying pan. Wash, then wet your hands and form small portions of the dough into small balls or oval shapes about the size of cherries. Add the dough balls as you shape them, repeatedly wetting your hands to prevent the dough sticking. Fry over moderate heat for about 5 minutes, until cooked through and golden brown. Use a spoon and fork to turn the pieces of dough as they cook, so that they brown evenly. The dough makes about 60 small balls.

Drain the cooked dough balls on absorbent kitchen paper and place in a soup tureen. Pour in the chicken stock and serve at once.

SERVES EIGHT

 FREEZER TIP

The cooked balls of dough may be frozen, ready for adding straight to hot soup or reheating briefly in a hot oven before serving.

CREAM OF ALMOND SOUP

The delicate flavour of this soup makes it the perfect introduction to a simple summer meal.

300 ml/½ pint milk
175 ml/6 fl oz single cream
pared rind of 1 lemon
50 g/2 oz butter
50 g/2 oz plain flour
1 litre/1¾ pints Chicken Stock (page 46)
salt and pepper
75 g/3 oz ground almonds
pinch of cayenne pepper
2.5 ml/½ tsp ground mace

Combine the milk, cream and lemon rind in a saucepan. Bring to just below boiling point, then remove from the heat.

Melt the butter in the top of a double saucepan, stir in the flour and cook for 2 minutes. Gradually add the stock, stirring all the time until the mixture boils and thickens. Add salt and pepper to taste.

Remove from the heat. Gradually stir in the milk mixture. When the mixture is smooth and creamy, add the ground almonds, cayenne and mace. Place the pan over simmering water and cook for 15 minutes, stirring frequently. Remove the lemon rind and serve.

SERVES FOUR TO SIX

COCONUT SOUP

This unusual soup is delicately flavoured but quite rich, with a very smooth, creamy texture.

25 g/1 oz desiccated coconut or 40 g/1½ oz
    shelled fresh coconut, grated
600 ml/1 pint good ham stock, preferably
    from a smoked gammon joint
1 small onion, thinly sliced
1 bay leaf
40 g/1½ oz butter
60 ml/4 tbsp plain flour
pinch of mace
2.5 ml/½ tsp sugar
pepper
300 ml/½ pint single cream

Place the coconut in a saucepan with the stock. Add the onion and bay leaf, and bring to the boil. Lower the heat so that the stock is barely simmering, cover the pan tightly and leave over low heat for 1 hour. Strain into a bowl, squeezing all the liquid from the coconut mixture.

Melt the butter in the rinsed-out pan. Stir in the flour and gradually add the strained stock, stirring all the time. Add a little mace, the sugar and pepper to taste – the soup is unlikely to need salt as ham stock is salty.

Bring to the boil, stirring, then lower the heat and simmer for 3 minutes. Add the cream, stir well and heat for a few seconds without boiling. Serve at once.

SERVES FOUR

CHESTNUT SOUP

Chestnuts have a robust flavour which combines well with beef stock in this unusual soup.

350 g/12 oz chestnuts
1.4 litres/2½ pints Rich Strong Stock (page 45) or Vegetable Stock (page 46)
salt and cayenne pepper
2.5 ml/½ tsp ground mace
150 ml/¼ pint single cream

Make a small slit in the shell of each chestnut. Place the chestnuts in a saucepan of boiling water and cook for 5 minutes. Drain, carefully removing the shells and skins while the chestnuts are still very hot.

Put the peeled chestnuts into a pan and cover with 400 ml/14 fl oz of the stock. Bring to the boil, lower the heat and simmer for 30–40 minutes or until the chestnuts break when touched with a fork. Drain the chestnuts thoroughly, reserving about 250 ml/8 fl oz of the chestnut-flavoured stock.

Rub the chestnuts through a sieve into a clean pan. Stir in the remaining stock, with enough of the chestnut–flavoured stock to give a good flavour (see Mrs Beeton's Tip). Add salt, cayenne and mace to taste.

Bring the soup to just below boiling point, stirring frequently, then remove from the heat and stir in the cream. Serve at once.

SERVES FOUR TO SIX

 MRS BEETON'S TIP

The stock in which the chestnuts have been cooked will have a sweetish flavour which may not be to everyone's taste, so add it with discretion.

CUCUMBER AND YOGURT SOUP

Low in calories, this is the ideal soup for a summer lunch party.

15 ml/1 tbsp butter or light olive oil
1 small onion, finely chopped
½ large cucumber, peeled and cut into 5 mm/¼ inch dice
450 ml/¾ pint plain yogurt
250 ml/8 fl oz Chicken or well-flavoured Vegetable Stock (page 46)
grated rind and juice of ½ lemon
10 ml/2 tsp finely chopped mint
salt and pepper
mint sprigs to garnish

Melt the butter in a saucepan, add the onion and cucumber and cook over very gentle heat for 8–10 minutes. Leave to cool.

Whisk the yogurt in a bowl until smooth. Add the onion mixture with the stock. Stir in the lemon rind and juice, with the mint. Add salt and pepper to taste. Cover the bowl and chill for several hours. Serve in chilled bowls, garnished with mint sprigs.

SERVES THREE TO FOUR

 MRS BEETON'S TIP

Omit the stock to make a creamy dip, ideal for serving with Grissini (page 57) or crisps.

CHILLED AVOCADO SOUP

4 ripe avocados
juice of 1 lemon
500 ml/18 fl oz Consommé (page 55) or
    canned consommé
250 ml/8 fl oz soured cream or fromage frais
salt and pepper
30 ml/2 tbsp snipped chives or spring onion
    green

Scoop the flesh from the avocados into a sieve set over a bowl. Spoon the lemon juice over the top and then rub the avocados through the sieve. Stir in the consommé and soured cream or fromage frais.

Add salt and pepper to taste, cover the bowl and refrigerate for 2–3 hours. Just before serving, stir in the chives or spring onions.

SERVES SIX

 MRS BEETON'S TIP

The soup can be made very quickly in a blender or food processor, but take care not to overprocess the avocado.

VICHYSOISSE

A simple soup which can be served hot, but tastes even better chilled.

25 g/1 oz butter
450 g/1 lb leeks, white parts only, trimmed,
    sliced and washed
2 onions, chopped
450 g/1 lb potatoes, cubed
900 ml/1½ pints Chicken Stock (page 46)
salt and pepper
150 ml/¼ pint milk
150 ml/¼ pint single cream
snipped chives to garnish

Melt the butter in a saucepan, add the leeks, onions and potatoes and fry gently for 10 minutes without browning. Stir in the stock, with salt and pepper to taste. Bring to the boil, lower the heat and simmer for about 30 minutes or until the vegetables are soft.

Purée the mixture in a blender or food processor, or press through a sieve into a bowl. Cool quickly, then stir in the milk and cream. Add more salt and pepper if required. Cover and chill for 4–6 hours. Serve in chilled individual bowls, sprinkled with chives.

SERVES FOUR TO SIX

 FREEZER TIP

Make the soup as above, but use only 1 onion and 600 ml/1 pint chicken stock. After puréeing the vegetables and stock, cool the mixture quickly and freeze in a rigid container. Thaw overnight in the refrigerator. Stir in the remaining stock with the milk and cream, then chill for at least 2 hours more before serving.

JELLIED TOMATO SOUP

2 spring onions, finely chopped
2-3 celery leaves, finely chopped
250 ml/8 fl oz tomato juice
few drops of Worcestershire sauce
3 cloves
pinch of sugar
few drops of lemon juice
salt and pepper
cayenne pepper
15 ml/1 tbsp gelatine
250 ml/8 fl oz Chicken Stock (page 46),
  chilled

GARNISH
30-45 ml/2-3 tbsp soured cream
freshly ground black pepper

Combine the spring onions, celery leaves and tomato juice in a large saucepan. Add the Worcestershire sauce, cloves, sugar and lemon juice, with salt, pepper and cayenne to taste. Bring to simmering point, half cover the pan, and simmer for 10 minutes. Strain into a bowl.

Put 30 ml/2 tbsp water in a small bowl. Sprinkle the gelatine on top. Set aside for 15 minutes until the gelatine is spongy. Stand the bowl over a saucepan of hot water and stir until the gelatine has dissolved completely. Add a little of the strained tomato liquid and stir well.

Pour the gelatine mixture into the remaining tomato liquid and mix thoroughly. Add the chilled chicken stock, stir until well mixed, then refrigerate for about 2 hours or until set.

To serve, whisk the jellied soup until frothy. Spoon into 4 chilled individual bowls. Garnish with the soured cream and a generous grinding of black pepper.

SERVES FOUR

GAZPACHO

2 thick slices of bread, cubed
1 litre/1¾ pints tomato juice
1 small onion, finely chopped
2 garlic cloves, crushed
¼ cucumber, finely chopped
1 green pepper, seeded and chopped
6 tomatoes, peeled and chopped
75 ml/3 fl oz olive oil
30 ml/2 tbsp red wine vinegar
1.25 ml/¼ tsp dried oregano
1.25 ml/¼ tsp dried mixed herbs
salt and pepper

TO SERVE
croûtons (see Mrs Beeton's Tip, below)
diced cucumber
diced onion
black olives

Put the bread cubes in a large bowl with the tomato juice. Leave to soak for 5 minutes, then add the chopped vegetables. Stir in the olive oil, cover and leave to stand for 1 hour.

Purée the soup in a blender or food processor, then rub through a sieve into a clean bowl. Stir in the vinegar and herbs, with salt and pepper to taste. Cover the bowl closely and chill for 2-3 hours. Serve with the suggested accompaniments, in separate bowls.

SERVES FOUR

 MRS BEETON'S TIP

To make croûtons, fry small cubes of bread in a mixture of olive oil and butter, turning them frequently, until golden brown all over.

APPLE SOUP

450 g/1 lb cooking apples
1.75 litres/3 pints White Stock (page 46)
3 cloves
2.5 ml/½ tsp white pepper
ground ginger to taste

Peel the apples, cut them into quarters and remove the cores. Put them into a large saucepan with the stock. Add the cloves. Cook over moderate heat until tender.

Rub the mixture through a sieve into a clean pan. Add the pepper with ground ginger to taste. Bring to the boil, stirring frequently, then remove from the heat and serve.

SERVES SIX

 MRS BEETON'S TIP

In Mrs Beeton's day there were said to be upwards of 1,500 varieties of apple. She specifically recommended Colvilles for this recipe, but Bramleys will serve equally well. Some of the old varieties are once again being cultivated; it is worth looking out for them.

SWEET FRUIT SOUPS

Popular in Eastern European and Scandinavian countries, sweetened soups made from tangy fruit do not replace light savoury soups for the first course of a meal but are rather served between courses. More often, a fruit soup will be served as a light meal or snack, perhaps with light, sweetened curd cheese dumplings as an accompaniment. A fruit soup can also make an unusual and refreshing dessert course.

Tangy, full-flavoured fruit, such as sour cherries, plums, damsons and redcurrants, are all suitable ingredients for soup. The basic method is straightforward: the fruit is cooked with water and sugar to taste until tender, then puréed and sieved. Reserved fruit may be added to the soup which can be enriched by the addition of cream or yogurt.

Spices such as cinnamon, cloves or allspice berries may be cooked with the fruit and red or white wine may be used instead of part of the water. Arrowroot is a suitable thickening agent, if required.

Fruit soups are usually chilled if they are to be served for dessert or between courses; however, many are equally palatable hot, especially when served with slices of toasted sweet or rich bread, such as brioche.

First Courses, Canapés, Snacks and Savouries

Striking the right note is all important with the opening dish of the meal – the flavours and textures should stimulate the palate without dulling the appetite for what follows.

The choice of appetizer depends on the remaining courses. Plain, refreshing starters are ideal before a hearty main course and rich dessert; alternatively, you may prefer to present an array of mixed hors d'oeuvre and keep the rest of the meal fairly light.

Serve thin, crisp toast; hot bread rolls; sliced wholemeal or Granary bread; or slices or chunks of French bread as accompaniments.

SIMPLE FRUIT STARTERS

Light fruit starters are ideal for lunch or summer dinners. Several ways of serving fruit are also appropriate for the canapé tray.

Avocado Avocado must be ripe but not mushy. Unripe fruit is hard, bitter and has a poor flavour. Test by gently pressing the outside of the avocado: it should give slightly, feeling tender but not soft enough to be able to compress the flesh. Avoid fruit which is very hard as it may never ripen. If the avocado feels firm but not hard, leave it in a warm room for a day or two until it feels tender. Soft avocados are perfectly suitable for making dips; however, very soft fruit with loose skin which may be dented or bruised should be avoided as the flesh will probably be blackened and stringy.

Serve avocado very plain, with a vinaigrette dressing, or use it in simple salads, with leafy vegetables or tomato. Chunks of avocado, wrapped in bacon and grilled, may be served 'en brochette' or skewered as miniature kebabs, or offered on cocktail sticks with before-dinner drinks.

Banana Thickly sliced, wrapped in bacon and grilled, banana may be stuck with cocktail sticks to serve with drinks.

Citrus Fruit Grapefruit is an old favourite, especially when halved and sprinkled with sugar well in advance of serving, so that the fruit is very juicy; or combined with orange in a simple cocktail. To prepare the fruit, cut it in half and use a serrated knife or grapefruit knife to loosen the flesh from the shell, then cut between the segments and remove any central core of pith and membrane. The combination of grapefruit, orange and crisp grilled bacon or cooked ham makes an excellent first-course salad with eye appeal.

Dates Fresh dates may be stoned and filled with soft cheese for serving with canapes. Soft cheese with garlic and herbs is a good choice.

Figs Fresh figs are delicious with Parma ham or with soft cheese – particularly goat's cheese. Peel the figs thinly, then cut them almost through into quarters, opening out the segments, flower-fashion, on individual plates. Serve with freshly ground black pepper.

Melon The many types of melon are all suitable for serving plain or in cocktails. Cut melons in half and remove the seeds. Serve small melons in halves or wedges. Alternatively, use a melon baller to scoop out the flesh or cut it into neat pieces. Dress less sweet varieties with a little caster sugar and dust with a pinch of ground ginger. Port, sherry, vermouth or ginger wine are all useful simple marinades or dressings for melon.

MIXED HORS D'OEUVRE

A selection of complementary prepared and dressed ingredients for sampling in small portions.

Artichoke Bottoms or Hearts Fresh, cooked and prepared or canned, these may be served plain with an oil-based dressing.

Cheese Fine slices of Gruyère, Gouda or other mild, and not too rich, cheese may be included.

Cooked Meats and Poultry Ham, roast meat, smoked poultry, salami and other cured meats should be served finely sliced and attractively arranged.

Eggs Hard-boiled and halved, quartered or sliced. These may be dressed with mayonnaise or stuffed and garnished. Quail's eggs, smoked or plain, are ideal for hors d'oeuvre. Pickled eggs may also be used.

Tomatoes Take advantage of the different types but always select for flavour; serve with an oil-based dressing. Plum tomatoes may be sliced or quartered lengthways. Mix red and yellow cherry tomatoes.

Vegetable Salads Keep these simple, dressing plain well-prepared vegetables and allowing them to marinate. Suitable candidates include grated carrots with a little spring onion, finely sliced cucumber, tiny new potatoes cooked in their skins and shredded fennel or celery. Grill, peel and slice the flesh of red or green peppers for a delicious addition. Button mushrooms marinated in olive oil, garlic, seasoning and lemon juice may be added to the hors d'oeuvre tray.

GRAPEFRUIT COCKTAIL

2 grapefruit
caster or soft brown sugar (optional)
30 ml/2 tbsp medium-dry sherry (optional)

DECORATION
2 maraschino cherries, halved
8 mint leaves

Cut the grapefruit across in half; remove visible pips. Using a serrated stainless steel knife (preferably a grapefruit knife) cut around each half between the flesh and the pith, to loosen the flesh. Cut between the membranes which divide the segments, but leave the flesh in the halved skins as if uncut. Sprinkle with sugar, if required, and/or with sherry. Decorate with cherries and mint leaves.

SERVES FOUR

AVOCADO VINAIGRETTE

2 ripe avocados
60 ml/4 tbsp Vinaigrette Dressing (page 469)

Prepare the avocados just before serving. Cut in half lengthways; remove the stones. Arrange the halves on individual plates or in avocado-shaped dishes. Spoon a little dressing into each hollow and serve at once.

SERVES TWO TO FOUR

 MRS BEETON'S TIP

The easiest way to remove the stone from an avocado is to spear it with a strong knife. Take care to avoid slipping the knife into your hand. Stab the blade down firmly into the stone, then lift the knife and the stone should come away cleanly.

MELON BOATS

1 large ripe melon, cut into 6-8 segments
1 lemon or lime, sliced
sherry or ginger wine (optional)

Using a sharp knife, slice between the melon skin and flesh on each segment to free the flesh but do not remove it. Cut the flesh across into bite-size sections. Gently ease the first row of chunks forward, then move the next row back. Continue moving neighbouring rows in this fashion so that all the pieces are staggered attractively. Three rows are the typical number in melon wedges.

Cut into the centre of each lemon or lime slice, then twist each slice and use a cocktail stick to secure the twists in the melon boats. Sprinkle each portion with sherry or ginger wine, if liked. Serve lightly chilled.

SERVES SIX TO EIGHT

MELON WITH PARMA HAM

This simple starter is always popular.

1 ripe green-fleshed melon, halved
  lengthways
12 slices of Parma ham

Cut the melon flesh into 16 sticks, each measuring about 7.5 × 2 cm/3 × ¾ inch. Roll the Parma ham loosely. Arrange the ham and melon alternately on individual plates.

SERVES FOUR

ASPARAGUS WITH HOT BUTTER SAUCE

48 asparagus spears, trimmed
175 g/6 oz butter
white pepper
lemon juice

Cook the asparagus in simmering water in a tall narrow saucepan or on a rack over boiling water in a roasting tin for about 10 minutes, until tender. Meanwhile, melt the butter. Add pepper and lemon juice to taste and pour over the drained asparagus.

SERVES SIX

VARIATIONS

Asparagus Hollandaise Cook as above. Serve hot, with Hollandaise sauce (page 480).

Asparagus Polonaise Cook as above. Melt 45 ml/3 tbsp butter in a frying pan, add 60 g/2 oz fresh white breadcrumbs and cook until golden. Stir in the chopped yolks of 4 hard-boiled eggs, with 30 ml/2 tbsp chopped parsley. Spoon over the asparagus.

ASPARAGUS ROLLS

12 thin slices of white or brown bread,
  crusts removed
50 g/2 oz butter, softened
12 cold cooked asparagus spears
salt and pepper

Flatten the bread slices lightly with a rolling pin. Spread them with butter. Lay an asparagus spear diagonally across each slice of bread. Season to taste, then roll up. Arrange the rolls in a shallow dish, seams underneath. Cover with cling film until required.

SERVES FOUR

TARAMASALATA

A food processor may be used to make taramasalata in a few seconds.

100 g/4 oz smoked cod's roe, skinned
1 garlic clove, halved
30 ml/2 tbsp lemon juice
60 ml/4 tbsp olive oil
black pepper

Pound the cod's roe and garlic in a mortar with the lemon juice until smooth. Add the olive oil and 30 ml/2 tbsp water alternately in small amounts, beating well after each addition, until the paste is smooth and completely blended. Grind in black pepper to taste and serve with warm pitta bread, lemon wedges and olives.

SERVES FOUR

✳ MICROWAVE TIP

Warm the contents of a packet of pitta bread on several sheets of absorbent kitchen paper for 1–2 minutes on High.

POTTED LOBSTER

This rich mixture is delicious with crisp thin toast or with thin slices of rye bread. It also makes a luscious topping for canapés.

450 g/1 lb boiled lobster
125 ml/4 fl oz single cream
1.25 ml/¼ tsp ground white pepper
pinch of ground mace
pinch of cayenne pepper
salt
100 g/4 oz unsalted butter, melted

Pick the lobster meat from the shell and dice it finely. Put it in a bowl. Heat the cream, white pepper, mace and cayenne without boiling. Add salt to taste.

Pour the spiced cream over the lobster meat and mix well. Gradually stir in the melted butter. Turn the mixture into a large dish or 4 individual dishes. Refrigerate until firm.

MAKES ABOUT 575 G/1¼ LB

POTTED SALMON

450 g/1 lb cold cooked salmon, skinned and
    boned
salt and pepper
pinch of cayenne pepper
pinch of ground mace
anchovy essence
50 g/2 oz softened clarified butter, plus extra
    for sealing (page 424)

Pound the salmon flesh in a mortar or process roughly in a blender or food processor. Add salt, pepper, cayenne, mace and anchovy essence to taste. Blend in the softened clarified butter thoroughly.

Rub the mixture through a fine sieve into a bowl. Turn into small pots. Cover with a layer of clarified butter and refrigerate until the butter is firm.

MAKES ABOUT 450 G/1 LB

POTTED HERRING FILLETS

This makes an excellent starter with Melba toast.

1 (198 g/7 oz) can herring fillets in tomato
  sauce
25 g/1 oz butter
pinch of ground mace
salt and pepper
melted clarified butter (page 424)

Mash the herring fillets with any sauce from
the can. Melt the butter in a small saucepan.
Add the mashed herrings, the mace and salt
and pepper to taste. Stir until the mixture is just
heated.

Cool slightly, then turn into small pots. Cover
with a layer of clarified butter and refrigerate
until the butter is firm.

MAKES ABOUT 200 G/7 OZ

SPRAT PASTE

450 g/1 lb sprats, cleaned
10 ml/2 tsp butter
pinch of cayenne pepper
black pepper
1.25 ml/¼ tsp ground mace
5 ml/1 tsp anchovy essence
15 ml/1 tbsp lemon juice
melted clarified butter (page 424)

Set the oven at 180°C/350°F/gas 4. Place the
sprats on a large sheet of foil supported on a
baking sheet. Dot the fish with butter and fold
the foil over to make a loose parcel. Bake for
10–15 minutes.

While still warm, remove the heads, tails, skin
and backbones from the fish. Pound the flesh
well in a mortar, then rub through a sieve into a
small mixing bowl.

Add cayenne, black pepper and mace to taste,
then beat in the anchovy essence and lemon
juice. Turn into small pots. Cover with a layer
of clarified butter and refrigerate until the
butter is firm.

MAKES ABOUT 450 G/1 LB

POTTED SHRIMPS OR PRAWNS

225 g/8 oz unsalted butter
450 g/1 lb peeled cooked shrimps or prawns
1.25 ml/¼ tsp ground white pepper
1.25 ml/¼ ground mace
1.25 ml/¼ ground cloves
dill sprigs to garnish

Melt the butter in a saucepan, add the shrimps
or prawns and heat very gently, without boiling. Add the pepper, mace and cloves.

Using a slotted spoon, transfer the shrimps or
prawns to small pots. Pour a little of the hot
spiced butter into each pot.

Set the remaining spiced butter aside until the
residue has settled, then pour over the shrimps
or prawns. Chill until the butter is firm. Store in
a refrigerator for no more than 48 hours.
Garnish with dill.

MAKES ABOUT 675 G/1½ LB

 MRS BEETON'S TIP

Look out for small brown shrimps, sold
unshelled, particularly in good fishmongers or coastal towns. They have an
excellent flavour which warrants the time
and effort of peeling them. Buy double the
quantity to allow for shell wastage.

GRAVAD LAX

**2 pieces unskinned salmon fillet, total
weight about 1 kg/2¼ lb, scaled**
200 g/7 oz salt
90 g/3½ oz caster sugar
50 g/2 oz white peppercorns, crushed
90 g/3½ oz fresh dill, plus extra to garnish

MUSTARD SAUCE
**30 ml/2 tbsp Swedish mustard (or other mild
mustard)**
10 ml/2 tsp caster sugar
15 ml/1 tbsp chopped fresh dill
45–60 ml/3–4 tbsp sunflower oil
lemon juice to taste
salt and pepper

Score the skin on each salmon fillet in 4 places.
Mix the salt, sugar and peppercorns in a bowl.

Sprinkle a third of the salt mixture on the base
of a shallow dish. Place one salmon fillet, skin
side down, on the mixture. Cover with a further
third of the salt mixture and add half the dill.
Arrange the second fillet, skin side up, on top.
Cover with the remaining salt mixture and dill.

Cover with foil. Place a plate or oblong baking
sheet or tin on top of the fish and weight it
down. Leave in the refrigerator for 36 hours,
during which time the salt mixture will become
a brine solution. Turn the whole fillet 'sandwich' every day and baste with the liquor.

For the sauce, mix the mustard, sugar and dill.
Add the oil very slowly, beating all the time to
make a thick sauce. Stir in a little lemon juice
with salt and pepper to taste.

Drain off the brine, scape away the dill and
peppercorns before serving. Serve thinly
sliced, garnished with fresh dill, with the
mustard sauce.

SERVES FOUR TO SIX

PRAWN COCKTAIL

4 lettuce leaves, shredded
225 g/8 oz peeled cooked prawns
75 ml/5 tbsp mayonnaise
15 ml/1 tbsp tomato purée
few drops of Tabasco sauce
**5 ml/1 tsp chilli vinegar or tarragon vinegar
(optional)**
4 whole cooked prawns to garnish

Place a little shredded lettuce on the base of 4
glass dishes. Put the prawns on top. Mix the
mayonnaise with the tomato purée and add a
few drops of Tabasco sauce. Stir in the vinegar,
if liked. Spoon the mayonnaise mixture over
the prawns and garnish each dish with a whole
cooked prawn, preferably in the shell. Serve
with brown bread and butter, if liked.

SERVES FOUR

VARIATIONS

Avocado Ritz   Serve the prawns and mayonnaise on avocado halves. Cut the avocados in
half and remove the stones just before topping
and serving. If there is likely to be any delay,
brush the avocado flesh with lemon juice to
prevent discoloration.

Prawn and Horseradish Cocktail   Omit
the Tabasco sauce and vinegar from the receipe
above and add 5 ml/1 tsp grated fresh horseradish or 15 ml/1 tbsp creamed horseradish.

HERRING ROLLS

25 g/1 oz butter, softened
2 hard-boiled eggs, yolks and whites
   separated and finely chopped
8 anchovy fillets, finely chopped
cayenne pepper
4 rollmop herrings, each divided into 2
   fillets
lemon juice

GARNISH
8 lemon slices
4-6 sliced gherkins
1 small diced beetroot
chopped parsley

Cream the butter in a bowl with the hard-boiled egg yolks and anchovies. Add a pinch of cayenne and mix well.

Spread most of the butter mixture on the rollmops and roll up firmly. Spread the remaining mixture thinly on the round ends of each roll and dip in the chopped egg white. Sprinkle the rolls with lemon juice and arrange on a plate, garnished with lemon slices, gherkins, beetroot and parsley.

SERVES FOUR

VARIATION

Salted Herring Rolls Use salted herrings instead of rollmops. Soak them in cold water for several hours before use, then fillet, being careful to remove all the bones.

CHOPPED HERRINGS

3 salted herrings, soaked in cold water
   overnight
1 large cooking apple
1 small mild onion
2 hard-boiled eggs, yolks and whites
   separated
1 slice of white bread, crust removed
10-15 ml/2-3 tsp white wine vinegar
15-30 ml/1-2 tbsp caster sugar

Drain the herrings and remove the skin and bones. Rinse well and drain again. Quarter the apple and remove the skin and core.

Mince together the herrings, onion, apple, hard-boiled egg whites, 1 hard-boiled egg yolk and the bread. Turn the mixture into a bowl and stir in vinegar and sugar to taste. Mix well and spoon into a serving dish. Sieve the remaining egg yolk over the surface to serve.

SERVES SIX TO EIGHT

 MRS BEETON'S TIP

Herring fillets in oil may be used in this recipe. They are ready to use when drained and give delicious results.

CRAB AU GRATIN

25 g/1 oz butter
25 g/1 oz plain flour
300 ml/½ pint milk
salt and pepper
400 g/14 oz white crab meat, flaked
100 g/4 oz Gruyère cheese, grated
50 g/2 oz fresh white breadcrumbs
30 ml/2 tbsp grated Parmesan cheese

GARNISH
tomato slices
parsley sprigs

Melt the butter in a saucepan. Stir in the flour and cook over low heat for 2–3 minutes, without allowing the mixture to colour. Gradually add the milk, stirring constantly until the sauce boils and thickens. Add salt and pepper to taste.

Stir the crab meat and Gruyère into the sauce. Spoon into individual ramekins, sprinkle with the breadcrumbs and Parmesan and brown under a moderate grill for 2–3 minutes. Garnish with tomato slices and parsley sprigs and serve at once.

SERVES SIX

 MRS BEETON'S TIP

The crab meat mixture may be served in crab shells, if liked. Make sure the shells are scrupulously clean and dry. Give them an attractive gloss by buffing them with a piece of absorbent kitchen paper dipped in oil.

SARDINE CASSOLETTES

3 large slices of stale bread, each about
  2 cm/¾ inch thick
oil for shallow frying
1 (65 g/2½ oz) can sardines in oil, drained
15 ml/1 tbsp Greek yogurt
15 ml/1 tbsp tomato purée
salt and pepper
few drops of lemon juice
10 ml/2 tsp grated Parmesan cheese
watercress sprigs to garnish

Set the oven at 180°C/350°F/gas 4. Using a 5 cm/2 inch biscuit cutter, stamp out 8–10 rounds from the bread. Mark an inner circle on each bread round, using a 3.5 cm/1¼ inch cutter.

Heat the oil in a large frying pan, add the bread rounds and fry until lightly browned on both sides, turning once. Remove the rounds with a slotted spoon and drain on absorbent kitchen paper. With the point of a knife, lift out the inner ring on each round to form a hollow case. Put the cases on a baking sheet and place in the oven for a few minutes to crisp the insides. Cool completely.

Make the filling by mashing the sardines thoroughly and mixing them with the yogurt and tomato purée. Add salt and pepper to taste and stir in the lemon juice and Parmesan. Spoon into the prepared cases and garnish with watercress.

MAKES EIGHT TO TEN

VARIATIONS

Canned Skippers (smoked sprats), tuna or salmon may be used instead of sardines. Reduce the quantity of tomato purée to 5 ml/1 tsp to balance the lighter flavour of these fish.

TUNA SAUCE

Serve with cooked pasta as a quick and easy starter before a light main course. The sauce may also be served with rice, ladled into split baked potatoes or into scooped-out crusty rolls for a simple snack supper.

25 g/1 oz butter or margarine
1 (200 g/7 oz) can tuna
1 onion, chopped
25 g/1 oz plain flour
450 ml/¾ pint milk
100 g/4 oz mushrooms, sliced
50 g/2 oz Cheddar cheese, grated
salt and pepper
30 ml/2 tbsp chopped parsley

Melt the butter in a saucepan. If the tuna is canned in oil, drain the oil into the pan with the butter. Drain and flake the tuna and set it aside. Add the onion and cook gently, stirring occasionally, for about 15 minutes or until soft. Stir in the flour and cook for 1 minute, then reduce the heat to low and slowly pour in the milk, stirring constantly. Bring to the boil, lower the heat again and simmer for 3 minutes.

Stir the mushrooms and cheese into the sauce with salt and pepper to taste. Cook over low heat until the cheese melts, then add the parsley and flaked drained tuna. Stir for 1-2 minutes until the tuna is hot. Serve at once.

SERVES FOUR

ANGELS ON HORSEBACK

8 large shelled oysters
8 rindless streaky bacon rashers
2-3 slices of bread
butter for spreading

Wrap each oyster in a bacon rasher. Fasten the rolls with small poultry skewers, place in a grill pan and grill for 4-6 minutes.

Meanwhile toast the bread. Spread with butter and cut into small fingers. Remove the skewers and serve on toast fingers.

MAKES EIGHT

SAUCY ANGELS

6 rindless streaky bacon rashers
5 ml/1 tsp finely chopped onion
2.5 ml/½ tsp chopped parsley
125 ml/4 fl oz thick White Sauce (page 479)
2.5 ml/½ tsp lemon juice
paprika
salt
800 g/1¾ lb canned or bottled mussels,
    drained
12 small rounds of fried bread

Set the oven at 180°C/350°F/gas 4. Using a rolling pin, stretch and flatten each rasher of bacon. Cut them in half. Stir the onion and parsley into the white sauce, add the lemon juice and season with paprika and a little salt. Stir in the mussels.

Spoon 2 or 3 mussels with sauce on to each piece of bacon. Roll up carefully, securing each bacon roll with a small skewer. Place on a baking sheet and bake for 7-8 minutes. Serve hot on fried bread.

MAKES TWELVE

OYSTER FRITTERS

12 small oysters
10ml/2tsp lemon juice
cayenne pepper
6 rindless back bacon rashers, each rasher
    cut into 4 pieces
oil for deep frying

BATTER
100g/4oz plain flour
1.25ml/¼tsp salt
1 egg, beaten
125ml/4floz milk
5ml/1tsp grated onion
10ml/2tsp chopped parsley

TO SERVE
5 slices of white bread
50g/2oz Herb Butter (page 492)

Make the batter. Mix the flour and salt in a bowl. Make a well in the centre, and add the beaten egg and 60ml/4tbsp of the milk. Mix well, gradually incorporating the flour. Beat until smooth, then stir in the remaining milk, with the onion and parsley.

Open the oyster shells (see page 117), remove the oysters and dry gently on absorbent kitchen paper. Season an oyster with lemon juice and cayenne. Place between 2 bacon pieces and press together firmly. Repeat with remaining oysters and bacon.

Put the oil for frying into a deep wide saucepan and heat to 180-190°C/350-375°F or until a cube of bread added to the oil browns in 30 seconds. If using a deep-fat fryer, follow the manufacturer's instructions.

Dip the bacon and oyster fritters in the batter, a few at a time, and deep fry for 2-3 minutes until golden brown. Drain well on absorbent kitchen paper and keep hot in a warmed dish in a low oven or under the grill.

Reheat the oil before putting in each fresh batch of fritters.

Toast the bread. Using a biscuit cutter, cut each slice into 2 rounds and spread with parsley butter. Serve 1 fritter on each toast round.

SERVES FOUR TO SIX

SCALLOPS ON SKEWERS

12 shallots or small onions, peeled but left
    whole
2 courgettes cut in 2cm/¾ inch cubes
8 rindless streaky bacon rashers
16 scallops
12 button mushrooms
40g/1½oz butter, melted
salt and pepper

Put the shallots or onions in a small saucepan with water to cover. Bring to the boil, lower the heat and simmer for 4 minutes. Add the courgettes and simmer for 2 minutes more. Drain thoroughly.

Stretch the bacon over the back of a knife and cut each rasher in half. Wrap half a rasher around each scallop. Thread the onions, courgettes, mushrooms and bacon-wrapped scallops alternately on 4 skewers.

Melt the butter and brush it over the kebabs. Sprinkle with salt and pepper to taste. Grill under moderate heat for 5-7 minutes, turning frequently.

SERVES FOUR

CHICKEN AND HAM SCALLOPS

25 g/1 oz butter
250 g/9 oz cooked chicken
100 g/4 oz cooked ham
salt and pepper
good pinch of grated nutmeg
60 ml/4 tbsp fine dried white breadcrumbs

SAUCE
25 g/1 oz butter
25 g/1 oz plain flour
300 ml/½ pint milk, chicken stock or a
  mixture

Butter 6 deep scallop shells, reserving the remaining butter. Set the oven at 190-200°C/375-400°F/gas 5-6.

To make the sauce, melt the butter in a saucepan. Stir in the flour and cook over low heat for 2-3 minutes, without colouring. Over very low heat, gradually add the liquid, stirring constantly. Bring to the boil, stirring, and simmer for 1-2 minutes until smooth and thickened. Add salt and pepper to taste. Cool.

Remove any skin and bone from the chicken. Chop the meat coarsely and place in a bowl. Chop the ham finely and add it to the chicken. Moisten the mixture well with some of the sauce. Add salt and pepper to taste and a good pinch of grated nutmeg.

Divide the chicken mixture between the prepared scallop shells. Top with the remaining sauce, then sprinkle evenly with breadcrumbs and flake the rest of the butter on top. Bake for about 20 minutes, until golden brown.

SERVES FOUR TO SIX

VARIATIONS

Chicken and Cheese Scallops Omit the ham, substitute 5 ml/1 tsp lemon juice for the grated nutmeg and add 5 ml/1 tsp chopped parsley to the mixture. Mix 20 ml/4 tsp grated cheese with the breadcrumbs. Bake as above or place under moderate grill for 4-6 minutes to brown.

Browned Chicken Scallops Heat the chicken and ham mixture gently in a saucepan before putting it into scallop shells. Cover with breadcrumbs and butter as before, then put under moderate grill for 4-6 minutes to brown the top.

STUFFED MUSHROOMS

fat for greasing
12 large flat mushrooms
25 g/1 oz butter or margarine
1 onion, finely chopped
50 g/2 oz cooked ham, finely chopped
15 ml/1 tbsp fresh white breadcrumbs
10 ml/2 tsp grated Parmesan cheese
10 ml/2 tsp chopped parsley
white wine
salt and pepper

Generously grease an ovenproof dish. Set the oven at 190°C/375°F/gas 5.

Clean the mushrooms and remove the stalks. Place the caps in the prepared dish, gills uppermost. Chop the stalks finely. Melt the butter or margarine in a pan and fry the mushroom stalks and onion gently for 5 minutes. Add the ham to the onion mixture together with the breadcrumbs, Parmesan and parsley. Add just enough white wine to bind the mixture together. Add salt and pepper to taste. Divide the stuffing mixture between the mushroom caps, heaping it up in the centre.

Cover and bake for 25 minutes.

SERVES SIX

WELSH RAREBIT

25 g/1 oz butter
15 ml/1 tbsp plain flour
75 ml/5 tbsp milk or 30 ml/2 tbsp milk and
　45 ml/3 tbsp ale or beer
5 ml/1 tsp French mustard
few drops of Worcestershire sauce
175 g/6 oz Cheddar cheese, grated
salt and pepper

Melt the butter in a saucepan, stir in the flour
and cook over gentle heat for 2–3 minutes,
stirring constantly. Do not let the flour colour.
Stir in the milk and blend to a smooth, thick
mixture, then stir in the ale or beer, if used.
Add the mustard and Worcestershire sauce.

Gradually add the cheese, stirring after each
addition. Remove from the heat as soon as the
mixture is smooth. Add salt and pepper to
taste. Place in a covered container and chill
when cool.

To use the rarebit, spread the mixture on
buttered toast and place under a preheated hot
grill for 2–3 minutes until bubbling and lightly
browned. Serve at once.

SERVES FOUR TO SIX

VARIATIONS

Buck Rarebit Make as for Welsh Rarebit,
but top each slice with a poached egg.

Yorkshire Rarebit Make as for Welsh Rarebit, but add 4 grilled rindless back bacon
rashers.

IRISH RAREBIT

100 g/4 oz mild Cheddar cheese, grated
60 ml/4 tbsp milk
25 g/1 oz butter
5 ml/1 tsp white wine vinegar
5 ml/1 tsp prepared English mustard
salt and pepper
10 ml/2 tsp chopped gherkin

Combine the cheese, milk and butter in a
saucepan. Cook over gentle heat, stirring constantly, until the cheese has melted and the
mixture is smooth and creamy.

Stir in the vinegar and mustard, with salt and
pepper to taste. Add the gherkin. Transfer to a
container, cover and chill when cold.

To use the rarebit, spread the mixture on
buttered toast and grill briefly under moderate
heat to brown the surface.

SERVES TWO

CURRY CHEESE TOPPER

15 ml/1 tbsp apricot or mango chutney
100 g/4 oz mature Cheddar cheese, grated
5 ml/1 tsp curry powder

Chop any large chunks in the chutney. Pound
the cheese, chutney and curry powder together
in a small bowl. Place the mixture in a covered
container in the refrigerator. To use the mixture, spread it on buttered toast and grill for 3–4
minutes until browned. Alternatively, serve on
plain crackers.

SERVES TWO

SCOTCH WOODCOCK

A modern version of this delicious savoury may be made by scrambling 2 whole eggs with the yolks and cream, then serving them instead of the softer sauce.

1 (50 g/2 oz) can anchovy fillets, drained
50 g/2 oz butter
freshly ground black pepper
150 ml/¼ pint single cream
3 egg yolks
4 slices of hot thick toast

Mash the anchovy fillets in a small bowl with the butter and pepper. Set aside. Heat the cream in a small heavy-bottomed saucepan but do not boil. Beat the egg yolks in a small bowl, then stir in the hot cream. Return the mixture to the pan. Cook over gentle heat, stirring until the sauce thickens. Do not boil or it will curdle.

Spread the anchovy butter on the toast, pour the sauce over and serve at once.

SERVES FOUR

ANCHOVY TOAST

1 (50 g/2 oz) can anchovy fillets
100 g/4 oz butter
cayenne pepper
1.25–2.5 ml/¼–½ tsp prepared mustard
6–8 slices of toast

Pound the anchovies and their oil to a paste, then mix with the butter, adding a little cayenne and mustard to taste. Spread on hot toast, cut into pieces and serve at once.

SERVES FOUR TO SIX

SCOTCH EGGS

1 egg
50 g/2 oz dried white breadcrumbs
350 g/12 oz sausagemeat
15 ml/1 tbsp plain flour
salt and pepper
4 eggs, hard-boiled
oil for deep frying

Beat the egg with 10 ml/2 tsp water in a small bowl. Spread out the breadcrumbs in a second, shallow bowl. Divide the sausagemeat into four equal portions. Pat out each portion into a burger-like shape.

Mix the flour with salt and pepper, and use to coat the hard-boiled eggs. Place an egg in the centre of each circle of sausagemeat. Mould the sausagemeat evenly around each egg, pinching it together to seal the joins.

Mould each Scotch egg to a good shape, roll in beaten egg, then roll in the breadcrumbs. Press the crumbs on well.

Put the oil for frying into a deep saucepan and heat to 160°C/325°F or until a cube of bread added to the oil browns in 2 minutes. If using a deep-fat fryer, follow the manufacturer's instructions. Add the eggs carefully and fry for about 10 minutes until golden brown. Lift out with a slotted spoon and drain on absorbent kitchen paper. Serve hot or cold, cutting each egg in half lengthways.

MAKES FOUR

 MRS BEETON'S TIP

Scotch eggs will keep for a day if chilled when cold; however, do not freeze them as the cooked egg becomes unpleasant, watery and rubbery during freezing and thawing.

MRS BEETON'S SCOTCH EGGS

**4 rindless back bacon rashers, finely
  chopped
50 g/2 oz shredded suet
75 g/3 oz wholemeal breadcrumbs
15 ml/1 tbsp grated lemon rind
5 ml/1 tsp finely chopped parsley
1.25 ml/¼ tsp dried oregano
pinch of ground mace
salt and cayenne pepper
Worcestershire sauce
2 eggs, beaten
75 g/3 oz fresh white breadcrumbs
15 ml/1 tbsp plain flour
salt and pepper
4 hard-boiled eggs
oil for deep frying**

Combine the bacon, suet, breadcrumbs, lemon
rind, herbs and mace in a bowl. Add salt,
cayenne and Worcestershire sauce to taste. Stir
in enough of the beaten egg to make a forcemeat which can be shaped.

Beat the remaining beaten egg with 10 ml/2 tsp
water in a small bowl. Spread out the breadcrumbs in a second, shallow bowl. Divide the
foremeat into 4 equal pieces. On a lightly
floured surface, pat each piece into a circle
about 13 cm/5 inches in diameter.

Mix the remaining flour with the salt and
pepper in a sturdy polythene bag. Add the
hard-boiled eggs and toss gently to coat evenly.
Place an egg in the centre of each circle of
forcemeat. Mould the forcemeat evenly round
the egg, making sure it fits snugly. Seal the
joins with a little of the beaten egg mixture and
pinch well together.

Mould each Scotch egg to a good shape, brush
all over with beaten egg, then roll in the
breadcrumbs until evenly coated. Press the
crumbs well in.

Put the oil for frying into a deep saucepan and
heat to 160°C/325°F or until a cube of bread
added to the oil browns in 2 minutes. If using a
deep fat fryer, follow the manufacturer's
instructions. Add the eggs carefully and fry for
about 10 minutes until golden brown. Lift out
with a slotted spoon and drain on absorbent
kitchen paper. Serve hot or cold.

SERVES FOUR

BURLINGTON CROUTES

**100 g/4 oz cooked chicken, finely chopped
30 ml/2 tbsp mayonnaise
2 tomatoes, each cut into 6 thin slices
salt and pepper
12 rounds of fried bread or crackers
butter (optional)
12 stuffed olives**

Mix the chicken with the mayonnaise in a
bowl. Sprinkle the tomato slices with salt and
pepper. If using fried bread, drain thoroughly
on absorbent kitchen paper. Butter crackers,
if using.

Place a slice of tomato on each bread round or
cracker. Pile the chicken mixture on top. Top
each croûte with a stuffed olive.

MAKES TWELVE

CHICKEN LIVER PATTIES

50 g/2 oz butter
1 onion, chopped
2 rindless bacon rashers, chopped
2.5 ml/½ tsp dried sage
1 bay leaf
225 g/8 oz chicken livers, trimmed and
  chopped
4 button mushrooms, chopped
30 ml/2 tbsp plain flour
100 ml/3½ fl oz chicken stock
salt and pepper
15 ml/1 tbsp marsala
225 g/8 oz Rough Puff Pastry (page 516)
beaten egg to glaze

Set the oven at 190°C/375°F/gas 5. Make the filling. Melt half the butter in a saucepan. Add the onion, bacon, sage and bay leaf and fry over gentle heat for about 6 minutes until the onion is golden brown and the bacon is beginning to crisp. Stir in the chopped liver and mushrooms and cook for about 5 minutes more, turning the mixture over from time to time.

Meanwhile, in a second pan, melt the remaining butter, stir in the flour and cook for 1 minute. Gradually add the stock, stirring until the mixture boils and thickens. Stir in the chicken liver mixture with the marsala and add plenty of salt and pepper. Remove the bay leaf.

Roll out the pastry on a lightly floured surface and cut out twelve 10 cm/4 inch rounds. Line 6 patty tins with the pastry rounds, divide the liver mixture among them and top with the pastry lids. Seal the edges well. Brush the patties with beaten egg, prick with a fork and bake for 20-30 minutes. Serve hot or cold.

MAKES TWELVE

MRS BEETON'S PASTRY RAMAKINS

These cheese savouries can be made with the odd pieces of cheese left from a cheeseboard. Mix a little strong cheese with any mild-flavoured leftovers.

oil for greasing
225 g/8 oz Puff Pastry (page 516)
175 g/6 oz Stilton or Cheshire cheese, or a
  mixture of Parmesan and mild cheese,
  grated or finely crumbled
1 egg yolk

Grease a baking sheet. Set the oven at 220°C/425°F/gas 7. Roll out the pastry into an oblong measuring about 20 × 10 cm/8 × 4 inches. Sprinkle half the cheese over the middle of the pastry. Fold the bottom third over the cheese, then fold the top third down. Give the pastry a quarter turn clockwise, then roll it out into an oblong about the same size as the original shape.

Sprinkle the remaining cheese over the pastry and repeat the folding and rolling. Finally, roll out the pastry to about 2.5 mm/⅛ inch thick, or slightly thicker. Use fancy cutters to stamp out shapes – fluted circles, diamonds, triangles or crescents – and place them on the baking sheet.

Stir 5 ml/1 tsp water into the egg and brush it over the pastries. Bake for 10-15 minutes, until puffed and browned. Serve freshly baked.

MAKES ABOUT 24

Pâtés, Terrines and Savoury Mousses

Home-made pâtés and potted foods have a character of their own, quite different from bought types and definitely superior to the majority of commercial varieties. With careful preparation, prompt cooling and chilling, they keep well in the refrigerator – ideal for impressing weekend guests, for picnics or holiday meals.

A pâté is a coarse or fine mixture, seasoned and flavoured for serving cold. Fish, meat, offal, poultry, game, cheese, vegetables or pulses may be potted or used to make pâtés. The term 'terrine' may be used to describe a lidded baking dish and, traditionally, a coarse pâté which is cooked in such a dish. Terrine is also now more broadly used for vegetable, fish or fruit recipes which are baked or set in a loaf-shaped container. Potted foods may be finely minced, cut up or whole, as in the case of shrimps, and served as for pâtés. This chapter includes a selection of popular recipes.

PREPARATION TECHNIQUES

Mincing or Puréeing When this is carried out, depends on the recipe. Some pâtés require the raw meat, offal, onions and bread to be processed until smooth, then combined and cooked. Other recipes parcook the meat or offal before processing. Potted foods are usually cooked, if necessary, before being puréed.

A mincer is the best appliance for puréeing raw meat, whereas a food processor or blender may be used for parcooked or cooked meat. Use a coarse blade first, followed by a fine one. For a very smooth result, the purée may be sieved.

Stretching Bacon for Lining Some pâtés are cooked in a tin, terrine or dish which is first lined with bacon rashers. Streaky bacon should be used and the rashers should be stretched with the back of a knife. When they are thin and long, lay them in the dish, overlapping each rasher and leaving extra length overhanging the edge. When the dish is filled with pâté, the ends of the bacon should be folded over the top of the mixture.

Baking in a Bain Marie To prevent the outside of the pâté from overcooking before the centre has cooked, the dish or container is placed in a roasting tin. Hot water is poured into the roasting tin to just below its rim, and the pâté is then baked. The water should be topped up during cooking.

Weighting To the give the pâté its characteristic dense texture it should be weighted after cooking. Cover the top of the pâté with greaseproof paper and foil, then place a heavy weight on top. If the pâté has been cooked in a round dish, place a plate on top before adding the weight; the plate should be slightly smaller in diameter than the dish. Leave the pâté until cold, then chill overnight.

Cans of food, scale weights or other suitable heavy items may be used to weight the pâté. Remember to stand the dish in an outer container to catch any juices that spill over.

Storage and Usage Always keep pâtés and potted foods covered on a low shelf in the refrigerator. Remove slices or portions as required and return the rest to the refrigerator promptly.

Most pâtés improve if they are allowed to mature for 1–2 days, but they should be eaten within a week. Pâtés made from poultry livers are the exception; they should be made and eaten within 2 days. Always use perfectly fresh ingredients for making pâtés.

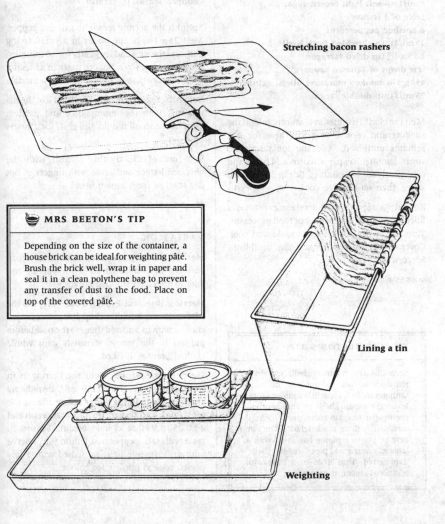

Stretching bacon rashers

> 🍲 **MRS BEETON'S TIP**
>
> Depending on the size of the container, a house brick can be ideal for weighting pâté. Brush the brick well, wrap it in paper and seal it in a clean polythene bag to prevent any transfer of dust to the food. Place on top of the covered pâté.

Lining a tin

Weighting

SMOKED MACKEREL PATE

25 g/1 oz clarified butter, plus extra for
    sealing (page 424)
2 shallots, finely chopped
75 g/3 oz tomato purée
5 ml/1 tsp soft light brown sugar
juice of ¼ lemon
8 crushed peppercorns
15 ml/1 tbsp shredded fresh basil
1.25 ml/¼ tsp dried tarragon
few drops of Tabasco sauce
450 g/1 lb smoked mackerel fillets, skinned
75 ml/5 tbsp double cream

Melt the clarified butter in a saucepan, add the
shallots and cook over gentle heat for 2-3
minutes until soft. Add the tomato purée,
sugar, lemon juice, peppercorns and herbs and
cook gently for 4-5 minutes. Stir in the Tabasco
sauce, then set aside to cool.

Roughly purée the shallot mixture, mackerel
fillets and cream in a blender or food processor.
Turn into a suitable dish or mould and cool.
Cover with clarified butter and chill until firm.
Serve with toast.

MAKES ABOUT 450 G/1 LB

 MRS BEETON'S TIP

Serve this pâté in tomato shells. Cut small
tomatoes in half and remove the pulp,
setting it aside for use in a soup or sauce.
Invert the tomato shells on absorbent kitchen paper to drain thoroughly, then fill
each shell with the mackerel pâté. The pâté
may be put in a piping bag fitted with a
large star nozzle and piped into the shells,
if preferred. Thin it down a little with
additional cream, if necessary.

HERRING ROE PATE

100 g/4 oz soft herring roes
salt and pepper
75 g/3 oz butter
30 ml/2 tbsp lemon juice
15 ml/1 tbsp chopped parsley
chopped lettuce to garnish

Sprinkle the herring roes with salt and pepper.
Melt 25 g/1 oz of the butter in a small frying
pan, add the roes and fry gently for 10 minutes.
Process the roes to a smooth paste in a blender
or food processor, or pound them in a mortar.

Soften the remaining butter and add it to the roe
mixture, with the lemon juice and parsley.
Turn into a small mould and chill for 2 hours
until set.

Turn out of the mould, garnish with the
chopped lettuce and serve with fingers of hot
dry toast or fresh brown bread.

MAKES ABOUT 175 G/6 OZ

VARIATION

Herbed Herring Roe Pâté Use 30 ml/2 tbsp
chopped fresh dill instead of the parsley and
add 15 ml/1 tbsp snipped chives.

Herring Roe and Prawn Pâté Prepare the
pâté as above. Roughly chop 100 g/4 oz peeled
cooked prawns and add them to the pâté before
putting in the mould. Garnish with whole
cooked prawns, if liked.

Herring Roe Sauce Cook the herring as in
the recipe above, frying 30 ml/2 tbsp finely
chopped onion in the butter before adding the
roes. Process to a paste, tip into a saucepan and
add 250 ml/8 fl oz double cream. Season to
taste with salt, pepper and lemon juice. Serve
with grilled white fish, garnished with a few
peeled cooked prawns for colour.

FISH TERRINE

450 g/1 lb plaice fillets, skinned
225 g/8 oz smoked salmon offcuts
600 ml/1 pint White Sauce (page 479)
6 eggs
30 ml/2 tbsp chopped parsley
30 ml/2 tbsp snipped chives
salt and pepper
Hollandaise Sauce (page 586), to serve

Set the oven at 160°C/325°F/gas 3. Prepare a bain marie: have a large roasting tin or dish and a kettle of boiling water ready. Base line and grease a 900 g/2 lb loaf tin.

Pick any tiny bones from the plaice and purée it in a food processor or blender. Transfer to a large bowl. Check that the smoked salmon offcuts are free of all bones and skin, then purée them and place in a separate, large bowl.

Add half the sauce to the plaice purée, the remainder to the smoked salmon. Beat 3 eggs and stir them into the plaice mixture; beat the remaining eggs and add to the smoked salmon mixture. Stir the parsley into the plaice, the chives into the smoked salmon. Add salt and pepper to taste to the plaice mixture; pepper only to the smoked salmon mixture.

Spoon half the plaice mixture into the prepared tin. Top with the salmon mixture then the remaining plaice mixture. Cover with foil and stand the terrine in the roasting tin. Pour boiling water into the outer tin to come almost up to the rim. Bake the fish terrine in the bain marie for 1¼ hours, or until it feels firm to the touch. If the middle feels soft, continue cooking for 10-15 minutes more.

Leave the cooked terrine to stand for 5 minutes before turning it out. Invert the tin on to a warmed platter. Serve in slices with the hollandaise sauce. Alternatively, the terrine may be served cold with mayonnaise or sourced cream and crisp Melba toast.

SERVES EIGHT

MOULDED SALMON SALAD

500 ml/17 fl oz White Wine Fish Stock
(page 48)
25 g/1 oz gelatine
salt and pepper
¼ unpeeled cucumber, sliced
2 firm tomatoes, sliced
225 g/8 oz cooked salmon or 1 (397 g/14 oz)
can salmon, drained

Heat the stock in a saucepan, stir in the gelatine and stir briskly until completely dissolved. Add salt and pepper to taste. Set aside to cool but do not allow to set.

Cover the bottom of a 600 ml/1 pint mould with some cool fish stock. Chill until set. Arrange a few cucumber and tomato slices on the jelly-lined mould, then pour a little more stock over the top to keep the garnish in place. Chill again until set. Add a layer of salmon and another layer of stock, and chill again until set.

Repeat these layers until the mould is full, then cover closely and chill until required. Invert the mould on to a wetted plate (see Mrs Beeton's Tip, page 98) to serve.

SERVES SIX TO EIGHT

FRESH SALMON MOUSSE

oil for greasing
450 g/1 lb salmon fillet or steak (a tail piece
  may be used)
1 litre/1¾ pints Court Bouillon (page 122)
15 g/½ oz gelatine
50 g/2 oz butter, softened
45 ml/3 tbsp double cream, lightly whipped
15 ml/1 tbsp medium-dry sherry

BECHAMEL SAUCE
½ small onion
½ small carrot
1 small celery stick
300 ml/½ pint milk
1 bay leaf
few parsley stalks
1 fresh thyme sprig
1 clove
5 white peppercorns
1 blade of mace
salt
25 g/1 oz butter
25 g/1 oz plain flour

Brush a glass or metal fish mould with oil. Leave upside down to drain. Make the sauce. Combine the onion, carrot, celery and milk in a saucepan. Add the herbs and spices, with salt to taste. Heat to simmering point, cover, turn off the heat and allow to stand for 30 minutes to infuse. Strain into a measuring jug.

Melt the butter in a saucepan. Stir in the flour and cook over a low heat for 2–3 minutes, without allowing the mixture to colour. Gradually add the flavoured milk, stirring constantly until the mixture boils and thickens. Remove the pan from the heat, cover the surface of the sauce with damp greaseproof paper and set aside until required.

Put the salmon in a large saucepan and cover with court bouillon. Bring to the boil, lower the heat and simmer for 15 minutes. Drain, cool

and remove the skin and bones. Pound to a paste in a mortar or process in a blender or food processor until smooth.

Place 30 ml/2 tbsp water in a small bowl and sprinkle the gelatine on to the liquid. Set aside for 15 minutes until the gelatine is spongy. Stand the bowl over a pan of hot water and stir the gelatine until it has dissolved completely.

Tip the salmon into a large bowl and add the cold Béchamel sauce. Mix until thoroughly blended, then add the softened butter, whipped cream, sherry and dissolved gelatine. Mix well, then spoon into the prepared mould. Smooth the top, cover closely and chill for 2–3 hours until set. Turn out (see Mrs Beeton's Tip), garnish with cucumber and radish slices and serve.

SERVES SIX TO EIGHT

VARIATION

Canned salmon may be used instead of fresh fish. Use one 213 g/7½ oz can. Drain the can liquid and use to sponge the gelatine instead of water.

 MRS BEETON'S TIP

Rinse the serving platter in cold water, draining off the excess. Run the point of a sharp knife around the edge of the salmon mousse to loosen it, then dip the mould in warm water. Invert the plate on top of the mould, then, holding mould and plate firmly, turn both right side up again. The mould should lift off easily. If necessary, move the mousse to the desired position on the platter – the skin of water remaining on the plate will make this possible. Repeat the process if the mousse does not come out first time, but avoid leaving it in the warm water for too long or the design on the mousse will be blurred.

KIPPER MOUSSE

fat for greasing
75 g/3 oz butter
3 mushrooms or 8 mushrooms stems,
   chopped
6 black peppercorns
1–2 parsley stalks
25 g/1 oz plain flour
250 ml/8 fl oz Fish Stock (page 48) or Chicken
   Stock
salt and pepper
lemon juice
1 small onion, finely sliced
575 g/1¼ lb kipper fillets, skinned and cut
   into 2.5 cm/1 inch pieces
250 ml/8 fl oz mayonnaise
75 ml/5 tbsp dry white wine
15 g/½ oz gelatine
250 ml/8 fl oz double cream

GARNISH
lemon slices
parsley sprigs

Melt 25 g/1 oz of the butter in a saucepan; add
the chopped mushrooms, peppercorns and
parsley stalks. Cook over gentle heat for 10
minutes. Add the flour and stir over low heat
for 2–3 minutes, without allowing the mixture
to colour. Gradually add the stock and simmer,
stirring, for 3–4 minutes. Rub the sauce
through a sieve into a clean saucepan. Add salt,
pepper and lemon juice to taste. Cover the
saucepan closely and set aside until cold.

Grease a soufflé dish or oval pâté mould. Melt
the remaining butter in a frying pan, add the
onion and fry gently for 2–3 minutes. Add the
fish and fry gently for 7 minutes more. Tip the
contents of the pan into a large bowl and stir in
the cold sauce and the mayonnaise. Process the
mixture in a blender or food processor or pound
to a smooth paste in a mortar. Using a rubber
spatula, scrape the purée into a large bowl.
Place the wine in a small bowl and sprinkle the

gelatine on to the liquid. Set aside for 15
minutes until the gelatine is spongy. Stand the
bowl over a saucepan of hot water and stir the
gelatine until it has dissolved completely. Add
it to the kipper purée and mix very thoroughly.
Blend in the cream and add salt, pepper and a
dash of lemon juice to taste.

Turn the mixture into the prepared dish or
mould, cover the surface closely and chill for at
least 2 hours. Serve from the dish or turn out on
to a serving dish (see Mrs Beeton's Tip, left).
Garnish with lemon slices and parsley sprigs
and serve.

SERVES FOUR TO SIX

VARIATIONS

Smoked Haddock Mousse Use smoked
haddock fillet instead of kipper fillets. Skin the
fillet and remove any bones. Add the haddock
to the onion, sprinkle with 45 ml/3 tbsp water
and cover the pan, then cook for 7-10 minutes
over gentle heat until the haddock flakes easily.
Purée the small amount of liquor with the fish.
Continue as in the main recipe.

Kipper and Egg Mousse Hard boil, shell
and chop 2 eggs. Place half the mousse in the
mould, cover with a layer of egg then top with
the remaining mousse.

 MICROWAVE TIP

Dissolve the gelatine in the microwave if
preferred. Sprinkle over the wine in a small
bowl, let stand until spongy, then cook on
High for 30-45 seconds.

CHICKEN OR TURKEY MOUSSE

225 g/8 oz cooked chicken or turkey breast
  meat
275 ml/9 fl oz double cream
275 ml/9 fl oz chicken stock with fat
  removed
15 ml/1 tbsp gelatine
3 egg yolks, beaten
salt and pepper
20 ml/4 tsp mayonnaise

GARNISH
watercress sprigs
small lettuce leaves

Remove any skin, gristle and fat from the poultry, mince it finely and put it in a bowl. In a second bowl, whip the cream lightly. Chill until required. Place a mixing bowl in the refrigerator to chill.

Put 100 ml/3½ fl oz of the stock in a heatproof bowl, sprinkle on the gelatine and set aside for 15 minutes until spongy. Put the rest of the stock in the top of a double saucepan and stir in the beaten egg yolks, with salt and pepper.

Place the pan over simmering water and cook gently, stirring frequently, until the mixture thickens slightly. Remove from the heat and pour into the chilled bowl. Stand the bowl containing the gelatine over a saucepan of hot water and stir the gelatine until it has dissolved completely. Stir into the egg mixture, mixing well. Add the minced chicken or turkey and stir until thoroughly mixed.

Stand the bowl in a basin of cold water or crushed ice, or place in the refrigerator until the mousse mixture begins to thicken at the edges. Fold in the chilled whipped cream and the mayonnaise. Turn into a wetted 1 litre/1¾ pint mould and chill until set. To serve, turn out on to a platter and garnish.

SERVES FOUR

CHICKEN JELLY

1.5 litres/2¾ pints vegetable stock
1 (1.1 kg/2½ lb) chicken, skinned and jointed
2 celery sticks, sliced
1 onion, thickly sliced
1 carrot, thickly sliced
salt
15 ml/1 tbsp white wine vinegar
2 bay leaves
5 peppercorns
white and crushed shell of 1 egg
30 ml/2 tbsp gelatine

Bring the stock to the boil in a large saucepan. Put in the chicken pieces, vegetables, salt, vinegar, bay leaves and peppercorns. Bring back to the boil and skim well. Lower the heat, cover the pan and simmer the chicken for 45 minutes until tender. Using a slotted spoon, remove the chicken pieces. Cut the meat off the bones in small pieces, cool and chill. Return the bones to the stock in the pan and boil until reduced by half. Strain, cool and chill the stock. Skim off the fat.

Scald a large enamel or stainless steel (not aluminium) saucepan, a piece of clean muslin or thin white cotton, a metal sieve and a whisk in boiling water. Pour the stock into the pan with the egg white, crushed shell and gelatine. Bring to the boil over moderate heat, whisking constantly with the whisk until a thick white crust of foam develops on the top of the liquid. Remove the whisk. As soon as the liquid rises to the top of the pan, remove it from the heat. Leave to stand briefly until the foam falls back into the pan, then heat the stock in the same way once or twice more, until the stock is crystal clear. Strain the stock through the muslin-lined sieve into a perfectly clean bowl.

Arrange the reserved chicken meat in a wetted 1 litre/1¾ pint mould. Pour the stock over gently, cool, then chill. Turn out to serve.

SERVES SIX TO EIGHT

POTTED HAM

butter for greasing
1.25 kg/2¾ lb cooked ham, not too lean
1.25 ml/¼ tsp ground mace
1.25 ml/¼ tsp grated nutmeg
pinch of cayenne pepper
1.25 ml/¼ tsp ground black pepper
melted clarified butter (page 424)

Grease a pie dish. Set the oven at 180°C/350°F/
gas 4. Mince the ham two or three times, then
pound well and rub through a fine sieve into a
clean bowl. Add the spices and peppers and
mix well. Spoon the ham mixture into the
prepared dish, cover with buttered greaseproof
paper and bake for about 45 minutes.

When cooked, allow to cool, then turn into
small pots and cover with clarified butter.
Refrigerate until the butter is firm.

MAKES ABOUT 1 KG/2¼ LB

POTTED VENISON

100–150 g/4–5 oz butter
1 kg/2¼ lb cooked venison, finely minced
60 ml/4 tbsp port or brown stock
1.25 ml/¼ tsp grated nutmeg
1.25 ml/¼ tsp ground allspice
salt
2.5 ml/½ tsp freshly ground black pepper
melted clarified butter (page 424)

Melt 100 g/4 oz of the butter in a saucepan. Add
the minced venison, port or stock, spices, salt
and pepper. If the meat is very dry, add the
remaining butter.

Cook the mixture gently until blended and
thoroughly hot. Immediately, turn into small
pots and leave to cool. Cover with clarified
butter. When cool, refrigerate until the butter is
firm.

MAKES ABOUT 1 KG/2¼ LB

POTTED BEEF

*A popular Victorian dish, potted beef will keep for up
to a week in the refrigerator when made from very
fresh meat and sealed with clarified butter. Chuck
and skirt steak are both ideal cuts to use.*

butter for greasing
450 g/1 lb lean braising steak, trimmed and
  cubed
blade of mace
pinch of ground ginger
30 ml/2 tbsp beef stock
75 g/3 oz butter
salt and pepper
melted clarified butter (page 424)

Set the oven at 150°C/300°F/gas 2. Combine
the beef cubes, mace, ginger and stock in a
casserole or ovenproof dish. Cover tightly with
buttered greaseproof paper and foil.

Bake for 3½–4 hours, until the meat is very
tender. Remove the mace. Mince the meat
twice, then pound it well with the butter and
any meat juices remaining in the casserole to
make a smooth paste. Add salt and pepper
to taste.

Turn into small pots and cover with clarified
butter. When cool, refrigerate the potted beef
until the butter is firm.

MAKES ABOUT 450 G/1 LB

POTTED GAME

A small amount of game, potted with cooked ham or bacon, makes a satisfying starter. Alternatively, try it with salad as the basis of a light lunch or picnic.

350 g/12 oz cooked boneless game meat, trimmed
100 g/4 oz cooked ham or boiled bacon, trimmed
75 g/3 oz butter, softened
pinch of cayenne pepper
salt
1.25 ml/¼ tsp ground black pepper
melted clarified butter (below)

GARNISH
bay leaves
juniper berries

Mince the game and ham or bacon very finely. Pound it to a smooth paste, gradually working in the butter. Alternatively, grind the meats in a food processor; add the butter and process briefly to combine. Mix in the cayenne, with salt and pepper to taste.

Turn the mixture into small pots and cover with clarified butter. Refrigerate the pots until the butter is firm.

MAKES ABOUT 450 G/1 LB

 MRS BEETON'S TIP

To clarify butter, heat gently until melted, then stand for 2–3 minutes. Carefully pour the clear yellow liquid on top into a clean bowl, leaving the residue behind. This is the clarified butter.

BAKED HARE PATE

fat for greasing
1 thick slice of white bread, crust removed
15 ml/1 tbsp milk
65 g/2½ oz butter
50 g/2 oz flat mushrooms, sliced
450 g/1 lb cooked boneless hare meat, chopped
2 egg yolks
60–90 ml/4–6 tbsp cooking brandy, Marsala or Madeira
gravy to moisten (optional)
salt and pepper
1 bay leaf to garnish

Soak the bread in the milk in a shallow bowl for 10 minutes. Meanwhile melt 15 g/½ oz of the butter in a small frying pan, add the mushrooms and fry gently until soft.

Mash the bread lightly and put it in the bowl of a blender or food processor with the mushrooms and hare meat. Process finely. Scrape the mixture into a bowl, using a rubber spatula.

Melt the remaining butter and stir it into the bowl with the egg yolks and liquor. Moisten with a little gravy if necessary and add salt and pepper to taste.

Set the oven 160°C/325°F/gas 3. Grease a terrine or pie dish. Centre the bay leaf on the base of the dish, scrape in the hare mixture and cover the dish tightly with foil.

Stand the terrine or dish in a roasting tin. Pour boiling water into the outer tin to come almost up to the rim of the dish. Bake the pâté for 2 hours, then weight and cool it. Chill for 12 hours. To serve, turn out on to a platter so that the bay leaf is on top. Serve in thin slices.

MAKES ABOUT 300 G/11 OZ

MARBLED RABBIT

**2 rabbits, jointed, liver and kidneys
reserved
salt and pepper
450 g/1 lb gammon or boiling bacon, sliced
1.1 litres/2 pints chicken stock
2.5 ml/½ tsp dried mixed herbs
5 ml/1 tsp chopped parsley
fresh white breadcrumbs (see method)
beaten egg to bind
fat for shallow frying
10 ml/2 tsp gelatine
2 hard-boiled eggs, sliced**

Put the rabbit joints into a shallow dish with strongly salted water to cover. Set aside for at least 1 hour. Rinse and drain thoroughly.

Chop half the gammon or bacon and set it aside. Pack the rabbit joints into a saucepan with the remaining gammon or bacon on top. Barely cover with stock. Cover the pan tightly. Simmer gently for 1¼–1½ hours, until the rabbit is tender. Check the level of the stock from time to time and top up as necessary.

Remove the rabbit joints with a slotted spoon. Cut the meat off the bones and chop it into large pieces. Trim into neat shapes and set aside.

Reserve the trimmings. Strain the stock into a clean saucepan. Finely chop any gammon or bacon pieces remaining in the strainer; put them in a bowl. Finely chop the reserved trimmings and add them to the bowl with the herbs. Add salt and pepper to taste. Weigh the mixture and add half its weight in breadcrumbs. Mix well. Bind the mixture with beaten egg and form into small forcemeat balls.

Add the remaining stock to the saucepan, bring to simmering point and poach the forcemeat balls for 10 minutes. Remove with a slotted spoon, drain and set aside.

Trim the rabbit liver and kidneys. Heat the fat for shallow frying in a small frying pan, add the liver and kidneys and fry until just tender. Remove with a slotted spoon and slice. Add the reserved chopped gammon or bacon to the fat remaining in the pan; fry until cooked.

Strain 300 ml/½ pint of the stock into a small bowl. Sprinkle the gelatine on to the liquid. Set aside until spongy, then stand the bowl over a saucepan of hot water; stir until the gelatine has dissolved completely. Allow to cool but not set.

Pour a little of the gelatine mixture into a wetted mould. Chill until set. Cover with pieces of rabbit, layered with the fried gammon or bacon, the forcemeat balls, slices of liver and kidney and slices of hard-boiled egg. Do not pack down tightly; fill up the mould with the remaining gelatine mixture, covering the ingredients completely. Chill for 3–4 hours until set, then turn out on to a serving dish.

SERVES EIGHT

LIVER PATE

Serve this flavoursome pâté in the dish in which it was cooked, with hot dry toast, or cut into slices and serve with salad.

fat for greasing
75 g/3 oz butter
100 g/4 oz lean rindless bacon rashers, chopped
225 g/8 oz calf's or pig's liver, trimmed and chopped
225 g/8 oz chicken livers, trimmed and chopped
1 small onion, finely chopped
a few gherkins, chopped (optional)
1–2 hard-boiled eggs, chopped
salt and pepper
5–10 ml/1–2 tsp dried mixed herbs
melted clarified butter (page 424)

Grease an ovenproof terrine or similar dish. Set the oven at 180°C/350°F/gas 4. Melt the butter in a frying pan, add the bacon, livers and onion and fry gently for 5-6 minutes. Mince finely twice or process in a blender or food processor to a smooth paste. Add the chopped gherkins and hard-boiled eggs, with salt, pepper and herbs to taste. Stir well. Spoon into the prepared dish; cover with buttered greaseproof paper.

Stand the dish in a roasting tin and add enough hot water to come to within 2.5 cm/1 inch of the rim of the tin. Bake for 30 minutes.

When cooked, cover immediately with a layer of clarified butter. Leave to cool, then chill before serving. Alternatively, place under a light weight and cover with clarified butter when cold.

MAKES ABOUT 675 G/1½ LB

PATE MAISON

8–10 rindless back bacon rashers
100 g/4 oz pig's liver, trimmed and coarsely chopped
100 g/4 oz rindless boned belly of pork, coarsely chopped
225 g/8 oz sausagemeat
225 g/8 oz cold cooked rabbit, finely chopped
1 onion, finely chopped
25 g/1 oz fresh white breadcrumbs
1 egg, beaten
15 ml/1 tbsp milk
75 ml/3 fl oz brandy
salt and pepper
3 bay leaves, to garnish

Set the oven at 180°C/350°F/gas 4. Arrange the bay leaves on the base of 1.25 litre/2¼ pint rectangular ovenproof dish or terrine. Lay the bacon rashers flat on a board, one at a time, and stretch them with the back of a knife until quite thin. Set aside two or three rashers for the topping and use the rest to line the dish, overlapping them neatly.

Combine the chopped liver, pork, sausagemeat, rabbit, onion and breadcrumbs in a mixing bowl. Stir in the egg, milk and brandy, with salt and pepper to taste. Spoon the mixture into the lined dish, cover with the reserved bacon rashers and then with a lid or foil. Stand the dish in a roasting tin and add enough hot water to come to within 2.5 cm/1 inch of the rim of the tin.

When cooked, weight the pâté and leave to cool. Chill for 18-24 hours. To serve, remove the top bacon rashers and invert the pâté on a platter.

MAKES ABOUT 1 KG/2¼ LB

RABBIT TERRINE

2 oven-ready pigeons
1 (1 kg/2¼ lb) rabbit, skinned and boned or
   450 g/1 lb boneless rabbit meat
100 g/4 oz pig's liver, trimmed and sliced
150 ml/¼ pint red wine
1 bay leaf
275 g/10 oz unsmoked rindless streaky bacon
   rashers
450 g/1 lb rindless boned belly of pork,
   coarsely chopped
1 garlic clove, crushed
30 ml/2 tbsp brandy
freshly ground black pepper

Remove the pigeon meat from the bones and place in a mixing bowl with the rabbit meat. Add the liver, wine and bay leaf. Cover tightly and marinate overnight in the refrigerator.

Stretch the bacon rashers lightly with the back of a knife and line a 2 litre/3½ pint terrine or pie dish. Set the oven at 160°C/325°F/gas 3.

Drain the meat, reserving the marinade. Mince the pork and marinated meats or process roughly in a food processor. Stir in the garlic, reserved marinade and brandy. Season with plenty of black pepper.

Spoon the mixture into the prepared terrine and cover with foil or a lid. Stand the dish in a roasting tin and add enough hot water to come to within 2.5 cm/1 inch of the rim of the tin. Bake for about 2 hours.

When cooked, pour off any excess liquid and weight the pâté. Cool, then chill before serving.

MAKES ABOUT 1.6 KG/3½ LB

TERRINE OF DUCK

450 g/1 lb boneless duck meat, minced
125 ml/4 fl oz brandy
450 g/1 lb thinly sliced pork back fat or
   rindless streaky bacon rashers
225 g/8 oz rindless boned belly of pork
275 g/10 oz boneless chicken breast
2 shallots, chopped
rind of 1 orange, cut into fine shreds
2.5 ml/½ tsp dried thyme
salt and pepper
3 eggs, beaten

Put the duck meat into a large bowl with the brandy, cover and marinate for 4–6 hours.

Set the oven at 180°C/350°F/gas 4. Line a 1.4 litre/2½ pint ovenproof serving dish with slices of pork fat or bacon, reserving enough to cover the top of the dish.

Mince the belly of pork and chicken together, then add to the duck meat in the bowl. Stir in the shallots, orange rind and herbs, with salt and pepper to taste. Stir in the eggs and mix well. Spoon into the lined dish, smooth and level the surface and cover with the reserved fat or bacon.

Cover the dish with foil and stand the terrine in a roasting tin. Pour boiling water into the outer tin to come almost up to the rim of the dish. Bake for 1¼ hours, or until the terrine shrinks slightly from the sides of the dish and any melted fat on the top is clear. Remove the foil and top layer of fat 15 minutes before the end of cooking time to let the pâté brown slightly.

When cooked, weight the terrine. Cool, then chill for 12 hours. Serve in slices.

MAKES ABOUT 1.4 KG/3 LB

Fish and Seafood

From humble herring to luxurious lobster, there is literally a fish for every occasion.
This chapter opens with notes on the variety which is commonly available, then moves on
to provide a guide to classic preparation techniques.

A GUIDE TO FISH AND SEAFOOD

Abalone A single-shelled relation of the limpet, this large shellfish has a reputation for being tough. It is beaten to tenderize the flesh, then cooked quickly to prevent it from toughening again. Soups and Oriental dishes incorporating abalone are available in cans; the frozen shellfish is sometimes sold at Oriental supermarkets.

Anchovy A relation of the herring, the fresh anchovy is a small round fish, 7.5-15 cm/3-6 inches in length. Canned anchovy fillets are salted for at least a month before being packed in either olive or vegetable oil.

Brill A large flat fish, similar to turbot but slightly more oval and smaller, weighing up to 4.5 kg/10 lb. Small brill may be cooked whole but the fish is usually sold as fillets. Brill is available from June to February and is at its best during June and July.

Carp There are many species of this round freshwater fish. Carp is popular in China and eastern Europe. Wild carp can have a muddy taste; the live fish should be kept in clean water for 24 hours before being killed. The carp available in specialist fishmongers comes from fish farms. The two farmed varieties are mirror carp, which is covered in scales, and leather carp which has a tough skin and fewer, large scales. They are available from June to March but not in April and May, the breeding season.

You will have to order carp well in advance to be sure of obtaining a fish for a specific occasion. Fish weighing less than 900 g/2 lb are not worth preparing and those above 3.5-4 kg/8-9 lb are very coarse. Farmed fish usually weigh between 1-2.5 kg/2¼-5½ lb, the best weight for eating. The firm white flesh has large flakes and a distinctive taste which is not to everyone's liking. Although carp is very bony, the bones are long and large, therefore easy to avoid.

Catfish There are both sea and freshwater species. The sea fish is the most common and it is also known as rock fish, wolf fish or spotted catfish. This fish has a long body which tapers towards the tail to resemble a large tadpole. The skin is brown-beige with a mottled, dark pattern of inverted 'V' shapes along its length. A long dorsal fin extends from the head to the tail. The flesh is white and fine flavoured as the catfish feeds on mussels and whelks. It is usually sold as fillets between February and July.

Freshwater catfish has dark skin and whiskers on either side of the head. Its white flesh resembles that of pike.

Caviar The soft roe, or eggs of sturgeon which are processed with speed and care. They are lightly salted to flavour and preserve them, then vacuum packed. Cans of Russian caviar are marked 'malossol', indicating that the contents are lightly salted.

Beluga caviar – the most expensive – is grey in colour; the eggs are large. It comes from the largest variety of sturgeon, the beluga, which can live for up to a century and may grow to be a huge fish.

Pressed caviar is made of very small immature eggs or those that may have been slightly crushed or damaged in production.

Clams There are many types of clam, ranging from the giant species to the small, striped Venus clam of the Mediterranean which is likely to be 2.5–4 cm/1–1½ inches long.

Fresh clams are available all year but you will have to order them in advance. Prepare as for mussels. Canned and frozen clams are also available.

Cockles Small molluscs with ridged shells which look heart-shaped when viewed from the side. Cockles are usually cooked and shelled before being sold in local markets. Fresh cockles must be purged overnight and prepared as for mussels. They are most readily available in jars, preserved in vinegar.

Cod Probably the most popular white fish, cod has firm, white flesh and a good flavour. This is a large fish which is sold prepared, either in fillets, cutlets or steaks. The fillets are thick and therefore versatile. Although the battered cod on sale at fish and chip shops is not often skinned, it is best to skin cod fillets before cooking. Codling are young cod.

Smoked cod fillet and smoked cod's roe are both readily available. See also Salt Cod.

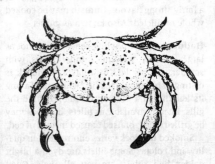

Coley A relative of the cod, coley has thicker skin, darker flesh, a coarse texture and stronger taste. Although it is not much favoured as a fish for grilling or frying, it makes good pies, fish cakes or sauced dishes. Coley is usually sold in fillets. Frozen, pre-formed coley steaks are also popular and quick to prepare.

Pollock is an American term for coley. In Britain, the fish is also known as saithe or coalfish.

Conger Eel A sea eel which grows to great length (up to 3 metres/9 feet). Sold skinned and cut in steaks, conger is firm and meaty with large bones. Unlike most fish, conger requires comparatively long cooking in sauce until tender, otherwise it can be tough. Conger steaks are used in Mediterranean fish stews, such as bouillabaisse or bourride.

Crab World-wide, there is an enormous variety of edible crabs. The brown crab is the species most often sold in Britain, both live and cooked. As with all live crustaceans, crabs should be lively when bought. Avoid limp-clawed specimens that look thoroughly dead. Live crabs should feel heavy for their size. Give the crabs a shake and avoid any that make swishing noises; a sign that they contain water.

When buying a cooked crab, make sure that it looks clean and fresh and that the legs and claws are tight against the body. Cooked crab is also sold ready dressed, with all meat removed and presented in the cleaned shell. Buy from a reputable source.

Soft shell crabs are small shore crabs that have shed their hard covering in spring or autumn and have not had time to acquire new ones. These are cooked and eaten whole.

Crawfish Also known as langouste or spiny lobster, this is a marine crustacean which looks rather like a large lobster without claws. It differs from the lobster in that the shell of the live animal is red, although some species are darker than others. A prized seafood, crawfish is not often found on the supermarket fish counter, although it may be available at a large wholesale fish market. The American use of the term crawfish to describe crayfish is confusing. Crayfish, a freshwater species, is not readily available.

Dab A small flat fish of the plaice family, in season all year. Dabs are cleaned (gutted), trimmed and cooked whole by grilling or frying.

Dover Sole Dover sole has a fine flavour and firm delicate flesh. The fish yields small fillets, so it is usually grilled or fried whole. The fishmonger will clean and skin the fish for you – the tough skin is slit at the tail end and easily pulled away from the flesh.

Eel Freshwater eel are considered superior to conger eel as they have rich, oily flesh. Although they are available all year, they are best during the winter months when fully mature, dark-skinned specimens are on sale. Young, yellow-coloured eels are inferior.

Since eels have to be cooked absolutely fresh, they are usually sold live. Fishmongers selling eels keep them in tanks or buckets of water and kill, then skin them as required. They should be cooked on the day of purchase.

Elvers, tiny eels resembling short spaghetti and measuring about 5 cm/2 inches in length, are a traditional West Country speciality, fried with bacon. Cold elver cake is cooked, pressed elvers, served in slices.

Smoked eel fillets are a speciality from the Netherlands and Scandinavian countries. They are also an East Anglian delicacy. Available from delicatessens and larger supermarkets, smoked eel is skinned and ready to serve. It has a delicate flavour and it is good served very simply with soured cream and chives, and thin, buttered bread.

Flounder A flat fish which is similar in size to plaice. It has brown and yellow blotchy markings and a rough patch on its head.

Flounder is available from March to November and it may be cooked whole or as fillets. The flesh is delicate but not outstanding.

Grayling A freshwater fish of the salmon and trout family. Grayling is seldom sold commercially but the firm white flesh and good flavour make for excellent eating.

Grey Mullet A round fish with large scales, grey mullet is available from September to February. This fish is not related to red mullet and it is quite different in size, appearance and taste.

Grey mullet vary in size, the largest farmed mullet being over 60 cm/24 inches long, although the majority are about 45 cm/18 inches long. The white flesh is of good quality but it bruises and becomes soft easily, so the fish should be handled and scaled with care. Mullet is usually cooked whole, by baking or poaching; it is also a good candidate for the barbecue.

Gurnard These are a group of ugly-looking fish with bony, angular heads. Both red and grey gurnard are available, the latter being slightly more brown-beige in colour than grey. Red gurnard, available from July to February, is better quality than the grey fish. Red gurnard must not be confused with red mullet which is usually smaller and not as ugly.

The flesh is firm and the flakes are large with a fairly strong flavour. Gurnard may be cooked whole or filleted. Also known as gurnet.

Haddock A firm white fish which is not as large as cod, yielding thinner fillets with smaller, slightly less firm flakes. Haddock is distinguished by a black line which runs along its length and a thumbprint mark behind the gills. Readily available as fillets, haddock may be grilled, fried, braised or used instead of cod.

Smoked haddock varies enormously in quality and colour. Some fillets are dyed a bright golden hue, others are naturally pale. Good fishmongers clearly distinguish between the different types.

Finnan haddock are small fish that are split and smoked on the bone over peat or oak. They are pale gold, with the tail still intact. They look slightly dry compared to smoked haddock fillets that are processed by other methods, but are actually superior in flavour. The name derives from the Scottish village, Findon, where the haddock were originally smoked by this method.

Hake From the same family as cod and haddock, hake is longer and slimmer in shape. It has a finer flavour than its relatives and firm, white flesh. Available from June to March, hake is most often sold as steaks or cutlets.

Halibut Available from June to March, halibut is the largest of the flat fish. It is sold fresh and frozen, as fillets or steaks. Its firm, white flesh has a fine flavour. Halibut may be cooked by almost any method but it should be kept moist during cooking, either by the addition of a sauce or by frequent basting.

Herring An oily fish of silvery appearance which is known for its tasty flesh and multitude of bones, herring is similar in size to small or medium mackerel. It is best to bone the fish before cooking. Herrings may be grilled, fried, baked or soused and are also available preserved as rollmops in brine or in vinegar. Salted herring fillets packed in oil have an excellent flavour. Herring fillets are also canned in oil, mustard sauce or a variety of other sauces.

Kippers are smoked herrings, either split and opened out or filleted. Bloaters are whole, lightly smoked herrings.

Huss Also known as dogfish, flake or tope, huss is a member of the shark family. It does not have bones but is a tough, cartilaginous fish with a characteristic, slightly chewy texture which is not to everyone's taste. Huss often appears on fish and chip shop menus; in some areas the battered and deep-fried form is greatly favoured.

At the wet fish shop it is usually sold skinned and prepared for cooking. The flesh has a very slight pink tinge. Huss may be barbecued or grilled on kebabs, but is also suitable for braising.

John Dory A deep-bodied fish which looks alarming, mainly because of its large mouth and long, prickle-like fins. When headless and cleaned, the fish is reduced to two-thirds of its original weight. The flesh has a good flavour and texture. Available all year, the fish is good grilled, poached or baked and served cold.

Laver Bread Cooked and puréed laver seaweed, a Welsh speciality. Resembles spinach in flavour but has a dark, almost black, colour. Oatmeal is added to thicken the purée which is coated in more oatmeal and fried in the shape of soft cakes. Served with bacon.

Lemon Sole This is not related to true sole (referred to as Dover sole in this book). Lemon sole is a flat fish, larger than Dover sole and not as expensive. Lemon sole has good flavour which, as the name suggests, has a hint of lemon. It may be cooked whole but it is also large enough to yield good fillets. Available from April to February.

Lobster Live lobsters are dark in colour – almost black – and turn red on cooking. Although cooked lobsters are available both fresh and frozen in ice, lives ones are only stocked by the busiest and most cosmopolitan fishmongers. However, most good fishmongers or fish counters at large supermarkets will order a live lobster on request.

Lobster meat, extracted from the tail and claws, is firm, white and sweet. If you are buying a live lobster, look for one which is quite perky and heavy for its size.

Cooked lobster should be clean and bright in appearance with a tightly curled tail. Always follow the instructions on the packaging for thawing and using frozen lobster.

Mackerel An oily fish with distinctive green-blue markings, mackerel are available all year.

Tasty dark flesh and large bones are typical of this fish which may be grilled, fried, poached, soused, baked or barbecued. The fish may be cooked whole, split or filleted.

Smoked mackerel fillets or whole smoked mackerel are widely available, sometimes with additional seasonings.

Megrim A small flat fish which is a pale brown-gold in colour. Available from May to March. The fillets are not exceptionally flavoursome; they tend to be slightly dry as well as bland.

Monkfish This weird-looking fish has a huge ugly head, so the tail flesh is usually sold skinned and prepared for cooking. The flesh is firm and has an excellent flavour; it is also expensive. It may be cooked by all methods and served either hot or cold. Available all year, also known as angler fish or angel fish.

Mussels Dark, oval bivalves, these shellfish are in season from September to March. Apart from the familiar dark-shelled mussels, there are also brown-shelled species and very large New Zealand mussels with green shells.

Smoked mussels vary in quality from small, shrunken offerings, sometimes canned in oil, to lightly smoked, large mussels that retain a delicate texture.

Pickled mussels in vinegar or brine are a poor substitute for fresh mussels; however frozen mussels are a good alternative. These are available frozen on the half shell.

Octopus These molluscs are popular in Mediterranean countries where they may be served stewed or fried whole when small. They are not so readily available as squid which is more versatile.

Oysters There are many varieties of oyster and they vary in size. In Britain, Colchester and Whitstable are known for their oyster beds and for the excellent quality of their shellfish. British oysters are known as 'native' to distinguish them from imported types.

Oysters are, of course, known for the fact that they are eaten raw, with a squeeze of lemon or perhaps a dash of Tabasco. To be served this way, they must be absolutely fresh and newly opened, displayed on ice.

Smoked oysters vary enormously in quality. The best are succulent and lightly smoked; the worst are strong, synthetic in flavour and oily.

Perch A freshwater fish, olive-green in colour with vertical black stripes. Good to eat but bony, perch is usually filleted, then poached or fried.

Pike A large, fierce freshwater fish of medium size. Those weighing up to 3 kg/6½ lb are best for cooking. Pike flesh is soft, with many fine bones. The flavour is valued for making traditional dishes such as quenelles, when the flesh is puréed and sieved. Not readily available.

Pilchards These are usually large sardines.

Plaice A familiar flat fish which is available either whole or as fillets. Fine, slightly soft flesh and a delicate flavour are characteristic of plaice. The fish may be fried, grilled, baked, stuffed or poached.

Pollack Not to be confused with the pollock (the American name for coley), pollack is a white-fleshed member of the cod family. Its flesh is slightly watery and not such good quality as cod.

Prawns See also Shrimps. Good fish-mongers usually sell two varieties of this crustacean: cold water prawns and Mediterranean prawns, also known as king prawns or jumbo prawns. The smaller, more familiar cold water prawns are available cooked, either peeled or in their shells. They are also readily available frozen. Mediterranean prawns are usually sold cooked and in their shells. Uncooked Mediterranean prawns are sometimes available. They are a grey colour and turn pink on cooking. The usual way of buying uncooked Mediterranean prawns is peeled and frozen.

Confusion arises over the terms prawn and shrimp because Americans use only the latter. American cooks refer to shrimp and jumbo shrimp; both are larger than those available in Britain.

Redfish Available all year, the redfish can grow up to 1 metre/3¼ feet long. Another ugly-looking specimen, the redfish is often displayed whole or filleted. The flesh is not noted for exceptional flavour.

Roe Roes are the testes of a male fish or the ovaries of the female.

Soft roes come from the herring. They are often cooked in butter and served on toast. Pressed roes are sold canned, for slicing and frying or grilling.

Smoked cod's roe is used for making Tara-masalata (page 82).

Lumpfish roe is served in the same way as caviar. It is salted and usually dyed. Norwegian types are less salty than some others.

Salmon Both farmed and wild salmon are available. Wild salmon, caught in rivers and lochs, is in season from February to the end of August. Excellent farmed salmon is available all year, as steaks, fillet portions or whole fish.

From June to the beginning of August small one-year-old farmed salmon are available.

Sea trout or salmon trout are in season from March to July. Smaller than salmon, these are caught in the sea. The flesh is similar in colour to salmon but has the flaky texture of trout. The bone structure is the same as for trout.

Salt Cod Also known as *bacalao*, this is cod fillet which is preserved by salting. Available from continental delicatessens, it is widely used in Mediterranean countries. The salted fillets must be soaked in cold water for 24 hours before use. Not to be confused with Italian dried cod (stockfish) which is unsalted.

Sardines These small flavoursome fish are available from February to July. They are also frozen and are of good quality. Usually cooked whole by grilling, sardines are delicious when barbecued. They may also be stuffed either whole or boned and rolled.

Scallops These shellfish are usually sold separated from their shells. They have a nugget of firm white flesh and a bright moon-shaped coral which should be a good red colour. Unopened scallops should be placed in a warm oven for a few moments until their shells begin to open. Place rounded shell down to catch precious juices. Carefully prise the white flesh and coral away from the shell, discarding the grey-brown frill and dark intestine.

Queen scallops are a small species, sold without roes as small rounds of very pale pink muscle. Canned queen scallops are also available but they are very disappointing.

Frozen scallops are often available from delicatessens or Oriental stores and they can be excellent. Scallops should be cooked gently and briefly; otherwise they become leathery.

Scampi Also known as langoustine, Dublin Bay prawns or Norway lobsters, these are orange-red crustaceans which look like miniature lobsters. They have long claws and curled tails. They must not be confused with Mediterranean prawns or crawfish, neither of which has claws. Remember, too, that uncooked Mediterranean prawns are grey rather than pink. Scampi are bright red-pink when alive; they retain this colour when cooked. The tail contains the meat. They are not readily available but an advance order at a good fishmonger may secure them.

Breaded scampi tails are available frozen. Check the wording on the packet to ensure that they are exactly that and not 'scampi-style' portions which are not the real thing.

Sea Bass A fine-flavoured, large scaly fish which is grey in colour, sea bass is in season from August to March. The fish may be baked, poached or barbecued whole. Although a fishmonger will fillet the fish, the fillets are surprisingly small.

Sea Bream Several types of bream (including a freshwater fish) are available from June to February. Known as porgy in America, bream has a good flavour. Look out for red bream, black bream and gilt head bream which is dark grey-blue with silvery lower sides. Also known as gilthead, the edge of the gill is scarlet and the fish has a bright golden stripe running across its forehead between the eyes.

Sea Trout See Salmon.

Shark Although many of the fish described here belong to the shark family, you can also buy shark steaks as such. Larger fishmongers may even display whole shark.

The tough, leather-like skin has to be removed before cooking as it shrinks and spoils the flesh. The flesh is firm, meaty and rather cartilaginous, a texture which not everyone likes. The flavour is not particularly noteworthy.

Shrimps Both brown and pink shrimps are available, although the brown ones are usually a regional speciality. They resemble very small prawns and are sold cooked in their shells. Peeling shrimps is a time-consuming task but the excellent flavour is ample reward. Shrimps are available canned but not frozen.

Skate A member of the shark family, also known as ray. Wings of skate are available from May to February. The flesh is cartilaginous and characteristically has a faint odour of ammonia which disappears when the fish is rinsed or blanched in acidulated water. Any strong smell of ammonia indicates that the fish is not as fresh as it should be.

Snails While snails are not, strictly speaking, seafood, they are members of the same family as periwinkles, limpets and whelks (right) and are habitually classified alongside these related molluscs. There are many types of snail. They are now commercially farmed. The wild snail (or 'garden snail') was traditionally collected but today the favoured variety is the Burgundy or Roman snail.

Processing live snails is a complicated business. They must be kept in a basket or ventilated box for a week to purge their systems. The next stage is salting, to remove all the slime. They are then washed, boiled, removed from their shells and boiled again until tender.

Prepared snails are sold in cans, often with clean shells as part of the packaging. The snails are placed in the shells, then topped with garlic butter. They are heated through in the oven and served in dimpled snail dishes with tongs to hold the shells and special forks for extracting the snails. The shells can be thoroughly washed, dried and used again and again.

Sprats Available from October to March, these small fish may be grilled or deep fried. They are usually gutted and their backbones are removed.

Squid Squid is sold prepared or whole from May to September. Many supermarkets sell battered squid rings, or *calamari*, ready for baking or frying.

Swordfish Available all year, swordfish steaks are firm and meaty. They have a good flavour and are ideal for grilling or barbecuing. Since it can become rather dry during cooking, swordfish benefits from frequent basting or cooking in butter or oil.

Trout A freshwater fish that is now inexpensive due to extensive farming. Available fresh and frozen, also as prepared fillets. Rainbow trout has pale pink, delicately flavoured flesh. For sea trout or salmon trout, see Salmon.

Tuna There are several different species of tuna, all large. It is available throughout the year, either fresh or frozen. The dark, sculptured flesh is dry; it benefits from marinating and frequent basting during cooking. Tuna is sold as portions or steaks and is ideal for barbecuing and for cooking in a sauce.

Canned tuna in oil or brine is a familiar – and useful – storecupboard item.

Turbot A large flat fish, turbot has firm white meat with a good flavour. It is available from April to February and is usually sold as steaks or fillets. Special turbot kettles are available for cooking whole fish.

Whelks and Winkles These are both sea snails. Whelks are carnivores and winkles are herbivores. Winkles, the smaller of the two, are traditionally picked from their shells by using a pin. Both are usually sold cooked and shelled. Whelks are available from February to August; winkles from September to April.

Whitebait Small young herrings and sprat fry, whitebait is available fresh from February to June. Frozen whitebait is on sale throughout the year. They are cooked whole by deep frying. The fish are eaten whole.

Whiting A member of the cod family, whiting has slightly soft white flesh which tends to be rather bland and uninteresting. It is usually sold filleted but is sometimes available whole. Available from June to February.

EXOTIC FISH

The following are just a few examples of the exotic fish which are sometimes available. Many are from tropical regions including the west coast of Africa, the Seychelles, the Pacific Ocean and the Indian Ocean. They make good eating and many look attractive when cooked and served whole.

Croakers or Drums Light brown fish with a red-tinged belly. Available all year.
Emperors or Emperor Bream A striking fish, available all year, this has golden fins, tail and nose on an otherwise grey-silver body.
Groupers A golden dorsal line, hints of orange-gold speckles and a bright orange-gold eye make this a decorative species. Available all year.
Jacks Colourful fish, tinged blue, yellow and red. Available all year.
Parrot Fish A striking fish, either blue or brightly coloured. Available all year.
Pomfret Available all year, a deep bodied fish with a small face. Tinged pale gold to grey.
Snappers Available all year. The red snapper is the most common.

PREPARATION TECHNIQUES

CLEANING COOKED CRAB

1. Twist off the claws and legs. Tap the edge of the shell firmly on a board to loosen the body slightly. Turn the crab upside down on a board with the mouth and eyes away from you. Pull off and discard the tail flap. Use both thumbs to ease the body up and out of the shell.

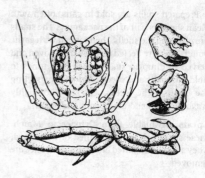

2. Discard the stomach sac, located just behind the mouth, and remove the soft gills around the body. The gills are known as dead men's fingers because of their appearance. Cut the body in half.

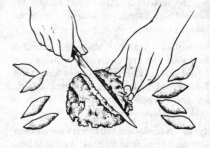

3. Pick out the white meat from the body and the brown meat from inside the shell. Crack the claws and legs, then pick out the white meat.

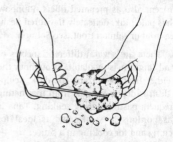

4. Trim the shell: tap away the shell edge around the groove and remove it. This gives a neat shell which should be thoroughly scrubbed in hot soapy water and rinsed with boiling water, then dried.

5. To dress crab, mix the brown meat with a small quantity of fresh breadcrumbs, a dash of lemon juice and salt and pepper to taste. Arrange it in the sides of the clean shell. Arrange the white meat in the middle. Chopped parsley, hard-boiled egg and lemon may be added as a garnish.

CLEANING LOBSTER

1. Twist off the claws and legs. Lay the lobster on a board with the shell down. Use a heavy, sharp knife and rolling pin or meat mallet to split the lobster down the middle.

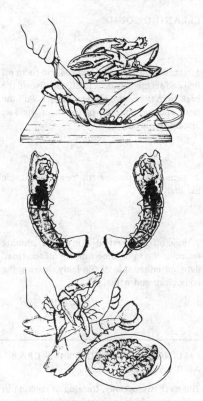

2. Discard the dark intestinal tract which runs down the length of the body. Discard the spongy gills from the head end. Scoop out and save any red coral. The soft, brown liver may be saved and used to flavour a sauce. Remove the firm white tail meat.

3. Clean out the head end of the shell, wash and dry it. The shell may be used to serve the cold dressed lobster, sauced lobster or lobster gratin. Crack the claws and pick out the meat.

PEELING PRAWNS

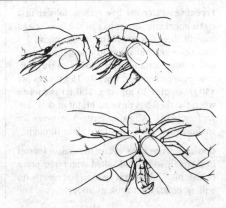

1. Break off and discard the head.

2. Pull the shell apart from underneath and slip it all off, leaving just the tail in place. Break off the tail.

CLEANING SQUID

1. If the tentacles are to be used, cut them off first and set them aside. Cut off and discard the beak from the centre of the tentacles. Pull the head and the attached parts out of the sac: discard the head parts.

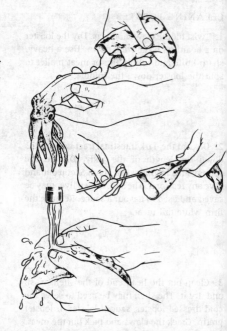

2. Remove the transparent 'pen' from inside the body.

3. Rub off the mottled skin under running water, at the same time rubbing off the small flaps on either side of the body, leaving the body clean and white.

KILLING AND COOKING LIVE CRAB AND LOBSTER

There are two options: freezing or cooking in cold water which is heated gradually.

Freezing Place the live crab or lobster in a clean polythene carrier bag in the freezer and leave it there for 5–7 hours or overnight.

Cover with cold water in a large saucepan, add a little salt and bring slowly to the boil. Lower the heat and simmer for 15 minutes per 450 g/1 lb, plus 10 minutes. Lobster is cooked when the shell has turned a bright pink. Drain well and cool. Allow an extra 5 minutes for shellfish that are frozen hard right through.

Cooking from Live Place the crab or lobster in a large pan of cold salted water and put a tight-fitting lid on the pan. Heat gently to boiling point, then cook as above.

Killing by Stabbing The method of stabbing lobsters behind the head or crabs between the eyes is not to be recommended. Freezing is much more humane.

PREPARATION OF SHELLS FOR SERVING

If empty shells are to be used for serving, they must first be thoroughly scrubbed and boiled in clean water for 5 minutes, then drained and dried. This applies particularly to shells from scallops or oysters which are not cooked with the shellfish.

STUNNING AND SKINNING EELS

Conger eel is sold skinned and cut into steaks. Freshwater eels are kept alive until they are prepared. The fishmonger will usually do this for you as it is not a pleasant task. If, however, you have to prepare an eel, the following may prove valuable.

First stun the eel by banging its head firmly against a hard surface. Then stab it through the back of the head to kill it.

Slit the skin around the head using a strong sharp knife. Using pliers, loosen the skin, then, holding the head firmly in a piece of cloth, pull back the skin from head to tail in one piece. Cut off and discard head.

The eel may be hung by the head from a meat hook and the skin pulled off.

PREPARING MUSSELS

Thoroughly scrub the shells and scrape off any barnacles. Discard any open shells which do not close when tapped. Pull away the dark hairy 'beard' which protrudes slightly from the shell.

Cook mussels in a small amount of boiling liquid over high heat. Put a tight-fitting lid on the saucepan. Shake the pan occasionally and cook for about 5 minutes, until all the shells have opened. The mussels cook in the steam of the liquid. They should not be overcooked or they will toughen. Discard any shells that have not opened after cooking.

Note: The above method is also used for cockles and clams. Bought farmed shellfish should not be sandy; however, leaving the shellfish in a cold place in a bucket of salted water overnight allows time for them to expel any sand they may contain.

OPENING OYSTERS

Ideally a special, short-bladed, tough oyster knife should be used. Do not use your favourite light kitchen knife as the blade may break. Select a fairly blunt, short, strong knife or similar implement. Hold the oyster with the curved shell down. Insert the point of the knife into the hinged end of the shell and prise it open. Take care as the tough shell is difficult to open and the knife can slip easily.

OPENING SCALLOPS

Scallops are usually sold prepared. To open them at home place them in a warm oven for a few moments, until the shells part slightly. Then prise the shells apart and cut the nugget of white muscle and coral free.

ASK THE FISHMONGER

Knowing the basics of fish preparation makes it easier when shopping. Always ask the fishmonger to clean (gut) whole fish (trout, mackerel, bass, mullet and so on), stating clearly whether you want the head and tail on or off. Filleting is a task for the fishmonger. Most will also bone, scale and skin fish. Some fishmongers may even cut large fillets into serving portions.

These are not attributes of the model fishmonger; they are services you can reasonably expect, for no extra charge, but you must be reasonable in making a request. At busy times, select your purchase, explain the preparation required and call back later. A polite request achieves a lot more than a haughty demand. Most fishmongers are highly skilled and only too ready to help.

SEAFISH QUALITY AWARD

Look out for the symbol above. It is displayed by fishmongers who have satisfied the judges that they not only sell quality fish, but also score in terms of quality and operation of premises, storage, equipment, staff, handling and presentation.

CLEANING FISH

If possible, ask the fishmonger or fisherman to clean (gut) fish for you. If you have to do this at home, lay several thicknesses of clean newspaper on the work surface and place the fish on greaseproof paper on top. Slit the fish down its belly, then scrape out the innards. Transfer the fish to a plate; repeat with other fish. Wrap the newspaper tightly around the innards at once, and place in an outdoor waste bin. Wash down all surfaces, utensils and your hands. Thoroughly rinse the fish, then pat it dry with absorbent kitchen paper.

Other methods Round fish may also be cleaned through the gills to avoid splitting the body open. Similarly, whole flat fish (plaice and Dover or lemon sole) have only small pockets of innards that are removed through a small slit below the head. The fishmonger will clean fish in this way for you but always remember to ask for a specific cleaning method, such as through the gills.

RULES TO REMEMBER

Buying Fish and Seafood

- Buy from a reputable source – the premises should look clean and smell fresh.
- Wet fish should look moist and bright. Eyes should be bright, gills red, markings on skin should be clear. Fish fillets should be moist, clean and unbroken.
- Ready-to-eat fish and seafood (for example, smoked mackerel) should never be handled immediately after raw fish. The fishmonger should pick up the ready-to-eat fish with an implement or in a bag. This rule is particularly important if the fishmonger has been cleaning raw fish. He should either wear gloves for this operation or wash his hands thoroughly when the fish has been cleaned.

- Make fish the last item you buy on a shopping trip, take it home quickly (in a chiller bag on hot days) and unpack it at once.
- Rinse and dry the fish, then put it in a dish and cover it with cling film. Place in the refrigerator and cook it within 24 hours.

Handling Fish

- Use a clean board, preferably made of plastic material. Wooden boards should always be scrubbed and rinsed in boiling water, then allowed to dry, after use.
- Use a sharp, narrow-bladed, pointed knife for preparing fish.
- Kitchen scissors are useful for snipping off fins and for cutting bones. Wash them well after use.
- Never prepare raw fish and cooked food using the same utensils, unless the utensils have been thoroughly washed and dried.
- Always keep fish covered and chilled before cooking.

Freezing Fish

- Bought frozen fish is frozen soon after it is taken from the sea. It is frozen speedily at low temperatures for best results.
- Fish for home freezing should be freshly caught or bought fresh from a reputable fishmonger. Do not freeze bought fish which has been frozen and thawed before sale. Freeze fish immediately after purchase. This applies particularly to oily fish such as mackerel.
- Always clean and prepare fish for cooking before freezing it.
- Pack fish in heavy polythene bags, excluding as much air as possible.
- White fish may be stored for 3-4 months;; oily fish keep for 2-3 months in a domestic freezer at $-18°C/0°F$.

Steamed, Sauced and Braised Fish

The wealth of international ingredients now at our disposal means that the plainest cooking techniques can be used to produce exciting, flavoursome results. Delicate herbs and crisp vegetables transform steamed fish from invalid food to a gourmet dish. As well as delicate sauces, colourful casseroles are created by the same, moist cooking method.

STEAMING

Steaming is a method of cooking food in water vapour, producing moist results and retaining the maximum flavour of the food.

EQUIPMENT

The traditional, and simplest, method of steaming fish and seafood is to sandwich it between two plates and to place it over a saucepan of boiling water; however, there are alternatives.

A saucepan-top steamer placed in or on a container over boiling water may be used to cook fish and seafood. Alternatively, foods such as rice may be cooked in the pan, with the seafood steamed directly on top so that its juices flavour the food below.

A bamboo steamer placed on a wok is ideal for cooking fish and seafood. Oriental-style techniques and seasonings perfectly complement the taste and texture of seafood.

Free-standing electric steamers come and go; all the rage one day and not available the next. Depending on the shape of the steaming compartment, an electric steamer can be useful for cooking fish.

Improvising is not difficult and a wire rack placed in a roasting tin of water makes a good platform on which to steam small whole salmon trout, whole trout or a small curved whole salmon. A foil covering with a tightly crumpled edge will usually keep in the steam.

SELECTING FISH FOR STEAMING

Fish fillets are ideal for this cooking method. Plaice, Dover or lemon sole, portions of cod or haddock fillet and smoked fish fillets are all suitable. Thin fillets may be rolled or folded, with herbs or other flavourings placed inside for flavour.

Shellfish, such as scallops, mussels and oysters, are excellent steamed.

Oily fish, on the other hand, do not benefit from being cooked by this method; mackerel, herring and sardines are better baked or grilled.

Size imposes restrictions on the choice of fish for this cooking method: whole fish do not fit well into the majority of steamers but it is worth improvising – curling a whole fish or steaming a fish in sections for later assembly – especially when it comes to fish like salmon and trout that benefit from being steamed.

FLAVOURING AND SEASONING

The choice of flavouring ingredients for any dish should be considered alongside the cooking method. Steaming produces fairly intense results, therefore strong ingredients (onion or garlic) can be rather overpowering in the finished dish.

Fresh Herbs There is a herb to flavour every food. Where fish is concerned the more delicate herbs are ideal. Dill and parsley are, of course, the classics; try fresh lemon thyme, basil, fennel, coriander leaves, lemon balm and lemon grass too. Fresh rosemary, savory, marjoram and oregano tend to be too strong for steamed fish; these herbs should be used judiciously with all seafood, however cooked.

Dried herbs can also be too intense with steamed fish and seafood; if you must use them, do so with caution.

Fresh Root Ginger   Ginger's reputation as a robust flavouring is based on the dried and ground product; fresh root ginger has a citrus-like tang and a hint of heat in its make-up. The preparation of fresh ginger plays an important role in determining its eventual impact in a dish: for just a touch of flavour a few slices of ginger may be added to a dish, then removed before serving. At the other end of the spectrum, grated ginger may be used liberally with other spices to maximize its warming properties. Peeled, thinly sliced and shredded ginger, added in carefully measured quantities are a compromise between the two, contributing plenty of zest with some heat.

Combine ginger with spring onions, soy sauce, carrots and celery to flavour strips of plaice, chunks of cod or mussels. Add a little ginger and lemon to scallops, lemon sole rolls or squid rings.

Lemon or Lime   Lemon is another favourite flavouring for fish. The rind (grated, cut in strips or shredded), the juice or just a slice or two of fruit may be used when steaming fish.

Lime also goes well with all types of fish and seafood. Use rind, juice and slices for steaming.

Soy Sauce   Combined with spring onions and fresh root ginger, soy sauce gives steamed fish a wonderful Oriental flavour that is the perfect foil to plain cooked rice. Whole fish such as plaice, grey mullet, bass or snapper may be cooked with this strong seasoning.

Vegetables   Celery, fennel, carrots and spring onions are useful for flavouring and adding colour to steamed fish. Cut the vegetables finely so that they give up their flavour and cook perfectly in the same time as the seafood.

STEAMING METHODS

Little by way of special preparation is needed for fish steamed between two plates. Lay fillets flat and add the chosen flavouring; a sprinkling of lemon juice, some chopped parsley or dill, seasoning and knob of butter produces excellent results.

If the fish is placed in a perforated, saucepan-top steamer or in a bamboo steamer, there are several options to consider. The cooking juices may be saved and served as a sauce or allowed to drip away into the water below. The flavouring ingredients may be placed on the fish or, in the plainest possible style of cooking, in the water below to scent the steam. The seafood may be put in a covered container or left uncovered so that some moisture collects to yield extra cooking liquor.

Allowing the cooking juices from white fish fillets or pieces to drip away tends to give bland results, unless the juices are absorbed by rice or couscous placed below the fish. Whole fish such as trout, salmon and bass cooked this way are protected from loss of flavour by their skin. In addition, flavouring ingredients may be tucked into the body cavity of whole fish.

Wrapping Seafood   Fish may be wrapped before being placed in a perforated steamer. Foil and roasting bags are ideal for retaining all the juices and flavourings. Greaseproof paper and cooking parchment may also be used but tend to become soft and allow loss of liquor and some flavour.

Leaves may be used to wrap seafood, imparting their own flavour as well as helping to retain the fish juices. Iceberg or cos lettuce leaves and vine leaves may be blanched to soften them before use as a wrapping for whole trout or red mullet. Herbs and other flavourings may be placed inside the fish or on the leaves before wrapping.

Cooking in Dishes The seafood may be placed in a suitable dish with the chosen flavouring ingredients. The dish may be covered or left open, in which case condensed steam will collect in it. The uncovered method is ideal when very brief cooking is required and when flavourings such as soy sauce are added, resulting in just the right amount of full-flavoured, thin sauce. Thinly cut strips of fish or shellfish may be cooked this way.

Cooking Directly on Other Food Fish can be steamed directly on other moist food with which it is being served. For example, fillets of smoked haddock may be laid on two-thirds cooked rice when making kedgeree. When the pan is covered the fish will cook in the steam from the rice. The fillets should be lifted off carefully at the end of cooking.

Similarly, fish may be laid on vegetables – a bed of spinach is ideal – and steamed gently in the cooking vapour.

POACHING

This is probably one of the most popular cooking methods for cooking fish and seafood. Poaching means cooking very gently in liquid. It is ideal for tender fish, allowing additional flavouring ingredients to be cooked with the fish to produce liquor, which may be thickened or reduced then served as a sauce.

Poaching is also used for cooking fish roes. Cod's roe is usually bought freshly boiled or smoked. Herring roes (soft roes, from the male fish) are not sold cooked. Poach them in Court Bouillon (page 122) for 15 minutes, then drain and press until cold, when they may be sliced and fried or grilled.

Very fresh trout may be cooked 'au bleu'. In this classic cooking method the natural slime on the skin of the fish is not rinsed off but is retained to give a soft slate blue covering to the lightly simmered fish.

FLAVOURING POACHED FISH

Poaching is often just one step in the overall cooking process. For example, fillets may be poached until barely cooked and the flesh flaked off them for adding to rice, pasta, pie fillings, croquettes and fish cakes. The poaching liquor is frequently saved and used to flavour the dish.

If poaching is to be the sole method of cooking used for the seafood, flavourings should be carefully chosen. Herbs and vegetables may be added to the poaching liquid. If the liquid is discarded or strained after poaching, these ingredients may be roughly cut and briefly simmered in the liquid before the fish is added. If the poaching liquid is reduced or thickened, then served without being strained, ingredients such as onion should be par-cooked in a little oil or butter to ensure they are completely cooked in the finished dish.

POACHING LIQUID

Fish Stock (page 48) or Court Bouillon (page 122) are used for poaching whole fish such as salmon, when the liquid is discarded after cooking and cooling.

Wine is usually combined with water or stock for poaching fish and seafood, with the resultant liquor thickened and served as a sauce. Dry cider may also be used in place of wine. Milk is used for poaching fish which is to be served in a creamy sauce or for cooking white fish for fish cakes.

Canned or fresh tomatoes may also be used for poaching or braising.

COURT BOUILLON

This is the traditional cooking liquid for poached fish and is discarded after use.

500 ml/17 fl oz dry white wine or dry cider
30 ml/2 tbsp white wine vinegar
2 large carrots, sliced
2 large onions, sliced
2–3 celery sticks, chopped
6 parsley stalks, crushed
1 bouquet garni
10 peppercorns, lightly crushed
salt and pepper

Put the wine in a large stainless steel or enamel saucepan. Add 1 litre/1¾ pints water, with the remaining ingredients. Bring to the boil, lower the heat and simmer for 30 minutes. Cool, then strain and use as required.

MAKES 1.5 LITRES/2¾ PINTS

CASSEROLES AND STEWS

Casseroles and stews are chunky and colourful compared to braised or sauced seafood, and they may be rich in the use of vegetables, herbs and spices. Vegetables, such as onion, celery and carrot, should be cooked in a little oil or butter before the seafood is added. Garlic, bay leaves and tomatoes are also excellent for flavouring mixed seafood casseroles. The cooking liquor may be derived from tomatoes or sautéed vegetables with a little added stock, wine or water. Cream, soured cream or yogurt may be swirled in before serving.

OVERCOOKING – THE ULTIMATE CRIME

Overcooking fish, particularly when steaming or poaching, ruins both flavour and texture. The plainer the cooking, the more important it is to ensure that the fish is cooked to perfection. The flesh should be just firm, still moist and just cooked. When steaming fish, always check part-way through the time to make sure that it is neither cooking too rapidly nor for too long.

When poaching fish the liquid should barely simmer. Boiling liquid will break delicate fillets and toughen seafood such as scallops or squid. The crucial words are time and temperature. Keep the cooking time short and the temperature low and check the fish frequently.

Poached fish which is to be served cold should be removed from the heat when it is three-quarters cooked, then allowed to cool in the liquid. The residual heat completes the cooking and ensures that the fish is moist.

MICROWAVE COOKING

The microwave produces results comparable with those achieved by steaming. It is a very quick cooking method which may be used successfully for fish. Mussels and scallops may be cooked in the microwave but take care not to overcook them or they will become rubbery.

It is most important to read and follow the microwave manufacturer's instructions and suggested timings for cooking fish.

COD WITH CREAM SAUCE

6 (100 g/4 oz) cod steaks or portions
75 g/3 oz butter
250 ml/8 fl oz Fish Stock (page 48)
milk (see method)
25 g/1 oz plain flour
30 ml/2 tbsp double cream
15 ml/1 tbsp lemon juice
salt and pepper

Rinse the fish and pat dry on absorbent kitchen paper. Melt half the butter in a frying pan, add the cod and fry quickly on both sides to seal without browning.

Add the stock, cover the pan and simmer gently for 20 minutes. Drain the fish, reserving the cooking liquid in a measuring jug, place on a warmed dish and keep hot. Make the cooking liquid up to 300 ml/½ pint with milk.

Melt the remaining butter in a saucepan, add the flour and cook for 1 minute, stirring. Gradually add the reserved cooking liquid and milk mixture, stirring constantly. Bring to the boil, lower the heat and simmer for 4 minutes, stirring occasionally.

Remove the pan from the heat and stir in the cream and lemon juice. Add salt and pepper to taste and spoon a little sauce over each fish portion. Serve at once.

SERVES SIX

 MRS BEETON'S TIP

The stock used as the basis for this recipe should be pale in colour. Avoid adding the skin of the fish when making it, as this would darken it.

CURRIED COD

800 g/1¾ lb cod fillets, skinned
50 g/2 oz butter
1 large onion, sliced
15 ml/1 tbsp plain flour
10 ml/2 tsp curry powder
500 ml/17 fl oz Fish Stock (page 48)
15 ml/1 tbsp lemon juice
salt and pepper
cayenne pepper

Rinse the fish and pat dry. Cut into pieces about 2.5 cm/1 inch square. Melt the butter in a saucepan and fry the cod lightly for 2-3 minutes. Using a slotted spoon, transfer the pieces to a warmed dish and keep hot.

Add the onion to the butter remaining in the pan and fry gently for 3-4 minutes until soft. Stir in the flour and curry powder and fry for 5 minutes, stirring constantly to prevent the onion from becoming too brown.

Pour in the stock and bring to the boil, stirring constantly. Lower the heat and simmer for 15 minutes. Strain the sauce into a clean saucepan, adding lemon juice, salt and pepper and cayenne to taste. Carefully add the fish to the pan, stir gently and bring to simmering point.

Simmer for about 10 minutes, until the fish has absorbed the flavour of the sauce. Stir occasionally to prevent sticking. Serve at once, with boiled rice if liked.

SERVES SIX

VARIATION
Quick Cod Curry Use cold cooked fish, omitting the preliminary frying. Serve with a mixture of plain yogurt and chopped cucumber.

COD PORTUGAISE

75 ml/5 tbsp oil
1 large onion, finely diced
2 garlic cloves, crushed
45 ml/3 tbsp plain flour
225 g/8 oz tomatoes, peeled, seeded and
  chopped
1 green pepper, seeded and diced
125 ml/4 fl oz dry white wine
2.5 ml/½ tsp dried thyme
10–12 stuffed green olives
salt and pepper
575 g/1¼ lb cod fillet, skinned and cut
  into 4 pieces

GARNISH
lemon wedges
fresh thyme sprigs

Heat 30 ml/2 tbsp of the oil in a saucepan. Add the onion and garlic and fry gently for 4–5 minutes until soft. Add half the flour and cook for 1 minute, stirring.

Add the tomatoes and green pepper and stir in the wine, with 125 ml/4 fl oz water. Add the thyme and bring to the boil, stirring. Reduce the heat, cover and simmer for 10 minutes, stirring occasionally. Add the olives, stir gently and simmer for 5 minutes.

Meanwhile, add salt and pepper to the remaining flour in a shallow bowl, add the pieces of fish and coat on all sides. Heat the remaining oil in a frying pan, add the fish and fry for 10 minutes, turning once.

Remove the pieces of fish with a fish slice and arrange on a warmed serving dish. Pour the sauce over, garnish and serve at once.

SERVES FOUR

FISH PUDDING

This old-fashioned pudding is light and delicately flavoured, rather similar to fish cakes made with breadcrumbs rather than potato.

fat for greasing
450 g/1 lb white fish fillet (cod, haddock,
  hake, ling), skinned and finely chopped
50 g/2 oz shredded suet
50 g/2 oz fresh white breadcrumbs
30 ml/2 tbsp chopped parsley
salt and pepper
few drops of anchovy essence
2 eggs, lightly beaten
125 ml/4 fl oz milk
lemon wedges to serve

Grease a 1.1 litre/2 pint pudding basin. Prepare a steamer or half fill a large saucepan with water and bring to the boil.

Combine the fish, suet, breadcrumbs and parsley in a bowl. Mix well and add salt, pepper and anchovy essence.

Stir in the eggs and milk. Spoon the mixture into the prepared basin, cover with greased greaseproof paper or foil and secure with string.

Put the pudding in the perforated part of the steamer, or stand it on an old saucer or plate in the saucepan of boiling water. The water should come halfway up the sides of the basin. Cover the pan tightly and steam the pudding for 1½ hours.

Leave for 5–10 minutes at room temperature to firm up, then turn out on to a warmed serving plate. Serve with a parsley or mushroom sauce, if liked, or with lemon wedges for their juice.

SERVES FOUR

HADDOCK FLORENTINE

50 g/2 oz butter
1 kg/2¼ lb fresh spinach
salt and pepper
100 ml/3½ fl oz Fish Stock (page 48)
100 ml/3½ fl oz dry white wine
1 kg/2¼ lb haddock fillets, skinned
1.25 ml/¼ tsp grated nutmeg
50 g/2 oz Parmesan cheese, grated

MORNAY SAUCE
1 small onion
1 small carrot
1 small celery stick
600 ml/1 pint milk
1 bay leaf
few parsley stalks
1 fresh thyme sprig
1 clove
6 white peppercorns
1 blade of mace
50 g/2 oz butter
50 g/2 oz plain flour
1 egg yolk
25 g/1 oz Gruyère cheese, grated
25 g/1 oz Parmesan cheese, grated
60 ml/4 tbsp single cream
pinch of grated nutmeg

Start by making the sauce. Combine the onion, carrot, celery and milk in a saucepan. Add the herbs and spices, with salt to taste. Heat to simmering point, cover, turn off the heat and allow to stand for 30 minutes to infuse. Strain into a measuring jug.

Melt the butter in a saucepan. Stir in the flour and cook over low heat for 2–3 minutes, stirring occasionally, without allowing the mixture to colour. Gradually add the flavoured milk, stirring constantly.

Continue to cook over moderate heat, stirring until the mixture boils and thickens to a thick coating consistency. When the mixture boils, lower the heat and simmer gently for 1–2 minutes, stirring occasionally to prevent a skin forming. Cool slightly.

Beat the egg yolk in a small bowl. Add a little of the sauce and mix well. Add the contents of the bowl to the sauce and heat gently, stirring. Do not allow the sauce to boil. Stir in the cheeses until melted. Add the cream and nutmeg. Cover the surface of the sauce closely with damp greaseproof paper and set aside.

Using 25 g/1 oz of the butter, grease a shallow ovenproof serving dish. Tear the spinach leaves from the stalks and place in a large saucepan with the remaining butter. Add salt and pepper to taste. Cover with a tight-fitting lid and cook gently for about 15 minutes, shaking the pan occasionally.

Meanwhile, combine the stock and white wine in a large saucepan. Bring to simmering point, add the fish and poach for 7–10 minutes.

Drain the spinach thoroughly in a colander, pressing out all free liquid with the back of a wooden spoon. Put the spinach on the base of the prepared dish. Remove the fish fillets with a slotted spoon and arrange them on top of the spinach. Keep hot.

Boil the fish stock until reduced by half. Reheat the sauce, stirring frequently. Add the reduced fish stock, season with salt, pepper and nutmeg and pour the sauce over the fish. Sprinkle with the grated Parmesan and brown under a hot grill. Serve at once.

SERVES FOUR

GEFILTE FISH

This mixture may also be used to stuff a whole fish such as carp, which is then poached whole.

1 large carrot, sliced
3 onions
10 ml/2 tsp salt
pinch of pepper
fish bones and fish head (if available)
1 kg/2¼ lb haddock, cod or whiting fillets
2 eggs, lightly beaten
30 ml/2 tbsp medium matzo meal or fresh white breadcrumbs
5 ml/1 tsp caster sugar

Put the carrot into a saucepan. Slice 1 onion and add it to the pan with 1 litre/1¾ pints water, the salt, pepper and fish bones. Bring to the boil, lower the heat and simmer for 30 minutes.

Meanwhile, mince the raw fish or process it roughly in a food processor. Put it into a large bowl. Mince or grate the remaining onions and add them to the bowl with the eggs, matzo meal or breadcrumbs and sugar. Stir in salt and pepper to taste.

With wet hands, form the mixture into 12–14 balls. Add to the fish stock and simmer gently for 1 hour.

Transfer the fish balls to a serving plate, using a slotted spoon. Set aside to cool. Strain the stock into a clean bowl, reserving the cooked carrot slices. Cool, then chill the stock.

When the fish balls are cold, garnish each one with a slice of cooked carrot. Serve with the chilled stock.

SERVES FOUR

PLAICE MORNAY

fat for greasing
350 ml/12 fl oz milk
1 onion, finely chopped
1 carrot, finely chopped
1 celery stick, finely chopped
1 bouquet garni
salt and pepper
8 plaice fillets
25 g/1 oz butter
25 g/1 oz plain flour
100 g/4 oz Gruyère cheese, grated
50 g/2 oz Parmesan cheese, grated
1.25 ml/¼ tsp mustard powder
fresh chervil sprigs to garnish

Grease a shallow flameproof dish. Combine the milk, vegetables and bouquet garni in a saucepan. Add salt and pepper to taste. Bring to the boil, lower the heat and simmer for 10 minutes. Set aside to cool.

Fold the plaice fillets in three, skin side inwards. Strain the flavoured milk into a deep frying pan and heat to simmering point. Add the fish and poach for 6–8 minutes or until the fish is cooked. Using a slotted spoon, transfer the fish to the prepared dish. Cover with buttered greaseproof paper and keep warm. Reserve the cooking liquid in a jug.

Melt the butter in a saucepan, add the flour and cook for 1 minute, stirring. Gradually add the reserved cooking liquid, whisking constantly until the sauce thickens.

Mix the cheeses and stir half the mixture into the sauce, with the mustard. Remove the buttered paper from the fish, pour the sauce over the top and sprinkle with the remaining cheese mixture. Brown briefly under a hot grill. Garnish and serve.

SERVES FOUR

SWEET AND SOUR HAKE

**450 g/1 lb hake fillet, skinned and cut into
2.5 cm/1 inch cubes
cornflour for coating
oil for deep frying
1 green pepper, seeded and finely chopped**

MARINADE

**2 spring onions, finely chopped
15 ml/1 tbsp medium-dry sherry
30 ml/2 tbsp soy sauce
15 ml/1 tbsp finely chopped fresh root ginger**

SAUCE

**1 (227 g/8 oz) can pineapple cubes in natural
juice
30 ml/2 tbsp cornflour
30 ml/2 tbsp soy sauce
15 ml/1 tbsp medium-dry sherry
5 ml/1 tsp malt vinegar
5 ml/1 tsp oil**

Make the marinade by combining all the ingredients in a shallow dish large enough to hold all the fish cubes in a single layer. Add the fish cubes, cover the dish and marinate for 1–2 hours, stirring several times.

Meanwhile make the sauce. Drain the pineapple cubes, reserving the juice in a measuring jug. Make up to 90 ml/6 tbsp with orange juice or water if necessary. Reserve the pineapple cubes.

Put the cornflour in a small saucepan. Add about 30 ml/2 tbsp of the pineapple juice and mix to a smooth paste, then stir in the remaining pineapple juice, soy sauce, sherry, vinegar and oil. Bring to the boil, stirring constantly, then reduce the heat and simmer for 3 minutes.

Drain the fish cubes, discarding the marinade. Spread the cornflour for coating in a shallow bowl, add the fish cubes and shake the bowl until all the cubes are well coated.

Put the oil for deep frying into a deep wide pan. Heat the oil to 180–190°C/350–375°F or until a cube of bread added to the oil browns in 30 seconds. If using a deep-fat fryer, follow the manufacturer's instructions.

Fry the fish cubes, a few at a time, for 2–3 minutes until evenly browned. Drain on absorbent kitchen paper and keep hot.

Add the reserved pineapple cubes to the sweet and sour sauce and heat through. Pour the sauce over the fish, sprinkle with the chopped green pepper and serve at once.

SERVES FOUR

PLAICE WITH GINGER

**25 g/1 oz butter
2 onions, sliced
8 plaice fillets, skinned and cut into 5 cm/
2 inch wide strips
salt and pepper
15 ml/1 tbsp ground ginger
juice of 3 lemons
4 eggs, beaten**

Melt the butter in a large frying pan, add the onions and cook until lightly browned. Add the fish, salt, pepper, ginger, lemon juice and 150 ml/¼ pint water. Heat until simmering, cover and cook gently for 20 minutes. Transfer the fish to a serving dish and keep hot.

Slowly beat the cooking liquor into the eggs. Pour the mixture back into the pan and cook gently, whisking all the time, until the eggs are creamy. Do not overcook or stop whisking. Pour over the fish and serve.

SERVES FOUR

MACKEREL NICOISE

4 small mackerel
25 g/1 oz butter
30 ml/2 tbsp olive oil
1 large onion, finely chopped
1 garlic clove, crushed
125 ml/4 fl oz medium-dry white wine
10 ml/2 tsp tomato purée
pinch of powdered saffron
salt and pepper
225 g/8 oz tomatoes, peeled, seeded and
    chopped

GARNISH
parsley sprigs
stoned black olives
lemon slices

Rinse the fish inside and out and pat dry on absorbent kitchen paper. Melt the butter in the oil in a large frying pan. Add the onion and garlic and fry for 3–4 minutes until soft but not coloured. Place the fish on top.

Mix the wine and tomato purée together and pour over the fish. Add the saffron, salt and pepper. Bring the liquid to simmering point and poach the fish for 10 minutes.

Using a slotted spoon and a fish slice, carefully transfer the fish to a warmed serving dish and keep hot. Add the chopped tomatoes to the cooking liquid and boil briskly for 5 minutes, stirring occasionally.

Pour the sauce over the fish, garnish with parsley, olives and lemon slices and serve at once.

SERVES FOUR

RED MULLET WITH TOMATOES AND OLIVES

150 ml/¼ pint olive oil
1 onion, finely chopped
1 garlic clove, crushed
25 g/1 oz parsley, chopped
225 g/8 oz tomatoes, peeled, seeded and
    chopped
5 ml/1 tsp tomato purée
salt and pepper
1 bouquet garni
4 (225 g/8 oz) red mullet, cleaned and scaled
8 black olives, stoned
75 ml/5 tbsp dry white wine
lemon slices, to garnish

Heat 100 ml/3½ fl oz of the olive oil in a saucepan, add the onion and fry for 3–4 minutes until lightly browned. Add the garlic and parsley, with the chopped tomatoes. Stir in the tomato purée, with salt and pepper to taste, and add the bouquet garni. Simmer for 15 minutes.

Heat the remaining oil in a deep frying pan and fry the fish gently for 5 minutes, turning once.

When the sauce is cooked, remove the bouquet garni and add the olives and wine. Drain the excess oil from the frying pan. Pour the sauce over the fish, cover the pan and cook for 10 minutes more.

Carefully transfer the fish and sauce to a warmed serving dish. Serve at once, garnished with lemon slices.

SERVES FOUR

SCALLOPED HADDOCK

fat for greasing
450 g/1 lb potatoes, halved and cooked
salt and pepper
75 g/3 oz butter
15-30 ml/1-2 tbsp single cream
250 ml/8 fl oz milk
30 ml/2 tbsp chopped onion
1 blade of mace
225 g/8 oz smoked haddock
25 g/1 oz plain flour
30 ml/2 tbsp chopped parsley
30 ml/2 tbsp double cream
browned breadcrumbs

Grease 4 shallow individual ovenproof dishes.
Set the oven at 200°C/400°F/gas 6. Mash the
potatoes until smooth. Beat in 25 g/1 oz of the
butter and the single cream.

Combine the milk, onion and mace in a deep
frying pan. Bring to simmering point, add the
fish and poach gently for 5-8 minutes. Using a
slotted spoon, transfer the fish to a large plate.
Remove any skin and flake the fish, then divide
it between the dishes. Reserve the cooking
liquid.

Melt half the remaining butter in a saucepan,
add the flour and cook for 1 minute, stirring.
Gradually add the reserved cooking liquid and
boil, stirring. Add seasoning, parsley and
double cream. Pour the sauce over the fish.
Sprinkle with the breadcrumbs.

Spoon the creamed potato into a piping bag
fitted with a large star nozzle and pipe a border
of mashed potato around the edge of each dish.
Stand the dishes on a large baking sheet and
bake for 4-5 minutes until browned.

SERVES FOUR

HAM AND HADDIE

125 ml/4 fl oz milk
575 g/1¼ lb Finnan haddock on the bone
25 g/1 oz butter
4 (100 g/4 oz) slices of cooked ham
pepper
45 ml/3 tbsp double cream

Pour the milk into a large frying pan. Heat to
just below boiling point, add the haddock,
lower the heat and simmer for 10-15 minutes
or until the fish is cooked.

Using a slotted spoon and a fish slice, transfer
the fish to a large plate. Remove the skin and
bones from the fish and flake the flesh. Reserve
the cooking liquid in a jug.

Melt the butter in a clean frying pan and add
the ham slices. Heat through, turning once,
then arrange the ham slices in a warmed
flameproof dish. Spoon the flaked fish over the
ham and pour the reserved cooking liquid over.
Add pepper to taste, then drizzle the cream
over the dish. Brown quickly under a hot grill.

SERVES FOUR

JUGGED HADDOCK

4 pieces of Finnan haddock fillet
2 bay leaves
4 thyme sprigs
4 parsley sprigs
75 g/3 oz butter, melted
freshly ground black pepper

Rinse a heatproof bowl with boiling water to
heat it. Lay the fish and herbs in the dish, then
pour in boiling water to cover. Cover and leave
for 10 minutes. Drain the haddock and serve
with hot melted butter and pepper.

SERVES FOUR

SKATE IN BLACK BUTTER

1-2 skate wings, total weight about
   800 g/1¾ lb
1 litre/1¾ pints Court Bouillon (page 122)
25 g/1 oz butter
salt and pepper
30 ml/2 tsp capers
30 ml/2 tbsp chopped parsley
75 ml/5 tbsp wine vinegar

Rinse and dry the skate and cut it into serving portions. Put the fish in a deep frying pan and cover with court bouillon. Bring to simmering point and simmer for 15-20 minutes or until the fish is cooked.

Using a slotted spoon and a fish slice, lift out the fish and transfer to a platter or board. Scrape away the skin. Place the fish in a warmed ovenproof dish and keep hot.

Pour off the court bouillon from the frying pan, add the butter to the pan and heat until it is a rich golden brown. Spoon over the fish, sprinkle with salt and pepper to taste and scatter the capers and parsley over the top. Pour the vinegar into the pan, swill it around while heating quickly, then pour it over the fish. Serve at once.

SERVES THREE TO FOUR

VARIATIONS

Skate with Caper Sauce Cook and skin the skate as above. Meanwhile, cut 30 ml/2 tbsp capers into quarters and mix them with 5 ml/1 tsp of the vinegar from the jar. Cut 100 g/4 oz butter into chunks and place in a small saucepan. Sprinkle 10 ml/2 tsp plain flour and 150 ml/¼ pint water over the butter. Stir steadily in the same direction over medium heat until the butter melts. Bring to the boil and remove from the heat. Stir in the capers, 15 ml/1 tbsp anchovy essence and pepper to taste. Pour over the skate.

Skate with Shrimp Sauce Cook and skin the skate as above. Cut 100 g/4 oz butter into chunks and place it in a small saucepan. Sprinkle 10 ml/2 tsp plain flour and 150 ml/¼ pint water over the butter. Stir steadily in the same direction over medium heat until the butter melts. Bring to the boil and remove from the heat. Stir in 100 g/4 oz peeled cooked shrimps and season with a little cayenne pepper. Pour over the skate and serve at once.

JUGGED KIPPERS

4 kippers
4 pats of chilled Maître d'Hôtel Butter (page 492)

Put the kippers, tail end up, in a tall heatproof jug. Pour boiling water into the jug to cover all but the tails of the fish. Cover the jug with a cloth and leave to stand for 5 minutes.

Tilt the jug gently over a sink and drain off the water (see Mrs Beeton's Tip). Put each kipper on a warmed plate and serve topped with a pat of maître d'hôtel butter.

SERVES FOUR

 MRS BEETON'S TIP

Do not attempt to pull the kippers out of the jug by their tails – they may well part company with the body of the fish.

ANGEVIN SALMON TROUT

fat for greasing
1 (1 kg/2¼ lb) salmon trout
1 onion, finely chopped
375 ml/13 fl oz rosé wine
15 g/½ oz butter
15 ml/1 tbsp plain flour
30 ml/2 tbsp double cream
salt and pepper
125 ml/4 fl oz Hollandaise Sauce (page 480)

GARNISH
fleurons (see Mrs Beeton's Tip, page 342)
watercress sprigs

Generously butter a fairly deep ovenproof dish large enough to hold the whole fish. Set the oven at 160°C/325°F/gas 3.

Cut the fins from the fish and thoroughly wash the body cavity. Put the fish in the dish, curling it round if necessary. Add the onion. Mix the wine with 100 ml/3½ fl oz water and pour over the fish. Oven-poach for 30 minutes.

Using a slotted spoon and a fish slice, carefully transfer the fish to a wooden board. Remove the skin and keep the fish hot. Strain the cooking liquid into a saucepan and boil until reduced by one third.

Melt the butter in a clean saucepan, add the flour and cook for 1 minute, stirring constantly. Gradually add the reduced cooking liquid, stirring all the time until the mixture comes to the boil. Remove from the heat and add the cream, with salt and pepper to taste. Beat in the hollandaise sauce.

Fillet the fish, placing the fillets on a warmed serving dish. Coat with half the sauce, pouring the rest into a sauceboat. Garnish with the pastry fleurons and the watercress and serve the fish at once, with the remaining sauce.

SERVES FOUR

TWEED KETTLE

575 g/1¼ lb middle cut salmon
500 g/17 fl oz Fish Stock (page 48)
250 ml/8 fl oz dry white wine
pinch of ground mace
salt and pepper
25 g/1 oz chopped shallots or snipped chives
5 ml/1 tsp chopped parsley
25 g/1 oz butter
30 ml/2 tbsp plain flour

Put the salmon in a saucepan with the fish stock, wine and mace. Add salt and pepper to taste. Bring the liquid to simmering point and simmer gently for 10-15 minutes or until the fish is just cooked through.

Using a slotted spoon and a fish slice, transfer the fish to a large plate. Remove the skin and bones and return them to the stock in the pan. Transfer the skinned fish to a warmed serving dish and keep hot.

Simmer the stock and fish trimmings for 10 minutes, then strain into a clean pan. Simmer gently, uncovered, until reduced by half. Stir in the shallots or chives and the parsley and remove from the heat.

In a small bowl, blend the butter with the flour. Gradually add small pieces of the mixture to the stock, whisking thoroughly after each addition. Return to the heat and simmer for 5 minutes, stirring. Pour the sauce over the fish and serve at once.

SERVES FOUR

TROUT HOLLANDAISE

6 trout, cleaned, heads left on
1 litre/1¾ pints Court Bouillon (page 122)
chopped parsley, to garnish
250 ml/8 fl oz Hollandaise Sauce (page 480),
    to serve

Put the trout in a saucepan large enough to hold them in a single layer. Add the court bouillon, bring to simmering point and poach the fish gently for 15 minutes.

Carefully remove the fish from the stock and arrange on a heated serving dish. Garnish with parsley and serve at once, with the sauce.

SERVES SIX

POACHED TROUT WITH PRAWN SAUCE

125 ml/4 fl oz red wine
1 clove
1 bay leaf
4 trout, cleaned, heads left on
salt and pepper
25 g/1 oz butter
25 g/1 oz plain flour
125 ml/4 fl oz milk
100 g/4 oz peeled cooked prawns
45 ml/3 tbsp double cream

GARNISH
parsley sprigs
lemon wedges

Set the oven at 160°C/325°F/gas 3. Combine the red wine, clove and bay leaf in a shallow ovenproof dish large enough to hold all the trout in a single layer. Add the fish, with salt and pepper to taste. Cover tightly with foil to keep in all the moisture and place in the oven

for 15-20 minutes, or until cooked. The fish poach in the wine and moisture in the gentle oven heat.

Using a slotted spoon and a fish slice, carefully transfer the fish one at a time to a platter or board. Remove the skin, then put the fish on a warmed serving dish, cover and keep hot. Strain the cooking liquid.

Melt the butter in a clean saucepan, add the flour and cook for 1 minute, stirring constantly. Gradually add the cooking liquid, stirring all the time until the mixture begins to thicken, then gradually add the milk, still stirring and bring to the boil. Lower the heat and simmer for 2-3 minutes, stirring occasionally.

Remove the sauce from the heat and stir in the prawns and cream. Pour the hot sauce over the fish, garnish and serve.

SERVES FOUR

 MICROWAVE TIP

The trout may be cooked in the microwave. Arrange them in alternate directions in a shallow dish. Pour over the wine and add the clove and bay leaf. Cover loosely and cook on High for 12 minutes, turning once. Strain off the cooking liquid as suggested above. Make the sauce in a large bowl by whisking the cooking liquid into the flour then adding the milk and finally the butter. Cook on High for 10 minutes, whisking twice during cooking. Whisk again and stir in the prawns and cream. Reheat the fish for 1 minute on High if necessary, pour over the sauce, garnish and serve.

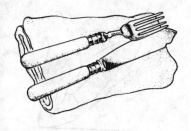

HOT POACHED SALMON

Serve hot poached salmon with Hollandaise Sauce (page 480). Cold poached salmon may be glazed with aspic jelly and garnished with cucumber slices. See Garnishing Salmon, page 135.

1 (1.6–3.25 kg/3½–7 lb) salmon
about 3.5 litres/6 pints Court Bouillon (page 122)

Cut the fins from the fish, remove the scales and thoroughly wash the body cavity. Tie the mouth of the fish shut. Tie the body of the fish loosely to keep it in shape during cooking – two or three bands of string around the fish to prevent the body cavity from gaping are usually sufficient. Weigh the fish and calculate the cooking time. Allow 5 minutes per 450 g/1 lb for salmon up to 2.25 kg/5 lb in weight; 4 minutes per 450 g/1 lb plus 5 minutes for salmon up to 3.25 kg/7 lb.

Put the fish in a fish kettle and pour over the court bouillon. Bring the liquid gently to just below boiling point. Lower the heat and simmer for the required cooking time. The court bouillon should barely show signs of simmering; if the liquid is allowed to bubble then it may damage the delicate salmon flesh. If serving the salmon cold, simmer for 5 minutes only, then leave the fish to cool in the cooking liquid.

Drain the salmon well and untie the body. Slide the salmon on to a large, heated platter. Slit the skin around the body immediately below the head and just above the tail of the fish. Carefully peel back the skin from the head towards the tail. Carefully turn the fish over and remove the skin from the second side. Untie the mouth.

Garnish the salmon with lemon slices and parsley sprigs. Freshly cooked vegetables (new potatoes and baby carrots) may be arranged around the fish. Serve at once.

SERVINGS FROM SALMON

Hot salmon served as a main course will yield the servings below. If the fish is served cold and dressed, as part of a buffet with other main dishes, then it will yield about 2 extra portions.

1.6 kg/3½ lb salmon – 4 portions
2.25 kg/5 lb salmon – 6 portions
3.25 kg/7 lb salmon – 10 portions

 MICROWAVE TIP

Provided it can be curled into a circular dish that will fit into your microwave, salmon may be cooked by this method. Prepare the fish, tuck 2 bay leaves, some peppercorns and a small sprig of parsley into the body cavity, then curl the fish into the dish (a 25 cm/10 inch quiche dish works well). Cover fish and dish with two layers of microwave-proof film to hold the fish securely and prevent it from losing its shape. Cook on High. A 2.25 kg/5 lb salmon will take about 12 minutes. If you do not have a turntable turn the dish three times while cooking. Allow to stand, covered, for 5 minutes. To serve hot, drain, remove the herbs from the body cavity and skin as suggested above. Allow to cool in the wrapping if serving cold.

DRESSING SALMON AND LARGE FISH

Although salmon is the most obvious choice for serving cold, carp, salmon trout and bass are equally well suited to this treatment. Also, it is worth remembering that dressed fish fillets or steaks are an excellent alternative to whole fish. Since the dressing of a whole fish often presents the cook with problems, the following techniques are worth noting.

BONING POACHED SALMON

Follow the recipe for Hot Poached Salmon (page 187). Cool the fish in the court bouillon, following the instructions for serving cold and removing the skin.

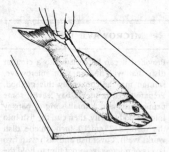

Using a sharp, pointed knife, cut the flesh around the head down to the bone. Cut the flesh down to the bone around the tail. Make a cut into the flesh along the length of the fish as far as the bone (above).

Cut horizontally into the flesh, along the backbone of the fish, from head to tail to loosen the top fillet.

Have a piece of foil on the work surface beside the fish ready to hold the fillets. You need a long palette knife or two fish slices to remove the fillet. Carefully slide the knife or slices under the fillet and lift it off in one piece. If the fish is large, cut the fillet in half or into three portions, then remove each piece neatly.

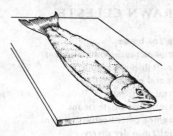

Carefully cut the flesh off the bone over the belly of the fish and lift it off, in one piece or several pieces, as before.

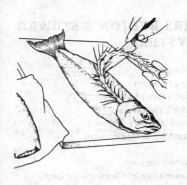

Now remove all the bones from the fish. If serving a salmon trout, snip the backbone at the head and tail end. The bones of salmon come away easily in sections.

When all the bones have been removed, carefully replace the fillets in their original position. There will be small gaps and untidy-looking areas but these will be covered by the garnish.

GARNISHING SALMON

The final dressing: cut the finest possible slices of cucumber. Thick slices will not do – they have to be thin enough to curve to the shape of the fish. Dip each slice in aspic, made using fish stock (see Mrs Beeton's Tip, page 191) and lay it on the salmon. Start at the tail, overlapping each row of cucumber to mimic scales.

When the fish is completely covered with cucumber, use a teaspoon to lightly glaze it with more aspic. At this stage the salmon may be chilled for a few hours until just before serving, when the final garnish should be added.

Pipe mayonnaise stars or shells around the tail and head of the fish, also along the top and base of the body if liked. Small triangles of lemon slices or sliced stuffed olives may be used to cover the eye of the fish. Sprigs of parsley may also be used as a garnish.

CURVED FISH

If the fish has been curved for cooking, it should be garnished with the bones in place.

PRAWN CELESTE

50 g/2 oz butter
100 g/4 oz mushrooms, sliced
15 ml/1 tbsp plain flour
salt and pepper
125 ml/4 fl oz milk
125 ml/4 fl oz single cream
225 g/8 oz peeled cooked prawns
15 ml/1 tbsp dry sherry
chopped parsley, to garnish
4 slices of toast, cut in triangles, to serve

Melt the butter in a saucepan, add the mushrooms and cook over moderate heat for 3-4 minutes. Stir in the flour, with salt and pepper to taste and cook gently for 3 minutes. Gradually add the milk and cream, stirring constantly until the sauce thickens. Add the prawns and sherry. Spoon into a warmed serving dish, garnish with the chopped parsley and serve with the toast triangles.

SERVES FOUR

SALMON TROUT WITH AVOCADO SAUCE

1 (1.8–2 kg/4–4¼ lb) salmon trout
Court Bouillon (page 122)

SAUCE
2 avocados
30 ml/2 tbsp lime or lemon juice
45 ml/3 tbsp oil
salt and pepper

Clean the salmon trout, if necessary, but leave the head and tail on.

Place the fish in a kettle or suitable pan and pour in the court bouillon to cover the fish by at least 3.5 cm/1¼ inches. Top up the water if necessary. Bring the liquid to a bare simmer, cover the pan tightly and cook for about 30 minutes or until the thickest part of the fish yields slightly when pressed.

Carefully transfer the fish to a board or platter. Skin as much of the fish as possible. Turn the fish on to a serving platter, or carefully turn it over, and strip off the remaining skin. Cover loosely with a cloth and set aside to cool.

Make the sauce by mashing the avocado flesh in a bowl with the remaining ingredients until it has the consistency of thick mayonnaise. A food processor or blender may be used, but take care not to over-process the mixture.

When the fish is cold, use a little of the sauce to mask it. Serve the remaining sauce separately.

SERVES SIX TO EIGHT

MRS BEETON'S STEWED OYSTERS

12–16 oysters
25 g/1 oz butter
15 ml/1 tbsp plain flour
1.25 ml/¼ tsp mace
grated rind of ¼ lemon
250 ml/8 fl oz single cream
salt
cayenne pepper
croûtons (see Mrs Beeton's Tip page 77)

Open the oysters (see page 117) and place in a small saucepan with the liquor from their shells. Bring just to the boil, strain and reserve the liquor. Melt the butter in the pan. Stir in the flour and cook for 3 minutes. Pour in the oyster liquor and bring to the boil, stirring all the time. Lower the heat.

Add the mace, lemon rind and cream, stir in the oysters and heat through gently for 1-2 minutes without boiling. Season with salt and cayenne and serve garnished with croûtons.

SERVES FOUR

SWEET AND SOUR PRAWNS

225 g/8 oz peeled cooked prawns
15 ml/1 tbsp medium-dry sherry
salt and pepper
30 ml/2 tbsp oil
2 onions, sliced in rings
2 green peppers, seeded and sliced in rings
125 ml/4 fl oz chicken or vegetable stock
1 (227 g/8 oz) can pineapple cubes, drained
15 ml/1 tbsp cornflour
30 ml/2 tbsp soy sauce
125 ml/4 fl oz white wine vinegar
75 g/3 oz sugar
whole cooked prawns, to garnish

Spread out the prawns on a large shallow dish. Sprinkle with the sherry, salt and pepper, cover and set aside to marinate for 30 minutes.

Towards the end of the marinating time, heat the oil in a frying pan or wok. Add the onions and peppers and fry gently for 5-7 minutes. Add the stock and pineapple cubes. Cover and cook for 3-5 minutes.

In a small bowl, blend the cornflour, soy sauce, vinegar and sugar together. Stir the mixture into the pan or wok and bring to the boil, stirring, then simmer for 2 minutes until thickened. Lower the heat, add the prawns with the marinating liquid and heat for 1 minute.

Serve hot on a bed of rice, if liked. Garnish with the whole cooked prawns, in their shells.

SERVES FOUR

PRAWN CURRY

15 ml/1 tbsp ground coriander
2.5 ml/½ tsp ground cumin
2.5 ml/½ tsp chilli powder
2.5 ml/½ tsp turmeric
1 garlic clove, crushed
250 ml/8 fl oz Fish Stock (page 48)
30 ml/2 tbsp oil
1 large onion, finely chopped
45 ml/3 tbsp tomato purée
2 tomatoes, peeled, seeded and chopped
450 g/1 lb peeled cooked prawns
juice of ¼ lemon
10 ml/2 tsp coconut cream (optional)
fresh coriander sprigs, to garnish

Mix all the spices in a small bowl. Add the garlic and mix to a paste with a little of the stock. Set aside.

Heat the oil in a frying pan, add the onion and fry for 4-5 minutes until golden brown. Add the tomato purée and spice mixture, then cook for 1-2 minutes. Stir in the remaining stock and tomatoes, cover the pan and simmer gently for 20 minutes.

Add the prawns and lemon juice to the pan, with the coconut cream, if used. Stir until the coconut cream dissolves, then simmer for 5 minutes more. Garnish with fresh coriander sprigs and serve with Basmati rice.

SERVES FOUR

STUFFED SQUID

8 squid, cleaned and trimmed
25 g/1 oz butter
1 small onion, finely chopped
1 garlic clove, crushed
grated rind and juice of ½ lemon
50 g/2 oz mushrooms, diced
50 g/2 oz fresh white breadcrumbs
30 ml/2 tbsp chopped parsley
5 ml/1 tsp dried marjoram
salt and pepper
a little oil for brushing
Fresh Tomato Sauce (page 483)
lemon wedges, to garnish

Rinse the squid well, drain and dry on absorbent kitchen paper. Set aside. Melt the butter in a frying pan, add the onion and garlic and cook, stirring occasionally, until the onion is soft but not browned.

Add the grated lemon rind and mushrooms to the pan and continue to cook until the mushrooms have reduced and most of the liquid has evaporated – this takes some time but it is important to avoid making the stuffing too moist.

Remove the pan from the heat and stir in the breadcrumbs and herbs, with salt and pepper to taste. Add lemon juice to taste but avoid making the stuffing too moist.

Use a teaspoon to fill the squid pouches with stuffing – they should not be too full as the breadcrumb mixture expands on heating. Thread a small meat skewer through the open end of each squid to keep the stuffing enclosed, then pass the skewer through the pointed end of the body.

Brush the squid with oil and grill under moderate heat, turning occasionally, until they are golden brown all over. This will take about 15 minutes. Do not let the squid cook too quickly or the stuffing will not be cooked.

Heat the tomato sauce if necessary, then pour it into a serving dish. Arrange the squid in it and add lemon wedges for garnish. Any remaining lemon juice may be drizzled over the squid. Offer a mill of black pepper with the squid.

SERVES FOUR

SCAMPI IN PAPRIKA CREAM

25 g/1 oz butter
15 ml/1 tbsp finely chopped onion
5 ml/1 tsp paprika
100 ml/3½ fl oz medium-dry sherry
450 g/1 lb peeled cooked scampi tails
3 egg yolks
200 ml/7 fl oz double cream
4 small tomatoes, peeled, seeded and cut in
    quarters
salt and pepper

Melt the butter in a saucepan, add the onion and cook gently for 8–10 minutes, stirring often, until the onion is softened but not browned.

Add the paprika and sherry to the onion and butter. Stir in and boil, uncovered, until reduced by half. Stir in the scampi tails, lower the heat and heat gently for 5 minutes.

Beat the egg yolks and cream in a small bowl. Stir in a little of the hot sauce and mix well. Add the contents of the bowl to the scampi and sauce mixture and heat gently, stirring. Do not allow the sauce to boil. Stir in the tomatoes and heat through gently, then spoon the mixture into a warmed serving dish. Serve at once, with boiled rice or chunks of French bread.

SERVES FOUR

SPANISH LOBSTER

Canned or frozen lobster meat may be used for this recipe.

30 ml/2 tbsp oil
1 large onion, chopped
4 tomatoes, peeled, seeded and chopped
125 ml/4 fl oz medium-dry sherry
salt and pepper
125 ml/4 fl oz Fish Stock (page 48)
350 g/12 oz lobster meat, roughly diced
1 small bunch of chives, snipped
juice of ½ lemon

Heat the oil in a large frying pan. Add the onion and fry gently for 15–20 minutes until softened but not browned. Add the tomatoes and sherry, with plenty of salt and pepper. Cook over moderate heat until soft, stirring occasionally.

Pour in the stock and heat until just boiling. Cook at a fast simmer, stirring occasionally, until the mixture is reduced and thickened. This will take 15–20 minutes. The larger the pan, the quicker the extra liquid will evaporate, so take care not to allow the mixture to become too dry.

Add the lobster meat and stir it with the sauce. Heat gently for about 5 minutes, until the lobster is hot, then stir in the snipped chives and lemon juice.

Serve at once with boiled rice or noodles, if liked.

SERVES THREE TO FOUR

LOBSTER THERMIDOR

45 ml/3 tbsp butter
2 shallots, finely chopped
150 ml/¼ pint dry white wine
5 ml/1 tsp chopped fresh tarragon
5 ml/1 tsp chopped fresh chervil
200 ml/7 fl oz Béchamel Sauce (page 481)
125 ml/4 fl oz double cream
30 ml/2 tbsp French mustard
30 ml/2 tbsp grated Parmesan cheese
salt and pepper
2 cooked lobsters

GARNISH
watercress sprigs
lemon slices

Set the oven at 200°C/400°F/gas 6. Melt the butter in a saucepan, add the shallots and fry gently for 5 minutes until soft. Add the wine and herbs, raise the heat and boil the mixture until reduced by half.

Stir the Béchamel sauce into the shallot mixture and remove from the heat. Add the cream and mustard, with half the Parmesan and salt and pepper to taste. Mix well. Set about 60 ml/4 tbsp of the sauce aside.

Twist off the lobster claws. Split the lobsters in half lengthways. Carefully remove the meat from the claws and body, keeping the lobster shells intact (see page 115). Chop the lobster meat coarsely and mix it with the sauce in the pan. Return the sauced lobster meat to the clean shells.

Place the filled shells on an ovenproof serving platter and spoon the reserved sauce over the top. Sprinkle with the remaining Parmesan. Brown in the oven for 10–15 minutes, garnish and serve very hot.

SERVES FOUR

QUEENS OF THE SEA

Queens are small scallops. They have good texture and flavour and are well worth looking for. They are usually sold shelled, as small round nuggets.

75 g/3 oz butter
30 ml/2 tbsp dry white wine
16 queen scallops
30 ml/2 tbsp plain flour
pinch of paprika
250 ml/8 fl oz milk
salt and pepper
4 hard-boiled eggs
1 egg yolk
15 ml/1 tbsp double cream

Melt half the butter in a large frying pan. Add the wine and scallops and cook very gently for 3 minutes or until just cooked. Do not boil. Set the pan aside.

Melt the remaining butter in a saucepan, add the flour and paprika and cook for 1 minute, stirring constantly. Gradually add the milk, stirring, and bring to the boil. Simmer for 2 minutes until the sauce thickens. Add salt and pepper.

Spoon 60 ml/4 tbsp of the sauce into a shallow dish. Add the remaining sauce to the scallop mixture and heat gently, shaking the pan to blend the ingredients. Cut each of the eggs into 8 segments and arrange them on the sauce in the dish.

Beat the egg yolk and cream in a small bowl. Add to the scallops in sauce and heat gently, stirring. Do not allow the sauce to boil. As soon as the sauce has heated through, pour it over the hard-boiled eggs and place under a hot grill to brown slightly. Serve at once.

SERVES FOUR

COQUILLES ST JACQUES MORNAY

Great care must be taken not to overcook the scallops. Their delectable flavour and texture is easily spoiled by high heat.

fat for greasing
450 g/1 lb potatoes, halved
salt and pepper
50 g/2 oz butter
90 ml/6 tbsp single cream
8-12 large scallops, shelled, with corals
1 small onion, sliced
1 bay leaf
45 ml/3 tbsp dry white wine
juice of ½ lemon
25 g/1 oz plain flour
125 ml/4 fl oz milk
75 ml/5 tbsp single cream
45 ml/3 tbsp dried white breadcrumbs
60 ml/4 tbsp grated Parmesan cheese
watercress sprigs to garnish

Cook the potatoes in a saucepan of salted boiling water for about 30 minutes or until tender. Drain thoroughly and mash with a potato masher, or beat with a hand-held electric whisk until smooth. Beat in 25 g/1 oz of the butter and 15 ml/1 tbsp of the cream to make a creamy piping consistency.

Grease 4 scallop shells or shallow individual ovenproof dishes. Spoon the creamed potato into a piping bag fitted with a large star nozzle and pipe a border of mashed potato around the edge of each shell. Set the oven at 200°C/400°F/gas 6.

Combine the scallops, onion, bay leaf, wine and lemon juice in a saucepan. Add 75 ml/5 tbsp water. Bring to simmering point and poach the scallops gently for 5 minutes. Using a slotted spoon, remove the scallops and cut into slices. Strain the cooking liquid into a jug.

Melt the remaining butter in a saucepan, add the flour and cook for 1 minute, stirring constantly. Gradually add the reserved cooking liquid, stirring all the time, until the sauce starts to thicken. Add salt and pepper to taste and stir in the milk. Bring to the boil, stirring, then lower the heat and simmer for 2–3 minutes. Remove from the heat and stir in the cream.

Divide the sliced scallops between the prepared scallop shells or dishes. Coat with the sauce and sprinkle lightly with the breadcrumbs and Parmesan

Stand the scallop shells or dishes on a large baking sheet and bake for 10 minutes until the breadcrumbs are crisp and the potatoes browned. Garnish with the watercress sprigs and serve at once.

SERVES FOUR

 MRS BEETON'S TIP

Scallops can be poached in the same way as oysters, following the recipe for Mrs Beeton's Stewed Oysters (see page 136). They may be served with croûtons, as for the oysters. Alternatively, serve with rice or pasta shells for a light lunch dish or as a main meal when served with additional vegetables or salad.

MOULES MARINIERE

1.6 kg/3½ lb mussels
1 onion, sliced
2 garlic cloves, cut in slivers
1 carrot, sliced
1 celery stick, sliced
1 bouquet garni
125 ml/4 fl oz white wine
25 g/1 oz butter
15 ml/1 tbsp plain flour
salt and pepper
chopped parsley to garnish

Wash, scrape and beard the mussels following the instructions on page 117. Put them in a large saucepan. Tuck the sliced vegetables among the mussels and add the bouquet garni.

Pour over 125 ml/4 fl oz water and the wine. Place over moderate heat and bring to the boil. As soon as the liquid begins to boil, shake the pan 2 or 3 times, cover it tightly and cook for about 5 minutes until the mussels have opened. Discard any that remain shut. With a slotted spoon transfer the mussels to a deep dish and keep hot.

Strain the cooking liquid through muslin or a very fine sieve into a smaller saucepan. In a cup, cream the butter with the flour.

Place the small pan over moderate heat and add the butter and flour in small pieces, whisking thoroughly. Bring to the boil, whisking, then add salt and pepper.

Pour the thickened cooking liquid over the mussels, sprinkle with chopped parsley and serve with plenty of chunky bread.

SERVES FOUR TO SIX

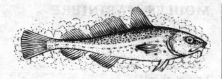

PIKE QUENELLES

450 g/1 lb pike fillets, skinned and finely
  diced
4–5 egg whites
500 ml/17 fl oz double cream
salt and pepper
pinch of grated nutmeg
1 litre/1¾ pints Court Bouillon (page 122)

Purée the fish with the egg whites in a blender or food processor, then rub the mixture through a sieve into a bowl.

In a clean bowl, whip the cream to the same consistency as the fish purée. Fold the cream into the puréed fish lightly but thoroughly. Add salt, pepper and nutmeg to taste, cover the bowl and chill for several hours.

The chilled quenelle mixture is shaped and cooked in one operation. Prepare a large saucepan of hot water and place a large dinner plate on top of it: this will be used to keep the quenelles hot as they are cooked and before they are served. As soon as the first quenelle is placed on the hot plate, turn the heat off under the pan to prevent further cooking.

Heat the court bouillon in a large saucepan until just simmering: the surface should just quiver. Using 2 rounded dessertspoons shape the chilled mixture into ovals, and gently lower these into the liquid. To obtain a neat oval, scoop a portion of mixture cleanly from the bowl. Use the second spoon to cup the top of the portion, then slide the spoon over the mixture to scoop it from the first spoon. This technique of passing the mixture from one spoon to another makes the oval shape.

Simmer the quenelles for 8–10 minutes, then carefully remove with a slotted spoon. Transfer the quenelles to the plate over the pan of hot water as they are cooked. Cover loosely with foil to keep hot until all the mixture is cooked.

Serve the quenelles immediately, with home-made tomato sauce.

SERVES FOUR TO SIX

BRAISED PIKE

40 g/1½ oz butter
225 g/8 oz rindless streaky bacon rashers, cut
  into small squares
1 (1 kg/2¼ lb) pike, cleaned, trimmed,
  filleted and cut into 5 cm/2 inch cubes
250 ml/8 fl oz Fish Stock (page 48)
10 ml/2 tsp lemon juice
salt and pepper
1 tablespoon plain flour
chopped parsley to garnish

Melt 25 g/1 oz of the butter in a saucepan and add the bacon. Fry until crisp, then add the fish cubes, turning until well coated in butter and bacon fat. Pour the stock and lemon juice into the pan and add plenty of salt and pepper. Bring to simmering point, cover the pan and poach the fish for 15 minutes.

Using a slotted spoon, transfer the fish and bacon to a warmed serving dish. Keep hot. Strain the cooking liquid into a clean saucepan.

In a small bowl, blend the remaining butter with the flour. Gradually add small pieces of the mixture to the stock, whisking thoroughly after each addition. Return the pan to the heat and simmer until the sauce thickens. Pour the sauce over the fish, garnish with parsley and serve at once.

SERVES FOUR

CARP WITH MUSHROOMS

butter for greasing
1.25 kg/2¾ lb carp fillets, skinned and cut
  into large pieces
salt and pepper
150 ml/¼ pint dry white wine
50 g/2 oz butter
1 onion, finely chopped
150 g/5 oz mushrooms, sliced
15 ml/1 tbsp chopped parsley
15 g/½ oz plain flour
150 ml/¼ pint double cream

Grease a large ovenproof dish. Set the oven at
160°C/325°F/gas 3. Arrange the fish fillets in
the dish. Sprinkle with salt and pepper, add the
wine and cover with a sheet of buttered greaseproof paper. Oven-poach for 25–35 minutes.

Using a slotted spoon and a fish slice, transfer
the fish to a serving dish and keep hot. Reserve
the cooking liquid.

Melt the butter in a frying pan, add the onion
and fry gently for 3–4 minutes until transparent. Add the mushrooms and fry gently for
3 minutes, then add the parsley. Sprinkle in the
flour, stir well and cook for 1 minute. Gradually
add the reserved poaching liquid, mixing well.
Simmer the sauce for 3–4 minutes until thick,
then stir in the cream. Heat gently, but do not
allow the sauce to boil.

Taste the sauce, add salt and pepper, then pour
it over the fish. Serve at once.

SERVES SIX

> **MRS BEETON'S TIP**
>
> Quickly toss a few small, whole button
> mushrooms in hot butter and sprinkle
> them with chopped parsley. Use to garnish
> the carp.

STUFFED CARP

1 (1.4 kg/3 lb) carp, cleaned
salt and pepper

STUFFING
50 g/2 oz butter
1 onion, diced
15 ml/1 tbsp chopped parsley
5 ml/1 tsp snipped chives
100 g/4 oz fresh white breadcrumbs
3 eggs, beaten
350 g/12 oz mushrooms, chopped
about 75 ml/3 fl oz red wine (optional)

GARNISH
lemon wedges
parsley sprigs

Scale the fish, cut off the fins and wash the body
cavity. Sprinkle with salt and pepper.

Make the stuffing. Melt the butter in a saucepan, add the onion and fry gently for 3–4
minutes until soft. Remove from the heat and
add the herbs and breadcrumbs, with the beaten
eggs. Set aside for 10 minutes. Stir in the
mushrooms and moisten with the red wine, if
necessary. Add plenty of salt and pepper, and
stir well. Do not leave the stuffing to stand or
the mushrooms will weep and make it too soft.

Stuff the cavity of the fish, secure the opening
with a skewer to keep it closed and wrap the
fish securely in greased foil. Place in a fish
kettle, large flameproof casserole or deep roasting tin and add water to cover. Bring to just
below boiling point, lower the heat, cover and
simmer for 25 minutes.

Lift out the fish, remove the foil and transfer to
a warmed serving dish. Garnish with lemon
wedges and parsley sprigs and serve at once. If
preferred, drain the package well and serve the
fish in the foil, opening it neatly.

SERVES FOUR

Grilled and
Fried Fish

Grilling and frying are probably the most familiar and popular methods of cooking fish.
This chapter offers some alternative ideas as well as all the basic information on how
to achieve perfection using simple techniques.

GRILLING

Grilling is a quick cooking method, particularly well suited to oily fish, such as mackerel and herring.

FISH FOR GRILLING

The practicalities of grilling as a cooking method mean that the choice of fish is limited to the more sturdy cuts and varieties. Thus cod fillet is more suitable than plaice fillets which tend to break more easily, and cod steaks are even better since they are thicker and less likely to break up.

Fillets should be firm and fairly thick for cooking on the grill rack; otherwise they may be grilled in a flameproof dish. All fish steaks are ideal for grilling. Similarly, small whole fish cook well by this method but larger fish may not cook through sufficiently. Chunks of firm fish (monkfish, huss, thick end of cod fillet) may be skewered.

Shellfish such as Mediterranean prawns and lobster are good grilled; other varieties – scallops, mussels and oysters – need protection. Grilled small squid can be delicious.

MARINATING

Marinating is the process of soaking food before cooking. Its purpose is to flavour and to moisten food, also to tenderize meat. Fish is marinated before cooking principally for flavour, but also to moisten certain types.

Swordfish, tuna, shark, halibut and turbot all benefit from being marinated before grilling. Cubed monkfish and peeled uncooked prawns may also be marinated to keep them moist when skewered.

Oil is an important ingredient in marinades for fish – sunflower, grapeseed and groundnut oils are all light; olive oil contributes its own distinctive flavour. Fresh herbs, garlic, grated citrus rind, grated fresh root ginger, ground coriander, cumin and other curry spices may be used. Tomatoes, chopped onion, olives and capers are also worth remembering.

Unlike meat, fish does not require lengthy marinating for tenderizing. A couple of hours is usually sufficient.

TURNING AND BASTING

During cooking the fish should be basted to keep it moist. A marinade may be drained and used for this purpose; otherwise oil may be used. Melted butter is another option but it tends to burn easily so should be reserved for seafood such as boiled lobster which grills very quickly. A mixture of melted butter and oil may be used.

Handle fish carefully to prevent it from breaking up. Check the cooking progress often and regulate the heat so that the fish is only turned once. Use a fish slice and palette knife or slotted spoon, or two slices to avoid the fish breaking. Turn skewered fish carefully.

USING FOIL

Fish often benefits from being cooked on foil. Fillets stay moist, but it is wise to be aware of the possible danger of flaming. Using foil to support the fish, but pricking holes all over the foil to drain the fat, is a good compromise.

TOPPINGS FOR GRILLED FISH

Flavoured butters are by far the easiest topping – have neat pats ready to place on each portion of cooked fish.

Other toppings can be placed on the fish before cooking. Here are a few ideas.

Cheese One of the simplest toppings and delicious on cod steaks. Cook the steaks on one side in a flameproof dish. Turn them over and partially cook the second side, then top each steak with a slice of cheese such as creamy mozzarella. Cook under moderate heat until golden.

Tomatoes Sliced peeled tomatoes are good under cheese. If they are added on their own, place them on top towards the end of grilling and baste them with oil.

Peppers Thin rings of red or green pepper are tasty and colourful – good with olive oil, garlic and chopped marjoram on meaty fish.

Breadcrumbs – gratin style Fresh breadcrumbs may be added to make a gratin topping on fish which is almost cooked. Trickle melted butter over or mix the crumbs with grated cheese first – Parmesan is robust. Chopped walnuts and herbs are other tasty additions.

FRYING FISH

All three methods of frying may be used for seafood – deep, shallow and stir frying.

DEEP FRYING

Fish for frying must be coated, either in breadcrumbs, flour or batter. It is important to follow the rules of frying if results are to be crisp and light.

Temperature Vegetable oil used for frying should be heated to 180°C/350°F. Check the temperature by using a sugar thermometer or by dropping a small cube of bread into the oil. The bread should brown in 30–60 seconds. If the oil is hot enough, it seals the coating on the food rapidly to give crisp, light results. If the oil is too cool, some of it is absorbed by the food before the outside becomes crisp and sealed. If the oil is too hot, the outside will brown before the inside of the food is cooked.

When the oil is heated and the food added, the heat should be kept at a fairly high level for about a minute before it is reduced to prevent the oil from overheating. The cold food cools down the oil when it is added and a common mistake is to reduce the heat under the pan at this stage. The time taken for the oil to come back to temperature will, of course, vary with the amount of food added.

By far the best way to deep fry is in an electric deep-fat fryer which automatically controls the temperature of the oil.

Draining Once fried, the food should be lifted from the pan and held over it for a few moments so that excess oil drips off. Then it should be placed on a plate or dish covered with a double thickness of absorbent kitchen paper. The paper absorbs the excess oil, leaving the fried food crisp. Deep fried food should be served freshly cooked.

If you must keep fried fish hot for a short time, perhaps while cooking subsequent batches, place it on a thick pad of absorbent kitchen paper under a grill on low heat.

Choice of Seafood Options include thick fish fillets coated in batter, cooked mussels or prawns in batter, squid rings in batter, whitebait coated in seasoned flour, fish cakes or croquettes in egg and breadcrumbs and white fish fillets coated in egg and breadcrumbs.

Oily fish, such as mackerel and herring, are not at their best when deep fried.

SHALLOW FRYING

Most fish may be cooked by this method but the choice of cooking fat is important.

Fat There are two options: either the cooking fat is discarded or it is served with the fish. For example, fish shallow fried in oil is drained before serving, whereas butter used for cooking may be poured over the fish as an accompaniment. Although it is not practical to check the exact temperature of the fat before adding the fish, it is important that it is hot enough to prevent absorption. Remember that butter overheats at a lower temperature than oil. A combination of oil and butter may be used for flavour, as when olive oil and butter is used as a basis for a sauce.

Turning and Draining The fish should be turned once during shallow frying. A large spatula or slice should be used along with a palette knife, fork or slotted spoon to prevent the fish from breaking.

Choice of Fish and Coating Small whole fish (trout, mackerel, red mullet and sardines), fillets or portions of fillets, steaks and cutlets are all suitable for shallow frying. Batter is not a good coating as it should be submerged completely in hot oil for successful cooking. Egg and breadcrumbs or seasoned flour are both suitable coatings.

Draining and Serving Fish coated in egg and breadcrumbs should be drained on absorbent kitchen paper. Fish coated in seasoned flour should be drained over the pan and absorbent kitchen paper used if it is very crisp. Butter used in cooking may be flavoured with lemon juice, herbs or chopped capers and poured over the fish.

STIR FRYING

This is a quick method of moving food around in a large pan containing a small amount of very hot oil. All the ingredients should be cut to a similar size and should be of a type that will cook quickly.

Fish is usually stir fried with vegetables. Onions, carrots and celery, for example, should quickly be stirred around in the pan before the fish is added.

Choice of Fish Strips of whiting, plaice and other thin fillets are suitable. You might also like to try shellfish or squid. If using strips of fish, avoid stirring them so vigorously that they disintegrate.

COATING FOR FRYING

EGG AND BREADCRUMBS

The fish or seafood should be trimmed and dry. Coat it first in seasoned flour, then in beaten egg and lastly in fine, dried, white breadcrumbs. Use two forks to lift the food. Make sure the egg is in a wide dish which allows room to hold the fish. The breadcrumbs are best placed in a thick layer on a sheet of greaseproof paper or foil. The paper can be lifted and used to tease the crumbs over the egg-coated fish. Press a thick layer of crumbs on the fish, then gently shake off any excess.

BATTER

Recipes for suitable batters are on pages 440–443. The batter should be freshly made. The fish or seafood is first coated in seasoned flour, then dipped in the batter just before being submerged in the hot oil. Use two forks to turn the food in the batter, taking care not to knock the air out of a very light mixture. Have the container near the pan, then lift the food and allow excess batter to drip off. Give the food a twist to catch the drips of batter, then lower it carefully into the hot oil.

BACALAO DOURADO

Bacalao – salt cod – looks like a skateboard but tastes delicious when properly soaked and cooked. Skimping on the soaking time leads to disaster.

450 g/1 lb salt cod
125 ml/4 fl oz olive oil
2 onions, finely chopped
450 g/1 lb potatoes, very finely sliced
6 eggs, lightly beaten
salt and pepper
10 ml/2 tsp chopped parsley to garnish

Place the cod in a large bowl, cover with cold water and leave to soak for 24 hours in a cold place, changing the water occasionally.

Drain the fish and put it in a large saucepan with fresh water to cover. Bring to the boil, then drain again. Skin the fish, remove the bones and flake the flesh finely.

Heat 30 ml/2 tbsp of the olive oil in a large frying pan. Add the onions and fry over medium heat until golden – this will take 20–30 minutes depending on the type of pan and the heat. Do not be tempted to increase the heat under the pan so as to save time; this results in burning not browning. Add the flaked fish, cook for 3 minutes more, then pour off any excess oil. Set the pan aside.

Heat the remaining oil in a saucepan or second frying pan, add the sliced potatoes and fry gently for 10–15 minutes until tender but not crisp. Remove the slices from the oil with a slotted spoon, drain on absorbent kitchen paper and add to the fish. Mix well.

Return the pan to moderate heat and cook, stirring lightly so as not to break up the potatoes, until heated through. Add the beaten eggs with salt and pepper to taste and continue cooking until the eggs have the consistency of creamy scrambled egg.

Turn the mixture out on to a heated serving dish, sprinkle with chopped parsley and serve.

SERVES FOUR TO SIX

SPICY FISH SLICES

675 g/1½ lb cod or hake fillets
7.5 ml/1½ tsp salt
5 ml/1 tsp turmeric
5 ml/1 tsp chilli powder
90 ml/6 tbsp oil
fresh coriander sprigs to garnish

Cut the fish into 2 cm/¾ inch slices and spread them out in a shallow dish large enough to hold all the slices in a single layer. Mix the salt and spices in a bowl. Stir in enough water to make a thick paste. Rub the paste into the fish, cover and leave to marinate for 1 hour.

Heat the oil in a large frying pan. Add as much of the spiced fish as possible, but do not overfill the pan. Fry the fish for 5–10 minutes until golden brown all over, then remove from the pan with a slotted spoon. Drain on absorbent kitchen paper and keep hot while cooking the rest of the fish.

Garnish and serve hot, with rice or a small salad, if liked.

SERVES FOUR TO FIVE

COD CUTLETS WITH SHRIMP STUFFING

4 cod cutlets
15 ml/1 tbsp oil

STUFFING
25 g/1 oz butter
1 onion, chopped
50 g/2 oz fresh white breadcrumbs
15 ml/1 tbsp chopped parsley
150 g/5 oz peeled cooked shrimps or prawns, chopped
juice of ½ lemon
salt and pepper

GARNISH
lemon twists
watercress sprigs
whole prawns

Make the stuffing. Melt the butter, add the onion and fry gently for 10 minutes until soft but not browned. Remove from the heat and stir in the breadcrumbs and parsley, with the shrimps or prawns and lemon juice. Add salt and pepper to taste.

Rinse the fish cutlets, pat them dry with absorbent kitchen paper and remove their bones. Arrange the fish neatly on a flameproof platter or baking sheet and fill the centre spaces with the stuffing.

Sprinkle the oil over the stuffed fish and cook under a moderate grill for 15-20 minutes or until the fish is cooked through. If the stuffing begins to brown too fiercely before the fish is cooked, then reduce the heat. Garnish with lemon twists, watercress sprigs and whole prawns, and serve at once.

SERVES FOUR

JAMAICAN FRIED FISH

225 g/8 oz fish bones and trimmings
3 green peppers, seeded and sliced
3 onions, sliced
3 carrots, sliced
2 bay leaves, split in half
2 cm/¾ inch fresh root ginger, peeled and finely chopped
8 peppercorns
1 blade of mace
salt
30 ml/2 tbsp groundnut oil
90 ml/6 tbsp malt vinegar
45 ml/3 tbsp sunflower or corn oil
1 kg/2¼ lb white fish fillets

Put the fish bones and trimmings in a large saucepan with the peppers, onions, carrots, bay leaves and ginger. Add the peppercorns and mace, with salt to taste. Pour in 350 ml/12 fl oz water, bring to the boil and simmer uncovered for 35 minutes. Add the groundnut oil and vinegar and simmer for 2 minutes more. Strain the stock, reserving the vegetables as accompaniments for the fish, if liked. Keep hot.

Heat the sunflower or corn oil in a large frying pan, add the fish fillets and fry for 7-8 minutes, turning once, until just browned. Remove the fish from the oil with a slotted spoon and drain on absorbent kitchen paper.

Place the fish fillets in a warmed serving dish, pour the reserved stock over and serve at once, with the reserved vegetables.

SERVES SIX

VARIATION

Jamaican Fish Salad Cook as suggested above, but let the fish fillets cool down in the stock. Chill. Garnish with olives and strips of pepper before serving.

HERRINGS WITH MUSTARD SAUCE

4 herrings
10 ml/2 tsp lemon juice
salt and pepper
10 ml/2 tsp mustard powder
2 egg yolks
50 g/2 oz butter
30 ml/2 tbsp double cream
15 ml/1 tbsp chopped capers
15 ml/1 tbsp chopped gherkin

Scale the herrings, cut off the heads and remove the bones. Sprinkle the flesh with the lemon juice and plenty of salt and pepper. Grill under moderate heat for 3–5 minutes on each side. Transfer to a warmed serving dish and keep hot.

Combine the mustard and egg yolks in the top of a double saucepan, place over hot water and whisk until creamy. Add the butter, a small piece at a time, whisking well after each addition.

When the sauce thickens, remove the pan from the heat and stir in the cream, capers and gherkin. Add salt and pepper to taste, pour into a sauceboat and serve with the fish.

SERVES FOUR

HADDOCK AND FENNEL FLAMBE

dried fennel stalks (see method)
225 g/8 oz butter
60 ml/4 tbsp brandy
1 kg/2¼ lb haddock or hake fillets
salt and pepper
15 ml/1 tbsp chopped fresh fennel
lemon wedges to garnish

Have ready a metal serving dish large enough to accommodate the rack of your grill pan. Pile dried fennel stalks on the dish to a depth of 5 cm/2 inches. Melt 200 g/7 oz of the butter in a small saucepan. Keep it warm over a candle burner at the table. Have the brandy ready in a small jug. You will also need an all-metal soup ladle and a long match or taper.

Place the fish, skin side up, on the rack of the grill pan. Grill under moderate heat for 5 minutes, then carefully remove the skin. Turn the fillets over carefully, using a fish slice. Sprinkle with salt, pepper and chopped fennel, and dot with the remaining butter. Grill for a further 10 minutes.

Place the rack containing the cooked fish over the fennel and carry it to the table. Pour the brandy into the soup ladle and warm it over the candle burner. Pour the warm brandy over the fish, then light the brandy and dried fennel.

When the flames have died down, transfer the fish to individual plates. Garnish with the lemon wedges. Serve with the melted butter.

SERVES FOUR

VARIATIONS

Mackerel Flambé Slash the sides of 4 mackerel and tuck a few fennel leaves inside each. Season the fish, grill for 10–12 minutes, then flambé as suggested above.

GRILLED SMOKED HADDOCK

450–575 g/1–1¼ lb smoked haddock fillet,
trimmed and cut into serving portions
melted butter or oil for brushing
4 pats of Herb Butter (page 492) to serve

Place the fish in a large frying pan and pour in boiling water to cover. Leave to stand for 5 minutes. Carefully remove each portion with a fish slice, drain well and arrange, skin side up, in a grill pan.

Grill under moderate heat for 3–5 minutes, depending on the thickness of the fish. Turn the fish over, brush the uncooked sides generously with melted butter or oil and grill for 4 minutes more or until tender.

Serve on individual warmed plates, topping each portion with a pat of chilled herb butter.

SERVES FOUR

FRENCH FRIED HADDOCK

1 kg/2¼ lb haddock fillets, skinned
250 ml/8 fl oz milk
100 g/4 oz plain flour
salt and pepper
oil for deep frying
lemon wedges, to serve

Cut the fish into 4–5 portions. Pour the milk into a shallow bowl. Spread out the flour in a second bowl; add salt and pepper. Dip the pieces of fish first into milk and then into flour, shaking off the excess.

Put the oil for frying into a deep wide pan. Heat the oil to 180–190°C/350–275°F or until a cube of bread added to the oil browns in 30 seconds.

If using a deep-fat fryer, follow the manufacturer's instructions.

Carefully lower the fish into the hot oil and fry for 3–5 minutes until evenly browned. Drain on absorbent kitchen paper and serve on a warmed platter, with lemon wedges.

SERVES FOUR TO FIVE

 MRS BEETON'S TIP

The fish should be of uniform thickness for frying. Any thin pieces, such as tail ends, should be folded double before flouring the fish.

GRILLED KIPPERS

4 kippers
20 ml/4 tsp butter
4 pats of butter, chilled, to serve
chopped parsley to garnish

Lay the kippers flat, skin side up, in the base of the grill pan. Do not place on a rack. Grill under moderate heat for 3 minutes.

Turn the kippers over, dot each one with 5 ml/1 tsp butter and grill for 3 minutes more.

Serve on individual warmed plates, topping each portion with a pat of chilled butter and a sprinkling of chopped parsley.

SERVES FOUR

FRIED WHITING

25–50g/1–2oz plain flour
salt and pepper
2 eggs
50g/2oz dried white breadcrumbs for
  coating
12 small whiting fillets
oil for deep frying
150 ml/¼ pint Tartare Sauce (page 469)
  to serve

Mix the flour with salt and pepper on a large plate. Beat the eggs in a shallow bowl. Spread out the breadcrumbs on a sheet of foil. Coat each whiting fillet first in flour, then in egg and finally in breadcrumbs. Roll up the fillets and secure with a skewer or wooden cocktail stick.

Put the oil for frying into a deep wide pan. Heat the oil to 180–190°C/350–375°F or until a cube of bread added to the oil browns in 30 seconds.

Carefully lower the whiting rolls into the hot oil and fry for 3–5 minutes. Drain on absorbent kitchen paper and serve on a warmed platter. Hand the tartare sauce separately.

SERVES SIX

VARIATIONS

Whiting with Avocado Sauce Instead of serving tartare sauce, mash a ripe avocado with 30 ml/2 tbsp soured cream. Mix in 30 ml/2 tbsp snipped chives, salt and pepper to taste.

Whiting with Tomato Salsa Finely chop 4 ripe tomatoes. Mix with 1 crushed garlic clove, 30 ml/2 tbsp finely chopped onion, 1 small seeded and finely chopped green chilli, 5 ml/1 tsp caster sugar, salt and pepper to taste. Add 2–3 shredded sprigs of fresh basil if available. Serve instead of tartare sauce.

GOUJONS OF PLAICE

12 (100g/4oz) plaice fillets
50g/2oz plain flour
salt and pepper
100 ml/3½ fl oz milk
oil for deep frying
Tartare Sauce (page 469) to serve

GARNISH
lemon wedges
parsley sprigs

Cut the fish fillets lengthways into short strips about 4cm/1½ inches wide. Mix the flour with salt and pepper and spread out in a shallow bowl. Pour the milk into a second bowl. Coat the strips of plaice first in milk and then in seasoned flour, shaking off any excess.

Put the oil for frying into a deep wide pan. Heat the oil to 180–190°C/350–375°F or until a cube of bread added to the oil browns in 30 seconds. If you are using a deep-fat fryer, follow the manufacturer's instructions.

Carefully add the strips of fish, a few at a time, to the hot oil. Fry for 2–3 minutes until golden brown. Drain on absorbent kitchen paper and keep hot on a warmed dish. Reheat the oil before putting in each fresh batch of goujons. Garnish and serve with tartare sauce.

SERVES SIX

SOLE COLBERT

200 g/7 ox Maître d'Hôtel butter (page 492)
10 ml/2 tsp finely chopped fresh tarragon
6 Dover soles
100 g/4 oz plain flour
salt and pepper
2 eggs, lightly beaten
50 g/2 oz fresh white breadcrumbs
oil for deep frying

GARNISH
lemon wedges
fresh tarragon sprigs

Mix the maître d'hôtel butter and tarragon. Remove the dark skin of the fish. Cut down the backbone on the skinned side and slice under the flesh, following the bones to make a pocket on each side. Cut the backbone in three places with sharp scissors to allow removal after cooking.

Mix the flour with salt and pepper and spread out in a shallow bowl. Put the beaten eggs in a second shallow bowl and spread out the breadcrumbs on a sheet of foil. Coat each fish in flour, then in egg and breadcrumbs.

Put the oil for frying into a deep wide pan. Heat the oil to 180-190°C/350-375°F or until a cube of bread added to the oil browns in 30 seconds. If using a deep-fat fryer, follow the manufacturer's instructions. Deep fry the fish, one at a time, until golden brown, reheating the oil as necessary.

Drain the fish on absorbent kitchen paper, remove the bone where cut and arrange on a warmed serving dish. Fill the pockets of the fish with the tarragon-flavoured butter and serve immediately, garnished with lemon and tarragon.

SERVES SIX

SOLE ANTHONY

100 g/4 oz butter
225 g/8 oz dried white breadcrumbs
6 (150 g/5 oz) Dover sole fillets
6 slices of fresh or canned pineapple
25 g/1 oz sugar
parsley sprigs to garnish

SAUCE
50 g/2 oz butter
25 g/1 oz plain flour
300 ml/½ pint Fish Stock (page 48)
60 ml/4 tbsp dry white wine
2 egg yolks
juice of ½ lemon
salt and pepper
75 g/3 oz mushrooms, chopped

Make the sauce. Melt 25 g/1 oz of the butter in a saucepan. Stir in the flour and cook over low heat for 2-3 minutes, without allowing the mixture to colour. Gradually add the fish stock, stirring constantly.

Increase the heat to moderate and cook, stirring, until the mixture boils and thickens to a coating consistency. Stir in the wine, reduce the heat and simmer for 10 minutes.

Heat the sauce to just below boiling point and whisk in the remaining butter, a little at a time. Remove the pan from the heat.

Beat the egg yolks and lemon juice in a small bowl. Add a little of the sauce and mix well. Add the contents of the bowl to the sauce and heat gently, stirring. Do not allow the sauce to boil. Add salt and pepper to taste and the mushrooms. Cover the sauce closely with damp greaseproof paper and keep warm.

Melt the butter in a small pan. Use some of it to grease a shallow flameproof dish. Pour the rest into a shallow bowl. Spread the breadcrumbs on a sheet of foil. Coat the fish in melted butter and then in breadcrumbs. Arrange in the prepared dish.

Grill the fish for 3 minutes on each side. Brush the pineapple slices with melted butter, sprinkle with sugar and brown under the grill.

Spoon the sauce into a flameproof serving dish. Arrange the fish on top and place a slice of pineapple on each. Grill for 5 minutes. Serve very hot, garnished with parsley sprigs.

SERVES SIX

FRITTO MISTO

50 g/2 oz plain flour
salt and pepper
225 g/8 oz fresh sardines or sprats, cleaned
oil for deep-frying
225 g/8 oz scampi tails, thawed if frozen
100 g/4 oz cauliflower sprigs, parboiled for 5
  minutes and drained
2 courgettes
1 large onion, cut in thin rings
lemon wedges, to serve

BATTER
1 egg
30 ml/2 tbsp corn oil
100 g/4 oz plain flour
pinch of salt
15 ml/1 tbsp chopped parsley
1 garlic clove, crushed

Make the batter. Combine the egg and oil in a 600 ml/1 pint jug. Add 300 ml/½ pint water and mix well. Mix the flour and salt in a bowl. Make a well in the centre, add the egg mixture and mix well, gradually incorporating the flour to make a smooth batter. Leave to stand for 15 minutes, then add the parsley and garlic.

Add salt and pepper to the flour and spread some of it out in a shallow bowl. Coat the sardines or sprats in the seasoned flour.

Put the oil for frying into a deep wide pan. Heat the oil to 180–190°C/350–375°F or until a cube of bread added to the oil browns in 30 seconds. If using a deep-fat fryer, follow the manufacturer's instructions.

Carefully add the fish to the hot oil and fry for 1–2 minutes. Drain on absorbent kitchen paper and keep hot in a warmed dish. Reheat the oil. Dry the scampi and coat in seasoned flour. Dip in the batter, a few at a time, and deep fry for 3–4 minutes until crisp. Drain and keep hot with the fish. Reheat the oil.

Coat the cauliflower sprigs in seasoned flour, dip in the batter and deep fry for 2–3 minutes. Drain and keep hot.

Using a canelle knife, score the skin of the courgettes deeply. Cut them in half across, then lengthways into quarters. Coat in seasoned flour, dip in batter and deep fry as for the cauliflower. Drain and keep hot with the fish. Repeat the procedure with the onion rings, reheating the oil as necessary.

Pile the mixture of fritters on a serving platter, sprinkle with salt and serve at once with lemon wedges.

SERVES SIX

 MRS BEETON'S TIP

Fritto Misto, meaning 'mixed fry', is a classic Italian dish often served as the opening course of the meal or antipasto. Although, as here, it is frequently linked with fish and seafood, authentically there are many regional versions which may include poultry or meat as well as vegetables. Indeed, the mixture of food is not always limited to savoury ingredients, and fruit or even pieces of sponge cake may form part of the surprise combination.

FILLETS OF SOLE ORLY

Fresh Tomato Sauce (page 483) is the perfect accompaniment for this dish.

6 (175 g/6 oz) lemon sole fillets
oil for deep frying
lemon wedges to serve

MARINADE
30 ml/2 tbsp chopped parsley
30 ml/2 tbsp chopped onion
salt and pepper
15 ml/1 tbsp lemon juice
15 ml/1 tbsp corn oil

BATTER
50 g/2 oz plain flour
salt
15 ml/1 tbsp corn oil
1 egg white

Mix all the ingredients for the marinade in a shallow bowl large enough to hold all the sole fillets in a single layer (see Mrs Beeton's Tip, below). Add the fish, cover and marinate for 1 hour. Drain the fish and pat dry on absorbent kitchen paper.

Make the batter. Mix the flour and salt in a bowl. Make a well in the centre, add 60 ml/4 tbsp water and the oil. Mix well, gradually incorporating the flour to make a smooth batter. In a clean, dry bowl whisk the egg white until stiff. Fold it into the batter.

Put the oil for frying into a deep wide pan. Heat the oil to 180–190°C/350–375°F or until a cube

of bread added to the oil browns in 30 seconds. If using a deep-fat fryer, follow the manufacturer's instructions.

Dip the fish fillets in the batter, carefully lower them into the hot oil and fry for 3–5 minutes until golden brown. Drain on absorbent kitchen paper, arrange on a warmed platter and serve at once, garnished with lemon wedges.

SERVES SIX

SOLE MEUNIERE

50 g/2 oz plain flour
salt and pepper
4 large sole fillets
75 g/3 oz butter
30 ml/2 tbsp chopped parsley
juice of 1 lemon
lemon wedges to garnish

Mix the flour with salt and pepper and spread out in a shallow bowl. Lightly coat the fish fillets in the seasoned flour.

Melt the butter in a frying pan and fry the fillets over moderate heat for about 7 minutes, turning once, until golden brown.

Using a slotted spoon and a fish slice, carefully transfer the fish to a warmed serving dish and keep hot. Continue heating the butter until it is nut brown. Add the parsley.

Pour the butter over the fish, sprinkle with lemon juice and serve at once, garnished with lemon wedges.

SERVES FOUR

> 🥄 **MRS BEETON'S TIP**
>
> A lasagne dish may be used for marinating the fish. Alternatively, line a roasting tin with foil.

FISH CAKES

Tasty, nutritious, easy to make and popular with children, home-made fish cakes are perfect for midweek family meals.

350 g/12 oz cooked white fish, flaked
450 g/1 lb potatoes
25 g/1 oz butter
30 ml/2 tbsp single cream or milk
15 ml/1 tbsp finely chopped parsley
salt and pepper
50 g/2 oz plain flour
oil for shallow frying

Remove any bones from the fish. Cook the potatoes in a saucepan of salted boiling water for about 30 minutes or until tender. Drain thoroughly and mash with a potato masher, or beat with a hand-held electric whisk until smooth. Beat in the butter and cream or milk. Add the flaked fish and parsley, with salt and pepper to taste. Set aside until cold.

Form the fish mixture into 8 portions, shaping each to a flat round cake. Spread out the flour in a shallow bowl, add salt and pepper and use to coat the fish cakes.

Heat the oil in a frying pan, add the fish cakes and fry for 6–8 minutes, turning once. Drain on absorbent kitchen paper, arrange on a warmed serving dish and serve.

SERVES FOUR

 MRS BEETON'S TIP

For extra flavour, try adding chopped anchovy fillets, fried finely chopped onion, grated Cheddar cheese or crumbled fried bacon to the basic mixture above.

MRS BEETON'S DRESSED WHITEBAIT

50 g/2 oz plain flour
salt and pepper
125 ml/4 fl oz milk
100 g/4 oz whitebait
oil for deep frying
cayenne pepper

GARNISH
parsley sprigs
lemon wedges

Mix the flour, salt and pepper in a sturdy polythene bag. Pour the milk into a shallow bowl. Dip the whitebait into the milk, then toss them in the seasoned flour in the bag. Shake off excess flour and make sure that all the fish are separate.

Put the oil for frying into a deep wide pan. Heat the oil to 180–190°C/350–375°F or until a cube of bread added to the oil browns in 30 seconds. If using a deep-fat fryer, follow the manufacturer's instructions.

Carefully add the fish, a few at a time, in a chip basket to the hot oil and fry for 30 seconds to 1 minute. Drain on absorbent kitchen paper and keep hot in a warmed dish. Reheat the oil before putting in each fresh batch of fish.

When all the fish are fried, pile them on a serving platter, sprinkle with salt and cayenne and serve at once, garnished with parsley and lemon wedges.

SERVES THREE TO FOUR

FRIED SMELTS

Small silvery fish, related to salmon, smelts are too often overlooked.

200 g/7 oz plain flour
salt
15 ml/1 tbsp olive oil
1 egg, separated
30–45 ml/2–3 tbsp milk
oil for deep frying
18 smelts, cleaned, heads removed
watercress to garnish

Mix the flour and salt in a bowl. Make a well in the centre, add the oil, egg yolk and 30 ml/2 tbsp of the milk. Mix well, gradually incorporating the flour to make a stiff batter. Add the extra 15 ml/1 tbsp milk if necessary. Cover the batter and let it stand for 15 minutes.

In a clean, dry bowl whisk the egg white until stiff. Fold it into the batter.

Put the oil for frying into a deep wide pan. Heat the oil to 180–190°C/350–375°F or until a cube of bread added to the oil browns in 30 seconds. If using a deep-fat fryer, follow the manufacturer's instructions.

Dip the fish in the batter, a few at a time, and deep fry for 1–2 minutes until crisp. Drain on absorbent kitchen paper and keep hot in a warmed dish. Reheat the oil before putting in each fresh batch of fish.

When all the fish are fried, pile them on a serving platter, garnish with watercress and serve at once.

SERVES SIX

MONKFISH AND BACON KEBABS

125 ml/4 fl oz olive oil
1 garlic clove, crushed
5 ml/1 tsp lemon juice
5 ml/1 tsp dried oregano
800 g/1¾ lb monkfish, cleaned, trimmed and
   cut into 2 cm/¾ inch cubes
225 g/8 oz rindless streaky bacon rashers
200 g/7 oz small mushrooms
salt and pepper

Combine the olive oil, garlic, lemon juice and oregano in a shallow bowl large enough to hold all the monkfish cubes in a single layer. Mix well, add the fish, and marinate for 15 minutes. Drain the monkfish, reserving the marinade.

Thread a piece of bacon on to a kebab skewer. Add a cube of fish, then a mushroom, weaving the bacon between them. Continue to add the fish and mushrooms, each time interweaving the bacon, until the skewer is full. Add a second rasher of bacon if necessary. Fill five more skewers in the same way. Sprinkle with salt and pepper.

Grill the monkfish kebabs under moderate heat for 10–15 minutes, basting frequently with the reserved marinade.

SERVES SIX

 MICROWAVE TIP

Thread the mixture on wooden skewers. Put the skewers on a large plate. Spoon a little of the marinade over each kebab and cook on High for 8 minutes, turning and rearranging the kebabs once during cooking.

MACKEREL WITH GOOSEBERRY SAUCE

Gooseberry sauce is such a classic accompaniment to mackerel that in France the fruit is known as groseille à maquereau.

50 g/2 oz plain flour
salt and pepper
8 mackerel fillets
50 g/2 oz butter
juice of 1 lemon
45 ml/3 tbsp chopped parsley

SAUCE
450 g/1 lb gooseberries, topped and tailed
45 ml/3 tbsp dry still cider
25 g/1 oz butter
15 ml/1 tbsp caster sugar

Make the sauce by combining the gooseberries, cider and butter in a small saucepan. Bring the liquid to simmering point and poach the fruit, stirring occasionally, until soft. Purée the mixture by passing it through a sieve set over a small pan. Stir in the sugar.

Spread out the flour in a shallow bowl, add salt and pepper, and coat the fish lightly all over.

Melt the butter in a large frying pan, add the fish and fry gently for 5–7 minutes or until browned, turning once. Using a slotted spoon and a fish slice, transfer the fish to a warmed serving dish and keep hot.

Heat the gooseberry sauce. Continue to heat the butter in the frying pan until it becomes light brown. Stir in the lemon juice and parsley and pour over the fish. Pour the gooseberry sauce into a jug or sauceboat and serve at once, with the fish.

SERVES FOUR

SABO-NO-TERIYAKI

This dish can also be made with herring, salmon or bream.

150 ml/¼ pint soy sauce
45 ml/3 tbsp mirin (see Mrs Beeton's Tip)
pinch of chilli powder
15 ml/1 tbsp grated fresh root ginger
2 garlic cloves, crushed
4 mackerel fillets

Mix the soy sauce, mirin, chilli powder, ginger and garlic in a bowl. Stir well. Arrange the mackerel fillets in a shallow dish large enough to hold them all in a single layer. Pour the soy sauce mixture over, cover the dish and marinate for 2 hours.

Drain the fish, reserving the marinade. Cook under a hot grill for 5–10 minutes, brushing the fish several times with the reserved marinade during cooking. Serve at once.

SERVES FOUR

 MICROWAVE TIP

The gooseberries can be cooked in the microwave. Combine the cider and butter in a mixing bowl and heat for 1 minute on High. Add the fruit, stir, cover the bowl and cook for 5–7 minutes or until soft. Stir once or twice during cooking.

 MRS BEETON'S TIP

If you cannot obtain mirin, which is a sweet Japanese rice wine, use a mixture of 45 ml/3 tbsp of dry sherry and 10 ml/2 tsp sugar.

MARINATED FRIED HERRINGS

Serve as a starter with brown bread and butter.
Soured cream makes a good accompaniment.

8 herrings
30 ml/2 tbsp plain flour
2.5 ml/½ tsp salt
2.5 ml/½ tsp pepper
butter for shallow frying

MARINADE
300 ml/½ pint cider vinegar
90 g/3½ oz sugar
1 onion, thinly sliced
1 bay leaf
6 peppercorns

Make the marinade by combining the vinegar and sugar in a saucepan. Add 300 ml/½ pint water and bring to the boil, stirring until the sugar has dissolved. Set aside to cool.

Split the herrings and remove the backbones. Spread out the flour in a shallow bowl, add salt and pepper, and use to coat the fish lightly all over.

Melt the butter in a large frying pan, add the fish and fry for 7-8 minutes or until golden brown, turning once. Using a slotted spoon and a fish slice, transfer the herrings to a dish large enough to hold them all in a single layer.

Tuck the onion slices, bay leaf and peppercorns around the herrings and pour the cold vinegar mixture over. Cover the dish and set aside in a cool place for about 6 hours. Serve with brown bread and butter, if liked.

SERVES FOUR

FRIED SKATE

50 g/2 oz plain flour
salt and pepper
1 egg, lightly beaten
50 g/2 oz dried white breadcrumbs
4 skate wings, total weight about 575 g/1¼ lb
75 g/3 oz butter
Tartare Sauce (page 469)

GARNISH
lemon slices · watercress sprigs

Mix the flour with salt and pepper and spread out in a shallow bowl. Put the egg in a second bowl and spread out the breadcrumbs on a sheet of foil. Coat each skate wing first in seasoned flour, then in egg and breadcrumbs.

Melt the butter in a large frying pan, add the fish and fry gently for 5 minutes on each side or until golden and cooked through. Garnish and serve with tartare sauce.

SERVES FOUR

MARINATED SKATE

4 skate wings, total weight about 575 g/1¼ lb
1 onion, sliced
small bunch of parsley
salt and pepper
juice of ½ lemon
150 ml/¼ pint cider vinegar
50 g/2 oz plain flour
50 g/2 oz butter

TO SERVE
45 ml/3 tbsp chopped parsley
grated rind of 1 lemon
15 ml/1 tbsp finely chopped onion

Lay the skate wings in a large shallow dish. Sprinkle with the onion slices, parsley sprigs, salt and pepper. Pour the lemon juice, vinegar and 60 ml/4 tbsp water over. Cover and leave in a cool place for 1½ hours.

Drain the skate and pat it dry on absorbent kitchen paper. Dust all over with the flour. Melt the butter in a large frying pan, add the fish and fry gently for 5 minutes on each side or until lightly browned and cooked.

Meanwhile, mix the parsley, lemon rind and onion for serving. Transfer the skate wings to warmed plates and pour the pan juices over. Sprinkle with the parsley and lemon mixture and serve at once with thinly sliced bread and butter.

SERVES FOUR

TROUT WITH ALMONDS

100 g/4 oz butter
4 trout, cleaned and trimmed
salt and pepper
juice of ½ lemon
50 g/2 oz flaked almonds
125 ml/4 fl oz double cream
3 egg yolks

Melt the butter in a grill pan under moderate heat. Lay the trout in the pan and sprinkle with salt and pepper and lemon juice. Grill for 5 minutes.

Carefully turn the trout over. Sprinkle most of the almonds over the fish, spreading out the rest at the side of the pan. Grill for 3–5 minutes more until the trout are tender and the almonds browned. Using a fish slice and slotted spoon, transfer the trout and almonds to absorbent kitchen paper to drain. Tip the grill pan juices into a small saucepan. Arrange the trout on a warmed serving platter and keep hot. Set the browned almonds aside.

Add the cream and egg yolks to the pan juices and mix well. Heat gently, stirring constantly until the sauce thickens. Do not let the mixture boil. Spoon the sauce over the trout, garnish with the reserved almonds and serve at once.

SERVES FOUR

TROUT MEUNIERE

4 trout
50 g/2 oz plain flour
salt and pepper
50 g/2 oz butter
juice of ½ lemon
10 ml/2 tsp chopped parsley
lemon twists to garnish

Dry the fish well with absorbent kitchen paper. Spread out the flour in a shallow bowl and add salt and pepper. Add the fish and coat well on all sides.

Melt the butter in a large frying pan. When it foams, add the trout. Fry gently for 6–7 minutes on each side or until the skin is golden and crisp.

Using a slotted spoon and a fish slice, transfer the fish to a warmed serving dish. Keep hot. Add salt and pepper to the butter remaining in the pan and heat until it is nut brown. Add the lemon juice and chopped parsley and pour over the trout. Garnish with lemon twists and serve at once.

SERVES FOUR

Baked Fish Dishes

*Baking is an easy, versatile cooking method for fish, as this chapter shows. Most types of
seafood may be baked in some way or other, either very simply, with herbs and lemon juice or
mixed with a sauce, layered with vegetables topped with breadcrumbs or made into a pie.
Baking is one of the easiest cooking methods because, to a large extent, it takes care
of itself. As with other methods, it is important to avoid overcooking the fish.
Here are a few simple suggestions.*

BAKING IN FOIL

Individual portions of fish cook well in closed
foil packages. Steaks and small whole fish are
ideal for baking by this method, and portions of
thick fillet (from cod or monkfish) are also
suitable.

Cut pieces of foil large enough to hold the
fish. Brush the middle of the foil with oil or
melted butter and place the fish on it. Add herb
sprigs – parsley, thyme or bay – and a trickle of
oil or knob of butter. Sprinkle salt and pepper
over the fish and fold the foil around it. Fold the
edges of the foil over to seal in the fish, then
place the package on a baking sheet. To check
whether the fish is cooked open a very small
gap in the foil and test with a thin skewer.

Serve the foil packages on individual plates
to be opened at the table.

COOKING EN PAPILLOTTE

A traditional method of baking in paper, this
works well for fish. Cut neat pieces of double
thick greaseproof paper, large enough to hold
the fish. The paper may be cut in various ways;
oblong or square shapes, circles or heart-
shaped pieces may be used.

Brush the paper with oil or melted butter and
lay the fish in the middle. Bring the paper up
over the fish and crumple the edges together

firmly to seal in the contents. The edges of the
paper must be closed over the top of the fish so
that the package may be opened easily on the
plate, revealing the contents ready to eat. Once
cooked the paper becomes very brittle.

Non-stick baking parchment may be used
instead of greaseproof paper for strength.

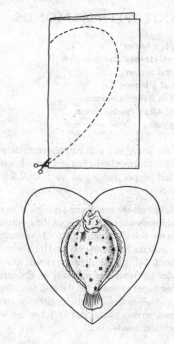

COOKING IN FILM

Roasting bags and film may be used for enclosing fish in sealed packages for baking. The large bags make practical containers for larger whole fish – redfish, grey mullet or a curved salmon trout. Several smaller fish (red mullet or mackerel) may be arranged in the same bag placed in a dish or roasting tin. This is useful if you do not have a suitable baking dish large enough to hold the fish.

BAKING IN SHELLS

Scrubbed scallop shells may be used for baking fish and seafood in sauce or with gratin toppings. The deep shells should be saved, thoroughly scrubbed, boiled, rinsed and dried (see also page 116). Some fishmongers sell the cleaned shells.

Smaller shells are also useful. Mussels may be 'stuffed' in their shells. Larger deep oyster shells and clam shells are suitable both for holding fish and seafood during baking and as attractive serving vessels, particularly for appetizers.

FLAVOURING BAKED FISH

Whether the fish is enclosed in a package or placed in a covered dish, the choice of seasonings and flavourings is important. Herbs, pared or grated lemon rind and cloves of garlic (whole, chopped or crushed) are typical additions. A moistening agent of some kind is usually added. This may be butter or margarine, a little oil or a squeeze of lemon juice. A couple of spoonfuls of milk or single cream may be used with white fish fillets, while a little white wine, dry cider or dry white vermouth can contribute flavour and moisture.

Vegetables should be selected with care. Onion added to a sauce can taste raw even after baking unless it is quickly cooked in oil or butter first. Carrots and celery also benefit from brief pre-cooking before being baked with fish. Cooked chopped spinach makes an excellent base on which to bake skinned fish fillets or steaks.

TOPPINGS

Baked fish is often finished off with a gratin topping of breadcrumbs. Chopped parsley, grated cheese (Cheddar or Parmesan) and a little melted butter may be mixed with the crumbs.

Other toppings include chopped nuts mixed with breadcrumbs, sliced boiled potatoes, diced boiled potatoes tossed with melted butter or sliced mozzarella cheese.

Creamy mixtures of yogurt or fromage frais with beaten egg also make good toppings, but care must be taken not to bake these mixtures at too high a temperature or for too long or they may curdle.

The stage at which the topping is added depends on the ingredients and the cooking time. Fish and seafood which bakes very quickly may be topped when first placed in the oven. If the main part of the dish requires slightly longer, and the topping is light, as when a sprinkling of breadcrumbs is added, it is often best to add the topping halfway through cooking.

COD AU GRATIN

fat for greasing
4 (100 g/4 oz) portions of cod fillet
25 g/1 oz butter
2 large onions, finely chopped
100 g/4 oz mushrooms, sliced
salt and pepper
1 green pepper, seeded and diced
450 g/1 lb tomatoes, peeled, seeded and
    sliced
50 g/2 oz Cheddar cheese, grated
75 g/3 oz fresh white breadcrumbs

Grease a fairly deep ovenproof dish. Set the oven at 190°C/375°F/gas 5. Arrange the cod portions on the base of the dish.

Melt the butter in a frying pan, add the onions and fry gently for 4–5 minutes until slightly softened. Remove the onions with a slotted spoon and place on top of the fish. Cook the mushrooms in the same way.

Meanwhile bring a small saucepan of salted water to the boil, add the diced green pepper and blanch for 2 minutes. Drain and add to the fish, followed by the mushrooms. Top with the tomato slices, generously sprinkled with salt and pepper.

Combine the cheese and breadcrumbs in a bowl, mix well, then sprinkle over the fish and vegetables. Bake for 30 minutes. Serve at once.

SERVES FOUR

SMOKED COD AND CORN CASSEROLE

1 (326 g/11½ oz) can sweetcorn kernels,
    drained
450 g/1 lb smoked cod fillet, skinned and cut
    in 1 cm/½ inch strips
pepper
25 g/1 oz butter
125 ml/4 fl oz single cream

Set the oven at 180°C/350°F/gas 4. Drain the corn and spread a layer on the base of an ovenproof dish. Add a layer of cod strips. Season with pepper and dot with butter.

Repeat the layers until all the corn and cod have been used, then pour over the cream. Cover and bake for 25 minutes. Serve at once.

SERVES THREE TO FOUR

VARIATION

Corn 'n Cod Poach the smoked cod fillets, then drain and flake. Make a white sauce, using 50 g/2 oz each of butter and plain flour and 600 ml/1 pint milk (or milk mixed with the drained liquid from the can of sweetcorn). Add salt and pepper to taste and stir in the flaked cod and the corn. Spoon into a dish, top with grated Cheddar cheese and bake for 15–20 minutes at 180°C/350°F/gas 4.

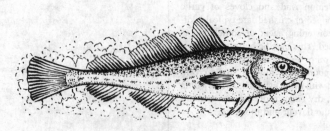

COLEY PROVENCALE

fat for greasing
15 ml/1 tbsp oil
2 onions, chopped
1 green pepper, seeded and chopped
3 large tomatoes, peeled, seeded and
  chopped
2 garlic cloves, crushed
salt and pepper
575 g/1¼ lb coley fillet, skinned and cut into
  2 cm/¾ inch cubes
8 green olives, stoned
8 black olives, stoned, to garnish

Grease a shallow ovenproof dish. Set the oven
at 180°C/350°F/gas 4.

Heat the oil in a large frying pan, add the
onions and pepper and fry gently for 5
minutes, stirring frequently. Add the tomatoes
and garlic, lower the heat and simmer for 10
minutes, stirring occasionally. Remove from
the heat and add salt and pepper to taste.

Put the fish cubes in the prepared dish. Add the
green olives, then pour the tomato mixture
over the top. Cover loosely with greased greaseproof paper or foil and bake for 30 minutes.
Garnish with the black olives and serve at once.

SERVES FOUR TO FIVE

 MRS BEETON'S TIP

The finest green olives generally come
from Spain. They should be large and firm,
with a good colour. Greek black olives are
considered to be the best, but it is always
worth buying loose olives rather than the
canned or bottled variety, so that you can
try before you buy.

BAKED MURRAY COD

oil for greasing
4 portions of cod fillet, total weight about
  450 g/1 lb, skinned
2 rindless fat back bacon rashers, chopped
1 large onion, finely chopped
250-350 ml/8-12 fl oz milk
1 bay leaf
salt and pepper
25 g/1 oz dried white breadcrumbs

Grease an ovenproof baking dish just large
enough to hold all the fish in a single layer. Set
the oven at 230°C/450°F/gas 8. Cook the bacon
and onion together in a heavy-bottomed pan
until the fat runs from the bacon and the onion
is slightly softened. Spread the mixture out in
the dish. Top with the fish.

Pour the milk into a saucepan, add the bay leaf
and bring to the boil. Remove the bay leaf, add
salt and pepper to taste and pour the hot milk
into the dish to the depth of the fish. The tops of
the fish fillets should be exposed.

Cover the fish thickly with the breadcrumbs.
Bake for 20 minutes or until the fish is tender
and the topping browned. Serve piping hot
with peas or spinach.

SERVES FOUR

 MRS BEETON'S TIP

Bacon complements a variety of seafood
dishes: wrap around chucks of white fish
or scallops before skewering and grilling
them; wrap streaky rashers around trout
before baking; or add diced bacon to fish
and seafood casseroles.

HADDOCK IN CIDER

fat for greasing
575 g/1¼ lb haddock fillet, skinned and
    cubed
225 g/8 oz tomatoes, peeled and sliced
150 g/5 oz mushrooms, sliced
125 ml/4 fl oz dry cider
salt and pepper
30 ml/2 tbsp chopped parsley
25 g/1 oz Cheddar cheese, grated
30 ml/2 tbsp fresh white breadcrumbs

Grease a large ovenproof baking dish. Set the
oven at 230°C/450°F/gas 8. Spread out the fish
cubes in an even layer on the base of the dish
and top with the tomatoes and mushrooms.

Pour the cider over the fish and sprinkle with
salt and pepper. Mix the parsley, cheese and
breadcrumbs together in a small bowl. Scatter
over the fish and bake for 20-25 minutes. Serve
at once.

SERVES FOUR

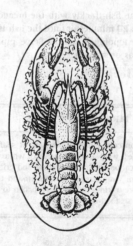

HADDOCK WITH SOURED CREAM

margarine or butter for greasing
25 g/1 oz butter
1 lemon, thinly sliced
575 g/1¼ lb haddock fillet, skinned and cut
    into serving portions
salt and pepper
125 ml/4 fl oz soured cream
paprika

GARNISH
2 hard-boiled eggs, chopped
30 ml/2 tbsp chopped parsley

Grease an ovenproof baking dish large enough
to hold all the fish. Set the oven at 200°C/
400°F/gas 6.

Melt the butter in a large frying pan. Add the
lemon slices and cook them for about 3
minutes on each side, until just beginning to
brown. Remove from the heat.

Spread out the lemon slices and their cooking
liquor on the base of the dish, top with the fish
and sprinkle with salt and pepper. Cover the
dish with foil and bake for 20-25 minutes.

Remove the foil and pour the soured cream
over the fish. Sprinkle with salt and paprika
and place under a moderate grill until lightly
browned on top. Garnish with eggs and parsley
and serve at once.

SERVES FOUR

 MRS BEETON'S TIP

If commercially soured cream is not available, stir 5 ml/1 tsp lemon juice into
125 ml/4 fl oz single cream. Set aside for
10-15 minutes before use.

BAKED HADDOCK FILLETS

fat for greasing
1 onion, finely chopped
150 g/5 oz mushrooms, sliced
15 ml/1 tbsp chopped parsley
800 g/1¾ lb haddock fillets, skinned and cut
   into 4 portions
100 ml/3½ fl oz dry white wine
50 g/2 oz fresh white breadcrumbs
50 g/2 oz butter

Grease an ovenproof dish. Set the oven at 190°C/375°F/gas 5. Spread the onion and mushrooms over the base of the prepared dish. Sprinkle with the parsley and top with the fish.

Pour the wine into the dish, sprinkle the fish with the breadcrumbs and dot with butter. Bake for 30–35 minutes. Serve at once.

SERVES FOUR

BRILL AND POTATO MORNAY

800 g/1¾ lb potatoes
75 g/3 oz butter
575 g/1¼ lb brill fillets, skinned
salt and pepper
juice of 1 lemon
50 g/2 oz Cheddar cheese, grated

MORNAY SAUCE
50 g/2 oz butter
50 g/2 oz plain flour
600 ml/1 pint milk, Fish Stock (page 48) or a
   mixture
salt and pepper
50 g/2 oz Cheddar cheese, grated

Boil the potatoes in their skins in a large saucepan of salted water for 20–30 minutes,

until tender. Drain and keep warm (see Mrs Beeton's Tip). Set the oven at 180°C/350°F/gas 4.

Make the sauce. Melt the butter in a saucepan. Stir in the flour and cook over low heat for 2–3 minutes, without allowing the mixture to colour. Remove the pan from the heat and gradually add the liquid, stirring constantly.

Return the pan to moderate heat, stirring until the mixture boils and thickens. Stir in the grated cheese. Cover the surface of the sauce with damp greaseproof paper and set aside until required.

Use a little of the butter to grease a shallow ovenproof baking dish and a sheet of greaseproof paper. Lay the fish in the dish. Add salt and pepper to taste, dot with the remaining butter and sprinkle with lemon juice. Cover the dish with the sheet of buttered greaseproof paper and bake for 15 minutes.

Meanwhile peel the potatoes and cut them into rounds. Reheat the cheese sauce, stirring constantly. Overlap the potato rounds to make a decorative topping for the fish. Pour the cheese sauce over the top, top with the grated cheese and brown under a hot grill.

SERVES SIX

 MRS BEETON'S TIP

An easy way to keep the potatoes warm is to drain off the water, cover the potatoes with crumpled absorbent kitchen paper and replace the saucepan lid. This method also works well for boiled peeled potatoes, which will then become perfectly dry.

BAKED WHITING

50 g/2 oz butter
4 whiting, cleaned and trimmed
salt and pepper
75 g/3 oz dried white breadcrumbs
lemon twists to serve

Use a little of the butter to grease an ovenproof baking dish. Melt the remaining butter in a small saucepan. Set the oven at 190°C/375°F/gas 5.

Brush the whiting all over with melted butter, season with salt and pepper and sprinkle liberally with breadcrumbs. Place in the prepared dish and bake for 20 minutes. Garnish with lemon twists and serve.

SERVES FOUR

JOHN DORY AU GRATIN

fat for greasing
8 John Dory fillets
salt and pepper
60 ml/4 tbsp milk
50 g/2 oz Gruyère cheese, grated
100 g/4 oz dried white breadcrumbs
25 g/1 oz butter

Grease an ovenproof baking dish. Set the oven at 190°C/375°F/gas 5.

Roll up the fish fillets and place them in the prepared dish. Sprinkle with salt and pepper and pour over the milk. Mix the cheese and breadcrumbs in a bowl and sprinkle the mixture over the fish.

Dot with butter and bake for 20 minutes. Serve at once.

SERVES THREE TO FOUR

IRISH BAKE

A simple supper dish that goes down well with the younger members of the family.

butter or margarine for greasing
450 g/1 lb potatoes, thinly sliced
450 g/1 lb firm white fish fillet, skinned and
   cut in 2 cm/¾ inch cubes
1 small onion, grated
50 g/2 oz mushrooms, sliced
salt and pepper
1 (298 g/11 oz) can ready-to-serve tomato
   soup
chopped parsley to garnish

Grease a shallow ovenproof dish. Set the oven at 200°C/400°F/gas 5. Cook the potatoes in boiling salted water for 10 minutes, then drain well.

Lay the fish in the prepared dish. Top with the grated onion and mushrooms, then add a layer of sliced potatoes. Pour the soup over the potatoes, then bake for 25-30 minutes, or until the fish is cooked and the mixture is bubbling hot.

Sprinkle with chopped parsley and serve.

SERVES FOUR

 MRS BEETON'S TIP

If preferred, canned cream-style corn or cream of mushroom soup may be used instead of tomato soup. For an equally speedy, more sophisticated dish, trickle 300 ml/½ pint single cream over instead of the soup. Add extra seasoning.

BAKED GRAYLING

Grayling are freshwater members of the salmon family (see page 108). They have firm white flesh and a flavour similar to, though not as pronounced as trout.

2 (450 g/1 lb) grayling
25 g/1 oz butter
2 large onions, thinly sliced
30 ml/2 tbsp chopped parsley
salt and pepper
250 ml/8 fl oz dry white wine
250 ml/8 fl oz double cream
juice of ¼ lemon
watercress sprigs to garnish

Clean the fish and remove the heads and fins. Use half the butter to grease a large ovenproof dish generously. Set the oven at 200°C/400°F/gas 6.

Cover the base of the prepared dish with the onions. Sprinkle with parsley, salt and pepper. Lay the fish side by side in the dish.

Melt the remaining butter in a small saucepan. Brush it over the fish and bake for 10 minutes. Add the wine to the dish, baste the fish and bake for 15 minutes more.

Pour the cream into the dish and bake for a further 5 minutes. Squeeze the lemon juice over the fish, garnish with watercress sprigs and serve at once.

SERVES TWO TO THREE

BAKED MULLET

25 g/1 oz butter
225 g/8 oz onions, thinly sliced
225 g/8 oz tomatoes, peeled, seeded and sliced
4 (225 g/8 oz) grey mullet, cleaned and trimmed
100 ml/3½ fl oz dry white wine
salt and pepper
15 ml/1 tbsp chopped fresh tarragon or 5 ml/1 tsp dried tarragon
1 lemon, sliced
sippets (see Mrs Beeton's Tip), to garnish

Use the butter to grease a shallow ovenproof baking dish and a sheet of greaseproof paper. Set the oven at 190°C/375°F/gas 5.

Spread out the onion rings on the base of the dish and top with the sliced tomatoes. Lay the fish on top of the vegetables and pour the wine over. Sprinkle with salt, pepper and tarragon.

Arrange the lemon slices on top of the fish and cover loosely with the buttered greaseproof paper. Bake for 30 minutes. Garnish with sippets and serve from the dish.

SERVES FOUR

> 🥄 **MRS BEETON'S TIP**
>
> To make sippets, toast white or granary bread until golden. Cut into triangles, cubes or fancy shapes.

RED MULLET BAKED IN FOIL

6 red mullet, cleaned and trimmed
50 g/2 oz butter
salt and pepper
juice of ½ lemon

GARNISH
lemon wedges
parsley sprigs

Set the oven at 190°C/375°F/gas 5. Lay each mullet on a piece of foil large enough to enclose it completely. Dot with butter, sprinkle with salt and pepper and add a little lemon juice. Fasten the packages by folding the edges of the foil firmly together over the fish.

Put the fish packages on a baking sheet and bake for 20–30 minutes. Remove from the foil, taking care to save the cooking juices. Transfer the fish to a warmed platter, pour over the cooking juices and serve at once, garnished with lemon and parsley.

SERVES SIX

BAKED HERRINGS

butter for greasing
4 herrings, cleaned and scaled
salt and pepper
25 g/1 oz butter
2 onions, finely sliced
450 g/1 lb tomatoes, peeled and sliced
30 ml/2 tbsp malt vinegar
parsley sprigs to garnish

Grease an ovenproof baking dish. Set the oven at 190°C/375°F/gas 5. Make three shallow cuts on either side of each herring and sprinkle with salt and pepper.

Melt half the butter in a frying pan. Add the onions and fry gently for 5 minutes. Place the tomato slices on the base of the prepared dish. Add the onions, salt, pepper and vinegar.

Arrange the fish on top and dot with the remaining butter. Cover and bake for 45 minutes. Garnish with parsley sprigs.

SERVES FOUR

RED MULLET WITH MUSHROOMS

25 g/1 oz butter
6 small red mullet, cleaned and trimmed

STUFFING
25 g/1 oz butter
1 large onion, chopped
225 g/8 oz mushrooms, finely chopped
50 g/2 oz fresh white breadcrumbs
25 g/1 oz parsley, chopped
salt and pepper

GARNISH
baby tomatoes
watercress sprigs

Use the butter to grease an ovenproof baking dish large enough to hold all the fish in a single layer. Set the oven at 190°C/375°F/gas 5.

Make the stuffing. Melt the butter in a small saucepan and fry the onion for 3–4 minutes or until soft. Transfer to a bowl and add the chopped mushrooms, breadcrumbs and parsley, with salt and pepper to taste. Stuff the fish with this mixture.

Place the stuffed fish in the prepared baking dish, cover and bake for 30 minutes. Garnish with baby tomatoes and watercress sprigs and serve at once.

SERVES SIX

HERRINGS STUFFED WITH SHRIMPS

4 herrings
salt and pepper
1 egg, beaten
browned breadcrumbs
25 g/1 oz butter

STUFFING

15 ml/1 tbsp fresh white breadcrumbs
15 ml/1 tbsp milk
50 g/2 oz peeled cooked shrimps, chopped
cayenne pepper
few drops of anchovy essence

Set the oven at 190°C/375°F/gas 5. Scale the herrings, cut off the heads and remove the bones without breaking the skin. Sprinkle with plenty of salt and pepper.

Make the stuffing by combining all the ingredients in a small bowl. Mix well. Spread the filling on the flesh side of the fillets and roll up tightly. Fasten each with a small skewer.

Pack the herrings tightly in an ovenproof dish. Brush with the egg, sprinkle with the browned breadcrumbs, dot with butter and bake for 30–35 minutes. Serve at once.

SERVES FOUR

STUFFED HERRINGS

butter for greasing
4 large herrings

STUFFING

50 g/2 oz butter
225 g/8 oz onions, finely chopped
225 g/8 oz cooking apples
15 ml/1 tbsp cider or white wine vinegar
salt and pepper

Grease a flat ovenproof dish and a piece of foil large enough to cover it. Set the oven at 190°C/375°F/gas 5. Scale the herrings, cut off the heads and remove the bones without breaking the skin.

Make the stuffing. Melt the butter in a large frying pan, add the onions and fry gently for about 10 minutes until soft. Peel, core and grate the apples and add them to the pan. Mix well, then add the vinegar, with salt and pepper to taste.

Divide the stuffing between the herrings, filling the cavities and then reshaping the fish. Lay them on the prepared dish, cover loosely with the foil and bake for 25 minutes. Serve at once.

SERVES FOUR

 MICROWAVE TIP

Arrange the stuffed herrings in alternate directions in a suitable dish. Cover with microwave film and cook on High for 7–8 minutes.

PLAICE STUFFED WITH PRAWNS

fat for greasing
8 (75 g/3 oz) plaice fillets, skinned
100 ml/3½ fl oz white wine
250 ml/8 fl oz Fish Stock (page 48)
25 g/1oz butter
100 g/4 oz button mushrooms, halved if
   large
25 g/1 oz plain flour
juice of 1 lemon
salt and pepper
100 ml/3½ fl oz double cream
fleurons (see Mrs Beeton's Tip, page 342)
chopped parsley

STUFFING
50g/2oz fresh white breadcrumbs
50g/2oz butter, softened
50g/2oz peeled cooked prawns, chopped

Grease a shallow ovenproof baking dish and a piece of foil large enough to cover it. Set the oven at 190°C/375°F/gas 5. Make the stuffing by mixing all the ingredients in a bowl.

Spread the stuffing over the plaice and roll up. Place the plaice rolls in the prepared dish and pour the wine and fish stock over. Cover loosely with the foil and bake for 20 minutes. Using a slotted spoon, transfer the fish to a warmed

---

 MICROWAVE TIP

The sauce can be made in the microwave. Slice the mushrooms. Put the butter and flour in a bowl. Whisk in the cooking liquid, then cook on High for 6 minutes, whisking thoroughly once during cooking and again when cooking is complete. Add the mushrooms and lemon juice and cook for 2–3 minutes more. Remove from the microwave, cool slightly, then stir in the cream.

---

serving dish. Keep hot. Tip the cooking liquid into a jug.

Meanwhile melt the butter in a saucepan. Add the mushrooms and fry gently for 3–4 minutes. Stir in the flour and cook for 1 minute. Gradually add the cooking liquid, stirring constantly until the mixture boils and thickens. Lower the heat and stir in the lemon juice, with salt and pepper to taste.

Remove the pan from the heat, cool slightly, then stir in the cream. Pour the sauce over the fish, garnish with the pastry fleurons and sprinkle with chopped parsley. Serve at once.

SERVES FOUR

PLAICE PORTUGAISE

fat for greasing
25 g/1oz butter
2 shallots, sliced
4 tomatoes, peeled, seeded and chopped
100 g/4 oz mushrooms, halved if large
8 (75 g/3 oz) plaice fillets
100 ml/3½ fl oz dry white wine
salt and pepper

Grease a shallow ovenproof baking dish and a piece of foil large enough to cover it. Set the oven at 190°C/375°F/gas 5.

Melt the butter in a frying pan, add the shallots and fry for 2–3 minutes until slightly softened. Stir in the tomatoes and mushrooms and fry for 3–4 minutes. Spread the mixture in the prepared dish.

Fold each fillet into 3, skin side in, and arrange on the tomato mixture. Pour the wine over the fish, sprinkle with salt and pepper to taste and cover loosely with the foil. Bake for 25 minutes. Spoon the sauce mixture over the fish and serve at once.

SERVES FOUR

DUNWICH PLAICE

25 g/1 oz butter
4 (275 g/10 oz) plaice, cleaned and trimmed

STUFFING
100 g/4 oz mild Cheddar cheese, grated
50 g/2 oz fresh white breadcrumbs
5 ml/1 tsp mustard powder
salt and pepper
10 ml/2 tsp shredded fresh basil or 5 ml/1 tsp
  dried basil
juice of ½ lemon
30 ml/2 tbsp beaten egg

GARNISH
2 halved tomatoes
4 rolled anchovies

Use most of the butter to grease a shallow oven-proof baking dish and a piece of foil large enough to cover it. Set the oven at 190°C/375°F/gas 5. Make a cut down the entire length of each fish as though for filleting. Remove the bone to make a pouch.

Make the stuffing by mixing all the ingredients together in a small bowl. Lift the two loose flaps on one of the fish and fill the pouch with a quarter of the stuffing. Repeat with the remaining fish.

Place the fish in the prepared dish, dot with the remaining butter, cover with the foil and bake for 20–30 minutes. Garnish each portion with half a tomato and a rolled anchovy. Serve at once.

SERVES FOUR

PLAICE AND OYSTER PIE

12 oysters
6 plaice fillets, skinned
salt and pepper
75 g/3 oz fresh white breadcrumbs
30 ml/2 tbsp chopped parsley
freshly grated nutmeg
75 g/3 oz butter, melted, plus extra for
  greasing

Set the oven at 190°C/375°F/gas 5. Butter an ovenproof dish. Open the oysters (see page 117), reserving the liquor.

Check that the plaice fillets are free of bones, then lay half of them in the dish. Top with half the oysters and sprinkle with salt and pepper. Sprinkle about a third of the breadcrumbs, half the parsley and a little nutmeg over the top. Add a second layer of plaice and oysters.

Pour the reserved oyster liquor over the fish, then trickle half the butter over before adding the remaining breadcrumbs, parsley and a little nutmeg. Trickle the remaining butter over the top. Bake for 40–45 minutes, until golden and cooked.

SERVES FOUR TO SIX

VARIATIONS

Lattice Puff Pie Reduce the final layer of breadcrumbs by half. Press a strip of puff pastry around the rim of the dish, then top the pie with a lattice of puff pastry strips and glaze with beaten egg. Bake at 220°C/425°F/gas 7 for 15 minutes, then reduce the temperature to 190°C/375°F/gas 5 and bake for a further 15-20 minutes.

Creamy Potato-top Pie Omit the second layer of breadcrumbs. Instead of butter, pour about 300 ml/½ pint Béchamel Sauce (page 481) over the fish. Top with mashed potato.

SOLE DIEPPOISE

In this classic dish, the sole is poached in white wine with mussels and shrimps.

fat for greasing
1 (800 g/1¾ lb) sole, cleaned and trimmed
1 small onion, thinly sliced
1 bouquet garni
150 ml/¼ pint dry white wine
12 mussels, scrubbed and bearded
15 ml/1 tbsp white wine vinegar
12 peeled cooked prawns or shrimps
15 ml/1 tbsp butter
15 ml/1 tbsp plain flour
1 egg yolk
90 ml/6 tbsp single cream
salt and pepper
pinch of grated nutmeg
juice of ½ lemon
pinch of cayenne pepper or paprika

Grease a shallow ovenproof baking dish and a piece of foil large enough to cover it. Set the oven at 190°C/375°F/gas 5.

Skin and fillet the sole. Put the bones, skin and head in a saucepan with the onion, bouquet garni and white wine. Put the mussels into the pan, bring to the boil, lower the heat and simmer for 6 minutes.

Using a slotted spoon, remove the mussels. Discard any that remain shut. Shell the mussels and set them aside. Add 150 ml/¼ pint water to the pan and stir in the vinegar. Reduce the liquid by boiling gently for 15 minutes, uncovered, then strain into a jug.

Fold each fillet in half and place in a single layer in the prepared dish. Pour in the reserved cooking liquid and arrange the shelled mussels and prawns or shrimps around the fish. Cover with the foil and bake for 20 minutes.

Drain the stock from the fish into a saucepan and heat to simmering point. Keep the fish and shellfish hot. In a small bowl, cream the butter to a paste with the flour.

Add the butter and flour paste to the fish stock, a little at a time, whisking after each addition. Raise the heat and bring the sauce to the boil, whisking constantly. Boil for 10 minutes. Lower the heat.

Mix the egg yolk and cream in a bowl and stir in about 100 ml/3½ fl oz of the thickened sauce. Add the contents of the bowl to the sauce and bring the mixture to just below boiling point. Add salt, pepper and nutmeg and pour the sauce evenly over the fish and shellfish. Sprinkle with the lemon juice and dust with the cayenne or paprika. Serve at once.

SERVES FOUR

FILLET OF SOLE BONNE FEMME

fat for greasing
16 lemon sole fillets
275 g/10 oz mushrooms
50 g/2 oz butter
12 black peppercorns
2–3 parsley stalks
25 g/1 oz plain flour
300 ml/½ pint Fish Stock (page 48)
salt and pepper
lemon juice
2 shallots, slices
15 ml/1 tbsp chopped parsley
250 ml/8 fl oz dry white wine

Grease a shallow ovenproof baking dish and a piece of foil large enough to cover it. Arrange the sole fillets on the base. Set the oven at 180°C/350°F/gas 4. Cut off the mushroom stems and set them aside. Slice the mushroom caps and scatter them over the fish.

Melt 25 g/1 oz of the butter in a saucepan, add the mushroom stems, peppercorns and parsley stalks. Cook over gentle heat for 10 minutes. Add the flour and cook over a low heat for 2-3 minutes, without allowing the mixture to colour. Gradually add the stock and simmer, stirring for 3-4 minutes. Rub the sauce through a sieve into a clean pan. Add salt, pepper and lemon juice to taste. Cover the surface with damp greaseproof paper and set aside.

Sprinkle the shallots and parsley over the fish, sprinkle with salt and pepper and pour in the wine. Cover with the foil and bake for 20 minutes.

Using slotted spoon and fish slice, transfer the fish to a warmed serving dish and keep hot. Strain the cooking liquid into a saucepan. Boil it rapidly until reduced by half.

Meanwhile return the sauce to a gentle heat and bring to simmering point. Stir the sauce into the reduced cooking liquid with the remaining butter. As soon as the butter has melted, pour the sauce over the fish. Place under a hot grill until lightly browned. Serve at once.

SERVES EIGHT

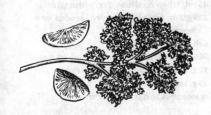

SOLE WITH PRAWNS

100 g/4 oz peeled cooked prawns, finely chopped
50 g/2 oz fresh white breadcrumbs
1 egg
salt and pepper
12 Dover sole or lemon sole fillets
125 ml/4 fl oz dry white wine
125 ml/4 fl oz Fish Stock (page 48)
50 g/2 oz butter
50 g/2 oz plain flour
250 ml/8 fl oz milk
salt and pepper

GARNISH
whole cooked prawns
parsley sprigs
lemon slices or wedges

Set the oven at 190°C/375°F/gas 5. Mix the prawns, breadcrumbs and egg in a bowl, with salt and pepper to taste. Spread the mixture over each fillet, roll up and place in an oven-proof baking dish. Pour over the wine and stock and bake for 20 minutes.

Using a slotted spoon, transfer the stuffed fish rolls to a warmed serving dish and keep hot. Tip the cooking juices into a jug.

Melt the butter in a saucepan. Stir in the flour and cook over low heat for 2-3 minutes, without allowing the mixture to colour. Gradually add the reserved cooking juices and the milk, stirring constantly until the sauce boils and thickens. Add salt and pepper to taste.

Pour the sauce over the fish and garnish before serving.

SERVES SIX

BAKED GREY MULLET

2 (1 kg/2¼ lb) grey mullet, scaled, cleaned
  and trimmed
2-3 rindless streaky bacon rashers

FORCEMEAT
50 g/2 oz margarine, melted
100 g/4 oz fresh white breadcrumbs
pinch of grated nutmeg
15 ml/1 tbsp chopped parsley
5 ml/1 tsp chopped mixed fresh herbs
grated rind of ½ lemon
salt and pepper
1 egg, beaten

GARNISH
lemon wedges
fresh herb sprigs

Set the oven at 180°C/350°F/gas 4. Make the
forcemeat by combining all the ingredients
except the egg in a bowl. Mix well, adding
enough of the egg to moisten. The forcemeat
should not be sloppy.

Stuff the fish with the forcemeat and place
them in an ovenproof dish or on a baking sheet.
Lay the bacon rashers over the top of each and
bake for 25-30 minutes.

Transfer to a warmed platter, garnish with the
lemon wedges and fresh herb sprigs and serve
at once.

SERVES FOUR TO SIX

 MRS BEETON'S TIP

A yogurt and cucumber sauce goes well
with this dish. Combine a 225 g/8 oz carton
of Greek yogurt with ½ unpeeled cucumber,
diced. Add plenty of salt and pepper, a
pinch of dill and a squeeze of lime or lemon
juice.

BAKED SMELTS

12 smelts, cleaned and trimmed
100 g/4 oz dried white breadcrumbs
50 g/2 oz butter
salt
cayenne pepper
squeeze of lemon juice

GARNISH
fried parsley
lemon wedges

Set the oven at 190°C/375°F/gas 5. Arrange the
fish in a shallow ovenproof baking dish.

Cover the fish with the breadcrumbs and dot
with the butter. Sprinkle with plenty of salt and
cayenne and bake for 15 minutes.

Just before serving, add a squeeze of lemon
juice. Serve garnished with fried parsley and
lemon wedges.

SERVES THREE

BAKED FRESH SARDINES

fat for greasing
45 ml/3 tbsp olive oil
2 large onions, finely chopped
45 ml/3 tbsp medium-dry white wine
225 g/8 oz tomatoes, peeled, seeded and
  chopped
salt and pepper
900 g/2 lb sardines, cleaned and trimmed
50 g/2 oz fresh white breadcrumbs
25 g/1 oz butter
watercress sprigs to garnish

Grease a shallow ovenproof baking dish. Set
the oven at 180°C/350°F/gas 4.

Heat the oil in a small saucepan, add the onions
and fry gently for about 5 minutes until lightly
browned. Add the wine and boil until the

volume is reduced by two thirds. Stir in the tomatoes, with salt and pepper to taste. Cook for 3–4 minutes.

Pour the tomato mixture into the prepared dish, arrange the sardines on top and sprinkle with the breadcrumbs. Dot with the butter and bake for 25 minutes. Serve hot, garnished with watercress.

SERVES SIX

BAKED TURBOT

3 shallots, chopped
6 (150 g/5 oz) turbot fillets
150 g/5 oz mushrooms, sliced
salt and pepper
250 ml/8 fl oz Fish Stock (page 48)
juice of 1 lemon
250 ml/8 fl oz double cream
3 egg yolks
12 fleurons (see Mrs Beeton's Tip, page 342)

Spread out the chopped shallots on the base of a shallow ovenproof baking dish. Arrange the fish on the top and add the mushrooms. Sprinkle with salt and pepper to taste and pour over the stock and lemon juice. Cover and bake for 30 minutes.

Using a slotted spoon, transfer the fish and mushrooms to a dish; keep hot. Tip the cooking juices into a clean saucepan.

Mix the cream and egg yolks in a bowl. Add to the cooking liquid and heat very gently until thickened, stirring constantly. Do not boil. Pour the sauce over the fish and top with the fleurons.

SERVES SIX

TURBOT MARENGO

fat for greasing
4 (1 cm/½ inch thick) turbot steaks
350 ml/12 fl oz Fish Stock (page 48)
50 g/2 oz butter
1 onion, sliced
1 carrot, sliced
1 turnip, sliced
5 ml/1 tsp dried mixed herbs
25 g/1 oz plain flour
1 (70 g/12½ oz) can tomato purée
salt and pepper

GARNISH
stuffed green olives
chopped parsley
lemon slices

Grease a shallow ovenproof baking dish. Set the oven at 180°C/350°F/gas 4. Arrange the fish in the dish, add 75 ml/5 tbsp of the fish stock and bake for 20 minutes.

Meanwhile melt 25 g/1 oz of the butter in a frying pan. Add the onion, carrot and turnip and fry gently for 5 minutes until soft. Sprinkle over the herbs, add the remaining stock and cover the pan. Simmer for 20 minutes. Strain the stock into a jug, discarding the solids in the strainer.

Melt the remaining butter in a saucepan, add the flour and cook for 1 minute. Gradually add the reserved cooking liquid, stirring constantly, then stir in the tomato purée and seasoning. Simmer the sauce, stirring occasionally, for 10 minutes.

When the fish is cooked, transfer it to a warmed serving dish. Pour over the sauce, garnish with olives, parsley and lemon slices and serve at once.

SERVES FOUR

TURBOT DUGLERE

fat for greasing
1 (1.5 kg/3¼ lb) turbot, cleaned and trimmed
40 g/1½ oz butter
30 ml/2 tbsp oil
1 small onion, finely chopped
225 g/8 oz tomatoes, peeled and chopped
30 ml/2 tbsp white wine vinegar
200 ml/7 fl oz dry white wine
salt and pepper
1 bouquet garni
10 ml/2 tsp plain flour

Skin and fillet the turbot, reserving the trimmings in a saucepan. Grease a shallow ovenproof baking dish. Set the oven at 190°C/375°F/gas 5.

Melt 25 g/1 oz of the butter in the oil in a frying pan. Add the onion and fry for 2–3 minutes until soft but not coloured. Add the chopped tomatoes, vinegar and white wine. Simmer for 10 minutes; set aside.

Lay the fish fillets in the prepared dish. Sprinkle with salt and pepper and pour over the tomato mixture. Cover the dish with a lid or foil and bake for 20 minutes.

Meanwhile add 300 ml/½ pint water and the bouquet garni to the fish trimmings. Bring to the boil, lower the heat and simmer for 15 minutes. Remove from the heat. Strain the liquid into a small pan. In a small bowl, cream the remaining butter to a paste with the flour.

Add the butter and flour paste to the fish stock, a little at a time, whisking after each addition. Return to the heat and bring the sauce to the boil, whisking constantly until the sauce thickens. Add salt and pepper to taste and pour the sauce over the fish.

SERVES FOUR

BAKED TROUT WITH OLIVES AND TOMATOES

4 (225 g/8 oz) trout
50 g/2 oz plain flour
salt and pepper
125 ml/4 fl oz oil
1 large onion, sliced
25 g/1 oz stuffed green olives, sliced
225 g/8 oz tomatoes, peeled, seeded and
    chopped
30 ml/2 tbsp white wine vinegar
juice of 1 lemon
15 ml/1 tbsp capers
25 g/1 oz butter
fresh herbs to garnish

Wash and scale the trout. Cut off the fins and wipe the fish with a cloth. Mix the flour with salt and pepper, spread out in a shallow bowl and coat the trout well on all sides. Shake off excess flour.

Heat the oil in a large frying pan and brown the trout on both sides for 2–3 minutes. Using a slotted spoon and a fish slice, transfer the trout to a shallow ovenproof baking dish large enough to hold them all in a single layer. Set aside.

Add the onion and olives to the oil remaining in the pan and fry for 4 minutes until golden. Remove with a slotted spoon and spread over the fish. Top with the tomatoes. Sprinkle with the vinegar and lemon juice. Scatter the capers on top, add salt and pepper to taste and bake for 15 minutes.

Meanwhile melt the butter in a small frying pan until foaming. Pour it over the cooked fish, garnish with fresh herbs and serve at once.

SERVES FOUR

APRICOT-STUFFED TROUT

The apricots for the stuffing need to be soaked overnight, so start preparation the day before cooking – or use ready-to-eat fruit.

fat for greasing
6 trout, cleaned and trimmed
2 onions, finely chopped
salt and pepper
250 ml/8 fl oz dry white wine
75 g/3 oz butter
25 g/1 oz plain flour
250 ml/8 fl oz Fish Stock (page 48)
60 ml/4 tbsp dry white wine
2 egg yolks
juice of ½ lemon
chopped parsley to garnish

STUFFING
75 g/3 oz dried apricots
75 g/3 oz fresh white breadcrumbs
pinch of dried thyme
pinch of ground mace
pinch of grated nutmeg
1 celery stick, finely chopped
25 g/1 oz butter

Make the stuffing. Soak the apricots overnight in a small bowl with water to cover. Next day, drain the fruit, reserving the soaking liquid, and chop finely. Mix the apricots in a bowl with the breadcrumbs, salt, pepper, herbs, spices and celery. Melt the butter in a small saucepan and stir it into the mixture. Moisten further with a little of the reserved soaking liquid (see Mrs Beeton's Tip).

Grease a shallow ovenproof baking dish. Set the oven at 180°C/350°F/gas 4. Fill the trout with the apricot stuffing. Spread out the onions on the base of the prepared dish, arrange the trout on top and sprinkle with plenty of salt and pepper. Pour the wine into the dish, dot the fish with 25 g/1 oz of the butter, cover and oven-poach for 25 minutes.

Meanwhile, melt 25 g/1 oz of the remaining butter in a pan. Stir in the flour and cook over low heat for 2-3 minutes, without allowing the mixture to colour. Gradually add the fish stock, stirring constantly until the sauce boils and thickens. Add salt and pepper to taste. Reduce the heat, add the wine and the sauce simmer for 10 minutes.

Bring the sauce to just below boiling point and whisk in the remaining butter, a little at a time. Remove the pan from the heat. Blend the egg yolks and lemon juice in a small bowl, add a little of the hot sauce and mix well. Add the contents of the bowl to the sauce and mix well. Cover with damp greaseproof paper and set aside.

Using a slotted spoon and fish slice, carefully transfer the fish to a wooden board. Strain the cooking liquid into a pan. Skin the trout, then arrange them on a warmed flameproof serving dish and keep hot.

Boil the cooking liquid until it is reduced by a quarter, then add it to the white wine sauce. Place over moderate heat and warm through, stirring the sauce until it thickens. Do not allow it to boil. Pour the hot sauce over the fish. Place under a moderate grill for 4-5 minutes to brown lightly. Garnish with chopped parsley and serve at once.

SERVES SIX

 MRS BEETON'S TIP

If you use ready-to-eat dried apricots, moisten the stuffing with a little chicken stock.

BAKED SALMON

800 g/1¾ lb middle cut salmon
salt and pepper
grated nutmeg
2 small shallots, chopped
15 ml/1 tbsp chopped parsley
25 g/1 oz butter
100 ml/3½ fl oz dry white wine

Set the oven at 190°C/375°F/gas 5. Wash and dry the fish and lay it on a sheet of heavy-duty foil large enough to enclose it completely. Lift the edges of the foil and pinch the corners together to make a shallow case. Sprinkle the fish with salt, pepper and a little grated nutmeg. Add the chopped shallots and sprinkle the parsley over the fish. Dot with the butter and pour over the wine.

Carefully lift the edges of the foil and pinch them together to enclose the fish and the wine. Carefully transfer the foil parcel to an ovenproof dish. Cook for 25 minutes.

Drain the fish and serve hot with Hollandaise Sauce (page 480) or leave to cool in the cooking juices, drain and serve with green salad, thinly sliced cucumber and mayonnaise.

SERVES SIX TO EIGHT

SALMON AURORE

50 g/2 oz butter
1 shallot, finely chopped
4 salmon steaks
salt and pepper
125 ml/4 fl oz dry white wine
125 ml/4 fl oz tomato juice
15 ml/1 tbsp plain flour
125 ml/4 fl oz Hollandaise Sauce (page 480)
5 ml/1 tsp snipped chives
fleurons (see Mrs Beeton's Tip, page 342)

Using 15 g/½ oz of the butter, grease an oven-proof dish (large enough to hold all the steaks in a single layer) and a piece of foil large enough to cover it. Set the oven at 190°C/375°F/gas 5.

Sprinkle the shallot over the base of the dish and add the salmon steaks. Add salt and pepper to taste and pour over the wine and tomato juice. Cover loosely with the foil and bake for 20 minutes.

Using a fish slice, transfer the salmon to a warmed serving dish. Cover loosely with the foil and keep hot. Strain the cooking liquid into a small pan, bring to the boil; cook for 10 minutes. Remove from the heat.

Meanwhile cream 25 g/1 oz of the remaining butter to a paste with the flour in a small bowl. Add the butter and flour paste to the reduced cooking liquid, a little at a time, whisking after each addition. Return the pan to the heat and boil the sauce, stirring constantly until it thickens. Remove from the heat.

Stir in the remaining butter, the Hollandaise sauce and the chives. Pour the sauce over the fish and serve at once, garnished with puff pastry fleurons.

SERVES FOUR

CAPE COD PIE

fat for greasing
450 g/1 lb potatoes, halved
salt and pepper
90 g/3½ oz butter
30–45 ml/2–3 tbsp single cream
25 g/1 oz plain flour
300 ml/½ pint milk
450 g/1 lb cooked cod, skinned, boned and
 flaked
50 g/2 oz Cheddar cheese, grated
few grains of cayenne pepper
1 egg, beaten
pinch of grated nutmeg

Grease a 1 litre/1¾ pint pie dish. Cook the potatoes in a saucepan of salted boiling water for about 20 minutes or until tender. Drain and mash until smooth. Beat in 25 g/1 oz of the butter and the cream. Set aside until cold.

Set the oven at 190°C/375°F/gas 5. Melt 25 g/1 oz of the remaining butter in a saucepan. Stir in the flour and cook over low heat for 2–3 minutes, without allowing the mixture to colour. Gradually add the milk, stirring constantly until the sauce boils and thickens. Add salt and pepper to taste. Stir in the flaked cod, half the cheese and 15 g/½ oz of the remaining butter. Add the cayenne. Remove from the heat.

Set aside about 10 ml/2 tsp of the beaten egg for glazing. Stir the remaining egg into the cold mashed potato. Melt the remaining butter and stir it into the potato with the nutmeg. Line the prepared dish with half the potato mixture.

Heat the fish mixture until it bubbles. Pour it into the lined pie dish and cover evenly with the rest of the potato. Press the edge with the tines of a fork. Glaze with the reserved egg and sprinkle with the remaining cheese. Bake for 8–12 minutes until well browned.

SERVES FOUR TO FIVE

OYSTERS ROCKEFELLER

24 oysters
3 shallots, finely chopped
100 g/4 oz fresh spinach, finely chopped
2 celery sticks, finely chopped
10 ml/2 tsp chopped fresh thyme
15 ml/1 tbsp Worcestershire sauce
100 g/4 oz butter
30 ml/2 tbsp pastis or other aniseed-flavour
 liquor
50 g/2 oz fresh white breadcrumbs

Open the oysters (see page 117), reserving the liquor. Arrange the oysters on the half shell, in an ovenproof dish. Set the oven at 220°C/450°F/gas 7.

Combine the chopped vegetables and thyme in a saucepan. Add the oyster liquor and 100 ml/3½ fl oz water. Boil for 5–7 minutes, then add the Worcestershire sauce and butter. Beat until the butter melts and the mixture is well blended, then add the pastis. Mix well.

Pour the sauce over the oysters, sprinkle with the breadcrumbs and bake for 5–10 minutes.

SERVES TWO

✳ FREEZER TIP

Uncooked oysters freeze well. Open the oysters and place them in a rigid container, pouring in the liquor from their shells. Freeze only when really fresh. Thaw at room temperature until the liquor is just thawed and use promptly.

CREAMED SALMON IN PASTRY

125 ml/4 fl oz white wine
1 bouquet garni
1 onion, sliced
salt and pepper
450 g/1 lb salmon pieces or steaks
50 g/2 oz butter
25 g/1 oz plain flour
150 g/5 oz mushrooms, sliced
75 ml/5 tbsp double cream
450 g/1 lb puff pastry, thawed if frozen
plain flour for rolling out
beaten egg for glazing

GARNISH
lemon wedges · dill sprigs

Put the wine in a saucepan with 125 ml/4 fl oz water. Add the bouquet garni and onion slices, with salt and pepper to taste. Bring to the boil, lower the heat and simmer for 5 minutes. Strain into a clean pan, add the salmon and poach gently for 10–15 minutes or until cooked. Using a slotted spoon, transfer the fish to a wooden board. Remove the skin and any bones; flake the flesh. Reserve the cooking liquid.

Melt half the butter in a saucepan. Stir in the flour and cook over low heat for 2–3 minutes, without allowing the mixture to colour. Gradually add the reserved cooking liquid, stirring constantly until the sauce boils and thickens. Lower the heat and simmer for 3–4 minutes. Stir in the flaked salmon and remove from the heat.

Melt the remaining butter in a frying pan. Add the mushrooms and fry for 3–4 minutes. Using a slotted spoon, add the mushrooms to the salmon mixture. Stir in the cream, cover the surface of the mixture with damp greaseproof paper and set aside.

Set the oven at 200°C/400°F/gas 6. Roll out the pastry 3 mm/⅛ inch thick on a floured surface. Cut to a 25 cm/10 inch square, reserving the pastry trimmings. Place the salmon mixture in the middle and brush the edges of the pastry with beaten egg. Lift the corners of the pastry to the middle, enclosing the filling. Seal with beaten egg. Make leaf shapes from the trimmings and use to hide the seal on the top of the pastry envelope. Glaze with egg.

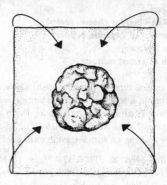

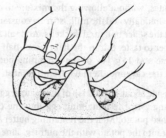

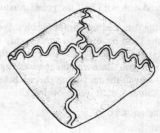

Place the pastry envelope on a baking sheet and bake for 15 minutes. Lower the temperature to 190°C/375°F/gas 5 and bake for 20 minutes more. Serve hot, garnished with lemon wedges and dill.

SERVES FOUR TO SIX

SALTBURN FISH PIE

Although haddock is traditionally used for this dish, cod or any other firm white fish is equally suitable.

butter for greasing
450g/1lb haddock fillet
60ml/4tbsp grated onion
salt and pepper
30ml/2tbsp lemon juice
2 gammon steaks, trimmed and cut into
  7.5cm/3 inch squares
3 hard-boiled eggs, sliced
30ml/2tbsp chopped parsley

SHORT CRUST PASTRY
150g/5oz plain flour
1.25ml/¼tsp salt
65g/2½oz margarine
plain flour for rolling out

Grease a 750ml/1¼ pint pie dish. Set the oven at 200°C/400°F/gas 6. Make the pastry. Sift the flour and salt into a bowl, then rub in the margarine until the mixture resembles fine breadcrumbs. Add enough cold water to make a stiff dough. Press the dough together with your fingertips, wrap in a polythene bag and chill until required.

Put the haddock in a large frying pan. Sprinkle the onion over the top, with salt and pepper to taste, and add the lemon juice. Pour almost enough water into the pan to cover the fish. Heat the liquid to simmering point and simmer for 8-15 minutes or until the fish is just tender.

Using a fish slice and slotted spoon, transfer the fish to a wooden board. Remove any fins, bones or skin and flake the fish. Reserve the cooking liquid.

Put a layer of fish into the prepared pie dish. Cover with a layer of gammon, then a layer of sliced egg. Sprinkle with salt and parsley. Continue layering until all the ingredients have been used. Moisten with a little of the reserved cooking liquid.

Roll out the pastry on a lightly floured surface and use to make a crust for the pie. Dampen the edges of the dish, lay the pastry crust on the dish and press down firmly to seal. Bake for 25-30 minutes. Serve hot.

SERVES FOUR

 MRS BEETON'S TIP

When the pastry has been rolled to a round large enough to cover the pie, place the rolling pin in the middle of the pastry, lop half the pastry over it, then use the rolling pin to lift the pastry into position.

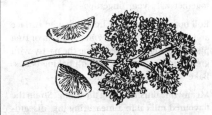

PRAWN QUICHE

1 small onion, thickly sliced
1 small carrot, thickly sliced
½ celery stick, thickly sliced
300 ml/½ pint milk
1 bay leaf
1 parsley stalk
1 fresh thyme sprig
4 white peppercorns
salt
25 g/1 oz butter
25 g/1 oz plain flour
30 ml/2 tbsp single cream
150 g/5 oz Cheddar cheese, grated
200 g/7 oz peeled cooked prawns
juice of ½ lemon

SHORT CRUST PASTRY
100 g/4 oz plain flour
1.25 ml/¼ tsp salt
50 g/2 oz margarine
flour for rolling out

Combine the onion, carrot, celery and milk in a saucepan. Add the herbs and spices, with salt to taste. Heat to simmering point, cover, turn off the heat and allow to stand for 30 minutes to infuse.

Set the oven at 200°C/400°F/gas 6. Make the pastry. Sift the flour and salt into a bowl, then rub in the margarine until the mixture resembles fine breadcrumbs. Add enough cold water to make a stiff dough. Press the dough together with your fingertips.

Roll out the pastry on a lightly floured surface and use to line an 18 cm/7 inch flan tin or ring placed on a baking sheet. Line the pastry with greaseproof paper and fill with baking beans. Bake 'blind' for 20 minutes.

Meanwhile finish making the filling. Strain the flavoured milk into a measuring jug, discarding the solids in the strainer. Melt the butter in a saucepan. Stir in the flour and cook over low

heat for 2–3 minutes without allowing the mixture to colour. Gradually add the flavoured milk, stirring constantly.

Raise the heat to moderate, stirring until the mixture thickens. Stir in the cream and half the cheese, then add the prawns. Mix well. Finally add the lemon juice.

Remove the flan tin from the oven, take out the paper and beans and return the flan shell to the oven for 5 minutes. Pour the prawn mixture into the flan shell, top with the remaining cheese and brown under a moderate grill. Serve the quiche hot.

SERVES FOUR

 MRS BEETON'S TIP

Ceramic baking beans for baking 'blind' may be purchased from cookware shops. Ordinary dried beans or peas may be used instead. These are sprinkled over the greaseproof paper to weight the pastry slightly. After use, the beans or peas are cooled and stored in an airtight container. They may be used again and again, but may not be cooked to be eaten in another recipe.

STARGAZEY PIE

This is a traditional Cornish recipe. Its appearance may be a bit off-putting and it is not a recipe for anyone who is deterred by fish bones but it tastes delicious. The top crust is traditionally glazed with thick Cornish cream, but single cream or top-of-the-milk may be used instead.

5 even-sized pilchards or herrings, scaled and cleaned
1 onion, finely chopped
1 small sharp cooking apple
90 ml/6 tbsp fresh white breadcrumbs
salt and pepper
150-175 ml/5-6 fl oz dry still cider
2 hard-boiled eggs
2 rindless back bacon rashers, finely chopped
10 ml/2 tsp cider vinegar
6 parsley sprigs to garnish

SHORT CRUST PASTRY
150 g/5 oz plain flour
1.25 ml/¼ tsp salt
65 g/2½ oz margarine
plain flour for rolling out
cream for glazing

Make the pastry. Sift the flour and salt into a bowl, then rub in the margarine until the mixture resembles fine breadcrumbs. Add enough cold water to make a stiff dough. Press the dough together with your fingertips, wrap in a polythene bag and chill.

Rinse in cold water a pie dish or ovenproof plate that will just hold two fish placed end to end across the centre, with their tails overlapping in the centre and their heads sticking over the edge. Turn the pie dish upside down to drain until required.

Set the oven at 160°C/325°F/gas 3. Split the fish, without removing the heads or tails, and ease out the backbones. Set 30 ml/2 tbsp of the

chopped onion aside and put the rest in a bowl. Peel and grate the apple and add it to the bowl with the breadcrumbs. Add salt and pepper to taste and moisten the stuffing with 45-60 ml/3-4 tbsp of the cider. Stuff the fish with the mixture and reshape neatly. Reserve any leftover stuffing.

Roll out the pastry on a lightly floured surface and use just over half of it to line the chosen dish. Arrange the fish in a star shape with heads right on the edge of the dish and tails overlapping in the centre. Lift the tails and form them into an upright cluster, securing them with wooden cocktail sticks if necessary. Twist a piece of foil over and around them.

Fill the triangular spaces between the fish with egg, bacon, the reserved onion and any leftover stuffing. Sprinkle with the vinegar and pour the remaining cider into the dish.

Roll out the remaining pastry on a floured surface and make a crust for the pie. Make a hole in the centre of the crust large enough to fit around the fish tails. Dampen the edges of the pastry.

Very carefully lift the pastry on the rolling pin and lay it on the pie, with the fish tails sticking through the middle. Press the pastry crust between the fish heads, pushing it back slightly around the heads so that they stick out. Brush the top crust with cream and bake for 1 hour. Garnish with sprigs of parsley around the tails and serve very hot.

SERVES SIX

Poultry

Poultry is ideal for all occasions, for light everyday dishes or celebration meals; from popular chicken and festive turkey to the traditional Christmas goose, duck and guineafowl. The recipes in this chapter range from homely favourites to exotic new ideas.

Poultry is the term used for domestic birds specially bred for food, as opposed to birds caught in the wild, which are game. Except at small country markets, when birds may be 'rough-plucked', all poultry is sold ready for cooking; plucked and drawn. If you do have to carry out any such basic preparation, follow the information given for game birds. Unlike game, poultry should be plucked and drawn when freshly killed and the birds are not hung for lengthy periods.

CHICKEN

Chicken is lean, tender and easy to digest. The majority of the fat content is found in or under the skin, so trimming and skinning renders chicken meat ideal for low-fat meals. The vast majority of chickens are roasting birds, under a year old; birds over this age are referred to as boiling fowl but these are no longer popular. Although they taste good, boiling fowl require 1½-2 hours boiling to tenderize the meat, after which time they have to be sauced for pies or similar recipes or used in soup.

Chickens are sold ready for cooking, most often without their giblets. If the giblets are included, they will be sealed in a packet in the body cavity of the bird; this will be clearly marked on the outside of the packaging.

Corn Fed Chicken This has a distinct yellow tinge when raw and the skin browns to a golden colour when roasted. The meat has a fine flavour, resulting from the high proportion of corn in the birds' feed.

Poulet Noir A popular French breed of black-feathered bird. Poulet noir has a mild gamey flavour.

Poussins Young birds, 4-8 weeks old, these are ideal for grilling, steaming or speedy roasting. They are usually served as individual portions, but larger birds (up to 675 g/1½ lb) may be split to provide two servings.

Spring Chickens Small chickens, weighing 900 g-1.4 kg/2-3 lb, these are 8-12 weeks old.

Chicken Portions There is a good choice of prepared portions, including skinned boneless breasts or thin fillets of breast meat, chicken quarters, drumsticks, thighs and wings.

TURKEY

Uncooked turkey portions, whole birds and turkey products are available throughout the year. Significantly larger than other poultry, weighing 2.25-11.3 kg/5-25 lb, turkey has a high meat yield for the carcass. The white, tender, delicately flavoured breast meat is the prized portion. Leg meat is dark and tougher, also veined with sinews. Like chicken, whole birds are sold ready for cooking, with or without giblets. Larger birds are not as popular as they were when turkey was reserved as a Christmas speciality.

In addition to whole birds, whole breast fillets are sold boned and tied into neat joints. These are usually barded with a thin coating of fat, or rolled so that the skin forms a neat covering. Breast fillets and a variety of white-meat products are available. Drumsticks are also sold separately; these are useful for casseroling.

Cubed and diced turkey (trimmed of all skin) is sold in many larger supermarkets. It is economical and useful for braising dishes, pies and risottos. Minced turkey is also available.

DUCKS AND DUCKLINGS

Although larger than chickens, duck do not have a high yield of meat for their carcass size. They range in weight from 1.5 kg/3¼ lb to 2.5 kg/5½ lb and yield 2–4 servings. Duck has a higher fat content than either turkey or chicken. However, birds are now reared to have far less fat so this once off-putting characteristic of duck is no longer as relevant as it once was. It is, however, advisable to prick the skin on a whole bird all over before roasting to release the fat.

As well as whole birds, which are mainly sold frozen (usually with giblets), quarters, breast portions and legs are available.

GOOSE

Goose is probably the most expensive of the poultry birds. Available all year, most often to order, goose yields little meat and a large quantity of fat for its carcass size of 3–7 kg/6½–15¼ lb. The main area of meat is on the breast, where it is dark and flavoursome. The high fat content means that goose requires long roasting to render the fat; small birds are therefore not the the best buy.

GUINEAFOWL

Although guineafowl is a domestic bird, originally from West Africa, it does have a hint of game to its flavour. Available all year, the birds range from 675 g/1½ lb to 2 kg/4½ lb, depending on maturity. Sold ready for cooking, guineafowl should be treated in the same way as chicken.

FREEZING AND THAWING POULTRY

Poultry for freezing should be absolutely fresh. Never buy poultry and allow the use-by date to expire before freezing it; when buying from a butcher always check that the bird is suitably fresh for freezing, or that portions have not previously been frozen.

Never re-freeze poultry once it has been thawed.

Prepare birds as for cooking and pack them in heavy-quality airtight bags, labelled with the date and weight or number of portions. Breasts, drumsticks, fillets or other portions may be individually wrapped in freezer film before being packed in bags. Cubed meat or strips of meat should be loosely packed in sealed bags. The bags should then be spread out thinly on a baking sheet until the meat is hard. When hard the meat may be shaken down in the bag and any extra air extracted – this method creates a 'free-flow' pack, permitting some of the meat to be used as required and the rest replaced in the freezer without thawing. If available, use the fast freeze facility on your freezer to process the poultry as speedily as possible. Follow the freezer manufacturer's instructions.

Always allow sufficient time for thawing poultry in the refrigerator before cooking. It is also possible to thaw poultry in the microwave oven following the appliance manufacturer's instructions. Both chicken and turkey must be cooked through before serving; if the whole bird or portions are not thoroughly thawed before cooking, thick areas of meat may not cook through. Due to its size, whole turkey is the most difficult poultry to thaw.

Always unwrap poultry and place it in a covered deep dish in the refrigerator, preferably on a low shelf, ensuring that it will not drip on any other food. Occasionally, drain off the liquid which seeps from the poultry as it thaws. Allow several hours or up to 24 hours for portions and smaller birds to thaw. Large poultry such as turkeys are usually purchased fresh; when buying frozen birds always read and follow the recommendations listed on the wrapping. The following is a guide to recommended thawing times by weight in the refrigerator: these times are not exact and they can only act as a guide. As soon as it is possible to do so, remove the giblets, and cook them to make stock. Cool the stock and freeze it until required. This is preferable to storing the stock in the refrigerator for several days while the turkey continues to thaw.

Weight of turkey	Thawing time in refrigerator
2.5–3.5 kg/5½–8 lb	up to 2½ days
3.5–5.5 kg/8–12 lb	2½–3 days
5.5–7.25 kg/12–16 lb	3–4 days
7.25–9 kg/16–20 lb	4–4½ days

PREPARING POULTRY FOR COOKING

Ensure that the bird is free from any small feathers or hairs. If necessary, singe the bird to remove hairs: use long matches or a taper and allow the flame to burn for a few seconds until it has stopped smoking. Trim away any lumps of fat from the body cavity. Rinse the bird inside and out under cold water and dry it well on absorbent kitchen paper.

HYGIENE NOTE

Always thoroughly wash surfaces, the sink and all utensils that come in contact with raw poultry immediately after use. Scrub cutting boards after use. Wash your hands well, paying attention to nails, and dry them thoroughly before preparing other food.

STUFFING POULTRY

Never stuff a bird more than an hour before cooking it. The stuffing may be prepared in advance and kept separately in a covered container in the refrigerator. Stuffing may be placed in the body cavity of the bird or under the skin covering the breast.

To insert stuffing under the skin, first loosen the skin by inserting the point of a knife between it and the flesh at the neck end of the bird. Once the skin is loosened, wash and dry your hands, then work your fingers up between the flesh and skin to form a pocket over the breast meat. Take care not to split the skin. Thoroughly clean your hands.

Use a spoon to insert the stuffing into the prepared pocket, easing it in place by moulding it with the skin on the outside. When the stuffing is in place, use a skewer to secure the end of the skin to the bird.

PREPARATION TECHNIQUES

The majority of poultry is sold ready for cooking. If any special preparation is required, a good butcher will almost certainly do this willingly, given sufficient notice, but it is useful to know the basics of trussing and jointing poultry.

JOINTING

You need a large, heavy cook's knife. A pair of poultry shears or strong kitchen scissors are also useful and a meat mallet or rolling pin may be necessary to tap the blade of the knife through areas of bone. There are many ways of jointing poultry; this is one method.

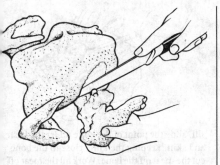

Pull the leg away from the body, cut through the skin, then break the joint away above the thigh.

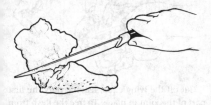

Cut through the meat between the thigh and drumstick and separate the two portions.

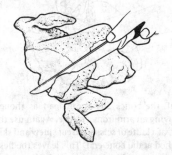

Cut through the breast down to the wing joint, taking a portion of breast meat and removing it with the whole wing joint.

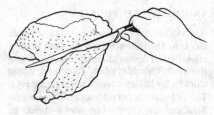

Turn the bird over, so that the breast is down. Cut the carcass in half through the middle, tapping the knife with a meat mallet. Cut away the ends of the breast bone and any small pieces of bone. Turn the breast over and split it in half.

SPATCHCOCK

Turn the bird breast down. Cut off the parson's nose. Using a heavy cook's knife, cut through the skin, flesh and bone down the length of the bird to open the carcass. Do not cut right through to the breast. Open the carcass out and turn it over so that the breast is uppermost.

Place the palm of your hand on the top of the breast and flatten the bird by pressing down firmly with your other hand. The spatchcocked bird may be kept flat by threading two metal skewers through it.

SKINNING RAW POULTRY

It is occasionally necessary to skin a whole chicken. The technique is sometimes used to allow the full flavour of a marinade to permeate the flesh, notably when spicing a whole chicken for baking covered and serving cold. The technique is not difficult and there are no hard and fast rules about how it should be done. The method described below, however, is an organized and practical approach to the task, which avoids damaging the meat.

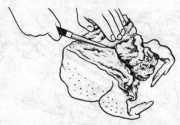

Use a sharp knife to slit the skin down the back of the bird. Pull it off, using a pointed knife to separate the skin from the membrane covering the flesh. Use scissors to cut the skin free around the joints. Turn the bird over and loosen the skin at the neck end, then pull it away from the breast meat, easing it off and cutting it free around the joints and at the parson's nose.

Skin the drumsticks individually with the help of scissors or a sharp pointed knife. Do the same with the first part of the wing joint, nearest the body. It is not easy to remove the skin from the wing ends, and they are best removed. The parson's nose may be left in place or cut off as required.

BONING A BIRD

Have ready a sharp, pointed cook's knife. A pair of kitchen scissors is also useful for snipping flesh and sinew free from joint ends.

Lay the bird breast down. Cut through the skin and flesh right in to the bone along the length of the back. Beginning at one end of the slit, slide the point of the knife under the flesh and skin. Keeping the knife close to the bone, cut the meat off the bone. Work all the meat off the bone on one side of the carcass, going down the rib cage as far as the breast. Leave the breast meat attached to the soft bone.

Cut off the wing ends, leaving only the first part of the joint in place. To free the flesh from the wing joint, carefully scrape the meat off the first part, using scissors or the point of the knife to cut sinews.

Pull the bones and meat apart as though removing an arm from a sleeve. Again use the point of a knife or scissors to cut sinew and skin attached at the bone end. This leaves the flesh and skin turned inside-out and the bones free but attached to the carcass. Turn the flesh and skin back out the right way. Repeat the process with the leg.

Turn the bird around and repeat the process on the second side, again leaving the breast meat attached to the soft bone.

When all the meat is removed from the second side, and the joints have been boned, the carcass will remain attached along the breast bone. Taking care not to cut the skin, lift the carcass away from the meat and cut along the breast bone, taking the finest sliver of soft bone to avoid damaging the skin.

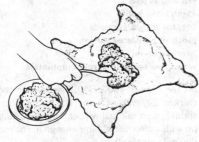

Spread out the boned bird. It is now ready for stuffing. To reshape it, simply fold the sides over the stuffing and sew them with a trussing needle and cooking thread. Turn the bird over with the seam down and plump it up into a neat shape, tucking the boned joint meat under.

ROASTING POULTRY

The cooking time should be calculated according to the weight of the prepared bird, with stuffing, if used. Place the bird in a roasting tin; using a rack or trivet if liked. A goose should always be cooked on a rack over a deep tin so that the large amount of fat drips away. Brush the bird with a little melted butter or oil if required and sprinkle with seasoning (see individual recipes for more detailed information). A large chicken or turkey may have its breast covered with streaky bacon to prevent the meat from drying out. Turkey should be covered with foil for part of the cooking time to prevent overbrowning.

Chicken does not usually require turning during cooking. Duck may be turned once or twice but this is not essential. Goose and turkey should be turned several times, depending on size, to promote moist, even cooking. All poultry should be basted during cooking. The following times are a general guide but may vary according to the exact ingredients used and the oven temperature, as when a bird is marinated and coated with seasonings that affect the browning.

Chicken and Guineafowl Allow 20 minutes per 450 g/1 lb plus 20 minutes at 180°C/350°F/gas 4.

Duck Prick the duck all over with a fork or skewer to release the fat. Roast on a rack, allowing 15-20 minutes per 450 g/1 lb at 190-200°C/375-400°F/gas 5-6.

Goose Allow 20-25 minutes per 450 g/1 lb at 180°C/350°F/gas 4.

Turkey This requires long, slow cooking to ensure that the meat is thoroughly cooked. This is particularly important if the body cavity of the bird is stuffed. The following times are at 180°C/350°F/gas 4. Keep the bird covered with foil until the final 30-45 minutes of cooking. These times are a guide only, based upon the bird's weight excluding stuffing, since it is not easy to weigh a stuffed turkey. Birds without stuffing will take slightly less time to cook.

Weight (before stuffing)	Time at 180°C/350°F/gas 4
2.5 kg/5½ lb	2½–3 hours
2.75–3.5 kg/6–8 lb	3–3¾ hours
3.5–4.5 kg/8–10 lb	3¾–4½ hours
4.5–5.5 kg/10–12 lb	4½–5 hours
5.5–11.4 kg/12–25 lb	20 minutes per 450 g/1 lb plus 20 minutes

Microwave Cooking   Lean, tender poultry cooks well in the microwave, although whole chickens and ducks benefit from being partially cooked by this method, then placed in a conventional oven to crisp the skin. See the Microwave Chapter and charts for more information.

TESTING FOR COOKING PROGRESS

It is essential that chicken and turkey are thoroughly cooked right through. With large birds, increasing the cooking temperature will not necessarily speed up the process as lengthy cooking must be allowed to ensure the thick areas of meat and the body cavity reach a high temperature.

To test, pierce the meat at a thick point – for example on the thigh behind the drumstick. Check for any signs of blood in the juices and for any meat that appears pink or uncooked. When the bird is cooked, the juices will run clear and the meat will be firm and white right through to the bone. On a large bird test in at least two places to ensure that all the meat is well cooked.

CARVING

The same rules apply to all poultry: the breast meat is carved in neat slices, working at an angle to the carcass to yield several slices of a similar size from each side. The wings and legs are then removed. To make it easier to carve the breast meat on chickens and smaller birds, the wings and legs are usually cut off first and served as individual portions. This is not necessary when carving larger birds, such as turkey, as the breast meat can easily be sliced off with the joints still in place.

ROAST CHICKEN WITH HONEY AND ALMONDS

1 (1.5–1.8 kg/3½–4 lb) oven-ready roasting chicken
½ lemon
salt and pepper
45 ml/3 tbsp honey
50 g/2 oz flaked almonds
pinch of powdered saffron
30 ml/2 tbsp oil
watercress sprigs to garnish (optional)

Set the oven at 180°C/350°F/gas 4. Rub the chicken all over with the cut lemon, then sprinkle with salt and pepper. Line a roasting tin with a piece of foil large enough to enclose the bird completely.

Put the bird into the foil-lined tin, then brush it all over with the honey. Sprinkle the nuts and saffron over, then trickle the oil very gently over the top. Bring up the foil carefully, tenting it over the bird so that it is completely covered. Make sure that the foil does not touch the skin. Seal the package by folding the edges of the foil over.

Roast for 1½–2 hours or until the chicken is cooked through. Open the foil for the last 10 minutes to allow the breast of the bird to brown. Transfer the chicken to a heated serving dish and garnish it with watercress if liked.

SERVES FOUR TO SIX

When it is on the point of setting but still tepid, whisk in half the mayonnaise until smooth.

Place the chicken portions on a wire rack. As soon as the mayonnaise mixture reaches a good coating consistency, pour it over the chicken portions to coat thoroughly.

Arrange the lettuce leaves on a serving dish and place the chicken portions on top. Surround with celery and hard-boiled egg slices and garnish with the olives and tomatoes.

SERVES SIX

CHAUDFROID OF CHICKEN

Chaudfroid of chicken may be made with portions (boneless breast portions, neat thigh joints or meaty quarters) or with a whole bird, as for the galantine (overleaf). This recipe illustrates the method of preparing a chaudfroid coating based on mayonnaise: either make your own mayonnaise or buy a good-quality brand. Alternatively, the coating may be made using a Béchamel Sauce and this option is used on the galantine. Whichever coating is used, it is important to ensure that it is evenly applied and attractively garnished before serving.

6 cooked chicken joints
125 ml/4 fl oz aspic jelly (see Mrs Beeton's
 Tip)
375 ml/13 fl oz mayonnaise
lettuce leaves
3 celery sticks, sliced
2 hard-boiled eggs, sliced

GARNISH
stoned olives
tomato slices

Remove the skin, excess fat and bones from the chicken joints, keeping the pieces in neat shapes. Melt the aspic jelly and leave to cool.

 MRS BEETON'S TIP

To make 500 ml/17 fl oz aspic jelly you require 500 ml/17 fl oz chicken stock from which all fat has been removed. Remove all traces of grease from a large enamel or stainless steel saucepan by scalding it in boiling water. Also scald a piece of clean muslin, a metal sieve and a whisk. Put the stock into the pan with 60 ml/4 tbsp white wine, 15 ml/1 tbsp white wine vinegar, 20–25 g/¾–1 oz gelatine, 1 bouquet garni and the white and crushed shell of 1 egg. Heat gently, whisking, until the gelatine dissolves, then bring the liquid to just below boiling point, whisking constantly. A thick white foam crust will form on top of the liquid. When this happens, remove the pan from the heat so that the foam falls back into the pan. Heat the stock in the same way one or twice more, until the liquid is crystal clear. Line the sieve with muslin and place it over a perfectly clean bowl. Strain the crust and liquid through the muslin into the bowl, trying not to break the crust. The aspic should be sparkling clear. If necessary, repeat the process, scalding the equipment again. Use aspic as directed in recipes or freeze in clean containers.

GALANTINE OF CHICKEN

1 (2.25 kg/5 lb) chicken
salt and pepper
450 g/1 lb sausagemeat
100 g/4 oz cooked ham, cut in 1 × 2.5 cm/½ × 1
  inch strips
2 hard-boiled eggs, sliced
6 flat mushrooms, chopped
25 g/1 oz pistachio nuts, blanched, skinned
  and chopped
750 ml/1¼ pints chicken stock

CHAUDFROID SAUCE
125 ml/4 fl oz aspic jelly (see Mrs Beeton's
  Tip, page 191)
10 ml/2 tsp gelatine
300 ml/½ pint Béchamel sauce (page 587),
  cooled until tepid
5 ml/1 tsp white wine vinegar or lemon juice
15 ml/1 tbsp double cream

GARNISH
125 ml/4 fl oz aspic jelly
canned or boiled pimiento strips
lemon rind strips
hard-boiled egg slices

Using a sharp knife, cut down the back of the
bird, then remove all the bones neatly, using
the technique described on pages 188–189.
Open out the boned bird and season with plenty
of salt and pepper.

Spread half the sausagemeat evenly over the
inner surface of the bird. Arrange the ham
strips, egg slices, chopped mushrooms and
nuts on top. Add salt and pepper to taste, then
top with the remaining sausagemeat. Carefully
lift the two halves of the bird and bring them
together so that it is as near the original shape
as possible. Wrap the bird tightly in foil.

Heat the chicken stock in a saucepan large
enough to hold the stuffed bird. Carefully lower
the bird into the hot stock and simmer gently

for 2½ hours. Allow to cool for 30 minutes in
the stock. Remove and drain the package,
tighten the foil to allow for any shrinkage
during cooking, then press the foil-wrapped
chicken between two large plates or boards and
cool. Chill until quite cold.

Meanwhile make the chaudfroid sauce. Melt
the aspic jelly in a bowl placed over hot water.
Add the gelatine and continue to stir over heat
until dissolved. Cool the mixture until tepid,
then fold it into the Béchamel sauce. Add salt
and pepper to taste. Stir in the vinegar or lemon
juice. Rub the sauce through a fine sieve into a
clean bowl, then fold in the cream. Leave to
cool and thicken slightly but do not allow the
sauce to set.

Unwrap the chicken, remove the skin from the
bird and wipe away any excess grease. Place
the chicken on a wire rack and stand this on a
sheet of foil. Slowly spoon the chaudfroid
sauce over the chicken, teasing it down the
sides to coat the bird evenly. Work quickly
before the sauce sets and use a spatula to
retrieve the excess which drops on the foil. If
the sauce becomes too thick to coat the chicken
evenly, stand the bowl over hot water for a few
seconds and stir the sauce until it is smooth and
more fluid. Chill until the coating is set.

For the garnish, have the aspic jelly cooled and
just beginning to set: it should resemble syrup
in consistency. The chaudfroid coating must be
chilled. Dip the strips of pimiento and lemon
rind in the aspic, then arrange them on the
chicken. Carefully arrange the egg slices on the
chicken, then spoon the aspic all over the bird
to coat it in a thin even glaze. Catch the excess
aspic as before, tip it into a small pan, and
warm it until just fluid. Pour it into a small
rectangular dish. Chill the chicken and remaining aspic until set. Chop the aspic and arrange
it around the chicken on a serving platter.

SERVES FOUR TO SIX

CHICKEN KIEV

The original chicken Kiev was a boned and flattened chicken breast with a simple herb – usually chive – butter filling. Today the butter is frequently flavoured with garlic, as in the version below.

4 chicken breast and wing joints
salt and pepper
plain flour for coating
1 egg, beaten
about 75 g/3 oz dried white breadcrumbs
oil for deep frying

BUTTER FILLING
100 g/4 oz butter, softened
finely grated rind of ½ lemon
15 ml/1 tbsp chopped parsley
2 small garlic cloves, crushed

GARNISH
lemon wedges
parsley sprigs

Make the butter filling. Beat the butter lightly in a bowl. Gradually work in the lemon rind, parsley and garlic, with salt and pepper to taste. Form the butter into a roll, wrap it in grease-proof paper and chill well.

To prepare the chicken, cut off the wing ends and remove the skin from the breast meat. Turn the joints flesh side up and cut out all bones except the wing bone, which is left in place. Do not cut right through the flesh. To flatten the boned meat slightly, place it between grease-proof paper and beat lightly with a cutlet bat or rolling pin.

Cut the flavoured butter into four long pieces and place one on each piece of chicken. Fold the flesh over the butter to enclose it completely and secure with wooden cocktail sticks. The wing bone should protrude at one end of each chicken cutlet.

Spread out the flour in a shallow bowl and add salt and pepper. Put the beaten egg in a second bowl and stir in a little water. Place the bread-crumbs on a sheet of foil. Coat the chicken in flour, then in egg and breadcrumbs. Repeat the coating at least once more, using more egg and breadcrumbs, so that the chicken and butter filling are well sealed. Chill lightly.

Heat the oil to 160°C/325°F or until a cube of bread added to the oil browns in 2 minutes. Deep fry the chicken, turning or basting the cutlets until golden brown and firm to the touch, as necessary for even cooking. Allow 15–20 minutes to ensure the flesh is cooked through. Drain thoroughly and keep hot, if necessary, while frying any remaining cutlets. To serve, place the cutlets on a heated serving dish. Remove the cocktail sticks and garnish with lemon wedges and parsley.

SERVES FOUR

VARIATIONS

Alternative Fillings Instead of using butter, flavoured soft cheese makes a deliciously creamy filling. For example, try bought soft cheese with herbs and garlic or mix some chopped fresh herbs with plain cream or curd cheese. Finely chopped ham or crumbled crisply grilled bacon also makes an excellent filling when combined with soft cheese.

Baked Kiev The coated chicken may be baked instead of being deep fried. It is essential to make the breadcrumb coating even and fairly thick. Place the portions in a well-greased roasting tin and dot with a little butter or trickle a little oil over the top. Bake at 190°C/375°F/gas 5 for 45–50 minutes, until the coating is well browned and crisp. The chicken must be fully cooked – pierce one portion towards one end near the bone to check.

SPATCHCOCKED CHICKENS WITH BACON AND CORN FRITTERS

2 spring chickens
50 g/2 oz butter
salt and pepper
bacon rolls (see Mrs Beeton's Tip) and
    parsley sprigs to garnish

CORN FRITTERS
1 (275 g/10 oz) can sweetcorn, drained
2 eggs, separated
75 g/3 oz self-raising flour
2.5 ml/½ tsp salt
oil for frying

Split the birds through the back only, following the instructions on page 187. Flatten out each bird, removing the breast bone if necessary. Break the joints and remove the tips from the wings, to make flattening easier. Use skewers to keep the birds in shape while cooking.

Melt the butter and brush it on both sides of the birds. Sprinkle lightly with salt and pepper. Grill under moderate heat – or over medium coals – for about 20 minutes on each side, or until cooked through. Brush the chickens with more butter and turn occasionally while grilling to ensure even cooking.

Meanwhile make the corn fritters. Combine the corn, egg yolks and flour in a bowl. Whisk the egg whites and the salt until they form soft peaks, then fold them into the corn mixture.

Pour oil to a depth of about 1 cm/½ inch into a large deep saucepan. Heat to 180-190°C/ 350-375°F or until a cube of bread browns in 30 seconds. Gently drop in spoonfuls of the corn mixture, a few at a time. As each corn fritter browns, turn it over with a slotted spoon and cook the other side. When cooked, remove the fritters, drain on absorbent kitchen paper and keep hot while cooking the remainder.

When the chickens are cooked, remove the skewers, arrange on a heated platter and serve, surrounded by the corn fritters, bacon rolls and parsley sprigs.

SERVES FOUR

 MRS BEETON'S TIP

To make the bacon rolls, roll up 8 rindless streaky bacon rashers, threading them in pairs on short metal skewers. Grill for about 5 minutes, turning frequently, until the rolls are crisp.

BARBECUED CHICKEN DRUMSTICKS

75 g/3 oz butter
12 chicken drumsticks
60 ml/4 tbsp vinegar
15 ml/1 tbsp Worcestershire sauce
15 ml/1 tbsp tomato purée
5 ml/1 tsp soy sauce
5 ml/1 tsp grated onion
5 ml/1 tsp paprika
2.5 ml/½ tsp salt

Melt the butter in a small saucepan. Brush a little of it over the chicken drumsticks to coat them thoroughly, then arrange on a rack in a grill pan.

Stir the remaining ingredients into the leftover butter in the pan. Simmer for 2 minutes, then brush a little of the mixture over the chicken. Grill or barbecue over medium coals, turning occasionally and brushing with more sauce until cooked through. Serve with rice or salad.

SERVES FOUR

CHICKEN CHASSEUR

butter for greasing
1 (1.6 kg/3½ lb) roasting chicken
25 g/1 oz plain flour
salt and pepper
50 g/2 oz butter
15 ml/1 tbsp oil
1 small onion, finely chopped
175 g/6 oz button mushrooms, sliced
150 ml/¼ pint dry white wine
15 ml/1 tbsp tomato purée
275 ml/9 fl oz chicken stock
1 sprig each of fresh tarragon, chervil and
    parsley, chopped

Divide the chicken into 8 serving portions. Mix the flour, salt and pepper in a sturdy polythene bag. Add the chicken portions and toss until well coated. Shake off excess flour.

Melt the butter in the oil in a large frying pan. When hot, add the chicken pieces and fry until browned all over and cooked through, (see Mrs Beeton's Tip). Using a slotted spoon, remove the chicken pieces from the pan, drain on absorbent kitchen paper and transfer to a warmed serving dish. Cover and keep hot.

Add the onion to the fat remaining in the pan and fry gently until soft but not coloured. Add the mushrooms and fry briefly. Pour in the wine and add the tomato purée and stock. Stir until well blended, then simmer gently for 10 minutes. Stir in two-thirds of the chopped herbs, with salt and pepper to taste.

Pour the sauce over the chicken portions and sprinkle with the remaining herbs. Serve hot.

SERVES FOUR

 MRS BEETON'S TIP

Do not rush the cooking process when frying chicken. Keep the heat moderate to prevent the butter from burning and turn the chicken portions frequently to ensure they cook evenly. The cooking temperature and size of the portions affects the timing – even the size of the pan contributes to the result. Allow at least 15-20 minutes but always check the thickest areas of meat to ensure they are cooked before serving.

DEVILLED CHICKEN

4 chicken breasts
30 ml/2 tbsp oil
50 g/2 oz butter, softened
15 ml/1 tbsp tomato purée
2.5 ml/½ tsp mustard powder
few drops of Tabasco sauce
10 ml/2 tsp Worcestershire sauce
lemon or lime wedges to serve

Place the chicken breasts on a rack in a grill pan. Brush generously with oil and grill under moderate heat for 5 minutes on each side.

Meanwhile, prepare the devilled mixture. Beat the butter in a small bowl and gradually work in the tomato purée, mustard powder, Tabasco and Worcestershire sauce. Spread half the mixture over the chicken and grill for 5 minutes more, then turn the breasts over carefully, spread with the remaining mixture and grill for a further 5 minutes or until the chicken is thoroughly cooked. Transfer the chicken to plates or a serving dish and add lemon or lime wedges: the fruit juice may be squeezed over just before the chicken is eaten. Serve with baked jacket potatoes and a salad.

SERVES FOUR

FRITOT OF CHICKEN

1 (1.4–1.6 kg/3–3½ lb) cooked chicken
oil for deep frying
watercress to garnish

MARINADE
¼ onion, finely chopped
1 parsley sprig, finely chopped
30 ml/2 tbsp olive oil
15 ml/1 tbsp lemon juice
2.5 ml/½ tsp dried mixed herbs
salt and pepper

BATTER
15 ml/1 tbsp oil
100 g/4 oz plain flour · 5 ml/1 tsp salt
2 egg whites

Cut the chicken into 8 serving portions. Remove the skin and any fat, then place the pieces in a bowl large enough to hold them all in a single layer. Mix all the ingredients for the marinade in a bowl, pour over the chicken, cover and marinate for 1½ hours.

Make the batter. Mix the oil with 125 ml/4 fl oz tepid water in a jug. Mix the flour and salt in a bowl. Make a well in the centre, add the liquid and mix well, gradually incorporating the flour until smooth. Leave to stand for 1 hour.

Drain the chicken portions and pat dry with absorbent kitchen paper. Whisk the egg whites in a clean, grease-free bowl until stiff; fold into the batter.

Heat the oil for deep frying to 180–190°C/ 350–375°F or until a cube of bread browns in 30 seconds.

Dip each piece of chicken in batter, add to the hot oil and fry until golden on all sides. Turn once or twice during cooking. Drain on absorbent kitchen paper and keep hot while frying any remaining portions, reheating the oil if necessary. Garnish with watercress. Serve with courgettes and plain boiled or baked potatoes, if liked. Alternatively, add some fresh orange segments to a plain green salad to accompany.

SERVES FOUR TO SIX

CHICKEN AND BACON CASSEROLE

25 g/1 oz plain flour
salt and pepper
1 (1.6 kg/3½ lb) chicken, cut in serving
  portions
30 ml/2 tbsp cooking oil
100 g/4 oz rindless streaky bacon rashers, cut
  into strips
100 g/4 oz mushrooms, sliced
1 onion or 100 g/4 oz shallots, finely
  chopped
500 ml/17 fl oz chicken stock

Mix the flour, salt and pepper in a sturdy polythene bag. Add the chicken portions and toss until well coated. Shake off and reserve excess flour.

Heat the oil in a flameproof casserole. Add the chicken pieces and fry them until golden on all sides, turning frequently. Remove from the pan, then add the bacon, mushrooms and onion or shallots to the fat remaining in the pan. Cook for 5 minutes, stirring frequently, then stir in the reserved flour and half the stock. Replace the chicken in the pan.

Stir in enough stock to cover the chicken pieces. Bring to the boil, then lower the heat. Cover the casserole and simmer for 1–1½ hours or until the chicken portions are cooked through. Taste and add more seasoning if required. Serve from the casserole, with Potatoes Lyonnaise (page 353) and peas if liked. Alternatively, serve buttered noodles and plain green beans with the casserole.

SERVES FOUR TO SIX

BRAISED CHESTNUT CHICKEN

1 (1.4-1.6 kg/3-3½ lb) chicken
flour for coating
salt and pepper
45 ml/3 tbsp oil
1 onion, sliced
3 rindless streaky bacon rashers, cut into
  strips
300 ml/½ pint chicken stock
30 ml/2 tbsp plain flour
25 g/1 oz butter
450 g/1 lb chipolata sausages, fried or grilled,
  to garnish

STUFFING
450 g/1 lb chestnuts
250-300 ml/8-10 fl oz chicken stock
50 g/2 oz cooked ham, finely chopped
100 g/4 oz fresh white breadcrumbs
grated rind of 1 lemon
2-3 parsley sprigs, chopped
25 g/1 oz butter, melted
1 egg, beaten

Start by making the stuffing. Remove the shells and skins of the chestnuts (see Mrs Beeton's Tip). Place the cleaned nuts in a saucepan, just cover with stock and bring to the boil. Cover, lower the heat until the liquid is only just boiling, and cook for about 20 minutes or until the nuts are tender. Drain and mash them, or press them through a fine sieve into a bowl.

Stir in the ham, breadcrumbs, lemon rind and parsley, with salt and pepper to taste. Add the melted butter with enough of the beaten egg to bind. Stuff the chicken with this mixture and truss it.

Spread out the flour in a large shallow bowl. Season with salt and pepper. Add the chicken, turning and rolling it in the mixture until well coated. Heat the oil in a large, heavy-bottomed flameproof casserole or saucepan with a lid.

Fry the bird on all sides until lightly browned, then remove it.

Add the onion and bacon to the oil remaining in the pan and fry for 4-5 minute over gentle heat until the onion is slightly softened but not coloured. Replace the chicken in the pan. Pour in the stock, cover the pan and bring just to the boil. Lower the heat and simmer for 1½ hours or until the chicken is cooked through, adding more chicken stock or water as necessary.

Carefully remove the chicken from the pan. Use a large spoon to skim the fat from the cooking liquid, then process the remaining juices in a blender or food processor, or push them through a sieve into a clean saucepan. In a small bowl, blend the flour with the butter. Bring the sieved liquid to the boil, then reduce the heat so it simmers steadily. Gradually add small pieces of the flour and butter mixture to the cooking juices remaining in the pan, whisking thoroughly after each addition. Whisk until the sauce is thickened. Simmer for 3 minutes, whisking occasionally, add salt and pepper to taste and pour into a sauceboat.

Serve the chicken surrounded by fried or grilled chipolatas. Offer the sauce separately.

SERVES FOUR TO SIX

 MRS BEETON'S TIP

To shell chestnuts, make a small slit in the shell of each, then place the nuts in a saucepan of boiling water. Cook for 5 minutes. Drain, carefully removing the shells and skins while the chestnuts are still hot.

CHICKEN WINGS WITH GINGER

oil for greasing
12 chicken wings
juice of 1 lemon
2.5 ml/½ tsp sesame oil
45 ml/3 tbsp plain flour
10 ml/2 tsp ground ginger
salt and pepper

SAUCE
60 ml/4 tbsp preserved ginger in syrup,
   drained and chopped
30 ml/2 tbsp medium-dry sherry
25 g/1 oz butter

Remove and discard the ends from the chicken wings. Mix the lemon and oil together in a small bowl. Brush the mixture all over the chicken wings. Reserve the remaining lemon/oil mixture.

Spread out the flour in a shallow bowl and flavour with the ginger, salt and pepper. Add the chicken wings and turn them in the mixture until well coated.

Set the oven at 190°C/375°F/gas 5. Spread out the chicken wings on a greased baking sheet and bake for 50-60 minutes, or until crisp and golden. Turn the wings occasionally during cooking.

Meanwhile, make the sauce. Add the ginger, sherry and butter to the remaining lemon/oil mixture, tip into a small saucepan and bring to the boil. Arrange the cooked chicken wings on a heated serving platter and pour the sauce over them. Serve with noodles or rice, if liked, and some stir-fried mixed vegetables.

SERVES FOUR

LEMON CHICKEN

6 chicken breasts
salt and pepper
50 g/2 oz butter
15 ml/1 tbsp oil
1 onion, sliced
1 lemon, sliced
60 ml/4 tbsp plain flour
250 ml/8 fl oz chicken stock
2-3 bay leaves
5 ml/1 tsp caster sugar

Set the oven at 190°C/375°F/gas 5. Season the chicken breasts with salt and pepper. Melt the butter in the oil in a large frying pan, add the chicken and fry until golden brown all over. Using tongs or a slotted spoon, transfer to a casserole.

Add the onion and lemon slices to the fat remaining in the pan and fry over very gentle heat for about 15 minutes. Using a slotted spoon, transfer the onion and lemon to the casserole.

Sprinkle the flour into the fat remaining in the pan. Cook for 1 minute, then blend in the stock. Bring to the boil, stirring all the time. Add the bay leaves and sugar, with salt and pepper to taste. Pour over the chicken breasts in the casserole, cover and bake for about 45 minutes or until the chicken is tender. Remove the casserole lid 5 minutes before the end of the cooking time.

Remove the bay leaves before serving or reserve them as a garnish.

SERVES SIX

COQ AU VIN

The best coq au vin is made by marinating the chicken overnight in the red wine before cooking.

1 (1.6 kg/3½ lb) chicken with giblets
1 bouquet garni
salt and pepper
75 g/3 oz unsalted butter
15 ml/1 tbsp oil
150 g/5 oz belly of pickled pork or green
   (unsmoked) bacon rashers, rind removed
   and chopped
150 g/5 oz button onions or shallots
30 ml/2 tbsp brandy
175 g/6 oz small button mushrooms
2 garlic cloves, crushed
575 ml/19 fl oz burgundy or other red wine
15 ml/1 tbsp tomato purée
25 g/1 oz plain flour
croûtes of fried bread, to serve

Joint the chicken and skin the portions if liked. Place the giblets in a saucepan with 450 ml/¾ pint water. Add the bouquet garni, salt and pepper. Cook gently for about 1 hour, then strain. Measure the stock and set aside 275 ml/9 fl oz.

Set the oven at 150°C/300°F/gas 2. Melt 40 g/1½ oz of the butter in the oil in a flame-proof casserole. Add the pork or bacon, with the onions. Cook over gentle heat for about 10 minutes until the onions are lightly coloured. Using a slotted spoon, transfer the bacon and onions to a plate.

Add the chicken portions to the fat remaining in the pan and brown lightly all over. Ignite the brandy (see Mrs Beeton's Tip). When the flames die down, pour it into the casserole. Add the reserved bacon and onions, with the mushrooms and garlic. Stir in the wine, giblet stock and tomato purée. Cover and cook in the oven for 1-1½ hours or until the chicken is cooked through and tender.

Using a slotted spoon, transfer the chicken portions to a heated serving dish. Arrange the bacon, mushrooms and onions over them. Cover with buttered greaseproof paper and keep hot. Return the casserole to the hob and simmer the liquid until reduced by about one-third.

Meanwhile make a beurre manié by blending the remaining butter with the flour in a small bowl. Gradually add small pieces of the mixture to the stock, whisking thoroughly after each addition. Continue to whisk the sauce until it thickens. Pour it over the chicken. Garnish with croûtes of fried bread and serve.

SERVES FOUR TO SIX

 MRS BEETON'S TIP

To flame the brandy, either pour it into a soup ladle and warm over low heat or warm it in a jug in the microwave for 15 seconds on High. Ignite the brandy (if warmed in a soup ladle it may well ignite spontaneously) and when the flames die down, pour it into the casserole.

SPRING CHICKENS WITH PARSLEY

50 g/2 oz parsley sprigs
100 g/4 oz butter
salt and pepper
2 spring chickens
300 ml/½ pint double cream

GARNISH
1 lemon, cut in wedges
4 parsley sprigs

Strip the leaves from the parsley sprigs and chop them roughly. Soften half the butter in a bowl, beat well, then mix in half the parsley, with salt and pepper to taste. Place half the mixture in the body cavity of each bird.

Melt the remaining butter in a large frying pan, add the chickens and brown them lightly all over. Add 150 ml/¼ pint water, bring just to the boil, cover and cook gently for 40 minutes or until the chickens are cooked through. Transfer the chickens to a plate and cut them in half. Arrange on a heated serving dish and keep hot.

Add the cream to the stock remaining in the pan and cook over low heat, stirring until the sauce is hot. Do not allow it to boil. Add the remaining parsley, taste the sauce, and add more salt and pepper if required. Pour the sauce over the chicken and garnish with lemon wedges and parsley sprigs.

SERVES FOUR

 MRS BEETON'S TIP

If spring chickens are not available, substitute 1 (1.4 kg/3 lb) roasting chicken. Stuff it with the parsley butter. Cook for about 1½ hours, adding extra water as necessary. When cooked, cut into quarters.

CHICKEN SUPREME

1 (1.4–1.6 kg/3–3½ lb) chicken
1 litre/1¾ pints chicken or vegetable stock
chopped truffles or poached mushrooms to garnish

SAUCE
50 g/2 oz butter
4 button mushrooms, finely chopped
6 black peppercorns
4–5 parsley stalks
25 g/1 oz plain flour
salt and pepper
lemon juice (see method)
150 ml/¼ pint single cream
1 egg yolk
grated nutmeg

Truss the chicken neatly, put it into a large saucepan and pour over the stock. Bring the liquid to the boil, lower the heat, cover the pan and simmer for 1½–2 hours or until tender. After 1 hour, strain off 250 ml/8 fl oz of the chicken stock. Blot the surface with a piece of absorbent kitchen paper to remove excess fat, then set the stock aside for use in the sauce.

Melt half the butter in a saucepan. Add the mushrooms, peppercorns and parsley stalks. Cook gently for 10 minutes, then stir in the flour. Cook over gentle heat for 2–3 minutes. Gradually add the reserved stock, stirring well to prevent the formation of lumps. Raise the heat and cook the sauce, stirring constantly, until it thickens. Rub through a sieve into a clean pan, add salt, pepper and lemon juice to taste and stir in half the cream. Cool the sauce slightly.

Beat the egg yolk and remaining cream with a little of the cooled sauce in a bowl. Add the contents of the bowl to the sauce and stir over gentle heat until heated. The yolk and cream enrich, rather than thicken the sauce. Do not boil or the yolk and cream will curdle. Whisk in the remaining butter, adding a knob at a time. Add nutmeg to taste.

Drain the cooked chicken, joint it into serving portions and transfer these to a heated serving dish. Pour the sauce over, garnish with truffles or mushrooms and serve.

SERVES FOUR TO SIX

 MRS BEETON'S TIP

The stock remaining in the pan when the chicken has been removed may be cooled, then chilled, so that the fat solidifies and can be removed easily. The skimmed stock may then be used for soup or in another recipe.

POACHED CHICKEN WITH OYSTERS

24 oysters
1 (1.4–1.6 kg/3–3½ lb) chicken
1 blade of mace
salt and pepper

SAUCE
50 g/2 oz plain flour
50 g/2 oz butter
1 egg, beaten
30 ml/2 tbsp single cream

Open the oysters (see page 117), reserving the liquor. Reserve 12 of the oysters. Put the rest inside the chicken, then truss the bird and put it in a large saucepan with a tight-fitting lid. Add water to a depth of about 2.5 cm/1 inch, then add the mace, salt and pepper. Bring the liquid to the boil, lower the heat, cover the pan and cook for 1½ hours or until the chicken is cooked through, adding more water during cooking if required.

Remove the trussing string from the chicken, put the bird on a heated platter and keep hot while making the sauce. Strain the cooking liquid into a measuring jug and make up to 600 ml/1 pint with water, if necessary.

Place the flour in a saucepan. Gradually whisk in the chicken stock and add the butter, then whisk over moderate heat until the mixture comes to the boil. Lower the heat and simmer for 3–4 minutes, whisking constantly until the sauce is thick, smooth and glossy. Add salt and pepper to taste. Cool the sauce slightly.

Beat the egg and cream with a little of the cooled sauce in a bowl. Add the contents of the bowl to the sauce and stir over gentle heat until the mixture thickens a little more. Do not allow it to boil. Carve the chicken.

Meanwhile, put the reserved oysters in a small saucepan with the oyster liquor and poach very gently for 10 minutes. To assemble the dish, pour half the sauce over the chicken portions. Stir the oysters and their liquor into the remaining sauce and serve separately, in a sauceboat.

SERVES FOUR TO SIX

VARIATION

If preferred, boneless breast portions may be used instead of a whole chicken. Cut a small slit into each portion to make a pocket, then slip an oyster into each pocket and secure the opening with a wooden cocktail stick. Poach the chicken in chicken stock (instead of water) for about 45 minutes, or until cooked. Continue as above. The individual portions are easy to serve and this method uses fewer oysters.

shallow dish, cover tightly with foil and a lid and marinate for 12 hours or overnight.

Set the oven at 180°C/350°F/gas 4. Put the chicken on a rack in a shallow roasting tin. Baste it with the oil and any remaining paste. Bake for 1½–2 hours, spooning over the oil and pan juices from time to time. When cooked, sprinkle with the toasted cumin seeds. Serve with rice and a tomato and onion salad.

SERVES FOUR

 MRS BEETON'S TIP

There are many versions of garam masala. The spice mix is usually dry, although some are mixed to a paste with water. They vary according to region and the cook's preference but the sweet spices are used to make the fragrant mixtures. Garam masala may be used in a wide variety of dishes, either added towards the end of the cooking time or combined with other spices in a paste. It may be sprinkled over the food during the final stages before serving. To make your own garam masala, toast 60 ml/4 tbsp coriander seeds in a small ungreased frying pan, stirring all the time for a few minutes until they give off their aroma. Tip the seeds into a bowl and repeat the process with 30 ml/2 tbsp cumin seeds, 30 ml/2 tbsp cumin seeds, 15 ml/1 tbsp black peppercorns, 10 ml/2 tsp cardamom seeds, 3 cinnamon sticks and 5 ml/1 tsp whole cloves, toasting each spice separately. When all the spices have been toasted and cooled, grind them to a powder in a coffee grinder (reserved for the purpose) or in a mortar with a pestle. Stir in 30 ml/2 tbsp freshly grated nutmeg. Store in an airtight jar.

TANDOORI CHICKEN

1 (1.4–1.6 kg/3–3½ lb) chicken
15 ml/1 tbsp cumin seeds
30 ml/2 tbsp grated fresh root ginger
1 onion, grated
4 garlic cloves, crushed
5 ml/1 tsp salt
5 ml/1 tsp chilli powder
2.5 ml/½ tsp turmeric
5 ml/1 tsp garam masala
few drops of red food colouring (optional)
juice of 2 lemons
150 ml/¼ pint plain yogurt
30 ml/2 tbsp oil

Skin the chicken. Keep it whole or cut it into 4 or 8 pieces. Toast the cumin seeds in a small ungreased frying pan over moderate heat for 1 minute. Grind them in a pepper mill, or use a pestle and mortar. Set the seeds aside.

Combine the ginger, onion, garlic, salt, chilli powder, turmeric and garam masala in a small bowl. Add the colouring, if used, then stir in the lemon juice and yogurt.

Prick the chicken with a fork and cut a few slits in the legs and breast. Rub the bird with the paste, pressing it deeply into the slits. Place in a

MRS BEETON'S CHICKEN PIE

fat for greasing
1 (1.6 kg/3½ lb) chicken with giblets
1 onion, halved
salt and pepper
1 bouquet garni
1 blade of mace
2.5 ml/½ tsp grated nutmeg
2.5 ml/½ tsp ground mace
6 slices of lean cooked ham
3 hard-boiled eggs
flour for dredging
150 g/5 oz puff pastry, thawed if frozen
beaten egg for glazing

HERB FORCEMEAT
50 g/2 oz shredded beef suet or margarine
100 g/4 oz fresh white breadcrumbs
pinch of grated nutmeg
15 ml/1 tbsp chopped parsley
5 ml/1 tsp chopped fresh mixed herbs
grated rind of ½ lemon
1 egg, beaten

Lightly grease a 1.5 litre/2¾ pint pie dish. Make the herb forcemeat. Melt the margarine, if using. Mix the breadcrumbs with the suet or margarine in a bowl. Add the nutmeg, herbs and lemon rind. Add salt and pepper to taste, then bind with the beaten egg.

Skin the chicken and cut it into small serving joints. Put the leftover bones, neck and gizzard into a small pan with 250 ml/8 fl oz water. Add the onion to the pan with salt, pepper, bouquet garni and blade of mace. Half cover and simmer gently for about 45 minutes until the liquid is well reduced and strongly flavoured. Set the pan aside.

Set the oven at 220°C/425°F/gas 7. Put a layer of chicken joints in the bottom of the prepared dish. Sprinkle with salt, pepper, nutmeg and ground mace. Cover with a layer of ham, then

with forcemeat; add salt and pepper to taste. Slice the eggs, place a layer over the forcemeat, and season again. Repeat the layers until the dish is full and all the ingredients are used, ending with a layer of chicken joints. Pour in 150–200 ml/5–7 fl oz water and dredge lightly with flour.

Roll out the pastry on a lightly floured surface to the same shape as the dish but 2.5 cm/1 inch larger all round. Cut off the outside 2 cm/¾ inch of the pastry. Lay the pastry strip on the rim of the dish. Dampen the strip and lay the lid on top. Knock up the edge, trim, then use any trimmings to decorate the crust with pastry leaves. Make a pastry rose and put to one side. Brush the pastry with the beaten egg. Make a small hole in the centre of the pie.

Bake for 15 minutes to set the pastry, then reduce the oven temperature to 180°C/350°F/gas 4, and cover the pastry loosely with grease-proof paper. Bake for 1–1¼ hours. Bake the pastry rose with – but not on – the pie for the final 20 minutes. Test whether the joints are cooked through by running a small heated skewer into the pie through the central hole. It should come out clean with no trace of blood.

Just before the pie is cooked, reheat the stock and strain it. When the pie is cooked, pour the stock in through the central hole, then cover with the pastry rose.

SERVES SIX TO EIGHT

 MRS BEETON'S TIP

If the pie is to be served cold, substitute boneless chicken breasts for the jointed bird. Sausagemeat may be used instead of the forcemeat. In both cases increase the cooking time by about 30 minutes, covering loosely with foil if necessary.

CHICKEN RAMEKINS

butter for greasing
175 g/6 oz raw chicken or turkey meat,
  minced
2 eggs, separated
50 g/2 oz mushrooms, chopped
salt and pepper
45 ml/3 tbsp double cream
milk (see method)

Grease eight small ramekins. Set the oven at
190°C/375°F/gas 5. Put the minced chicken or
turkey in a bowl and gradually add the egg
yolks, stirring to make a very smooth mixture.
Stir in the mushrooms and set aside.

Whisk the egg whites with salt and pepper to
taste in a clean, dry bowl until very stiff. In
another bowl, whip the cream lightly. Fold the
cream into the chicken mixture, then fold in
the whisked egg whites. If the mixture is very
stiff, add a little milk.

Divide the mixture between the prepared
ramekins. Bake for about 30 minutes or until
well risen, firm to the touch and browned.
Serve at once.

SERVES FOUR TO EIGHT

CHICKEN MARENGO

30 ml/2 tbsp plain flour
salt and pepper
1 (1.4 kg/3 lb) chicken, jointed
60 ml/4 tbsp oil
2 garlic cloves, crushed
100 g/4 oz small button mushrooms
2 tomatoes, peeled and chopped
15 ml/1 tbsp tomato purée
150 ml/¼ pint dry white wine

Mix the flour with salt and pepper, then use to
coat the chicken portions. Heat the oil in a large
flameproof casserole, add the chicken and fry

until golden on all sides. Stir in the garlic,
mushrooms, tomatoes and tomato purée, with
the wine.

Bring just to the boil, lower the heat so that the
mixture simmers and cover with a tight-fitting
lid. Cook over gentle heat for about 45 minutes
until the chicken is cooked through. Sprinkle
with parsley and serve.

SERVES FOUR

SPICED DRUMSTICKS

15 ml/1 tbsp oil
1 onion, grated
1 garlic clove, crushed
5 ml/1 tsp curry powder
salt and pepper
60 ml/4 tbsp mango chutney
8 chicken drumsticks

Heat the oil in a small saucepan, then add the
onion and garlic. Cook, stirring, for 5 minutes.
Add the curry powder and plenty of salt and
pepper; stir for another minute or so. Remove
from the heat. Chop any large pieces of fruit in
the mango chutney, add it to the onion mixture
and stir well. Set the oven at 200°C/400°F/
gas 6.

Make two or three slashes into the skin and
flesh on both sides of the drumsticks, then
place them in an ovenproof dish. Spoon the
onion mixture over and cover with foil. Bake
for 30 minutes.

Turn the drumsticks over and base them with
the cooking juices, then continue to cook,
uncovered, for a further 20–30 minutes, turning once more, until cooked through and well
browned. Serve at once. To serve cold, transfer
to a cold dish, cover and cool quickly, then chill
until required.

SERVES FOUR

CHICKEN AND RICE CROQUETTES

200 g/7 oz risotto rice
450 ml/¾ pint cold chicken stock
salt (optional)
75 g/3 oz butter
1 egg
50 g/2 oz dried white breadcrumbs
oil for deep frying

FILLING
175 g/6 oz minced cooked chicken
1 hard-boiled egg, finely chopped
1.25 ml/¼ tsp cayenne pepper
1.25/¼ tsp ground mace
30 ml/2 tbsp double or single cream or milk

Put the rice in a saucepan. Pour in the cold stock. Add a little salt if the chicken stock is unseasoned, then bring to the boil. Cover the pan tightly and reduce the heat to the lowest setting. Leave the rice for 15 minutes, turn off the heat and leave for a further 15 minutes without removing the lid.

Add the butter to the rice in the pan and cook over gentle heat until it has all been absorbed and the rice is creamy. Set aside to cool.

Mix the ingredients for the filling in a bowl, adding the cream or milk to bind the mixture. Wash, then wet your hands in cold water. Take a spoonful of rice and flatten it on one palm, then place a small portion of the chicken mixture on top. Mould the rice over the chicken mixture, smoothing it around it to enclose the filling completely. The balls should be about the size of small eggs or tomatoes. Chill the rice balls for about 1 hour to firm up.

Beat the egg in a shallow bowl with 15 ml/1 tbsp water. Spread the breadcrumbs on a sheet of foil. Roll each croquette in egg, then in breadcrumbs. Heat the oil to 180°C/350°F and fry the croquettes, a few at a time, until golden brown. Remove with a slotted spoon, drain on absorbent kitchen paper and keep hot while frying successive batches.

MAKES ABOUT FOURTEEN

FRENCH CUTLETS

50 g/2 oz dried white breadcrumbs
grated rind of ½ lemon
salt and pepper
pinch of cayenne pepper
1.25 ml/¼ tsp ground mace
1 egg yolk
4 boneless chicken breasts, skinned
30 ml/2 tbsp oil
50 g/2 oz butter
2 shallots or ½ small onion, chopped
1 small carrot, diced
30 ml/2 tbsp plain flour
300 ml/½ pint chicken stock
1 bouquet garni
100 g/4 oz mushrooms, diced
4 fried bread croûtes to serve (optional)

Mix the breadcrumbs, lemon rind, salt, cayenne pepper and mace on a plate. Brush the egg yolk over the chicken portions, then coat them in the breadcrumb mixture. Heat the oil and half the butter in a frying pan and fry the chicken for about 15 minutes on each side, until golden and cooked through.

Meanwhile, heat the remaining butter in a small saucepan. Add the shallots or onion and carrot, then cook for 5 minutes. Stir in the flour, gradually stir in the stock and bring to the boil, stirring. Add the bouquet garni and mushrooms, cover and simmer for 20 minutes. Serve the chicken on bread croûtes, if used. Remove the bouquet garni and offer the sauce separately.

SERVES FOUR

HOT CHICKEN LIVER MOUSSES

fat for greasing
15 ml/1 tbsp butter
30 ml/2 tbsp plain flour
150 ml/¼ pint milk
salt and pepper
225 g/8 oz chicken livers, trimmed
1 egg, plus 1 yolk
5 ml/1 tsp Worcestershire sauce
45 ml/3 tbsp double cream
15 ml/1 tbsp dry sherry
30 ml/2 tbsp snipped chives

Grease four 150 ml/¼ pint ovenproof dishes. Set the oven at 180°C/350°F/gas 4. Combine the butter, flour and milk in a small saucepan. Whisk over moderate heat until the mixture comes to the boil. Lower the heat and simmer for 3–4 minutes, whisking constantly, until the sauce is thick, smooth and glossy. Add salt and pepper to taste. Cover the surface with buttered greaseproof paper and cool.

Purée the livers in a blender or food processor or put them through a mincer twice. Scrape the purée into a bowl and beat in the egg and egg yolk. Add the Worcestershire sauce, cream and dry sherry; stir in the sauce and chives.

Divide the liver mixture between the prepared dishes, place them in a deep baking tin and pour in enough boiling water to come halfway up the sides of the dishes. Bake for 25–30 minutes until a fine skewer inserted in the centre of one of the mousses comes out clean. Remove from the water and stand for 2–3 minutes before serving.

SERVES FOUR

MRS BEETON'S ROAST TURKEY

The recipe that follows is based upon a 6 kg/13 lb bird. Timings for birds of different weights are given in the introduction to this section, which also includes information on thawing frozen birds, tips for successful cooking and advice on carving.

fat for basting
1 turkey
450 g/1 lb Mrs Beeton's Forcemeat (page 475)
675 g/1½ lb seasoned sausagemeat
225 g/8 oz rindless streaky bacon rashers

Set the oven at 220°C/425°F/gas 7. Weigh the turkey. Trim it, and wash it inside and out in cold water. Pat dry with absorbent kitchen paper. Immediately before cooking, stuff the neck of the bird with forcemeat. Put the sausagemeat inside the body cavity. Cover the breast of the bird with the bacon rashers.

Place the prepared turkey in a roasting tin. Cover with foil and roast for 15 minutes. Lower the oven temperature to 180°C/350°F/gas 4 and roast for 20 minutes per 450 g/1 lb (unstuffed weight) plus 20 minutes, or until cooked through. Remove the foil for the last hour of cooking and the bacon strips for the final 20 minutes to allow the breast to brown.

Serve on a heated platter, with roasted or grilled chipolata sausages, bacon rolls (see page 194) and bread sauce.

SERVES FOURTEEN TO SIXTEEN

 MRS BEETON'S TIP

Lemons, cut in half and with all flesh and pulp removed, make ideal containers for individual portions of cranberry sauce. Arrange them around the turkey.

ROAST TURKEY WITH CHESTNUTS

1 (4.5–5.5 kg/10–12 lb) turkey
salt and pepper
225 g/8 oz rindless streaky bacon rashers

HERB FORCEMEAT
50 g/2 oz margarine
100 g/4 oz fresh white breadcrumbs
pinch of grated nutmeg
15 ml/1 tbsp chopped parsley
5 ml/1 tsp chopped fresh mixed herbs
grated rind of ½ lemon
salt and pepper
1 egg, beaten

CHESTNUT STUFFING
1 kg/2¼ lb chestnuts
275 ml/9 fl oz turkey or chicken stock
50 g/2 oz butter
1 egg, beaten
single cream or milk (see method)

Make the chestnut stuffing first. Shell and skin the chestnuts (see Mrs Beeton's Tip, page 197). Put them in a saucepan, add the stock and simmer for 20 minutes or until tender. Drain the chestnuts and chop them finely, or press through a sieve into a clean bowl. Melt the butter in a small saucepan. Remove from the heat and add to the bowl containing the chestnuts. Stir in the beaten egg, with enough cream or milk to moisten the mixture.

Make the forcemeat. Melt the margarine in a small saucepan. Add the breadcrumbs, nutmeg, herbs and lemon rind. Stir in salt and pepper to taste and sufficient beaten egg to bind the mixture.

Set the oven at 180°C/350°F/gas 4. Trim the turkey and wash it inside and out in cold water. Pat dry with absorbent kitchen paper and season inside with salt and pepper. Immediately before cooking, fill the neck end of the bird with chestnut stuffing and the body with the forcemeat. Truss if wished, and cover the bird with the bacon.

Place the bird in a roasting tin and roast for 4½–5 hours or until cooked through, removing the bacon towards the end to allow the breast to brown. (For a larger bird, see the chart on page 258 for cooking times.) Serve with giblet gravy.

SERVES FOURTEEN TO SIXTEEN

IDEAS FOR LEFTOVER ROAST TURKEY

Hashed Turkey Make stock from turkey bones and trimmings, a sliced carrot, a diced turnip, a blade of mace and a bouquet garni. Cover with water and simmer for 1 hour. Strain. Cook 1 chopped onion in a knob of butter. Add 40 g/1½ oz plain flour and cook for 2 minutes. Pour in 600 ml/1 pint strained stock and bring to the boil. Add 30 ml/2 tbsp mushroom ketchup, 45 ml/3 tbsp port or sherry and salt and pepper. Gently poach sliced cooked turkey in the sauce, adding any leftover stuffing cut in neat portions, for 15 minutes until thoroughly heated.

Turkey Croquettes Mince or finely chop cooked turkey – this is ideal for dark meat and small pieces which do not slice well. For every 225 g/8 oz turkey, allow 50 g/2 oz diced or minced cooked ham and ½ small finely chopped onion. Cook the onion in a little butter, stir in 15 ml/1 tbsp plain flour and 150 ml/¼ pint turkey gravy or stock. Bring to the boil. Off the heat add the turkey, ham, 1 egg yolk and plenty of seasoning. Cool, then chill. Shape the mixture into croquettes. Coat in flour, egg and breadcrumbs, then deep or shallow fry until golden. Originally, the mixture was shaped into small mounds by pressing it into a small, greased wine glass before coating.

TURKEY WITH WALNUTS

Serve this nutty, Oriental-style turkey dish with plain cooked rice and a fresh green salad topped with diced avocado.

60 ml/4 tbsp cooking oil
225 g/8 oz shelled walnuts, roughly chopped
4 thick turkey fillets, skinned and diced
15 ml/1 tbsp cornflour
pinch of salt
pinch of sugar
45 ml/3 tbsp soy sauce
45 ml/3 tbsp dry sherry
100 g/4 oz button mushrooms, sliced

Heat the oil in a heavy-bottomed frying pan, add the walnuts and fry for 2–3 minutes until browned. Using a slotted spoon, remove them from the pan and drain well on absorbent kitchen paper.

Add the diced turkey to the oil remaining in the pan. Fry, stirring gently, until pale golden and cooked. Mix the cornflour, salt, sugar, soy sauce and sherry to a smooth paste in a small bowl. Stir in 30 ml/2 tbsp water and pour the mixture into the pan; add the mushrooms.

Cook the mixture, stirring, over moderate heat until the sauce boils. Simmer for 2–3 minutes, stirring frequently to prevent the mixture from sticking to the base of the pan. Remove from the heat, stir in the walnuts and serve at once.

SERVES FOUR

TURKEY LOAF

fat for greasing
50 g/2 oz long-grain rice
225 g/8 oz cooked turkey meat
4 rindless streaky bacon rashers
salt and pepper
1 onion, finely chopped
about 50 ml/2 fl oz turkey or chicken stock
grated rind and juice of ½ lemon
50 g/2 oz fresh white breadcrumbs
2.5 ml/½ tsp chopped fresh thyme
5 ml/1 tsp chopped parsley
15 ml/1 tbsp milk

Grease a 450 g/1 lb loaf tin. Set the oven at 190°C/375°F/gas 5. Cook the rice in a saucepan of boiling salted water for 20 minutes, then drain and set aside.

Mince the turkey meat with the bacon. Put the mixture in a bowl and add plenty of salt and pepper. Stir in the onion, stock, lemon rind and rice.

In a separate bowl, mix the breadcrumbs, thyme, parsley and lemon juice. Add a little salt and pepper and mix in the milk to bind this stuffing.

Put half the turkey mixture in the prepared tin, spread with the stuffing, then cover with the remaining turkey mixture. Bake for about 35 minutes, until firm and browned on top. Turn out and serve hot or cold.

SERVES SIX TO EIGHT

TURKEY AND CHIPOLATA HOTPOT

This is an excellent way of using up leftovers from a roast turkey. Cooked chicken may be used instead of turkey and the chipolatas will extend a small amount of meat to serve four.

15 ml/1 tbsp oil
225 g/8 oz cocktail or chipolata sausages
1 onion, halved and sliced
2 carrots, diced
2 parsnips, diced
1 bay leaf
5 ml/1 tsp dried sage
45 ml/3 tbsp plain flour
300 ml/½ pint medium cider
300 ml/½ pint turkey or chicken stock
350 g/12 oz cooked turkey, diced
salt and pepper
100 g/4 oz frozen peas

Heat the oil in a large flameproof casserole until it runs easily over the base. Add the cocktail sausages or chipolatas and turn them in the oil. Sprinkle the onion into the pan and cook, turning occasionally, until the sausages are evenly and lightly browned but not necessarily cooked through.

Add the carrots, parsnips, bay leaf and sage to the casserole. Cover and cook gently for 15 minutes. Stir in the flour, then gradually stir in the cider and stock and bring to the boil. Add the turkey, with salt and pepper to taste, then cover and simmer for 10 minutes, or until the vegetables are tender.

Stir in the peas, replace the cover and simmer for a further 10-15 minutes, until the vegetables are all tender. Taste and adjust the seasoning before serving. If using chipolatas, cut them into bite-sized chunks.

SERVES FOUR

ENGLISH ROAST DUCK

fat for basting
Sage and Onion Stuffing (page 474)
1 (1.8 kg/4 lb) oven-ready duck
salt and pepper
30 ml/2 tbsp plain flour
300 ml/½ pint duck or chicken stock (see
    Mrs Beeton's Tip)

Set the oven at 190°C/375°F/gas 5. Spoon the stuffing into the duck and truss it. Weigh the duck and calculate the cooking time at 20 minutes per 450 g/1 lb. Sprinkle the breast with salt. Put the duck on a wire rack in a roasting tin and prick the skin all over with a fork or skewer to release the fat. Roast for the required time, basting the duck occasionally with the pan juices and pouring away the excess fat as necessary. Test by piercing the thickest part of the thigh with the point of a sharp knife. The juices should run clear.

Transfer the duck to a heated platter, remove the trussing string and keep hot. Pour off most of the fat from the roasting tin, sprinkle in the flour and cook, stirring, for 2 minutes. Blend in the stock. Bring to the boil, then lower the heat and simmer, stirring, for 3-4 minutes. Add salt and pepper to taste. Serve in a gravyboat, with the duck.

SERVES FOUR

 MRS BEETON'S TIP

If you have the duck giblets, use them as the basis of your stock. Put them in a saucepan with 1 sliced onion and 1 sliced carrot. Add 600 ml/1 pint water. Simmer, covered, for 1 hour, then strain.

DUCK WITH ORANGE SAUCE

1 (1.6–1.8 kg/3½–4 lb) oven-ready duck
salt and pepper
5 oranges
15 ml/1 tbsp caster sugar
15 ml/1 tbsp white wine vinegar
30 ml/2 tbsp brandy
15 ml/1 tbsp plain flour

Set the oven at 190°C/375°F/gas 5. Weigh the duck and calculate the cooking time at 20 minutes per 450 g/1 lb. Sprinkle the breast with salt. Put the duck on a wire rack in a roasting tin and prick the skin all over with a fork or skewer to release the fat. Roast for the required time, basting the duck occasionally with the pan juices and pouring away the excess fat as necessary.

Meanwhile, thinly peel the rind from one of the oranges, taking care not to include any of the bitter pith. Cut the rind into strips, then cook these in boiling water for 1 minute. Drain and set aside on absorbent kitchen paper. Slice one of the remaining oranges and set the slices aside for the garnish. Squeeze the rest of the oranges, including the one with the rind removed, and set the juice aside.

Put the sugar in a saucepan with the vinegar. Heat gently, stirring until the sugar has dissolved, then bring to the boil and boil rapidly without stirring until the syrup turns a golden caramel colour. Remove from the heat and carefully add the orange juice and brandy. Return to the heat and stir until just blended, then add the blanched orange rind strips.

When the duck is cooked, transfer it to a platter, remove the trussing string and cut it into serving portions. Transfer to a heated serving dish and keep hot. Pour off the fat from the roasting tin, sprinkle in the flour and cook, stirring, for 2 minutes. Blend in the orange mixture. Bring to the boil, then lower the heat and simmer, stirring, for 3–4 minutes. Add the salt and pepper to taste. Spoon the sauce over the duck, garnish with the reserved orange slices and serve.

SERVES FOUR

SALMIS OF DUCK

1 (2.25 kg/5 lb) duck
1 Spanish onion, sliced
1 carrot, quartered
25 g/1 oz butter
25 g/1 oz plain flour
350 ml/12 fl oz well-flavoured duck or
   chicken stock
150 ml/¼ pint burgundy
12 stoned green olives
salt and pepper

Set the oven at 200°C/400°F/gas 6. Prick the duck all over with a fork. Spread the onion slices on the base of a roasting tin, add the carrot quarters and put the duck on top. Roast for 1–1½ hours or until tender. Cut the duck into portions and keep hot. Discard the vegetables.

Pour off the fat from the roasting tin, add the butter and melt over gentle heat. Stir in the flour and cook for 1 minute, then gradually add the stock and wine, stirring until the sauce boils and thickens. Stir in the olives, with salt and pepper to taste.

Return the duck to the sauce and heat through gently for 10–15 minutes, stirring frequently. Serve at once. Potato croquettes and broccoli would be suitable accompaniments.

SERVES FOUR

FILLETS OF DUCK WITH RICH CHERRY DRESSING

Creamy mashed potatoes or plain cooked noodles and crisp, lightly cooked green beans are suitable accompaniments for this simple, yet rich dish.

4 boneless duck breasts
salt and pepper
2.5 ml/½ tsp ground mace
4 bay leaves
4 fresh thyme sprigs
125 ml/4 fl oz red wine
60 ml/4 tbsp port
25 g/1 oz butter
15 ml/1 tbsp finely chopped onion
225 g/8 oz cherries, stoned
5 ml/1 tsp grated lemon rind
10 ml/2 tsp arrowroot

Prick the skin on the duck breasts all over, or remove it, if preferred. Rub plenty of salt, pepper and mace into the breasts, then place them in a shallow dish, skin uppermost, with a bay leaf and thyme sprig under each. Pour the wine and port over the duck, cover and allow to marinate for at least 2 hours; it may be chilled overnight.

Melt the butter in a frying pan and add the onion with the herbs from the duck. Cook over low heat for 5 minutes. Meanwhile, drain the duck breasts, reserving the marinade. Place them skin down in the pan and increase the heat to moderate. Cook until the skin is well browned, then turn the breasts and cook the second side. Allow about 15 minutes on each side to cook the duck breasts.

Using a slotted spoon, transfer the cooked duck to a heated serving dish or individual plates. Keep hot. Leaving the herbs in the pan, add the cherries and lemon rind. Toss the cherries in the cooking juices for about a minute, until the heat causes them to begin to change colour.

Pour in the reserved marinade and heat gently until just boiling. While the sauce is heating, put the arrowroot in a cup and blend to a paste with 15–30 ml/1–2 tbsp cold water. Add it to the pan, stirring. Bring to the boil and remove the pan from the heat.

Discard the thyme sprigs but arrange the bay leaves on the duck. Use a slotted spoon to divide the cherries between the duck breasts, then pour the sauce over and serve at once.

SERVES FOUR

VARIATION

Fillets of Duck Bigarade   Cut the pared rind from 1 Seville orange into fine strips and simmer these in water until tender; drain and set aside. Marinate the duck as above, adding the juice of the orange but omitting the port. Continue as above, stirring 30 ml/2 tbsp plain flour into the cooking juices from the duck, then add 250 ml/8 fl oz duck or chicken stock and 5 ml/1 tsp tomato purée. Bring to the boil, stirring, then add the reserved marinade. Lower the heat and simmer rapidly for 10 minutes. Stir in the juice of ½ lemon and 5 ml/1 tsp redcurrant jelly. Taste for seasoning and pour over the duck.

 MRS BEETON'S TIP

For presentation purposes, cut each cooked duck fillet across into thick slices. Separate the slices slightly on individual plates before finishing with bay leaves, cherries and sauce.

DUCK AND ORANGE CURRY

1 (2.25 kg/5 lb) duck, jointed
salt
30 ml/2 tbsp ghee, clarified butter (page 424)
   or oil
2 large onions, chopped
2 garlic cloves, crushed
2.5 ml/½ tsp cardamom seeds
10 ml/2 tsp finely grated fresh root ginger
5 ml/1 tsp ground cumin
5 ml/1 tsp turmeric
10 ml/2 tsp ground coriander
5 cm/2 inch cinnamon stick
6 cloves
750 ml/1¼ pints unsweetened orange juice

Sprinkle the duck generously with salt. Heat the ghee, fat or oil in a large deep frying pan, add the duck and fry over moderate heat for 15-20 minutes, turning frequently. Using tongs, transfer the duck portions to a plate and set aside.

Add the onions and garlic to the fat remaining in the pan and fry for 4-6 minutes until transparent. Add the spices and fry for 2-3 minutes, stirring constantly, then pour in the juice. Bring to the boil, stirring.

Replace the duck in the pan, cover and simmer for 1¼-1½ hours. Add a little salt if required. Serve with rice.

SERVES FOUR

 MRS BEETON'S TIP

Cardamom seeds are the tiny black seeds found inside the pale green pods. Slit each pod with the point of a knife, holding it over a small bowl, then scrape out the seeds.

DUCK ON CROUTES

50 g/2 oz butter
2 onions, finely chopped
25 g/1 oz plain flour
600 ml/1 pint well-flavoured stock
2 cloves
1 blade of mace
6 allspice berries
6 small mushrooms
salt and pepper
350 g/12 oz cold roast duck, cut into neat
   pieces
oil for shallow frying
8 rounds of bread, crusts removed
Apple Sauce (page 490), to serve

Melt the butter in a saucepan, add the onions and fry until lightly browned. Stir in the flour and cook slowly until nut brown, then add the stock. Bring to the boil, stirring constantly, then lower the heat and simmer for 10 minutes.

Tie the spices in muslin and add with the mushrooms to the pan. Stir in salt and pepper to taste. Add the duck pieces to the sauce, then simmer gently for 20 minutes.

Just before serving, make the croûtes. Heat the oil in a large frying pan. Add the rounds of bread and fry quickly until golden on both sides. Remove from the heat, drain on absorbent kitchen paper and arrange the croutes on four heated plates.

Arrange the pieces of duck on the croûtes, discarding the spices from the sauce. Spoon the remaining sauce over the duck. Serve the apple sauce separately.

SERVES FOUR

ROAST GOOSE WITH FRUIT STUFFING AND RED CABBAGE

1 goose with giblets
½ lemon
salt and pepper
350 g/12 oz prunes, soaked overnight in
  water to cover
450 g/1 lb cooking apples
15 ml/1 tbsp redcurrant jelly

RED CABBAGE
50 g/2 oz butter
1.5 kg/3¼ lb red cabbage, finely shredded
50 g/2 oz demerara sugar
75 ml/5 tbsp malt or cider vinegar
salt and pepper

Remove the giblets from the goose and put them in a saucepan. Add 1.5 litres/2¾ pints water and bring to the boil. Lower the heat and simmer until the liquid is reduced by half. Strain and set aside.

Set the oven at 230°C/450°F/gas 8. Weigh the goose and calculate the cooking time at 20 minutes per 450 g/1 lb. Remove the excess fat usually found around the vent. Rinse the inside of the bird, then rub the skin with lemon. Season with salt and pepper.

Drain the prunes, remove the stones and roughly chop the flesh. Put it in a bowl. Peel, core and chop the apples. Add them to the prunes, with salt and pepper to taste. Use the mixture to stuff the body of the bird. Put the goose on a rack in a roasting tin. Place in the oven, immediately lower the temperature to 180°C/350°F/gas 4 and cook for the calculated time. Drain away fat from the roasting tin occasionally during cooking.

Meanwhile, melt the butter in a large flame-proof casserole, add the red cabbage and sugar and stir well. Pour in 75 ml/5 tbsp water and the vinegar, with salt and pepper to taste. Cover and cook in the oven for about 2 hours, stirring occasionally.

When the goose is cooked, transfer it to a heated serving platter and keep hot. Drain off the excess fat from the roasting tin, retaining the juices. Stir in the reserved giblet stock and cook over fairly high heat until reduced to a thin gravy. Stir in the redcurrant jelly until melted. Serve the gravy and red cabbage separately.

SERVES SIX TO EIGHT

DUCK AND RED CABBAGE

The trimmings from two roast ducks should yield enough meat for this flavoursome dish.

50 g/2 oz butter
450 g/1 lb red cabbage, shredded
salt and pepper
well-flavoured stock (see method)
about 400 g/14 oz cold roast duck, shredded
15 ml/1 tbsp red wine vinegar
15 ml/1 tbsp demerara sugar

Melt the butter in a heavy-bottomed saucepan and add the red cabbage. Stir lightly to coat the cabbage in butter, then add salt and pepper. Cover the pan tightly and simmer for 1 hour. Shake the pan from time to time to prevent the cabbage from sticking to the base, and add just enough stock to prevent it from burning.

In another pan, combine the duck with enough stock to moisten. Place over gentle heat until the duck is heated through. Add the vinegar and sugar to the cabbage, mix well, then turn on to a heated dish. Drain the duck and arrange it on the top. Serve with a mixture of brown rice and wild rice, if liked.

SERVES FOUR TO SIX

ROAST GOOSE WITH APPLES AND ONIONS

1 goose with giblets
salt and pepper
1 orange
1 lemon
13 small onions
7 bay leaves
1 large fresh thyme sprig
30 ml/2 tbsp dried sage
1 cinnamon stick
4 cloves
50 g/2 oz butter
12 Cox's Orange Pippin apples
5 ml/1 tsp lemon juice
45 ml/3 tbsp port
45 ml/3 tbsp crab apple or redcurrant jelly
25 g/1 oz plain flour

Remove the giblets from the goose and put them in a saucepan. Add 1.5 litres/2¾ pints water and bring to the boil. Lower the heat and simmer until the liquid is reduced by half. Strain and set aside.

Set the oven at 230°C/450°F/gas 8. Weigh the goose and calculate the cooking time at 20 minutes per 450 g/1 lb. Trim away excess fat and rinse the bird, then rub it all over with plenty of salt and pepper. Pare the rind from the fruit and place it in the body cavity with 1 onion, 2 bay leaves and the thyme sprig. Rub the sage over the outside of the bird and tuck a bay leaf behind each of the wing and leg joints.

Place the goose on a rack in a roasting tin. Place it in the oven and immediately reduce the heat to 180°C/350°F/gas 4. Cook for the calculated time, draining away fat from the roasting tin occasionally.

Peel the remaining onions but leave them whole. Place them in a saucepan and pour in boiling water to cover. Add a little salt. Simmer for 15 minutes, then drain well. Squeeze the juice from the orange and lemon, and mix together in a small saucepan. Add the cinnamon, cloves and remaining bay leaf, then heat gently until simmering. Cover and cook for 15 minutes. Off the heat, stir in the butter.

Peel and core the apples. As each apple is prepared, place it in a bowl of iced water to which the lemon juice has been added. This will prevent discoloration. Drain the apples, put them in an ovenproof dish and spoon the fruit juice and spice mixture over them to coat them completely. Add the onions, then toss them with the apples so all are coated in juices.

Place the dish of apples and onions in the oven 1 hour before the goose is cooked. Turn them occasionally during cooking so that they are evenly browned and tender. About 10 minutes before the goose is cooked, heat the port and jelly gently in a saucepan or in a bowl in the microwave until the jelly has melted. Spoon this over the apple and onion mixture for the final 5 minutes.

When the goose is cooked, transfer it to a heated serving platter and keep hot. Drain off the fat from the tin. Stir the flour into the cooking juices and cook over low heat for 5 minutes, scraping in all the sediment from the base of the pan. Pour in the reserved giblet stock and bring to the boil, stirring all the time. Taste for seasoning and pour or strain into a sauceboat.

Serve the goose surrounded by the glazed apples and onions, with their juices.

SERVES SIX (with meat to spare, depending on the size of the goose)

GUINEAFOWL WITH GRAPES

The guineafowl may be stuffed with Wild Rice Stuffing (page 475), if liked. Select the longer cooking time. Guineafowl is a farmed bird which is hung to give a mild, game-like flavour.

1 guineafowl with giblets
1 bouquet garni
salt and pepper
50 g/2 oz butter
1 parsley sprig
6 rindless streaky bacon rashers
30 ml/2 tbsp plain flour
125 ml/4 fl oz dry white wine
225 g/8 oz seedless white grapes
lemon juice (see method)

GARNISH
filled lemon cups (see Mrs Beeton's Tip,
   page 278) seedless red grapes or
   redcurrant jelly

Put the guineafowl giblets in a saucepan. Add 250 ml/8 fl oz water, the bouquet garni, salt and pepper. Bring to the boil, lower the heat and simmer for 40 minutes to make a good stock. Strain the stock and reserve 150 ml/¼ pint.

Set the oven at 180°C/350°F/gas 4. Put a knob of butter and the parsley inside the bird; spread the rest of the butter over the breast. Cover with the bacon.

Put the bird in a roasting tin and roast for 1-1½ hours, basting frequently. Remove the bacon rashers for the last 15 minutes to allow the breast to brown.

Remove the guineafowl from the roasting tin. Cut it into neat serving portions, arrange on a heated serving dish and keep hot. Drain the fat from the tin, leaving just sufficient to absorb the flour. Sprinkle the flour into the tin and brown it lightly. Stir in the wine and reserved stock. Bring the gravy to the boil, stirring constantly, then add the grapes. Add a little lemon juice to bring out the flavour and heat through, stirring all the time. Taste the sauce and add more salt and pepper if required. Pour the sauce over the guineafowl. Garnish with lemon cups filled with small red seedless grapes or redcurrant jelly and serve.

SERVES THREE TO FOUR

ROAST GUINEAFOWL

50 g/2 oz butter
salt and pepper
1 guineafowl
2 rindless fat bacon rashers
flour for dredging

GARNISH
watercress sprigs
130 ml/2 tbsp French Dressing

Set the oven at 180°C/350°F/gas 4. Mix the butter in a small bowl with plenty of salt and pepper. Put most of the seasoned butter inside the body of the bird. Spread the rest on the thighs. Lay the bacon rashers over the breast.

Put the bird in a roasting tin and roast for 1-1½ hours or until cooked through, basting frequently. When the bird is almost cooked, remove the bacon rashers, dredge the breast with flour, baste with the juices and finish cooking.

Wash and dry the watercress. Put it in a bowl, add about 30 ml/2 tbsp French dressing and toss lightly. Remove any trussing strings from the bird, place it on a serving dish and garnish.

SERVES TWO TO THREE

POULTRY PILAU

350g/12oz basmati rice
50g/2oz butter
4 boneless poultry breast fillets, skinned
6 cardamoms
4 cloves
15ml/1 tbsp coriander seeds, crushed
15ml/1 tbsp allspice berries, crushed
1 cinnamon stick
1 blade of mace
salt and pepper
1.1 litres/2 pints chicken stock
15ml/1 tbsp oil
4 onions, thinly sliced
8 thin rindless bacon rashers
2 eggs, hard-boiled and quartered

Wash the basmati rice in several changes of water, then drain it in a sieve. Melt half the butter in a flameproof casserole or heavy-bottomed saucepan. Add the poultry breasts and brown them well all over. Sprinkle all the spices, salt and pepper around the poultry and cook for 2 minutes, then add the rice. Pour in the stock and bring to the boil. Reduce the heat, cover the pan tightly and cook the pilau gently for about 30 minutes, until the chicken is cooked and the stock is absorbed. Leave to stand, covered, off the heat for 5 minutes before removing the lid.

Meanwhile, melt the remaining butter with the oil in a large frying pan. Add the onions and a little salt and pepper. Then cook, turning the slices occasionally, until golden brown. Roll the bacon rashers and thread them on metal skewers. Cook under a hot grill until crisp and golden, then drain on absorbent kitchen paper.

Mound the cooked pilau on a heated serving dish. Top with the browned onions. Garnish with the bacon rolls and eggs.

SERVES FOUR

POULTRY WITH PEAS

350g/12oz cooked chicken, turkey, duck or
  goose, cut in neat pieces
salt and pepper
2.5ml/½ tsp ground mace
30ml/2 tbsp plain flour
50g/2oz butter or 25g/1oz butter and
  15ml/1 tbsp oil
300ml/½ pint poultry or giblet stock
450g/1lb shelled peas
5ml/1 tsp sugar

Place the poultry in a small bowl. Add plenty of salt and pepper, the mace and flour. Mix well. Melt the butter, or heat the butter and oil, in a heavy-bottomed saucepan. Add the poultry, reserving any flour in the bowl, and brown the pieces lightly.

Stir in any remaining flour, then gradually pour in the stock and bring to the boil, stirring. Add the peas, reduce the heat so that the sauce simmers and cover the pan. Cook for 20 minutes, until the peas are tender. Stir in the sugar and check the seasoning before serving.

SERVES FOUR

POULTRY FRITTERS

These fritters may be garnished with parsley and bacon rolls. Originally, gravy or a sauce may have been offered with them; however, they are best served with lemon wedges for their juice and a crisp salad to complement the rich batter.

225–350 g/8–12 oz cooked chicken, turkey,
   duck or goose, cut in neat pieces
salt
cayenne pepper
5 ml/1 tsp wine vinegar
2–3 shallots or ¼ onion, finely chopped
5 ml/1 tsp grated lemon rind
ground mace or grated nutmeg
oil for deep frying

BATTER
100 g/4 oz plain flour
25 g/1 oz butter, melted
1 egg white

Place the poultry in a bowl. Add plenty of salt, a pinch of cayenne, the vinegar, shallots or onion and a pinch of mace or a little grated nutmeg. Mix well, then leave to marinate for 1 hour.

Heat the oil for deep frying to 190°C/375°F or until a cube of bread browns in 30 seconds. To make the batter, sift the flour into a bowl. Stir in 200 ml/7 fl oz hand-hot water and the butter, then beat well until smooth. In a separate bowl, whisk the egg whites until stiff. Fold the whites into the batter.

Coat pieces of the marinated poultry in the batter, then deep fry them until crisp and golden. Very small offcuts may be cooked together to make bite-sized fritters. Drain on absorbent kitchen paper. Serve piping hot.

SERVES FOUR

POULTRY A LA BECHAMEL

If you have only a small amount of leftover roast poultry, add some sliced mushrooms or diced cooked ham to the sauce as well.

leftovers from a roast chicken or turkey, cut
   into neat pieces
600 ml/1 pint Béchamel Sauce (page 481)
salt and pepper
2 eggs, separated
25 g/1 oz butter, melted
60 ml/4 tbsp dried white breadcrumbs
30 ml/2 tbsp grated Parmesan cheese

Set the oven at 200°C/400°F/gas 6. Stir the poultry into the sauce and add salt and pepper to taste. Stir in the egg yolks and the butter, then turn the mixture into an ovenproof dish – a pie dish is ideal.

In a perfectly clean bowl, whisk the egg whites until stiff. Gently fold in the breadcrumbs and Parmesan cheese – do not be too fussy about thoroughly combining the ingredients, it is more important to retain air in the egg white.

Turn the egg white mixture out on top of the poultry in sauce and spread it out evenly. Bake for 20 minutes, until the topping is golden brown and the chicken mixture is thoroughly heated. Serve at once.

SERVES FOUR

GAME

Game refers to wild birds and animals which are hunted for sport as well as for food. The hunting, killing and selling of game is strictly controlled in Great Britain and the majority of game is protected by law, the exceptions being rabbits and woodpigeons.

There are certain times of the year when game cannot be shot and these 'seasons' vary slightly according to the nesting and mating patterns of the individual species. Outside of the season, not only is it illegal to kill game but it is also an offence to sell game: unless it has been imported into the country when already dead. Only licensed butchers and poulterers are allowed to deal in game and it can be offered for sale up to 10 days after the end of the season. The restrictions on the sale of home-reared game apply to frozen animals as well as to fresh ones. However, there are companies that specialize in importing game for out-of-season sale. Some game, notably venison, is now farmed. Certain birds must not be killed and these include wild geese, Garganey teal, Long-tailed duck and Scaup duck.

A note of the season for each type of game is given in the following pages, along with advice on identifying birds and the best cooking methods to use. In the section which follows, the details of preparing and cooking game are outlined; however you will find that game is readily available dressed for the oven, not only from specialist butchers but also from good supermarkets where it is often sold frozen.

CAPERCAILLIE

Season: October 1st to January 31st.

The capercaillie is a member of the grouse family, originating from Scandinavia. It is found today in small numbers in the northern areas of Scotland where it has been re-introduced following previous extinction from Britain. It is not a common game bird but when available it should be treated in the same way as grouse, and grouse can be substituted for it in recipes. This is a large bird which can weigh up to 4 kg/9 lb. It should be hung for 3-4 days, depending on conditions and personal preference.

GROUSE

Season: August 12th to December 10th.

In addition to the capercaillie (left) there are several other members of the grouse family, including the blackcock (also known as the heathpoult or black grouse) and the ptarmigan which comes from Europe and North America. However, the smaller Scottish grouse or red grouse (weighing about 675 g/1½ lb each) is considered to be the finest for flavour.

Young grouse shot early in the season are the most tender. They can be slightly tough at the beginning of December, just before the season ends. Look for birds with pointed flight feathers and soft pliable feet, also a downy breast. Hang for about 3-4 days, depending on conditions and preference. The young birds are ideal for roasting or grilling and the older ones can be casseroled. An average-sized grouse serves 1-2.

PARTRIDGE

Season: September 1st to February 1st.

This bird is related to the pheasant. There are two main varieties: the grey partridge which is the most common and considered to be the better bird and the red-legged, or French, partridge. When selecting birds, look for pliable, yellow-brown feet as they turn grey when the bird is older. The flight feathers should have pointed tips and the under feathers should be rounded. The beak of a young bird is fairly sharp. The best birds are obtained in October and November.

As a guide, partridges should be hung for about a week. Young birds can be roasted, older ones should be casseroled. It is usual to serve one partridge per person or one bird can be split before cooking to serve 2. The average weight for a partridge is 350-400 g/12-14 oz.

PHEASANT

Season: October 1st to February 1st.

The pheasant is probably the best known and most readily obtainable of the game birds. Pheasants are sold dressed, ready for the oven, or they can be purchased in the traditional brace, consisting of a male and female bird. The male bird is easily distinguished by its bright plumage but the hen pheasant is rather dull by comparison, with pale brown feathers. However, the hen pheasant is the most tender and has the best flavour; the cock pheasant can be rather dry and slightly tough.

When looking for a bird, notice the feet which should be fairly smooth on a young bird. They tend to become scaly in appearance as the pheasant ages. The breast of a young bird should still be downy. Pheasants can be hung for some time, anything from a few days to two weeks, but this is a matter of taste and a source of great controversy among gourmets and cooks alike. The best months for buying pheasant are November and December.

The younger birds or tender hen pheasants can be roasted but if they are older or likely to be tough, they should be braised or casseroled. An average weight for pheasant is about 1.4 kg/3 lb and the hen is smaller than the cock. A smaller bird will serve 3; a larger one can be made to serve 4, depending on the way in which it is prepared and served.

PIGEON

Season: Available all year.

There are two types of pigeon: the woodpigeon which is larger and has dark flesh and the stronger flavour, and the tame pigeon which has pale flesh and resembles young chicken more than game. The average weight for a pigeon is just over 450 g/1 lb and they are at their best from August to October. Look for birds with pink legs as they tend to be younger. Pigeons are best cooked by moist methods.

QUAIL

Season: Available all year.

Quail are protected by law in Britain and are not shot in the wild; however, they are farmed and are therefore available all year round, both fresh and frozen. They are very small birds, weighing about 150 g/5 oz, and are often sold – and served – in pairs.

They are tender and delicate in flavour and much esteemed by gourmets. Suitable for grilling or roasting, quails are not hung. They are usually cooked whole, without being drawn.

SNIPE

Season: August 12th to January 31st.

Small birds, not widely available in shops, and best killed when plump, in November. Related to woodcock, snipe live only in marshy land.

Weighing about 100g/4oz each, snipe are considered a delicacy. They are cooked whole, trussed with their long, pointed beaks skewered through their legs. Hang the birds for a few days, or up to a week. The gizzard can be removed before roasting or grilling. Serve 1 snipe per person.

WILD DUCK

Season: September 1st to January 31st.

There are many varieties of wild duck. The mallard is the most common and is also the largest. Other common varieties include the pintail, teal and widgeon; the teal being the smallest. The best months for wild duck are November and December. They should be eaten fresh, without hanging. A mallard will serve 2-3; the teal serves 1.

WOODCOCK

Season: October 1st to January 31st.

A relative of the snipe, the woodcock is found in woodland as well as marshy land. Seldom available in the shops, this bird is prized for its flavour. Weighing about 150g/5oz, serve 1 woodcock per person. Hang these birds for up to a week, then cook them by roasting or braising.

VENISON

Season: England and Wales

Red deer, stags: August 1st to April 30th.
   hinds: November 1st to February 28/29th.
Fallow deer, bucks: August 1st to April 30th.
   does: November 1st to April 30th.
Roe deer, bucks: April 1st to September 30th.
   does: November 1st to February 28/29th.

Scotland

Red deer, stags: July 1st to October 20th.
   hinds: October 21st to February 15th.
Fallow deer, bucks: August 1st to April 30th.
   does: October 21st to February 15th.
Roe deer, bucks: April 1st to October 20th.
   does: October 21st to March 31st.

The red deer is the largest and most splendid-looking beast; the meat of the roe deer is paler and the least gamey; and the fallow deer is considered to have the best flavour. The meat of any type should be fine-grained and dark, with firm white fat. Young animals or fawns up to 18 months old produce delicate meat which should not be marinated before cooking. The meat of the male is preferred to that of the female and older vension is usually marinated, larded or barded before cooking as it is dry.

Vension is always hung, otherwise it would have little flavour. The whole carcass is hung for 10-14 days, depending on the weather and the strength of flavour required. Small cuts need hanging for about a week; however, if you buy the meat from a butcher, it will have been hung in advance. If you prefer well-hung venison, ask your butcher if he advises hanging the meat for a while longer before cooking.

If you have fresh venison, inspect the meat thoroughly before hanging it. If there is any musty smell, the meat should be washed in lukewarm water and dried thoroughly. Rub the meat with a mixture of ground ginger and black pepper, then hang it in a cool, dry, well-ventilated place. Check the venison daily and wipe off any moisture. To test if the meat is ready, run a sharp knife into the flesh near the bone. If it smells very strong, cook the meat at once or wash it with warm milk and water, then dry it and cover it with plenty of ginger and pepper. Wash the spices off before cooking. Haunch, saddle and loin are the prime cuts for roasting, or they can be cut into cutlets or steaks for grilling. Shoulder is a fairly tender cut which can be roasted or braised. The neck and other pieces of meat are either stewed, minced or made into sausages. The fat should always be removed from venison before cooking as it has an unpleasant flavour.

HARE

Two types of hare are fairly common in Britain, the English or brown hare and the Scottish or blue hare; the brown hare is considered to have the best flavour. An animal under a year old is known as a leveret. It is distinguished by a small bony knot near the foot, a short neck, long joints, smooth sharp claws, a narrow cleft in its lip and soft ears.

Hare should be hung, whole, for 7–10 days, depending on the weather. It should hang from the back legs in a cool, dry, well-ventilated place. Catch its blood in a dish. Add one or two drops of vinegar to the blood to prevent clotting; store, covered, in the refrigerator.

The back, saddle and the hind legs can be roasted; the shoulders or forelegs are better cooked by braising or casseroling, or they can be jugged.

RABBIT

Wild and tame (farmed) rabbit are closely related but the difference in flavour is derived from the diet and habitat. The meat of wild rabbit is darker and it has a more gamey flavour.

Three-to-four-month-old rabbit is best, with thick foot joints, smooth claws, a flexible jaw

and soft ears. The eyes should be bright, the fat whitish and the liver bright red. Average weight is 2–2.25 kg/4½–5 lb but can be up to 4 kg/9 lb.

PREPARING AND COOKING GAME

All water birds should be eaten as fresh as possible but most other game birds of any size should be hung to tenderize the meat and to give the characteristic gamey flavour. Birds which are over-hung have a distinct greenish or blueish tinge to the skin. In this case they should be washed with salted water which contains a little vinegar, then rinsed.

ROASTING TIMES FOR GAME BIRDS

The following times are a guide for roasting unstuffed birds. For a small stuffed bird up to 375 g/13 oz in weight allow up to 10 minutes extra; for a larger stuffed bird allow between 15–18 minutes extra cooking time.

Blackcock 40–50 minutes
Grouse 25–30 minutes
Pheasant 45–60 minutes
Partridge 20–30 minutes
Teal 15–20 minutes
Widgeon 25–30 minutes
Pintail 20–30 minutes
Mallard 30–45 minutes
Tame pigeon 30–40 minutes
Squab 15–25 minutes
Woodpigeon 35–45 minutes
Other small birds 10–15 minutes

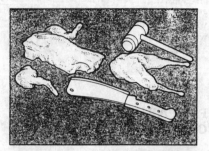

JOINTING HARE OR RABBIT

1 The head should be removed. Cut off each foreleg in one piece. Cut off the hind legs where they join on to the back (or saddle) of the animal. First cut straight across. You will need a heavy cook's knife and a mallet or rolling pin to tap the knife through the bones.

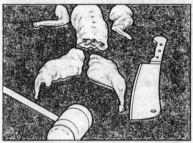

2 Cut between the hind legs to make two separate joints. The hind legs of rabbit are usually left whole unless they are to be used in a pie in which case they can be cut into two portions.

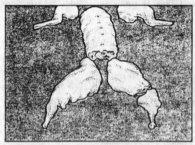

3 The hind legs of a hare should be split into thigh portions and lower leg portions, cutting through at the joint, again tapping the knife through the bones if necessary.

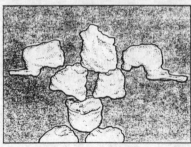

4 Separate the rib cage from the saddle, cutting through the spine as before, about a third of the way down the back. Cut the saddle across to give two joints. The front joint from the saddle can be chopped in half lengthways to split it into two joints.

LARDING VENISON

Larding is the term used for threading strips of fat through meat before cooking. The fat is cut from belly of pork in neat slices, then the slices are cut into strips. A special larding needle is available, with a grip to hold a strip of fat at one end. Larding is used for very lean cuts of meat that tend to become dry on cooking. The strips of fat moisten the meat as it cooks.

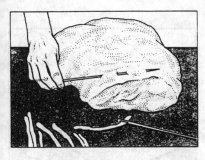

1 Cut neat strips of fat: they do not have to be too long but they should be fairly even in thickness. Larding is made easier if a fine skewer is first used to pierce the meat; this helps to prevent the fat from breaking as you pull it through with the larding needle. Pierce the meat as though sewing running stitches, inserting a fine skewer, then pushing it out about 2.5-5 cm/1-2 inches along.

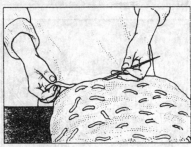

2 Put a piece of fat in the larding needle, then thread it through the meat, following the line cut by the skewer. Leave a short piece of fat protruding at each end of the stitch, then continue to lard the piece of meat all over, keeping the spaces between the fat even.

🥄 **MRS BEETON'S TIP**

The process of larding meat is not a difficult one but it is time-consuming. The fat should be evenly cut into narrow strips measuring about 5 mm/¼ inch wide and up to 5 cm/2 inches long. Larding bacon is specially prepared without saltpetre but pork fat can be used. Pierce and lard a small area at a time, working in a methodical pattern over the joint.

PREPARING A HAUNCH OF VENISON FOR COOKING

A haunch of venison can be boned out completely, then tied neatly in place before cooking. The butcher will usually do this for you but should you want to attempt the task yourself, it is not very difficult but it is time-consuming. You will need a very sharp pointed knife.

1 If the butcher has not already done so, chop off the bone end close to the meat and pull away any tendons. Trim all fat off the meat, cutting it away thinly using a sharp knife.

2 Once the meat is trimmed it should be larded, then marinated. Recipes for suitable marinades are in the chapter on Salad Dressings, Marinades, Stuffings and Savoury Sauces. Place the joint in a suitable dish, one which is large enough to hold the venison and deep enough to hold the marinade. A large gratin dish, lasagne dish or similar is ideal. During marinating the meat should be turned frequently and basted.

Start from the wide end, cutting the meat off the bone. Work very closely to the bone, easing the meat away with your fingers. Alternatively, split the haunch down one side, then cut out the bone.

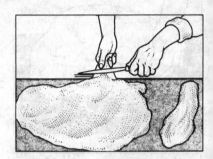

ROASTING TIMES FOR VENISON

The following is a guide to cooking at 180°C/350°F/gas 4. Allow 15 minutes per 450g/1 lb for large joints. Increase the time to 20 minutes per 450g/1 lb for smaller joints weighing 1.5 kg/3¼ lb or less.

CARVING GAME

CARVING HARE OR RABBIT

1 Carve the hare before arranging it on a plate for serving. Make short cuts across the spine in two or three places, then cut through down the length of the spine, from head to tail.

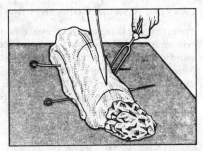

2 Cut across the spine towards the hind-quarters, then cut between the legs to make two serving portions. This releases any stuffing in the body cavity and it can be scooped out at this stage.

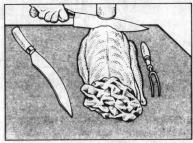

3 Divide the thigh and lower leg from the body meat to cut each of the two hind portions into two separate pieces.

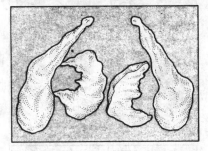

4 Cut across the spine just behind the shoulders to separate the saddle from the forequarters. The saddle can be cut across into two or three portions. Cut off the head and cut forelegs into two further portions if preferred.

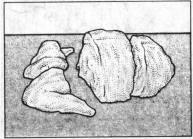

CARVING A SADDLE OF VENISON

The easiest way to prepare and serve saddle of venison is to ask the butcher for a boned and rolled joint which will include the tender fillet. Boned and rolled joints can be obtained in a variety of sizes, to cater for individual requirements. However, joints on the bone tend to be far larger and they may have the fillets left on. The fillets should be cut off in one piece and sliced. A rolled joint can be cut across into thick slices. The following steps are a guide to the more difficult process of carving the whole, unboned, saddle joint.

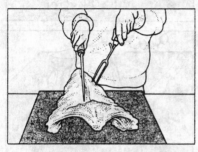

1 First carve the meat off the top, or loin, of the saddle. Starting in the middle to one side of the bone, cut downwards as near to the bone as possible.

2 The next cut should be at a slight angle but down to meet the base of the first cut and release the first slice of meat.

3 When one slice has been removed the carving is simplified and the rest of the same side of the haunch should be carved in neat, long slices. Carve the opposite side of the saddle in the same way.

4 If the fillets were not removed before cooking, remove each in one piece: to do this, first slice down as near to the bone as possible, then cut outwards from the base to remove the fillet in one piece. Remove the fillet from the second side in the same way.

5 Cut the fillets into neat slices and serve them with the long slices taken from the top of the saddle.

CARVING A HAUNCH OF VENISON

A haunch of venison on the bone is not as difficult to carve as a saddle joint. The meat is taken off the sides, working on both sides of the joint to cut away large, even slices. The remaining small pieces of meat can be sliced off in small pieces but these are not prime portions. A boned haunch can be cut across into slices. Venison differs from beef in that the meat should be cut into fairly thick slices.

1 Holding the joint firmly by the bone end, cut neat slices off one side, then turn the leg slightly to carve the meat off the other side. The remaining meat can be cut off in small slices.

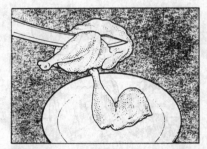

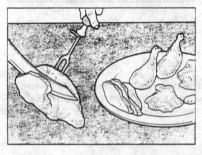

CARVING ROAST PHEASANT

1 Remove the legs by cutting between the breast and the point where the legs join the body. The bones should be cleanly cut and a pair of stout kitchen scissors may be useful. The legs can be cut into 2 portions, the thigh and the lower leg, although they are best left whole.

2 Next the wings should be removed, cutting them off close to the body and again using a pair of kitchen scissors to snip through awkward bones.

3 Lastly the breast meat should be carved off, first one side, then the other. Cut the meat into neat, even slices, as thinly as possible.

ACCOMPANIMENTS FOR GAME

The traditional accompaniments for roast game are the same for all types.
- Fried breadcrumbs may be served with large birds. Small to medium birds may be served on a croûte of fried bread.
- Thin gravy or giblet gravy.
- Bread Sauce (page 588) for grouse, pheasant and partridge.

- Sharp fruit jelly such as redcurrant or crab apple jelly.
- Watercress sprigs for garnish.
- Green vegetables, particularly Brussels sprouts, or a crisp salad.
- Game chips. These are made by thinly slicing potatoes, rinsing and patting dry, then frying in hot deep fat until golden. Before serving, drain game chips thoroughly on absorbent kitchen paper.

HIGHLAND GROUSE

The availability of frozen raspberries allows for this dish to be prepared while grouse is in season – even if the fresh fruit is long finished.

50 g/2 oz butter
2 young grouse
salt and pepper
225 g/8 oz raspberries
grated rind of 1 lemon

GARNISH
whole raspberries (optional)
herb sprigs or watercress

Set the oven at 200°C/400°F/gas 6. Place half the butter inside each bird and sprinkle well with salt and pepper. Mix the raspberries and lemon rind together in a bowl and fill the cavities in the birds with the mixture. Put 5 mm/¼ inch water in a deep ovenproof dish with a lid which will just hold the birds. Place the birds and any remaining raspberry mixture in the dish, and cover. Cook for 35-45 minutes. Remove the lid and cook for a further 10 minutes, to brown the birds.

Serve with creamed potatoes and a green vegetable. Garnish with a few whole raspberries and herb sprigs or watercress.

SERVES FOUR

NORMANDY PARTRIDGES

Serve simple, but interesting, vegetables to accompany this old-fashioned French dish. Tiny scrubbed potatoes, baked in their jackets, lightly steamed French beans and carrots cut into thin julienne strips are all ideal.

100 g/4 oz unsalted butter
2 young partridges
salt and pepper
2 rindless streaky bacon rashers
675 g/1½ lb eating apples
125 ml/4 fl oz double cream
30 ml/2 tbsp Calvados or brandy
chopped parsley to garnish

Set the oven at 180°C/350°F/gas 4. Heat half the butter in a flameproof casserole, add the partridges and brown them on all sides. Sprinkle with salt and pepper. Place a bacon rasher on each bird's breast. Peel, core and cut the apples into wedges. Melt the remaining butter in a frying pan, add the apples and cover the pan. Cook gently for 5 minutes, then add to the casserole.

Cook in the oven for 20-30 minutes. Transfer the partridges and apples to a hot serving dish.

Mix the cream and the Calvados or brandy, then add salt and pepper to taste. Heat the mixture over a low heat, stirring well, and taking great care that the mixture does not boil. Pour this sauce over the partridges and apples, and sprinkle with chopped parsley before serving.

SERVES TWO

 MRS BEETON'S TIP

Calvados is a French brandy made by distilling cider. It is a speciality of the Pays d'Auge.

RAISED PHEASANT PIE

450 g/1 lb plain flour
2.5 ml/½ tsp salt
225 g/8 oz butter or margarine
2 egg yolks
1 hen pheasant, boned (see page 188)
  carcass retained
grated nutmeg
1.25 ml/¼ tsp ground allspice
salt and pepper
2 quantities Mrs Beeton's Forcemeat (page
  475)
2 veal escalopes
1 thick slice of cooked ham (about
  50–75 g/2–3 oz)
beaten egg for glazing
1 small onion, quartered
1 bay leaf
1 carrot, quartered lengthways
10 ml/2 tsp gelatine

To make the pastry, mix the flour and salt in a large bowl. Add the butter or margarine and rub it into the flour until the mixture resembles fine breadcrumbs. Make a well in the middle and add the egg yolks with about 60 ml/4 tbsp water. Mix the pastry to a smooth, fairly soft dough, adding extra water as necessary. The pastry should have a little more water than ordinary short crust dough but it must not be sticky.

Set the oven at 160°C/325°F/gas 3. Grease a 23 cm/9 inch raised pie mould with a little oil and place it on a baking sheet. Set aside one-third of the pastry for the lid, then roll out the remainder into an oblong shape, about twice the size of the top of the mould. Do not be tempted to roll the pastry out into a sheet large enough to completely line the mould as it may break when you lift it into the mould. Carefully lift the pastry into the mould, then use the back of your fingers and knuckles to press it into the base of the mould, smoothing it up the sides to line the mould completely. Take plenty of time to ensure that the mould is well lined with pastry and that there are no breaks in the lining.

Open out the pheasant and sprinkle it with a little nutmeg, the allspice, salt and pepper. Set aside half the forcemeat, then divide the remainder into two portions. Spread one portion over the middle of the pheasant and lay the veal escalopes on top. Lay the cooked ham on top of the veal, then spread the second portion of forcemeat over the ham. Fold the sides of the boned pheasant around the stuffing to enclose it completely.

Put half the reserved forcemeat into the base of the pie, particularly around the edges. Put the pheasant in the pie, placing the join in the skin downwards (there is no need to sew up the opening as the pie will keep the filling inside the bird). Use the remaining forcemeat to fill in around the pheasant, packing it neatly into all the gaps.

Cut off a small piece of the remaining pastry and set it aside to make leaves for the pastry lid. Roll out the rest to a shape slightly larger than the top of the pie. Dampen the rim of the pastry lining with a little water, then lift the lid on top of the pie and press the edges to seal in the filling. Trim off any excess pastry – you may find that snipping it off with a pair of kitchen scissors is the easiest method. Pinch up the pastry edges. Roll out the trimmings with the reserved pastry and cut out leaves for the top of the pie. Cut a small hole to allow steam to escape, then glaze the pie with beaten egg.

Bake the pie for 3 hours. Check it frequently and cover it loosely with a piece of foil after the first hour to prevent the pastry from overcooking. Increase the oven temperature to 190°C/375°F/gas 5, uncover the pie and glaze it with a little more egg. Cook for a further 20-30 minutes, until the pastry is golden and glossy.

While the pie is cooking, simmer the pheasant carcass in a saucepan with the onion, bay leaf and carrot for 1½ hours. Make sure that there is plenty of water in the pan to cover the carcass and keep the pan covered. Strain the stock into a clean pan, then boil it hard, uncovered, until it is reduced to 300 ml/½ pint. Strain it through a muslin-lined sieve, then taste and season it.

When the pie is cooked, heat the stock and sprinkle the gelatine into it. Remove the pan from the heat and stir until the gelatine has dissolved completely. Set this aside to cool. When the pie has cooled until it is just hot and the stock is cold, pour the stock slowly in through the vent in the top crust.

Leave the pie to cool in the tin, then carefully remove the clips which hold the sides of the tin together; ease the sides away from the pie. Have a small pointed knife ready to ease away any small pieces of pastry that are stuck.

SERVES SIX TO EIGHT

PHEASANT WITH MUSHROOM STUFFING

2 pheasants
½ onion
50 g/2 oz butter

STUFFING
25 g/1 oz butter or margarine
100 g/4 oz finely chopped onion
100 g/4 oz mushrooms, chopped
50 g/2 oz cooked ham, chopped
75 g/3 oz fresh white breadcrumbs
salt and pepper
15 ml/1 tbsp game or chicken stock
  (optional)
watercress sprigs to garnish

Wash the pheasant giblets. Put them in a saucepan, and cover with cold water. Add the half onion and simmer gently for 40 minutes to make stock for the gravy.

Make the stuffing. Melt the butter or margarine in a frying pan and cook the onion until soft. Add the mushrooms to the onion; cook for a few minutes. Stir in the ham and breadcrumbs, then add salt and pepper. If the stuffing is too crumbly, add the stock.

Set the oven at 190°C/375°F/gas 5. Divide the stuffing between the birds, filling the body cavities only. Truss the birds neatly and put them in a roasting tin; spread with the butter. Roast for 45–60 minutes, depending on the size of the birds. Baste occasionally while roasting. Transfer the birds to a heated serving dish and remove the trussing strings. Garnish with watercress and serve with gravy made from the giblet stock (see page 488). Wild mushrooms, tossed in butter, are good with this dish.

SERVES SIX

PHEASANT VERONIQUE

2 pheasants
salt and pepper
75 g/3 oz butter
600 ml/1 pint chicken stock
7.5-10 ml/1½-2 tsp arrowroot
225 g/8 oz seedless white grapes, peeled
60 ml/4 tbsp double cream
5 ml/1 tsp lemon juice

Set the oven at 180°C/350°F/gas 4. Wipe the pheasants, season and rub well all over with butter. Put a knob of butter inside each bird. Place the pheasants, breast side down, in a deep pot roaster or flameproof casserole. Cover with stock and buttered paper. Cook for 1-1¼ hours, until tender, turning the birds breast side up after 25 minutes.

When cooked, remove the pheasants from the stock and cut into convenient portions for serving; keep hot. Boil the liquid in the casserole to reduce it a little. Strain into a saucepan. Blend the arrowroot with a little water, then stir it into the hot stock. Bring to the boil and stir until the sauce thickens and clears. Add the grapes, cream and lemon juice, then heat through without boiling. Check the seasoning. Arrange the pheasants on a serving dish, spoon the sauce over and serve.

SERVES FOUR

 MRS BEETON'S TIP

When seedless grapes are not available, halve ordinary fruit and remove all the pips. Unfortunately, this is a tedious task which is essential. Use a small, pointed knife to peel the grapes.

PIGEONS IN RED WINE

75 g/3 oz butter
3 woodpigeons
salt and pepper
1 large onion or 3 shallots, sliced

SAUCE
25 g/1 oz dripping or lard
1 small carrot, sliced
1 onion, sliced
25 g/1 oz plain flour
600 ml/1 pint game or chicken stock
salt and pepper
300 ml/½ pint red wine

Start by making the sauce. Melt the dripping or lard in a saucepan. Fry the vegetables slowly for about 10 minutes until the onion is golden brown. Stir in the flour and cook very gently until golden, then gradually add the stock, stirring constantly until the sauce boils and thickens. Lower the heat and simmer for 30 minutes, then strain the sauce into a large clean pan. Add salt and pepper to taste, stir in the red wine and bring the mixture slowly to simmering point.

Meanwhile melt two-thirds of the butter in a large frying pan and fry the pigeons, turning as required, until browned on all sides. Add the pigeons to the wine sauce and simmer with the pan half-covered for about 45 minutes, or until the birds are tender. Taste and season towards the end of the cooking time.

Melt the remaining butter in a frying pan and fry the onion or shallots. Drain well and keep hot. Split the cooked pigeons in half. Serve with the onions and the sauce poured over.

SERVES SIX

PIGEON PIE

2 pigeons
45 ml/3 tbsp plain flour
salt and pepper
45 ml/3 tbsp corn oil
100 g/4 oz chuck steak, cubed
100 g/4 oz button onions
30 ml/2 tbsp sage and onion stuffing mix
1 small cooking apple, peeled, cored and
  sliced
250 ml/8 fl oz beef stock
225 g/8 oz prepared puff pastry, thawed if
  frozen
flour for rolling out
beaten egg for glazing

Cut the pigeons into quarters. Remove the feet and backbone. Put the flour in a stout polythene bag, with salt and pepper to season. Add the pigeon joints and shake the bag to coat them in seasoned flour. Heat the oil and fry the joints for about 10 minutes, turning as required, until lightly browned all over.

Add the steak to the bag and coat in the remaining seasoned flour. Remove the pigeons from the pan and drain on absorbent kitchen paper. Add the steak and onions to the pan and cook for 5 minutes, turning frequently.

Make up the stuffing according to the packet directions. Form into small balls and fry in the pan until lightly browned. Remove and drain.

Set the oven at 220°C/425°F/gas 7. In a large casserole or pie dish, layer all the filling ingredients, adding salt and pepper to taste. Pour in the stock. Roll out the pastry on a lightly floured surface to fit the dish. Moisten the rim of the pie dish and cover the pie with the pastry. Brush the crust with the egg.

Cook for 20 minutes, until the pastry is risen and golden. Lower the heat to 180°C/350°F/gas 4, and cook for a further 2 hours, or until the pigeons are tender when pierced with a skewer

through the the crust. Cover the pie crust with buttered greaseproof paper if necessary to prevent it overbrowning or drying out.

SERVES FOUR TO FIVE

ROAST QUAIL IN A VINE-LEAF COAT

8 oven-ready quail
8 fresh or canned vine leaves
8 rindless streaky bacon rashers
4 large slices of bread from a tin loaf
butter for spreading
small bunches of black and green grapes to
  garnish

Set the oven at 200°C/400°F/gas 6. Wrap each quail in a vine leaf. Wrap one bacon rasher around each quail. Secure with thread or use wooden cocktail sticks. Place on a rack in a roasting tin and roast for 10–20 minutes.

Meanwhile, cut the crusts off the bread, cut each slice in half and toast lightly on both sides. Spread the toast with drippings from the quail and a little butter. Serve each quail on toast and garnish with grapes.

SERVES FOUR

ORANGE-SCENTED BRAISED VENISON

1-1.25 kg/2-2¾ lb haunch or shoulder of
    venison
25 g/1 oz dripping
1 onion, thickly sliced
2 carrots, thickly sliced
2 celery sticks, thickly sliced
1 orange
game or chicken stock (see method)
25 g/1 oz butter
45 ml/3 tbsp plain flour
30 ml/2 tbsp redcurrant jelly
salt and pepper

RED WINE MARINADE
1 onion, chopped
1 carrot, chopped
1 celery stick, sliced
6-10 parsley sprigs, chopped
1 garlic clove, crushed
5 ml/1 tsp dried thyme
1 bay leaf
6-8 peppercorns
1-2 cloves
2.5 ml/½ tsp ground coriander
2.5 ml/½ tsp juniper berries
250 ml/8 fl oz chicken stock
150 ml/¼ pint each red wine and oil

GARNISH
watercress sprigs
orange slices
Mrs Beeton's Forcemeat Balls (page 475)

Combine all the ingredients for the marinade in
a deep dish. Stir in 150 ml/¼ pint water and add
the venison. Leave for about 12 hours or
overnight, basting and turning occasionally.
Dry the venison on absorbent kitchen paper
and trim if required. Reserve the marinade.

Set the oven at 190°C/375°F/gas 5. Melt the
dripping in a large frying pan and brown the
venison on all sides. Remove and set aside.

Add the vegetables to the fat remaining in the
pan and cook briefly, then place in a large
casserole. Pare off a few thin strips of rind from
the orange and add to the casserole. Strain in
the marinade and add enough stock just to
cover the vegetables. Place the venison on top,
cover with a well-greased piece of greaseproof
paper and a lid. Cook for 1¼ hours. Meanwhile
cream the butter and flour together in a small
bowl. Set aside.

Carve the meat into slices. Arrange them on a
heated serving dish and keep hot. Strain the
stock from the casserole into a small saucepan,
discarding the vegetables. Squeeze the orange
and strain the juice into the pan. Add the
redcurrant jelly, salt and pepper, and bring to
the boil. Lower the heat and stir until the jelly
has melted, then add knobs of the prepared
butter and flour paste, whisking well after each
addition. Simmer for 2-3 minutes, whisking.

Pour the sauce over the venison and garnish
with the watercress, orange slices and forcemeat balls. Serve at once.

SERVES SIX TO EIGHT

 MRS BEETON'S TIP

Instead of braising a whole joint of
venison, the same ingredients and method
may be used for steaks. Alternatively, the
joint may be cut into serving portions
before cooking.

ROAST VENISON WITH BAKED APPLES

4 small sharp cooking apples
juice of 1 lemon
30 ml/2 tbsp gooseberry, rowanberry or
    redcurrant jelly
15 ml/1 tbsp butter
10 ml/2 tsp soft light brown sugar
1 kg/2¼ lb young venison
about 45 ml/3 tbsp oil

SAUCE
150 ml/¼ pint game or beef stock
30 ml/2 tbsp gooseberry, rowanberry or
    redcurrant jelly
small pinch of ground cloves
salt and pepper
10 ml/2 tsp cornflour
30 ml/2 tbsp sherry

Set the oven at 190°C/375°F/gas 5. Peel and core the apples. Put them in a saucepan, add a little water and the lemon juice and simmer for 10-15 minutes. Drain and arrange in an oven-proof dish. Fill the core holes with the jelly. Top each apple with butter and brown sugar.

Put the venison in a roasting tin. Brush with 30 ml/2 tbsp of the oil and roast for 40 minutes, basting with extra oil from time to time. Bake the apples at the same time.

Meanwhile make the sauce. Combine the stock, jelly, ground cloves, salt and pepper in a small pan. Heat gently to dissolve the jelly. In a cup, blend the cornflour with 15 ml/1 tbsp water, add to the stock and bring to the boil, stirring all the time. Cook for 2 minutes.

Slice the meat and arrange it on a warm dish with the apples; keep both hot. Place the roasting tin over the heat, add the sauce and the sherry and stir vigorously. Strain over the meat and serve at once.

SERVES FOUR TO SIX

MARINATED VENISON STEAKS

4 slices of venison (from haunch)
salt and pepper
25 g/1 oz plain flour
butter or dripping
1 small onion, chopped
6-8 juniper berries, crushed
150 ml/¼ pint game or chicken stock
chopped parsley to garnish

MARINADE
about 300 ml/½ pint red wine
1 bouquet garni
6 peppercorns
4 onion slices
30 ml/2 tbsp olive oil
10 ml/2 tsp red wine vinegar

Make the marinade. Mix all the ingredients in a saucepan and boil for 1 minute. Cool completely. Put the venison in a large dish. Pour the marinade over; leave overnight.

Set the oven at 180°C/350°F/gas 4. Drain the venison and pat dry. Reserve the marinade. Snip the edges of the venison slices to prevent curling. Season the flour and rub it over the steaks. Heat the fat in a flameproof casserole. Sear the steaks; add the onion when searing the second side.

Pour off all but a film of fat from the pan. Sprinkle the steaks with the crushed juniper. Pour the stock and a little of the marinade round them, to a depth of about 1 cm/½ inch. Cover the casserole or tin tightly with foil and bake for 30 minutes, or until the steaks are tender. Drain and serve, sprinkled with parsley. Drain off the excess fat from the stock and serve the stock with the steaks.

SERVES SIX TO EIGHT

BIGOS

There are many ways of preparing what is in effect Poland's national dish. The essence of them all is that they should consist of a mixture of sauerkraut and smoked sausage and the game secured by the hunter. Duck or any type of game can be used instead of venison.

1 kg/2¼ lb sauerkraut
450 g/1 lb boneless shoulder of venison
175–225 g/6–8 oz smoked pork sausage
50 g/2 oz lard
1 large onion, sliced
30 ml/2 tbsp tomato purée
125 ml/4 fl oz red wine
salt and pepper
1 large green apple
2 bay leaves
250 ml/8 fl oz game or chicken stock
25 g/1 oz butter
15 ml/1 tbsp plain flour

Thoroughly squeeze the sauerkraut, then shred it. Wipe the venison, trim off all the fat and cut into 2.5 cm/1 inch cubes. Slice the sausage into pieces 1 cm/½ inch thick.

Melt half the lard in a large frying pan and brown the onion until golden. Add the venison

and cook, stirring for 5 minutes. Stir in the tomato purée and the wine. Season to taste and mix in the sausage.

Set the oven at 180°C/350°F/gas 4. Place half the sauerkraut in a large casserole, then top with the meat. Peel, core and dice the apple. Add it to the casserole with the bay leaves and place the remaining sauerkraut on top. Pour half the stock over the bigos. Dot with flakes of butter, cover and cook for 2½–3 hours, or until the venison is tender. Stir the bigos occasionally during cooking.

About 10 minutes before the end of cooking time, melt the remaining lard in a frying pan, add the flour and stir over low heat for 2–3 minutes, without allowing the mixture to colour. Gradually add the remaining stock, stirring all the time, until the sauce boils and thickens. Simmer for 2 minutes, stirring, then season to taste. Mix the sauce into the bigos, which should be moist. Serve piping hot.

SERVES FOUR

 MRS BEETON'S TIP

Use a large Polish boiling sausage for bigos, for example *wiejska*, available from larger supermarkets and delicatessens. The sauerkraut is usually squeezed and shredded before being added to the stew; however, if preferred it may be rinsed and squeezed first. Another traditional ingredient is dried mushrooms: soak 2–4 in boiling water to cover for 15 minutes, then drain and chop them before adding to the bigos at the beginning of cooking. Strain the soaking water through muslin and add that too.

JUGGED HARE

Jugged hare is thickened with the blood which is saved when the animal is paunched.

1 hare
liver of the hare (optional)
blood of the hare
5 ml/1 tsp vinegar (see method)
30 ml/2 tbsp plain flour
salt and pepper
100 g/4 oz butter or margarine
3 whole cloves
1 onion
1 bouquet garni
good pinch of ground mace
good pinch of freshly grated nutmeg
beef stock to moisten
150 ml/¼ pint port or claret
50 g/2 oz redcurrant jelly
lemon juice (optional)

GARNISH
heart-shaped or triangular sippets of toasted bread
Mrs Beeton's Forcemeat Balls (page 475)

Joint the hare. Reserve the liver and the blood in a bowl, adding the vinegar to the blood to prevent it coagulating. Set the oven at 180°C/350°F/gas 4. Put the flour in a bowl, season with salt and pepper, then dust the hare joints with it. Melt the butter or margarine in a frying pan and brown the hare joints all over. Remove the hare joints from the pan and put them in a deep ovenproof pot or cooking jar, preferably earthenware. Press the cloves into the onion. Add the onion, bouquet garni, spices and just enough stock to cover about a quarter of the joints. Cover the pot or jar very securely with foil and stand it in a roasting tin. Add boiling water to the tin to come halfway up the sides of the pot or jar and cook for about 3 hours, depending on the age and toughness of the hare.

Meanwhile, prepare the liver. When the hare is cooked, remove the meat to a serving dish and keep hot. Pour off the juices into a saucepan. If using the hare's liver, mash it into the hot liquid. Add the port or claret and redcurrant jelly. Add the hare's blood to the liquids in the pan and reheat, stirring all the time; do not allow the sauce to boil. If the blood is not available, thicken the sauce with a beurre manié (see Mrs Beeton's Tip). Sharpen with a few drops of lemon juice, if liked.

Pour the thickened sauce over the hare joints and serve garnished with the sippets and forcemeat balls.

SERVES SIX

 MRS BEETON'S TIP

To thicken the sauce without using the blood, blend 15 ml/1 tbsp butter with 15 ml/1 tbsp plain flour in a bowl. Gradually add small pieces of the mixture to the sauce, whisking thoroughly after each addition. Bring the sauce to the boil, lower the heat and simmer for 5 minutes, stirring.

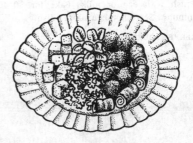

DURHAM RABBIT PIE

200 g/7 oz cooked rabbit
50 g/2 oz boiled bacon, without rinds
4 eggs
salt and pepper
beaten egg or milk for glazing

SHORT CRUST PASTRY
225 g/8 oz plain flour
2.5 ml/½ tsp salt
100 g/4 oz margarine (or half butter, half lard)
flour for rolling out

Set the oven at 200°C/400°F/gas 6. To make the pastry, sift the flour and salt into a bowl, then rub in the margarine until the mixture resembles fine breadcrumbs. Add enough cold water to make a stiff dough. Press the dough together with your fingertips.

Roll out the pastry on a lightly floured surface and use half of it to line a 20 cm/8 inch pie plate. Use the remainder for the lid.

Chop the rabbit meat and bacon finely and mix together in a bowl. Place the mixture on the pastry in the form of a cross, leaving the outside 1 cm/½ inch of pastry uncovered. Break an egg carefully into each uncovered pastry triangle, taking care not to break the yolks. Add salt and pepper to taste. Dampen the edges of the pastry and cover with the remaining pastry. Brush with egg or milk. Bake for 30-40 minutes. Serve hot as a supper dish.

SERVES FOUR

CASSEROLE OF RABBIT

1 rabbit
salt and pepper
60 ml/4 tbsp plain flour
65 g/2½ oz butter
1 onion, sliced
225 g/8 oz cooking apples, peeled, cored and sliced
1 (213 g/7½ oz) can prunes
1 chicken stock cube

GARNISH
chopped parsley
crescents of fried bread

Set the oven at 180°C/350°F/gas 4. Joint the rabbit and discard the lower forelegs and rib-cage, or keep for stock. Put half the flour in a shallow bowl, season and coat the rabbit lightly. Melt 50 g/2 oz butter in a flameproof casserole and brown the rabbit on all sides; transfer to a plate. Add the onion and fry until soft. Stir in the apples.

Drain the prunes and make the juice up to 250 ml/8 fl oz with water. Add the stock cube, crumbling it finely. Return the rabbit to the casserole with the prunes and stock. Cover and cook in the oven for 1½ hours, or until the rabbit is tender.

When the rabbit is cooked, arrange the joints on a warmed serving dish with the apples and prunes; keep hot. In a small bowl, blend the remaining butter with the remaining flour. Gradually add small pieces of the mixture to the liquid in the casserole, whisking thoroughly after each addition. Bring to the boil and stir all the time until the sauce thickens. Check the seasoning before pouring the sauce over the rabbit. Garnish and serve.

SERVES FOUR

Moules Marinière (page 141)

Gravad Lax (page 84) **and Potted Shrimps** (page 83)

Roast Chicken with Honey and Almonds (page 190)

Herbed Shoulder of Lamb (page 277)

Pheasant Veronique (page 232) **and Pigeons in Red Wine** (page 232)

Fillets of Duck Bigarade (page 211) **and
Roast Quail in a Vine-Leaf Coat** (page 233)

Noisettes Jardinère (page 280) **and Lamb Shish Kebab** (page 280)

Boiled Dressed Ham (page 298) **with**
Strawberry and Tomato Salad (page 383) **and new potatoes**

Pasticcio di Lasagne Verde (page 418) **and
Cannelloni with Mushroom Stuffing** (page 419)

Spaghetti alla Carbonara (page 417) **and
Pasta, Anchovy and Sweetcorn Salad** (page 382)

Boston Roast (page 389) **and Cauliflower with Beans** (page 340)

Pastry Horns and Vol-au-Vent Cases (both on page 538)

Leek Tart (page 345) **and Quiche Lorraine** (page 520)

Cornish Pasties (page 521)

Blackberry and Apple Pie (page 522)

Eccles Cakes (page 543) **and Cream Eclairs** (page 549)

RABBIT A LA MINUTE

Mrs Beeton's version used 600 ml/1 pint water instead of stock but this slight variation gives a moist dish, ideal to serve with plain cooked potatoes and green vegetables or with rice.

1 oven-ready rabbit, cut into small serving
  portions
salt and pepper
30 ml/2 tbsp plain flour
2.5 ml/½ tsp ground mace
25 g/1 oz butter or 30 ml/2 tbsp oil
100 g/4 oz mushrooms, sliced
300 ml/½ pint chicken or vegetable stock
60 ml/4 tbsp sherry
30 ml/2 tbsp chopped parsley

Coat the rabbit portions with the salt, pepper, flour and mace. Melt the butter or heat the oil in a large deep frying pan. Add the rabbit portions and cook, turning frequently, for about 20 minutes, or until well cooked.

Add the mushrooms, distributing them among the rabbit portions, pour in the stock and sherry. Sprinkle the parsley over the rabbit, bring to the boil, then lower the heat and simmer, uncovered, for 15 minutes. Taste for seasoning and serve.

SERVES FOUR

VARIATION

Quick Mild Curried Rabbit Substitute 15 ml/1 tbsp curry powder for an equal quantity of flour. Omit the mace. Cook 1 chopped onion with the rabbit. Add 1 peeled, cored and diced cooking apple instead of the mushrooms. Stir in 15 ml/1 tbsp mango chutney, 10 ml/2 tsp desiccated coconut, 25 g/1 oz sultanas and 25 g/1 oz blanched almonds. Increase stock to 450 ml/¾ pint; omit sherry. Cooking times as in the main recipe above.

RAGOUT OF RABBIT

1 oven-ready rabbit, cut into small serving
  portions
salt and pepper
45 ml/3 tbsp plain flour
50 g/2 oz butter
3 onions, sliced
4 rindless streaky bacon rashers, diced
450 ml/¾ pint chicken or vegetable stock
2 slices of lemon
1 bay leaf
150 ml/¼ pint port or sherry

Coat the rabbit portions with the salt, pepper and flour. Melt the butter in a heavy-bottomed saucepan or flameproof casserole. Add the rabbit portions and cook, turning frequently, until lightly browned all over. Use a slotted spoon to remove the portions from the pan.

Add the onions to the fat remaining in the pan and cook, stirring occasionally, until the slices are well browned. Stir in any leftover flour from the rabbit, then add the bacon and cook for 2 minutes. Pour in the stock and bring to the boil, stirring all the time.

Replace the rabbit portions in the pan. Add the lemon slices and bay leaf and cover the pan. Simmer for about 30 minutes, or until the rabbit portions are cooked. Stir in the port or sherry and taste for seasoning. Add a little more salt and pepper if necessary, then bring to the boil and serve.

SERVES FOUR

Meat Dishes

This chapter concentrates on the essential aspects of meat cookery, from hints on buying and storing or carving to classic dishes and contemporary, International favourites.

Always buy meat from a reputable supplier to ensure that it has been properly handled and prepared before sale. Local butchers offer a personal service and expert advice. They will prepare exactly the amount or cut you want, or offer advice on the best buy if you are not sure what you need, and trim, truss or bone the meat for you, often more economically than the pre-packed product.

All meat should look moist and fresh. Fat should be firm and pale. There should be no unpleasant smell, slimy texture, softening or wet feel or appearance to the fat, nor any tinge of green or yellow to either meat or fat. Beef ranges from bright red to a darker colour when well hung. Lamb is neither as bright nor as dark as beef and it tends to be slightly drier. Its skin should look clean and pale and any fat should be creamy-white. Pork is a paler meat and the fat is softer and creamier in appearance. Liver, kidney and heart should all be firm, moist and evenly coloured and they should smell fresh without any hint of a strong or 'off' smell.

Bacon and ham should be firm and even in colour, with pale, creamy, firm fat. Avoid any fat which is yellowing, soft or slightly slimy in appearance; and meat which has a yellow-green tint or sheen.

Remember that meat should be kept chilled until sold – either in a butcher's cold room or refrigerator or in a refrigerated display cabinet. It should not be displayed unchilled (pre-packed or otherwise).

Chill meat as soon as possible after purchase. Leave sealed packs closed; transfer wrapped meat to a large covered container. Place the meat on a low shelf in the refrigerator, making sure that it does not drip over the edges of the container. Cook the meat before the date on the packet, or within 1–2 days if bought loose. Use minced meat and offal within a day of purchase.

COOKING METHODS

The selection of meat depends on the cooking method; some methods are suitable for certain cuts and not appropriate to others.

Roasting This is a dry cooking method for tender cuts. Originating from spit roasting over an open fire, the traditional method is to cook the joint uncovered on a rack in a tin. Modern cooks may dispense with the rack, placing the meat directly in the tin. It may be loosely covered for part of the cooking time to prevent overbrowning.

Grilling A quick cooking method for tender, small cuts such as steak and chops.

Frying Shallow, deep or stir frying are all suitable methods for tender cuts. Deep frying, like stir frying, is used only for meat which has been cut into small pieces. Chops and steaks are typical candidates for shallow frying, whereas tender pork, trimmed and cut into small pieces, is perfect for stir frying.

Pot Roasting This is a form of roasting, usually on a bed of vegetables, in a tightly covered container. A little liquid may be added to the container. This is not strictly necessary; the condensation from the ingredients will be retained in the cooking pot. This method is suitable for less tender cuts but it is not a moist method and will not be successful with tough cuts.

Braising This is a part-moist method. The meat is cooked with some liquid, usually on a bed of vegetables, but is not submerged in liquid. It is suitable for less tender cuts as well as chops and steak but not for tough meats.

Stewing This is a moist cooking method for tough cuts of meat. The meat should be submerged in liquid and the container covered. Stews may be cooked on the hob or in the oven but it is important that the process is slow and lengthy, allowing time for the meat to become perfectly tender.

Casseroling This is a slightly ambiguous term used for moist cooking. It is similar to braising, but usually has more liquid; however it is not usually used to denote cooking periods as long as for stewing.

Microwave Cooking The majority of meat does not cook particularly well in the microwave oven. Sauces, such as Bolognese, which are based upon minced meat, can be cooked by this method, but microwave cooking is not suitable for any of the cuts that require long, slow cooking. See the microwave chapter and charts for more information.

CUTS OF MEAT

A wide variety of cuts is available, including the traditional portions listed here and Continental-style cuts which are cut quite differently, often with the grain of the meat instead of across it. Most supermarkets and butchers also offer a range of trimmed meats which are ready for grilling, frying or baking. These include skewered meats, rolled portions, thin escalopes or slices of meat and fine strips or cubes.

The value of becoming familiar with different cuts is in learning how best to cook them. Meat is muscle tissue: if it is taken from the most active part of the animal, for example the leg, it will have more connective tissue and be tougher than meat from less active muscles on the back and around the rib areas. Long, moist cooking is necessary to soften connective tissue and make the meat tender. Tender cuts which do not have much connective tissue may be cooked by the quicker, fiercer and dry methods.

CARVING MEAT

A sharp, long-bladed knife is essential for carving and a two-pronged carving fork is useful but not vital.

Remove any trussing string and skewers. Holding the joint with the fork, use a sawing action to slice across the grain of the meat. Cutting across the grain is important as it makes the meat more tender to eat. If the joint has an 'L' shaped bone (such as in a rib of beef), then cut between the meat and bone, as close to the bone as possible, on the shortest side of the bone. Carve the meat in slices down towards the bone, either straight down or at an angle, whichever is best for giving large, neat slices. When the majority of the meat is removed from one side, turn the joint, if necessary, and remove meat from the other side. Any remaining small areas of meat should be cut in small neat pieces.

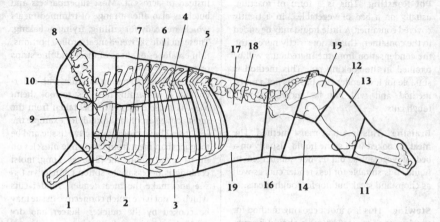

BEEF

1 **Shin** A tough cut with much gristle, this must be cooked by a slow moist method. It is ideal for flavoursome stews, soups and stocks, particularly on the bone, when it will yield stock which sets well on chilling.

2 **Brisket** Usually sold boned and rolled. This used to be a fatty cut, but modern breeding methods have reduced the fat content considerably. Suitable for pot roasting or braising, brisket may also be casseroled or boiled. It has good flavour.

3 **Flank** A comparatively fatty joint which requires long, slow cooking, by boiling, stewing or braising.

4 **Flat Rib** Taken from between the flank and forerib, this is not commonly available. If found it should be pot roasted or braised, as it is not a tender cut.

5 **Wing Rib** Cut from between the rib and sirloin, this is a succulent cut for roasting.

6 **Forerib** A roasting joint, at its best cooked on the bone. A well-hung joint, roasted fairly slowly will yield full-flavoured, tender results. Since a joint on the bone has to be large in order to be practical, forerib is often sold boned and rolled.

7 **Top Rib** With back rib, this is also known as middle rib, thick rib or, traditionally, leg-of-mutton cut. Top rib and back rib may be sold separately, the former being an excellent cut for braising to soften the gristle which runs through the meat.

8 **Chuck and Bladebone** Both braising cuts, also used for making succulent stews. Chuck steak may also be purchased in one piece and pot roasted to give excellent results. In some areas chuck may also be known as chine. In Scotland chuck and blade combined are known as shoulder.

9/10 **Clod or Front Chest and Sticking or Neck of Beef** Although these inexpensive cuts do not have a lot of connective tissue, they contain significant amounts of gristle. Use for boiling or stewing.

11 **Leg** Suitable for long slow stewing and boiling, leg has good flavour and yields tender results when cooked correctly. Leg may be sliced across the muscle in large round nuggets of meat. It may be stewed in this form, or cut into cubes before cooking.

12 **Topside** This is taken from the inside of the leg. It is lean and boneless and the rolled joint is usually wrapped in a thin sheet of fat (barded) to keep it moist during cooking. Although topside is often regarded as a roasting joint, it is best pot roasted.

13 **Silverside** From the thigh and buttock, this is suitable for roasting, but benefits from pot roasting or braising. Silverside is also suitable for boiling; salted silverside is an excellent boiling joint.

14 **Top Rump or Thick Flank** Although this is generally regarded as a braising joint (whole or in slices) it may be pot roasted to give full-flavoured results.

15 **Aitchbone** This is a large joint on the bone lying over the rump. It is an old-fashioned cut which can be boned and rolled and prepared in smaller joints. It may be roasted or braised.

16 **Rump** Next to the sirloin, this is a popular cut for grilling and frying, but it is not the most tender of steaks. Rump has a thin covering of fat but it is free of gristle.

17 **Sirloin** The prime, traditional roasting joint, sirloin includes the fillet. Tender and flavoursome, sirloin is one of the most expensive cuts of beef. A well-hung rib of beef is less expensive and offers equal if not better flavour when cooked with care.

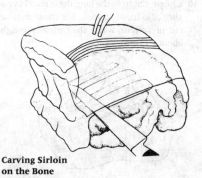

**Carving Sirloin
on the Bone**

18 **Fillet** Tucked underneath the bone, the fillet is a long, slim piece of very tender meat with a good flavour. As it is expensive it is usually reserved for special dishes, such as Beef Wellington, or it may be sliced into small, thick steaks for grilling or frying.

19 **Hindquarter Flank** The belly of the animal. A braising and stewing cut which has a high fat content and is therefore often trimmed and minced.

BEEF STEAKS

Fillet Small steaks off the fillet which cook quickly to give succulent, tender results.

Tournedos A 2.5 cm/1 inch thick slice off the fillet, trimmed and tied neatly.

Châteaubriand A thick centre cut from the fillet, weighing about 250 g/9 oz and measuring about 5 cm/2 inches thick, this may be served as a portion for two.

Rump Flavoursome steak for grilling, frying, or braising, this is not the most tender but it is economical with good texture.

Sirloin Large tender steak on the bone, this may be cut in several ways and served under several names.

Porterhouse A 2.5 cm/1 inch thick steak from the thick end of the sirloin, this is tender and ideal for grilling.

T-bone On the T-shaped bone, this large steak cut through the sirloin includes a slice each of the loin meat and of the fillet.

Entrecôte A boneless steak consisting of the eye of the loin meat from the sirloin, but without fillet. Usually cut 2.5-4 cm/1-1½ inches thick.

Minute Steak A thin slice of steak of good quality which may be fried or grilled very quickly. This may be taken from the sirloin, or even from the fillet. It is trimmed of all fat and may be beaten out very thinly.

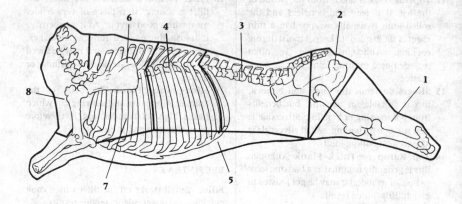

VEAL

1 Leg The lower part of the leg, the knuckle or shin, this is jointed on the bone for stewing or boned and cubed to be sold as pie veal. The upper part of the leg provides a large roasting joint. Continental escalopes are cut along the muscle on the topside area of the joint; however British escalopes may be cut across the grain of the meat on the fleshy part of the leg in the form of steaks which are beaten out thinly to make escalopes.

2 Fillet The most expensive and tender cut, either sliced into steaks or cooked whole.

3 Loin For roasting on the bone or boned, this may be cut into chops for grilling or frying. The leg end of the loin may be referred to as the chump end.

4 Best End of Neck For roasting or braising, this is also chopped into cutlets for grilling and frying.

5 Breast Usually boned for stuffing, rolling and roasting. An economical cut with a good flavour.

6 Shoulder On the bone or boned and rolled, for roasting. If the fore knuckle is removed, this is called the oyster of veal.

7/8 Middle Neck and Scrag For stewing and braising, these have a high proportion of bone to meat.

9 Cutlets Cut from the best end of neck, providing 6 per carcass, each weighing about 175 g/6 oz.

10 Chops Cut from the loin, these may have a slice of kidney included. The chops may be cut in various ways; they usually weigh about 225 g/8 oz each.

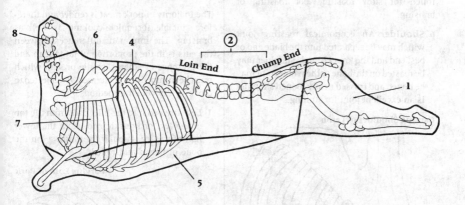

Loin End

Chump End

LAMB

1 Leg Known as gigot in Scotland, the leg may be divided into fillet and shank end. Leaner than shoulder, the leg may be roasted whole or boned and stuffed. Slices chopped off the leg are known as lamb steaks.

Carving Leg of Lamb

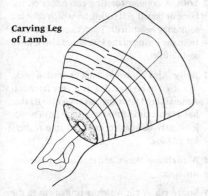

2 Loin A roasting joint for cooking on the bone or boned and rolled. Divided into loin and chump ends, the joint may be separated into loin and chump chops.

3 Saddle The whole loin from both sides of the lamb, with a central bone.

Carving Saddle of Lamb

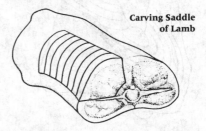

4 Best End of Neck This may be boned and rolled, then sliced into noisettes. The individual bones may be separated with their eye of meat to make cutlets or the whole rack roasted on the bone. Two racks may be interlocked to make a guard of honour, or they may be trussed into a circular crown roast.

5 Breast One of the most economical cuts of meat, the breast may be separated into riblets on the bone for treating like pork spare ribs.

More commonly, the boned joint is stuffed and rolled for slow roasting, pot roasting or braising.

6 Shoulder An economical roasting joint which may be separated into the blade end or best end and the knuckle end. Shoulder may be roasted on the bone or the whole joint may be boned and trussed neatly. Boned shoulder is an excellent joint for stuffing.

Carving Shoulder of Lamb

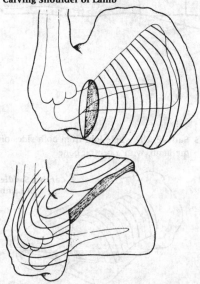

7 Middle Neck Usually chopped into portions for stewing; however 2–3 chops of grilling quality may be taken from the meat closest to the best end of neck.

8 Scrag End of Neck Economical for stews and casseroles.

9 Chops Each carcass yields 4–6 chump chops, 6 loin chops and 4–6 neck chops (cutlets with the rib bone removed). Leg chops or cutlets, also known as steaks, may be cut from the fillet end of the leg.

PORK

The majority of pork meat is tender and therefore suitable for quick cooking as well as braising. The important differences between the cuts is in the proportion of fat to lean and the presence of sinews, gristle or skin which must be trimmed before the meat is subjected to quick or dry cooking methods.

1 Leg Divided into the fillet end, from the top of the leg, or knuckle end, from the lower half of the leg. Popular for roasting, on the bone or boned and rolled.

Carving Loin of Pork

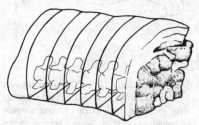

2 Loin A popular roasting cut, either on the bone or boned and rolled (in which case the joint may be stuffed). Tenderloin is the meat from the inside of the loin bone, also known as the fillet.

3 Belly Also known as flank or draft of pork, this used to be regarded as a very fatty cut. Animals bred for leaner meat yield belly that has a better proportion of lean to fat. The flat joint may be roasted or sliced into rashers for grilling.

4 Bladebone Boned and stuffed or roasted on the bone.

5 Spare rib A cut which is equivalent to the middle neck of lamb. This is marbled with fat, but overall it provides a lean roasting joint or slices (known as spare rib chops) for grilling and frying.

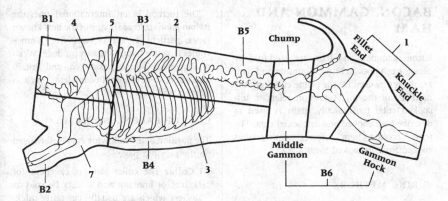

Note 'B' numbers refer to bacon and gammon cuts, see following page.

6 Spare Ribs These are cut from the belly once the main joint has been removed to include only the bones with their covering of meat. The amount of meat left on the bone can vary considerably, so always look for meaty ribs when buying.

7 Hand and Spring A large, economical cut which yields a generous amount of meat. Ideal for slow roasting, it can be divided into hand which may be boned and stuffed, and spring which may be trimmed and cubed for braising. With careful trimming of sinews, the joint provides a large quantity of meat which may be used for different purposes: a fair-sized portion for roasting, cubes for braising and strips or small cubes for frying and stir frying.

8 Head The head contains a considerable quantity of meat, notably the cheeks which are traditionally boiled and crumbed to be sold as Bath Chaps, small hams on the bone. The whole head may be boiled and cleaned for making brawn, or a prepared half head purchased from butchers.

9 Trotters or Pettitoes These may be boiled,

skinned and the meat removed. The meat is flavoursome and the stock sets to a firm jelly. Unskinned trotters may be boned and stuffed, then roasted.

10 Chops Taken from the loin or spare rib. Chump chops are the first 2–3 chops from the leg-end of the loin. They are large and meaty. Middle loin chops are sometimes sold with the kidney, whereas foreloin chops have a curved shape and no kidney.

Chump Chop

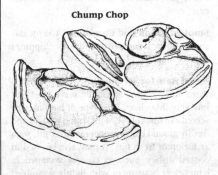

Middle Loin Chop

BACON, GAMMON AND HAM

Bacon, gammon and ham are produced by curing fresh pork in brine. Gammon and ham are the terms used for the prime cuts from the hind leg of the pig. Gammon refers to un-cooked cuts; traditionally, ham is used to describe both cooked and uncooked cuts. The term 'cooked ham' clearly distinguishes cooked from uncooked meat.

CURING METHODS

There are many variations on curing methods, including traditional techniques giving full-flavoured bacon and modern methods for milder, less-salty cuts.

The most popular curing method, based on an old Wiltshire technique, involves injecting the meat with brine, then soaking it in brine. It is matured for two to four days.

Modern quick-cure methods may be used on some cuts of meat such as gammon. In this case the various parts of the carcass are cured separately.

Sweet, tender and mild cure bacon has had sugar or other sweetening added during curing, and a fruit-based tenderizing agent is often added, particularly to 'tender-sweet' or 'tender-cure' cuts.

Smoked Bacon and Gammon   The meat is smoked over wood sawdust or oak chippings after curing.

Cured Ham for Serving Raw   Ham which is cured and air-dried is usually served raw, cut into very thin slices. This type of ham may be served as a first course, with lemon wedges and freshly ground black pepper or with fruit, such as melon or fresh figs. It may also be used in cooked dishes, such as chicory wrapped in ham before braising or with lightly scrambled eggs to serve with pasta.

The method is an International one; the Italian *prosciutto crudo* is one of the best known types, particularly Parma ham; from France comes Bayonne ham; Germany produces West-phalian ham, which is smoked, and Britain also offers some regional equivalents, such as Cumberland ham.

CUTS OF BACON AND HAM

The position of the following cuts is illustrated on the previous page.

B1 Collar   The collar joint is excellent for boiling or braising and it may be sold as rashers which are usually cut fairly thick. Collar is also good diced or cubed for pie fillings, pasta and rice dishes. A collar joint may need soaking before cooking, tradition-ally for several hours or overnight.

B2 Forehock   Sometimes referred to as gam-mon hock. The forehock may be boiled as a base for soups, stews and casseroles. The meat is flavoursome and excellent for dicing and mincing. The butt end of the forehock is the meaty part which is suitable for cooking whole and slicing. The thinner end of the hock joint is ideal for making excellent stock and soup. The meat should be cut off the bone, trimmed of fat and rind and diced. Well prepared, hock provides flavoursome inexpensive meat for a variety of dishes.

B3 Back Rashers and Chops   Back rashers may also be cut from the portion of meat between the middle rashers and the middle gammon. These are prime rashers with a good nugget of lean tender meat and they are ideal for grilling or frying.

Chops are cut thicker than bacon rashers, each providing an individual portion. They may be served plain grilled or fried. Alter-natively, they can be browned, then braised.

B4 Streaky   Streaky is a tasty cut which is striped with fat as well as lean. Streaky rashers are ideal for chopping and using in cooked dishes and they yield the best crispy bacon bits for garnishing soups or tossing into salad. Streaky bacon may also be bought as a joint for boiling, and it is excellent when pressed and served cold.

B5 Middle Rashers These are economical and meaty. They may be cooked by grilling or frying.

Throughcut Rashers These are rashers cut from the complete side of bacon, including the streaky and the middlecut or back rashers.

B6 Gammon This is the prime, lean and tender, cut for boiling or baking, or cooking by a combination of both methods. The gammon may be purchased whole, as a large joint on the bone including the middle gammon down to the hock end of the joint. The whole joint is ideal for a large party or gathering, such as a wedding. Some butchers boil their own gammons (or hams) and will provide a whole joint to order.

However, the gammon is usually boned and rolled, then cut into smaller joints or steaks.

Middle Gammon The large round of meat; the prime joint for serving hot or cold.

Gammon Steaks These large, round slices, usually sliced about 1 cm/½ inch thick, are cut from the middle gammon joint. They are ideal for grilling or frying. Since they provide large individual portions, many butchers sell the steaks cut in half.

Gammon Slipper and Corner Gammon Small lean joints of prime meat cut from the hock.

Gammon Hock A meaty, well-shaped joint which may be cooked on the bone. This is the end of the gammon and, when cooked on the bone, it provides an impressive joint of practical size for small gatherings, Christmas or other festive occasions.

Bacon Offcuts These are the trimmings and bits left from cutting joints and slicing bacon rashers. They usually consist of a mixture of bits from all parts of the carcass and they can include a lot of fat. However, provided that there is not too much fat in the pack or tray of offcuts, they are an excellent, economical buy for dicing and chopping. The offcuts may also be trimmed and minced, then combined with breadcrumbs, egg, herbs and seasoning to make delicious burgers.

Bacon Rind Pre-packed bacon is often sold with the rind removed and many prime cuts which are sold loose are trimmed of rind.

COOKING METHODS

Frying For rashers, steaks and chops. Remove the rind, if liked, and snip the fat to prevent the rashers curling up during cooking. Lay the bacon in a heavy-bottomed frying pan and place over medium heat. As the bacon heats and the fat runs, turn the rashers over and cook for 1–2 minutes on each side, until lightly browned. Drain; serve on heated plates.

Grilling For rashers, steaks and chops. Lay the rashers on a rack in the grill pan, then place them under a hot grill for 2–3 minutes on each side, turning once, until lightly browned.

Boiling For joints. Weigh the joint and allow 20 minutes per 450g/1 lb, plus 20 minutes. This timing applies whether the joint is cooked completely by boiling or boiled for half to three quarters of the time, then baked. The rind may be removed and the fat scored and glazed or browned in the oven.

Baking For joints, usually in combination with boiling. However, gammon joints may be baked from raw, allowing 20 minutes per 450g/1 lb, plus 20 minutes. Very large joints, over 4.5 kg/10 lb, require 15 minutes per 450g/1 lb, plus 15 minutes.

OFFAL

Offal is the term used for internal organs and other, less valuable, edible parts of the carcass. The term embraces brains, tongue, head, sweetbreads, heart, liver, kidneys, lights, tripe, melts, caul, marrow bones, tail and feet. Most offal is highly nutritious and low in fat, and many types cook quickly.

Liver Calf's liver is considered to have the best and most delicate flavour, followed by lamb's, pig's and ox liver, in that order. Calf's liver and lamb's liver are both suitable for grilling, frying or braising. Although pig's liver has a fine texture, its flavour is strong, so it is usually used in pâtés or combined with other ingredients in mixed dishes. Ox liver is the least popular since it is both strongly flavoured and coarse-textured. It is seldom used except in casseroles which include plenty of other ingredients.

Liver is covered with a fine membrane which should be removed before cooking. When rinsed and dried on absorbent kitchen paper, the liver may be sliced, cut in strips or diced. All sinews and any blood vessels should be removed. Before frying or grilling, liver is usually coated in well-seasoned flour.

Kidneys These have a distinct flavour, strongest in ox and pig's kidneys. Lamb's kidneys are milder. Lamb's, pig's and calf's kidneys may be grilled, fried or braised; ox kidney is suitable for stewing and for adding to pies and savoury puddings.

Kidneys are usually sold with the outer covering of fat removed. The fine membrane surrounding them should be removed and they should then be cut open so that the core, tubes and sinews may be cut out. A pair of kitchen scissors is the best implement for this.

Hearts Ox, calf's, lamb's and sheep's hearts are all lean and firm. They require careful preparation to remove all tubes, then long,

slow cooking. The outer covering of fat and any membrane should be removed, then the tubes, fat and tough tissue should be cut away to leave only the trim, dark meat. The heart may be split and stuffed, then neatly sewn to enclose the stuffing before long slow braising.

Sweetbreads The thymus gland. Ox, calf's and lamb's sweetbreads are sold in pairs, each pair serving two people. Sweetbreads should be soaked in cold water for 15 minutes, then thoroughly washed in several changes of cold water. They must be simmered gently until firm – 2–5 minutes, depending on type – then drained and rinsed in cold water. The outer membrane should be removed and the sweetbreads pressed by placing in a dish, covering with scalded muslin and placing a weight on top. Chill until firm – this takes several hours. The sweetbreads will then be ready for cooking: they may be cut into pieces or sliced and coated in egg and breadcrumbs for frying. Alternatively, they may be coated in well-seasoned flour, browned in butter and served in a creamy sauce.

Oxtail This is sold ready jointed. Excess fat should be trimmed off and the joints stewed with vegetables and stock or water for several hours, until tender. The meat may be served on the bone or the joints may be picked over for meat and the bones discarded. Oxtail has a rich, beefy flavour, ideal for winter stews and soups.

Tongue Lamb's, ox and calf's tongues require boiling, skinning and trimming. Ox tongue may be purchased pickled in brine or unsalted, the former requiring soaking before cooking. Tongue should be simmered gently with vegetables, bay leaves, mace and other herbs in plenty of water to cover until tender. This will take about 45 minutes for lamb's tongues, 1 hour for a calf's tongue and 2 or more hours for an ox tongue. For detailed instructions on how to prepare (and press) tongue, see page 407. Pressed tongue may be served with mustard. Hot Béchamel sauce flavoured with mustard is the ideal accompaniment for a freshly boiled tongue.

Tripe This is the lining of the stomach. Smooth, or blanket tripe comes from the first stomach cavity and honeycomb tripe comes from the second stomach cavity. The latter has a distinct honeycomb texture. Tripe is usually sold prepared, blanched and cleaned, or dressed, ready for cooking in a sauce. The preparation process is long, involving much washing, scrubbing, blanching and rinsing. The prepared tripe is white with a glutinous texture. It should be further cooked for anything from 30 minutes to 2 hours, depending on the dish.

Brains Lamb's and calf's brains have a delicate flavour, although they are not a popular food. Their preparation is similar to that of sweetbreads, involving soaking and rinsing, blanching and removing all the covering membrane, then pressing and chilling before coating or cooking as required.

Heads Pig's head is used for making brawn and is the only head sold with the animal carcass to the butcher. They are easily obtainable from proper butchers (as opposed to meat sellers). The boiled head is used to make brawn, although a half head may be a more practical buy in view of its size. Calf's heads are also traditionally, although less commonly, used for brawn. Sheep's head may be split, boiled, casseroled and served in a variety of ways but these are not popular in British cookery.

Feet Pig's and calf's trotters and cow heel are all traditionally boiled for their jellied stock. Pig's trotters, both fresh or smoked, are more readily available than calf's. They are delicious for making soups and stews and yield a good portion of flavoursome meat.

Bones and Other Offal Marrow bones should be chopped by the butcher ready for baking and boiling at home to make stock.

In various countries and regions many other animal parts are eaten, including the lungs (lights) and melts (spleen) or even the testicles, ears and intestines. However, these are not popular for home cooking, even though they may be encountered as well-seasoned specialities at Continental charcuteries. Perhaps the nearest British equivalent is the Scottish haggis, although the modern version makes less use of offal than the old-fashioned stuffed sheep's stomach did.

Internal fat from carcasses also has a number of uses. Beef suet is taken from fat surrounding kidneys. Lard is derived from fat deposits inside the carcass of a pig. Caul is a fatty membrane which covers and supports internal organs as well as the head of the foetus. The fatty deposits distributed over it give it a lacy appearance. Traditionally, caul is used as a casing for lean joints, pâtés, faggots and their French equivalent, crepinette. It requires careful preparation, including soaking in warm water with a little vinegar added, and thorough rinsing several times before use.

Sausages are a familiar food which use offal as a casing. Natural sausage skins are prepared from the intestines of animals. They are cleaned and salted. Before use the skins have to be soaked and rinsed several times. Synthetic alternatives are now commonly used.

Availability of Offal Greater awareness of food safety has led to separate preparation of offal and meat products. The process varies according to the animal; however, the retail butcher no longer receives a whole carcass. Pig carcasses are bought complete with heads, so most independent butchers will provide a prepared head at a few days' notice. Less-popular offal is sometimes sold frozen. Unprocessed internal fat, such as caul, is difficult to obtain.

ROASTING TIMES FOR MEAT

The following times are a guide for roasting meat at 180°C/350°F/gas 4. Weights and timings are for oven-ready joints, including any stuffing. Small joints weighing less than 1 kg/2¼ lb may need an extra 5 minutes per 450 g/1 lb.

Personal preferences play an important role when roasting, and there are many methods. For example, the joint may be placed in an oven preheated to a higher temperature than that recommended for general roasting. The temperature may be reduced immediately or after the first 5-15 minutes. This method is popular for pork (to crisp the rind) and for sealing and browning the outside of larger joints of beef or lamb. Small to medium joints may need less time than that calculated below, if they are started off at a high temperature, but thick or large joints will still require the full calculated time to ensure they are cooked.

Attitudes towards roasting pork have changed considerably, based on professional guidance on food safety. Pork is usually served cooked through, not rare or medium; however, the meat may be roasted until it is succulent rather than very dry; hence the choice of two recommended timings.

BEEF

Rare   – 20 minutes per 450 g/1 lb
            plus 20 minutes
Medium   – 25 minutes per 450 g/1 lb
            plus 25 minutes
Well Done   – 30 minutes per 450 g/1 lb
            plus 30 minutes

LAMB

Medium   – 20-25 minutes per 450 g/1 lb
            plus 20-25 minutes
Well Done   – 25-30 minutes per 450 g/1 lb
            plus 25-30 minutes

PORK

Medium   – 20-25 minutes per 450 g/1 lb
            plus 25-30 minutes
Well Done   – 25-30 minutes per 450 g/1 lb
            plus 25-30 minutes

VEAL

Well Done   – 30 minutes per 450 g/1 lb
            plus 30 minutes

USING A MEAT THERMOMETER

A meat thermometer may be inserted into the joint before cooking, ready to register the internal temperature and indicate the extent of cooking. Preheat the thermometer in the oven from cold. Pierce the meat at the thickest point with a skewer and insert the hot thermometer into it. At any stage during cooking the reading on the thermometer may be checked to assess cooking progress (see chart below). When the meat is cooked, remove the thermometer and place it on a plate to cool.

BEEF

Rare   –   60°C/140°F
Medium   –   70°C/158°F
Well Done   –   80°C/176°F

LAMB

Medium   –   70-75°C/158-167°F
Well Done   –   75-80°C/167-176°F

PORK

Medium   –   75-80°C/167-176°F
Well Done   –   80-85°C/176-185°F

VEAL

Well Done   –   80-85°C/176-185°F

meat; $2\frac{1}{4}$ hours for well-done meat. Baste frequently during cooking.

Meanwhile make the Yorkshire pudding batter. Sift the flour into a bowl and add a pinch of salt. Make a well in the centre of the flour and add the beaten egg. Stir in the milk, gradually working in the flour. Beat vigorously until the mixture is smooth and bubbly, then stir in 150 ml/$\frac{1}{4}$ pint water.

About 30 minutes before the end of the cooking time, spoon off 30 ml/2 tbsp of the dripping and divide it between six 7.5 cm/3 inch Yorkshire pudding tins. Place the tins in the oven for 5 minutes or until the fat is very hot, then carefully divide the batter between them. Bake above the meat for 15–20 minutes.

ROAST RIBS OF BEEF WITH YORKSHIRE PUDDING

This impressive joint is also known as a standing rib roast. Ask the butcher to trim the thin ends of the bones so that the joint will stand upright. The recipe below, as in Mrs Beeton's day, uses clarified dripping for cooking, but the roast may be cooked without any additional fat, if preferred. There will be sufficient fat from the meat for basting.

2.5 kg/5$\frac{1}{2}$ lb forerib of beef
50–75 g/2–3 oz beef dripping
salt and pepper
vegetable stock or water (see method)

YORKSHIRE PUDDING
100 g/4 oz plain flour
1 egg, beaten
150 ml/$\frac{1}{4}$ pint milk

Set the oven at 230°C/450°F/gas 8. Wipe the meat but do not salt it. Melt 50 g/2 oz of the dripping in a roasting tin, add the meat and quickly spoon some of the hot fat over it. Roast for 10 minutes.

Lower the oven temperature to 180°C/350°F/gas 4. Baste the meat thoroughly, then continue to roast for a further 1$\frac{3}{4}$ hours for rare

When the beef is cooked, salt it lightly, transfer it to a warmed serving platter and keep hot. Pour off almost all the water in the roasting tin, leaving the sediment. Pour in enough vegetable stock or water to make a thin gravy, then heat to boiling point, stirring all the time. Season with salt and pepper and serve in a heated gravyboat with the roast and Yorkshire puddings.

SERVES SIX TO EIGHT

 MRS BEETON'S TIP

Yorkshire pudding is traditionally cooked in a large tin below the joint, so that some of the cooking juices from the meat fall into the pudding to give it an excellent flavour. In a modern oven, this means using a rotisserie or resting the meat directly on the oven shelf. The pudding should be cooked in a large roasting tin, then cut into portions and served as a course on its own before the meat course. Gravy should be poured over the portions of pudding.

BEEF WELLINGTON

This classic Beef Wellington differs from beef en croûte in that the meat is covered with fine pâté – preferably pâté de foie gras – before it is wrapped.

800 g–1 kg/1¾ lb–2¼ lb fillet of beef
freshly ground pepper
25 g/1 oz butter
15 ml/1 tbsp oil
100 g/4 oz button mushrooms, sliced
5 ml/1 tsp chopped fresh mixed herbs
5 ml/1 tsp chopped parsley
75 g/3 oz fine liver pâté

PUFF PASTRY
225 g/8 oz plain flour
2.5 ml/½ tsp salt
225 g/8 oz butter
3.75 ml/¾ tsp lemon juice
beaten egg for glazing

Make the pastry. Sift the flour and salt into a mixing bowl and rub in 50 g/2 oz of the butter. Add the lemon juice and mix to a smooth dough with cold water. Shape the remaining butter into a rectangle on greaseproof paper. Roll out the dough on a lightly floured surface to a strip a little wider than the butter and rather more than twice its length. Place the butter on one half of the pastry, fold the other half over it, and press the edges together with the rolling pin. Leave in a cool place for 15 minutes to allow the butter to harden.

Roll out the pastry into a long strip. Fold the bottom third up and the top third down, press the edges together with the rolling pin and turn the pastry so that the folded edges are on the right and left. Roll and fold again, cover and leave in a cool place for 15 minutes. Repeat this process until the pastry has been rolled out six times. Chill the pastry well between each rolling, wrapping it in cling film to prevent it drying on the surface. After the final rolling,

leave the wrapped pastry in the refrigerator until required.

Set the oven at 230°C/450°F/gas 8. Wipe, trim and tie the meat into a neat shape. Season with pepper. Melt the butter in the oil in a large frying pan, add the fillet and brown it quickly all over. Carefully transfer the fillet to a roasting tin, reserving the fat in the pan, and roast it for 10-20 minutes (for rare to medium result). Remove and cool. Leave the oven on.

Heat the fat remaining in the frying pan, add the mushrooms and fry over moderate heat for 2-3 minutes. Remove from the heat, add the herbs and leave to cool.

Roll out the pastry on a lightly floured surface to a rectangle large enough to enclose the fillet. Using a slotted spoon, transfer the mushroom mixture to one half of the pastry. Lay the beef on top and spread the pâté over the meat. Wrap the pastry around the beef to form a neat parcel, sealing the edges well. Place on a baking sheet with the join underneath. Top with leaves and/or a lattice of strips cut from the pastry trimmings, glaze with beaten egg and bake for about 30 minutes. Serve hot or cold.

SERVES SIX

VARIATION

To make individual beef wellingtons, use six portions of raw fillet. Wrap individually, including mushrooms and pâté, bringing up the pastry sides to make neat parcels. Glaze and bake, allowing 15-20 minutes for rare beef; 25-30 minutes for medium-cooked beef.

GRILLING STEAKS AND SMALL CUTS

Only prime cuts of tender meat are suitable for grilling. Best results are obtained from meat which has a natural layer of fat on it as this melts slightly to baste and flavour the meat during this extremely dry cooking method. It is best not to sprinkle salt directly on meat before grilling (see Mrs Beeton's Tip, right); however, pepper, herbs and seasoned marinades may be used to flavour the meat.

Providing firm guidelines for grilling times is difficult as the performance of individual appliances varies enormously. Equally, the exact thickness and shape of the food, its position under the heat and personal preferences all determine the cooking time. The following timings are intended as a guide only. They are based upon initial cooking under a grill preheated to the hottest setting, the temperature being reduced partway through cooking once the outside of the meat is sealed.

Meat	Thickness	Time for Each Side
Beef Steak, rare	2 cm/¾ inch	2½ minutes
Beef Steak, medium	as above	4 minutes
Beef Steak, well done	as above	6 minutes
Minute Steak	5 mm/¼ inch	1 minute
Pork Chop	2.5 cm/1 inch	10 minutes
Lamb Chop	2.5 cm/1 inch	5–8 minutes
Lamb Cutlet	2.5 cm/1 inch	4–5 minutes

CHATEAUBRIAND STEAK

Châteaubriand is a luxury cut, from the thickest part of the beef fillet. It may be served simply with maître d'hôtel butter, or with Béarnaise Sauce (page 481)

1 double fillet steak, not less than 4 cm/
   1½ inches thick, trimmed
melted butter
freshly ground black pepper
maître d'hôtel butter (page 492), to serve

Brush the steak generously all over with melted butter, season with pepper and place on a rack in a grill pan. Cook under a very hot grill for 2–3 minutes until browned and sealed. Turn the steak over, using a palette knife or spoons, and grill until browned. Lower the heat slightly and continue grilling, turning the steak once or twice, until cooked to taste. Rare meat will require a total cooking time of about 20 minutes; for medium-rare add an extra 5 minutes.

Cut the meat downwards at a slight angle into four even slices. Put two slices on each of two heated plates, top with maître d'hôtel butter and serve at once.

SERVES TWO

 MRS BEETON'S TIP

Salt is not sprinkled directly on meat before grilling as it tends to toughen the surface slightly, also it encourages the meat juices to seep out slightly on standing and during cooking. Herbs, spices and pepper may be used. Salt may be added to flour before coating and frying meat and it may be combined with liquid seasonings. Heavily salted marinades draw out meat juices.

STEAKS WITH MUSTARD SAUCE

4 (150–175 g/5–6 oz) fillet or sirloin steaks,
  trimmed
freshly ground black pepper
25 g/1 oz unsalted butter
30 ml/2 tbsp oil
150 ml/¼ tsp pint soured cream
5 ml/1 tsp lemon juice
10 ml/2 tsp French mustard
salt
watercress to garnish

Beat each steak lightly on both sides with a cutlet bat or rolling pin. Season with pepper (see Mrs Beeton's Tip). Melt the butter in the oil in a heavy-bottomed frying pan. When hot, add the steaks to the pan and fry quickly on both sides, allowing 2–3 minutes a side for rare steak, 3½–4 minutes for medium-rare and 5-6 minutes a side for well done.

Lift out the steaks, transfer them to a warmed serving dish and keep hot. Stir the soured cream into the juices remaining in the pan and heat through gently, without boiling. Stir in the lemon juice, mustard and salt to taste.

Pour the mustard sauce over the steak, garnish with watercress and serve at once.

SERVES FOUR

 MRS BEETON'S TIP

Do not salt the steaks before frying as this draws out the juices.

STEAK AU POIVRE

20 ml/4 tsp whole black and white peppercorns, mixed
4 (150–200 g/5–7 oz) steaks (fillet, sirloin or
  entrecôte), wiped and trimmed
1 garlic clove, cut in half
60 ml/4 tbsp olive oil
50 g/2 oz butter

PARSLEY BUTTER
50 g/2 oz butter, softened
30 ml/2 tbsp chopped parsley
salt and pepper

Make the parsley butter. Beat the butter until creamy in a small bowl. Add the parsley, beating until well combined, then season the mixture with salt and a small pinch of pepper. Form into a roll, wrap in greaseproof paper, and refrigerate until required.

Crush the peppercorns in a mortar with a pestle. Set aside. Rub the steaks on both sides with the cut clove of garlic, then brush both sides generously with olive oil. With the heel of your hand, press the crushed peppercorns into the surface of the meat on each side.

Melt the butter with any remaining olive oil in a heavy-bottomed frying pan. When hot, add the steaks to the pan and fry quickly on both sides, allowing 2–3 minutes a side for rare steak; 3½–4 minutes for medium-rare and 5-6 minutes a side for well done.

Using a palette knife or two spoons, transfer the steaks to a warmed serving dish. Slice the parsley butter into rounds and place one on top of each steak. Serve at once.

SERVES FOUR

TOURNEDOS ROSSINI

Tournedos is a slice from the fillet, usually about 2 cm/¾ inch thick and a neat round shape. In the classic version of this recipe, foie gras and truffles are used instead of liver pâté and mushrooms, and the dish is served with a brown sauce enriched with Madeira.

4 (175 g/6 oz) tournedos steaks, trimmed
4 slices of white bread
100 g/4 oz butter
15 ml/1 tbsp cooking oil
salt and pepper

GARNISH
4 rounds of good quality liver pâté, 5 mm/
  ¼ inch thick
4 small flat mushrooms
20 ml/4 tsp chilled butter
watercress sprigs

Tie the tournedos to a neat shape. Cut the bread slices into 4 rounds, each large enough to accommodate one of the steaks. Melt half the butter in the oil in a large, deep frying pan and fry the bread rounds over moderate heat until pale gold and crisp on both sides. Transfer to a warmed serving dish, cover with buttered greaseproof paper and keep warm.

Add half the remaining butter to the pan. When hot, add the steaks to the pan and fry quickly for 2–3 minutes on each side, or until well seared and browned all over, but rare inside. Remove them from the pan, using a palette knife or two spoons, and place one on each fried bread round. Keep hot.

Heat the remaining butter in a small frying pan, add the pâté slices and mushrooms and turn over high heat until the mushrooms are soft and the pâté is lightly browned but still holds its shape.

Place a slice of pâté on each tournedos and cap it with a mushroom, gill side down. Top each mushroom with 5 ml/1 tsp chilled butter. Garnish with watercress and serve at once, with freshly ground black pepper.

SERVES FOUR

STEAK CHASSEUR

75 g/3 oz butter
30 ml/2 tbsp finely chopped shallots or
  spring onions
100 g/4 oz mushrooms, sliced
125 ml/4 fl oz dry white wine
4 (150 g/5 oz) fillet steaks
125 ml/4 fl oz good quality beef stock
15 ml/1 tbsp tomato purée
15 ml/1 tbsp finely chopped parsley

Melt 25 g/1 oz of the butter in a small saucepan. Add the shallots or spring onions and cook gently until softened but not browned. Add the mushrooms and shake over high heat for 2–3 minutes. Pour in the wine. Boil it rapidly uncovered, until reduced to about half. Set aside while cooking the steaks.

Melt the remaining butter in a frying pan. When hot, add the steaks to the pan and fry quickly on both sides, allowing 2–3 minutes a side for rare steaks; 3½–4 minutes for medium-rare and 5–6 minutes a side for well done. Arrange on a heated dish.

Pour off most of the fat from the pan and add the beef stock and tomato purée. Boil rapidly, stirring to incorporate any sediment on the base of the pan, until reduced to about half. Stir in the mushroom mixture and parsley, pour over the steaks and serve.

SERVES FOUR

STEAK AND ONIONS

Serve creamy mashed potatoes, fine potato chips or French fries or plain boiled potatoes sprinkled with a little parsley with this traditional dish of fried steak with onions.

beef dripping for cooking
2 large onions, thinly sliced
1 bay leaf
1 fresh thyme sprig
4 (225-350 g/8-12 oz) slices of rump steak
salt and pepper
60 ml/4 tbsp plain flour
15 ml/1 tbsp tomato purée
300 ml/½ pint beef stock
dash of Worcestershire sauce

GARNISH (OPTIONAL)
4 small tomatoes, halved or quartered
fresh herb sprigs

Melt a knob of dripping in a large frying pan. Add the onions, bay leaf and thyme, and cook the onions over moderate heat, stirring occasionally, until they are evenly browned. This takes up to 25 minutes – do not increase the heat to hurry the browning; the secret of a good flavour is the long cooking.

Meanwhile, trim any gristle and excess fat from the steak, then beat the pieces with a meat mallet or rolling pin to tenderize them. Avoid beating the meat in such a way that the steaks are thinned. Place the steaks on a plate. Add plenty of salt and pepper to the flour, then sprinkle half over the steaks, dusting them evenly. Turn the meat over and sprinkle the remaining flour over the second sides.

Use a slotted spoon to remove the onions from the pan. Drain them on absorbent kitchen paper and transfer to a heated serving dish or individual plates. Keep hot. Leave the bay leaf and thyme in the pan and add a little extra dripping if necessary. When the fat is hot, add

the steaks and brown them quickly on both sides. Allow about 3 minutes on each side for rare steaks. For medium or well done steaks, lower the heat slightly once the meat is sealed and continue to cook for 4-7 minutes on each side. The exact time depends on the thickness of the meat.

Transfer the steaks to the dish or plates, cover loosely and keep hot. Stir any remaining flour into the juices in the pan, then stir in the tomato purée and the stock. Bring to the boil, stirring, and boil rapidly to reduce the sauce by about a third. Add a little Worcestershire sauce and taste for seasoning.

Spoon the sauce and onion over the steaks. Garnish with tomatoes and herbs, if liked. Serve at once.

SERVES FOUR

SCOTCH COLLOPS

Collop is said to be derived from escalope, meaning slice. It was also used as an everyday term for veal, so sliced veal could equally well have been used in this old-fashioned dish. Minced collops, a less extravagant variation on this recipe, uses hand-minced, or diced steak in place of sliced meat.

50 g/2 oz dripping, lard or butter
675 g/1½ lb rump steak, beaten and cut into
 thin slices, about 7.5 cm/3 inches long
25 g/1 oz plain flour
salt and pepper
½ small onion or 1 shallot, finely chopped
250 ml/8 fl oz good beef stock
5 ml/1 tsp chopped capers
1 pickled walnut, chopped

Heat the fat in a deep frying pan. In a bowl or stout polythene bag, toss the meat with the flour, salt and pepper, then add the slices to the hot fat and fry until browned on all sides. With a slotted spoon, remove the meat from the pan.

Add the onion or shallot to the fat remaining in the pan and fry gently until softened but not browned. Stir in any flour left from dusting the meat and cook for about 5 minutes, stirring all the time, until the flour begins to brown.

Gradually add the stock, stirring constantly, then add the capers, pickled walnut and salt and pepper to taste. Bring to the boil, stirring constantly, then lower the heat and replace the meat. Simmer very gently for 10 minutes and serve piping hot.

SERVES FOUR TO SIX

VARIATION

Minced Collops Braising steak may be used instead of rump. Trim and chop the meat by hand (minced beef is too fine) – it should be finely chopped. Use 1 chopped onion and fry it in the fat, then add the beef tossed in flour, and cook until browned. Add the stock and seasoning, as above, without removing the meat from the pan. Omit the capers and walnut but add a bouquet garni and a dash of Worcestershire sauce or mushroom ketchup instead. Bring just to the boil, then cover and simmer gently for 1-1½ hours, until tender. Garnish with sippets.

 MRS BEETON'S TIP

To make sippets, toast white or granary bread until golden. Cut into triangles or cubes.

CARPET BAG STEAK

fat for roasting
1-1.5 kg/2¼-3¼ lb piece of rump steak or
   topside, not less than 5 cm/2 inches thick,
   trimmed
30 ml/2 tbsp butter
12 fresh oysters, shelled
100 g/4 oz mushrooms, sliced
grated rind of ½ lemon
150 g/5 oz fresh white breadcrumbs
15 ml/1 tbsp chopped parsley
salt and paprika
1 egg, beaten

Set the oven at 160°C/325°F/gas 3. Slit the meat through the middle horizontally, leaving three edges joined, to make a deep pocket.

Melt the butter in a frying pan, add the oysters and mushrooms and cook gently for 3 minutes. Tip the contents of the pan into a bowl and mix in the lemon rind, breadcrumbs and parsley. Add salt and paprika to taste and stir in enough of the beaten egg to bind the mixture.

Fill the pocket in the steak with the oyster stuffing, skewering or stitching the open edge closed. Melt a little fat in a roasting tin. When hot, add the stuffed steak and baste it, then roast it for 1-1½ hours or until the meat is tender. Alternatively, cook under a preheated hot grill, brushing the steak with oil from time to time. Allow 5-6 minutes on each side under a hot grill, then lower the heat to moderate and grill for about 10-15 minutes more on each side, or until the steak and stuffing are cooked.

SERVES SIX

 MRS BEETON'S TIP

Keep a stock of breadcrumbs in the freezer. They thaw very swiftly.

BEEF STROGANOFF

675 g/1½ lb thinly sliced rump steak,
  trimmed
45 ml/3 tbsp plain flour
salt and pepper
50 g/2 oz butter
225 g/8 oz onions, thinly sliced
225 g/8 oz mushrooms, thinly sliced
250 ml/8 fl oz soured cream

Beat the steak slices with a cutlet bat or rolling pin, then cut them into thin strips. Put the flour in a shallow bowl, season with plenty of salt and pepper and coat the beef strips.

Melt half the butter in a large heavy-bottomed saucepan, add the onion slices and fry for about 10 minutes until golden. Stir in the mushrooms and continue cooking for a further 2–3 minutes. Using a slotted spoon, transfer the vegetables to a dish. Set aside.

Melt the remaining butter in the pan, add the meat and fry rapidly for 2–3 minutes, turning frequently. Return the vegetables to the pan and heat through for 1 minute. Pour in the soured cream, stir once or twice, and heat for 1–2 minutes until all the ingredients are heated through (see Mrs Beeton's Tip). Serve at once, with noodles, boiled new potatoes or rice.

SERVES FOUR

 MRS BEETON'S TIP

Do not allow the sauce to approach boiling point after the soured cream has been added, or it will curdle.

BEEF CREOLE

4 rindless streaky bacon rashers
1 kg/2¼ lb rump steak, trimmed
salt and pepper
2 small red chillies, seeded and very finely
  chopped
2 garlic cloves, crushed
575 g/1¼ lb onions, sliced
1 each red and green peppers, seeded and
  sliced
575 g/1¼ lb tomatoes, sliced
225 g/8 oz long-grain rice

Set the oven at 160°C/325°F/gas 3. Lay the bacon rashers on the base of a casserole large enough to hold the meat snugly. Place the meat on top and season well. Sprinkle the chillies and garlic on top.

Smother the meat with onions, then top with a layer of peppers and tomato slices. Cover with foil or a tight-fitting lid. Bake for 3–3½ hours, until the beef is tender.

About 20 minutes before the beef is cooked, place the rice in a saucepan and pour in 600 ml/1 pint water. Add a little salt, then bring just to the boil. Stir once, cover and turn the heat to the lowest setting. Leave the rice to cook for 20 minutes. Turn the heat off but leave the rice with the lid on the pan for a further 5–10 minutes.

Fork up the rice and turn it out on a large heated platter or shallow dish. Use a slotted spoon to transfer the onions, peppers and tomatoes to the bed of rice. Slice or cut up the meat and arrange it over the vegetables. Cut up the bacon and sprinkle over the meat. Cover and keep hot. Boil the cooking juices until reduced by half. Season; pour over beef and serve at once.

SERVES FOUR TO SIX

BEEF OLIVES

This makes an excellent main course for a casual dinner party and has the advantage that the meat is prepared in individual portions and needs very little last-minute attention.

450 g/1 lb rump or chuck steak, trimmed
45 ml/3 tbsp dripping or oil
1 large onion, sliced
45 ml/3 tbsp plain flour
600 ml/1 pint beef stock
1 tomato, peeled and sliced
1 carrot, sliced
15 ml/1 tbsp Worcestershire sauce
salt and pepper
30 ml/2 tbsp chopped parsley
fresh herb sprigs to garnish

STUFFING
50 g/2 oz margarine
100 g/4 oz fresh white breadcrumbs
pinch of grated nutmeg
15 ml/1 tbsp chopped parsley
5 ml/1 tsp chopped fresh mixed herbs
grated rind of ½ lemon
1 egg, beaten

Make the stuffing. Melt the margarine in a small saucepan. Add the breadcrumbs, nutmeg, herbs and lemon rind, with salt and pepper to taste. Add enough beaten egg to bind the mixture.

Cut the meat into four slices and flatten each with a cutlet bat or rolling pin. Divide the stuffing between the meat slices, spreading it out evenly. Roll each piece of meat up tightly and tie securely with fine string or cotton.

Heat the dripping or oil in a large saucepan and fry the beef olives, turning them frequently until browned. Using a slotted spoon, transfer them to a plate.

Add the onion slices to the fat remaining in the pan and fry until golden brown. Using a slotted spoon, transfer to the plate with the beef olives. Add the flour to the pan and cook until golden brown, stirring constantly. Gradually add the stock, stirring until the mixture boils, then lower the heat and simmer for 5 minutes.

Return the beef olives and onion slices to the pan. Add the tomato, carrot and Worcestershire sauce, with salt and pepper to taste. Cover the pan with a tight-fitting lid and simmer for 1-2 hours.

Having removed the strings from the beef olives, serve them on a bed of mashed potato or rice. Strain the sauce and pour it over the beef olives. Sprinkle with chopped parsley and garnish with fresh herbs (the same types as used in the stuffing). Serve at once.

SERVES FOUR

VARIATIONS

Hanover Rouladen Omit the stuffing. Instead lay a strip of gherkin on each portion of beef, with 15 ml/1 tbsp finely chopped onion, 15 ml/1 tbsp chopped ham and 5 ml/1 tsp capers. Proceed as in the recipe above but cook for 1½ hours only.

Mushroom Paupiettes Use a mushroom stuffing instead of herb. Chop 1 rindless bacon rasher and fry without additional fat for 2 minutes. Add 100 g/4 oz finely chopped mushrooms and fry over gentle heat for 5 minutes, stirring. Stir in 100 g/4 oz fresh white breadcrumbs, a knob of butter and pinch of grated nutmeg. Add salt and pepper to taste. Bind with beaten egg. Prepare and cook the paupiettes as for the beef olives in the recipe above, but stir 250 ml/8 fl oz soured cream into the sauce just before serving.

BRAISED BRISKET

1.25-1.5 kg/2¾-3¼ lb brisket of beef, trimmed
25 g/1 oz dripping or 30 ml/2 tbsp oil
25 g/1 oz rindless streaky bacon rashers,
  chopped
1 large carrot, thickly sliced
1 small turnip, thickly sliced
1 large onion, chopped, or 15 button onions
2 celery sticks, thickly sliced
1 bouquet garni
salt and pepper
250-300 ml/8-10 fl oz beef stock

GRAVY
30 ml/2 tbsp dripping or oil
10 ml/2 tsp plain flour
450 ml/¾ pint beef stock
10 ml/2 tsp tomato purée

Tie the meat into a neat shape if necessary.
Heat the dripping or oil in a large flameproof
casserole, add the meat and brown it on all
sides. Remove the meat and set it aside.

Add the bacon and vegetables, and fry gently
until beginning to soften. Tuck in the bouquet
garni and add salt and pepper to taste. Place the
meat on top of the vegetables and pour the
stock over. Cover with a tight-fitting lid and
cook over gentle heat for 2 hours or until the

meat is tender. Baste occasionally and add
more stock if required. Alternatively, cook in a
preheated 160°C/325°F/gas 3 oven for about
2 hours.

To make the gravy, heat the dripping or oil in a
saucepan. Stir in the flour and cook gently until
pale brown. Gradually add the stock, stirring
constantly, then add the tomato purée. Bring to
the boil, stirring all the time, then lower the
heat and simmer uncovered for 15-20
minutes.

When the meat is cooked, transfer it to a heated
serving dish, remove the string, if used, and
keep hot. Strain any stock remaining in the
casserole into the gravy. Garnish the meat with
the vegetables and serve the gravy separately.

SERVES TEN TO TWELVE

VARIATION

If liked, slivers of garlic may be inserted into
the meat and red wine used in place of part or
all of the beef stock. For a rich and tasty gravy
made from the pan juices, combine
30 ml/2 tbsp tomato purée, 15 ml/1 tbsp soy
sauce, 5 ml/1 tsp Worcestershire sauce and a
pinch of brown sugar in a bowl. Mix well and
spread over the surface of the meat about 45
minutes before it is cooked. Leave for 15
minutes, then remove the pan lid and baste the
meat with the stock so that the spicy mixture
combines with it. Serve as suggested above, but
use the pan gravy as an accompaniment, skimming any fat from the surface before serving.

BRAISED BEEF WITH PEPPERS

1 kg/2¼ lb topside or brisket of beef
25 g/1 oz dripping or 30 ml/2 tbsp oil
2 rindless streaky bacon rashers, chopped
1 large carrot, sliced
1 small turnip, sliced
12 button onions, peeled but left whole
100 g/4 oz button mushrooms
2 celery sticks, thickly sliced
2 leeks, trimmed, sliced and washed
1 bouquet garni
salt
6 black peppercorns
250 ml/8 fl oz beef stock

GRAVY
15 ml/1 tbsp dripping or oil
30 ml/2 tbsp plain flour
250 ml/8 fl oz beef stock
5 ml/1 tsp tomato purée

GARNISH
3 red peppers, seeded and sliced into 1 cm/
½ inch wide strips
12 black olives (optional)

Tie the meat into a neat shape if necessary. Heat the dripping or oil in a large flameproof casserole or heavy-bottomed saucepan, add the meat and brown it on all sides. Remove the meat and set it aside.

Add the bacon and vegetables to the fat remaining in the casserole or pan. Fry gently until beginning to soften. Tuck in the bouquet garni and add salt to taste. Stir in the peppercorns. Place the meat on top of the vegetables and pour the stock over. Cover with a tight-fitting lid and cook over a gentle heat for 2½–3 hours or until the meat is tender. Baste occasionally and add more stock if required. Alternatively, cook in a preheated 160°C/325°F/gas 3 oven for about 2½ hours.

Meanwhile make the gravy. Heat the dripping or oil in a saucepan. Stir in the flour and cook gently until pale brown. Gradually add the stock, stirring constantly, then add the tomato purée. Bring to the boil, stirring all the time, then lower the heat and simmer, uncovered, for 15–20 minutes.

Lift out the meat from the casserole or pan. Add the pepper strips to the remaining stock and simmer for 10 minutes. Meanwhile remove the string from the meat, carve it into neat slices and arrange on a heated serving dish. Use a slotted spoon to arrange the pepper strips and vegetables around the meat slices. Complete the garnish with the black olives, if liked. Pour the cooking juices from the meat into the gravy and spoon a little over the meat. Serve at once, offering the remaining gravy separately.

SERVES SIX

 MRS BEETON'S TIP

It is hard to believe that the sweet bell peppers, used here, come from the same family as the fiery chillies that enliven Mexican and Indian cooking. Sweet peppers come in a variety of shapes, sizes and colours. Raw fresh peppers contain significant amounts of vitamin C.

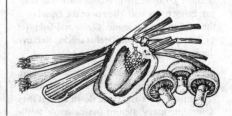

CARBONNADE OF BEEF

Brown ale and long, slow cooking combine to make this classic, full-flavoured stew with its crunchy topping of mustard-seasoned French bread.

50 g/2 oz butter or margarine
675 g/1½ lb stewing steak, trimmed and cut
    into 4 cm/1½ inch cubes
2 large onions, sliced
1 garlic clove, crushed
15 ml/1 tbsp plain flour
250 ml/8 fl oz beef stock
375 ml/13 fl oz brown ale
salt and pepper
1 bouquet garni
pinch of grated nutmeg
pinch of soft light brown sugar
5 ml/1 tsp red wine vinegar
6 thin slices of French bread
15 ml/1 tbsp French mustard

Set the oven at 160°C/325°F/gas 3. Melt the butter or margarine in a heavy-bottomed frying pan, add the beef and fry quickly until browned on all sides. Using a slotted spoon, transfer the beef to a casserole and keep hot. Add the onions to the fat remaining in the pan and fry until lightly browned, then stir in the garlic and fry over gentle heat for 1 minute.

Pour off any excess fat from the pan to leave about 15 ml/1 tbsp. Add the flour to the onions and garlic and cook, stirring constantly, until lightly browned. Gradually stir in the stock and ale, with salt and pepper to taste. Add the bouquet garni, nutmeg, brown sugar and vinegar. Bring to the boil, then pour the liquid over the beef in the casserole. Cover and bake for 1½–2 hours or until the beef is tender. Remove the bouquet garni.

Spread the French bread slices with mustard. Arrange them, mustard side up, on top of the carbonnade, pressing them down so that they absorb the gravy. Return the casserole to the oven, uncovered, for about 15 minutes or until the bread browns slightly. Alternatively, place under a hot grill for a few minutes. Serve immediately, straight from the casserole.

SERVES SIX

 PRESSURE COOKER TIP

Follow the recipe left, removing the open pressure cooker from the heat before adding the stock and ale. The cooker should not be more than half full. Close the cooker, bring to 15 lb pressure and cook for 20 minutes. Reduce the pressure quickly. Transfer the stew to a casserole, top with the bread slices as left, and grill until golden.

MRS BEETON'S BOEUF A LA MODE

2 rindless back bacon rashers
1 kg/2¼ lb thick flank of beef (see Mrs
    Beeton's Tip opposite)
100 ml/3½ fl oz red wine vinegar
25 g/1 oz butter
1 onion, sliced
2 celery sticks, sliced
1 carrot, chopped
½ turnip, chopped
75 ml/5 tbsp port
salt and pepper

SEASONING MIXTURE
1 clove
4 black peppercorns
3 allspice berries
3 parsley sprigs, finely chopped
1 fresh thyme sprig, leaves finely chopped
    or 1.25 ml/¼ tsp dried thyme
1 bay leaf, finely crumbled

Cut the bacon crossways into 2 cm/¾ inch strips, including fat and lean in each strip. Trim the meat and, using a sharp knife, make sufficient deep slits in the flesh to accommodate all the bacon strips.

Make the seasoning mixture. Pound the clove, peppercorns and allspice in a mortar with a pestle. Add all the remaining ingredients and mix well.

Pour the vinegar into a shallow bowl. Dip the bacon strips into the vinegar and then into the spice mixture. Insert a bacon strip into each slit in the meat. Rub any remaining spice mixture over the surface of the meat, then tie the beef into a neat shape.

Melt the butter in a flameproof casserole large enough to hold the piece of beef. Add the onion and fry gently until golden brown, then stir in the celery, carrot and turnip. Place the meat on the vegetables. Gently pour in the vinegar, with 250 ml/8 fl oz water, and cover the pan closely. Heat to boiling point, lower the heat and simmer very gently for about 1¾ hours, turning the meat over after 40 minutes' cooking time, and again after a further 30 minutes.

When cooked, transfer the meat to a warmed serving dish and keep hot. Strain the cooking liquid into a pan, skim off the fat, and add the port. Bring to the boil over gentle heat. Add salt and pepper if required. Remove the strings from the meat and pour a little of the sauce over. Serve the remaining sauce in a warmed sauceboat.

SERVES FOUR TO SIX

 MRS BEETON'S TIP

Thick flank or top rump, as it is often called, is usually sold with extra fat tied around it. The quantity of meat stipulated left is without the added fat.

BEEF AND POTATO PIE

This is simple country cooking with no frills. Salt and pepper are the only condiments used; the pie deriving its flavour from long slow cooking of meat and vegetables. It is therefore important that the stewing steak is of good quality. Remember that stewing steak gives a better flavour than braising steak in a recipe of this type.

675 g/1½ lb stewing steak, trimmed and cut into 2 cm/¾ inch cubes
3 onions, sliced
3 large carrots, sliced
1 kg/2¼ lb potatoes, sliced
salt and pepper
hot beef stock (see method)

Set the oven at 160°C/325°F/gas 3. Layer the meat with the onion, carrot and potato slices in an ovenproof casserole, finishing with a neat layer of potatoes. Add salt and pepper.

Pour in enough hot stock to three-quarters cover the contents of the casserole, reserving some stock for adding if the dish begins to dry out during cooking. Cover with a tight-fitting lid or foil and bake for 3-3½ hours, or until the beef is very tender.

About 30-40 minutes before the end of the cooking time, remove the casserole lid to allow the top layer of potato to brown. Serve straight from the casserole.

SERVES SIX

 MRS BEETON'S TIP

If liked, the top layer of potato may be sprinkled with paprika before browning. Use a sweet Hungarian rose paprika if possible.

MOCK HARE

30 ml/2 tbsp plain flour
salt and pepper
675 g/1½ lb chuck steak or shin of beef,
    trimmed and cut into 2 cm/¾ inch cubes
100 g/4 oz rindless fat bacon, diced
1 onion
3 cloves
400 ml/14 fl oz well-flavoured stock
1 bouquet garni
15 ml/1 tbsp redcurrant jelly
125 ml/4 fl oz port
10 ml/2 tsp chopped gherkins

GARNISH
Mrs Beeton's Forcemeat Balls (page 475)
parsley sprigs

Mix the flour, salt and pepper in a sturdy polythene bag. Add the beef cubes and toss until well coated. Shake off excess flour. Put the bacon in a large flameproof casserole and heat gently until the fat runs. Add the floured meat cubes, a few at a time, turning them until evenly browned. As the cubes brown push them to the sides of the casserole, or use a slotted spoon to transfer them to a plate, replacing them in the casserole when all the cubes have been browned.

Peel the onion and press the cloves into it. Add it to the casserole with the stock and bouquet garni. Bring to the boil, lower the heat, cover and cook gently for 1½–2 hours for chuck steak, 2–2½ hours for shin. Remove the onion and bouquet garni.

Add the redcurrant jelly, port and gherkins to the casserole, stirring until the jelly melts. Serve the meat from the casserole, garnished with forcemeat balls and parsley.

SERVES SIX

BEEF AND BEAN STEW

Stews and casseroles improve if cooked a day ahead. Cool the cooked stew as quickly as possible, cover and store in the refrigerator. Next day, remove any fat from the surface of the stew and reheat on top of the stove or in the oven at 180°C/350°F/gas 4.

675 g/1½ lb leg of beef, trimmed and cut in
    neat 2 cm/¾ inch thick pieces
seasoned flour
60 ml/4 tbsp oil
1 large onion, chopped
2 carrots, chopped
1 small turnip, chopped
750 ml/1¼ pints beef stock
30 ml/2 tbsp tomato purée
salt and pepper
75 g/3 oz haricot beans, soaked in water
    overnight
100 g/4 oz mushrooms, sliced

Toss the beef cubes in seasoned flour until well coated. The easiest way to do this is in a tightly closed stout polythene bag. Tip the contents of the bag into a sieve; shake off excess flour.

Heat the oil in a flameproof casserole and fry the onion, carrots and turnip until golden. With a slotted spoon, transfer the vegetables to a bowl and set aside. Add the floured beef cubes

---

 PRESSURE COOKER TIP

Follow the recipe above, but add only 600 ml/1 pint beef stock. After adding the beans, close the cooker, bring to 15 lb pressure and cook for 20 minutes. Reduce the pressure quickly. Stir the stew, taking care to incorporate any sediment on the bottom of the pan, then add the mushrooms, if time permits. Cook in the open pan for 15–20 minutes over gentle heat. Proceed as above.

to the fat remaining in the pan and cook until browned on all sides. Pour off any excess fat and return the partially cooked vegetables to the pan. Gradually stir in the stock and tomato purée, with salt and pepper to taste. Simmer.

Drain the beans and place them in a separate saucepan with cold water to cover. Bring to the boil, boil vigorously for 10 minutes, then drain. Add the beans to the stew and simmer gently for about 2-2½ hours or until the meat and beans are tender. Stir occasionally during cooking, never allowing the liquid to boil as this will toughen the meat.

Add the mushrooms and cook for 20-30 minutes more. Serve at once, or transfer to a suitable covered container to cool, chill and refrigerate for reheating the next day.

SERVES SIX

STEW WITH SAVOURY PARSLEY DUMPLINGS

30 ml/2 tbsp dripping or oil
675 g/1½ lb chuck or blade steak, trimmed and cut into 5 cm/2 inch cubes
3 onions, chopped
45 ml/3 tbsp plain flour
600 ml/1 pint beef stock
5 ml/1 tsp vinegar
salt and pepper

PARSLEY DUMPLINGS
175 g/6 oz self-raising flour
2.5 ml/½ tsp salt
75 g/3 oz shredded beef suet
15 ml/1 tbsp finely chopped parsley

Heat the dripping or oil in a large heavy-bottomed saucepan. Add the meat and fry until browned on all sides, then remove with a slotted spoon and set aside. Add the onions to the fat remaining in the pan and fry gently until

golden brown. Stir in the flour and cook until lightly browned.

Gradually stir in the stock. Bring to the boil, stirring, then lower the heat to simmering point. Stir in the vinegar, with salt and pepper to taste. Return the beef cubes, cover the pan and simmer gently for 1½ hours, or until the meat is tender.

To make the parsley dumplings, sift the flour and salt into a mixing bowl and stir in the suet and parsley. Add about 90 ml/6 tbsp water and mix lightly to make a firm elastic dough. Divide the dough into 12 equal pieces, shaping each into a ball.

Bring the stew to boiling point and arrange the parsley dumplings on top. Lower the heat, half cover the pan and simmer for a further 20 minutes or until the dumplings are cooked. To serve, arrange the dumplings around a heated serving dish, then ladle the meat in the centre.

SERVES SIX

 PRESSURE COOKER TIP

The stew can be made very successfully in a pressure cooker. Follow the recipe above, removing the pan from the heat before adding the stock. The pan should not be more than half full. Close the cooker, bring to 15 lb pressure and cook for 20 minutes. Return the cooker – without the lid – to the heat and bring to the boil. Add the dumplings and lower the heat. Place the lid lightly on top to serve as a cover, but do not close or add weights. Simmer gently until the dumplings are cooked. Serve the stew as suggested above.

STEWED STUFFED BEEF

about 1.4 kg/3 lb top rib of beef or braising
  steak in one piece
1 quantity Mrs Beeton's Forcemeat (page
  475)
salt and pepper
50 g/2 oz plain flour
50 g/2 oz butter
2 blades of mace
30 ml/2 tbsp lemon juice
1.1 litres/2 pints weak veal or beef stock
60 ml/4 tbsp dry sherry
50 g/2 oz small button mushrooms

Slit the beef three-quarters of the way through
horizontally. Fold the top portion open and lay
the meat on double-thick greaseproof paper.
Cover with more paper and beat out the meat to
thin it slightly.

Spoon the forcemeat down the length of the
meat, then fold the top portion over the stuffing
to enclose it completely. Tie the meat firmly in
shape. Season the meat well and dust it all over
with half the flour.

Melt half the butter in a large flameproof
casserole. Add the meat and brown it lightly all
over. Add the mace and lemon juice, then pour
the stock into the pan. Bring only just to the
boil, lower the heat and cover the pan tightly.
Simmer the stuffed beef very gently for 3 hours,
until the meat is very tender. Turn the meat
over halfway through cooking.

Cream the remaining butter and flour to a paste
in a small bowl.

Transfer the meat to a heated serving plate. Boil
the cooking juices to reduce them by about a
third. Meanwhile, remove the string from the
meat and slice it, overlapping the slices on the
serving plate.

Remove the mace from the cooking liquor. Add
the sherry, then allow to simmer. Whisking all

the time, gradually add knobs of the butter and
flour mixture. Bring to the boil, whisking, to
thicken the sauce. Add the mushrooms and
simmer for 3 minutes. Taste for seasoning.

Ladle some of the sauce over the meat. Pour the
rest into a warmed sauceboat and offer separately. Serve at once, with a colourful array of
vegetables.

SERVES SIX

BOILED BEEF AND DUMPLINGS

1–1.25 kg/2½–2¾ lb beef brisket or silverside,
  trimmed
5 ml/1 tsp salt
3 cloves
10 peppercorns
1 bouquet garni
3 onions, quartered
4 potatoes, halved or quartered
4 large carrots, cut lengthways in quarters,
  then in thick slices
4 small turnips, halved
1 small swede, cut in chunks

DUMPLINGS
225 g/8 oz self-raising flour
2.5 ml/½ tsp salt
100 g/4 oz shredded beef suet

Weigh the meat and calculate the cooking time,
allowing 25 minutes per 450 g/1 lb plus 20
minutes over. Tie the meat to a neat shape with
string, if necessary. Put it into a large heavy-
bottomed saucepan, cover with boiling water
and add the salt. Bring to the boil again and boil
for 5 minutes to seal the surface of the meat.
Lower the heat to simmering point, skim, then
add the cloves, peppercorns and bouquet garni.
Cover and simmer for the rest of the calculated
cooking time.

About 45 minutes before the end of the cooking time, add the onions; 15 minutes later add the potatoes and carrots. Make the dumplings by sifting the flour and salt into a mixing bowl. Stir in the suet and add enough cold water to make a firm elastic dough. Divide the dough into walnut-sized pieces, shaping each into a neat ball.

Twenty minutes before the end of the cooking time, add the turnips and swede, and bring the stock around the beef to boiling point. Drop in the dumplings. Lower the heat, half cover the pan and simmer until the dumplings are cooked, turning them over once with a slotted spoon during this time.

To serve, remove the dumplings from the pan and arrange them as a border on a large heated serving dish. Remove and discard the bouquet garni, then lift out the vegetables with a slotted spoon and arrange them with the dumplings, placing excess vegetables in a separate dish. Remove any strings from the meat, skewer it if necessary to retain the shape, and set it in the centre of the dish. Serve some of the cooking liquid separately in a sauceboat.

SERVES EIGHT TO TEN

GOULASH

It is the paprika that gives this hearty Hungarian stew its delicious flavour. Serve simply, with crusty bread.

50 g/2 oz dripping or lard
675 g/1½ lb chuck or blade steak, trimmed
   and cut into 2 cm/¾ inch cubes
2 onions, sliced
30 ml/2 tbsp plain flour
125 ml/4 fl oz beef stock
125 ml/4 fl oz red wine
450 g/1 lb tomatoes, peeled and diced or
   1 (397 g/14 oz) can chopped tomatoes
2.5 ml/½ tsp salt
15 ml/1 tbsp paprika
1 bouquet garni
450 g/1 lb potatoes
150 ml/¼ pint soured cream

Heat the dripping in a flameproof casserole and fry the meat until browned on all sides. Using a slotted spoon, remove the meat and set aside. Add the onions to the fat remaining in the casserole and fry gently until just beginning to brown. Add the flour and cook, stirring until browned. Gradually add the stock and wine, with the tomatoes, salt, paprika and bouquet garni. Bring to the boil, stirring, then lower the heat and simmer for 1½–2 hours or until the meat is tender. Alternatively, transfer the goulash to a casserole and bake at 160°C/325°F/gas 3 for 1½–2 hours.

Thirty minutes before the end of the cooking time, peel the potatoes, cut them into cubes and add them to the goulash. When cooked they should be tender but not broken. Just before serving, remove the bouquet garni and stir in the soured cream.

SERVES SIX

BOILED BRISKET

15 ml/1 tbsp red wine vinegar
5 ml/1 tsp salt
1.25-1.5 kg/2¾-3¼ lb boned and rolled beef
  brisket
150 g/5 oz rindless streaky bacon rashers
2 carrots, thickly sliced
2 onions, thickly sliced
1 turnip, chopped
1-2 celery sticks, sliced
1 blade of mace
10 black peppercorns
1 bouquet garni
25 g/1 oz butter
25 g/1 oz plain flour
salt and pepper

Mix the vinegar with half the salt in a small bowl. Rub the mixture over the meat. Set aside in a cool place, covered, for 2-3 hours.

Cover the base of a heavy-bottomed saucepan with half the bacon rashers. Place the meat on top and lay the remaining rashers over the meat. Add the vegetables, mace, peppercorns and bouquet garni to the pan and pour in enough water to cover. Bring to the boil, skim well, then lower the heat, cover the pan tightly, and cook very gently for 2½ hours, checking the level of water occasionally. The liquid should always two-thirds to three-quarters cover the meat.

When cooked, remove the meat from the pan and place it on a warmed serving dish. Remove any strings and keep the meat hot. Using a slotted spoon, remove the vegetables and arrange them around the meat on the dish.

Make the sauce. Strain the stock remaining in the pan, skim off excess fat from the surface and measure 350 ml/12 fl oz. Melt the butter in a small saucepan, stir in the flour and cook for 1 minute. Gradually stir in the stock, then bring to the boil, stirring constantly, and cook until

thickened. Add salt and pepper to taste. Serve in a sauceboat with the meat and vegetables.

SERVES TEN TO TWELVE

MRS BEETON'S RUMP STEAK PIE

225 g/8 oz plain flour
75 g/3 oz beef dripping
900 g/2 lb rump steak
salt and pepper · 1 egg yolk

Place the flour in a bowl. Gradually mix in enough water to make a soft but not too sticky dough – about 150 ml/¼ pint. On a lightly floured surface, roll out the dough into a 28 × 15 cm (11 × 6 inch) oblong. Dot a third of the dripping over the top two-thirds of the dough, fold the bottom third of the dough over the middle portion of fat, then fold the top third over that. Give the dough a quarter turn to the right, roll it out and repeat the process twice more to incorporate all the fat. Roll and fold the dough a fourth time without fat, then wrap it in polythene and chill for 30 minutes.

Set the oven at 180°C/350°F/gas 4. Cut the steak into thin slices measuring about 7.5 × 5 cm/3 × 2 inches, then layer it in a 1.1 litre/2 pint pie dish, mounding it up in the middle and pressing down neatly. Season each layer very generously. Slowly pour in enough water to come just below the rim of the dish.

Roll out the dough thickly. Dampen the rim of the dish and press a strip of dough on it. Dampen the dough rim, then cover the pie and seal the edge well. Decorate the top with pastry trimmings. Beat the egg yolk with 5 ml/1 tsp water; brush it over the pie. Bake for about 2½ hours, covering loosely with foil after 1¼-1½ hours. Pierce the pie with a knife to check that the meat is tender.

SERVES FOUR

STEAK PIE

575 g/1¼ lb chuck or blade steak, trimmed
   and cut into 1 cm/½ inch cubes
45 ml/3 tbsp seasoned flour
2 onions, chopped
about 250 ml/8 fl oz beef stock
beaten egg or milk for glazing

ROUGH PUFF PASTRY
200 g/7 oz plain flour
1.25 ml/¼ tsp salt
150 g/5 oz butter or half butter, half lard,
   well chilled
2.5 ml/½ tsp lemon juice
flour for rolling out

Make the pastry. Sift the flour and salt into a bowl. If butter and lard are used, blend them together evenly with a round-bladed knife and chill. Cut the fat into pieces the size of walnuts and add to the flour. Make a well in the centre, mix in the lemon juice, then gradually add enough cold water to make an elastic dough. On a lightly floured surface, roll into a long strip, keeping the edges square.

Fold the bottom third over the centre third, then fold the top third over. With the rolling pin, press to seal the edges. Turn the pastry so that the folded edges are on the left and right. Repeat the rolling and folding three more times, allowing the pastry to rest in a cool place for 10 minutes between the second and third rollings. Finally, wrap the pastry in foil and store in the refrigerator until required.

In a stout polythene or paper bag, toss the beef cubes in seasoned flour until well coated. Shake off excess flour, then transfer the cubes to a 1 litre/1¾ pint pie dish, piling them higher in the centre than at the sides and sprinkling chopped onion between the layers. Pour in enough of the stock to quarter-fill the dish. Reserve the remaining stock.

Set the oven at 230°C/450°F/gas 8. Roll out the pastry on a lightly floured surface. Cut a strip of pastry from around the outside of the piece. Dampen the rim of the pie dish and press the pastry strip on it, trimming off any extra length. Use the remaining pastry to cover the dish. Trim the edge, knock up with the back of a knife and flute the edge. Make a small hole in the centre of the lid and surround it with pastry leaves made from the trimmings. Make a pastry tassel or rose to cover the hole after baking, if liked. Brush the pastry with the beaten egg or milk.

Place the pie on a baking sheet, with the pastry tassel, if made, next to it. Bake for about 10 minutes until the pastry is risen and golden brown. Lower the oven temperature to 180°C/350°F/gas 4 and, if necessary, move the pie to a lower shelf. Cover loosely with foil to prevent overbrowning and continue to cook for about 2 hours or until the meat is tender when tested through the crust with a skewer.

Heat the reserved beef stock in a small saucepan. Pour it into the pie through a funnel inserted in the hole in the crust. Cover the hole with the pastry tassel or rose, if made, and serve at once.

SERVES SIX

VARIATIONS

Steak and Kidney Pie   As above, but add 2 sheep's or 150 g/5 oz ox kidneys. Skin, core and slice the kidneys before mixing with the steak and onions.

Steak and Mushroom Pie   As above, but add 100 g/4 oz sliced mushrooms to the meat in the pie dish.

Steak and Oyster Pie   As above, but add 12 oysters to the meat. Open the oysters (page 117) and save the liquor from the shells, adding it to the pie.

STEAK AND KIDNEY PUDDING

The original recipe was contributed by a lady who lived in Sussex, a county renowned for its savoury puddings in those days. Prepared in a dish, rather than a basin, it would have contained more meat and ox kidney. Onion was not added and the suet pastry was mixed with milk. Apart from these minor variations, this classic British dish has survived generations of changing tastes to remain a firm favourite.

fat for greasing
150 g/5 oz lamb's, pig's or ox kidney(s)
575 g/1¼ lb stewing steak, trimmed and cut
    into 1 cm/½ inch cubes
1 onion, chopped
45 ml/3 tbsp plain flour
5 ml/1 tsp salt
1.25 ml/¼ tsp freshly ground black pepper
45 ml/3 tbsp beef stock or water

SUET CRUST PASTRY
225 g/8 oz self-raising flour
2.5 ml/½ tsp salt
100 g/4 oz shredded beef suet

Grease a 1.1 litre/2 pint pudding basin. Make the pastry. Sift the flour and salt into a mixing bowl. Stir in the suet and add cold water (about 150 ml/¼ pint) to make a firm dough.

Wash the kidney(s) and remove the membrane and white core. Cut into 2.5 cm/1 inch chunks. In a bowl, mix the beef cubes, kidney and onion with the flour, salt and pepper.

Set aside one quarter of the pastry for the lid. Roll out the remaining pastry on a lightly floured surface to a round 1 cm/½ inch larger than the rim of the prepared basin. The pastry should be about 5 mm/¼ inch thick. Press the pastry round well into the basin.

Half fill the lined basin with the steak mixture,

add the stock, then spoon in the rest of the meat. Roll out the reserved pastry to make a lid. Put the lid on the pudding, tucking its edges down around the meat. Dampen the top edge of the lid, then fold the top of the lining pastry over it. Cut a large piece of greaseproof paper, fold a pleat in it and grease it. Cover the pudding with the pleated paper, top with pleated foil and tie down securely.

Prepare a steamer or half fill a large saucepan with water and bring to the boil. Put the pudding in the perforated part of the steamer, or stand it on an old saucer or plate in the saucepan of boiling water. The water should come halfway up the sides of the basin. Cover the pan tightly and steam the pudding over boiling water for about 5 hours, topping up the steamer or pan with boiling water frequently to prevent it from boiling dry.

Serve the pudding from the basin. Fold a clean tea-towel or large table napkin in half or thirds, then wrap it neatly around the side and up to the rim of the basin. Beef gravy may be served with the pudding.

SERVES SIX

 PRESSURE COOKER TIP

To save time, the steak and kidney mixture may be precooked with 300 ml/½ pint beef stock. Cook in a pressure cooker, allowing 15 minutes at 15 lb pressure. Cool the mixture, then fill the pastry-lined pudding basin, using only enough of the gravy to half cover the meat. Steam gently without weights for 10 minutes, then bring to 5 lb pressure and cook for 35 minutes. Reduce the pressure slowly. Reheat the remaining gravy, add more salt and pepper if required, then pour it into the pudding through a hole cut in the crust.

HAMBURGERS

If you intend serving the burgers less than well cooked, buy good-quality steak and mince it at home. Bought minced steak should be cooked through before serving.

450 g/1 lb minced steak
2.5 ml/½ tsp salt
2.5 ml/½ tsp freshly ground black pepper
5–10 ml/1–2 tsp grated onion (optional)

Combine the meat, salt and pepper in a bowl. Add the onion, if used, and mix well. Shape the mixture lightly into four flat round cakes, about 2 cm/¾ inch thick.

Heat a frying pan or griddle until very hot, add the hamburgers and cook for 2 minutes on each side for rare meat; 4 minutes per side for well done meat. Alternatively, cook under a pre-heated grill or over coals on a barbecue grill for 6–8 minutes, turning once. Serve plain or in buns, with toppings or fillings as desired.

SERVES FOUR

VARIATIONS

Offer any or all of the following: lettuce leaves; sliced cucumber; sliced tomatoes; sliced gherkins; sliced raw or fried onions; hamburger relish; German or French mustard; tomato ketchup; mayonnaise; soured cream.

Lamb burgers Use good quality minced lamb instead of steak. Add 2.5 ml/½ tsp dried oregano to the mixture.

Cheese burgers Top each hamburger with a slice of processed cheese during the final minute of grilling.

Pitta burgers Make 8 burgers instead of 4 and serve them in warm pitta bread pockets, with shredded lettuce, chopped cucumber and chopped tomatoes. Add a dollop of Greek yogurt, if liked.

BOLOGNESE SAUCE

15 g/½ oz butter
15 ml/1 tbsp olive oil
75 g/3 oz unsmoked rindless streaky bacon rashers, diced
1 onion, finely chopped
2 garlic cloves, crushed
1 carrot, finely diced
¼ celery stick, thinly sliced
225 g/8 oz lean minced beef
100 g/4 oz chicken livers, trimmed and cut into small shreds
1 (397 g/14 oz) can chopped tomatoes
200 ml/7 fl oz beef stock
15 ml/1 tbsp tomato purée
125 ml/4 fl oz dry white or red wine
5 ml/1 tsp dried marjoram
salt and pepper
pinch of grated nutmeg

Melt the butter in the oil in a saucepan. Add the bacon and cook it gently until brown. Add the onion, garlic, carrot and celery. Cook over gentle heat for about 10 minutes until the onion is soft and just beginning to brown. Add the beef and cook, stirring, until browned and broken up.

Add the chicken livers to the pan and cook for 3 minutes, turning the livers over gently to brown them on all sides. Stir in the tomatoes, stock, tomato purée, wine and marjoram. Add to taste salt, pepper and nutmeg. Bring to simmering point and cook, covered, for about 1 hour, stirring occasionally.

Remove the lid for the final 20 minutes of the cooking time to allow some of the liquid to evaporate. Taste and add extra salt and pepper if necessary. Serve with pasta, rice or baked potatoes.

SERVES FOUR WITH PASTA OR RICE

COTTAGE PIE

50 g/2 oz butter
575 g/1¼ lb minced beef
1 onion, chopped
2 carrots, finely chopped
100 g/4 oz mushrooms, chopped
30 ml/2 tbsp plain flour
300 ml/½ pint beef stock
5 ml/1 tsp Worcestershire sauce
salt and pepper
900 g/2 lb potatoes, halved
30 ml/2 tbsp milk
pinch of grated nutmeg

Melt half the butter in a saucepan and fry the minced beef until browned, stirring to break up any lumps. Add the chopped onion, carrots and mushrooms and cook for 10 minutes or until softened slightly.

Stir in the flour, then pour in the beef stock and Worcestershire sauce, with salt and pepper to taste. Bring to the boil, stirring, then cover the pan and simmer for 30 minutes.

Cook the potatoes in a saucepan of salted boiling water for about 20 minutes or until tender. Drain thoroughly and mash with a potato masher. Beat in the remaining butter and the milk to make a creamy consistency. Add salt, pepper and nutmeg to taste.

Set the oven at 200°C/400°F/gas 6. Spoon the meat mixture into an ovenproof dish. Cover with the potato and mark the top with a fork. Bake for about 25 minutes until the potato topping is browned.

SERVES FOUR TO SIX

BEEF RISSOLES

In Mrs Beeton's day, when large beef roasts were more common than they are now, this was a popular way of using up leftovers.

450 g/1 lb cold lean roast beef
350 g/12 oz fresh white breadcrumbs
2.5 ml/½ tsp chopped fresh summer savory
2.5 ml/½ tsp chopped fresh thyme or
  1.25 ml/¼ tsp dried thyme
grated rind and juice of ½ lemon
salt and pepper
1-2 eggs, beaten
oil for shallow frying
fried parsley (see Mrs Beeton's Tip), to
  garnish

Mince the beef finely. Put it in a bowl with the breadcrumbs, herbs, lemon rind and juice, with salt and pepper to taste. Add enough beaten egg to bind the mixture, then shape into balls or cones.

Heat the oil in a large deep frying pan and fry the rissoles until they are a rich brown colour. Garnish with fried parsley and serve with a rich gravy, creamed onions and Anna Potatoes (page 354).

SERVES FOUR

 MRS BEETON'S TIP

Fried parsley makes a colourful garnish. Select perfectly fresh parsley sprigs, wash swiftly and lightly and dry thoroughly on absorbent kitchen paper. Heat oil for deep frying to 180-190°C/350-365°F. Put a double layer of absorbent kitchen paper on a plate. Drop the parsley carefully into the hot oil and cook for a few seconds until bright green and crisp. Drain on the paper and serve at once.

BEEF GALANTINE

The browned breadcrumbs and aspic improve the appearance of the galantine but are not essential.

200 g/7 oz lean rindless back bacon, minced
450 g/1 lb chuck or blade steak, minced
150 g/5 oz fresh white or brown breadcrumbs
salt and pepper
1 egg, beaten
75 ml/3 fl oz beef stock
60 ml/4 tbsp browned breadcrumbs
margarine or lard for greasing
125 ml/4 fl oz chopped aspic jelly, to garnish
   (optional)

The galantine may either be steamed or boiled in stock. If the former, prepare a steamer. Alternatively, half fill a large saucepan with stock and bring to the boil.

Combine the bacon, meat and breadcrumbs in a bowl. Add salt and pepper to taste and mix together well. Mix the egg and measured stock together and combine this thoroughly with the meat mixture. Shape into a short, thick roll, then wrap in greased greaseproof paper. Wrap in a scalded pudding cloth or foil, tying or twisting the ends securely.

Put the roll on the perforated part of the steamer, curving it round if necessary, and steam for 2½ hours, or lower it gently into the fast-boiling stock, lower the heat and simmer for 2 hours. Check the volume of water frequently if using a steamer, and top it up with boiling water from a kettle as necessary.

When cooked, lift out the roll, unwrap it, and then roll up tightly in a clean dry pudding cloth. Press the roll between two plates until just cold. Then remove the cloth, roll the meat in the breadcrumbs; chill until ready to serve. Place on a plate and garnish with aspic jelly, if liked.

SERVES SIX TO EIGHT

CHILLI CON CARNE

225 g/8 oz red kidney beans, soaked
   overnight in water to cover
225 g/8 oz rindless smoked streaky bacon
   rashers, chopped
1 Spanish onon, chopped
2 garlic cloves, crushed
30 ml/2 tbsp ground coriander
15 ml/1 tbsp ground cumin
15 ml/1 tbsp chilli powder or to taste
450 g/1 lb minced beef
1 beef stock cube
30 ml/2 tbsp tomato purée
salt and pepper
30 ml/2 tbsp chopped fresh coriander or
   parsley

Drain the beans and put them in a large saucepan. Add plenty of water and bring to the boil. Boil vigorously for 10 minutes, then lower the heat, cover the pan and simmer gently for 30 minutes.

Put the bacon in a large heavy-bottomed saucepan. Heat gently until the fat runs. Add the onion and fry, stirring frequently for about 5 minutes until the onion is soft but not browned. Stir in the garlic, ground coriander, cumin and chilli powder. Cook for 1 minute, stirring, then add the meat and cook until lightly browned. Crumble in the stock cube and pour in 600 ml/1 pint water. Stir in the tomato purée and add salt and pepper to taste. Bring to the boil.

Drain the beans. Add them to the saucepan and bring the stock back to the boil. Cover the pan, lower the heat and simmer gently for about 1 hour or until the beans are tender and the liquid has been absorbed. Stir in the coriander or parsley. Serve at once, with rice, crusty bread or as a filling for baked jacket potatoes.

SERVES FOUR

LAMB PROVENCALE

butter for greasing
4 canned anchovy fillets
1 (2.5–3 kg/5½–6½ lb) leg of lamb
lardons of fat bacon
4 parsley sprigs
2 garlic cloves, halved lengthways

MARINADE
1 small onion, chopped
3 fresh parsley sprigs
3 fresh thyme sprigs
2–3 bay leaves
salt and pepper
250 ml/8 fl oz olive oil
30 ml/2 tbsp vinegar

Cut the anchovy fillets in half lengthways, then across into 4 thin strips. Weigh the meat and calculate the cooking time. Allow 25 minutes per 450 g/1 lb plus 25 minutes over; slightly less time if you like your lamb 'pink'. Carefully use a pointed knife to make 4 cuts under the skin, taking care not to damage the meat underneath. Tuck the lardons, anchovy strips, parsley and garlic under the skin.

Make the marinade by combining all the ingredients in a bowl large enough to hold the lamb. Mix well, then add the lamb, cover and marinate for 2–3 hours, turning frequently.

Set the oven at 180°C/350°F/gas 4. Line a roasting tin with a large sheet of foil, making sure that there is enough foil to enclose the leg of lamb. Remove the lamb from the marinade and put it in the tin, cover with the onion and herbs from the marinade and bring up the side of the foil to make a neat parcel. Roast for the calculated cooking time, opening the parcel for the final 20 minutes to brown the meat. Serve on a heated platter.

SERVES SIX TO TEN

ROAST RACK OF LAMB

1 rack of lamb
45 ml/3 tbsp plain flour
salt and pepper
30 ml/2 tbsp redcurrant jelly

Set the oven at 180°C/350°F/gas 4. Weigh the joint of lamb and calculate the cooking time at 25 minutes per 450 g/1 lb, plus 25 minutes. This gives a medium result; for a well-done joint allow 30 minutes per 450 g/1 lb plus 30 minutes.

Dust the joint with flour and plenty of seasoning. Place it in a roasting tin and cook for three-quarters of the time, basting occasionally. Pour off excess fat and pour in 600 ml/1 pint boiling water. Finish roasting the meat.

Meanwhile, melt the jelly in a small saucepan. Transfer the meat to a serving plate and glaze it with the jelly. Tent with foil to keep hot. Boil the cooking liquor until reduced by about a third, taste for seasoning, pour into a gravyboat and serve with the lamb.

SERVES FOUR TO SIX

VARIATIONS

Crown Roast or Guard of Honour A pair of racks of lamb may be trussed into a crown roast or a guard of honour. For a crown, the racks are sewn end to end, then trussed (sewn) into a ring with the fat side inwards and trimmed bones forming the top of the crown. For a guard of honour, the racks are arranged opposite each other with bone ends interlocked. Both joints are sold ready prepared; both may be stuffed. Stuffing is spooned into the middle of the crown roast or packed between the racks for a guard of honour.

HERBED SHOULDER OF LAMB

This recipe may be used for leg as well as for shoulder of lamb.

1 shoulder of lamb, boned
4 garlic cloves, peeled and quartered
    lengthways
about 6 each small fresh rosemary and
    thyme sprigs
4 bay leaves
2 oranges
60 ml/4 tbsp olive oil
salt and pepper
300 ml/½ pint red wine

GARNISH
orange slices
fresh herbs

Trim any lumps of fat from the lamb, then tie it in a neat shape if the butcher has not already done this. Weigh the joint and calculate the cooking time at 30 minutes per 450 g/1 lb plus 30 minutes (see guide to cooking times, page 340). Use a small pointed knife to make short cuts into the lamb, at an angle running under the skin, all over the joint. Insert pieces of garlic and the rosemary and thyme sprigs into the cuts. Place the joint in a deep dish, with two bay leaves underneath and two on top.

Pare two long strips of rind off one orange and add them to the dish, next to or on top of the lamb. Squeeze the juice from the oranges, then mix it with the olive oil, salt and pepper. Pour this mixture over the lamb, cover and marinate for several hours or overnight. Turn the joint at least once during marinating.

Set the oven at 180°C/350°F/gas 4. Transfer the joint to a roasting tin, adding the bay leaves and orange rind but reserving the marinade. Cook for half the calculated time, brushing occasionally with the reserved marinade and basting with cooking juices from the tin. Pour the remaining marinade and the wine over the joint and continue roasting. Baste the lamb occasionally and add a little water to the juices in the tin if they begin to dry up – if the roasting tin is large they will evaporate more speedily.

Transfer the cooked joint to a serving dish, cover with foil and set aside. Pour 300 ml/½ pint boiling water or vegetable cooking water into the roasting tin. Boil the cooking juices rapidly, stirring and scraping the sediment off the base and sides of the pan, until they are reduced by half. Taste for seasoning, then strain the sauce into a heated sauceboat.

Garnish the lamb with orange slices and fresh herbs and serve at once, carving it into thick slices. Offer the sauce separately.

SERVES SIX

 MRS BEETON'S TIP

Once it has been reduced, the sauce may be thickened by whisking in small knobs of beurre manié, then boiling for 2 minutes, whisking all the time. To make beurre manié cream 25 g/1 oz butter with 30–45 ml/2–3 tbsp plain flour.

LOIN OF LAMB WITH LEMON AND PARSLEY STUFFING

Adapted from one of Mrs Beeton's first edition recipes for a loin of mutton, this lightly spiced roast joint was originally part baked and part stewed. It was justifiably described as 'very excellent'. The same combination of ingredients and stuffing will complement a leg or shoulder joint.

1 (1.4–1.6 kg/3–3½ lb) boned and rolled double loin of lamb, bones reserved, trimmed
salt and pepper
1.25 ml/¼ tsp each ground allspice and mace, and grated nutmeg
6 cloves
600 ml/1 pint lamb, chicken or vegetable stock
30 ml/2 tbsp plain flour
25 g/1 oz butter
125 ml/4 fl oz port
30 ml/2 tbsp mushroom ketchup
100 g/4 oz button mushrooms, sliced

STUFFING
50 g/2 oz shredded beef suet
50 g/2 oz cooked ham, chopped
15 ml/1 tbsp finely chopped parsley
5 ml/1 tsp chopped fresh thyme
grated rind of ½ lemon
175 g/6 oz fresh white breadcrumbs
2.5 ml/½ tsp grated nutmeg or ground mace
pinch of cayenne pepper
1 egg, beaten
a little milk

Open out the lamb and sprinkle the inside lightly with salt and pepper. Mix the allspice, mace and nutmeg, then rub the spices all over the meat, outside and on the cut surface. Cover and allow to marinate for at least 1 hour, or up to 24 hours.

Make the stuffing. Combine the suet, ham, parsley, thyme, lemon rind, breadcrumbs and nutmeg or mace in a bowl. Add salt and pepper to taste, and the cayenne. Stir in the egg and add enough milk to bind the mixture lightly together. Spread the stuffing evenly over the inside of the lamb, carefully roll it up again and tie it neatly. Stick the cloves into the joint, piercing it first with the point of a knife.

Set the oven at 180°C/350°F/gas 4. Put the lamb bones in the bottom of a roasting tin and pour over just enough stock to cover them. Weigh the meat and calculate the cooking time. Allow 30 minutes per 450 g/1 lb plus 30 minutes over. Place the stuffed lamb on top of the bones in the tin. Cook for the calculated time, adding extra stock or water during cooking to maintain the level of liquid just below the top of the bones and joint. Baste the joint occasionally with the cooking juices.

When the lamb is cooked, transfer it to a heated serving platter and allow to rest under tented foil. Remove the bones and skim off most of the fat from the liquid in the roasting tin. Beat the flour and butter to a smooth paste. Place the roasting liquid over medium heat, stir in the port and mushroom ketchup, then bring the mixture to simmering point. Whisking all the time, gradually add small lumps of the butter and flour mixture. Continue whisking well after each addition, then until the sauce boils and thickens. Stir in the mushrooms and simmer for 3 minutes.

Taste the sauce for seasoning before serving it with the lamb, which should be carved into thick slices. Redcurrant jelly, new potatoes and fresh peas are excellent accompaniments.

SERVES SIX

LAMB CUTLETS EN PAPILLOTE

oil for greasing
4-6 slices of cooked ham
6 lamb cutlets, trimmed
15 ml/1 tbsp oil
1 onion, finely chopped
25 g/1 oz button mushrooms, finely chopped
10 ml/2 tsp finely chopped parsley
grated rind of ½ lemon
salt and pepper

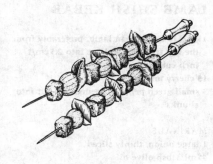

Set the oven at 190°C/375°F/gas 5. Cut out 12 small rounds of ham, each large enough to cover the round part of a cutlet. Heat the oil in a small saucepan and fry the onion for 4-6 minutes until slightly softened. Remove from the heat and stir in the mushrooms, parsley and lemon rind, with salt and pepper to taste. Leave to cool.

Cut out six heart-shaped pieces of double thickness greaseproof paper or foil large enough to hold the cutlets. Grease the paper generously with oil. Centre one of the ham rounds on the right half of one of the prepared paper hearts, spread with a little of the mushroom mixture and lay a cutlet on top. Spread the cutlet with a little more of the mushroom mixture and add another round of ham so that the round part of the cutlet is neatly sandwiched. Fold over the paper and twist the edges well together.

Lay the wrapped cutlets on a greased baking sheet and bake for 30 minutes. Transfer, still in their wrappings, to heated individual plates and serve at once.

SERVES SIX

LAMB SHASHLIK

50 g/2 oz butter
450 g/1 lb boned leg of lamb, cut into 2 cm/¾ inch cubes
200 g/7 oz lean bacon, cut into 1 cm/½ inch cubes
8 button onions
8 bay leaves
salt and pepper

Heat 25 g/1 oz of the butter in a large frying pan, add the lamb cubes and brown on all sides. Bring a small saucepan of water to the boil, add the onions and cook for 3 minutes; drain thoroughly.

Divide the meat, bacon, onions and bay leaves into 4 portions. Thread each portion on to a long skewer. Season with salt and pepper. Melt the remaining butter in a small pan and brush the meat and vegetables generously all over.

Cook the shashlik under a hot grill or over medium coals for 8–10 minutes, turning the skewers occasionally, until the meat is well browned. Serve with rice and Cucumber in Yogurt (page 374).

SERVES FOUR

LAMB SHISH KEBAB

1 kg/2¼ lb boned lean lamb, preferably from
the leg, trimmed and cut into 2.5 cm/1
inch cubes
18 cherry tomatoes
3 small green peppers, seeded and cut into
chunks

MARINADE
1 large onion, thinly sliced
45 ml/3 tbsp olive oil
45 ml/3 tbsp lemon juice
15 ml/1 tbsp salt
2.5 ml/½ tsp freshly ground black pepper

Make the marinade by combining all the ingredients in a shallow dish large enough to hold all the meat cubes in a single layer. Add the cubes and stir well to coat them thoroughly. Cover the dish and leave the meat to marinate for several hours, stirring occasionally.

Drain the lamb cubes, reserving the marinade. Thread the tomatoes, lamb cubes and pepper chunks alternately on to six kebab skewers.

Grill the shish kebabs under high heat or over medium coals, turning occasionally, until the vegetables are well browned and the lamb is done to taste. Baste occasionally with the reserved marinade. For pink lamb, allow about 10 minutes; for well-done lamb, allow about 15 minutes.

SERVES SIX

NOISETTES JARDINIERE

1 kg/2¼ lb boned best end of neck of lamb
30 ml/2 tbsp oil
salt and pepper
50 g/2 oz green beans, diced
1 carrot, diced
1 small turnip, diced
2 celery sticks, diced
450 g/1 lb potatoes, halved and cooked
25 g/1 oz butter
15–30 ml/2–3 tbsp single cream
gravy to serve

Wipe the meat. Roll it up and tie with fine string at 2.5 cm/1 inch intervals. Cut through the roll between the string.

Brush the noisettes with oil, season generously with salt and pepper and cook for 6–7 minutes under a moderate grill until cooked through and browned on both sides. Meanwhile, cook each vegetable except the potatoes separately in boiling salted water until just tender. Drain and mix.

Mash the potatoes until smooth. Beat in the butter and single cream. Spoon the creamed potato into a piping bag fitted with a large star nozzle and pipe a border of mashed potato around the edge of a heated serving dish. Arrange the noisettes and vegetables on the dish. Serve at once with hot gravy made using the cooking juices.

SERVES SIX

 MRS BEETON'S TIP

If preferred, the noisettes may be cooked in a frying pan. Heat the oil, add the noisettes and fry for about 3 minutes on each side.

EPIGRAMS OF LAMB

1 breast of lamb, about 450 g/1 lb
1 onion, thickly sliced
½ turnip, thickly sliced
1 carrot, thickly sliced
1 bouquet garni
salt and pepper
15 g/½ oz gelatine
500 ml/17 fl oz Béchamel Sauce (page 481)
1 egg, lightly beaten
90 ml/6 tbsp fresh white breadcrumbs
oil for deep frying

ONION SAUCE
1 onion, chopped
20 g/¾ oz butter
45 ml/3 tbsp plain flour
150 ml/¼ pint milk
salt and pepper
few drops of lemon juice

Put 1 litre/1¾ pints water in a large saucepan. Bring to the boil, add the meat and boil for 5 minutes. Add the onion, turnip and carrot with the bouquet garni. Season with salt and pepper. Lower the heat, cover the pan and simmer gently for about 1 hour or until the meat is tender. When cooked, take the meat out of the pan. Remove the skin, bones and gristle, and press the meat between two plates until cold and firm.

Place 30 ml/2 tbsp water in a small bowl. Sprinkle the gelatine on to the liquid. Set aside for 15 minutes until the gelatine is spongy. Stand the bowl over a saucepan of hot water and stir the gelatine until it has dissolved completely. Mix it with the hot Béchamel sauce, then set the sauce aside until cold and beginning to thicken.

Cut the cold meat into neat pieces for serving. Season the meat well with salt and pepper, then coat it completely with the Béchamel sauce. Repeat the coating if necessary to give a thick

covering of sauce. Chill these epigrams until the sauce is set.

Meanwhile make the onion sauce. Put the onion in a small saucepan with 250 ml/8 fl oz water. Bring to the boil, lower the heat and simmer for 10–15 minutes until softened. Drain thoroughly, reserving the onion and 150 ml/¼ pint of the cooking liquid. Melt the butter in a saucepan and add the flour. Cook for 1 minute, stirring, then gradually add the reserved onion liquid and milk, stirring until the mixture boils and thickens. Add salt and pepper to taste. Stir in the reserved onion and sharpen the flavour with the lemon juice. Set aside until required.

Put the beaten egg in a shallow dish. Spread out the breadcrumbs on a sheet of foil. When the sauce-coated lamb epigrams are set and firm, dip them into beaten egg and then into breadcrumbs.

Put the oil for frying into a deep wide saucepan. Heat the oil to 180–190°C/350–375°F or until a cube of bread added to the oil browns in 30 seconds. If using a deep-fat fryer, follow the manufacturer's instructions. Fry the epigrams quickly until golden brown. Drain on absorbent kitchen paper. Reheat the sauce.

Serve the epigrams in a circle around the edge of a heated serving dish, with the onion sauce in a sauceboat in the centre.

SERVES FOUR TO SIX

BRAISED LEG OF LAMB

fat for greasing
25 g/1 oz dripping or 30 ml/2 tbsp oil
2 onions, thickly sliced
1 turnip, thickly sliced
2 carrots, thickly sliced
vegetable stock (see method)
1 bouquet garni
10 black peppercorns
1.8–2.25 kg/4–5 lb leg of lamb
30 ml/2 tbsp butter
2 shallots, finely chopped
45 ml/3 tbsp plain flour
salt and pepper

Heat the dripping or oil in a large flameproof casserole, add all the vegetables, except the shallots, cover the pan and sweat them gently for 5–10 minutes. Add enough stock to almost cover the vegetables, tuck the bouquet garni among them and sprinkle in the peppercorns. Put the meat on top and cover with a piece of greased greaseproof paper, greased side down. Cover the pan with a tight-fitting lid. Cook over low heat for 2½–3 hours or until the lamb is cooked. Baste the lamb occasionally with the stock, and add more stock as necessary.

When the meat is cooked, transfer it to a warmed serving dish and keep hot. Strain the stock into a measuring jug and make up to 500 ml/17 fl oz with water if necessary.

Melt the butter in a small saucepan, add the shallots and fry gently for about 4 minutes until softened. Stir in the flour and cook until well browned. Gradually add the reserved stock, stirring until the mixture boils and thickens. Add salt and pepper to taste. Pour a little of the sauce over the meat and serve the rest in a sauceboat.

SERVES SIX TO TEN

OXFORD JOHN

575 g/1¼ lb boned leg of lamb, trimmed
salt and pepper
15 ml/1 tbsp finely chopped ham
5 ml/1 tsp finely chopped onion
5 ml/1 tsp chopped parsley
2.5 ml/½ tsp dried mixed herbs
50 g/2 oz butter or margarine
25 g/1 oz plain flour
250 ml/8 fl oz lamb or beef stock
5 ml/1 tsp lemon juice

Cut the meat into neat, thin round slices, about 10 cm/4 inches in diameter. Season with salt and pepper. Put the ham in a bowl and add the onion, herbs and a little salt and pepper. Use this filling to sandwich the rounds of meat together in pairs. Place them on a baking sheet, cover and leave for 1 hour to absorb the flavours.

Melt the butter in a large frying pan and fry the meat 'sandwiches', a few at a time, until browned and cooked. As they cook, transfer the 'sandwiches' to a heated dish; keep hot.

Stir the flour into the fat remaining in the pan and cook until it is well browned. Gradually add the stock, stirring until the mixture boils and thickens. Add the lemon juice and return the meat. Simmer for 10 minutes. Serve hot.

SERVES SIX

STUFFED BREAST OF LAMB WITH PILAFF

1 breast of lamb, about 675 g/1½ lb
salt and pepper
350 g/12 oz pork sausagemeat
15 ml/1 tbsp oil
2 rindless streaky bacon rashers, chopped
1 large carrot, chopped
1 large onion, chopped
1 bouquet garni
250 ml/8 fl oz lamb or chicken stock

PILAFF
30 ml/2 tbsp oil (preferably olive oil)
1 large onion, chopped
1 bay leaf
1 cinnamon stick
1 garlic clove, crushed
225 g/8 oz long-grain rice
750 ml/1¼ pints vegetable stock
50 g/2 oz sultanas
50 g/2 oz blanched almonds, cut into slivers
    and toasted
250 ml/8 fl oz Fresh Tomato Sauce (page 483)

Set the oven at 180°C/350°F/gas 4. Remove all the bones from the meat and trim off any excess fat. Flatten it, if necessary, with a cutlet bat or rolling pin, season with salt and pepper and spread the sausagemeat over the surface. Roll up tightly and tie the meat neatly.

Heat the oil in a frying pan, add the bacon and cook until the fat runs. Add the vegetables and fry quickly until lightly browned, then place them in a large casserole. Add the bouquet garni, sprinkle with salt and pepper, and pour in just enough stock to cover the vegetables. Put the rolled breast of lamb on top of the vegetables and cover the casserole with a tight-fitting lid. Bake for 2-2½ hours, until tender.

Prepare the pilaff about 30 minutes before the lamb is ready. Heat the oil in a saucepan, add the onion, bay leaf, cinnamon stick and garlic,

then fry gently for about 10 minutes until the onion is slightly softened but not browned. Add the rice, stir well, then pour in the stock. Add salt and pepper to taste, bring the stock to the boil and stir once. Cover, lower the heat and simmer for 15 minutes. Sprinkle the sultanas and almonds over the rice, replace the lid (without stirring) and cook for a further 5 minutes. Turn the heat off and leave for 5 minutes. Heat the tomato sauce.

Turn out the pilaff on a warmed serving dish. Cut the lamb into thick slices and lay them on the pilaff, then pour the tomato sauce over the meat. Serve at once.

SERVES SIX

IRISH STEW

1 kg/2¼ lb middle neck or scrag end of neck
    of lamb
2 large onions, thinly sliced
1 kg/2¼ lb potatoes, thinly sliced
salt and pepper
well-flavoured lamb or chicken stock
30 ml/2 tbsp chopped parsley to garnish

Set the oven at 190°C/375°F/gas 5. Cut the meat into neat cutlets or pieces, trimming off any excess fat. Layer the meat, onions, and potatoes in a casserole, sprinkling each layer with salt and pepper, and ending with potatoes.

Add enough stock to half fill the casserole. Cover with a lid and bake for about 2-2½ hours, removing the lid for the last 30 minutes of the cooking time, to allow the potato topping to brown. Sprinkle with chopped parsley to serve.

SERVES FOUR TO SIX

COLLARED LAMB

2 breasts of lamb, total weight about
    1.5 kg/3¼ lb
30–45 ml/2–3 tbsp oil
10 ml/2 tsp grated lemon rind
salt and pepper
pinch of ground allspice
10 ml/2 tsp anchovy essence
50 g/2 oz gherkins, chopped
30 ml/2 tbsp chopped parsley
5 ml/1 tsp dried thyme
5 ml/1 tsp snipped chives
100 g/4 oz fresh white breadcrumbs
750 ml/1¼ pints well-flavoured lamb or
    chicken stock

Set the oven at 160°C/325°F/gas 3. Remove the
bones from the meat without piercing through
the flesh. Set the bones aside. Brush the boned
sides of the lamb with the oil, and sprinkle with
the lemon rind, seasoning, spice and anchovy
essence.

In a bowl, mix the gherkins with the herbs and
breadcrumbs. Use a little of the stock to bind
the mixture, then spread it over the seasoned
sides of the lamb.

Place the breasts end to end, overlapping
slightly, and roll up together like a Swiss roll.
Tie with string at regular intervals. Cover the
meat tightly with muslin. Secure with string.

Put the collared lamb into a large casserole, add
the reserved lamb bones and the remaining
stock. Cover the casserole with foil or a lid and
cook for 3 hours, until the lamb is tender and
cooked through. Remove the collared lamb
from the casserole, take off the muslin wrapping and serve thickly sliced. Strain the stock,
discarding the bones, and use as the basis of a
sauce or gravy, if liked.

SERVES SIX TO TEN

LANCASHIRE HOT POT

fat for greasing
1 kg/2¼ lb potatoes
1 kg/2¼ lb middle neck of lamb or mutton,
    trimmed and cut into neat cutlets
3 lambs' kidneys, skinned, cored and sliced
2 large onions, sliced
salt and pepper
250 ml/8 fl oz hot lamb or vegetable stock
25 g/1 oz lard or dripping

Set the oven at 180°C/350°F/gas 4. Slice half
the potatoes and cut the rest into chunks.
Arrange half the sliced potatoes in the bottom
of a greased large deep casserole. Layer the
meat, kidneys, onions and potato chunks on
top, seasoning each layer lightly with salt and
pepper. Finish with the remaining potato
slices.

Pour in the hot stock. Melt the lard or dripping
and brush it over the top layer of potatoes.
Cover the casserole with a tight-fitting lid and
bake for about 2 hours or until the meat and
potatoes are tender.

Remove the lid, increase the oven temperature
to 220°C/425°F/gas 7 and cook for 20 minutes
more or until the top layer of potatoes is brown
and crisp. Serve from the casserole.

SERVES SIX

VARIATION

Lamb and Oyster Hotpot Add a central
layer, consisting of 8 sliced flat mushrooms
and 18 shelled fresh oysters. Proceed as in the
recipe above.

FRICASSEE OF LAMB

1 breast of lamb, about 800g/1¾lb, boned
25g/1oz dripping or 30ml/2tbsp oil
1 onion, sliced
2 bay leaves · 2 cloves
1 blade of mace
6 white peppercorns
salt and pepper
600ml/1 pint lamb or chicken stock, or
   water
1kg/2¼lb potatoes, halved
50g/2oz butter
30ml/2tbsp plain flour
15ml/1tbsp milk
10ml/2tsp roughly chopped capers

Cut the meat into 5cm/2 inch squares, trimming off any excess fat. Melt the dripping or heat the oil in a heavy-bottomed saucepan. Add the meat, onion, bay leaves, cloves, mace and peppercorns, with salt to taste. Half cover the pan and cook the mixture very gently for about 30 minutes, stirring frequently. Add the stock or water and bring to the boil. Lower the heat, cover the pan and simmer for about 1½ hours more, until the meat is tender.

About 30 minutes before the end of the cooking time, cook the potatoes in a saucepan of salted boiling water. When the meat is tender, strain the stock into a clean saucepan and place over medium heat. Set the meat aside. In a small bowl, blend 25g/1oz of the butter with the flour. Gradually add small pieces of the mixture to the simmering stock, whisking in each addition. Continue whisking until the sauce boils. Add the meat and heat through.

Meanwhile drain and mash the potatoes. Beat in the remaining butter and the milk. Spoon the creamed potato into a piping bag fitted with a large star nozzle and pipe a border on a heated serving dish. Spoon the meat into the middle. Sprinkle with capers and serve.

SERVES FOUR TO SIX

BLANQUETTE OF LAMB

1kg/2¼lb best end of neck of lamb
salt and pepper
1 onion, sliced
1 bouquet garni
6 black peppercorns
pinch of grated nutmeg
30ml/2tbsp butter
30ml/2tbsp plain flour
100g/4oz small button mushrooms
90ml/6tbsp single cream
1 egg yolk

Bone the meat and cut it into pieces about 5cm/2 inches square. Put it into a heavy-bottomed saucepan with salt to taste. Add water to cover and bring to the boil. Add the onion, bouquet garni, peppercorns and nutmeg. Lower the heat, cover the pan tightly and simmer for 1½–2 hours until tender. Keep meat hot. Strain 250ml/8floz stock.

Melt the butter in a saucepan, stir in the flour and cook for 1 minute. Gradually add the reserved stock, stirring the mixture until it boils and thickens. Lower the heat and simmer the sauce for 2–3 minutes.

Meanwhile prepare the garnish by heating the button mushrooms in a small saucepan with 60ml/4tbsp of the single cream. Add salt and pepper to taste. Cook gently, without allowing the cream to boil.

Beat the egg yolk and remaining cream in a small bowl. Stir in a little of the hot sauce and mix well. Add the contents of the bowl to the sauce mixture and heat gently, stirring. Do not allow the sauce to boil. Add salt and pepper to taste. Strain the liquid from the mushrooms into the sauce, then pour it over the meat. Garnish with the poached mushrooms and serve at once.

SERVES FOUR TO SIX

BOILED LAMB WITH CAPER SAUCE

1 (2kg/4½lb) leg of lamb, trimmed
5ml/1tsp salt
1 bay leaf
10 black peppercorns
2 onions, quartered
4 carrots, cut into large chunks
2 turnips or 1 large parsnip, cut into chunks
1-2 leeks, trimmed, sliced and washed

CAPER SAUCE
50g/2oz butter
40g/1½oz plain flour
450ml/¾ pint lamb stock
450ml/¾ pint milk
30ml/2tbsp chopped capers
15ml/1tbsp pickling vinegar from the jar of capers

Put the lamb into a large heavy-bottomed saucepan with the salt, bay leaf and peppercorns. Pour in enough cold water to cover. Bring to the boil. Skim, lower the heat, cover the pan with a tight-fitting lid and simmer for 2½-3 hours or until the meat is tender, adding the vegetables about 45 minutes before the end of the cooking time.

When the lamb is almost cooked, make the caper sauce. Melt the butter in a saucepan, stir in the flour and cook for 1-2 minutes. Gradually add the lamb stock, stirring constantly, then add the milk in the same way. Bring the sauce to the boil, stirring until it thickens. Add the capers and vinegar; stir well.

Drain the meat and vegetables from the cooking liquid. Place the meat on a heated serving dish, coat with the caper sauce, and surround with the vegetables. Serve at once.

SERVES EIGHT TO TEN

LAMB CURRY

1 kg/2¼lb boneless leg or shoulder lamb, cut into 2.5cm/1 inch cubes
60ml/4tbsp lemon juice
450ml/¾ pint plain yogurt
salt and freshly ground black pepper
75g/3oz ghee (see Mrs Beeton's Tip)
2 onions, finely chopped
3 garlic cloves, crushed
5cm/2 inch fresh root ginger, grated
5ml/1tsp chilli powder
10ml/2tsp each ground coriander and cumin
8 green cardamom pods
150g/5oz tomato purée

Put the lamb cubes into a large non-metallic bowl and sprinkle with the lemon juice. Stir in the yogurt and salt. Cover and marinate for 24 hours or for up to 3 days. Stir the mixture occasionally.

Heat the ghee in a large saucepan, add the onions, garlic and ginger and fry for 4-6 minutes until the onion is soft but not coloured. Add the chilli powder, coriander, cumin and black pepper and fry for 2 minutes, then stir in the lamb, with its marinade. Stir in the cardamom pods and tomato purée, with 300ml/½ pint water. Bring to the boil, reduce the heat and simmer for about 1 hour or until the meat is tender. Serve with rice, chopped tomato and onion, and diced cucumber in yogurt.

SERVES FOUR TO SIX

 MRS BEETON'S TIP

Ghee is clarified butter made from the milk of the water buffalo or goat. It can be bought commercially. For more information and instructions on making clarified butter, see page 424.

CUMBERLAND LAMB PIES

300g/11oz minced lamb
10ml/2tsp dripping or oil
1 onion, chopped
100g/4oz mushrooms, chopped
1.25ml/¼ tsp grated nutmeg
10ml/2tsp chopped parsley
pinch of dried thyme
salt and pepper
5ml/1tsp Worcestershire sauce
60ml/4tbsp chicken or vegetable stock
beaten egg or milk for glazing

PASTRY
300g/10oz plain flour
pinch of salt
150g/5oz margarine (or half butter, half
  lard)
flour for rolling out

Set the oven at 190°C/375°F/gas 5. To make the pastry, sift the flour and salt into a bowl, then rub in the margarine until the mixture resembles fine breadcrumbs. Add enough cold water to make a stiff dough. Press the dough together with your fingertips. Place the dough in a polythene bag and refrigerate while making the filling.

Put the minced lamb in a bowl. Heat the dripping or oil in a small frying pan, add the onion and fry for 4-6 minutes until soft but not coloured. Stir into the lamb with the chopped mushrooms, nutmeg, parsley and thyme. Add salt and pepper to taste, stir in the Worcestershire sauce and mix well.

Roll out half the pastry on a lightly floured surface and use to line six individual Yorkshire pudding or flan tins, or ovenproof saucers. Divide the lamb mixture between them, adding 10ml/2tsp stock to each. Roll out the remaining pastry and cut out six lids. Dampen the edges of the pies, put on the lids and seal well. Brush with beaten egg or milk. Make a hole in

the lid of each pie to allow steam to escape. Bake for 40-45 minutes, covering the tops of the pies with foil if they begin to overbrown. Serve hot or cold.

MAKES SIX

CHINA CHILO

450g/1lb minced lamb
2 onions, finely chopped
1 Iceberg lettuce, shredded
5ml/1tsp salt
2.5ml/½ tsp freshly ground black pepper
150ml/¼ pint stock (lamb, vegetable or
  chicken)
450g/1lb fresh peas, shelled or 225g/8oz
  frozen peas
30-45ml/2-3tbsp chopped fresh mint,
  tarragon or parsley

Heat the minced lamb in a heavy-bottomed saucepan until the fat runs. Remove the pan from the heat and drain off the fat. Add the onions, then continue to cook, stirring constantly, until the meat is well browned.

Stir in the lettuce with the salt and pepper. Cook, turning the mixture, for 2-3 minutes, then pour in the stock. Bring to the boil, lower the heat, cover the pan with a tight-fitting lid and simmer very gently for 30 minutes. Add the peas and stir well, then replace the lid and cook for a further 30 minutes. Check the pan from time to time and add more stock or water if the mixture is too dry.

Stir in the chopped mint, tarragon or parsley and serve the china chilo hot. Baked or boiled potatoes (particularly new potatoes) are simple accompaniments; alternatively, cooked rice or pasta makes a practical base on which to serve the meat mixture.

SERVES FOUR

LAMB PILAFF WITH EGGS

450g/1lb minced lamb
1 large onion, chopped
10ml/2tsp ground coriander
2.5ml/½tsp ground cinnamon
1.25ml/¼tsp ground cloves
5ml/1tsp cumin seeds (optional)
salt and pepper
225g/8oz long-grain rice
15ml/1tbsp tomato purée
600ml/1 pint lamb or chicken stock
50g/2oz shelled pistachio nuts or blanched
  almonds, roughly chopped
50g/2oz ready-to-eat dried apricots, sliced,
  or raisins
4 eggs, poached, fried or soft boiled

Fry the lamb, onion, coriander, cinnamon, cloves and cumin seeds (if used) in a flame-proof casserole or heavy-bottomed saucepan over gentle heat until the meat is lightly cooked. Add salt and pepper, the rice, tomato purée and stock, stirring well, then bring to the boil.

Reduce the heat, cover the casserole or pan tightly and cook very gently for 20 minutes. Sprinkle the nuts and apricots or raisins over the meat mixture, replace the cover and continue to cook gently for 10 minutes. Turn the heat off and leave the pilaff to stand for 5–10 minutes before serving.

Cook the eggs by the chosen method. Fork the meat and rice mixture to mix in the fruit and nuts, taste for seasoning and serve at once. Top each portion with an egg.

SERVES FOUR

MOUSSAKA

fat for greasing
1 aubergine
salt and pepper
30ml/2tbsp olive oil
1 large onion, chopped
1 garlic clove, crushed
450g/1lb minced lamb or beef
10ml/2tsp chopped parsley
2 tomatoes, peeled, seeded and chopped
150ml/¼ pint dry white wine
300ml/½ pint milk
1 egg, plus 2 egg yolks
pinch of grated nutmeg
75g/3oz Kefalotiri or Parmesan cheese,
  grated

Grease a 20 × 10 × 10cm (8 × 4 × 4 inch) baking dish. Set the oven at 180°C/350°F/gas 4. Cut the aubergine into 1cm/½ inch slices, put them in a colander, and sprinkle generously with salt. Set aside.

Heat the olive oil, and gently fry the onion and garlic for about 10 minutes until the onion is soft. Add the mince and continue cooking, stirring with a fork to break up any lumps in the meat. When the meat is thoroughly browned, add salt, pepper, parsley and tomatoes. Mix well, then add the white wine.

In a bowl, beat the milk, whole egg, egg yolks, salt and a good pinch of grated nutmeg together. Add about half the cheese to the egg mixture, then beat again briefly.

Rinse and drain the aubergine slices and pat dry with absorbent kitchen paper. Place half in the bottom of the prepared dish and cover with the meat mixture. Lay the remaining aubergine slices on the meat and pour the milk and egg mixture over them. Sprinkle the remaining cheese on top. Bake for 30–40 minutes, until golden brown.

SERVES FOUR

DORMERS

225 g/8 oz cold roast lamb
75 g/3 oz cooked rice
50 g/2 oz fresh white breadcrumbs
salt and pepper
30 ml/2 tbsp chopped fresh mint
about 60 ml/4 tbsp gravy, stock or milk
1 egg
50 g/2 oz dried white breadcrumbs
oil for shallow frying

Finely chop the lamb and rice, using a food processor if possible. Add the breadcrumbs with plenty of salt and pepper, and the mint. Stir in just enough gravy, stock or milk to bind the mixture.

Form the mixture into six sausage shapes or patties. Beat the egg with 15 ml/1 tbsp water in a shallow bowl. Spread out the breadcrumbs on a sheet of foil. Coat the dormers in egg, then in breadcrumbs. If time permits, chill the crumbed dormers on a plate in the refrigerator for about 1 hour to firm up.

Heat the oil in a large shallow frying pan and fry the dormers for 10-15 minutes until golden brown. Drain on absorbent kitchen paper. Serve with a flavoursome gravy or rich tomato sauce.

MAKES SIX

 MRS BEETON'S TIP

The dormers can be as simple – or as spicy – or as you like. Add any of the following, singly or in combinations of three or four: 1 small onion, finely chopped or minced; 2 crushed garlic cloves; 5 ml/1 tsp chopped fresh thyme; 5 ml/1 tsp ground mace; 10 ml/2 tsp ground coriander; 15 ml/1 tbsp green peppercorns, lightly crushed; 15 ml/1 tbsp capers, chopped.

SHEPHERD'S PIE

butter for greasing
50 g/2 oz butter
2 onions, roughly chopped
15 ml/1 tbsp plain flour
250 ml/8 fl oz well-flavoured lamb stock
575 g/1¼ lb lean cooked lamb, minced
salt and pepper
5 ml/1 tsp Worcestershire sauce
675 g/1½ lb potatoes, halved
15-30 ml/1-2 tbsp milk
pinch of grated nutmeg

Melt half the butter in a saucepan and fry the onions until softened but not coloured. Stir in the flour and cook gently for 1-2 minutes, stirring all the time. Gradually add the stock. Bring to the boil, stirring until the sauce thickens.

Stir in the lamb, with salt and pepper and Worcestershire sauce to taste. Cover the pan and simmer for 30 minutes.

Meanwhile cook the potatoes in a saucepan of salted boiling water for about 30 minutes or until tender. Drain thoroughly and mash with a potato masher, or beat them with a hand-held electric whisk until smooth. Beat in the rest of the butter and the milk to make a creamy consistency. Add salt, pepper and nutmeg to taste.

Set the oven at 220°C/450°F/gas 7. Spoon the meat mixture into a greased pie dish or shallow oven-to-table dish. Cover with the potato, smooth the top, then flick it up into small peaks or score a pattern on the surface with a fork. Bake for 10-15 minutes until browned on top. Serve at once.

SERVES FOUR TO SIX

COLLOPS WITH ASPARAGUS

450 g/1 lb cold pink-cooked roast lamb
30 ml/2 tbsp plain flour
salt and pepper
2.5 ml/½ tsp grated lemon rind
1.25 ml/¼ tsp dried mixed herbs
1 (340 g/12 oz) can asparagus tips
30 ml/2 tbsp butter
250 ml/8 fl oz well-flavoured lamb or
  chicken stock

Cut the meat into 7.5 cm/3 inch slices, about 1 cm/½ inch thick. Mix half the flour with the salt and pepper, lemon rind and herbs in a small bowl. Sprinkle the mixture over the collops and stand for 1 hour.

Heat the asparagus tips in their liquid in a small saucepan. Melt the butter in a large frying pan, add the collops and cook them quickly over moderate heat until lightly browned on both sides. Remove them with a fish slice and arrange in a close circle on a heated serving dish. Keep hot.

Stir the remaining flour into the fat remaining in the pan and cook until browned. Gradually add the stock, stirring until the mixture boils and thickens. Add salt and pepper to taste.

Drain the asparagus tips and place them in the centre of the collops. Spoon the sauce over.

SERVES FOUR

 MRS BEETON'S TIP

When fresh asparagus is available, trim off its tough stalk ends, then cook it in boiling water for 10–15 minutes. If you do not have a tall asparagus pan, place the bundle of spears in a saucepan and tent a piece of foil over the top, crumpling it around the rim of the pan to seal in the steam.

SAVOURY LOIN OF PORK

1–1.5 kg/2¼–3¼ lb loin of pork on the bone
15 ml/1 tbsp finely chopped onion
2.5 ml/½ tsp dried sage
2.5 ml/½ tsp salt
1.25 ml/¼ tsp freshly ground pepper
pinch of dry mustard
30 ml/2 tbsp sieved apricot jam, melted
125 ml/4 fl oz Apple Sauce (page 490)

Set the oven at 220°C/425°F/gas 7. Weigh the meat and calculate the cooking time at 30 minutes per 450 g/1 lb plus 30 minutes over. Mix the onion, sage, salt, pepper and mustard in a small bowl. Rub the mixture well into the surface of the meat.

Put the meat in a roasting tin and roast for 10 minutes, then lower the oven temperature to 180°C/350°F/gas 4 and roast for the remainder of the calculated cooking time. About 30 minutes before serving, remove the pork from the oven and brush with melted apricot jam. Continue cooking to crisp the crackling.

Serve the pork on a heated serving dish, offering the apple sauce separately. Serve with roast potatoes, broad beans and Celeriac Purée (page 342).

SERVES SIX

 MRS BEETON'S TIP

If a savoury glaze is preferred for the crackling, brush with oil and sprinkle with salt. Raise the oven temperature to 220°C/435°F/gas 7, return the pork to the oven and continue cooking for 15–20 minutes.

ROAST PORK WITH MUSHROOM AND CORN STUFFING

If the whole joint is taken to the table, you may like to add a garnish of baby sweetcorn cobs (cook them in boiling water for 3-5 minutes) and button mushrooms tossed in hot butter.

1.5 kg/3 lb boned bladebone of pork, scored
   (see Mrs Beeton's Tip)
45 ml/3 tbsp oil
15 ml/1 tbsp cooking salt

STUFFING
25 g/1 oz butter or margarine
1 onion, finely chopped
1 celery stick, finely chopped
100 g/4 oz mushrooms, finely chopped
50 g/2 oz thawed frozen sweetcorn, drained
50 g/2 oz fresh white breadcrumbs
15 ml/1 tbsp chopped parsley
2.5 ml/½ tsp ground mace
5 ml/1 tsp lemon juice
salt and pepper

Set the oven at 230°C/450°F/gas 8. Make the stuffing. Melt the butter or margarine in a small saucepan. Add the onion and celery and fry for 4-6 minutes until soft but not browned. Remove from the heat and add the remaining ingredients.

Spoon the stuffing evenly into the 'pocket' left when the meat was boned. Roll up the joint and tie with thin string at regular intervals. Generously brush 15 ml/1 tbsp of the oil over the rind. Sprinkle with the salt, rubbing it well in.

Heat the remaining oil in a roasting tin, add the meat, turning it in the hot fat, and roast for 20-30 minutes until the crackling crisps. Do not cover the meat or the crackling will soften again. Lower the heat to 180°C/350°F/gas 4 and cook for about 1½ hours more or until the pork is cooked.

Transfer the meat to a warmed serving dish, remove the string and keep hot. If liked, pour off the fat from the roasting tin, using the sediment for gravy (see page 488).

SERVES SIX

 MRS BEETON'S TIP

If the butcher has not already scored the pork rind, do this yourself, using a very sharp knife and making the cuts about 3 mm/⅛ inch deep and 1 cm/½ inch apart.

LOIN OF PORK STUFFED WITH PRUNES

1.25-1.5 kg/2¾-3¼ lb boned loin of pork
200 g/7 oz ready-to-eat prunes
juice of 1 lemon
salt and pepper

Set the oven at 180°C/350°F/gas 4. Weigh the meat and calculate the cooking time at 30 minutes per 450 g/1 lb plus 30 minutes over. Spread the prunes over the pork flesh, roll up the meat and tie it securely. Pour the lemon juice all over the meat, rubbing it well in.

Put the meat in a roasting tin, season with salt and pepper and roast for the calculated cooking time, basting occasionally. Serve on a heated platter, accompanied with a thickened gravy made from the sediment in the roasting tin (see page 488).

SERVES SIX

MRS BEETON'S ROAST GRISKIN OF PORK

fat for greasing
1 kg/2¼ lb neck end of chine of pork or
    griskin (see Mrs Beeton's Tip)
flour for dredging
50 g/2 oz lard
15 ml/1 tbsp dried sage
30 ml/2 tbsp plain flour
salt and pepper

Set the oven at 220°C/425°F/gas 7. Dredge the meat lightly with flour. Melt the lard in a roasting tin. When hot, add the meat and spoon the melted fat over the top. Season well. Roast for 20 minutes, baste well then cover the meat loosely with greased greaseproof paper.

Reduce the oven temperature to 180°C/350°F/gas 4. Roast the meat for a further 1¼-1½ hours, basting often. Ten minutes before the end of the cooking time, remove from the oven, sprinkle with the sage, and return to the oven, uncovered.

Pour off most of the fat from the roasting tin. Sprinkle in the flour. Cook, stirring for 3-4 minutes until lightly browned. Gradually add 600 ml/1 pint water, stirring until the mixture boils. Season, simmer for 5 minutes, then strain, if liked, and serve with the pork.

SERVES FOUR

 MRS BEETON'S TIP

The griskin is the backbone, spine or chine of a pig, cut away when preparing a side for bacon. The term is also used for a shoulder of pork, stripped of fat. As it is sold without rind or fat, it needs frequent basting.

ROAST PORK WITH SAGE AND ONION STUFFING

Use the pan juices from the pork to make a gravy and offer Apple Sauce (page 490) as an accompaniment.

4 large onions
100 g/4 oz fresh breadcrumbs
45 ml/3 tbsp chopped fresh sage or
    15 ml/1 tbsp dried sage
salt and pepper
40 g/1½ oz butter, melted
1 egg
1.5 kg/3 lb boned joint from leg of pork,
    boned and scored
30 ml/2 tbsp oil

Place the onions in a saucepan, cover with water and bring to the boil. Cook for 5 minutes, then drain, cool slightly and chop. Mix the onions with the breadcrumbs. Add the sage, plenty of seasoning, the butter and the egg.

Set the oven at 180°C/350°F/gas 4. Make sure the pork rind is well scored. Fill the cavity left by the bone with some stuffing, then tie the joint into a neat shape. Place the remaining stuffing in a buttered, ovenproof dish; set aside.

Place the joint in a roasting tin and rub plenty of salt into the rind, then trickle the oil over. Roast for about 2 hours, basting the joint occasionally, until cooked through. Place the dish of stuffing in the oven halfway through cooking.

SERVES SIX

CIDERED PORK CHOPS

4 pork loin chops, trimmed
oil (optional)
60 ml/4 tbsp dry cider
1 bouquet garni
2 cooking apples
2 onions, chopped
pinch of ground cinnamon
salt and pepper
100 g/4 oz flat mushrooms, thickly sliced
200 g/7 oz fresh peas
25 g/1 oz butter
200 g/7 oz cooked small whole beetroot
225 g/8 oz tagliatelle, cooked

Set the oven at 160°C/325°F/gas 3. Heat a frying pan. Brown the chops on both sides, adding a little oil if the chops are very lean. Remove the chops and place them in a casserole. Pour the cider over the chops and add the bouquet garni. Cover the casserole and start cooking it in the oven.

Peel, core and chop the apples. Add them with the onions to the fat remaining in the frying pan and fry gently for 5 minutes. Stir in the cinnamon, with just enough water to cover the onion mixture. Cover the pan and simmer for about 15 minutes, until the onions and apples are soft. Rub the mixture through a sieve into a bowl, add salt and pepper to taste, then spoon the mixture over the chops in the casserole. Return to the oven for 45 minutes.

Add the mushrooms and peas to the casserole and cook for 30 minutes more. Towards the end of the cooking time, melt the butter in a small saucepan, add the beetroot and heat gently, turning often. Arrange the tagliatelle and chops on a heated serving dish with the chops on top. Arrange the mushrooms, peas and beetroot around them.

SERVES FOUR

BARBECUED SPARE RIBS

2 kg/4½ lb pork spare ribs
1 lemon, cut in wedges
herb sprigs to garnish (optional)

BARBECUE SPICE MIXTURE
90 ml/6 tbsp soft light brown sugar
15 ml/1 tbsp grated lemon rind
15 ml/1 tbsp paprika
salt and pepper

BASTING SAUCE
200 ml/7 fl oz tomato juice
45 ml/3 tbsp tomato ketchup
15-30 ml/1-2 tbsp Worcestershire sauce
30 ml/2 tbsp soft light brown sugar
5 ml/1 tsp mustard powder
1.25 ml/¼ tsp chilli powder

Cut the ribs into individual portions. Mix all the ingredients for the barbecue spice mixture and rub into the ribs.

Meanwhile make the basting sauce. Combine all the ingredients in a small saucepan. Add 100 ml/3½ fl oz water, bring to the boil, then lower the heat and simmer for 15 minutes. Spread out the ribs in a large shallow dish or roasting tin and brush generously with the basting sauce. Cover and set aside for 30 minutes at cool room temperature. Brush again and leave for a further 30 minutes.

Cook the ribs on a grid placed high over medium coals for 1-1¼ hours, turning frequently and basting with the sauce. Alternatively, bake in a preheated 150°C/300°F/gas 2 oven for about 1 hour or until nearly cooked. Baste frequently. Finish by cooking under a hot grill – or over the fire. Serve with lemon wedges, and garnish with fresh herbs.

SERVES SIX TO EIGHT

BRAISED PORK

1 pork spare rib joint, about 2 kg/4½ lb,
   trimmed
45 ml/3 tbsp oil
1 large onion, sliced
2 large carrots, sliced
1 garlic clove, crushed
125 ml/4 fl oz dry cider
125 ml/4 fl oz well-flavoured chicken or
   vegetable stock
1 bouquet garni
salt and pepper

Weigh the pork and calculate the cooking time
at 30–35 minutes per 450 g/1 lb. Heat the oil in
a large, flameproof casserole and fry the joint,
turning frequently, until browned on all sides.
Remove the meat and set aside.

Add the vegetables and garlic to the fat remaining in the casserole. Fry gently for 5 minutes.
Pour in the cider and stock, and add the
bouquet garni. Return the meat to the pan and
season it with plenty of salt and pepper. Bring
the liquid to the boil, lower the heat, cover the
casserole and simmer gently for the calculated
cooking time. Turn the meat occasionally.

When cooked, transfer the meat to a heated
serving dish. Strain the liquid from the casserole into a clean saucepan. Skim off the excess
fat from the surface, then boil the liquid until
reduced to a thin gravy. Serve in a heated
gravyboat.

SERVES EIGHT TO TEN

PORK AND APPLE HOT POT

fat for greasing
1 cooking apple
45 ml/3 tbsp oil
1 onion, thinly sliced
100 g/4 oz mushrooms, thinly sliced
4 pork loin chops, trimmed
2.5 ml/½ tsp dried sage or savory
450 g/1 lb potatoes, cut into 2 cm/¾ inch
   cubes
salt and pepper

GARNISH (OPTIONAL)
1–2 slices of eating apple, cored and halved
parsley sprigs

Set the oven at 180°C/350°F/gas 4. Peel, core
and slice the apple. Heat the oil in a large frying
pan, add the apple and onion and fry over
moderate heat until golden brown.

Put the mushrooms on the base of a large
shallow greased casserole. Add the chops and
cover with the apple and onion. Sprinkle the
herbs over the top. Cover with the potatoes,
brushing them with the fat remaining in the
pan. Sprinkle with salt and pepper to taste.
Pour in enough water to come halfway up the
meat and vegetables.

Cover the casserole with foil or a tight-fitting
lid. Bake for 1½ hours, removing the covering
30 minutes before the end of the cooking time
to allow the potatoes to brown. Garnish with
apple and parsley (if used), then serve from the
casserole. Carrots with Cider (page 339) may be
served as an accompaniment, if liked.

SERVES FOUR

SWEET AND SOUR PORK

675 g/1½ lb pork, trimmed and cut into
2 cm/¾ inch cubes
oil for deep frying

MARINADE
1 egg white
40 g/1½ oz cornflour
30 ml/2 tbsp soy sauce
30 ml/2 tbsp dry sherry
salt and pepper

BATTER
1 egg
45 ml/3 tbsp plain flour
45 ml/3 tbsp cornflour
45-60 ml/3-4 tbsp light beer

SAUCE
30 ml/2 tbsp oil
3 spring onions, finely chopped
1 small red pepper, seeded and cut into thin
strips
3 canned pineapple rings, chopped
500 ml/17 fl oz chicken stock
30 ml/2 tbsp vinegar
45 ml/3 tbsp tomato ketchup
45 ml/3 tbsp soy sauce
25 g/1 oz caster sugar
30 ml/2 tbsp cornflour

Make the marinade. Beat the egg white in a bowl with the cornflour. Stir in the soy sauce and sherry, with salt and pepper to taste. Add the meat cubes and marinate for 15 minutes, turning frequently. Remove from the marinade and drain well.

Meanwhile make the sauce. Heat the oil in a saucepan, add the spring onions, peppers and pineapple and fry for 2 minutes, stirring all the time. Add the chicken stock, vinegar, tomato ketchup and soy sauce, with sugar and salt to taste. Simmer for 5 minutes.

To make the batter, mix the egg, flour, cornflour and beer in a bowl. Add a pinch of salt and whisk the mixture.

Heat the oil for deep frying to 180-190°C/350-375°F or until a cube of bread added to the oil browns in 30 seconds. If using a deep-fat fryer, follow the manufacturer's instructions. Dip the meat cubes in the batter and fry a few at a time until golden brown. As each batch of cubes browns, remove them with a slotted spoon and keep warm on a serving dish.

Finish the sauce. Put the cornflour in a cup and mix to a paste with a little cold water. Stir the paste into the sweet and sour sauce and bring to the boil, stirring until it thickens. Pour the sauce over the pieces of pork and serve at once.

SERVES FOUR

VARIATION

Sweet and Sour Pork Stir Fry Mix the marinade as suggested above, add the pork cubes and turn to coat in the mixture. Do not allow to stand. Heat 75 ml/5 tbsp oil in a wok. Add the pork cubes and stir fry over high heat until cooked and crisp. Transfer to a bowl with a slotted spoon and serve with the sweet and sour sauce.

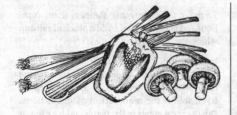

PORK CHOW MEIN

3 dried Chinese mushrooms (optional)
225 g/8 oz lean boneless pork
60 ml/4 tbsp soy sauce
60 ml/4 tbsp dry sherry
225 g/8 oz Chinese egg noodles
90 ml/6 tbsp oil (preferably groundnut oil)
4 spring onions, shredded
1 small green pepper, seeded and cut into
   thin strips
1 small red pepper, seeded and cut into thin
   strips
2 celery sticks, thinly sliced at a slant
50 g/2 oz mushrooms, sliced (optional)
150 g/5 oz drained canned bamboo shoots,
   cut into strips

If using the dried mushrooms, place them in a small bowl or mug and add just enough boiling water to cover them. Put a saucer or second mug on the mushrooms to keep them submerged. Leave to soak for 15 minutes. Drain, discard the tough stalks and thinly slice the mushroom caps.

Slice the pork thinly against the grain, then cut it into strips. Place in a bowl with the soy sauce and sherry. Mix well, cover and marinate for 30 minutes, stirring occasionally.

Meanwhile bring a large saucepan of water to the boil, add the noodles and cook for 2–3 minutes or according to packet instructions. Drain, rinse under cold water until cool, then drain again. Set aside.

Heat half the oil in a large frying pan or wok and add the noodles. Press them out and cook quickly for 2–3 minutes until lightly browned. Turn and cook for another 2–3 minutes, or until the noodles are crisp in places and hot. Turn the noodles out on to a serving plate and keep hot.

Heat the remaining oil. Using a slotted spoon, remove the pork strips from the marinade and add them to the hot oil. Stir fry for 3–5 minutes or until browned; add the spring onions, peppers and celery slices and stir fry for 4 minutes. Add the mushrooms (including dried mushrooms if used) and bamboo shoots with the reserved marinade. Cook, stirring occasionally, for 4–5 minutes, then spoon the mixture over the noodles and serve at once. The noodles and stir fry may be mixed as the chow mein is served.

SERVES FOUR TO SIX

 MRS BEETON'S TIP

Stir frying is a quick cooking method and the pan with the cooking oil should be shimmering hot before the meat is added. Groundnut oil is ideal as it reaches a high temperature before smoking, so the pork cooks quickly and browns easily, but other cooking oils may be used. Dried Chinese mushrooms (shiitake) give the chow mein an excellent flavour; however, they are expensive. Look out for fresh shiitake and use them instead of the fresh mushrooms – they have a good flavour. The soaking liquid from the mushrooms may be added to the chow mein or reserved for another Chinese dish.

SAUSAGES

Making your own sausages is highly satisfying. Not only is the flavour vastly superior to that of many commercially sold sausages, but you control the contents and can tailor the fillings to your family's own tastes.

You may be able to buy skins from a family butcher who makes his own sausages, but this may mean buying in bulk. Natural sausage skins will keep in an airtight container in the bottom of the refrigerator for 2–3 months – and the filled sausages may be frozen – but it may be simplest to forego skins altogether, and simply shape the sausagemeat into patties, dip these in flour, and fry or grill them.

Some of the larger food mixers have sausage-filling attachments, which are easy to use. If you do not own one of these, try the following method, which is quite successful. Cut the sausage skin into manageable lengths – each no longer than 0.9 m/1 yd – and soak in cold water for at least 30 minutes, preferably overnight. Drain, rinse and drain again, repeating this process until all the salt has been removed. Finally put the lengths of skin in a bowl and cover with fresh water.

Have the sausagemeat ready. Fit a large piping bag with a large (1–2.5 cm/½–1 inch) nozzle. Put some of the sausagemeat into the bag and press down to fill the nozzle. Carefully open the end of one of the sausage skins. With the filled bag resting on the work surface, carefully push the sausage skin as far up the nozzle and the outside of the piping bag as possible. When most of the skin is on the nozzle, start squeezing out the mixture. When a little of the skin has been filled, tie a neat knot in the end.

Continue to fill the sausage skin, keeping up a low steady pressure on the piping bag, at the same time allowing the skin to flow off the end of the nozzle, so that the skin fills evenly without bursting. The length of sausage may either be twisted at regular lengths to make conventional sausages, or looped round, pinwheel fashion, to make a single large sausage.

When cooking home-made sausages, do not prick the skins. Bake them slowly in the oven until the centres are cooked and the skins crisp. Alternatively, fry or grill them, using moderate heat so that the skins do not burst. Drain on absorbent kitchen paper before serving.

OXFORD SAUSAGES

Choose pork which consists of two-thirds lean meat to one-third fat, without skin or gristle.

1.5 kg/3¼ lb pork, minced
450 g/1 lb fresh white breadcrumbs
5 ml/1 tsp freshly ground black pepper
grated rind of ½ lemon
2.5 ml/½ tsp grated nutmeg
6 fresh sage leaves, chopped
2.5 ml/½ tsp chopped fresh winter savory
2.5 ml/½ tsp dried marjoram

Mix the pork with the other ingredients in a large bowl. Add enough water to make a mixture with a soft piping consistency. Fill sausage skins, following the instructions above, or shape into small patties. If possible, allow the sausages to mature overnight in the refrigerator before cooking.

MAKES 36 SAUSAGES

BOILED DRESSED HAM

1 leg of ham
250 ml/8 fl oz cider or white wine (optional)
1 large onion, roughly chopped
3–4 celery sticks, roughly chopped
1 large turnip, roughly chopped
1 large carrot, roughly chopped
1 bouquet garni

GARNISH
browned breadcrumbs
demerara sugar · cloves
small bunches of watercress

Weigh the ham. Depending on how salty the ham is, it may be necessary to soak it in cold water for up to 12 hours. Soaking is not usually necessary with modern curing, however, since less salt is used. Check with your butcher.

Drain the ham if necessary. Place it in a large saucepan, cover with fresh water and bring to the boil. Skim off any scum that rises to the surface, lower the heat and simmer for 20 minutes per 450 g/1 lb, or until the bone at the knuckle end sticks out about 2.5 cm/1 inch and starts to feel loose.

Pour off the water from the pan and add the cider or wine, if used. Add fresh tepid water to cover, together with the prepared vegetables and bouquet garni. Bring the liquid to simmer-

ing point, half cover the pan and simmer gently for 10 minutes per 450 g/1 lb.

When the ham is cooked, lift it out of the pan. Remove the rind and score the fat into a diamond pattern, using a sharp knife and making the cuts about 5 mm/¼ inch deep.

Cover the fat with equal quantities of browned breadcrumbs and demerara sugar. Press a clove into the centre of each diamond pattern. Place small bunches of watercress at either end of the ham and cover the knuckle with a pie frill. Serve hot or cold.

TOAD-IN-THE-HOLE

450 g/1 lb pork sausages

BATTER
100 g/4 oz plain flour
1.25 ml/¼ tsp salt
1 egg beaten
300 ml/½ pint milk, or milk and water

Make the batter. Sift the flour and salt into a bowl, make a well in the centre and add the beaten egg. Stir in half the milk (or all the milk, if using a mixture of milk and water), gradually working in the flour.

Beat vigorously until the mixture is smooth and bubbly, then stir in the rest of the milk (or the water). Pour the batter into a jug and set aside.

Set the oven at 220°C/425°F/gas 7. Arrange the sausages, spoke-fashion, in a shallow 1.1 litre/2 pint circular dish. Stand the dish on a baking sheet and cook the sausages for 15 minutes.

Pour the batter over the sausages and bake for 40–45 minutes more until golden brown and well risen. Serve at once with a rich gravy or home-made tomato sauce.

SERVES FOUR

 MRS BEETON'S TIP

Whole hams vary considerably in size and in the relation of meat to bone. It is therefore difficult to give exact servings. As a general guide, a 4.5 kg/10 lb ham should feed 30 people.

PORK SAUSAGES WITH CABBAGE

1 large hard white cabbage, about 1 kg/2¼ lb
75 g/3 oz butter
1 small onion, finely chopped
6 juniper berries, crushed
salt and pepper
50 ml/2 fl oz vegetable or chicken stock
450 g/1 lb pork sausages

Trim the cabbage and cut it into quarters. Shred it finely lengthways. Melt the butter in a large saucepan, add the onion and fry over gentle heat for about 5 minutes until transparent. Add the cabbage and juniper berries, with salt and pepper to taste. Pour in the stock, cover with a tight-fitting lid and cook gently for 1 hour. Stir occasionally and top up the liquid if it threatens to evaporate, leaving the cabbage dry.

Meanwhile grill, bake or fry the sausages until cooked through. Pile the cooked cabbage in a heated serving dish. Arrange the hot sausages on top and serve at once.

SERVES FOUR

 MRS BEETON'S TIP

Juniper berries have a sweet, aromatic flavour reminiscent of pine. Their principal use is as a flavouring for gin, but they are also used in marinades, pâtés and in game cookery.

HAM WITH RAISIN AND ORANGE SAUCE

2 kg/4½ lb ham, boiled for 20 minutes per 450 g/1 lb
225 g/8 oz soft dark brown sugar
cloves
100 ml/3½ fl oz white wine vinegar

RAISIN SAUCE
50 g/2 oz soft dark brown sugar
2.5 ml/½ tsp prepared mustard
15 ml/1 tbsp cornflour
75 g/3 oz seedless raisins
15 ml/1 tbsp grated orange rind
100 ml/3½ fl oz fresh orange juice

Set the oven at 160°C/325°F/gas 3. Drain the ham. Put it in a shallow baking tin. Bake for 10 minutes per 450 g/1 lb. Thirty minutes before the end of the calculated cooking time, lift the ham out of the tin, reserving the juices in a measuring jug. Remove the rind and score the fat into a diamond pattern. Cover with brown sugar and stud with cloves.

Return the ham to the pan and trickle the vinegar over the top, taking care not to wash off the sugar. Continue baking, basting once or twice with the juices, until the ham is fully cooked.

Meanwhile make the sauce. Mix the brown sugar, mustard and cornflour in a small saucepan. Stir in the remaining ingredients with 200 ml/7 fl oz water. Cook over very gentle heat for about 10 minutes or until syrupy.

When the ham is cooked, transfer it to a heated platter. Serve the sauce separately.

SERVES EIGHT TO TEN

HONEY GLAZED HAM

1.5-2 kg/3¼-4½ lb ham
500 ml/17 fl oz dry cider
5 ml/1 tsp prepared mustard
45 ml/3 tbsp set honey
generous pinch of ground cloves
1 (227 g/8 oz) can pineapple chunks,
    drained, juice reserved
maraschino cherries, halved
20 ml/4 tsp softened butter
15 ml/1 tbsp double cream
watercress sprigs to garnish

Parboil the ham for 20 minutes per 450 g/1 lb, then drain and place in a large baking tin. Set the oven at 180°C/350°F/gas 4.

Pour the cider over the ham, cover the tin tightly with foil and bake for 30 minutes. Meanwhile make the glaze by mixing the mustard, honey and ground cloves together in a small bowl.

When the ham is cooked, lift it out of the tin, reserving the juices in a measuring jug. Remove the rind and score the fat into a diamond pattern. Brush generously with about half the honey glaze. Place pineapple chunks and halved cherries, cut side down, in alternate diamonds on the ham. Brush with a little more glaze, taking care not to disturb the garnish. Return the ham to the tin and bake, loosely covered with foil, for about 20 minutes or until the glaze is set.

Meanwhile add the reserved pineapple juice to the cooking juices. Make up to 600 ml/1 pint with water, if necessary. Pour into a small saucepan and bring to simmering point. Add the butter, in small pieces, stirring after each addition until melted. Simmer until well reduced and flavoured, then remove from the heat, add the cream and pour into a heated sauceboat. Garnish the ham with watercress and serve hot, with the sauce. The sauce may be omitted, and the ham served cold, if preferred.

SERVES EIGHT TO TEN

VARIATION

Marmalade Glaze Heat 250 ml/8 fl oz marmalade with 30 ml/2 tbsp cider vinegar and 30 ml/2 tbsp orange juice. Use as suggested above. Instead of studding the ham with pineapple and cherries, use thin slices of sweet orange, secured with cloves.

BAKED HAM LOAF

fat for greasing
100 g/4 oz dried breadcrumbs
350 g/12 oz cooked ham, minced
50 g/2 oz sultanas
1 large cooking apple
15 ml/1 tbsp chopped parsley
5 ml/1 tsp grated lemon rind
pinch of ground allspice
pinch of grated nutmeg
salt and pepper
2 eggs, beaten
milk (see method)

Grease a 450 g/1 lb loaf tin and coat it with some of the breadcrumbs. Set the oven at 150°C/300°F/gas 2.

Put the remaining breadcrumbs in a mixing bowl and add the minced ham and sultanas. Peel, core and grate the apple. Add it to the bowl with the parsley, lemon rind, spices, and salt and pepper to taste. Bind with the beaten eggs, adding a little milk if necessary.

Spoon the mixture into the prepared tin, taking care not to disturb the breadcrumb coating. Bake for 40 minutes. Allow to cool for 5 minutes, then turn out on to a heated serving dish. Serve hot, or cold.

SERVES SIX

HAM AND EGGS

4 gammon steaks
4 eggs

Trim the rind from the gammon steaks. Put it in a large cold frying pan. Heat, gently at first, until the fat runs, pressing the rind to extract the fat. Tilt the pan to grease it thoroughly, then discard the rind.

Snip the fat around the gammon steaks at intervals, add them to the pan and cook for about 20 minutes, turning several times.

Using tongs, transfer the gammon to a heated platter. Fry the eggs in the fat remaining in the pan, spooning the fat over the top from time to time until the whites are firm and yolks set. Alternatively poach the eggs. Serve on top of the ham.

SERVES FOUR

MIXED GRILL

4 lamb cutlets
4 pork sausages
4 lambs' kidneys, skinned, cored and
halved
a little oil
2 gammon rashers, rind removed and
halved or 8 rindless bacon rashers
salt and pepper
8 flat mushrooms
4 tomatoes

GARNISH (OPTIONAL)
fried bread (see Mrs Beeton's Tip)
parsley sprigs

Trim excess fat from the cutlets. Place the sausages on the rack in the grill pan. Cook for 5 minutes, turning once, before adding the cutlets and lambs' kidneys to the rack. Brush with a little oil. If serving gammon, lay the steaks on the rack at the same time and brush with a little oil. If serving bacon, add after about 5 minutes.

Continue cooking, turning the sausages often and turning the cutlets, kidneys and gammon when browned on one side. Allow about 5 minutes on each side for the cutlets, depending on thickness. Brush occasionally with juices from the pan and rearrange the food so that it all cooks at the same rate, pushing the sausage to a cooler part of the grill when they are browned. Have a heated serving dish ready and transfer cooked items to it promptly.

Lastly, brush the mushrooms and tomatoes with cooking juices and sprinkle them with a little salt and pepper. Place them on the grill rack when the meats are almost cooked. Grill the mushrooms for 1–2 minutes on each side, so that they are very lightly cooked, and grill the tomatoes cut sides up for 2 minutes.

Arrange the grilled foods on a serving plate, adding fried bread and parsley sprigs if liked. Serve freshly cooked.

SERVES FOUR

 MRS BEETON'S TIP

For fried bread, cut medium thick slices of bread. Trim off the crusts, if preferred, then cut the slices crossways in half or into quarters in the shape of triangles. Heat some dripping (ideally from bacon or gammon) or a mixture of oil and butter, add the bread and turn the slices almost immediately. This allows both sides to absorb a little fat and reduces the overall quantity of fat required to cook the bread. Cook until crisp and golden, then turn and cook the second side. Serve immediately.

MRS BEETON'S SAUSAGEMEAT CAKES

The original recipe did not have any breadcrumbs but they do help to give the mixture a workable consistency, avoiding hours of hard pounding in a mortar. Also, in Mrs Beeton's day the pork would have been considerably more fatty; she called for fat bacon in the first edition recipe to give a mixture of a binding consistency.

450 g/1 lb boneless belly of pork, skinned
350 g/12 oz rindless bacon (offcuts will do
   very nicely)
15 g/½ oz salt
freshly ground black pepper
1.25 ml/¼ tsp grated nutmeg
15 ml/1 tbsp chopped parsley
50 g/2 oz fresh breadcrumbs
flour for shaping
oil for frying

Finely chop the pork and bacon, then place them in a bowl. A food processor is ideal for this, otherwise use a large, very sharp knife or cleaver. Add the salt, plenty of pepper, nutmeg, parsley and breadcrumbs. Pound the mixture until the ingredients bind together.

Wet your hands and shape the mixture into 8 neat round cakes. Knead the mixture together so that it binds firmly, then dust the cakes with flour. Heat a very small amount of oil in a frying pan (just enough to stop the cakes from sticking), then cook the cakes fairly slowly so that they are thoroughly cooked through by the time they are well browned on both sides. Allow about 30 minutes' total cooking time. Serve at once.

MAKES EIGHT

BACON AND APPLE PATTIES

This is a good recipe for inexpensive bacon offcuts or for turning a comparatively small amount of bacon into an interesting meal. Serve the patties with baked potatoes and cabbage or a salad.

225 g/8 oz rindless bacon rashers, chopped
   (see Mrs Beeton's Tip)
1 onion, finely chopped
75 g/3 oz fresh breadcrumbs
salt and pepper
5 ml/1 tsp chopped fresh thyme or
   2.5 ml/½ tsp dried thyme
15 ml/1 tbsp chopped fresh sage or 5 ml/1 tsp
   dried sage
1 cooking apple, peeled, cored and grated
15 ml/1 tbsp sugar
1 egg
oil for frying

In a bowl, mix the bacon, onion, breadcrumbs, a little salt and plenty of pepper, the thyme, sage, apple and sugar. When the ingredients are well combined, mix in the egg to bind the mixture.

Wet your hands and shape the mixture into 8 small round patties. Heat a little oil in a frying pan and cook the patties fairly slowly so that they cook through. Allow 25–30 minutes, or until the patties are well browned on both sides. Serve freshly cooked.

MAKES EIGHT

 MRS BEETON'S TIP

An easy way of cutting bacon rashers into small pieces is by using kitchen scissors. Cut 2 or 3 rashers at a time, first into narrow strips, then across into small pieces.

PORK CHEESE

Originally presented as an excellent breakfast dish, this pâté-style recipe for cooked pork may be served with bread or toast and a salad for lunch or supper. Scoop it out of the baking dish rather than attempt to unmould the mixture or bottom-line the dish with greased greaseproof paper to turn out and slice the pork cheese. Bake the mixture in small pots or ramekins for taking on a picnic.

1.4 kg/3 lb belly of pork, boned
salt and pepper
30 ml/2 tbsp chopped parsley
5 ml/1 tsp chopped fresh thyme or
  2.5 ml/½ tsp dried thyme
2.5 ml/½ tsp chopped rosemary
15 ml/1 tbsp chopped fresh sage or 5 ml/1 tsp
  dried sage
2.5 ml/½ tsp ground mace
a little grated nutmeg
grated rind of ½ lemon
300 ml/½ pint pork gravy (see Mrs Beeton's
  Tip)
butter for greasing

Set the oven at 180°C/350°F/gas 4. Place the pork in a roasting tin and cook for 1½ hours, until cooked through. Leave to cool for about 30 minutes, or until the meat is just cool enough to handle.

Set the oven at 180°C/350°F/gas 4 again. Use a sharp paring knife or fine-bladed knife to cut all the rind off the pork. Chop the meat and fat, either by hand or in a food processor. Do not overprocess the mixture as the pieces should resemble very fine dice. Place the pork in a large bowl. Add plenty of salt and pepper, all the herbs, the mace, nutmeg and lemon rind. If you have a large pestle, then use it to pound the meat with the flavouring ingredients; if not, use the back of a sturdy mixing spoon. The more you pound the mixture, the better the texture.

When all the ingredients are thoroughly mixed, work in the gravy to bind them together loosely. Good thick gravy is best as it will not make the mixture too runny, more can be incorporated and the cheese will have a good flavour.

Grease a 1.1 litre/2 pint ovenproof dish, for example a soufflé dish or terrine. Turn the mixture into the dish, smooth it down and cover with foil. Bake for 1½ hours, then leave to cool completely. Chill overnight before serving.

SERVES TEN TO TWELVE

 MRS BEETON'S TIP

After roasting the pork, pour off excess fat, then use the cooking juices to make gravy. Allow 40 g/1½ oz plain flour to 600 ml/1 pint chicken or vegetable stock. Stir the flour into the residue in the roasting tin and cook, stirring, for 3 minutes. Gradually stir in the stock, bring to the boil and simmer for 5 minutes, stirring occasionally.

PORK BRAWN

*Although the idea of cooking a pig's head may be
anathema to modern cooks, the butcher prepares the
'joint' beyond immediate recognition and it is worth
the effort of cooking brawn to experience the full
flavour of long-cooked meat jellied in a stock rich
with aromatics. The beef in the recipe that follows is
an optional extra, mainly for bulk; the flavour is
excellent without it. You will need a large saucepan
for this, or a stainless steel preserving pan with a
makeshift foil cover. The meat must be kept covered
with plenty of water during cooking.*

½ pig's head, ears, brain and snout removed
1 pig's trotter, split
350 g/12 oz shin of beef (optional)
15 ml/1 tbsp salt
6 black peppercorns
6 cloves
5 ml/1 tsp dried marjoram or oregano
5 ml/1 tsp ground mace or 2 blades of mace
2 bay leaves
1 large fresh sage sprig
2 fresh thyme sprigs
1 fresh rosemary sprig
1 fresh savory sprig (optional)
4 parsley sprigs, with long stalks
2 onions, cut into chunks
2 large carrots, sliced
1 small turnip, cubed

Pig's heads are sold as part of the carcass, so
any good butcher or supermarket which
butchers its own meat (rather than taking
prepacked deliveries) will be able to supply a
head within a few days of ordering. Ask for the
ears, snout and brain to be removed, and for the
half head to be chopped into two pieces so that
it fits easily into a large saucepan. Have the
trotter split in half.

Wash the head well in salted cold water, then
rinse it under clear water and place the pieces
in a large pan. Add the shin of beef, if used, the
trotter, salt, peppercorns, cloves, marjoram
and mace. Tie the bay leaves and herb sprigs
into a neat bouquet garni and add them to the
pan. A dried bouquet garni is no replacement
for fresh herbs as their flavour is important.

Add the onions, carrots and turnip to the pan,
then pour in cold water to cover the meat
amply. Bring to the boil, then use a slotted
spoon to skim the surface of the liquid for the
first 5–10 minutes' cooking, or until the scum
has stopped forming. Take care to avoid removing any onion or too much of the dried herb and
mace. Reduce the heat so that the liquid is just
boiling and cover the pan. Cook for 3 hours.

Have a very large bowl or saucepan, metal
colander and two large meat plates ready, then
lift the head and shin, if used, from the pan on
to one plate. A large fish slice and barbecue
forks are ideal for this. Strain the cooking
liquid through a colander into the bowl or pan.
Replace the trotters in the bowl or pan but
discard the vegetables and herbs. If the stock
has been strained into a bowl, pour it back into
the clean pan. Bring it just to the boil.

Transfer a piece of meat to the clean plate for
preparation. Use a sharp pointed knife to cut off
the rind, leaving a thin layer of fat over the
meat. Cut all the meat off the bones, using the
point of the knife to scrape the crevices – this is
an easy task as the meat literally falls away
from the carcass.

Do not discard all the fat as it contributes
flavour and moistens the finished brawn; however, remove all blood vessels and any small,
dark and hard portions that are offal-like in
appearance and texture. The meat is easy to
distinguish as it is quite stringy and plentiful.
Cut the meat into small pieces, across the grain,
and chop the fat. Return any bones to the pan of
stock for further boiling. Continue until all the
carcass is cleaned. Trim any fat and gristle from
the beef, if used, and chop the meat. Mix it with
the pork.

Cook the stock with the bones in the open pan until well reduced to less than half its original volume, then strain it again. You should aim to reduce the stock to 1.1–1.25 litres/2–2½ pints as this concentrates the flavour and gives a firm brawn. Although further reduction will intensify the flavour, the resultant brawn would set more firmly than is desirable. Lastly, strain the stock through a sieve lined with scalded muslin.

Mix the pork and fat well with the beef, if used, and place it in a 1.1 litre/2 pint basin. Stir in about 450 ml/¾ pint of the strained stock, mixing well at first, until all the meat is evenly distributed and the top just covered with stock (see Mrs Beeton's Tip). Cover and cool, then chill for at least 3 hours, or until set.

To serve, slide the point of a knife around the rim of the brawn, between it and the basin. Cover with a plate and invert both the basin and the plate, giving them a firm jerk to release the jellied meat. Cut into slices and serve the brawn with ripe tomatoes or salad and baked or fried potatoes. Alternatively, offer it with plain chunks of bread. Any leftover brawn makes a delicious sandwich filling.

SERVES FOUR TO SIX

 MRS BEETON'S TIP

The leftover stock makes delicious soup or it may be used in casseroles: cool, then freeze it in usable quantities.

SALT PORK WITH SAUERKRAUT

675 g/1½ lb salted belly pork
1 onion, peeled but left whole
1 garlic clove, peeled but left whole
1 carrot, quartered
50 g/2 oz unsalted butter
675 g/1½ lb sauerkraut
15 ml/1 tbsp caraway seeds (optional)
45 ml/3 tbsp vegetable or chicken stock
salt and pepper

Put the pork in a bowl with cold water to cover. Soak for 1 hour, then drain and put into a large saucepan. Add fresh water to cover, bring to the boil and skim well. Add the onion, garlic and carrot. Half cover the pan, lower the heat and simmer gently for 1 hour. Remove from the heat and leave to cool in the liquid. Slice the onion thickly.

Set the oven at 180°C/350°F/gas 4. Grease a casserole with half the butter, put the sauerkraut on the base, sprinkle with the caraway seeds, if used, and top with the flavouring vegetables from the pork. Add the pork. Pour the measured stock over and season with salt and pepper. Cover with buttered greaseproof paper and a tight-fitting lid. Cook for about 1½ hours, by which time all the stock should have evaporated. Take out the pork and set it aside. Stir the remaining butter into the sauerkraut.

Spoon the sauerkraut on to a heated serving platter. Slice the pork and arrange it on top. Serve at once.

SERVES FOUR TO SIX

FAGGOTS

fat for greasing
800 g/1¾ lb pig's liver
2 onions, quartered
2.5 ml/½ tsp dried thyme
10 ml/2 tsp dried sage
generous pinch of grated nutmeg
2.5 ml/½ tsp ground mace
salt and pepper
1 egg, lightly beaten
100 g/4 oz fresh white breadcrumbs
caul fat, pork dripping, lard or butter

Remove the skin and any tubes from the liver and slice it thinly. Put it in a saucepan with the onions. Add just enough water to cover. Bring to the boil, lower the heat, cover and simmer for 30 minutes. Drain. Mince the liver and onions finely or process in a food processor. Add the herbs, spices, seasoning, egg and enough breadcrumbs to make a firm mixture.

Divide the mixture into 8 equal portions and shape into balls. Wrap in caul fat, if used. Lay the faggots side by side in a greased baking tin and dot with fat if caul is not used. Cover the tin loosely with foil. Bake for 25 minutes, then remove the foil and bake for a further 10–15 minutes to brown the tops of the faggots. Serve hot, with a thickened gravy.

SERVES FOUR TO SIX

 MRS BEETON'S TIP

Caul fat is a tough membrane laced with fat. Salted caul is seldom available; however should it be obtained, it must be soaked in cold water for 30 minutes, then thoroughly rinsed and soaked in fresh water with a little vinegar added. Finally, it should be rinsed and spread out on a perfectly clean tea-towel ready for use.

LIVER HOT POT

fat for greasing
450 g/1 lb lamb's liver, sliced
45 ml/3 tbsp plain flour
salt and pepper
2 large onions, thinly sliced
800 g/1¾ lb potatoes, thinly sliced
500 ml/18 fl oz beef stock
6–8 rindless streaky bacon rashers

Set the oven at 180°C/350°F/gas 4. Remove the skin and any tubes from the liver. Mix the flour with salt and pepper in a shallow bowl. Coat the liver slices in the seasoned flour. Shake off excess flour.

Arrange layers of liver, onion and potatoes in a greased casserole, ending with a layer of potatoes. Heat the stock in a small saucepan and pour in just enough to cover the potatoes. Cover the casserole with a lid or foil and bake for 1 hour or until the liver is tender.

Remove the lid and arrange the bacon rashers on top of the potatoes. Return the casserole to the oven for about 15 minutes or until the bacon is browned. Serve immediately, straight from the casserole.

SERVES SIX

KIDNEYS IN ITALIAN SAUCE

450 g/1 lb lambs' kidneys
45 ml/3 tbsp plain flour
salt and pepper
30 ml/2 tbsp beef dripping
8 young fresh sage leaves (optional)
1 small onion, finely chopped
25 g/1 oz butter or margarine
375 ml/13 fl oz beef stock
100 g/4 oz mushrooms, sliced
15-30 ml/1-2 tbsp sherry
75 g/3 oz mange tout, lightly cooked, to garnish

Wash the kidneys, halve and remove the membrane and white core from each. Cut into slices. Mix the flour with salt and pepper in a shallow bowl. Coat the kidneys in seasoned flour, shake off excess flour and reserve.

Heat the dripping in a frying pan, add the kidney slices and sage, if using, and fry quickly, stirring, until firm. Add the onion, lower the heat, cover and fry gently for 20 minutes.

Meanwhile, melt the butter or margarine in a saucepan, stir in the reserved flour and cook until nut brown in colour. Gradually add the stock, stirring constantly, and bring to the boil. Lower the heat and simmer for 5 minutes.

With a slotted spoon, transfer the kidney slices and onions to the sauce. Half cover the pan and simmer the mixture for 45 minutes, then add the mushrooms and sherry, with extra salt and pepper if liked. Simmer for 15 minutes more. Serve at once, garnished with mange tout.

SERVES FOUR

DEVILLED KIDNEYS

8 lambs' kidneys
30 ml/2 tbsp oil
15 ml/1 tbsp chopped onion
2.5 ml/½ tsp salt
1.25 ml/¼ tsp cayenne pepper
5 ml/1 tsp Worcestershire sauce
10 ml/2 tsp lemon juice
2.5 ml/½ tsp prepared mustard
125 ml/4 fl oz beef stock
2 egg yolks
fresh white breadcrumbs
buttered wholemeal toast, to serve

Skin, halve and core the kidneys, then chop them into small pieces. Heat the oil in a small saucepan, add the onion and cook gently for 4-6 minutes until softened but not browned. Add the kidneys, salt, cayenne, Worcestershire sauce, lemon juice, mustard and stock. Bring to the boil, lower the heat and simmer for 15-20 minutes, until the kidneys are cooked. Cool slightly.

Beat the egg yolks lightly and stir them quickly into the kidney mixture. Sprinkle in enough of the breadcrumbs to give the mixture a soft consistency. Add more salt and pepper if required. Serve on buttered wholemeal toast.

SERVES FOUR

KIDNEYS TURBIGO

15 ml/1 tbsp oil
225 g/8 oz cocktail sausages
1 small onion, finely chopped
450 g/1 lb lambs' kidneys, halved and cored
salt and pepper
100 g/4 oz small button mushrooms
15 ml/1 tbsp plain flour
30 ml/2 tbsp tomato purée
150 ml/¼ pint dry white wine
150 ml/¼ pint vegetable or chicken stock
45 ml/3 tbsp chopped parsley

Heat the oil in a large frying pan, add the sausages and cook them over moderate heat until evenly golden. Using a slotted spoon, transfer them to a dish and set aside.

Pour off any excess fat from the pan, leaving enough to cook the remaining ingredients. Add the onion and cook, stirring, for 10 minutes, until softened. Add the kidneys, with salt and pepper to taste. Cook them, turning often, until browned all over and just cooked.

Add the mushrooms to the pan and continue cooking for about 5 minutes, so that the mushrooms are lightly cooked. Use a slotted spoon to transfer the kidneys and mushrooms to the dish with the sausages.

Stir the flour into the fat remaining in the pan. Stir in the tomato purée, then gradually stir in the wine and stock. Bring to the boil, stirring all the time, then lower the heat and return the sausages, mushrooms and kidneys to the pan. Simmer gently for 5 minutes.

Add the parsley and seasoning to taste before serving with cooked pasta or rice.

SERVES FOUR

STUFFED HEARTS

butter for greasing
4 lambs' hearts (see Mrs Beeton's Tip)
50 g/2 oz dripping or 60 ml/4 tbsp oil
30 ml/2 tbsp plain flour
salt and pepper
350 ml/12 fl oz strong lamb or beef stock

STUFFING
50 g/2 oz margarine
100 g/4 oz fresh white breadcrumbs
30 ml/2 tbsp chopped parsley
2.5 ml/½ tsp chopped fresh thyme
grated rind of ½ lemon

Set the oven at 180°C/350°F/gas 4. Melt the margarine and stir in the remaining stuffing ingredients, with seasoning. Divide between the hearts. Skewer or sew together the flaps at the top to seal.

Heat the dripping or oil in a small baking tin. Put in the hearts and baste well. Bake for 45 minutes, basting several times. Transfer to a serving dish, remove the skewers if necessary, and keep hot.

Drain off most of the fat from the baking tin, retaining any meat juices. Transfer the tin to the top of the stove and stir in the flour over low heat. Cook for 1 minute, then gradually add the stock, stirring until the mixture boils. Add seasoning and serve with the hearts.

SERVES FOUR

 MRS BEETON'S TIP

Wash lambs' hearts under running water. Cut off the lobes, flaps and gristle. Cut away membranes which separate the cavities inside. Soak in cold water for 30 minutes, then dry on absorbent kitchen paper.

TONGUE WITH RAISIN SAUCE

1 fresh ox tongue, about 2 kg/4½ lb, or
   6 lambs' tongues
1 onion, chopped
1 carrot, diced
1 turnip, diced
1 celery stick, sliced
1 bouquet garni
6 whole allspice
4 whole cloves
6 black peppercorns
chopped parsley to garnish

RAISIN SAUCE
50 g/2 oz butter
25 g/1 oz plain flour
600 ml/1 pint cider
100 g/4 oz seedless raisins
5 ml/1 tsp grated lemon rind
2.5 ml/½ tsp French mustard

Weigh the tongue(s), then wash thoroughly. Soak in cold water for 2 hours. Drain and put in a large saucepan. Cover with fresh cold water, bring to the boil, then drain again. Repeat the process with fresh cold water.

Return the tongue to the pan again, cover with cold water once more and add the vegetables, bouquet garni and spices. Bring to the boil, cover with a tight-fitting lid, lower the heat and simmer gently until tender. An ox tongue will take about 3 hours; lambs' tongues 1–1½ hours (see Mrs Beeton's Tip).

When cooked, lift out the tongue(s) and plunge into cold water. Drain. Remove the skin carefully and take out the small bones at the root of the tongue, together with any excess fat, glands and gristle. Carve the tongue in slices and arrange on a large platter. Keep hot while making the sauce.

Melt the butter in a saucepan, stir in the flour and cook for 1 minute. Add the cider and raisins, stirring until the mixture boils and thickens. Lower the heat and simmer for 5 minutes, the stir in the lemon rind and mustard. Spoon the sauce over the tongue slices and serve at once.

SERVES NINE TO TWELVE

VARIATION

Pressed Tongue To serve an ox tongue cold, cook, skin and trim as above. While it is hot, curl the tongue into an 18 cm/7 inch straight-sided dish or tin. Spoon over a little of the stock in which the tongue was cooked, to fill up the crevices. Put a flat plate, just large enough to fit inside the dish, on top of the tongue, and add a heavy weight. Chill overnight to set, then run a knife around the edge of the tongue and turn it out. Cut in thin slices and serve with salad.

 MRS BEETON'S TIP

To test whether the tongue is cooked, attempt to pull out one of the small bones near the root. If it comes away easily, the tongue is ready.

TRIPE AND ONIONS

Tripe is the muscular lining of the four stomachs of cattle or sheep. It varies in consistency and appearance, depending on the source. Honeycomb tripe is the most delicate type. It is usually sold blanched and parboiled. It is highly perishable and should always be cooked as soon as possible after purchase.

450 g/1 lb dressed tripe
600 ml/1 pint milk
salt and pepper
3 large onions, chopped
25 g/1 oz butter
30 ml/2 tbsp plain flour

GARNISH
15 ml/1 tbsp chopped parsley
toast triangles

Wash the tripe and cut it into 5 cm/2 inch squares. Put it in a heavy-bottomed saucepan. Add the milk, with salt and pepper to taste. Stir in the onions. Bring the milk to the boil, lower the heat, cover with a tight-fitting lid and simmer for about 2 hours (see Mrs Beeton's Tip) or until the tripe is tender.

Knead the butter and flour together until evenly blended. Add it in small pieces to the contents of the pan. Stir until smooth, then continue cooking for a further 30 minutes. Serve on a heated dish, garnished with parsley and toast triangles.

SERVES FOUR

 MRS BEETON'S TIP

Cooking time for tripe varies, depending on type and preliminary preparation. Ask the butcher's advice.

FRIED SWEETBREADS

3 pairs lamb's sweetbreads, total weight about 675 g/1½ lb
chicken or lamb stock (see method)
40 g/1½ oz butter
2.5 ml/½ tsp lemon juice
30 ml/2 tbsp plain flour
salt and pepper
1 egg, lightly beaten
fresh white breadcrumbs for coating

CUCUMBER SAUCE
15 g/½ oz butter
½ cucumber, chopped
15 ml/1 tbsp chicken or lamb stock
125 ml/4 fl oz Béchamel Sauce (page 481)
pinch of sugar
grated nutmeg
lemon juice
30 ml/2 tbsp single cream

Soak the sweetbreads in cold water to cover for 1–2 hours to remove all the blood.

Meanwhile, make the sauce. Melt the butter in a saucepan, add the cucumber and cook gently for 10 minutes. Add the stock and continue cooking until the cucumber is very soft. Rub it through a fine sieve into a clean pan, then simmer until slightly reduced. Stir in the Béchamel sauce and heat through if necessary. Add salt, pepper, sugar and nutmeg to taste; sharpen the flavour with lemon juice. Cover the surface of the sauce closely with buttered greaseproof paper and set aside.

Drain the sweetbreads. Put them in a saucepan with fresh water to cover. Bring to the boil, then pour off the liquid. Rinse the sweetbreads under cold water; remove the black veins and as much as possible of the membranes which cover them.

Put the sweetbreads in a saucepan with just enough stock to cover them; add 5 ml/1 tsp of the butter and the lemon juice. Bring the stock to the boil, lower the heat, cover the pan and simmer for 15–20 minutes. Leave the sweetbreads to cool in the stock, then drain.

Spread out the flour in a shallow bowl and season with salt and pepper. Put the egg into a second bowl and the breadcrumbs on a sheet of foil. Dip the sweetbreads in flour, then in egg and finally in breadcrumbs. Heat the remaining butter in a frying pan, add the crumbed sweetbreads and fry for about 8 minutes until golden brown on all sides. Remove with a slotted spoon and drain on absorbent kitchen paper. Arrange on a serving dish.

Reheat the sauce; off the heat, stir in the cream. Serve with the sweetbreads.

SERVES SIX

OXTAIL HOT POT

1 kg/2¼ lb oxtail, jointed
30 ml/2 tbsp plain flour
salt and pepper
2 large onions, thinly sliced
800 g/1¾ lb potatoes, sliced
5 ml/1 tsp dried mixed herbs
beef stock (see method)
6 rindless streaky bacon rashers, cut in
    small squares

Set the oven at 180°C/350°F/gas 4. Wash the oxtail, dry it thoroughly and trim off any excess fat. Mix the flour with salt and pepper, and use to coat the oxtail.

Place alternate layers of onions, oxtail and potatoes in a pie dish or casserole, sprinkling each layer with salt, pepper and dried mixed herbs, and ending with a layer of potatoes. Pour in just enough beef stock to cover the meat. Cover the casserole and bake for 2½–3 hours, or

until the meat is tender. Check the hot pot from time to time, and add more stock if necessary.

Remove the lid from the casserole, lay the bacon rashers over the top and bake for 30 minutes more. Serve.

SERVES FOUR

WIENER SCHNITZEL

plain flour
salt and pepper
1 egg
2–3 drops of oil
dried white breadcrumbs for coating
6 thin escalopes of veal, each measuring
    about 13 × 7.5 cm/5 × 3 inches
oil and butter for shallow frying

GARNISH
6 lemon slices
15 ml/1 tbsp chopped parsley

Spread out the flour in a shallow bowl and season with salt and pepper. Put the egg in a second bowl, add the oil and beat lightly. Spread out the breadcrumbs on a sheet of foil. Coat the escalopes in flour, then in egg and finally in breadcrumbs, pressing them on well.

Heat the oil and butter in a large frying pan. Put in the escalopes and fry over gentle to moderate heat for 7–10 minutes, turning them over once only with two fish slices or spatulas.

Remove the escalopes and place them, overlapping slightly, on a heated flat serving dish. Garnish the middle of each escalope with a slice of lemon sprinkled with parsley.

SERVES SIX

CALF'S LIVER WITH SAVOURY RICE

450 g/1 lb calf's liver, sliced
40 g/1½ oz butter or margarine
1 onion, finely chopped
2 garlic cloves, crushed
150 g/5 oz long-grain rice
375 ml/13 fl oz well-flavoured chicken or
    vegetable stock
salt and pepper
1.25–2.5 ml/¼–½ tsp powdered saffron
plain flour for coating
oil for frying
bacon rolls (see Mrs Beeton's Tip, page 194)
    to garnish

SAUCE

15 ml/1 tbsp dripping or lard
1 carrot, thinly sliced
1 small onion, thinly sliced
30 ml/2 tbsp plain flour
300 ml/½ pint lamb or vegetable stock
30 ml/2 tbsp tomato purée
15 ml/1 tbsp shredded fresh sage or
    1.25 ml/¼ tsp dried sage

Remove the skin and any tubes from the liver. Melt 25 g/1 oz of the butter or margarine in a frying pan, add the onion and garlic and sauté without colouring for 2–3 minutes. Stir in the rice and cook over gentle heat for 3 minutes.

Add the stock, with salt and pepper to taste, then sprinkle in the saffron. Cover the pan and cook for about 20 minutes until the rice is soft and has absorbed all the stock. Add the remaining butter or margarine, mix well, then press into a ring mould. Set aside until set.

Set the oven at 160°C/325°F/gas 3. Make the sauce. Melt the dripping or lard in a saucepan. Add the carrot and onion and fry over gentle heat until the onion is golden brown. Stir in the flour, lower the heat and cook for 1 minute. Gradually add the stock, tomato purée and sage, stirring constantly. Bring to the boil, stirring all the time, then lower the heat, cover and simmer for 15 minutes. Strain into a clean pan and add salt and pepper to taste. Cover the surface of the sauce with dampened greaseproof paper and set aside.

Place the flour for coating in a shallow bowl, add salt and pepper and coat the slices of liver on both sides. Heat the oil for frying in a large frying pan, add the liver and fry quickly for about 4 minutes, turning once, until browned and crisp on the outside but still pink in the centre. Drain the liver, then cut the slices into strips.

Turn the rice ring on to a heated serving dish, cover lightly with buttered greaseproof paper and heat through in the oven for 10–12 minutes. Meanwhile reheat the sauce until just below boiling point. Stir in the liver, lower the heat and simmer for 2–3 minutes until heated through. Spoon the liver mixture into the centre of the rice ring, garnish with the bacon rolls and serve at once.

SERVES SIX

FRIED FILLETS OF VEAL WITH LEMON SAUCE

275 g/10 oz fillet of veal, trimmed and cut
   into 4 slices
1 egg, lightly beaten
2.5 ml/½ tsp chopped parsley
1.25 ml/¼ tsp chopped fresh thyme
5 ml/1 tsp grated lemon rind
5 ml/1 tsp lemon juice
dried white breadcrumbs for coating
50 g/2 oz butter

LEMON SAUCE
15 ml/1 tbsp plain flour
250 ml/8 fl oz chicken stock
2.5 ml/½ tsp lemon juice
salt and pepper
15-30 ml/1-2 tbsp single cream

Place the veal slices between greaseproof paper and flatten them with a cutlet bat or rolling pin. Put the egg in a shallow bowl with the herbs, lemon rind and juice. Add the veal slices, turn them in the egg, then cover and marinate in the refrigerator for 30 minutes. Spread out the breadcrumbs on a sheet of foil and use to coat the veal slices, pressing the crumbs in well.

Heat the butter in a large frying pan and fry the veal slices over moderate heat until golden brown on both sides, then lower the heat and cook more slowly for 7-10 minutes. Drain on absorbent kitchen paper and keep hot.

Make the lemon sauce. Stir the flour into the fat remaining in the frying pan. Cook gently for about 2 minutes. Gradually add the stock, stirring the mixture until it boils and thickens. Add the lemon juice with salt and pepper to taste. Simmer the sauce for 3 minutes, then remove from the heat.

Pour some of the lemon sauce over the veal and serve the rest in a heated sauceboat.

SERVES THREE TO FOUR

ESCALOPES WITH HAM AND CHEESE

6 thin escalopes of veal
plain flour
salt and pepper
1 egg
2-3 drops of oil
dried white breadcrumbs for coating
butter and oil for shallow frying
6 thin slices of lean cooked ham
6 thin slices of Gruyère cheese

Set the oven at 180°C/350°F/gas 4. Wipe the escalopes, place them between greaseproof paper and flatten them with a cutlet bat or rolling pin. Coat them in seasoned flour, egg (with oil) and breadcrumbs as described for Wiener Schnitzel (page 409).

Heat the butter and oil in a large frying pan. Put in the escalopes and fry over gentle to moderate heat for about 3 minutes on each side.

Remove the escalopes and lay them in a flat ovenproof dish. Cover each escalope with a slice of ham and top with a slice of cheese. Spoon a little of the pan juices over the top of each escalope, put the dish in the oven and bake until the cheese melts – about 20 minutes. Serve at once.

SERVES SIX

VARIATION

Veal Cordon Bleu In this popular dish, the veal escalopes are folded over, with the ham and cheese sandwiched in the middle, before the escalopes are coated in breadcrumbs.

OSSO BUCO

450 g/1 lb tomatoes, peeled, seeded and
    chopped or 1 (397 g/14 oz) can chopped
    tomatoes
30 ml/2 tbsp tomato purée
200 ml/7 fl oz beef stock
salt and pepper
50 g/2 oz plain flour
4 veal knuckles or 4 veal shank slices,
    about 2 cm/¾ inch thick
60 ml/4 tbsp oil
1 onion, finely chopped
2 garlic cloves, crushed
2 carrots, finely chopped
2 celery sticks, sliced
juice of 1 lemon
150 ml/¼ pint dry white wine
2 bay leaves
2 fresh thyme sprigs

GREMOLADA
45 ml/3 tbsp chopped parsley
1 garlic clove, chopped
grated rind of ½ lemon

Set the oven at 180°C/350°F/gas 4. Put the
tomatoes, with any juices, into a bowl. Stir in
the tomato purée and stock, with salt and
pepper to taste. Set the mixture aside.

Put the flour in a stout polythene or paper bag.
Season with salt and pepper. Add the veal
knuckles or shank slices and toss until well
coated. Shake off excess flour. Heat the oil in a
large flameproof casserole, add the meat and
fry for about 8 minutes, turning once or twice,
until browned all over. With tongs, transfer the
meat to a plate and set aside.

Add the onion, garlic, carrots and celery to the
fat remaining in the casserole. Fry over gentle
heat for 6-8 minutes or until the onion is
golden brown. Add the reserved tomato mixture and bring to the boil, scraping in any
sediment on the base of the pan. Remove from

the heat and add the lemon juice and wine,
with the bay leaves and thyme.

Return the veal to the casserole, pushing the
pieces well down so that they are completely
covered by the sauce. Cover the dish tightly
with foil and a lid and bake for 1½-2 hours or
until the meat is very tender. Remove the bay
leaves and thyme sprigs. If necessary, place the
casserole over moderate heat for 5-10 minutes,
stirring occasionally, to reduce the sauce.

Make the *gremolada* by mixing all the ingredients together in a small bowl. Sprinkle over
the osso buco just before serving. Serve with
Risotto Milanese (page 407) and Italian
Spinach (page 359) if liked.

SERVES FOUR

FRICADELLES OF VEAL

275 g/10 oz fresh white breadcrumbs
60 ml/4 tbsp milk
450 g/1 lb lean pie veal, trimmed (see Mrs
    Beeton's Tip) or minced veal
100 g/4 oz shredded beef suet
grated rind of 1 lemon
generous pinch of grated nutmeg
salt and pepper
3 eggs
750 ml/1¼ pints veal or chicken stock
oil for deep frying
400 ml/14 fl oz Fresh Tomato Sauce (page
    483)

GARNISH
lemon slices
black olives

Put 175 g/6 oz of the breadcrumbs in a shallow
bowl, sprinkle the milk over and leave to stand
for 5 minutes. Squeeze out as much milk as
possible; rub out any lumps. Mince the pie veal

or process it roughly in a food processor. Scrape it into a bowl and add the soaked bread, suet, lemon rind and nutmeg, with plenty of salt and pepper. Beat 2 of the eggs lightly and stir into the mixture. Shape into balls about the size of large walnuts.

Bring the stock to the boil in a large saucepan, add the veal balls and cook for 6 minutes, until firm and cooked. Remove with a slotted spoon and drain well. Cool slightly before coating. Beat the remaining egg lightly in a shallow bowl. Spread out the remaining breadcrumbs on a sheet of foil. Coat the fricadelles in egg and breadcrumbs.

Heat the oil for deep frying to 180–190°C/ 350–375°F or until a cube of bread added to the oil browns in 30 seconds. Fry the fricadelles until golden brown.

Meanwhile, reheat the tomato sauce to simmering point in a large saucepan. As the fricadelles cook, remove them with a slotted spoon and drain them on absorbent kitchen paper. Serve piping hot, with the tomato sauce, garnished with lemon and black olives. Offer cooked rice or pasta with the fricadelles.

SERVES SIX

 MRS BEETON'S TIP

If the veal is boned by the butcher, ask him for the bones. These may be used for stock.

MRS BEETON'S BAKED VEAL OR HAM LOAF

Leftover roast veal would have been commonplace in Mrs Beeton's day but the recipe will work equally well if cooked ham or other cold cooked meat or poultry is used.

fat for greasing
200 g/7 oz cold roast veal or cooked ham
4 rindless streaky bacon rashers
175 g/6 oz fresh white breadcrumbs
250 ml/8 fl oz veal or chicken stock
2.5 ml/½ tsp grated lemon rind
2.5 ml/½ tsp ground mace
1.25 ml/¼ tsp cayenne pepper
30 ml/2 tbsp chopped parsley
salt
2 eggs, lightly beaten

Thoroughly grease a 450 g/1 lb loaf tin or 750 ml/1¼ pint ovenproof dish. Set the oven at 160°C/325°F/gas 3. Mince the veal or ham and bacon together finely or process in a food processor. Scrape into a bowl and add the breadcrumbs, stock and lemon rind, mace, cayenne and parsley with salt to taste. Mix in the eggs.

Spoon the mixture into the prepared tin or dish and bake for 1 hour, or until the mixture is firm and lightly browned. Serve hot, with gravy or tomato sauce, if liked.

SERVES THREE TO FOUR

 MRS BEETON'S TIP

If the loaf tin has a tendency to stick, line the base with baking parchment or grease-proof paper so that the loaf will turn out easily.

MEATBALLS IN CELERIAC SAUCE

200 g/7 oz minced veal
200 g/7 oz minced pork
1 egg, lightly beaten
50 g/2 oz plain flour
125 ml/4 fl oz milk
2 onions
salt and pepper
2.5 ml/½ tsp ground allspice
600 ml/1 pint vegetable stock
1 large celeriac, diced
25 g/1 oz butter
30 ml/2 tbsp chopped fresh dill or
   15 ml/1 tbsp chopped fresh tarragon
triangles of fried bread to garnish

Put the veal and pork in a large bowl. Stir in the egg with 45 ml/3 tbsp of the flour. Bring the milk to the boil in a small saucepan. Add it gradually to the minced meat mixture, stirring until all the milk has been absorbed. Grate 1 onion and add it to the meat with salt and pepper to taste. Add the allspice and mix well. Chill for 30 minutes in the bottom of the refrigerator. Wet your hands, then form the mixture into small balls, about 2 cm/¾ inch in diameter.

Bring the vegetable stock to the boil in a large saucepan. Add the meatballs, boil for about 5 minutes, then transfer to a bowl, using a slotted spoon. Add the celeriac to the pan and cook for 5 minutes or until just tender but not soft. Again using a slotted spoon, transfer the cooked celeriac to the bowl with the meatballs. Pour the vegetable stock into a jug and make it up to 450 ml/¾ pint with water. Set aside.

Melt the butter in a saucepan. Chop the remaining onion and add it to the pan. Cook, stirring, over very low heat for 15-20 minutes, until softened. Stir in the remaining flour and cook for 1 minute. Gradually add the reserved vegetable stock, stirring, then raise the heat and

cook until the mixture boils and thickens. Add the celeriac and meatballs to the sauce and simmer gently for 5 minutes. Add the dill or tarragon, with salt and pepper to taste. Serve at once with triangles of fried bread, or cool, cover and refrigerate for serving hot next day.

SERVES FOUR TO FIVE

 FREEZER TIP

Cool the meatballs quickly in the sauce. Freeze in a sealed container for up to 6 weeks. Reheat from frozen in a preheated 190°C/375°F/gas 5 oven for 45-60 minutes.

MEATLOAF

oil for greasing
450 g/1 lb minced beef or pork, or a mixture
   of both
50 g/2 oz fresh breadcrumbs
1 large onion, finely chopped
15 ml/2 tbsp chopped parsley
5 ml/1 tsp chopped fresh thyme
5 ml/1 tsp chopped fresh sage
1 egg
15 ml/1 tbsp Worcestershire sauce
salt and pepper

Grease a 450 g/1 lb loaf tin. Set the oven at 180°C/350°F/gas 4. Place all the ingredients in a bowl, adding plenty of salt and pepper. Pound the ingredients with the back of a mixing spoon until thoroughly combined and well bound together.

Turn the mixture into the tin, press it down well and cover the top with a piece of greased greaseproof paper. Bake for 1 hour, until firm and shrunk away from the tin slightly. Turn out and serve hot or cold.

SERVES FOUR

Vegetable Dishes

Variety and quality are all-important in the selection and use of vegetables. This chapter offers traditional and contemporary ideas to ensure that, whatever their role, the vegetables will complement the rest of the menu.

BUYING VEGETABLES

Although most vegetables are on sale all year, it is still worth taking advantage of locally grown produce in season, both for flavour and economy. Look out for home-grown produce in supermarkets and take advantage of any local market gardens and farms. Remember, too, that markets are an excellent place to shop for value – in some rural areas they can be the best place to buy really fresh produce.

Whatever and wherever you buy, always look for good-quality produce. Vegetables should look fresh – firm, crisp and bright. Avoid limp, yellowing and wrinkled produce; onions that are soft or sprouting; and items that have been excessively trimmed. Do not buy green potatoes as they are inedible; this should be brought to the attention of the seller.

The fact that vegetables have been cleaned is not necessarily an indication of their quality – for example, vegetables that have a certain amount of earth on them or retain their leaves are often better quality than thoroughly washed, trimmed and prepacked items.

When buying packs of vegetables always check that they are not sweating, with moisture inside the bag causing rapid deterioration in quality. Turn items over, feel them and inspect them for soft spots or bad patches.

STORING

Vegetables should be used as fresh as possible. The majority of vegetables should be stored in the refrigerator: salad vegetables should be polythene-wrapped or stored in the salad drawer. Carrots, parsnips and similar vegetables soon deteriorate if they are stored in polythene bags, so thick paper bags are the best wrapping in the salad drawer. Similarly, mushrooms go off quickly if they are stored in polythene. Green vegetables and cauliflower should be stored in polythene bags.

Potatoes should be stored only if suitable conditions are available, that is a cool, dry place where the tubers may be kept in a thick brown paper bag to exclude all light. They should not be stored in warm, light, moist conditions for any length of time. So only buy large polythene bags of potatoes if you can use them within a few days.

As a general rule, buy little and often for best quality and food value.

FROZEN VEGETABLES

Frozen vegetables are excellent quality, in terms of food value as well as flavour. They are also easy to prepare at home. Take advantage of pick-your-own farms or farm shops if you do not grow your own vegetables, and freeze only good quality produce which is freshly picked and processed as quickly as possible.

COOKING METHODS

British cooking is given a bad name by the characteristic overboiling of vegetables, rendering high-quality produce unpalatable and lacking in nutrients. Happily, attitudes are changing and a far broader range of cooking methods is now commonly used, with shorter cooking times and greater appreciation of the value of raw vegetables, for their texture and flavour as well as for their food value. Flavourings have become more adventurous and salt, once added automatically to every pan of boiling vegetables, is now very much a matter of personal choice.

Boiling   This is an easy and practical cooking method for many vegetables including potatoes, carrots, swedes, parsnips, beans, cauliflower and cabbage. However, it is important that the boiling process is only long enough to make the vegetables tender.

There are two methods of boiling. The first involves covering vegetables with water, which is then brought to the boil. The heat is then reduced and the pan covered so that the water just boils. For the second method, a comparatively small amount of water is brought to the boil, the vegetables are added and are cooked more fiercely with or without a lid on the pan. This takes less time.

The first method is used for potatoes, swedes and similar vegetables which require to be covered with liquid to make them tender in the shortest possible time. The liquid from cooking may be used for sauces, such as gravy, or in soups.

The second method is suitable for quick-cooking vegetables such as cabbage, green beans, Brussels sprouts and cauliflower. Once the vegetables are added to the pan, the liquid should be brought back to the boil quickly, then the heat controlled so that the cooking is fairly rapid. Cooking times will vary, depending on the vegetables.

Salt may be added to the cooking water. This is a matter for personal choice but the water should not be heavily salted.

Never add bicarbonate of soda to the cooking water for green vegetables. In the days when vegetables were regularly overcooked, this was regarded as a good way of preserving the colour; however it destroys the vitamin C content of the food and should be avoided.

Stewing and Braising   Ratatouille is one of the best-known, classic vegetable stews. Stewing and braising are used for vegetables which require moderate to lengthy cooking. or which benefit from a moist cooking method. They are also used to combine vegetable flavours and create a mixed vegetable dish.

Celery, fennel, cucumber and carrots are typical examples of vegetables that respond well to braising, with the addition of a little onion, some stock or wine and herbs. The braising process should be fairly slow so that the vegetables are tender throughout. The cooking juices are either reduced or thickened, then poured over the vegetables to serve.

Steaming   This is a good, plain method which gives results similar to boiling. Nutrients are lost from the vegetables by seepage via the steam into the water below. To conserve as much food value as possible steam vegetables over a main dish such as a stew so that the nutrients are retained.

Although a perforated container is usually used, vegetables that require light cooking, such as courgettes, may be steamed in a dish, on a plate over a saucepan of water or wrapped in foil.

The flavour of some vegetables is heightened by steaming rather than boiling. Cauliflower, broccoli and cabbage are all examples.

Frying   Shallow frying, under the guise of sautéing, is a popular method for vegetables that require little cooking. Courgettes are often cooked by this method. The thinly cut vegetables are tossed in a little butter or oil over moderate to high heat.

Deep frying is not a practical way of cooking many vegetables but it is used for potato chips and for making fritters or vegetable croquettes. In the latter case, the portions of vegetable are protected by a coating, such as batter.

Stir Frying A comparatively modern method for Western cooks, this is suitable for most vegetables. The results are crisp, flavoursome and colourful. Many stir-fried vegetables are ideal for grilled dishes but are not the best accompaniment for casseroles or roasts.

Grilling This method is not often used for vegetables other than mushrooms or tomatoes. However, courgettes, aubergines and peppers may be grilled.

Microwave Cooking Microwave cooking is excellent for the majority of vegetables, particularly when small to medium quantities are cooked. The chapter on Microwave Cooking gives detailed information. Here are a few reminders:

- Never add salt before cooking.
- Cook vegetables with a small amount of water or liquid.
- Use a covered microwave-proof container or roasting bag, closed loosely to allow steam to escape.
- Arrange tougher areas, such as stalks, towards the outside of a dish, where they receive most energy.
- Turn and rearrange vegetables at least once during cooking.
- Spinach, peas, French beans, cauliflower florets, new potatoes, Jerusalem and globe artichokes are just a few examples which cook very well in the microwave.
- Less successful vegetables include celery (unless as part of a dish), old carrots in chunks, large quantities of 'boiled' potatoes – particularly for mashing – and larger quantities of green cabbage.

A GUIDE TO VEGETABLES

ARTICHOKES

Globe At their best and least expensive during late summer, these are the flower buds of a large thistle. They should be thoroughly washed and drained. Trim off loose leaves around the base of the head. Snip off the ends of the leaves and the top of the head. Place in acidulated water to prevent discoloration and cook promptly in boiling salted water with lemon juice added. Allow 25–45 minutes, depending on size. To check if the artichokes are cooked, pull off one of the base leaves: it should come away easily. Drain well and cool.

Separate the leaves slightly to reveal the group of leaves that form the central part of the artichoke. Pull these out to reveal the 'choke', a cushion of fine hairs seated in the centre of the vegetable. Use a teaspoon to scrape the choke away carefully, leaving a pad of pale, tender flesh known as the bottom, base or *fond*. Trim off the stalk so that the artichoke sits neatly and fill the centre with an oil and vinegar dressing or a stuffing.

Like asparagus, artichokes are eaten with the fingers. Each leaf is pulled off individually and the small portion of pale flesh at the base dipped in dressing before being eaten. The rest of the tough leaf is discarded.

Artichoke bottoms (or *fonds*) are regarded as a delicacy and frequently form the basis of more sophisticated dishes. If only the artichoke bottoms ae required, the leaves, chokes and stalks may be removed and the artichoke bottoms carefully peeled before being cooked in boiling water until tender.

Jerusalem These look like small, knobbly new potatoes, but have a delicate nutty flavour. They should be scrubbed and peeled or cooked with the peel left on. Jerusalem artichokes discolour quickly, so should be placed in acidulated water. Boil them for 10–15 minutes until tender or cook by steaming.

They may be served gratinéed, with a crumb topping, mashed, coated in sauce, tossed in melted butter or sliced and topped with cheese, then grilled. They also make good soup.

ASPARAGUS

Although greengrocers have supplies throughout the year, home-grown asparagus is a summer vegetable, ready in May and June. Look for bright, firm but slim spears that are not woody. On larger spears, make sure that there is a good length of tender green stalk once the tougher end is trimmed. Allow 6–8 spears per portion.

Trip off the woody ends and scrape or peel any remaining tough spear ends. Tie the asparagus in bundles. Cook them in a special asparagus pan or stand them in a saucepan of boiling water, with the tender tips exposed. Tent with foil and simmer for about 15 minutes, or until tender. The tips will steam while the stalks cook in the simmering water.

Alternatively, asparagus may be steamed over boiling water on a rack in a wok or on a wire rack over boiling water in a roasting tin, with the tips towards the outside of the wok or tin so that they do not overcook.

Serve with melted butter poured over. The trimmings may be used to flavour soups or sauces.

AUBERGINES

Also known as eggplants (in America) and brinjals (in India), these vegetables have pale, tender but firm flesh. The shiny skins are usually purple, although white varieties are also available. They should be firm and shiny outside, with a bright green calyx. Aubergines are cooked in a wide variety of ways: they may be stewed in ratatouille; cubed and grilled on skewers; braised with meat or poultry; roasted and mashed to make a dip; stuffed and baked; sliced, fried and layered with meat in moussaka; or spiced in a variety of Indian or Mediterranean dishes.

Since the flesh can be rather bitter, aubergine flesh should be salted and allowed to stand in a colander or sieve over a bowl for 15–30 minutes before use. This process, which is also sometimes used for cucumbers, is known as *degorging*.

BEANS

Broad Available from early spring through to autumn, broad beans are best when young and small. Allow about 225 g/8 oz pods per person, selecting firm plump pods with a good green colour. Shrivelled, blackened or largely empty pods are not a good buy. Equally, very large hard pods yield tough old beans.

Shell the beans and cook them in boiling water for 5–15 minutes, depending on their age and your personal taste. Add a sprig of summer savory to the cooking water if liked.

Serve the beans with butter and pepper. They are excellent with diced cooked ham or crisp grilled bacon, or they may be sauced with Hollandaise sauce or soured cream.

French These require little preparation. Buy bright, firm beans which are not damaged or shrivelled. Trim off their ends and wash them well. Add to a pan of boiling water and cook for 2–10 minutes, depending on size and use. A crunchy result can quickly be achieved if the beans are very slim.

Serve French beans topped with butter or fried breadcrumbs. Chopped hard-boiled egg and chopped parsley is another popular topping.

Lightly cooked and cooled, these beans are good in salads. They may be stir fried.

Runner These are best freshly picked. It is usually necessary to remove the strings, or trim these beans down both sides, before cooking.

Some varieties do not need stringing. Avoid very large beans or any that have shrivelled.

Slice the beans at an angle into long thin pieces, add these to a saucepan of boiling water and cook for 3-10 minutes, depending on taste. About 5 minutes is average; any longer and the beans become soft. Toss with butter and serve freshly cooked.

BEAN SPROUTS

These are usually mung beans, although a variety of dried beans may be sprouted. Bean sprouts provide a useful amount of protein and are therefore ideal for adding to vegetable stir fries which contain little meat or fish.

The bean sprouts should be rinsed and drained, then cooked very briefly – stir frying for 3 minutes or less is the best method. The bean sprouts may be added to sauced mixtures and braised for 1-2 minutes, but avoid over-cooking them or they will become limp and unpleasant.

BEETROOT

Do not peel raw beetroot before boiling. Simply wash away dirt and twist off the leaves above stalk level. Put the beetroot in a large saucepan with water to cover. Add some salt, if liked. Bring to the boil, lower the heat and simmer, covered, for 45-60 minutes for small to medium young beetroot. Larger, older vegetables can take up to 1½-2 hours to cook but these are not often sold. Beetroot is cooked when it feels tender and the skin rubs off easily.

Drain off the cooking water and replace it with cold water to cover the beetroot. Working under water while the beetroot is still hot, rub off the skins. These should slip off easily with their stalks. Place the peeled beetroot in a dish, cover and leave until cool.

Beetroot may be served hot with fried bread-crumbs and chopped onion. It combines well with other vegetables in hot bakes, or it may be allowed to cool before being used in salads or served with soured cream or fromage frais.

Beetroot may be sliced or preserved whole in vinegar. It is a traditional accompaniment for cold roast meats. The uncooked vegetable is also used to make a delicious soup, known as *borsch*.

BROCCOLI

The two main types are sprouting broccoli, with long stalks, a few leaves and small heads in purple or pale green, and calabrese with larger heads and shorter stalks. The stalks on young sprouting broccoli are tender when cooked and may be included as part of the vegetable; discard slightly older stalks.

Broccoli should be washed and trimmed, then broken if the heads are large. Cook in a saucepan of boiling water. Tender young sprouting broccoli cooks quite quickly and it will be tender after 3-5 minutes but larger heads may require 10-15 minutes. Broccoli may also be steamed or stir fried, and makes an excellent soup.

Serve plain with butter or coated with a sauce, such as cheese sauce. Broken into small florets, broccoli may be cooked in a little olive oil with garlic and onion for tossing with pasta and serving with grated Parmesan cheese.

Broccoli is useful as a filling for pies, with chicken or fish, and it also makes a first class pancake filling.

BRUSSELS SPROUTS

This winter vegetable is one of the traditional accompaniments to roast turkey. Look for small firm sprouts which are slightly shiny and green. Avoid very loose, yellowing or insect-nibbled sprouts.

Wash the vegetables thoroughly. Cut a cross in the stalk of larger ones so that they cook evenly. Add to a saucepan of boiling water and cook for 5-10 minutes.

Small, young sprouts may be steamed; halved sprouts may be stir fried. Cooked sprouts may be served plain or tossed with cooked chestnuts (see page 435) or browned blanched almonds.

CABBAGE

There are many varieties, the key differences being that they may be hard or loose-packed. The following are some of the varieties most commonly sold in Britain:

White Cabbage   A hard creamy-white to pale green cabbage with tightly packed leaves.

Red Cabbage   Resembles white cabbage but has dark red leaves.

Savoy Cabbage   A large cabbage with a neat firm heart and slightly crinkly leaves.

Winter Cabbage   A term used for cabbage with a firm heart and looser outer leaves, similar to Savoy but without the characteristic crinkly, deeply veined leaves.

Spring Green   The new growth of loose leaves which do not have a heart.

There are many cooking methods for cabbage; all types may also be eaten raw. For salads, white and red cabbage are the most popular; they are also ideal for stir frying or braising. Red cabbage is also suitable for pickling in vinegar and white cabbage is traditionally salted to make sauerkraut.

Green cabbages may be boiled, steamed or stir fried. Individual leaves may be blanched until soft, then stuffed and braised. Shredded green cabbage may be blanched, drained, then deep fried and tossed in sugar and soy sauce to be served Chinese style as 'seaweed'.

Wedges of cabbage heart may be steamed or braised. Shredded cabbage may be combined with rice in risottos or added to soups.

To boil cabbage, add the trimmed leaves to the minimum of boiling water, pressing them down well. Cover the pan tightly and cook quickly for 3–7 minutes, according to taste. Drain and roughly chop the cabbage before tossing it with butter and pepper.

Steaming times vary according to the method of preparation: if the cabbage is cut in chunks allow up to 15 minutes. Braised cabbage may be cooked for anything from 15 minutes to 1½ hours (for red cabbage cooked with onions and apples).

CARROTS

Young, or baby, carrots have the best flavour. Look out for firm, unblemished carrots, preferably sold in bundles with leaves. If you do buy carrots prepacked in polythene, check that they are not wet from condensation; in damp conditions, they deteriorate very rapidly.

Young carrots do not require peeling; a good scrub or scrape is sufficient. Whether older carrots are peeled or scrubbed is a matter of taste. Small carrots are best cooked whole by boiling or steaming briefly. Medium and large carrots may be halved, quartered, cut in sticks or slices. Boil, steam or stir fry them. To glaze carrots, cut them into fine strips and cook them in a little water with a knob of butter. By the time the carrots are just tender the water should have evaporated, leaving the vegetables coated in a glossy glaze. A little sugar may be added when cooking old carrots. The carrots should be stirred or the pan shaken often to prevent them burning.

Small new carrots take about 5–7 minutes to boil until tender; older carrots take 10–15 minutes, depending on size. Carrots may be cooked for slightly longer, then mashed with swede or potatoes. Well cooked carrots may also be rubbed through a sieve or puréed in a food processor, then enriched with a little butter and cream.

Carrots are an essential flavouring vegetable for soups, stocks and stews. They are also valuable in mince dishes and they make delicious soup. Grated carrot is a useful salad ingredient and this versatile vegetable may also be used in preserves and sweet dishes, such as carrot cake or a lightly spiced Indian dessert. Carrot marmalade was a clever war-time invention as a substitute for orange preserve: the finely cut carrots were flavoured with orange rind and juice and cooked in syrup.

CAULIFLOWER

Green and purple cauliflowers are now available in addition to the more familiar white-headed vegetables, and very small cauliflowers are cultivated as individual portions.

Look for firm, white unblemished vegetables that are neatly packed with a small amount of green leaves. Avoid soft, rubbery cauliflowers or any that have very long stalks and loose heads. Cauliflowers that are not perfectly white are not necessarily inferior in flavour, provided that they are good quality in other respects. It is as well, however, to avoid any that have softening brown patches or have been trimmed.

Cauliflowers may be cooked whole or divided into florets. Boiling, steaming or stir frying are the most common cooking methods. Used raw or briefly blanched, cauliflower florets make very good additions to salads, and they may be coated in cheese-flavoured choux pastry, then deep fried to make delicious savoury fritters.

Overcooked cauliflower is soft, watery and tasteless. About 5-7 minutes is sufficient boiling time for florets and a whole cauliflower should not be boiled for more than 10-15 minutes. Steaming is a particularly good cooking method for cauliflower. For florets allow the same time as for boiling; when steaming a whole cauliflower increase the cooking time to 20-30 minutes, depending on size.

Serve cauliflower plain, with a little butter; coated with a cheese sauce; or topped with fried breadcrumbs. Cauliflower is excellent in vegetable curry, it makes good soup (particularly topped with cheese) or it may be puréed and enriched with cream or fromage frais.

CELERIAC

This is a cream-coloured root vegetable, about the same size as a swede and with a similarly thick skin. It has a delicate flavour reminiscent of celery. To prepare celeriac, peel and trim it, then plunge it straight into a bowl of acidulated water as it discolours quickly.

Cut celeriac into neat cubes or sticks and cook in a saucepan of boiling water until tender, about 8-10 minutes for small pieces. If preferred, the vegetable may be cut into large chunks and boiled for 15-20 minutes, then mashed with butter and pepper. Boiling is a better option than steaming, although finely cut celeriac may be steamed in packets of mixed vegetables or as a flavouring for fish and poultry.

Celeriac may also be served raw, usually coarsely grated or finely shredded. If adding it to long-cooked soups and stews, put it in towards the end of the cooking time or it may become very soft. It also makes good soup. Plain cooked celeriac (in chunks or slices) is delicious coated with cheese sauce.

CELERY

A versatile vegetable for serving raw or cooked, or using as a flavouring ingredient. Look for firm, unblemished heads of celery with leaves that are bright and crisp. Stalks with large ribs may be stringy. Trimmed celery hearts are also available for braising whole. Canned celery hearts are a useful storecupboard standby for wrapping in cooked ham and coating in cheese sauce as a supper dish.

The top of the head and stalk ends should be cut off but not discarded. The leaves and stalk tops may be used as part of a bouquet garni or they may be reserved for garnish. Cut up small, they are perfectly good in salads, soups and stews, as are the chopped stalks.

Remove stalks from the celery as required, scrub them well and cut off any blemished parts. Slice the celery or cut it into lengths for cooking. If a recipe calls for diced or chopped celery, cut the stalks into thin strips lengthways before slicing them across into small pieces. Cut into very thin strips, about 5 cm/2 inches long, then soaked for about 30 minutes in iced water, celery is excellent in salads.

Serve lengths of raw celery with dips or cheese. Braise lengths or hearts with a small amount of sautéed onion and diced carrot in a little stock or wine. Cook for about 40-60 minutes, depending on size and age, until the celery is tender. The cooking juices may be thickened with beurre manié to serve as an accompanying sauce.

Stir frying is a good cooking method for celery. The sticks should be sliced thinly or cut into fine strips. Slicing at an angle is an Oriental technique popular for stir fries.

Celery may also be cooked by boiling and steaming. Boil for 10-20 minutes, depending on size and age; or allow up to 30 minutes' steaming time.

CHICORY

Small oval heads of pale, closely packed leaves tipped with yellow, chicory has a slightly bitter flavour. It may be used raw in salads or braised until tender.

Trim off the stalk end of each head and wash well. Cut the head across into slices for mixing into salads or separate the leaves and use them as a base for serving a variety of dishes. The whole leaves may also be served with dips.

Chicory may be boiled in a saucepan of acidulated water until tender – about 15-20 minutes – but the preferred cooking method is braising. Cook a small amount of finely chopped onion in butter or oil, then turn the chicory heads in the fat. Pour in stock or wine to come about a third to halfway up the heads. Cover and braise for 30-60 minutes depending on the size of the chicory heads, until tender throughout. Turn once or twice. The cooking juices may be thickened and poured over the chicory heads.

The American name for chicory is endive.

CHINESE LEAVES

Also known as Chinese cabbage. A tall, fairly loosely packed vegetable consisting mainly of tender crunchy stalks edged by pale green-yellow leaves. The vegetable has a mild, cabbage-like flavour. It may be shredded for use in salads or stir fries. Thicker slices may be added to sauced dishes, usually well-seasoned Chinese braised mixtures, and cooked very briefly.

Overcooking gives limp, tasteless results.

COURGETTES

Both green and yellow varieties are available. Look for firm, unblemished vegetables. Trim off the ends and peel the courgettes if liked, although they may be cooked with the peel on. Cut courgettes into slices, chunks or sticks, or grate them. They may be halved and baked with a topping, or their centres scooped out and a stuffing added.

Basic cooking methods include steaming, braising, baking, sautéing, stir frying and shallow frying. Although courgettes may be boiled, this cooking method does not do them justice as even brief boiling tends to oversoften the delicate flesh. Coated in batter or breadcrumbs, courgettes are also delicious deep fried. In Italy and America, where the vegetable is known as *zucchini*, the flowers are regarded as a delicacy and are frequently coated in light batter and deep fried.

For steaming, wrap sliced courgettes in foil; cook for about 10 minutes. Sautéing and stir frying are excellent methods. Thinly cut vegetables will require 2–5 minutes. Baking is a practical method when the courgettes are served with a baked dish; simply dot them with butter, sprinkle them with salt and pepper and cook in a covered dish for 15–30 minutes at 180°C/350°F/gas 4. Braise courgettes with onions and tomatoes or other vegetables, allowing about 20 minutes' cooking, or up to 45 minutes depending on the way in which the vegetables are cut and the other ingredients.

CUCUMBER

Although they are usually eaten raw in salads, cucumbers are also good braised. Buy firm, bright green medium-sized cucumbers. Avoid any with very dark, thick-looking skins, as these may have large seeds, poor texture and a strong unacceptable flavour.

Cucumbers may be peeled, partially peeled or served with the peel on for salads. The classic preparation is to slice the cucumber very thinly, sprinkle it with a little salt and allow it to drain in a colander for 10 minutes before use. This extracts the excess liquid from the vegetable. Having been prepared in this way, the cucumber slices may be dried on absorbent kitchen paper and used to make delicious sandwiches. They may also be topped with a little chopped mint or snipped chives for serving as a plain salad. An oil and vinegar dressing, or cider vinegar, are classic additions.

Grated or diced cucumber may be mixed with plain yogurt to make a dip or side dish for spicy food. Add garlic and a little chopped onion to make *tzatziki*, a Greek starter served with plenty of crusty bread.

Peel cucumber before cooking, then cut it into 5 cm/2 inch lengths. The seeds are usually scooped out. Braise trimmed cucumber in stock for about 20 minutes. Dill or mint may be added before serving and the sauce may be enriched with soured cream. Sticks of cucumber may be stir fried briefly.

ENDIVE

This resembles a curly lettuce. It has firm leaves which are usually pale yellow-green with darker green tips. To prepare endive, trim off the stalk, wash well and use in salads.

The American term for endive is chicory.

FENNEL

Florence fennel is a bulbous vegetable with a texture like that of celery and an aniseed flavour. There are usually a few fronds of feathery leaves attached to the trimmed stalks at the top of the bulbs – these may be reserved for garnishing or used in cooking.

Trim away tough stalk ends, then thoroughly wash and slice fennel for use in salads. Fennel discolours easily when cut, so always use a stainless steel knife and use the vegetable as soon as possible after cutting. The bulbs may be braised as for celery, either whole or as halves and cook in about 1–1¼ hours.

KOHLRABI

This is the swollen stem of a member of the cabbage family. It has a flavour slightly similar to swede. Either purple or green skinned, and ranging in size from that of a large potato to a small swede, kohlrabi may be served raw or cooked.

Peel the vegetable and place it in a bowl of acidulated water. For serving raw, kohlrabi should be grated or cut into small pieces. Small kohlrabi may be boiled whole; larger vegetables should be sliced or cut into chunks. Cook in boiling water for 15–45 minutes or until tender. Follow the longer time if cooking whole vegetables.

Sticks of kohlrabi may be stir fried with other vegetables, such as leeks or onions. Diced or cubed kohlrabi may be added to soups, stews or casseroles.

LEEKS

These vary considerably in size. Look for firm, well-formed vegetables with a good ratio of white to green. Trim off the ends and slice, then wash in a colander, separating the slices into rings. Alternatively, slit the leeks three-quarters through down their length, then open each one out and hold it under cold running water to wash away all the grit.

Leeks may be boiled, steamed, fried, stewed, braised or baked. Allow 10-20 minutes for boiling or steaming, the longer time for large lengths or small whole vegetables. Drain well and serve coated with cheese sauce. Alternatively, top with grated cheese and breadcrumbs and grill until brown.

Fry sliced leeks in butter until tender but not soft – about 15 minutes – or stir fry them with other vegetables. Add leeks to soups and stews or use them to flavour stocks.

LETTUCE

There is a wide variety of lettuces on offer all year. These are the most common types:

Round The traditional British salad leaf; a loosely packed bright vegetable with a small heart. Flavour and texture are not particularly interesting.

Cos Lettuce A tall, dark-leafed lettuce with crisp firm leaves and a good flavour.

Webb's Wonderful A round lettuce with slightly wrinkled, crisp dark leaves, and a firm heart.

Iceberg A tightly packed, pale green lettuce with very crisp leaves and a good flavour.

Lamb's Lettuce Small oval-leafed plants, resembling immature round lettuce but darker.

Lollo Rosso/Lollo Biondo A frilly, firm-textured lettuce which is loosely packed. The lollo rosso variety has dark leaves fringed with

deep red, whereas the biondo type has pale-edged leaves.

Wash all lettuce well and discard any tough or damaged stalks. It is traditional to shred lettuce by hand rather than to cut it with a knife, but this is a matter for personal taste. Never prepare lettuce a long time before serving.

Although lettuce is usually served raw, it is also delicious when braised with a little finely chopped onion in stock or wine. Fresh peas braised with lettuce is a classic French dish. Allow about 30 minutes' gentle cooking in a small amount of liquid and use a covered pan or dish.

MARROW

From the same family as courgettes and pumpkin, marrow has a tough skin and soft, fibrous centre with lots of seeds surrounded by firm flesh. Cut the vegetable in half or slice it into rings, then remove the soft flesh and seeds before peeling thickly.

Marrow may be baked, braised, steamed, stir fried or boiled, the latter being the least interesting cooking method. Overcooked marrow is watery and mushy, particularly when boiled. Baking or braising with onions and herbs are the best methods. Chunks of marrow (about 5 cm/2 inches in size) take about 40 minutes to bake at 180°C/350°F/gas 4, depending on the other ingredients added. They may also be braised for about 30 minutes with onions and herbs, either in their own juice or with the addition of tomatoes or a little wine or cider.

Stuffings for marrow range from meat mixtures to rice or breadcrumb fillings. Rings or halves may be stuffed, or the vegetable may be laid on its side and a thick slice removed from the top as a lid. The hollowed-out marrow may then be stuffed and the 'lid' replaced. Bake the stuffed marrow until tender, then remove the 'lid' to allow the stuffing to brown. At 180°C/

350°F/gas 4, a medium-sized whole marrow will require 1¼-1¾ hours to bake, whereas rings cook in 45 minutes-1¼ hours, depending on size and filling.

Marrow may also be used as a key ingredient for making chutney. It is usually combined with fruit, such as apples, and lots of onions for flavour. It may also be cooked with ginger and used to add bulk to jam.

MUSHROOMS

Most of the mushrooms available in green-grocers and supermarkets are the same variety, differing only in the stage of development at which they have been harvested. Fully open or flat mushrooms traditionally known as field mushrooms are the most mature. They may be recognized by their dark gills and large heads. Flat mushrooms have good flavour but tend to discolour dishes to which they are added, so are usually used for grilling and stuffing.

Wild mushrooms are a separate issue from cultivated varieties. Before they are gathered, a specialist source of information should be consulted to avoid any danger of consuming a poisonous species. Some specialist stores sell wild mushrooms but they are most commonly available dried from delicatessens.

Cultivated mushrooms do not require peeling. Trim tough stalks from shiitake or oyster mushrooms. Rinse mushrooms, gills down under slowly running cold water, rubbing them gently. Alternatively, simply wipe them with dampened absorbent kitchen paper. Never leave mushrooms to soak as they will absorb water, ruining both texture and flavour.

Mushrooms may be brushed with a little fat and grilled, flat or on skewers. They may also be poached in a little milk, stock or wine for a few minutes. Alternatively, whole or cut-up mushrooms may be shallow fried or stir fried in oil or butter, either whole or cut up. Coated with egg and breadcrumbs, dipped in choux pastry or batter, button mushrooms are delicious deep fried. They are also excellent baked particularly when topped with breadcrumbs and cheese.

For frying or poaching, allow about 5-15 minutes' cooking time. Allow 15-30 minutes for baking, depending on the topping or stuffing. Grill mushrooms briefly for about 5 minutes, gills uppermost.

Pale mushrooms may be added to sauces and soups; all types are suitable for flavouring stews, the choice depending on the colour of the stew.

Cup mushrooms or open mushrooms are slightly paler in colour and they have a lip around the edge. Useful for stuffing.

Button mushrooms may be fully closed or partially closed, with little of the gill area showing. They vary in size; very small buttons are perfect for adding whole to casseroles and sauces. Button mushrooms are ideal for sauces and pale dishes which require a delicate colour and flavour.

In addition to the grades of cultivated mushroom described above, at least three other types of fresh mushroom are commonly available.

Chestnut mushrooms have a darker skin than ordinary mushrooms and a more pronounced flavour. They are usually sold as large buttons.

Oyster mushrooms are flat and pale creamy-yellow in colour with a soft texture and delicate flavour. They break easily and require very little cooking.

Shiitake are strongly flavoured mushrooms from China and Japan. They are popular in Oriental cooking. They are usually sold dried in delicatessens and Oriental supermarkets, when their flavour is very pronounced, but are also available fresh. The fresh mushrooms are darker than cultivated British field mushrooms and they tend to have a firmer, slightly more rubbery texture.

OKRA

Also known as ladies' fingers, these pale green ridged pods vary in size, the smaller ones being the most tender. Look for unblemished whole vegetables with the stalks intact. Trim off the stalk ends and wash well. The okra pods may be cooked whole or sliced before cooking. Do not prepare the vegetable too far in advance of cooking as slices may discolour.

Okra contains a gum-like substance that seeps out of the pods during long cooking to thicken stews and braised dishes. Typical dishes with okra include *gumbo*, a classic Creole stew, and spiced okra with onions, which is often served as a side dish in Indian restaurants. Okra may also be stuffed and braised or baked.

Cooking times for okra should either be brief, using fierce heat, or long enough to tenderize the pods. Sliced okra may be coated in flour and seasonings or spices, then shallow or deep fried for a few minutes until browned. Slices may also be braised briefly or added to casseroles and stews towards the end of cooking; however, the vegetable quickly becomes slimy when sliced and long-cooked by moist methods. Whole pods may be braised with onions, tomatoes and garlic until tender – about 15-30 minutes, depending on the size and age of the pods.

ONIONS

Large Spanish onions are the mildest variety. These are ideal for boiling whole and serving with butter or a sauce, or for stuffing. The medium-sized common onions, most often used in cooking, are stronger in flavour. Small, pickling or button onions have a strong flavour. They may be boiled and coated with sauce or peeled and added whole to casseroles. Cocktail, or silverskin, onions are tiny. They are sometimes available fresh but are most often sold pickled in vinegar. Spring- or salad onions have not formed bulbs. They have a dense white base leading to hollow green ends. Once trimmed, the whole of the onion may be used raw or in cooking. Shallots and Welsh onions are small onions. Each shallot consists of two or three cloves, similar in shape to garlic cloves, clumped together inside the papery skin. They are mild in flavour and may be peeled and chopped or used whole. The tops from fresh young shallots may also be used in cooking, rather like chives.

Onions are often fried briefly as a preliminary cooking stage in more complicated dishes. The aim is to soften the onion but not brown it, and the cooking process will only be completed when the onion has been incorporated with other ingredients and cooked until tender. Browning onions by frying requires significantly longer cooking, depending on the number cooked. Onions shrink significantly when fried until brown, and this should be done over moderate heat, turning occasionally, for about 20-30 minutes until the onions are golden and evenly cooked. If fried by this method they will be tender and flavoursome. Onions that are browned quickly over too high a heat will not be cooked through, but simply scorched outside.

Onions may also be boiled or steamed. Allow 30 minutes for small onions or up to $1\frac{1}{4}$ hours for large ones. Large onions may be baked whole, washed but unpeeled, until very tender, then split and filled or topped with butter.

PARSNIPS

Look for firm, unblemished parsnips. To prepare them, peel, then cut them in half, in chunks or slices. They may be boiled, steamed or roasted.

Chunks of parsnip will be tender when boiled for 10 minutes; larger pieces require about 20 minutes. When tender, drain well and serve with a soured cream sauce, or mash with butter and pepper.

To roast parsnips arrange them around a joint of meat or in a separate dish and brush with fat. Allow about 45 minutes-1¼ hours at 180-190°C/350-375°F/gas 4-5, until tender and golden.

Parsnips are delicious in mixed vegetable curry and may also be added to soups and stews. Parsnip fritters may be made by coating par-boiled vegetables in batter and deep frying them until golden.

PEAS

Fresh peas are in season from May to September. Look for bright, fresh plump pods. The peas inside should not be bullet-hard nor very large as they can become very dry in texture and particularly dull in flavour. Allow about 350-400 g/12-14 oz per person as a good deal of weight is lost to the pods.

Split the pods over a colander and slide the peas out using a fingertip. Wash well, then add to a small amount of just boiling water. Cook for 7-10 minutes, until the peas are tender. Alternatively, peas may be steamed for 15-20 minutes. It is traditional to add a sprig of mint to the water when cooking peas which are to be served with lamb.

Mange Tout The name means 'eat all', a fitting description. Mange tout are flat pea pods with tiny peas just forming inside. The entire pod is edible, excluding the stalk, which is trimmed. Mange tout may be cooked in boiling water for 2-3 minutes, or steamed for up to 5 minutes, but are at their best when stir fried for 3-5 minutes.

Sugar Snaps These are small peas enclosed in edible pods. They have an excellent flavour. Everything is edible except the stalk, which should be trimmed. Cook sugar snaps in a saucepan of boiling water for 3-5 minutes, or by steaming for about 5 minutes. They are a more substantial and flavoursome vegetable than mange tout.

PEPPERS

Large sweet or bell peppers come from the capsicum family. They are also known as pimento (or pimientos when bottled). The most common type is the green pepper, which changes colour as it ripens, first to yellow and then to red. A variety of other colours is also available, including white and purple-black.

To prepare a pepper, remove the stalk end and cut out the core from the inside. Discard the ribs, pith and seeds. The pepper shell may then be rinsed free of seeds and drained.

Peppers are used in a variety of ways: they may be eaten raw in salads or crudités; lightly cooked in stir fries; stuffed and baked or braised; grilled on skewers; or stewed slowly with meat, poultry or other vegetables.

When raw they have a crunchy texture and fresh flavour, but when cooked they soften and their flavour mellows. Some salad recipes require peppers to be charred, then skinned.

POTATOES

These may be loosely divided into new and old, the former being the thin-skinned, spring crop for immediate consumption and the latter being the second crop of thicker-skinned potatoes grown for winter storage. The choice is always changing, with imported varieties and new strains constantly being developed.

Avoid buying or eating potatoes that have turned green. Cut out any eyes and sprouting areas from potatoes in preparation. Store potatoes in a cool, dry place in thick brown paper bags that exclude all light.

Although new potatoes are now available all year, Jerseys are the traditional 'first' new potatoes in the shops. Imported early in the year, from Christmas or even before, these have a fine flavour but are expensive. Small, waxy and firm, they are ideal for steaming or boiling. Small, waxy 'salad' potatoes are also available all year at a price.

The following are good all round, old potatoes for boiling, mashing, baking and frying: King Edward, Redskin, Maris Piper, Pentland Hawk, Pentland Ivory and Desirée. Majestic tend to break up easily when boiled, so they are better for baking and frying. Pentland Squire are floury and good for baking, as are Cara, because they are large and even in size and shape.

Boiling Peel the potatoes, if liked, or scrub them well. Remove all eyes and blemishes and any green areas. Cut large potatoes in half or into quarters and place in a saucepan. Cover with cold water, add salt if wished, and bring to the boil. Reduce the heat, partly cover the pan and cook for about 20 minutes. Small chunks cook in about 10-15 minutes (useful for mashing); larger, unpeeled, potatoes take somewhat longer. New potatoes cook more quickly, in 10-15 minutes.

Baking An easy cooking method, this is discussed, with serving suggestions, on page 456. Floury potatoes – the sort that do not boil well – give best results for baking. Scrub the potatoes well and prick them all over to prevent them from bursting. Potatoes may be brushed with oil if wished.

Roasting Peeled potatoes, cut in halves or quarters, may either be roasted from raw or parboiled for 5-10 minutes, dusted with plain flour, and then added to the hot fat in the roasting tin. They should be coated in hot fat and turned once or twice during cooking. For crisp results, raw potatoes will take 1-1½ hours, depending on the size of the potatoes and the oven temperature. Parboiled potatoes require about 1 hour at 190°C/375°F/gas 5.

Chipped Potatoes Cut the thoroughly scrubbed, or washed and peeled, potatoes into thick fingers and deep fry in oil at 190°C/375°F until just beginning to brown. Lift the chips out of the oil and drain them well. Bring the oil back to the original cooking temperature. Lower the chips into the oil again and cook for a couple of minutes more, until crisp and golden. Drain well on absorbent kitchen paper and serve at once.

PUMPKIN

Pumpkin belongs to the same family as marrow. Pumpkins vary enormously in size. Small ones may be sold whole, but you are more likely to encounter wedges cut from a large vegetable.

The central soft core of seeds should be removed and the orange-coloured flesh thickly peeled. The flesh is firmer than marrow and is delicious roasted, baked or braised with onions, herbs and bacon and a cheese topping for about an hour. Pumpkin may also be boiled and mashed or steamed for 30-45 minutes and puréed for use in savoury and sweet dishes, particularly the American sweet and spicy pumpkin pie. Pumpkin also makes good soup.

RADISHES

These are usually eaten raw in salads or as crudités; however, large white radishes are also combined with other ingredients in stir fries and steamed Oriental-style dishes.

Small round red radishes are the most common, but the long white radish known as mooli or daikon (in Japanese cooking) is becoming increasingly popular. Red radishes require no preparation other than washing, topping and tailing. Large white radishes must be peeled. Very large, old white radishes can be fibrous, stringy and unpleasant even when cut finely.

SALSIFY AND SCORZONERA

These root vegetables are in season from October to May. Salsify is a creamy colour and scorzonera is black. Although both have a delicate flavour, scorzonera is considered to be salsify's superior.

Do not use a carbon steel knife to prepare these vegetables and cook them as soon as possible after preparation, or they may discolour. The moment the vegetables have been trimmed and peeled, put them into acidulated water. To cook, cut into lengths or fingers and add to a saucepan of salted boiling water to which a little lemon juice has been added. Cook for 20-30 minutes, or until tender. Drain and serve with butter or with a coating sauce such as Béchamel or Hollandaise.

Salsify or scorzonera which is three-quarters cooked by boiling, may be drained and fried in butter before serving or coated in a light batter and deep fried to make fritters.

SEAKALE

Resembling celery stalks surrounded by dark green, tough, frilly leaves, seakale grows wild on the beaches of South East England between December and May and is also found in Western Europe. Although it is also cultivated, it is seldom available. Cultivated, blanched, seakale has tender stalks, picked before the leaf shoots develop. To prepare wild seakale, wash it and trim off the thick, tough stalk. Cook in a small amount of boiling water for 15 minutes, or until tender, drain and serve like spinach.

SORREL

Sorrel is used both as a vegetable and a herb. There are many varieties, some quite bitter. Treat as spinach, adding a little sugar during cooking to counteract the natural acidity.

SPINACH

There are winter and summer varieties of this versatile, easy-to-cook vegetable. Since it shrinks considerably on cooking, allow about 225 g/8 oz fresh spinach per portion.

Wash the leaves well and trim off any tough stalk ends. Pack the wet leaves into a large saucepan and cover with a tight-fitting lid. Place over moderate to high heat and cook for about 3 minutes, shaking the pan often, until the spinach has wilted. Lower the heat slightly, if necessary, and cook for 3-5 minutes more, or until the spinach is tender. Drain well in a sieve, squeezing out all the liquid if the vegetable is to be chopped.

Serve spinach tossed with butter and pepper or a little nutmeg. It may be used in a variety of pasta dishes, pies, quiches, soufflés and soups. Spinach is delicious topped with scrambled or poached eggs, poached fish or grilled chicken.

SQUASHES

Squash is an American term applied to marrow and a wide variety of vegetables of the same family. Availability in Britain and Europe is somewhat unpredictable; however these are a few of the main types:

Butternut Squash A small vegetable with pale, beige-peach coloured skin and deep orange-coloured flesh. The halved vegetable has a small central hollow for seeds, so that it resembles a large avocado. The whole or halved squash is usually baked or roasted.

Crookneck This is a large, rough-skinned, long-bodied yellow squash. As its name suggests it has a long narrow, curved neck. The flesh may be treated as marrow.

Custard Marrow A pale, flat, fluted squash.

Hubbard Squash A melon-shaped gourd with rough green skin, this may be treated as marrow once peeled.

Spaghetti Squash Oval, yellow-skinned squash about the size of a large yellow melon. It gets its name from the flesh, which resembles spaghetti when cooked. The squash should be boiled or steamed whole, or halved and wrapped in foil, for 20-50 minutes, depending on size. When cooked, halve the squash if necessary, discard the seeds from the middle and use a fork to scoop out the strands of flesh. These are at their best when still slightly crunchy. They have plenty of flavour and are delicious topped with butter and cheese or any sauce suitable for pasta.

SWEDES

Large, inexpensive root vegetables with thick skin and pale orange flesh. Wash, trim and peel thickly, then cut into chunks for cooking. Boil for 20–30 minutes, or until tender, then drain thoroughly and mash with butter and pepper. This is the traditional accompaniment for haggis. Swedes may also be mashed with carrots or potatoes.

The diced vegetable is excellent in soups and stews. Puréed cooked swede may be used in soufflé mixtures.

SWEETCORN

Corn cobs are surrounded by silky threads and an outer covering of leafy husks, which must be removed before cooking unless the corn is to be cooked on a barbecue. The kernels are pale when raw, becoming more yellow in colour on cooking.

Place the corn cobs in a pan with water to cover and bring to the boil. Do not add salt as this toughens the kernels. Simmer for about 10 minutes, or until the corn kernels are tender and come away easily from the cob. Drain well and serve topped with a little butter. Corn holders – pronged utensils inserted at either end of the cob – make it possible to eat these tasty vegetables without burning your fingers.

For using in salads or other dishes, the cooked kernels may be scraped off the cobs using a kitchen knife. It is usually simpler, however, to use frozen or canned sweetcorn kernels, both of which are of excellent quality.

Whole cobs may be baked in their husks or barbecued. Carefully fold back the husks and remove the silky threads, then wash well and drain. Fold the husks back over the corn. Cook over medium coals or roast in the oven at 190°C/375°F/gas 5 for about 40 minutes, or until the kernels are tender.

SWEET POTATOES

In spite of their name, these are not potatoes at all, but are red-skinned, large vegetables with pale orange flesh and a slightly sweet flavour. Sweet potatoes may be baked or boiled in their skins. To boil, allow about 30–40 minutes, depending on size. Bake as for ordinary potatoes (page 456). Once cooked, peel and cut into cubes, then toss with butter and a little nutmeg. Alternatively, mash with butter and nutmeg or a little mace.

Sweet potatoes are used in a variety of sweet and savoury dishes.

SWISS CHARD

The leaves of this vegetable may be cooked exactly as for spinach, giving very similar results. The tender stalks, which resemble thin, wide celery sticks, are delicious when lightly cooked in boiling water and served with butter. Allow about 5 minutes to cook tender stalks. Serve them as a separate vegetable or starter, perhaps with Hollandaise or with some grated Parmesan cheese.

TOMATOES

Although tomatoes are technically fruit, they are used as a vegetable. Of the many varieties available, all may be used raw and many are ideal for cooking. Freshly picked sun-ripened tomatoes are delicious, but it is worth investigating some of the other varieties.

Cherry Tomatoes Very small tomatoes, these can have an excellent sweet flavour when ripe. However, some purchased tomatoes can be sharp and lacking in flavour. Ideal for salads or for skewering with other ingredients for kebabs.

Marmande, Beef or Beefsteak Tomatoes Very large tomatoes that are ideal for stuffing. They should be a good deep red when ripe. Sun-ripened large tomatoes have an outstanding flavour. Sadly this is seldom found in purchased fruit, which is usually picked well before it is ripe.

Plum Tomatoes Deep red, oval, small to medium-sized fruit. Plum tomatoes have a good flavour and are valued for cooking and as the prime ingredient in tomato purée. They are also good in salads.

Yellow Tomatoes Large or cherry-sized, these tomatoes are sweet when ripe but can lack flavour when picked too early. They should be a rich yellow colour. Used mainly raw, yellow tomatoes may be cooked with yellow peppers, yellow courgettes and white aubergines in a pale version of ratatouille.

Cooking methods for tomatoes include grilling and frying. They are usually cut in half – or in slices for speed – and are traditionally served with grilled meat or fish, mixed grill or as part of a traditional cooked breakfast. Grilled or fried tomatoes on toast make a good snack or light meal.

Baked tomatoes are usually scooped out and filled with a rice- or breadcrumb-based stuffing or a minced meat mixture.

TURNIPS

Small, round summer turnips have delicate flavour. They are ideal for cooking whole and serving as a vegetable accompaniment. Larger main crop turnips are better suited to dicing or cutting into chunks and using in soups and stews or casseroles.

To prepare turnips, trim off the ends and remove the peel; small young vegetables need only be peeled thinly. Cook small whole turnips in a saucepan of boiling acidulated water for about 15 minutes, or until tender. Drain well and toss with butter and parsley or serve generously coated with cheese, Béchamel or Hollandaise sauce.

Larger turnips may be boiled, drained and mashed or puréed. Matchstick sticks of turnip are suitable for stir frying or baking in foil with parsnips and carrots cut to a similar size. Small, young turnips may also be parboiled, then glazed with the minimum of liquid and a little butter as for carrots.

The leaves of fresh young turnips may be trimmed from their stalks and cooked as for cabbage.

YAMS

These tubers resemble large potatoes, with white, floury flesh. Scrub and boil yams in their skin.

There are a number of vegetables available which belong to the yam and cassava family, including small dark and hairy eddoes. These vegetables must not be eaten raw as they contain natural toxins: in fact, prepared cassava should be soaked in water for about 30 minutes before cooking.

Note More information and methods of cooking, including microwave instructions are listed, where appropriate, under individual recipes.

ARTICHOKES AU GRATIN

675 g/1½ lb Jerusalem artichokes
50 g/2 oz Cheddar cheese, grated
25 g/1 oz fresh white breadcrumbs

CHEESE SAUCE
40 g/1½ oz butter
40 g/1½ oz plain flour
450 ml/¾ pint milk
salt and pepper
40 g/1½ oz Cheddar cheese, grated

Prepare the artichokes (see Mrs Beeton's Tip) and cook them in a saucepan of boiling water for 10–15 minutes until tender.

Meanwhile, make the sauce. Melt the butter in a saucepan. Stir in the flour and cook over low heat for 2–3 minutes, without allowing the mixture to colour. Gradually add the milk, stirring constantly until the mixture boils and thickens. Stir in salt and pepper to taste, then add the grated cheese.

Drain the artichokes, tip them into a flame-proof dish and pour the cheese sauce over the top. Mix lightly. Combine the cheese and

---

 MRS BEETON'S TIP

Wash the artichokes and peel them thinly. Artichokes discolour readily, so put them into acidulated water (water to which lemon juice has been added) as soon as they are peeled. It is a good idea to cook them in salted acidulated water too. Large artichokes may be cut into smaller pieces, or knobbles may be broken off, before cooking. They may be sliced or chopped, in which case they cook quite quickly – about 10 minutes. As with potatoes, it is not essential to peel artichokes before cooking; however they should be thoroughly scrubbed with a stiff brush.

---

breadcrumbs in a small bowl, sprinkle the mixture over the artichokes and place under a moderate grill until golden brown. Alternatively, brown the topping in a preheated 220°C/425°F/gas 7 oven for about 10 minutes.

SERVES FOUR

GARLANDED ASPARAGUS

30 asparagus spears
75 g/3 oz butter
salt and pepper
50 g/2 oz Parmesan cheese, grated
4 egg yolks, unbroken
butter for frying

Set the oven at 200°C/400°F/gas 6. Prepare and cook the asparagus (see page 320). Drain thoroughly and place in an ovenproof dish. Melt half the butter in a small frying pan and spoon it over the top. Sprinkle with salt and pepper to taste and top with the Parmesan. Bake for 15 minutes or until the topping is golden brown.

Meanwhile, add the remaining butter to the frying pan and melt over gentle heat. Add the egg yolks, taking care not to break them, and cook gently until just set outside, basting often. Using an egg slice, carefully lift them out of the pan, draining off excess fat, and arrange them around the asparagus. Serve at once.

SERVES FOUR

FRIED AUBERGINES WITH ONION

2 aubergines
salt and pepper
50 g/2 oz plain flour
cayenne pepper
oil for frying
1 onion, finely chopped
30 ml/2 tbsp chopped parsley to garnish

Cut the ends off the aubergines, slice them thinly and put them in a colander. Sprinkle generously with salt. Set aside for 30 minutes, then rinse, drain and dry thoroughly on absorbent kitchen paper.

Mix the flour with a pinch each of salt and cayenne. Add the aubergine slices, toss until lightly coated, then shake off excess flour.

Heat a little oil in a large frying pan, add the onion and cook over moderate heat for about 10 minutes until golden. Using a slotted spoon, transfer to a small bowl and keep hot.

Add the aubergine slices, a few at a time, to the hot oil in the pan. Fry until soft and lightly browned, turning once during cooking. As the slices brown, remove them from the pan with a fish slice, arrange on a heated serving dish and keep hot. Add extra oil and heat it as necessary between batches of aubergine slices.

When all the aubergine slices have been fried, sprinkle them with the fried onion and the chopped parsley. Serve at once.

SERVES SIX

BEANS WITH SOURED CREAM

fat for greasing
450 g/1 lb runner beans
150 ml/¼ pint soured cream
1.25 ml/¼ tsp grated nutmeg
1.25 ml/¼ tsp caraway seeds
salt and pepper
50 g/2 oz butter
50 g/2 oz fresh white breadcrumbs

Set the oven at 200°C/400°F/gas 6. Grease a 1 litre/1¾ pint baking dish. Wash the beans, string them if necessary and slice them thinly. Cook in boiling water for 3-7 minutes until cooked to taste. Alternatively, cook in a steamer over boiling water. Drain thoroughly.

Combine the soured cream, nutmeg and caraway seeds in a bowl. Stir in salt and pepper to taste. Add the beans and toss well together. Spoon the mixture into the baking dish.

Melt the butter in a small frying pan, add the breadcrumbs and fry over gentle heat for 2-3 minutes. Sprinkle the mixture over the beans. Bake for 20-30 minutes or until the topping is crisp and golden.

SERVES THREE TO FOUR

 MICROWAVE TIP

The first stage of this recipe – cooking the runner beans – may be done in the microwave. Put the beans in a dish with 60 ml/4 tbsp water. Cover loosely and cook on High for 10-12 minutes, stirring once or twice. Take care when removing the cover to avoid being scalded by the steam.

BROAD BEANS WITH CREAM SAUCE

250 ml/8 fl oz chicken stock
15 ml/1 tbsp chopped fresh herbs (parsley,
  thyme, sage, savory)
1 kg/2¼ lb broad beans, shelled
1 egg yolk
150 ml/¼ pint single cream
salt and pepper

Combine the stock and herbs in a saucepan. Bring to the boil, add the beans and cook for 5-15 minutes until tender. Lower the heat to a bare simmer.

Beat the egg yolk with the cream in a small bowl. Add 30 ml/2 tbsp of the hot stock and mix well, then pour the contents of the bowl into the pan. Heat gently, stirring all the time, until the sauce thickens slightly. Do not allow the mixture to boil or it will curdle. Add salt and pepper to taste and serve.

SERVES FOUR

STIR-FRIED BEANS WITH SAVORY

450 g/1 lb French beans, trimmed
salt and pepper
15 ml/1 tbsp butter
15 ml/1 tbsp oil
15 ml/1 tbsp finely chopped fresh summer
  savory
4 spring onions, thinly sliced

Cook the beans in boiling salted water for 2 minutes, then drain, refresh under cold running water and drain again.

Melt the butter in the oil in a large frying pan or wok. Add the beans and half the savory. Stir fry for 3 minutes. Add the spring onions, with salt and pepper to taste, and stir fry for 2-3 minutes more. The beans should be tender but still crisp. Sprinkle with the remaining savory and serve at once.

SERVES FOUR

VARIATION

Use only 225 g/8 oz beans and add 225 g/8 oz sliced button mushrooms with the onions. Substitute 10 ml/2 tsp fennel seeds for the savory, if liked. A few water chestnuts, thinly sliced, may be added for extra crunch.

POLISH BEETROOT

30 ml/2 tbsp butter
1 small onion, finely chopped
30 ml/2 tbsp plain flour
250 ml/8 fl oz plain yogurt
675 g/1½ lb cooked beetroot, peeled and
  grated
30 ml/2 tbsp finely grated horseradish
salt and pepper
sugar (optional)
15 ml/1 tbsp chopped parsley to garnish

Melt the butter in a saucepan, add the onion and fry for 4-6 minutes until soft but not coloured. Stir in the flour and cook for 1 minute, then lower the heat and gradually stir in the yogurt.

Bring to the boil, stirring constantly until the sauce thickens. Add the beetroot and horseradish and heat thoroughly. Season to taste with salt and pepper, and add a little sugar, if liked. Serve hot, garnished with the parsley.

SERVES SIX

BRUSSELS SPROUTS WITH CHESTNUTS

This is a classic accompaniment to the Christmas turkey. The slightly sweet flavour of the chestnuts is the perfect foil for the Brussels sprouts.

225 g/8 oz chestnuts, shelled (see Microwave Tip, below and Mrs Beeton's Tip on page 197)
1 kg/2¼ lb Brussels sprouts
75 g/3 oz cooked ham, finely chopped
60 ml/4 tbsp single cream
salt and pepper

Set the oven at 180°C/350°F/gas 4. Place the cleaned nuts in a saucepan, just cover with water and bring to the boil. Cover the pan, lower the heat, and simmer for about 20 minutes or until the nuts are tender. Drain, then cut each chestnut into quarters.

Trim the sprouts, pulling off any damaged leaves. Using a sharp knife, cut a cross in the base of each. Cook the sprouts in a saucepan of salted boiling water for 5-10 minutes until just tender. Drain well.

Combine the sprouts, chestnuts and ham in a small casserole. Stir in the cream and season with salt and pepper. Cover and bake for 15 minutes.

SERVES SIX

 MICROWAVE TIP

Shelling chestnuts is made a lot easier by using the microwave. Make a slit in the shell of each nut, then rinse them thoroughly but do not dry them. Put the damp nuts in a bowl, cover loosely and cook on High for 5 minutes. When cool enough to handle, remove the shells.

BAVARIAN CABBAGE

75 g/3 oz butter
1 onion, finely chopped
1.1 kg/2½ lb white cabbage, washed, quartered and shredded
1 cooking apple
salt and pepper
10 ml/2 tsp sugar
125 ml/4 fl oz vegetable stock or water
1.25 ml/¼ tsp caraway seeds
15 ml/1 tbsp cornflour
60 ml/4 tbsp white wine

Melt the butter in a heavy-bottomed saucepan. Add the onion and fry gently for 10 minutes until soft but not coloured. Stir in the cabbage, tossing it lightly in the fat.

Peel and core the apple, chop it finely and stir it into the pan. Add salt and pepper to taste, then stir in the sugar, stock or water, and caraway seeds. Cover the pan with a tight-fitting lid and simmer very gently for 1 hour.

Meanwhile mix the cornflour and wine together in a small bowl. Stir the mixture into the pan. Bring to the bowl, stirring the mixture constantly until it thickens. Cook for 2-3 minutes, still stirring. Serve at once.

SERVES SIX

VARIATION

For a slightly more fruity flavour, increase the number of apples to 2 and substitute cider for the stock and wine. Omit the caraway seeds.

STUFFED CABBAGE LEAVES

fat for greasing
8 large cabbage leaves

STUFFING
15 ml/1 tbsp oil
1 onion, finely chopped
400 g/14 oz minced beef
1 (397 g/14 oz) can tomatoes
10 ml/2 tsp cornflour
15 ml/1 tbsp Worcestershire sauce
2.5 ml/½ tsp dried mixed herbs
15 ml/1 tbsp chopped parsley
salt and pepper

SAUCE
15 ml/1 tbsp tomato purée
20 ml/4 tsp cornflour

Remove the thick centre stems from the cabbage leaves, then blanch them in boiling water for 2 minutes. Drain well.

To make the stuffing, heat the oil in a saucepan and gently fry the onion for 5 minutes. Add the beef and cook, stirring, until the meat has browned. Drain the tomatoes and reserve the juice. Roughly chop the tomatoes and add them to the meat mixture. Mix the cornflour with the Worcestershire sauce in a cup; stir into the meat mixture with the herbs and salt and pepper. Cover and cook for 20 minutes, stirring occasionally.

Grease a shallow ovenproof dish. Set the oven at 190°C/375°F/gas 5. Divide the stuffing between the cabbage leaves and roll up, folding over the edges of the leaves to enclose the meat completely. Place in the prepared dish and cover with foil. Bake for 20 minutes.

Meanwhile make the sauce. Mix the reserved juice from the tomatoes with the tomato purée in a measuring jug; make up to 250 ml/8 fl oz

with water. In a cup, blend the cornflour with 15 ml/1 tbsp of the sauce. Pour the rest of the sauce into a saucepan and bring to the boil. Stir in the blended cornflour. Boil, stirring all the time, until the sauce has thickened. Add salt and pepper to taste. Pour the sauce over the stuffed cabbage leaves just before serving.

SERVES FOUR

RED CABBAGE WITH APPLES

45 ml/3 tbsp oil
1 onion, finely chopped
1 garlic clove, crushed
900 g/2 lb red cabbage, finely shredded
2 large cooking apples
15 ml/1 tbsp soft light brown sugar or golden syrup
juice of ½ lemon
30 ml/2 tbsp red wine vinegar
salt and pepper
15 ml/1 tbsp caraway seeds (optional)

Heat the oil in a large saucepan, add the onion and garlic and fry gently for 5 minutes. Add the cabbage. Peel, core and slice the apples and add them to the pan with the sugar or syrup. Cook over very gentle heat for 10 minutes, shaking the pan frequently.

Add the lemon juice and vinegar, with salt and pepper to taste. Stir in the caraway seeds, if used. Cover and simmer gently for 1-1½ hours, stirring occasionally and adding a little water if the mixture appears dry. Check the seasoning before serving.

SERVES SIX

SAUERKRAUT WITH JUNIPER BERRIES

One of the oldest forms of preserved food, sauerkraut is simply fermented cabbage. It is sometimes possible to buy it loose from a large barrel in a delicatessen, but is more generally sold in cans or jars.

400 g/14 oz sauerkraut
50 g/2 oz butter
4 rindless streaky bacon rashers, chopped
1 large onion, chopped
1 garlic clove, crushed
6 juniper berries, crushed
2 bay leaves
5 ml/1 tsp caraway seeds
250 ml/8 fl oz chicken stock
salt and pepper (optional)

Put the sauerkraut in a large bowl, add cold water to cover and soak for 15 minutes. Drain thoroughly, then squeeze dry.

Melt the butter in a saucepan, add the bacon and onion and fry over gentle heat for about 10 minutes. Add all the remaining ingredients, cover the pan and simmer for 1 hour. Add salt and pepper, if required, before serving.

SERVES FOUR

 MRS BEETON'S TIP

For a richer, creamier flavour, stir in 150 ml/¼ pint plain yogurt or soured cream just before serving the sauerkraut. Do not allow the mixture to approach boiling point after adding the yogurt or cream.

CARROTS WITH CIDER

This traditional way of cooking carrots was originally known as the 'conservation method' because it preserved as many of the nutrients as possible.

75 g/3 oz butter
675 g/1½ lb young carrots, trimmed and
  scraped
salt
60 ml/4 tbsp double cream
125 ml/4 fl oz dry cider
few drops of lemon juice
pepper

Melt 25 g/1 oz of the butter in a heavy-bottomed saucepan. Add the carrots and cook over very gentle heat for 10 minutes, shaking the pan frequently so that the carrots do not stick to the base. Pour over 100 ml/3½ fl oz boiling water, with salt to taste. Cover the pan and simmer the carrots for about 10 minutes more or until tender. Drain, reserving the liquid for use in soup or stock.

Melt the remaining butter in the clean pan. Gradually stir in the cream and cider. Add the lemon juice and salt and pepper to taste. Stir in the carrots, cover the pan and cook gently for 10 minutes more. Serve at once.

SERVES SIX

 MRS BEETON'S TIP

Another way of preserving as many nutrients as possible is to cook the carrots in the microwave, but the results will be more satisfactory if smaller quantities are used. Combine 225 g/8 oz young carrots with 30 ml/2 tbsp butter in a dish. Cover loosely and cook on High for 5–7 minutes, stirring once. Before serving, add salt and pepper to taste.

GLAZED CARROTS

50 g/2 oz butter
575 g/1¼ lb young carrots, scraped but left
   whole
3 sugar cubes, crushed
1.25 ml/¼ tsp salt
beef stock (see method)
15 ml/1 tbsp chopped parsley to garnish

Melt the butter in a saucepan. Add the carrots, sugar and salt. Pour in enough stock to half cover the carrots. Cook over gentle heat, without covering the pan, for 15-20 minutes or until the carrots are tender. Shake the pan occasionally to prevent sticking.

Using a slotted spoon, transfer the carrots to a bowl and keep hot. Boil the stock rapidly in the pan until it is reduced to a rich glaze. Return the carrots to the pan, two or three at a time, turning them in the glaze until thoroughly coated. Place on a heated serving dish, garnish with parsley and serve at once.

SERVES SIX

CAULIFLOWER POLONAISE

1 large cauliflower, trimmed
salt
50 g/2 oz butter
50 g/2 oz fresh white breadcrumbs
2 hard-boiled eggs
15 ml/1 tbsp chopped parsley

Put the cauliflower, stem down, in a saucepan. Pour over boiling water, add salt to taste and cook for 10-15 minutes or until the stalk is just tender. Drain the cauliflower thoroughly in a colander.

Meanwhile, melt the butter in a frying pan, add the breadcrumbs and fry until crisp and golden.

Chop the egg whites finely. Sieve the yolks and mix them with the parsley in a small bowl.

Drain the cauliflower thoroughly and place it on a heated serving dish. Sprinkle first with the breadcrumbs and then with the egg yolk mixture. Arrange the chopped egg white around the edge of the dish. Serve at once.

SERVES FOUR

CAULIFLOWER WITH BEANS

45 ml/3 tbsp oil
knob of butter (optional)
1 small onion, chopped
1 small cauliflower, broken in florets
225 g/8 oz French beans, trimmed and cut in
   pieces or thawed and drained if frozen
salt and pepper
15-45 ml/1-3 tbsp chopped fresh herbs

Heat the oil and butter (if used) in a large frying pan or wok. Stir fry the onion for 5 minutes, until slightly softened. Add the cauliflower and cook, stirring, for 5 minutes, until the florets are translucent and lightly cooked.

Add the beans and continue stir frying for a further 3-4 minutes or until all the vegetables are just cooked but still crunchy. Add salt and pepper to taste and stir in the herbs. Serve.

SERVES FOUR TO SIX

CAULIFLOWER CHEESE

salt and pepper
1 firm cauliflower
30 ml/2 tbsp butter
60 ml/4 tbsp plain flour
200 ml/7 fl oz milk
125 g/4½ oz Cheddar cheese, grated
pinch of dry mustard
pinch of cayenne pepper
25 g/1 oz dried white breadcrumbs

Bring a saucepan of salted water to the boil, add the cauliflower, cover the pan and cook gently for 20-30 minutes until tender. Drain well, reserving 175 ml/6 fl oz of the cooking water. Leave the cauliflower head whole or cut carefully into florets. Place in a warmed ovenproof dish, cover with greased greaseproof paper and keep hot.

Set the oven at 220°C/425°F/gas 7 or preheat the grill. Melt the butter in a saucepan, stir in the flour and cook for 1 minute. Gradually add the milk and reserved cooking water, stirring all the time until the sauce boils and thickens. Remove from the heat and stir in 100 g/4 oz of the cheese, stirring until it melts into the sauce. Add the mustard and cayenne, with salt and pepper to taste.

Pour the sauce over the cauliflower. Mix the remaining cheese with the breadcrumbs and sprinkle them on top. Brown the topping for 7-10 minutes in the oven or under the grill. Serve at once.

SERVES FOUR

VARIATIONS

A wide variety of vegetables can be cooked in this way. Try broccoli (particularly good with grilled bacon); small whole onions (see Mrs Beeton's Tip page 447 for microwave cooking); celery, celeriac; leeks or chicory (both taste delicious if wrapped in ham before being covered in the cheese sauce) and asparagus. A mixed vegetable gratin – cooked sliced carrots, green beans, onions and potatoes – also works well. Vary the cheese topping too: Red Leicester has good flavour and colour; Gruyère or Emmental is tasty with leeks or chicory; a little blue cheese mixed with the Cheddar will enliven celery or celeriac.

CAULIFLOWER AND CASHEW NUT STIR FRY

30 ml/2 tbsp oil
5 ml/1 tsp sesame oil (optional)
1 small cauliflower, broken into small florets
30 ml/2 tbsp grated fresh root ginger (optional)
1 bunch of spring onions, shredded
50 g/2 oz salted cashew nuts
5 ml/1 tsp cornflour
15 ml/1 tbsp soy sauce or salt
60 ml/4 tbsp dry sherry

Heat the oil in a large frying pan or wok. Add the sesame oil for a Chinese-style dish. Add the cauliflower and ginger – again for a Chinese flavour – and stir fry for 3 minutes. Add the spring onions and cashew nuts, then continue to cook for a further 3 minutes, until the cauliflower has lost its raw edge.

Blend the cornflour with the soy sauce, if you are opting for the Chinese flavour, otherwise add a little salt. In either case, stir in the sherry and 30 ml/2 tbsp water. Pour the cornflour mixture over the cauliflower and stir for 1-2 minutes, over high heat, until the juices thicken. Serve at once.

SERVES FOUR TO SIX

CELERIAC PUREE

15 ml/1 tbsp lemon juice
1 large celeriac root, about 1 kg/2¼ lb
salt and white pepper
90 ml/6 tbsp single cream
15 ml/1 tbsp butter
60 ml/4 tbsp pine nuts

Have ready a large saucepan of water to which the lemon juice has been added. Peel the celeriac root fairly thickly so that the creamy white flesh is exposed. Cut it into 1 cm/½ inch cubes. Add the cubes to the acidulated water and bring to the boil over moderate heat. Add salt to taste, if desired, and cook for 8–10 minutes or until the celeriac is tender.

Drain the celeriac and purée it with the cream and butter in a blender or food processor. Alternatively, mash until smooth, then press through a sieve into a bowl. Reheat the purée if necessary, adjust the seasoning, stir in the nuts and serve at once.

SERVES FOUR

VARIATION

Celeriac and Potato Purée Substitute potato for half the celeriac. Cook and purée as suggested above.

 MICROWAVE TIP

The celeriac can be cooked in the microwave. Toss the celeriac cubes in acidulated water, drain off all but 60 ml/4 tbsp, and put the mixture in a roasting bag. Close the bag lightly with an elastic band and cook on High for 15 minutes. Shake the bag once during cooking. It will be very hot, so protect your hand in an oven glove. Drain by snipping an end off the bag and holding it over the sink. Purée as above.

BRAISED CHESTNUTS WITH ONION AND CELERY

600 ml/1 pint beef stock
1 kg/2¼ lb chestnuts, peeled (see Mrs Beeton's Tip, page 197)
1 small onion stuck with 2 cloves
1 celery stick, roughly chopped
1 bay leaf · 1 blade of mace
pinch of cayenne pepper · salt
puff pastry fleurons (see Mrs Beeton's Tip) to garnish

Bring the stock to the boil in a saucepan. Add the chestnuts, onion, celery, bay leaf, mace and cayenne, with a little salt. Cover and simmer for about 30 minutes, until the nuts are tender.

Drain the chestnuts, reserving the cooking liquid, and keep them hot in a serving dish. Chop the onion, discarding the cloves, and add it to the chestnuts. Discard the bay leaf and mace. Return the cooking liquid to the clean pan. Boil the liquid rapidly until it is reduced to a thin glaze. Pour the glaze over the chestnuts and garnish with the pastry fleurons.

SERVES SIX

 MRS BEETON'S TIP

To make pastry fleurons, roll out 215 g/7½ oz puff pastry on a floured board. Cut into rounds, using a 5 cm/2 inch cutter. Move the cutter halfway across each round and cut in half again, making a half moon and an almond shape. Arrange the half moons on a baking sheet, brush with beaten egg and bake in a preheated 200°C/400°F/gas 6 oven for 8-10 minutes. The almond shapes may either be baked as biscuits or rerolled and cut to make more fleurons.

BRAISED CELERY

The celery is cooked on a bed of vegetables or mirepoix, which adds flavour, keeps the celery moist and prevents scorching.

15 ml/1 tbsp dripping or margarine
2 rindless bacon rashers, chopped
2 onions, finely chopped
1 carrot, finely chopped
½ turnip, finely chopped
chicken stock (see method)
4 celery hearts, washed but left whole
15 ml/1 tbsp chopped fresh coriander or
    parsley

Melt the dripping or margarine in a large heavy-bottomed saucepan. Add the bacon and fry for 2 minutes, then stir in the onions, carrot and turnip. Cook over gentle heat, stirring occasionally, for 10 minutes.

Pour over enough chicken stock to half cover the vegetables. Place the celery on top and spoon over some of the stock. Cover the pan tightly with foil and a lid and cook over very gentle heat for 1½ hours or until the celery is very tender. Baste the celery occasionally with the stock.

Using a slotted spoon, transfer the celery to a heated serving dish. Drain the cooking liquid into a small pan, reserving the *mirepoix* in a small heated serving dish.

Boil the cooking liquid rapidly until it is reduced to a thin glaze, then pour it over the celery. Sprinkle the *mirepoix* with the chopped coriander or parsley and serve it as a separate vegetable dish.

SERVES FOUR

COURGETTES IN TOMATO SAUCE

30 ml/2 tbsp olive or sunflower oil
450 g/1 lb courgettes, trimmed and sliced
6 spring onions, chopped
1 garlic clove, crushed
225 g/8 oz tomatoes, peeled, halved and
    seeded or 1 (227 g/8 oz) can chopped
    tomatoes, drained
15 ml/1 tbsp tomato purée
1 bay leaf
15 ml/1 tbsp dried basil
30 ml/2 tbsp dry white wine
salt and pepper

Heat the oil in a saucepan, add the courgettes, spring onions and garlic and cook over gentle heat for 5 minutes. Stir in the tomatoes, tomato purée, bay leaf, basil and wine, with salt and pepper to taste. Boil, lower the heat, cover and simmer for 15 minutes. Remove the bay leaf and serve.

SERVES FOUR

COURGETTES WITH DILL

A simple dish to go with fish.

25 g/1 oz butter
grated rind of ½ lemon
8 small courgettes, trimmed and sliced
salt and pepper
45 ml/3 tbsp chopped fresh dill
squeeze of lemon juice

Melt the butter in a large frying pan. Add the lemon rind and cook for a few seconds before adding the courgettes. Cook over medium to high heat for 2–3 minutes, then add salt and pepper, and the dill. Toss in a little lemon juice and serve.

SERVES FOUR

COURGETTES WITH ALMONDS

The cooked courgettes should be firm and full flavoured, not overcooked and watery.

25 g/1 oz butter
25 g/1 oz blanched almonds, split in half
450 g/1 lb courgettes, trimmed and thinly
  sliced
salt and pepper
30 ml/2 tbsp snipped chives or chopped
  parsley

Melt the butter in a large frying pan. Add the almonds and fry over moderate heat, stirring, until lightly browned. Tip the courgettes into the pan and cook, gently stirring and turning the slices all the time, for 3-5 minutes.

Tip the courgettes into a heated serving dish, add salt and pepper to taste and sprinkle the chives or parsley over them. Serve at once.

SERVES FOUR TO SIX

FENNEL WITH LEEKS

4 fennel bulbs, trimmed and halved
juice of ½ lemon
knob of butter or 30 ml/2 tbsp olive oil
4 leeks, sliced
1 bay leaf
2 fresh thyme sprigs
salt and pepper
150 ml/¼ pint chicken or vegetable stock
45 ml/3 tbsp dry sherry (optional)

Set the oven at 180°C/350°F/gas 4. As soon as the fennel is prepared, sprinkle the lemon juice over the cut bulbs. Heat the butter or oil in a frying pan and sauté the leeks for 2 minutes to soften them slightly. Add the pieces of fennel to the pan, pushing the leeks to one side. Turn

the pieces of fennel in the fat for a minute or so, then tip the contents of the pan into an oven-proof casserole.

Add the bay leaf and thyme to the vegetables and sprinkle in salt and pepper to taste. Pour the stock and sherry (if used) over the fennel and cover the dish. Bake for 1-1¼ hours, turning the fennel mixture over twice, until tender. Taste for seasoning, remove the bay leaf and serve.

SERVES FOUR

BUTTERED LEEKS

50 g/2 oz butter
675 g/1½ lb leeks, trimmed, sliced and
  washed
15 ml/1 tbsp lemon juice
salt and pepper
30 ml/2 tbsp single cream (optional)

Melt the butter in a heavy-bottomed saucepan. Add the leeks and lemon juice, with salt and pepper to taste. Cover the pan and cook the leeks over very gentle heat for about 30 minutes or until very tender. Shake the pan from time to time to prevent the leeks from sticking to the base. Serve in the cooking liquid. Stir in the cream when serving, if liked.

SERVES FOUR

 MRS BEETON'S TIP

Leeks can be very gritty. The easiest way to wash them is to trim the roots and tough green leaves, slit them lengthways to the centre, and hold them open under cold running water to flush out the grit.

LEEK TART

8 small leeks, trimmed and washed
2 eggs
salt and pepper
grated nutmeg
25 g/1 oz Gruyère cheese, grated

SHORT CRUST PASTRY
100 g/4 oz plain flour
1.25 ml/¼ tsp salt
50 g/2 oz margarine (or half butter, half lard)
flour for rolling out

SAUCE
15 g/½ oz butter
15 g/½ oz plain flour
150 ml/¼ pint milk or milk and leek cooking liquid

Set the oven at 200°C/400°F/gas 6. To make the pastry, sift the flour and salt into a bowl, then rub in the margarine until the mixture resembles fine breadcrumbs. Add enough cold water to make a stiff dough. Press the dough together.

Roll out the pastry on a lightly floured surface and use to line an 18 cm/7 inch flan tin or ring placed on a baking sheet. Line the pastry with greaseproof paper and fill with baking beans. Bake 'blind' for 20 minutes, then remove the paper and beans. Return to the oven for 5 minutes, then leave to cool. Reduce the oven temperature to 190°C/375°F/gas 5.

Using the white parts of the leeks only, tie them into two bundles with string. Bring a saucepan of salted water to the boil, add the leeks and simmer gently for 10 minutes. Drain, then squeeze as dry as possible. Cut the leeks into thick slices.

To make the sauce, melt the butter in a saucepan. Stir in the flour and cook over low heat for 2-3 minutes, without colouring. Gradually add the liquid, stirring constantly. Bring to the boil,

stirring, then lower the heat and simmer for 1-2 minutes.

Beat the eggs into the white sauce. Then add salt, pepper and nutmeg to taste. Stir in half of the Gruyère. Put a layer of sauce in the cooled pastry case, cover with the leeks, then with the remaining sauce. Sprinkle with the remaining Gruyère. Bake for 20 minutes or until golden on top.

SERVES EIGHT

LETTUCE WITH HERB SAUCE

salt and pepper
6 small heads of lettuce, trimmed
25 g/1 oz butter
25 g/1 oz plain flour
250 ml/8 fl oz chicken or vegetable stock
10 ml/2 tsp snipped chives
1 bay leaf
10 ml/2 tsp chopped parsley

Bring a large saucepan of salted water to the boil, add the lettuces and blanch for 2 minutes. Drain thoroughly, blotting off excess water with absorbent kitchen paper.

Melt the butter in a small saucepan, stir in the flour and cook for 1 minute. Gradually add the stock, stirring all the time until the mixture boils and thickens. Stir in the herbs, with salt and pepper to taste. Add the lettuces.

Cover the pan and cook the lettuces in the sauce for 20-30 minutes, stirring occasionally, but taking care not to break up the heads. Remove the bay leaf, add more salt and pepper if required, and serve.

SERVES SIX

BAKED STUFFED MARROW

fat for greasing
1 marrow
1 small onion, finely chopped or grated
225 g/8 oz minced beef
100 g/4 oz pork sausagemeat or 100 g/4 oz
    extra minced beef
25 g/1 oz fresh white breadcrumbs
15 ml/1 tbsp chopped parsley
15 ml/1 tbsp snipped chives
5 ml/1 tsp Worcestershire sauce
salt and pepper
1 egg, beaten

SAUCE
25 g/1 oz butter
25 g/1 oz plain flour
300 ml/½ pint milk, stock or mixture (see
    method)
75-100 g/3-4 oz Cheddar cheese, grated
pinch of dry mustard

Generously grease a large, shallow casserole. Set the oven at 180°C/350°F/gas 4. Halve the marrow lengthways and scoop out the seeds. Lay the halves side by side in the prepared casserole.

Put the onion into a bowl with the beef, sausagemeat, if used, breadcrumbs, parsley, chives, Worcestershire sauce and salt and pepper. Mix well. Bind the mixture with beaten egg. Avoid making it too moist.

Divide the stuffing between each marrow half. Cover the dish and bake for 1 hour.

Strain off most of the liquid in the casserole. Meanwhile make the sauce. Melt the butter in a saucepan. Stir in the flour and cook over low heat for 2-3 minutes, without colouring. Over very low heat, gradually add the liquid (the casserole juices may be used), stirring constantly. Bring to the boil, stirring, then lower the heat and simmer for 1-2 minutes until

smooth and thickened. Add the cheese, mustard and salt and pepper to taste. Pour the cheese sauce over the marrow and bake, uncovered, for a further 20 minutes, until the sauce topping is golden brown.

SERVES FOUR TO SIX

MARROW WITH TOMATOES

30 ml/2 tbsp olive or sunflower oil
1 onion, finely chopped
1-2 garlic cloves, crushed
450 g/1 lb ripe tomatoes, peeled and chopped
10 ml/2 tsp paprika
15 ml/1 tbsp tomato purée
1 (1 kg/2¼ lb) marrow, peeled, seeded and
    cubed
salt and pepper
45 ml/3 tbsp chopped parsley

Heat the oil in a flameproof casserole. Add the onion and garlic, and fry gently for about 15 minutes until soft but not coloured. Stir in the tomatoes, paprika and tomato purée and cook, stirring occasionally, for 10 minutes.

Add the marrow cubes, with salt and pepper to taste, stir well until simmering, then cover and cook gently for about 25 minutes, stirring occasionally, until tender but not watery. Add the parsley and taste for seasoning.

SERVES SIX

VARIATION

Marrow Montgomery Set the oven at 190°C/375°F/gas 5. Add the marrow as above, then stir in 40 g/1½ oz cubed dark rye bread. Buy an unsliced rye loaf for this recipe as the pre-sliced bread sold in packets is cut too thin. Bake the mixture, uncovered, for 30-40 minutes, sprinkle with parsley and serve.

SHERRIED MUSHROOMS

25 g/1 oz butter
30 ml/2 tbsp plain flour
250 ml/8 fl oz milk
45 ml/3 tbsp dry sherry
350 g/12 oz mushrooms, sliced
salt and pepper
toast triangles to serve

Melt the butter in a saucepan, add the flour and cook for 1 minute. Gradually add the milk, stirring all the time until the mixture boils and thickens.

Stir in the sherry, then add the mushrooms, with salt and pepper to taste. Cook over gentle heat, stirring frequently, for about 5 minutes or until the mushrooms are just cooked.

Spoon on to a heated serving dish and serve at once, with toast triangles.

SERVES FOUR TO SIX

MUSHROOMS IN CREAM SAUCE

50 g/2 oz butter
450 g/1 lb small button mushrooms
10 ml/2 tsp arrowroot
125 ml/4 fl oz chicken or vegetable stock
15 ml/1 tbsp lemon juice
30 ml/2 tbsp double cream
salt and pepper
30 ml/2 tbsp chopped parsley

Melt the butter in large frying pan, add the mushrooms and fry over gentle heat without browning for 10 minutes.

Put the arrowroot in a small bowl. Stir in 30 ml/2 tbsp of the stock until smooth. Add the remaining stock to the mushrooms and bring to

the boil. Lower the heat and simmer gently for 15 minutes, stirring occasionally. Stir in the arrowroot, bring to the boil, stirring, then remove the pan from the heat.

Stir in the lemon juice and cream, with salt and pepper to taste. Serve sprinkled with parsley.

SERVES FOUR TO SIX

MUSHROOMS WITH BACON AND WINE

6 rindless streaky bacon rashers, chopped
400 g/14 oz button mushrooms, halved or
    quartered if large
5 ml/1 tsp snipped chives
5 ml/1 tsp chopped parsley
10 ml/2 tsp plain flour
75 ml/5 tbsp white wine or cider
salt and pepper

Cook the bacon gently in a heavy-bottomed saucepan until the fat begins to run, then increase the heat to moderate and fry for 10 minutes. Add the mushrooms and herbs, tossing them in the bacon fat.

Sprinkle the flour over the mushrooms, cook for 1 minute, stirring gently, then add the wine or cider. Simmer for 10 minutes, stirring occasionally. Season and serve.

SERVES SIX

 MRS BEETON'S TIP

Store mushrooms in a paper bag inside a polythene bag. The paper absorbs condensation and the mushrooms keep for three days in the refrigerator.

OKRA AND AUBERGINE BAKE

1 aubergine
salt and pepper
400 g/14 oz okra
60 ml/4 tbsp olive oil
1 onion, finely chopped
2 garlic cloves, crushed
10 ml/2 tsp fennel seeds
3 tomatoes, peeled and sliced
10 ml/2 tsp chopped fresh marjoram
60 ml/4 tbsp wholemeal breadcrumbs
15 ml/1 tbsp butter

Set the oven at 190°C/375°F/gas 5. Cut the ends off the aubergine and cut it into cubes. Put the cubes in a colander and sprinkle generously with salt. Set aside for 30 minutes.

Meanwhile wash the okra in cold water. Pat dry on absorbent kitchen paper. Trim but do not completely remove the stems. Rinse the aubergines thoroughly, drain and pat dry.

Heat the oil in a flameproof casserole, add the onion, garlic, fennel seeds and aubergine and cook over gentle heat for about 20 minutes until the onion is soft but not coloured and the aubergine is tender. Stir in the okra, tomatoes and marjoram.

Sprinkle the breadcrumbs over the top of the casserole, dot with the butter and bake for 15-20 minutes. Serve at once.

SERVES SIX

 MRS BEETON'S TIP

When preparing the okra, take care not to split the pods or the sticky juices inside will be lost and the okra will lose their shape during cooking.

GLAZED ONIONS

Glazed onions make a tasty accompaniment to grilled steak, baked ham or bacon chops. They are often used as a garnish.

400 g/14 oz button onions
chicken stock (see method)
salt and pepper
15 ml/1 tbsp soft light brown sugar
25 g/1 oz butter
pinch of grated nutmeg

Skin the onions and put them in a single layer in a large saucepan. Add just enough stock to cover. Bring to the simmering point and cook for 15-20 minutes until the onions are just tender, adding a small amount of extra stock if necessary.

By the time the onions are cooked, the stock should have reduced almost to a glaze. Remove from the heat and stir in the remaining ingredients. Turn the onions over with a spoon so that the added ingredients mix well and the onions are coated in the mixture.

Return the pan to the heat until the onions become golden and glazed. Serve at once, with the remaining syrupy glaze.

SERVES FOUR

VARIATION

Citrus Glazed Onions   Melt 25 g/1 oz butter in a frying pan. Add 400 g/14 oz button onions. Sprinkle with 15 ml/1 tbsp soft light brown sugar. Add salt and pepper to taste and fry, turning the onions occasionally until golden brown. Stir in 150 ml/¼ pint orange juice and 10 ml/2 tsp lemon juice. Cover and simmer for 15 minutes.

ONIONS AND TOMATOES IN CIDER

6 large onions, peeled but left whole
50g/2oz butter or margarine
225g/8oz tomatoes, peeled and sliced
2 bay leaves
2 cloves
150ml/¼ pint medium cider
125ml/4floz vegetable stock
salt and pepper

Bring a saucepan of water to the boil. Add the onions and cook for 2 minutes, then drain thoroughly. Cool, cut into rings and dry on absorbent kitchen paper.

Melt the butter or margarine in a deep frying pan. Add the onion rings. Fry over gentle heat until golden. Add the tomatoes, bay leaves, cloves, cider and stock. Cover and simmer for 45 minutes. Remove the bay leaves and cloves, season and serve.

SERVES SIX

STUFFED ONIONS

salt and pepper
6 large onions
75g/3oz cooked ham, finely chopped
30ml/2tbsp fresh white breadcrumbs
2.5ml/½tsp finely chopped sage
beaten egg for binding
30ml/2tbsp butter
100g/4oz Cheddar cheese, grated (optional)

Bring a saucepan of salted water to the boil, add the unpeeled onions and parboil for 45 minutes or until almost tender. Drain, skin and remove the centres with a teaspoon.

Set the oven at 180°C/350°F/gas 4. Mix the ham, breadcrumbs and sage in a small bowl. Add salt and pepper to taste and stir in enough of the beaten egg to give a fairly firm mixture. Fill the centres of the onions with the mixture.

Put the onions in a baking dish just large enough to hold them snugly. Dot the tops with butter. Bake for 30–45 minutes or until tender, sprinkling the tops of the onions with the grated cheese, if used, 10 minutes before the end of the cooking time.

SERVES SIX

 MRS BEETON'S TIP

Peel the onions. Arrange them around the rim of a round shallow dish, add 45ml/3tbsp water and cover. Cook on High for 10–12 minutes or until the onions are tender. When cool enough to handle, scoop out the centres and fill as described above. Return the onions to the dry dish and cook for 4–6 minutes. If a cheese topping is required, sprinkle the grated cheese on top and brown under a grill for 3–4 minutes.

PANFRIED ONION AND APPLE

40g/1½oz butter
350g/12oz onions, sliced in rings
450g/1lb cooking apples
10ml/2tsp caster sugar
salt and pepper

Melt the butter in a heavy-bottomed frying pan. Add the onions and fry gently. Peel, core and slice the apples into the pan. Mix lightly to coat the apples in the melted butter. Sprinkle the sugar over the top, cover and simmer for 30 minutes or until the onions and apples are tender. Add salt and pepper to taste before serving.

SERVES FOUR

CREAMED ONIONS

fat for greasing
1 kg/2¼ lb small onions, peeled but left
  whole
100 ml/3½ fl oz double cream
Béchamel sauce (page 481) made using
  300 ml/½ pint milk
grated nutmeg
salt and pepper
25 g/1 oz butter
50 g/2 oz dried white breadcrumbs
30 ml/2 tbsp chopped parsley

Grease a 1 litre/1¾ pint casserole. Set the oven
at 160°C/325°F/gas 3. Bring a saucepan of
water to the boil. Add the onions and cook for
10–15 minutes until just tender. Drain well.

Add the double cream to the Béchamel sauce
and reheat gently without boiling. Stir in the
nutmeg with salt and pepper to taste, add the
onions and mix lightly.

Spoon the mixture into the prepared casserole.
Top with the breadcrumbs and dot with the
butter. Bake for 20 minutes. Serve hot, sprinkled with the parsley.

SERVES SIX TO EIGHT

 MRS BEETON'S TIP

To make about 100 g/4 oz dried breadcrumbs, cut the crusts off six slices
(175 g/6 oz) of bread, then spread the bread
out on baking sheets. Bake in a preheated
150°C/300°F/gas 2 oven for about 30
minutes until dry but not browned. Cook,
then crumb in a food processor or blender.
Alternatively, put the dried bread between
sheets of greaseproof paper and crush with
a rolling pin.

ONIONS ITALIAN-STYLE

675 g/1½ lb button onions
30 ml/2 tbsp olive oil
2 bay leaves
2 cloves
4 white peppercorns
30 ml/2 tbsp white wine vinegar
5 ml/1 tsp caster sugar

Cook the onions in their skins in a saucepan of
boiling water for 15–20 minutes, until just
tender. Drain. When cool enough to handle,
slip off the skins.

Heat the oil in a saucepan. Put in the bay leaves,
cloves and peppercorns and shake the pan over
moderate heat for 2–3 minutes. Add the onions
to the pan and cook very gently for 5 minutes.
Stir in the vinegar and sugar. Continue cooking
until the liquid is reduced to a syrup. Serve hot.

SERVES SIX

 MRS BEETON'S TIP

Try to find silverskin or small white onions
for this recipe. Slices of the deep reddish-
purple Italian onions may also be used, in
which case substitute red wine vinegar for
the white.

PARSNIP SOUFFLE

butter for greasing
200 g/7 oz parsnips
salt and pepper
65 g/2¼ oz butter
30 ml/2 tbsp grated onion
45 ml/3 tbsp plain flour
100 ml/3½ fl oz parsnip cooking water
100 ml/3½ fl oz milk
30 ml/2 tbsp chopped parsley
pinch of grated nutmeg
4 eggs, separated
125 ml/4 fl oz Béchamel sauce (page 481)

Grease a 1 litre/1¾ pint soufflé dish. Cook the parsnips in a saucepan with a little boiling salted water for 20-30 minutes until tender. Mash and sieve them, working to a smooth purée. Measure out 150 g/5 oz purée, and keep the rest on one side. Melt 15 g/½ oz of the butter in a frying pan and gently cook the onion until soft. Mix it with the 150 g/5 oz parsnip purée.

Set the oven at 190°C/375°F/gas 5. Melt the remaining butter in a saucepan, stir in the flour and cook over low heat for 2-3 minutes, without colouring, stirring all the time. Mix the stock or water and the milk. Over very low heat, gradually add the liquid to the pan, stirring constantly. Bring to the boil, stirring, and simmer for 1-2 minutes until thickened. Stir in the measured parsnip purée and parsley. Add salt, pepper and nutmeg to taste. Cool slightly.

Beat the yolks into the mixture one by one. In a clean, grease-free bowl, whisk all the egg whites until stiff. Using a metal spoon, fold into the mixture. Spoon the mixture into the prepared dish. Bake for 25-30 minutes, until risen and set. Meanwhile, mix the remaining parsnip purée with the Béchamel sauce, and heat gently. Serve with the soufflé.

SERVES FOUR

SWEET PARSNIP BAKE

fat for greasing
450 g/1 lb parsnips, sliced
250 ml/8 fl oz apple purée
75 g/3 oz soft light brown sugar
salt
2.5 ml/½ tsp grated nutmeg
15 ml/1 tbsp lemon juice
75 g/3 oz butter
75 g/3 oz fresh white breadcrumbs
1.25 ml/¼ tsp paprika

Grease an ovenproof dish. Set the oven at 190°C/375°F/gas 5. Put the parsnips in a saucepan of cold water, bring to the boil and cook for 15-20 minutes or until tender. Drain thoroughly, then mash the parsnips by hand or purée in a blender or food processor.

Arrange alternate layers of parsnip purée and apple purée in the prepared dish, sprinkling each layer with brown sugar, salt, nutmeg, lemon juice and flakes of butter. Top with the breadcrumbs and a dusting of paprika. Bake for 30 minutes.

SERVES SIX

 MRS BEETON'S TIP

Horseradish sauce or creamed horseradish make interesting condiments for parsnips. Beat a couple of spoonfuls into mashed, boiled parsnips, adding a knob of butter. Taste as you add, and remember that horseradish sauce is far hotter than creamed horseradish.

PETITS POIS A LA FRANCAISE

50g/2oz butter
1 lettuce heart, shredded
1 bunch of spring onions, finely chopped
675g/1½lb fresh shelled garden peas or
   frozen petits pois
pinch of sugar
salt and pepper

Melt the butter in a heavy-bottomed saucepan
and add the lettuce, spring onions, peas and
sugar, with salt and pepper to taste. Cover and
simmer very gently until the peas are tender.
Frozen petits pois may be ready in less than 10
minutes, but fresh garden peas could take 25
minutes.

SERVES SIX

PEASE PUDDING

575g/1¼lb split peas, soaked overnight in
   cold water to cover
1 small onion, peeled but left whole
1 bouquet garni
salt and pepper
50g/2oz butter, cut into small pieces
2 eggs, beaten

Drain the peas, put them in a saucepan and add
cold water to cover. Add the onion, the bouquet
garni and salt and pepper to taste. Bring to the
boil, skim off any scum on the surface of the
liquid, then reduce the heat to very low and
simmer the peas for 2–2½ hours or until tender.

Drain the peas thoroughly. Press them through
a sieve or purée in a blender or food processor.
Add the pieces of butter with the beaten eggs.
Beat well.

Spoon the mixture into a floured pudding cloth
and tie tightly. Suspend the bag in a large

saucepan of boiling salted water and simmer
gently for 1 hour. Remove from the pan, take
the pudding out of the cloth and serve very hot.

SERVES SIX

 MRS BEETON'S TIP

Modern cooks, unfamiliar with pudding
cloths, can bake this nutritious pudding in
a greased casserole. It will need about 30
minutes to cook in a preheated 180°C/
350°F/gas 4 oven.

BAKED STUFFED PEPPERS

fat for greasing
4 green peppers
1 small onion, finely chopped
400g/14oz lean minced beef
100g/4oz cooked rice
salt and pepper
good pinch of dried marjoram
250ml/8floz tomato juice
strips of green pepper to garnish

Grease an ovenproof dish. Set the oven at
180°C/350°F/gas 4. Cut a slice off the top of
each pepper, then remove the membranes and
seeds. Blanch in a saucepan of boiling water for
2 minutes.

Mix the onion, beef, rice, salt, pepper and
marjoram together in a bowl. Stand the peppers
upright in the prepared dish; if they do not
stand upright easily, cut a thin slice off the
base. Divide the stuffing mixture between the
peppers. Pour the tomato juice around the base
of the peppers.

Cover and bake for 1 hour. Garnish with strips
of pepper.

SERVES FOUR

PEPERONATA

A delicious starter from Italy, peperonata is perfect for serving with prosciutto or salami.

45 ml/3 tbsp olive oil
1 large onion, sliced
2 garlic cloves, crushed
350 g/12 oz tomatoes, peeled, seeded and cut in quarters
2 large red peppers, seeded and cut in thin strips
1 large green pepper, seeded and cut in thin strips
1 large yellow pepper, seeded and cut in thin strips
2.5 ml/½ tsp coriander seeds, lightly crushed (optional)
salt and pepper
15 ml/1 tbsp red wine vinegar (optional)

Heat the oil in a large frying pan, add the onion and garlic and fry over gentle heat for 10 minutes. Add the tomatoes, peppers and coriander seeds, if used, with salt and pepper to taste. Cover and cook gently for 1 hour, stirring from time to time. Add more salt and pepper before serving if necessary. To sharpen the flavour, stir in the red wine vinegar, if liked.

SERVES FOUR

POTATOES LYONNAISE

This is a very good way of using up leftover boiled new potatoes. A crushed garlic clove may be added to the onion, if liked.

1 kg/2¼ lb potatoes, scrubbed but not peeled
75 g/3 oz butter or margarine
225 g/8 oz onions, thickly sliced
salt and pepper
15 ml/1 tbsp chopped parsley

Boil or steam the potatoes in their jackets until tender. When cool enough to handle, peel and cut into slices 5 mm/¼ inch thick.

Melt the butter or margarine in a large frying pan. Add the onions and fry over moderate heat until just golden. Using a slotted spoon, transfer the onions to a plate; keep warm. Add the potatoes to the fat remaining in the pan and fry on both sides until crisp and golden.

Return the onions to the pan and mix with the potatoes. Add salt and pepper to taste, turn into a serving dish and sprinkle with the parsley.

SERVES SIX

 MRS BEETON'S TIP

Use an electric frying pan, if you have one, for this recipe. The size and depth means that the onions and potatoes will be easy to cook, and the readily-controlled temperature will be an asset when frying the potatoes.

DUCHESSE POTATOES

butter or margarine for greasing
450g/1lb old potatoes
salt and pepper
25g/1oz butter or margarine
1 egg or 2 egg yolks
grated nutmeg (optional)
beaten egg for brushing

Grease a baking sheet. Cut the potatoes into pieces and cook in a saucepan of salted water for 15-20 minutes. Drain thoroughly, then press the potatoes through a sieve into a large mixing bowl.

Set the oven at 200°C/400°F/gas 6. Beat the butter or margarine and egg or egg yolks into the potatoes. Add salt and pepper to taste and the nutmeg, if used. Spoon the mixture into a piping bag fitted with a large rose nozzle. Pipe rounds of potato on to the prepared baking sheet. Brush with a little beaten egg. Bake for about 15 minutes, until golden brown.

SERVES SIX

ANNA POTATOES

fat for greasing
1 kg/2¼lb even-sized potatoes
salt and pepper
melted clarified butter (page 424)

Grease a 20cm/8 inch round cake tin and line the base with greased greaseproof paper. Set the oven at 190°C/375°F/gas 5.

Trim the potatoes so that they will give equal-sized slices. Slice them very thinly using either a sharp knife or a mandoline. Arrange a layer of potatoes, slightly overlapping, in the base of the tin. Add salt and pepper to taste, then spoon a little clarified butter over them. Make a second layer of potatoes and spoon some more butter over them. Complete these layers until all the potatoes have been used. Cover the tin with greased greaseproof paper and foil.

Bake for 1 hour. Check the potatoes several times during cooking and add a little more clarified butter if they become too dry. Invert the tin on to a warm serving dish to remove the potatoes. Serve at once.

SERVES SIX

GRATIN DAUPHINOIS

25g/1oz butter
1kg/2¼lb potatoes, thinly sliced
1 large onion, about 200g/7oz, thinly sliced
200g/7oz Gruyère cheese, grated
salt and pepper
grated nutmeg
125ml/4floz single cream

Butter a 1.5 litre/2¾ pint casserole, reserving the remaining butter. Set the oven at 190°C/375°F/gas 5. Bring a saucepan of water to the boil, add the potatoes and onion, then blanch for 30 seconds. Drain.

Put a layer of potatoes in the bottom of the prepared casserole. Dot with a little of the butter, then sprinkle with some of the onion and cheese, a little salt, pepper and grated nutmeg. Pour over some of the cream. Repeat the layers until all the ingredients have been used, finishing with a layer of cheese. Pour the remaining cream on top.

Cover and bake for 1 hour. Remove from the oven and place under a hot grill for 5 minutes, until the top of the cheese is golden brown and bubbling.

SERVES SIX

POTATOES SAVOYARDE

1 small garlic clove, cut in half
75 g/3 oz Gruyère cheese, grated
1 kg/2¼ lb potatoes, thinly sliced
salt and pepper
freshly grated nutmeg
40 g/1½ oz butter
about 375 ml/13 fl oz chicken or vegetable
  stock

Set the oven at 190°C/375°F/gas 5. Rub the cut garlic all over the inside of a 2 litre/3½ pint baking dish. Set aside 30 ml/2 tbsp of the grated cheese.

Put the potatoes into a mixing bowl. Add salt, pepper and a little nutmeg to taste, then mix in the remaining cheese. Use a little of the butter to grease the baking dish generously, add the potato mixture and pour in just enough stock to cover the potatoes.

Dot the remaining butter over the potatoes and sprinkle with the reserved grated cheese. Bake for 1¼ hours or until golden brown and the potatoes are tender.

SERVES SIX

POTATO CROQUETTES

450 g/1 lb potatoes, halved or quartered
25 g/1 oz butter or margarine
2 whole eggs plus 2 egg yolks
salt and pepper
15 ml/1 tbsp chopped parsley
flour for dusting
dried white breadcrumbs for coating
oil for deep frying

Cook the potatoes in boiling water for about 20 minutes until tender. Drain thoroughly and rub through a sieve into a mixing bowl. Beat in the butter or margarine with the egg yolks and add salt and pepper to taste. Add the parsley.

Spread out the flour for dusting in a shallow bowl. Put the whole eggs in a second bowl and beat them lightly with a fork. Spread the breadcrumbs on a plate or sheet of foil.

Form the potato mixture into balls or cylindrical rolls. Coat them first in flour, then in egg and finally in breadcrumbs. Repeat the operation so that they have a double coating, then place them on a baking sheet and chill for 1 hour to firm the mixture.

Heat the oil for deep frying to 180-190°C/350 -375°F or until a cube of bread added to the oil browns in 30 seconds. Fry the potato croquettes, a few at a time, until golden brown. Drain on absorbent kitchen paper and keep the croquettes hot while cooking successive batches.

MAKES TWELVE TO FIFTEEN

VARIATIONS

The basic potato mixture may be used as a base for making a variety of firm-textured croquettes. These are easier to handle in preparation than classic sauce-based croquette mixtures.

Ham Croquettes Add 100 g/4 oz chopped ham to the basic mixture.

Tuna Croquettes Add 100 g/4 oz drained flaked tuna to the basic mixture, with 10 ml/2 tsp finely chopped capers.

Cheese Croquettes Omit the parsley in the basic recipe, if liked, and add 50-100 g/2-4 oz grated Cheddar cheese. Alternatively, use about 25-50 g/1-2 oz Cheddar and 30 ml/2 tbsp grated Parmesan cheese.

Nut Croquettes Add 50 g/2 oz ground almonds to the basic mixture, increasing the amount of liquid by adding a little milk if necessary. Roll the croquettes in a mixture of breadcrumbs and finely chopped blanched almonds.

POTATOES DAUPHINE

575 g/1¼ lb potatoes
salt and pepper
oil for deep frying

CHOUX PASTRY
100 g/4 oz plain flour
pinch of salt
50 g/2 oz butter or margarine
2 whole eggs, plus 1 yolk

Scrub the potatoes, but do not peel them. Steam them or cook in a large saucepan of boiling water for 20–30 minutes, or until tender. Drain, peel and press through a sieve into a mixing bowl. Beat in salt and pepper to taste. Set aside.

Make the choux pastry. Sift the flour and salt on to a sheet of greaseproof paper. Put 250 ml/8 fl oz water in a saucepan and add the butter or margarine. Heat gently until the fat melts. When the fat has melted, bring the liquid rapidly to the boil and add all the flour at once. Immediately remove the pan from the heat and stir the flour into the liquid to make a smooth paste which leaves the sides of the pan clean. Set aside to cool slightly.

Add the egg yolk and beat well. Add the whole eggs, one at a time, beating well after each addition. Continue beating until the paste is very glossy. Add the potato purée to the choux pastry mixture and beat well.

 MRS BEETON'S TIP

Although Potatoes Dauphine are traditionally deep fried, they may also be baked. Using 2 teaspoons, place rounds of the mixture on to greased baking sheets. Bake in a preheated 220°C/425°F/gas 7 oven for 10 minutes, then lower the heat to 180°C/350°F/gas 4 and bake for 20 minutes.

Put the oil for frying into a deep wide saucepan. Heat the oil to 180–190°C/350–375°F or until a cube of bread added to the oil browns in 30 seconds. If using a deep-fat fryer, follow the manufacturer's instructions.

Drop small spoonfuls of the potato mixture, a few at a time, into the hot oil, and cook until they are puffed up and golden brown. Remove from the pan, drain on absorbent kitchen paper and keep hot while cooking successive batches. Serve freshly cooked.

SERVES SIX

SCALLOPED POTATOES WITH ONIONS

fat for greasing
675 g/1½ lb potatoes, peeled and cut into
  5 mm/¼ inch slices
450 g/1 lb onions, sliced in rings
salt and pepper
125 ml/4 fl oz milk or cream
20 ml/4 tsp butter

Grease a baking dish. Set the oven at 190°C/375°F/gas 5. Layer the potatoes and onions in the prepared dish, sprinkling salt and pepper between the layers and ending with potatoes. Pour the milk or cream over the top. Dot the surface with butter and cover with foil or a lid. Bake for 1½ hours, removing the cover for the last 20–30 minutes of the cooking time to allow the potatoes on the top to brown.

SERVES FOUR TO SIX

MRS BEETON'S POTATO RISSOLES

Mrs Beeton suggests that these rissoles may be made very simply, without the onion, or that their flavour may be improved by adding a little chopped cooked tongue or ham.

50 g/2 oz butter
1 large onion, finely chopped
350 g/12 oz hot mashed potato
salt and pepper
10 ml/2 tsp chopped parsley
2 eggs, beaten
75 g/3 oz dried white breadcrumbs
oil for shallow frying

Melt half the butter in a frying pan. Cook the onion, stirring often, until soft but not browned. Season the mashed potato generously, then stir in the parsley and onion with all the butter from the pan. Allow the mixture to cool completely. When cold, shape the mixture into small balls.

Put the beaten egg in a shallow bowl and the breadcrumbs on a plate or sheet of foil. Dip the potato rissoles in the egg, then coat them thoroughly in breadcrumbs. Place them on a baking sheet and chill for 15 minutes to firm the mixture.

Heat the remaining butter with the oil for shallow frying in a deep frying pan. Put in the rissoles and turn them in the hot fat for 6-9 minutes until golden brown all over. Drain on absorbent kitchen paper and serve hot.

MAKES ABOUT TEN

POTATO SOUFFLE

butter for greasing
450 g/1 lb potatoes
salt and pepper
grated nutmeg
100 g/4 oz Cheddar cheese, finely grated
50 g/2 oz butter
125 ml/4 fl oz top-of-the-milk
30 ml/2 tbsp chopped parsley
3 eggs, separated, plus 1 egg white

Grease a 1 litre/1¾ pint soufflé dish. Cook the potatoes in a saucepan of boiling salted water for 20-30 minutes.

Set the oven at 190°C/375°F/gas 5. Mash the potatoes and rub them through a sieve. Add a generous amount of salt, pepper and nutmeg. Stir in the remaining ingredients except the egg whites. Beat well with a wooden spoon until the mixture is smooth.

In a clean, grease-free bowl, whisk all the egg whites until stiff. Using a metal spoon, stir one spoonful of the whites into the potato mixture to lighten it, then fold in the rest until evenly distributed. Spoon the mixture into the prepared dish.

Bake for 30-35 minutes, until well risen and browned. Serve at once.

SERVES FOUR

BAKED JACKET POTATOES

4 large, even-sized baking potatoes
oil for brushing (optional)
butter or flavoured butter, to serve

Set the oven at 200°C/400°F/gas 6. Scrub the potatoes, dry them with absorbent kitchen paper and pierce the skin several times with a skewer. If you like soft jackets, brush the potatoes all over with oil.

Bake the potatoes directly on the oven shelf for 1–1½ hours. Test by pressing gently with the fingers. To serve, cut a cross in the top of each potato with a sharp knife. Squeeze the sides of the potato so that the top opens up. Add a pat of plain or flavoured butter and serve.

SERVES FOUR

FILLINGS

Make a meal of baked jacket potatoes by cutting them in half, scooping out the centres and mashing them with selected ingredients. Pile the fillings back into the potato shells and heat through, if necessary, in a 180°C/350°F/gas 4 oven for about 20 minutes. Alternatively, reheat in the microwave oven or under a moderate grill.

Cheese and Ham Mash the potato. Grate in 100 g/4 oz Cheddar cheese, add 50 g/2 oz chopped ham (use trimmings for economy) and mix with 25 g/1 oz softened butter. Replace in oven until golden.

Kipper Mash the potato with 75 g/3 oz flaked cooked kipper. Add 1 chopped hard-boiled egg, with salt and pepper to taste. Thin with a little milk, if necessary. Reheat.

Frankfurter Mash the potato with butter. For each potato, add 2 heated chopped frankfurters and 15 ml/1 tbsp tomato relish. Add chopped parsley.

TOPPINGS

The easy option. Cut the potatoes almost but not quite in half and open out. Top with any of the mixtures suggested below.

Blue Cheese and Yogurt Mash 100 g/4 oz ripe Danish blue cheese. Mix with 150 ml/¼ pint Greek yogurt.

Sausage and Chutney Mix hot or cold sliced cooked sausage with diced eating apple, chopped spring onions and a little of your favourite chutney.

Egg Mayonnaise Mash hard-boiled eggs with a little mayonnaise or plain yogurt. Add 5 ml/1 tsp tomato ketchup or tomato purée and some snipped chives.

Sardine Mash canned sardines in tomato sauce and mix with diced cucumber. Serve with shredded lettuce.

Chick-pea Mash 100 g/4 oz drained canned chick-peas. Mix with 1 crushed garlic clove and 15–30 ml/1–2 tbsp Greek yogurt. Top with chopped spring onion and sesame seeds.

Cheese Soufflé Combine 100 g/4 oz grated Cheddar cheese and 1 beaten egg. Cut potatoes in half, pile some of the mixture on each half and grill until topping puffs up and turns golden brown.

Peas and Bacon Combine 100 g/4 oz cooked petits pois and 3 crumbled grilled rindless bacon rashers. Top with a knob of butter.

Broccoli and Asparagus Mix 175 g/6 oz cooked broccoli and 100 g/4 oz drained canned asparagus tips. Stir in 150 ml/¼ pint soured cream, with salt and pepper to taste.

Southern Special Warm 100–150 g/4–5 oz creamed sweetcorn. Spoon on to potatoes. Top each portion with 2 grilled rindless bacon rashers and 3–4 banana slices.

 MICROWAVE TIP

Cooking jacket potatoes in the microwave has practically become a national pastime. Prick the potatoes several times with a skewer or they may burst. Cook directly on the microwave rack or wrap in absorbent kitchen paper if a very soft potato is preferred. For crisper potatoes, brush with oil or butter after microwave cooking, then crisp under a hot grill, turning once. Jacket potatoes also cook extremely well in a combination microwave oven. Follow the instructions in your handbook.

MICROWAVE COOKING TIMES ON HIGH (600–650 WATT OVENS)

Large potatoes (350 g/12 oz)

1 potato	8 minutes
2 potatoes	15 minutes
4 potatoes	27 minutes

Medium potatoes (150 g/5 oz)

1 potato	4 minutes
2 potatoes	5–6 minutes
4 potatoes	10 minutes
6 potatoes	18–19 minutes

ITALIAN SPINACH

25 g/1 oz sultanas
1 kg/2¼ lb spinach
30 ml/2 tbsp oil
1 garlic clove, crushed
salt and pepper
25 g/1 oz pine nuts

Put the sultanas in a small bowl or mug, pour on boiling water to cover and set aside for 2–3 minutes until plumped. Drain well and set the sultanas aside.

Wash the fresh spinach several times and remove any coarse stalks. Put into a saucepan with just the water that clings to the leaves, then cover the pan. Put the pan over high heat for 2–3 minutes, shaking it frequently. Lower the heat, stir the spinach and cook for a further 5 minutes, turning the spinach occasionally, until cooked to your liking. Drain thoroughly, then chop the spinach coarsely.

Heat the oil in a large frying pan. Add the spinach and garlic, with salt and pepper to taste. Turn the spinach over and over in the pan with a wide spatula to heat it thoroughly without frying. Turn into a heated serving bowl, add the sultanas and nuts and mix lightly. Serve at once.

SERVES FOUR

 MRS BEETON'S TIP

Pine nuts – or pine kernels as they are sometimes known – are produced inside the cones of a pine tree that grows in North America and in the southern Mediterranean. White and waxy in appearance, they are used extensively in the cooking of the Middle East and are also an important ingredient in the Italian sauce, *pesto*.

RATATOUILLE

Traditionally, the vegetable mixture is cooked gently for about 45–60 minutes and it is richer, and more intensely flavoured if prepared ahead, cooled and thoroughly reheated. This recipe suggests cooking for slightly less time, so that the courgettes and aubergines still retain a bit of bite; the final simmering time may be shortened, if liked, to give a mixture in which the courgettes contribute a slightly crunchy texture.

2 aubergines
salt and pepper
125–150 ml/4–5 fl oz olive oil
2 large onions, finely chopped
2 garlic cloves, crushed
2 peppers, seeded and cut into thin strips
30 ml/2 tbsp chopped fresh marjoram or
    10 ml/2 tsp dried marjoram
450 g/1 lb tomatoes, peeled and chopped
4 courgettes, thinly sliced
30 ml/2 tbsp finely chopped parsley or mint

Cut the ends off the aubergines and cut them into cubes. Put the cubes in a colander and sprinkle generously with salt. Set aside for 30 minutes, then rinse thoroughly, drain and pat dry on absorbent kitchen paper.

Heat some of the oil in a large saucepan or flameproof casserole, add some of the aubergine cubes and cook over moderate heat, stirring frequently, for 10 minutes. Using a slotted spoon, transfer the aubergine to a bowl; repeat until all the cubes are cooked, adding more oil as necessary. Add the onions to the oil remaining in the pan and fry for 5 minutes, until slightly softened. Stir in the garlic, peppers and marjoram, with salt and pepper to taste. Cook, stirring occasionally for 15–20 minutes, or until the onions are thoroughly softened.

Stir the tomatoes and courgettes into the vegetable mixture. Replace the aubergines, heat until bubbling, then cover and simmer for a further 15–20 minutes, stirring occasionally. Serve hot, sprinkled with parsley, or cold, sprinkled with mint.

SERVES FOUR TO SIX

MIXED VEGETABLE CASSEROLE

45 ml/3 tbsp oil
2 onions, finely chopped
2 garlic cloves, crushed
4 rindless streaky bacon rashers, diced
2 celery sticks, chopped
1 green pepper, seeded and diced
1 small red pepper, seeded and diced
45 ml/3 tbsp tomato purée
750 ml/1¼ pints chicken stock
salt and pepper
1 kg/2¼ lb potatoes, quartered
225 g/8 oz tomatoes, seeded and roughly
    chopped
15 ml/1 tbsp chopped mixed fresh herbs
150 g/5 oz Parmesan cheese, grated

Heat the oil in a flameproof casserole, add the onion, garlic and bacon and fry over gentle heat for 4–6 minutes until the vegetables are soft but not coloured. Add the celery and peppers and cook, stirring occasionally, for 5 minutes more.

Stir the tomato purée and stock into the pan, with salt and pepper to taste. Bring to the boil and add the potatoes, tomatoes and herbs. Mix well. Lower the heat and cover the casserole.

Cook gently for 20–30 minutes, or until the potatoes are tender but not mushy. Sprinkle the cheese on top and brown under a preheated grill. Serve at once.

SERVES SIX

VEGETABLE CHILLI

1 large aubergine, trimmed and cut into
  2.5 cm/1 inch cubes
salt and pepper
60 ml/4 tbsp oil
1 large onion, chopped
4 celery sticks, sliced
1 green pepper, seeded and chopped
2 garlic cloves, crushed
1 large potato, cut into 2.5 cm/1 inch cubes
1 large carrot, diced
5–10 ml/1–2 tsp chilli powder
15 ml/1 tbsp ground coriander
15 ml/1 tbsp ground cumin
100 g/4 oz mushrooms, sliced
2 (397 g/14 oz) cans chopped tomatoes
2 (425 g/15 oz) cans red kidney beans,
  drained
2 courgettes, halved lengthways and cut
  into chunks
100 g/4 oz frozen cut green beans or peas

Place the aubergine cubes in a colander, sprinkling each layer with salt. Stand the colander over a bowl or in the sink and leave for 30 minutes. Rinse the aubergine and dry the cubes on absorbent kitchen paper.

Heat the oil and fry the onion, celery, pepper and garlic until the onion is slightly softened. Stir in the aubergine and cook, stirring, until the outside of the cubes are lightly cooked. Stir in the potato, carrot, chilli, coriander and cumin. Stir for a few minutes to coat all the vegetables in the spices, then lightly mix in the mushrooms and tomatoes. Bring to the boil, lower the heat so that the mixture simmers and cover. Cook, stirring occasionally, for 30 minutes.

Add the kidney beans, courgettes, beans or peas, with salt and pepper to taste. Cover and continue to cook for a further 30 minutes, stirring occasionally, or until all the vegetables are tender. The juice from the vegetables, combined with the canned tomatoes, should be sufficient to keep the mixture moist. If the mixture cooks too quickly the liquid will evaporate and the vegetables may stick to the pan.

SERVES FOUR

WINTER VEGETABLE CASSEROLE

This simple casserole may be simmered very slowly on the hob, if preferred.

50 g/2 oz butter
30 ml/2 tbsp oil
2 onions, sliced
1 garlic clove, crushed (optional)
2 leeks, trimmed, sliced and washed
225 g/8 oz swede, cubed
100 g/4 oz turnip, cubed
3 carrots, sliced
100 g/4 oz mushrooms, sliced
100 g/4 oz pearl barley, washed
5 ml/1 tsp dried thyme
1 bay leaf
salt and pepper
450 ml/¾ pint vegetable stock
30 ml/2 tbsp chopped parsley to garnish

Set the oven at 180°C/350°F/gas 4. Melt the butter in the oil in a large flameproof casserole. Add the onions, garlic, leeks, swede, turnip and carrots and fry for about 10 minutes, stirring frequently.

Stir in the mushrooms, barley, thyme and bay leaf, with plenty of salt and pepper. Pour in the stock. Cover the casserole and transfer it to the oven. Bake for 1–1½ hours until all the vegetables are cooked and the barley is tender. Fluff up the grains with a fork, sprinkle the parsley over the top and serve at once.

SERVES FOUR

Salads

Crisp and refreshing or full-flavoured and satisfying, salads play many roles in the modern menu.
The section on Vegetable Dishes includes a guide to lettuce varieties and other salad vegetables, while this
chapter provides traditional and contemporary recipes for all meal occasions.

The British attitude to salad has changed enormously over the past century or more. In Mrs Beeton's day, the dish was likely to consist of the few raw vegetables that were cultivated in summer and cold cooked root vegetables in winter. Raw vegetables were considered to be indigestible and unsuitable for consumption in quantity, certainly not for anyone of a delicate digestive disposition. Although lettuce was used in season for dainty luncheon dishes, cooked vegetables, such as potatoes, celery, beans and potatoes, were preferred.

Today an excellent choice of salad leaves and vegetables is available in most supermarkets throughout the year. Recipes are more adventurous than ever before; salads are interesting and satisfying to eat and they play an essential role in a healthy, balanced diet.

TOSSING AN EXCELLENT SALAD

- Ingredients both raw and cooked must be fresh and in prime condition.
- Select ingredients which complement each other in flavour and texture.
- Do not use so many ingredients that the salad ends up as a kaleidoscope of unrecognizable, clashing flavours.
- Ingredients such as cut beetroot, which discolour or shed colour, should be prepared and added just before serving.
- Salads, salad leaves and greens which become limp quickly should be dressed at the last minute.

- The salad dressing should moisten, blend and develop the flavour of the main ingredients. It should not dominate the dish in any way.

SIDE SALADS

If the salad is served to accompany a main food, for example as a garnish for a starter or to complement a main course dish, choose ingredients and a dressing which complement the main food. Side salads should be simple, with clearly defined flavours and a light dressing.

Plain Green Salad Do not underestimate the value of a good, crisp, really fresh lettuce lightly tossed with a well-seasoned, oil-based dressing. This makes an ideal accompaniment for grilled fish, meat or poultry, or may be served with the cheese course. This classic green salad accentuates the richness of the main dish and refreshes the palate.

Mixed Green Salad This should consist of green ingredients, for example salad leaves, cucumber, green pepper, celery, spring onions, watercress, mustard and cress, and avocado. These flavours go together well; a mixed green salad is ideal for serving with foods such as a quiche, with baked potatoes (topped with low-fat soft cheese, butter, soured cream or fromage frais) and with cold roast meats or grilled pork sausages.

Mixed Salad This type of side salad usually consists of a base of leaves, with other green ingredients, topped with raw items, such as tomatoes, radishes and red or yellow peppers. A mixed salad goes well with cold meats and poultry, cheese or eggs. The ingredients should complement the main dish – grated carrots, shredded cabbage and beetroot may replace some of the other basic ingredients.

Satisfying Side Salads Pasta, rice, beans, grains and potatoes all make good salads, and do not have to be mixed with a cornucopia of ingredients. They should be perfectly cooked, then tossed with selected herbs, such as parsley, mint, basil or tarragon. Additional ingredients should be kept to the minimum: chopped spring onions, diced tomato, and/or chopped olives perhaps. In keeping with the main dish, mayonnaise, yogurt, fromage frais, soured cream or an oil-based mixture may be used to dress the salad.

MAIN COURSE SALADS

Fish and seafood, poultry, meat, game and dairy produce all make excellent salads. Beans and pulses are also suitable. The main food should feature in the same way as for a hot dish, with supporting ingredients and a full-flavoured dressing. It should stand out clearly as the star of the salad, without competition from other ingredients. The salad may be served on a base of shredded lettuce and a garnish of herbs, nuts or croûtons of fried bread may be included to balance the texture where necessary. Main course salads often have very plain accompaniments – chunks of crusty bread (or a baked potato for larger appetites) are usually all that is required.

MARINATED HERRING

3 salted herrings, cleaned

MARINADE
2 onions, chopped
12 bay leaves
30 ml/2 tbsp caster sugar
60 ml/4 tbsp distilled vinegar (see Mrs Beeton's Tip)
45 ml/3 tbsp tomato purée

Pat the herrings dry with absorbent kitchen paper. Lay them in a shallow glass or enamel bowl. Pour over cold water to cover, then cover the bowl tightly. Set aside for 6 hours in a cold place.

Make the marinade by combining all the ingredients in a large shallow dish. Add 15 ml/1 tbsp water and mix well.

Drain the herrings and pat dry with absorbent kitchen paper. Cut them into small pieces, discarding the bones. Add the herring pieces to the marinade and mix well. Cover the dish and marinate for 48 hours, stirring several times.

SERVES SIX

 MRS BEETON'S TIP

Vinegars vary considerably in the percentage of acetic acid they contain. Malt and cider vinegars are milder than wine vinegars. The strongest vinegars are labelled fortified or distilled. Distilled vinegar is usually made from malt. It is colourless. If you find it difficult to obtain, use pickling vinegar instead.

MACKEREL SALAD

500 ml/17 fl oz Court Bouillon (page 174)
8 mackerel fillets, cleaned
45 ml/3 tbsp cider vinegar
15 ml/1 tbsp gelatine
75 ml/5 tbsp mayonnaise

GARNISH
fresh tarragon, chervil or parsley sprigs
tomato wedges
watercress sprigs

Bring the court bouillon to simmering point in a saucepan, add the mackerel and poach gently for 15 minutes. Using a slotted spoon, transfer the fish to a wooden board. When cool enough to handle, remove the skin neatly, then leave until cold.

Meanwhile place the vinegar in a small bowl and sprinkle the gelatine on to the liquid. Set aside for 15 minutes until the gelatine is spongy. Stand the bowl over a saucepan of hot water and stir the gelatine until it has dissolved completely. Alternatively, dissolve the gelatine in the microwave. Mix with the mayonnaise and chill until on the point of setting.

Arrange the mackerel fillets, skinned side up, on a serving dish. Coat each fish with the semi-set mayonnaise and garnish with fresh herb sprigs, tomato wedges and watercress.

SERVES FOUR

CAMARGUE MUSSELS

2 kg/4½ lb mussels
1 onion, sliced
2 garlic cloves, cut in slivers
1 carrot, sliced
1 celery stick, sliced
1 bouquet garni
125 ml/4 fl oz white wine
chopped parsley to garnish

MAYONNAISE
1 egg yolk
5 ml/1 tsp French mustard
salt · cayenne
5 ml/1 tsp white wine vinegar
100 ml/3½ fl oz sunflower oil
20 ml/4 tsp lemon juice

Wash, scrape and beard the mussels following the instructions on page 117. Put them in a large saucepan. Tuck the sliced vegetables among the mussels and add the bouquet garni.

Pour over the wine and add 125 ml/4 fl oz water. Place the pan over moderate heat and bring to the boil. As soon as the liquid bubbles up over the mussels, shake the pan several times, cover, lower the heat and simmer until the mussels have opened. Discard any that remain shut. With a slotted spoon remove the mussels from the stock. Arrange them, on their half shells, on a large flat dish. Strain the cooking liquid into a jug and set aside to cool.

Make the mayonnaise. Blend the egg yolk, mustard, salt, cayenne and vinegar in a bowl. Using a balloon whisk, beat in the oil very gradually, drop by drop. When about half the oil has been added and the mixture looks thick and shiny, add the rest of the oil in a slow thin stream. Stir in the lemon juice and cooking liquid. Spoon the mayonnaise over the mussels and sprinkle with parsley. Serve chilled.

SERVES FIVE TO SIX

SHRIMP OR PRAWN SALAD

½ cucumber
5 ml/1 tsp salt
2 lettuce hearts or 1 Iceberg lettuce, finely
  shredded
60 ml/4 tbsp mayonnaise
30 ml/2 tbsp plain yogurt
225 g/8 oz peeled cooked shrimps or prawns
2 hard-boiled eggs, halved or sliced
  lengthways
black pepper

Slice the unpeeled cucumber thinly. Put the slices in a colander, sprinkle over the salt and leave for 30 minutes to drain. Rinse the cucumber slices, drain well, then pat dry with absorbent kitchen paper. Use the slices to line a glass salad bowl.

Lay the lettuce in the lined bowl. Sprinkle lightly with salt. Mix the mayonnaise and yogurt in a bowl, then spoon the mixture over the lettuce. Pile the shrimps or prawns in the centre of the dish with the hard-boiled egg halves or slices in a circle around them. Grind black pepper over the egg slices just before serving the salad.

SERVES FOUR

 MRS BEETON'S TIP

Place the cucumber slices side by side, just touching but not overlapping. A layer of radish slices may be added.

CRAB AND MANDARIN SALAD

50 g/2 oz shelled whole walnuts or walnut
  halves
400 g/14 oz drained canned or thawed frozen
  crab meat
75 g/3 oz celery, sliced
100 g/4 oz drained canned mandarin
  segments
1 lettuce, separated into leaves

DRESSING
50 g/2 oz blue cheese
125 ml/4 fl oz soured cream
2.5 ml/½ tsp grated lemon rind
salt and pepper
75 ml/5 tbsp sunflower oil
20 ml/4 tsp lemon juice

Make the dressing. Crumble the cheese into a bowl. Gradually work in the soured cream until smooth. Add the remaining ingredients and whisk until completely blended. Pour into a jug, cover and chill.

Set half the walnuts aside to use as a garnish. Chop the remaining walnuts finely and place them in a large bowl. Add the crab meat, celery and mandarin orange segments. Toss lightly, breaking up any large pieces of crab meat with a fork.

Arrange the lettuce leaves on a flat salad platter. Pile the crab mixture in the centre. Trickle a little of the dressing over the crab mixture and garnish with the reserved walnuts. Serve the rest of the dressing separately.

SERVES FOUR

SEA BREAM MAYONNAISE

Sea bream is not one of the most common fish but it is caught around the British coast. As well as the dark-skinned fish (black bream or sea bream), there is a red-skinned variety known as red sea bream.

butter for greasing
575 g/1¼ lb red sea bream fillets, skinned
lemon juice
salt and pepper
125 ml/4 fl oz mayonnaise
1 hard-boiled egg, chopped
10 ml/2 tsp chopped parsley
8 lettuce leaves
tomato wedges to garnish

Grease a shallow ovenproof dish. Set the oven at 190°C/375°F/gas 5. Arrange the fish fillets in the dish, sprinkle with lemon juice, salt and pepper and cover loosely with greaseproof paper. Bake for 20 minutes. Flake the fish with a fork, remove any bones and leave to cool.

Mix the mayonnaise, hard-boiled egg and parsley lightly in a bowl. Stir in the cold flaked fish. Spread out the lettuce leaves on a flat salad platter, top with the fish mixture and garnish with the tomato wedges. Serve.

SERVES FOUR

 MRS BEETON'S TIP

White fish is underrated as a salad ingredient, yet it can produce excellent results. Always use fresh fish which is freshly cooked and cooled; never overcook the fish. Cod, hake and haddock may all be used for salads.

SALAD NICOISE

salt and pepper
225 g/8 oz French beans, topped and tailed
2 hard-boiled eggs, cut in quarters
3 small tomatoes, cut in quarters
1 garlic clove, crushed
1 (198 g/7 oz) can tuna, drained and flaked
50 g/2 oz black olives
1 large lettuce, separated into leaves
1 (50 g/2 oz) can anchovy fillets, drained, to garnish

DRESSING
45 ml/3 tbsp olive oil or a mixture of olive and sunflower oil
salt and pepper
pinch of English mustard powder
pinch of caster sugar
15 ml/1 tbsp wine vinegar

Bring a small saucepan of salted water to the boil. Add the beans and cook for 5-10 minutes or until just tender. Drain, refresh under cold water and drain again.

Make the dressing by mixing all the ingredients in a screw-topped jar. Close the jar tightly; shake vigorously until well blended.

Put the beans into a large bowl with the eggs, tomatoes, garlic, tuna and most of the olives. Pour over the dressing and toss lightly. Add salt and pepper to taste.

Line a large salad bowl with the lettuce leaves. Pile the tuna mixture into the centre and garnish with the remaining olives and the anchovy fillets. Serve at once.

SERVES FOUR TO SIX

BEAN SALAD WITH TUNA

450 g/1 lb dry flageolet beans, soaked
  overnight in water to cover
150 g/5 oz tomatoes, peeled, seeded and
  chopped
2 spring onions, finely chopped
1 (198 g/7 oz) can tuna, drained and flaked

DRESSING
90 ml/6 tbsp sunflower oil
45 ml/3 tbsp white wine vinegar
1 garlic clove, crushed
15 ml/1 tbsp chopped parsley

Drain the beans and put them into a saucepan
with fresh cold water to cover. Boil briskly for
at least 10 minutes, then lower the heat and
simmer for about 1 hour or until tender.

Meanwhile make the dressing by mixing all
the ingredients in a screw-topped jar. Close the
jar tightly; shake vigorously until well blended.

Drain the beans and put them in a bowl. Add
the tomatoes, spring onions and tuna and mix
well. Pour the cold dressing over the hot beans
and the other ingredients and serve at once on
small warmed plates.

SERVES FOUR

 MRS BEETON'S TIP

A variety of beans may be combined with
tuna: haricot, borlotti, butter and red kidney beans are all suitable. Remember that
canned beans are excellent for speedy,
highly successful salads.

SEAFOOD SALAD

*The cod fillet must be fresh, firm and of excellent
quality if the salad is to be first rate.*

450 g/1 lb cod fillet, skinned
30 ml/2 tbsp lemon juice
2.5 ml/½ tsp sugar
salt and pepper
75 ml/5 tbsp olive oil or other salad oil
15 ml/1 tbsp chopped capers
30 ml/2 tbsp chopped spring onion
225 g/8 oz peeled cooked prawns, thawed if
  frozen
100 g/4 oz shelled freshly cooked mussels
4 ripe tomatoes, peeled and diced
30 ml/2 tbsp chopped parsley
1 courgette, diced
¼ Iceberg lettuce, shredded

Steam the cod between two plates over a
saucepan of boiling water for 10–15 minutes,
until the flesh is firm and white but still moist.

While the fish is cooking, place the lemon juice
in a bowl. Whisk in the sugar, with salt and
pepper to taste. When the sugar and salt have
dissolved, whisk in the oil. Stir in the capers
and chopped spring onion.

Flake the cod into large pieces, discarding all
skin and bones.

Place in a dish and pour the dressing over. Add
the prawns, mussels, tomatoes and parsley,
then mix lightly, taking care not to break up the
cod flakes.

Toss the courgette and lettuce together and
arrange on four plates. Top with the seafood
mixture and serve at once, with hot fresh toast,
Melba toast or crusty bread.

SERVES FOUR

VEAL AND TUNA SALAD

1.8 kg/4 lb fillet of veal
1 carrot, cut into quarters
1 small onion, cut into quarters
1 celery stick, roughly chopped
4 black peppercorns
5 ml/1 tsp salt

SAUCE
1 (198 g/7 oz) can tuna, drained
4 anchovy fillets
125 ml/4 fl oz olive oil
2 egg yolks
black pepper
15–30 ml/1–2 tbsp lemon juice

GARNISH
capers
sliced gherkins
fresh tarragon (optional)

Trim the veal. Tie it into a neat shape, if necessary. Place in a large saucepan with the carrot, onion, celery, peppercorns and salt. Pour over enough water to cover the meat. Bring to the boil, lower the heat, cover the pan and simmer for 1½ hours or until the meat is very tender. Carefully lift it out of the liquid and set it aside on a plate to cool. Boil the cooking liquid quickly to reduce it by half, strain through a fine sieve and reserve.

Make the sauce. Put the tuna in a bowl with the anchovies. Add 15 ml/1 tbsp of the oil. Pound to a smooth paste by hand or use a blender or food processor. Blend in the egg yolks and season with pepper. Add half the lemon juice, then gradually add the remaining oil, as when making mayonnaise. When the sauce is thick and shiny, add more lemon juice to taste. Stir in about 30 ml/2 tbsp of the reserved cooking liquid from the veal to make a thin coating sauce.

Cut the cold veal into thin slices and arrange them in a dish. Coat completely with the sauce, then cover the dish and refrigerate for up to 24 hours. Before serving, garnish with capers, sliced gherkins and fresh tarragon, if liked.

SERVES SIX

HALIBUT, ORANGE AND WATERCRESS SALAD

600 ml/1 pint Court Bouillon (page 122)
4–6 halibut steaks
8 large lettuce leaves, shredded
125 ml/4 fl oz mayonnaise

GARNISH
orange slices
watercress sprigs

Bring the court bouillon to simmering point in a large saucepan. Add the halibut steaks and poach gently for 7–10 minutes until cooked. Using a slotted spoon transfer the fish to a plate and leave to cool. Remove the skin.

Arrange most of the shredded lettuce on a flat salad platter. Coat the fish in mayonnaise and arrange it on the lettuce. Garnish with orange slices, watercress and the remaining lettuce.

SERVES FOUR TO SIX

MRS BEETON'S TIP

Do not discard the remaining veal cooking liquid, Use it as the basis of a soup or sauce.

CHICKEN AND CELERY SALAD

1 large lettuce, separated into leaves
1 celery heart
350g/12oz cooked chicken, cut into serving
  pieces
10ml/2tsp tarragon or white wine vinegar
salt and pepper
150ml/¼ pint mayonnaise

GARNISH
lettuce leaves
2 hard-boiled eggs, sliced or chopped
stoned black olives and/or gherkin strips

Wash the lettuce leaves and dry them thoroughly. Shred the outer leaves with the celery. Put in a bowl with the chicken and vinegar. Toss lightly and add salt and pepper to taste.

Spoon the chicken mixture into a bowl or on to a platter. Coat with the mayonnaise. Garnish with lettuce leaves, sliced or chopped egg and olives and/or gherkin strips.

SERVES SIX

VARIATION

If preferred, keep the lettuce heart as a base for the chicken and celery mixture. For a substantial, meal-in-one salad, toss in some cooked pasta shapes or cooked rice.

PORK AND SALAMI SALAD

1 lettuce, separated into leaves
200g/7oz cold roast pork, diced
200g/7oz cold boiled potatoes, diced
100g/4oz boiled beetroot, diced
2-3 gherkins, sliced
15ml/1tbsp capers
salt and pepper
100ml/3½fl oz mayonnaise
12 slices of salami
1 lemon, sliced
12 stoned green olives to garnish

Wash the lettuce leaves and dry them thoroughly. Use them to line a salad bowl. Mix the pork, potatoes, beetroot, gherkins and capers lightly. Add salt and pepper to taste. Then pile the mixture into the lined bowl.

Pour the mayonnaise over the top, and arrange alternate slices of salami and lemon around the rim. If the salami is sliced thinly, roll each slice into a neat cone shape; alternatively, overlap the slices as they are arranged flat. Garnish with the olives. Serve at once.

SERVES FOUR

 MRS BEETON'S TIP

It has to be said that the quality of salami varies enormously. Luckily, there is a good choice of well-flavoured salami but the lurid, soft and fatty types are best avoided. Ask for salami to be sliced very thinly.

FRENCH BEAN AND TOMATO SALAD

salt and pepper
225 g/8 oz French beans, trimmed
3 tomatoes, peeled, seeded and quartered
15 ml/1 tsp snipped chives

DRESSING
45 ml/3 tbsp walnut or sunflower oil
10 ml/2 tsp white wine vinegar
5 ml/1 tsp lemon juice
pinch of caster sugar
pinch of mustard powder
1 garlic clove, crushed

Make the dressing by mixing all the ingredients in a screw-topped jar. Add salt and pepper to taste, close the jar tightly and shake vigorously until well blended.

Bring a small saucepan of salted water to the boil. Add the beans and cook for 5-10 minutes or until just tender. Drain, rinse briefly under cold water, drain again, then tip into a bowl. Immediately add the dressing and toss the beans in it. Leave to cool.

Add the tomatoes and toss lightly. Taste the salad and add more salt and pepper if required. Turn into a salad bowl, sprinkle with the chives and serve.

SERVES FOUR

 MICROWAVE TIP

Wash the beans. Drain lightly, leaving some moisture on the pods. Place them in a roasting bag, tie the top loosely with an elastic band and microwave on High for 5 minutes. Shake the bag carefully, set it aside for 1 minute, then transfer the contents to a bowl and add the dressing and remaining ingredients.

BEETROOT AND CELERY SALAD

450 g/1 lb cooked beetroot
1 celery heart
2 green-skinned eating apples
50 g/2 oz walnuts, roughly chopped
15 ml/1 tbsp chopped parsley
watercress to garnish

DRESSING
30 ml/2 tbsp olive or sunflower oil
15 ml/1 tbsp cider vinegar
pinch of mustard powder
1.25 ml/¼ tsp brown sugar
salt and pepper

Peel the beetroot and cut a few neat rounds for the garnish. Dice the rest neatly. Use one stick of the celery to make curls (see Mrs Beeton's Tip) and chop the rest.

Mix the dressing ingredients together in a screw-topped jar. Close tightly and shake well. Quarter, core and dice the apples and put them in a salad bowl. Add the dressing, tossing the apples to prevent discoloration. Add the beetroot, celery, walnuts and parsley. Toss lightly.

Pile the salad into a serving dish and garnish with the reserved beetroot rounds, the celery curls and watercress.

SERVES SIX

 MRS BEETON'S TIP

The easiest way to make celery curls is to cut the celery stick into 7.5 cm/3 inch pieces. Make thin slits in each piece, almost to the end, then place in iced water until the ends curl up. Drain well.

FLEMISH WINTER SALAD

450 g/1 lb cooked potatoes, sliced
350 g/12 oz cooked beetroot, sliced
60 ml/4 tbsp French dressing (page 470)
1 (50 g/2 oz) can anchovy fillets
2 radishes, sliced
dill sprigs to garnish

Layer the potatoes and beetroot in a glass bowl, sprinkling each layer with a little of the French dressing, and ending with a layer of potatoes. Arrange a lattice of anchovy fillets on top of the salad, filling each square with a slice of radish. Garnish with dill sprigs.

SERVES SIX

VARIATION

Reduce the quantities of potatoes and beetroot to 225 g/8 oz each. Add 1 red-skinned and 1 green-skinned eating apple, diced but not peeled. Toss these ingredients with the French dressing.

BEAN SPROUT SALAD

225 g/8 oz bean sprouts
1 small orange, peeled and sliced
100 g/4 oz Chinese leaves, shredded
2 celery sticks, thinly sliced
salt and pepper

DRESSING
45 ml/3 tbsp olive oil or a mixture of olive
    and sunflower oil
15 ml/1 tbsp white wine vinegar
1 garlic clove, crushed
2.5 ml/½ tsp soy sauce
pinch of caster sugar

Pick over the bean sprouts, wash them well, then dry. Cut the orange slices into quarters.

Make the dressing by mixing all the ingredients in a screw-topped jar. Close the jar tightly and shake vigorously.

Combine the bean sprouts, Chinese leaves, celery and orange in a bowl. Pour over the dressing and toss lightly. Season to taste and serve at once.

SERVES FOUR

 MRS BEETON'S TIP

Bean sprouts are highly nutritious. To grow your own, place dried soya beans, mung beans or alfalfa seeds in a clean glass jar. The jar should be no more than one-sixth full. Cover the jar with a piece of muslin held in place by an elastic band. Fill the jar with cold water, then drain off the liquid. Store in a cool dark place. Rinse the beans in fresh water every day. They should start to sprout in 2–3 days and will be ready to eat in 5–6 days.

COLESLAW

Coleslaw looks marvellous in a natural cabbage bowl. Use a sharp knife to cut out the centre of a Savoy cabbage, using the cut portion for the coleslaw. Rinse the cabbage bowl under cold water, shake off excess moisture and dry between the leaves with absorbent kitchen paper. Trim the base of the cabbage bowl so that it stands neatly.

450 g/1 lb firm white or Savoy cabbage,
  finely shredded
100 g/4 oz carrots, coarsely grated
2 celery sticks, thinly sliced
½ small green pepper, seeded and thinly
  sliced
150 ml/¼ pint mayonnaise or plain yogurt
salt and pepper
lemon juice (see method)

Mix all the ingredients in a salad bowl, adding enough lemon juice to give the mayonnaise or yogurt a tangy taste. Chill before serving.

SERVES FOUR

VARIATION

Fruit and Nut Slaw Core and dice, but do not peel, 1 red-skinned eating apple. Toss in 15 ml/1 tbsp lemon juice, then add to the slaw with 25 g/1 oz seedless raisins or sultanas and 25 g/1 oz chopped walnuts, almonds or hazelnuts.

CABBAGE CRUNCH

100 g/4 oz white cabbage, shredded
225 g/8 oz red cabbage, shredded
4 celery sticks, chopped
2 carrots, cut into matchsticks
1 green pepper, seeded and thinly sliced
4 ready-to-eat dried apricots, thinly sliced
100 g/4 oz pecan nuts or walnuts, chopped
50 g/2 oz sunflower seeds

DRESSING
1 hard-boiled egg yolk
salt and pepper
1.25 ml/¼ tsp prepared mustard
dash of Worcestershire sauce
pinch of caster sugar
10 ml/2 tsp cider vinegar
15 ml/1 tbsp sunflower oil
30 ml/2 tbsp double cream

Make the dressing. Sieve the egg yolk into a bowl. Gradually work in the salt and pepper, mustard, Worcestershire sauce, caster sugar and vinegar. Add the oil gradually, beating constantly. Whip the cream in a clean bowl, then fold it into the dressing. Mix all the salad ingredients and toss in the dressing.

SERVES SIX

 MRS BEETON'S TIP

Remember that full-flavoured, firm-textured salads like Coleslaw and Cabbage Crunch make excellent fillings for piping-hot baked potatoes. Not only does the flavour of the salad complement potatoes but the textures also marry well.

GRAPEFRUIT AND CHICORY SALAD

3 grapefruit
3 small heads of chicory
50 g/2 oz seedless raisins
15 ml/1 tbsp grapefruit juice
45 ml/3 tbsp oil
2.5 ml/½ tsp French mustard
salt and pepper
mustard and cress to garnish

Cut the grapefruit in half. Cut the fruit into segments and put them into a bowl. Remove all the pulp and pith from the grapefruit shells; stand the shells upside down on absorbent kitchen paper to drain. Shred the chicory, reserving some neat rounds for the garnish, and add to the grapefruit segments with all the remaining ingredients except the garnish. Toss the mixture lightly together, then pile back into the grapefruit shells. Garnish with the cress and reserved chicory and serve at once.

SERVES SIX

CELERY AND CHESTNUT SALAD

1 small lettuce, separated into leaves
225 g/8 oz cooked chestnuts, halved or
    quartered
6 celery sticks, finely chopped
1 eating apple
100 ml/3½ fl oz mayonnaise

Wash the lettuce leaves and dry them thoroughly. Line a salad bowl. Put the chestnuts in a bowl with the celery. Peel, core and dice the apple and add it to the bowl with the mayonnaise. Mix well. Pile the celery mixture into the lettuce-lined bowl. Serve at once.

SERVES FOUR

FENNEL AND CUCUMBER SALAD

½ large cucumber, diced
6 radishes, sliced
1 fennel bulb, sliced
1 garlic clove, crushed
5 ml/1 tsp chopped mint
2 eggs, hard-boiled and quartered, to
    garnish

DRESSING
30 ml/2 tbsp olive oil
15 ml/1 tbsp lemon juice
salt and pepper

Combine the cucumber, radishes, fennel and garlic in a salad bowl. Sprinkle with the mint. Make the dressing by shaking all the ingredients in a tightly-closed screw-topped jar. Pour over the salad, toss lightly and serve with the hard-boiled egg garnish.

SERVES SIX

RUSSIAN CUCUMBER SALAD

4 hard-boiled egg yolks
250 ml/8 fl oz soured cream
few drops of vinegar
1 large cucumber, chilled
salt and pepper
dill sprigs to garnish

Sieve the egg yolks into a bowl, stir in the cream and vinegar and mix well. Chill for 30 minutes. Dice the cucumber, pat it dry with absorbent kitchen paper and place in a dish. Season well, stir in the cream mixture. Garnish and serve.

SERVES FOUR

CUCUMBER IN YOGURT

1 large cucumber
salt and pepper
300 ml/½ pint plain or Greek strained
 yogurt, chilled
15 ml/1 tsp vinegar (optional)
30 ml/2 tbsp chopped mint
pinch of sugar

Cut the cucumber into small dice and place it in a colander. Sprinkle with salt, leave for 3-4 hours, then rinse and drain thoroughly. Pat the cucumber dry on absorbent kitchen paper.

Stir the yogurt, vinegar (if used), mint and sugar together in a bowl. Add the cucumber and mix well. Taste and add salt and pepper if required.

SERVES FOUR TO SIX

VARIATION

Tzatziki The combination of cucumber and yogurt is an Internationally popular one. This is a Greek-style variation. Grate the cucumber instead of dicing it. Omit the vinegar. The mint is optional but a crushed garlic clove and 15 ml/1 tbsp finely chopped onion are essential. Mix all the ingredients and serve with warm, fresh bread for a refreshing first course.

 MRS BEETON'S TIP

Serve within 1 hour of making, or the liquid in the cucumber may thin the yogurt and spoil the consistency of the salad.

ORANGE AND ORTANIQUE SALAD

3 oranges, peeled and sliced
3 ortaniques, peeled and sliced (see Mrs
 Beeton's Tip)
1 mild Italian or Spanish onion, cut
 in rings
12 black olives
30 ml/2 tbsp chopped mint to garnish

DRESSING
75 ml/5 tbsp olive oil
30 ml/2 tbsp orange juice
15 ml/1 tbsp red wine vinegar
5 ml/1 tsp soy sauce
5 ml/1 tsp liquid honey
salt and pepper

Make the dressing by mixing all the ingredients in a screw-topped jar. Close the jar tightly and shake vigorously until well blended.

Put the dressing in a large bowl and add the orange, ortanique and onion slices. Cover the bowl and set aside for 1-2 hours.

When ready to serve, arrange the fruit and onion slices on a large platter, add the olives and drizzle the remaining dressing over the top. Sprinkle with the mint.

SERVES SIX

 MRS BEETON'S TIP

The ortanique – a cross between an orange and a tangerine – was developed in Jamaica. The fruit is easy to peel and segment, and is very sweet and juicy. If unavailable, substitute tangerines, grapefruit or limes.

CAESAR SALAD

As the egg in this salad is only lightly cooked, it is very important that it be perfectly fresh, and purchased from a reputable source.

3 garlic cloves, peeled but left whole
2 cos lettuces, separated into leaves
150 ml/¼ pint olive oil
4 large thick slices of bread, crusts removed
    and cubed
1 egg
juice of 1 lemon
1 (50 g/2 oz) can anchovy fillets, drained
50 g/2 oz Parmesan cheese, grated
salt and pepper

Cut 1 garlic clove in half and rub it all around a salad bowl. Wash the lettuce leaves and dry them thoroughly. Tear into small pieces and put in the salad bowl.

Heat 60 ml/4 tbsp of the olive oil in a small frying pan, add the remaining garlic cloves and fry over gentle heat for 1 minute. Add the bread cubes and fry until golden on all sides. Remove from the pan with a slotted spoon and drain on absorbent kitchen paper. Discard the garlic and oil in the pan.

Add the remaining olive oil to the lettuce and toss until every leaf is coated. Bring a small saucepan of water to the boil, add the egg and cook for 1 minute. Using a slotted spoon remove it from the water and break it over the lettuce. Add the lemon juice, anchovies, cheese, salt and pepper and toss lightly.

Add the croûtons of fried bread and toss again. Serve as soon as possible, while the croûtons ar still crisp.

SERVES SIX

RICE SALAD

200 g/7 oz long-grain rice
salt
60 ml/4 tbsp olive oil
30 ml/2 tbsp white wine vinegar
2 spring onions, finely chopped
1 carrot, finely diced and blanched
1 small green pepper, seeded and finely
    diced
2 gherkins, finely diced
30 ml/2 tbsp snipped chives
watercress to serve

Place the rice in a saucepan. Pour in 450 ml/¾ pint cold water. Add a little salt, then bring to the boil. Cover the pan tightly and reduce the heat to the lowest setting. Leave the rice for 15 minutes, turn off the heat and leave for a further 15 minutes without removing the lid. The rice should have absorbed all the liquid. Drain if necessary.

Stir in the oil and vinegar while the rice is still hot. Add the vegetables and chives; mix well. Pile on a dish and garnish with watercress. Serve at once.

SERVES FOUR TO SIX

 MRS BEETON'S TIP

This looks good in tomato shells. Cut the tops off 4–6 beefsteak tomatoes and reserve as lids. Hollow out the centres, saving the pulp for use in soup or another recipe. Turn the tomatoes upside down on absorbent kitchen paper to drain. When ready to serve, fill the tomatoes with the rice mixture and replace the lids at an angle.

POTATO SALAD

salt and pepper
6 large new potatoes or waxy old potatoes
150 ml/¼ pint mayonnaise
3 spring onions, chopped
30 ml/2 tbsp chopped parsley

Bring a saucepan of salted water to the boil, add the potatoes in their jackets and cook for 20–30 minutes until tender. Drain thoroughly. When cool enough to handle, peel and dice the potatoes. Put them in a bowl and add the mayonnaise while still warm. Lightly stir in the spring onions and parsley, with salt and pepper to taste. Cover, leave to become quite cold and stir before serving.

SERVES SIX

VARIATIONS

French Potato Salad Substitute 100 ml/3½ fl oz French dressing for the mayonnaise. Omit the spring onions, increase the parsley to 45 ml/3 tbsp and add 5 ml/1 tsp chopped fresh mint and 5 ml/1 tsp snipped chives.

German Potato Salad Omit the mayonnaise and spring onions. Reduce the parsley to 5 ml/1 tsp and add 5 ml/1 tsp finely chopped onion. Heat 60 ml/4 tbsp vegetable stock in a saucepan. Beat in 15 ml/1 tbsp white wine vinegar and 30 ml/2 tbsp oil. Add salt and pepper to taste. Pour over the diced potatoes while still hot and toss lightly together. Serve at once, or leave to become quite cold.

Potato Salad with Apple and Celery Follow the basic recipe above, but add 2 sliced celery sticks and 1 diced red-skinned apple tossed in a little lemon juice.

MRS BEETON'S POTATO SALAD

This should be made two or three hours before it is to be served so that the flavours have time to mature. Cold beef, turkey or other poultry may be thinly sliced or cut into chunks and combined with the potato salad to make a light main course dish.

10 small cold cooked potatoes
60 ml/4 tbsp tarragon vinegar
90 ml/6 tbsp salad oil
salt and pepper
15 ml/1 tbsp chopped parsley

Cut the potatoes into 1 cm/½ inch thick slices. For the dressing, mix the tarragon vinegar, oil and plenty of salt and pepper in a screw-topped jar. Close the jar tightly and shake vigorously until well blended.

Layer the potatoes in a salad bowl, sprinkling with a little dressing and the parsley. Pour over any remaining dressing, cover and set aside to marinate before serving.

SERVES SIX

VARIATIONS

Potato and Anchovy Salad Drain a 50 g/2 oz can of anchovy fillets, reserving the oil. Chop the fillets. Use the oil to make the dressing. Sprinkle the chopped anchovies between the layers of potato with the dressing.

Potato and Olive Salad Thinly slice 50 g/2 oz stoned black olives. Chop 2 spring onions, if liked, and mix them with the olives. Sprinkle the olives between the potato layers.

Potato Salad with Pickles Dice 1 pickled gherkin and 1–2 pickled onions. Reduce the vinegar to 15–30 ml/1–2 tbsp when making the dressing. Sprinkle the pickles between the layers of potato with the dressing.

SPINACH AND BACON SALAD

450 g/1 lb fresh young spinach
150 g/5 oz button mushrooms, thinly sliced
1 small onion, thinly sliced
15 ml/1 tbsp oil
6 rindless streaky bacon rashers, cut into
strips
75 ml/5 tbsp French dressing (page 576)

Remove the stalks from the spinach, wash the leaves well in cold water, then dry thoroughly on absorbent kitchen paper. If time permits, put the leaves in a polythene bag and chill for 1 hour.

Tear the spinach into large pieces and put into a salad bowl with the mushrooms and onion.

Heat the oil in a small frying pan and fry the bacon until crisp. Meanwhile toss the salad vegetables with the French dressing. Pour in the hot bacon and fat, toss lightly to mix and serve at once.

SERVES FOUR

 MRS BEETON'S TIP

If preferred, the bacon may be grilled until crisp and crumbled into the salad just before serving.

TOMATO SALAD

Sun-warmed tomatoes, freshly picked, are perfect for this salad. In the classic Italian version, olive oil is the only dressing, but a little red wine vinegar may be added, if preferred.

450 g/1 lb firm tomatoes, peeled and sliced
salt and pepper
pinch of caster sugar (optional)
45 ml/3 tbsp olive oil
5 ml/1 tsp chopped fresh basil
fresh basil sprigs to garnish

Put the tomatoes in a serving dish and sprinkle lightly with salt and pepper. Add the sugar, if used. Pour over the olive oil and sprinkle with chopped basil. Garnish with basil sprigs.

SERVES FOUR TO SIX

VARIATIONS

Mozzarella and Tomato Salad Interleave the sliced tomatoes with sliced mozzarella cheese. Cover and leave to marinate for at least an hour before serving.

Tomato and Onion Salad A popular salad to serve with cold meats. Omit the basil. Thinly slice 1 red or white onion and separate the slices into rings. Sprinkle these over the tomatoes. Sprinkle with sugar, salt and pepper, and a few drops of cider vinegar as well as the oil.

Minted Tomato Salad with Chives Omit the basil. Sprinkle 15 ml/1 tbsp chopped fresh mint and 45 ml/3 tbsp snipped chives over the tomatoes before adding the oil. Garnish with sprigs of mint.

CHEF'S SALAD

½ cos lettuce, separated into leaves
50 g/2 oz cold cooked chicken, cut in strips
50 g/2 oz cold cooked tongue, cut in strips
50 g/2 oz Gruyère cheese, cut in strips
1 hard-boiled egg, thinly sliced
15 ml/1 tbsp chopped onion
8 black olives

DRESSING
90 ml/6 tbsp olive oil
30 ml/2 tbsp red wine vinegar
2.5 ml/½ tsp lemon juice
2.5 ml/½ tsp French mustard
salt and pepper

Make the dressing by mixing all the ingredients in a screw-topped jar. Close the jar tightly and shake vigorously until blended.

Wash the lettuce leaves, dry them thoroughly and arrange in a large salad bowl. Add a little of the dressing and toss. Arrange the cold meats and cheese on the lettuce, with the egg, onion and olives. Serve remaining dressing separately.

SERVES FOUR

WALDORF SALAD

4 sharp red dessert apples
2 celery sticks, thinly sliced
25 g/1 oz chopped or broken walnuts
75 ml/5 tbsp mayonnaise
30 ml/2 tbsp lemon juice
pinch of salt
lettuce leaves (optional)

Core the apples, but do not peel them. Cut them into dice. Put them in a bowl with the celery and walnuts. Mix the mayonnaise with the lemon juice. Add salt to taste and fold into the apple mixture. Chill. Serve on a bed of lettuce leaves, if liked.

SERVES FOUR

VARIATION

Waldorf Salad with Chicken Make as above, but use only 2 apples. Add 350 g/12 oz diced cold cooked chicken. For extra flavour and colour, add 50 g/2 oz small seedless green grapes.

PEPPER SALAD

2 large green peppers
2 large red peppers
2 large yellow peppers
1 mild Italian or Spanish onion, thinly
   sliced in rings
100 ml/3½ fl oz olive oil
salt and pepper (optional)

Wash the peppers and pat dry with absorbent kitchen paper. Grill under moderate heat, turning the peppers frequently with tongs until the skins blister, then char all over. Immediately transfer the peppers to a large bowl and cover with several layers of absorbent kitchen paper. Alternatively, put the grilled peppers in a polythene bag. When cold, rub off the skin under cold water. Remove cores and seeds and cut or tear the peppers into thin strips.

Put the pepper strips on a serving platter, arrange the onion rings around the rim, and drizzle the olive oil over the top. Add salt and pepper to taste, if liked. Serve at once.

SERVES SIX TO EIGHT

MRS BEETON'S WINTER SALAD

Adding milk to an oil and vinegar dressing gives an unusual, slightly creamy mixture. The milk may be omitted, or mayonnaise thinned with single cream, yogurt or milk may be used instead.

1 head of endive, washed and shredded
1 punnet of mustard and cress
2 celery sticks, thinly sliced
4 hard-boiled eggs, sliced
225 g/8 oz cooked beetroot, sliced

DRESSING
5 ml/1 tsp French mustard
5 ml/1 tsp caster sugar
30 ml/2 tbsp salad oil
30 ml/2 tbsp milk
30 ml/2 tbsp cider vinegar
salt
cayenne

Arrange the endive, mustard and cress and celery in a salad bowl. Top with the eggs and beetroot, overlapping the slices or interleaving them with the endive but keeping them separate from each other.

For the dressing, put the mustard and sugar in a small basin. Gradually add the oil, whisking all the time. Add the milk very slowly, whisking vigorously to prevent the mixture curdling. Continue adding the vinegar in the same way – if the ingredients are added too quickly the dressing will curdle. Add salt and a hint of cayenne. Spoon this dressing over the salad just before serving.

SERVES SIX

COURGETTE AND AVOCADO SALAD

salt and pepper
450 g/1 lb courgettes, thickly sliced
1 Lollo Rosso lettuce, separated into leaves
2 avocados
3 rindless streaky bacon rashers, grilled, to garnish

DRESSING
75 ml/5 tbsp olive oil
30 ml/2 tbsp tarragon or white wine vinegar
pinch of caster sugar
1 garlic clove, crushed
salt and pepper

Make the dressing by mixing all the ingredients in a screw-topped jar. Close the jar tightly and shake vigorously until well blended.

Bring a saucepan of salted water to the boil, add the courgettes, lower the heat and simmer for 1 minute. Drain the courgettes and put them in a bowl. While still warm, pour the dressing over. Allow the mixture to cool, then cover and marinate in the refrigerator for 2-3 hours.

Wash the Lollo Rosso leaves and dry them thoroughly. Divide between six salad bowls. Drain the courgettes, reserving the dressing, and divide between the bowls.

Peel and slice the avocados, toss them lightly in the reserved dressing, then arrange on top of the salads, using a slotted spoon. Crumble a little bacon over each salad and serve, with the remaining dressing in a small jug.

SERVES SIX

PEAR, NUT AND DATE SALAD

1 small crisp lettuce, separated into leaves
3 ripe dessert pears
15 ml/1 tbsp lemon juice
100 g/4 oz stoned dates
50 g/2 oz walnuts
10 ml/2 tsp chopped parsley
45 ml/3 tbsp French dressing (page 470)

Wash the lettuce leaves and dry them thoroughly. Reserve 6 outer leaves, shred the rest and put them in a bowl. Peel and halve the pears, put them in a second bowl and add the lemon juice. Toss lightly to preserve the colour.

Add the dates, walnuts and parsley to the shredded lettuce, pour over the dressing and toss lightly. Arrange the outer lettuce leaves on six individual plates. Put a pear half on each plate, cut side up. Pile the date mixture into the centre of each fruit, cover and chill for 1 hour before serving.

SERVES SIX

MRS BEETON'S BOILED SALAD

Halving the quantities given in the original recipe makes this workable for today's households. Chopped tarragon, chervil or burnet may be added to the salad.

1 head of celery, trimmed
1 small onion, chopped
¼ cauliflower, broken into florets
350 g/12 oz French beans, trimmed
1 lettuce heart, shredded (optional)
dressing as for Mrs Beeton's Winter Salad
    (page 379) or mayonnaise

Cut the celery into 5 cm/2 inch lengths. Bring a large saucepan of water to the boil. Add the celery and onion, bring back to the boil and cook for 2 minutes. Add the cauliflower, bring back to the boil again and cook for a further 2 minutes.

Meanwhile, cut the French beans into 5 cm/ 2 inch lengths. Add the beans to the other vegetables. Bring back to the boil, cook for 2 minutes, then drain the vegetables and cool until just warm. Arrange the lettuce in a salad bowl and top with the boiled vegetables. Pour the dressing over and serve at once.

SERVES SIX TO EIGHT

RICE AND ARTICHOKE SALAD

Basmati rice gives this salad the best flavour. Make the vinaigrette at least 1 hour before use, to allow the flavours to develop.

200 g/7 oz long-grain rice
salt
100 ml/3½ fl oz Vinaigrette Dressing (page
    469)
1 garlic clove, crushed
1 (397 g/14 oz) can artichoke hearts, drained
    and halved
30 ml/2 tbsp snipped chives to garnish

Place the rice in a saucepan and pour in 450 ml/¾ pint cold water. Cover the pan tightly and reduce the heat to the lowest setting. Leave the rice for 15 minutes, turn off the heat and leave for a further 15 minutes without lifting the lid.

Mix the dressing and garlic, add to the hot rice and fork it in lightly. Leave to cool.

Just before serving, fork the artichoke hearts into the rice. Sprinkle with the chives.

SERVES FOUR

LENTIL AND ONION SALAD

225 g/8 oz brown or green lentils, soaked for
  2-3 hours in water to cover
1 salt-free vegetable or onion stock cube
sea salt
1 red onion, thinly sliced in rings
30 ml/2 tbsp finely chopped parsley

DRESSING
45 ml/3 tbsp light olive oil
salt and pepper
pinch of mustard powder
pinch of caster sugar
5 ml/1 tsp soy sauce
15 ml/1 tbsp red wine vinegar

Put the lentils in a saucepan with cold water to cover. Bring to the boil, add the crumbled stock cube, lower the heat and simmer for 30-40 minutes until tender but not mushy.

Meanwhile make the dressing by mixing all the ingredients in a screw-topped jar. Close the jar tightly and shake vigorously until well blended.

Drain the cooked lentils thoroughly, tip into a serving bowl and immediately add the dressing. Toss lightly, then add the onion rings with half the parsley.

Allow the salad to stand for at least 1 hour before serving to allow the flavours to blend. Sprinkle with the remaining parsley.

SERVES FOUR TO SIX

 MRS BEETON'S TIP

Italian red onions are at their best in late spring. Mild, sweet and crisp, they are ideal for stuffing, roasting whole or in salads.

TABBOULEH

This delicious salad is served all over the Middle East. It central ingredient is bulgur or cracked wheat, which has been hulled and parboiled. It therefore needs little or no cooking.

125 g/4½ oz bulgur wheat
2 tomatoes, peeled, seeded and diced
1 small onion, finely chopped
2 spring onions, finely chopped
50 g/2 oz parsley, very finely chopped
45 ml/3 tbsp lemon juice
30 ml/2 tbsp olive oil
salt and pepper
crisp lettuce leaves to serve

Put the bulgur wheat in a large bowl, add water to generously cover and set aside for 45-60 minutes. Line a sieve or colander with a clean tea-towel and strain the bulgur. When most of the liquid has dripped through, scoop the bulgur up in the tea-towel and squeeze it strongly to extract as much of the remaining liquid as possible. Tip the bulgur into a bowl.

Add the tomatoes, onion, spring onions, parsley, lemon juice and oil, with salt and pepper to taste. Mix well.

Dome the tabbouleh in the centre of a large platter. Arrange the lettuce leaves around the rim to be used as scoops.

SERVES SIX TO EIGHT

VARIATION

Tabbouleh in Peppers or Tomatoes Serve tabbouleh in halved, boiled and well-drained pepper shells or in scooped-out tomato shells.

PASTA, ANCHOVY AND SWEETCORN SALAD

150 g/5 oz pasta shells
salt and pepper
60 ml/4 tbsp mayonnaise
1 (50 g/2 oz) can anchovies, drained and
  finely chopped
225 g/8 oz drained canned sweetcorn kernels
2 spring onions, finely chopped, to garnish

Cook the pasta in a large saucepan of boiling salted water for 10–12 minutes or until tender but still firm to the bite. Drain thoroughly. While still warm, stir in the mayonnaise. Set aside to cool.

Add the anchovies and sweetcorn, with salt and pepper to taste. Toss the salad lightly and garnish with the chopped spring onions.

SERVES FOUR TO SIX

 MRS BEETON'S TIP

Use any decorative pasta for this dish. Spirals, bows or tiny cartwheels are all suitable. For a touch of colour, use tomato or spinach-flavoured pasta shapes.

FLAGEOLET BEAN SALAD

The fresh green colour and tender flavour of flageolets makes them an ideal candidate for a light summer salad. Add a little crumbled grilled bacon or drained flaked tuna and serve with French bread for a simple summer lunch.

225 g/8 oz dried flageolet beans, soaked
  overnight in water to cover
1 bouquet garni
150 ml/¼ pint mayonnaise
1 onion, finely chopped
15 ml/1 tbsp finely chopped parsley
salt

Drain the beans, put them in a clean saucepan with the bouquet garni and add fresh water to cover. Bring the water to the boil, boil briskly for 10 minutes, then lower the heat and simmer the beans for 1¼–1½ hours until tender.

Drain the beans thoroughly, remove the bouquet garni and tip into a bowl. While the beans are still warm, stir in the mayonnaise, onion and parsley, with salt to taste. Toss lightly.

Allow the salad to stand for at least 3 hours before serving to allow the flavours to blend.

SERVES FOUR TO SIX

 MRS BEETON'S TIP

Do not add salt to the water when cooking pulses such as dried flageolet beans as it toughens them. Pulses are delicious when cooked in vegetable stock, but take care to use a salt-free variety.

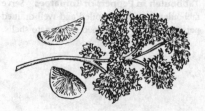

CHERRY SALAD

This is delicious with roast duck or game.

450g/1lb black cherries
15ml/1tbsp olive oil
5ml/1tsp lemon juice
2.5ml/½tsp tarragon or red wine vinegar
10ml/2tsp brandy or kirsch
5ml/1tsp finely chopped fresh tarragon
5ml/1tsp finely chopped fresh chervil
2.5ml/½tsp caster sugar
salt and pepper

Stone the cherries and put them in a bowl. Combine the other ingredients in a screw-topped jar. Close the jar tightly and shake vigorously until well blended. Pour over the cherries, cover and leave for 1-2 hours.

SERVES FOUR TO SIX

STRAWBERRY AND TOMATO SALAD

450g/1lb firm tomatoes, peeled
salt · pinch of paprika
15ml/1tbsp lemon juice
350g/12oz firm strawberries, hulled and
   quartered
30ml/2tbsp salad oil

GARNISH
a few whole strawberries
¼ cucumber, thinly sliced

Cut the tomatoes in half and remove the seeds and pulp, reserving these for use in another recipe. Cut the tomato flesh into thin slices, place in a bowl and add salt and paprika to taste. Sprinkle with lemon juice; set aside.

Just before serving, add the strawberries and transfer the mixture to a serving platter or dish. Drizzle with the oil and garnish with the whole strawberries and cucumber slices.

SERVES SIX

TRUFFLES DRESSED IN CHAMPAGNE

Finally, the ultimate in salads, not so much a practical recipe as a culinary day-dream – even when the original quantities are halved!

6 large black truffles, scrubbed
4 rindless streaky bacon rashers
1 small carrot, diced
½ turnip, diced
1 onion, thinly sliced
1 bouquet garni
2 cloves
1 blade of mace
300ml/½ pint champagne or sparkling dry
   white wine
150ml/¼ pint vegetable stock

The truffles should be perfectly clean and free from grit. Lay the bacon in a saucepan and place the truffles on top. Add all the vegetables, herbs and spices. Pour in the champagne and stock. Heat gently until just simmering. Cover the pan and leave to cook gently for 1 hour. Turn the heat off and leave until cold.

Remove the truffles from their cooking liquor and slice them. Place in a saucepan with a little of the liquor and warm them briefly. Use a slotted spoon to remove them from the pan and serve. The juices from reheating may be poured over or the truffles may be served on a stark white napkin.

SERVES SIX

Beans and Pulses

This chapter serves as an excellent introduction to a broad culinary topic: International, versatile and nutritious, beans and pulses may be used in many exciting dishes.

Whether you prepare them yourself, or save time by using a canned variety, beans and pulses are nutritious and inexpensive. In many diets they are a valued protein food (along with most nuts and some seeds) and soya beans in particular compare well with animal foods (fish, poultry, meat and dairy produce) as a source of protein. Tofu, or bean curd, is produced from soya beans, so it too is a valuable protein food, especially in a vegetarian diet.

As well as their essential role in a vegetarian diet, beans and pulses feature in many traditional meat and poultry soups and stews. They are also used extensively in ethnic cooking, often to extend small amounts of more expensive meat or to balance spicy seasonings.

Apart from hot dishes, the cooked pulses are used to make tempting dips. Puréed and combined with other ingredients, they may be formed into patties or loaves to serve hot and cold, for main meals, picnics, buffets and nutritious snacks.

SOYA MILK

Soya milk, as its name suggests, is produced from soya beans. Available in long-life packs, it may be used instead of cow's milk in drinks, on cereals and in cooking. It is a useful product for anyone who is allergic to dairy produce as it gives excellent results and its flavour is very mild, making it an ideal substitute for cow's milk in sauces, custards and so on. Soya milk is not as rich as whole cow's milk, so results may be slightly 'weaker', as with skimmed milk.

COOKING BEANS AND PULSES

The majority of dried beans and pulses should be soaked for several hours or overnight before cooking. Lentils and many brands of dried peas do not require soaking before cooking; however, the following notes apply to other pulses.

- Rinse the pulses, then leave them in plenty of cold water to soak, preferably in a cool place and never for longer than 24 hours.
- Drain, then transfer to a large saucepan and cover with fresh cold water.
- Do not add salt – this toughens the pulses if added before they are thoroughly tender, and they cannot be tenderized once seasoned.
- Bring to the boil and boil rapidly for 10 minutes. This is important as it destroys natural toxins in the pulses.
- Lower the heat, cover and keep the water just boiling.
- The cooking time varies but is usually between 40-60 minutes. Some pulses take longer, up to $1\frac{1}{2}$ hours, and soya beans take $2\frac{1}{2}$ hours or slightly longer.
- Make sure the pulses are covered with water all the time they cook. Drain when tender and use as required.
- When pulses are parboiled, then added to a stew to finish cooking, the stew must not be highly salted or the pulses will toughen.
- Pulses may be added to soups for cooking after the initial boiling period.

PRESSURE COOKING

The pressure cooker is excellent for cooking dried beans and pulses. First soak the beans in boiling water, allowing 15 minutes for aduki beans, butter beans, mung beans or similar; 1 hour for kidney beans, soya beans or yellow split peas; and 2–3 hours for chick peas. Drain and put in the pressure cooker with plenty of water to cover. Cook at 15 lb pressure, allowing 12–15 minutes for aduki, mung and kidney beans, and split peas; chick peas and soya beans take about 15 minutes. Lentils cook without soaking in 8 minutes.

MICROWAVE COOKING

Not an ideal method for pulses which require large quantities of cooking liquid; however, lentils cook well in the microwave, particularly the red type which absorb all the cooking liquid. A quantity of 225 g/8 oz lentils take about 15–20 minutes to cook.

TYPES OF BEANS AND PULSES

Aduki Small, round red beans with a nutty flavour. Cooking time: 30 minutes.

Black-eyed Beans Small kidney-shaped whole beans with a prominent black spot. Cooking time: 30 minutes.

Borlotti Beans Mottled pink beans, often used in Italian cooking. Cooking time: 45 minutes.

Brown Beans Medium, oval beans, often used in Mediterranean cuisines. Cooking time: 30 minutes.

Butter Beans Large white beans which cook comparitively quickly when soaked and become mushy if overcooked. Cooking time: 40 minutes.

Chick-peas Also known as *garbanzos*. They resemble small, light brown nuts and have an affinity for spices. Cooking time: 1 hour.

Flageolet Beans Small, oval, pale green beans with a delicate flavour. Cooking time: 30 minutes.

Haricot Beans There are many varieties and sizes, but the name is generally used for small, oval white beans. Cooking time: 40 minutes.

Lentils Several different varieties are available. Unlike most other pulses, lentils do not need to be soaked before being cooked. For more information, see Boiled Lentils, page 488. Cooking time: 20–45 minutes.

Peas Dried green peas are not as popular as they once were, but make a tasty soup or purée, especially when flavoured with onion and bacon or ham. Cooking time: 35–45 minutes.

Pinto Beans Mottled, pink beans often confused with borlotti beans from the same family. Cooking time: 40 minutes.

Processed Peas Bright green in colour and slightly sweet, they are usually sold in cans. Mushy peas are processed marrowfat peas.

Red Kidney Beans Dark red, oval beans, an essential ingredient of Chilli con Carne. Also delicious when cooked with Indian spices, onions and tomatoes. Cooking time: 50 minutes.

Soya Beans Creamy-beige small beans, rounded in shape. They require long soaking and cooking. Highly nutritious. Cooking time: 2–2½ hours.

Split Peas The basis of pea soup and pease pudding. They require less cooking time than whole dried peas. Although both yellow and green varieties are available, the former are most widely used. Like split lentils, they lose their shape when cooked. Cooking time: 20 minutes.

CURRIED BEANS

200 g/7 oz dried haricot beans, soaked
  overnight in water to cover
30 ml/2 tbsp oil
1 onion, finely chopped
2.5 cm/1 inch fresh root ginger, peeled and
  finely chopped
2 garlic cloves, crushed
pinch of cayenne pepper
15 ml/1 tbsp ground coriander
2.5 ml/½ tsp turmeric
30 ml/2 tbsp brown sugar
1 (397 g/14 oz) can chopped tomatoes
1 bay leaf
salt and pepper
50 g/2 oz raisins
1 eating apple, peeled, cored and diced

Drain the beans, put them in a clean saucepan
and add fresh water to cover. Bring the water to
the boil, boil briskly for 10 minutes, then lower
the heat and simmer the beans for about 40
minutes or until just tender.

Meanwhile heat the oil in a large saucepan. Fry
the onion, ginger and garlic over gentle heat for
about 10 minutes. Stir in cayenne to taste, with
the coriander, turmeric and sugar. Fry for 5
minutes more, stirring constantly.

Drain the beans and add them, with the canned
tomatoes and bay leaf, to the onion mixture.
Add salt and pepper to taste and stir well. Bring
just to the boil, then lower the heat and simmer
for 30 minutes. Add the raisins and apple, recover and cook gently for a further 30 minutes.

SERVES FOUR

SPICED LENTILS

450 g/1 lb red lentils
2.5 ml/½ tsp sea salt
45 ml/3 tbsp oil
1 onion, chopped
1 small cooking apple, chopped
1.25 ml/¼ tsp turmeric
1.25 ml/¼ tsp ground ginger
5 ml/1 tsp garam masala
5 ml/1 tsp ground cumin
3 tomatoes, peeled and chopped

GARNISH
chopped fresh coriander leaves
chopped onion or fried onion rings

Put the lentils in a large saucepan with
900 ml/1½ pints water. Bring to the boil, lower
the heat and cover the pan. Simmer gently for
20 minutes. Add the sea salt and simmer for 5
minutes more or until the lentils are soft and all
the water has been absorbed.

Meanwhile, heat the oil in a large deep frying
pan and add the onion, apple and spices. Fry
gently for about 10 minutes until the vegetables
are soft and lightly browned. Stir the tomatoes
into the pan and cook for 5 minutes, then pour
in the lentils.

Stir thoroughly, then serve very hot, sprinkled
with the coriander leaves and onion.

SERVES FOUR TO SIX

 MRS BEETON'S TIP

To peel tomatoes, cut a small cross in the
top of each fruit and place them in a bowl.
Pour on freshly boiling water. Leave for
about 45 seconds, depending on ripeness,
then drain. Peel back and remove the skins.

FELAFEL

Serve felafel in pitta pockets, or omit the tahini and serve with Greek yogurt and salad for a simple and satisfying lunch.

**200 g/7 oz chick peas, soaked overnight or
  for several hours in water to cover**
75 g/3 oz fine matzo meal or wholemeal flour
5 ml/1 tsp salt
5 ml/1 tsp ground cumin
10 ml/2 tsp ground coriander
1 garlic clove, crushed
oil for deep frying

TAHINI
50 g/2 oz ground sesame seeds
1 garlic clove, crushed
1.25 ml/¼ tsp salt
15 ml/1 tbsp lemon juice
pinch of pepper

Drain the chick peas, put them in a clean saucepan and add fresh water to cover. Bring to the boil, lower the heat and simmer for 1-1½ hours until very tender. Drain, mince the chick peas finely or chop and sieve them.

Combine the minced chick peas, matzo meal, salt, cumin, coriander and garlic in a bowl. Form into small balls, adding 15-30 ml/1-2 tbsp water if necessary.

Heat the oil to 170°C/338°F or until a cube of bread added to the oil browns in 1½ minutes. Add the felafel, a few at a time, and fry until golden brown. Drain on absorbent kitchen paper; keep the felafel hot while cooking successive batches.

To make the tahini, mix all the ingredients together and add 75 ml/5 tbsp water. Sieve to a smooth purée or process in a blender or food processor for a few minutes. Add more salt and pepper if required.

MAKES 36

HUMMUS

Serve as a starter or snack, with French bread, pitta or crispbreads.

150 g/5 oz chick peas
1 garlic clove, chopped
salt
90 ml/6 tbsp olive oil
**60 ml/4 tbsp Tahini (bought or see recipe
  left)**
60 ml/4 tbsp lemon juice
chopped parsley to garnish

Soak and cook the chick peas, following the method given for Felafel, left. Drain thoroughly, then mash and sieve or crush in a mortar with a pestle to a smooth paste. An alternative, and much easier method, is to process the chick peas in a blender or food processor.

Add the garlic and salt to taste. Stir briskly until well mixed, then gradually work in the olive oil, as when making mayonnaise. The chick peas should form a creamy paste. Work in the tahini slowly, adding it a teaspoonful at a time at first. When the mixture is creamy work in lemon juice to taste.

Transfer the hummus to a shallow serving bowl and sprinkle with chopped parsley.

SERVES SIX TO EIGHT

 MRS BEETON'S TIP

Hummus makes a delicious filling for baked potatoes. Serve with a crisp salad for a contrast in texture.

HARICOT BEANS WITH ONION AND CARAWAY

200 g/7 oz haricot beans, soaked overnight in
  cold water to cover
25 g/1 oz butter
2 onions, finely chopped
5 ml/1 tsp caraway seeds
salt and pepper
125 ml/4 fl oz soured cream
30 ml/2 tbsp chopped parsley

Drain the beans. Put them in a saucepan with
fresh water to cover. Bring to the boil, boil
vigorously for 10 minutes, then lower the heat,
cover the pan and simmer for about 40 minutes
or until the beans are tender. Drain thoroughly.

Melt the butter in a saucepan. Add the onions
and caraway seeds and fry for about 10 minutes
until just transparent. Add the beans, with salt
and pepper to taste, and toss together until
heated through.

Spoon into a heated serving dish, top with the
soured cream and parsley and serve at once.
Alternatively, serve on a bed of red cabbage.

SERVES FOUR TO SIX

 MRS BEETON'S TIP

To give the haricot beans extra flavour,
cook them in vegetable stock. If you are
making your own stock (page 86), omit the
salt, since this would toughen the beans.

HARICOT BEANS WITH PARSLEY SAUCE

200 g/7 oz haricot beans, soaked overnight in
  cold water to cover
30 ml/2 tbsp butter
1 onion, finely chopped
100 g/4 oz mushrooms, thinly sliced
15 ml/1 tbsp lemon juice
Pesto Genovese (page 491), to serve

PARSLEY SAUCE
25 g/1 oz butter
25 g/1 oz plain flour
300 ml/½ pint milk
salt and pepper
60 ml/4 tbsp chopped parsley

Drain the beans. Put them in a saucepan with
fresh water to cover. Bring to the boil, boil
vigorously for 10 minutes, then lower the heat,
cover the pan and simmer for about 40 minutes
or until the beans are tender.

When the beans are almost cooked, melt the
butter in a small frying pan, add the onion and
fry over gentle heat for 10 minutes until the
onion is soft and transparent. Add the mushrooms and cook for a further 5 minutes. Set the
pan aside.

Make the parsley sauce. Melt the butter in a
saucepan, stir in the flour and cook for 1
minute. Gradually add the milk, stirring constantly, and cook until the mixture boils and
thickens. Add salt and pepper to taste, then stir
in the parsley.

Drain the haricot beans. Add them to the
parsley sauce with the lemon juice. Toss
together lightly. Stir in the reserved mushroom
mixture, with salt and pepper to taste. Heat
through gently. Serve in individual bowls,
topped with pesto.

SERVES SIX

BOSTON ROAST

fat for greasing
300 g/11 oz haricot beans, soaked overnight
   in cold water to cover
salt and pepper
15 ml/1 tbsp oil
1 onion, chopped
150 g/5 oz Cheddar cheese, grated
60 ml/4 tbsp vegetable stock
1 egg, beaten
100 g/4 oz fresh white breadcrumbs
5 ml/1 tsp dried thyme
2.5 ml/½ tsp grated nutmeg

Drain the beans, put them in a saucepan and add fresh water to cover. Do not add salt. Bring to the boil, cook for 10 minutes, then lower the heat and simmer for about 40 minutes or until tender. Drain the beans. Mash with seasoning or purée in a food processor.

Set the oven at 180°C/350°F/gas 4. Heat the oil in a frying pan, add the onion and fry for about 10 minutes, or until softened. Tip the onion into a large bowl and add the mashed or puréed beans with the rest of the ingredients.

Spoon the mixture into a well greased 900 g/2 lb loaf tin. Cover the surface with greased greaseproof paper. Bake for 45 minutes, until firm and slightly shrunk. Serve with Fresh Tomato Sauce (page 483).

SERVES SIX

 FREEZER TIP

Boston Roast freezes very well. Cool quickly, then slice. Separate individual slices with freezer film and wrap in an airtight polythene bag.

LENTIL PASTIES

100 g/4 oz split red lentils
300 ml/½ pint vegetable stock
25 g/1 oz butter
salt and pepper
pinch of grated nutmeg
4 button mushrooms, sliced
15 ml/1 tbsp double cream
beaten egg or milk for glazing

SHORT CRUST PASTRY
225 g/8 oz plain flour
2.5 ml/½ tsp salt
100 g/4 oz margarine
flour for rolling out

Make the pastry. Sift the flour and salt into a bowl, then rub in the margarine until the mixture resembles fine breadcrumbs. Add enough cold water to make a stiff dough. Press the dough together with your fingertips. Wrap in greaseproof paper and chill until required.

Put the lentils in a saucepan with the vegetable stock. Bring to the boil, lower the heat and cover the pan. Simmer for 20 minutes or until the lentils are soft and all the liquid is absorbed. Beat in the butter and season with salt, pepper and nutmeg. Stir in the mushrooms and cream. Set aside. Set the oven at 200°C/400°F/gas 6.

Roll out the pastry very thinly on a floured surface, and cut into eight 13 cm/5 inch rounds. Divide the lentil filling between the rounds, dampen the edges and fold over to form half circles. Press the edges together and seal firmly, then brush with a little beaten egg or milk. Place on baking sheets and bake for about 15 minutes, or until the pastry is cooked and browned.

MAKES EIGHT

SOYA BEAN BAKE

fat for greasing
450 g/1 lb soya beans, soaked for 24 hours in
   cold water to cover
2 onions, finely chopped
1 green pepper, seeded and chopped
1 carrot, coarsely grated
1 celery stick, sliced
45 ml/3 tbsp molasses
45 ml/3 tbsp chopped parsley
5 ml/1 tsp dried thyme
5 ml/1 tsp dried savory or marjoram
salt and pepper
2 (397 g/14 oz) cans chopped tomatoes
175 g/6 oz medium oatmeal
50 g/2 oz Lancashire or Caerphilly cheese,
   finely crumbled or grated
45 ml/3 tbsp snipped chives
50 ml/2 fl oz olive oil

Grease a large ovenproof dish – a lasagne dish
is ideal. Set the oven at 180°C/350°F/gas 4.
Drain the beans. Put them in a saucepan with
fresh water to cover. Bring to the boil, boil
vigorously for 45 minutes, then lower the heat,
add more boiling water if necessary, cover the
pan and simmer for 1½-2 hours until tender.
Top up the water as necessary.

Drain the beans and put them in a mixing bowl
with the onions, green pepper, carrot and
celery. Warm the molasses in a small saucepan
and pour it over the bean mixture. Stir in the
herbs, with salt and pepper. Mix in the canned
tomatoes.

Spoon the mixture into the prepared dish. Mix
the oatmeal, cheese and chives. Spoon the
oatmeal mixture over the beans, then drizzle
the olive oil over the top. Cover the dish with
foil or a lid and bake for 45 minutes. Remove
the lid and bake for a further 15 minutes. Serve
hot, from the dish.

SERVES SIX

BOILED LENTILS

*Red lentils are readily available. This type needs no
presoaking and quickly cooks to a pale gold mass.
They do not retain their shape when cooking, a
characteristic which makes them ideal for purées,
vegetarian pâtés, soups and layer bakes. Continental
lentils (green or brown lentils) take slightly longer to
cook. They do not lose their shape and are useful for
adding texture to dishes. The black lentilles de Puy
from the Auvergne in France have the finest flavour.*

*Measure the liquid for red lentils as it should all
be absorbed at the end of cooking, leaving the pulses
soft and moist – rather like mashed potato when
stirred. Allow 600 ml/1 pint liquid to 225 g/8 oz red
lentils, checking two-thirds of the way through
cooking and adding a little extra liquid if necessary.
It is important that the lentils do not dry before they
are tender. Bring to the boil, lower the heat, cover
and simmer until tender. Red lentils will take about
20 minutes. Green and brown lentils take 30–45
minutes and Puy lentils 40–50 minutes.*

*Allow 50 g/2 oz per person as a side dish; 75 g/3 oz
with vegetables; 100 g/4 oz served simply as a main
course.*

1 onion stuck with 2 cloves
450 g/1 lb split red lentils
1 bouquet garni
25 g/1 oz butter
salt and pepper

Put the onion into a saucepan with the lentils
and bouquet garni. Add 1.1 litres/2 pints water
and bring to the boil. Lower the heat, cover
tightly and simmer for 20 minutes or until the
lentils are soft. Check that the water is not
absorbed completely before the lentils are
tender. Discard the onion and bouquet garni.
Stir in the butter with salt and pepper to taste.
Serve at once.

SERVES FOUR TO SIX

LENTIL AND STILTON LASAGNE

This makes a delicious vegetarian main course which is full flavoured and usually enjoyed by non-vegetarians as well. Serve with a fresh, good mixture of green salad ingredients.

225 g/8 oz green lentils
8 sheets of lasagne
salt and pepper
30 ml/2 tbsp olive oil
1 large onion, chopped
1 garlic clove, crushed
5 ml/1 tsp dried marjoram
225 g/8 oz mushrooms, sliced
2 (397 g/14 oz) cans chopped tomatoes
225 g/8 oz ripe blue Stilton cheese (without rind)
30 ml/2 tbsp plain flour
300 ml/½ pint milk

Cook the lentils in plenty of boiling water for 35 minutes, until just tender. Cook the lasagne in boiling salted water with a little oil added for 12–15 minutes, or until just tender. Drain both and set the lentils aside; lay the lasagne out to dry on absorbent kitchen paper.

Heat the remaining oil in a large saucepan. Add the onion, garlic and marjoram, and cook for 10 minutes, or until slightly softened. Stir in the mushrooms and cook for 5 minutes before adding the tomatoes. Stir in the cooked lentils with plenty of salt and pepper and bring to the boil. Reduce the heat and cover the pan, then simmer for 5 minutes.

Set the oven at 180°C/350°F/gas 4. Grease a lasagne dish or large ovenproof dish. Pour half the lentil mixture into the base of the dish and top it with half the lasagne. Pour the remaining lentil mixture over the pasta, then end with the remaining pasta.

Mash the Stilton in a bowl with a sturdy fork or process it in a food processor. Sprinkle a little of the flour over the cheese and work it in, then add the remaining flour in the same way to make the mixture crumbly. Gradually work in the milk, a little at a time, pounding the cheese at first, then beating it as it softens. When the mixture is soft and creamy, the remaining milk may be incorporated more quickly. Add some pepper and just a little salt. Pour the mixture over the lasagne, scraping the bowl clean. Bake for 40–45 minutes, or until the top of the lasagne is well browned and bubbling.

SERVES SIX

VARIATION

Lentil and Leek Lasagne Omit the onion in the main recipe and use 450 g/1 lb sliced leeks. Cook them with an additional knob of butter until well reduced. Continue as above. Cheddar may be substituted for the Stilton: it should be finely grated or chopped in a food processor.

LENTIL AND BROCCOLI GRATIN

225 g/8 oz green or brown lentils
2 onions, chopped
1 bay leaf
750 ml/1¼ pints vegetable stock
450 g/1 lb broccoli, broken into small florets
30 ml/2 tbsp oil
6 tomatoes, peeled and quartered
150 ml/¼ pint medium cider
salt and pepper
225 g/8 oz mozzarella cheese, diced

Place the lentils in a saucepan with 1 onion, the bay leaf and the stock. Bring to the boil, then lower the heat and cover the pan. Simmer the lentils for 40–50 minutes, until they are tender and most of the stock has been absorbed. Check that they do not become dry during cooking. Replace the cover, remove from the heat and leave to stand.

Meanwhile, cook the broccoli in a saucepan of boiling water for 2–3 minutes, until just tender. Drain. Heat the oil in a large flameproof casserole and add the remaining onion. Cook, stirring, for 10–15 minutes, or until softened. Stir in the broccoli, tomatoes and cider with salt and pepper. Cook, stirring occasionally, for 15 minutes.

Discard the bay leaf from the lentils, then tip them into the pan with the broccoli mixture. Stir to combine all the ingredients. Taste and add more salt and pepper if required. Top with the mozzarella cheese and grill until the cheese is bubbling, crisp and golden. Serve piping hot.

SERVES FOUR TO SIX

THREE-BEAN SAUTE

A quick and easy dish for a light meal, this sauté tastes delicious when served on a base of mixed green salad – crunchy Iceberg lettuce, some thinly sliced green pepper and sliced cucumber.

100 g/4 oz shelled broad beans
juice of 2 oranges
2 carrots, cut into matchstick strips
225 g/8 oz fine French beans
salt and pepper
30 ml/2 tbsp oil
1 onion, halved and thinly sliced
2 (425 g/15 oz) cans butter beans, drained
30 ml/2 tbsp chopped parsley
4 tomatoes, peeled, seeded and cut into
  eighths

Place the broad beans in a saucepan with the orange juice. Add just enough water to cover the beans, then bring to the boil. Lower the heat slightly so that the beans simmer steadily. Cook for 5 minutes.

Add the carrots and French beans, mix well and sprinkle in a little salt and pepper. Continue to cook, stirring often, until the carrots are just tender and the liquid has evaporated to leave the vegetables juicy. Set aside.

Heat the oil in a clean saucepan and cook the onion until softened but not browned – about 10 minutes. Stir in the butter beans and parsley, and cook for 5 minutes, stirring until the beans are hot. Tip the carrot mixture into the pan, add the tomatoes and mix well. Cook for 1–2 minutes before serving.

SERVES FOUR

TAGLIATELLE WITH BORLOTTI BEANS

350 g/12 oz tagliatelle
salt and pepper
25 g/1 oz butter
30 ml/2 tbsp olive oil
1 garlic clove, crushed
1 onion, chopped
100 g/4 oz button mushrooms, sliced
2 (425 g/15 oz) cans borlotti beans, drained
225 g/8 oz tomatoes, peeled and chopped
5 ml/1 tsp dried oregano
45 ml/3 tbsp chopped parsley
grated Parmesan cheese, to serve

Bring a large saucepan of salted water to the boil and cook the pasta. Allow 3 minutes for fresh pasta or about 12 minutes for the dried type. Drain well and set aside.

Heat the butter, oil and garlic in a large frying pan. Add the onion and fry it over gentle heat, stirring, for about 15 minutes or until softened. Add the mushrooms and cook for 5 minutes before stirring in the beans and tomatoes with the herbs. Add salt and pepper to taste and cook for 10 minutes.

Tip the tagliatelle into the pan and toss it with the bean mixture until piping hot – about 5 minutes. Divide between four large bowls and serve with freshly grated Parmesan cheese.

SERVES FOUR

BLACK-EYED BEAN AND TOMATO GOULASH

225 g/8 oz black-eyed beans, soaked in cold
  water overnight
1 large aubergine, trimmed and diced
salt and pepper
45 ml/3 tbsp oil
2 large onions, chopped
1 garlic clove, crushed
4 celery sticks, diced
1 large red pepper, seeded and diced
1 bay leaf
2 fresh thyme sprigs
15 ml/1 tbsp paprika
15 ml/1 tbsp sugar
2 (397 g/14 oz) cans chopped tomatoes
150 ml/¼ pint plain yogurt

Drain the soaked beans. Put them in a saucepan with plenty of fresh water. Bring to the boil, boil vigorously for 10 minutes, then lower the heat and cover the pan. Simmer for 30–40 minutes, or until tender.

Meanwhile, place the aubergine in a colander. Sprinkle with salt, then leave over a bowl or in the sink for 30 minutes. Rinse and drain well.

Heat the oil in a saucepan. Add the chopped onion, garlic, celery, pepper, bay leaf and thyme. Cook, stirring often, for 15–20 minutes, or until the onion is soft but not brown. Add the aubergine. Cook, stirring often, for 15 minutes until tender.

Add salt and pepper to taste, stir in the paprika and sugar, then pour in the tomatoes and bring the mixture to the boil. Drain the black-eyed beans and add them to the pan. Mix well and simmer for 5 minutes, then taste for seasoning. Top each portion with a little yogurt.

SERVES FOUR TO SIX

ADUKI PILAFF

45 ml/3 tbsp olive oil
1 garlic clove, crushed
1 cinnamon stick
4 cloves
1 bay leaf
2 onions, sliced
225 g/8 oz brown rice
600 ml/1 pint vegetable stock
300 ml/½ pint dry white wine
salt and pepper
100 g/4 oz aduki beans, soaked, drained and
    cooked
100 g/4 oz blanched almonds, split
2 celery sticks, diced
1 eating apple, peeled, cored and diced
100 g/4 oz ready-to-eat dried apricots, diced
grated rind of 1 lemon
30 ml/2 tbsp chopped fresh mint

Heat 30 ml/2 tbsp of the oil in a heavy-bottomed saucepan. Add the garlic, cinnamon, cloves, bay leaf and half the onion slices. Cook for 5 minutes, stirring, then add the rice.

Stir in the stock. Pour in the wine and add salt and pepper. Bring to the boil, lower the heat and cover the pan. Cook for 15 minutes.

Drain the beans if necessary. Tip them into the pan but do not mix them into the rice. Replace the lid quickly and continue cooking for a further 15 minutes over low heat. Turn the heat off and leave the pan covered.

Meanwhile, heat the remaining oil in a frying pan. Add the almonds and brown them all over, then, using a slotted spoon, transfer them to a plate. Add the remaining onion and the celery to the oil remaining in the pan and cook until the onion is browned – about 20-30 minutes. Stir occasionally to prevent the onion from burning.

Stir the apple and apricots into the onion, with a little salt and pepper. Cook for 5 minutes

more. Lastly stir in the browned almonds, lemon rind and mint.

Fork the beans into the rice, then turn it into a large serving dish. Sprinkle the onion mixture over the pilaff and serve at once.

SERVES FOUR

FLAGEOLET AND FENNEL STIR FRY

30 ml/2 tbsp oil
1 large onion, halved and sliced
1 bay leaf
2 fennel bulbs, thinly sliced
2 (425 g/15 oz) cans flageolet beans, drained
salt and pepper
2 avocados
juice of ¼ lemon
30 ml/2 tbsp chopped fresh mint

Heat the oil in a wok or large frying pan. Add the onion, bay leaf and fennel. Stir fry the vegetables for about 20 minutes, or until they are slightly tender.

Add the flageolets with salt and pepper to taste. Stir well, then lower the heat and leave to cook gently for 5 minutes, or until the beans are hot. Meanwhile, halve, stone and peel the avocados. Dice the flesh, put it into a bowl, add the lemon juice and toss lightly.

Stir the avocado into the bean mixture, add the mint and cook for 1 minute. Serve at once, with a plain risotto or warmed crusty bread and a crisp green salad, if liked.

SERVES FOUR

CHICK-PEA CASSEROLE

A few fresh herb sprigs used as a garnish improve the appearance of individual portions.

300 g/11 oz chick-peas, soaked overnight in
    cold water to cover
30 ml/2 tbsp olive oil
1 onion, chopped
1 garlic clove, crushed
1 bay leaf
1 green pepper, seeded and sliced
200 g/7 oz white cabbage, shredded
100 g/4 oz mushrooms, sliced
1 (397 g/14 oz) can chopped tomatoes
2.5 ml/½ tsp ground ginger
pinch of ground cloves
salt and pepper
30 ml/2 tbsp chopped fresh mint
60 ml/4 tbsp chopped parsley

Drain the chick-peas, put them in a saucepan and add fresh water to cover. Do not add salt. Bring to the boil, cook for 10 minutes, then lower the heat and simmer for 1 hour or until tender. Drain the chick-peas, reserving the cooking liquor.

Heat the olive oil in a large saucepan, add the onion, garlic, bay leaf, green pepper and cabbage and fry over moderate heat for 10 minutes. Add the mushrooms, chick-peas and tomatoes. Stir in 125 ml/4 fl oz of the reserved cooking liquor, with the ginger and ground cloves. Add salt and pepper to taste. Bring to the boil, lower the heat and cook very gently for 1 hour, adding more liquid, if required, during cooking. The cooked casserole should be moist, but there should not be too much liquid. Before serving, stir in the mint, parsley and more seasoning if necessary.

SERVES FOUR

SPICY SPINACH AND CHICK-PEAS

The use of canned chick-peas makes this delicious dish a quick-cook option.

25 g/1 oz butter
30 ml/2 tbsp cumin seeds
15 ml/1 tbsp coriander seeds, crushed
15 ml/1 tbsp mustard seeds
1 large onion, chopped
2 garlic cloves, crushed
2 (425 g/15 oz) cans chick-peas, drained
5 ml/1 tsp turmeric
1 kg/2¼ lb fresh spinach, cooked
salt and pepper

Melt the butter in a saucepan, add the cumin, coriander and mustard seeds and cook gently, stirring, for about 3 minutes, or until the seeds are aromatic. Keep the heat low to avoid burning the butter.

Add the onion and garlic to the pan and continue to cook for about 15 minutes, until the onion is softened. Stir in the chick-peas and turmeric and cook for 5 minutes, until thoroughly hot. Tip the spinach into the pan and stir it over moderate heat until heated through. Season and serve.

SERVES FOUR TO SIX

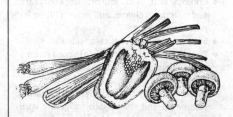

TOFU

Tofu (bean curd) is made by soaking and crushing soya beans, then coagulating the liquid. The result is a creamy-white, flavourless curd which may be soft, with a custard-like texture, or firm enough to sauté. It is widely used in Chinese and Japanese cooking and, being an excellent source of protein, is valued in the vegetarian diet.

Tofu absorbs flavours readily and is a versatile ingredient for all types of cooking, from plain frying or baking with vegetables and sauces, to making dips, spreads and sauces. It may be used to make sweet dishes similar to cheesecakes. It is available in several forms, including a powder mix, long-life packs or fresh, and the ready-made types may be plain, flavoured or smoked.

Packet mixes often give a soft-textured tofu, whereas many of the ready-made types are very firm. Soft tofu is ideal for dips, sauces and puréed mixtures; the firm blocks are suitable for frying or stir-frying.

Store tofu in a covered container in the refrigerator and use within 2 days unless otherwise stated.

USING TOFU

- Marinate chunks with olive oil, garlic and marjoram, then coat with tomato sauce, top with grated cheese and bake.
- Combine with leeks, mushrooms, courgettes and walnuts or cheese, and use as a filling for pastries and pies.
- Smoked tofu makes a tasty salad.
- Purée tofu with a little milk to make a creamy sauce, then pour over a layer of cooked vegetables and bake until golden.
- Marinate firm tofu in soy sauce, garlic, sesame oil and sherry. Stir fry gently with shredded vegetables, adding the marinade to make a sauce.

- Marinate firm tofu with herbs and oil or with a Chinese-style mixture as above. Coat with egg and breadcrumbs or flour and deep fry or bake until crisp and golden. Serve with a crisp green salad.

TOFU PARCELS

fat for greasing
1 carrot, diced
100 g/4 oz fine French beans, thinly sliced
salt and pepper
2 spring onions, chopped
30 ml/2 tbsp chopped parsley
4 large sheets of filo pastry
50 g/2 oz butter, melted or 60 ml/4 tbsp olive oil
100 g/4 oz low-fat soft cheese with garlic and herbs
275 g/10 oz smoked tofu, quartered

WATERCRESS CREAM
1 bunch of watercress, trimmed and chopped
5 ml/1 tsp grated lemon rind
150 ml/¼ pint soured cream, fromage frais or Greek-style yogurt

Blanch the carrot and French beans in a saucepan of boiling salted water for 2 minutes, then drain and mix with the spring onions and parsley. Set the oven at 200°C/400°F/gas 6. Grease a baking sheet.

Work on 1 sheet of filo at a time, keeping the others covered. Brush the pastry with butter or olive oil and fold it in half. Place a quarter of the soft cheese in the middle, spreading it slightly but taking care not to tear the pastry. Divide the vegetable mixture into quarters. Use a teaspoon to sprinkle half of one portion over the cheese.

Top with a quarter of the tofu, diced, then sprinkle the remainder of the vegetable portion over.

Fold one side of the filo over the filling, brush lightly with butter or oil, then fold the opposite side over, pressing the pastry together. Brush with more fat and fold the two remaining sides over as before to make a neat parcel. Brush the top with a little oil or butter, then invert the parcel on the prepared baking sheet, so that the thicker layers of pastry are underneath. Brush the top with more fat. Repeat with the remaining pastry and filling.

Bake the parcels for about 30 minutes, until golden and crisp. Meanwhile, mix the watercress, lemon rind and soured cream, fromage frais or yogurt in a bowl. Add a little salt and pepper. Use a metal slice to transfer the parcels to serving plates and serve at once, with the watercress cream.

SERVES FOUR

 MRS BEETON'S TIP

Instead of making individual parcels, use the same filling ingredients to make a pie. Increase the number of filo pastry sheets to line a flan dish, overlapping them and ensuring the pastry is at least two layers thick. Dice the tofu and spread it out with the rest of the filling. Top with more filo, then fold over the excess from lining the dish. Bake at 180°C/350°F/gas 4 for about 45 minutes, to allow the filo base to cook through.

TOFU AND SPRING ONION STIR FRY

This tasty stir fry goes well with cooked rice or Oriental noodles.

350 g/12 oz firm tofu cut into 2.5 cm/1 inch
   cubes
1 garlic clove, crushed
45 ml/3 tbsp soy sauce
5 cm/2 inch fresh root ginger, peeled and
   chopped
5 ml/1 tsp sesame oil
5 ml/1 tsp cornflour
30 ml/2 tbsp dry sherry
60 ml/4 tbsp vegetable stock
30 ml/2 tbsp oil
1 red pepper, seeded and diced
1 bunch of spring onions, trimmed and
   sliced diagonally
100 g/4 oz button mushrooms, sliced
salt and pepper

Place the tofu in a large, shallow dish. Mix the garlic, soy sauce, ginger and sesame oil in a bowl, then sprinkle the mixture evenly over the tofu. Cover and leave to marinate for 1 hour. In a jug, blend the cornflour to a paste with the sherry, then stir in the stock and set aside.

Heat the oil in a wok or large frying pan. Add the tofu and stir fry until lightly browned. Add the pepper and continue cooking for 2–3 minutes before stirring in the spring onions. Once the onions are combined with the tofu, make a space in the middle of the pan and stir fry the mushrooms for 2 minutes. Pour in the cornflour mixture and stir all the ingredients together. Bring the juices to the boil, stirring all the time, then lower the heat and simmer for 2 minutes. Taste the mixture for seasoning, then serve.

SERVES FOUR

Rice, Cereals
and Other Grains

*Rice, grains and cereals have had an enormous impact on savoury dishes in the British diet as
there has been a move away from traditional meat-and-two-veg meals. These ingredients make
a wide variety of dishes, from traditional kedgeree to polenta and buttery gnocchi.*

TYPES OF RICE

There are many types available in most good
supermarkets and even more on offer in
specialist stores. Information on pudding rice
is included in the chapter on Rice Puddings and
Cooked Milk Puddings.

Long-grain White Rice   The most basic rice,
found even in the smallest shop. White rice has
had all the outer husk removed to leave white
grains. Price is a good indication of quality,
with some very cheap packets holding broken
grains.

Easy-cook Rice   There are many brands of
easy-cook rice, both white and brown. This
type of rice has been treated and partially
cooked. The grains cook quickly and remain
separate and whole. Always follow the packet
instructions closely.

Brown Rice   Brown rice retains some of the
outer covering on the grain. The types vary
according to the brand; the cooking time varies
too. Brown rice usually takes nominally longer
to cook than white rice; however overcooking
is a common fault with this grain. When
cooked, brown rice should be nutty in flavour
and slightly chewy (not soft). The grains
should be separate – more so than with a fluffy
white rice (such as Basmati). Brown rice is
overcooked if the grains have burst and
softened.

Basmati Rice   Both brown and white are
now available, the latter being more traditional
and providing marginally more flavour. Most
often served with Indian dishes, Basmati rice is
a delicious grain with a distinct, very delicate,
aroma and flavour. Open a new packet of good
Basmati rice and take the trouble to smell the
delicate scent of the grains. It is far superior to
the easy-cook and plain types of rice and well
worth buying. However, to overcook Basmati is
a crime because the flavour is diminished.

Risotto Rice   Italian risotto rice has rounder,
shorter grains than other types of rice used for
savoury cooking. When cooked, the grains
should be creamy, not separate. This type of
rice is essential for making authentic risotto.

Sushi Rice or Japanese Rice   A short-
grained rice which is similar to risotto rice. The
grains become quite sticky when cooked, a
characteristic useful when shaping sushi.

Glutinous Rice   Short-grain Chinese rice
which becomes very sticky on cooking. It is
also used for making congee, a cross between
soup and porridge.

Convenience Types   Frozen cooked rice,
canned rice and a broad range of flavoured rice
or rice mixtures are available (in cans, packets
or frozen). The best advice is to sample and
decide for yourself – frozen cooked rice and
canned cooked rice are undeniably quick and
easy, but rather mean on flavour.

CEREALS AND GRAINS

Barley Pot barley is whole grain and pearl barley is the husked, polished grain. Both are cooked by boiling and are traditionally added to soups or stews. However, they may be served or used in place of rice. Barley flakes are also available and are used in muesli.

Buckwheat The seed of a plant which is thought to have originated in China, buckwheat is nutritious and high in fibre. Commonly sold hulled and roasted, the grain must be cooked very gently to avoid reducing it to mush. Dark, buckwheat flour is made from the ground grain. It is used in some Eastern European puddings and pancakes known as blini.

Corn/Maize The familiar vegetable is also cultivated as a cereal crop. When ground, it is sold as maize flour, corn meal or polenta.

Couscous See Semolina.

Rye This grain is cultivated extensively, especially in Northern Europe. It is milled to make rye flour, which is used in breadmaking; also for crackers and crispbreads.

Millet Fine yellow grain which is available from wholefood shops. It cooks quickly and rapidly overcooks to a porridge, so it should be treated similarly to buckwheat. Not particularly popular but may be used instead of rice as an accompaniment.

Oats The whole grain is not used in the same way as rice, barley or wheat in cooking. Hulled and ground grain is known as oatmeal and it ranges from fine ground (pinhead) oatmeal to coarse meal. Used in baking and for coating savoury food before frying or cooking. Oatmeal may also be used for porridge, although processed rolled oats are more popular.

Sago Derived from the starchy pith of several varieties of palm. The starch extracted from the pith is dried, then made into granules. It is used in puddings, some soups, and as a general thickener.

Tapioca Similar to sago in terms of usage, this cereal is derived from the cassava root.

Wheat A widely distributed cereal crop, the basis of most of the flour used in the West for baking. The whole wheat grain requires lengthy boiling to tenderize it. Cracked wheat is the uncooked grain which has been split. It is added to breads for its texture or may be cooked by boiling or by adding to moist dishes. Burghul (or bulgar) is a hulled and cooked wheat-grain product which must not be confused with cracked wheat. It may be softened by soaking, then used in salads or it may be briefly cooked for hot dishes. Wheatgerm, the embryo of the wheat, is highly nutritious. It is used as a thickener and as a dietary supplement.

Semolina is a cereal derived from hard (durum) wheat. It is used as a thickener, especially in milk puddings, and is the basis of a type of porridge. A form of soaked semolina, couscous, is very popular in North Africa. The pearl-like pellets are steamed, traditionally over a pan of stew. Sold ready prepared, couscous cooks and swells quickly when soaked in boiling water.

Wild Rice Not a rice at all, but a species of aquatic grass, this consists of dark, long, thin grains (almost black in colour) which do not become soft on cooking, but remain firm and chewy. Packets often contain a mixture of different types of wild rice, or wild rice mixed with brown, cultivated grain. Wild rice is good when mixed with other ingredients (for example, in a stuffing) or scented with herbs and lemon as an accompaniment. Served solo, wild rice is satisfying; you will not need as much as if you were serving white or brown rice.

COOKING RICE

225 g/8 oz long-grain rice
salt and pepper

If using Basmati rice, plain, untreated long-grain rice or wild rice, start by placing the grains in a bowl. Wash the rice in several changes of cold water, taking care not to swirl the grains vigorously as this may damage them. Pour off most of the water each time, then add fresh water and swirl the rice gently with your fingertips. Finally drain the rice in a sieve and turn it into a saucepan.

Add cold water: 600 ml/1 pint for white rice; 750 ml/1¼ pints for brown or wild rice. Add a little salt and bring to the boil. Stir once, then lower the heat and put a tight-fitting lid on the pan. Cook very gently until the grains are tender: 15–20 minutes for easy-cook varieties and white rice; 20 minutes for Basmati rice; 25–35 minutes for brown rice; 40–50 minutes for wild rice.

Remove the pan from the heat and leave, covered, for 5 minutes, then fork up the grains, add salt and pepper if liked, and serve the rice.

SERVES FOUR

VARIATIONS

Saffron Rice Add 3 green cardamom pods and a bay leaf to the rice. Reduce the amount of water by 50 ml/2 fl oz. Pound 2.5–5 ml/½–1 tsp saffron strands to a powder in a mortar with a pestle. Add 50 ml/2 fl oz boiling water and stir well until the saffron has dissolved. Sprinkle this over the rice after it has been cooking for 15 minutes, then replace the lid quickly and finish cooking. Fork up the rice before serving, removing the bay leaf and cardomons.

Pilau Rice Cook 1 chopped onion in a little butter or ghee in a large saucepan, then add 1 cinnamon stick, 1 bay leaf, 4 green cardomoms and 4 cloves. Stir in 225 g/8 oz Basmati rice and 600 ml/1 pint water and cook as in the main recipe. In a separate pan, cook a second onion, this time thinly sliced, in 50 g/2 oz butter or ghee until golden brown. Add 30 ml/2 tbsp cumin seeds (preferably black seeds) when the onion has softened and before it begins to brown. Add half the sliced onion mixture to the rice and fork it in. Pour the remaining onion mixture over the top of the rice before serving. Saffron may be added to pilau.

Brown and Wild Rice Mix different grains for an interesting texture. Start by cooking the wild rice for 10 minutes, then add the brown rice and continue cooking until the brown rice is tender.

Walnut Rice Cook the chosen rice; add 100 g/4 oz chopped walnuts and 30 ml/2 tbsp chopped parsley before serving.

Lemon Rice Add the grated rind of 1 lemon to the rice: if it is added at the beginning of cooking it gives a deep-seated flavour; added just before serving it adds a fresh, zesty tang to the rice.

Rice with Herbs Add bay leaves, sprigs of rosemary, thyme, savory or sage to the rice at the beginning of cooking. Alternatively, sprinkle chopped parsley, fresh tarragon, dill, mint or marjoram over the rice at the end of cooking. Match the herb to the flavouring in the main dish, with which the rice is to be served.

Tomato Rice Add 1 finely chopped onion, 1 bay leaf and 30 ml/2 tbsp tomato purée to the rice before cooking.

RICE MOULDS

A rice mould may be large or small and it may be served hot or cold. Making a rice ring is the popular form of moulding rice so that the middle may be filled with a hot sauced mixture or cold dressed salad. Typical fillings are salmon, tuna, or mixed seafood in a white sauce, or chicken in sauce. Salads of seafood or poultry, dressed with mayonnaise, soured cream or fromage frais, turn a rice ring into a rich main dish; light vegetable mixtures, such as tomato or courgette salad, are ideal for moulds which are intended as a side dish.

For best results, and particularly when making large moulds, avoid easy-cook rice and mixtures with a high proportion of wild rice as the grains tend not to cling together well. The basic recipe opposite or any of the flavoured variations may be used to make the moulds and rings that follow.

Mrs Beeton's Rice Mould Here is a slight adaptation of the original recipe (referred to as a rice casserole) which suggested beating the overcooked (by our standards) rice until it formed a paste. Use plain rice and cook a double quantity of the basic recipe, using stock if liked instead of water. While the rice is cooking, set the oven at 230°C/450°F/gas 8 and thoroughly butter an 18 cm/7 inch round tin. Prepare a pad of absorbent kitchen paper, about 13 cm/5 inches across and 5 cm/2 inches (or slightly less) shallower than the tin. Wrap this completely in foil and grease it well with oil.

Stir the cooked rice well, then allow to cool for 5 minutes. Beat in an egg, then press a layer of mixture firmly into the base of the tin. Line the sides of the tin with about a 2.5 cm/1 inch thickness of mixture, then put the foil pad in the middle, filling around it with rice. Cover the top of the foil thickly with rice and press down well. Bake for 15 minutes. Grease a baking sheet, then invert the mould on it. Use a knife to cut a circle inside the top of the mould, for a lid, then bake for a further 15 minutes, until lightly browned and firm. Carefully cut out the lid and use a palette knife to remove it. Remove the foil pad and the rice mould is ready for filling.

Hot Ring Mould Cook 1 quantity of the rice. Set the oven at 180°C/350°F/gas 4. Meanwhile, thoroughly grease a 1.1 litre/2 pint metal ring mould with either butter or oil. Stir 45 ml/3 tbsp single cream or milk into the rice, then press it into the mould and cover the top with foil. Bake for 30 minutes. Turn out on a warmed serving dish.

Cold Rice Ring Cook 1 quantity of rice. Grease a 1.1 litre/2 pint ring mould with oil. Press the cooked rice into it, cover and cool. Chill lightly before inverting the mould on a serving dish.

Individual Moulds These may be either hot or cold, using tins or individual ovenproof basins for hot moulds. Grease the moulds well, using oil for cold rice. Dariole moulds, individual basins and ramekin dishes are all ideal. Follow the instructions for ring moulds, reducing the cooking time to 20 minutes for a hot mould.

Multi-layered Moulds With contrasting layers which are visually pleasing, the shape of the mould can be extremely simple, such as a plain round tin or soufflé dish. Combine two or three layers, remembering that the layer in the base of the dish will be on top when the rice is unmoulded. For example, begin by placing a layer of Lemon Rice in the mould, then add a layer of Tomato Rice and finally add a layer of Rice with Herbs, mixing in plenty of chopped parsley after cooking. This combination is excellent with plain grills, such as barbecued foods.

SCAMPI JAMBALAYA

25 g/1 oz butter
15 ml/1 tbsp oil
2 onions, finely chopped
100 g/4 oz cooked ham, diced
3 tomatoes, peeled and chopped
1 green pepper, seeded and finely chopped
1 garlic clove, crushed
pinch of dried thyme
salt and pepper
cayenne pepper
5 ml/1 tsp Worcestershire sauce
225 g/8 oz long-grain rice
125 ml/4 fl oz hot chicken stock
450 g/1 lb peeled cooked scampi tails
100 g/4 oz shelled cooked mussels (optional)
30 ml/2 tbsp medium-dry sherry
fresh thyme sprigs to garnish

Melt the butter in the oil in a deep frying pan. Add the onions and fry gently for 4–5 minutes until soft. Add the ham, tomatoes, green pepper and garlic, then stir in the thyme, with salt, pepper and cayenne to taste. Add the Worcestershire sauce and rice. Stir well. Pour in the hot chicken stock, cover the pan and cook for 12 minutes.

Add the scampi to the pan, with the mussels, if used. Lower the heat, cover and simmer for 5 minutes more or until the rice is perfectly cooked. Stir in the sherry, garnish with thyme and serve at once.

SERVES FOUR

 MRS BEETON'S TIP

Peeled cooked prawns may be substituted for the scampi. Large Mediterranean prawns are delicious in Jambalaya but ordinary prawns are quite suitable.

FISH AND RICE SOUFFLE

fat for greasing
500 ml/17 fl oz milk
1 onion slice
6 peppercorns
1 small bay leaf
piece of lemon rind
450 g/1 lb cod or haddock fillets
50 g/2 oz cooked rice
salt and pepper
3 eggs, separated, plus 1 egg white

Grease a 1 litre/1¾ pint soufflé dish. Set the oven at 190°C/375°F/gas 5.

Put the milk in a large shallow saucepan or frying pan with the onion, peppercorns, bay leaf and lemon rind. Bring to simmering point, add the fish and poach gently for about 15 minutes or until cooked. Using a slotted spoon and a fish slice, transfer the haddock to a wooden board. Strain the cooking liquid into a bowl and stir in the rice.

Remove the skin and any bones from the haddock. Flake the flesh finely and add it to the rice mixture with plenty of salt and pepper. Add the egg yolks one by one, stirring well after each addition.

In a clean, grease-free bowl, whisk all the egg whites until stiff. Using a metal spoon, fold the whites into the fish and rice. Spoon into the prepared dish and bake for 30–35 minutes until well risen and browned. Serve immediately.

SERVES FOUR

PAELLA VALENCIANA

1 kg/2¼ lb mussels, washed, scraped and
   bearded
30 ml/2 tbsp plain flour
1 (1.5 kg/3½ lb) roasting chicken, cut into
   portions
90 ml/6 tbsp olive oil
2 garlic cloves
675 g/1½ lb risotto rice
pinch of saffron threads
salt

GARNISH
450 g/1 lb cooked shellfish (prawns, crayfish,
   lobster or crab; see Mrs Beeton's Tip)
strips of canned pimiento
green or black olives
chopped parsley

Wash, scrape and beard the mussels, following
the instructions on page 169. Put them in a
large saucepan with 125 ml/4 fl oz water. Place
over moderate heat and bring to the boil. As
soon as the liquid bubbles up over the mussels,
shake the pan two or three times, cover, lower
the heat and simmer until the mussels have
opened. Discard any that remain shut. Remove
the mussels with a slotted spoon and shell
them, retaining the best half shells. Strain the

mussel liquid through muslin into a large
measuring jug, add the cooking liquid and
make up to 1.25 litres/2¼ pints with water. Set
aside.

Put the flour in a stout polythene bag, add the
chicken portions and shake until well coated.
Heat 45 ml/3 tbsp of the olive oil in a large frying pan, add the chicken and fry until golden
brown on all sides. Using tongs, transfer the
chicken to a plate and set aside.

Heat the remaining oil in a large deep frying
pan or paella pan. Slice half a garlic clove
thinly and add the slices to the oil. Fry until
golden brown, then discard the garlic. Add the
rice to the pan and fry very gently, turning
frequently with a spatula. Crush the remaining
garlic. Pound the saffron to a powder with a
pestle in a mortar and sprinkle it over the rice
with the garlic. Add salt to taste.

Add the reserved cooking liquid to the pan and
heat to simmering point, stirring frequently.
Cook for 5 minutes, still stirring. Add the
chicken pieces, cooking them with the rice for
15–20 minutes until they are tender and the
rice is cooked through.

Garnish with the shellfish, pimiento, olives
and parsley. Replace the mussels in the half
shells and arrange them on top of the rice
mixture. Remove the pan from the heat, cover
with a clean cloth and set aside for 10 minutes
before serving. Serve from the pan.

SERVES EIGHT

 MRS BEETON'S TIP

The weight of shellfish depends on the
types included: increase the quantity if
adding lots of crab claws or lobster.

KOULIBIAC

Koulibiac is a large oblong pastry filled with a mixture of cooked rice and salmon. Smoked salmon offcuts or canned salmon may be used instead of fresh salmon. Instead of following the method described below, cook the fish on a covered plate which fits tightly over the saucepan, if preferred. This is good either hot or cold and is therefore ideal for formal meals, buffets or picnics.

fat for greasing
450 g/1 lb salmon fillet or steaks
salt and pepper
juice of ½ lemon
175 g/6 oz long-grain rice
50 g/2 oz butter
1 onion, chopped
60 ml/4 tbsp chopped parsley
4 hard-boiled eggs, roughly chopped
15 ml/1 tbsp chopped fresh tarragon
   (optional)
450 g/1 lb puff pastry
1 egg, beaten, to glaze
150 ml/¼ pint soured cream to serve

Lay the salmon on a piece of greased foil large enough to enclose it completely. Sprinkle with salt, pepper and a little of the lemon juice, then wrap the foil around the fish, sealing the edges.

Place the rice in a large saucepan and add 450 ml/¾ pint water. Bring to the boil, lower the heat and cover the pan. Simmer the rice for 10 minutes, then place the foil-wrapped fish on top of the rice. Cover the pan again and cook for about 10 minutes more or until the grains of rice are tender and all the water has been absorbed.

At the end of the cooking time, remove the foil-packed salmon from the pan. Transfer the fish to a board, reserving all the cooking juices, then discard the skin and any bones. Coarsely flake the flesh and set the fish aside. Tip the cooked rice into a bowl.

Melt half the butter in a small saucepan. Add the onion and cook over low heat for about 15 minutes until it is soft but not browned. Mix the cooked onion with the rice and add the salmon and parsley, with salt and pepper to taste. Put the chopped hard-boiled eggs in a bowl. Stir in the remaining lemon juice and add the tarragon, if used. Melt the remaining butter and trickle it over the eggs.

Set the oven at 220°C/425°F/gas 7. Cut a large sheet of foil, at least 30 cm/12 inches long. On a floured board, roll out the pastry to a rectangle measuring about 50 × 25 cm/20 × 10 inches. Trim the pastry to 43 × 25 cm/17 × 10 inches. Cut the trimmings into long narrow strips. Set aside.

Lay the pastry on the foil. Spoon half the rice mixture lengthways down the middle of the pastry. Top with the egg mixture in an even layer, then mound the remaining mixture over the top. Fold one long side of pastry over the filling and brush the edge with beaten egg. Fold the other side over and press the long edges together firmly. Brush the inside of the pastry at the ends with egg and seal them firmly.

Use the foil to turn the koulibiac over so that the pastry seam is underneath, then lift it on to a baking sheet or roasting tin. Brush all over with beaten egg and arrange the reserved strips of pastry in a lattice pattern over the top. Brush these with egg too.

Bake the koulibiac for 30–40 minutes, until the pastry is well puffed and golden. Check after 25 minutes and if the pastry looks well browned, tent a piece of foil over the top to prevent it from overcooking.

Serve a small dish of soured cream with the koulibiac, which should be cut into thick slices.

SERVES EIGHT

MUSSEL RISOTTO

1.6 kg/3½ lb mussels
50 g/2 oz butter
30 ml/2 tbsp olive oil
1 onion, finely chopped
2 garlic cloves, crushed
225 g/8 oz risotto rice
grated rind of ½ lemon
1 bay leaf
300 ml/½ pint dry white wine
salt and pepper
300 ml/½ pint hot Fish Stock (page 48) or
   water
75 g/3 oz Parmesan cheese, grated
60 ml/4 tbsp chopped parsley
8 lemon wedges to serve

Wash, scrape and beard the mussels following the instructions on page 117. Discard any that are open and do not shut when tapped. Put the mussels in a large saucepan. Add 125 ml/4 fl oz water and place over moderate heat to bring to the boil. As soon as the liquid boils, shake the pan and put a tight-fitting lid on it. Cook for about 5 minutes until all the mussels have opened, shaking the pan a couple of times.

Heat half the butter with the olive oil in a separate saucepan. Add the onion and garlic, then cook gently, stirring occasionally, for 10 minutes. Stir in the rice, lemon rind and bay leaf. Cook for a few minutes, stirring gently, until all the rice grains are coated in fat.

Pour in the wine, with salt and pepper to taste. Bring to the boil. Stir once, lower the heat and cover the pan tightly. Leave over low heat for 15 minutes.

Meanwhile, strain the mussels and reserve the cooking liquid. Discard any mussels that have not opened. Reserve a few mussels in shells for garnish and remove the others from their shells.

Pour the mussel cooking liquid and the hot stock or water into the rice mixture. Stir lightly, then cover the pan again. Continue to cook for 15-20 minutes more until the rice is cooked, creamy and moist. Stir in the remaining butter and the cheese. Taste the risotto, adding more salt and pepper if required, then sprinkle in the parsley and place all the mussels on top. Cover the pan tightly and leave off the heat for 5 minutes.

Lightly fork the mussels and parsley into the risotto, turn it into 4 serving bowls and add a couple of lemon wedges to each. Garnish with the reserved mussels.

SERVES FOUR

SAVOURY RICE

200 g/7 oz long-grain rice
1 onion, chopped
salt and pepper
50 g/2 oz mature Cheddar cheese, grated
45 ml/3 tbsp Fresh Tomato Sauce (page 483)
30 ml/2 tbsp chopped parsley
1.25 ml/¼ tsp dried mixed herbs
pinch of cayenne pepper
50 g/2 oz butter, chopped
25 g/1 oz Parmesan cheese, grated, to serve

Place the rice and onion in a saucepan and pour in 450 ml/¾ pint cold water. Add a little salt. Bring to the boil, cover the pan tightly and lower the heat to the lowest setting. Leave for 15 minutes, turn off the heat and leave for a further 15 minutes without removing the lid.

Mix in the Cheddar and the tomato sauce, with the parsley, herbs, cayenne and salt and pepper to taste. Stir in the butter. Heat through, stirring, for 3-4 minutes, then pile on to a warmed serving dish. Sprinkle with Parmesan cheese and serve at once.

SERVES THREE TO FOUR

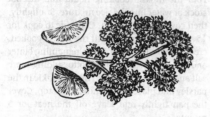

KEDGEREE

No Victorian country-house breakfast would have been complete without kedgeree. Hard-boiled egg and parsley are the traditional garnish, sometimes arranged in the shape of the cross of St Andrew.

salt and pepper
150 g/5 oz long-grain rice
125 ml/4 fl oz milk
450 g/1 lb smoked haddock
50 g/2 oz butter
15 ml/1 tbsp curry powder
2 hard-boiled eggs, roughly chopped
cayenne pepper

GARNISH
15 g/½ oz butter
1 hard-boiled egg, white and yolk sieved
　separately
15 ml/1 tbsp chopped parsley

Bring a saucepan of salted water to the boil. Add the rice and cook for 12 minutes. Drain thoroughly, rinse under cold water and drain again. Place the strainer over a saucepan of simmering water to keep the rice warm.

Put the milk in a large shallow saucepan or frying pan with 125 ml/4 fl oz water. Bring to simmering point, add the fish and poach gently for 4 minutes. Using a slotted spoon and a fish slice, transfer the haddock to a wooden board. Discard the cooking liquid.

Remove the skin and any bones from the haddock and break up the flesh into fairly large flakes. Melt half the butter in a large saucepan. Blend in the curry powder and add the flaked fish. Warm the mixture through. Remove from the heat, lightly stir in the chopped eggs; add salt, pepper and cayenne.

Melt the remaining butter in a second pan, add the rice and toss until well coated. Add salt, pepper and cayenne. Add the rice to the haddock mixture and mix well. Pile the kedgeree on to a warmed dish.

Dot the kedgeree with the butter, garnish with sieved hard-boiled egg yolk, egg white and parsley and serve at once.

SERVES FOUR

SHRIMP AND RICE STIR

salt and pepper
200 g/7 oz long-grain rice
100 g/4 oz butter
100 g/4 oz mushrooms, sliced
100 g/4 oz cooked ham, cut in thin strips
225 g/8 oz peeled cooked shrimps

Bring a saucepan of salted water to the boil. Add the rice and cook for 15 minutes. Drain thoroughly, rinse under cold water and drain again. Place the strainer over a pan of simmering water to keep the rice warm.

Melt the butter in a frying pan, add the mushrooms and fry for 3–4 minutes until golden. Stir in the rice and fry for 4 minutes, then add the ham and shrimps. Lower the heat and simmer for 2–3 minutes. Add salt and pepper to taste, pile on to a warmed serving dish and serve at once.

SERVES FOUR

PHEASANT PILAFF

The day before making the pilaff, roast the pheasant and soak the dried fruit. Leftover pheasant may be used; roast two birds, serve the breast meat only when freshly cooked, and use the remaining meat for the pilaff.

75 g/3 oz prunes, soaked overnight in water
  to cover
1 pheasant, roasted and cooled
225 g/8 oz long-grain rice
salt and pepper
50 g/2 oz butter
75 g/3 oz blanched almonds
1 large onion, chopped
75 g/3 oz ready-to-eat dried apricots, diced
75 g/3 oz seedless raisins
5 ml/1 tsp clear honey
30 ml/2 tbsp chopped parsley

Drain the soaked prunes and stone them if necessary. Remove the pheasant meat from the bones and dice it. Cook the rice in boiling salted water for 12-15 minutes until tender. Drain well.

Heat the butter in a frying pan and brown the almonds lightly. Remove and set aside. Add the onion to the butter remaining in the pan. Cook, stirring often, until thoroughly softened. Stir in the apricots, prunes and raisins. Add the pheasant meat and cover. Continue cooking gently, stirring occasionally, for 15 minutes.

Stir in the hot rice, browned almonds, honey and parsley. Stir well, then check the seasoning and serve at once.

SERVES FOUR

RISOTTO MILANESE

75 g/3 oz butter
30 ml/2 tbsp olive oil
1 onion, finely chopped
350 g/12 oz risotto rice
600 ml/1 pint vegetable stock
2.5 ml/½ tsp saffron threads
300 ml/½ pint dry white wine
salt and pepper
150 g/5 oz Parmesan cheese, grated

Heat 25 g/1 oz of the butter with the olive oil in a large saucepan. Add the onion and fry gently, stirring occasionally for 10 minutes. Add the rice and cook for a few minutes, stirring gently until all the rice grains are coated in fat. Meanwhile heat the stock to simmering point in a separate pan.

Put the saffron threads in a mortar and pound them with a pestle. Stir in a little of the hot stock to dissolve the saffron, then set aside.

Add the wine and half the remaining stock to the rice, with salt and pepper to taste. Bring to the boil. Stir once, lower the heat and cover the pan tightly. Leave over low heat for 10 minutes. Pour in half the remaining hot stock, do not stir, then cover and cook for 5 minutes, shaking the pan occasionally to prevent sticking. Finally, add the remaining stock and saffron liquid. Stir once or twice, cover and cook for about 10 minutes, until the rice is cooked, creamy and moist.

Stir in the remaining butter and the cheese. Taste the risotto, adding more salt and pepper if required. Cover tightly and leave to stand for 5 minutes before serving.

SERVES FOUR

POLENTA WITH SMOKED SAUSAGE

The sausages used in this satisfying dish are dried continental ones. They have a high meat content and require a little cooking before eating.

400 g/14 oz polenta
salt and pepper
400 g/14 oz chorizo, cabanos or other small smoked sausages
200 g/7 oz tomato purée
50 g/2 oz Parmesan cheese, grated
25 g/1 oz dried white breadcrumbs
25 g/1 oz butter

Bring 500 ml/17 fl oz water to the boil in a large saucepan. Stir in the polenta and salt and pepper to taste. Cook for 10-15 minutes, stirring all the time. Leave to cool.

Cook the sausages in boiling water for 10 minutes. Remove from the pan and leave to cool. Remove the skins and cut into 2 cm/¾ inch slices.

Set the oven at 180°C/350°F/gas 4. Put a layer of polenta in the bottom of an ovenproof dish, cover with a layer of sausages, some tomato purée, Parmesan, salt and pepper. Repeat the layers until all the ingredients have been used. Sprinkle the breadcrumbs over the mixture. Dot with the butter. Bake for 25-30 minutes.

SERVES THREE TO FOUR

POLENTA WITH CHEESE

5 ml/1 tsp salt
200 g/7 oz polenta
50 g/2 oz butter
50 g/2 oz Parmesan cheese, grated

Bring 500 ml/17 fl oz water to the boil in a saucepan with the salt. Add the polenta and stir well with a wooden spoon. Cook for 20-30 minutes, stirring all the time. When the mixture leaves the sides of the pan cleanly, stir in the butter and Parmesan quickly and thoroughly.

Spread the mixture on a dish which has been sprinkled with cold water. Cut into slices to serve.

SERVES THREE TO FOUR

VARIATION

Cut cold polenta into pieces, 1 cm/½ inch thick. Place in a pie dish and cover with a thick layer of grated cheese. Continue layering the polenta and cheese until all the polenta has been used up. Top with a thick layer of cheese and dot with butter. Bake in the oven at 190°C/375°F/gas 5 for 20-25 minutes.

SEMOLINA GNOCCHI

Serve this Italian-style dish with a tomato sauce or spicy savoury sauce. The gnocchi may be cooked in the oven or under the grill.

fat for greasing
500 ml/17 fl oz milk
100 g/4 oz semolina
salt and pepper
1.25 ml/¼ tsp grated nutmeg
1 egg
100 g/4 oz Parmesan cheese, grated
25 g/1 oz butter

Grease a shallow ovenproof dish. Bring the milk to the boil in a saucepan. Sprinkle in the semolina and stir over low heat until the mixture is thick. Mix in the salt, pepper, nutmeg, egg and 75 g/3 oz of the Parmesan. Beat the mixture well until smooth. Spread on a shallow dish and leave to cool.

Set the oven at 200°C/400°F/gas 6, if using. Cut the cooled semolina mixture into 2 cm/¾ inch squares or shape into rounds. Place in the prepared ovenproof dish and sprinkle with the remaining Parmesan; dot with butter. Brown under the grill or in the oven for 8-10 minutes.

SERVES FOUR

 MRS BEETON'S TIP

Canned chopped tomatoes make a quick sauce. Add them to a chopped onion cooked in butter or oil until soft. Simmer for 5 minutes, then add salt, pepper and plenty of chopped parsley. Herbs, such as bay and marjoram, and garlic may be added; with a little red wine and longer simmering the sauce is rich and excellent.

CORN PUDDING

fat for greasing
100 g/4 oz plain flour
5 ml/1 tsp salt
2.5 ml/½ tsp black pepper
2 eggs, beaten
500 ml/17 fl oz milk
400 g/14 oz fresh or frozen sweetcorn kernels

Grease a 1.5 litre/2¾ pint pie or ovenproof dish. Set the oven at 180°C/350°F/gas 4. Sift the flour, salt and pepper into a bowl. Add the beaten eggs, stirring well. Beat together with the milk and then the corn to form a batter. Turn into the prepared dish. Bake for 1 hour. Serve.

SERVES SIX

BUCKWHEAT BAKE

fat for greasing
200 g/7 oz roasted buckwheat
1 egg
75 g/3 oz butter
salt and pepper
75 g/3 oz Parmesan cheese, grated

Grease a 900 ml/1½ pint baking dish. Set the oven at 190°C/375°F/gas 5. Put the buckwheat into a large saucepan with 600 ml/1 pint cold water. Bring to the boil, lower the heat to the lowest setting and cover the pan tightly. Leave for 15 minutes, by which time the grains should have absorbed the liquid.

Tip the buckwheat into a bowl, add the egg and beat well. Stir in 25 g/1 oz of the butter and seasoning. Melt the remaining butter. Pour alternate layers of buckwheat and grated cheese in the prepared baking dish. Pour the remaining butter over the top. Bake for 20-30 minutes, until browned.

SERVES THREE TO FOUR

COUSCOUS

50 g/2 oz chick-peas, soaked overnight in
  plenty of cold water
45 ml/3 tbsp olive oil
8 chicken thighs, skinned if preferred
2 garlic cloves, crushed
1 large onion, chopped
1 green pepper, seeded and sliced
1 green chilli, seeded and chopped
  (optional)
15 ml/1 tbsp ground coriander
5 ml/1 tsp ground cumin
100 g/4 oz carrots, sliced
100 g/4 oz turnips, cut into chunks
450 g/1 lb pumpkin, peeled, seeds removed
  and cut into chunks
450 g/1 lb potatoes, cut into chunks
1 bay leaf
2 (397 g/14 oz) cans chopped tomatoes
50 g/2 oz raisins
150 ml/¼ pint chicken stock or water
salt and pepper
225 g/8 oz courgettes, sliced
45 ml/3 tbsp chopped parsley
350 g/12 oz couscous
50 g/2 oz butter, melted

Drain the chick-peas, then cook them in plenty of fresh boiling water for 10 minutes. Lower the heat, cover the pan and simmer for 1½ hours, or until the chick-peas are just tender. Drain.

Heat the oil in a very large flameproof casserole or saucepan. Add the chicken pieces and brown them all over, then use a slotted spoon to remove them from the pan and set aside. Add the garlic, onion, pepper and chilli, if used, to the oil remaining in the pan and cook for 5 minutes, stirring.

Stir in the coriander and cumin, then add the carrots, turnips, pumpkin, potatoes, bay leaf, tomatoes, raisins, stock or water with salt and pepper to taste. Stir in the drained chick-peas. Bring to the boil, then lower the heat and replace the chicken thighs, tucking them in among the vegetables. Cover and simmer gently for 1 hour. Stir in the courgettes and parsley, cover the pan and continue to cook gently for a further 30 minutes.

There are two options for preparing the couscous. The first is to line a steamer with scalded muslin, then sprinkle the couscous into it. Place the steamer over the simmering stew for the final 30 minutes' cooking, covering it tightly to keep all the steam in. Alternatively – and this is the easier method – place the couscous in a deep casserole or bowl and pour in fresh boiling water from the kettle to cover the grains by 2.5 cm/1 inch. Cover and set aside for 15 minutes. The grains will absorb the boiling water and swell. If the couscous cools on standing, it may be reheated over a pan of boiling water or in a microwave for about 2 minutes on High.

To serve, transfer the couscous to a very large serving dish and pour the hot melted butter over it. Fork up the grains and make a well in the middle. Ladle the chicken and vegetable stew into the well, spooning cooking juices over the couscous.

SERVES EIGHT

 MRS BEETON'S TIP

Cubes of boneless lamb may be used instead of the chicken. The vegetables may be varied according to what is freshly available – marrow or green beans may be added or substituted for other ingredients.

Couscous is usually accompanied by a hot, spicy condiment known as *harissa*. This paste, made from chillies, cumin, coriander, garlic, mint and oil, is deep red in colour and fiery of flavour. It is added to individual portions to taste but should be treated with respect.

Pasta

As versatile as the British potato, pasta is an International food with origins in many countries and favoured all over the world. This chapter serves as an introduction to a broad culinary topic.

Although Italy is usually the country that comes to mind when pasta is mentioned, many other nations have developed some form of pasta dough, and the ways in which this versatile food is used are legion. Oriental pasta dough is utilized to make noodles, popular in both Chinese and Japanese cooking, and small filled dumplings which are served as dim sum, or snacks, in the Chinese tradition. Filled dumplings from Poland and other European countries share more in common with their Italian relatives, ravioli, than they do with the suet dumplings of British fame.

The recipes in this chapter are basics which may be varied to make a broad selection of dishes. Pasta dishes are included throughout this book; a general list can be found in the Index, under 'Pasta'.

In many recipes, the specific shape of pasta mentioned is merely a suggestion; experiment with alternatives and discover, for instance, that tagliatelle is delicious with Bolognese Sauce; shells can be substituted for macaroni in Macaroni Cheese.

SAUCES FOR PASTA

Sauces are the natural partners for pasta, whether you choose a plain tomato or rich meat sauce to serve Italian style; or toss a succulent, sauced stir fry with Chinese egg noodles to produce a tempting chow mein.

Simple milk-based sauces, such as cheese, mushroom or egg sauce, are sufficient to turn a bowl of cooked pasta into a meal. Tossed together, topped with cheese, then grilled until golden and bubbling, the combination is deliciously satisfying. Seafood, poultry and meat sauces take pasta beyond the realms of snack and supper cookery to dinner-party status. Meat-free dishes are quickly conjured up by combining braised vegetable mixtures with fresh cooked pasta.

PASTA SIMPLICITY

One of the most appealing aspects of pasta cookery is that it can be ultra simple, extremely stylish and absolutely mouthwatering. One classic Italian snack is a dish of piping hot pasta, generously dressed with olive oil in which a few crushed cloves of garlic have been lightly cooked. Sprinkled with some shredded basil or chopped parsley, topped with several grindings of black pepper and a few spoonfuls of freshly grated Parmesan cheese, this is indeed a snack to set before the hungriest gourmet. Here are a few equally simple combinations to toss into freshly cooked pasta.

- Flaked canned tuna, chopped spring onion and chopped black olives.
- Diced tomato, shredded fresh basil, a few chopped capers and crisp grilled bacon bits.
- Chopped hard-boiled egg with peeled cooked prawns, a knob of butter and pepper.
- Diced and sautéed courgettes with grated Gruyère cheese.

FILLED PASTA

Raw fillings may be used for small pasta shapes and dumplings. The rolled dough is filled, sealed and cooked. Enough time must be allowed for the filling to cook through. The drained cooked pasta is then tossed with a simple sauce; oil or butter and Parmesan cheese may be offered with Italian dishes.

On occasion, as when preparing cannelloni, the pasta and filling are cooked separately, then combined and coated with sauce for the final baking.

SWEET PASTA

The popularity of pasta as a savoury food outshines interest in its potential as an ingredient in sweet dishes; however, there are many traditional, International sweet pasta recipes, including macaroni pudding.

TYPES OF PASTA

Fresh Pasta   Available chilled or frozen, this has the best flavour. It cooks very quickly (except when filled). Fresh pasta is also easy to make and it freezes well. It may be flavoured and coloured with a variety of ingredients, such as spinach, tomato or beetroot.

Dried Pasta   The shapes and forms of dried pasta are too numerous to mention; the list is always increasing. Some of the traditional shapes are illustrated on page 516; others include large shapes for stuffing and novelty shapes for children. Dried pasta is manufactured in many colours and flavours.

Quick-Cook Dried Pasta   There are several forms, including shapes which require brief boiling and lasagne sheets which do not require any pre-cooking before they are layered

with a sauce for baking. Quality varies enormously. In general, these products are inferior to more traditional forms of pasta as their texture tends to be softer and slightly more 'jellied', lacking the bite which is characteristic of pasta (fresh or dried), which is cooked 'al dente'.

USES FOR PASTA

Serving with Sauce   Shapes, noodles, spaghetti, Chinese egg noodles.

Layering and Baking or Grilling   Lasagne, medium-sized shapes, cut macaroni.

Filling   Fresh pasta dough, cannelloni, large shells, large elbow shapes or other large shapes with a pocket or hollow for stuffing.

Soups   Very small shapes, cut macaroni, vermicelli, Oriental rice noodles.

As a Stuffing   For filling scooped out tomatoes and other vegetables, such as peppers, soup pasta, macaroni and small shapes are all suitable.

PASTA

Home-made pasta dough may be used to make noodles, lasagne or stuffed pasta (such as ravioli). Alternatively, it may be cut into small squares for cooking.

400 g/14 oz strong white flour
2.5 ml/½ tsp salt
30 ml/2 tbsp olive oil or 40 g/1½ oz butter, melted
3 eggs, beaten
about 15 ml/1 tbsp oil for cooking
about 50 g/2 oz butter
freshly ground black pepper

Put the flour and salt in a large bowl and make a well in the middle. Add the oil or butter and the eggs, then gradually mix in the flour to make a stiff dough. As the mixture clumps together use your hands to knead it into one piece. If necessary add 15–30 ml/1–2 tbsp water, but take care not to make the mixture soft. It should be quite hard at this stage as it will become more pliable on kneading.

Knead the dough thoroughly on a very lightly floured surface for 10–15 minutes, or until it is very smooth and pliable. Ideally you should be able to work without dusting the surface with flour more than once, provided you keep the dough moving fairly fast all the time.

Cut the dough in half and wrap one piece in polythene to prevent it from drying out. Roll out the dough, adding a dusting of flour as necessary, into a large thin oblong sheet.

To cut noodles, dust the dough with flour and fold it in half, dust it again and fold over once more. Cut the folded dough into 1 cm/½ inch wide strips, then shake them out and place on a floured plate. Cover loosely with polythene to prevent them from drying out until they are cooked. Repeat with the remaining dough.

Bring a very large saucepan of salted water to the boil. Add a little oil. Tip all the noodles into the pan and bring the water back to the boil rapidly, stir once, then regulate the heat so that the water boils but does not froth over. Cook for about 3 minutes. The pasta should be tender but not soft.

Drain the pasta and turn it into a heated bowl. Toss a knob of butter and plenty of freshly ground black pepper with the noodles, then serve piping hot.

MAKES ABOUT 450 G/1 LB

VARIATIONS

Pasta Verde Cook 225 g/8 oz fresh spinach, or 100 g/4 oz frozen chopped spinach. Drain the spinach thoroughly and purée in a blender or food processor. When making the pasta, use an extra 50 g/2 oz plain flour. Add the spinach purée to the well in the flour and mix it in with the eggs. It will not be necessary to add any water.

Tomato Pasta Mix 30 ml/2 tbsp tomato purée with the oil or butter, then stir in the eggs before incorporating the mixture with the flour.

** FREEZER TIP**

Roll out and cut up the pasta, then freeze it in practical quantities. Fresh pasta freezes very well and cooks from frozen, taking 2–3 minutes longer than usual.

SEAFOOD LASAGNE

butter for greasing
12 sheets of lasagne
25 g/1 oz butter
1 onion, chopped
1 celery stick, diced
25 g/1 oz plain flour
300 ml/½ pint red wine
45 ml/3 tbsp tomato purée
1 bay leaf
60 ml/4 tbsp chopped parsley
salt and pepper
450 g/1 lb white fish fillet, skinned and cut
    into small pieces
225 g/8 oz peeled cooked prawns, thawed if
    frozen
225 g/8 oz shelled cooked mussels, thawed if
    frozen
100 g/4 oz mushrooms, sliced
100 g/4 oz mozzarella cheese, diced
600 ml/1 pint White Sauce (page 479)

Grease a large lasagne dish with butter. Cook the lasagne if necessary (if using lasagne which requires no pre-cooking, follow package instructions). Leave to dry.

Melt the butter in a saucepan. Add the onion and celery, then cook, stirring occasionally, for 10 minutes. Stir in the flour, then gradually pour in the wine, stirring all the time. Add 125 ml/4 fl oz water and bring to the boil, stirring. Stir in the tomato purée, bay leaf and parsley. Lower the heat and simmer for 5 minutes. Taste the sauce; add salt and pepper as required.

Set the oven at 180°C/350°F/gas 4. Remove the wine sauce from the heat. Add the fish, prawns and mussels. Make sure that any frozen seafood is well drained. Lastly, stir in the mushrooms.

Place a layer of lasagne in the prepared dish, then top with half the seafood sauce. Lay half the remaining lasagne over the sauce, then pour on all the remaining seafood mixture. Top with the rest of the lasagne. Stir the mozzarella into the white sauce, then pour this over the lasagne.

Bake for 20–40 minutes until golden brown and bubbling hot. (The type of pasta used will dictate the exact timing.) If liked, serve with salad and crusty bread to mop up the sauce.

SERVES SIX

A SELECTION OF PASTA SHAPES

 1 spaghetti
 2 cannelloni tubes
 3 shells
 4 long thin spirals (fusilli)
 5 twists
 6 lasagne sheet
 7 cartwheels
 8 bows
 9 macaroni
10 elbow macaroni
11 tagliatelle

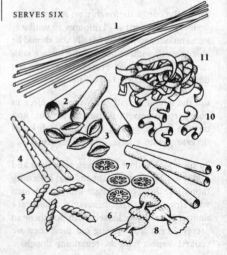

RAVIOLI WITH CHICKEN AND HAM

100 g/4 oz cooked chicken
25 g/1 oz cooked ham
15 ml/1 tbsp chopped parsley
45 ml/3 tbsp double cream
1.25 ml/¼ tsp grated nutmeg
salt and pepper
50 g/2 oz Parmesan cheese, grated
300 ml/½ pint Fresh Tomato Sauce (page 483)
15 g/½ oz butter

PASTA DOUGH
225 g/8 oz strong white flour
1.25 ml/¼ tsp salt
40 g/1½ oz butter, softened
2 eggs, plus extra for sealing dough
cornflour for rolling out

Mince the chicken and ham together. Transfer to a bowl and stir in the parsley, cream and nutmeg. Stir in salt and pepper to taste and add half the Parmesan. Pound well, then rub through a coarse sieve. Alternatively, grind the chicken and ham in a food processor, then add the remaining ingredients and process until almost smooth.

To make the pasta dough, sift the flour and salt into a large bowl. Make a well in the centre and put in the butter and eggs. Mix well, adding a little water if necessary to make a stiff dough. Knead well for about 15 minutes or until the dough is perfectly smooth and elastic.

Divide the dough into 2 equal portions. Roll a portion of dough into a 30 cm/12 inch square. Set aside, covered with polythene, and roll out the second portion to the same size. Place small balls (cherry-sized) of the chicken mixture about 2 cm/¾ inch apart on the dough in neat rows. You should have 36 small balls.

Brush beaten egg between the balls of filling. Cover with the second sheet of dough and press down well around each mound of filling. Using a pastry wheel or small fluted cutter, cut between the filling to make neat squares. A long, clean, ruler as a guide helps to make neat ravioli. Set the oven at 200°C/400°F/gas 6.

Bring a large saucepan of water to the boil. Drop the ravioli into the water and boil for 10–15 minutes. Drain thoroughly, then place in an ovenproof dish and pour the tomato sauce over the pasta. Mix well to coat all the ravioli in the sauce.

Sprinkle the remaining Parmesan over the top and dot with the butter. Bake for about 20 minutes. Serve at once.

SERVES SIX

VARIATION

If preferred, serve the cooked ravioli tossed with cream. Heat 300 ml/½ pint soured cream very gently until just warm. Toss into the pasta with plenty of shredded fresh basil and snipped chives. Sprinkle with Parmesan and serve.

LASAGNE AL FORNO

150 g/5 oz lasagne (7 sheets) or 200 g/7 oz (12 sheets) no-precook lasagne
30 ml/2 tbsp oil
2 onions, finely chopped
2 garlic cloves, chopped
225 g/8 oz minced beef
225 g/8 oz minced pork
100 g/4 oz mushrooms, sliced
2 (397 g/14 oz) cans chopped tomatoes
2.5 ml/½ tsp dried basil
2.5 ml/½ tsp dried oregano
150 ml/¼ pint red wine
salt and pepper
900 ml/1½ pints cold White Sauce (page 479)
50 g/2 oz Parmesan cheese, grated

Cook the lasagne, if necessary, in plenty of boiling salted water. Add the lasagne a sheet at a time, then boil for about 12 minutes until tender but not soft. Drain well, rinse under cold water and lay out to dry on absorbent kitchen paper.

Heat the oil in a heavy-bottomed saucepan, add the onions and garlic and fry over medium heat for 10 minutes. Stir in the beef and pork. Cook, stirring, for 5-10 minutes.

Stir in the mushrooms, tomatoes, herbs and wine. Add salt and pepper. Bring just to the boil, stirring. Reduce the heat, then simmer the sauce steadily, uncovered, stirring occasionally. Allow 1¼-1½ hours until the meat is tender and the sauce thick when stirred.

Set the oven at 180°C/350°F/gas 4. Spread a thin layer of the white sauce over the base of a 30 × 20 cm/12 × 8 inch baking dish. Arrange a layer of lasagne in the dish. Top with a layer of meat sauce. Add a thin layer of white sauce, but do not worry too much about spreading the sauce perfectly; the next layer of lasagne will smooth it out. Repeat the layers, ending with white sauce. Sprinkle the top with Parmesan.

Bake for 40-50 minutes, until golden brown. Allow the lasagne to stand for 10 minutes before serving.

SERVES SIX TO EIGHT

CRAB-STUFFED CANNELLONI

fat for greasing
12 cannelloni
salt and pepper
225 g/8 oz crab meat
50 g/2 oz fresh white breadcrumbs
3 spring onions, chopped
225 g/8 oz ricotta cheese
600 ml/1 pint Fresh Tomato Sauce (page 483)
225 g/8 oz mozzarella cheese, sliced

Grease a large, shallow baking dish with butter. Alternatively, prepare 4 individual gratin dishes. Cook the cannelloni in boiling salted water for 10-15 minutes, until tender. Drain and rinse in cold water, then lay out to dry on a clean tea-towel.

Set the oven at 190°C/375°F/gas 5. Place the crab meat in a bowl and shred it with two forks. If using brown meat as well as white, add it after the white has been shredded. Mix in the breadcrumbs, spring onions and ricotta, with salt and pepper.

There are two ways of filling cannelloni: either put the crab mixture into a piping bag fitted with a large plain nozzle and force the mixture into the tubes, or use a teaspoon to fill the tubes. For those who are confident about using a piping bag the former method is less messy.

Lay the filled cannelloni in the prepared baking dish or dishes. Pour the tomato sauce over. Top with the mozzarella and bake for about 40 minutes, until golden.

SERVES FOUR

SPAGHETTI ALLA CARBONARA

450g/1lb spaghetti
salt and pepper
15ml/1tbsp oil
100g/4oz rindless streaky bacon rashers, cut into fine strips
4 eggs
30ml/2tbsp double cream
75g/3oz Pecorino or Parmesan cheese, grated

Cook the spaghetti in a large saucepan of boiling salted water for 8-10 minutes or until tender but still firm to the bite.

Meanwhile heat the oil in a large frying pan and fry the bacon until the fat is transparent. Draw the pan off the heat. In a bowl, beat the eggs with the cream, adding a little salt and a generous grinding of pepper.

Drain the cooked spaghetti thoroughly and mix it with the bacon. Return to moderate heat for 1-2 minutes to heat through. Stir the egg mixture rapidly into the pan. As it begins to thicken, tip in the cheese. Do not stir it in. Serve immediately on hot plates.

SERVES FOUR

 MRS BEETON'S TIP

Use fresh pasta with this sauce, if preferred. It will cook in considerably less time than dried pasta and will be ready as soon as it rises to the surface of the boiling water. Test after 1 minute.

NOODLES WITH WALNUT SAUCE

4-6 fresh marjoram sprigs or 6-8 parsley sprigs
100g/4oz walnut pieces
100ml/3½floz double cream
olive oil (see method)
salt and pepper
450g/1lb tagliatelle or other flat ribbon noodles
50g/2oz butter
50g/2oz Parmesan cheese, grated (optional)

Pick the leaves off the marjoram or parsley. Grind the walnuts to a paste in a blender or food processor, then add the leaves and process until finely chopped; the mixture need not be completely smooth. Gradually add the cream, procesing briefly after each addition, then work in just enough oil to make a thick, creamy, pale green purée. Add salt and pepper to taste. Cover the bowl and chill for at least 1 hour.

Cook the noodles in a large saucepan of boiling salted water for 8-10 minutes or until tender but still firm to the bite. Drain well, place in a large bowl and toss with the butter. Spoon the cold walnut sauce over the pasta. Serve at once, with grated Parmesan cheese, if liked.

SERVES FOUR

 MRS BEETON'S TIP

If you do not have a food processor or blender, make the sauce as follows: grind the walnuts in a mortar with a pestle, add the finely chopped leaves and pound to a paste. Transfer the mixture to a bowl and gradually add the cream, beating after each addition. Proceed as in the recipe above.

PASTICCIO DI LASAGNE VERDE

fat for greasing
250 g/9 oz green lasagne
60 ml/4 tbsp oil
50 g/2 oz onion, chopped
1 garlic clove, chopped
50 g/2 oz celery, chopped
50 g/2 oz carrot, chopped
500 g/18 oz lean minced beef
300 ml/½ pint beef stock
50 g/2 oz tomato purée
salt and pepper
75 g/3 oz walnut pieces, finely chopped
50 g/2 oz sultanas
250 g/9 oz tomatoes, peeled, seeded and
    chopped
50 g/2 oz red pepper, seeded and chopped
150 ml/¼ pint cold Cheese Sauce (page 480)

Grease a shallow ovenproof dish. Cook the lasagne if necessary (if using lasagne which requires no pre-cooking, follow package instructions). Leave to dry.

Heat the oil in a frying pan and cook the onion, garlic, celery and carrot for 5 minutes. Add the minced meat and brown it lightly all over. Add the stock, tomato purée and salt and pepper to taste. Bring to the boil, lower the heat and simmer for 30 minutes. Set the oven at 180°C/350°F/gas 4.

Line the bottom of the dish with half the pasta and cover with the meat mixture, then sprinkle with the nuts, sultanas, tomatoes and red pepper. Cover with the remaining pasta. Coat with the cold sauce and bake for 20 minutes.

SERVES FOUR

STUFFED BAKED CANNELLONI

butter for greasing
12-16 cannelloni
15 ml/1 tbsp olive oil
300 g/11 oz frozen chopped spinach
salt and pepper
1.25 ml/¼ tsp grated nutmeg
150 g/5 oz ricotta or cottage cheese
50 g/2 oz cooked ham, finely chopped
600 ml/1 pint Cheese Sauce (page 586)
25 g/1 oz dried white breadcrumbs
25 g/1 oz Parmesan cheese, grated

Butter an ovenproof dish. Set the oven at 180°C/350°F/gas 5. Cook the cannelloni in a saucepan of boiling salted water with the oil for 10–15 minutes until tender but still firm to the bite. Drain well.

Place the spinach in a saucepan. Cook over low heat for about 10 minutes or until the spinach has thawed completely. Raise the temperature and heat the spinach thoroughly. Drain. Mix the spinach, salt, pepper, nutmeg, soft cheese and ham in a bowl. Spoon the mixture into the cannelloni. Place in the prepared ovenproof dish. Pour the sauce over the cannelloni.

Bake for 15-20 minutes. Mix together the crumbs and Parmesan, then sprinkle over the dish. Place under a hot grill for 2-3 minutes to brown the top.

SERVES FOUR

CANNELLONI WITH MUSHROOM STUFFING

Illustrated on page 399

butter for greasing
12–16 cannelloni
15 ml/1 tbsp olive oil
750 ml/1¼ pints White Sauce (page 479)
50 g/2 oz butter
200 g/7 oz button mushrooms, thinly sliced
50 g/2 oz Parmesan cheese, grated
50 g/2 oz Gruyère cheese, grated
50 g/2 oz Parma ham, finely shredded
15 ml/1 tbsp fine dried white breadcrumbs
15 ml/1 tbsp single cream or top of the milk

Butter a shallow ovenproof dish. Set the oven at 180°C/350°F/gas 5. Cook the cannelloni in a saucepan of boiling salted water with the oil for 10–15 minutes until al dente. Drain well. Simmer 500 ml/18 fl oz of the sauce until well reduced and very thick. Put the sauce on one side.

Melt 25 g/1 oz of the butter in a pan and gently cook the mushrooms for 2 minutes. Add to the sauce with 25 g/1 oz of the Parmesan. Leave to cool for 10 minutes.

Spoon the cooled mixture into the cannelloni. Place in the prepared ovenproof dish. Sprinkle the Gruyère and ham over the cannelloni, then sprinkle with the breadcrumbs. Add the cream or top of the milk to the remaining sauce and pour over the pasta. Top with the remaining Parmesan and dot with the remaining butter.

Bake for 15–20 minutes, until lightly browned. Cover with greased foil if browning too much before the end of cooking.

SERVES FOUR

MACARONI CHEESE

An old favourite, Macaroni Cheese may be served solo or with grilled bacon or sausages. A layer of sliced tomato may be added to the topping before being baked or grilled, if liked.

fat for greasing
150 g/5 oz elbow macaroni
salt and pepper
600 ml/1 pint hot White Sauce (page 479)
100 g/4 oz Cheddar cheese, grated

Grease a 750 ml/1¼ pint pie dish. Set the oven at 200°C/400°F/gas 6. Cook the macaroni in a large saucepan of boiling salted water for 10–12 minutes or until tender but still firm to the bite.

Drain the macaroni thoroughly and stir it gently into the white sauce. Add three-quarters of the cheese, with salt and pepper to taste. Spoon the mixture into the prepared pie dish. Sprinkle with the remaining cheese and bake for 15–20 minutes.

Alternatively, place under a preheated grill for 2–4 minutes to melt and brown the cheese topping.

SERVES THREE TO FOUR

MACARONI SAVOURY

*Mrs Beeton served this simple dish as a savoury with
the cheese course; however, today it is better classed as
a quick, delicious but rich, supper dish. Good with a
crisp green salad or a tomato salad. Cheshire cheese
may be used instead of fresh Parmesan and a few
shredded basil leaves may be added.*

225 g/8 oz macaroni
salt and pepper
100-175 g/4-6 oz fresh Parmesan cheese,
   grated
75-100 g/3-4 oz butter, melted
50 g/2 oz fresh breadcrumbs

Cook the macaroni in boiling salted water until
just tender. Drain well and layer in a warmed
fireproof dish, sprinkling each layer with pepper, Parmesan and a little butter.

Top with the breadcrumbs and remaining butter, then brown under a hot grill. Serve at once.

SERVES FOUR

CREAMED PASTA

175 g/6 oz macaroni or tagliatelle
300 ml/½ pint milk
300 ml/½ pint chicken or vegetable stock
3 egg yolks
salt and pepper
60 ml/4 tbsp single cream
100 g/4 oz fresh Parmesan or Cheshire
   cheese, grated
25 g/1 oz butter

Place the pasta in a large saucepan with the
milk and stock. Bring to the boil, stirring,
reduce the heat so that the pasta simmers
without boiling over and cover the pan. Simmer for 20 minutes, or until the pasta is tender.
Stir occasionally to prevent the pasta sticking.

Drain the pasta, reserving the cooking liquid
and place in a flameproof serving dish. Return
the liquid to the pan. Beat the egg yolks,
seasoning and cream, then pour this into the
liquid in the pan and heat gently without
boiling. Stir in most of the cheese and pour over
the pasta. Toss well, sprinkle with the remaining cheese and dot with butter. Brown under
the grill and serve at once.

SERVES FOUR

NOODLES WITH
MUSHROOMS

15 g/½ oz butter
30 ml/2 tbsp oil
2 rindless streaky bacon rashers, chopped
450 g/1 lb open mushrooms, sliced
salt and pepper
350 g/12 oz noodles
150 ml/¼ pint single cream

Melt the butter in the oil in a large frying pan.
Add the bacon and fry for 2 minutes, then stir
in the mushrooms. Add salt and pepper to taste
and cook over moderately high heat, stirring
occasionally, for about 10 minutes.

Meanwhile cook the noodles in a large saucepan of boiling salted water for 8-10 minutes or
until tender but still firm to the bite.

Stir the cream into the mushrooms and heat
through over low heat. Drain the noodles thoroughly, pour the mushroom mixture over the
top and toss lightly. Serve at once.

SERVES FOUR

SPAGHETTI ALLA MARINARA

100 g/4 oz butter
1 garlic clove, crushed
10 ml/2 tsp chopped parsley
15 ml/1 tbsp shredded fresh basil or
    5 ml/1 tsp dried basil
salt and pepper
225 g/8 oz spaghetti, broken into short
    lengths
50 g/2 oz Parmesan cheese, grated
25 g/1 oz plain flour
225 g/8 oz peeled cooked scampi tails
oil for shallow frying
pinch of grated nutmeg

SAUCE
45 ml/3 tbsp oil
2 rindless streaky bacon rashers, finely
    chopped
½ onion, finely chopped
1 garlic clove, crushed
½ red pepper, seeded and finely chopped
25 g/1 oz plain flour
45 ml/3 tbsp tomato purée
4 large tomatoes, peeled, seeded and
    chopped or 1 (397 g/14 oz) can chopped
    tomatoes
300 ml/½ pint chicken stock
salt and pepper
5 ml/1 tsp thick honey
15 ml/1 tbsp chopped fresh herbs (oregano,
    basil, rosemary, parsley)

Make the sauce. Heat the oil in a large saucepan, add the bacon and fry for 2 minutes. Add the onion, garlic and pepper and cook gently for 5 minutes, stirring occasionally. Stir in the flour and tomato purée and cook for 5 minutes more.

Add the chopped tomatoes and chicken stock. Bring to the boil, stirring occasionally, then lower the heat and simmer for 30 minutes. Add salt and pepper to taste, stir in the honey and herbs and keep warm.

Cream 50 g/2 oz of the butter with the garlic, parsley and basil in a small bowl. Set aside. Bring a large saucepan of salted water to the boil, add the spaghetti and boil for 10-12 minutes or until tender. Drain in a colander, rinse with hot water and drain again. Turn on to a sheet of greaseproof paper and pat dry.

Tip the spaghetti into a clean pan. Add the remaining butter and half the Parmesan, with plenty of salt and pepper and heat through. Transfer to a large shallow flameproof dish and keep warm.

Put the flour in a stout polythene bag with salt and pepper to taste. Add the scampi and toss until well coated. Shake off excess flour. Heat the oil in a large frying pan and shallow fry the scampi for 5 minutes. Drain off the oil and add the scampi to the spaghetti. Stir in the herb butter.

Spoon the tomato sauce over the pasta and shellfish, sprinkle with the remaining Parmesan and brown under a moderate grill for 3-5 minutes. Serve at once.

SERVES FOUR

 MRS BEETON'S TIP

Fresh basil is used extensively with pasta. Never attempt to chop basil in the same way as parsley as it rapidly loses its flavour, becoming limp and damp. Instead shred the leaves and tender sprig ends using a pair of kitchen scissors.

Dairy Foods

Recipes using dairy foods feature throughout the book; however, this chapter serves as an introduction to their cooking properties and uses.

Dairy food is the term for milk and cream and their products: butter, cheese, yogurt and buttermilk. It also covers eggs. These are all highly nutritious protein foods which play an important part in the diet.

MILK

Milk is an important source of nutrients for everyone and for children in particular. Apart from the protein and vitamins it provides, it is one of the key sources of calcium in the diet.

Milk is now available in many forms, from whole milk which yields a creamy layer on standing (top-of-the-milk) to skimmed milk, long-life milk and dried milk powders or granules. The following is a brief guide to fresh and preserved types of cow's milk. Production methods and laws relating to fat contents of different types of milk vary and up-to-date information is available from the milk marketing authority.

TYPES OF FRESH MILK

Most fresh milk is heat treated by pasteurisation to destroy unwanted bacteria and to increase its shelf life. Untreated milk is available; however, it may only be sold under licence and the governing board point out that it may contain organisms which can be harmful to health. A green top is used for bottles of untreated milk; any cartons must be labelled as such.

Whole Milk This contains an average of 3.9% fat. On standing it has a noticeable line of creamy milk on its surface and the traditional bottle top is silver.

Homogenized Milk The process of homogenization distributes and suspends the cream throughout the milk, so it does not separate out on standing. The bottle top is red.

Guernsey or Jersey Milk From the Guernsey or Jersey breed of cow, this has a fat content averaging at 5.1%; the traditional bottle top is gold. Traditionally, gold-top milk was known for its creamy 'top-of-the-milk' which was skimmed from the surface of the new pint and served instead of single cream – a treat for one or two persons.

Semi-skimmed Milk Some of the fat is removed to give an average content of 1.6%. A red and silver stripped bottle top is used for semi-skimmed milk.

Skimmed Milk With an average fat content of 0.1% or lower, this is sold in blue and silver checked top bottles.

Sterilized Milk Whole milk which has been sterilized, this is not common but it may be distinguished by a blue bottle top or crown cap.

LONG-LIFE MILK PRODUCTS

UHT Milk Whole, semi-skimmed or skimmed, this is processed by heating to a high temperature for a brief, precise, period, then packing in sealed sterile containers excluding air. It has a shelf life of 6 months and does not require refrigeration; however, it is best not to store it in a warm place.

Dried Milk Available as a powder or granules, in skimmed, semi-skimmed and whole forms. An excellent storecupboard item, this is useful for sauces, puddings and other dishes made with milk.

Evaporated Milk Canned milk which is heat treated to evaporate some of the water content. It is homogenized and canned. Evaporated milk is two-and-a-half-times more concentrated than fresh milk, it has a distinct taste and is used mainly in cooking or as a dessert topping.

Condensed Milk This is treated in the same way as evaporated milk but it is more concentrated and it is sweetened. The finished product contains about 55% sugar, therefore it is very sweet. Its main use is in sweet cookery.

BUTTERMILK

A by-product from the manufacture of butter. Butter made from fresh cream yields buttermilk which is similar to skimmed milk; if the butter is made from cream to which an acid culture has been added, then the buttermilk will have a sour taste.

Commercial buttermilk is usually made by introducing a culture to skimmed milk to give it a fresh, sharp taste.

CREAM

There are nine types of fresh pasteurized cream:

Half Cream Contains 12% butterfat. Half cream can be used in place of single cream. It cannot be whipped.

Single Cream Contains 18% butterfat. Single cream is often homogenized to give a thicker consistency. It can be poured over puddings or stirred into sweet or savoury mixtures but it is not suitable for whipping.

Soured Cream Contains 18% butterfat. Soured cream is fresh cream which has had a culture added to give a slightly acidic taste. It is thicker than single cream but it is not suitable for whipping. A little lemon juice may be stirred into single cream for a similar result.

Whipping Cream Contains 35-38% butterfat. This can be poured or it can be whipped to give soft peaks. When whipped it can be piped but it does not hold its shape as well as double cream or for the same length of time. The whipped cream may be frozen.

Whipped Cream Contains 35% butterfat. This is a ready whipped dairy product, used for topping desserts. Available frozen as well as fresh.

Crème Fraiche Contains 30-35% butterfat. Richer than soured cream, this has had a culture added to give the slightly acidic taste. It is not suitable for whipping.

Double Cream Contains 48% butterfat. Double cream is suitable for pouring and it whips well to give the consistency required when filling and decorating gâteaux or piping on other desserts. Whipped double cream freezes well.

Extra Thick Double Cream Contains 35-48% butterfat, this is homogenized to create a thick cream which may be spooned over desserts. It is not suitable for whipping or piping.

Clotted Cream Contains 55% butterfat. Thick enough to spoon over fruit or to spread on scones. Not suitable for whipping or piping. Clotted cream will freeze successfully.

Other fresh cream products include the following:

Aerosol Cream Fresh cream which is ready to squirt on to desserts. Suitable only for topping, this collapses quickly.

Long-life Cream Half, single, whipping and double creams are available in cartons or packets. These products have been heat treated or sterilized. They have a shelf life of up to three months without refrigeration. Once opened they chould be treated as fresh cream.

Frozen Cream Single, whipping, double, clotted and ready whipped creams are all available frozen. Usually frozen in small pieces for thawing in small quantities.

NON-DAIRY CREAMS

Several non-dairy creams and dessert toppings are available. These may be long-life, perishable, in the form of mixes or as aerosols. Although these are not dairy cream, they may contain buttermilk or a certain amount of butterfat. Always read the label if you are unfamiliar with a product – it may not be all that it seems.

CANNED CREAM

Sterilized dairy cream is sold in cans. It is not suitable for whipping but it is thick enough to spoon over desserts. It can also be stirred into mixtures. It has a distinctive flavour which distinguishes it from fresh cream or long-life cream.

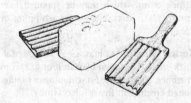

YOGURT

Yogurt is a dairy product produced by souring cows', sheep's or goats' milk. It varies greatly from a low-fat product which may be thickened with starch to the increasingly popular, naturally thick and creamy variety which was originally imported from Greece and neighbouring countries but is now also made in Britain. Yogurt can also be made at home. (See page 427.)

BUTTER

There are two types of butter to choose from: the first is sweet cream butter which is salted or slightly salted. The second is lactic butter which is slightly salted or unsalted and may be referred to as the continental type.

Traditionally, the sweet cream varieties are the most popular and they form the largest proportion of butter produced in the United Kingdom, the Republic of Ireland and New Zealand. This type of butter is produced by churning cream which has been allowed to stand for approximately twelve hours. The addition of salt produces the characteristic flavour and improves the keeping quality.

A certain amount of lactic butter is produced in the United Kingdom but the majority is imported. A culture of lactic acid is added to the cream before it is churned; this results in a slightly acidic flavour.

In addition a number of regional butters are produced in the United Kingdom. These have subtle individual flavour qualities that are appreciated on bread. These are not usually specified for use in recipes.

When buying butter always check the sell-by date which is given on the packet. (Remember that sell-by dates are for guidance only and they are not a compulsory feature.) Store butter in the refrigerator, neatly packed in its original wrapping. The keeping quality of butter does vary according to its type and packaging. Butter in foil packaging keeps slightly better than butter in parchment packing, and salted butter keeps nominally better than the unsalted type. The foil-wrapped butter can be kept for up to eleven weeks in the refrigerator; butter in parchment can be kept for seven weeks.

Butter can be frozen, when the unopened pack should be enclosed in a sealed polythene bag. The unsalted type will keep best in the freezer and it can be stored for up to six months. Salted butter can be frozen for shorter periods of up to three months.

All butter should be well wrapped during storage as it absorbs flavours and odours.

To clarify butter, heat gently until melted, then stand for 2–3 minutes. Pour off the clear yellow liquid on top and allow to solidify. This is the clarified butter.

EGGS

Eggs play many vital roles in cooking. They are used to enrich, set or lighten mixtures, both sweet and savoury. In some recipes, where a high proportion of eggs are used, they are the only raising agent; for example in baked soufflés or whisked sponge cakes. Eggs may be fully cooked, partially cooked (as used in custards) or used raw (for mayonnaise or mousse).

The eggs can be used whole or they may be separated before they are added to a mixture. Whisked with sugar, they may form the basis for a sweet mixture and the other ingredients will be folded into them. For some recipes the egg yolks are incorporated first, then the whisked whites are folded in; this is typical of soufflés or continental-style cake mixtures. In this case a little of the white should be stirred in first to soften the bulk of the mixture before the remainder is folded in.

In some recipes just the whites or yolks are used; for example, mayonnaise can be made with yolks alone, meringues require the whites only and biscuits often use just yolks. Other recipes may call for more whites than yolks in order to produce a very light mixture.

Buying Eggs Eggs come in different sizes and they are also categorized by quality. Two quality grades of whole eggs are sold, either A or B quality, and this is clearly stated on the box. There are regulations that have to be observed for the sale of pre-packed eggs, and certain information has to be included on the outside of the box.

Firstly, the class of eggs must be clearly marked and the number of eggs must also be shown along with the registered number of the packing station, the name and address of those responsible for packing and the date on which the eggs were packed. In addition there may be a sell-by-date, although this is optional – always look out for this and make sure that it has not expired if it is included.

It makes sense to buy eggs from a reputable supplier. Particular care should be taken if eggs are to be used raw, as in mayonnaise or chocolate mousse.

Egg Sizes Class A eggs are graded in sizes from 1–7. The sizes most commonly available are 2–4.

Size 1 – 70g and over
Size 2 – 65g and under 70g
Size 3 – 60g and under 65g
Size 4 – 55g and under 60g
Size 5 – 50g and under 55g
Size 6 – 45g and under 50g
Size 7 – under 45g

Size 3 are the most suitable for baking unless otherwise stated; for example if large eggs are called for, then size 2 should be used.

Storing Eggs Eggs should be stored in the refrigerator, preferably in their box, and the pointed end of each egg should be kept downwards to help to prevent breakages, to reduce evaporation and to help to prevent any odours being absorbed through the shell.

Using Eggs   For many recipes it is best if eggs are used at room temperature so they should be removed from the refrigerator about 30 minutes before they are to be used. However this is not essential. It is very important that eggs are clean and they should be washed under cool water and dried before they are cracked, taking care not to break them, of course. It is best to crack eggs individually into a mug, cup or small basin before adding them to mixtures and any traces of broken shell should be removed.

Eggs are a protein food and they should be treated with the same standards of hygiene that are adopted for all raw meat, fish and poultry. All utensils must be thoroughly clean before use and hands should be washed before and after breaking eggs, particularly if cooked food is handled after raw eggs. Any unused beaten egg should be kept in a tightly covered container and placed in the refrigerator. It should be used within 24 hours. Egg whites can be frozen in a clean, airtight, rigid container. Remember to label the container with the number of whites which it contains. Whole eggs (yolk and white; not in shells) or yolks may be frozen if beaten with a little salt or sugar but they are not as successful as whites alone. Once thawed, egg should always be used immediately.

MAKING YOGURT OR CHEESE

When preparing any food that requires long standing, straining or fermentation, always make sure that all ingredients are absolutely fresh and equipment is scrupulously clean. Do not try to rush the process of straining curds or fermenting yogurt; equally, do not leave the food in a warm place, or without covering and chilling, for any length of time after the process is complete.

EQUIPMENT

You do not need a stack of specialist equipment to make soft cheese or yogurt. The instructions for making yogurt outline the process clearly; although a yogurt maker is useful, a vacuum flask serves just as well.

For straining curds you will need a fine muslin cloth, some form of stand or a fine sieve and a large bowl.

A thermometer is useful to check the temperature of milk but it is not essential; most sugar thermometers will serve the purpose well enough.

All equipment should be thoroughly cleaned, then scalded in boiling water for 5 minutes before use.

TECHNIQUES

Hanging or Straining   Since few modern homes have a cold room with a marble slab and convenient hook above, hanging curds to separate them from the whey may mean devising a special contraption.

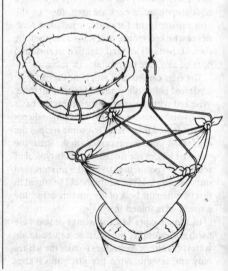

A jelly bag and stand for preserving is ideal. If this is not available, use a pair of metal coat hangers, slotted together and bound in place with wire. The jelly bag or cloth may be hung from the four corners.

Alternatively, if you have a very large mixing bowl with a rim, a length of muslin may be secured loosely over it with elastic. Tie the length of elastic first, then slip it over the edge of the bowl so that it fits under the rim when the muslin is in place.

Squeezing Whey To reduce the amount of moisture in curds, gather up the muslin and squeeze out extra whey by twisting the ends of the fabric. Take care not to squeeze too hard as this may cause the soft cheese to be pressed through the muslin.

Weighting The curds may be placed in a dish and weighted to give a closer-textured cheese. Line a suitable dish or container with scalded muslin, then spoon in the curds and press them down. Cover with more muslin, or fold over the ends, and weight the cheese with a heavy object wrapped in polythene. Stand the dish in a container. Chill overnight, then remove the weight and turn out the cheese.

HOME-MADE YOGURT

Yogurt can easily be made at home. It will not always have the consistency of the commercial product, but the results will be successful if a few simple rules are followed. The yogurt will keep for 4–5 days in a refrigerator. A new carton of commercial yogurt will be needed for the next incubation.

The yogurt can be incubated in one of three ways:
- In an electric, thermostatically controlled incubator. These are very useful if the family eats a lot of yogurt.

- In a wide-necked vacuum flask (a narrow-necked flask is not suitable as the yogurt is broken up when it is removed). This is suitable for smaller quantities of yogurt.
- In a home-made incubator made from a large biscuit or cake tin with a lid. Line the base and sides with an insulating material such as woollen fabric or cotton wool and have a piece of material large enough to fit inside the top. Use 4 or 5 screw-topped glass jars that will fit inside the incubator.

METHOD

- Sterilize all the equipment by immersion in boiling water for at least 3 minutes or by using a commercial sterilizing solution.
- Heat 500 ml/17 fl oz UHT or sterilized milk to 43°C/108°F in a saucepan (use a cooking thermometer) and blend in 5 ml/1 tsp *fresh* natural yogurt. Alternatively, use a yogurt starter culture (obtainable with full instructions from dairy laboratories).
- Pour into pots or glasses, if using. Place in the vacuum flask or prepared incubator, seal, and leave for 6–8 hours.
- Turn the yogurt into a cold bowl and cool rapidly, standing the bowl in cold water and whisking the yogurt until creamy.
- Cover the bowl and chill for about 4 hours when the yogurt will have thickened further.
- When serving, gently stir in sugar. Flavour with stewed fruit or jam.

 MICROWAVE TIP

Yogurt can be made in the microwave. Heat 600 ml/1 pint milk in a large bowl on High for 6 minutes. Cool until tepid (about 46°C/115°F) and stir in 15 ml/1 tbsp plain yogurt. Add 30 ml/2 tbsp dried full-cream powdered milk. Beat well. Cover the bowl and heat on Low for 70 minutes. Cool, then chill until required.

USING YOGURT

- Plain yogurt may be used in place of cream in savoury and sweet cooking. When heated it may curdle, so stir it into hot sauces, soups and other dishes at the end of cooking.
- Use plain yogurt in salad dressings, dips and savoury mousses.
- Yogurt combined with flour is less likely to curdle on cooking, for example in quiche fillings or as a topping for savoury bakes.
- Substitute plain yogurt for cream to give a lighter texture and sharper flavour in cold desserts.
- Spread a thick layer of plain yogurt or Greek yogurt over drained canned apricots in a shallow gratin dish. Top with a generous coating of brown sugar and flash under a hot grill to make a wonderful fruit brûlée.
- Stir clear honey into plain yogurt. Add toasted almonds just before serving.
- Make a tangy fruit jelly by dissolving a jelly tablet in a half quantity of hot water. Allow the jelly to cool before stirring it into an equal quantity of plain yogurt. Pour into a mould or individual dishes and chill until set.

JUNKET

The temperature is important in the making of junket; if it is too hot or too cold, it will not set. Also it is important to use fresh milk. Homogenised milk gives a very light set but UHT and sterilized milk will not set. This is due to the processing causing slight changes to the structure of the milk and preventing the rennet culture from working.

600 ml/1 pint milk
15 ml/1 tbsp sugar
few drops of vanilla essence
5 ml/1 tsp rennet essence
grated nutmeg or ground cinnamon

In a saucepan, warm the milk to blood-heat (about 37°C/98°F) with the sugar and vanilla essence. Stir in the rennet essence.

Pour the mixture into 1 large or 4 small dishes. Cover and leave to stand in a warm place for about 1 hour or until set. Do not move the junket at this stage.

Sprinkle the junket with spice and serve cold but not chilled.

SERVES FOUR

VARIATIONS

Almond or Rum Junket Instead of the vanilla essence, add 2.5 ml/½ tsp almond or rum essence to the milk. Decorate with toasted almonds, if liked.

Lemon or Orange Junket Infuse the pared rind of 1 lemon or orange in the milk. Using a few drops of food colouring, tint the junket pale yellow or orange. Do not use any other flavouring.

Rich Junket Run a layer of single cream, flavoured with brandy, if liked, over the top of the junket. Flavour in any of the ways given above.

SIMPLE SOFT CHEESE

Strictly speaking this is not a cheese at all – it is strained yogurt which becomes thick and similar in texture to a soft cheese. It can be used in place of soft cheese in many recipes or flavoured to serve as a spread.

1.1 litres/2 pints yogurt or low-fat fromage frais

30 ml/2 tbsp lemon juice

Have ready a large piece of double-thick scalded muslin. Put the yogurt or fromage frais in a bowl and stir in the lemon juice. Pour the mixture into the muslin and gather up the corners, then hang the yogurt or fromage frais overnight in a cool place.

Discard the liquid, then squeeze the muslin lightly. Use a spatula to scrape the 'cheese' into a bowl. Cover and chill.

MAKES ABOUT 225 G/8 OZ

VARIATIONS

- Add salt and pepper to taste. Mix in chopped parsley, a little chopped fresh tarragon, some chopped fresh thyme and a little crushed garlic (if liked). Press neatly into a dish and chill until ready to serve with crackers or crusty bread.
- Mix 50 g/2 oz finely chopped walnuts and 45 ml/3 tbsp snipped chives into the cheese.
- Finely chop ½ seeded red pepper, then add it to the cheese with 30 ml/2 tbsp grated onion and salt and pepper to taste.
- Make a sweet cheese by adding grated orange rind and sugar to taste.

SOFT CHEESE

The perfect way to use up excess milk, soft cheese can be flavoured with finely chopped herbs, ground or crushed whole spices or finely drained chopped fruit. The quantity of flavouring used will vary, but as a general rule, 1.25 ml/¼ tsp crushed spice or 5 ml/1 tsp solid flavouring is sufficient for 200 g/7 oz cheese. Pay particular attention to hygiene when making soft cheese; ensure all equipment is scrupulously clean and hang the cheese in a cold place.

2.6 litres/4½ pints fresh milk
20 ml/4 tsp rennet essence
salt   ·   30–60 ml/2–4 tbsp single cream

Warm the milk to tepid (30–35°C/86–95°F) and pour into a bowl. Stir in the rennet essence and leave to stand at room temperature until a curd forms. Meanwhile, line a metal sieve with a scalded piece of muslin about 25 cm/10 inches square. Stand the sieve over a bowl.

Gently tip the curdled milk into the cloth, bring the corners of the cloth up and tie securely with string. Hang above the bowl to catch the dripping whey. Leave for 6–8 hours; longer if a fairly thick cloth is used.

Open the bag and scrape down any curd on the sides of the cloth to form one mass. Cut any solid curd into small pieces. Tie the bag up again, hang it up and continue draining. Repeat the scraping down and cutting once or twice more until the cheese reaches the required consistency. This can be judged by squeezing the bag gently.

Turn the curd into a bowl. Mix in salt to taste gently but thoroughly. Blend in cream. Form the cheese into pats or turn into pots or cartons. Cover and chill until required. Use within 36 hours; 24 hours if solid fresh flavourings such as herbs have been added.

MAKES ABOUT 500 G/18 OZ

CHEESE

FOOD VALUE OF CHEESE

Cheese is one of our most nourishing foods. Full-fat cheese contains almost all the nourishment of whole milk except the milk sugar (lactose), and a few vitamins and minerals. It consists of the solid parts of the milk solidified into clots or curd, separated from the whey, which is drained off. The curd is usually pressed or heated, or both, to expel more whey, and as it dries becomes firm and will keep for some time without spoiling.

Depending on how much whey is removed from it, cheese may be classed as hard, semi-hard, semi-soft or soft.

Cheese of any type is most valuable for its protein content. It contains more protein, weight for weight, than prime raw beef. It is a good source of calcium, and contains vitamins A and D, and some B vitamins. Most cheeses, certainly the hard and semi-hard ones, are also rich in fat. A hard cheese like Cheddar is made up of about one-third fat, one-third protein, and one-third water. Cheese made from skimmed or defatted milk contains less fat and therefore a higher proportion of protein.

Cheese does not contain any carbohydrate, but is generally eaten with foods which supply carbohydrate, eg bread and biscuits, vegetables or pasta.

HOW CHEESE IS MADE

Most cheese in Britain is now made from cows' milk, although the milk of goats, sheep, asses, and other animals is also used in some parts of the world.

Commercially, it is made from fresh milk which is first heat-treated. It is then cooled before being pumped into vats where a starter culture is added. When the acidity in the ripened milk reaches 0.02% lactic acid, the milk is heated to 30°C/86°F and rennet is added to clot the milk.

Most semi-hard and hard cheeses are made in much the same general way as soft ones; but they are drained more thoroughly, pressed, and moulded in a variety of ways which all help to give them an individual character. Some are heat-treated a second time. Some are quick-ripening, others are hard pressed and matured for several months after being made. Some are made from skimmed or partly skimmed milk, other have cream or herbs added. Moulds are another way of making cheese.

Soft cheeses such as Camembert and other soft-paste cheeses, are made like hard cheeses, but are less fully drained and may have a mould added which gives them their particular flavour and rind.

Besides these different ways of making cheese, the variations in climate, pasture, temperature, the breed of cow or goat, even the time of milking, all affect the final product, so cheeses can be almost infinitely varied in flavour and texture.

Many are farmhouse cheeses made by hand, or local cheeses, made only in one particular area. Most British hard and semi-hard cheeses are now made for mass sale in big creameries, although the most full-flavoured and individual in style are still made on farms. Both the creamery and farmhouse-made cheeses were traditionally large, drum-shaped, rinded, and matured in cloth bandages. But, increasingly, both kinds have come to be made in a block for easier storage, and are waxed instead of having a rind and bandages. There is said to be no loss in the quality and flavour of these cheeses compared with rinded, round ones of the same age.

Soft, fresh, and slightly salted curd cheeses are the ones most frequently made at home. They consist of curds (sometimes with cream added), and are drained so that some of the liquid whey has run off; they may be lactic cheeses made with a starter alone, or renneted.

They all still contain a good deal of whey, and must therefore be refrigerated and eaten soon after production.

Cottage cheese is more difficult to make than curd cheese because it is heat-treated and washed, and is made from ripened milk which has stood for some time.

BUYING AND STORING CHEESE

It is much easier to assess the quality of cheese in the block, free of wrappings, as both the texture and condition can be seen.

The cut surface of any cheese is a good guide to its quality and condition. A hard or semi-hard cheese for eating raw (or for grating) should be firm, even slightly flaky in a cheese such as Cheddar, but must not have cracks in the surface. Equally, it must not be sweaty or show beads of fat, which indicate it has been kept too long in a warm place, uncovered. It should be more or less the same colour throughout; a darker colour near the rind may be a sign that the cheese is old; any white specks or blue sheen indicate mould and a musty flavour. Even a strong cheese should not taste harsh or acidic.

A milder cheese for eating or cooking should be firm or crumbly and still have a definite cheesy taste; it should not be soapy.

The blander semi-soft cheeses such as Edam or Port Salut should be velvety when cut, neither moist nor flaky, and should be the same creamy colour thoroughout. They should yield slightly when pressed with the finger.

Soft cheeses such as Camembert and Brie can quickly ripen and spoil but are tasteless when under-ripe. The crust of Brie should be white and even with signs of red at the edges; the curd pale yellow and creamy throughout, although not spilling out. If it is running when purchased, it may well be inedible by the time it is needed. A hard cake-like white strip in the centre is unlikely to ripen before the outer cheese goes bad.

The same applies to soft-paste cheeses, such as the creamy French cheeses. Like soft fresh cheeses, they spoil within a few days. They should be clean and well-shaped, neither discoloured nor dented, and the inside should be even in texture, without seeping moisture but soft enough to cut with a spoon.

Blue cheeses should also be even-coloured, without greyish patches, and with clear-cut veins of colour. They should be crumbly or moist, not grainy. Milder ones such as Dolcelatte may look creamy. All blue cheeses are fairly pungent, and may become unpleasantly harsh with age, so that colour and texture should be noted carefully before buying.

None of these pointers to quality can be checked in the case of prepacked cheeses. There are, however, one or two ways of telling whether they are good value and have been well cared for:

On any cheese counter, or in a chilled cabinet, cheeses should be on their own shelf or rack, separate from other foods, so that cross-flavouring cannot occur. Ideally, each cheese should have its separate place; strong and mild cheeses should not be stacked together.

Any semi-soft cheese should yield to the touch. It should always fill its box or wrapping, and never be sunken in the middle. All cheese wrappings should be fresh and clean. Sticky, stained or torn wrappings are always a warning not to buy.

Whenever possible, cheese should be bought in a compact block, not a long, thin slice or section. A thin slice is less easy to package, and keeps less well.

Cheese should be bought in small quantities, preferably just enough for 1 or 2 servings. Although the harder cheeses keep well, and it is tempting to keep a quantity in stock, any cheese tends to lose surface texture and flavour in storage, especially in a refrigerator. If it must be stored in a refrigerator, it should be kept in the least cold part, closely wrapped in grease-proof or waxed paper, and enclosed in a moisture-proof outer container or polythene bag. Cheeses should be removed and unwrapped at least 1 hour before use, to let them regain their full flavour. Any refrigerator-stored hard or semi-hard cheese should be used within 2 weeks, semi-soft and blue cheeses within 1 week. Soft cheeses must be used as soon as possible. To prevent ripe, soft, crusted cheeses oozing when a wedge has been cut out, wrap closely.

Any blue mould which develops on the surface of a hard or semi-hard cheese may be cut-off; the cheese itself is unharmed; the flavour, especially of mature cheeses, will however become stronger the longer they are kept.

Most cheeses can be frozen successfully but tend to crumble after being frozen. Cream cheese tends to separate on thawing; it is best blended with double cream before freezing, to be used as a dip. Freeze cheeses in small quantities, wrapped in greaseproof or waxed paper and overwrapped in polythene. See also the Freezing Chapter.

COOKING CHEESE

Cheese must always be cooked gently and as briefly as possible. Even if cooked with extra fat, it should never spit, or bubble quickly.

Gentle cooking prevents the cheese becoming rubbery or ropey. If the fat globules melt due to quick or fierce heating, the fat runs off, leaving a stringy mass of curd and separate fat instead of a creamy mass.

Hard and semi-hard cheeses are most often used for cooking. Cheeses with a high fat content and well-aged, mature cheeses melt and blend better with other ingredients than low-fat or less ripened cheeses. Less is needed too, since they are richer and better flavoured. Matured Cheddar and Parmesan cheeses are good for this reason. Processed cheeses melt easily but their flavour is usually very bland. Most cheese will retain its creamy texture if it is first grated and mixed with breadcrumbs, flour or extra fat. This coats the fat globules and will absorb some of the cooking heat, thereby preventing the fat from melting too soon.

A good way to melt cheese by itself is to place it in a bowl over a pan of simmering water. Another way is to add it to a hot mixture after the main cooking is completed, eg to sprinkle it into a cooked omelette just before folding and serving it.

When grilling cheese, it should be kept about 10 cm/4 inches below the heat, which should be as low as possible. Cheese used for a topping should be grated; it can be mixed with breadcrumbs before being sprinkled on the dish.

When cheese is mixed into a casserole or similar dish, whether cooked over heat or in the oven, the heat should also be kept as low as possible throughout the cooking time.

TYPES OF BRITISH CHEESE

Caerphilly is a mild, white, close-textured, slightly salty cheese. The new cheese is lightly brined, then dried, and allowed to ripen for about 14 days. Caerphilly is good with salads and in packed meals and sandwiches, but is not an ideal cooking cheese. It can be crumbled instead of grated.

Cheddar is the best known and most widely used British cheese, and is copied in many parts of the world. Its flavour varies in strength a great deal. British Cheddar is of two main kinds: farmhouse and creamery. Farmhouse Cheddar is still made by individual families and small dairies, usually from a single herd of cows, although creameries do produce it also. It is of high quality, is matured slowly for at least 6 months, preferably much longer, and is slightly more expensive than creamery Cheddar. This may be a quickly ripened, quite mild cheese; or it may be sold as mature, having been allowed to ripen for 6–8 months. Like most British cheese, Cheddar is a full-fat, hard cheese made from cows' milk only. All Cheddar should be close in texture, with a clean, nutty flavour. It is a first-class eating cheese, but is also excellent for grating and cooking.

Cheshire may also be farmhouse or creamery-made. It is more salty than Cheddar, due to the salt in the Cheshire soil where most of it is still made. It is also slightly more acid, and more crumbly. It is naturally white, but a reddish type, dyed with a harmless vegetable dye, is also popular. There is also a fuller-flavoured, creamy-textured **Blue Cheshire**, yellow in colour with broad blue streaks. Modern Cheshire cheese has a $33\frac{1}{2}$% fat content, and is usually medium-ripened for 4–8 weeks. It is a good eating cheese, especially with gingerbread, cake or apples. It is also widely used for cooking.

Derby is a pale honey-coloured, smooth-textured cheese, mild when young but with a certain tang when mature at 4–6 months old. It is good with biscuits, as a lunch cheese, and with fruit. **Sage Derby** has green threads or a broad band of green through it, and a flavour of the sage leaves which provide the colouring.

Double Gloucester is akin to Cheddar. It is straw-coloured or light red, close in texture, and mellow or pungent in flavour when mature; it ripens in 3–4 months as a rule. It is good after a meat meal or with beer, and is also good for cooking.

Dunlop is a Cheddar-style cheese from Scotland; so are the small **Orkney** and **Islay** cheeses.

Lancashire is a semi-hard cheese which may be farmhouse-made. It is the strongest farmhouse cheese in flavour, although the creamery-made cheese is mild. Both are white and crumble easily, and are good for toasted dishes (it was once called the 'Leigh Toaster'). It is also good crumbled into stews, or eaten, uncooked, with sharp salads or with sweet fruits. It is traditionally eaten with oatcakes.

Leicester a rich orange-red cheese, is fairly mild in flavour, but with a tang when mature at about 2 months old. It is soft and crumbly, and may be slightly flaky. It makes a good cooking as well as an eating cheese.

Stilton is considered the king of British cheeses. It is rich and creamy, and slowly matured to let the blue veins develop properly. It is best eaten with bread or plain biscuits, and is an excellent accompaniment to wine, especially Madeira or port. The rind is wrinkled and crusty, and the creamy interior is slightly darker near the crust. Top-quality Stilton is still made, as a rule, in cylindrical hoops, although jars of Stilton are widely available; it is sold too in film-wrapped or vacuum-packed wedges. Aged Stilton, past its prime, can be potted for storage, and used later as a spread.

If you buy a whole Stilton or part of a round, do not scoop the cheese out of the centre or pour port into the cheese. It will be difficult to store and may go sour. The correct way to care for a Stilton is to cut off the top crust in a thin layer; keep this aside. When serving the cheese, cut wedges of equal depth from all round the cheese so that it keeps a flat top. To store the cheese, replace the top crust, wrap in greaseproof or waxed paper, put in a polythene bag or box and keep in a cool place.

The younger **White Stilton** is crumbly, with a strong aroma, and a mild, slightly sour flavour.

Wensleydale is a white, softish, close-textured cheese, not unlike Caerphilly in taste when young, being mild and slightly salty. It matures in 12–14 days. It is better for eating than for cooking. **Blue Wensleydale** has finer, more diffuse threads of blue veining than blue Cheshire, and, as a rule, is less creamy and more salty than either blue Cheshire or Stilton.

Soft Cheeses of various kinds are made on farms and at home as well as in creameries. **Colwick** cheese and **York** cheese are both now made only on farms, for private use.

Caboc and **Crowdie** are creamery cheeses. They differ in appearance, flavour, and texture according to the area in which they are made, the type of moulds used, and the method of making. They may be lactic (sweet milk) or acid-curd cheeses, and are normally graded according to their butterfat content as follows:

skimmed milk soft cheese (less than 2% fat)
low-fat soft cheese (2–10% fat)
medium-fat soft cheese (10–20% fat)
full-fat soft cheese (20–45% fat)
cream cheese (46–65% fat)
double cream cheese (at least 65% fat)

Curd cheeses of various types which are often made in the home, may be low, medium or full-fat. Like cream cheese, they have a closer texture than cottage cheese which contains about 4% butterfat but also more whey. All these cheeses keep for only about 4 days chilled.

Other cheeses available include **Red Windsor** which is based on Cheddar and flavoured with an English red wine. It has a creamier taste and a slightly more acid flavour than mature Cheddar. **Ilchester**, another Cheddar-based cheese, flavoured with beer and garlic, is a soft-textured cheese with a full flavour; the garlic is well subdued. **Walton** is a softer cheese based on Cheddar mixed with Stilton, with walnuts added; the taste of Stilton is mild. **Cotswold** is based on Double Gloucester and is flavoured with chives. **Sherwood** is another cheese based on Double Gloucester. It is flavoured with sweet pickle. **Blue Shropshire** cheese has a deep golden taste and clear-cut blue veining. It is lighter in flavour than blue Cheshire or Stilton, but fuller than blue Wensleydale, with its own character. **Melbury** is a mild soft cheese with a white surface mould coat.

Traditional hard cheeses are also available with a reduced fat content. Additionally, there are vegetarian hard cheeses; these are made with rennet of microbial origin.

POPULAR INTERNATIONAL CHEESES

Bel Paese is one of the best known Italian cheeses. It is a full-fat, ivory-coloured cheese, semi-soft and bland. It is used mostly as a table cheese although it melts easily, and is therefore useful in cooked dishes and for toasted sandwiches.

Boursin is French fresh cheese. The basic light-flavoured cheese can have either garlic added or a coat of crushed black peppercorns.

Brie, with a recorded history from 1217, is the most famous French cheese. It is often sold in prepacked wedges, so that its quality cannot be checked; it is best to buy it cut to order, from a whole 35 cm/14 inch wheel, since Brie must be eaten in peak condition. Brie varies widely in flavour, depending on how long it is ripened. **Brie du Coulommiers** for instance, generally has a delicate, mild flavour whereas **Brie de Melun** is well-ripened and tastes much stronger, more like Camembert.

Camembert is France's most plentiful and popular cheese. It is widely sold prepacked, in whole or half rounds, or in small sections. One has to take a chance on its quality, since it is usually kept very cool in a store and is firmer than it will be when eaten. An unwrapped Camembert should have an even, light brownish crust level with the rim, with no sunken centre. Inside, it should be creamy-yellow throughout, like Brie. Its aroma and flavour is, however, a good deal stronger. Camembert matures and becomes inedible even more quickly than Brie, and is distinctly unpleasant when over-ripe.

Chèvre is the term for small, rich, French goats' milk cheeses, often shaped like small cylinders. Unless the words *pur chèvre* appear on the label, the cheese may be made from a mixture of goats' and cows' milk. Goats' milk cheeses vary in flavour with their type and area of origin; but they should all have a pale crust with only a light mould, and should be crumbly or creamy inside, not grainy.

Danish Blue   is of two types; the usual type, sometimes called **Danablu**, is white with bluish-green veins; **Mycella**, which is less common, is yellowish with green veins, more aromatic and subtle. Both are rich in cream, buttery in texture, and are table cheeses. Danablu is sometimes over-salted for export.

Demi-sel and Petit-Suisse   are two of the family of French soft cream cheeses. Rich and mild in flavour, all these cream cheeses should be eaten as soon as possible after purchase.

Dolcelatte   is a mild, creamy, Italian cheese using milk from valley herds, and made in a similar way to Gorgonzola.

Edam   is Holland's most widely exported cheese. It is made from partly skimmed cows' milk, and has a cannonball shape and a bright red rind or wax coating. Its texture is smooth, and its flavour bland. It is not good for cooking, but is popular for eating, especially with slimmers. It tastes fuller when cut in thin slivers or slices.

Emmental   is Swiss in origin, and the best Emmental cheese still comes from Switzerland. It is one of the most difficult cheeses to make, requiring high-quality raw milk and considerable skill in manufacture. It has a hard golden-brown rind, and a yellow-ivory curd with cherry-sized holes. It has a sweet, dry flavour, and an aroma like hazelnuts. Famous as a cooking cheese, it is often used with Parmesan; and it is one of the cheeses traditionally used for a classic cheese fondue. It takes 7–10 months to mature fully.

Esrom, Havarti and Samsøe   are hard Danish cheeses, all versatile, with a pale or golden-yellow taste, mild when young but gaining piquancy with age. All have tiny holes, yet are distinctly different; Esrom is the sweetest and most fragrant.

Feta   is a Greek fresh sheeps' milk cheese or mixed milk cheese. It ripens in its own whey mixed with brine, so tastes piquant and salty. It should be eaten as soon as it is purchased, with salads, cold meats or black olives.

Gorgonzola   is an ancient Italian blue cheese, widely exported. The curd varies from cream to straw-yellow with blue-green veining, and it should be elastic rather than crumbly. It is used mainly as a table cheese although its mildness makes it suitable for a number of cooked dishes.

Gouda   is a full-fat Dutch cheese, made in both farmhouses and creameries. There is a good deal of difference between the two products, although both are good. Factory-made Gouda is relatively bland, not unlike Edam, although cartwheel in shape with a yellowish rind. Farmhouse Gouda has a noticeably variable flavour depending on where it comes from. An old one has a hard rind, a firm paste, and a full flavour. A farmhouse Gouda may be matured for as much as 12–14 months.

Gruyère   is another Swiss cheese, although it is now widely copied because it is so popular. It is a classic cooking cheese, used for fondues and quiches. Wheel-shaped, with a warm brown rind, its curd is ivory-yellow, pocked with small holes, moister than that of Emmental, and therefore still better for hot dishes.

Jarlsberg   is an old Norwegian full-fat cheese, revived and popularized in modern times. Its curd is pale and smooth with large, cherry-sized holes; its flavour is slightly sweet, mild, and nutty.

Monterey Jack   is an American cheddar-type cheese. It ranges from mild to mature in flavour.

Mozzarella   is a soft, fresh cheese, originally made from buffalo milk, now more usually from cows' milk. Its shape varies, but the commonest is an oval ball. It should be very moist and yield slightly when bitten; it should be eaten as soon as possible after purchase.

Parmesan is the most famous and widely used Italian cheese. It is piquant, hard, and grainy due to long, slow maturing, although a milder, elastic, younger Parmesan is sold for table use in Italy. The Parmesan which reaches foreign markets, either in the block or ready-grated for cooking use, is at least 2–3 years old. The flavour of Parmesan bought ungrated is very much better than that of the factory-grated product.

Pipo Crème is a mild, creamy, fairly modern French blue cheese.

Pont l'Évêque is a semi-hard French cheese from Normandy, with a fat content of 50%. The cheese has a smooth, creamy consistency, golden rind, a savoury taste and some bouquet.

Port Salut is a small, round, French cheese with a pale yellow rind and a mild flavour. It is closely related to **St Paulin**. Both are mild table cheeses, not generally well suited to cooking.

Roquefort is easily the best known French blue cheese, with an old and noble history. Originally a sheeps' milk cheese, it is not always so today. Genuine Roquefort cheeses still come from the same Tarn area and are matured in mountain caves where the bacteria *penicillium roqueforti* give them their particular mould veining and flavour. The rind of a Rouquefort cheese is wrinkled, its paste white and fairly crumbly, its veining dark blue-green and delicate. Matured in a thin coating of salt, its high but fine flavour can only be tasted fully when it is mature. Exported Roquefort cheeses, sometimes prepacked in wedges, are often too young and salty.

CHEESE PUDDING

fat for greasing
100–150 g/4–5 oz Cheddar or Gruyère cheese, grated
2 eggs, beaten
250 ml/8 fl oz whole or skimmed milk
100 g/4 oz fresh white breadcrumbs
salt (optional)

Butter an ovenproof dish. Set the oven at 180°C/350°F/gas 4. Combine the cheese, eggs and milk in a bowl. Add the breadcrumbs, with a little salt, if required. Mix thoroughly, then pour into the dish. Bake for 25–30 minutes, until set in the centre and browned on top.

SERVES TWO TO FOUR

MRS BEETON'S CHEESE PUDDINGS

75 g/3 oz butter, melted
50 g/2 oz fresh breadcrumbs
60 ml/4 tbsp milk
4 eggs, separated
salt and pepper
100 g/4 oz Cheshire cheese, finely grated
100 g/4 oz Parmesan cheese, grated

Set the oven at 190°C/375°F/gas 5. Grease 4 individual soufflé dishes or an ovenproof dish with some of the butter. Place the bread in a bowl and sprinkle the milk over. Leave for 5 minutes, then beat in the egg yolks, salt and pepper and both types of cheese.

Whisk the egg whites until stiff. Stir the remaining melted butter into the cheese mixture, then fold in the egg whites. Turn into the dishes and bake for about 30 minutes for individual puddings or 40–45 minutes for a large pudding. Serve at once.

SERVES FOUR

CHEESE AND POTATO PIE

fat for greasing
675 g/1½ lb potatoes, halved
175 g/6 oz Cheddar cheese, finely grated
salt and pepper · milk (see method)

Grease a pie dish. Cook the potatoes in a saucepan of boiling water for about 20 minutes or until tender. Drain thoroughly and mash with a potato masher, or beat with a hand-held electric whisk until smooth.

Add 150 g/5 oz of the grated cheese, with salt and pepper to taste, then beat well with enough milk to make a creamy mixture. Spoon into the dish, sprinkle with the remaining cheese and brown under a moderate grill for 3–5 minutes. Serve at once.

SERVES FOUR

SWISS CHEESE FONDUE

Cheese fondue is traditionally made in an open ceramic or earthenware pan called a caquelon. The pan is set on a spirit lamp or burner, which can be regulated to prevent the cheese mixture from burning. Long-handled fondue forks enable each guest to spear a cube of bread and dip it into the fondue mixture. The golden crust which forms in the bottom of the pan is a traditional, end-of-fondue treat.

1 garlic clove
300 ml/½ pint light dry white wine
350 g/12 oz Emmental cheese, grated
450 g/1 lb Gruyère cheese, grated
10 ml/2 tsp cornflour or potato flour
15 ml/1 tbsp kirsch
white pepper and grated nutmeg
2 long French sticks, cubed

Cut the garlic clove in half; rub the cut sides over the inside of a fondue pan or flameproof casserole.

Pour the wine into the pan or casserole and heat until steaming but not simmering. Gradually add the grated cheese, a little at a time, stirring constantly. Allow each addition of cheese to melt before adding the next. Remove the pan from the heat.

Mix the cornflour or potato flour to a paste with the kirsch and stir this into the fondue. Return to the heat and cook, stirring constantly, until the mixture is smooth, thick and creamy. Add pepper and nutmeg to taste.

Set the pan over a burner or hotplate at the table. Serve at once, with the bread.

SERVES SIX TO EIGHT

MRS BEETON'S CHEESE FONDUE

Mrs Beeton's fondue has little in common with the Swiss variety. It is baked in the oven, in much the same way as a soufflé.

fat for greasing
4 eggs, separated
50 g/2 oz Parmesan cheese, finely grated
50 g/2 oz butter, finely grated
salt and pepper

Set the oven at 180°C/350°F/gas 4. Grease a soufflé dish.

Beat the egg yolks until pale in colour. Stir in the grated cheese and butter, with salt and pepper to taste. In a separate, grease-free bowl, whisk the egg whites to soft peaks. Fold them into the cheese mixture.

Scrape the mixture into the prepared dish or tin, which should be no more than half full as the mixture will rise considerably. Bake for about 45 minutes. Serve at once, as the fondue will sink if allowed to stand.

SERVES FOUR

BRILLAT SAVARIN'S FONDUE

The interesting formula for this recipe is to use one egg per person and one third of the total weight of the eggs in the shell in cheese. The quantity of butter required is one sixth of the weight of the cheese.

6 eggs
100 g/4 oz Gruyère cheese, grated
20 g/¾ oz butter, grated
salt and pepper

Put the eggs in a large bowl and beat them well. Beat in the cheese and butter, with salt and pepper.

Transfer the mixture to a large heavy-bottomed saucepan and cook over gentle heat, whisking constantly until the mixture is thick and creamy: stirring is not vigorous enough to make the mixture creamy. Do not stop whisking or the eggs will scramble as they set.

Remove the pan from the heat when the fondue is slightly runny and whisk for a few seconds while the heat of the pan continues to set the mixture. Do not overcook the fondue or the eggs will scramble or, worse, curdle. Serve at once, with rounds of French bread or cubes of crusty bread to dip.

SERVES SIX

LANCASHIRE CHEESE AND ONIONS

5 large onions, thickly sliced
125 ml/4 fl oz milk
salt and pepper
150 g/5 oz Lancashire cheese, grated or
  crumbled
15 ml/1 tbsp butter
hot buttered toast to serve

Put the onions in a saucepan with water to cover. Boil for 20–25 minutes, or until the onions are tender and the water has almost evaporated. Add the milk, with salt and pepper to taste, and bring to the boil again.

Remove from the heat and add the grated or crumbled cheese. Stir in the butter. Leave to stand for 7–10 minutes or until the cheese has fully melted. Stir once; reheat without boiling. Serve at once, with hot buttered toast.

SERVES FOUR

MRS BEETON'S BAKED CHEESE SANDWICHES

8 slices of bread
butter
4 large thick slices of Cheshire or Cheddar
  cheese

Set the oven at 200°C/400°F/gas 6 and heat a baking sheet. Spread the bread with the butter and make 4 cheese sandwiches.

Spread the top of each sandwich very lightly with butter, then invert them on the hot baking sheet. Spread the top of each sandwich very lightly with butter. Bake for 5 minutes, turn the sandwiches and bake for a further 5 minutes, until golden. Serve at once.

SERVES FOUR

TOASTED CHEESE

A traditional savoury to serve at the end of the meal, this would have been kept hot at the table in a hot-water cheese dish, which consisted of a metal container (for the cheese) set over a reservoir of hot water.

175 g/6 oz mature Cheddar cheese, grated
5-10 ml/1-2 tsp prepared English mustard
freshly ground black pepper
15-30 ml/1-2 tbsp port
hot toast to serve

Heat the grill. Place the cheese in a bowl over a saucepan of simmering water. Stir occasionally until melted, then add the mustard, pepper and port to taste. Pour into a flameproof dish and brown the top under the grill. Serve at once with hot toast.

SERVES FOUR

CROQUE MONSIEUR

These classic hot ham and cheese sandwiches may be grilled or baked (as for Mrs Beeton's Baked Cheese Sandwiches, left) if preferred, in which case the outside of the sandwiches should be spread with a little butter before cooking. A little French mustard may be spread on the buttered bread when assembling the sandwiches. If a poached, baked or fried egg is served on top of the whole cooked sandwiches they become Croque Madame.

8 slices of bread, crusts removed
butter
4 thin slices of lean cooked ham
4 slices of Gruyère cheese

Spread the bread with butter and make 4 ham and cheese sandwiches, pressing them together firmly.

Heat a knob of butter in a large frying pan and fry the sandwiches for about 2 minutes on each side, until crisp and golden. Transfer to a platter and cut diagonally in half or into quarters.

SERVES FOUR

EGGY BREAD AND CHEESE

8 thin slices of white bread, crusts removed
butter
175 g/6 oz Cheshire or Cheddar cheese, thinly sliced
3 eggs, beaten
salt
oil for shallow frying

Spread the bread thinly with butter. Top four of the slices with cheese, leaving a narrow border all around. Add the remaining slices of bread to make four sandwiches, then press the edges of each sandwich lightly with a rolling pin to seal in the filling.

Put the eggs with a little salt in a shallow dish large enough to hold all the sandwiches in a single layer. Add the sandwiches and soak for 20 minutes, turning them over carefully half-way through.

Heat the oil in a large fring pan, add the sandwiches and fry for 2-3 minutes on each side until crisp and golden. Drain on absorbent kitchen paper before serving.

SERVES FOUR

BATTER

A batter is made by combining flour with egg and liquid, usually milk or milk and water. Some savoury coating batters are a simple combination of flour and liquid; however the majority of recipes are enriched by the addition of eggs. These also serve to lighten the mixture.

SMOOTH BATTERS

A good batter should be perfectly smooth and light. To achieve this, a whole egg is added to a well in the flour and a little of the milk (or liquid) is poured in. A wooden spoon is used to combine the egg with the milk and the flour is gradually worked in to make a smooth, thick mixture. This mixture should be thoroughly beaten to get rid of any lumps. When the thick batter is perfectly smooth, the remaining liquid is stirred in. The batter should be used immediately for baked puddings.

Alternatively, all the ingredients may be combined in a blender or food processor and processed until smooth.

If the batter is to be used for coating fritters, the eggs are separated. The yolks are combined with the flour and liquid to make a smooth, fairly thick batter. The egg whites are whisked until stiff, then folded into the batter. The batter should be used at once. When fried this type of batter is very crisp and light.

PERFECT PANCAKES

A thin batter should be used for pancakes; it should be allowed to stand for at least 30 minutes so that all the air may escape. The batter may thicken slightly on standing and a little extra liquid may have to be added halfway through making the pancakes.

A good pan is essential for making successful pancakes. A heavy non-stick pan usually gives good results if the base is in good condition. The best pan is a heavy, cast-iron pan that has become well seasoned with years of use. It is a good idea to set aside a pan specifically for pancakes. It is possible to buy a heavy flat, non-stick pan with a shallow rim for just this purpose.

To prevent the batter sticking, stir in a little cooking oil – about 15 ml/1 tbsp per 600 ml/1 pint of batter is sufficient. The pan should be hot and greased with oil or a mixture of butter and oil in equal proportions. Have a small bowl of oil or melted butter and oil to one side. Spoon a little into the pan and heat it, then pour out the excess and heat the pan again for a few seconds before pouring in the batter.

Use a ladle to pour the batter into the hot pan. Tilt the pan as your pour in the batter to coat the base thinly and evenly. The pan should be hot enough to set the batter immediately. Place the pan over moderate heat until the pancake has completely set and is browned underneath. Check that it is cooked underneath by lifting the edge with a palette knife or slice.

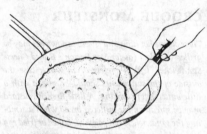

When the base of the pancake has browned and the edges are just beginning to turn crisp, slide a palette knife or slice under it and turn it over. To toss a pancake, first loosen it all around the edge, then give the pan a firm jolt upwards to flip the pancake up and over in one movement. Practice makes perfect!

As the pancakes are cooked, stack them, sprinkling each sweet pancake with a little caster sugar. Absorbent kitchen paper may be layered between savoury pancakes to prevent them sticking.

FREEZING PANCAKES

Stack cold pancakes on a double thickness of foil, layering freezer film between each one. Pack tightly, label and freeze. They keep for up to 6 months. Individual pancakes thaw quickly; if you want to thaw the whole stack quickly separate them and spread them on a clean board. Keep the pancakes covered while they are thawing. See also individual recipes.

MAKING WAFFLES

Unlike pancake batter, the mixture for waffles is made from self-raising flour. As it cooks and sets, the batter rises in the waffle iron to give a crisp, slightly spongy result.

Batter for making waffles should be the consistency of thick cream and it should be cooked as soon as it is prepared. Serve waffles freshly cooked.

WAFFLE IRONS

To shape the waffles you will need a special utensil known as a waffle iron. This is a hinged metal mould which should be greased and heated over a gas flame or electric ring. Plug-in electric waffle cookers are also on sale, usually with non-stick plates that may be removed for

easy cleaning. Always follow the manufacturer's instructons when using an electric appliance.

When using a hand-held waffle iron, pour enough batter into one side of the greased mould to cover it. Close the iron and cook the waffle on both sides until it has stopped steaming. Open the iron carefully – if the waffle is cooked it should come away from the metal plate quite easily. If you have to keep waffles hot, place them in a single layer on a wire rack in a low oven. Do not stack them or they will become soggy.

YORKSHIRE PUDDING BATTER

Yorkshire pudding can be made in a large baking tin or in individual tins. For more information see Roast Ribs of Beef with Yorkshire Pudding on page 341.

100g/4oz plain flour
pinch of salt
1 egg, beaten
150ml/¼ pint milk

Sift the flour into a bowl and add a pinch of salt. Make a well in the centre and add the beaten egg. Stir in the milk, gradually working in the flour. Beat vigorously until the mixture is smooth and bubbly, then stir in 150ml/¼ pint water. Pour into a jug. The mixture may be left to stand at this stage, in which case it should be covered and stored in the refrigerator.

MAKES ABOUT 300ML/½ PINT

COATING BATTER

This is a stiff batter, suitable for cod fillets, meat, poultry or other firm foods.

100 g/4 oz plain flour
pinch of salt
1 egg
125 ml/4 fl oz milk

Sift the flour and salt into a bowl and make a well in the centre.

Add the egg and a little milk, then beat well, gradually incorporating the flour and the remaining milk to make a smooth batter.

MAKES ABOUT 150 ML/¼ PINT

LIGHT BATTER

This light, thin batter is ideal for delicate or sweet foods.

100 g/4 oz plain flour
pinch of salt
15 ml/1 tbsp oil
2 egg whites

Sift the flour and salt into a bowl and make a well in the centre.

Pour 125 ml/4 fl oz cold water into the well in the flour and add the oil. Gradually beat the liquid into the flour to make a smooth, thick batter. Beat really well so that the batter is light.

Just before the batter is to be used, whisk the egg whites until stiff in a clean dry bowl. Fold the egg whites into the batter and use at once.

MAKES ABOUT 175 ML/6 FL OZ

BAKED BATTER PUDDING

The batter that is the basis of Yorkshire pudding may also be used to make a simple sweet.

25 g/1 oz cooking fat or 30 ml/2 tbsp oil
caster sugar for sprinkling

BATTER
100 g/4 oz plain flour
1.25 ml/¼ tsp salt
1 egg, beaten
250 ml/8 fl oz milk, or half milk and half water

Make the batter. Sift the flour and salt into a bowl, make a well in the centre and add the beaten egg. Stir in half the milk (or all the milk, if using a mixture of milk and water), gradually working the flour down from the sides.

Beat vigorously until the mixture is smooth and bubbly, then stir in the rest of the milk (or the water). Pour into a jug. The mixture may be left to stand at this stage, in which case it should be covered and stored in the refrigerator.

Set the oven at 220°C/425°F/gas 7. Put the fat or oil into a 28 × 18 cm/11 × 7 inch baking tin and heat in the oven for 15 minutes.

Stir the batter and immediately pour it into the baking tin. Return to the oven and bake for 30–35 minutes, until the pudding is brown and well risen.

Cut into squares and serve at once, sprinkled with caster sugar or with a suitable sauce.

SERVES FOUR

EVERYDAY PANCAKES

Pancakes are much too good to be reserved exclusively for Shrove Tuesday. Simple, versatile, and always popular, they lend themselves to a wide range of savoury and sweet fillings. For more recipes see the chapter on Sweet Batter Puddings.

100 g/4 oz plain flour
1.25 ml/¼ tsp salt
1 egg, beaten
250 ml/8 fl oz milk, or half milk and half
   water
oil for frying

Make the batter. Sift the flour and salt into a bowl, make a well in the centre and add the beaten egg. Stir in half the milk (or all the milk, if using a mixture of milk and water), gradually working the flour down from the sides.

Beat vigorously until the mixture is smooth and bubbly, then stir in the rest of the milk (or the water), Pour into a jug. The mixture may be left to stand at this stage, in which case it should be covered and stored in the refrigerator.

Heat a little oil in a clean 18 cm/7 inch pancake pan. Pour off any excess oil, leaving the pan covered with a thin film of grease. Stir the batter and pour about 30-45 ml/2-3 tbsp into the pan. There should be just enough to thinly cover the base. Tilt and rotate the pan so that the batter runs over the surface evenly.

Cook over moderate heat for about 1 minute until the pancake is set and golden brown underneath. Make sure the pancake is loose by shaking the pan, then either toss it or turn it with a palette knife or fish slice. Cook the second side for about 30 seconds or until golden.

Slide the pancake out on to a warmed plate. Serve at once, with a suitable filling or sauce, or keep warm over simmering water while mak-

ing 7 more pancakes in the same way. Add more oil to the pan when necessary.

MAKES EIGHT

VARIATIONS

Rich Pancakes Add 15 g/½ oz cooled melted butter or 15 ml/1 tbsp oil to the batter with 1 egg yolk. Alternatively, enrich the batter by adding 1 whole egg.

Cream Pancakes Use 150 ml/¼ pint milk and 50 ml/2 fl oz single cream instead of 250 ml/8 fl oz milk. Add 2 eggs and 25 g/1 oz cooled melted butter, then stir in 15 ml/1 tbsp brandy with caster sugar to taste. The mixture should only just coat the back of a spoon as the pancakes should be very thin.

SAVOURY PANCAKE FILLINGS

Reheat savoury pancakes in a 180°C/350°F/ gas 4 oven for 30 minutes if they have a cold filling; 20 minutes if the filling is hot. Pancakes topped with grated cheese may be browned under the grill.

Asparagus Add 30 ml/2 tbsp thawed frozen chopped spinach to the pancake batter, if liked. Place a trimmed slice of ham on each pancake, top with a large asparagus spear and roll up. Cover the rolled pancakes with 600 ml/1 pint Béchamel sauce (page 481), reheat, then sprinkle with grated Gruyère cheese and grill to brown.

Chicken and Mushroom Sauté 175 g/6 oz sliced mushrooms in 45 ml/3 tbsp butter for 2-3 minutes. Stir in 15 ml/1 tbsp plain flour and cook for 1 minute, then gradually add 150 ml/¼ pint chicken stock. Bring to the boil, stirring. Add 5 ml/1 tsp mushroom ketchup, if liked. Stir in 75 g/3 oz chopped cooked chicken. Fill the pancakes and reheat.

Poached Haddock Poach 300 g/11 oz smoked haddock fillets in a little water for 10–15 minutes. Drain and flake the fish. Make 250 ml/8 fl oz Béchamel sauce (page 481). Add the fish and 2 chopped hard-boiled eggs, 5 ml/1 tsp chopped capers, 5 ml/1 tbsp chopped parsley, 15 ml/1 tbsp lemon juice and salt and pepper. Fill the pancakes, sprinkle with 25 g/1 oz grated cheese and reheat.

Spinach Pancakes Cook 300 g/11 oz frozen spinach; drain well. Add 200 g/7 oz cottage cheese, 50 g/2 oz grated mature Cheddar cheese; 100 ml/3½ fl oz double cream, a pinch of nutmeg and seasoning. Fill the pancakes, sprinkle with 25 g/1 oz grated cheese and reheat.

SWEET PANCAKE FILLINGS

Lemon juice and caster sugar share the honours with warmed jam as the most common fillings for pancakes. Here are a few more ideas: Spoon the chosen filling on to the pancakes and roll up. If liked, sprinkle the rolled pancakes with caster sugar, and glaze in a very hot oven or under a hot grill.

Apple In a bowl, mix together 250 ml/8 fl oz sweetened thick apple purée, 50 g/2 oz sultanas and a pinch of cinnamon.

Apricot Add 15 ml/1 tbsp cinnamon to the batter when making the pancakes. Soak 50 g/2 oz dried apricots in 60 ml/4 tbsp water in a saucepan, then simmer with 50 g/2 oz sugar and a generous squeeze of lemon juice until soft and pulpy. Add 25 g/1 oz chopped toasted almonds.

Banana In a bowl, mash 4 bananas with 50 g/2 oz softened butter, 30 ml/2 tbsp sugar and the grated rind and juice of 1 lemon.

Chocolate and Whipped Cream Whip 150 ml/¼ pint double cream with 15–30 ml/1–2 tbsp icing sugar until it stands in soft peaks. Gently fold in 100 g/4 oz grated chocolate and 30 ml/2 tbsp finely chopped toasted hazelnuts. Swirl this on the pancakes, fold into quarters and serve at once.

Curd Cheese In a bowl, beat 100 g/4 oz curd cheese with 45 ml/3 tbsp double cream, 30 ml/2 tbsp caster sugar and the grated rind of ½ lemon. Add 40 g/1½ oz sultanas.

Dried Fruit Put 100 g/4 oz chopped raisins, dates and cut mixed peel into a small saucepan with 100 ml/3½ fl oz apple juice. Simmer until syrupy.

Ginger and Banana Add 15 ml/1 tbsp ground ginger to the batter when making the pancakes, if liked. For the filling, mash 4 bananas in a bowl with 30 ml/2 tbsp double cream. Add a few pieces of chopped preserved ginger.

Maple Syrup and Ice Cream Trickle about 10 ml/2 tsp maple syrup over each pancake and roll up. Arrange on serving plates and top with good-quality Cornish ice cream. Sprinkle with chopped walnuts.

Pineapple Drain 1 (227 g/8 oz) can crushed pineapple. Combine the fruit with 250 ml/8 fl oz soured cream in a bowl. Fill the pancakes with this mixture and serve with a sauce made by heating the fruit syrup with a few drops of the lemon juice.

Rum Warmers Place 45 ml/3 tbsp brown sugar in a saucepan with 5 ml/1 tsp ground cinnamon and 90 ml/6 tbsp orange juice. Heat until the sugar melts, then bring to the boil and boil for 1 minute. Remove from the heat and stir in 60 ml/4 tbsp rum. Moisten the pancakes with a little rum syrup before rolling them up, then trickle the remainder over the top. Serve with whipped cream.

Surprise Spoon ice cream into the centre of each pancake and fold in half like an omelette. Serve at once with a jam sauce or Melba Sauce (page 501).

APPLE FRITTERS

450 g/1 lb apples
5 ml/1 tsp lemon juice
oil for deep frying
caster sugar for sprinkling
St Clement's Sauce (page 496) or single
   cream to serve

BATTER
100 g/4 oz plain flour
1.25 ml/¼ tsp salt
15 ml/1 tbsp vegetable oil
60 ml/4 tbsp milk
2 egg whites

Make the batter. Sift the flour and salt into a bowl. Make a well in the centre of the flour and add the oil and milk. Gradually work in the flour from the sides, then beat well until smooth. Stir in 75 ml/5 tbsp cold water. The mixture may be left to stand at this stage, in which case it should be covered and stored in the refrigerator.

Peel and core the apples. Cut them into 5 mm/¼ inch slices and place in a bowl of cold water with the lemon juice added.

Whisk the egg whites in a clean, grease-free bowl until stiff. Give the batter a final beat, then lightly fold in the egg whites.

Set the oven at 150°C/300°F/gas 2. Put the oil for frying in a deep wide saucepan. Heat the oil to 185°C/360°F or until a bread cube immersed in the oil turns pale brown in 45 seconds. If using a deep-fat fryer, follow the manufacturer's instructions.

Drain the apples thoroughly and dry dry with soft absorbent kitchen paper. Coat the apple slices in batter and fry 5 or 6 pieces at a time for 2–3 minutes until golden. Lift out the fritters with a slotted spoon and dry on absorbent kitchen paper. Keep hot on a baking sheet in the oven while cooking the next batch.

When all the fritters have been cooked, sprinkle them with caster sugar and serve with St Clement's Sauce or cream.

SERVES FOUR

VARIATIONS

Apricot Fritters Prepare batter as above. Sprinkle drained canned apricot halves with rum and leave for 15 minutes. Coat in batter, then fry. Dredge with caster sugar and serve with custard or cream.

Banana Fritters Prepare batter as above. Peel 4 small bananas, cut in half lengthways, then in half across. Coat in batter, then fry. Serve with custard or liqueur-flavoured cream.

Orange Fritters Prepare batter as above. Remove the peel and pith from 4 oranges. Divide them into pieces of about 2 or 3 segments each. Carefully cut into the centre to remove any pips. Coat in batter, then fry. Serve with custard or cream.

Pear Fritters Prepare batter as above. Peel and core 4 pears. Cut into quarters, sprinkle with sugar and kirsch and leave to stand for 15 minutes. Finely crush 4 almond macaroons and toss the pear pieces in the crumbs. Coat in batter, then fry. Serve with a lemon sauce.

Pineapple Fritters Prepare batter as above. Drain 1 (556 g/19 oz) can pineapple rings, pat dry on absorbent kitchen paper, and sprinkle with 20 ml/4 tsp kirsch. Leave to stand for 15 minutes. Coat in batter, then fry. Serve with the pineapple juice, thickened with arrowroot.

SOUFFLES AND MOUSSES

The principles involved in making cold soufflés and mousses are the same. The difference
between the two dishes is mainly in the way in
which they are set and served.

Soufflés and mousses are mixtures that are
lightened with egg. Hot soufflés rely on
whisked egg whites to make the mixture rise
and set; cold soufflés and mousses are lightened with egg whites and set with gelatine.

Recipes for savoury soufflés follow. For
sweet soufflés see the chapter on Sweet Soufflés and Mousses.

HOT SOUFFLES

A hot soufflé ought to make an impressive
entrance at the end of a meal, so to ensure
success you must be confident and well organized. The flavoured base mixture for the
soufflé should be prepared in advance, ready
for the egg whites to be whisked and folded in
just before cooking. Timing is crucial, so work
out a timetable and plan exactly when you
intend to finish preparing the soufflé and place
it in the oven. When the soufflé is cooked it
should be taken immediately to the table and
served.

You will need an ovenproof, straight-sided
soufflé dish or individual soufflé or ramekin
dishes. These should be buttered. For sweet
soufflés, dishes may be sprinkled with a little
caster sugar, according to the recipe. This
helps the mixture to cling to the sides of the
dish as it rises.

For easy removal from the oven, stand individual dishes on a baking sheet once they are
prepared. As soon as the dish, or dishes, have
been filled with mixture, quickly wash and dry
your hands and run your thumb around the
inside edge of the dish, cleaning away the
mixture, to create a gutter. This ensures that the
mixture rises evenly and high instead of sticking to the top edge of the dish, which would
make it dome and crack.

ADDING THE FINISHING TOUCHES
TO SWEET SOUFFLES

Hot soufflés may be dredged with a thick
covering of icing sugar before serving. The
icing sugar may be caramelized with a hot
skewer in a criss-cross pattern. The best way to
do this is to preheat two metal skewers under
the grill until they are red hot. Alternatively,
hold the skewers in a gas flame or on a solid
electric hot plate. As soon as the soufflé has
been thickly dredged with icing sugar, mark it
by pressing the hot skewer into it; remove the
skewer quickly. Having a second hot skewer in
reserve means the decoration may be finished
swiftly and the soufflé will be served speedily.

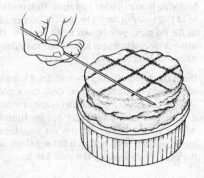

COLD SOUFFLES

Cold soufflés are easier to make than hot ones and may be prepared in advance. The basic flavouring mixture is usually enriched with cream, lightened with whisked egg whites and set with gelatine. The egg yolks may be creamed with sugar or mixed with a savoury sauce base. The dissolved gelatine is usually stirred into the mixture just before any whipped cream is added. The egg whites are folded in last, just before the mixture is poured into the prepared dish.

When the cold soufflé mixture is poured into the dish it should come over the top of the rim. Level the mixture gently and keep the dish level in the refrigerator while the soufflé sets.

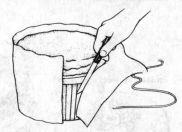

When the soufflé has set, untie the string that holds the paper. Carefully peel the paper from the set soufflé, at the same time gently running the blade of a knife between the soufflé mixture and the paper. This ensures that the soufflé mixture standing above the side of the dish keeps its shape.

PREPARING A SOUFFLE DISH

This method is used for all cold, set mixtures which stand above the rim of the dish. Although it is not necessary to prepare dishes in this way for baked soufflés, some cooks prefer to do so. In the event, the inside of the paper should be well greased.

1 Using a piece of string, measure the height of the dish and its circumference.

2 Cut a strip from two thicknesses of greaseproof paper or non-stick baking parchment that exceeds the height of the dish by 7.5 cm/3 inches and is long enough to go right around the dish with an overlap.

3 Tie the paper around the dish with string. If the dish has sloping sides or a projecting rim, secure the paper above and below the rim with gummed tape or pins. Make sure the paper has no creases and forms a neat round shape.

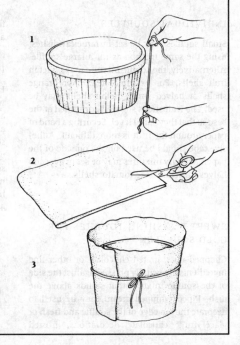

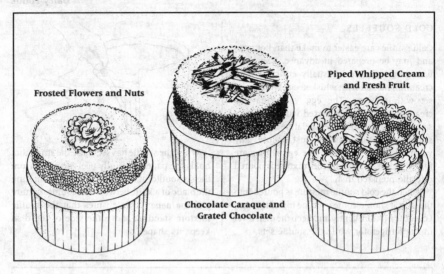

Frosted Flowers and Nuts

Piped Whipped Cream and Fresh Fruit

Chocolate Caraque and Grated Chocolate

INDIVIDUAL SOUFFLES

Small soufflés may be set in ramekin dishes, using the same method as for a large soufflé. Alternatively, the soufflé mixture may be set in fruit shells. For example, lemon or orange shells or halved small melon shells may be used. The fruit shells should be trimmed at the base so that they stand level. Securing a band of paper around the fruit is more difficult. Adhesive tape should be used on the outside of the paper. Savoury mixtures may be set in avocado halves, artichokes or tomato shells.

SWEET FINISHING TOUCHES FOR COLD SOUFFLES

Chopped nuts, grated chocolate or other fine ingredients are usually pressed against the side of the soufflé mixture that stands above the dish. Piped whipped cream may be used to decorate the top edge of the soufflé and fresh or glacé fruit, chocolate decorations, frosted flowers or other suitable ingredients may be added for decoration.

ICED SOUFFLES

Light and creamy cold soufflé mixtures freeze well to make a dessert which is a cross between a soufflé and an ice cream. Individual soufflés are particularly practical for freezing as they soften to a pleasant eating consistency fairly quickly and are easy to serve. Prepare the soufflé as usual, then place it in the freezer, making sure that it is level. Freeze for several hours or overnight. Allow to soften for about 45 minutes in the refrigerator.

HOT CHEESE SOUFFLE

Individual hot soufflés make a very good starter, light main course or savoury finish to a meal. The quantity of mixture below will make 6 individual soufflés in 200 ml/7 fl oz dishes, and will take 20 minutes to bake.

fat for greasing
50 g/2 oz butter
25 g/1 oz plain flour
250 ml/8 fl oz milk
100–150 g/4–5 oz Cheddar cheese, grated, or
    75–100 g/3–4 oz mixed grated Parmesan
    and Gruyère cheese
2.5 ml/½ tsp dry mustard
pinch of cayenne pepper
salt and pepper
4 eggs, separated, plus 1 egg white

Grease a 1 litre/1¾ pint soufflé dish. Set the oven at 190°C/375°F/gas 5.

Melt the butter in a saucepan, stir in the flour and cook over low heat for 2–3 minutes without colouring, stirring all the time. Over very low heat, gradually add the milk, stirring constantly. Bring to the boil, stirring, and simmer 1–2 minutes more until smooth and thickened. Remove from the heat and beat hard until the sauce comes away cleanly from the sides of the pan. Cool slightly and put into a bowl. Stir in the cheese, mustard, cayenne, salt and pepper.

Beat the yolks into the mixture one by one. In a clean, grease-free bowl, whisk the egg whites until stiff. Using a metal spoon, stir one spoonful of the whites into the mixture to lighten it, then fold in the rest until evenly distributed.

Spoon the mixture into the prepared dish and bake for 30–35 minutes, until well risen and browned. Serve the soufflé immediately with hot buttered toast.

SERVES FOUR

VARIATIONS

Cheese and Onion Soufflé   Add 50 g/2 oz very finely chopped onion cooked in the butter for 2–3 minutes until transparent, to the grated cheese.

Cheese and Watercress Soufflé   Chop the leaves from half a bunch of watercress and add to the cheese.

Layered Cheese Soufflé   Put half the soufflé mixture into the dish and add a layer of 75 g/3 oz sautéed mushrooms, or 100 g/4 oz cooked flaked fish, or 45 ml/3 tbsp spinach purée and then the remaining mixture.

Oeufs Mollets en Soufflé   Soft boil 4 small eggs. Put one-third of the soufflé mixture into the dish. Arrange the eggs on top. Add the remainder of the mixture and bake.

Chicken Soufflé   Add 200 g/7 oz cooked minced chicken, 25 g/1 oz chopped sautéed onion, 30 ml/2 tbsp lemon juice and 5 ml/1 tsp chopped parsley.

 MRS BEETON'S TIP

The flavour of some soufflés, such as those made with fish or white meat, can be bland, so it is a good idea to infuse the milk with plenty of flavouring as when making a Bèchamel sauce.

AVOCADO RAMEKINS

These individual savoury soufflés make a spectacular start to a special meal.

butter for greasing
50 ml/2 fl oz milk
about 25 g/1 oz fresh white breadcrumbs
50 g/2 oz Cheshire or Cheddar cheese, finely
  grated
25 g/1 oz unsalted butter, melted
1 egg, separated
1 avocado, halved, stoned, peeled and
  finely diced
salt and pepper
pinch of ground mace

Grease 4 small ovenproof pots or ramekins. Set the oven at 200°C/400°F/gas 6.

Heat the milk and pour it over the breadcrumbs to cover them. Leave to stand for 5–10 minutes. Stir in the cheese and butter. Beat the yolk into the cheese mixture. Add the avocado, with salt, pepper and mace to taste. Mix lightly.

In a clean, grease-free bowl, whisk the egg white until stiff. Using a metal spoon, stir one spoonful of the egg white into the cheese mixture to lighten it, then fold in the rest. Spoon into the prepared pots or ramekins.

Bake for 25–30 minutes until risen and lightly browned. Serve immediately.

SERVES FOUR

CRAB SOUFFLE

fat for greasing
50 g/2 oz butter
45 ml/3 tbsp plain flour
250 ml/8 fl oz milk
salt and pepper
4 eggs, separated, plus 1 white
200 g/7 oz flaked crab meat
2–3 drops Tabasco sauce
30 ml/2 tbsp dry white wine

Grease a 900 ml/1½ pint soufflé dish. Set the oven at 190°C/375°F/gas 5.

Melt the butter in a saucepan, stir in the flour and cook slowly for 2–3 minutes without colouring, stirring all the time. Add the milk gradually and beat until smooth. Cook for 1–2 minutes more, still stirring. Remove from the heat and beat hard until the sauce comes away cleanly from the sides of the pan. Cool slightly, put into a bowl and add salt and pepper to taste.

Beat the yolks into the flour mixture one by one. Stir in the crab meat and add the Tabasco sauce and wine.

In a clean, grease-free bowl, whisk all the egg whites until stiff. Using a metal spoon, stir 1 spoonful of the whites into the crab meat mixture to lighten it, then fold in the rest until evenly distributed.

Spoon into the prepared dish and bake for 30–35 minutes until well risen and browned. Serve immediately, with hot buttered toast if liked.

SERVES FOUR

COOKING EGGS

Boiling Bring the eggs to room temperature before cooking to avoid cracking the shells if they are very cold. If an egg does crack, add 15 ml/1 tbsp vinegar or lemon juice to the cooking water to set the white quickly as it escapes.

Bring a small saucepan of water to the boil, allowing enough water to cover the eggs. Place an egg on a spoon and lower it into the water. Begin timing the cooking as soon as the egg is in the water. Regulate the heat so that the water is just boiling. Timing for boiled eggs is very personal but the following provides a guide when cooking average-sized eggs (sizes 3-4):

Soft boiled (soft set white) 3¼ minutes. Medium (soft yolk, firm white) 4-4¾ minutes. Hard (firm white, just firm yolk) 10 minutes.

Poaching Pour 5 cm/2 inches water into a pan – a frying pan is ideal. Add 15 ml/1 tbsp cider vinegar and bring just to simmering point. Crack a fresh egg on to a saucer. Use a draining spoon to swirl the water in the pan, then slide the egg into the middle of the gentle swirl. (The swirling water gives the egg a good shape.) Simmer for about 3 minutes, or until the egg is set. Spoon the simmering water over the egg to set it evenly. Up to four eggs may be cooked at the same time in a frying pan. Use a slotted spoon to drain the eggs as they are cooked. Trim the edges of the whites and serve at once.

Scrambled Eggs Allow two eggs per person. Put the requisite number of eggs in a bowl. Add 15–30 ml/1–2 tbsp milk for each pair of eggs. Sprinkle in some salt and pepper to taste and beat the mixture lightly until it is well mixed.

Melt a little butter in a small saucepan. There should be just enough butter to cover the bottom of the pan; do not allow it to become too hot. Pour in the eggs. Cook gently, stirring or whisking all the time, until the eggs are lightly set and creamy. Remove from the heat and serve at once. If the eggs are allowed to stand in the hot pan or left on the heat, they set firmly and separate into curds and a thin liquid.

A variety of flavourings may be stirred into the cooked eggs. They may be enriched by using single cream instead of milk or by stirring in a little extra cream as the eggs begin to thicken. Diced smoked salmon or a little grated cheese may be added just before serving.

Fried Eggs Heat a thin layer of oil or half oil and half butter in a frying pan. Bacon fat may be used instead or this may be combined with oil. Crack an egg into a saucer, then slide it into the hot fat. Cook over moderate heat, spooning fat over the egg, until the white is set and the yolk is covered with a lightly set white film. For a firmer set use a fish slice to turn the egg over as soon as the white is set firmly underneath. Cook for a further 30-60 seconds before serving – this gives a yolk which is partially set. A soft fried egg is usually ready in 2-3 minutes, slightly sooner if basted often.

Baking Plain baked eggs should be cooked in individual ovenproof dishes, such as ramekins or the slightly deeper, rounded cocotte dishes. Eggs which are baked with additional ingredients also cook successfully in a large dish; for example, eggs may be baked in hollows among vegetables such as spinach or ratatouille.

For the basic method of baking eggs, follow the recipe for Eggs in Cocottes (page 558).

Deep Fried Eggs These are well puffed, crisp and golden outside, with a soft centre. Heat oil for deep frying to 180°C/350°F or until a cube of day old bread browns in 30 seconds. Crack an egg into a mug or saucer. Standing back, slide the egg into the hot oil – it will bubble and spit. Use a slotted spoon to gently move the egg off the bottom of the pan if it does not rise to the surface quickly. The egg will quickly turn brown and crisp outside, and will be cooked with a soft centre in less than a minute. Drain well on the slotted spoon.

EGGS IN COCOTTES

25 g/1 oz butter
4 eggs
salt and pepper
60 ml/4 tbsp milk or cream

Butter 4 ramekins or cocottes at least 3.5 cm/1¼ inches deep, and stand them in a baking tin containing enough warm water to come half-way up their sides. Set the oven at 180°C/350°F/gas 4.

Break an egg into each warm dish and add salt and pepper to taste. Top with any remaining butter, cut into flakes. Spoon 15 ml/1 tbsp milk or cream over each egg.

Bake for 6-10 minutes, depending on the thickness of the dishes. The whites of the eggs should be just set. Wipe the outsides of the dishes and serve at once.

SERVES FOUR

VARIATIONS

- Shake ground nutmeg or cayenne pepper over the eggs before cooking.
- Sprinkle the eggs with very finely grated cheese before cooking.
- Put sliced, fried mushrooms, chopped ham, cooked diced chicken or lightly sautéed, diced Italian sausage in the bottom of each dish before adding the eggs.
- Put 15-30 ml/1-2 tbsp spinach purée in the dishes before adding the eggs.

MOULDED EGGS

50 g/2 oz butter
30 ml/2 tbsp finely chopped parsley
4 eggs
4 slices of white bread

Butter 4 dariole moulds generously, reserving the remaining butter. Set the oven at 180°C/350°F/gas 4.

Coat the insides of the moulds lightly with the parsley. Break an egg into each, then put them in a baking tin. Pour in enough warm water to come halfway up the sides of the moulds. Bake for 10-12 minutes, until the egg whites are just firm.

Meanwhile, cut a circle 7.5 cm/3 inches in diameter from each slice of bread and fry in the remaining butter, until golden brown on each side. Loosen the cooked eggs in the moulds, turn out on to the fried bread, and serve immediately.

SERVES FOUR

VARIATIONS

- About 15 ml/1 tbsp finely snipped chives can be used instead of the parsley.
- Use 25 g/1 oz mushrooms, finely chopped, cooked in butter and drained, instead of the parsley.
- Use 25 g/1 oz minced ham mixed with 10 ml/2 tsp chopped parsley instead of the parsley alone.
- The bread can be toasted and buttered instead of fried.
- The eggs can be turned out on to rounds of pastry or into shallow pastry cases.
- Large flat mushrooms, lightly cooked in butter, can be used instead of the bread.
- Tomatoes, peeled, cut in half and seeded, can be used instead of the bread

SHIRRED EGGS

butter for greasing
4 eggs
salt
1.25 ml/¼ tsp paprika
10 ml/2 tsp snipped chives or chopped
  parsley

Grease a shallow ovenproof dish, about 30 cm/12 inches across. Set the oven at 180°C/350°F/gas 4. Separate the eggs, keeping each yolk intact and separate.

Put the egg whites into a clean, dry bowl. Add 2.5 ml/½ tsp salt and whisk to very stiff peaks. Spread the whites lightly over the prepared dish – they should form a layer about 5 cm/2 inches deep.

Using the back of a spoon, make 4 hollows in the egg white. Space the hollows as evenly as possible and do not make them too near the edge. Slip 1 egg yolk into each hollow.

Bake for about 10 minutes or until the eggs are just set. Sprinkle with paprika and chives, or parsley and serve.

SERVES FOUR

VARIATION

Shirred Eggs on Toast Use four egg yolks but only two whites. Whisk the whites with 1.25 ml/¼ tsp salt until very stiff and fold in 50 g/2 oz finely grated Cheddar cheese. Lightly toast 4 slices of bread. Pile the cheesy meringue mixture on the toast, make a depression in each and slip in an egg yolk. Sprinkle about 15 ml/1 tbsp grated cheese over each egg yolk and cook under a low grill until the meringue is golden and the egg yolks are cooked. Serve.

FRAMED EGGS

4 thick slices of white bread
oil for shallow frying
4 eggs

Cut each slice of bread into a 10 cm/4 inch round, then cut a second 6 cm/2½ inch round from the centres, so that four bread rings are left.

Heat the oil in a large frying pan and fry the bread rings until brown and crisp on one side. Turn them over, lower the heat and break an egg into the centre of each ring. Fry gently, spooning the oil over the top from time to time, until the eggs are set. Using a fish slice, remove the framed eggs from the pan, draining excess oil, and serve at once.

SERVES FOUR

EGGS A LA MAITRE D'HOTEL

100 g/4 oz butter
30 ml/2 tbsp plain flour
300 ml/½ pint milk
salt and pepper
30 ml/2 tbsp chopped parsley
6 eggs, hard boiled and quartered
juice of ½ lemon

Melt half the butter in a small saucepan. Stir in the flour and cook for a few seconds, then gradually pour in the milk, stirring all the time. Bring to the boil, stirring, reduce the heat and leave the sauce to simmer gently for 5 minutes. Gradually beat in the remaining butter, add the parsley and remove from the heat.

Arrange the eggs in a dish or in four individual dishes. Stir the lemon juice into the sauce, pour it over the eggs and serve.

SERVES FOUR

PEASANTS' EGGS

salt and pepper
575 g/1¼ lb potatoes, cubed
60 ml/4 tbsp oil
8 rindless back bacon rashers, cut into
  strips
1 onion, chopped
30 ml/2 tbsp chopped parsley
30 ml/2 tbsp butter
4 eggs

Bring a large saucepan of salted water to the boil, add the potatoes and bring back to the boil. Cook for 1 minute, then drain thoroughly.

Heat the oil in a large deep frying pan. Add the bacon and fry for 2–3 minutes until crisp. Using a slotted spoon, remove and drain on absorbent kitchen paper. Add the onion to the oil remaining in the pan and fry for 3–4 minutes until golden; remove with the slotted spoon and put in the baking dish with the bacon. Keep hot.

Add the potatoes to the frying pan and fry gently for 5–6 minutes, turning occasionally, until cooked and brown. Drain and add to the bacon and onion mixture with plenty of salt, pepper and parsley. Mix lightly and keep hot.

Melt the butter in the remaining oil. Fry the eggs. Arrange on the potato mixture and serve at once.

SERVES FOUR

EGGS MORNAY

1 kg/2¼ lb potatoes, halved
salt and pepper
8 eggs
300 ml/½ pint Béchamel Sauce (page 481)
75 g/3 oz Cheddar cheese, grated
2.5 ml/½ tsp French mustard
30 ml/2 tbsp butter
45 ml/3 tbsp milk

Cook the potatoes in a saucepan of salted boiling water for 20 minutes until tender.

Meanwhile bring a small saucepan of water to the boil, carefully add the eggs and cook them for 5 minutes. Plunge them into cold water, leave for 5 minutes, then remove their shells carefully under the water. Leave the shelled eggs under the water. Reheat the Béchamel sauce gently with most of the cheese and stir in the mustard.

Drain the cooked potatoes thoroughly and mash with a potato masher, or beat with a hand-held electric whisk until smooth. Beat in the butter and milk to make a creamy piping consistency. Spoon the creamed potato into a piping bag fitted with a star nozzle and pipe a border of mashed potato around the edge of a large shallow dish to go under the grill.

Using a slotted spoon, drain the shelled eggs well and arrange in the dish. Coat with the hot sauce. Sprinkle the remaining cheese over and grill until brown.

SERVES FOUR

 MRS BEETON'S TIP

When reheating the Béchamel sauce with the cheese, do not allow the mixture to boil or the cheese may become stringy.

EGGS FLORENTINE

butter for greasing
1 kg/2¼ lb fresh spinach or 2 (225 g/8 oz)
    packets frozen leaf spinach
15 ml/1 tbsp butter
salt and pepper
4 eggs
100 g/4 oz Fontina or Cheddar cheese, finely
    grated

Set the oven at 190°C/375°F/gas 5. Wash the fresh spinach several times and remove any coarse stalks. Put into a saucepan with just the water that clings to the leaves, then cover the pan with a tight-fitting lid. Place over moderate heat for about 3 minutes, shaking the pan often until the spinach has wilted. Lower the heat slightly and cook for 3–5 minutes more. (Cook frozen spinach according to the directions on the packet.)

When the spinach is tender, drain it thoroughly in a colander. Cut through the leaves several times with a knife to chop them roughly. Melt the butter in the clean pan, add the spinach with salt and pepper to taste, and heat through gently.

Spoon into a greased ovenproof dish and, using the back of a spoon, make 4 small hollows in the surface. Break an egg into each hollow, add salt and pepper to taste, then sprinkle the grated cheese over the eggs. Bake for 12–15 minutes until the eggs are lightly set. Serve at once.

SERVES FOUR

CURRIED EGGS

60 ml/4 tbsp oil
2 onions, finely chopped
1 cooking apple
15–30 ml/1–2 tbsp mild curry powder
30 ml/2 tbsp plain flour
10 ml/2 tsp tomato purée
500 ml/17 fl oz vegetable stock
30 ml/2 tbsp mango chutney
15 ml/1 tbsp soft light brown sugar
30 ml/2 tbsp lemon juice
salt
6 eggs, hard boiled, shelled and cut into
    quarters
30 ml/2 tbsp plain yogurt

Heat the oil in a saucepan, add the onions and sauté for 4–6 minutes until soft but not coloured. Peel, core and chop the apple. Add it to the onions, and continue cooking for 5 minutes.

Stir in the curry powder and flour and fry for 2–3 minutes, then add the tomato purée, vegetable stock, chutney, sugar, lemon juice and a pinch of salt. Bring to the boil, stirring constantly, then lower the heat, cover and simmer for 30 minutes, stirring occasionally.

Add the hard-boiled eggs and warm through over gentle heat. To serve, remove from the heat and gently stir in the yogurt, taking care not to break up the curried eggs.

SERVES FOUR

 MRS BEETON'S TIP

Cook some Basmati rice according to the instructions on page 502, adding a few frozen peas halfway through cooking. Serve the rice and peas with the eggs.

ANCHOVY EGGS

4 slices of white bread
75 g/3 oz butter
anchovy paste (see method)
4 eggs
10 ml/2 tsp tarragon vinegar
20 ml/4 tsp chopped parsley

Toast the bread on both sides and cut off the crusts. Spread each slice with butter and a little anchovy paste.

Melt the remaining butter in a frying pan and fry the eggs until set. Put one egg on each slice of toast and keep hot.

Continue heating the butter with the vinegar until the mixture browns. Pour it over the eggs, top with parsley and serve.

SERVES FOUR

OEUFS AU PLAT

50 g/2 oz butter
4 eggs
salt and white pepper

Set the oven at 180°C/350°F/gas 4 or heat the grill. Butter a shallow ovenproof or flameproof dish (for grilling) quite generously. The lid of an ovenproof glass casserole or a medium quiche dish will do instead of a gratin dish.

Break the eggs into the dish and sprinkle with salt and white pepper. Dot with the remaining butter. Bake for about 12 minutes, or until the eggs are cooked to taste. Alternatively, place them under the grill on a low rack. Cook for about 5 minutes, or until the eggs are set.

SERVES FOUR

EGGS BENEDICT

2 muffins, split, or 4 slices of white bread
30 ml/2 tbsp butter
4 slices of ham
4 eggs

HOLLANDAISE SAUCE
45 ml/3 tbsp white wine vinegar
6 peppercorns
½ bay leaf
1 blade of mace
3 egg yolks
100 g/4 oz butter, softened
salt and pepper

Make the Hollandaise sauce. Combine the vinegar, peppercorns, bay leaf and mace in a small saucepan. Boil rapidly until the liquid is reduced to 15 ml/1 tbsp. Strain into a heatproof bowl and leave to cool. Add the egg yolks and a nut of butter to the vinegar and place over a saucepan of gently simmering water. Heat the mixture gently, beating constantly until thick. Do not allow it to approach boiling point. Add the remaining butter, a little at a time, beating well after each addition. When all the butter has been added the sauce should be thick and glossy. Season lightly.

Toast the muffins or bread slices, then butter them. Trim the ham slices to fit the bread. Put the trimmings on the hot muffins or toast and cover with the ham slices. Put on a large heated platter or individual plates and keep hot.

Poach the eggs and drain well. Put an egg on each piece of ham, cover with about 15 ml/1 tbsp of the Hollandaise sauce and serve the remaining sauce separately.

SERVES FOUR

OMELETTE

The secret of a light omelette is to add water, not milk, to the mixture, beating it only sufficiently to mix the yolks and whites. The mixture must be cooked quickly until evenly and lightly set, then served when still moist. Have everything ready before you start to cook, including the diner, so that the omelette can be taken to the table as soon as it is ready.

**2 eggs
salt and pepper
15 ml/1 tbsp unsalted butter or margarine**

Break the eggs into a bowl, add 15 ml/1 tbsp cold water, salt and pepper. Beat lightly with a fork. Thoroughly heat a frying pan or omelette pan. When it is hot, add the butter or margarine, tilting the pan so that the whole surface is lightly greased. Without drawing the pan off the heat, add the egg mixture. Leave to stand for 10 seconds.

Using a spatula, gently draw the egg mixture from the sides to the centre as it sets, allowing the uncooked egg mixture to run in to fill the gap. Do not stir or the mixture will scramble.

When the omelette is golden and set underneath, but still slightly moist on top, remove it from the heat. Loosen the edges by shaking the pan, using a round-bladed knife or the edge of a spatula, then flip one-third of the omelette towards the centre. Flip the opposite third over towards the centre. Tip the omelette on to a hot plate, folded sides underneath. Alternatively, the cooked omelette may be rolled out of the pan after the first folding, so that it is served folded in three. A simpler method is to fold the omelette in half in the pan, then slide it out on to the plate.

SERVES ONE

FILLINGS

Cheese Add 40 g/1½ oz grated cheese to the beaten eggs. Sprinkle a further 15 g/½ oz over the omelette.

Fine Herbes Add 2.5 ml/½ tsp chopped fresh tarragon, 2.5 ml/½ tsp chopped fresh chervil, 5 ml/1 tsp chopped parsley and a few snipped chives to the beaten eggs.

Ham Add 50 g/2 oz chopped ham to the egg mixture.

Fish Add 50 g/2 oz flaked cooked fish to the omelette just before folding.

Bacon Grill 2 rindless bacon rashers until crisp; crumble into the centre of the omelette just before folding.

Mushroom Fry 50 g/2 oz sliced mushrooms in butter. Spoon into the centre of the omelette just before folding.

Shrimp or Prawn Sauté 50 g/2 oz shrimps or prawns in a little butter in a saucepan. Add a squeeze of lemon juice and spoon into the omelette before folding.

Chicken Chop 25 g/1 oz cooked chicken. Mix with 60 ml/4 tbsp white sauce. Heat gently in a small saucepan. Spoon into the centre of the omelette before folding.

 MRS BEETON'S TIP

In Mrs Beeton's day, most households would have a special omelette pan. When new, this would be 'seasoned' by melting a little butter in the pan, sprinkling it with salt, and rubbing vigorously with a soft cloth. This process helped to prevent the egg mixture from sticking. The omelette pan would not be washed after use; instead it would be rubbed all over with a soft cloth. Salt would be used, if necessary, to remove any egg still sticking to the pan.

OMELETTE ARNOLD BENNETT

150 g/5 oz smoked haddock
25 g/1 oz unsalted butter
60 ml/4 tbsp single cream
2 eggs, separated
salt and pepper
30 ml/2 tbsp grated Parmesan cheese
parsley sprigs to garnish

Bring a saucepan of water to simmering point, add the haddock and poach gently for 10 minutes. Using a slotted spoon transfer the fish to a large plate. Remove any skin or bones. Flake the fish into a large bowl and add half the butter and 15 ml/1 tbsp of the cream. Mix well.

In a separate bowl mix the egg yolks with 15 ml/1 tbsp of the remaining cream. Add salt and pepper to taste. Add to the fish mixture and stir in half the cheese.

In a clean dry bowl, whisk the egg whites until stiff. Fold them into the fish mixture.

Heat half the remaining butter in an omelette pan. Pour in half the fish mixture and cook quickly until golden brown underneath (see Mrs Beeton's Tip). Sprinkle over half the remaining cheese, spoon over 15 ml/1 tbsp of the remaining cream and brown quickly under a hot grill. Do not fold. Very quickly make a second omelette in the same way. Garnish and serve at once.

SERVES TWO

 MRS BEETON'S TIP

Use a slim spatula to lift one side of the omelette in order to check the colour underneath.

BREADCRUMB OMELETTE

Some people find this more digestible than a conventional omelette as it is less rich.

25 g/1 oz fresh white breadcrumbs
250 ml/8 fl oz milk
4 eggs, separated
salt and pepper
20 ml/4 tsp butter

Put the breadcrumbs in a bowl, add the milk and leave to stand for 10 minutes. Stir in the egg yolks, with salt and pepper to taste. In a clean, dry bowl, whisk the egg whites until stiff; fold them into the breadcrumb mixture.

Place a frying pan or omelette pan over gentle heat. When it is hot, add the butter or margarine, tilting the pan so that the whole surface is lightly greased. Without drawing the pan off the heat, add the egg mixture. Leave to stand for 10 seconds. Preheat the grill.

Using a spatula, gently draw the egg mixture from the sides to the centre as it sets, allowing the uncooked egg mixture to run in to fill the gap. Do not stir or the mixture will scramble.

When the omelette is set and browned underneath, but still moist on top, remove it from the heat. Place under the hot grill for a few seconds to cook the top. Using a spatula, fold the omelette over in half and slide it out of the pan on to a heated plate.

SERVES ONE

SPANISH OMELETTE

Known as tortilla, a Spanish omelette is quite different from filled and folded omelettes or feather-light soufflé omelettes. It is a thick cake of potato and onion set in eggs, cut into wedges and served hot or cold. This classic potato omelette is quite delicious without any additional ingredients; however, the recipe is often varied to include red and green peppers or a mixture of vegetables, such as peas and green beans.

675 g/1½ lb potatoes
225 g/8 oz onions, thinly sliced
salt and pepper
45 ml/3 tbsp olive oil
6 eggs, beaten

Cut the potatoes into 1 cm/½ inch cubes and mix them with the onions in a basin. Add plenty of seasoning and mix well.

Heat the oil in a heavy-bottomed frying pan which has fairly deep sides. Add the potatoes and onions, then cook, stirring and turning the vegetables often, until both potatoes and onions are tender. This takes about 25 minutes.

Pour the eggs over the potatoes and cook over medium heat, stirring, until the eggs begin to set. Press the vegetables down evenly and leave to set. Lower the heat to prevent the base of the omelette overbrowning before the eggs have set sufficiently.

Lay a large plate over the omelette and invert the pan to turn the omelette out on the plate. The base of the pan should be well greased but if it looks a little dry, then add a little extra olive oil and heat it. Slide the omelette back into the pan and cook over medium to high heat for 3–5 minutes, until crisp and browned. Serve the omelette hot, warm or cold.

SERVES FOUR TO SIX

THE CURE'S OMELETTE

Brillat Savarin provides a colourful account of the origins of this recipe in his Physiology of Taste. It was served to Madame Récamier, a Parisienne beauty who took great interest in benevolent work, when she visited the Curé. Mrs Beeton quotes Brillat Savarin's recipe; this is a contemporary version.

50 g/2 oz soft roes (carp's roe was used originally)
salt and pepper
about 50 g/2 oz fresh tuna steak
½ shallot, chopped
50 g/2 oz butter
10 ml/2 tsp chopped parsley
5 ml/1 tsp chopped fresh tarragon
5 ml/1 tsp chopped dill
2.5 ml/½ tsp chopped fresh thyme
6 eggs, beaten
juice of ½ lemon

Bring some water to the boil in a small saucepan. Add a little salt, then add the roe and lower the heat. Simmer for 5 minutes, then drain and roughly chop the roes. Chop the tuna and mix with the roes and shallot. Melt half the butter with the herbs in a small saucepan; keep hot. Melt the remaining butter in a large omelette pan. Add the tuna mixture and cook, stirring, until the tuna is cooked and well mixed with the butter.

Add a little salt and pepper to the eggs, pour them over the tuna mixture and cook, stirring occasionally, until the omelette begins to set. Leave to cook until just set and creamy. The omelette should be thick, light and oval in shape, rather than round. Turn it on a warmed serving platter. Add the lemon juice to the hot butter mixture, pour this over the omelette and serve at once.

SERVES TWO TO THREE

SWEET SOUFFLE OMELETTE

Soufflé omelettes are quick and easy to make – the perfect finale for the busy cook. Fill simply with 30 ml/2 tbsp warmed jam or try any of the exciting fillings that follow.

2 eggs, separated
5 ml/1 tsp caster sugar
few drops of vanilla essence
15 ml/1 tbsp unsalted butter or margarine
icing sugar for dredging

In a large bowl, whisk the yolks until creamy. Add the sugar and vanilla essence with 30 ml/2 tbsp water, then whisk again. In a clean, grease-free bowl, whisk the egg whites until stiff and matt.

Place an 18 cm/7 inch omelette pan over gentle heat and when it is hot, add the butter or margarine. Tilt the pan to grease the whole of the inside. Pour out any excess.

Fold the egg whites into the yolk mixture carefully until evenly distributed, using a metal spoon (see Mrs Beeton's Tip). Heat the grill to moderate.

Pour the egg mixture into the omelette pan, level the top very lightly, and cook for 1–2 minutes over moderate heat until the omelette is golden brown on the underside and moist on top. (Use a palette knife to lift the edge of the omelette to look underneath).

Put the pan under the grill for 5–6 minutes until the omelette is risen and lightly browned on the top. The texture of the omelette should be firm yet spongy. Remove from the heat as soon as it is ready, as over-cooking tends to make it tough. Run a palette knife gently round the edge and underneath to loosen it. Make a mark across the middle at right angles to the pan handle but do not cut the surface. Put the chosen filling on one half, raise the handle of the pan and double the omelette over. Turn gently on to a warm plate, dredge with icing sugar and serve at once.

SERVES ONE

 MRS BEETON'S TIP

When folding the beaten egg whites into the omelette mixture, be very careful not to overmix, as it is the air incorporated in the frothy whites that causes the omelette to rise.

FILLINGS

Apricot Omelette Add the grated rind of 1 orange to the egg yolks. Spread 30 ml/2 tbsp warm, thick apricot purée over the omelette.

Cherry Omelette Stone 100 g/4 oz dark cherries, or use canned ones. Warm with 30 ml/2 tbsp cherry jam and 15 ml/1 tbsp kirsch. Spread over the omelette.

Creamy Peach Omelette Stone and roughly chop 1 ripe peach, then mix it with 45 ml/3 tbsp cream cheese. Add a little icing sugar to taste and mix well until softened. Spread over the omelette.

Jam Omelette Warm 45 ml/3 tbsp fruity jam and spread over the omelette.

Lemon Omelette Add the grated rind of ½ lemon to the egg yolks. Warm 45 ml/3 tbsp lemon curd with 10 ml/2 tsp lemon juice, and spread over the omelette.

Orange Chocolate Omelette Warm 15 ml/1 tbsp orange marmalade and mix with 30 ml/2 tbsp chocolate spread. Spread over the omelette.

Raspberry Omelette Spread 30 ml/2 tbsp warm, thick, raspberry purée or Melba Sauce (page 501) over the omelette.

Rum Omelette Add 15 ml/1 tbsp rum to the egg yolks.

Strawberry Omelette Hull 5 ripe strawberries and soak in a bowl with a little kirch. Mash slightly with icing sugar to taste. Put in the centre of the omelette.

Surprise Omelette Put ice cream into the centre of the omelette before folding. Work quickly to prevent the ice cream from melting and serve the omelette immediately.

SPECIAL EFFECTS

Flambé Omelette Warm 30 ml/2 tbsp rum or brandy. Put the cooked omelette on to a warm plate, pour the warmed spirit round it, ignite, and serve immediately.

Branded Omelettes Soufflé omelettes are sometimes 'branded' for a special occasion. A lattice decoration is marked on the top using hot skewers. Heat the pointed ends of three metal skewers until red-hot. When the omelette is on the plate, dredge with icing sugar. Protecting your hand in an oven glove, quickly press the hot skewers, one at a time, on to the sugar, holding them there until the sugar caramelizes. Make a diagonal criss-cross design. Each skewer should make two marks if you work quickly.

BAKED SOUFFLE OMELETTE

fat for greasing
60 ml/4 tbsp jam or stewed fruit
4 eggs, separated
50 g/2 oz caster sugar
pinch of salt
caster or icing sugar for dredging

Grease a shallow 23 cm/9 inch ovenproof dish and spread the jam or fruit over the base. Set the oven at 190°C/375°F/gas 5.

In a mixing bowl, beat the eggs yolks with the sugar and 30 ml/2 tbsp water.

In a clean, grease-free bowl, whisk the egg whites with the salt until stiff, then fold into the yolk mixture. Pour over the jam or fruit and bake for 15–20 minutes. Dredge with sugar and serve at once.

SERVES TWO

 MRS BEETON'S TIP

A little water is often added to omelette mixtures to lighten them. Never add milk or cream, which would make the texture of the omelette tough.

CUSTARDS

The introduction to this chapter provides a guide to the different dairy products used to make custards. Many of these dishes are particularly delicate and require a little extra care in the preparation and cooking. If you have experienced problems when making custards, the following notes may be of some help.

It is most important that all dairy foods are perfectly fresh. Eggs, in particular, should be purchased from a reputable source as they are only lightly cooked. Dishes that are to be served chilled should be covered and cooled quickly, then stored in the refrigerator.

MAKING PERFECT SWEET CUSTARDS

A common problem when making custard is that the mixture curdles. Follow a few simple rules to ensure this does not happen. Custard may be baked or cooked in a bowl over hot water to make a pouring custard. When cold and chilled a pouring custard may set, for example on the top of a trifle. The eggs in a custard curdle when the mixture has been overcooked. This may be due to cooking the custard for too long or at too high a temperature.

Pouring custards may be cooked in a double saucepan or in a heatproof bowl over a pan of water. The water should only just simmer; if it boils, the custard may well curdle. Stir the mixture all the time it cooks, until it thickens enough to coat the back of a spoon. A common mistake is to expect the custard to look thicker when it is cooked; remember that it will thicken on cooling and become creamy on chilling (depending on the number of eggs used).

Rich custards are made by using cream instead of milk. Single cream is the most common option; double is used for very rich desserts.

When the custard is cooked it should be removed from over the water and allowed to cool. To prevent the formation of a skin, the custard may be stirred as it cools or the surface may be covered with dampened greaseproof paper or microwave cling film. Alternatively, a little caster sugar may be sprinkled all over the surface to prevent a skin from forming.

BAKING SWEET OR SAVOURY CUSTARDS IN A BAIN MARIE

A bain marie is simply a container of water in which to stand the dish of custard (or any other delicate mixture that requires careful cooking). A roasting tin or any fairly deep ovenproof dish that is large enough to hold the container of custard will do. Very hot, not boiling, water should be poured into the outer container. Ideally, the water in the outer container should come halfway up the outside of the dish of custard.

The bain marie protects the custard from overcooking; the water barrier moderates the heat which reaches the outside of the dish. If the recipe requires very lengthy cooking the water must be topped up.

SWEET CORNFLOUR CUSTARD

An easy alternative to custard thickened solely with egg is one with a little cornflour added. When cornflour and egg yolks are combined the custard may be brought to the boil in a saucepan. The resulting custard is significantly thicker and, with sufficient cornflour, it sets to a more creamy, or even firm, consistency when chilled, for example when used as a topping for trifle. This type of mixture (using plain flour in place of cornflour) and method is used for making crème pâtissière, a thick custard enriched with cream which is used as a filling for flans or gâteaux. It also provides a quick alternative for topping trifles or as a basis for a variety of desserts.

PRESSURE COOKING

Surprisingly, set custards cook very well in the pressure cooker and far quicker than when baked. General guidance on using pressure cookers is given in the section on equipment. See also Baked Custard (page 465).

MICROWAVE COOKING

Set and pouring custards both cook successfully in the microwave. Individual set custards cook more evenly than large ones. Stand the custards in a microwave-proof bain marie.

To prevent it curdling, a pouring custard must be stirred or whisked frequently during cooking. With care, custards cooked in the microwave are less likely to curdle than conventionally-cooked custards that are not watched constantly when cooking.

FREEZING

Custards and desserts thickened or lightened with eggs do not freeze successfully as they tend to separate and curdle on thawing.

FISH CUSTARD

fat for greasing
450g/1lb sole or plaice fillets, skinned
500ml/17fl oz milk
4 eggs
grated rind of ½ lemon
30ml/2tbsp chopped parsley
salt and pepper

Grease an ovenproof dish. Set the oven at 150°C/300°F/gas 2. Arrange the fish fillets on the base of the dish.

Warm the milk in a saucepan, but do not allow it to approach boiling point. Beat the eggs, lemon rind, parsley, salt and pepper in a large bowl. Stir in the milk. Strain the custard into the dish.

Stand the dish in a roasting tin. Pour in enough boiling water to come halfway up the sides of the dish. Bake for 1½ hours or until the custard is set in the centre.

SERVES FOUR

VARIATION

Smoked Cod Custard Bring the milk to simmering point in a saucepan, add 450g/1lb smoked cod and poach for 10 minutes. Drain, reserving the milk in a measuring jug. Remove any skin or bones from the fish and flake the flesh into the prepared dish. Make up the milk to 500ml/17fl oz if necessary. Use the warm (not hot) fish-flavoured milk to make the custard. Proceed as above.

CHEESE AND ASPARAGUS CUSTARD

It is desirable to cook asparagus upright, so that the stalks are poached while the delicate tips are gently steamed. If the asparagus is too tall for the saucepan, cover it with a dome of foil, crumpled around the pan's rim, instead of using the lid. You can buy special asparagus pans from specialist kitchen shops.

butter for greasing
1 bundle of small or sprue asparagus, trimmed or 225 g/8 oz canned or frozen asparagus
100 g/4 oz cheese, grated
4 eggs
salt and pepper
500 ml/17 fl oz milk

Butter a 750 ml/1¼ pint ovenproof dish. Tie fresh asparagus in small bundles. Add enough salted water to a deep saucepan to come three-quarters of the way up the stalks. Bring to the boil. Wedge the bundles of asparagus upright in the pan, or stand them in a heatproof container in the pan. Cover and cook gently for about 10 minutes, depending on the thickness of the stalks. Drain carefully. Drain canned asparagus or cook frozen asparagus according to the directions on the packet.

Set the oven at 150°C/300°F/gas 2. Cut the asparagus into short lengths and put into the prepared dish, with the tips arranged on the top. Sprinkle the grated cheese over the asparagus. Beat the eggs, salt and pepper together lightly and stir in the milk. Strain the custard into the dish.

Stand the dish in a shallow tin containing enough warm water to come halfway up the sides of the dish. Bake for 1½ hours, until the custard is set in the centre.

SERVES FOUR

STEAMED CUSTARD

butter for greasing
500 ml/17 fl oz milk
4 eggs or 3 whole eggs and 2 yolks
25 g/1 oz caster sugar
vanilla essence

Grease a baking dish. Prepare a steamer or half fill a large saucepan with water and bring to the boil.

In a second pan, warm the milk to just below boiling point. Put the eggs and sugar into a bowl, mix well, then stir in the scalded milk and vanilla essence to taste. Strain the custard mixture into the prepared baking dish, cover with greased greaseproof paper or foil and secure with string.

Put the dish in the perforated part of the steamer, or stand it on an old saucer or plate in the pan of boiling water. The water should come halfway up the sides of the dish. Cover the pan tightly and steam the custard very gently for about 40 minutes or until just firm in the centre.

Serve hot or cold with jam sauce.

SERVES FOUR

 MICROWAVE TIP

Cook individual set custards in the microwave. Pour the custard into six ramekin dishes. Stand these in a large dish and pour boiling water around them. Cook on High for 5-7 minutes, rearranging the dishes twice until the custard is set.

BAKED CUSTARD

Egg dishes should be cooked by gentle heat. If the custard is allowed to boil, the protein will no longer be able to hold moisture in suspension and the resultant pudding will be watery. It is therefore a wise precaution to use a bain marie or water bath.

fat for greasing
500 ml/17 fl oz milk
3 eggs
25 g/1 oz caster sugar
grated nutmeg

Grease a baking dish. Set the oven at 140-150°C/275-300°F/gas 1-2.

In a saucepan, bring the milk to just below boiling point. Put the eggs and sugar into a bowl, mix well, then stir in the scalded milk. Strain the custard mixture into the prepared dish. Sprinkle the nutmeg on top.

Stand the dish in a roasting tin and add enough hot water to come halfway up the sides of the dish. Bake for 1 hour or until the custard is set in the centre.

SERVES FOUR

 PRESSURE COOKER TIP

Make the custard as described above, using a dish that will fit inside your pressure cooker. Pour 300-600 ml/½-1 pint water into the cooker. Stand the dish on a trivet in the cooker, close the lid and bring to 15 lb pressure. Cook for 5 minutes. Reduce the pressure slowly.

BANANA CUSTARD

500 ml/17 fl oz milk
3 eggs plus 2 yolks
25 g/1 oz caster sugar
few drops of vanilla essence
3 bananas (about 400 g/14 oz)

DECORATION
30 ml/2 tbsp crushed butterscotch or grated
chocolate or toasted flaked almonds

In a saucepan, bring the milk to just below boiling point. Put the eggs and sugar into a bowl, mix well, then stir in the scalded milk and vanilla essence. Strain the custard mixture into a heavy-bottomed saucepan or a heatproof bowl placed over a saucepan of simmering water. Alternatively, use a double saucepan, but make sure the water does not touch the upper pan.

Cook the custard over very gentle heat for 15-25 minutes, stirring all the time with a wooden spoon, until the custard thickens to the consistency of single cream. Stir well around the sides as well as the base of the pan or bowl to prevent the formation of lumps, especially if using a double saucepan. Do not let the custard boil or it may curdle.

As soon as the custard thickens, pour it into a jug to stop further cooking. Peel and slice the bananas and stir them into the custard. Stand the jug in a bowl of hot water for 5 minutes to allow the flavours to blend. Spoon into a serving dish or individual dishes and decorate with butterscotch, grated chocolate or flaked almonds.

If the custard is to be served cold, pour it into a bowl and cover the surface with a piece of dampened greaseproof paper to prevent discoloration and a skin forming. When cold, pour into a serving dish and decorate as desired.

SERVES FOUR

PINEAPPLE CUSTARD

1 (376 g/13 oz) can crushed pineapple
25 g/1 oz cornflour
400 ml/14 fl oz milk
2 eggs, separated
25 g/1 oz caster sugar

Drain the pineapple, pouring the juice into a jug and spreading the fruit out in an ovenproof dish.

In a bowl, blend the cornflour to a smooth paste with a little of the milk. Heat the rest of the milk in a saucepan until it is just below boiling point, then pour on to the blended cornflour. Stir in well.

Return the mixture to the clean saucepan and bring to the boil, stirring all the time. Boil gently for 1–2 minutes. Remove from the heat and stir in the reserved pineapple juice.

Add the egg yolks to the cornflour sauce. Stir well. Return to the heat and cook very gently, without boiling, stirring all the time, until the mixture thickens. Remove from the heat and leave to cool; stir from time to time to prevent the formation of a skin. Set the oven at 140°C/275°F/gas 1.

Pour the cooled custard over the crushed pineapple. In a clean, grease-free bowl, whisk the egg whites until stiff, then whisk in most of the sugar. Spread the meringue mixture over the custard, making sure that it is completely covered. Sprinkle with the remaining sugar. Bake for 30 minutes until the meringue is crisp and browned.

SERVES FOUR

ZABAGLIONE

4 egg yolks
40 g/1½ oz caster sugar
60 ml/4 tbsp Marsala or Madeira

Put the egg yolks into a deep heatproof bowl and whisk lightly. Add the sugar and wine, and place the bowl over a saucepan of hot water. Whisk for about 10 minutes or until the mixture is very thick and creamy (see Mrs Beeton's Tip).

Pour the custard into individual glasses and serve while still warm, with sponge fingers.

SERVES FOUR

VARIATION

Zabaglione Cream Dissolve 50 g/2 oz caster sugar in 60 ml/4 tbsp water in a saucepan and boil for 1–2 minutes until syrupy. Whisk with the egg yolks until pale and thick. Add 30 ml/2 tbsp Marsala or Madeira and 30 ml/2 tbsp single cream while whisking. The finely grated rind of ½ lemon can be added, if liked. Spoon into individual glasses. Chill before serving.

 MRS BEETON'S TIP

When the whisk is lifted out of the bowl, the trail of the whisk should lie on top of the mixture for 2–3 seconds.

Salad Dressings, Marinades, Stuffings and Savoury Sauces

Clever use of dressings, marinades, sauces, stuffings and butters can transform plain ingredients into special meals, so it is worth having chilled or frozen preparations in stock always. Even items that are partially prepared, such as flavoured vinegars and oils or stuffing bases, reduce preparation and serve as an inspiration when time is at a premium.

SALAD DRESSINGS

When making dressings for long storage, remember that the flavour of garlic, spices or other strong ingredients will become very pronounced on standing, so they are often best added just before use. However, oils and vinegars flavoured with herbs and spices are a good standby. Recipes for horseradish and fruit vinegars are given on pages 925 and 926; here are some alternative suggestions.

Herbs Use sprigs of fresh herbs to flavour oil or vinegar. Trim off excess stalk or use the leaves only if they are large (such as bay or sage). Wash thoroughly and dry on absorbent kitchen paper. Place several herb sprigs or leaves in a clean dry bottle, bending and crushing bay or sage to bring out the flavour. Cover with a light oil, such as grapeseed or sunflower, or use vinegar. Wine or cider vinegar is ideal for tarragon and other herbs. A strong vinegar, such as balsamic, may be used with bay, thyme, marjoram, rosemary and other herbs which have a pronounced flavour.

Cover the bottles tightly and leave in a cool, dark place for at least 2 weeks to allow the flavour to infuse.

Spices Chilli and garlic are popular flavourings for oil and vinegar. Dried red chillies should be added sparingly to bottles of oil or vinegar and allowed to infuse for a couple of weeks. One or two chillies to 600 ml/1 pint gives plenty of flavour but this can be increased for very hot results. This is a particularly useful way of flavouring oil for stir frying or for use in spicy dishes. Opt for a versatile oil, such as sunflower, which may be used in cooking as well as dressings.

Whole peeled garlic cloves may be added to vinegar for flavouring salad dressings at a later stage. Garlic-flavoured oil is useful for cooking.

A spiced vinegar recipe for pickling is given on page 925 but individual spices may be added to bottles of oil or vinegar, if liked. Try adding a cinnamon stick, a few cloves, crushed coriander seeds or crushed allspice berries.

USING FLAVOURED OILS AND VINEGARS

- Toss a little flavoured oil or vinegar into a salad before dressing with soured cream or mayonnaise.
- Use to make salad dressings, either on their own or with unflavoured oil. A little flavoured oil may be used to make mayonnaise but should be blended with plain oil or the result may be too strongly flavoured.
- Trickle garlic or chilli oil over slices of French bread, bake until golden, then serve as a snack or with soup.
- Flavour cider vinegar strongly with herbs; use sparingly in sauces, adding it to taste just before serving. For example, make a sweetened apple sauce to serve with pork, then give it a herby sweet-sour tang by adding rosemary or sage vinegar.
- Mint vinegar may be used to flavour sweetened fruit drinks or dessert sauces.

MAYONNAISE

Buy eggs from a reputable supplier and make sure they are perfectly fresh. Immediately before using wash the eggs in cold water and dry them on absorbent kitchen paper.

2 egg yolks
salt and pepper
5 ml/1 tsp caster sugar
5 ml/1 tsp Dijon mustard
about 30 ml/2 tbsp lemon juice
250 ml/8 fl oz oil (olive oil or a mixture of
    olive and grapeseed or sunflower oil)

Place the egg yolks in a medium or large bowl. Add salt and pepper, the sugar, mustard and 15 ml/1 tbsp of the lemon juice. Whisk thoroughly until the sugar has dissolved. An electric whisk is best; or use a wire whisk and work the mixture vigorously.

Whisking all the time, add the oil drop by drop so that it forms an emulsion with the egg yolks. As the oil is incorporated, and the mixture begins to turn pale, it may be added in a slow trickle. If the oil is added too quickly before it begins to combine with the eggs, the sauce will curdle.

The mayonnaise may be made in a blender or food processor. The egg mixture should be processed first, with 10 ml/2 tsp of the oil added right at the beginning. With the machine running, add the rest of the oil drop by drop at first, then in a trickle as above.

When all the oil has been incorporated the mayonnaise should be thick and pale. Taste the mixture, then stir in more lemon juice, salt and pepper, if necessary. Keep mayonnaise in a covered container in the refrigerator for up to 5 days.

MAKES ABOUT 300 ML/½ PINT

VARIATIONS

Aïoli   Add 2 fresh large crushed garlic cloves to the yolks with the seasonings.

Rouille   Add 2 fresh large crushed garlic cloves to the yolks. Omit the mustard. Add 15 ml/1 tbsp paprika and 1.25 ml/¼ tsp cayenne pepper to the yolk mixture before incorporating the oil.

 MRS BEETON'S TIP

All is not lost if the mixture curdles. Stop adding the oil immediately the sauce shows any sign of curdling. Take a clean bowl and place a fresh egg yolk in it. Whisk the yolk well with 5 ml/1 tsp of the curdled mixture. Whisking vigorously, add the remaining curdled mixture drop by drop. Make sure each drop of curdled mixture is incorporated before adding more.

VINAIGRETTE DRESSING

90 ml/6 tbsp light olive oil
salt and pepper
pinch of mustard powder
pinch of caster sugar
30 ml/2 tbsp white wine vinegar
10 ml/2 tsp finely chopped gherkin
5 ml/1 tsp finely chopped onion or chives
5 ml/1 tsp finely chopped parsley
5 ml/1 tsp finely chopped capers
5 ml/1 tsp finely chopped fresh tarragon or
   chervil

Mix all the ingredients in a screw-topped jar. Close the jar tightly and shake vigorously until well blended; then allow to stand for at least 1 hour. Shake again before using.

MAKES ABOUT 125 ML/4 FL OZ

CLARET DRESSING

1 garlic clove, crushed
125 ml/4 fl oz claret
5 ml/1 tsp lemon juice
5 ml/1 tsp finely chopped shallot or onion
salt and pepper

Mix all the ingredients in a screw-topped jar. Close the jar tightly and shake vigorously until well blended; then allow to stand overnight. Shake, strain and pour over a salad tossed in a little oil.

MAKES ABOUT 150 ML/¼ PINT

TARTARE SAUCE

2 hard-boiled egg yolks
2 egg yolks
salt and pepper
15 ml/1 tbsp white wine vinegar
300 ml/½ pint oil (olive oil or a mixture of
   olive with grapeseed or sunflower oil)
15 ml/1 tbsp chopped capers
15 ml/1 tbsp chopped gherkin
30 ml/2 tbsp chopped parsley
15 ml/1 tbsp snipped chives

Sieve the hard-boiled egg yolks into a bowl. Add one of the raw yolks and mix thoroughly, then work in the second raw yolk. Stir in salt and pepper to taste and mix to a paste with the vinegar.

Beating vigorously, gradually add the oil, drop by drop, as for making mayonnaise (left). When all the oil has been incorporated and the mixture is thick, stir in the capers, gherkin and herbs.

MAKES ABOUT 300 ML/½ PINT

CHIFFONADE DRESSING

2 hard-boiled eggs, finely chopped
¼ small red pepper, seeded and finely
   chopped
30 ml/2 tbsp finely chopped parsley
5 ml/1 tsp very finely chopped shallot
125 ml/4 fl oz French dressing (page 470)

Mix all the ingredients in a small bowl. Whisk with a balloon whisk to blend thoroughly.

MAKES 150 ML/¼ PINT

FRENCH DRESSING

salt and pepper
pinch of mustard powder
pinch of caster sugar
30 ml/2 tbsp wine vinegar
90 ml/6 tbsp olive oil or a mixture of olive
   and sunflower oil

Mix the salt and pepper, mustard and sugar in a small bowl. Add the vinegar and whisk until the sugar has dissolved. Whisk in the oil and check the dressing for salt and pepper before using.

MAKES ABOUT 125 ML/4 FL OZ

VARIATIONS

Almost every cook has his or her favourite way of preparing French dressing. Garlic, whole or crushed, is a favourite addition, while others swear that a few drops of soy sauce sharpen the flavour. Lemon juice frequently replaces all or part of the vinegar. The recipe above may be doubled or trebled, if liked, but the proportions should always remain the same.

 MRS BEETON'S TIP

The ingredients for French Dressing may be mixed in a screw-topped jar and shaken but the result is not as good as when the sugar is dissolved in the vinegar before the oil is mixed in.

MARINADES

Marinades are used to add moisture to dry meats before roasting. They also impart flavour and can help to tenderize the joint.

RED WINE MARINADE

1 onion, chopped
1 carrot, chopped
1 celery stick, chopped
6-10 parsley sprigs, chopped
1 garlic clove, crushed
5 ml/1 tsp dried thyme
1 bay leaf
6-8 peppercorns
1-2 cloves
5 ml/1 tsp ground coriander
2.5 ml/½ tsp juniper berries, lightly crushed
salt and pepper
250 ml/8 fl oz Rich Strong Stock (page 45)
150 ml/¼ pint red wine
150 ml/¼ pint oil

Mix all the ingredients in a large bowl. Stir in 150 ml/¼ pint water. Use as required.

MAKES ABOUT 600 ML/1 PINT

COOKED RED WINE MARINADE

1 carrot, thinly sliced
1 onion, thinly sliced
3 bay leaves
12 black peppercorns
15 ml/1 tbsp salt
250 ml/8 fl oz red wine
juice of 1 lemon
5 ml/1 tsp sugar
6 juniper berries

Put the carrot and onion in a saucepan. Add 1.1 litres/2 pints water, with the bay leaves, peppercorns and salt. Bring to the boil, then lower the heat and simmer until the vegetables are tender.

Add the remaining ingredients. Put the meat or game in a deep dish just large enough to hold it snugly. Pour over the hot marinade, cover and marinate for as long as required, see Mrs Beeton's Tip.

MAKES ABOUT 1.25 LITRES/2¼ PINTS

 MRS BEETON'S TIP

For a large piece of meat left to marinate for 36 hours or longer, strain off the marinade on the second day. Boil it again, leave to cool completely, then pour back over the meat. This can be done a second time over a 4–5 day period, if required. The marinade should not be reboiled more than twice.

STUFFINGS

The simplest stuffing combination to store or freeze consists of breadcrumbs with parsley and thyme. Unless both herbs and crumbs are thoroughly dried, they should be frozen. Add milk or egg to bind, if necessary, when thawed. When freezing any stuffing always include a detailed label. Although you may be convinced you will remember how the aromatic lemon and raisin stuffing was made, three months later you will probably have difficulty in deciding whether or not it is appropriate for fish.

The best types of stuffings to freeze in large quantities are the ones that go well with everything. Consider these combinations:

• Breadcrumbs or cooked rice with lemon rind, chopped parsley, raisins and lightly cooked diced onion. Good with cod steaks, chicken, duck, pork chops or lamb.
• Wholemeal breadcrumbs with marjoram, peeled and chopped tomato, and par-cooked finely chopped onion. Open freeze the mixture to prevent it from forming a lump, then break it up and pack. Use with pork, lamb or in beef olives (rolled slices of meat). The stuffing may also be mixed with minced beef, lamb or pork to make meat loaf, burgers or meatballs.
• Lightly cooked finely chopped onion and garlic mixed with grated fresh root ginger and a little chopped green chilli makes a good flavouring. Mix with breadcrumbs, a sprinkling of ground coriander and a little chopped fresh coriander to create an excellent spicy stuffing for chicken breasts or lamb breast. Mixed with minced lamb, it makes delicious meatballs.
• Breadcrumbs or cooked lentils, grated orange rind, thyme or rosemary, parsley and cooked finely chopped onion is another winning mixture. Open freeze, then pack in

chunks. Use with pork, lamb, duck or vegetables. Add some finely chopped nuts and use to make vegetarian burgers.

- Mixed with grated cheese, breadcrumb stuffing mixes make excellent gratin toppings or toppings for savoury crumble.
- Use breadcrumb mixes to coat chicken breasts, then bake until cooked and golden.

HERB STUFFING

Keeping a stock of stuffing in the freezer means that chicken, fish fillets and boned joints can be prepared swiftly for the oven. Use double the quantity below to stuff the neck end of a 5-6 kg/11-13 lb turkey.

50 g/2 oz butter or margarine
100 g/4 oz soft white or Granary
   breadcrumbs
pinch of grated nutmeg
15 ml/1 tbsp chopped parsley
5 ml/1 tsp chopped fresh mixed herbs
grated rind of ½ lemon
salt and pepper
1 egg, beaten

Melt the butter or margarine in a small saucepan and stir in the breadcrumbs, nutmeg, herbs and lemon rind. Add salt and pepper to taste. Stir in enough of the beaten egg to bind the mixture.

SUFFICIENT FOR 1 (1.5-2 KG/3¼-4½ LB)
CHICKEN, A BONED JOINT OF VEAL OR
8 (75 G/3 OZ) FISH FILLETS

 MRS BEETON'S TIP

A bird, joint of meat or fish should always be stuffed just before being cooked. If preferred, the stuffing may be shaped into 12 or 16 small balls and baked in a preheated 180°C/350°F/gas 4 oven for 15-20 minutes.

CHESTNUT AND ONION STUFFING

Use double the quantity listed below when stuffing the neck end of a 5-6 kg/11-13 lb turkey.

1 large onion, thickly sliced
125 ml/4 fl oz chicken stock or water
450 g/1 lb chestnuts, prepared and cooked
   (see Mrs Beeton's Tip) or 300 g/11 oz
   canned chestnuts
salt and pepper
1 egg, beaten

Combine the onion and stock or water in a small saucepan. Bring the liquid to the boil, lower the heat and simmer for about 10 minutes until the onion is tender; drain and chop finely.

Meanwhile mince the chestnuts or chop them finely. Combine the chestnuts and onion in a bowl, stir in salt and pepper to taste and add enough of the egg to bind the stuffing.

SUFFICIENT FOR 1 (2.5 KG/5½ LB DUCK

 MRS BEETON'S TIP

To prepare chestnuts, make a slit in the rounded side of each nut, then bake them in a preheated 180°C/350°F/gas 4 oven for 30 minutes or cook them in boiling water for 20 minutes. Remove the shells and skins while still hot. Put the shelled nuts in a saucepan with just enough stock to cover. Bring the liquid to the boil, lower the heat and simmer for 45-60 minutes or until the nuts are tender.

APPLE AND CELERY STUFFING

3 rindless streaky bacon rashers, chopped
1 onion, finely chopped
1 celery stick, finely sliced
3 large cooking apples
75 g/3 oz fresh white breadcrumbs
15 ml/1 tbsp grated lemon rind
salt and pepper

Heat the bacon gently in a frying pan until the fat runs, then increase the heat and fry until browned, stirring frequently. Using a slotted spoon, transfer the bacon to a bowl. Add the onion and celery to the fat remaining in the frying pan and fry over moderate heat for 5 minutes. Remove with a slotted spoon, add to the bacon and mix lightly.

Peel, core and dice the apples. Add them to the pan and fry until soft and lightly browned. Add to the bacon mixture with the breadcrumbs and lemon rind. Mix well, adding salt and pepper to taste.

SUFFICIENT FOR 1 (4–5 KG/9–11 LB) GOOSE,
2 (2.5 KG/5½ LB) DUCKS OR 1 BONED PORK
JOINT

 MRS BEETON'S TIP

Many delicatessens and deli counters in supermarkets sell packets of bacon bits – the trimmings left after slicing. These are ideal for a recipe such as this, and may also be used in quiches, on pizzas and to flavour soups and stews.

WALNUT STUFFING

15 g/½ oz butter
1 small onion, finely chopped
12 whole walnuts or 24 halves, chopped
50 g/2 oz sausagemeat
50 g/2 oz fresh white breadcrumbs
2.5 ml/½ tsp dried mixed herbs
1 large cooking apple
salt and pepper
1 egg, lightly beaten
milk (see method)

Melt the butter in a saucepan, add the onion and cook over very gentle heat for about 10 minutes until soft and pale golden.

Combine the walnuts, sausagemeat, breadcrumbs and herbs in a bowl. Peel, core and chop the apple. Add it to the bowl, with salt and pepper to taste. Stir in the onion with the melted butter and mix well. Bind with the egg, adding a little milk if necessary.

SUFFICIENT FOR 1 (2.5 KG/5½ LB) DUCK;
DOUBLE THE QUANTITY FOR 1
(4–5 KG/8–11 LB) GOOSE

LEMON AND HERB STUFFING

50 g/2 oz butter
100 g/4 oz fresh white breadcrumbs
30 ml/2 tbsp chopped parsley
2.5 ml/½ tsp chopped fresh thyme
grated rind of ½ lemon
salt and pepper

Melt the butter in a small saucepan. Add the breadcrumbs, herbs and lemon rind. Add salt and pepper to taste, then use as required.

SUFFICIENT FOR 8 (75 G/3 OZ) THIN FISH
FILLETS

SAGE AND ONION STUFFING

2 onions, thickly sliced
4 young fresh sage sprigs or 10 ml/2 tsp
   dried sage
100 g/4 oz fresh white breadcrumbs
50 g/2 oz butter or margarine, melted
salt and pepper
1 egg, lightly beaten (optional)

Put the onions in a small saucepan with water to cover. Bring to the boil, cook for 2–3 minutes, then remove the onions from the pan with a slotted spoon. Chop them finely. Chop the sage leaves finely, discarding any stalk.

Combine the breadcrumbs, onions and sage in a bowl. Add the melted butter or margarine, with salt and pepper to taste. Mix well. If the stuffing is to be shaped into balls, bind it with the beaten egg.

SUFFICIENT FOR 1 (2.5 KG/5½ LB) DUCK;
DOUBLE THE QUANTITY FOR 1
(4–5 KG/9–11 LB) GOOSE

TOMATO STUFFING

2 large ripe tomatoes, peeled, seeded and
   chopped
1 red pepper, seeded and chopped or 2
   canned pimientos, chopped
1 garlic clove, crushed
50-75 g/2-3 oz fresh wholemeal breadcrumbs
salt and pepper

Mix the tomatoes, pepper or pimientos and garlic in a bowl. Add enough breadcrumbs to absorb the juice from the tomatoes. Add salt and pepper to taste, then use as required.

SUFFICIENT FOR 1.5 KG/3¼ LB WHITE FISH

CHESTNUT STUFFING

800 g/1¾ lb chestnuts, shelled (see Mrs
   Beeton's Tip, page 472).
150–250 ml/5–8 fl oz chicken or vegetable
   stock
50 g/2 oz butter, softened
pinch of ground cinnamon
2.5 ml/½ tsp sugar
salt and pepper

Put the shelled chestnuts in a saucepan and add the stock. Bring to the boil, lower the heat, cover and simmer until the chestnuts are tender. Drain, reserving the stock.

Rub the chestnuts through a fine wire sieve into a bowl. Add the butter, cinnamon and sugar, with salt and pepper to taste. Stir in enough of the reserved stock to bind.

SUFFICIENT FOR THE NECK END OF 1
(5–6 KG/9–11 LB) TURKEY; USE HALF THE
QUANTITY FOR 1 (1.5 KG/3¼ LB) CHICKEN

 MRS BEETON'S TIP

Canned chestnuts may be used for the stuffing. You will require about 450 g/1 lb.

MRS BEETON'S FORCEMEAT

100 g/4 oz gammon or rindless bacon, finely
   chopped
50 g/2 oz shredded beef suet
grated rind of 1 lemon
5 ml/1 tsp chopped parsley
5 ml/1 tsp chopped mixed herbs
salt and cayenne pepper
pinch of ground mace
150 g/5 oz fresh white breadcrumbs
2 eggs, lightly beaten

Combine the gammon or bacon, suet, lemon
rind and herbs in a bowl. Add salt, cayenne and
mace to taste, mix well with a fork, then stir in
the breadcrumbs. Gradually add enough beaten
egg to bind.

MAKES ABOUT 350G/12OZ

VARIATION

Mrs Beeton's Forcemeat Balls Roll the
mixture into 6-8 small balls. Either cook the
forcemeat balls around a roast joint or bird, or
fry them in a little oil until browned and cooked
through.

SAUSAGEMEAT STUFFING

1 chicken or turkey liver, trimmed
   (optional)
450 g/1 lb pork sausagement
50 g/2 oz fresh white breadcrumbs
15 ml/1 tbsp chopped parsley
5 ml/1 tsp dried mixed herbs
1 egg, lightly beaten
salt and pepper

If using the liver, chop it finely and put it in a
mixing bowl. Add the sausagemeat and breadcrumbs, with the herbs. Stir in enough of the
beaten egg to bind the mixture. Add plenty of
salt and pepper.

SUFFICIENT FOR 1 (1.5 KG/3¼ LB) CHICKEN;
TREBLE THE QUANTITY FOR 1
(5-6 KG/9-11 LB) TURKEY

WILD RICE STUFFING

*This stuffing is particularly recommended for game
birds.*

350 ml/12 fl oz stock
150 g/5 oz wild rice
50 g/2 oz butter
2 shallots, finely chopped
½ small green pepper, finely chopped
1 small celery stick, finely sliced
100 g/4 oz mushrooms, chopped
30 ml/2 tbsp tomato purée

Bring the stock to the boil in a saucepan and
add the wild rice. Lower the heat, cover and
cook gently for 40 minutes until the rice is
almost tender and the majority of the stock is
absorbed. Cover and set aside.

Melt the butter in a saucepan, add the shallots,
green pepper, celery and mushrooms and fry
over gentle heat for 3 minutes. Remove from
the heat, add to the wild rice with the tomato
purée and mix well.

SUFFICIENT FOR 2 PHEASANTS OR 1 LARGE
GUINEAFOWL

RICE AND OLIVE STUFFING

50 g/2 oz butter
1 onion, finely chopped
2 celery sticks, finely chopped
50 g/2 oz stuffed green olives, chopped
100 g/4 oz cooked long-grain rice
1.25 ml/¼ tsp dried sage
1.25 ml/¼ tsp dried thyme
salt and pepper

Melt the butter in a small saucepan. Add the onion and celery and fry gently for 3–4 minutes until soft.

Stir in the olives, rice and herbs. Cook gently for 3 minutes, then add salt and pepper to taste. Use as required.

SUFFICIENT FOR 1 (1.4 KG/3 LB) WHOLE FISH

 MRS BEETON'S TIP

As a guide, 50 g/2 oz uncooked rice will yield 100–150 g/4–5 oz cooked rice.

EGG STUFFING

15 g/½ oz butter, softened
1 hard-boiled egg, finely chopped
75 ml/5 tbsp fresh white breadcrumbs
2.5 ml/½ tsp chopped parsley
salt and pepper
milk

Cream the butter in a small bowl. Add the egg, breadcrumbs and parsley, with salt and pepper to taste. Mix well, adding just enough milk to bind the mixture. Use as required.

SUFFICIENT FOR 2 (75 G/3 OZ) THIN WHITE FISH FILLETS

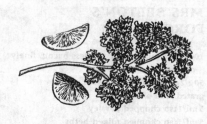

APRICOT STUFFING

This stuffing is particularly good with pork, but may also be used with lamb, any poultry or game birds. Use double the quantity listed below when stuffing 1 (4–5 kg/9–11 lb) goose.

75 g/3 oz dried apricots, soaked overnight in water to cover
75 g/3 oz soft white or Granary breadcrumbs
25 g/1 oz butter, melted
1.25 ml/¼ tsp salt
1.25 ml/¼ tsp freshly ground black pepper
pinch each of dried thyme, ground mace and grated nutmeg
1 celery stick, finely chopped

Drain the apricots, reserving the liquid, and chop finely. Put in a bowl with the breadcrumbs, butter, salt, pepper, thyme and spices. Stir in the celery and moisten the mixture with a little of the reserved apricot liquid.

SUFFICIENT FOR A BONED JOINT OF PORK OR 1 (2.5 KG/5½ LB) DUCK

 MRS BEETON'S TIP

Ready-to-eat dried apricots may be used for this stuffing, in which case the mixture should be moistened with a little vegetable or chicken stock.

PRUNE AND APPLE STUFFING

Use double the quantity listed below when stuffing a 4-5 kg/9-11 lb goose.

100 g/4 oz prunes, soaked overnight and drained
1 large cooking apple
100 g/4 oz boiled long-grain white or brown rice
50 g/2 oz flaked almonds
50 g/2 oz butter, softened
salt and pepper
grated rind and juice of ½ lemon
1 egg, beaten

Stone and chop the prunes. Peel, core and roughly chop the apple. Combine the chopped fruits in a bowl with the rice, almonds and butter. Add salt and pepper to taste and stir in the lemon rind and juice. Add enough of the beaten egg to moisten the stuffing.

SUFFICIENT FOR A BONED JOINT OF PORK OR 1 (2.5 KG/5½ LB) DUCK

 MRS BEETON'S TIP

Canned prunes may be used for this stuffing. Choose the variety canned in natural juice and substitute a little of the juice for half the lemon juice in the recipe above.

MUSHROOM STUFFING

Although this stuffing is recommended for fish, it is also very good with all poultry and game birds.

1 rindless streaky bacon rasher, chopped
100 g/4 oz button mushrooms with stalks, chopped
100 g/4 oz fresh white breadcrumbs
knob of butter or margarine
pinch of grated nutmeg
salt and pepper
1 egg

Put the bacon in a heavy-bottomed saucepan over moderate heat for about 2 minutes or until the fat runs.

Add the mushrooms and fry very gently for 3-5 minutes, stirring frequently. When the mushrooms soften, remove the pan from the heat and stir in the breadcrumbs, butter or margarine and nutmeg. Add salt and pepper to taste.

Beat the egg in a cup until it is just liquid, then stir enough of the beaten egg into the stuffing to bind it. Use as required.

SUFFICIENT FOR 8 (75 G/3 OZ) THIN FISH FILLETS

 MRS BEETON'S TIP

It is a good idea to keep a stock of breadcrumbs in a sealed polythene bag in the freezer. They thaw swiftly and can be used in a wide variety of sweet and savoury dishes.

OYSTER STUFFING

Once a common food, oysters are central to many traditional English dishes. Rich in protein and full of flavour, they make an excellent stuffing for a whole fish such as grey mullet or could be used as a stuffing for steak.

6 fresh or canned oysters
100 g/4 oz fresh white breadcrumbs
50 g/2 oz shredded suet or melted butter
5 ml/1 tsp chopped mixed fresh herbs
pinch of grated nutmeg
salt and pepper
1 egg

If using fresh oysters, open them over a saucepan (see Mrs Beeton's Tip), then simmer them very gently in their own liquor for 10 minutes. Canned oysters need no cooking.

Drain the oysters, reserving the liquor, and cut into small pieces.

In a bowl, mix the breadcrumbs with the suet or melted butter. Add the oysters, herbs and nutmeg, with salt and pepper to taste.

Beat the egg in a cup until it is just liquid, then stir it into the oyster mixture, adding a little of the reserved oyster liquor, if necessary, to bind.

SUFFICIENT FOR 1 (1.1 KG/2½ LB) WHOLE FISH

 MRS BEETON'S TIP

Use a strong knife or special oyster knife to open the oysters (see page 169), working it between the shells to cut the ligament hinge which keeps the shells together.

FISH FORCEMEAT

25 g/1 oz plain flour
125 ml/4 fl oz Fish Stock (page 48)
25 g/1 oz butter
salt and pepper
1 egg
225 g/8 oz white fish fillet, skinned and
    finely flaked
grated rind and juice of ½ lemon

Sift the flour on to a sheet of greaseproof paper. Bring the stock and the butter to the boil in a small saucepan. Heat gently until the butter melts.

When the butter has melted, bring the liquid rapidly to the boil and add all the flour at once. Immediately remove the pan from the heat and stir the flour into the liquid to make a smooth paste which leaves the sides of the pan clean. Add salt and pepper to taste. Cool slightly.

Beat the egg in a cup until it is just liquid, then add it gradually to the cooled mixture, beating well after each addition.

Beat the raw flaked fish into the mixture with the grated lemon rind. Add lemon juice to taste. Use as required.

SUFFICIENT FOR 12 (75 G/3 OZ) THIN FISH FILLETS, 8 FISH CUTLETS OR 4 (350-450 G/12 OZ-1 LB) WHOLE FISH

 MRS BEETON'S TIP

When grating citrus fruit, work over a sheet of foil, using a clean pastry brush to extricate all the rind from the grater. Tip the rind into the bowl or saucepan, then use the brush to sweep in any lingering shreds.

SAVOURY SAUCES AND BUTTERS

Many fresh sauces keep for 3–5 days if cooled and chilled promptly after cooking. This can be useful if you intend making several dishes over a long weekend for example, when a basic tomato sauce can be adapted to pizza topping, seafood casserole or a meaty goulash. In the long term, frozen tomato sauce may be thawed in the microwave or in a covered pan over the lowest possible heat. Once thawed, the sauce can be heated and used as a side dish or as the basis for a more complicated recipe.

This chapter includes one sauce that should reside in every herb-lover's refrigerator: pesto. Grow a huge tub of basil outdoors in the summer to use as required and at the end of the summer you should still have enough to make a few pots of pesto. Olive oil is the essential preservative, so do not skimp on quantity. Make sure jars are perfectly clean and check the sauce after a couple of days to ensure it has a good layer of oil on the surface. In this state it will keep at the bottom of the refrigerator for several months, although once opened and partially used it should be eaten quickly.

Another sauce of Italian origin, tonnato or tuna sauce, is the ideal emergency recipe. It consists of tuna creamed to a mayonnaise-like consistency and can be used to coat cooked veal, chicken, pasta, eggs or vegetables.

Savoury butters should be stored, well covered, in the refrigerator. They may also be frozen in individual portions, or in rolls, to be sliced and required. Savoury butters are frequently served in pats or slices on grilled fish or steak to replace a pouring sauce. They are also used as spreads on sandwiches, canapés or snacks.

WHITE SAUCE

The recipe that follows is for a thick coating sauce. See Chart (page 480) for variations.

50 g/2 oz butter
50 g/2 oz plain flour
600 ml/1 pint milk, stock or a mixture
salt and pepper

Melt the butter in saucepan. Stir in the flour and cook over low heat for 2–3 minutes, without browning.

With the heat on the lowest setting, gradually add the liquid, stirring constantly. If lumps begin to form, stop pouring in liquid and stir the sauce vigorously, then continue pouring in the liquid when smooth. Increase the heat to moderate and cook the sauce, stirring, until it boils and thickens.

Lower the heat and simmer for 1–2 minutes, beating briskly to give the sauce a gloss. Add salt and pepper to taste.

MAKES 600 ML/1 PINT

VARIATION

Pouring Sauce   Follow the recipe above, but use only 40 g/1½ oz each of butter and flour.

 MRS BEETON'S TIP

White Sauce can be made by the all-in-one method. Simply combine the butter, flour and liquid in a saucepan and whisk over moderate heat until the mixture comes to the boil. Lower the heat and simmer for 3–4 minutes, whisking constantly until the sauce is thick, smooth and glossy. Add salt and pepper to taste.

	Cheese, grated (Cheddar)	Eggs, hard-boiled and chopped	Anchovy essence	Parsley, chopped	Tomato purée	Mush-rooms, sliced and cooked in butter	Mustard, made mild	Capers, chopped
White Sauce	100 g/4 oz	3–4		60 ml/ 4 tbsp		175 g/6 oz	45–60 ml/ 3–4 tbsp	
Béchamel Sauce		3	30 ml/ 2 tbsp		30 ml/ 2 tbsp	100 g/4 oz		45 ml/ 3 tbsp
Hollandaise Sauce					15 ml/ 1 tbsp			15 ml/ 1 tbsp
Mayonnaise			15 ml/ 1 tbsp	30 ml/ 2 tbsp	15 ml/ 1 tbsp		10–15 ml/ 2–3 tsp	15 ml/ 1 tbsp

SIMPLE VARIATIONS ON BASIC SAUCES

Add one of the ingredients shown to the basic recipe (in this chapter), when the sauce is cooked.

HOLLANDAISE SAUCE

This is the classic sauce to serve with poached salmon or other firm fish.

45 ml/3 tbsp white wine vinegar
6 peppercorns
½ bay leaf
1 blade of mace
3 egg yolks
100 g/4 oz butter, softened
salt and pepper

Combine the vinegar, peppercorns, bay leaf and mace in a small saucepan. Boil rapidly until the liquid is reduced to 15 ml/1 tbsp. Strain into a heatproof bowl and leave to cool.

Add the egg yolks and a nut of butter to the vinegar and place over a pan of gently simmering water. Heat the mixture gently, beating constantly until thick. Do not allow it to approach boiling point.

Add the remaining butter, a little at a time, beating well after each addition. When all the butter has been added the sauce should be thick and glossy. If the sauce curdles, whisk in 10 ml/2 tsp cold water. If this fails to bind it, put an egg yolk in a clean bowl and beat in the sauce gradually. Add a little salt and pepper and serve the sauce lukewarm.

MAKES ABOUT 125 ML/4 FL OZ

 MICROWAVE TIP

A quick and easy Hollandaise Sauce can be made in the microwave oven. Combine 30 ml/2 tbsp lemon juice with 15 ml/1 tbsp water in a large bowl. Add a little salt and white pepper and cook on High for 3–6 minutes or until the mixture is reduced by about two-thirds. Meanwhile place 100 g/4 oz butter in a measuring jug. Remove the bowl of lemon juice from the microwave oven, replacing it with the jug of butter. Heat the butter on High for 2½ minutes. Meanwhile add 2 large egg yolks to the lemon juice, whisking constantly. When the butter is hot, add it in the same way. Return the sauce to the microwave oven. Cook on High for 30 seconds, whisk once more and serve.

BECHAMEL SAUCE

Marquis Louis de Béchameil is credited with inventing this French foundation sauce. For a slightly less rich version, use half white stock and half milk.

1 small onion, thickly sliced
1 small carrot, sliced
1 small celery stick, sliced
600 ml/1 pint milk
1 bay leaf
few parsley stalks
1 fresh thyme sprig
1 clove
6 white peppercorns
1 blade of mace
salt
50 g/2 oz butter
50 g/2 oz plain flour
60 ml/4 tbsp single cream (optional)

Combine the onion, carrot, celery and milk in a saucepan. Add the herbs and spices, with salt to taste. Heat to simmering point, cover, turn off the heat and allow to stand for 30 minutes to infuse, then strain.

Melt the butter in a saucepan. Stir in the flour and cook over low heat for 2–3 minutes, without browning. With the heat on the lowest setting, gradually add the flavoured milk, stirring constantly.

Increase the heat to moderate, stirring until the mixture boils and thickens to a coating consistency. Lower the heat when the mixture boils and simmer the sauce for 1–2 minutes, beating briskly to give the sauce a gloss. Stir in the cream, if used, and remove the sauce from the heat at once. Do not allow the sauce to come to the boil again. Add salt if required.

MAKES ABOUT 600 ML/1 PINT

BEARNAISE SAUCE

The classic accompaniment to grilled beef steak, especially tournedos, Béarnaise Sauce is also delicious with vegetables such as broccoli.

60 ml/4 tbsp white wine vinegar
15 ml/1 tbsp chopped shallot
5 black peppercorns, lightly crushed
1 bay leaf
2 fresh tarragon stalks, chopped, or
   1.25 ml/¼ tsp dried tarragon
1.25 ml/¼ tsp dried thyme
2 egg yolks
100 g/4 oz butter, cut into small pieces
salt and pepper

Combine the vinegar, shallot, peppercorns and herbs in a small saucepan. Boil until the liquid is reduced to 15 ml/1 tbsp, then strain into a heatproof bowl. Cool, then stir in the egg yolks.

Place the bowl over a saucepan of simmering water and whisk until the eggs start to thicken. Gradually add the butter, whisking after each addition, until the sauce is thick and creamy. Add salt and pepper to taste.

MAKES ABOUT 175 ML/6 FL OZ

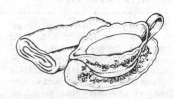

BREAD SAUCE

600 ml/1 pint milk
1 large onion studded with 6 cloves
1 blade of mace
4 peppercorns
1 allspice berry
1 bay leaf
100 g/4 oz fine fresh white breadcrumbs
15 ml/1 tbsp butter
salt and pepper
freshly grated nutmeg
30 ml/2 tbsp single cream (optional)

Put the milk in a small saucepan with the studded onion, mace, peppercorns, allspice and bay leaf. Bring very slowly to boiling point, then remove from the heat, cover the pan and set it aside for 30 minutes.

Strain the flavoured milk into a heatproof bowl, pressing the onion against the sides of the strainer to extract as much of the liquid as possible. Stir in the breadcrumbs and butter, with salt, pepper and nutmeg to taste.

Set the bowl over simmering water and cook for 20 minutes, stirring occasionally until thick and creamy. Stir in the cream, if using, just before serving.

MAKES ABOUT 250 ML/8 FL OZ

 MICROWAVE TIP

There is no need to infuse the onion in the milk if the sauce is to be made in the microwave. Simply put the clove-studded onion in a deep bowl, cover and cook on High for 2 minutes. Add the spices, bay leaf and milk, cover loosely and cook on High for 6–6½ minutes. Stir in the remaining ingredients, except the cream, and cook for 2 minutes more. Remove the studded onion, whole spices and bay leaf. Whisk the sauce, adding the cream if liked.

FOUNDATION BROWN SAUCE

25 g/1 oz dripping or lard
1 small carrot, sliced
1 onion, sliced
25 g/1 oz plain flour
600 ml/1 pint Rich Strong Stock (page 45)
salt and pepper

Melt the dripping or lard in a saucepan. Add the carrot and onion and fry over gentle heat for 10–15 minutes, until the onion is golden brown.

Stir in the flour, lower the heat and cook very gently, stirring, until the flour is also golden brown. Gradually add the stock, stirring constantly until the sauce boils and thickens. Add salt and pepper to taste. Strain into a heated sauceboat and serve hot.

MAKES ABOUT 300 ML/½ PINT

BLACK BUTTER

Black butter is a bit of a misnomer. The beurre noir so beloved of the French should be a rich golden brown. It is the perfect accompaniment to fried or poached skate.

150 g/5 oz butter
30 ml/2 tbsp chopped parsley
15 ml/1 tbsp chopped capers
10–15 ml/2–3 tsp wine vinegar

Heat the butter in a heavy-bottomed frying pan until deep golden brown but not burnt. Add the parsley and capers. Pour into a heated jug.

Add the vinegar to the frying pan and bring to the boil. Immediately add it to the butter mixture. Stir and use at once.

MAKES ABOUT 200 ML/7 FL OZ

BUTTER SAUCE

This classic sauce, rich in the use of butter, is delicious with plain, lightly poached white fish or some shellfish. For example, serve with fresh cod, rolled plaice fillets or poached scallops. It is a last-minute sauce – make it only when you are ready to serve it.

30 ml/2 tbsp finely chopped onion or shallot
30 ml/2 tbsp white wine vinegar
225 g/8 oz unsalted butter, chilled
salt and white pepper
lemon juice

Place the onion or shallot and vinegar in a saucepan. Add 45 ml/3 tbsp water and bring to the boil. Boil until the liquid is reduced by half.

Meanwhile, cut the butter into chunks. Reduce the heat to the lowest setting so that the liquid is below simmering point. Whisking constantly, add a piece of butter. Continue adding the butter, one piece at a time, whisking to melt each piece before adding the next.

The sauce should be pale, creamy in appearance and slightly thickened – rather like single cream. Take care not to let the mixture become too hot or it will curdle.

Remove the pan from the heat when all the butter has been incorporated. Taste the sauce, then add salt, white pepper and lemon juice to taste. Serve at once with poached fish.

MAKES ABOUT 250 ML/8 FL OZ

FRESH TOMATO SAUCE

Fresh tomato sauce has a multitude of uses in savoury cookery. It is one of the simplest accompaniments for plain cooked pasta, it is included in many baked dishes and it is, of course, excellent with grilled fish, poultry and meat.

30 ml/2 tbsp olive oil
1 onion, finely chopped
1 garlic clove, crushed
1 bay leaf
1 rindless streaky bacon rasher, chopped
800 g/1¾ lb tomatoes, peeled and chopped
60 ml/4 tbsp stock or red wine
salt and pepper
generous pinch of sugar
15 ml/1 tbsp chopped fresh basil or 5 ml/1 tsp
    dried basil

Heat the oil in a saucepan and fry the onion, garlic, bay leaf and bacon over gentle heat for 15 minutes.

Stir in the remaining ingredients except the basil. Heat until bubbling, then cover the pan and simmer gently for 30 minutes or until the tomatoes are reduced to a pulp.

Rub the sauce through a sieve into a clean saucepan or purée in a blender or food processor until smooth, then rub it through a sieve to remove seeds, if required.

Reheat the sauce. Add the basil. Add more salt and pepper if required before serving.

MAKES ABOUT 600 ML/1 PINT

ESPAGNOLE SAUCE

50 g/2 oz butter
50 g/2 oz lean raw ham or bacon, chopped
1 small onion, sliced
1 small carrot, sliced
50 g/2 oz mushrooms, sliced
50 g/2 oz plain flour
600 ml/1 pint Rich Strong Stock (page 45)
1 bouquet garni
6 black peppercorns
1 bay leaf
150 ml/¼ pint canned tomatoes, puréed or
    15 ml/1 tbsp tomato purée
60 ml/4 tbsp sherry (optional)

Melt the butter in a saucepan and fry the ham or bacon for 2–3 minutes. Add the vegetables and fry very gently for 8–10 minutes, until golden brown.

Stir in the flour until smooth. Cook over gentle heat, stirring frequently until the flour is a rich brown colour. Gradually add the stock, stirring constantly until the mixture boils and thickens.

Add the bouquet garni, peppercorns and bay leaf. Half cover the pan, lower the heat and simmer the sauce for 30 minutes. Stir in the tomatoes or tomato purée and simmer for 30 minutes more. Rub through a fine nylon sieve into a clean saucepan and stir in the sherry, if using. Reheat before serving.

MAKES 300–450 ML/½–¾ PINT

VELOUTE SAUCE

50 g/2 oz butter
6 button mushrooms, finely chopped
12 black peppercorns
a few parsley sprigs
50 g/2 oz plain flour
600 ml/1 pint White Stock (page 46) or
    Chicken Stock (page 46)
salt and pepper
lemon juice
60–125 ml/2–4 fl oz single cream

Melt the butter in a saucepan and add the mushrooms, peppercorns and parsley. Fry over gentle heat for 10 minutes, stirring occasionally.

Stir in the flour and cook over gentle heat for 2–3 minutes. Do not allow the flour to colour. Gradually add the stock, stirring until the mixture boils and thickens. Lower the heat and simmer, still stirring, for 3–4 minutes.

Rub the sauce through a sieve into a clean saucepan. Add salt, pepper and lemon juice to taste. Reheat to just below boiling point, remove from the heat and stir in enough cream to give the desired flavour and consistency. Pour into a sauceboat and serve at once.

MAKES ABOUT 600 ML/1 PINT

CUMBERLAND SAUCE

A rich, zesty sauce that may be served hot or cold with plain roast or grilled game.

grated rind and juice of 1 orange
grated rind and juice of 1 lemon
75 ml/5 tbsp port
30 ml/2 tbsp red wine vinegar
100 g/4 oz redcurrant jelly
1.25 ml/¼ tsp prepared mustard
salt and cayenne pepper

Combine the orange and lemon rind in a small saucepan. Add 75 ml/5 tbsp water and heat to simmering point. Simmer gently for 10 minutes. Add the port, vinegar, redcurrant jelly and mustard, stirring until the jelly melts. Stir in the citrus juices and add salt and cayenne to taste. Simmer for 3-4 minutes, pour into a sauceboat and serve.

MAKES ABOUT 250 ML/8 FL OZ

PIQUANT SAUCE

1 small onion or 2 shallots, finely chopped
1 bay leaf
1 blade of mace
30 ml/2 tbsp vinegar
300 ml/½ pint Foundation Brown Sauce
   (page 482)
3 button mushrooms, roughly chopped
15 ml/1 tbsp capers, halved
15 ml/1 tbsp gherkins, finely chopped
10 ml/2 tsp mushroom ketchup
2.5 ml/½ tsp sugar (optional)

Combine the onion or shallots, bay leaf, mace and vinegar in a saucepan. Simmer for 10 minutes.

Heat the brown sauce in a separate pan if necessary. Stir in the onion mixture, with the mushrooms. Simmer for 12-15 minutes, until the mushrooms have softened.

Using a slotted spoon, remove the bay leaf and mace from the sauce. Stir in the capers, gherkins, mushroom ketchup and sugar, if using. Reheat gently, pour into a sauceboat and serve.

MAKES ABOUT 300 ML/½ PINT

CREAMY MUSHROOM SAUCE

For a simple mushroom sauce – a variation on a basic white sauce – see the chart on page 480. This version owes its rich creamy flavour to the addition of full fat soft cheese.

50 g/2 oz butter
175 g/6 oz button mushrooms, sliced
25 g/1 oz plain flour
300 ml/½ pint milk
75 g/3 oz full fat soft cheese, cubed
salt and pepper
5-10 ml/1-2 tsp lemon juice (optional)

Melt 25 g/1 oz of the butter in a small saucepan. Add the mushrooms and fry over very gentle heat for 10 minutes until soft but not browned.

In a second saucepan, melt the remaining butter. Stir in the flour and cook for 1-2 minutes. Gradually add the milk, stirring constantly until the mixture boils and thickens.

Remove the pan from the heat and beat in the cheese, a few cubes at a time. Fold in the mushrooms, with the pan juices, and add salt and pepper to taste. Stir in the lemon juice, if using, and reheat the sauce gently without boiling. Serve in a sauceboat.

MAKES ABOUT 350 ML/12 FL OZ

OYSTER SAUCE

8–10 large oysters
250 ml/8 fl oz Fish Stock (page 48)
25 g/1 oz butter
25 g/1 oz plain flour
salt and pepper
lemon juice

Open the oysters (see page 169) and strain the liquor into a saucepan. Add the fish stock. Set aside 6 oysters; add the rest to the saucepan. Simmer for 10 minutes. Strain the oyster-flavoured fish stock into a jug.

Melt the butter in a clean saucepan. Add the flour and cook for 1 minute, stirring. Gradually add the fish stock, stirring constantly until the sauce boils and thickens.

Cut the reserved oysters into 3–4 pieces. Add to the hot sauce and simmer for 2–3 minutes. Add salt, pepper and lemon juice to taste. Serve at once in a sauceboat.

MAKES ABOUT 300 ML/½ PINT

 MRS BEETON'S TIP

Canned oysters, provided they are not smoked, can be used for this sauce. Add the liquid from 1 (225 g/8 oz) can to the fish stock, simmering the mixture until it is reduced to 300 ml/½ pint. Strain and use to make the sauce. Slice the oysters and add them as described above.

PRUNE SAUCE

Prune sauce is rich and dark. Its sweet taste complements meats which are traditionally fatty, such as lamb or pork, and it also marries very well with venison. The prunes may be soaked in red wine or a mixture of half-and-half wine and water.

225 g/8 oz prunes, soaked overnight in water
  to cover
strip of lemon rind
25 g/1 oz sugar
pinch of ground cinnamon
15 ml/1 tbsp rum or brandy (optional)
lemon juice

Transfer the prunes, with the soaking water, to a saucepan. Add the lemon rind and simmer for 10–15 minutes until tender. Strain the prunes, reserving the liquid. Remove the stones and discard the lemon rind.

Purée the prunes with the reserved liquid in a food processor or blender. Alternatively, rub the mixture through a sieve into a clean saucepan. Stir in the sugar and cinnamon. Reheat gently, stirring until all the sugar has dissolved. Stir in the rum or brandy (if using) and add lemon juice to taste. Serve at once, in a sauceboat.

MAKES ABOUT 350 ML/12 FL OZ

BIGARADE SAUCE

½ Seville orange
juice of ½ lemon
250 ml/8 fl oz Espagnole Sauce (page 484)
60 ml/4 tbsp red wine
5 ml/1 tsp redcurrant jelly
salt and cayenne pepper
sugar

Peel the orange, taking care not to remove any of the pith. Cut the rind into neat, thin strips. Put the strips in a saucepan with cold water to cover. Simmer until the rind is just tender. Drain, setting the orange rind aside.

Squeeze the juice from the orange. Add it to the saucepan of Espagnole Sauce with the lemon juice and reserved orange rind. Stir in the wine and redcurrant jelly. Add salt, cayenne and sugar to taste. Serve in a sauceboat.

MAKES ABOUT 300 ML/½ PINT

CELERY SAUCE

This is a very good accompaniment to roast turkey or chicken.

1 head of celery, sliced
300 ml/½ pint Chicken Stock (page 46) or
   Vegetable Stock (page 46)
2 blades of mace
1 bay leaf
25 g/1 oz butter
25 g/1 oz plain flour
salt and pepper
150 ml/¼ pint single cream
5-10 ml/1-2 tsp lemon juice

Put the celery in a saucepan with the stock, mace and bay leaf. Simmer for about 20 minutes or until tender, then drain, reserving the celery in a bowl and the stock in a jug.

Melt the butter in a clean pan, add the flour and cook for 1 minute. Gradually add the reserved stock, stirring until the mixture boils and thickens. Add salt and pepper to taste.

Remove the sauce from the heat and stir in the celery, with the cream and lemon juice. Reheat gently without boiling, if necessary.

MAKES ABOUT 450 ML/¾ PINT

CHESTNUT SAUCE

Serve this creamy sauce instead of chestnut stuffing with turkey. It also goes well with roast, grilled or pan-fried chicken.

225 g/8 oz chestnuts
300 ml/½ pint Chicken Stock (page 46)
2 strips of lemon rind
salt and pepper
cayenne pepper
150 ml/¼ pint single cream
lemon juice

Make a small slit in the shell of each chestnut. Place the chestnuts in a saucepan of boiling water and cook for 15 minutes. Drain, carefully removing the shells and skins while the chestnuts are still very hot.

Put the peeled chestnuts in a pan and add the stock and lemon rind. Bring to the boil, lower the heat and simmer for 15 minutes.

Purée the chestnuts with the stock in a blender or food processor, or press through a fine sieve into a clean pan. Add salt, pepper and cayenne to taste. Stir in the cream and heat through without boiling. Add lemon juice to taste to sharpen the sauce. Serve at once.

SERVES SIX (MAKES ABOUT 600 ML/1 PINT)

GRAVY

**giblets, carcass bones or trimmings from
    meat, poultry or game
1 bay leaf
1 thyme sprig
1 clove
6 black peppercorns
½ onion, sliced
pan juices from roasting (see Mrs Beeton's
    Tip)
25 g/1 oz plain flour (optional)
salt and pepper**

Place the giblets, bones, carcass and/or trimmings (for example wing ends) in a saucepan.
Pour in water to cover, then add the bay leaf,
thyme, clove, peppercorns and onion. Bring to
the boil and skim off any scum, then lower the
heat, cover the pan and simmer for about
1 hour.

Strain the stock and measure it. You need about
600–750 ml/1–1¼ pints to make gravy for up to
six servings. If necessary, pour the stock back
into the saucepan and boil until reduced.

Pour off most of the fat from the roasting tin,
leaving a thin layer and all the cooking juices.
Place the tin over moderate heat; add the flour
if the gravy is to be thickened. Cook the flour,

 MRS BEETON'S TIP

The quality of the sediment on the base of
the cooking tin determines the quality of
the gravy. If the meat was well seasoned
and roasted until well browned outside, the
sediment should have a good colour and
flavour. Any herbs (other than large
stalks), onions or flavouring roasted under
the meat should be left in the pan until the
gravy is boiled, then strained out before
serving.

---

stirring all the time and scraping all the sediment off the tin, for about 3 minutes, until it is
browned. If the gravy is not thickened, pour in
about 300 ml/½ pint of the stock and boil,
stirring and scraping, until the sediment on the
base of the tin is incorporated.

Slowly pour in the stock (or the remaining
stock, if making thin gravy), stirring all the
time. Bring to the boil and cook for 2–3 minu-
tues to reduce the gravy and concentrate the
flavour slightly. Taste and add more salt and
pepper if required.

SERVES FOUR TO SIX

GRAVY NOTES

- If making gravy for a meal other than a roast,
  for example to accompany sausages or toad-
  in-the-hole, use a little fat instead of the pan
  juices and brown the flour well over low to
  moderate heat. Meat dripping gives the best
  flavour but butter or other fat may be used.
- To make onion gravy, slowly brown 2 thinly
  sliced onions in the fat before adding the
  flour – this is excellent with grilled sausages
  or toad-in-the-hole.
- Gravy browning may be added if necessary;
  however, it can make the sauce look artificial
  and unpleasant. Pale gravy is perfectly
  acceptable, provided it has good flavour.
- Always taste gravy when cooked. It should
  be well seasoned. If it lacks flavour, or is
  rather dull, a dash of Worcestershire sauce,
  mushroom ketchup or about 5–15 ml/1–3 tsp
  tomato purée may be whisked in.
- Gravy may be enriched by adding up to half
  wine instead of stock.
- Add 60 ml/4 tbsp port or sherry, and
  15 ml/1 tbsp redcurrant jelly to make a rich
  gravy for duck, game, lamb, pork or venison.
- Add 2 chopped pickled walnuts and
  15 ml/1 tbsp walnut oil to the pan juices to
  make a delicious walnut gravy.

- Use vegetable stock to make vegetable gravy. Cook a finely diced carrot and 2 thinly sliced onions in butter or margarine instead of using meat juices. Add 1.25 ml/¼ tsp ground mace and 30 ml/2 tbsp chopped parsley.
- Add 100 g/4 oz thinly sliced mushrooms to the pan juices to make a mushroom gravy. The sauce may be further enriched by adding a little mushroom ketchup.

BARBECUE SAUCE

This is a very adaptable sauce. It can be used as a marinade, as a basting sauce for chicken portions, steaks, chops and similar foods being cooked on the barbecue grill, or as a side sauce to serve with grilled meats.

30 ml/2 tbsp oil
1 onion, finely chopped
2 garlic cloves, crushed
1 (397 g/14 oz) can chopped tomatoes
45 ml/3 tbsp red wine vinegar
30 ml/2 tbsp soft dark brown sugar
30 ml/2 tbsp tomato ketchup
10 ml/2 tsp soy sauce
10 ml/2 tsp Worcestershire sauce
salt and pepper

Heat the oil in a saucepan. Add the onion and garlic and fry over gentle heat for 4-6 minutes, until the onion is soft but not coloured. Stir in the remaining ingredients and bring to the boil. Lower the heat and simmer for 30-45 minutes, until the sauce is thick and well flavoured.

MAKES ABOUT 150 ML/¼ PINT

BROWN APPLE SAUCE

In Mrs Beeton's day, this tangy, apple-flavoured gravy was frequently served as an accompaniment to roast pork or goose. It is also suitable for grilled pork chops or gammon steaks.

350 g/12 oz Bramley apples
300 ml/½ pint Gravy (opposite), made with poultry or pork cooking juices
45 ml/3 tbsp sugar
salt and pepper
cayenne pepper

Quarter, peel, core and slice the apples. Put them in a saucepan with the gravy. Bring to the boil, reduce the heat and cover the pan. Simmer for 10-15 minutes until the apple is reduced to a pulp.

Beat the pulp into the gravy until smooth. Add the sugar with salt, pepper and cayenne to taste. Serve hot.

MAKES ABOUT 600 ML/1 PINT

BENTON SAUCE

Fresh horseradish is very useful. Not only is it the basis of an excellent sauce to serve with roast beef, but it also adds piquancy to seafood cocktail sauces and dips. In Mrs Beeton's day, a little horseradish was also added to apple sauce, which was served with pork or beef.

30 ml/2 tbsp freshly grated horseradish
10 ml/2 tsp prepared mustard
10 ml/2 tsp caster sugar
125 ml/4 fl oz malt vinegar

Pound the horseradish with the mustard and sugar in a small bowl. Gradually add the vinegar, mixing well.

MAKES ABOUT 150 ML/¼ PINT

APPLE SAUCE

450g/1lb apples
4 cloves
15g/½oz butter
rind and juice of ½ lemon
sugar (see method)

Peel, core and slice the apples. Put them in a saucepan with 30ml/2tbsp water, add the cloves, butter and lemon rind. Cover and cook over low heat until the apple is reduced to a pulp. Remove the cloves. Beat until smooth, rub through a sieve or process in a blender or food processor. Return the sauce to the clean pan, stir in the lemon juice and add sugar to taste. Reheat gently, stirring until the sugar has dissolved. Serve hot or cold.

MAKES ABOUT 350ML/12FLOZ

CRANBERRY SAUCE

150g/5oz sugar
225g/8oz cranberries

Put the sugar in a heavy-bottomed saucepan. Add 125ml/4floz water. Stir over gentle heat until the sugar dissolves. Add the cranberries and cook gently for about 10 minutes until they have burst and are quite tender. Leave to cool.

MAKES ABOUT 300ML/½ PINT

VARIATIONS

Cranberry and Apple Use half cranberries and half tart cooking apples.

Cranberry and Orange Use orange juice instead of water. Add 10ml/2tsp finely grated orange rind.

Cranberry and Sherry Add 30–45ml/2–3 tbsp sherry with the cranberries.

CHRISTOPHER NORTH'S SAUCE

Serve this potent sauce as a relish with roast beef, veal or game, or use it to pep up gravies and other sauces.

175 ml/6 fl oz port
30 ml/2 tbsp Worcestershire sauce
10 ml/2 tsp Mushroom Ketchup (page 923)
10 ml/2 tsp caster sugar
15 ml/1 tbsp lemon juice
1.25 ml/¼ tsp cayenne pepper
2.5 ml/½ tsp salt

Mix all the ingredients together in the top of a double saucepan or a heatproof bowl set over simmering water. Heat gently, without boiling. Serve at once or cool quickly and refrigerate in a closed jar until required.

MAKES ABOUT 250ML/8FLOZ

HORSERADISH SAUCE

60ml/4tbsp grated horseradish
5ml/1tsp caster sugar
5ml/1tsp salt
2.5ml/½ tsp pepper
10ml/2tsp prepared mustard
malt vinegar (see method)
45–60/3–4 tbsp single cream (optional)

Mix the horseradish, sugar, salt, pepper and mustard in a non-metallic bowl. Stir in enough vinegar to make a sauce with the consistency of cream. The flavour and appearance will be improved if the quantity of vinegar is reduced, and the single cream added.

MAKES ABOUT 150ML/¼ PINT

PESTO GENOVESE

A little pesto goes a long way to flavour pasta. Put the pasta in a heated serving bowl or individual dishes add the pesto and toss lightly. Serve at once.

2 garlic cloves, roughly chopped
25–40 g/1–1½ oz fresh basil leaves, roughly
  chopped
25 g/1 oz pine nuts, chopped
40 g/1½ oz Parmesan cheese, grated
juice of 1 lemon
salt and pepper
75–100 ml/3–3½ fl oz olive oil

Combine the garlic, basil leaves, nuts, Parmesan, lemon juice, salt and pepper in a mortar. Pound with a pestle until smooth. Alternatively, process in a blender or food processor. While blending, trickle in the oil as when making mayonnaise, until the sauce forms a very thick paste.

SERVES FOUR

 MRS BEETON'S TIP

Basil has a particular affinity with Italian dishes and it is worth growing it in a large pot on the patio during summer. For a simple starter with a wonderful taste, try sliced tomatoes topped with mozzarella cheese, a drizzle of olive oil and chopped fresh basil leaves.

TUNA SAUCE

The pantry furnishes all the ingredients for this excellent sauce. It is traditionally used to coat cold cooked veal, but is equally good with hard-boiled eggs, cold cooked chicken, pasta or over brown rice.

1 (198 g/7 oz) can tuna in oil
juice of 1 lemon
2 anchovy fillets, roughly chopped
100 ml/3½ fl oz olive oil
15 ml/1 tbsp capers, chopped

Place the tuna, with the oil from the can, in a mixing bowl. Add the lemon juice and anchovy fillets and mash finely with a wooden spoon until smooth. Alternatively, process in a blender or food processor.

When the mixture is smooth, trickle in the oil gradually, as when making mayonnaise, whisking vigorously or blending at high speed until the mixture thickens. Add the salt and pepper to taste and fold in the capers.

MAKES ABOUT 200 ML/7 FL OZ

 MRS BEETON'S TIP

There is a wide range of olive oils on the market, from the rich green extra-virgin oil to light, mild but equally flavoursome oils specially formulated for frying, cooking and baking. It is always worth buying a good quality oil and experimenting to find the flavour that suits your family best. Store olive oil in a cool dark place, if necessary decanting it into a clean green glass wine bottle with cork to protect it from ultra-violet rays.

SAVOURY BUTTERS

MAITRE D'HOTEL BUTTER

100 g/4 oz butter
4–5 large parsley sprigs, finely chopped
salt and pepper
2.5 ml/½ tsp lemon juice

Beat the butter until creamy in a small bowl. Add the parsley, a little at a time, beating until well combined. Add salt to taste and a small pinch of pepper. Add a few drops of lemon juice to intensify the flavour. Use at once or press into small pots, tapping the pots while filling to knock out all the air. Cover with foil and refrigerate until required. Use within 2 days.

MAKES 100G/4OZ

 FREEZER TIP

A convenient way to freeze this butter is to shape it into a roll on a piece of foil or freezer paper. Roll it up in the paper, overwrap in a polythene bag, seal, label and freeze. The frozen butter can then be cut into slices as required, using a warm knife.

GARLIC BUTTER

1 garlic clove, crushed
50–75 g/2–3 oz butter, softened

Put the crushed garlic in a bowl and add enough butter to give the desired flavour. Use at once or press into small pots, tapping the pots while filling to knock out all the air. Cover with foil and refrigerate until required. Use within 2 days.

MAKES 50–75G/2–3OZ

HERB BUTTER

Herb butter may be prepared using one or more herbs. When mixing herbs, balance strong and mild types. Although dried herbs may be used, fresh ones give a superior flavour. Parsley and dill work well.

100 g/4 oz butter, softened
45 ml/3 tbsp chopped parsley
5 ml/1 tsp chopped fresh thyme or
  2.5 ml/½ tsp dried thyme
salt and pepper

Beat the butter until creamy in a small bowl. Add the herbs, beating until well combined. Add salt to taste and a small pinch of pepper. Use at once or press into small pots, tapping the pots while filling to knock out all the air. Cover with foil and refrigerate until required. Use within 2 days.

MAKES 100G/4OZ

DEVILLED BUTTER

A pat of this butter, placed on fish steaks while grilling, imparts a delicious flavour.

100 g/4 oz butter, softened
generous pinch of cayenne pepper
generous pinch of white pepper
1.25 ml/¼ tsp curry powder
1.25 ml/¼ tsp ground ginger

Beat all the ingredients together in a small bowl, using the back of the spoon to combine them thoroughly. Check the seasoning. Use at once or press into small pots, tapping the pots while filling to knock out all the air. Cover with foil and refrigerate until required. Use within 2 days.

MAKES 100G/4OZ

EPICUREAN BUTTER

2 hard-boiled egg yolks
4 anchovy fillets, finely chopped
5 ml/1 tsp chopped fresh tarragon
4 cocktail gherkins, finely chopped
10 ml/2 tsp snipped chives
75 g/3 oz butter, softened
5 ml/1 tsp French mustard

Mash the egg yolks with a pestle in a mortar. Add the anchovy fillets, tarragon, gherkins and chives. Add a little of the butter and pound to a paste. Alternatively process all these ingredients together in a blender until smooth.

In a bowl, beat the remaining butter until light; beat in the mustard. Add the pounded or blended ingredients and mix thoroughly. Chill the mixture until firm but still workable. Form into pats or press into small pots.

MAKES 90 G/3½ OZ

HORSERADISH BUTTER

15 ml/1 tbsp grated fresh or bottled
  horseradish
50 g/2 oz butter, softened
lemon juice

If using bottled horseradish, put it in a colander, rinse it under cold water, then pat dry with absorbent kitchen paper.

Beat the butter in a small bowl until light and fluffy. Gradually work in the horseradish. Add lemon juice to taste. Use at once or cover and chill until required.

MAKES ABOUT 65 G/2½ OZ

OLIVE BUTTER

50 g/2 oz butter, softened
30 ml/2 tbsp stoned chopped green olives
a few drops of onion juice (optional)

Beat the butter in a small bowl until light and fluffy. Pound the olives in a mortar with a pestle. Stir the olives and onion juice, if using, into the butter. Use at once or cover and chill.

MAKES ABOUT 65 G/2½ OZ

MONTPELIER BUTTER

60 ml/4 tbsp mixed chopped leaves (spinach,
  parsley, cress, tarragon, and chives),
  blanched and drained
2 small garlic cloves, crushed
15 ml/1 tbsp chopped capers
a few drops of anchovy essence
2 hard-boiled egg yolks
100 g/4 oz butter, softened

Mix all the ingredients except the butter in a mortar. Pound to a paste with a pestle, gradually adding the butter until a smooth green paste is obtained. Rub through a sieve into a bowl. Use at once or cover and chill.

MAKES ABOUT 150 G/5 OZ

Dessert Sauces

A well-chosen, perfectly prepared sauce adds a professional touch to a dessert.

Many recipes offer guidance as to the type of sauce to serve but you may wish to use a little imagination when selecting the accompaniments for a pudding. For example a lively, cold fruit sauce contrasts well with a piping hot steamed sponge pudding; or a spicy sauce flavoured with ginger will enliven a delicate fruit mousse.

Caramel and chocolate are two dessert sauces that have long refrigerator lives; they are always useful as toppings for ice cream, sponge cake, meringues or fresh fruit.

When serving a cold sauce, prepare it in advance, cool and chill it until it is needed. If you are preparing a hot sauce that requires last-minute attention weigh all the ingredients and set out all the utensils beforehand. Some hot sauces may be made and put on one side ready for last-minute reheating. To prevent the formation of a skin on a sauce, cover it with a piece of dampened greaseproof paper; alternatively, sprinkle a little caster sugar over the surface.

REDCURRANT SAUCE

100 g/4 oz redcurrant jelly
45 ml/3 tbsp port

Combine the jelly and port in a small saucepan and cook over gentle heat until the jelly melts. Pour over steamed puddings or serve with hot milk puddings such as semolina. The sauce also makes a good glaze for cheesecakes topped with berry fruits.

MAKES ABOUT 150 ML/¼ PINT

APPLE AND ORANGE SAUCE

Rich and full of flavour, this is an ideal accompaniment to steamed fruit puddings. Cold, it makes a good filling for apple meringue pie or cake.

450 g/1 lb cooking apples
15 g/½ oz butter or margarine
finely grated rind and juice of ½ orange
sugar (see method)

Peel and core the apples and slice them into a saucepan. Add 30 ml/2 tbsp water with the butter and orange rind. Cover the pan and cook over low heat until the apple is reduced to a pulp.

Beat the pulp until smooth, then rub through a sieve. Alternatively, purée the mixture in a blender or food processor.

Return the purée to the clean pan and reheat. Stir in the orange juice, with sugar to taste. Serve hot or cold.

MAKES 375 ML/13 FL OZ

 MICROWAVE TIP

Place the sliced apples in a large dish or bowl with the water, butter and orange rind. Make sure there is room for the apples to boil up. Cover and cook on High for 5–7 minutes, stirring once. Continue as above.

CARAMEL CUSTARD SAUCE

25 g/1 oz granulated sugar
250 ml/8 fl oz milk
few drops of vanilla essence or a strip of
  lemon rind
3 egg yolks
50 g/2 oz caster sugar

Start by making the caramel. Mix the granulated sugar with 15 ml/1 tbsp water in a small saucepan. Heat gently until the sugar dissolves, then boil the syrup until it is golden brown. Remove the syrup from the heat and immediately add 30 ml/2 tbsp cold water (see Mrs Beeton's Tip). Leave in a warm place to dissolve.

Meanwhile, make the sauce. Combine the milk and chosen flavouring in a saucepan. Warm gently but do not let the liquid boil.

In a bowl, beat the egg yolks and sugar together until creamy. Remove the lemon rind, if used, from the pan and add the milk to the eggs.

Strain the custard into a double saucepan or a heatproof bowl placed over a saucepan of simmering water. Cook, stirring constantly, until the custard thickens and coats the back of the spoon.

Stir the caramel. Add enough to the finished custard sauce to give a good flavour and colour. Serve warm or cold.

MAKES ABOUT 300 ML/½ PINT

 MRS BEETON'S TIP

Take care when adding the cold water to the hot caramel. The mixture may spit, so it is wise to protect your hand by wearing an oven glove.

SWEET WHITE SAUCE

20 ml/4 tsp cornflour
250 ml/8 fl oz milk
15–30 ml/1–2 tbsp sugar
vanilla essence or other flavouring

Put the cornflour in a bowl. Stir in enough of the cold milk to form a smooth, thin paste.

Heat the remaining milk in a small saucepan. When it boils, stir it into the cornflour paste, then return the mixture to the clean pan and stir until boiling.

Lower the heat and cook, stirring frequently, for 3 minutes. Stir in sugar to taste and add the chosen flavouring. Serve hot.

MAKES ABOUT 250 ML/8 FL OZ

VARIATIONS

Almond Sauce Add 10 ml/2 tsp ground almonds to the cornflour when blending with the milk. When the sauce is cooked, stir in 2–3 drops of almond essence with vanilla essence to taste.

Brandy Sauce When the sauce is cooked, stir in 15–30 ml/1–2 tbsp brandy.

Chocolate Sauce When the sauce is cooked, stir in 15 ml/1 tbsp cocoa dissolved in 15 ml/1 tbsp boiling water.

Coffee Sauce To the cooked sauce add 10 ml/2 tsp instant coffee dissolved in 15 ml/1 tbsp boiling water.

Ginger Sauce Stir in 10 ml/2 tsp ground ginger with the cornflour. For extra taste and texture, 50 g/2 oz crystallized ginger, finely chopped, may be added to the cooked sauce.

SWEET ARROWROOT SAUCE

The advantage in using arrowroot is that it creates a clear sauce that will not mask the pudding over which it is poured. A thinner sauce may be made by increasing the water in the saucepan to 250 ml/8 fl oz.

thinly pared rind of 1 lemon or other solid
    flavouring
100 g/4 oz sugar
lemon juice
10 ml/2 tsp arrowroot

Put 125 ml/4 fl oz water in a saucepan. Add the lemon rind or other flavouring and bring to the boil. Lower the heat and simmer the sauce gently for 15 minutes.

Remove the lemon rind, if used, and stir in the sugar. Return the liquid to the boil and boil steadily for 5 minutes. Stir in lemon juice to taste.

In a cup, mix the arrowroot with 10 ml/2 tsp water until smooth. Stir into the hot liquid. Heat gently for 1–2 minutes, stirring constantly as the sauce thickens. Remove from the heat once the sauce has boiled.

MAKES ABOUT 175 ML/6 FL OZ

VARIATIONS

St Clement's Sauce Use the rind of ½ lemon or ½ orange and add 125 ml/4 fl oz lemon or orange juice.

Rich Lemon Sauce Beat 125 ml/4 fl oz sherry with 1 egg yolk. Add the mixture to the thickened sauce and heat gently. Do not allow the sauce to boil once the egg yolk mixture has been added.

CORNFLOUR CUSTARD SAUCE

15 ml/1 tbsp cornflour
250 ml/8 fl oz milk
1 egg yolk
15 ml/1 tbsp sugar
few drops of vanilla essence

Mix the cornflour with a little of the cold milk in a large bowl. Bring the rest of the milk to the boil in a saucepan, then stir into the blended mixture. Return the mixture to the clean pan.

Bring the cornflour mixture to the boil and boil for 3 minutes to cook the cornflour. Remove from the heat.

When the mixture has cooled a little, stir in the egg yolk and sugar. Return to low heat and cook, stirring carefully, until the sauce thickens. Do not let it boil. Flavour with a few drops of vanilla essence and pour into a jug.

MAKES ABOUT 250 ML/8 FL OZ

 MICROWAVE TIP

Mix the cornflour with all the milk in a bowl. Cook on High for 3–5 minutes, whisking twice. Whisk well, then whisk in the yolk, sugar and vanilla. Cook for a further 30–45 seconds on High.

CREME ANGLAISE

The classic egg custard sauce; and an essential ingredient of many desserts.

250 ml/8 fl oz milk
few drops of vanilla essence or a strip of
    lemon rind
3 egg yolks
50 g/2 oz caster sugar

Combine the milk and chosen flavouring in a saucepan. Warm gently but do not boil.

In a bowl, beat the egg yolks and sugar together until creamy. Remove the lemon rind, if used, from the saucepan and add the milk to the eggs.

Strain the custard into a double saucepan or a heatproof bowl placed over a saucepan of simmering water. Cook, stirring constantly, until the custard thickens and coats the back of the spoon. Serve hot or cold.

MAKES 300 ML/½ PINT

VARIATIONS

Liqueur Sauce Stir 125 ml/4 fl oz lightly whipped double cream and 30 ml/2 tbsp orange-flavoured liqueur into the sauce.

Chocolate Custard Sauce Use vanilla essence instead of lemon rind and add 100 g/4 oz coarsely grated plain chocolate to the milk. Warm until the chocolate melts, stir, then add to the egg yolks and proceed as in the main recipe.

CREAM CUSTARD SAUCE

4 egg yolks or 2 whole eggs
50 g/2 oz caster sugar
125 ml/4 fl oz milk
grated rind of 1 orange
125 ml/4 fl oz single cream

In a mixing bowl, beat the egg yolks or the whole eggs with the sugar and milk. Stir in the orange rind and cream.

Pour into a double saucepan or into a heatproof bowl placed over a saucepan of simmering water. Cook, stirring all the time, until the sauce thickens. Serve hot or cold.

MAKES ABOUT 250 ML/8 FL OZ

 MRS BEETON'S TIP

Do not allow the sauce to boil or it will curdle.

SWEET MOUSSELINE SAUCE

Serve this frothy sauce over light steamed or baked puddings, fruit desserts or Christmas pudding.

2 whole eggs plus 1 yolk
40 g/1½ oz caster sugar
75 ml/5 tbsp single cream
15 ml/1 tbsp medium-dry sherry

Combine all the ingredients in a double saucepan or in a heatproof bowl placed over a saucepan of simmering water. Cook and whisk until pale and frothy and of a thick, creamy consistency. Pour into a bowl and serve at once.

MAKES ABOUT 300 ML/½ PINT

VANILLA CUSTARD

*Adding cornflour stabilizes the custard and makes it
less inclined to curdle.*

10 ml/2 tsp cornflour
500 ml/17 fl oz milk
25 g/1 oz caster sugar
2 eggs
vanilla essence

In a bowl, mix the cornflour to a smooth paste
with a little of the cold milk. Heat the rest of the
milk in a saucepan and when hot pour it on to
the blended cornflour, stirring.

Return to the mixture to the pan, bring to the
boil, and boil for 1–2 minutes, stirring all the
time, to cook the cornflour. Remove from the
heat and stir in the sugar. Leave to cool.

Beat the eggs together lightly in a small bowl.
Add a little of the cooked cornflour mixture,
stir well, then pour into the pan. Heat gently for
a few minutes until the custard has thickened,
stirring all the time. Do not boil. Stir in a few
drops of vanilla essence.

Serve hot or cold as an accompaniment to a
pudding or pie.

MAKES ABOUT 600 ML/1 PINT

SIMPLE CUSTARD SAUCE

*The addition of cornflour makes it unnecessary to use
a double saucepan to make this sauce, provided care
is taken to avoid excessive heat and the custard is
constantly stirred.*

500 ml/17 fl oz milk
few drops of vanilla essence
6 egg yolks
100 g/4 oz caster sugar
10 ml/2 tsp cornflour

Combine the milk and vanilla essence in a
saucepan. Warm gently but do not boil.

In a bowl, beat the egg yolks, sugar and
cornflour together until creamy. Add the warm
milk.

Strain the mixture back into the clean pan and
cook, stirring constantly, until the custard
thickens and coats the back of the spoon. Serve
hot or cold.

MAKES ABOUT 600 ML/1 PINT

CLASSIC EGG CUSTARD SAUCE

This recipe may be used as the basis for ice cream or for Vanilla Bavarois (page 590).

500 ml/17 fl oz milk
few drops of vanilla essence or other
  flavouring
6 egg yolks
100 g/4 oz caster sugar

Put the milk in a saucepan with the vanilla or other flavouring. Warm gently but do not let the liquid boil. If a solid flavouring such as a strip of citrus rind is used, allow it to infuse in the milk for 5 minutes, then remove.

In a bowl, beat the egg yolks and sugar together until creamy. Add the warm milk to the egg mixture.

Strain the mixture into a double saucepan or a heatproof bowl placed over a saucepan of simmering water. Cook, stirring constantly with a wooden spoon for 20–30 minutes, until the custard thickens and coats the back of the spoon. Take care not to let the custard curdle. Serve hot or cold.

MAKES ABOUT 500 ML/17 FL OZ

VARIATIONS

Classic Lemon Custard Infuse a thin strip of lemon rind in the milk, removing it before adding to the eggs.

Classic Orange Custard Substitute orange rind for lemon rind.

Classic Liqueur Custard Add 15 ml/1 tbsp kirsch or curaçao at the end of the cooking time.

Praline Stir in crushed Praline (see Mrs Beeton's Tip, page 720) just before serving.

COLD SHERRY SABAYON SAUCE

50 g/2 oz caster sugar
2 egg yolks
15 ml/1 tbsp medium-sweet sherry or brandy
45 ml/3 tbsp double cream

Put the sugar in a saucepan with 75 ml/5 tbsp water. Warm gently until the sugar is completely dissolved, then bring to the boil and boil for 3 minutes.

Mix the egg yolks with the sherry or brandy in a bowl. Whisk in the syrup gradually, and continue whisking until the mixture is cool, thick and foamy.

In a second bowl, whip the cream lightly. Fold it gently into the egg mixture. Chill.

Pour into tall glasses and serve with ratafias. The sauce may also be served with cold desserts or fresh fruit.

MAKES ABOUT 400 ML/14 FL OZ

CHANTILLY CREAM

250 ml/8 fl oz double cream
25 g/1 oz icing sugar
few drops of vanilla essence

Pour the cream into a mixing bowl and chill it for several hours.

Just before serving, whip the cream with the sugar and vanilla essence to taste.

MAKES ABOUT 250 ML/8 FL OZ

SABAYON SAUCE

The French version of that Italian favourite, Zabaglione, Sabayon is usually served warm as an accompaniment to steamed pudding.

3 egg yolks
25 g/1 oz caster sugar
50 ml/2 fl oz Marsala, Madeira, sweet sherry
  or sweet white wine
small strip of lemon rind

Beat the yolks and sugar together in a heatproof bowl until thick and pale. Gradually whisk in the chosen wine. Add the lemon rind.

Pour the mixture into a double saucepan or stand the bowl over a saucepan of simmering water. Cook until thick and creamy, whisking all the time. When the whisk is lifted out of the mixture it should leave a trail that lasts for 2–3 seconds. Remove the lemon rind and serve at once.

MAKES ABOUT 200 ML/7 FL OZ

 MICROWAVE TIP

Whisk the yolks and sugar as above, in a bowl which may be used in the microwave. In a jug, heat the chosen wine on High for 30–45 seconds, until hot but not boiling, then whisk it into the yolks. Cook on High for about 1–1½ minutes, whisking thoroughly two or three times, until creamy.

PLUM PUDDING SAUCE

A thin sauce with a rich, buttery flavour to make a potent impression on Christmas pudding or a variety of other desserts.

100 g/4 oz caster sugar
75 ml/3 fl oz brandy
50 g/2 oz unsalted butter, diced
175 ml/6 fl oz Madeira

Put the sugar in a heatproof bowl with 30 ml/2 tbsp of the brandy. Add the butter. Set over simmering water and stir until the mixture is smooth. Gradually stir in the rest of the brandy with the Madeira and warm through. Either serve over the pudding or in a sauceboat.

MAKES 350 ML/12 FL OZ

CARAMEL

200 g/7 oz caster sugar

Put the sugar in a heavy-bottomed saucepan. Add 125 ml/4 fl oz water and stir over low heat for 3–4 minutes until the sugar has dissolved. Increase the heat and boil, without stirring, until the syrup is a light golden brown. Do not allow it to darken too much or it will taste bitter.

Immediately plunge the bottom of the pan into warm water to prevent further cooking. Allow the caramel mixture to cool slightly, then carefully add a further 75 ml/3 fl oz water. Return the pan to a low heat and stir constantly until the mixture becomes smooth. Remove from the heat, cool slightly, then use as required.

SERVES FOUR

APRICOT SAUCE

This fruity sauce may be served hot or cold, with set custards, sponge puddings, pancakes or ice cream. It also makes an unusual, lively accompaniment to plain apple pie.

225 g/8 oz fresh apricots
25–50 g/1–2 oz soft light brown sugar
15 ml/1 tbsp lemon juice
10 ml/2 tsp maraschino or apricot brandy
   (optional)
5 ml/1 tsp arrowroot

MELBA SAUCE

Although this sauce is principally used for Peach Melba, it is equally delicious when served with meringues, sorbet or any raspberry flavoured dessert.

225 g/8 oz fresh raspberries
45 ml/3 tbsp icing sugar
white wine (optional)

Put the raspberries in a sieve over a heatproof bowl. Crush them lightly with the back of a wooden spoon, then add the sugar and rub the raspberries through the sieve into the bowl.

Place the bowl over a saucepan of simmering water, and stir for 2–3 minutes to dissolve the sugar.

Remove from the heat, and stir in a little white wine if a thinner consistency is preferred. The sauce should only just coat the back of a spoon. Pour into a bowl or jug and chill before use.

MAKES ABOUT 125 ML/4 FL OZ

Stone the apricots, reserving the stones. Put the fruit into a saucepan with 125 ml/4 fl oz water. Cover the pan and simmer the fruit until softened. Rub through a sieve, or purée in a blender or food processor.

Crack the reserved apricot stones and remove the kernels. Cover the kernels with boiling water and leave for 2 minutes. Drain the kernels, and when cool enough to handle, skin them. Add to the apricots with sugar to taste and stir in the lemon juice with the liqueur, if used. Reheat the sauce.

In a cup, mix the arrowroot with 15 ml/1 tbsp water. Add to the sauce and bring to the boil, stirring until the sauce thickens. Serve.

MAKES ABOUT 375 ML/13 FL OZ

 MRS BEETON'S TIP

If time is short, subsitute 1 (425 g/15 oz) can apricots for fresh fruit. Purée the drained fruit with 125 ml/4 fl oz of the can syrup. Sugar need not be added, but lemon juice and liqueur, if used, should be added before the sauce is reheated.

 MICROWAVE TIP

Mix the fruit and sugar in a bowl. Cover and cook on High for 2 minutes, until the fruit is pulpy. Rub the sauce through a sieve. Continue as above, thinning the sauce with wine if liked.

THICKENED FRUIT SAUCE

450 g/1 lb ripe fruit (damsons, plums, berry fruits)
50–100 g/2–4 oz sugar
lemon juice
arrowroot (see method)

Put the fruit into a saucepan with about 30 ml/2 tbsp water. Cover the pan and cook over low heat until the fruit is reduced to a pulp. Remove any stones.

Beat the pulp until smooth, then rub through a sieve. Alternatively, purée the mixture in a blender or food processor. Pour the purée into a measuring jug; note the volume.

Return the purée to the clean pan and reheat. Stir in the sugar, with lemon juice to taste. To thicken the sauce, you will need 5 ml/1 tsp arrowroot for every 250 ml/8 fl oz fruit purée. Spoon the required amount of arrowroot into a cup or small bowl and mix to a paste with water. Add to the fruit mixture and bring to the boil, stirring constantly until the sauce thickens. Remove from the heat as soon as the sauce boils. Serve hot or cold.

MAKES ABOUT 400 ML/14 FL OZ

 FREEZER TIP

It is best to freeze the fruit purée before thickening. Pour into a rigid container, cover and seal. It will keep for up to 12 months. When required, thaw for 4 hours, reheat gently and thicken the sauce as described above.

COLD CHANTILLY APPLE SAUCE

450 g/1 lb cooking apples
25 g/1 oz butter
50 g/2 oz sugar
150 ml/¼ pint double cream

Peel, core and slice the apples, Put them into a saucepan with 30 ml/2 tbsp water. Add the butter and sugar. Cover the pan and simmer gently until the apple is reduced to a pulp.

Beat the pulp until smooth, then rub the mixture through a sieve. Alternatively, purée in a blender or food processor. Pour into a bowl and leave to cool.

In a separate bowl, whip the cream until stiff. Fold into the apple purée. Serve cold.

MAKES ABOUT 500 ML/17 FL OZ

FRUIT AND YOGURT SAUCE

Any fruit purée may be used for this sauce, provided it is not too acidic. Use fresh or canned fruit – apricots are particularly good.

150 ml/¼ pint plain yogurt
250 ml/8 fl oz fruit purée
sugar

Spoon the yogurt into a bowl and beat it lightly. Fold in the fruit purée. Add sugar to taste. Serve the sauce cold.

MAKES ABOUT 350 ML/12 FL OZ

CHOCOLATE CREAM SAUCE

Add a touch of luxury to rice pudding, poached pears or ice cream with this sauce. When cold, the sauce thickens enough to be used as a soft filling for eclairs or profiteroles.

75 g/3 oz plain chocolate, roughly grated
15 ml/1 tbsp butter
15 ml/1 tbsp single cream
5 ml/1 tsp vanilla essence

Put the grated chocolate in a heatproof bowl with the butter. Add 60 ml/4 tbsp water. Stand the bowl over a saucepan of simmering water and stir until the chocolate and butter have melted.

When the chocolate mixture is smooth, remove from the heat and immediately stir in the cream and vanilla essence. Serve at once.

MAKES ABOUT 125 ML/4 FL OZ

 MICROWAVE TIP

Combine the chocolate, butter and water in a bowl. Heat on High for about 1 minute, stirring once, until the chocolate has melted. Finish as above.

CHOCOLATE LIQUEUR SAUCE

75 g/3 oz plain chocolate or cooking chocolate
10 ml/2 tsp custard powder or cornflour
15 ml/1 tbsp orange-flavoured liqueur
15 ml/1 tbsp caster sugar

Break the chocolate into small pieces and put it in a heatproof bowl with 30 ml/2 tbsp cold water. Stand the bowl over a saucepan of simmering water and stir until the chocolate melts.

When the chocolate has melted, beat it until smooth, gradually adding 200 ml/7 fl oz water.

In a cup, mix the custard powder or cornflour with 30 ml/2 tbsp water, then stir into the chocolate sauce and cook for 3–4 minutes. Stir in the liqueur and the sugar.

MAKES ABOUT 400 ML/14 FL OZ

MOCHA SAUCE

100 g/4 oz plain chocolate
200 g/7 oz sugar
125 ml/4 fl oz strong black coffee
pinch of salt
2.5 ml/½ tsp vanilla essence

Break up the chocolate and put it into a saucepan with the other ingredients. Stir over gentle heat until the chocolate and sugar melt and the mixture becomes smooth.

Serve hot over ice cream, profiteroles or stewed pears.

MAKES ABOUT 150 ML/¼ PINT

RICH CHOCOLATE SAUCE

Plain ice cream becomes a party treat with this wickedly rich sauce. It also makes a very good topping for a chocolate Swiss Roll.

350 g/12 oz bitter-sweet dessert chocolate,
   roughly grated
45 ml/3 tbsp butter
30 ml/2 tbsp double cream
5 ml/1 tsp whisky

Put the grated chocolate in a saucepan with 200 ml/7 fl oz water. Heat gently, stirring all the time, until the chocolate melts. Do not let the sauce boil. Add the butter, 5 ml/1 tsp at a time, and continue stirring until it melts.

Remove the sauce from the heat and stir in the cream and whisky. Serve at once.

MAKES ABOUT 500 ML/17 FL OZ

✳ FREEZER TIP

The sauce may be poured into a heatproof container with a lid, cooled quickly and then frozen for up to 3 months. To use, thaw for 4 hours at room temperature, then stand the container in a saucepan of very hot water until warm.

RUM AND RAISIN CHOCOLATE SAUCE

25 g/1 oz cocoa
25 g/1 oz cornflour
25 g/1 oz caster sugar
450 ml/¾ pint milk
50 g/2 oz seedless raisins, chopped
30–45 ml/2–3 tbsp rum
30–45 ml/2–3 tbsp single cream

In a bowl, mix the cocoa, cornflour and sugar to a smooth paste with a little of the milk. Heat the rest of the milk until boiling. Stir it into the cocoa paste.

Return the mixture to the saucepan and stir until boiling; simmer for 3 minutes. Remove from the heat and stir in the raisins, rum and cream. Serve the sauce hot or cold.

MAKES ABOUT 250 ML/8 FL OZ

BUTTERSCOTCH SAUCE

1 (410 g/14 oz) can evaporated milk
100 g/4 oz soft light brown sugar
100 g/4 oz caster sugar
50 g/2 oz butter
15 ml/1 tbsp clear honey
2.5 ml/½ tsp vanilla essence
pinch of salt

Put the evaporated milk, sugars, butter, and honey into a heavy-bottomed saucepan. Stir over gentle heat until the sugar has dissolved. Stir in the vanilla essence and salt.

Pour into a jug and serve hot with steamed puddings.

MAKES ABOUT 500 ML/17 FL OZ

MARMALADE AND WINE SAUCE

Baked puddings can be somewhat dry. This zesty sauce is the perfect accompaniment.

90 ml/6 tbsp orange marmalade
90 ml/6 tbsp white wine

Combine the marmalade and wine in a saucepan and heat gently for 5 minutes.

Transfer to a jug and serve at once.

MAKES ABOUT 175 ML/6 FL OZ

GINGER SYRUP SAUCE

Warm a winter's evening with this sauce poured over Ginger Pudding (page 565)

strip of lemon rind
piece of fresh root ginger
125 ml/4 fl oz ginger syrup (from jar of preserved ginger)
100 g/4 oz soft light brown sugar, golden syrup or honey
5 ml/1 tsp lemon juice
10 ml/2 tsp arrowroot
2.5 ml/½ tsp ground ginger
15 ml/1 tbsp preserved ginger, chopped

Put the lemon rind, root ginger and syrup into a saucepan. Add 125 ml/4 fl oz water. Heat to boiling point. Lower the heat and simmer gently for 15 minutes.

Remove the lemon rind and root ginger. Add the brown sugar, syrup or honey, bring the mixture to the boil and boil for 5 minutes. Stir in the lemon juice.

In a cup, mix the arrowroot and ground ginger with a little cold water until smooth. Stir the arrowroot mixture into the hot liquid. Heat gently until the liquid thickens, stirring all the time.

Add the preserved ginger to the sauce and simmer for 2–3 minutes. Serve hot. .

MAKES ABOUT 300 ML/½ PINT

 MRS BEETON'S TIP

The syrup in a jar of preserved ginger makes a delicious addition to gingerbreads, steamed puddings and pancakes.

JAM SAUCE

Simple sauces can be highly successful. Try Jam Sauce on steamed or baked puddings.

60 ml/4 tbsp seedless jam
lemon juice
10 ml/2 tsp arrowroot
few drops of food colouring (optional)

Put the jam in a saucepan with 250 ml/8 fl oz water and bring to the boil. Add lemon juice to taste.

In a cup, mix the arrowroot with a little cold water until smooth. Stir into the hot liquid and heat gently until the sauce thickens, stirring all the time. Add a little colouring if necessary. Pour into a jug and serve at once.

MAKES ABOUT 300 ML/½ PINT

VARIATION

Marmalade Sauce Substitute marmalade for jam and use orange juice instead of water.

SWEET SHERRY SAUCE

75 ml/5 tbsp sherry
30 ml/2 tbsp seedless jam or jelly
lemon juice

Combine the sherry and jam in a saucepan. Add 75 ml/5 tbsp water with lemon juice to taste. Bring to the boil and boil for 2–3 minutes. Strain, if necessary, before serving in a jug or sauceboat.

MAKES ABOUT 150 ML/¼ PINT

SWEET BUTTERS

Sweet butters may be used to top pancakes, waffles, crumpets or drop scones. They are also used on fruit puddings, the best example being brandy butter, which is traditionally served with Christmas pudding.

BRANDY BUTTER

50 g/2 oz butter
100 g/4 oz caster sugar
15-30 ml/1-2 tbsp brandy

In a bowl, cream the butter until soft. Gradually beat in the sugar until the mixture is pale and light. Work in the brandy, a little at a time, taking care not to allow the mixture to curdle. Chill before using. If the mixture has separated slightly after standing, beat well before serving.

MAKES ABOUT 150 G/5 OZ

VARIATIONS

Sherry Butter   Make as for Brandy Butter but substitute sherry for the brandy. Add a stiffly beaten egg white, if a softer texture is preferred.

Vanilla Butter   Make as for Brandy Butter but substitute 5 ml/1 tsp vanilla essence for the brandy.

Orange or Lemon Butter   Cream the grated rind of 1 orange or ½ lemon with the butter and sugar, then gradually beat in 15 ml/1 tbsp orange juice or 5 ml/1 tsp lemon juice. Omit the brandy.

ALMOND BUTTER

100 g/4 oz butter, softened
100 g/4 oz ground almonds
about 30 ml/2 tbsp caster sugar
2.5-5 ml/½-1 tsp lemon juice
few drops of almond essence

Put the butter in a mixing bowl and work in the ground almonds thoroughly. Add the sugar, lemon juice and almond essence gradually. Use at once or pot (see Mrs Beeton's Tip) and chill.

MAKES ABOUT 225 G/8 OZ

 MRS BEETON'S TIP

Pots of Almond Butter make good gifts. Press the butter into small pots or cartons (mini yogurt pots are perfect) and cover. Chill in the refrigerator. Do not freeze.

CHESTNUT BUTTER

200 g/7 oz unsweetened chestnut purée
200 g/7 oz butter, softened
30-45 ml/2-3 tbsp caster sugar
15-30 ml/1-2 tbsp rum

Combine the chestnut purée and butter in a bowl and mix until thoroughly blended. Add the sugar and rum gradually, adjusting the flavour to taste. Chill until firm, then use at once, or pot and chill as for Almond Butter (above).

MAKES ABOUT 450 G/1 LB

BRANDY AND ALMOND BUTTER

100 g/4 oz unsalted butter
75 g/3 oz icing sugar
25 g/1 oz ground almonds
30 ml/2 tbsp brandy
few drops of lemon juice

In a mixing bowl, cream the butter until very light. Sift in the icing sugar, a little at a time, and beat in each addition lightly but throughly with a fork. Add the almonds in the same way. Lift the fork when beating to incorporate as much air as possible.

Beat in the brandy and lemon juice, a few drops at a time, taking care not to let the mixture separate. Taste, and add extra brandy if liked.

Pile the mixture into a dish and leave to firm up before serving; or turn lightly into a screw-topped jar and store in a cool place until required. Use within one week, or refrigerate for longer storage. Bring to room temperature before serving.

MAKES ABOUT 225 G/8 OZ

RUM BUTTER

50 g/2 oz butter
100 g/4 oz soft light brown sugar
30 ml/2 tbsp rum

In a bowl, cream the butter until soft, beating in the sugar gradually. When light and creamy, work in the rum, a little at a time. Chill the butter before using.

MAKES ABOUT 175 G/6 OZ

CUMBERLAND RUM BUTTER

100 g/4 oz unsalted butter
100 g/4 oz soft light brown sugar
30 ml/2 tbsp rum
2.5 ml/½ tsp grated orange rind
grated nutmeg

Put the butter in a bowl and cream it until very soft and light-coloured. Crush any lumps in the sugar. Work it into the butter until completely blended in.

Work the rum into the butter, a few drops at a time, take care not to let the mixture separate. Mix in the orange rind. Taste and add a little grated nutmeg.

Pile the rum butter into a dish, and leave to firm up before serving; or turn lightly into a screw-topped jar and store in a cool place until required. Use within 4 days, or refrigerate for longer storage. Bring to room temperature before serving.

MAKES ABOUT 225 G/8 OZ

ORANGE LIQUEUR BUTTER

grated rind of 2 oranges
4 sugar lumps
150 g/5 oz butter, softened
25 g/1 oz caster sugar
15 ml/1 tbsp orange juice, strained
20 ml/4 tsp Cointreau

Put the orange rind in a bowl and mix it with the sugar lumps. Work in the butter and caster sugar until well blended.

Stir in the juice and liqueur gradually, until fully absorbed. Use at once, or pot and chill as for Almond Butter (page 506).

MAKES ABOUT 175 G/6 OZ

STRAWBERRY BUTTER

100 g/4 oz butter, softened
225 g/8 oz icing sugar
175 g/6 oz fresh strawberries, hulled and
   crushed
50 g/2 oz ground almonds

In a bowl, beat the butter until light. Sift in the sugar and beat it in thoroughly.

Add the strawberries with the ground almonds. Mix thoroughly. Use at once.

MAKES ABOUT 575 G/1¼ LB

FAIRY BUTTER

Not a whipped butter, but a rich dessert composed of orange-flavoured strands. It looks very attractive and may also be used instead of whipped cream as a topping on a trifle or gâteau.

2 hard-boiled egg yolks
10 ml/2 tsp orange juice, strained
10 ml/2 tsp orange flower water
25 g/1 oz icing sugar, sifted
100 g/4 oz butter, softened
10 ml/2 tsp grated orange rind, to decorate

Sieve the egg yolks into a bowl. Using an electric whisk or rotary beater, gradually add the juice, orange flower water, sugar and butter until all the ingredients form a smooth paste.

To use, press the fairy butter through a sieve on to a decorative serving plate or individual plates in a pile of thin strands. Sprinkle with grated orange rind and serve at once.

MAKES ABOUT 175 G/6 OZ

 MRS BEETON'S TIP

The pile of butter strands should not be pressed down. Flick any stray strands into place with a fork.

Pastry

Put your pastry-making skills to the test and sample the delights this chapter has to offer: delicious quiches,
steaming hot sweet and savoury suet puddings, lightly layered puff pastry confections or crisply
crusted fruit flans are all here for the making. If you have any doubts about basic techniques,
simply read through the opening section first.

Good pastry should be light in texture. A few simple rules will help to ensure success with all types. Always weigh ingredients accurately as it is important that the correct proportions of fat, flour and liquid are used. Keep all ingredients, utensils and your hands as cool as possible.

RUBBING IN

The first stage in making several types of pastry is to rub the fat into the flour. This basic technique is used for other purposes in cookery so it is worth getting it right. Cut the fat into small pieces and mix it with the flour. Using just the tips of your fingers, lift a little of the mixture and rub the fat with the flour once or twice. Let the mixture fall back into the bowl before lifting another small portion and rubbing again. Continue in this way until the mixture has the texture of fine breadcrumbs.

It is important that you lift the mixture and rub it lightly to incorporate air into it. If you pick up too much mixture and push it back into the palms of your hands, air will not mix with it and the pastry will be heavy. Once you have mastered the technique you will find it quick and easy to perform; in fact, the quicker the process is completed, the lighter the pastry.

ADDING LIQUID TO SHORT PASTRIES

The term 'short' is used to describe pastry that is not made heavy by the addition of too much liquid. The 'melt-in-your-mouth' texture that

is characteristic of good 'short' pastry is the result of using the right proportion of fat to flour and just enough liquid to hold the pastry together as it is rolled.

When making sweet pastry dishes, various types of short pastry may be used and the difference may be in the liquid added to bind the ingredients. Plain short crust pastry is bound with a little water. The water should be very cold (preferably iced) and just enough should be added to bind the rubbed in mixture into lumps. The lumps are gently pressed together so that the pastry just holds its shape. It should not be sticky.

Sweet short crust or richer pastry for making flans may be bound with egg yolk instead of, or as well as, a little water. Egg yolk contains a high proportion of fat so the resulting pastry will be very short. Adding sugar to pastry also tends to give a short and crumbly texture. Some rich pastry is made very short by adding extra fat, usually butter, to give a good flavour as well as a short texture.

ADDING LIQUID TO PUFF PASTRY OR FLAKY PASTRY

The dough for this type of pastry has only a small proportion of the fat rubbed in, with the majority of the fat incorporated by rolling it with the pastry. A little extra liquid is added to make a dough that is just slightly sticky. This type of dough holds the fat which is added in lumps or a block during rolling. The resulting pastry is not short; it is crisp and it forms distinct layers. Puff pastry is lighter and has more layers than flaky pastry.

The layers in puff and flaky pastry trap air to make the pastry rise during cooking. A strengthening substance called 'gluten' is naturally present in flour; this is developed by rolling the pastry. The process of rolling and folding actually serves to toughen the basic dough. Adding the fat each time the pastry is rolled means that the dough does not form into a solid mass but retains very fine layers. The air trapped between these layers expands as the dough is heated and so the pastry rises. Because the dough itself is toughened by the gluten, the layers set and give the finished pastry its characteristic crisp texture.

ROLLING OUT

Whatever type of pastry you are handling, you should always roll it out very lightly. Use a very light dusting of flour on the work surface. There should be just enough to prevent the pastry from sticking; short pastries usually require less than puff or flaky pastries. Too much flour at this stage may spoil the balance of ingredients.

Never turn pastry over during rolling. The pastry should be lifted occasionally and turned round to prevent it sticking to the surface. Push the rolling pin away from you in short, quick strokes. Keep the rolling pin lightly dusted with flour.

When rolling out pastry, try to establish the shape as soon as you begin. For example, if you are lining a round flan dish start with a ball of pastry which is flattened into a roughly circular shape. If you want to end up with an oblong sheet of pastry, form the pastry into an oblong lump and flatten it slightly before rolling it.

LIFTING ROLLED-OUT PASTRY

To lift a sheet of pastry, dust the rolling pin lightly with flour and place it in the middle of the pastry. Fold half the pastry over it, then use the rolling pin to lift the pastry into position.

LINING A FLAN TIN OR DISH

Roll the pastry out to a size that wil cover the base and come up the sides of the dish with a little extra to spare. Lift the pastry on the rolling pin, then lower it loosely over the tin or dish.

Quickly work around the dish, lifting the edge of the pastry with one hand and pressing it down into the corner of the dish with the forefinger and knuckle of the other hand. When the pastry is pressed neatly all around the base of the dish, press the excess around the edge of the dish so that it falls backwards slightly.

Roll the rolling pin across the top of the dish to trim off excess pastry. If you are lining a tin its edge will cut off the pastry; if using a dish you will have to pull away the excess pastry edges gently.

BAKING BLIND

Pastry cases that are cooked and cooled before they are filled have a sheet of greaseproof paper and baking beans placed in them to prevent the base of the pastry from puffing up. This is known as baking blind. The paper and baking beans are usually removed once the pastry has

cooked enough to set, and the pastry case returned to the oven to allow it to brown slightly.

In some recipes, the pastry case is partially baked before it is filled, and the cooking is completed with the filling. The technique of baking blind would be used for this preliminary baking of the pastry case.

Clear instructions are given in individual recipes. Ceramic baking beans may be purchased for baking blind, or ordinary dried peas or beans may be used. These are sprinkled over the greaseproof paper to weight the pastry slightly. Dried peas or beans used for this purpose may be cooled and stored in an airtight container and used over and over again. However, they may not be cooked to be eaten in another recipe.

MAKING TURNOVERS

Turnovers may be cut in circles or squares. The size to which the pastry should be rolled depends on the quantities given in the recipe.

Use a saucer or plate to mark out circles; small turnovers are made by using large round biscuit cutters. When using a saucer or plate,

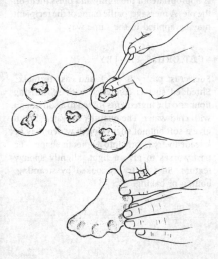

place it on the pastry and cut around it with a small pointed knife.

Put the filling on one half of the pastry. Dampen all around the pastry edge, then fold the pastry over the filling. Press the pastry edges together well to seal in the filling and to give a neat semi-circular turnover.

To make triangular turnovers, roll out the pastry into a large square. Use a large, clean ruler and a small, pointed knife to trim off the pastry edges.

Cut the pastry into four squares of equal size.

Place some filling on one half of each pastry square, in a corner, and dampen the edges.

Fold the corner of pastry opposite the filling over to enclose it completely and to make a neat triangle. Press the edges together to seal in the filling.

PASTRY PIES

Roll out the pastry about 5 cm/2 inches larger than the top of the dish. Cut off a strip from the edge of the pastry. Dampen the edge of the dish and press the strip of pastry on to it.

Fill the dish, dampen the pastry edge and lift the pastry lid over the top.

Press the edges of the pastry to seal in the filling. Holding the pie dish slightly raised in one hand, use a sharp knife to trim all around the edge of the dish. Keep the knife pointing outwards so that only the excess pastry is trimmed off.

KNOCKING UP

Knocking up is the term used for neatly sealing the pastry edges together. Press down and outwards on the pastry edge with the knuckle and forefinger of one hand, at the same time knocking the pastry edge inwards with the blunt edge of a round-bladed knife.

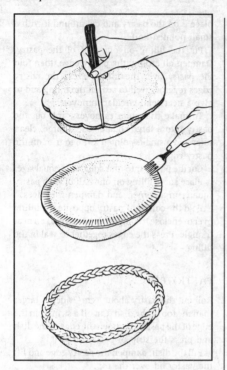

SCALLOPED EDGES

The traditional edge for a sweet pie is small scallops (large ones are used for savoury pies). Use the blunt edge of a knife to pull the pastry inwards as you push the edge out towards the rim of the dish with the finger of your other hand.

FORKED EDGE

A simple edging technique is to press all around the pastry with a fork. However, the edge does sometimes tend to become slightly too brown if the pastry is pressed very thin.

PLAITED EDGE

Re-roll leftover pastry and cut out three long, thin strips. Plait these together all around the edge of the pie.

DECORATIONS USING CUTTERS

Use small cocktail cutters to cut out pastry shapes. Dampen these and overlap them around the edge of the pie.

PASTRY LEAVES

Roll out a strip of pastry – the wider the strip, the longer the leaves – and cut it into diamond shapes. Mark veins on the leaves and pinch one end of each into a stalk.

IMAGINATIVE DESIGNS

Roll out pastry trimmings and cut out apples, pears, cherries or strawberry shapes to decorate the top of the pie. Dampen the pastry to keep the decorations in place. Alternatively, cut out letters to spell 'apple', 'pear' or whichever fruit is appropriate for the filling and press them on the pie. A message, or the name of the recipient may be applied in the same way.

SUET CRUST PASTRY

Suet crust pastry is quick and easy to make. Shredded suet is combined with self-raising flour and the ingredients mixed to a soft dough with cold water. The quantity of water should give a soft but not sticky dough which may be kneaded very lightly into a smooth shape. The pastry rises to give a light, slightly spongy texture. Suet pastry is cooked by steaming, boiling or baking.

CHOUX PASTRY

Although many people shy away from making choux pastry, it is not difficult. However, it is important that all the ingredients are accurately measured and that a few rules are observed.

The water and fat must be heated together gently until the fat melts, and the mixture brought to the boil as quickly as possible. Do not bring the water to the boil before the fat melts.

The flour must be tipped into the liquid all at once, the pan removed from the heat and the mixture stirred to make a smooth paste that comes away from the sides of the pan in a clean ball. Do not beat the mixture at this stage or it will become greasy. If the mixture is too wet put the pan back on the heat and stir gently until the paste comes away from the sides of the pan. This paste must be cooled slightly before the eggs are added.

Lastly, eggs are beaten into the paste. At this stage the mixture should be thoroughly beaten until it is smooth and glossy. The paste should be soft enough to pipe but it should not be runny. Use the choux pastry at once.

FILO PASTRY

This Greek pastry contains little fat. It is made with a strong flour. It is available both chilled and frozen, ready rolled in very thin sheets.

Two or three sheets are layered together before they are wrapped around a filling. Each sheet is brushed with melted butter. The pastry is very delicate to handle as it rapidly becomes brittle once unpacked. Always keep the pastry covered with cling film or under dampened tea-towels when you are not working with it as it dries rapidly if exposed to the air. Make sure the work surface is perfectly dry before unrolling the pastry. Any dampness will cause the pastry to stick, soften and break up.

TIPS FOR SUCCESS WITH PASTRY

- Work in a cool place; keep hands, utensils and all ingredients cool.
- Weigh and measure all ingredients accurately.
- Handle pastry as lightly as possible, and work as quickly as you can, at all stages.
- Use the minimum amount of flour for rolling out.
- Chill short crust, flaky and puff pastry for 20-30 minutes before rolling it out.
- Chill finished short crust, puff or flaky pastry goods for 15 minutes before baking.

SOME COMMON FAULTS WITH PASTRY AND HOW TO AVOID THEM

Short Crust Pastry   (or similar pastries)

Hard, tough pastry
- Too little fat used
- Too much liquid added
- Pastry handled too much or too heavily
- Too much flour used for rolling out

Grainy, flaky or blistered pastry
- Fat not rubbed in sufficiently
- Water not mixed in well
- Pastry rolled out twice
- Too much flour used for rolling

Pastry too short, very crumbly (collapses)
- Too much fat used
- Fat overworked into flour
- Too little liquid used

Puff or Flaky Pastry

Pastry Hard and Tough
- Warm fat used
- Too much water used
- Dough overkneaded
- Oven temperature too low during cooking

Unevenly Risen
- Fat not mixed in evenly during rolling
- Unevenly folded and rolled
- Pastry not chilled before use

Pastry flat, not light
- Warm fat used
- Dough not folded and rolled sufficiently

Soggy Pastry with a Hard Crust
- Oven too hot; pastry browned and hardened before it had time to rise

Suet Crust Pastry

Hard and Tough
- Too much water added
- Cooked in a low oven for too long

Solid, Lumpy Pastry
- Plain flour used in a recipe that stipulated self-raising flour or plain flour plus a raising agent
- Pastry cooked too quickly (suet has not melted)
- Pastry has got wet during steaming
- Home-grated suet was lumpy

HOT WATER CRUST PASTRY

By comparison with other pastries, hot water crust is a heavy dough. Plain flour is bound to a dough with a mixture of water and lard, heated together until boiling.

Hot water crust pastry should be mixed, then lightly kneaded until smooth. If it is over-worked it becomes greasy. Once mixed, the pastry should be kept warm in a bowl placed over hot (not simmering) water. To prevent the surface from drying, the dough should be closely covered with a polythene bag.

Hot water crust pastry is usually used for moulding pies, both large and small. When hot it is malleable and the surface of the dough is easily smoothed. Also, while hot the edges of the dough seal together easily and they may be pinched into a neat border.

As the pastry cools it becomes more difficult to manage and tends to crack on the surface. When moulding pie cases around the outside of a container, the pastry has to be cooled before it may be filled and covered; during this time the pastry for the lid should be kept just warm over hot water. The method which gives a better finish is to line a mould with pastry, then fill and cover it at once.

If the sides of a mould are removed so that the pastry may brown, it is important to work quickly once the mould is not supporting the pie, otherwise the soft pastry may collapse. Before removing the sides of the mould, have beaten egg ready to brush the pastry. Brush the pastry quickly and put the pie back into the oven. The egg helps to strengthen and seal the pastry quickly.

If the sides of a moulded pie begin to bulge, quickly wrap a double-thick band of foil around the pie, placing it halfway up the depth. Return the pie to the oven until the pastry sets.

SHORT CRUST PASTRY

225 g/8 oz plain flour
2.5 ml/½ tsp salt
100 g/4 oz margarine (or half butter, half lard)
flour for rolling out

Sift the flour and salt into a bowl, then rub in the margarine until the mixture resembles fine breadcrumbs. Add enough cold water to make a stiff dough.

Press the dough together with your fingertips. If time permits, wrap in greaseproof paper and rest in the refrigerator for 30 minutes. To use, roll out on a lightly floured surface.

MAKES ABOUT 225 G/8 OZ

VARIATION

Wholemeal Short Crust Pastry   Although wholemeal flour may be used on its own, this does tend to create a rather chewy pastry. Using 100 g/4 oz each of plain and wholemeal flour gives a very satisfactory result.

COMMON SWEET SHORT CRUST

This old-fashioned sweet pastry is firm, not crumbly – a sweet equivalent of hot water crust. It may be used as a topping for fruit pies.

225 g/8 oz plain flour
45 g/1½ oz butter
25 g/1 oz caster sugar
150 ml/¼ pint milk

Put the flour into a bowl. Rub in the butter until the mixture resembles fine breadcrumbs, then stir in the sugar.

Bring the milk to the boil in a small saucepan. Add the boiling milk to the flour mixture and knead until smooth. Use at once by rolling out thinly on a lightly floured surface.

MAKES ABOUT 350G/12OZ

BUTTER CRUST PASTRY

This excellent pastry forms crisp layers when cooked. It does not rise as high as puff or flaky pastry but it has a pleasing, filo-like texture to the separate flakes. It is ideal for topping savoury or sweet pies; for pasties or small items like sausage rolls and for plaits or slices.

225 g/8 oz plain flour, plus extra for rolling and dredging
75 g/3 oz butter

Put the flour in a bowl. Add sufficient water (about 150 ml/¼ pint) to make a smooth, soft dough, see Mrs Beeton's Tip.

Roll out the dough on a lightly floured surface into an oblong measuring 30 × 15 cm/12 × 6 inches. Mark roughly into thirds. Dot the middle third with the butter and dredge the fat lightly with flour.

Fold top and bottom thirds over the fat to enclose it completely, then roll it out again. If time permits, wrap in polythene and rest in the refrigerator for 15 minutes. Repeat the rolling and folding three times, so that the butter is evenly distributed. To use, roll out on a lightly floured surface.

MAKES ABOUT 350G/12OZ

> **MRS BEETON'S TIP**
>
> Use a round-bladed knife to mix the flour with the water.

PATE SUCREE

This sweet pastry may be used for flans, tarts and tartlets.

200 g/7 oz plain flour
1.25 ml/¼ tsp salt
90 g/3½ oz butter
50 g/2 oz caster sugar
1 egg yolk
flour for rolling out

Sift the flour and salt into a bowl. Cut the butter into small pieces and rub into the flour until the mixture resembles fine breadcrumbs. Mix in the sugar, then the egg yolk, and add enough cold water to make a stiff dough. Roll out on a lightly floured surface and use as required.

MAKES ABOUT 350G/12OZ

PUFF PASTRY

225 g/8 oz plain flour
1.25 ml/¼ tsp salt
225 g/8 oz butter, chilled
5 ml/1 tsp lemon juice
flour for rolling out

Sift the flour and salt into a bowl. Rub in 50 g/2 oz of the butter. Add the lemon juice and enough cold water to mix the ingredients to a smooth, fairly soft dough. The mixture should take about 125 ml/4 fl oz water but this must be added by the spoonful to avoid making the dough too wet. Wrap the dough in cling film and chill briefly.

Shape the remaining butter into a rectangle measuring about 10 × 7.5 cm/4 × 3 inches, then chill again. On a lightly floured surface, roll out the dough into an oblong measuring about 25 × 15 cm/10 × 6 inches, or slightly smaller. Place the butter in the middle of the dough, then fold the bottom third over it and fold the top third down to enclose the butter completely. The technique is illustrated on page 537, in relation to Mille-feuille Gâteau.

Press the edges of the dough together with the rolling pin. Give the dough a quarter turn in a clockwise direction. Roll out the dough into an oblong as before, fold it again, then wrap in cling film. Chill for 30 minutes. Roll and fold the pastry 6 times in all, chilling well each time. To remember the number of rollings, mark dents in the dough with your fingertips – 1 dent after the first rolling, 2 after the second and so on.

After the process of rolling and folding is complete, chill the pastry again before using it as required.

MAKES ABOUT 450 G/1 LB

ROUGH PUFF PASTRY

A slightly easier version of puff pastry; all the fat must be well chilled for success. For best results, chill the bowl of flour too; always make sure your hands are very cold by holding them under cold running water before handling the dough.

225 g/8 oz plain flour
1.25 ml/¼ tsp salt
175 g/6 oz butter, cut in chunks and chilled
5 ml/1 tsp lemon juice
flour for rolling out

Sift the flour and salt into a bowl. Add the butter and mix in lightly using a round-bladed knife. Mix in the lemon juice and enough ice-cold water to make a soft dough. The mixture should take about 125 ml/4 fl oz (or very slightly more) but add the water a spoonful at a time to avoid making the dough too wet. The dough should be soft and very lumpy.

On a lightly floured surface, roll out the dough into an oblong, keeping the corners square. Mark the oblong of dough into thirds, then fold and roll it as for flaky pastry (opposite). Repeat the process four times in all, chilling the dough between each rolling or as necessary.

The rolled dough should be smooth. Wrap it in cling film and chill well before rolling it out to use as required.

MAKES ABOUT 450 G/1 LB

FLAKY PASTRY

Flaky pastry does not have as many layers as puff pastry. It contains less fat to flour and the dough is rolled and folded fewer times.

225 g/8 oz plain flour
1.25 ml/¼ tsp salt
175 g/6 oz butter or 75 g/3 oz each butter and lard, chilled
5 ml/1 tsp lemon juice
flour for rolling out

Sift the flour and salt into a bowl. If using butter and lard, mix them together roughly. Rub in a quarter of the fat, keeping the remaining fat chilled. Stir in the lemon juice and enough cold water to mix the ingredients to a soft dough. The mixture should take about 125 ml/4 fl oz water but this should be added by the spoonful to avoid making the dough too wet.

On a lightly floured surface, roll out the dough into an oblong measuring about 25 × 15 cm/ 10 × 6 inches. Mark the dough into thirds. Cut the fat into 3 equal portions. Dot one portion of fat over the top two-thirds of the dough, in neat lumps.

Fold the bottom third of the dough up over the middle portion, then fold the top third down so that the lumps of fat are enclosed completely. Press the edges of the dough together with the rolling pin. Give the dough a quarter turn in a clockwise direction, then roll out as before.

Repeat the process of dotting the dough with fat, folding and rolling it, twice more. Chill the dough briefly between each rolling. Finally, fold and roll the pastry once more, without any fat, then chill again before using it as required.

MAKES ABOUT 450 G/1 LB

SUET CRUST PASTRY

200 g/7 oz plain flour
5 ml/1 tsp baking powder
pinch of salt
75 g/3 oz shredded suet
flour for rolling out

Sift the flour, baking powder and salt into a mixing bowl. Stir in the suet, then add enough cold water (about 150-175 ml/5-6 fl oz) to make a soft but not sticky dough. Use at once by rolling out on a lightly floured surface.

MAKES 200 G/7 OZ

CHOUX PASTRY

100 g/4 oz plain flour
50 g/2 oz butter or margarine
pinch of salt
2 whole eggs plus 1 yolk

Sift the flour on to a sheet of greaseproof paper. Put 250 ml/8 fl oz water in a saucepan and add the butter or margarine with the salt. Heat gently until the fat melts.

When the fat has melted, bring the liquid rapidly to the boil, then add all the flour at once. Immediately remove the pan from the heat and stir the flour into the liquid to make a smooth paste which leaves the sides of the pan clean. Set aside to cool slightly.

Add the egg yolk and beat well. Add the whole eggs, one at a time, beating well after each addition. Continue beating until the paste is very glossy. Use at once.

MAKES ABOUT 175 G/6 OZ

HOT WATER CRUST PASTRY

This pastry is used for pork, veal and ham, and raised game pies. It must be moulded while still warm.

200 g/7 oz plain flour
2.5 ml/½ tsp salt
75 g/3 oz lard
100 ml/3½ fl oz milk or water

Sift the flour and salt into a warm bowl and make a well in the centre. Keep the bowl in a warm place.

Meanwhile, heat the lard and milk or water until boiling. Add the hot mixture to the flour, mixing well with a wooden spoon until the pastry is cool enough to knead with the hands. Knead thoroughly and mould as required.

Bake at 220°C/425°F/gas 7 until the pastry is set, then reduce the oven temperature to 180°C/350°F/gas 4 until fully baked.

MAKES 350G/12OZ

TO MOULD A RAISED PIE

Hot Water Crust Pastry (above)
fat for greasing
flour

Use a jar, round cake tin or similar container, as a mould: grease and flour the sides and base of the mould and invert it.

Reserve a quarter of the warm pastry for the lid and leave in the bowl in a warm place, covered with a greased polythene bag.

Roll out the remainder to about 5 mm/¼ inch thick, in a round or oval shape. Lay the pastry over the mould, then ease the pastry round the sides. Take care not to pull the pastry and make sure that the sides and base are of an even thickness. Leave to cool.

When cold, remove the pastry case from the mould and put in the filling. Roll out the pastry reserved for the lid, dampen the rim of the case, put on the lid, pressing the edges firmly together. Tie 3 or 4 folds of greaseproof paper round the pie to hold it in shape during baking and to prevent it from becoming too brown.

MAKES ONE 13 CM/5 INCH PIE

Using a Raised Pie Mould Decorative pie moulds may be purchased from cookshops. Usually oval in shape, they range in size from those which provide up to 6 servings to others which make pies large enough to feed 40 people.

The two sides of the mould fit into a base and they are secured with clips. The sides should be secured and the inside of the mould should be well greased. The pastry should be rolled out to about two-thirds of the required size.

Lift the pastry into the mould and secure its edge just below the rim of the mould. Use your fingers to press the pastry into the mould, easing it upwards at the same time so that it comes above the rim of the mould when the lining is complete. The pie may be filled at once.

The sides of the mould should be removed about 15-30 minutes before the end of the cooking time. Brush the pastry with beaten egg immediately and return the pie to the oven promptly to prevent the sides from collapsing.

RAISED VEAL PIE

If preferred, these ingredients can be made into 6 individual pies. The eggs should be sliced and divided between the smaller pies.

Hot Water Crust Pastry (opposite), using
   400 g/14 oz flour
400 g/14 oz pie veal
400 g/14 oz lean pork
25 g/1 oz plain flour
7.5 ml/1½ tsp salt
1.25 ml/¼ tsp ground pepper
3 hard-boiled eggs
beaten egg for glazing
about 125 ml/4 fl oz well-flavoured, cooled
   and jellied stock or canned consommé

Set the oven at 230°C/450°F/gas 8. Line a 20 cm/8 inch round pie mould with three-quarters of the pastry, or use a round cake tin to mould the pie as described opposite. Use the remaining quarter for the lid.

Cut the meat into small pieces, removing any gristle or fat. Season the flour with the salt and pepper, then toss the pieces of meat in it. Put half the meat into the pastry case and put in the whole eggs. Add the remaining meat and 30 ml/2 tbsp water. Put on the lid and brush with beaten egg. Make a hole in the centre to allow steam to escape. Bake for 15 minutes, then reduce the oven temperature to 140°C/275°F/gas 1. Continue baking for 2½ hours. Remove the greaseproof paper or mould for the last 30 minutes of the cooking time and brush the top and sides of the pastry with beaten egg.

Heat the stock or consommé until melted. When the pie is cooked, pour it through the hole in the lid using a funnel until the pie is full. Leave to cool.

SERVES SIX

RAISED PORK PIES

about 400 g/14 oz pork bones
1 small onion, finely chopped
salt and pepper
300 ml/½ pint stock or cold water
Hot Water Crust Pastry (opposite), using
   400 g/14 oz flour
500 g/18 oz lean pork, minced
1.25 ml/¼ tsp dried sage
beaten egg for glazing

Simmer the pork bones, onion, salt, pepper and stock or water, covered, for 2 hours. Strain and cool. Make one 15 cm/6 inch pie (as described left) or divide three-quarters of the pastry into 6 portions. Mould each piece using a jam jar, as described opposite, keeping the pastry about 5 mm/¼ inch thick. Use the remainder for the lids. Set the oven at 220°C/425°F/gas 7.

Season the pork with salt, pepper and sage. Divide between the prepared pie case or cases and add 10 ml/2 tsp of the jellied stock to each. Put on the lids, brush with beaten egg, and make holes in the centres.

Bake for 15 minutes, then reduce the oven temperature to 180°C/350°F/gas 4. Continue baking for 45 minutes (1 hour for a large pie). Remove the greaseproof paper for the last 30 minutes and brush the top and sides of the pastry with egg.

When cooked, remove from the oven and leave to cool. Warm the remainder of the jellied stock. Using a funnel pour the stock through the hole in the pastry lids until the pies are full. Leave to cool.

SERVES SIX

VEGETABLE FLAN

200 g/7 oz plain flour
100 g/4 oz butter or margarine
salt and pepper
1 onion, chopped
50 g/2 oz button mushrooms, thinly sliced
250 ml/8 fl oz milk
100 g/4 oz Smoked Applewood cheese (or
    other hard cheese to taste)
2 eggs, separated
450 g/1 lb cauliflower florets, lightly cooked
30 ml/2 tbsp fine dried white breadcrumbs

Set the oven at 200°C/400°F/gas 6. Place 175 g/6 oz of the flour in a bowl and rub in 75 g/3 oz of the butter or margarine. Add enough cold water to bind the mixture to a short dough – about 30 ml/2 tbsp. Roll out the dough and use to line a 25 cm/10 inch flan tin or dish.

Prick the pastry all over, line with greaseproof paper and sprinkle with dried peas or baking beans. Bake 'blind' for 15 minutes. Remove the beans and paper and continue to cook for a further 15 minutes, until the pastry is cooked.

Melt the remaining butter or margarine in a small saucepan. Add the onion and mushrooms and cook, stirring, over medium heat until the onion is soft and the mushrooms well cooked – about 15 minutes. Add the remaining flour and stir well. Gradually stir in the milk and bring to the boil, stirring all the time, to make a smooth, thick sauce. Stir in the cheese and salt and pepper to taste. Remove from the heat and beat in the egg yolks. Whisk the egg whites until stiff, then fold them into the sauce.

Arrange the cauliflower evenly over the base of the pastry case, then spoon the sauce over, teasing it down between the florets. Sprinkle with the breadcrumbs and bake for about 15 minutes, until set and golden brown on top. Serve at once.

SERVES SIX TO EIGHT

QUICHE LORRAINE

225 g/8 oz rindless streaky bacon rashers
3 eggs
300 ml/½ pint single cream
2.5 ml/½ tsp salt
grinding of black pepper
pinch of grated nutmeg
25 g/1 oz butter, diced

SHORT CRUST PASTRY
100 g/4 oz plain flour
2.5 ml/½ tsp salt
50 g/2 oz margarine (or half butter, half lard)
flour for rolling out

Set the oven at 200°C/400°F/gas 6. To make the pastry, sift the flour and salt into a bowl, then rub in the margarine until the mixture resembles fine breadcrumbs. Add enough cold water to make a stiff dough. Press the dough together.

Roll out the pastry on a lightly floured surface and use to line an 18 cm/7 inch flan tin or ring placed on a baking sheet. Line the pastry with greaseproof paper and fill with baking beans. Bake 'blind' for 20 minutes until the rim of the pastry is slightly browned but the base still soft. Remove the paper and beans. Reduce the oven temperature to 190°C/375°F/gas 5.

Cut the bacon in 2 cm × 5 mm/¾ × ¼ inch strips. Dry fry for a few minutes. Drain and scatter the strips over the pastry base. Press in lightly. Beat the eggs, cream, salt, pepper and nutmeg. Pour the mixture into the pastry case and dot with butter. Bake for 30 minutes. Serve at once.

SERVES FOUR TO SIX

CORNISH PASTIES

FILLING
1 large or 2 small potatoes
1 small turnip
1 onion, chopped
salt and pepper
300 g/11 oz lean chuck steak, finely diced

PASTRY
500 g/18 oz plain flour
5 ml/1 tsp salt
150 g/5 oz lard
60 ml/4 tbsp shredded suet
flour for rolling out
beaten egg for glazing

Set the oven at 230°C/450°F/gas 8. To make the pastry, sift the flour and salt into a bowl. Rub in the lard, then mix in the suet. Moisten with enough cold water to make a stiff dough. Roll out on a lightly floured surface and cut into eight 16 cm/6½ inch rounds.

To make the filling, dice the potatoes and turnip, then mix with the onion and add salt and pepper to taste. Add the meat and 30 ml/2 tbsp water, and mix well. Divide between the pastry rounds, placing a line of mixture across the centre of each round.

Dampen the edges of each pastry round. Lift them to meet over the filling. Pinch together to seal, then flute the edges. Make small slits in both sides of each pasty near the top. Place the pasties on a baking sheet and brush with egg. Bake for 10 minutes, then lower the oven temperature to 180°C/350°F/gas 4. Continue baking for a further 45 minutes, or until the meat is tender when pierced by a thin, heated skewer through the top of a pasty.

MAKES EIGHT

LEEK TURNOVERS

These pasties make an ideal vegetarian snack.

10 large leeks, trimmed and washed
5 ml/1 tsp salt
5 ml/1 tsp lemon juice
5 ml/1 tsp sugar
125 ml/4 fl oz single cream
salt and pepper
beaten egg for glazing

SHORT CRUST PASTRY
450 g/1 lb plain flour
5 ml/1 tsp baking powder
100 g/4 oz lard
100 g/4 oz margarine
flour for rolling out

Set the oven at 200°C/400°F/gas 6. Remove the green part of the leeks and slice the white part only into 2 cm/¾ inch pieces. Put into a saucepan with just enough boiling water to cover. Add the salt, lemon juice and sugar. Cook for 5 minutes or until just tender. Drain the leeks and leave to cool.

To make the pastry, sift the flour, baking powder and a pinch of salt into a bowl. Rub in the lard and margarine. Mix to a stiff dough with cold water.

Roll out the pastry on a lightly floured surface to 1 cm/½ inch thick and cut into 10 oblong shapes, about 15 × 10 cm/6 × 4 inches. Lay the pieces of leek along the middle of each pastry piece. Moisten with a little cream and add salt and pepper to taste. Dampen the edges of the pastry and lift them to meet over the filling. Pinch and flute the edges to seal.

Place the pasties on a baking sheet and brush with egg. Bake for 25-30 minutes.

MAKES TEN

TRADITIONAL APPLE PIE

675 g/1½ lb cooking apples
100 g/4 oz sugar
6 cloves
caster sugar for dredging

SHORT CRUST PASTRY
350 g/12 oz plain flour
4 ml/¾ tsp salt
175 g/6 oz margarine (or half butter, half lard)
flour for rolling out

Set the oven at 200°C/400°F/gas 6. To make the pastry, sift the flour and salt into a bowl, then rub in the margarine until the mixture resembles fine breadcrumbs. Add enough cold water to make a stiff dough. Press the dough together with your fingertips.

Roll out the pastry on a lightly floured surface and use just over half to line a 750 ml/1¼ pint pie dish. Peel, core and slice the apples. Place half in the pastry-lined dish, then add the sugar and cloves. Pile the remaining apples on top, cover with the remaining pastry and seal the edges. Brush the pastry with cold water and dredge with caster sugar.

Bake for 20 minutes, then lower the oven temperature to 180°C/350°F/gas 4 and bake for 20 minutes more. The pastry should be golden brown. Dredge with more caster sugar and serve hot or cold.

SERVES SIX

VARIATIONS

Apricot Pie Use two 375 g/15 oz cans apricots, drained, instead of apples. Omit the sugar and cloves.

Blackberry and Apple Pie Use half blackberries and half apples and replace the cloves with 2.5 ml/½ tsp grated lemon rind.

Damson Pie Use damsons instead of apples, increase the sugar to 150 g/5 oz and omit the cloves.

Gooseberry Pie Use cleaned, topped and tailed gooseberries instead of apples. Omit the cloves.

Redcurrant and Raspberry Pie This is a winning combination. Use 450 g/1 lb redcurrants and 225 g/8 oz raspberries instead of apples. Reduce the sugar to 30 ml/2 tbsp and omit the cloves.

Rhubarb Pie Use rhubarb cut into 2 cm/¾ inch lengths instead of apples. Increase the sugar to 150 g/5 oz.

 FREEZER TIP

The pie may be frozen cooked or uncooked. If cooked, cool completely, wrap in foil and overwrap in a polythene bag. Wrap an uncooked pie in the same way. Reheat or cook the unwrapped pie from frozen. A cooked pie will require 20 minutes at 200°C/400°F/gas 6, followed by 15–20 minutes at 180°C/350°F/gas 4. For an uncooked pie, bake at 200°C/400°F/gas 6 for 30 minutes, then at 190°C/375°F/gas 5 for about a further 40 minutes. The exact timing will depend on the depth of the pie dish. Before transferring the pie from freezer to oven, make sure that the dish will withstand the sudden change in temperature.

MINCE PIES

Festive mince pies can also be made using flaky, rough puff or puff pastry with mouthwatering results. If using any of these pastries you will require 200 g/7 oz flour.

350 g/12 oz mincemeat
25 g/1 oz icing or caster sugar for dredging

SHORT CRUST PASTRY
300 g/10 oz plain flour
5 ml/1 tsp salt
150 g/5 oz margarine (or half butter, half lard)
flour for rolling out

Set the oven at 200°C/400°F/gas 6. To make the pastry, sift the flour and salt into a bowl, then rub in the margarine until the mixture resembles fine breadcrumbs. Add enough cold water to make a stiff dough. Press the dough together with your fingertips.

Roll out the pastry on a lightly floured surface and use just over half of it to line twelve 7.5 cm/3 inch patty tins. Cut out 12 lids from the rest of the pastry. If liked, make holly leaf decorations from the pastry trimmings.

Place a spoonful of mincemeat in each pastry case. Dampen the edges of the cases and cover with the pastry lids. Seal the edges well. Brush the tops with water and add any pastry decorations. Dredge with the sugar. Make 2 small cuts in the top of each pie. Bake for 15-20 minutes or until golden brown.

MAKES TWELVE

LEMON TARTLETS

50 g/2 oz butter
50 g/2 oz sugar
1 egg, beaten
grated rind and juice of ½ lemon
10 ml/2 tsp icing sugar

SHORT CRUST PASTRY
100 g/4 oz plain flour
1.25 ml/¼ tsp salt
50 g/2 oz margarine (or half butter, half lard)
flour for rolling out

Set the oven at 200°C/400°F/gas 6. To make the pastry, sift the flour and salt into a bowl, then rub in the margarine until the mixture resembles fine breadcrumbs. Add enough cold water to make a stiff dough. Press the dough together with your fingertips. Roll out and use to line twelve 7.5 cm/3 inch patty tins.

Cream the butter and sugar in a bowl until pale and fluffy. Beat in the egg. Add the lemon rind and juice. Fill the pastry cases with the mixture.

Bake for 15-20 minutes until set. Leave to cool. Sift the icing sugar over the tartlets.

MAKES TWELVE

PUMPKIN PIE

1 (425 g/15 oz) can pumpkin or 450 g/1 lb
  cooked mashed pumpkin
150 g/5 oz soft dark brown sugar
7.5 cm/1½ tsp cinnamon
2.5 ml/½ tsp salt
5 ml/1 tsp ground ginger
2.5 ml/½ tsp grated nutmeg
3 eggs
250 ml/8 fl oz milk

SHORT CRUST PASTRY
225 g/8 oz plain four
2.5 ml/½ tsp salt
100 g/4 oz margarine (or half butter, half
  lard)
flour for rolling out

Set the oven at 200°C/400°F/gas 6. To make the
pastry, sift the flour and salt into a bowl, then
rub in the margarine until the mixture resembles fine breadcrumbs. Add enough cold water
to make a stiff dough. Press the dough together
with your fingertips. Roll out on a lightly
floured surface and use to line a 25 cm/10 inch
pie plate. Chill in the refrigerator for 30
minutes.

In a large bowl, mix the pumpkin with the
sugar, cinnamon, salt, ginger and nutmeg. Beat
the eggs in a second bowl, add the milk and
mix well. Stir the egg mixture into the pumpkin mixture. Pour into the pastry case.

Bake for 15 minutes. Lower the temperature to
180°C/350°F/gas 4 and cook for a further
30–40 minutes, or until a knife inserted in the
centre of the pie comes out clean. Cool the pie
before serving.

SERVES SIX

SOUTHERN PECAN PIE

*Pecan nuts are oval and red-shelled when whole;
when shelled they resemble slim walnuts. Use
unbroken halves of pecan nuts in the filling
for this pie.*

50 g/2 oz butter
175 g/6 oz soft light brown sugar
3 eggs
225 g/8 oz shelled pecan nuts
150 g/5 oz golden syrup
15 ml/1 tbsp dark rum
2.5 ml/½ tsp salt
double cream, to serve

SHORT CRUST PASTRY
225 g/8 oz plain flour
2.5 ml/½ tsp salt
100 g/4 oz margarine (or half butter, half
  lard)
flour for rolling out

Set the oven at 200°C/400°F/gas 6. To make the
pastry, sift the flour and salt into a bowl, then
rub in the margarine until the mixture resembles fine breadcrumbs. Add enough cold water
to make a stiff dough. Press the dough together
with your fingertips. Roll out the pastry on a
lightly floured surface and use to line a
25 cm/10 inch pie plate. Prick the base well.

Bake the pie case for 5 minutes, then cool.
Lower the oven temperature to 180°C/350°F/
gas 4.

In a mixing bowl, cream the butter with the
sugar until light. Beat in the eggs, one at a time.
Stir in the rest of the ingredients. Fill the pastry
case with the mixture and bake for about 40
minutes or until a knife inserted in the centre
comes out clean. Serve warm or cold, with
double cream.

SERVES SIX

MINCEMEAT MERINGUE PIE

50 g/2 oz soft white breadcrumbs
30 ml/2 tbsp granulated sugar
2 eggs, separated
375 ml/13 fl oz milk
15 ml/1 tbsp butter
2.5 ml/½ tsp vanilla essence
225 g/8 oz mincemeat
75 g/3 oz caster sugar

SHORT CRUST PASTRY
100 g/4 oz plain flour
2.5 ml/½ tsp salt
50 g/2 oz margarine (or half butter, half lard)
flour for rolling out

Set the oven at 200°C/400°F/gas 6. To make the pastry, sift the flour and salt into a bowl, then rub in the margarine until the mixture resembles fine breadcrumbs. Add enough cold water to make a stiff dough. Press the dough together with your fingertips.

Roll out the pastry on a lightly floured surface and use to line an 18 cm/7 inch flan tin or ring placed on a baking sheet. Line the pastry with greaseproof paper and fill with baking beans. Bake 'blind' for 10 minutes, then remove the paper and beans. Return to the oven for 5 minutes, then remove. Lower the oven temperature to 180°C/350°F/gas 4.

Combine the breadcrumbs, sugar and egg yolks in a bowl and mix well. Warm the milk and butter together in a saucepan until the butter has just melted, then stir slowly into the breadcrumb mixture. Mix well, then stir in the vanilla essence. Leave to stand for 5 minutes.

Pour the breadcrumb filling into the flan case and bake for 35–45 minutes or until the custard is firm. Remove from the oven.

Raise the oven temperature to 200°C/400°F/gas 6. Spread the mincemeat over the crumb custard. Whisk the egg whites in a clean, grease-free bowl until stiff, gradually whisking in about 50 g/2 oz of the caster sugar. Pile or spoon the meringue over the pie filling, covering both the mincemeat and the pastry edge completely. Sprinkle with the remaining sugar. Bake for 5–10 minutes until the meringue is golden. Serve at once, with single cream.

SERVES FOUR TO SIX

JAM TART

60–90 ml/4–6 tbsp firm jam
beaten egg for glazing

SHORT CRUST PASTRY
150 g/5 oz plain flour
2.5 ml/½ tsp salt
65 g/2½ oz margarine (or half butter, half lard)
flour for rolling out

Set the oven at 200°C/400°F/gas 6. To make the pastry, sift the flour and salt into a bowl, then rub in the margarine until the mixture resembles fine breadcrumbs. Add enough cold water to make a stiff dough. Press the dough together lightly.

Roll out the pastry on a lightly floured surface and use to line a 20 cm/8 inch pie plate. Decorate the edge with any trimmings. Fill with jam and glaze the uncovered pastry with beaten egg.

Bake for 15 minutes or until the pastry is cooked. Serve hot or cold.

SERVES SIX

CRANBERRY RAISIN PIE

225 g/8 oz cranberries
175 g/6 oz raisins
150 g/5 oz sugar
30 ml/2 tbsp plain flour
1.25 ml/¼ tsp salt
25 g/1 oz butter, diced

SHORT CRUST PASTRY
225 g/8 oz plain flour
2.5 ml/½ tsp salt
100 g/4 oz margarine (or half butter, half
   lard)
flour for rolling out

Set the oven at 200°C/400°F/gas 6. To make the pastry, sift the flour and salt into a bowl, then rub in the margarine until the mixture resembles fine breadcrumbs. Add enough cold water to make a stiff dough. Press the dough together with your fingertips. Roll out on a lightly floured surface and use two-thirds of the pastry to line a 23 cm/9 inch pie plate.

In a bowl, combine the cranberries and raisins with the sugar, flour and salt. Mix lightly, then spoon into the pastry case. Dot with the butter.

Roll out the remaining pastry into a rectangle and cut into five 1 cm/½ inch strips. Arrange the strips in a lattice on top of the pie. Bake for 10 minutes, then reduce the oven temperature to 180°C/350°F/gas 4 and bake for 30–40 minutes more.

SERVES SIX

 MRS BEETON'S TIP

When rolling out pastry, use as little flour as possible. Flour worked in at this stage toughens the pastry.

GLAZED APPLE DUMPLINGS

6 cooking apples
1.25 ml/¼ tsp cinnamon
50 g/2 oz soft light brown sugar
12 cloves
15 ml/1 tbsp milk
25 g/1 oz caster sugar

SHORT CRUST PASTRY
175 g/6 oz plain flour
1.25 ml/¼ tsp salt
75 g/3 oz margarine (or half butter, half lard)
flour for rolling out

Set the oven at 200°C/400°F/gas 6. To make the pastry, sift the flour and salt into a bowl, then rub in the margarine until the mixture resembles fine breadcrumbs. Add enough cold water to make a stiff dough. Press the dough together with your fingertips.

Divide the pastry into 6 portions. On a lightly floured surface roll out each portion to a round. Peel and core the apples and put one on each round of pastry. Mix the cinnamon and sugar together in a bowl and fill each apple cavity with some of the mixture. Press 2 cloves in the top of each apple. Work the pastry around each apple to enclose it, moisten the edges and press well together.

Place the dumplings on a baking sheet, brush with milk and dredge with caster sugar. Bake for 30–35 minutes or until the apples are tender. Serve with cream or custard.

SERVES FOUR

Meanwhile mix 50 g/2 oz of the caster sugar, the cornflour, plain flour and salt in a saucepan. Stir in 300 ml/½ pint water and bring to the boil, stirring.

Draw the pan off the heat and add the butter, lemon rind and juice. Put the egg yolks in a bowl, add a little of the cooked mixture, then add to the mixture in the pan. Beat well, replace over the heat and cook, stirring constantly for 2 minutes. Remove the pan from the heat and set aside to cool. Remove the pie from the oven and reduce the oven temperature to 180°C/350°F/gas 4.

In a clean, grease-free bowl, whisk the egg whites until stiff. Fold in the remaining sugar. Pour the lemon custard into the baked pastry case and cover the top with the meringue, making sure that it covers the top completely. Bake for 12–15 minutes until the meringue is lightly browned. Cool before cutting.

SERVES SIX

LEMON MERINGUE PIE

300 g/11 oz caster sugar
45 ml/3 tbsp cornflour
45 ml/3 tbsp plain flour
pinch of salt
30 ml/2 tbsp butter
grated rind and juice of 2 lemons
3 eggs, separated

SHORT CRUST PASTRY
175 g/6 oz plain flour
2.5 ml/½ tsp salt
75 g/3 oz margarine (or half butter, half lard)
flour for rolling out

Set the oven at 200°C/400°F/gas 6. To make the pastry, sift the flour and salt into a bowl, then rub in the margarine until the mixture resembles fine breadcrumbs. Add enough cold water to make a stiff dough. Press the dough together lightly.

Roll out the pastry on a lightly floured surface and use to line a 23 cm/9 inch pie plate. Line the pastry with greaseproof paper and fill with baking beans. Bake 'blind' for 15 minutes; remove paper and beans. Return to the oven for 5 minutes.

 MRS BEETON'S TIP

Meringue-topped pies are notoriously difficult to cut. It will simplify matters if you use a sharp knife which is dipped in warm water before each cut is made.

MRS BEETON'S BAKEWELL PUDDING

strawberry or apricot jam
50 g/2 oz butter
50 g/2 oz caster sugar
1 egg
50 g/2 oz ground almonds
50 g/2 oz fine cake crumbs
few drops of almond essence
icing sugar for dusting

SHORT CRUST PASTRY
100 g/4 oz plain flour
1.25 ml/¼ tsp salt
50 g/2 oz margarine (or half butter, half lard)
flour for rolling out

Set the oven at 200°C/400°F/gas 6. To make the pastry, sift the flour and salt into a bowl, then rub in the margarine until the mixture resembles fine breadcrumbs. Add enough cold water to make a stiff dough. Press the dough together.

Roll out the pastry on a lightly floured surface and use to line an 18 cm/7 inch flan tin or ring placed on a baking sheet. Spread a good layer of jam over the pastry base.

In a mixing bowl, cream the butter with the sugar until pale and fluffy. Beat in the egg, then add the almonds, cake crumbs and essence. Beat until well mixed. Pour into the flan case, on top of the jam.

Bake for 30 minutes or until the centre of the pudding is firm. Sprinkle with icing sugar and serve hot or cold.

SERVES FOUR TO FIVE

VARIATIONS

Bakewell Tart Make as above, but use raspberry jam and only 25 g/1 oz bread or cake crumbs and 25 g/1 oz ground almonds. Bake for 25 minutes.

Almond Tartlets Line twelve 7.5 cm/3 inch patty tins with the pastry. Replace the cake crumbs with an extra 50 g/2 oz ground almonds and the almond essence with 2.5 ml/½ tsp lemon juice. Bake for 12–18 minutes.

West Riding Pudding Line a 500 ml/17 oz dish with the pastry. Make as for Bakewell Pudding but substitute 75 g/3 oz plain flour and 2.5 ml/½ tsp baking powder for the cake crumbs and ground almonds. If the mixture seems stiff, add a little milk. Bake at 190°C/375°F/gas 5 for 1 hour. Serve hot or cold.

BANANA FLAN

1 whole egg, separated, plus 1 yolk
50 g/2 oz caster sugar
30 ml/2 tbsp plain flour
30 ml/2 tbsp cornflour
300 ml/½ pint milk
2.5 ml/½ tsp vanilla essence
3 bananas
30 ml/2 tbsp Apricot Glaze (page 766)

SHORT CRUST PASTRY
100 g/4 oz plain flour
1.25 ml/¼ tsp salt
50 g/2 oz margarine (or half butter, half lard)
flour for rolling out

Set the oven at 200°C/400°F/gas 6. To make the pastry, sift the flour and salt into a bowl, then rub in the margarine until the mixture resembles fine breadcrumbs. Add enough cold water to make a stiff dough. Press the dough together with your fingertips.

Roll out the pastry on a lightly floured surface and use to line a 20 cm/8 inch flan tin or ring placed on a baking sheet. Line the pastry with greaseproof paper and fill with baking beans.

Bake 'blind' for 20 minutes, then remove the paper and beans. Return to the oven for 5–7 minutes, then cool completely.

Make the filling. In a bowl, mix both egg yolks with the sugar. Beat until thick and pale in colour, then beat in the flours. Add enough of the milk to make a smooth paste. Pour the rest of the milk into a saucepan and bring to just below boiling point. Pour on to the yolk mixture, stirring constantly, then return the mixture to the pan. Cook over low heat, stirring, until the mixture boils and thickens. Remove from the heat.

Whisk the egg white in a clean, grease-free bowl until stiff. Fold it into the custard with the vanilla essence. Return to the heat and cook for a couple of minutes, then cool. Cover the surface of the custard with dampened greaseproof paper while cooling.

Spoon the cold custard into the flan case and top with sliced bananas. Glaze immediately with hot apricot glaze and leave to set. Serve the flan cold.

SERVES SIX

PEACH FLAN

350 g/12 oz peaches
5 ml/1 tsp lemon juice
25 g/1 oz sugar
5 ml/1 tsp arrowroot
whipped cream to decorate

SHORT CRUST PASTRY
100 g/4 oz plain flour
1.25 ml/¼ tsp salt
50 g/2 oz margarine (or half butter, half lard)
flour for rolling out

Set the oven at 200°C/400°F/gas 6. To make the pastry, sift the flour and salt into a bowl, then rub in the margarine until the mixture resembles fine breadcrumbs. Add enough cold water to make a stiff dough. Press the dough together with your fingertips.

Roll out the pastry on a lightly floured surface and use to line an 18 cm/7 inch flan tin or ring placed on a baking sheet. Line the pastry with greaseproof paper and fill with baking beans. Bake 'blind' for 20 minutes, then remove the paper and beans. Return to the oven for 5–7 minutes, then leave to cool.

Skin the peaches (see Mrs Beeton's Tip), then halve and slice, discarding the stones. Put the fruit in a saucepan with 45 ml/3 tbsp water and stew gently until tender.

With a slotted spoon, carefully transfer the fruit to the cooled flan shell, shaking off as much of the liquid as possible. Make up the liquid in the saucepan to 75 ml/3 fl oz with the lemon juice and water, if necessary. Stir in the sugar. Simmer for a few minutes until the sugar has dissolved completely.

Meanwhile mix the arrowroot with 30 ml/2 tbsp water in a cup. Stir into the hot syrup and bring to the boil, stirring all the time until thick and smooth. Cool the mixture slightly, then spoon over the fruit. When cool, decorate the flan with piped whipped cream.

SERVES FIVE TO SIX

 MRS BEETON'S TIP

To skin peaches, place them in a heatproof bowl and pour over boiling water to cover. Leave to stand for 1–2 minutes. The skins will slip off easily.

FRESH PINEAPPLE FLAN

800 g/1¾ lb peeled fresh pineapple
250 ml/8 fl oz pineapple juice
25 g/1 oz caster sugar
10 ml/2 tsp arrowroot
lemon juice

SHORT CRUST PASTRY
225 g/8 oz plain flour
2.5 ml/½ tsp salt
100 g/4 oz margarine (or half butter, half
   lard)
flour for rolling out

Set the oven at 200°C/400°F/gas 6. To make the pastry, sift the flour and salt into a bowl, then rub in the margarine until the mixture resembles fine breadcrumbs. Add enough cold water to make a stiff dough. Press the dough together with your fingertips.

Roll out the pastry on a lightly floured surface and use to line a 20 cm/8 inch flan tin or ring placed on a baking sheet. Line the pastry with greaseproof paper and fill with baking beans. Bake 'blind' for 20 minutes, then remove the paper and beans. Return to the oven for 5–7 minutes. Set aside.

Dice the pineapple into a colander, removing the core and any remaining peel. Drain the pineapple well.

Bring the pineapple juice and sugar to the boil in a saucepan, then lower the heat and simmer for 10 minutes. In a cup, mix the arrowroot to a paste with a litte lemon juice, then stir it into the syrup. Cook gently, stirring, until the sauce boils, thickens and clears.

Put the drained pineapple dice in an even layer in the cooked flan case, pour the syrup over the top and cool completely.

SERVES EIGHT

TREACLE TART

An old favourite which is today as popular as ever. Try it with cornflakes or similar cereals for a tasty change.

45 ml/3 tbsp golden syrup
50 g/2 oz soft white breadcrumbs
5 ml/1 tsp lemon juice

SHORT CRUST PASTRY
150 g/5 oz plain flour
2.5 ml/½ tsp salt
65 g/2½ oz margarine (or half butter, half
   lard)
flour for rolling out

Set the oven at 200°C/400°F/gas 6. To make the pastry, sift the flour and salt into a bowl, then rub in the margarine until the mixture resembles fine breadcrumbs. Add enough cold water to make a stiff dough. Press the dough together with your fingertips.

Roll out the pastry on a lightly floured surface and use just over three quarters of it to line a 20 cm/8 inch pie plate, reserving the rest for a lattice topping.

Melt the syrup in a saucepan. Stir in the breadcrumbs and lemon juice, then pour the mixture into the prepared pastry case.

Roll out the reserved pastry to a rectangle and cut into 1 cm/½ inch strips. Arrange in a lattice on top of the tart. Bake for about 30 minutes.

SERVES SIX

VARIATION

Treacle Jelly Tart   Make as above, but omit the breadcrumbs and add 1 beaten egg to the syrup. Bake in a 180°C/350°F/gas 4 oven until golden brown. When cold, the filling sets like jelly.

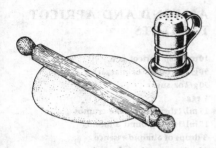

APRICOT MERINGUE FLAN

SHORT CRUST PASTRY
225 g/8 oz plain flour
2.5 ml/½ tsp salt
100 g/4 oz margarine (or half butter, half lard)
flour for rolling out

FILLING
1 (340 g/12 oz) can apricots
25 g/1 oz margarine
5 ml/1 tsp cornflour
2 eggs, separated
30 ml/2 tbsp brandy
75 g/3 oz caster sugar

single cream to serve (optional)

Set the oven at 200°C/400°F/gas 6. To make the pastry, sift the flour and salt into a bowl, then rub in the margarine until the mixture resembles fine breadcrumbs. Add enough cold water (about 45 ml/3 tbsp) to make a stiff dough. Press the dough together with your fingertips.

Roll out the pastry on a lightly floured surface and use to line a 20 cm/8 inch flan tin or ring placed on a baking sheet. Line the pastry with greaseproof paper and fill with baking beans.

Bake 'blind' for 10 minutes, then remove the paper and beans. Return to the oven for 5 minutes.

Meanwhile make the filling. Purée the apricots with their juice in a blender or food processor. Alternatively, press the apricots through a sieve into a bowl.

Combine the margarine, cornflour and 150 ml/¼ pint water in a small saucepan. Whisking constantly over moderate heat, bring to the simmering point, then simmer gently for 2–3 minutes until thick and smooth. Cool slightly, then stir in the egg yolks, brandy and apricot purée. Spoon the mixture into the cooked flan case.

In a clean, grease-free bowl, whisk the egg whites until fairly stiff. Gradually whisk in the sugar until stiff peaks form. Pile the meringue mixture on top of the apricot filling, covering it completely. Bake for 25–35 minutes until the meringue is set and the peaks tinged with gold.

Allow the flan to stand for at least 30 minutes before serving. It tastes best when just warm, with single cream if liked.

SERVES FOUR TO SIX

VARIATIONS

Other canned fruits may be substituted for the apricots. Crushed pineapple may be used, with rum instead of brandy, if preferred. Canned peaches, mango or plums work equally well. However, very delicate fruit, such as pears or gooseberries, do not contribute sufficient flavour to the filling.

MRS BEETON'S APPLE FLAN

6 eating apples
4 cloves
45 ml/3 tbsp medium-dry sherry
30 ml/2 tbsp soft light brown sugar
3 egg whites
45 ml/3 tbsp caster sugar

SHORT CRUST PASTRY
175 g/6 oz plain flour
2.5 ml/½ tsp salt
75 g/3 oz margarine (or half butter, half lard)

Peel and core the apples, cutting each into 8 sections. Place in a heatproof bowl, add the cloves and sherry and cover closely. Place the bowl in a deep saucepan. Add boiling water to come halfway up the sides of the bowl and cook for 20 minutes until the apple sections are tender but still intact.

Set the oven at 200°C/400°F/gas 6. Sift the flour and salt into a bowl, then rub in the margarine. Add enough cold water to make a stiff dough.

Roll out the pastry on a lightly floured surface and use to line a 23 cm/9 inch flan tin. Line the pastry with greaseproof paper and fill with baking beans. Bake for 10 minutes. Remove the paper and beans; cook for 5 minutes. Set aside.

Lower the oven temperature to 140°C/275°F/gas 1. Arrange the apples in the flan. Sprinkle with 30 ml/2 tbsp of the cooking liquid and the brown sugar.

In a clean, grease-free bowl, whisk the egg whites until stiff. Whisk in 10 ml/2 tsp of the caster sugar and spread lightly over the apples. Sprinkle the remaining sugar over. Bake for 1 hour. Serve warm or cold.

SERVES SIX

ALMOND AND APRICOT TARTLETS

10 ml/2 tsp apricot jam
50 g/2 oz butter or margarine
50 g/2 oz sugar
1 egg
15 ml/1 tbsp plain cake crumbs
15 ml/1 tbsp ground almonds
3 drops of almond essence
10 ml/2 tsp nibbed almonds
15 ml/1 tbsp Apricot Glaze (page 766)
10 ml/2 tsp chopped angelica

SHORT CRUST PASTRY
100 g/4 oz plain flour
1.25 ml/¼ tsp salt
50 g/2 oz margarine (or half butter, half lard)
flour for rolling out

Set the oven at 190°C/375°F/gas 5. To make the pastry, sift the flour and salt into a bowl, then rub in the margarine until the mixture resembles fine breadcrumbs. Add enough cold water to make a stiff dough. Press the dough together lightly.

Roll out the pastry on a lightly floured surface and use to line twelve 7.5 cm/3 inch patty tins. Put a little apricot jam in each.

In a bowl, cream the butter or margarine with the sugar until pale and fluffy. Gradually beat in the egg. Stir in the cake crumbs, ground almonds and almond essence. Half fill each pastry case with the mixture and smooth the tops. Sprinkle the nibbed almonds on top.

Bake for 15 minutes or until firm to the touch. Leave the tartlets to cool. Warm the apricot glaze, brush it on top of the tartlets, then sprinkle with the chopped angelica.

MAKES TWELVE

BALMORAL TARTLETS

50 g/2 oz butter
50 g/2 oz sugar
1 egg, separated
15 g/½ oz glacé cherries, chopped
25 g/1 oz plain cake crumbs
15 g/½ oz cut mixed peel
5 ml/1 tsp cornflour
icing sugar for dredging

SHORT CRUST PASTRY
100 g/4 oz plain flour
1.25 ml/¼ tsp salt
50 g/2 oz margarine (or half butter, half lard)
flour for rolling out

Set the oven at 200°C/400°F/gas 6. To make the pastry, sift the flour and salt into a bowl, then rub in the margarine until the mixture resembles fine breadcrumbs. Add enough cold water to make a stiff dough. Press the dough together with your fingertips.

Roll out the pastry on a lightly floured surface; use to line twelve 7.5 cm/3 inch patty tins.

In a bowl, cream the butter with the sugar until pale and fluffy. Beat in the egg yolk and add the chopped cherries with the cake crumbs, mixed peel and cornflour. Mix well.

Whisk the egg white in a clean, grease-free bowl until stiff, then fold lightly into the cherry mixture. Fill the pastry cases and bake for about 20 minutes. Cool on a wire rack.

Just before serving, sift a little icing sugar over the top of the tartlets.

MAKES TWELVE

CUSTARD TARTLETS

1 egg
15 ml/1 tbsp caster sugar
125 ml/4 fl oz milk
pinch of grated nutmeg

SWEET SHORT CRUST PASTRY
100 g/4 oz plain flour
1.25 ml/¼ tsp salt
50 g/2 oz margarine (or half butter, half lard)
5 ml/1 tsp caster sugar
flour for rolling out

Set the oven at 180°C/350°F/gas 4. To make the pastry, sift the flour and salt into a bowl, then rub in the margarine until the mixture resembles fine breadcrumbs. Stir in the caster sugar. Add enough cold water to make a stiff dough. Press the dough together with your fingertips. Roll out and use to line twelve 7.5 cm/3 inch patty tins.

Beat the egg lightly in a bowl and add the sugar. Warm the milk in a saucepan, then pour it on to the egg. Strain the custard mixture into the pastry cases and sprinkle a little nutmeg on top of each.

Bake for about 30 minutes, until the custard is firm and set. Leave to cool before removing from the tins.

MAKES TWELVE

VARIATION

Custard Meringue Tartlets Make as above, but omit the nutmeg and bake for 15 minutes only. Lower the oven temperature to 140°C/275°F/gas 1. Whisk 2 egg whites in a clean, grease-free bowl until stiff. Fold in 75 g/3 oz caster sugar. Pile the meringue on to the tartlets. Bake for about 30 minutes.

CHERRY ROSETTES

1 (375 g/13 oz) can red cherries in syrup
25 g/1 oz lump sugar
5 ml/1 tsp arrowroot
10 ml/2 tsp lemon juice
drop of red food colouring
125 ml/4 fl oz double cream

SHORT CRUST PASTRY
100 g/4 oz plain flour
1.25 ml/¼ tsp salt
50 g/2 oz margarine (or half butter, half lard)
flour for rolling out

Set the oven at 200°C/400°F/gas 6. To make the pastry, sift the flour and salt into a bowl, then rub in the margarine until the mixture resembles fine breadcrumbs. Add enough cold water to make a stiff dough. Press the dough together.

Roll out the pastry on a lightly floured surface and use to line twelve 7.5 cm/3 inch patty tins or boat-shaped moulds. Prick the pastry, then bake the tartlets for 10 minutes.

Drain and stone the cherries, reserving the syrup in a measuring jug. Make it up to 125 ml/4 fl oz with water, if necessary.

Put a layer of cherries in each pastry case. Pour the cherry syrup mixture into a saucepan, add the sugar and boil. Boil for 5 minutes.

Meanwhile mix the arrowroot to a paste with the lemon juice in a cup. Add to the syrup, stirring all the time, and bring to the boil. Add a little red food colouring. Cool the glaze slightly, then pour a little over the cherries in each tartlet. Leave to set.

In a bowl, whip the cream until stiff. Put it in a piping bag fitted with a 1 cm/½ inch nozzle and pipe a large rosette on each tartlet.

MAKES TWELVE

PARISIAN TARTLETS

50 g/2 oz butter
50 g/2 oz caster sugar
1 egg, beaten
15 ml/1 tbsp cornflour
15 ml/1 tbsp single cream or milk
25 g/1 oz ground almonds
25 g/1 oz plain cake crumbs
2.5 ml/½ tsp ground cinnamon
10 ml/2 tsp lemon juice
caster sugar for dredging

SHORT CRUST PASTRY
100 g/4 oz plain flour
1.25 ml/¼ tsp salt
50 g/2 oz margarine (or half butter, half lard)
flour for rolling out

Set the oven at 200°C/400°F/gas 6. To make the pastry, sift the flour and salt into a bowl, then rub in the margarine until the mixture resembles fine breadcrumbs. Add enough cold water to make a stiff dough. Press the dough together with your fingertips.

Roll out on a lightly floured surface and use to line twelve 7.5 cm/3 inch patty tins.

Cream the butter and sugar in a bowl until pale and fluffy. Add the egg and beat well. Blend the cornflour with the cream or milk, then stir this into the creamed mixture. Add the ground almonds, cake crumbs, cinnamon and lemon juice. Fill the pastry cases with the mixture.

Bake for 15-20 minutes until golden brown. Dredge with caster sugar when baked.

MAKES TWELVE

FILBERT TARTLETS

30 ml/2 tsp cornflour
60 ml/4 tbsp single cream or creamy milk
2 eggs
75 g/3 oz caster sugar
75 g/3 oz shelled filberts, skinned and
  chopped
25 g/1 oz ground almonds
milk and caster sugar for glazing

SHORT CRUST PASTRY
100 g/4 oz plain flour
1.25 ml/¼ tsp salt
50 g/2 oz margarine (or half butter, half lard)
flour for rolling out

Set the oven at 200°C/400°F/gas 6. To make the pastry, sift the flour and salt into a bowl, then rub in the margarine until the mixture resembles fine breadcrumbs. Add enough cold water to make a stiff dough. Press the dough together with your fingertips. Roll out on a lightly floured surface and use to line twelve 7.5 cm/3 inch patty tins, reserving a little pastry for decoration.

In a saucepan, mix the cornflour to a paste with the cream or milk. Stir over gentle heat until the mixture boils. Remove from the heat.

In a bowl, beat the eggs with the sugar until pale and fluffy. Add the chopped filberts, ground almonds and cornflour mixture. Spoon into the pastry cases. Cut the reserved pastry

---

> **MRS BEETON'S TIP**
>
> To skin filberts (or hazelnuts), place the nuts on a baking sheet and bake at 180°C/350°F/gas 4 for 5–6 minutes. Put the nuts in a paper bag and rub against each other. The skin fibres will break down and the skins will be removed.

---

into strips and place 2 strips across each tartlet in the form of a cross.

Brush the tartlets with milk and dredge with caster sugar. Bake for about 20 minutes or until the pastry is golden brown.

MAKES TWELVE

CREAM TARTLETS

30 ml/2 tbsp smooth apricot jam
250 ml/8 fl oz whipping cream
15 ml/1 tbsp icing sugar
30 ml/2 tbsp finely chopped pistachio nuts

SHORT CRUST PASTRY
100 g/4 oz plain flour
1.25 ml/¼ tsp salt
50 g/2 oz margarine (or half butter, half lard)
flour for rolling out

Set the oven at 200°C/400°F/gas 6. To make the pastry, sift the flour and salt into a bowl, then rub in the margarine until the mixture resembles fine breadcrumbs. Add enough cold water to make a stiff dough. Press the dough together with your fingertips.

Roll out the pastry on a lightly floured surface and use to line twelve 7.5 cm/3 inch patty tins. Prick the pastry, then bake the tartlets for 10 minutes. Cool completely.

When the tartlets are quite cold, put a little apricot jam in the base of each. In a bowl, whip the cream as stiffly as possible, gradually adding the sugar. Put the cream into a piping bag fitted with a 1 cm/½ inch nozzle and pipe in swirls and peaks over the jam. Sprinkle with the chopped pistachios.

MAKES TWELVE

CANADIAN CAKES

1 egg
100 g/4 oz currants
100 g/4 oz sugar
15 g/½ oz butter
125 ml/4 fl oz whipping cream
15 ml/1 tbsp caster sugar

SHORT CRUST PASTRY
100 g/4 oz plain flour
1.25 ml/¼ tsp salt
50 g/2 oz margarine (or half butter, half lard)
flour for rolling out

Set the oven at 200°C/400°F/gas 6. To make the pastry, sift the flour and salt into a bowl, then rub in the margarine until the mixture resembles fine breadcrumbs. Add enough cold water to make a stiff dough. Press the dough together with your fingertips. Roll out on a lightly floured surface and use to line twelve 7.5 cm/3 inch patty tins.

In a bowl, beat the egg lightly and stir in the currants and sugar. Melt the butter in a saucepan and stir into the fruit mixture. Spoon the mixture into the pastry cases.

Bake for 15–20 minutes, then set aside to cool before removing from the tins. Whip the cream with the caster sugar in a bowl until stiff, put it into a piping bag and pipe a rosette on each tartlet.

MAKES TWELVE

 MRS BEETON'S TIP

If you do not have a pastry cutter, use an upturned glass, dipping the rim lightly in flour to prevent it sticking to the pastry.

COVENTRY TURNOVERS

30 ml/2 tbsp raspberry jam
15 ml/1 tbsp caster sugar

SHORT CRUST PASTRY
150 g/5 oz plain flour
1.25 ml/¼ tsp salt
65 g/2½ oz margarine (or half butter, half lard)
flour for rolling out

Set the oven at 200°C/400°F/gas 6. To make the pastry, sift the flour and salt into a bowl, then rub in the margarine until the mixture resembles fine breadcrumbs. Add enough cold water to make a stiff dough. Press the dough together with your fingertips.

Roll out the pastry on a lightly floured surface to a thickness of 3 mm/⅛ inch. Cut out 8 rounds using a 10 cm/4 inch cutter. Place spoonfuls of jam in the centre of each pastry round. Moisten the edges with water and fold the pastry over the filling. Press the edges well together and crimp or decorate with a fork.

Place the turnovers on a baking sheet, brush with water and dredge with the caster sugar. Bake for about 20 minutes or until the pastry is golden brown.

MAKES EIGHT

 FREEZER TIP

When cold, open freeze on clean baking sheets, then wrap individually in freezer wrap and pack in a rigid container.

MILLE-FEUILLE GATEAU

PUFF PASTRY
200g/7oz plain flour
1.25 ml/¼ tsp salt
200g/7oz butter
2.5 ml/½ tsp lemon juice
flour for rolling out

FILLING AND TOPPING
300ml/½ pint double cream
100g/4oz icing sugar, sifted
100g/4oz raspberry jam

Make the pastry. Sift the flour and salt into a mixing bowl and rub in 50g/2oz of the butter. Add the lemon juice and mix to a smooth dough with cold water.

Shape the remaining butter into a rectangle on greaseproof paper. Roll out the dough on a lightly floured surface to a strip a little wider than the butter and rather more than twice its length. Place the butter on one half of the pastry, fold the other half over it, and press the edges together with the rolling pin. Leave in a cool place for 15 minutes to allow the butter to harden.

Roll the pastry out into a long strip. Fold the bottom third up and the top third down, press the edges together with the rolling pin and turn the pastry so that the folded edges are on the right and left. Roll and fold again, cover and leave in a cool place for 15 minutes. Repeat this process until the pastry has been rolled out 6 times (see Mrs Beeton's Tip). Chill the pastry

well between each rolling, wrapping it in cling film to prevent it drying on the surface. The pastry is now ready for use.

Set the oven at 230°C/450°F/gas 8. Roll out the pastry on a lightly floured surface to a thickness of 3 mm/⅛ inch. Cut into six 15 cm/6 inch rounds. If work surface space is limited, it is best to cut the pastry into portions to do this. Either cut the pastry into six portions or cut it in half and cut out three circles from each half.

Place the pastry circles on baking sheets, prick well and bake for 8–10 minutes until crisp and golden brown. Lift the rounds off carefully and cool on wire racks.

In a bowl, whip the cream until thick. Make glacé icing by mixing the icing sugar with enough cold water to form an icing that will coat the back of the spoon. Coat one pastry layer with icing and set aside for the lid. Sandwich the remaining layers together lightly with the jam and cream. Put the iced layer on top. Serve as soon as possible.

SERVES SIX TO EIGHT

 MRS BEETON'S TIP

Never rush the process of making puff pastry: always chill it if the fat begins to melt. It is a good idea to mark the pastry each time it is rolled, as it is easy to lose track of the number of times this process has been carried out.

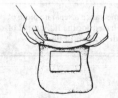 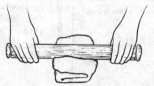

PASTRY HORNS

Puff Pastry (page 516), using 100 g/4 oz flour
flour for rolling out
beaten egg and milk for glazing

Roll out the pastry 5 mm/¼ inch thick on a
lightly floured surface, then cut into strips
35 cm/14 inches long and 2 cm/¾ inch wide.
Moisten the strips with cold water.

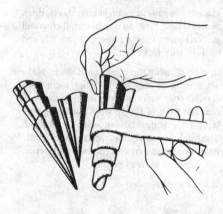

Wind each strip around a cornet mould, working from the point upward, keeping the moistened surface on the outside. Lay the horns on a
dampened baking sheet, with the final overlap
of the pastry strip underneath. Leave in a cool
place for 1 hour.

Set the oven at 220°C/425°F/gas 7. Brush the
horns with beaten egg and milk. Bake for
10-15 minutes or until golden brown. Remove
the moulds and return the horns to the oven for
5 minutes. Cool completely on a wire rack.
When cold, fill the horns with a sweet or
savoury filling.

MAKES EIGHT

VOL-AU-VENT CASES

Puff Pastry (page 516), using 200 g/7 oz flour
flour for rolling out
beaten egg for glazing

Set the oven at 220°C/425°F/gas 7. Roll out the
pastry on a lightly floured surface about 2 cm/¾
inch thick (1 cm/½ inch thick for bouchées).
Cut into round or oval shapes as liked. Place on
a baking sheet and brush the top of the pastry
with beaten egg.

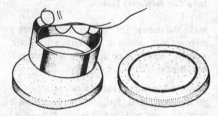

With a smaller, floured cutter, make a circular
or oval cut in each case, to form an inner ring,
cutting through about half the depth of the
pastry. Bake for 20-25 minutes until golden
brown and crisp.

When baked, remove the inner circular or oval
lid, then scoop out the soft inside while still
warm to make room for the filling.

MAKES TWENTY-FOUR 5 CM/2 INCH OR
TWELVE 7.5 CM/3 INCH BOUCHEES OR EIGHT
9 CM/3½ INCH OR TWO 15 CM/6 INCH VOL-
AU-VENT CASES

 MRS BEETON'S TIP

For a better appearance a separate piece of
pastry can be baked for the lid instead of
using the centre portion of the case.

LARGE DEEP VOL-AU-VENT

A large deep vol-au-vent should be made for serving with a hot, savoury sauced filling, a hot dessert filling, such as stewed fruit, or a pile of strawberries topped with whipped cream. The pastry should be prepared as for the previous recipe and the oven preheated. The pastry should be rolled to a thickness of 3.5 cm/1½ inches. Use a plate to stamp out the vol-au-vent. It is possible to buy large cutters, plain and fluted, from specialist cookshops and catering suppliers. Bake as for small vol-au-vent cases, allowing an extra 5 minutes' cooking if necessary.

FILLINGS FOR PASTRY HORNS AND VOL-AU-VENT CASES

The basic pastry cases may be filled in a variety of ways, both savoury and sweet.

Seafood Filling For vol-au-vent cases. Melt 25 g/1 oz butter in a saucepan. Stir in 25 g/1 oz plain flour, then cook for 1 minute. Pour in 300 ml/½ pint milk, stirring all the time, and bring to the boil. Simmer for 3 minutes. Add a 200 g/7 oz can tuna (drained), 100 g/4 oz frozen peeled cooked prawns and seasoning to taste. Stir in 30 ml/2 tbsp chopped parsley and simmer for 3 minutes, stirring occasionally until the prawns are thawed. Spoon into the pastry cases and serve hot.

Hot Chicken Make the sauce as for seafood filling, using half milk and half chicken stock. Instead of adding tuna, add 225 g/8 oz diced cooked chicken meat and 50 g/2 oz sliced button mushrooms. Season with a little nutmeg, then simmer gently for 5 minutes. Stir in 60 ml/4 tbsp single cream and a little chopped tarragon or parsley. Heat gently but do not boil.

Ham and Tomato Mix 50 g/2 oz diced cooked ham with 2 peeled and diced tomatoes, 1 chopped spring onion and 100 g/4 oz soft cheese (full-fat soft cheese, ricotta, quark or low-fat soft cheese). Add salt and pepper to taste, then spoon into the cold pastry cases.

Chicken Mayonnaise Dice 100 g/4 oz cooked chicken and bind with mayonnaise to a creamy mixture. Add 30 ml/2 tbsp snipped chives and salt and pepper to taste, then spoon the mixture into the cold pastry cases.

Spiced Turkey Dice 100–175 g/4–6 oz cooked turkey and mix with 15 ml/1 tbsp mango chutney. Cook ½ chopped onion in 25 g/1 oz butter until soft, stir in 5 ml/1 tsp curry powder and cook for 2 minutes. Stir into the turkey, then bind with mayonnaise.

Stewed Fruit Filling Apples, plums or other fresh fruit may be used to fill a large hot dessert vol-au-vent. Heat 50–75 g/2–3 oz sugar and 300 ml/½ pint water until the sugar dissolves. Bring to the boil. Add the chosen prepared fruit and cook gently, turning occasionally, until tender. Use a slotted spoon to transfer the fruit to a dish. Boil the syrup until well reduced and thickened. Spoon the fruit into the vol-au-vent, then pour the thick syrup over. Dust the filling with icing sugar and serve at once.

Jam and Cream Place 5 ml/1 tsp jam in each pastry case, then top with whipped cream. The cream may be flavoured with a little liqueur (such as Grand Marnier) or sherry and sweetened with a little caster or icing sugar before whipping. Sprinkle chopped nuts over the cream filling, if liked.

Fruit Horns Roughly chopped fresh fruit, such as strawberries or peaches, may be mixed with lightly sweetened whipped cream to fill the pastry cases.

Chocolate Cream Stir 45 ml/3 tbsp boiling water into 15 ml/1 tbsp cocoa. Add 30 ml/2 tbsp brandy or chocolate liqueur. Mix in 300 ml/½ pint double cream and 30 ml/2 tbsp icing sugar. Whip the cream until it stands in soft peaks. Pipe or spoon it into the pastries.

MRS BEETON'S MANCHESTER PUDDING

250 ml/8 fl oz milk
2 strips of lemon rind
75 g/3 oz fresh white breadcrumbs
2 whole eggs plus 2 egg yolks
50 g/2 oz butter, softened
45 ml/3 tbsp caster sugar
45 ml/3 tbsp brandy
45-60 ml/3-4 tbsp jam
extra caster sugar for sprinkling

PUFF PASTRY
150 g/5 oz plain flour
1.25 ml/¼ tsp salt
150 g/5 oz butter
2.5 ml/½ tsp lemon juice
flour for rolling out

Heat the milk in a saucepan with the lemon rind, then remove from the heat and leave to infuse for 30 minutes. Put the breadcrumbs in a bowl, strain the flavoured milk over them and return the mixture to the clean pan. Simmer for 2–3 minutes or until the crumbs have absorbed all the milk.

Beat the eggs and yolks until liquid, then stir into the breadcrumbs with the butter, sugar and brandy. Mix thoroughly; the butter should melt in the warm mixture. Cover the surface with dampened greaseproof paper and leave to cool.

Set the oven at 200°C/400°F/gas 6. Make the pastry. Sift the flour and salt into a mixing bowl and rub in 50 g/2 oz of the butter. Add the lemon juice and mix to a smooth dough with cold water.

Shape the remaining butter into a rectangle on greaseproof paper. Roll out the dough on a lightly floured surface to a strip a little wider than the butter and rather more than twice its length. Place the butter on one half of the pastry, fold the other half over it, and press the

edges together with the rolling pin. Leave in a cool place for 15 minutes to allow the butter to harden.

Roll out the pastry into a long strip. Fold the bottom third up and the top third down, press the edges together with the rolling pin and turn the pastry so that the folded edges are on the right and left. Roll and fold again, cover and leave in a cool place for 15 minutes. Repeat this process until the pastry has been rolled out 6 times.

Line a 750 ml/1¼ pint pie dish with the pastry. If liked, cut a strip out of the pastry trimmings to fit the rim of the pie dish. Dampen the rim of the lining and fit the extra strip. Wrap any remaining pastry and reserve in the refrigerator for another purpose.

Spread the jam over the base of the pastry. Spoon the cooled breadcrumb mixture into the pastry case and bake for 15 minutes, then lower the heat to 180°C/350°F/gas 4 and cook for 45–60 minutes more. The pudding should be set in the centre. Leave to cool. Serve cold, sprinkled with caster sugar.

SERVES SIX

 MRS BEETON'S TIP

When transferring the pastry to the pie dish, lop it over the rolling pin. Lift into the dish, easing half the pastry in first, then gently flick the rolling pin so that the other half falls into the dish.

GATEAU DE PITHIVIERS

225 g/8 oz plain flour
1.25 ml/¼ tsp salt
225 g/8 oz butter
2.5 ml/½ tsp lemon juice
flour for rolling out
Apricot Glaze (page 766)
1 egg, beaten with 15 ml/1 tbsp water
icing sugar

FILLING
50 g/2 oz butter
50 g/2 oz caster sugar
1-2 drops of almond essence
1 egg
20 ml/4 tsp plain flour
50 g/2 oz ground almonds

Start by making the filling. Cream the butter with the sugar in a large bowl, adding the essence. Add the egg and mix until smooth. Mix the flour and ground almonds in a bowl, then add them to the butter mixture to make a smooth pastry cream.

Make the pastry. Sift the flour and salt into a mixing bowl and rub in 50 g/2 oz of the butter. Add the lemon juice and mix to a smooth dough with cold water.

Shape the remaining butter into a rectangle on greaseproof paper. Roll out the dough on a lightly floured surface to a strip a little wider than the butter and rather more than twice its length. Place the butter on one half of the pastry, fold the other half over it, and press the

edges together with the rolling pin. Leave in a cool place for 15 minutes to allow the butter to harden.

Roll the pastry out into a long strip. Fold the bottom third up and the top third down, press the edges together with the rolling pin and turn the pastry so that the folded edges are on the right and left. Roll and fold again, cover and leave in a cool place for 15 minutes. Repeat this process until the pastry has been rolled out 6 times.

Roll out the pastry again and cut 2 rounds, measuring 18 cm/7 inches and 20 cm/8 inches in diameter. Place the smaller round on a baking sheet. Cover with apricot glaze to within 1 cm/½ inch of the edge. Spread with the glaze and then add the almond cream in an even layer. Moisten the edge of the pastry. Lay the larger round on top and press the edges to seal.

Make 5 curved cuts in the pastry lid, radiating from the centre at equal intervals. Brush the surface with the egg and water mixture. Let the pastry rest for 20 minutes.

Set the oven at 190°C/375°F/gas 5. Bake the pastry for 30 minutes or until risen and set. Dust the surface with icing sugar and return to the oven for 5 minutes to glaze. Cool on the baking sheet.

SERVES EIGHT TO TEN

CREAM SLICES

Puff Pastry (page 516), using 100 g/4 oz flour
flour for rolling out
white Glacé Icing (page 771), using
  225 g/8 oz icing sugar
30 ml/2 tbsp smooth seedless jam
125 ml/4 fl oz sweetened whipped cream

Set the oven at 220°C/425°F/gas 7. Roll out the pastry 1 cm/½ inch thick on a lightly floured surface into a neat rectangle. Cut into 8 oblong pieces, each measuring 10 × 2 cm/4 × ¾ inch. Place on a baking sheet and spread the tops thinly with half of the icing.

Bake for 20 minutes or until the pastry is well risen and the icing is slightly browned. Leave to cool completely.

When cold, split each pastry in half crossways. Spread the top of each bottom half with jam, and the bottom of each top half with cream; then sandwich the halves together again. Spread a little icing on top of each slice, over the browned icing.

MAKES EIGHT

VARIATION

Vanilla Slices Make as for Cream Slices but without the baked icing. When the slices are cold, fill with Confectioners' Custard or Crème St Honoré (page 778) instead of cream. Ice the tops with white Glacé Icing (page 771).

 MRS BEETON'S TIP

The pastry can be cooked and baked with royal icing using 100 g/4 oz icing sugar, instead of the glacé icing.

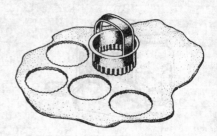

MAIDS OF HONOUR

These cakes are supposed to date back to Elizabethan times, when they were a great favourite of the court. Orange flower water is a fragrantly scented flavouring essence. It is prepared by distilling the spring blossom of the bitter Seville or Bigarade orange.

Puff Pastry (page 516), using 200 g/7 oz flour
flour for rolling out
200 g/7 oz ground almonds
100 g/4 oz caster sugar
2 eggs, beaten
25 g/1 oz plain flour
60 ml/4 tbsp single cream
30 ml/2 tbsp orange flower water

Set the oven at 200°C/400°F/gas 6. Roll out the pastry on a lightly floured surface and use to line twenty 7.5 cm/3 inch patty tins.

Mix the ground almonds and sugar in a bowl. Add the eggs, then mix in the flour, cream and orange flower water. Put the mixture into the pastry cases.

Bake for about 15 minutes or until the filling is firm and golden brown.

MAKES TWENTY

MRS BEETON'S CUSTARD TARTLETS

Puff Pastry (page 516), using 200 g/7 oz flour
flour for rolling out
25 g/1 oz butter
scant 75 ml/5 tbsp icing sugar
15 ml/1 tbsp plain flour
3 eggs
250 ml/8 fl oz milk
few drops of vanilla essence
30 ml/2 tbsp whole fruit strawberry or
    blackcurrant jam, plus extra to decorate

Roll out the pastry on a lightly floured surface to 5 mm/¼ inch thick. Leave to rest while preparing the custard.

Cream the butter and sugar in a bowl, then mix in the flour until well blended. Whisk the eggs into the milk and add the vanilla essence. Blend the mixture gradually into the butter and sugar, breaking down any lumps. Heat gently in a heavy saucepan, stirring all the time, until the mixture reaches simmering point and thickens. Remove from the heat, cover with damp greaseproof paper and leave to cool while preparing the pastry cases. Set the oven at 190°C/375°F/gas 5.

Line twelve 7.5 cm/3 inch patty tins, about 1 cm/½ inch deep, with the pastry, pressing it in well. Put a little of the jam in the bottom of each pastry case. Spoon the custard mixture over the jam, almost filling the cases.

Bake for 20-25 minutes, until the custard is firm. Cool in the tins. Before serving, decorate each tartlet with a small dab of additional jam in the centre.

MAKES TWELVE

ECCLES CAKES

Rough Puff Pastry (page 516) using
    200 g/7 oz flour
flour for rolling out
25 g/1 oz butter or margarine
15 ml/1 tbsp sugar
75 g/3 oz currants
25 g/1 oz chopped mixed peel
1.25 ml/¼ tsp ground mixed spice
1.25 ml/¼ tsp ground nutmeg
caster sugar for dusting

Set the oven at 200°C/425°F/gas 7. Roll out the pastry on a lightly floured surface to 3 mm/⅛ inch thick. Cut into rounds using a 10 cm/ 4 inch pastry cutter.

Cream the butter or margarine and sugar in a bowl. Add the currants, peel and spices. Place spoonfuls of the mixture in the centre of each pastry round. Gather the edges of each round together to form a ball. With the smooth side uppermost, form into a flat cake. Make 2 cuts in the top of each cake with a sharp knife. Brush with water and dust with caster sugar.

Put on a baking sheet and bake for 20 minutes or until golden brown.

MAKES TWELVE TO FOURTEEN

SUET PUDDING

This plain pudding to serve with roast meat may be cooked in a basin if preferred. Slices of cooked pudding may be added to the roasting tin around a joint of meat for 2-5 minutes before serving. Traditionally, the slices of pudding would have been served before the meat to fill up a hungry family.

fat for greasing
350g/12oz plain flour
10ml/2tsp baking powder
2.5ml/½tsp salt
150g/5oz shredded suet
about 150ml/¼ pint milk
meat juices or melted butter to serve

Grease a large piece of greaseproof paper and lay it on a large sheet of foil. Sift the flour, baking powder and salt into a mixing bowl. Stir in the suet, then add enough milk to make a soft, but not sticky, dough.

Gently knead the dough into an oblong shape measuring about 25cm/10 inches long. Place it on the greaseproof paper. Fold the paper edges together several times, then seal the foil in the same way. Keep the wrapping loose to allow room for the pudding to rise. Twist or fold the ends of the paper and foil to seal them.

Bring a large saucepan or deep roasting tin of water to the boil and add the pudding. Cook for 3 hours, topping up the water with fresh boiling water as necessary. If using a roasting tin, tent foil over the top of it and seal it on the rim to keep in the steam, and top up the water frequently.

To serve, open the package and slice the pudding. Arrange the slices on a heated serving plate and trickle meat juices or melted butter over. Serve promptly.

SERVES SIX TO EIGHT

PORK AND ONION ROLY POLY

fat for greasing
400g/14oz lean pork, finely chopped
3 small onions, finely chopped
1.25ml/¼tsp dried sage
salt and pepper

SUET CRUST PASTRY
300g/10oz plain flour
7.5ml/1½tsp baking powder
2.5ml/½tsp salt
150g/5oz shredded suet
flour for rolling out

Combine the pork, onions and sage, with salt and pepper to taste, in a bowl. Mix well.

Make the pastry. Sift the flour, baking powder and salt into a mixing bowl. Stir in the suet, then add enough cold water (about 75-125ml/3-4floz) to make a soft but not sticky dough.

Roll out the suet crust pastry on a lightly floured surface to a rectangle measuring 40 × 25cm/16 × 10 inches. Spread the pork mixture over the rectangle, leaving a 1cm/½ inch border all round. Roll up from the narrow side, like a Swiss roll, and press the end and sides to seal in the filling.

Wrap the roly poly firmly in a sheet of greased greaseproof paper and then in foil or a scalded pudding cloth. Bring a large saucepan of water to the boil, add the pork and onion roly poly and cook for 3 hours. Turn out on to a heated dish and serve.

SERVES SIX

DUMPLINGS

100 g/4 oz self-raising flour
50 g/2 oz shredded beef suet
salt and pepper

Mix the flour and suet in a bowl. Add salt and pepper to taste and bind with enough cold water to make a soft, smooth dough. With floured hands, divide the dough into 16 portions; roll into balls. Drop into simmering salted water, stock, soup or stew, lower the heat and simmer for 15–20 minutes. Serve with the liquid or with boiled meat, stew or vegetables.

MAKES ABOUT SIXTEEN

VARIATION

Herb Dumplings Add 25 g/1 oz grated onion and 5 ml/1 tsp chopped fresh herbs to the flour and suet.

STRAWBERRY TABLE DUMPLINGS

These are great fun. As their name implies, they are cooked at the table. Guests help themselves to suitable accompaniments.

800 g/1¾ lb fresh strawberries, hulled
100 g/4 oz caster sugar
15 ml/1 tbsp kirsch
1 whole egg, separated, plus 2 egg yolks
salt
about 225 g/8 oz plain flour
flour for rolling out
extra caster sugar to serve

Prepare the strawberries by spreading them in a shallow dish, covering them with sugar and kirsch and leaving to stand for 1 hour. Drain thoroughly, reserving any syrup. Mash the fruit lightly and put to one side.

Combine all the egg yolks in a bowl and beat lightly with a pinch of salt. Gradually add 100 ml/3½ fl oz water. Then add the flour, about 50 g/2 oz at a time, until a light firm dough is formed.

Roll out the dough on a lightly floured surface and cut into rounds, using a 5 cm/2 inch cutter. Brush the edges of each round with some of the egg white. Put about 2.5 ml/½ tsp strawberry filling in the centre of each round, then fold over to make small turnovers. Press the edges of each turnover with a fork, to seal.

At the table, have ready a large saucepan of lightly salted boiling water over a burner or hot tray. Lower the dumplings gently into the water, a few at a time, and cook for about 4 minutes until they rise to the surface. Lift out with a slotted spoon, drain over the pan, and serve on to the diners' plates.

A bowl of caster sugar and a sauceboat containing the strained fruit syrup should be placed by the pan so that diners may help themselves. Soured or fresh whipped cream may also be offered. The dumplings should be sprinkled with sugar before the fruit syrup is poured over them.

SERVES FOUR TO SIX

BOILED APPLE DUMPLINGS

6 cooking apples
75 g/3 oz demerara sugar
6 cloves

SUET CRUST PASTRY
150 g/5 oz plain flour
3.75 ml/¾ tsp baking powder
pinch of salt
65 g/2½ oz shredded suet
flour for rolling out

Make the pastry. Sift the flour, baking powder and salt into a mixing bowl. Stir in the suet, then add enough cold water (about 75–125 ml/3–4 fl oz) to make a soft but not sticky dough.

Divide the suet pastry into 6 portions. On a lightly floured surface, roll out each portion to a round. Core and peel the apples, and put one in the centre of each round. Work the pastry around each apple until it almost meets at the top. Fill each core hole with sugar and stick a clove upright in the middle of each apple.

Dampen the edges of the pastry, work it up to cover the apple and seal well, leaving the clove exposed. Tie each dumpling in a small well-floured pudding cloth.

Bring a large saucepan of water to the boil, add the dumplings and boil gently for 40–50 minutes. Drain well and serve with cream or custard.

SERVES SIX

GREENGAGE SUET PUDDING

fat for greasing
450 g/1 lb greengages
50 g/2 oz caster sugar

SUET CRUST PASTRY
200 g/7 oz plain flour
5 ml/1 tsp baking powder
pinch of salt
75 g/3 oz shredded suet
flour for rolling out

Grease a 750 ml/1¼ pint pudding basin. Prepare a steamer or half fill a large saucepan with water and bring to the boil.

Make the pastry. Sift the flour, baking powder and salt into a mixing bowl. Stir in the suet, then add enough cold water (about 150–175 ml/5–6 fl oz) to make a soft but not sticky dough. Cut off one quarter of the pastry and set aside for the lid. Roll out the rest on a lightly floured surface to a round 1 cm/½ inch larger than the top of the basin, then place the round in the basin. Pressing with the fingers, work the pastry evenly up the sides of the basin to the top.

To make the filling, halve the greengages and remove the stones. Put the fruit in a bowl and stir in the sugar. Spoon the fruit into the pastry-lined basin and add 30 ml/2 tbsp water. Roll out the reserved pastry to make the lid, dampen the rim and place the lid of top of the filling. Press the rim of the lid against the edge of the lining to seal the crust.

Cover the pudding with a well-floured cloth, greased greaseproof paper or foil and secure with string. Put the pudding in the perforated part of the steamer, or stand it on an old saucer or plate in the pan of boiling water. The water should come halfway up the sides of the basin. Cover the pan tightly and steam the pudding over gently simmering water for 2½-3 hours. Remove the cooked pudding from the steamer. Serve from the basin or leave to stand for a few minutes, then turn out on to a warmed serving dish. Serve with the custard.

SERVES SIX

VARIATIONS

Apples, blackberries, red and blackcurrants, cranberries, loganberries, damsons, gooseberries, plums and rhubarb may be used instead of greengages. Prepare the fruit according to type.

APPLE AND BLACKBERRY PUDDING

fat for greasing
Simple Custard Sauce (page 498) to serve

SUET CRUST PASTRY
200 g/7 oz plain flour
5 ml/1 tsp baking powder
pinch of salt
75 g/3 oz shredded suet
flour for rolling out

FILLING
350 g/12 oz cooking apples
75 g/3 oz sugar
350 g/12 oz blackberries

Grease a 750 ml/1¼ pint pudding basin. Prepare a steamer or half fill a large saucepan with water and bring to the boil.

Make the pastry. Sift the flour, baking powder and salt into a mixing bowl. Stir in the suet, then add enough cold water (about 150-175 ml/5-6 fl oz) to make a soft but not sticky dough. Cut off one quarter of the pastry

and set aside for the lid. Roll out the rest on a lightly floured surface to a round 1 cm/½ inch larger than the top of the basin, then place the round in the basin. Pressing with the fingers, work the pastry evenly up the sides of the basin to the top.

To make the filling, peel and core the apples and slice into a bowl. Stir in the sugar and blackberries. Spoon the fruit into the pastry-lined basin and add 30 ml/2 tbsp water. Roll out the reserved pastry to make the lid, dampen the rim and place the lid on top of the filling. Press the rim of the lid against the edge of the lining to seal the crust.

Cover the pudding with a well-floured cloth, greased greaseproof paper or foil and secure with string. Put the pudding in the perforated part of the steamer, or stand it on an old saucer or plate in the pan of boiling water. The water should come halfway up the sides of the basin. Cover the pan tightly and steam the pudding over gently simmering water for 2½-3 hours.

Remove the cooked pudding from the steamer. Serve from the basin or leave to stand for a few minutes, then turn out on to a warmed serving dish. Serve with the custard.

SERVES SIX

 MRS BEETON'S TIP

The method of lining a basin and preparing the pastry lid for a suet pudding as explained above is the basic technique, which may also be used for savoury puddings.

CHEESE ECLAIRS

Serve these savoury eclairs as cocktail snacks or at a buffet party.

CHOUX PASTRY
100 g/4 oz plain flour
50 g/2 oz butter or margarine
pinch of salt
2 whole eggs plus 1 yolk
salt and pepper
pinch of cayenne pepper

FILLING
25 g/1 oz butter
25 g/1 oz plain flour
300 ml/½ pint milk
75–100 g/3–4 oz Cheddar cheese, grated
pinch of mustard powder

Lightly grease a baking sheet. Set the oven at 220°C/425°F/gas 7. To make the pastry, sift the flour on to a sheet of greaseproof paper. Put 250 ml/8 fl oz water in a saucepan and add the butter or margarine with the salt. Heat gently until the fat melts.

When the fat has melted, bring the liquid rapidly to the boil and add all the flour at once. Immediately remove the pan from the heat and stir the flour into the liquid to make a smooth paste which leaves the sides of the pan clean. Set aside to cool slightly.

Add the egg yolk and beat well. Add the whole eggs, one at a time, beating well after each addition. Add salt, pepper and cayenne with the final egg. Continue beating until the paste is very glossy.

Put the pastry into a piping bag fitted with a 1 cm/½ inch nozzle and pipe it in 5 cm/2 inch lengths on the prepared baking sheet. Cut off each length with a knife or scissors dipped in hot water.

Bake for 10 minutes, then lower the oven temperature to 180°C/350°F/gas 4 and bake for 20 minutes, or until risen and browned. Split the eclairs open and cool on a wire rack.

Meanwhile, to make the filling, melt the butter in a saucepan. Stir in the flour and cook over low heat for 2–3 minutes, without colouring. Over very low heat, gradually add the milk, stirring constantly. Bring to the boil, stirring, and simmer for 1–2 minutes until smooth and thickened. Stir in the cheese, mustard and salt and pepper to taste.

Cool the eclairs on a wire rack. Fill with the cheese sauce.

MAKES 20-24

VARIATIONS

Ham and Egg Eclairs Omit the cheese. Add 2 chopped hard-boiled eggs, 15 ml/1 tbsp chopped tarragon and 75 g/3 oz diced cooked ham to the sauce for the filling.

Smoked Salmon Eclairs Omit the cheese. Add 75 g/3 oz roughly chopped smoked salmon and 2.5 ml/½ tsp grated lemon rind to the sauce for the filling. Smoked salmon offcuts are ideal: up to 100 g/4 oz may be added, depending on flavour and the saltiness of the salmon.

Turkey Eclairs Omit the cheese. Add 100 g/4 oz diced cooked turkey and 30 ml/2 tbsp chopped parsley to the sauce.

CREAM ECLAIRS

fat for greasing
250 ml/8 fl oz whipping cream
25 g/1 oz caster sugar and icing sugar, mixed
3–4 drops of vanilla essence

CHOUX PASTRY
100 g/4 oz plain flour
50 g/2 oz butter or margarine
pinch of salt
2 whole eggs plus 1 yolk

CHOCOLATE GLACE ICING
50 g/2 oz plain chocolate
10 ml/2 tsp butter
100 g/4 oz icing sugar, sifted

Lightly grease a baking sheet. Set the oven at 220°C/425°F/gas 7. To make the pastry, sift the flour on to a sheet of greaseproof paper. Put 250 ml/8 fl oz water in a saucepan and add the butter or margarine with the salt. Heat gently until the fat melts.

When the fat has melted, bring the liquid rapidly to the boil and add all the flour at once. Immediately remove the pan from the heat and stir the flour into the liquid to make a smooth paste which leaves the sides of the pan clean. Set aside to cool slightly.

Add the egg yolk and beat well. Add the whole eggs, one at a time, beating well after each addition. Continue beating until the paste is very glossy.

Put the pastry into a piping bag fitted with a 2 cm/¾ inch nozzle and pipe it in 10 cm/4 inch lengths on the prepared baking sheet. Cut off each length with a knife or scissors dipped in hot water.

Bake for 10 minutes. Lower the oven temperature to 180°C/350°F/gas 4. Bake for a further 20 minutes, or until risen and browned. Remove the eclairs from the oven and split them open.

Cool completely on a wire rack.

Meanwhile, to make the glacé icing, break the chocolate into a heavy-bottomed pan. Add 15 ml/1 tbsp water and the butter. Warm gently, stirring until smooth and creamy. Stir in the icing sugar, a little at a time.

Whip the cream until it holds its shape, adding the mixed sugars gradually. Add the vanilla essence while whipping.

Fill the eclairs with the cream and close neatly. Cover the tops with the glacé icing.

MAKES TEN TO TWELVE

VARIATION

Cream Buns Pipe the pastry in 5 cm/2 inch balls. Fill as above, and sift icing sugar over the tops instead of glacé icing.

✳ **FREEZER TIP**

When cool, the unfilled choux eclairs or buns may be packed in sealed polythene bags and frozen. Thaw in wrappings for 1–1½ hours at room temperature, then place on baking sheets and crisp in a 180°C/350°F/gas 4 oven for 5 minutes. Cool before filling and topping.

PROFITEROLES

CHOUX PASTRY PUFFS
100 g/4 oz plain flour
50 g/2 oz butter or margarine
pinch of salt
2 whole eggs plus 1 yolk

FILLING
250 ml/8 fl oz double cream, chilled
25 g/1 oz caster sugar
vanilla essence

TOPPING
200 g/7 oz icing sugar, sifted
15 ml/1 tbsp cocoa

Lightly grease 2 baking sheets. Set the oven at 220°C/425°F/gas 7.

Make the choux pastry. Sift the flour on to a sheet of greaseproof paper. Put 250 ml/8 fl oz water in a saucepan and add the butter or margarine with the salt. Heat gently until the fat melts.

When the fat has melted, bring the liquid rapidly to the boil and add all the flour at once. Immediately remove the pan from the heat and stir the flour into the liquid to make a smooth paste which leaves the sides of the pan clean. Set aside to cool slightly.

Add the egg yolk and beat well. Add the whole eggs, one at a time, beating well after each addition. Continue beating until the paste is very glossy.

Put the pastry into a piping bag fitted with a 2 cm/¾ inch nozzle and pipe it in 2 cm/¾ inch balls on the baking sheets, leaving room for them to puff up. Bake for 10 minutes, then lower the oven temperature to 180°C/350°F/ gas 4 and bake for 20 minutes more until crisp, golden and puffed.

Remove the puffs from the oven, slit them with a sharp knife, and remove any uncooked paste. If necessary, return them to the oven for a few minutes to dry out. Cool the puffs completely on a wire rack.

Just before serving, whip the cream lightly. Whip in the sugar with a few drops of vanilla essence to taste. Put into a piping bag and fill the choux puffs.

Make the chocolate topping by mixing the icing sugar and cocoa in a bowl with enough warm water (about 15–30 ml/1–2 tbsp) to form an icing that will coat the back of the spoon. Glaze the tops of the puffs with this mixture, reserving a little for assembling the dish.

Let the icing on the puffs harden, then arrange them in a pyramid, sticking the buns together with small dabs of the remaining icing. Serve 3 or 4 buns per person, with a chocolate sauce, if liked.

SERVES EIGHT

VARIATIONS

The filling may be varied to taste. Sweetened whipped cream, confectioners' custard or chocolate buttercream may be used. Instead of the icing, melted chocolate may simply be poured over the choux.

 **FREEZER TIP**

When cool, the unfilled choux puffs may be packed in sealed polythene bags and frozen. Thaw in wrappings for 1–1½ hours at room temperature, then place on baking sheets and crisp in a 180°C/350°F/gas 4 oven for 5 minutes. Cool before filling and topping.

CROQUEMBOUCHE

This spectacular gâteau is often used as a wedding cake in France.

1 Madeira cake (20 cm/8 inches in diameter
   6 cm/2¼ inches high)
200 g/7 oz Almond Paste (page 767)
Apricot Glaze (page 766)
white Glacé Icing (page 771)
marzipan flowers, to decorate

CHOUX PUFFS
butter for greasing
Choux Pastry (page 517), using 225 g/8 oz
   flour
Confectioners' Custard (page 778)

CARAMEL
500 g/18 oz granulated sugar
juice of 1 lemon

If the Madeira cake is peaked, cut out a thin strip of almond paste and put it round the edge of the cake to level the top. Brush off any loose crumbs, then brush the whole cake with warmed apricot glaze. Roll out the remaining almond paste, and use it to cover the top and sides of the cake. Place the cake on a 30 cm/12 inch serving board.

Lightly butter a baking sheet. Set the oven at 220°C/425°F/gas 7. Put the choux pastry into a piping bag fitted with a 5 mm/¼ inch nozzle and pipe small choux puffs on the prepared baking sheet. Bake for 10 minutes, then reduce the oven temperature to 180°C/350°F/gas 4 and bake for a further 15 minutes, or until risen, browned and crisp. Split the puffs open and cool on a wire rack. When cold, fill with confectioners' custard.

Make a strong paper cone, from heavy cartridge paper which is covered with non-stick baking parchment. Tape the parchment to the inside of the cone around the base to prevent it from slipping. The cone should measure about 30 cm/12 inches high and 15 cm/6 inches diameter at the base.

To make the caramel, dissolve the sugar in 300 ml/½ pint water and the lemon juice in a heavy-bottomed pan, then boil, without stirring, until deep golden. Immediately the caramel colours, plunge the bottom of the pan into iced water to prevent further cooking and darkening.

Stick the filled choux on the cone by dipping each in caramel and pressing it on to the cone. Begin with a circle of choux at the bottom, and work upwards. At the top, stick on the decorative marzipan flowers, using dabs of caramel.

Leave the caramel to harden; then slide out the paper lining and lift the cone very carefully on to the Madeira cake. Ice the exposed sections of the Madeira cake quickly with glacé icing. Serve on the same day as stacking the choux buns. The caramel softens if left to stand for a longer period and the cone will collapse.

SERVES ABOUT TWENTY

 MRS BEETON'S TIP

There is a quicker and easier way of achieving a similar result. Instead of making a hollow cone, stack the choux buns in a pyramid on top of the cake, dipping them in caramel to secure them in place. The cone may not stand quite as high but it will be more secure and easier for the non-professional cook to handle.

FILO AND FETA TRIANGLES

225 g/8 oz feta cheese
5 ml/1 tsp dried oregano
1 spring onion, chopped
pepper
4 sheets of filo pastry
50 g/2 oz butter, melted

Set the oven at 190°C/375°F/gas 5. Mash the feta with the oregano in a bowl, then mix in the spring onion and pepper to taste.

Lay a sheet of filo pastry on a clean, dry surface and brush it with melted butter. Cut the sheet widthways into 9 strips. Place a little feta mixture at one end of the first strip, leaving the corner of the pastry without filling. Fold the corner over the feta to cover it in a triangular shape, then fold the mixture over and over to wrap it in several layers of pastry, making a small triangular-shaped pasty.

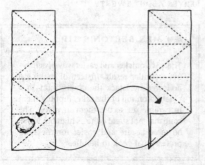

Repeat with the other strips of pastry. Cut and fill the remaining sheets in the same way to make 36 triangular pastries. Place these on baking sheets and brush any remaining butter over them.

Bake for about 10 minutes, until the filo pastry is crisp and golden. Transfer the triangles to a wire rack to cool. They are best served warm.

MAKES 36

SHAPES AND FILLINGS

The feta filling used in the triangles is a Greek speciality. A variety of other fillings may be used and the pastry shaped in other ways.

Instead of cutting strips, the pastry may be cut into squares (about 6 per sheet). The filling should be placed in the middle of the squares, and the pastry may be gathered up to form a small bundle. The butter coating keeps the bundle closed when the filo is pressed together. For strength, the filo may be used double.

Alternatively, squares of filo may be filled and folded into neat oblong parcels. Oblong pieces of filo (about 4 per sheet) may be folded into neat squares.

FILLINGS

Spinach and Cheese Thoroughly drained cooked spinach may be used with or without the cheese. Flavour plain spinach with chopped spring onion and grated nutmeg.

Sardine Mashed canned sardines in tomato sauce make a good filling for filo triangles.

Chicken or Ham Chopped cooked chicken or ham are both tasty fillings for filo. Combine them with a little low-fat soft cheese.

Apricot Apricot halves (drained canned or fresh) topped with a dot of marmalade make good sweet filo pastries. Dust them with icing sugar after baking.

Apple and Almond Mix some ground almonds into cold, sweetened apple purée. Use to fill triangles or squares.

BEIGNETS

oil for deep frying
icing sugar for dredging

CHOUX PASTRY
100g/4oz plain flour
50g/2oz butter or margarine
pinch of salt
2 whole eggs plus 1 yolk
vanilla essence

Start by making the choux pastry. Sift the flour on to a sheet of greaseproof paper. Put 250ml/8floz water in a saucepan and add the butter or margarine with the salt. Heat gently until the fat melts.

When the fat has melted, bring the liquid rapidly to the boil and add all the flour at once. Immediately remove the pan from the heat and stir the flour into the liquid to make a smooth paste which leaves the sides of the pan clean. Set aside to cool slightly.

Add the egg yolk and beat well. Add the whole eggs, one at a time, beating well after each addition (see Mrs Beeton's Tip). Continue beating until the paste is very glossy.

Put the oil for frying in a deep wide saucepan. Heat the oil to 185°C/360°F or until a bread cube immersed in the oil turns pale brown in 45 seconds.

Flavour the choux pastry with vanilla essence to taste. Dip a metal dessertspoon into the hot oil and use it to drop spoonfuls of the mixture gently into the hot oil, a few at a time. Fry slowly until crisp and golden, then drain on absorbent kitchen paper. Serve dredged in icing sugar.

SERVES FOUR

SPANISH FRITTERS

oil for deep frying
caster sugar and cinnamon for dredging

CHOUX PASTRY
100g/4oz plain flour
50g/2oz butter or margarine
pinch of salt
2 whole eggs plus 1 yolk
15ml/1tbsp caster sugar
vanilla essence

Make the choux pastry, following the instructions in the recipe for Beignets (left). Stir in the caster sugar and flavour with vanilla essence to taste.

Put the oil for frying in a deep wide saucepan. Heat the oil to 185°C/360°F or until a bread cube immersed in the oil turns pale brown in 45 seconds.

Put the choux pastry into a piping bag fitted with a 1cm/½ inch star nozzle. Press out 7.5cm/3 inch lengths of pastry and drop carefully into the hot oil. They will form twists. Fry slowly until crisp and golden, then drain on absorbent kitchen paper. Served dredged in sugar and cinnamon.

SERVES FOUR

 MRS BEETON'S TIP

The choux pastry may not accept all the egg. Add just enough to give a thick smooth paste with a glossy appearance.

APPLE STRUDEL

Anyone who has ever watched an Austrian pastry-cook at work will know that the best strudel is coaxed out to the correct size by hand. Using a rolling pin is no disgrace, however, and the recipe below gives very good results.

200 g/7 oz plain flour
1.25 ml/¼ tsp salt
30 ml/2 tbsp oil
1 egg
flour for rolling out

FILLING
450 g/1 lb cooking apples
50 g/2 oz butter
50 g/2 oz soft light brown sugar
5 ml/1 tsp ground cinnamon
50 g/2 oz sultanas

To make the strudel pastry, sift the flour and salt into a mixing bowl. Add the oil and egg, with 60 ml/4 tbsp warm water. Mix to a firm dough, cover with foil and leave in a warm place for about an hour. Set the oven at 190°C/375°F/gas 5.

Peel and core the apples. Chop them finely and put them into a bowl. Melt the butter in a small saucepan. Have the brown sugar, cinnamon and sultanas ready.

Lightly flour a clean tablecloth or sheet, placed on a work surface. Place the pastry on the cloth and roll it out very thinly to a rectangle measuring 50 × 25 cm/20 × 10 inches.

 **MRS BEETON'S TIP**

Work on a table that allows clear access all round if possible, and have all the filling ingredients ready before you begin.

Brush the strudel pastry with some of the melted butter and sprinkle with the brown sugar, cinnamon and sultanas. Top with the chopped apple. Starting from a long side, roll the strudel up like a Swiss roll, using the sheet as a guide.

Slide the strudel on to a large baking sheet, turning it to a horseshoe shape if necessary. Position it so that the join is underneath. Brush the top with more melted butter.

Bake for 40 minutes or until golden brown. To serve, cut the strudel in wide diagonal slices. It tastes equally good hot or cold, with or without cream.

SERVES EIGHT

VARIATIONS

Filo pastry may be used for a quick strudel. Brush each sheet generously with melted butter, covering any filo not in use with a clean damp tea-towel or cling film to prevent it from drying out.

Savoury Strudel Savoury fillings may be used instead of apples in the strudel. Chopped onion, cooked in oil or butter until soft, with shredded cabbage, a little grated carrot and grated eating apple is tasty. Diced cooked ham or lean bacon may be added and the mixture may be seasoned with a little grated nutmeg.

Alternatively, drained cooked spinach with lightly toasted pine nuts, cooked onion and crumbled Lancashire or Wensleydale cheese is delicious. A few sultanas or raisins may be added to the spinach which may be spiced with a good sprinkle of ground coriander.

LINZERTORTE

Linzertorte improves in flavour if kept for two to three days before cutting.

100 g/4 oz butter
75 g/3 oz caster sugar
1 egg yolk
1.25 ml/¼ tsp almond essence
grated rind of 1 small lemon
juice of ½ lemon
100 g/4 oz plain flour
5 ml/1 tsp ground cinnamon
50 g/2 oz ground almonds
flour for rolling out
200 g/7 oz raspberry jam
15 ml/1 tbsp icing sugar

In a mixing bowl, cream the butter with the sugar until pale and fluffy. Beat in the egg yolk, almond essence, lemon rind and juice. Add the flour, cinnamon and ground almonds and mix to a smooth dough. Wrap in foil and chill for 1 hour.

Set the oven at 160°C/325°F/gas 3. Roll out three quarters of the pastry on a lightly floured surface and use to line an 18 cm/7 inch flan tin. Spread the jam over the base.

Roll out the remaining pastry to a rectangle 18 cm/7 inches long and cut into strips about 5 mm/¼ inch wide. Arrange the strips in a lattice on top of the jam. Bake for about 1 hour or until the pastry is golden brown. Leave to cool.

Remove from the flan tin, dredge with icing sugar and serve cold, with whipped cream.

SERVES SIX

STUFFED MONKEY

fat for greasing
45 ml/3 tbsp margarine
50 g/2 oz cut mixed peel
50 g/2 oz blanched almonds, chopped
50 g/2 oz sultanas
25 g/1 oz sugar
2.5 ml/½ tsp mixed spice
50 g/2 oz flaked almonds

PASTRY
150 g/5 oz plain flour
2.5 ml/½ tsp ground cinnamon
100 g/4 oz margarine
100 g/4 oz brown sugar
1 egg, beaten
flour for rolling out

Grease an 18 cm/7 inch square tin. Set the oven at 190°C/375°F/gas 5.

Make the pastry. Sift the flour and cinnamon into a bowl, then rub in the margarine until the mixture resembles fine breadcrumbs. Stir in the sugar. Add enough of the beaten egg to form a soft dough, reserving a little. Halve the dough. Roll out one portion to fit the prepared tin. Lay it in the tin.

For the filling, melt the margarine in a saucepan and stir in the mixed peel, almonds, sultanas, sugar and mixed spice. Cool. Spread the filling over the pastry, leaving a 2 cm/¾ inch clear border all around. Dampen the clear edge with water.

Roll out the second portion of pastry to the same size as the first. Lay it on the filling and press the edges together to seal. Brush with the reserved beaten egg and sprinkle with the flaked almonds. Bake for 30 minutes, then cool in the tin. Cut into squares and serve.

SERVES NINE

Steamed Sweet Puddings

The steaming-hot puddings in this chapter are perfect for winter days, from homely
Treacle Layer Pudding to traditional Rich Christmas Pudding or lighter Snowdon Pudding.
Treat the family to a delicious Chocolate Crumb Pudding or surprise them with a steamed sponge pudding
cooked in minutes in the microwave.

Traditional steamed puddings take a while to cook and there are a few points to remember for safety and success. In Mrs Beeton's day steaming was a popular cooking method for both savoury and sweet puddings, fish and fowl. The food would be allowed to steam over a pot of boiling water on the kitchen fire or coal-burning stove. When gas and electric cookers became popular, they led to a decline in the use of long, hob-top cooking methods.

Recent trends in healthy eating and cooking have brought steaming right back into fashion, although this method of cooking is used primarily for savoury foods. There are many types of steamer available in the shops, from the metal saucepan-top steamer to the oriental-style bamboo steamer to fit over a wok. Here are a few key features to look out for if you are buying a steamer:

The steamer should have a large base, enabling it to hold plenty of water without needing constant topping up, and it should fit neatly on top of the base to prevent steam escaping around the sides. The top of the steamer should have a tight-fitting lid to keep the steam in during cooking. The following notes outline the types of steamers available and their usefulness for cooking puddings.

SAUCEPAN AND STEAMER SET

This usually comprises a double-handled saucepan base with one, two or more steamers that fit on top. The steaming sections have perforated bases to allow the steam to pass through and they are slightly smaller in diameter at the bottom to fit neatly into the base. Usually made of stainless steel, this type of steamer may be built up to include several cooking tiers. This is ideal for cooking puddings, and the main course or vegetables for the meal may be cooked in separate tiers at the same time.

BAMBOO STEAMERS

Bamboo steamers with tight-fitting lids are available in different sizes. These are designed to fit in a wok. They are perfect for cooking vegetables, oriental-style dishes and any suitable food which can be placed in a fairly shallow container. Some bamboo steamers are deep enough to hold pudding basins; however most woks will only hold sufficient water for comparatively short periods of steaming and need frequent topping up with boiling water. This type of steamer is not recommended for puddings that require hours of steaming.

EXPANDING STEAMERS

This type of steamer is made from small stainless steel plates that fold up into a compact shape for storage. The steamer opens out as large as is necessary to hold the food. It stands on short legs in the base of a saucepan. The boiling water must be kept below the level of the steamer and the saucepan must have a tight

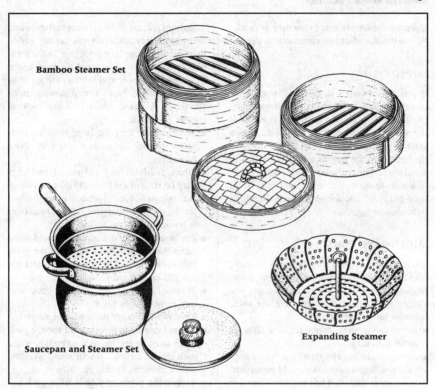

Bamboo Steamer Set

Saucepan and Steamer Set

Expanding Steamer

fitting lid. This type of steamer is ideal for vegetables and it may be used for puddings. Since only a small amount of water may be placed in the pan beneath the steamer it is not suitable for cooking puddings that require many hours of steaming.

ALUMINIUM STEAMERS WITH GRADUATED BASES

These are very common and are designed to fit on top of saucepans of different sizes. Ensure that the steamer has a tight-fitting lid and that it sits neatly on top of the pan.

ELECTRIC STEAMER

This is a plug-in, work-top appliance. A heating element in the base is thermostatically controlled to keep the water boiling or steaming at the right temperature. One or two tiers are supplied to fit over the base, with a tight-fitting lid for the top. In comparison with the other types of steamers, this is an expensive option. However, if you intend to steam a lot of foods it may be a worthwhile purchase. Depending on the individual steamer, this type may lose a lot of steam during cooking, creating puddles on the work surface or condensation on surrounding fittings. Check the steaming layers on the base to make sure they fit neatly. Follow the manufacturer's instructions closely.

IMPROVISING

If you do not own a steamer it is possible to steam puddings by standing them in a saucepan and adding boiling water to come part of the way up the outside of the container. Place a suitable saucer or cereal bowl upside down in the bottom of the pan as a base on which to stand the pudding, allowing for a greater depth of water. Make sure that the saucepan has a tight-fitting lid and follow the instructions in individual recipes.

MICROWAVE COOKING

The microwave oven may be used to make excellent steamed puddings. For more information, and a sponge pudding recipe, see Canary Pudding (page 562). Here are some hints for safety and success:

- Never use a metal container or dish with metal trimmings.
- Sponge puddings rise rapidly and to a considerable height, so make sure the basin used is not more than half full before microwave steaming.
- When cooked, sponge puddings should be slightly sticky on top.
- Use microwave cling film or a suitable plate to cover the pudding during cooking.

PRESSURE COOKING

A pressure cooker may be used to cook steamed puddings quickly and very successfully. It may also be used to cook certain other puddings, for example set custards, and notes are given where applicable.

Information on pressure cookers is included in the section on equipment. Always read and follow the manufacturer's instructions for your cooker. In particular, check information on the minimum volume of water to use in the cooker, notes about pressure levels and specific advice on cooking sponge-type puddings in the pressure cooker. Selected recipes have been tested in a pressure cooker and timings are given in Pressure Cooker Tips. The following rules should be followed when pressure cooking sponge puddings.

- Traditional recipes for large steamed puddings should be cooked on Low (5 lb) pressure.
- Small puddings and individual puddings may be cooked on High (15 lb) pressure.
- Add at least 900 ml/$1\frac{1}{2}$ pints of water to allow for the pre-steaming time before the cooker is brought to pressure.
- The basin used for the pudding should withstand the temperature reached in the pressure cooker; it should be watertight and not cracked or chipped.
- Thoroughly grease the pudding basin and half or two-thirds fill it.
- Tie down the cover on the basin securely.
- Before bringing to pressure, all sponge puddings must be pre-steamed in boiling water with the lid on but without using weights. This allows the raising agent to work.
- Reduce the pressure slowly after cooking, following the manufacturer's instructions.

BROWN BREAD PUDDING

fat for greasing
175 g/6 oz dried brown breadcrumbs
75 g/3 oz raisins
75 g/3 oz sultanas
100 g/4 oz shredded suet
75 g/3 oz caster sugar
2 eggs, beaten
milk (see method)

Grease a 750 ml/1¼ pint pudding basin. Prepare a steamer or half fill a large saucepan with water and bring to the boil.

Place the breadcrumbs, dried fruit, suet and sugar in a mixing bowl. Stir in the eggs, with enough milk to give a dropping consistency. Mix well.

Spoon the mixture into the prepared basin, cover with greased greaseproof paper and foil and secure with string.

Put the pudding in the perforated part of the steamer, or stand it on an old saucer or plate in the pan of boiling water. The water should come halfway up the sides of the basin. Cover the pan tightly and steam the pudding over gently simmering water for 2½–3 hours.

Serve from the basin or leave for 5–10 minutes at room temperature to firm up, then turn out on to a serving plate. Serve with a vanilla custard or Apricot Sauce (page 501).

SERVES SIX

 PRESSURE COOKER TIP

Pour 1.1 litres/2 pints boiling water into the cooker. Steam the pudding without weights on the cooker for 15 minutes. Bring to 15 lb pressure and cook for 25 minutes. Reduce pressure slowly.

DRIED FRUIT PUDDING

This pudding is boiled, not steamed, so the water in the saucepan should at all times cover the pudding basin. Top the pan up as necessary with boiling water.

fat for greasing
100 g/4 oz dried white breadcrumbs
100 g/4 oz plain flour
pinch of salt
10 ml/2 tsp baking powder
100 g/4 oz shredded suet
100 g/4 oz raisins
100 g/4 oz currants
100 g/4 oz soft light brown sugar
1.25 ml/¼ tsp ground mace
1.25 ml/¼ tsp grated nutmeg
1 egg
about 125 ml/4 fl oz milk

Grease a 1 litre/1¾ pint pudding basin. Three-quarters fill a large saucepan with water and bring to the boil.

Combine all the ingredients in a mixing bowl and beat well, adding sufficient milk to give a dropping consistency. Spoon the mixture into the basin, cover with greased greaseproof paper and foil and a floured cloth. Secure with string.

Carefully lower the basin into the pan of boiling water. Cover the pan and lower the heat so that the water is kept at a steady simmer. Cook the pudding for 4–5 hours.

Serve from the basin or leave for 5–10 minutes at room temperature to firm up, then turn on to a serving plate. Serve with warmed golden syrup and whipped cream or with a citrus-flavoured sauce.

SERVES SIX

APPLE PUDDING

*It is important to use dried white breadcrumbs, not
fresh breadcrumbs, for this pudding. Dried breadcrumbs absorb more fruit juice during cooking to
give the cooked pudding the correct consistency.*

fat for greasing
150 g/5 oz cooking apples
100 g/4 oz shredded suet
100 g/4 oz dried white breadcrumbs
100 g/4 oz soft light brown sugar
1.25 ml/¼ tsp grated nutmeg
pinch of salt
2 eggs, beaten
about 125 ml/4 fl oz milk

Peel, core and roughly chop the apples. Mix
them in a large bowl with the suet, breadcrumbs, sugar, nutmeg and salt.

Add the beaten eggs with enough milk to make
a soft, dropping consistency. Leave to stand for
1 hour.

Meanwhile grease a 1 litre/1¾ pint pudding
basin. Prepare a steamer or half fill a large
saucepan with water and bring to the boil.

Stir the pudding mixture, adding a little more
milk if very stiff. Pour the mixture into the
basin, cover with greased greaseproof paper
and foil and secure with string.

Put the pudding in the perforated part of the
steamer, or stand it on an old saucer or plate in

 PRESSURE COOKER TIP

Pour 900 ml/1½ pints boiling water into the
pressure cooker. Stand the pudding on the
trivet and steam it with the lid on, without
weights, for 10 minutes. Bring to 15 lb
pressure and cook for 25 minutes. Reduce
pressure slowly.

---

the pan of boiling water. The water should
come halfway up the sides of the basin. Cover
the pan tightly and steam the pudding over
gently simmering water for 1¾–2 hours.

Serve from the basin or leave for 5–10 minutes
at room temperature to firm up, then turn out
on to a serving plate.

SERVES FIVE TO SIX

VARIATIONS

The recipe works equally well with a wide
variety of other fruits. Try damsons, gooseberries, greengages, plums or rhubarb, adjusting
the quantity of sugar as required.

MOUSSELINE PUDDING

*It is vital to serve this lovely light pudding as soon as
it is turned out of the basin. It will collapse if left
to stand.*

butter for greasing
50 g/2 oz butter
50 g/2 oz icing sugar
3 eggs, separated
grated rind and juice of ½ lemon or few
    drops of vanilla essence

Grease a 1 litre/1¾ pint pudding basin. Prepare
a steamer or half fill a large saucepan with
water and heat gently.

Cream the butter with the icing sugar in a large
heatproof bowl. Add the egg yolks, one at a
time, beating well after each addition. Stir in
the lemon rind and juice or add a few drops of
vanilla essence.

Stand the bowl over a small saucepan of hot
water or use a double saucepan. Heat for 10–12
minutes, stirring constantly until the mixture

is thick enough to hold the mark of a trail for 1-2 seconds (see Mrs Beeton's Tip). Remove from the heat and continue stirring until the mixture is cold.

In a clean, grease-free bowl, whisk the egg whites until stiff. Fold them into the egg yolk mixture, then spoon the mixture into the prepared pudding basin. Cover with greased greaseproof paper and foil and secure with string. Bring the steamer or pan of water to the boil.

Put the pudding in the perforated part of the steamer, or stand it on an old saucer or plate in the pan of boiling water. The water should come halfway up the sides of the basin. Cover the pan tightly and steam the pudding over gently simmering water for 45 minutes. Serve the pudding at once, inverting it on a warmed serving plate.

SERVES FOUR

 MRS BEETON'S TIP

When the egg yolk mixture is heated in the double saucepan, it may separate. It will also become runny as the butter melts. Persevere – it will bind again and thicken as the egg yolks cook.

CUMBERLAND PUDDING

fat for greasing
225 g/8 oz cooking apples
100 g/4 oz shredded suet
200 g/7 oz plain flour
10 ml/2 tsp baking powder
pinch of salt
150 g/5 oz currants
75 g/3 oz soft light brown sugar
1.25 ml/¼ tsp grated nutmeg
2 eggs, beaten
about 75 ml/3 fl oz milk
soft light brown sugar for dredging

Peel, core and roughly chop the apples. Put them in a large bowl with the suet, flour, baking powder, salt, currants, brown sugar and nutmeg. Mix well.

Add the beaten eggs with enough milk to make a soft, dropping consistency. Cover the bowl and leave to stand for 1 hour.

Meanwhile grease a 750 ml/1¼ pint pudding basin. Prepare a steamer or half fill a large saucepan with water; bring to the boil.

Stir the pudding mixture, adding a little more milk if very stiff. Pour the mixture into the basin, cover with greased greaseproof paper and foil and secure with string.

Put the pudding in the perforated part of the steamer, or stand it on an old saucer or plate in the pan of boiling water. The water should come halfway up the sides of the basin. Cover the pan tightly and steam the pudding over gently simmering water for 1¾-2 hours.

Leave the pudding for 5-10 minutes at room temperature to firm up, then turn out on to a serving plate. Dredge with brown sugar before serving.

SERVES FIVE TO SIX

CANARY PUDDING

fat for greasing
150g/5oz butter or margarine
150g/5oz caster sugar
3 eggs, beaten
150g/5oz plain flour
grated rind of ½ lemon
5ml/1tsp baking powder

Grease a 1 litre/1¾ pint pudding basin. Prepare a steamer or half fill a large saucepan with water and bring to the boil.

Cream the butter or margarine with the sugar in a mixing bowl until light and fluffy. Beat in the eggs gradually, adding a little of the flour if the mixture begins to curdle. Add the lemon rind.

Sift the flour and baking powder together and fold lightly into the creamed mixture. Spoon the mixture into the prepared basin, cover with greased greaseproof paper and foil and secure with string.

Put the pudding in the perforated part of the steamer, or stand it on an old saucer or plate in the pan of boiling water. The water should come halfway up the sides of the basin. Cover the pan tightly and steam the pudding over gently simmering water for 1¼–1½ hours. Leave for 3–5 minutes at room temperature to firm up, then turn out on to a serving plate.

SERVES SIX

 MICROWAVE TIP

To make a light sponge pudding in the microwave, use 50g/2oz each of butter or margarine, sugar and self-raising flour with 1 egg and 30ml/2tbsp milk. Prepare the pudding as above and put it into a greased 1.1 litre/2 pint basin. Cook on High for 3–5 minutes.

VARIATIONS

Date Sponge Pudding Add 150g/5oz chopped stoned dates. Substitute orange rind for lemon rind.

Dried Fruit Sponge Pudding Add to the basic recipe 150g/5oz mixed dried fruit. Serve with a vanilla custard.

Chocolate Sponge Pudding Substitute 25g/1oz cocoa for the same quantity of the flour and stir 75g/3oz chocolate chips into the mixture.

Ginger Sponge Pudding Add 10ml/2tsp ground ginger with the flour and stir 50g/2oz chopped preserved ginger into the mixture.

PARADISE PUDDING

fat for greasing
225g/8oz cooking apples, peeled, cored and minced
3 eggs, beaten
75g/3oz sugar
75g/3oz currants
grated rind of 1 lemon
100g/4oz fresh white breadcrumbs
2.5ml/½tsp grated nutmeg
60ml/4tbsp brandy

Grease a 1 litre/1¾ pint soufflé dish or basin. Prepare a steamer or half fill a large saucepan with water and bring to the boil.

Mix all the ingredients in a bowl and beat well. Turn into the dish, cover with greased greaseproof paper and foil and secure with string. Put the pudding in the perforated part of the steamer, or stand it on an old saucer or plate in the pan of boiling water. Steam over boiling water for 1¼ hours, until set to the middle. Serve with a vanilla custard.

SERVES SIX

RICH CHRISTMAS PUDDING

fat for greasing
225 g/8 oz plain flour
pinch of salt
5 ml/1 tsp ground ginger
5 ml/1 tsp mixed spice
5 ml/1 tsp grated nutmeg
50 g/2 oz blanched almonds, chopped
400 g/14 oz soft dark brown sugar
225 g/8 oz shredded suet
225 g/8 oz sultanas
225 g/8 oz currants
200 g/7 oz seedless raisins
175 g/6 oz cut mixed peel
175 g/6 oz dried white breadcrumbs
6 eggs
75 ml/5 tbsp stout
juice of 1 orange
50 ml/2 fl oz brandy
125–250 ml/4–8 fl oz milk

Grease four 600 ml/1 pint pudding basins. Three-quarters fill four saucepans, each deep enough to hold a single pudding, with water.

Sift the flour, salt, ginger, mixed spice and nutmeg into a very large mixing bowl. Add the almonds, sugar, suet, dried fruit, peel and breadcrumbs.

In a second bowl, combine the eggs, stout, orange juice, brandy and 125 ml/4 fl oz milk. Mix well.

Stir the liquid mixture into the dry ingredients, adding more milk if necessary to give a soft dropping consistency. Divide the mixture between the pudding basins, covering each with greased greaseproof paper and a floured cloth or foil. Secure with string.

Carefully lower the basins into the pans of boiling water. Cover the pans and lower the heat so that the water is kept at a steady simmer. Cook the puddings for 6–7 hours, topping up each pan with boiling water as required. The pudding basins should be covered at all times with boiling water.

To store, cover each pudding with a clean dry cloth, wrap in greaseproof paper and store in a cool, dry place until required. To reheat, boil or steam each pudding for 1½–2 hours. Serve with Brandy Butter (page 506) or Brandy and Almond Butter (page 507).

EACH PUDDING SERVES SIX

STORING CHRISTMAS PUDDING

The large quantity of sugar and dried fruit together act as a preservative in Christmas pudding. After cooking, make sure that the pudding is dry and wrap it in clean paper, then place it in an airtight container or seal it in a polythene bag. Foil may be used as an outer covering, over paper, but it should not come in direct contact with the pudding as the fruit acid causes it to break down and disintegrate to a coarse foil powder which ruins the surface of the pudding. Kept in a cool, dry, place, Christmas pudding will remain excellent for up to a year. 'Feed' it occasionally with a little brandy.

 PRESSURE COOKER TIP

Pour 1.5 litres/2¾ pints boiling water into the pressure cooker. Stand one pudding on the trivet and steam it, without weights, for 20 minutes. Bring to 15 lb pressure and cook for 1¾ hours. Allow the pressure to reduce slowly. To reheat, cook at 15 lb pressure for 20 minutes, reduce pressure slowly and serve.

PLUM PUDDING

Christmas pudding became known as plum pudding in Tudor times, when dried plums (prunes) were the popular prime ingredient.

fat for greasing
100g/4oz cooking apple
200g/7oz dried figs, chopped
100g/4oz currants
225g/8oz seedless raisins
200g/7oz blanched almonds, chopped
25g/1oz shelled Brazil nuts, chopped
100g/4oz pine kernels
175g/6oz dried white breadcrumbs
5ml/1tsp mixed spice
100g/4oz soft light brown sugar
100g/4oz cut mixed peel
pinch of salt
grated rind and juice of 1 lemon
100g/4oz butter or margarine
100g/4oz honey
3 eggs, beaten

Grease two 750ml/1¼ pint pudding basins. Prepare two steamers or three-quarter fill two saucepans with water. Each pan should hold one pudding.

Peel, core and chop the apple. Put it in a large mixing bowl with the dried fruits, nuts, breadcrumbs, spice, sugar, peel, salt and the lemon rind and juice.

Combine the butter and honey in a saucepan and warm gently until the butter has melted. Beat in the eggs.

Stir the liquid mixture into the dry ingredients and mix well. Spoon the mixture into the basins, cover with greased greaseproof paper and a floured cloth or foil. Secure with string.

Place the basins in the steamers or carefully lower them into the pans of boiling water. Cover the pans and lower the heat so that the water is kept at a steady simmer. Boil the puddings for 3 hours or steam for 3½-4 hours, topping up each pan with boiling water as required.

To store, cover each pudding with a clean dry cloth, wrap in greaseproof paper and store in a cool, dry place until required. To reheat, boil or steam each pudding for 1½-2 hours.

EACH PUDDING SERVES SIX

 MRS BEETON'S TIP

Plum puddings are traditionally flamed when served. To do this, warm 30-45ml/2-3tbsp brandy, either in a soup ladle over a low flame or in a measuring jug in the microwave for 15 seconds on High. Ignite the brandy (if warmed in a soup ladle it may well ignite spontaneously) and carefully pour it over the hot pudding. Do not use holly to decorate the top of a pudding that is to be flamed.

MRS BEETON'S DELHI PUDDING

fat for greasing
400g/14oz cooking apples
150g/5oz currants
75g/3oz soft light brown sugar
1.25ml/¼tsp grated nutmeg
grated rind of 1 lemon

SUET CRUST PASTRY
400g/14oz plain flour
2.5ml/½tsp salt
10ml/2tsp baking powder
175g/6oz shredded suet

Grease a 750ml/1¼ pint pudding basin. Prepare a steamer or half fill a large saucepan with water and bring to the boil.

Make the pastry. Sift the flour, salt and baking powder into a mixing bowl. Add the suet and enough cold water (about 300 ml/½ pint) to make an elastic dough. Divide the dough in two equal portions.

On a floured surface, roll out one portion of the suet pastry to a round 1.5 cm/¾ inch larger than the top of the prepared pudding basin. Put the pastry into the basin and, pressing with the fingers, ease it evenly up the sides to the top. Thinly roll out the rest of the pastry and cut three rounds in graduated sizes to fit the basin at different levels.

Peel and core the apples. Slice into a bowl and mix with the remaining ingredients. Put layers of fruit and pastry into the basin, finishing with a layer of pastry. Seal the pastry edges firmly by pinching together.

Cover the pudding with greased greaseproof paper and foil and secure with string. Put the pudding in the perforated part of the steamer or stand it on an old saucer or plate in the pan of boiling water. The water should come halfway up the sides of the basin. Cover the pan tightly and steam the pudding over gently simmering water for 2½–3 hours.

Serve from the basin or leave for 5–10 minutes at room temperature to firm up, then turn out on to a serving plate. Serve with a vanilla custard.

SERVES FIVE TO SIX

GINGER PUDDING

fat for greasing
200 g/7 oz plain flour
5 ml/1 tsp ground ginger
pinch of salt
5 ml/1 tsp bicarbonate of soda
100 g/4 oz shredded suet
75 g/3 oz caster sugar
15 ml/1 tbsp black treacle
1 egg, beaten
50–100 ml/2–3½ fl oz milk

Grease a 1 litre/1¾ pint pudding basin. Prepare a steamer or half fill a large saucepan with water and bring to the boil.

Sift the flour, ginger, salt and bicarbonate of soda into a mixing bowl. Add the suet and sugar. Mix lightly.

In a second bowl, beat the treacle and egg with 50 ml/2 fl oz of the milk. Stir the liquid mixture into the dry ingredients, adding more milk if necessary to give a soft dropping consistency.

Spoon the mixture into the prepared basin, cover with greased greaseproof paper and foil and secure with string.

Put the pudding in the perforated part of the steamer, or stand it on an old saucer or plate in the pan of boiling water. The water should come halfway up the sides of the basin. Cover the pan tightly and steam the pudding over gently simmering water for 1¾–2 hours.

Serve from the basin or leave for 5–10 minutes at room temperature to firm up, then turn out on to a serving plate. Serve with Ginger Syrup Sauce (page 505) or Classic Egg Custard Sauce (page 499).

SERVES SIX

GOLDEN SYRUP PUDDING

fat for greasing
45 ml/3 tbsp golden syrup
150 g/5 oz plain flour
5 ml/1 tsp bicarbonate of soda
pinch of salt
5 ml/1 tsp ground ginger
150 g/5 oz dried white breadcrumbs
100 g/4 oz shredded suet
50 g/2 oz caster sugar
1 egg
15 ml/1 tbsp black treacle
75–100 ml/3–3½ fl oz milk

Grease a 1 litre/1¾ pint pudding basin and put 15 ml/1 tbsp golden syrup in the bottom. Prepare a steamer or half fill a large saucepan with water and bring to the boil.

Sift the flour, bicarbonate of soda, salt and ginger into a mixing bowl. Add the breadcrumbs, suet and sugar and mix lightly.

In a second bowl, combine the egg, remaining syrup and treacle. Beat in 75 ml/3 fl oz of the milk. Stir into the dry ingredients, adding more milk if necessary to give a soft dropping consistency.

Spoon the mixture into the prepared basin, cover with greased greaseproof paper and foil and secure with string.

Put the pudding in the perforated part of the steamer, or stand it on an old saucer or plate in the pan of boiling water. The water should come halfway up the sides of the basin. Cover

the pan tightly and steam the pudding over gently simmering water for 1½–2 hours.

Leave for 5–10 minutes at room temperature to firm up, then turn out on to a serving plate. Serve with additional warmed golden syrup and whipped cream.

SERVES SIX TO EIGHT

TREACLE LAYER PUDDING

fat for greasing
65 g/2½ oz dried white breadcrumbs
grated rind of 1 lemon
200 g/7 oz treacle or golden syrup or a
    mixture

SUET CRUST PASTRY
300 g/11 oz plain flour
pinch of salt
10 ml/2 tsp baking powder
150 g/5 oz shredded suet
flour for rolling out

Grease a 1 litre/1¾ pint pudding basin. Prepare a steamer or half fill a large saucepan with water and bring to the boil.

Make the pastry. Sift the flour, salt and baking powder into a mixing bowl. Add the suet and enough cold water (about 250 ml/8 fl oz) to make an elastic dough. Divide the dough in two equal portions.

On a floured surface, roll out one portion of the suet pastry to a round 1 cm/½ inch larger than the top of the prepared pudding basin. Put the pastry into the basin and, pressing with the fingers, ease it evenly up the sides to the top.

Use half the remaining pastry to make a lid to fit the top of the basin. Thinly roll out the rest and cut two rounds in graduated sizes to fit the basin at two different levels.

✳ FREEZER TIP

Keep a bag of breadcrumbs in the freezer for sweet and savoury toppings, puddings and stuffings.

In a bowl, mix the breadcrumbs and lemon rind. Put a layer of treacle or golden syrup on the base of the pastry-lined basin and sprinkle generously with the breadcrumb mixture. Cover with the smaller pastry round, moistening the edges with water and pressing them to join them to the pastry at the side of the basin. Layer the remaining ingredients and pastry, finishing with the pastry lid.

Cover the pudding with greased greaseproof paper and foil and secure with string. Put the pudding in the perforated part of the steamer or stand it on an old saucer or plate in the pan of boiling water. The water should come halfway up the sides of the basin. Cover the pan tightly and steam the pudding over gently simmering water for $2\frac{1}{4}$–$2\frac{1}{2}$ hours.

Serve from the basin or leave for 5-10 minutes at room temperature to firm up, then turn out on to a serving plate. Serve with warmed golden syrup and single cream.

SERVES SIX TO EIGHT

SNOWDON PUDDING

Mix the cherries and raisins used in the pudding thoroughly with the dry ingredients before adding the marmalade and liquids. This will prevent the fruit from sinking to the bottom of the pudding.

fat for greasing
25 g/1 oz glacé cherries, halved
100 g/4 oz raisins
100 g/4 oz dried white breadcrumbs
100 g/4 oz shredded suet
25 g/1 oz ground rice
grated rind of 1 lemon
100 g/4 oz caster sugar
pinch of salt
30 ml/2 tbsp marmalade
2 eggs, beaten
about 75 ml/3 fl oz milk

Grease a 1 litre/1¾ pint pudding basin and decorate the base with some of the cherry halves and raisins. Prepare a steamer or half fill a large saucepan with water. Bring to the boil.

Mix the breadcrumbs, remaining cherries and raisins, suet, ground rice, grated lemon rind, sugar, salt and marmalade in a mixing bowl. Stir in the beaten eggs with enough milk to give a dropping consistency. Spoon the mixture into the prepared basin, cover with greased greaseproof paper and foil and secure with string.

Put the pudding in the perforated part of the steamer, or stand it on an old saucer or plate in the pan of boiling water. The water should come halfway up the sides of the basin. Cover the pan tightly and steam the pudding over gently simmering water for 2–2½ hours.

Leave for 5–10 minutes at room temperature to firm up, then turn out on to a serving plate. Serve the pudding with Marmalade and Wine Sauce (page 504).

SERVES SIX

┌─────────────────────────────────────┐
│ 🗄 **PRESSURE COOKER TIP** │
├─────────────────────────────────────┤
│ Pour 1.1 litres/2 pints boiling water into the cooker. Steam the pudding without weights on the cooker for 15 minutes. Bring to 15 lb pressure and cook for 25 minutes. Reduce pressure slowly. │
└─────────────────────────────────────┘

PADDINGTON PUDDING

fat for greasing
100 g/4 oz dried white breadcrumbs
100 g/4 oz sultanas
100 g/4 oz shredded suet
100 g/4 oz self-raising flour
grated rind of 1 lemon
50 g/2 oz caster sugar
pinch of salt
60 ml/4 tbsp marmalade
2 eggs, beaten
about 75 ml/3 fl oz milk

Grease a 1 litre/1¾ pint pudding basin. Prepare a steamer or half fill a large saucepan with water and bring to the boil.

Mix the breadcrumbs, sultanas, suet, flour, grated rind, sugar, salt and marmalade in a mixing bowl. Stir in the beaten eggs with enough milk to give a dropping consistency. Spoon the mixture into the prepared basin, cover with greased greaseproof paper and foil and secure with string.

Put the pudding in the perforated part of the steamer, or stand it on an old saucer or plate in the pan of boiling water. The water should come halfway up the sides of the basin. Cover the pan tightly and steam the pudding over gently simmering water for 1½–2 hours.

Leave for 5–10 minutes at room temperature to firm up, then turn out on to a serving plate. Serve with single cream or custard.

SERVES SIX

TANGY LEMON PUDDING

fat for greasing
50 g/2 oz plain flour
pinch of salt
5 ml/1 tsp baking powder
175 g/6 oz dried white breadcrumbs
100 g/4 oz caster sugar
100 g/4 oz shredded suet
grated rind and juice of 2 lemons
2 eggs, beaten
150–175 ml/5–6 fl oz milk

Grease a 750 ml/1¼ pint pudding basin. Prepare a steamer or half fill a large saucepan with water and bring to the boil.

Sift the flour, salt and baking powder into a mixing bowl. Stir in the breadcrumbs, sugar, suet and lemon rind. Mix lightly.

In a second bowl, beat the eggs with the lemon juice and about 150 ml/¼ pint of the milk. Stir into the dry ingredients, adding more milk if necessary to give a soft dropping consistency. Spoon the mixture into the prepared basin, cover with greased greaseproof paper and foil and secure with string.

Put the pudding in the perforated part of the steamer, or stand it on an old saucer or plate in the pan of boiling water. The water should come halfway up the sides of the basin. Cover the pan tightly and steam the pudding over gently simmering water for 1½–2 hours.

Serve from the basin or leave for 5–10 minutes at room temperature to firm up, then turn out on to a serving plate. Serve the pudding with a rich lemon sauce.

SERVES SIX

WASHINGTON RIPPLE

fat for greasing
150 g/5 oz butter or margarine
150 g/5 oz caster sugar
3 eggs, beaten
150 g/5 oz plain flour
5 ml/1 tsp baking powder
30 ml/2 tbsp raspberry jam or jelly

Grease a 1 litre/1¾ pint pudding basin. Prepare a steamer or half fill a large saucepan with water and bring to the boil.

Cream the butter or margarine with the sugar in a mixing bowl until light and fluffy. Beat in the eggs gradually, adding a little of the flour if the mixture begins to curdle.

Sift the flour and baking powder together and fold lightly into the creamed mixture. Add the jam or jelly, using a skewer to draw it lightly through the mixture to create a ripple effect.

Spoon the mixture into the prepared basin, cover with greased greaseproof paper and foil and secure with string.

Put the pudding in the perforated part of the steamer, or stand it on an old saucer or plate in the pan of boiling water. The water should come halfway up the sides of the basin. Cover the pan tightly and steam the pudding over gently simmering water for 1¼–1½ hours.

Leave for 3–5 minutes at room temperature to firm up, then turn out on to a serving plate. Serve with a vanilla custard.

SERVES SIX

APRICOT AND ALMOND PUDDING

fat for greasing
75 g/3 oz butter or margarine
75 g/3 oz caster sugar
2 eggs, beaten
75 g/3 oz plain flour
30 ml/2 tbsp grated orange rind
2.5 ml/½ tsp baking powder
6 canned apricot halves, chopped
25 g/1 oz ground almonds
1 slice of orange, halved, to decorate

Grease a 750 ml/1¼ pint pudding basin. Prepare a steamer or half fill a large saucepan with water and bring to the boil.

Cream the butter or margarine with the sugar in a mixing bowl until light and fluffy. Beat in the eggs gradually, adding a little of the flour if the mixture begins to curdle. Add the orange rind.

Sift the flour and baking powder together and fold lightly into the creamed mixture with the chopped apricots and ground almonds. Spoon the mixture into the prepared basin, cover with greased greaseproof paper and foil and secure with string.

Put the pudding in the perforated part of the steamer, or stand it on an old saucer or plate in the pan of boiling water. The water should come halfway up the sides of the basin. Cover the pan tightly and steam the pudding for 1¼–1½ hours.

Leave for 5 minutes at room temperature to firm up. Turn the pudding out on to a serving plate, decorate with the orange slice and serve with Apricot Sauce (page 501).

SERVES SIX

BACHELOR PUDDING

fat for greasing
1 cooking apple (about 150 g/5 oz)
100 g/4 oz dried white breadcrumbs
grated rind of ½ lemon
100 g/4 oz currants
75 g/3 oz caster sugar
pinch of salt
1.25 ml/¼ tsp grated nutmeg
2 eggs, beaten
125 ml/4 fl oz milk
2.5 ml/½ tsp baking powder

Peel, core and grate the apple. Put it into a mixing bowl with the breadcrumbs, lemon rind, currants, sugar, salt and nutmeg. Add the eggs with enough of the milk to give a soft dropping consistency. Leave to stand for 30 minutes.

Grease a 1 litre/1¾ pint pudding basin. Prepare a steamer or half fill a large saucepan with water and bring to the boil.

Stir the baking powder into the pudding mixture. Spoon the mixture into the prepared basin, cover with greased greaseproof paper and foil and secure with string.

Put the pudding in the perforated part of the steamer, or stand it on an old saucer or plate in the pan of boiling water. The water should come halfway up the sides of the basin. Cover the pan tightly and steam the pudding over gently simmering water for 2½–3 hours.

Serve from the basin or leave for 5–10 minutes at room temperature to firm up, then turn out on to a serving plate. Serve with Redcurrant Sauce (page 494) or Cold Chantilly Apple Sauce (page 502).

SERVES SIX

CHOCOLATE CRUMB PUDDING

The mixture is particularly suitable for making individual puddings and the results are so light that they are ideal for 'dressing up' for dinner party occasions. Simple finishing touches, such as the cream feathered through the sauce, or serving fresh fruit with the puddings, make the dinner party dessert very special.

fat for greasing
50 g/2 oz plain chocolate
125 ml/4 fl oz milk
40 g/1½ oz butter or margarine
40 g/1½ oz caster sugar
2 eggs, separated
100 g/4 oz dried white breadcrumbs
1.25 ml/¼ tsp baking powder

DECORATION
Chocolate Caraque or grated chocolate (page 784)
strawberries, halved (optional)

Grease a 750 ml/1¼ pint pudding basin or six dariole moulds. Prepare a steamer or half fill a large saucepan with water and bring to the boil.

Grate the chocolate into a saucepan, add the milk and heat slowly to melt the chocolate.

Cream the butter or margarine with the sugar in a mixing bowl. Beat in the egg yolks with the melted chocolate mixture. Add the breadcrumbs and baking powder.

In a clean, grease-free bowl, whisk the egg whites until fairly stiff. Fold them into the pudding mixture. Spoon the mixture into the prepared basin or dariole moulds, cover with greased greaseproof paper and foil, and secure with string.

Put the pudding or puddings in the perforated part of the steamer, or stand it (them) on an old plate in the pan of boiling water. The water should come halfway up the sides of the basin or moulds. Cover the pan tightly and steam the pudding over gently simmering water for 1 hour for a large pudding, or 30 minutes for individual moulds.

Leave for 3–5 minutes at room temperature to firm up, then turn out on to a serving plate. Serve with Chocolate Cream Sauce (page 503), Mocha Sauce (page 503) or whipped cream. Top the puddings with chocolate caraque or grated chocolate and decorate with fresh strawberries when in season.

SERVES SIX

 MRS BEETON'S TIP

Feather a little single cream through the sauce. Put a few drops of cream on to the chocolate or mocha sauce, then drag the tip of a cocktail stick through it.

EVERYDAY CHOCOLATE PUDDING

fat for greasing
200 g/7 oz plain flour
5 ml/1 tsp baking powder
pinch of salt
25 g/1 oz cocoa
100 g/4 oz butter or margarine
100 g/4 oz caster sugar
2 eggs
1.25 ml/¼ tsp vanilla essence
milk (see method)

Grease a 1 litre/1¾ pint pudding basin. Prepare a steamer or half fill a large saucepan with water and bring to the boil.

Sift the flour, baking powder, salt and cocoa into a mixing bowl. Rub in the butter or margarine and stir in the sugar.

In a second bowl, beat the eggs with the vanilla essence. Add to the dry ingredients with enough milk to give a soft dropping consistency.

Spoon the mixture into the prepared basin, cover with greased greaseproof paper and foil and secure with string.

Put the pudding in the perforated part of the steamer, or stand it on an old saucer or plate in the pan of boiling water. The water should come halfway up the sides of the basin. Cover the pan tightly and steam the pudding over gently simmering water for 1¾–2 hours.

Leave for 5–10 minutes at room temperature to firm up, then turn out on to a serving plate. Serve with Mocha Sauce (page 503) or, on special occasions, with Chocolate Liqueur Sauce (page 503).

SERVES SIX

 MRS BEETON'S TIP

When rubbing the fat into the flour, use only the tips of your fingers, lifting the mixture above the surface of the bowl and letting it drop back naturally to incorporate as much air as possible.

NEWCASTLE PUDDING

fat for greasing
25 g/1 oz glacé cherries, halved
100 g/4 oz butter or margarine
100 g/4 oz caster sugar
2 eggs, beaten
150 g/5 oz plain flour
pinch of salt
5 ml/1 tsp baking powder
about 45 ml/3 tbsp milk

Grease a 1 litre/1¾ pint pudding basin. With the cherries, make a pattern on the base of the basin. Prepare a steamer or half fill a large saucepan with water and bring to the boil.

Cream the butter or margarine with the sugar in a mixing bowl. Gradually beat in the eggs, adding a little flour if the mixture begins to curdle.

Sift the flour with the salt and baking powder and stir into the pudding mixture with enough milk to give a soft dropping consistency.

Spoon the mixture into the prepared basin, cover with greased greaseproof paper and foil and secure with string.

Put the pudding in the perforated part of the steamer, or stand it on an old saucer or plate in the pan of boiling water. The water should come halfway up the sides of the basin. Cover the pan tightly and steam the pudding over gently simmering water for 1½-2 hours.

Leave for 5-10 minutes at room temperature to firm up, then turn out on to a serving plate. Serve with single cream.

SERVES SIX

PATRIOTIC PUDDING

fat for greasing
45 ml/3 tbsp red jam
200 g/7 oz plain flour
pinch of salt
10 ml/2 tsp baking powder
100 g/4 oz butter or margarine
100 g/4 oz caster sugar
1 egg, beaten
about 75 ml/3 fl oz milk

Grease a 1 litre/1¾ pint pudding basin and cover the base with the jam. Prepare a steamer or half fill a large saucepan with water and bring to the boil.

Sift the flour, salt and baking powder into a mixing bowl. Rub in the butter or margarine and add the sugar. Stir in the egg and milk to give a soft dropping consistency. Spoon the mixture into the prepared basin, cover with greased greaseproof paper and foil and secure with string.

Put the pudding in the perforated part of the steamer, or stand it on an old saucer or plate in the pan of boiling water. The water should come halfway up the sides of the basin. Cover the pan tightly and steam the pudding over gently simmering water for 1½-2 hours.

SERVES SIX

 PRESSURE COOKER TIP

Pour 1.1 litres/2 pints boiling water into the cooker. Steam the pudding without weights on the cooker for 15 minutes. Bring to 15 lb pressure and cook for 25 minutes. Reduce pressure slowly.

PRINCE ALBERT'S PUDDING

Prunes – those 'plums' so beloved of the Victorians – feature strongly in this pudding, which looks most effective when turned out.

fat for greasing
400 g/14 oz prunes, soaked overnight in
    water to cover
grated rind of 1 lemon
25 g/1 oz soft light brown sugar
100 g/4 oz butter or margarine
100 g/4 oz caster sugar
2 eggs, separated
40 g/1½ oz rice flour
100 g/4 oz fresh brown breadcrumbs

SAUCE
5 ml/1 tsp arrowroot
250 ml/8 fl oz prune liquid (see method)
10 ml/2 tsp granulated sugar
2-3 drops of red food colouring

Drain the prunes and transfer them to a saucepan. Add half the lemon rind, the brown sugar and 500 ml/17 fl oz water. Simmer gently until soft, stirring lightly from time to time to dissolve the sugar.

As soon as the prunes are soft, drain them, reserving 250 ml/8 fl oz of the cooking liquid. When the prunes are cool enough to handle, halve and stone them.

Grease a 1 litre/1¾ pint pudding basin. Use the prunes, skin side out, to line the basin. Chop any remaining prunes and set aside. Prepare a steamer or half fill a large saucepan with water and bring to the boil.

Cream the butter or margarine with the caster sugar in a mixing bowl. Beat in the egg yolks with the remaining lemon rind, the rice flour and breadcrumbs. Stir in any remaining chopped prunes.

In a clean, grease-free bowl, whisk the egg whites until fairly stiff. Fold into the pudding mixture. Spoon the mixture into the prepared basin, cover with greased greaseproof paper and foil and secure with string.

Put the pudding in the perforated part of the steamer, or stand it on an old saucer or plate in the pan of boiling water. The water should come halfway up the sides of the basin. Cover the pan tightly and steam the pudding over gently simmering water for 1½-1¾ hours.

Meanwhile make the sauce. In a bowl, mix the arrowroot to a smooth paste with some of the reserved prune liquid. Put the remaining liquid into a saucepan and bring it to the boil. Gradually pour the hot liquid over the arrowroot paste, stirring constantly. Return the mixture to the clean pan and bring to the boil, stirring all the time. Lower the heat and simmer for 2-3 minutes. Add the sugar and stir until dissolved. Add the colouring.

When the pudding is cooked, leave for 5-10 minutes at room temperature to firm up, then carefully turn out on to a serving plate. Pour the sauce over the top and serve at once.

SERVES SIX

 MICROWAVE TIP

No time to soak the prunes overnight? Place in a suitable bowl with water or tea to cover. Cover the bowl and microwave for 6-8 minutes on High. Stand for 10 minutes before using.

CLOUTIE DUMPLING

300 g/11 oz self-raising flour
5 ml/1 tsp baking powder
100 g/4 oz shredded suet
5 ml/1 tsp mixed spice
5 ml/1 tsp ground ginger
5 ml/1 tsp ground cinnamon
2.5 ml/½ tsp salt
100 g/4 oz soft light brown sugar
50 g/2 oz muscatel raisins, seeded
100 g/4 oz sultanas
50 g/2 oz cut mixed peel
1 carrot, grated
100 g/4 oz black treacle
200 ml/7 fl oz milk
1 egg, beaten
flour for dusting or fat for greasing

Mix the flour, baking powder, suet, spices, salt and sugar in a mixing bowl. Stir in the raisins, sultanas and mixed peel with the carrot.

Put the treacle in a saucepan with the milk and dissolve over low heat. Stir into the dry ingredients with the egg to give a fairly soft dropping consistency. Mix thoroughly.

Put the mixture into a scalded and floured cloth and tie with string, allowing room for expansion. Place on a plate in a pan and add sufficient boiling water to come three-quarters of the way up the dumpling. Simmer for 3 hours.

Alternatively spoon the mixture into a greased 1.5 litre/2¾ pint basin, cover with greased greaseproof paper and foil and secure with string. Cook in a steamer or on an old saucer or plate in a pan of boiling water. The water should come halfway up the sides of the basin. Simmer as above.

Turn out on to a serving dish and serve hot or cold with Classic Egg Custard Sauce (page 499) or Sweet Sherry Sauce (page 505).

SERVES FOUR TO SIX

VICARAGE PUDDING

Pepped up with orange and adapted to use less suet or block margarine, this is delicious.

175 g/6 oz self-raising flour
50 g/2 oz suet or block margarine, chilled
    and grated
100 g/4 oz currants
50 g/2 oz soft light brown sugar
5 ml/1 tsp ground ginger
grated rind and juice of 1 orange
about 50 ml/2 fl oz milk (see method)

Grease a 1 litre/1¾ pint pudding basin. Prepare a steamer or half fill a large saucepan with water and bring to the boil.

Beat all the ingredients together in a mixing bowl until thoroughly combined, adding a little milk, if necessary to give the mixture a firm dropping consistency.

Turn into the prepared pudding basin. Cover with greaseproof paper and foil and secure with string. Put the pudding in the perforated part of the steamer, or stand it on an old saucer or plate in the pan of boiling water. Cover the pan tightly and steam the pudding over simmering water for 1½ hours. Serve piping hot with a vanilla custard or cream.

SERVES FOUR TO SIX

 MRS BEETON'S TIP

To save transferring the sticky treacle, measure it in the saucepan, weighing the empty pan first and then adding sufficient treacle to increase the weight by 100 g/4 oz.

Rice Puddings and Cooked Milk Puddings

Milk puddings are as versatile as the occasions on which they may be served are varied. You will find recipes ranging from an inexpensive, nutritious weekday pudding to a splendid fruity concoction for special occasions.

Plain milk puddings fit very well into a day-to-day diet as they are inexpensive, satisfying and nutritious. Remember that you may always use semi-skimmed or skimmed milk if you are following a low-fat diet. Although white rice is the traditional ingredient for making puddings, brown rice may be used to provide a certain amount of fibre. Between the supermarkets, ethnic shops and healthfood stores we are provided with many different types of rice, not all of which is suitable for making puddings.

TYPES OF RICE

In Mrs Beeton's day the choice of rice for making a boiled rice pudding was limited compared to the varieties now available. However, Mrs Beeton distinguished between the qualities of rice on offer:

'Of the varieties of rice brought to our market, that from Bengal is chiefly of the species denominated cargo rice, and is of a coarse reddish-brown cast, but peculiarly sweet and large-grained; it does not readily separate from the husk, but it is preferred by the natives to all the others. Patna rice is more esteemed in Europe, and is of very superior quality; it is small-grained, rather long and wiry, and is remarkably white. The Carolina rice is considered as the best, and is likewise the dearest in London.'

Modern supermarkets stock several varieties of rice and the choice is widened by others sold in healthfood shops and ethnic stores. Brown rice, wild rice, Basmati rice, Italian risotto rice, easy-cook rice, long-grain rice, round-grain rice, pudding rice and flaked rice are all readily available and they all have different characteristics. The greater interest in savoury dishes using rice, and the different grains that may be used for them, has detracted attention from pudding rice. The Carolina rice that Mrs Beeton favoured is still the most common type of polished, unprocessed white rice although it is now grown in other parts of America as well as Carolina. Varieties of rice that are popular for savoury dishes are not necessarily suitable for making puddings. Unprocessed long-grain rice, Patna rice, pudding rice or flaked rice should be used. Short-grain or round-grain are other terms for pudding rice and you will find brown types as well as polished rice.

Processed, or easy-cook, rice is not suitable for making puddings as the grains do not break down to give a creamy result.

Other popular ingredients used to make milk puddings include semolina, macaroni, tapioca and sago.

Baked milk puddings are easy to prepare but they require slow cooking. For a creamy result stir in the skin which forms on the top of the pudding after the first two-thirds of the cooking time has elapsed. It is possible to cook rice pudding by simmering it very gently on the hob. The heat must be on the lowest setting and the pudding should be stirred often.

PRESSURE COOKING

Milk puddings may be cooked in a pressure cooker. This gives good, creamy results in a fraction of the time needed for baking or simmering. Do not use less than 600 ml/1 pint of milk and keep the heat at a steady temperature which is low enough to prevent the milk from rising too high in the cooker and blocking the vent. For the same reason the cooker should not be more than a quarter full when cooking a milk pudding. General guidance on the types of pressure cookers available and their use is given in the section on equipment (page 19).

MICROWAVE COOKING

The microwave oven may be used to cook milk puddings. Semolina cooks particularly well; however puddings using rice, tapioca, macaroni or semolina boil over very readily. For this reason a medium or low microwave power setting should be used and the pudding should be cooked in a very large dish – a mixing bowl covered with a suitable dinner plate or very deep casserole is ideal. The advantage of cooking milk puddings thickened with rice in the microwave is a matter of personal opinion. Since a low power setting has to be used the time saving is not enormous and this cooking method demands attention to ensure that the pudding does not boil over. As an alternative to traditional recipes, the following is an excellent microwave method for making an extravagant, deliciously creamy rice pudding.

Put 50 g/2 oz short-grain rice in a covered dish. Add 600 ml/1 pint water and cook on High for 20–25 minutes. At the end of the cooking time all the water should have been absorbed and the grains of rice should be swollen and sticky. Immediately stir in sugar to taste and 300 ml/½ pint double or single cream. The pudding may be dotted with butter and sprinkled with a little grated nutmeg, then lightly browned under a moderate grill.

RICE PUDDING

This basic recipe works equally well with flaked rice, sago or flaked tapioca.

butter for greasing
100 g/4 oz pudding rice
1 litre/1¾ pints milk
pinch of salt
50–75 g/2–3 oz caster sugar
15 g/½ oz butter (optional)
1.25 ml/¼ tsp grated nutmeg

Butter a 1.75 litre/3 pint pie dish. Wash the rice in cold water, drain and put it into the dish with the milk. Leave to stand for 30 minutes.

Set the oven at 150°C/300°F/gas 2. Stir the salt and sugar into the milk mixture and sprinkle with flakes of butter, if used, and nutmeg.

Bake for 2–2½ hours or until the pudding is thick and creamy, and brown on the top. The pudding is better if it cooks even more slowly, at 120°C/250°F/gas ½ for 4–5 hours.

SERVES FOUR TO FIVE

 PRESSURE COOKER TIP

Bring all the ingredients to the boil in the open cooker, stirring. Reduce the heat so that the milk just bubbles. Put the lid on and bring to 15 lb pressure without increasing the heat. Cook for 12 minutes. Reduce pressure slowly.

SEMOLINA PUDDING

Use coarsely ground rice, oatmeal, small sago or cornmeal instead of semolina, if preferred.

1 litre/1¾ pints milk
flavouring (see Mrs Beeton's Tip)
75 g/3 oz semolina
pinch of salt
50–75 g/2–3 oz caster sugar
butter for greasing (optional)

Warm the milk in a heavy-bottomed saucepan. Add any solid flavouring, if used, to the milk and infuse for about 10 minutes; then remove.

Sprinkle the semolina on to the milk, stirring quickly to prevent the formation of lumps. Bring to simmering point, stirring all the time. Continue stirring, and simmer for 15–20 minutes or until the grain is transparent and cooked through.

Stir in the salt, sugar, and any flavouring essence used. Serve the creamed semolina hot or cold or pour into a well-buttered 1.75 litre/3 pint pie dish, and bake at 180°C/350°F/gas 4, for 20–30 minutes until the top has browned.

SERVES SIX

VARIATION

Semolina Pudding with Eggs Cook the semolina as above, but do not add the flavouring or the salt. Leave to cool slightly. Separate 3 eggs. Stir the egg yolks, salt, sugar, and any flavourings into the semolina mixture. Whisk the egg whites to the same consistency as the pudding, and fold into the mixture. Pour into a well-buttered 1.75 litre/3 pint pie dish, and bake at 160°C/325°F/gas 3, for about 30 minutes until the top has browned. Sprinkle with brown sugar and/or butter flakes before baking, if liked.

RICE PUDDING WITH EGGS

Any suitable large grain may be used instead of pudding rice.

butter for greasing
100 g/4 oz pudding rice
1 litre/1¾ pints milk
2–3 eggs, separated
pinch of salt
50–75 g/2–3 oz caster sugar
1.25 ml/¼ tsp grated nutmeg

Butter a 1.75 litre/3 pint pie dish. Wash the rice in cold water, drain and put it into the top of a double saucepan with the milk. Cook slowly for about 1 hour, or until the grain is tender. Remove from the heat and cool slightly.

Set the oven at 160°C/325°F/gas 3. Stir the egg yolks, salt, sugar and nutmeg into the cooked rice mixture.

In a clean, grease-free bowl, whisk the egg whites to the same consistency as the pudding. Fold the egg whites into the mixture. Pour into the pie dish and bake for 40–45 minutes until creamy and browned.

SERVES SIX

 MRS BEETON'S TIP

Grated citrus rind, ground cinnamon, allspice or grated nutmeg may be added to all these puddings. Flavouring essences or liqueurs are equally suitable. A pinch of salt improves the flavour of all puddings.

BLANCMANGE MOULD

Blancmange may be made using ground rice or arrowroot instead of the cornflour given below. The quantities will be the same. Traditionally, blancmange was a white mould which was flavoured with sweet and bitter almonds. Use natural almond essence to give this mould the best flavour.

75 g/3 oz cornflour
1 litre/1¾ pints milk
50 g/2 oz sugar
a little almond essence

In a bowl, blend the cornflour to a smooth paste with a little of the cold milk. Bring the remaining milk to the boil in a saucepan.

Pour the boiling milk on to the cornflour mixture, stirring all the time. Pour the mixture back into the pan and heat gently, stirring all the time until the mixture simmers and thickens. Allow to simmer for 5-10 minutes, stirring occasionally.

Remove the pan from the heat and stir in the sugar. Add almond essence to taste, stir well, then pour the blancmange into a wetted 1.1 litre/2 pint mould. Press dampened greaseproof paper or microwave cooking film on to the surface of the blancmange and cool.

Chill the cooled blancmange for at least 2 hours, or until set. Unmould the blancmange just before serving.

SERVES SIX

FLAVOURINGS

To keep the mould a creamy colour, vanilla, grated lemon rind or a good knob of butter with 125 ml/4 fl oz sherry may be added instead of the almond essence. However, the mixture may also be flavoured with ingredients that add colour although the result is not strictly a blancmange.

Chocolate Either add 30 ml/2 tbsp cocoa to the cornflour and mix it to a paste or add 175 g/6 oz plain chocolate, broken into squares, to the cooked mixture. Stir the mixture until the chocolate has melted before pouring it into the wetted mould.

Coffee Dissolve 15 ml/1 tbsp instant coffee in 15 ml/1 tbsp boiling water, then stir in 30 ml/2 tbsp rum. Stir this essence into the cooked mixture before pouring it into the mould.

Strawberry Substitute 300 ml/½ pint fresh strawberry purée for the same volume of milk, adding it to the cornflour mixture before stirring in the boiling milk.

 MRS BEETON'S TIP

If arrowroot is used instead of cornflour, the pan should be removed from the heat as soon as the mixture has reached a full boil. If arrowroot is cooked for any length of time after boiling, it tends to thin down.

CHOCOLATE SEMOLINA

800 ml/27 fl oz milk
65 g/2¼ oz semolina
75 g/3 oz plain chocolate
50 g/2 oz caster sugar
few drops of vanilla essence

Heat 750 ml/1¼ pints of the milk in a heavy-bottomed saucepan. Sprinkle in the semolina, stir well, and simmer for 15-20 minutes or until the semolina is cooked.

Meanwhile, grate the chocolate into a second pan, add the remaining milk and heat until the chocolate has melted. Stir into the semolina with the sugar and essence, and serve at once.

SERVES FOUR TO FIVE

ARROWROOT PUDDING

The method below is suitable for all powdered grains, including cornflour, custard powder, finely ground rice or fine oatmeal.

1 litre/1¾ pints milk
flavouring (see Blancmange Mould, opposite)
65 g/2½ oz arrowroot
pinch of salt
50–75 g/2–3 oz caster sugar
butter for greasing (optional)

Warm the milk in a heavy-bottomed saucepan. Add any solid flavouring, if used, to the milk and infuse for 30 minutes; then remove.

Put the arrowroot in a bowl and blend with a little of the milk. In a saucepan bring the remaining milk to boiling point with the salt, and pour on to the blended paste, stirring briskly to prevent the formation of lumps.

Return the mixture to the clean pan, heat until it thickens, and simmer for 2–3 minutes to cook the grain completely, stirring all the time. Add the sugar and any liquid flavouring used.

Serve the arrowroot pudding as it is, hot or cold, or pour into a well-buttered 1.75 litre/3 pint pie dish, and bake for 20–30 minutes at 180°C/350°F/gas 4 until the top has browned.

SERVES SIX

GENEVA PUDDING

butter for greasing
75 g/3 oz long-grain rice
750 ml/1¼ pints milk
pinch of salt
75 g/3 oz caster sugar
1 kg/2¼ lb cooking apples
50 g/2 oz butter
1.25 ml/¼ tsp ground cinnamon

Butter a 1.5 litre/2¾ pint pie dish. Wash the rice and put it into a saucepan with the milk. Add the salt and simmer for about 1 hour or until the rice grains are tender.

Set the oven at 180°C/350°F/gas 4. Stir 25 g/1 oz of the sugar into the rice mixture. Set aside.

Peel, core, and chop the apples. Put them into a second saucepan with the butter and cinnamon. Add 45 ml/3 tbsp water. Simmer gently until soft, then purée in a blender or food processor or push through a sieve. Stir in the remaining sugar.

Arrange the rice and apple in alternate layers in the pie dish, with rice on the top and bottom. Bake for 20–30 minutes.

SERVES SIX

WINDSOR PUDDING

butter for greasing
40 g/1½ oz long-grain rice
350 ml/12 fl oz milk
450 g/1 lb cooking apples
grated rind of ½ lemon
50 g/2 oz caster sugar
3 egg whites

Butter a 1 litre/1¾ pint pudding basin or soufflé dish. Wash the rice, drain thoroughly and place in a saucepan with the milk. Simmer for 45–60 minutes or until the rice is tender and all the milk has been absorbed. Cool slightly.

Peel, core and roughly chop the apples. Stew in a covered, heavy-bottomed saucepan until soft. Shake the pan from time to time to prevent the apples from sticking. Prepare a steamer or half fill a large saucepan with water. Bring to the boil.

Purée the apples with the lemon rind in a blender or food processor. Alternatively, rub the apples through a sieve into a bowl, in which case add the grated lemon rind afterwards. Stir in the cooked rice and sugar.

In a clean, grease-free bowl, whisk the egg whites until fairly stiff and stir them into the apple mixture. Spoon the mixture into the prepared pudding basin or soufflé dish, cover with greased greaseproof paper or foil and secure with string.

Put the pudding in the perforated part of the steamer, or stand it on an old saucer or plate in the pan of boiling water. The water should come halfway up the sides of the basin. Cover the pan tightly and steam the pudding over gently simmering water for 45 minutes. Serve the pudding hot.

SERVES SIX

> **MRS BEETON'S TIP**
>
> Windsor pudding is very light and it can be difficult to turn out. Placing a small circle of non-stick baking parchment in the bottom of the basin helps. Alternatively, serve the pudding straight from the basin or dish.

CARAMEL RICE PUDDING

125 g/4½ oz long-grain rice
750 ml/1¼ pints milk
pinch of salt
75 g/3 oz lump sugar
2 eggs, beaten
40 g/1½ oz caster sugar

Wash the rice, drain thoroughly and put into a saucepan with the milk and salt. Simmer for about 1 hour or until the rice is soft and all the milk has been absorbed.

Meanwhile prepare a 1 litre/1¾ pint charlotte mould to receive a caramel coating (see Mrs Beeton's Tip). Prepare a steamer or half fill a large saucepan with water and bring to the boil.

Make the caramel by heating the lump sugar with 75 ml/5 tbsp water in a heavy-bottomed saucepan. Stir constantly until the sugar dissolves and the mixture comes to the boil.

Continue to boil, without stirring, until the mixture is golden brown. Immediately pour the caramel into the warmed mould, twisting and turning it until the sides and the base are evenly coated. Leave the coating to harden for a few minutes.

Stir the beaten eggs into the cooked rice with the caster sugar. Turn into the caramel-coated mould, cover with greased greaseproof paper or foil and secure with string.

Put the pudding in the perforated part of the steamer, or stand it on an old saucer or plate in the pan of boiling water. The water should come halfway up the sides of the charlotte mould. Cover the pan tightly and steam the pudding over gently simmering water for 1 hour or until firm.

Serve from the mould or turn out on to a serving plate. Serve hot or cold, with Caramel Custard Sauce (page 495), if liked.

SERVES SIX

 MRS BEETON'S TIP

Hot caramel can cause a nasty burn if it accidentally splashes on to exposed skin. The best way to safeguard yourself is by using a newspaper holder: Prepare a thickly folded band of newspaper long enough to encircle the chosen mould. Heat the mould in boiling water or in the oven, then wrap the newspaper around it, twisting the ends tightly to form a handle. Make sure that the band of paper is secure and that the ends are tightly twisted to prevent the mould from slipping. Hold the paper, not the side of the mould, when tilting it to distribute the caramel, and, as an additional safeguard, work over the sink.

LEMON RICE

A meringue topping gives this simple pudding a touch of class.

butter for greasing
50 g/2 oz long-grain rice
500 ml/17 fl oz milk
pinch of salt
pared rind and juice of 1 lemon
75 g/3 oz granulated sugar
2 eggs, separated
45 ml/3 tbsp smooth seedless jam
50 g/2 oz caster sugar
caster sugar for dredging

Butter a 1 litre/1¾ pint pie dish. Set the oven at 160°C/325°F/gas 3. Wash the rice and put it in a double saucepan with the milk, salt and lemon rind; simmer for about 1 hour or until tender. Remove the rind and stir in the granulated sugar. Cool slightly.

Stir the egg yolks and lemon juice into the rice. Pour into the pie dish and bake for 20–25 minutes. Lower the oven temperature to 140°C/275°F/gas 1.

Spread the jam on top of the pudding. In a clean, grease-free bowl, whisk the egg whites until stiff, and fold in the caster sugar. Pile on top of the pudding, dredge with a little extra caster sugar, and return to the oven. Bake for 20–30 minutes until the meringue is set and coloured.

SERVES SIX

EMPRESS PUDDING

butter for greasing
100g/4oz long-grain rice
1 litre/1¾ pints milk
pinch of salt
50g/2oz butter or margarine
50g/2oz caster sugar
200g/7oz jam or stewed fruit

SHORT CRUST PASTRY
75g/3oz plain flour
pinch of salt
40g/1½oz margarine (or half butter, half lard)
flour for rolling out

Butter the base of a 1.25 litre/2¼ pint ovenproof dish. Make the pastry. Sift the flour and salt into a bowl, then rub in the margarine until the mixture resembles fine breadcrumbs. Add enough cold water to make a stiff dough. Press the dough together with your fingertips. Set the pastry aside in a cool place while preparing the rice filling.

Wash the rice, drain and place in a heavy-bottomed saucepan. Add the milk and salt and simmer for about 1 hour or until tender. Stir in the butter or margarine and sugar.

Set the oven at 180°C/350°F/gas 4. Roll out the pastry on a lightly floured surface and line the sides of the baking dish. Spread a layer of the rice mixture on the base of the dish and cover with jam or fruit. Repeat the layers until the dish is full, finishing with a layer of rice. Bake for 25–30 minutes. Serve with Apricot Sauce (page 501).

SERVES SIX

PEAR AND RICE MERINGUE

butter for greasing
75g/3oz long-grain rice
750ml/1¼ pints milk
pinch of salt
1 bay leaf
40g/1½oz granulated sugar
25g/1oz butter
2 eggs, separated
6 fresh or canned pear halves
50g/2oz caster sugar
caster sugar for dredging

Butter a 1.5 litre/2¾ pint pie dish. Wash the rice, drain and place in a heavy-bottomed saucepan with the milk, salt and bay leaf. Simmer for about 1 hour, until the rice is tender. Remove the bay leaf.

Set the oven at 140°C/275°F/gas 1. Stir the granulated sugar and butter into the rice mixture. Cool slightly, then add the egg yolks, mixing well. Pour into the prepared pie dish. Arrange the pear halves, cut side down, on top.

In a clean, grease-free bowl, whisk the egg whites until stiff and fold in the caster sugar in spoonfuls. Pile on top of the rice and pears. Dredge the meringue with a little caster sugar and bake for about 20 minutes or until the meringue is crisp and golden brown. Serve.

SERVES SIX

 MRS BEETON'S TIP

Bay leaves are a valuable addition to the store cupboard or freezer. Although primarily used in stews, stocks and fish dishes, they add a subtle flavour to milk puddings.

SWEDISH RICE

300 g/11 oz long-grain rice
pinch of salt
625 g/1¼ lb cooking apples
pared rind of 1 lemon
375 ml/13 fl oz milk
75 g/3 oz caster sugar
1.25 ml/¼ tsp ground cinnamon
100 ml/3½ fl oz sweet sherry
100 g/4 oz raisins
single cream to serve

Wash the rice, drain it and put it in a saucepan. Add boiling salted water to cover and cook for 3 minutes; drain well.

Peel and core the apples and slice them thinly into a second pan. Add the rice, lemon rind and milk and simmer gently for about 45 minutes until tender. Remove the rind.

Stir the sugar, cinnamon, sherry, and raisins into the mixture and cook for a further 4–5 minutes. Spoon into individual bowls and serve with cream.

SERVES SIX

ICED RICE PUDDING

Serve cooled poached fruit, such as plums, apricots or pears, or a fruit salad with this frozen dessert. Spoon the fruit around the base of the unmoulded rice.

1 litre/1¾ pints milk
175 g/6 oz pudding rice
225 g/8 oz sugar
6 egg yolks
5 ml/1 tsp vanilla essence

Pour the milk into a heavy-bottomed saucepan, then stir in the rice and sugar. Bring to the boil, stirring occasionally to make sure the sugar dissolves and the rice does not stick, then lower the heat and cover the pan. Cook gently for 2 hours, stirring occasionally, or until the rice is thick and creamy. Remove from the heat and beat well.

Lightly whisk the egg yolks, then strain them through a fine sieve into the hot rice and beat well. Stir in the vanilla, then pour the rice into a mould, cake tin or container for freezing.

Cover the surface of the rice with dampened greaseproof paper and leave until cold. Freeze until firm, preferably overnight.

Leave the rice in a cool room or on a high shelf in the refrigerator for about 40 minutes before turning it out on to a serving platter.

SERVES EIGHT

CHILLED RICE MOULD

150 g/5 oz pudding rice
1 litre/1¾ pints milk
75 g/3 oz sugar
vanilla essence
25 g/1 oz butter

Wash the rice in cold water, drain and place in the top of a double saucepan with the milk. Cover the pan and cook the mixture gently over simmering water for 2–2½ hours until the grain is tender and the milk almost absorbed. Stir occasionally to prevent the grain from settling on the bottom of the pan.

Stir the sugar, vanilla essence to taste and the butter into the mixture and pour into a wetted 1 litre/1¾ pint mould or basin. Chill until set. Turn out and serve with stewed fruit or jam.

SERVES FOUR TO SIX

HOT TIMBALE OF SEMOLINA

butter for greasing
500 ml/17 fl oz milk
75 g/3 oz semolina
50 g/2 oz caster sugar
few drops of vanilla essence
2 eggs, separated
30 ml/2 tbsp single cream

DECORATION
1 (397 g/14 oz) can apricot halves in syrup
1 strip of angelica
3 glacé cherries
10 ml/2 tsp chopped almonds

Butter a 750 ml/1¼ pint timbale mould or 6 small dariole moulds.

Heat the milk in a heavy-bottomed saucepan, sprinkle in the semolina, stirring all the time, and simmer for 10–15 minutes until it is cooked. Cool slightly.

Stir the sugar and vanilla essence into the semolina mixture, with the egg yolks. Beat with an electric or rotary whisk until the mixture is nearly cold. Prepare a steamer or half fill a large saucepan with water and bring to the boil.

In a clean, grease-free bowl, beat the egg whites until just stiff, and fold into the semolina mixture with the cream. Three-quarters fill the timbale mould or small moulds with the mixture. Cover with greased greaseproof paper or foil and secure with string. Put the timbale or dariole moulds in the perforated part of the steamer or stand on a large plate in the pan of boiling water. Cover the pan tightly. Steam the large mould for about 45 minutes and small moulds for 30 minutes or until set.

Meanwhile, drain the apricots, reserving 250 ml/8 fl oz of the syrup in a small saucepan. Warm the fruit between 2 plates over a pan of simmering water. Boil the apricot syrup until well reduced. When the pudding is cooked and set, turn out on to a hot dish and decorate with the warmed apricot halves, the angelica, glacé cherries and chopped almonds. Pour the syrup around and serve.

SERVES SIX

RUM AND CHOCOLATE SEMOLINA MOULD

500 ml/17 fl oz milk
50 g/2 oz semolina
50 g/2 oz plain chocolate, grated
10 ml/2 tsp gelatine
50 g/2 oz caster sugar
2.5 ml/½ tsp rum

Bring the milk to the boil in a heavy-bottomed saucepan. Sprinkle in the semolina and cook gently, stirring all the time, for 15–20 minutes until soft and smooth. Stir in the grated chocolate and mix well.

Place 30 ml/2 tbsp water in a small bowl and sprinkle the gelatine on to the liquid. Stand the bowl over a saucepan of hot water and stir the gelatine until it has dissolved completely. Stir the dissolved gelatine into the semolina mixture with the sugar and rum.

Leave the mixture to cool, stirring from time to time. When tepid, pour into a wetted 600 ml/1 pint mould and leave for about 2 hours to set. Turn out on to a serving plate to serve.

SERVES THREE TO FOUR

HONEY PUDDING

butter for greasing
125 ml/4 fl oz milk
25 g/1 oz semolina
2 eggs, separated
25 g/1 oz butter
100 g/4 oz honey
grated rind of ½ lemon
2.5 ml/½ tsp ground ginger
150 g/5 oz dried white breadcrumbs

Butter a 600–750 ml/1–1¼ pint pudding basin. Prepare a steamer or half fill a large saucepan with water and bring to the boil.

Heat the milk in a heavy-bottomed saucepan. Sprinkle in the semolina and cook for 10 minutes, stirring all the time.

Remove the pan from the heat and add the egg yolks, butter, honey, lemon rind, ginger and breadcrumbs. Beat well.

In a clean, grease-free bowl, whisk the egg whites until fairly stiff. Fold into the semolina mixture. Pour the mixture into the prepared basin, cover with greased greaseproof paper or foil and secure with string.

Put the pudding in the perforated part of the steamer, or stand it on an old saucer or plate in the pan of boiling water. The water should come halfway up the sides of the basin. Cover the pan tightly and steam the pudding over gently simmering water for 1¾–2 hours.

Serve from the basin or leave for 5–10 minutes at room temperature to firm up, then turn out on to a serving plate. Serve with Almond Sauce (page 495).

SERVES FIVE TO SIX

TAPIOCA CREAM PUDDING

butter for greasing
75 g/3 oz tapioca
750 ml/1¼ pints milk
pinch of salt
15 g/½ oz butter or margarine
15 ml/1 tbsp caster sugar
1.25 ml/¼ tsp almond essence
3 eggs, separated
75 g/3 oz ratafias or small macaroons, crushed

Butter a 1.1 litre/2 pint pie dish. Wash the tapioca, drain and place in a saucepan with the milk and salt. Soak for 1–2 hours.

Heat the tapioca mixture and simmer for about 1 hour until the grain is soft and all the milk has been absorbed. Set the oven at 180°C/350°F/gas 4.

Remove the tapioca mixture from the heat and stir in the butter, sugar and essence. Cool slightly, then stir in the egg yolks. Pour the mixture into the prepared pie dish and bake for 15–30 minutes.

Lower the oven temperature to 140°C/275°F/gas 1. In a clean, grease-free bowl, whisk the egg whites until stiff. Fold in the crushed ratafias or macaroons. Pile on top of the tapioca mixture, return to the oven and bake for 20–30 minutes until the meringue topping is crisp and golden brown. Serve at once.

SERVES SIX

AMERICAN INDIAN PUDDING

fat for greasing
750 ml/1¼ pints milk
75 g/3 oz white or yellow cornmeal
100 g/4 oz caster sugar
1.25 ml/¼ tsp ground cinnamon or nutmeg
25 g/1 oz butter
maple syrup to serve

Grease a 1 litre/1¾ pint pie dish. Set the oven at 140-150°C/275-300°F/gas 1-2. Bring the milk to the boil in a heavy-bottomed saucepan, then pour in the cornmeal. Cook over gentle heat for 5 minutes, stirring all the time, until thickened.

Remove the pan from the heat and stir in the sugar, spice and butter. Pour into the prepared pie dish.

Bake the pudding for 1 hour until browned on top. Serve with maple syrup.

SERVES FOUR

CORNMEAL PUDDING

fat for greasing
500 ml/17 fl oz milk
75 g/3 oz white or yellow cornmeal
75 g/3 oz caster sugar
50 g/2 oz seedless raisins
grated rind and juice of ½ lemon
2 eggs, beaten

Grease a 900 ml/1½ pint pie dish. Set the oven at 180°C/350°F/gas 4. Bring the milk to just below boiling point in a heavy-bottomed saucepan. Pour in the cornmeal. Cook over gentle heat for 5 minutes, stirring all the time, until the mixture thickens. Remove from the heat and stir in the sugar and raisins with the lemon rind and juice. Cool slightly.

Add the beaten eggs to the mixture, transfer to the prepared pie dish and level the top.

Bake for 50-60 minutes until risen and browned on top. Serve with cream or ice cream.

SERVES FOUR

OATMEAL FLUMMERY

150 g/5 oz fine oatmeal
juice of 1 orange
15 ml/1 tbsp caster sugar or honey

Put the oatmeal in a large bowl. Add 500 ml/17 fl oz water and soak for 24 hours.

Transfer the oatmeal mixture to a large measuring jug. Measure an equal volume of water. Place the oatmeal mixture and measured water in a large bowl, and soak for a further 24 hours.

Strain the mixture through a fine sieve into a heavy-bottomed saucepan, squeezing or pressing the oatmeal to extract as much of the floury liquid as possible. Add the orange juice and sugar or honey.

Stir over gentle heat for 15-30 minutes or until the mixture boils and is very thick. Serve warm.

SERVES FOUR TO SIX

Creams, Whips and Custard Puddings

Creams, whips and custards are rich desserts that make perfect summer puddings. The selection here is merely representative of these soft desserts that were popular in Mrs Beeton's day.

Dairy produce is discussed at the beginning of the Dairy Foods Chapter. The recipes in this chapter rely on the use of cream – sometimes eggs – for delicate results. For special occasions creamy desserts are easy to make and simple to serve; however, if you wish to lighten some of the desserts for everyday use, remember that fromage frais makes an excellent substitute for cream in set dishes. Using a full-fat fromage frais does not make the dessert less rich, so look for medium-fat or low-fat fromage frais. The same applies to yogurt as some types are full fat.

It is worth emphasizing that eggs should be chosen very carefully for recipes in which they are used raw. Always buy from a reputable source and ensure the eggs are perfectly fresh. Very young children and the infirm are probably best advised to avoid dishes containing raw eggs.

SERVING SOFT DESSERTS

Elegant glasses, dainty dishes and pretty bowls always make the best of soft creamy desserts. Swirl those desserts that are not set firm by lightly dragging a spoon through them. If you are short of dessert glasses, then substitute large wine glasses instead.

Chilling soft desserts so that they are just firm and nicely cold is important; however take care not to leave syllabubs that may separate in the refrigerator for too long. Offer crisp biscuits as the perfect finishing touch.

FRENCH CHOCOLATE CREAMS

This is incredibly rich, so a little goes a long way.

150 ml/¼ pint milk
60 ml/4 tbsp caster sugar
pinch of salt
100 g/4 oz plain chocolate, coarsely grated
100 g/4 oz unsalted butter, in small pieces
8 egg yolks

Warm the milk, sugar and salt in a small saucepan and stir until the sugar dissolves. Set the pan aside.

Combine the chocolate and butter in a large heatproof bowl and place over hot water. Heat gently, stirring constantly, until the mixture is quite smooth and all the solids have melted.

Add the milk to the chocolate mixture, stirring it in thoroughly. Using a balloon whisk if possible, beat in the egg yolks one at a time. On no account allow the mixture to curdle.

Divide the cream between 6 small pots or ramekins and chill well before serving.

SERVES SIX

SWISS CREAM

100 g/4 oz ratafias or sponge fingers or
   sponge cake
60 ml/4 tbsp sweet sherry
35 g/1¼ oz arrowroot
500 ml/17 fl oz milk
1.25 ml/¼ tsp vanilla essence
pinch of salt
30–45 ml/2–3 tbsp caster sugar
grated rind and juice of 1 lemon
150 ml/¼ pint double cream

DECORATION
10 ml/2 tsp flaked almonds
4 glacé cherries, halved

Break the biscuits or cake into small pieces and
place on the base of a glass dish or individual
dishes. Pour over the sherry.

Put the arrowroot in a bowl and mix to a paste
with a little of the milk. Mix the remaining
milk with the vanilla essence and salt in a
heavy-bottomed saucepan. Bring to the boil,
then pour on to the blended paste, stirring
briskly to prevent the formation of lumps.

Return the mixture to the clean pan and heat
until it thickens and boils, stirring all the time.
Stir in the caster sugar until dissolved. Remove
the pan from the heat, cover the surface of the
mixture with greased greaseproof paper to
prevent the formation of a skin, and set aside
until cold.

Stir the lemon rind and juice into the cold
arrowroot mixture. In a bowl, whip the cream
until soft peaks form, then stir lightly into the
pudding mixture. Pour over the soaked biscuits
or cake and refrigerate for about 2 hours to
set. Decorate with almonds and cherries.

SERVES FOUR TO SIX

QUICK JELLY CREAM

1 (127 g/4½ oz) tablet orange jelly
45 ml/3 tbsp orange juice
30 ml/2 tbsp custard powder
250 ml/8 fl oz milk
125 ml/4 fl oz double cream

Chop the jelly tablet roughly. Heat 100 ml/
3½ fl oz water in a saucepan, add the jelly, and
stir until dissolved. Add the orange juice and
leave to cool.

Meanwhile, in a bowl, blend the custard
powder with a little of the milk. Put the rest of
the milk into a saucepan and bring to the boil.
Pour it slowly on to the blended custard
powder, stirring all the time. Return to the
clean pan, bring to the boil and boil for 1–2
minutes, stirring all the time, until the custard
thickens.

Cool the custard slightly, then stir into the jelly.
Cool until beginning to set.

In a bowl, whip the cream until it leaves a trail,
then fold into the setting mixture. Pour into 4
individual glasses and chill for about 1 hour.
Decorate as desired.

SERVES FOUR

VARIATIONS

Pineapple Jelly Cream Use a pineapple
jelly tablet and the juice from a 376 g/13 oz can
of crushed pineapple. Fold the fruit into the
setting mixture.

Berry Jelly Cream Use a raspberry or strawberry jelly tablet and the juice from a
219 g/7½ oz can of raspberries or strawberries.
Fold the fruit into the setting mixture.

VELVET CREAM

This basic recipe produces one of the simplest and most delicious of desserts, the full cream. It lends itself to a wide range of variations and may be served in glasses or as a decorative mould (see Mrs Beeton's Tip).

10 ml/2 tsp gelatine
50 g/2 oz caster sugar
30 ml/2 tbsp sherry or a few drops of vanilla
    essence
250 ml/8 fl oz double cream
250 ml/8 fl oz single cream

Place 45 ml/3 tbsp water in a small bowl and sprinkle the gelatine on to the liquid. Set aside for 15 minutes until the gelatine is spongy. Stand the bowl over a saucepan of hot water and stir the gelatine until it has dissolved completely. Add the sugar and sherry or vanilla essence and continue to stir until the sugar has dissolved. Set aside.

Combine the creams in a mixing bowl and whip lightly. Fold the flavoured gelatine mixture into the cream and divide between 4 glasses or individual dishes. Refrigerate for 1-2 hours or until set. When the cream has set, a thin top layer of fresh fruit jelly may be added, if liked.

SERVES FOUR

VARIATIONS

In each of the variations below, omit the sherry or vanilla essence.

Almond Cream Flavour with 1.25 ml/¼ tsp almond essence. Decorate with browned almonds.

Berry Cream Use 375 ml/13 fl oz double cream and fold in 125 ml/4 fl oz raspberry or strawberry purée instead of single cream. Decorate with fresh berry fruits.

Chocolate Cream Flavour with 75 g/3 oz melted plain chocolate. Decorate the top with chocolate curls.

Coffee Cream Flavour with 15 ml/1 tbsp instant coffee dissolved in 15 ml/1 tbsp boiling water and cooled. Add 15 ml/1 tbsp rum, if liked, and decorate with coffee beans.

Highland Cream Flavour with 15 ml/1 tbsp whisky and serve with a whisky-flavoured apricot sauce.

Lemon and Almond Cream Flavour with 30 ml/2 tbsp lemon juice, 5 ml/1 tsp grated lemon rind and 25 g/1 oz ground almonds.

Liqueur Cream Flavour with 15 ml/1 tbsp Tia Maria, curaçao, kirsch or Advocaat.

Pistachio Cream Blanch, skin and finely chop 100 g/4 oz pistachio nuts and fold into the mixture before adding the gelatine. Tint the cream pale green with food colouring.

 MRS BEETON'S TIP

The cream may be made in a mould, if preferred. Make up one quantity of Clear Lemon Jelly (page 820). Use some of the jelly to line a 750 ml/1¼ pint mould, decorating it with cut shapes of angelica and glacé cherry (see page 802). When the jelly lining has set, carefully add the prepared cream and refrigerate for 2-3 hours until set. The remaining jelly may be set in a shallow tray, then chopped for use as a decoration.

VANILLA BAVAROIS

*A bavarois, or Bavarian Cream, as it is sometimes
known, consists of a cup custard combined with
cream and flavouring, with gelatine as the setting
agent.*

oil for greasing
4 egg yolks or 1 whole egg and 2 yolks
50 g/2 oz caster sugar
250 ml/8 fl oz milk
2.5 ml/½ tsp vanilla essence
10 ml/2 tsp gelatine
150 ml/¼ pint double cream
150 ml/¼ pint single cream

Oil a 750 ml/1¼ pint mould. In a bowl, beat the
eggs and sugar together until fluffy and pale.

Warm the milk in a saucepan; do not let it boil.
Slowly stir it into the egg mixture, then strain
the custard back into the clean pan or into a
double saucepan or heatproof bowl placed over
hot water. Cook over very low heat until the
custard thickens.

Strain the thickened custard into a bowl, stir in
the vanilla essence and leave to cool.

Place 15 ml/1 tbsp water in a small bowl and
sprinkle the gelatine on to the liquid. Set aside
for 15 minutes until the gelatine is spongy.
Stand the bowl over a saucepan of hot water
and stir the gelatine until it has dissolved
completely. Cool until tepid and add to the
custard. Leave in a cool place until the mixture
thickens at the edges, stirring from time to time
to prevent the formation of a skin.

Combine the creams in a bowl and whip
lightly. Fold into the custard mixture, and pour
into the prepared mould. Refrigerate for about
2 hours until set, then turn out on to a flat
wetted plate to serve.

SERVES FOUR TO SIX

VARIATIONS

Caramel Bavarois Dissolve 100 g/4 oz
granulated sugar in 15 ml/1 tbsp water. Heat
until the syrup turns a rich brown colour.
Carefully add 60 ml/4 tbsp hot water, remove
from the heat, and stir until all the caramel
dissolves. Stir into the warm custard.

Chocolate Bavarois Grate 100 g/4 oz plain
chocolate and add with the milk. It will melt in
the warm custard. Add 5 ml/1 tsp vanilla
essence.

Coffee Bavarois Dissolve 15 ml/1 tbsp
instant coffee in 15 ml/1 tbsp boiling water.
Cool, then stir in 15 ml/1 tbsp rum. Add this
essence with the milk.

Crème Diplomate Soak 100 g/4 oz chopped
crystallized fruit in 30 ml/2 tbsp kirsch. Pour
the vanilla Bavarian cream into the mould to a
depth of 1.5 cm/¾ inch and leave to set. Spread
half the fruit over it and cover with a little of the
cream. Leave to set. Continue alternating layers
of fruit and cream, finishing with a layer of
cream. Allow each layer to set before adding
the next.

Crème Tricolore Divide the mixture into
three portions. Flavour the first with vanilla
essence, the second with chocolate, the third
with strawberry purée. Line the mould with
vanilla cream in the same way as when lining
with jelly (page 672). When this is completely
set, fill alternately with equal layers of the
chocolate and strawberry creams, allowing
each layer to set before adding the next.

Ribbon Bavarois Divide the mixture into
two portions, and flavour and colour each half
separately; for example, with vanilla and
chocolate, vanilla and orange, or ginger and
chocolate. Do not decorate the mould but oil it
lightly. Pour in one of the creams to a depth of
1.5 cm/¼ inch, leave to set, then repeat with the
second cream. Continue in this way until all the
mixture is used.

FRIED CREAMS

butter for greasing
1 whole egg, plus 4 yolks
50g/2oz fine cake crumbs
40g/1½oz plain flour
40g/1½oz cornflour
500ml/17floz milk
40g/1½oz caster sugar
pinch of salt
few drops of vanilla essence
15ml/1tbsp liqueur or brandy (optional)
oil for deep frying
caster sugar for dredging

Grease a shallow 600ml/1 pint ovenproof dish. Beat the whole egg in a shallow bowl and spread the cake crumbs in a similar bowl.

Put the 4 remaining egg yolks into a bowl and beat until liquid. In a second bowl, blend the flour and cornflour with enough of the milk to make a smooth paste. Bring the rest of the milk to the boil in a saucepan. Add slowly to the blended mixture, stirring all the time. Return to the pan and bring to the boil, still stirring. Cook for 2–3 minutes.

Remove the pan from the heat and gradually add the sugar, salt and beaten egg yolks. The mixture will be very thick, to take care to stir thoroughly to keep it smooth. Return to the heat and warm through, but do not allow the sauce to approach boiling point. Stir in the vanilla essence and liqueur or brandy, if used. Spread the mixture in the prepared dish to a depth of about 2cm/¾ inch. Leave until set.

Cut the set custard into neat shapes about 3cm/1¼ inches across. Dip in the beaten whole egg and then in cake crumbs to coat. Set the coated shapes on a plate and place in the refrigerator for 15–30 minutes or until firm.

Put the oil for frying in a deep wide saucepan. Heat the oil to 185°C/360°F or until a bread cube immersed in the oil turns pale brown in 45 seconds. If using a deep-fat fryer, follow the manufacturer's instructions.

Fry the coated shapes in the hot oil until golden brown, drain on absorbent kitchen paper and serve dredged in caster sugar.

SERVES FOUR

DAMASK CREAM

600ml/1 pint single cream
1 blade of mace
10cm/4 inch piece of cinnamon stick
20ml/4tsp icing sugar, sifted
triple-strength rose-water
15ml/1tbsp rennet essence

DECORATION
deep pink rose petals or 1 red rose

Pour 500ml/17floz of the cream into a saucepan, add the mace and cinnamon stick, and heat almost to boiling point. Remove from the heat and infuse for 20–30 minutes.

Strain the cream into a clean bowl, discarding the spices. Add 10ml/2tsp icing sugar to the cream with rose-water to taste. Cool to blood-heat, and stir in the rennet. Pour gently into a decorative 750ml/1¼ pint serving bowl and leave to set in a warm room until cold and firm.

Pour the remaining cream into a jug. Flavour with rose-water and very gently pour the flavoured cream over the set cream to a depth of 5mm/¼ inch. Sprinkle lightly all over with the remaining icing sugar.

Strew deep pink rose-petals around the edge of the dish or set one perfect red rosebud in the centre. Serve with thin, crisp, plain or almond biscuits.

SERVES FOUR

MRS BEETON'S DUTCH FLUMMERY

This is best made the day before it is to be served.

25 g/1 oz gelatine
grated rind and juice of 1 lemon
4 eggs, beaten
500 ml/17 fl oz dry sherry
50 g/2 oz caster sugar

Place 125 ml/4 fl oz water in a small bowl and sprinkle the gelatine on to the liquid. Set aside for 15 minutes until the gelatine is spongy. Stand the bowl over a saucepan of hot water and stir the gelatine until it has dissolved completely. Pour the mixture into a measuring jug and make up to 500 ml/17 fl oz with cold water. Add the grated lemon rind and strain in the juice.

In a second bowl, beat the eggs, sherry and sugar together. Add to the gelatine mixture. Pour into the top of a double saucepan, place over simmering water and cook over low heat, stirring all the time, until the mixture coats the back of the spoon. Do not let the mixture boil.

Strain the mixture into a wetted 1.75 litre/3 pint mould and refrigerate until set. Turn out on to a plate to serve.

SERVES FOUR TO SIX

 MRS BEETON'S TIP

It is often difficult to centre a moulded dessert on a serving plate. Wet the plate first, shaking off excess moisture. When the dessert is inverted on to the plate, the thin skin of liquid on the plate will make it easy to move it into the desired position.

HONEYCOMB MOULD

2 eggs, separated
25 g/1 oz caster sugar
500 ml/17 fl oz milk
5 ml/1 tsp vanilla essence
20 ml/4 tsp gelatine

FILLING
375 g/13 oz chopped fresh fruit or
  1 (425 g/15 oz) can fruit, well drained

In a bowl, combine the egg yolks, sugar and milk. Mix lightly. Pour into the top of a double saucepan and cook over simmering water until the custard coats the back of a spoon, stirring all the time. Do not allow the custard to boil. Stir in the essence.

Place 45 ml/3 tbsp water in a small bowl and sprinkle the gelatine on to the liquid. Set aside for 15 minutes until the gelatine is spongy. Stand the bowl over a saucepan of hot water and stir the gelatine until it has dissolved completely. Stir the gelatine mixture into the custard. Leave to cool.

In a clean, grease-free bowl, whisk the egg whites until just stiff. When the custard is just beginning to set, fold in the egg whites.

Pour the mixture into a wetted 1 litre/1¾ pint ring mould and refrigerate for 2–3 hours until set. Turn out on to a serving plate and fill the centre with fruit.

SERVES FOUR TO SIX

PINEAPPLE BUTTERMILK WHIP

This is a very good dessert for slimmers.

400 ml/14 fl oz unsweetened pineapple or orange juice
15 ml/1 tbsp gelatine
150 ml/¼ pint buttermilk

Place 60 ml/4 tbsp of the fruit juice in a small bowl and sprinkle the gelatine on to the liquid. Set aside for 15 minutes until the gelatine is spongy. Stand the bowl over a saucepan of hot water and stir the gelatine until it has dissolved completely.

Combine the gelatine mixture with the remaining fruit juice. Pour a little of the mixture into each of 4 stemmed glasses.

Chill the rest of the juice mixture for about 1 hour. When it is on the point of setting, whisk in the buttermilk until frothy. Spoon into the glasses and chill.

SERVES FOUR

 MRS BEETON'S TIP

Take care when adding the creamy mixture to the glasses, not to disturb the jelly layer. The two-tone effect is most attractive.

COFFEE WHIP

500 ml/17 fl oz milk
15 ml/1 tbsp coffee essence
25 g/1 oz sugar
20 ml/4 tsp gelatine
1 egg white
15 ml/1 tbsp flaked almonds to decorate

In a saucepan, heat together the milk, coffee essence and sugar, stirring until the sugar dissolves. Leave for about 30 minutes to cool. Place 30 ml/2 tbsp water in a small bowl and sprinkle the gelatine on to the liquid. Set aside for 15 minutes until the gelatine is spongy. Stand the bowl over a saucepan of hot water and stir the gelatine until it has dissolved completely. Stir into the cooled milk mixture.

In a clean, grease-free bowl, whisk the egg white lightly and add to the liquid milk jelly. Whisk very well until thick and frothy. Pile into a serving dish and decorate with the flaked almonds. Chill until set.

SERVES FOUR TO SIX

BRANDY WHIP

400 ml/14 fl oz double cream
100 ml/3½ fl oz brandy
juice of ¼ lemon
caster sugar (optional)
ground nutmeg

In a large bowl, whip the cream to soft peaks, adding the brandy and the lemon juice gradually. Taste, and add the caster sugar, if required.

Spoon the mixture into 4 individual glasses. Sprinkle with a little nutmeg and chill before serving.

Serve with sponge fingers.

SERVES FOUR

LEMON FLUFF

30 ml/2 tbsp lemon juice
30 ml/2 tbsp cornflour
75 ml/5 tbsp caster sugar
5 ml/1 tsp grated lemon rind
2 eggs, separated
125 ml/4 fl oz single cream

In a bowl, blend the lemon juice with the cornflour. Bring 150 ml/¼ pint water to the boil in a saucepan. Stir a little of the boiling water into the cornflour mixture, then add the contents of the bowl to the remaining boiling water. Bring the mixture back to the boil, stirring constantly, then boil for 1-2 minutes until the mixture thickens. Stir in 45 ml/3 tbsp of the caster sugar with the lemon rind. Remove the pan from the heat.

Add the egg yolks to the lemon mixture, stirring them in vigorously. Cover the mixture with dampened greaseproof paper to prevent the formation of a skin, and cool until tepid.

Stir the cream into the cooled lemon custard. In a clean, grease-free bowl, whisk the egg whites until stiff, add the remaining sugar and whisk until stiff again. Fold the egg whites into the lemon mixture until evenly distributed. Spoon into 4 glasses and chill before serving.

SERVES FOUR

 MRS BEETON'S TIP

When grating the lemon, be sure to remove only the outer rind and not the bitter pith.

CRANACHAN

125 g/4½ oz coarse oatmeal
400 ml/14 fl oz double cream
50 g/2 oz caster sugar
15 ml/1 tbsp rum
150 g/5 oz fresh raspberries

Toast the oatmeal under a low grill until lightly browned (see Mrs Beeton's Tip). Set aside to cool.

In a bowl, whip the cream until stiff. Stir in the toasted oatmeal and flavour with the sugar and rum.

Hull the raspberries. Stir them into the cream or layer with the Cranachan mixture, reserving 4 perfect fruit for decoration, if liked. Serve in 4 individual glass dishes.

SERVES FOUR

 MRS BEETON'S TIP

When toasting the oatmeal, shake the grill pan frequently so that the mixture browns evenly.

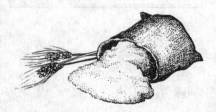

CIDER SYLLABUB

A syllabub was originally a sweet, frothy drink made with cider or mead mixed with milk straight from the cow. Mrs Beeton's original syllabub recipe combined 600 ml/1 pint of sherry or white wine with 900 ml/1½ pints of fresh, frothy milk. Nutmeg or cinnamon and sugar was stirred in, and clotted cream may have been added. When cider was used instead of wine, brandy was added to enrich the syllabub. It is now a rich creamy dessert, often made light and frothy by the addition of egg whites.

grated rind and juice of ½ lemon
50 g/2 oz caster sugar
125 ml/4 fl oz sweet cider
15 ml/1 tbsp brandy
250 ml/8 fl oz double cream

In a large bowl, mix the lemon rind and juice with the caster sugar, cider and brandy. Stir until the sugar is dissolved.

Put the cream in a mixing bowl. Whip until it stands in stiff peaks. Gradually fold in the lemon and cider mixture.

Pour the mixture into stemmed glasses and refrigerate for about 2 hours. Remove 20 minutes before serving to allow the flavours to 'ripen'.

SERVES FOUR

WHIPPED SYLLABUB

50 ml/2 fl oz sweet red wine or ruby port
250 ml/8 fl oz double cream
50 ml/2 fl oz medium dry sherry
juice of ½ orange
grated rind of ½ lemon
50 g/2 oz caster sugar

Divide the wine or port between 4 chilled stemmed glasses, and keep chilled.

In a bowl, whip the cream, adding the remaining ingredients gradually, in order, until the mixture just holds firm peaks.

Pile the cream mixture into the chilled glasses (see Mrs Beeton's Tip). Serve as soon as possible.

SERVES FOUR

 MRS BEETON'S TIP

When adding the cream mixture to the chilled wine take care not to mix the two. The wine should clearly be seen in the bottom of each glass.

WINE SYLLABUB

This syllabub has a frothy head, with the lemon juice and wine settling in the bottom of the glasses.

200 ml/7 fl oz double cream
2 egg whites
75 g/3 oz caster sugar
juice of ½ lemon
100 ml/3½ fl oz sweet white wine or sherry
crystallized lemon slices to decorate

In a large bowl, whip the cream until it just holds its shape. Put the egg whites in a clean, grease-free mixing bowl and whisk until they form soft peaks. Fold the sugar into the egg whites, then gradually add the lemon juice and wine or sherry.

Fold the egg white mixture into the whipped cream. Pour into glasses and refrigerate for about 2 hours. Remove 20 minutes before serving. Serve decorated with the crystallized lemon slices.

SERVES FOUR

COLD CABINET PUDDING

250 ml/8 fl oz Clear Lemon Jelly (page 686)
glacé cherries
angelica
10–12 sponge fingers
350 ml/12 fl oz milk
2 eggs, plus 1 yolk
15 ml/1 tbsp caster sugar
25 g/1 oz ratafias, crumbled
10 ml/2 tsp gelatine
few drops of vanilla essence
125 ml/4 fl oz double cream

Make up the jelly and use half of the mixture to line a 750 ml/1¼ pint soufflé dish. Cut the cherries into quarters and the angelica into leaf shapes and decorate the jelly lining as described on page 802, dipping each piece in liquid jelly before setting it in place. Refrigerate until set. Chill the remaining jelly in a shallow baking tin.

Line the sides of the prepared dish with the sponge fingers, trimming one end of each so that they stand evenly on top of the jelly. Trim the fingers level with the top of the soufflé dish. Set the lined dish aside. Reserve the trimmings from the sponge fingers.

In a saucepan, bring the milk to just below boiling point. Put the eggs and caster sugar into a bowl, mix well, then stir in the scalded milk. Strain the custard mixture into a heavy-bottomed saucepan or a heatproof bowl placed over a saucepan of simmering water. Alternatively, use a double saucepan, but make sure the water does not touch the upper pan.

Cook the custard over very gentle heat for 15–25 minutes, stirring all the time with a wooden spoon, until the custard thickens to the consistency of single cream. Stir well around the sides as well as the base of the pan or bowl to prevent the formation of lumps, especially if using a double saucepan. Do not let the custard approach boiling point.

As soon as the custard thickens, remove it from the heat and whisk in the crumbled ratafias with the sponge finger trimmings.

Place 30 ml/2 tbsp water in a small bowl and sprinkle the gelatine on to the liquid. Set aside for 15 minutes until the gelatine is spongy. Stand the bowl over a saucepan of hot water and stir the gelatine until it has dissolved completely, then add the gelatine to the custard mixture with vanilla essence to taste.

In a bowl, whip the cream until just stiff. Fold into the crumb custard, then pour into the prepared mould. Cool, then refrigerate for 1–2 hours to set. When ready to serve, chop the reserved jelly. Turn the mould out on to a serving dish and decorate with the chopped lemon jelly.

SERVES SIX

 MRS BEETON'S TIP

A commercial lemon jelly may be used to line the mould. Make up according to packet directions.

CABINET PUDDING

butter for greasing
75 g/3 oz seedless raisins, halved
3–4 slices of white bread, crusts removed
400 ml/14 fl oz milk
3 eggs
25 g/1 oz caster sugar
5 ml/1 tsp grated lemon rind

Grease a 1 litre/1¾ pint pudding basin. Decorate the sides and base of the basin by pressing on some of the halved raisins. Chill.

Cut the bread slices into 5 mm/¼ inch dice.

Place in a bowl. In a saucepan, warm the milk to about 65°C/150°F; do not let it come near to the boil.

Meanwhile mix the eggs and sugar in a bowl. Beat with a fork and stir in the milk, with the lemon rind and remaining raisins. Pour the custard mixture over the bread, stir, and leave to stand for at least 30 minutes. Meanwhile prepare a steamer or half fill a large saucepan with water and bring to the boil.

Spoon the bread mixture into the prepared basin, cover with greased greaseproof paper or foil and secure with string.

Put the pudding in the perforated part of the steamer, or stand it on an old saucer or plate in the pan of boiling water. The water should come halfway up the sides of the basin. Cover the pan tightly and steam the pudding over gently simmering water for 1 hour or until firm in the centre.

Remove the cooked pudding from the steamer, leave to stand for a few minutes, then turn out on to a warmed serving dish. Serve with a jam or fruit sauce.

SERVES FOUR TO SIX

 FREEZER TIP

Crumb the bread crusts in a food processor and store in a polythene bag in the freezer. Next time you make a fruit pie, sprinkle a thin layer of crumbs into the pie shell before adding the fruit; they will prevent the fruit juices from making the crust soggy.

BREAD AND BUTTER PUDDING

When the weather is dull and dreary, lift the spirits with this comforting old favourite.

butter for greasing
4 thin slices of bread (about 100 g/4 oz)
25 g/1 oz butter
50 g/2 oz sultanas or currants
pinch of ground nutmeg or cinnamon
400 ml/14 fl oz milk
2 eggs
25 g/1 oz granulated sugar

Grease a 1 litre/1¾ pint pie dish. Cut the crusts off the bread and spread the slices with the butter. Cut the bread into squares or triangles and arrange in alternate layers, buttered side up, with the sultanas or currants. Sprinkle each layer lightly with nutmeg or cinnamon. Arrange the top layer of bread in an attractive pattern.

Warm the milk in a saucepan to about 65°C/ 150°F. Do not let it approach boiling point. Put the eggs in a bowl. Add most of the sugar. Beat with a fork and stir in the milk. Strain the custard mixture over the bread, sprinkle some nutmeg and the remaining sugar on top, and leave to stand for 30 minutes. Set the oven at 180°C/350°F/gas 4.

Bake for 30–40 minutes until the custard is set and the top is lightly browned.

SERVES FOUR

 PRESSURE COOKER TIP

Use a dish that fits in the pressure cooker. Cover the pudding with foil or greased greaseproof paper, tied down securely. Cook at 15 lb pressure for 9 minutes. Reduce pressure slowly, then brown the pudding under the grill.

QUEEN MAB'S PUDDING

oil for greasing
400 ml/14 fl oz milk
pared rind of 1 lemon
3 eggs
75 g/3 oz caster sugar
few drops of almond essence
10 ml/2 tsp gelatine
50 g/2 oz glacé cherries, halved
25 g/1 oz cut mixed peel or whole citron
   peel, finely chopped
125 ml/4 fl oz double cream

DECORATION
whipped cream · glacé cherries

Lightly oil a 750 ml/1¼ pint mould. In a sauce-pan warm the milk with the lemon rind. Beat the eggs with the sugar in a mixing bowl until fluffy and pale, and slowly stir in the warm milk. Strain the custard back into the clean pan or into a double saucepan or bowl placed over hot water. Cook over very low heat for 15–20 minutes, stirring all the time, until the custard thickens. Do not let it approach the boil. Strain the custard into a bowl, stir in the almond essence, and cool.

Place 15 ml/1 tbsp water in a small bowl and sprinkle the gelatine on to the liquid. Set aside for 15 minutes until the gelatine is spongy. Stand the bowl over a saucepan of hot water and stir the gelatine until it has dissolved completely. Cool the mixture slightly, then stir it into the custard. Leave in a cool place until it begins to set, stirring occasionally to prevent a skin forming.

Stir the cherries and chopped peel into the setting custard. In a separate bowl, whip the cream until it is semi-stiff, then fold it into the mixture. Pour the pudding into the prepared mould and refrigerate for about 2 hours until set. Turn out on to a flat, wetted plate. Decorate and serve.

SERVES FOUR TO SIX

SHAHI TUKRA

3 medium slices of white bread
2 cardamoms
2 whole unblanched almonds
4 whole unblanched pistachio nuts
40 g/1½ oz ghee or butter
250 ml/8 fl oz milk
few strands of saffron
45 ml/3 tbsp sugar
75 ml/3 fl oz double cream
30 ml/2 tbsp single cream
pinch of grated nutmeg

Cut the crusts off the bread. Cut each slice into 4 triangular pieces. Split the cardamom pods, pick out and crush the seeds, discarding the outer husk. Crush the almonds and pistachio nuts with their skins.

Heat the ghee or butter in a frying pan, and fry the bread until golden brown on both sides. Drain on absorbent kitchen paper.

Heat the milk slowly in a shallow saucepan over moderate heat. When it begins to steam, add the saffron strands and sugar. Reduce to very low heat, and cook gently for 20 minutes.

Add the double cream to the saffron mixture and cook for a further 10 minutes. The sauce should be thickened but runny. Drop the fried bread triangles into the sauce. Turn them over after 5 minutes. Cook very slowly until the sauce is absorbed by the fried bread.

Serve hot or cold, covered with the single cream. Top each portion with a generous sprinkling of the crushed nuts and cardamom, adding a pinch of grated nutmeg.

SERVES FOUR TO FIVE

POOR KNIGHTS

'Poor Knights' originated in England, in the Middle Ages, but soon became popular all over Europe. Every country has its own traditional variation, and some have more elaborate versions called 'Rich Knights'. Some are made with sweet bread or stale cake, others are moistened with red wine.

4 thick slices of white bread
2 eggs, beaten
200 ml/7 fl oz milk or white wine
1.25 ml/¼ tsp cinnamon
15 ml/1 tbsp sugar
oil for shallow frying
caster sugar and ground cinnamon to serve

Cut the crusts off the bread, then cut each slice into quarters. Put into a deep dish.

In a bowl, mix the eggs with the milk or wine, cinnamon and sugar. Pour the liquid over the bread, cover, and leave to soak for 2-3 minutes.

Heat oil to a depth of 5 mm/¼ inch in a frying pan. Using a palette knife or fish slice, drain a square of bread from the dish. Slide the bread into the hot oil. Add 1 or 2 more squares, drained in the same way. Fry until golden brown on both sides, turning once.

Drain the 'poor knights' on absorbent kitchen paper, then keep uncovered in a warm place until needed. Fry the remaining bread squares in the same way. Serve sprinkled with caster sugar and cinnamon.

SERVES FOUR

BUTTERSCOTCH PUDDING

25 g/1 oz cornflour
500 ml/17 fl oz milk
2 eggs, separated
100 g/4 oz soft light brown sugar
25 g/1 oz butter
5 ml/1 tsp vanilla essence
25 g/1 oz walnuts, chopped, to decorate

In a bowl, mix the cornflour to a paste with a little of the cold milk. Bring the rest of the milk to the boil in a saucepan, and pour on to the blended cornflour, stirring to prevent the formation of lumps.

Return the mixture to the clean pan and bring to simmering point, stirring all the time. Simmer for 2-3 minutes. Cool for 3-4 minutes.

Add the egg yolks to the pan. Stir thoroughly, and cook without boiling for a further 2-3 minutes.

Melt the sugar in a heavy-bottomed saucepan and add the butter. When the butter has melted, stir the mixture into the cornflour sauce.

In a clean, grease-free bowl whisk the egg whites until fairly stiff and fold lightly into the pudding mixture. Add the essence. Pile into a serving dish and refrigerate for about 1 hour to set. Sprinkle the dessert with the walnuts before serving.

SERVES SIX

CREME BRULEE

fat for greasing
15 ml/1 tbsp cornflour
250 ml/8 fl oz milk
250 ml/8 fl oz single cream
few drops of vanilla essence
3 eggs
50 g/2 oz caster sugar

Grease a 600 ml/1 pint flameproof dish. In a bowl, blend the cornflour to a smooth paste with a little of the milk. Bring the rest of the milk to the boil in a saucepan.

Pour the boiling milk on to the blended cornflour, stirring well. Return the mixture to the clean pan, bring to the boil, and boil for 1 minute, stirring all the time. Remove from the heat and set the pan aside to cool.

Combine the cream, vanilla essence and eggs in a bowl and beat well. Stir into the cooled cornflour mixture. Whisk over low heat for about 30 minutes or until the custard thickens; do not boil. Add 25 g/1 oz of the sugar and pour into the prepared dish. Sprinkle the pudding with the rest of the sugar.

Place under a preheated hot grill for 10 minutes or until the sugar has melted and turned brown. Keep the custard about 10 cm/4 inches from the heat. Serve hot or cold.

SERVES FOUR

 MRS BEETON'S TIP

The brûlée may be browned in a 200°C/400°F/gas 6 oven if preferred. It will require about 15 minutes.

CREME BRULEE A LA GRANDE CATELET

An ideal dinner party dish. If serving cold, tap the caramel crust sharply with the back of a spoon to break it up.

250 ml/8 fl oz single cream or milk
250 ml/8 fl oz double cream
1 vanilla pod or a few drops of vanilla essence or 15 ml/1 tbsp brandy
6 egg yolks
about 75 g/3 oz caster sugar

Put the cream or milk and the double cream in a double saucepan or a bowl over a saucepan of hot water. Add the vanilla pod, if used, and warm very gently. Meanwhile mix the egg yolks with 25 g/1 oz of the caster sugar in a large bowl. Beat together thoroughly.

When the cream feels just warm to the finger, remove the pod, if used. Pour the cream on to the yolks, stir, and return to the double saucepan or bowl.

Continue to cook gently for about 40 minutes, stirring all the time with a wooden spoon, until the custard thickens to the consistency of single cream (see Mrs Beeton's Tip). Do not let the custard approach the boiling point. If a vanilla pod has not been used, add a few drops of vanilla essence or the brandy. Set the oven at 160°C/325°F/gas 3.

Strain the custard into a shallow 600 ml/1 pint flameproof dish, stand it on a baking sheet and

---

 MRS BEETON'S TIP

When cooking the custard scrape down the sides of the saucepan frequently with a spatula to prevent the formation of lumps.

bake for 5–10 minutes until a skin has formed on the top. Do not allow the custard to colour. Leave to cool, then refrigerate for at least 2–3 hours, or preferably overnight.

Heat the grill. Sprinkle enough of the remaining caster sugar over the surface of the custard to cover it entirely with an even, thin layer. Place the dish under the hot grill for 10–15 minutes or until the sugar melts and turns to caramel. Keep the top of the custard about 10 cm/4 inches from the heat. Serve hot or cold.

SERVES FOUR

HOUSE OF COMMONS PUDDING

butter for greasing
50 g/2 oz seedless raisins
30 ml/2 tbsp medium sherry
4 trifle sponges
9 ratafias or 2 almond macaroons
400 ml/14 fl oz milk
3 eggs
25 g/1 oz caster sugar
few drops of vanilla essence

DECORATION
glacé cherries, halved
angelica, cut in strips

Put the raisins in a small bowl with the sherry and macerate for 15 minutes. Meanwhile grease a 13 cm/5 inch round cake tin and line the base with greased greaseproof paper. Decorate the base of the tin with the cherries and angelica.

Cut the sponges into 1 cm/½ inch dice and put into a bowl. Add the crumbled ratafias or macaroons and mix lightly. Drain the raisins, discarding the sherry.

Add a layer of the sponge mixture to the prepared tin, taking care not to spoil the design. Top with a few of the drained raisins. Repeat the layers until all the sponge mixture and raisins have been used.

In a saucepan, bring the milk to just below boiling point. Put the eggs and sugar into a bowl, mix well, then stir in the scalded milk. Add a few drops of vanilla essence. Slowly strain the custard mixture into the cake tin, allowing it to seep down to the base of the tin gradually, so as not to disturb the pattern on the base. Leave to stand for 1 hour.

Prepare a steamer or half fill a large saucepan with water and bring to the boil. Cover the cake tin with greased greaseproof paper or foil and secure with string.

Put the pudding in the perforated part of the steamer, or stand it on an old saucer or plate in the pan of boiling water. The water should come halfway up the sides of the cake tin. Cover the pan tightly and steam the pudding over gently simmering water for 1 hour.

Remove the pudding from the steamer, leave to stand for a few minutes, then turn out on to a warmed dish and peel off the lining paper. Serve with Sabayon Sauce (page 500), if liked.

SERVES FOUR

MARQUISE ALICE

oil for greasing
4 eggs or 1 whole egg and 2 yolks
75 g/3 oz caster sugar
250 ml/8 fl oz milk
few drops of vanilla essence
10 ml/2 tsp gelatine
50 g/2 oz Praline (see Mrs Beeton's Tip), crushed
5-6 sponge fingers
60 ml/4 tbsp kirsch
125 ml/4 fl oz double cream
125 ml/4 fl oz single cream

DECORATION
200 ml/7 fl oz double cream, whipped
redcurrant jelly

Oil a 750 ml/1¼ pint mould. Beat the eggs and sugar until fluffy and pale.

Warm the milk in a saucepan; do not let it boil. Slowly stir it into the egg mixture, then strain the custard into a heatproof bowl placed over hot water. Cook over very low heat until the custard thickens.

Strain the thickened custard into a bowl, stir in the vanilla essence and leave to cool.

Place 60 ml/4 tbsp water in a small bowl and sprinkle the gelatine on to the liquid. Set aside for 15 minutes until the gelatine is spongy. Stand the bowl over a saucepan of hot water and stir the gelatine until it has dissolved completely. Add the praline and continue to stir until the sugar in the praline has similarly dissolved. Cool until tepid and add to the custard. Leave in a cool place until the mixture thickens at the edges, stirring from time to time.

Break the sponge fingers into small pieces and put into a mixing bowl. Add the kirsch and leave to soak. In a second bowl, combine the creams and whip until soft peaks form. Fold

into the setting praline custard. Pour half the mixture into the mould and leave until thickened and beginning to set.

Arrange the soaked sponge fingers in an even layer all over the custard, leaving a 5 mm/¼ inch clear border all around so that none of the sponge finger pieces will show when the pudding is turned out. Pour the rest of the mixture over the sponge finger pieces and refrigerate until set.

Turn out on to a wetted plate and decorate with lightly whipped cream. Warm the redcurrant jelly until it runs, then drizzle it over the cream. Serve at once.

SERVES FOUR TO SIX

 MRS BEETON'S TIP

To make praline, heat 100 g/4 oz sugar with 15 ml/1 tbsp water until dissolved, then boil until golden. Stir in 100 g/4 oz toasted blanched almonds and turn the mixture on to an oiled baking sheet to cool. Crush in a mortar with a pestle, or use a blender.

FLOATING ISLANDS

3 eggs, separated
200 g/7 oz caster sugar
500 ml/17 fl oz milk
few drops of vanilla essence

In a clean, grease-free bowl whisk the egg whites until very stiff. Fold in 150 g/5 oz of the caster sugar.

Pour the milk into a frying pan and add a few drops of vanilla essence. Heat gently until the surface of the milk is just shivering. It must not boil or the milk will discolour and form a skin. Using 2 dessertspoons, mould egg shapes from the meringue and slide them into the milk. Make only a few at a time, and leave plenty of space between them in the pan as they swell when cooking.

Cook the meringue shapes slowly for 5 minutes, then turn them over, using a palette knife and a spoon, and cook for 5 minutes more. They are very delicate and must be handled with care. Remove from the milk gently and place on a cloth or absorbent kitchen paper to drain. Continue making shapes from the meringue and poaching them in the milk, until all the meringue is used. Arrange the 'islands' in a flat serving dish.

In a bowl, blend the egg yolks with the rest of the sugar. Gradually stir in the warm milk. Strain the mixture into a saucepan and cook gently, stirring all the time, until the sauce thickens slightly. Do not let it approach boiling point or it will curdle. Pour the custard around the 'islands' and serve at once.

SERVES FOUR

CARAMEL CUSTARD CUPS

100 g/4 oz lump or granulated sugar
300 ml/½ pint milk
100 ml/3½ fl oz single cream
2 whole eggs and 2 yolks
25 g/1 oz caster sugar
few drops of vanilla essence

Prepare four 150 ml/¼ pint ovenproof moulds to receive a caramel coating (see Mrs Beeton's Tip, page 698).

Make the caramel by heating the lump sugar with 150 ml/¼ pint water in a heavy-bottomed saucepan. Stir constantly until the sugar dissolves and the mixture comes to the boil. Continue to boil, without stirring, until the mixture is golden brown. Pour a little of the caramel on to a metal plate and set aside. Immediately pour the remaining caramel into the warmed moulds, twisting and turning each mould in turn until the sides and the base are evenly coated. Leave until cold and set. Set the oven at 140–150°C/275–300°F/gas 1–2.

In a saucepan, bring the milk and cream to just below boiling point. Put the eggs and sugar into a bowl, mix well, then stir in the scalded milk. Add a few drops of vanilla essence. Strain the custard mixture into the prepared moulds.

Stand the moulds in a roasting tin and add hot water to come halfway up the sides of the moulds. Bake for 30 minutes or until the custard is set.

Remove the cooked custards and leave to stand for a few minutes, then invert each on an individual dessert plate. The caramel will run off and serve as a sauce. Break up the reserved caramel by tapping sharply with a metal spoon, and decorate the top of each custard with the pieces of broken caramel.

SERVES FOUR

NEWMARKET PUDDING

fat for greasing
4 individual trifle sponges
50 g/2 oz cut mixed peel
50 g/2 oz seedless raisins
25 g/1 oz currants
400 ml/14 fl oz milk
3 eggs, beaten
few drops of vanilla essence
45 ml/3 tbsp redcurrant jelly

Grease a 13 cm/5 inch round cake tin. Cut the sponges vertically into 1 cm/½ inch slices. In a bowl, mix the peel, raisins and currants together. Put the cake and fruit into the prepared cake tin in alternate layers.

In a saucepan, warm the milk to about 65°C/150°F; do not let it approach boiling point. Meanwhile, mix the beaten eggs with a few drops of vanilla essence in a bowl. Stir in the warm milk.

Strain the custard mixture over the cake and fruit layers. Leave to stand for 1 hour. Prepare a steamer or half fill a large saucepan with water and bring to the boil.

Cover the top of the cake tin with greased greaseproof paper or foil and secure with string. Put the tin in the perforated part of the steamer, or stand it on an old saucer or plate in the pan of boiling water. The water should come halfway up the sides of the tin. Cover the pan tightly and steam the pudding over gently simmering water for 1 hour.

Remove the cooked pudding from the steamer

and leave to stand for a few minutes. Meanwhile put the redcurrant jelly in a small pan and warm through until melted.

Turn the pudding out on to a warmed dish, pour the jelly over and serve at once.

SERVES FOUR TO SIX

FOREST PUDDING

fat for greasing
3 pieces of plain cake or trifle sponges
jam
5 ml/1 tsp grated lemon rind
500 ml/17 fl oz milk
2 eggs
25 g/1 oz caster sugar

Grease a 750 ml/1¼ pint pie dish. Cut the cake vertically into 1 cm/½ inch slices and sandwich in pairs with the jam. Place the cake sandwiches in the pie dish and sprinkle with lemon rind. Set aside.

In a saucepan, warm the milk to about 65°C/150°F; do not let it approach boiling point.

Put the eggs and sugar into a bowl, mix well, then stir in the warm milk. Strain the custard mixture into the dish and leave to stand for 1 hour. Meanwhile set the oven at 140–150°C/275–300°F/gas 1–2.

Bake the pudding for 1–1½ hours until the custard is set and the pudding browned on top. Serve hot.

SERVES FOUR

 MICROWAVE TIP

Melt the redcurrant jelly in a small bowl for a few seconds on High.

RING OF PEARS

fat for greasing
3 slices of plain cake or trifle sponges
400 ml/14 fl oz milk
25 g/1 oz butter
2 eggs
1 egg yolk
25 g/1 oz caster sugar
5 ml/1 tsp grated lemon rind
1 (425 g/15 oz) can pear halves in syrup
red food colouring (optional)

Grease a 600 ml/1 pint ring mould. Cut the cake vertically into 1 cm/½ inch slices and arrange these in the mould. Set the oven at 150°C/300°F/gas 2.

Warm the milk and butter in a saucepan until the butter just melts. In a bowl, mix together the whole eggs and yolk, the sugar and grated lemon rind. Stir in the warmed milk mixture and strain the mixture over the cake slices. Cover with greased greaseproof paper or foil.

Stand the pudding in a roasting tin. Add hot water to come halfway up the sides of the ring mould and bake for about 1 hour or until set.

Meanwhile drain the pears, reserving the fruit and boiling the syrup in a saucepan until slightly reduced. Add a few drops of red food colouring, if the fruit is very pale.

Leave the cooked pudding to stand for a few minutes, then carefully unmould the ring on to a warmed dish. Arrange the reserved pears in the centre, pouring the syrup over them. Serve at once.

SERVES FOUR

VARIATION

Use apricots or peaches instead of pears.

SAVOY PUDDING

fat for greasing
40 g/1½ oz cut mixed peel
125 g/4½ oz plain cake, finely crumbled
40 g/1½ oz butter, melted
300 ml/½ pint milk
45 ml/3 tbsp sweet sherry
2 eggs, separated
75 g/3 oz caster sugar

Grease a 750 ml/1¼ pint pie dish. Chop the mixed peel even more finely and put into a mixing bowl.

Add the cake crumbs, melted butter, milk and sherry to the chopped peel. Stir in the egg yolks and beat thoroughly. Leave to stand for 15 minutes. Set the oven at 160°C/325°F/gas 3.

Pour the pudding mixture into the prepared pie dish and bake for 35-40 minutes until lightly set. Remove from the oven and lower the oven temperature to 120°C/250°F/gas ½.

In a clean, grease-free bowl, whisk the egg whites until stiff. Add half the sugar and whisk again. Fold in all but 15 ml/1 tbsp of the remaining sugar, then pile the meringue on top of the pudding, making sure it is completely covered. Arrange in decorative peaks and sprinkle with the remaining sugar.

Return the pudding to the oven for 40-45 minutes until the meringue is set.

SERVES FOUR

 MICROWAVE TIP

Melt the butter in a small bowl on High for 1-1½ minutes.

SAXON PUDDING

Trifle sponges can be used in this pudding; however, far better results are obtained by using home-made cake or good-quality bought plain cake. If you have difficulty in obtaining ratafias, use double the quantity of almond macaroons instead.

oil for greasing
glacé cherries
angelica
25 g/1 oz flaked almonds
3 slices of plain cake or trifle sponges,
   crumbed
4 almond macaroons, crumbed
12 ratafias
2 eggs
100 ml/3½ fl oz single cream
25 g/1 oz caster sugar
300 ml/½ pint milk
45 ml/3 tbsp sherry

Grease a 13 cm/5 inch round cake tin and line the base with oiled greaseproof paper. Cut the cherries and angelica into small shapes and arrange them in a decorative pattern on the base of the prepared cake tin.

Spread out the almonds on a baking sheet and place under a hot grill for a few minutes until browned. Shake the sheet from time to time and watch the almonds carefully as they will readily scorch. Use the almonds to decorate the sides of the greased cake tin.

Mix the cake and macaroon crumbs with the ratafias in a mixing bowl. In a second bowl, combine the eggs, cream and sugar. Mix lightly, then stir in the milk. Strain on to the crumb mixture and add the sherry. Stir, then leave to stand for 1 hour.

Meanwhile prepare a steamer or half fill a large saucepan with water and bring to the boil. Stir the pudding mixture again, making sure the ratafias are properly soaked. Spoon the mixture into the prepared cake tin, taking care not to spoil the decoration. Cover with greased greaseproof paper or foil and secure with string.

Put the pudding in the perforated part of the steamer, or stand it on an old saucer or plate in the pan of boiling water. The water should come halfway up the sides of the tin. Cover the pan tightly and steam the pudding over gently simmering water for 1–1¼ hours.

Remove the cooked pudding from the steamer, leave to stand for 5–10 minutes at room temperature to firm up, then turn out on to a warmed serving plate. Peel off the lining paper. Serve hot, with Thickened Fruit Sauce (page 608) or cold with whipped cream.

SERVES FOUR

 PRESSURE COOKER TIP

Pour 900 ml/1½ pints boiling water into the cooker. Cook the pudding at 15 lb pressure for 10 minutes. Reduce pressure slowly.

QUEEN OF PUDDINGS

butter for greasing
75 g/3 oz fresh white breadcrumbs
400 ml/14 fl oz milk
25 g/1 oz butter
10 ml/2 tsp grated lemon rind
2 eggs, separated
75 g/3 oz caster sugar
30 ml/2 tbsp red jam

Grease a 750 ml/1¼ pint pie dish. Set the oven at 160°C/325°F/gas 3. Spread the breadcrumbs out on a baking sheet and put into the oven to dry off slightly.

Warm the milk and butter with the lemon rind in a saucepan. Meanwhile put the egg yolks in a bowl and stir in 25 g/1 oz of the sugar. Pour on the warmed milk mixture, stirring thoroughly. Add the breadcrumbs, mix thoroughly and pour into the prepared pie dish. Leave to stand for 30 minutes.

Bake the pudding for 40-50 minutes until lightly set, then remove from the oven. Lower the oven temperature to 120°C/250°F/gas ½. Warm the jam in a small saucepan until runny, then spread it over the top of the pudding.

In a clean, grease-free bowl, whisk the egg whites until stiff. Add half the remaining sugar and whisk again. Fold in all but 15 ml/1 tbsp of the remaining sugar. Spoon the meringue around the edge of the jam, drawing it up into peaks at regular intervals to resemble a crown. Sprinkle with the rest of the sugar.

Return the pudding to the oven and bake for 40-45 minutes more, until the meringue is set.

SERVES FOUR

 MICROWAVE TIP

Warm the jam for a few seconds on High.

CUSTARD TART

250 ml/8 fl oz milk
2 eggs
50 g/2 oz caster sugar
pinch of grated nutmeg

SHORT CRUST PASTRY
100 g/4 oz plain flour
1.25 ml/¼ tsp salt
50 g/2 oz margarine (or half butter, half lard)
flour for rolling out

Put an 18 cm/7 inch flan ring on a heavy baking sheet. Alternatively, line an 18 cm/7 inch sandwich cake tin with foil. Set the oven at 190°C/375°F/gas 5.

Make the pastry. Sift the flour and salt into a bowl, then rub in the margarine until the mixture resembles fine breadcrumbs. Add enough cold water to make a stiff dough. Press the dough together with your fingertips. Roll out on a lightly floured surface and use to line the flan ring or tin.

In a saucepan, bring the milk to just below boiling point. Put the eggs and caster sugar into a bowl, mix well, then stir in the scalded milk. Strain the mixture into the pastry case and sprinkle the top with grated nutmeg. Bake for 10 minutes.

Lower the oven temperature to 150°C/300°F/gas 2 and bake for 15-20 minutes more or until the custard is just set. Serve hot or cold.

SERVES FOUR TO SIX

PUDDING A L'AMBASSADRICE

1 Savarin (page 661)

CUSTARD FILLING
25 g/1 oz butter
25 g/1 oz plain flour
150 ml/¼ pint milk
1 egg yolk
45 ml/3 tbsp single cream
15 ml/1 tbsp caster sugar
rum or brandy essence

CARAMEL
100 g/4 oz granulated sugar

CREAM CUSTARD
350 ml/12 fl oz milk
3 eggs
150 ml/¼ pint single cream
15 ml/1 tbsp caster sugar

Prepare and bake the savarin following the recipe instructions, then turn it out on to a wire rack to cool. Do not soak the savarin with rum syrup and do not brush it with any glaze.

Meanwhile make the custard filling. Melt the butter in a saucepan. Stir in the flour and cook for 1 minute, then gradually stir in the milk. Bring to the boil, stirring constantly to make a thick paste. Cool slightly. In a bowl, beat the egg yolk, cream and sugar together, then add to the cooled mixture. Reheat and cook, stirring all the time, until the mixture boils and thickens. Add enough essence to give a definite flavour. Set aside to cool.

Prepare a thickly folded band of newspaper long enough to encircle an 18 cm/7 inch round cake tin. Heat the tin in boiling water or in the oven and wrap the newspaper around it. Prepare the caramel by putting the sugar in a saucepan with 150 ml/¼ pint water. Heat, stirring occasionally, until the sugar has completely dissolved. Bring to the boil and boil without stirring until the syrup is golden brown. Immediately pour the caramel into the warmed, dry tin. Using the paper as a handle, tilt and turn the tin until evenly coated. Leave until the coating is cold and set.

Prepare a steamer or half fill a large saucepan with water and bring to the boil. Cut the savarin into 1.5 cm/¾ inch slices, spread thickly with the custard filling, and arrange in layers in the caramel-coated tin.

Make the cream custard. Warm the milk in a saucepan, without allowing it to approach boiling point. Stir the eggs, cream and sugar together in a bowl, then stir in the milk. Strain the custard into the prepared tin, making sure that all the pieces of savarin are covered.

Put the pudding in the perforated part of the steamer, or stand it on an old saucer or plate in the pan of boiling water. The water should come halfway up the sides of the tin. Cover the pan tightly and steam the pudding for 1-1¼ hours, until the custard is set and the pudding is firm.

Leave for 10 minutes at room temperature to firm up, then turn the pudding out on to a serving plate. Alternatively, the pudding may be allowed to cool completely before turning out. Serve with cream.

SERVES FOUR

Sweet Soufflés and Mousses

A perfect hot dessert soufflé really is the crowning glory of any meal. Light, yet luscious, chilled soufflés and mousses are equally impressive, prepare-ahead alternatives. Basic techniques for preparing hot and cold soufflés, savoury and sweet, are included in the chapter on Dairy Foods (page 524)

VANILLA SOUFFLE

40 g/1½ oz butter
40 g/1½ oz plain flour
250 ml/8 fl oz milk
4 eggs, separated, plus 1 white
50 g/2 oz caster sugar
2.5 ml/½ tsp vanilla essence
caster or icing sugar for dredging

Grease a 1 litre/1¾ pint soufflé dish. Set the oven at 180°C/350°F/gas 4.

Melt the butter in a saucepan, stir in the flour and cook slowly for 2-3 minutes without colouring, stirring all the time. Add the milk gradually and beat until smooth. Cook for 1-2 minutes more, still stirring. Remove from the heat and beat hard until the sauce comes away cleanly from the sides of the pan. Cool slightly and put into a bowl.

Beat the yolks into the flour mixture one by one. Beat in the sugar and vanilla essence.

In a clean, grease-free bowl, whisk all the egg whites until stiff. Using a metal spoon, stir 1 spoonful of the whites into the mixture to lighten it, then fold in the rest until evenly distributed.

Spoon into the prepared dish and bake for 45 minutes until well risen and browned.

Dredge with caster or icing sugar and serve immediately from the dish, with a jam sauce.

SERVES FOUR TO SIX

VARIATIONS

Almond Soufflé Add 100 g/4 oz ground almonds, 15 ml/1 tbsp lemon juice and a few drops of ratafia essence to the mixture before adding the egg yolks. Reduce the sugar to 40 g/1½ oz. Omit the vanilla essence.

Coffee Soufflé Add 30 ml/2 tbsp instant coffee dissolved in a little hot water before adding the egg yolks, or use 125 ml/4 fl oz strong black coffee and only 125 ml/4 fl oz milk. Omit the vanilla essence.

Ginger Soufflé Add a pinch of ground ginger and 50 g/2 oz chopped preserved stem ginger before adding the egg yolks. Omit the vanilla essence. Serve each portion topped with double cream and ginger syrup.

Lemon Soufflé Add the thinly grated rind and juice of 1 lemon before adding the egg yolks. Omit the vanilla essence. Serve with a rich lemon sauce.

Liqueur Soufflé Add 30 ml/2 tbsp Cointreau, kirsch or curaçao instead of vanilla essence and make as for Soufflé au Grand Marnier below. Serve with sweetened cream flavoured with the liqueur.

Orange Soufflé Thinly pare the rind of 2 oranges. Put in a saucepan with the milk and bring slowly to the boil. Remove from the heat, cover, and leave to stand for 10 minutes, then remove the rind. Make up the sauce using the flavoured milk. Reduce the sugar to 40 g/1½ oz and omit the vanilla essence. Add the strained juice of ½ orange.

Praline Soufflé Dissolve 30–45 ml/2–3 tbsp almond Praline (see Mrs Beeton's Tip, page 602) in the milk before making the sauce, or crush and add just before the egg yolks. Omit the vanilla essence.

Soufflé au Grand Marnier Add 30–45 ml/ 2–3 tbsp Grand Marnier to the orange soufflé mixture. Serve with an orange sauce made by boiling 125 ml/4 fl oz orange juice and a few drops of liqueur with 50 g/2 oz caster sugar until syrupy. Add very fine strips of orange rind to the mixture.

Soufflé Ambassadrice Crumble 2 almond macaroons; soak them in 30 ml/2 tbsp rum with 50 g/2 oz chopped blanched almonds. Stir into a vanilla soufflé mixture.

Soufflé Harlequin Make up 2 half quantities of soufflé mixture in different flavours, eg chocolate and vanilla, or praline and coffee. Spoon alternately into the dish.

Soufflé Rothschild Rinse 50 g/2 oz mixed glacé fruit in hot water to remove any excess sugar. Chop the fruit and soak it in 30 ml/2 tbsp brandy or kirsch for 2 hours. Make up 1 quantity vanilla soufflé mixture. Put half the vanilla soufflé mixture into the dish, add the fruit, and then the rest of the soufflé mixture.

Soufflé Surprise Crumble 3 sponge fingers or almond macaroons into a bowl. Soak the biscuits in 30 ml/2 tbsp Grand Marnier or Cointreau. Add 30 ml/2 tbsp of the same liqueur to an orange soufflé mixture. Put half the mixture into the dish, sprinkle the biscuits on top, and add the rest of the soufflé mixture.

HOT FRUIT SOUFFLES

For fruit-flavoured soufflés a thick, sweet purée is added to the basic vanilla soufflé. It is important that the purée should have a strong flavour, otherwise the taste will not be discernible. If extra purée is added, the soufflé will be heavy and will not rise.

Apple Soufflé Add 125 ml/4 fl oz thick sweet apple purée, 15 ml/1 tbsp lemon juice, and a pinch of powdered cinnamon to the soufflé before adding the egg yolks. Dust the soufflé with cinnamon before serving.

Apricot Soufflé Before adding the egg yolks, add 125 ml/4 fl oz thick fresh apricot purée and 15 ml/1 tbsp lemon juice. If using canned apricots – 1 (397 g/14 oz) can yields 125 ml/4 fl oz purée – use half milk and half can syrup for the sauce. A purée made from dried apricots makes a delicious soufflé.

Pineapple Soufflé Before adding the egg yolks, add 125 ml/4 fl oz crushed pineapple or 75 g/3 oz chopped fresh pineapple, and make the sauce using half milk and half pineapple juice.

Raspberry Soufflé Before adding the egg yolks, add 125 ml/4 fl oz raspberry purée – 1 (397 g/14 oz) can yields 125 ml/4 fl oz purée – and 10 ml/2 tsp lemon juice.

Strawberry Soufflé Before adding the egg yolks, add 125 ml/4 fl oz strawberry purée. Make the sauce using half milk and half single cream. Add a little pink food colouring, if necessary.

CHOCOLATE DREAM

fat for greasing
100g/4oz plain chocolate
400ml/14floz milk
50g/2oz caster sugar
50g/2oz plain flour
15ml/1tbsp butter
3 whole eggs, separated, plus 1 egg white
icing sugar for dusting

Grease a 1.1 litre/2 pint soufflé dish. Set the oven at 180°C/350°F/gas 4.

Break the chocolate into pieces and put into a saucepan. Reserve 60ml/4tbsp of the milk in a mixing bowl and pour the rest into the pan with the chocolate. Add the sugar and warm over low heat until the chocolate begins to melt. Remove from the heat and leave to stand until the chocolate is completely melted, stirring occasionally.

Add the flour to the bowl containing the milk and stir to a smooth paste. Stir in the chocolate-flavoured milk, return the mixture to the clean pan and bring to the boil. Cook for 1-2 minutes, stirring all the time, then remove from the heat and add the butter. Stir well, then set aside to cool slightly.

Beat the egg yolks into the chocolate mixture one at a time. In a clean, grease-free bowl, whisk the egg whites until stiff. Stir one spoonful of the egg whites into the chocolate mixture to lighten it, then fold in the rest until evenly blended.

Spoon into the prepared dish and bake for 45 minutes. Dust with icing sugar and serve immediately, with Mocha Sauce (page 503) or Chocolate Cream Sauce (page 503).

SERVES FOUR

SEMOLINA SOUFFLE

Banish all thoughts of semolina as something thick and porridge-like. This soufflé is light and lovely.

fat for greasing
pared rind of ¼ lemon
400ml/14floz milk
50g/2oz semolina
50g/2oz caster sugar
3 eggs, separated

Grease a 1 litre/1¾ pint soufflé dish. Set the oven at 180°C/350°F/gas 4.

Combine the lemon rind and milk in a saucepan and bring to the boil. Immediately remove from the heat and leave to stand for 10 minutes. Remove the rind and sprinkle in the semolina. Cook for 2-3 minutes, stirring all the time, until the semolina mixture thickens. Stir in the sugar and leave to cool.

Beat the egg yolks into the semolina mixture one by one. In a clean, grease-free bowl, whisk the egg whites until stiff, and fold into the semolina mixture.

Put into the prepared dish and bake for 45 minutes. Serve at once, with an apricot sauce or redcurrant sauce.

SERVES FOUR

COLD SOUFFLES AND MOUSSES

MILK CHOCOLATE SOUFFLE

Cold soufflés are prepared in much the same way as hot ones; the difference being that gelatine is used instead of heat to set the eggs. The dish is prepared in a similar fashion, too, with a paper collar enabling the mixture to be taken above the level of the dish to simulate a risen soufflé.

10 ml/2 tsp gelatine
2 eggs, separated
50 g/2 oz caster sugar
150 ml/¼ pint evaporated milk, chilled
75 g/3 oz milk chocolate

DECORATION
whipped cream
grated milk chocolate

Prepare a 500 ml/17 fl oz soufflé dish (see page 447) and stand it on a plate for easy handling.

Place 30 ml/2 tbsp water in a small bowl and sprinkle the gelatine on to the liquid. Set aside for 15 minutes until the gelatine is spongy. Stand the bowl over a pan of hot water and stir the gelatine until it has dissolved completely. Cool slightly.

Combine the egg yolks and sugar in a heatproof bowl and stand over a saucepan of hot water set over low heat. Do not let the water boil or touch the bowl. Whisk the mixture for 5-10 minutes until thick and pale, then remove the bowl from the heat.

In a bowl, whisk the chilled evaporated milk until thick, then whisk into the egg yolk mix-

ture. Melt the chocolate on a plate over simmering water and whisk into the mixture.

Fold a little of the chocolate mixture into the cooled gelatine, then whisk this into the rest of the chocolate mixture. Put in a cool place until the mixture starts to set.

Whisk the egg whites in a clean, grease-free bowl until stiff, then fold into the mixture. Tip the soufflé gently into the prepared dish and refrigerate for about 2 hours until set.

Carefully remove the paper from the crown of the soufflé and decorate with whipped cream and grated chocolate.

SERVES FOUR

MILANAISE SOUFFLE

15 ml/1 tbsp gelatine
3 eggs, separated
grated rind and juice of 2 lemons
100 g/4 oz caster sugar
125 ml/4 fl oz double cream

DECORATION
finely chopped nuts or cake crumbs
whipped double cream (optional)
crystallized lemon slices
angelica

Prepare a 500 ml/17 fl oz soufflé dish (see Mrs Beeton's Tip and page 447) and stand it on a plate for easy handling.

Place 45 ml/3 tbsp water in a small bowl and sprinkle the gelatine on to the liquid. Set aside for 15 minutes until the gelatine is spongy. Stand the bowl over a pan of hot water and stir the gelatine until it has dissolved completely. Cool slightly.

Combine the egg yolks, lemon rind and juice, and sugar in a heatproof bowl and stand over a saucepan of hot water set over low heat. Do not let the water boil or touch the bowl. Whisk the mixture for 10-15 minutes until thick and pale, then remove from the heat and continue whisking until cool. Fold a little of the yolk mixture into the cooled gelatine, then whisk this into the rest of the yolk mixture. Put in a cool place until the mixture starts to set.

In a bowl, whip the cream to soft peaks. Using a large metal spoon, fold into the yolk mixture until evenly blended. Whisk the egg whites in a clean, grease-free bowl until stiff, then fold into the mixture. Tip the soufflé gently into the prepared dish and refrigerate until set.

Carefully remove the paper from the crown of the soufflé and decorate the sides with chopped nuts or cake crumbs. Pipe whipped cream on top, if liked, and decorate with crystallized lemon slices and small pieces of angelica.

SERVES FOUR

VARIATIONS

In each of the variations below, omit the lemon rind and juice.

Cold Chocolate Soufflé Whisk the yolks with 30 ml/2 tbsp water and 75 g/3 oz caster sugar. Melt 75 g/3 oz grated plain chocolate over a saucepan of hot water. Add to the yolk mixture with the dissolved gelatine and whisk well.

Cold Orange Soufflé Whisk the yolks with the finely grated rind and juice of 2 oranges and use 75 g/3 oz caster sugar only. Add 30 ml/2 tbsp Grand Marnier or orange curaçao, if liked. Dissolve the gelatine in a mixture of 15 ml/1 tbsp water and 30 ml/2 tbsp lemon juice. Decorate the soufflé with crystallized orange slices, nuts and cream.

Cold Praline Soufflé Make 75 g/3 oz Praline (see Mrs Beeton's Tip, page 720) and crush it. Dissolve 5 ml/1 tsp instant coffee in 30 ml/

2 tbsp hot water, and add 30 ml/2 tbsp cold water. Whisk the liquid with the yolks. Add 50 g/2 oz of the crushed praline to the mixture with the whipped cream. Decorate with the remaining praline and additional cream.

Cold Fruit Soufflés The recipe below uses raspberries but other fresh, frozen or canned soft fruits, such as strawberries, blackcurrants or blackberries, may be substituted to produce a strongly flavoured soufflé.

Cold Raspberry Soufflé Soften the gelatine in 45 ml/3 tbsp of strained fruit syrup from 1 (440 g/15½ oz) can of raspberries. Add 15 ml/1 tbsp lemon juice and 150 ml/¼ pint sieved fruit to the yolk mixture (this can be made up with a little strained syrup, if necessary). Use only 75 g/3 oz sugar and 100 ml/3½ fl oz double cream. Decorate the sides of the soufflé with desiccated coconut, and the top with whipped cream and raspberries.

Cold Apricot Soufflé Dried apricots make a delicious soufflé: Soak 50 g/2 oz overnight in enough water to cover. Tip into a saucepan and simmer for 15-20 minutes until tender, then purée in a blender or food processor. Soften the gelatine in a mixture of 15 ml/1 tbsp water and 30 ml/2 tbsp lemon juice. Add the apricot purée (made up to 150 ml/¼ pint with water, if necessary) and proceed as in the recipe above.

 MRS BEETON'S TIP

The size of the soufflé dish is crucial, since the mixture must 'rise' above it. If in doubt as to the capacity of the dish, measure by pouring in 500 ml/17 fl oz water. If the dish is slightly too small, do not worry, since the crown will merely be a little taller. A larger dish, however, will not be suitable.

BLACKCURRANT MOUSSE

A sweet mousse is a creamy dessert which usually has either a fruit purée or a flavoured custard sauce as its base, with beaten egg whites (and sometimes whipped cream) added to lighten the texture. Fresh, frozen or canned fruit may be used, with the amount of sugar adjusted according to the sweetness of the fruit.

250 g/9 oz fresh blackcurrants
50 g/2 oz caster sugar
10 ml/2 tsp lemon juice
10 ml/2 tsp gelatine
125 ml/4 fl oz double cream
2 egg whites
whipped cream to decorate

Reserve a few whole blackcurrants for decoration. Rub the rest through a sieve into a measuring jug, then make up the purée to 150 ml/¼ pint with water.

Combine the blackcurrant purée, sugar and lemon juice in a mixing bowl. Place 30 ml/2 tbsp water in a small heatproof bowl and sprinkle the gelatine on to the liquid. Set aside for 15 minutes until the gelatine is spongy. Stand the bowl over a saucepan of hot water and stir the gelatine until it has dissolved completely. Cool slightly.

Fold a little of the blackcurrant purée into the cooled gelatine, then whisk this mixture into the bowl of blackcurrant purée. Leave in a cool place until the mixture starts to set.

In a deep bowl, whip the cream until it just holds its shape, then fold into the blackcurrant mixture with a metal spoon. Whisk the egg whites in a clean, grease-free bowl, and fold in. Make sure that the mixture is thoroughly and evenly blended but do not overmix.

Pour gently into a glass dish, a wetted 500 ml/17 fl oz mould or individual glasses.

Refrigerate for 1–2 hours until set, then turn out if necessary and decorate with whipped cream and the reserved blackcurrants.

SERVES FOUR

 FREEZER TIP

Frozen blackcurrant mousse is delicious. Omit the gelatine and freeze the mixture in ice trays. Thaw for 15 minutes in the refrigerator before serving.

CHOCOLATE MARQUISE

150 g/5 oz plain chocolate, coarsely grated
200 g/7 oz unsalted butter, cubed
6 eggs, separated

Put the chocolate into a large heatproof bowl and place over hot water. Heat gently until the chocolate melts.

Gradually beat the butter into the chocolate, a cube at a time. Stir in the egg yolks, one by one. When all have been added and the mixture is smooth, remove the bowl from the heat.

In a clean, grease-free bowl, whisk the egg whites until stiff. Fold them into the chocolate mixture. Pour gently into a glass bowl or 6 individual dishes and chill thoroughly before serving.

SERVES SIX

 MICROWAVE TIP

Melt the chocolate in a small bowl on High for 2½–3 minutes.

CHOCOLATE MOUSSE

150 g/5 oz plain chocolate, grated
4 eggs, separated
vanilla essence

DECORATION
whipped cream
chopped walnuts

Put the grated chocolate into a large heatproof bowl with 30 ml/2 tbsp water. Stand over a saucepan of simmering water until the chocolate melts. Remove from the heat and stir the mixture until smooth.

Beat the egg yolks into the chocolate with a few drops of vanilla essence. In a clean, grease-free bowl, whisk the egg whites until fairly stiff, then fold gently into the chocolate mixture until evenly blended.

Pour into 4 individual dishes and refrigerate for 1–2 hours until set. Decorate with whipped cream and chopped walnuts just before serving.

SERVES FOUR

VARIATIONS

Mocha Mousse Dissolve 5 ml/1 tsp instant coffee in 30 ml/2 tbsp hot water and stir this liquid into the chocolate with the egg yolks and vanilla essence.

Choc-au-Rhum Mousse Add 15 ml/1 tbsp rum to the mixture. Alternatively, use brandy, Grand Marnier or Tia Maria.

White Mousse Use white chocolate, melting it in single cream instead of water.

CHOCOLATE AND ORANGE MOUSSE

100 g/4 oz plain chocolate, grated
60 ml/4 tbsp fresh orange juice
10 ml/2 tsp gelatine
3 eggs, separated
vanilla essence
100 ml/3½ fl oz double cream

DECORATION
whipped cream
coarsely grated plain chocolate

Put the grated chocolate into a large heatproof bowl with the orange juice. Sprinkle the gelatine on to the liquid. Set aside for 15 minutes until the gelatine in spongy. Stand the bowl over a saucepan of simmering water until the chocolate melts and the gelatine dissolves. Remove from the heat and stir until smooth.

Beat the egg yolks into the chocolate mixture with a few drops of vanilla essence. Whip the cream in a separate bowl until it just holds its shape, then fold into the mixture.

Finally, in a clean, grease-free bowl, whisk the egg whites until fairly stiff, then fold gently into the chocolate mixture until evenly blended. Pour into a wetted 750 ml/1¼ pint mould or deep serving bowl and refrigerate for about 2 hours until set.

Turn out, if necessary, and decorate with whipped cream and coarsely grated chocolate.

SERVES FOUR

 MICROWAVE TIP

Dissolve the chocolate and gelatine in the orange juice in a suitable bowl on High for 2–3 minutes.

COFFEE MOUSSE

250 ml/8 fl oz milk
15 ml/1 tbsp instant coffee
2 eggs, separated
50 g/2 oz caster sugar
10 ml/2 tsp gelatine
75 ml/5 tbsp double cream

DECORATION
whipped cream
Praline (see Mrs Beeton's Tip, page 602),
    crushed

In a saucepan, warm the milk and stir in the coffee. Set aside. Put the egg yolks into a bowl with the caster sugar and mix well, then gradually add the flavoured milk. Strain through a sieve back into the pan. Stir over very gentle heat for about 10 minutes until the custard starts to thicken. Cool slightly.

Place 30 ml/2 tbsp water in a small bowl and sprinkle the gelatine on to the liquid. Set aside for 15 minutes until the gelatine is spongy. Stand the bowl over a pan of hot water and stir the gelatine until it has dissolved completely. Cool until the gelatine mixture is at the same temperature as the custard, then mix a little of the custard into the gelatine. Stir back into the bowl of custard and leave in a cool place until beginning to set.

Whip the cream in a deep bowl until it just holds its shape. In a separate, grease-free bowl, whisk the egg whites until stiff. Fold first the cream, and then the egg whites, into the coffee custard, making sure the mixture is fully blended but not over-mixed.

Pour into a wetted 500 ml/17 fl oz mould or glass dish and refrigerate for 1–2 hours until set. Turn out, if necessary, and decorate with whipped cream and crushed praline.

SERVES FOUR

VARIATIONS

In each of the variations that follow, omit the instant coffee.

Caramel Mousse Before making the mousse mixture, warm 100 g/4 oz granulated sugar and 15 ml/1 tbsp water in a heavy-bottomed saucepan. Stir until the sugar dissolves. Continue heating until the syrup turns a rich brown colour. Remove from the heat and carefully add 60 ml/4 tbsp hot water, stirring quickly until all the caramel has dissolved. Cool. Add 200 ml/7 fl oz milk to the caramel and heat this with the egg yolks to make the custard for the mousse.

Orange Praline Mousse Before making the mousse mixture, make and crush 100 g/4 oz praline. Add the finely grated rind of 1 orange to the custard, and use the juice to dissolve the gelatine. Fold half the crushed praline into the completed mousse mixture, and use the rest to decorate the top.

LEMON CHIFFON

3 eggs, separated
150 g/5 oz caster sugar
125 ml/4 fl oz lemon juice
10 ml/2 tsp gelatine
grated rind of 2 lemons

Combine the egg yolks, sugar and lemon juice in a heatproof bowl. Stand over a saucepan of gently simmering water and whisk the mixture until frothy, pale and the consistency of single cream. Remove from the heat.

Place 45 ml/3 tbsp water in a small bowl and sprinkle the gelatine on to the liquid. Set aside for 15 minutes until the gelatine is spongy. Stand the bowl over a pan of hot water and stir the gelatine until it has dissolved completely. Cool for 5 minutes.

Whisk the gelatine into the egg yolk mixture. Cool the mixture, then refrigerate until beginning to set. Stir in the lemon rind.

In a clean, grease-free bowl, whisk the egg whites until stiff. Fold into the lemon mixture. Spoon into 4 glasses. Return to the refrigerator until completely set.

SERVES FOUR

SOFT MAPLE MOUSSE

For the best flavour, it is important that genuine maple syrup be used for this dessert. For a firm set, gelatine may be added to the mixture.

200 ml/7 fl oz pure maple syrup
4 egg yolks
200 ml/7 fl oz double cream

Pour the maple syrup into a saucepan. Beat the egg yolks lightly in a bowl, then stir them into the syrup. Cook over very low heat, stirring all the time with a wooden spoon until the mixture thickens enough to coat the back of the spoon thinly.

Remove from the heat and leave to cool, covered with dampened greaseproof paper. Stir once or twice during cooling. When the maple syrup mixture is cold, cover and refrigerate until required.

Just before serving, whip the cream in a deep bowl to the same consistency as the maple custard. Fold the cream gently into the maple custard, then chill again until required.

SERVES FOUR

MANGO MOUSSE

1 kg/2¼ lb ripe mangoes
90 ml/6 tbsp fresh lime juice
100 g/3½ oz caster sugar
15 ml/1 tbsp gelatine
2 egg whites
pinch of salt
100 ml/3½ fl oz double cream
15 ml/1 tbsp light rum

Peel the fruit and cut the flesh off the stones. Purée with the lime juice in a blender or food processor (see Mrs Beeton's Tip). When smooth, blend in the sugar, then scrape the mixture into a bowl with a rubber spatula.

Place 45 ml/3 tbsp water in a small bowl. Sprinkle the gelatine on to the liquid. Set aside for 15 minutes until the gelatine is spongy. Stand the bowl over a pan of hot water and stir the gelatine until it has dissolved completely. Cool slightly, then stir into the mango purée.

In a clean, grease-free bowl, whisk the egg whites with the salt until they form fairly stiff peaks. Stir 15 ml/1 tbsp of the egg whites into the purée to lighten it, then fold in the rest.

Lightly whip the cream and rum together in a separate bowl, then fold into the mango mixture as lightly as possible. Spoon into a serving bowl. Refrigerate for about 3 hours until set.

SERVES SIX TO EIGHT

 MRS BEETON'S TIP

If you do not have a blender or food processor, rub the mango flesh through a sieve into a bowl and stir in the lime juice and sugar.

Cheesecakes and Cream Pies

Sample the variety of cheesecakes and cream pies on offer in this chapter, from a light and fruity Raspberry Yogurt Cheesecake to mouthwatering Coffee Chiffon Pie. Make them for a Sunday treat or add lavish creamy decoration for a dinner-party dessert.

The cheesecakes that are popular today tend to be American-style concoctions, with gelatine as the setting agent. However, the traditional cuisines of European countries offer alternative recipes for baked cheesecakes that are zesty with lemon and fruity with sultanas, delicate and creamy with Italian ricotta cheese, or more substantial in the tradition of British baking.

There are no rules for making cheesecakes. For uncooked recipes made with soft cheese, the cheese used may be varied according to individual requirements. Use cream cheese for a rich result or lighter curd cheese (or sieved cottage cheese) for a cheesecake with a lower fat content. Plain yogurt or fromage frais may be used instead of cream in some recipes.

Recipes for baked cheesecakes should be followed more closely as the type of cheese used may well affect the result and yogurt or fromage frais may separate out during cooking.

A CHOICE OF BASE

Which base, or case, to use to hold the cheese mixture depends on the type of cheesecake being made. Cooked cheesecakes may be set in a sweet pastry case or on a base of pastry; alternatively a sponge cake mixture may form the base. Uncooked cheesecakes are usually set in a case or on a base made of biscuit crumbs and butter.

BISCUIT BASE

Quick and easy to make, a biscuit base is ideal for uncooked cheesecakes. Although a biscuit base can be used for cooked cheesecakes, the biscuits tend to become slightly overcooked and the fat which binds them seeps out during cooking.

To line the base only of a 20 cm/8 inch container you will need about 100 g/4 oz crushed biscuits combined with 50 g/2 oz butter. Digestive biscuits or other plain sweet biscuits are usually used; however chocolate-coated biscuits, gingernuts or coconut cookies may be crushed to vary the flavour of the base.

Crush the biscuits in a food processor if you have one. Otherwise, place them in a strong polythene bag and use a rolling pin to crush them. It is best to close the bag loosely with a metal tie to allow air to escape. Crush the biscuits carefully to avoid breaking the bag and making a mess.

Melt the butter in a saucepan, then stir in the crushed biscuits off the heat. Alternatively, melt the butter in a mug or small bowl in the microwave, allowing about 1 minute on High, then pour it over the biscuits in a dish. Stir well.

When the mixture is pressed on to the base of the container, smooth it over with the back of a clean metal spoon. Allow the base to cool, then chill it before adding the topping.

To line the sides of the container as well as the base, double the quantity of biscuits and butter and turn all the mixture into the container. Use a metal spoon to press the mixture all over the base and up the sides. This is only practical for a shallow container, such as a flan dish or tin.

PASTRY CASE

A case of sweet pastry is often used for a baked cheesecake. The ingredients and method are included in the relevant recipes. To vary the pastry slightly, spices, a few finely chopped or ground nuts (almonds or hazelnuts), grated lemon or orange rind may be added.

CAKE BASE

This type of base is used for cooked cheesecakes. A one-stage mixture of fat, egg and flour may be used and spread in the container before the topping is added (as for Baked Coffee Cheesecake, page 738).

A cake base may be made for an uncooked cheesecake. Set the oven at 180°C/350°F/gas 4. In a mixing bowl, beat together 50 g/2 oz each of butter, caster sugar and self-raising flour with 1 egg and 5 ml/1 tsp baking powder. When all the ingredients are thoroughly combined, spread the mixture in a well-greased 20 cm/8 inch sandwich tin and bake for 20–25 minutes, until risen and golden. The cake should feel firm on top when cooked. Turn it out on to a wire rack to cool.

Trim the top of the cake level before placing it in the base of a 20 cm/8 inch deep cake tin. Set the cheesecake mixture on top. For a very thin base to a shallow cheesecake, slice through the cake horizontally and use one half. Pack and freeze the second slice for making a second cheesecake. The base may be frozen for up to 3 months.

TURNING OUT A CHEESECAKE

To remove a cheesecake from a loose-bottomed flan tin, have ready a storage jar or small soufflé dish. Make sure that the jar has a flat, heat-resistant lid if the cheesecake is fresh from the oven. Stand the tin containing the cheesecake on top of the jar, so that the loose base is well

supported and the side is free. Gently ease the side away from the cheesecake, then transfer the dessert on its base to a flat platter.

FREEZING CHEESECAKES

Baked and fairly firm uncooked cheesecakes freeze very well. Freeze the whole cheesecake before adding any decoration. A cheesecake which is decorated with piped cream should be open frozen, then put in a large, deep, rigid container and returned to the freezer.

Any leftover cheesecake may be frozen in slices. Arrange the slices in a rigid container or on a double thickness of foil, placing a piece of freezer film between each slice. Close the foil loosely around the slices or cover the container and place in a level place in the freezer.

A decorated cheesecake may be frozen successfully for 2–3 weeks ready to be served for a special dessert. Slices of cheesecake may be frozen for up to 2 or 3 months. They will not look their best but will taste good as an impromptu family pudding.

ALMOND CHEESECAKE

fat for greasing
75 g/3 oz curd cheese
50 g/2 oz butter, melted
2 eggs, separated
grated rind and juice of ½ lemon
50 g/2 oz ground almonds
50 g/2 oz caster sugar
30 ml/2 tbsp self-raising flour

Line and grease a 15 cm/6 inch sandwich cake tin. Set the oven at 220°C/425°F/gas 7.

Rub the curd cheese through a sieve into a mixing bowl. Add the melted butter, egg yolks, lemon rind and juice, almonds and caster sugar and mix thoroughly. Sift the flour over the mixture and fold in.

In a clean, grease-free bowl, whisk the egg whites until stiff. Fold into the almond mixture. Spoon the mixture into the prepared tin and bake for 10 minutes.

Lower the oven temperature to 180°C/350°F/gas 4 and cook for about 15 minutes more. Test to see whether the cake is cooked (see Mrs Beeton's Tip). If necessary, return the cake to the oven for a few minutes, covering the surface loosely with foil or greaseproof paper to prevent overbrowning.

SERVES FOUR

 MRS BEETON'S TIP

To test the cake, insert a thin heated skewer into the centre. If the skewer comes out dry, the cake is cooked.

LEMON CHEESECAKE

BASE
100 g/4 oz digestive biscuits
50 g/2 oz butter
25 g/1 oz caster sugar

FILLING
200 g/7 oz full-fat soft cheese
75 g/3 oz caster sugar
2 eggs, separated
125 ml/4 fl oz soured cream
15 g/½ oz gelatine
grated rind and juice of 1 lemon

Make the base. Crumb the biscuits (see page 736). Melt the butter in a small saucepan and mix in the crumbs and sugar. Press the mixture on to the base of a loose-bottomed 15 cm/6 inch cake tin. Put in a cool place to set.

Make the filling. In a mixing bowl, beat the cheese and sugar together. Add the egg yolks and beat well. Stir in the soured cream.

Place 45 ml/3 tbsp water in a small bowl. Sprinkle the gelatine on to the liquid. Set aside for 15 minutes until the gelatine is spongy. Stand the bowl over a pan of hot water and stir the gelatine until it has dissolved completely. Stir the lemon rind, juice and dissolved gelatine into the cheese mixture.

In a clean, grease-free bowl, whisk the egg whites until stiff and fold carefully into the mixture. Pour into the prepared tin and chill for 45–60 minutes until firm. When quite cold, remove from the tin, transfer to a plate and slice to serve.

SERVES FOUR TO SIX

CHEDDAR CHEESECAKE

BASE
175 g/6 oz plain flour
75 g/3 oz margarine
1 egg yolk
flour for rolling out

FILLING
1 egg, separated, plus 1 white
grated rind and juice of 1 lemon
75 ml/5 tbsp plain yogurt
25 g/1 oz self-raising flour
75 g/3 oz caster sugar
150 g/5 oz Cheddar cheese, grated

Set the oven at 200°C/400°F/gas 6. To make the pastry base, sift the flour into a bowl, then rub in the margarine until the mixture resembles fine breadcrumbs. Add the egg yolk and enough water (about 15–30 ml/1–2 tbsp) to mix the ingredients into a short pastry. Press the pastry together gently with your fingertips.

Roll out the pastry on a lightly floured surface and use to line a 20 cm/8 inch flan ring or dish. Bake 'blind' (see Mrs Beeton's Tip). Lower the oven temperature to 160°C/325°F/gas 3.

 MRS BEETON'S TIP

To bake blind, prick the base of the pastry case with a fork, then cover with a piece of greaseproof paper. Fill the pastry case with dried beans, bread crusts or rice and bake at 200°C/400°F/gas 6 for 10 minutes. Remove the paper and beans or other dry filling and return the case to the oven for 5 minutes to dry out the inside before adding the chosen filling and returning the case to the oven. If a fully cooked pastry case is required, as when a cold filling is to be added, bake the pastry case blind for 20–30 minutes, and dry out for 5–7 minutes.

In a mixing bowl, combine the egg yolk, lemon rind and juice, yogurt, flour and sugar. Mix well, then fold in the grated cheese.

In a clean, grease-free bowl, whisk both egg whites until stiff. Stir 15 ml/1 tbsp of the beaten egg whites into the cheese mixture to lighten it, then gently fold in the remaining egg white. Turn into the prepared pastry case.

Bake for 35–45 minutes or until firm in the centre and lightly browned. Serve cold.

SERVES SIX TO EIGHT

VARIATIONS

Cheshire Cheesecake Substitute Cheshire cheese for the Cheddar. Either grate it finely or crumble the Cheshire cheese, then crush it with a fork until it breaks down into fine crumbs. Cheshire is milder and slightly more tangy than Cheddar.

Apple and Cheddar Cheesecake Spread a layer of stewed apples or sweetened apple purée in the pastry case before adding the cheese filling.

Glacé Fruit Cheesecake Sprinkle a mixture of glacé and candied fruit and peel over the pastry case before adding the cheese mixture. Chopped angelica, cherries, candied peel and crystallized ginger are suitable.

Individual Cheesecakes Make individual cheesecakes in patty tins.

CLASSIC BAKED CHEESECAKE

BASE
75 g/3 oz butter
150 g/5 oz fine dried white breadcrumbs
50 g/2 oz caster sugar
7.5 ml/3 tsp ground cinnamon

FILLING
3 eggs, separated
100 g/4 oz caster sugar
375 g/13 oz full-fat soft cheese
grated rind and juice of 1 lemon
125 ml/4 fl oz soured cream
icing sugar for dusting

Set the oven at 180°C/350°F/gas 4. Make the base. Melt the butter in a frying pan and stir in the breadcrumbs. Cook over gentle heat, stirring until the crumbs are golden. Remove from the heat; stir in the sugar and cinnamon. Press the crumbs over the base of a loose-bottomed 18 cm/7 inch cake tin.

Beat the egg yolks in a mixing bowl until liquid. Add the sugar to the egg yolks, beating until creamy. Rub the cheese through a sieve into the bowl, then work in lightly. Add the lemon rind and juice to the mixture with the soured cream.

In a clean, grease-free bowl, whisk the egg whites to soft peaks. Stir 30 ml/2 tbsp into the cheese mixture, then fold in the rest lightly. Turn the mixture gently on to the prepared base in the tin. Bake for 45 minutes. Cover loosely with foil and bake for a further 15 minutes. Cool in the tin. Serve dusted with icing sugar.

SERVES TEN

APPLE CHEESECAKE

This is not a cheesecake in the modern sense, but a tart filled with apple cheese (or apple curd). It is refreshing and delicious.

1 quantity Butter Crust Pastry (page 515) or
    350 g/12 oz puff pastry, thawed if frozen
450 g/1 lb cooking apples, peeled, cored
    and sliced
100 g/4 oz caster sugar
100 g/4 oz butter, melted
grated rind and juice of 1 lemon
2 eggs plus 2 egg yolks

Set the oven at 200°C/400°F/gas 6. Roll out the pastry and use to line a 25 cm/10 inch flan dish or tin. Prick the pastry all over, then chill for 20 minutes in the bottom of the refrigerator or 10 minutes in the freezer. Bake for 20 minutes. Remove the pastry case from the oven. Reduce the oven temperature to 180°C/350°F/gas 4.

Place the apples in a saucepan and add 30 ml/2 tbsp water. Cook over medium heat, stirring, until the fruit begins to soften. Allow to simmer gently and cover the pan. Stir occasionally until the apples are reduced to a pulp, then press them through a sieve into a bowl.

Stir the sugar, butter and lemon rind and juice into the apples. Beat the eggs and yolks together, then strain them through a fine sieve into the apple mixture. Beat well and pour the mixture into the pastry case. Bake for 25-30 minutes, until the apple filling is set.

Leave to cool, then serve with fresh cream or fromage frais.

SERVES TWELVE

MARIGOLD CHEESECAKE

BASE
100 g/4 oz digestive biscuits
50 g/2 oz butter
25 g/1 oz caster sugar

FILLING
25 g/1 oz gelatine
2 eggs, separated
200 g/7 oz full-fat soft cheese
25 g/1 oz caster sugar
250 ml/8 fl oz milk
pared rind of 1 orange

DECORATION
orange segments
½ glacé cherry

Make the base. Crumb the biscuits (see page 618). Melt the butter in a small saucepan and mix in the crumbs and sugar. Press the mixture into a loose-bottomed 15 cm/6 inch cake tin. Chill while making the filling.

Place 30 ml/2 tbsp water in a small bowl. Sprinkle the gelatine on to the liquid. Set aside for 15 minutes until the gelatine is spongy. Stand the bowl over a pan of hot water and stir the gelatine until it has dissolved completely.

Combine the egg yolks, soft cheese, sugar, milk, orange rind and gelatine mixture in the bowl of a blender or food processor. Process for 45 seconds or until smooth, then scrape into a mixing bowl with a spatula. Alternatively, beat well by hand.

In a clean, grease-free bowl, whisk the egg whites to soft peaks, then gently fold into the cheese mixture. Spoon very gently on to the base and chill until firm.

Garnish with orange segments and the cherry.

SERVES FOUR TO SIX

MELOPITA

In Greece, this honey-flavoured dessert would be made from myzithra. Sieved cottage cheese is an acceptable substitute.

BASE
300 g/11 oz plain flour
7.5 ml/1½ tsp baking powder
pinch of salt
125 g/4½ oz butter
flour for rolling out

FILLING
675 g/1½ lb cottage cheese
150 g/5 oz caster sugar
10 ml/2 tsp ground cinnamon
200 g/7 oz clear honey
5 eggs

Set the oven at 180°C/350°F/gas 4. To make the pastry base, sift the flour, baking powder and salt into a bowl, then rub in the butter until the mixture resembles fine breadcrumbs. Add enough cold water to mix the ingredients to a stiff pastry.

Roll out the pastry on a lightly floured surface and use to line a 25 cm/10 inch flan tin or dish. Line with greaseproof paper and sprinkle with baking beans or dried peas. Bake for 20 minutes; remove paper and beans or peas.

Rub the cottage cheese through a sieve into a mixing bowl and add the sugar, half the cinnamon, and the honey. Mix lightly, then add the eggs, one at a time, beating well after each addition. Rub the mixture through a sieve into a clean bowl, then turn into the pastry shell.

Bake for 45 minutes, then leave to cool in the oven. Serve cold, sprinkled with the remaining cinnamon.

SERVES TEN TO TWELVE

TORTA DI RICOTTA

BASE
100 g/4 oz butter or margarine
75 g/3 oz icing sugar
2 egg yolks
pinch of ground cinnamon
250 g/9 oz plain flour
flour for rolling out

FILLING
675 g/1½ lb ricotta cheese
25 g/1 oz grated Parmesan cheese
2 eggs
25 g/1 oz plain flour
45 ml/3 tbsp plain yogurt
50 g/2 oz caster sugar
grated rind and juice of 1 lemon
pinch of salt
few drops of lemon essence

DECORATION AND SAUCE
225 g/8 oz fresh raspberries
15 ml/1 tbsp arrowroot
100 g/4 oz raspberry jam
60 ml/4 tbsp maraschino liqueur
125 ml/4 fl oz sweet red vermouth

Make the pastry. Cream the butter or margarine with the sugar in a mixing bowl until light and fluffy. Blend in the egg yolks, cinnamon and flour. Knead the mixture lightly and roll into a ball. Chill for 20 minutes.

Set the oven at 200°C/400°F/gas 6. Roll out the pastry on a lightly floured surface to line a 25 cm/10 inch flan ring set on a baking sheet (see Mrs Beeton's Tip). Prick the base with a fork and chill for 30 minutes. Line with grease-proof paper and sprinkle with baking beans or dried peas. Bake for 20 minutes; remove paper and beans or peas. Lower the oven temperature to 180°C/350°F/gas 4.

For the filling, rub the ricotta through a sieve, then beat it with the Parmesan in a bowl and gradually beat in the rest of the filling ingredients. Spoon into the partially cooked flan case, level the surface and bake for about 50 minutes. Cover loosely with foil if the top becomes too dark. The filling should be firmly set when cooked. Leave to cool in the tin.

Decorate the cooled flan with the raspberries, and chill while making the sauce. Put the arrowroot in a small bowl and mix to a thin cream with 125 ml/4 fl oz water. Melt the jam in a saucepan. When it boils, stir in the arrow-root mixture to thicken it. Flavour with the maraschino liqueur and vermouth. Remove from the heat and when cold, pour a little of the sauce over the raspberries. Serve the rest separately.

SERVES EIGHT

 MRS BEETON'S TIP

To line the flan ring, place on the baking sheet and roll the pastry to a round at least 5 cm/2 inches larger than the ring. The pastry should be about 3 mm/⅛ inch thick. Lift the pastry round over a rolling pin to prevent it breaking and stretching, and lay it in the flan ring. Press the pastry gently down on the baking sheet and into the base of the ring. Working from the centre outwards, press the pastry into the base and up the sides, making sure it fits snugly into the flutes, if present, and is of even thick-ness all round. Trim off any surplus pastry by rolling across the top of the ring with the rolling pin.

COEUR A LA CREME AU CITRON

150 ml/¼ pint double cream
pinch of salt
150 g/5 oz low-fat curd cheese
50 g/2 oz caster sugar
grated rind and juice of 1 lemon
2 egg whites

Line a 400 ml/14 fl oz heart-shaped coeur à la crème mould with greaseproof paper. In a bowl whip the cream with the salt until it holds soft peaks. Break up the curd cheese with a fork, and whisk it gradually into the cream with the sugar. Do not let the mixture lose stiffness.

Fold the lemon rind and juice into the cream as lightly as possible.

In a clean, grease-free bowl, whisk the egg whites until they hold stiff peaks. Fold them into the mixture, then very gently turn the mixture into the mould, filling all the corners.

Stand the mould in a large dish or roasting tin to catch the liquid which seeps from the mixture. Chill for at least 2 hours or overnight. Turn out and serve with single cream.

SERVES SIX

 MRS BEETON'S TIP

Individual coeur à la crème moulds may be used. If these are unavailable, clean yogurt pots, with several drainage holes punched in the base of each, make an acceptable substitute.

COCONUT CREAM PIE

PIE SHELL
100 g/4 oz digestive biscuits
50 g/2 oz butter
25 g/1 oz sugar

FILLING
40 g/1½ oz cornflour
pinch of salt
40 g/1½ oz caster sugar
300 ml/½ pint milk
1 egg yolk
25 g/1 oz butter
few drops of vanilla essence
75 g/3 oz desiccated coconut

Make the pie shell. Place the biscuits between two sheets of greaseproof paper (or in a stout polythene bag) and crush finely with a rolling pin. Alternatively, crumb in a food processor.

Melt the butter in a small saucepan and mix in the crumbs and sugar. Press the mixture in an even layer all over the base and sides of a shallow 18 cm/7 inch pie plate. Put in a cool place until the shell has set.

Make the filling. Put the cornflour, salt and sugar in a bowl and stir in enough of the milk to make a smooth cream. Bring the rest of the milk to the boil in a saucepan. Pour it on to the cornflour mixture, stirring constantly, then return the mixture to the pan.

Bring the filling to the boil again, stirring constantly. Cook, still stirring vigorously, for 1-2 minutes, until the sauce thickens. Beat in the egg yolk, butter, vanilla essence and coconut.

Cool the filling until tepid, then spoon into the pie shell. When cold, refrigerate for 1-2 hours before serving.

SERVES FOUR

PEPPERMINT CREAM PIE

Decorate this delectable pie with crushed peppermint crisp for a party or other special occasion.

PIE SHELL
100 g/4 oz gingernut biscuits
50 g/2 oz plain chocolate
50 g/2 oz butter

FILLING
2 egg yolks
75 g/3 oz caster sugar
few drops of peppermint essence
10 ml/2 tsp gelatine
125 ml/4 fl oz double cream

Make the pie shell. Place the biscuits between two sheets of greaseproof paper (or in a stout polythene bag) and crush finely with a rolling pin. Alternatively, crumb in a food processor.

Melt the chocolate and butter in a heatproof bowl over gently simmering water. Stir in the crumbs thoroughly. Press the mixture in an even layer all over the base and sides of a shallow 18 cm/7 inch pie plate. Put in a cool place until the shell has set.

Make the filling. Combine the egg yolks and sugar in a heatproof bowl. Stir in 45 ml/3 tbsp cold water and stand the bowl over a saucepan of simmering water. Whisk the mixture until thick and pale, then whisk in the peppermint essence. (see Mrs Beeton's Tip).

 MRS BEETON'S TIP

Peppermint essence is very strong, so use sparingly. The best way to do this is to dip a cocktail stick or thin wooden skewer into the essence, then add just one drop at a time to the mixture.

Place 30 ml/2 tbsp water in a small bowl, and sprinkle the gelatine on to the liquid. Set aside for 15 minutes until the gelatine is spongy. Stand the bowl over a pan of hot water and stir the gelatine until it has dissolved completely. Cool for 5 minutes, then whisk into the peppermint mixture.

In a bowl, whisk the cream lightly. Fold it into the peppermint mixture, then turn into the chocolate crumb shell and refrigerate for about 1 hour until set.

SERVES FOUR

COFFEE CHIFFON PIE

PIE SHELL
75 g/3 oz digestive biscuits
50 g/2 oz butter
25 g/1 oz walnuts, chopped
25 g/1 oz sugar

FILLING
100 g/4 oz caster sugar
10 ml/2 tsp gelatine
15 ml/1 tbsp instant coffee
2 eggs, separated
pinch of salt
10 ml/2 tsp lemon juice
whipped cream to decorate

Make the pie shell. Place the biscuits between two sheets of greaseproof paper (or in a stout polythene bag) and crush finely with a rolling pin. Alternatively, crumb the biscuits in a food processor.

Melt the butter in a small saucepan and mix in the crumbs, chopped nuts and sugar. Press the mixture in an even layer all over the base and sides of a shallow 18 cm/7 inch pie plate. Put in a cool place until set.

To make the filling, mix 50 g/2 oz of the sugar

with the gelatine in a cup. Put the coffee into a measuring jug, add 45 ml/3 tbsp boiling water, and stir until dissolved. Make up the liquid with cold water to 250 ml/8 fl oz.

Pour the coffee liquid into a heatproof bowl or the top of a double saucepan. Add the egg yolks, mix well, then place over gently simmering water. Stir in the gelatine mixture, with a pinch of salt. Cook over gentle heat for about 15 minutes, stirring constantly until the custard thickens slightly. Do not let the mixture boil. Pour into a cold bowl, cover with dampened greaseproof paper and chill until on the point of setting, then stir in the lemon juice.

In a clean, grease-free bowl, whisk the egg whites until foamy. Gradually whisk in the remaining sugar and continue whisking until stiff and glossy. Fold the coffee custard into the meringue, pour into the pie shell and chill for at least 1 hour until set. Serve decorated with whipped cream.

SERVES FOUR

SHERRY CREAM PIE

PIE SHELL
150 g/5 oz plain chocolate digestive biscuits
50 g/2 oz butter

FILLING
125 ml/4 fl oz milk
2 eggs, separated
50 g/2 oz sugar
10 ml/2 tsp gelatine
30 ml/2 tbsp medium dry or sweet sherry
grated nutmeg
125 ml/4 fl oz double cream

Make the pie shell. Place the biscuits between two sheets of greasproof paper (or in a stout polythene bag) and crush finely with a rolling pin. Alternatively, crumb in a food processor.

Melt the butter in a small saucepan and mix in the crumbs. Press the mixture in an even layer all over the base and sides of a shallow 18 cm/7 inch pie plate. Put in a cool place until the shell has set.

To make the filling, warm the milk in a saucepan but do not let it boil. Beat the egg yolks with the sugar in a bowl, then lightly stir in the hot milk. Strain the custard into the clean pan or the top of a double saucepan. Cook over low heat, stirring, for about 15 minutes, until thickened. Do not allow the custard to boil. Cool slightly.

Meanwhile place 30 ml/2 tbsp water in a small bowl and sprinkle the gelatine on to the liquid. Set aside for 15 minutes until the gelatine is spongy. Stand the bowl over a pan of hot water and stir the gelatine until it has dissolved completely. Remove from the heat, stir in a spoonful of the custard, then mix into the rest of the custard. Add the sherry, a little at a time to prevent the custard from curdling. Stir in nutmeg to taste, then cool until just setting.

In a deep bowl, whip the cream to soft peaks, then stir into the custard. Whisk the egg whites in a clean, grease-free bowl until stiff, and fold in. Pour the mixture gently into the pie shell and refrigerate for 1½-2 hours until set.

SERVES FOUR

 MICROWAVE TIP

Dissolve the gelatine in the microwave; stir it into the water, let stand until spongy, then cook on High for 30-45 seconds.

LEMON CHIFFON PIE

PIE SHELL
100 g/4 oz digestive biscuits
50 g/2 oz butter
25 g/1 oz sugar

FILLING
100 g/4 oz caster sugar
10 ml/2 tsp gelatine
3 eggs, separated
grated rind and juice of 2 lemons

Make the pie shell. Place the biscuits between two sheets of greaseproof paper (or in a stout polythene bag) and crush finely with a rolling pin. Alternatively, crumb the biscuits in a food processor.

Melt the butter in a small saucepan and mix in the crumbs and sugar. Press the mixture in an even layer all over the base and sides of a shallow 18 cm/7 inch pie plate. Put in a cool place until the shell has set.

To make the filling, mix 50 g/2 oz of the caster sugar with the gelatine in a small bowl. Combine the egg yolks, lemon juice and 50 ml/ 2 fl oz water in a heatproof bowl or the top of a double saucepan. Mix lightly, then stir in the gelatine mixture.

Cook over gently simmering water for 10 minutes, stirring all the time, until the custard thickens. Do not let it boil. Pour into a cold bowl, cover with dampened greaseproof paper and chill until on the point of setting. Stir in the lemon rind.

In a clean, grease-free bowl, whisk the egg whites until foamy. Gradually whisk in the remaining sugar and continue to whisk until stiff and glossy. Fold the lemon custard mixture into the meringue, pile into the pie shell and chill for at least 1 hour until set.

SERVES FOUR

VARIATIONS

Chocolate Orange Chiffon Pie Make the pie shell using plain chocolate digestive biscuits. Follow the instructions for Orange Chiffon Pie (below).

Lime Chiffon Pie Make the pie shell. For the filling substitute 3 limes for the lemons. If the limes are very small and not over juicy, add an additional 30 ml/2 tbsp lemon juice.

Orange Chiffon Pie Make the pie shell. For the filling, substitute oranges for the lemons, but use the grated rind of a single fruit. Add 15 ml/1 tbsp lemon juice to the orange juice and enough water to make the liquid up to 150 ml/¼ pint. Use this with the egg yolks, gelatine and 15 ml/1 tbsp sugar, to make a custard. When whisking the egg whites, add only 40 g/1½ oz sugar.

Sweet Batter Puddings

Different types of batter are used to create several styles of sweet course, from flimsy pancakes to hearty baked puddings and crisp, light fritters. Hot or cold, traditional or modern, this chapter offers an interesting selection of recipes. For more general information on batters, see the Dairy Foods chapter.

APPLE BATTER PUDDING

25 g/1 oz cooking fat
450 g/1 lb cooking apples
50 g/2 oz sugar
grated rind of ½ lemon

BATTER
100 g/4 oz plain flour
1.25 ml/¼ tsp salt
1 egg, beaten
250 ml/8 fl oz milk, or half milk and half water

Make the batter. Sift the flour and salt into a bowl, make a well in the centre and add the beaten egg. Stir in half the milk (or all the milk, if using a mixture of milk and water), gradually working in the flour.

Beat vigorously until the mixture is smooth and bubbly, then stir in the rest of the milk (or the water).

Set the oven at 220°C/425°F/gas 7. Put the fat into a 28 × 18 cm/11 × 7 inch baking tin and heat in the oven for 5 minutes.

Meanwhile peel, core and thinly slice the apples. Remove the baking tin from the oven and swiftly arrange the apples on the base. Sprinkle with the sugar and lemon rind. Pour the batter over the top and bake for 30-35 minutes until brown and risen.

Cut into 4 pieces and serve at once, with golden syrup or a Rich Lemon Sauce (page 496) if liked.

SERVES FOUR

VARIATIONS

Apricot Batter Pudding Put 100 g/4 oz dried apricots in a bowl and add just enough water to cover. Soak until soft, preferably overnight. Transfer the apricots and soaking liquid to a pan and simmer for 15 minutes. Drain. Make the batter as left, heat the fat, and layer the apricots on the base of the baking tin. Proceed as left. Serve an apricot jam sauce.

Dried Fruit Batter Pudding Make the batter and heat the fat as left, then spread 50 g/2 oz mixed dried fruit over the base of the tin. Sprinkle with 2.5 ml/½ tsp mixed spice or cinnamon. Proceed as in the main recipe and serve with St. Clement's Sauce (page 496).

Black Cap Puddings Make the batter as left. Grease 12 deep patty tins and divide 50 g/2 oz currants between them. Pour in enough batter to half fill each tin and bake for 15–20 minutes. Turn out to serve, and pass round Ginger Syrup Sauce (page 505).

CLAFOUTI AUX CERISES

There are several versions of this classic French recipe. If preferred, the cherries may be placed in the dish first, then all the batter poured over them. Traditionally, the stones are left in the cherries but it makes for awkward, less enjoyable eating.

15 g/½ oz lard
15 g/½ oz butter
2 whole eggs, plus 1 egg yolk
75 g/3 oz granulated sugar
250 ml/8 fl oz milk
150 g/5 oz plain flour, sifted
pinch of cinnamon
450 g/1 lb Morello cherries, stoned
25 g/1 oz caster sugar
15 ml/1 tbsp kirsch

Mix the lard with the butter in a small bowl and use to grease an ovenproof dish, about 18 cm/7 inches in diameter, or a shallow baking tin. Set the oven at 200°C/400°F/gas 6.

In a bowl, beat the eggs and egg yolk with the sugar until light. Heat the milk in a saucepan until steaming. Gradually blend the flour into the egg mixture alternately with a little of the hot milk to make a batter. Stir in the cinnamon and remaining milk. Pour a thin layer of the batter into the prepared mould and bake for 5-7 minutes. Meanwhile drain the cherries thoroughly on absorbent kitchen paper.

Pour the remaining batter into the mould, add the cherries and sprinkle with caster sugar. Return to the oven for 10 minutes then lower the oven temperature to 190°C/375°F/gas 5 and cook for 20 minutes more.

Invert the pudding on to a warmed plate. The bottom of the batter should be crusty and the top should resemble thick custard. Serve warm, sprinkled with the kirsch.

SERVES SIX

QUICK BATTER PUDDINGS

Serve poached fruit, such as plums, cherries or apricots, with these puffy puddings.

25 g/1 oz butter plus extra for greasing
150 ml/¼ pint milk
50 g/2 oz plain flour
25 g/1 oz caster sugar
grated rind of 1 lemon
1 egg

Set the oven at 220°C/425°F/gas 7. Butter four ramekin dishes or small baking dishes and place them on a baking sheet.

Heat the butter and milk in a small saucepan until the butter has melted; cool. Mix the flour, sugar and lemon rind in a bowl, then make a well in the centre and add the egg. Add a little milk and beat the egg with a little of the flour mixture. Work in the flour, adding a little of the milk, to make a thick batter and beat until smooth. Gradually beat in the rest of the milk.

Divide the batter between the dishes and bake for 20-30 minutes, until the puddings are risen, golden and set. Serve at once.

SERVES FOUR

CHOCOLATE PANCAKE PIE

100 g/4 oz plain chocolate
50 g/2 oz icing sugar
whipped cream to serve

PANCAKES
100 g/4 oz plain flour
1.25 ml/¼ tsp salt
1 egg, beaten
250 ml/8 fl oz milk, or half milk and half water
oil for frying

Make the pancakes. Sift the flour and salt into a bowl, make a well in the centre and add the beaten egg. Stir in half the milk (or all the milk, if using a mixture of milk and water), gradually working the flour down from the sides.

Beat vigorously until the mixture is smooth and bubbly, then stir in the rest of the milk (or the water). Pour into a jug. The mixture may be left to stand at this stage, in which case it should be covered and stored in the refrigerator.

Grate the chocolate into a small bowl. Have the icing sugar ready in a sifter. Heat a little oil in a clean 18 cm/7 inch pancake pan. Pour off any excess oil, leaving the pan covered with a thin film of grease.

Stir the batter and pour about 30–45 ml/2–3 tbsp into the pan. There should be just enough to cover the base thinly. Tilt and rotate the pan so that the batter runs over the surface evenly.

Cook over moderate heat for about 1 minute until the pancake is set and golden brown underneath. Make sure the pancake is loose by shaking the pan, then either toss it or turn it with a palette knife or fish slice. Cook the second side for about 30 seconds or until golden.

Slide the pancake out on to a warmed plate. Sprinkle generously with grated chocolate and dredge lightly with icing sugar. Cook a second pancake and stack on top of the first, adding a chocolate and icing sugar topping as before. Continue until 8 pancakes have been made and topped. Dredge the top pancake on the stack with icing sugar only.

To serve the pancake pie, cut in wedges and top with whipped cream.

SERVES FOUR

 MRS BEETON'S TIP

The chocolate will be easy to grate if it is first chilled in the refrigerator. Chill the metal grater, too, if liked.

CREPES SUZETTE

100 g/4 oz unsalted butter
75 g/3 oz caster sugar
grated rind and juice of 1 lemon
5 ml/1 tsp lemon juice
15 ml/1 tbsp orange liqueur
45 ml/3 tbsp brandy for flaming

CREPES
100 g/4 oz plain flour
1.25 ml/¼ tsp salt
1 egg, beaten
250 ml/8 fl oz milk, or half milk and half
 water
15 g/½ oz butter, melted and cooled
oil for frying

Make the crêpe batter. Sift the flour and salt into a bowl, make a well in the centre and add the beaten egg. Stir in half the milk (or all the milk, if using a mixture of milk and water), gradually working the flour down from the sides of the bowl.

Beat vigorously until the mixture is smooth and bubbly, then stir in the rest of the milk (or the water). Pour into a jug. The mixture may be left to stand at this stage, in which case it should be covered and stored in the refrigerator.

Heat a little oil in a clean 18 cm/7 inch pancake pan. Pour off any excess oil, leaving the pan covered with a thin film of grease.

Stir the melted butter into the batter and pour about 30–45 ml/2–3 tbsp into the pan. There should be just enough to cover the base thinly. Tilt and rotate the pan so that the batter runs over the surface evenly.

Cook over moderate heat for about 1 minute until the crêpe is set and golden brown underneath. Make sure the crêpe is loose by shaking the pan, then either toss it or turn it with a palette knife or fish slice. Cook the second side for about 30 seconds or until golden.

Slide the crêpe out on to a plate and keep warm over simmering water while making 7 more crêpes in the same way. Add more oil to the pan when necessary.

Make the filling by creaming the unsalted butter with the sugar in a bowl. Beat in the orange rind, lemon juice and liqueur, with enough of the orange juice to give a soft, creamy consistency.

Spread the filling over the cooked crêpes, dividing it evenly between them. Fold each crêpe in half, then in half again to make a quarter circle.

Return half the crêpes to the pan and warm through for 1–2 minutes. As the orange butter melts and runs out, spoon it over the crêpes. Pour in half the brandy, tip the pan to one side and increase the heat. Ignite the brandy and serve at once, with the pan sauce. Repeat with the remaining crêpes and brandy.

SERVES FOUR

MRS BEETON'S POTATO FRITTERS

These fritters are very light and easily eaten in quantity with the complementary sherry sauce. The secret to success when cooking them is to keep the oil at just the right temperature.

450 g/1 lb potatoes, boiled and mashed
40 g/1½ oz plain flour
3 eggs
30 ml/2 tbsp double cream
30 ml/2 tbsp cream sherry
10 ml/2 tsp lemon juice
2.5 ml/½ tsp grated nutmeg
oil for deep frying
caster sugar for dredging

SHERRY SAUCE
200 ml/7 fl oz sweet sherry
juice of 1 lemon, strained
sugar to taste

Rub the mashed potatoes through a sieve placed over a bowl, to remove any lumps. Beat in the flour, then gradually beat in the eggs, cream, sherry, lemon juice and nutmeg. Continue to beat the batter until it is extremely smooth and light.

Heat the oil for frying in a deep wide saucepan to 180°C/350°F or until a bread cube immersed in the oil turns pale brown in 45 seconds. Use two dessertspoons to drop small portions of batter into the oil and fry for about 1 minute, until puffed and golden. Drain well on absorbent kitchen paper and dredge with caster sugar. Keep hot under a warm grill until all the batter is cooked.

Meanwhile, warm the sherry and lemon juice in a small saucepan. Stir in sugar to taste. Pour into a jug. Serve the fritters with the warmed sherry sauce.

SERVES SIX TO EIGHT

CURRANT FRITTERS

50 g/2 oz long-grain rice (not the easy-cook type)
50 g/2 oz plain flour
2 eggs, beaten
30 ml/2 tbsp milk
50 g/2 oz currants
25 g/1 oz caster sugar
1.25 ml/¼ tsp grated nutmeg
oil for deep frying
caster or icing sugar for dredging
lemon wedges to serve

Put the rice in a small saucepan and cover with plenty of water. Bring to the boil, then lower the heat and simmer for 25 minutes. Leave to drain in a sieve until cool.

Place the flour in a bowl, making a well in the centre. Add the eggs and gradually beat them into the flour. Add the milk slowly, beating all the time to make a smooth batter. Stir in the rice, currants, caster sugar and nutmeg until thoroughly mixed.

Heat the oil for deep frying in a deep, wide saucepan to 180°C/350°F or until a bread cube immersed in the oil turns pale brown in 45 seconds. Drop spoonfuls of the batter into the hot oil and fry until puffed, crisp and golden. Drain on absorbent kitchen paper, keeping the fritters hot under a warm grill while all the batter is cooked. Dredge with caster or icing sugar and serve with lemon wedges.

SERVES SIX TO EIGHT

Sweet Cobblers and Baked Puddings

These hearty puddings combine seasonal fruits with sponge toppings, light crumbly coverings or delicious scones. As well as the more satisfying hot puddings, the chapter also includes Baked Apples and Apple Meringue.

When making crumbles and scone toppings for puddings, quick, light handling of the ingredients plays an important part in achieving success. Follow the notes given at the beginning of the chapter on pastry making (page 509) when rubbing fat into flour. Here are just a few additional notes and hints which apply to this chapter.

COBBLERS

A cobbler is usually a fruit pudding with a topping of sweet scone dough. The basic scone mixture is made of self-raising flour (or plain flour with baking powder, or a mixture of bicarbonate of soda and cream of tartar) with a little fat and sugar. The dry ingredients are bound with milk.

Scone dough should be soft but not too sticky and it should be kneaded very lightly into a smooth ball before it is rolled out. It should not be handled heavily or for too long, otherwise the result will be heavy.

CRUMBLES

Crumbles are quick and easy to make and the basic mixture of flour, fat and sugar may be varied in many ways. Spices, nuts and cereals may be stirred in to add texture and flavour to the cooked crumble. When served, the topping should be browned and crisp, crumbly and cooked through.

Handle the crumble mixture lightly, sprinkling it over the fruit and spreading it evenly without pressing down too firmly.

FREEZING

Both cobblers and crumbles freeze well. The scone topping for cobblers must be cooked before freezing. The complete cobbler may be frozen or prepared scone toppings may be frozen separately for thawing and reheating on a base of cooked fruit.

Crumbles may be frozen when cooked or they may be prepared ready for cooking, frozen and cooked just before serving. Alternatively, the raw crumble mix may be frozen in a suitable bag, ready to be sprinkled over the fruit before cooking.

If you are freezing a pudding in its dish do make sure that the dish is suitable.

OTHER BAKED PUDDINGS

As well as puddings with crumble or cobbler toppings, this chapter offers recipes for fruits cooked with sponge or meringue toppings. There are light mixtures baked with fruit and other flavourings or substantial puddings using bread. A recipe for a self-saucing lemon pudding is also featured: a light cake batter separates during baking to give a delicate spongy top with a tangy lemon sauce below. In addition there are a few classic British suet puddings and others that make the most of tart cooking apples, such as Bramleys.

PEAR AND ORANGE COBBLER

This is an excellent pudding for using up a glut of home-grown pears.

grated rind and juice of 2 large oranges
30 ml/2 tbsp clear honey
5 ml/1 tsp cornflour
8 ripe pears, peeled, cored and sliced

TOPPING
175 g/6 oz plain wholemeal flour
15 ml/1 tbsp baking powder
50 g/2 oz butter or margarine
50 g/2 oz soft light brown sugar
75 g/3 oz walnuts, chopped
about 75 ml/3 fl oz milk, plus extra to glaze

Set the oven at 230°C/450°F/gas 8. Combine the orange rind and juice in a small saucepan. Stir in the honey and cornflour. Heat gently until boiling, stirring all the time. Lower the heat, add the pears and poach them for 2–5 minutes or until tender. Transfer the mixture to an ovenproof dish.

Make the topping. Mix the flour and baking powder in a bowl, then rub in the butter until the mixture resembles fine breadcrumbs. Stir in the sugar and walnuts. Mix in enough milk to make a soft dough.

Turn the dough out on to a lightly floured surface and knead it very lightly into a ball. Roll or pat out to an 18 cm/7 inch round and cut this into equal wedges.

Arrange the scone wedges, set slightly apart, on top of the pears and brush the top of the dough with a little milk. Bake for about 15 minutes, until the scones are well risen and browned. Serve the cobbler freshly cooked, with a vanilla custard.

SERVES SIX

APPLE AND BANANA COBBLER

900 g/2 lb cooking apples
75–100 g/3–4 oz sugar
50 g/2 oz raisins

TOPPING
225 g/8 oz self-raising flour
5 ml/1 tsp baking powder
50 g/2 oz butter or margarine
50 g/2 oz sugar, plus extra for sprinkling
1 banana
about 125 ml/4 fl oz milk, plus extra for
   brushing

Peel and core the apples. Slice them into a saucepan and add the sugar, raisins and 30 ml/2 tbsp water. Cook gently, stirring occasionally, until the apples are just soft. Transfer to an ovenproof dish.

Set the oven at 230°C/450°F/gas 8. Make the topping. Sift the flour and baking powder into a bowl. Rub in the butter or margarine until the mixture resembles fine breadcrumbs, then stir in the sugar. Peel and slice the banana and add to the mixture, with enough milk to bind the dough.

Turn the dough out on to a lightly floured surface and knead it very lightly into a smooth ball. Cut the dough into quarters, then cut each piece in half to make eight scones. Flatten each portion of dough into a round about 5 cm/2 inches in diameter.

Place the scones around the edge of the dish on top of the apples, overlapping them slightly. Brush the scones with a little milk and sprinkle them with sugar.

Bake the cobbler for about 15 minutes, until the scones are well risen and browned.

SERVES SIX TO EIGHT

GOOSEBERRY COBBLER

450 g/1 lb gooseberries, topped and tailed
100 g/4 oz sugar

TOPPING
100 g/4 oz self-raising flour
25 g/1 oz margarine
about 60 ml/4 tbsp milk, plus extra for
** brushing**
40 g/1½ oz glacé cherries, chopped
40 g/1½ oz blanched almonds, chopped
30 ml/2 tbsp sugar

Place the gooseberries in a saucepan with the sugar. Cook gently, stirring occasionally, until the fruit is soft. Transfer to an ovenproof dish.

Set the oven at 220°C/425°F/gas 7. Sift the flour into a bowl and rub in the margarine until the mixture resembles fine breadcrumbs. Stir in enough milk to make a soft dough.

In a small bowl, mix the cherries with the almonds and sugar. Turn the dough out on to a lightly floured surface and knead it gently into a smooth ball. Roll or pat the dough to a 15 cm/6 inch square and spread the cherry mixture over the top, leaving a 1 cm/½ inch border around the edge.

Brush the edge of the dough with milk, then roll it up to enclose the filling. Press the join together. Cut the roll into 8 equal pinwheels and arrange these on top of the gooseberries. Bake for about 15 minutes, until the topping is risen and cooked. Serve at once.

SERVES FOUR

SPICED RHUBARB COBBLER

Scones flavoured with spices and dried fruit make a hearty topping for tart stewed rhubarb.

675 g/1½ lb rhubarb, trimmed and sliced
100 g/4 oz sugar

TOPPING
175 g/6 oz self-raising flour
5 ml/1 tsp baking powder
40 g/1½ oz butter or margarine
30 ml/2 tbsp sugar
5 ml/1 tsp ground mixed spice
50 g/2 oz mixed dried fruit
grated rind of 1 orange (optional)
about 75 ml/3 fl oz milk, plus extra for
** brushing**

Place the rhubarb and sugar in a heavy-bottomed saucepan and cook gently until the juice begins to run from the fruit and the sugar dissolves. Stirring occasionally, continue to cook the rhubarb gently for 15-20 minutes, until tender. Transfer to an ovenproof dish.

Set the oven at 230°C/450°F/gas 8. Make the topping. Sift the flour into a bowl with the baking powder. Rub in the butter or margarine until the mixture resembles fine breadcrumbs, then stir in the sugar, spice, dried fruit and orange rind (if used). Mix in enough of the milk to make a soft dough.

Turn the dough out on to a lightly floured surface, knead it gently into a ball and roll it out to about 1 cm/½ inch thick. Use a 5 cm/2 inch round cutter to cut out scones. Arrange the scones on top of the fruit.

Brush the scones with milk and bake for 12-15 minutes, until risen and golden.

SERVES FOUR

UPSIDE-DOWN COBBLER

Take the scone topping that makes a traditional cobbler and use it as the base for a fruity topping.

225 g/8 oz self-raising flour
5 ml/1 tsp baking powder
50 g/2 oz butter or margarine
25 g/1 oz sugar
about 125 ml/4 fl oz milk
2 cooking apples
50 g/2 oz black grapes, halved and seeded
1 (227 g/8 oz) can peach slices, drained
30 ml/2 tbsp liquid honey
15 ml/1 tbsp orange juice
25 g/1 oz flaked almonds

Grease a large baking sheet. Set the oven at 220°C/425°F/gas 7. Sift the flour and baking powder into a mixing bowl. Rub in the butter or margarine until the mixture resembles fine breadcrumbs. Stir in the sugar, then mix in enough milk to make a soft dough.

Turn the dough out on to a lightly floured surface and knead it very gently into a smooth ball. Roll or pat out the dough to a 25 cm/10 inch circle, then lift it on to the baking sheet.

Peel and core the apples. Slice them into rings and arrange them, overlapping, around the outer edge of the scone base. Arrange the grapes in a circle inside the ring of apple slices. Arrange the peach slices in the middle.

Stir the honey and orange juice together in a cup, then brush a little over the apples; reserve most of the honey and orange juice glaze. Sprinkle the apples with the flaked almonds and bake for about 15–20 minutes, until the base is risen and cooked and the nuts on top are lightly browned. Remove the cobbler from the oven and brush the apples with the reserved glaze. Serve at once.

SERVES SIX TO EIGHT

NUTTY PLUM CRUMBLE

Tangy plums and toasted hazelnuts make a tasty combination in this tempting pudding. Apples, rhubarb, gooseberries, or a mixture of fruit may be used instead of the plums.

675 g/1½ lb plums, halved and stoned
50 g/2 oz sugar

TOPPING
175 g/6 oz plain flour
75 g/3 oz butter or margarine
25 g/1 oz demerara sugar
5 ml/1 tsp ground cinnamon
75 g/3 oz hazelnuts, toasted and chopped

Set the oven at 180°C/350°F/gas 4. Place the plums in an ovenproof dish and sprinkle with the sugar.

Make the topping. Sift the flour into a mixing bowl and rub in the butter or margarine until the mixture resembles fine breadcrumbs. Stir in the sugar, cinnamon and hazelnuts.

Sprinkle the topping evenly over the plums, pressing it down very lightly. Bake the crumble for about 45 minutes, until the topping is golden brown and the plums are cooked. Serve with custard, cream or vanilla ice cream.

SERVES FOUR TO SIX

APPLE CRUMBLE

fat for greasing
675 g/1½ lb cooking apples
100 g/4 oz granulated sugar
grated rind of 1 lemon
150 g/5 oz plain flour
75 g/3 oz butter or margarine
75 g/3 oz caster sugar
1.25 ml/¼ tsp ground ginger

Grease a 1 litre/1¾ pint pie dish. Set the oven at 180°C/350°F/gas 4.

Peel and core the apples. Slice into a saucepan and add the granulated sugar and lemon rind. Stir in 50 ml/2 fl oz water, cover the pan and cook until the apples are soft. Spoon the apple mixture into the prepared dish and set aside.

Put the flour into a mixing bowl and rub in the butter or margarine until the mixture resembles fine breadcrumbs. Add the caster sugar and ginger and stir well. Sprinkle the mixture over the apples and press down lightly. Bake for 30–40 minutes until the crumble topping is golden brown.

SERVES SIX

VARIATIONS

Instead of apples, use 675 g/1½ lb damsons, gooseberries, pears, plums, rhubarb or raspberries.

 MICROWAVE TIP

Put the apple mixture in a large bowl, adding only 30 ml/2 tbsp water, cover and cook for 7 minutes on High. Add the crumble topping and cook for 4 minutes more, then brown the topping under a preheated grill.

EVE'S PUDDING

fat for greasing
450 g/1 lb cooking apples
grated rind and juice of 1 lemon
75 g/3 oz demerara sugar
75 g/3 oz butter or margarine
75 g/3 oz caster sugar
1 egg, beaten
100 g/4 oz self-raising flour

Grease a 1 litre/1¾ pint pie dish. Set the oven at 180°C/350°F/gas 4. Peel and core the apples and slice them thinly into a large bowl. Add the lemon rind and juice, with the demerara sugar. Stir in 15 ml/1 tbsp water, then tip the mixture into the prepared pie dish.

In a mixing bowl, cream the butter or margarine with the caster sugar until light and fluffy. Beat in the egg. Fold in the flour lightly and spread the mixture over the apples.

Bake for 40–45 minutes until the apples are soft and the sponge is firm. Serve with melted apple jelly and single cream or Greek yogurt.

SERVES FOUR

VARIATIONS

Instead of apples, use 450 g/1 lb apricots, peaches, gooseberries, rhubarb, raspberries or plums.

APPLE MERINGUE

500 ml/17 fl oz thick apple purée
15 ml/1 tbsp lemon juice
3 eggs, separated
about 250 g/9 oz caster sugar

DECORATION
glacé cherries
angelica

Set the oven at 180°C/350°F/gas 4. Put the apple purée in a bowl and beat in the lemon juice and egg yolks with about 75 g/3 oz of the sugar. Spoon into a 750 ml/1¼ pint baking dish, cover, and bake for 15 minutes.

In a clean, grease-free bowl, whisk the egg whites to stiff peaks. Gradually whisk in 150 g/5 oz of the remaining sugar, adding 15 ml/1 tbsp at a time. Pile the meringue on top of the apple mixture and sprinkle with the remaining sugar. Return to the oven and bake for a further 15 minutes or until the meringue is pale golden brown in colour. Serve at once with a vanilla custard or single cream.

SERVES FOUR

MARMALADE MERINGUE PUDDING

fat for greasing
75 g/3 oz fresh white breadcrumbs
45 ml/3 tbsp marmalade
200 ml/7 fl oz milk
25 g/1 oz butter
2 eggs, separated
75 g/3 oz caster sugar

Grease a 750 ml/1¼ pint pie dish. Set the oven at 140°C/275°F/gas 1. Spread the breadcrumbs out on a baking sheet and put into the oven to dry off slightly.

Warm the marmalade in a small saucepan, then spread half of it over the base of the prepared pie dish. Warm the milk and butter in a second saucepan.

Meanwhile put the egg yolks in a bowl and stir in 25 g/1 oz of the sugar. Pour on the warmed milk mixture, stirring thoroughly. Add the breadcrumbs, mix thoroughly and leave to stand for 30 minutes.

Raise the oven temperature to 160°C/325°F/gas 3. Pour half the breadcrumb mixture into the prepared pie dish, spoon on another layer of marmalade, and put the rest of the crumb mixture on top. Smooth the surface, if necessary. Bake for 40–45 minutes until the pudding is lightly set.

Remove the pudding from the oven, then lower the oven temperature to 120°C/250°F/gas ½. In a clean, grease-free bowl, whisk the egg whites until stiff, add half the remaining sugar and whisk again. Fold in all but 15 ml/1 tbsp of the remaining sugar, then pile the meringue on top of the pudding mixture, making sure it is completely covered. Draw the mixture into peaks (see Mrs Beeton's Tip) and sprinkle with the reserved sugar.

Return to the oven for 40–45 minutes until the meringue is set and the tops of the peaks are brown. Serve at once.

SERVES FOUR

 MRS BEETON'S TIP

To draw the meringue into peaks, use a slim spatula or flat-bladed knife, setting the blade down flat upon the meringue, then flicking it upwards.

BAKED APPLES

6 cooking apples
75 g/3 oz sultanas, chopped
50 g/2 oz demerara sugar

Wash and core the apples. Cut around the skin of each apple with the tip of a sharp knife two-thirds of the way up from the base. Put the apples into an ovenproof dish, and fill the centres with the chopped sultanas.

Sprinkle the demerara sugar on top of the apples and pour 75 ml/5 tbsp water around them. Bake for 45-60 minutes, depending on the cooking quality and size of the apples.

Serve with a vanilla custard, ice cream, Brandy Butter (page 506) or with whipped cream.

SERVES SIX

VARIATIONS

Fill the apple cavities with a mixture of 50 g/2 oz Barbados or other raw sugar and 50 g/2 oz butter, or use blackcurrant, raspberry, strawberry or apricot jam, or marmalade. Instead of sultanas, chopped stoned dates, raisins or currants could be used. A topping of toasted almonds looks effective and tastes delicious.

 MICROWAVE TIP

Baked apples cook superbly in the microwave. Prepare as suggested above, but reduce the amount of water to 30 ml/2 tbsp. Cook for 10-12 minutes on High.

APPLE CHARLOTTE

butter for greasing
400 g/14 oz cooking apples
grated rind and juice of 1 lemon
100 g/4 oz soft light brown sugar
pinch of ground cinnamon
50-75 g/2-3 oz butter
8-10 large slices of white bread, about
   5 mm/¼ inch thick
15 ml/1 tbsp caster sugar

Generously grease a 1 litre/1¾ pint charlotte mould or 15 cm/6 inch cake tin with butter. Set the oven at 180°C/350°F/gas 4. Peel and core the apples. Slice them into a saucepan and add the lemon rind and juice. Stir in the brown sugar and cinnamon and simmer until the apples soften to a thick purée. Leave to cool.

Melt the butter in a saucepan, then pour into a shallow dish. Cut the crusts off the bread, and dip 1 slice in the butter. Cut it into a round to fit the bottom of the mould or tin. Fill any spaces with extra butter-soaked bread, if necessary. Dip the remaining bread slices in the butter. Use 6 slices to line the inside of the mould. The slices should touch one another to make a bread case.

Fill the bread case with the cooled apple purée. Complete the case by fitting the top with more bread slices. Cover loosely with greased grease-proof paper or foil, and bake for 40-45 minutes. To serve the charlotte turn out and dredge with caster sugar. Serve with bramble jelly and cream.

SERVES FIVE TO SIX

 MRS BEETON'S TIP

The mould or tin may be lined with slices of bread and butter, placed buttered side out.

BROWN BETTY

fat for greasing
1 kg/2¼ lb cooking apples
150 g/5 oz dried wholewheat breadcrumbs
grated rind and juice of 1 lemon
60 ml/4 tbsp golden syrup
100 g/4 oz demerara sugar

Grease a 1 litre/1¾ pint pie dish. Set the oven at 160°C/325°F/gas 3.

Peel and core the apples. Slice them thinly into a bowl. Coat the prepared pie dish with a thin layer of breadcrumbs, then fill with alternate layers of apples, lemon rind and breadcrumbs. Put the syrup, sugar and lemon juice into a saucepan. Add 30 ml/2 tbsp water. Heat until the syrup has dissolved, then pour the mixture over the layered pudding.

Bake for 1–1¼ hours until the pudding is brown and the apple cooked. Serve with single cream or a custard.

SERVES SIX

 MRS BEETON'S TIP

Use a tablespoon dipped in boiling water to measure the golden syrup. The syrup will slide off easily.

BAKED APPLES STUFFED WITH RICE AND NUTS

6 medium cooking apples
25 g/1 oz flaked almonds or other nuts
40 g/1½ oz seedless raisins
25–50 g/2–3 oz boiled rice (preferably boiled in milk)
50 g/2 oz sugar or to taste
1 egg, beaten
30 ml/2 tbsp butter
raspberry or blackcurrant syrup

Set the oven at 190°C/375°F/gas 5. Wash and core the apples but do not peel them. With a small rounded spoon, hollow out part of the flesh surrounding the core hole. Do not break the outside skin.

In a bowl, mix together the nuts, raisins and rice, using enough rice to make a stuffing for all the apples. Add the sugar, with enough egg to bind the mixture. Melt the butter and stir it into the mixture.

Fill the apples with the rice mixture. Place in a roasting tin and add hot water to a depth of 5 mm/¼ inch. Bake for 40 minutes or until the apples are tender. Remove the roasting tin from the oven and transfer the apples to a warmed serving platter, using a slotted spoon. Warm the fruit syrup and pour it over the apples.

SERVES SIX

 MICROWAVE TIP

The rice may be cooked in the microwave. Place 50 g/2 oz pudding rice in a large bowl with 30 ml/2 tbsp sugar. Stir in 600 ml/1 pint water, cover and cook on High for 25 minutes. Stir well, then stir in 300 ml/½ pint top-of-the-milk or single cream. Use 25–50 g/1–2 oz of the cooked rice for the above pudding and reserve the remainder.

FRIAR'S OMELETTE

fat for greasing
1 kg/2¼ lb cooking apples
grated rind and juice of 1 lemon
75 g/3 oz butter
100 g/4 oz sugar
2 eggs, beaten
100 g/4 oz dried white breadcrumbs

Grease a 1 litre/1¾ pint pie dish. Set the oven at 220°C/425°F/gas 7.

Peel and core the apples. Slice them into a saucepan and add the lemon rind and juice, 50 g/2 oz of the butter, and sugar. Cover the pan and cook the apples until very soft. Remove the pan from the heat and cool slightly.

Stir the eggs into the apple mixture and beat well. Put half the breadcrumbs into the prepared pie dish, cover with the apple mixture, and sprinkle with the remaining breadcrumbs. Dot with the remaining butter and bake for 20–25 minutes.

Serve with a vanilla custard.

SERVES FOUR TO FIVE

CHERRY PUDDING

fat for greasing
450 g/1 lb cherries
75 g/3 oz soft light brown sugar
50 g/2 oz cornflour
375 ml/13 fl oz milk
50 g/2 oz caster sugar
3 eggs, separated
grated rind of 1 lemon
1.25 ml/¼ tsp ground cinnamon

Grease a 1 litre/1¾ pint ovenproof dish. Set the oven at 190°C/375°F/gas 5.

Stone the cherries and put them into a saucepan. Add 600 ml/4 tbsp water and stir in the brown sugar. Stew very gently until the fruit is just soft. Leave to cool.

In a bowl, mix the cornflour to a paste with a little of the milk. Bring the rest of the milk to the boil in a saucepan, then pour it on to the cornflour mixture. Mix well. Return the mixture to the clean pan and bring to the boil, stirring vigorously all the time to make a very thick sauce. Simmer for 2–3 minutes. Stir in the caster sugar, remove from the heat and leave to cool.

Beat the egg yolks, lemon rind and cinnamon into the cornflour sauce. In a clean, grease-free bowl, whisk the egg whites until stiff but not dry, then fold them into the sauce.

Arrange the cherries in the base of the prepared dish, then top with the sauce mixture. Bake for 35–45 minutes or until risen, just set and golden. Serve at once with single cream.

SERVES FIVE TO SIX

 MRS BEETON'S TIP

A cherry stoner makes short work of preparing the fruit. For more information about this utensil, see page 28).

ALMOND CASTLES

fat for greasing
75 g/3 oz butter
75 g/3 oz caster sugar
3 eggs, separated
45 ml/3 tbsp single cream or milk
15 ml/1 tbsp brandy
150 g/5 oz ground almonds

Grease 8 dariole moulds. Set the oven at 160°C/325°F/gas 3.

In a mixing bowl, cream the butter and sugar until light and fluffy. Stir in the egg yolks, cream or milk, brandy and ground almonds.

In a clean, grease-free bowl, whisk the egg whites until just stiff, and fold lightly into the mixture. Three-quarters fill the dariole moulds and bake for 20-25 minutes, until the puddings are firm in the centre and golden brown.

Turn out on to individual plates and serve with a vanilla custard.

SERVES FOUR TO EIGHT

CASTLE PUDDINGS

fat for greasing
100 g/4 oz butter or margarine
100 g/4 oz caster sugar
2 eggs
1.25 ml/¼ tsp vanilla essence
100 g/4 oz plain flour
5 ml/1 tsp baking powder

Grease 6-8 dariole moulds. Set the oven at 180°C/350°F/gas 4.

In a mixing bowl, cream the butter or margarine with the sugar until light and creamy. Beat in the eggs and vanilla essence. Sift the flour and baking powder into a bowl, then fold into the creamed mixture.

Three-quarters fill the prepared dariole moulds. Bake for 20-25 minutes, until set and well risen. Serve with a vanilla custard or a jam sauce.

SERVES THREE TO FOUR

VARIATION

Somerset Puddings Serve the puddings cold, with the inside of each scooped out, and the cavity filled with stewed apple or jam. Serve with whipped cream.

COTTAGE PUDDING

butter for greasing
200 g/7 oz plain flour
pinch of salt
10 ml/2 tsp baking powder
100 g/4 oz butter or margarine
75 g/3 oz soft light brown sugar
100 g/4 oz raisins
1 egg, beaten
45-75 ml/3-5 tbsp milk

Grease a 25 × 20 cm/10 × 8 inch baking dish. Set the oven at 190°C/375°F/gas 5.

Sift the flour, salt and baking powder into a mixing bowl. Rub in the butter or margarine and add the sugar and raisins. Stir in the egg, with enough milk to make a soft dropping consistency.

Spoon the mixture into the prepared baking dish and bake for 35-40 minutes until firm in the centre and golden brown.

Serve with Redcurrant Sauce (page 494), or a vanilla custard.

SERVES FIVE TO SIX

COLLEGE PUDDINGS

fat for greasing
100g/4oz plain flour
2.5ml/½tsp baking powder
pinch of salt
1.25ml/¼tsp mixed spice
100g/4oz dried white breadcrumbs
75g/3oz shredded suet
75g/3oz caster sugar
50g/2oz currants
50g/2oz sultanas
2 eggs, beaten
100–125ml/3½–4floz milk

Grease 6–8 dariole moulds. Set the oven at 190°C/375°F/gas 5.

Sift the flour, baking powder, salt and spice into a mixing bowl. Add the crumbs, suet, sugar, currants and sultanas, and mix well. Stir in the eggs with enough milk to form a soft dropping consistency.

Half fill the prepared dariole moulds with the mixture and bake for 20–25 minutes.

Turn out and serve with Rich Lemon Sauce (page 496) or Thickened Fruit Sauce (page 502).

SERVES SIX TO EIGHT

EXETER PUDDING

butter for greasing
100g/4oz dried white breadcrumbs
25g/1oz ratafias or small almond
   macaroons
75g/3oz shredded suet
50g/2oz sago
75g/3oz caster sugar
grated rind and juice of 1 lemon
3 eggs
30ml/2tbsp milk
2 individual sponge cakes or trifle sponges,
   sliced
75g/3oz jam (any type)

Grease a 1 litre/1¾ pint pie dish. Coat with some of the crumbs, and cover the base with half the ratafias or macaroons. Set the oven at 180°C/350°F/gas 4.

Put the remaining crumbs into a mixing bowl with the suet, sago, sugar, lemon rind and juice. In a separate bowl, beat together the eggs and milk. Stir the liquid mixture into the dry ingredients.

Spoon a layer of the suet mixture into the prepared pie dish and cover with some of the slices of sponge cake. Add a layer of jam and some of the remaining ratafias. Repeat the layers until all the ingredients are used, finishing with a layer of suet mixture.

Bake for 45–60 minutes. Serve with a jam sauce using the same jam as that used in the recipe.

SERVES FIVE TO SIX

BAKED SPONGE PUDDING

fat for greasing
100 g/4 oz butter or margarine
100 g/4 oz caster sugar
2 eggs, beaten
150 g/5 oz plain flour
5 ml/1 tsp baking powder
1.25 ml/¼ tsp vanilla essence
about 30 ml/2 tbsp milk

Grease a 1 litre/1¾ pint pie dish. Set the oven at 180°C/350°F/gas 4. In a mixing bowl, cream the butter or margarine with the sugar until light and fluffy. Gradually beat in the eggs. Sift the flour and baking powder together into a bowl, then fold them into the creamed mixture. Add the essence and enough milk to form a soft dropping consistency.

Spoon the mixture into the prepared pie dish and bake for 30–35 minutes until well risen and golden brown.

Serve from the dish with a vanilla custard or any sweet sauce.

SERVES FOUR TO SIX

VARIATIONS

Jam Sponge Put 30 ml/2 tbsp jam in the base of the dish before adding the sponge mixture. Serve with a jam sauce made with the same type of jam.

Orange or Lemon Sponge Add the grated rind of 1 orange or 1 lemon to the creamed mixture. Serve the pudding with Rich Lemon Sauce (page 496).

Spicy Sponge Sift 5 ml/1 tsp mixed spice, ground ginger, grated nutmeg or cinnamon with the flour. Serve with Ginger Syrup Sauce (page 505).

Coconut Sponge Substitute 25 g/1 oz desiccated coconut for 25 g/1 oz flour. Serve with Apricot Sauce (page 501).

Chocolate Sponge Substitute 50 g/2 oz cocoa for 50 g/2 oz flour. Serve with Chocolate Cream Sauce (page 503) or Chocolate Liqueur Sauce (page 503).

HONESTY PUDDING

fat for greasing
50 g/2 oz fine oatmeal
15 ml/1 tbsp plain flour
750 ml/1¼ pints milk
1 egg, beaten
pinch of salt
2.5 ml/½ tsp grated orange rind

Grease a 750 ml/1¼ pint pie dish. Set the oven at 180°C/350°F/gas 4. Put the oatmeal and flour in a bowl and mix to a smooth paste with a little of the milk. Bring the rest of the milk to the boil in a saucepan, then pour it over the oatmeal mixture, stirring all the time.

Return the mixture to the clean pan and cook over low heat for 5 minutes, stirring all the time. Remove from the heat, and cool for 5 minutes.

Beat the egg into the cooled oatmeal mixture. Flavour with the salt and orange rind. Pour the mixture into the prepared pie dish, and bake for 35–40 minutes.

Serve hot from the dish, with single cream and brown sugar.

SERVES FOUR

DEVONSHIRE RUM

fat for greasing
about 225 g/8 oz cold Christmas pudding or
   rich fruit cake
10 ml/2 tsp cornflour
250 ml/8 fl oz milk
10 ml/2 tsp soft light brown sugar
1 egg, beaten
45 ml/3 tbsp rum or a few drops of rum
   essence

Grease a 750 ml/1¼ pint pie dish. Set the oven
at 180°C/350°F/gas 4.

Cut the pudding or cake into fingers, and
arrange in the prepared pie dish. In a bowl, mix
the cornflour to a paste with a little of the milk.
Heat the remaining milk in a saucepan to just
below boiling point, then pour it slowly on to
the cornflour mixture, stirring to prevent the
formation of lumps. Pour the mixture back into
the pan, return the pan to the heat and cook the
sauce gently for 2 minutes; then stir in the
sugar, egg, and rum or rum essence.

Pour the rum sauce over the pudding or cake
and bake for about 30 minutes or until firm.
Serve with Fairy Butter (page 508).

SERVES THREE TO FOUR

LEMON DELICIOUS PUDDING

*This pudding has a light spongy top with lemon
sauce underneath.*

butter for greasing
3 eggs, separated
75 g/3 oz caster sugar
200 ml/7 fl oz milk
15 ml/1 tbsp self-raising flour, sifted
grated rind and juice of 2 large lemons
pinch of salt
15 ml/1 tbsp icing sugar

Grease a deep 1 litre/1¾ pint ovenproof dish.
Set the oven at 180°C/350°F/gas 4.

In a mixing bowl, beat the egg yolks with the
caster sugar until light, pale and creamy.
Whisk the milk, flour, rind and lemon juice
into the egg yolks. In a clean, grease-free bowl,
whisk the egg whites with the salt, adding the
icing sugar gradually. Continue to whisk until
stiff but not dry. Fold into the lemon mixture.

Pour the mixture into the prepared dish and
stand the dish in a roasting tin. Add hot water
to come halfway up the sides of the dish. Bake
for 1 hour.

SERVES FOUR

 MRS BEETON'S TIP

If a fragment of shell drops into the egg
white, the easiest way to remove it is to use
another piece of shell.

BAKED JAM ROLL

butter for greasing
300 g/11 oz plain flour
5 ml/1 tsp baking powder
pinch of salt
150 g/5 oz shredded suet
flour for rolling out
200-300 g/7-11 oz jam

Grease a baking sheet. Set the oven at 190°C/375°F/gas 5.

Sift the flour, baking powder and salt into a mixing bowl. Add the suet and enough cold water to make a soft, but firm dough. On a lightly floured surface, roll the dough out to a rectangle about 5 mm/¼ inch thick. Spread the jam almost to the edges. Dampen the edges of the pastry rectangle with water and roll up lightly. Seal the edges at either end.

Place the roll on the prepared baking sheet with the sealed edge underneath. Cover loosely with greased greaseproof paper or foil and bake for 50-60 minutes until golden brown. Transfer to a warm platter, slice and serve with warmed jam of the same type as that used in the roll.

SERVES SIX

VARIATIONS

Instead of the jam, use 200-300 g/7-11 oz marmalade, or 225 g/8 oz dried fruit mixed with 50 g/2 oz demerara sugar. Serve with a vanilla custard or a lemon sauce.

SALZBURGER NOCKERL

50 g/2 oz butter
10 ml/2 tsp caster sugar
5 eggs, separated
15 ml/1 tbsp plain flour
125 ml/4 fl oz milk
icing sugar for dredging

Set the oven at 200°C/400°F/gas 6. Beat the butter and sugar together in a mixing bowl until light and fluffy. Stir in the egg yolks one at a time.

In a clean, grease-free bowl, whisk the egg whites until stiff, and fold lightly into the egg yolk mixture with the flour.

Pour the milk into a shallow flameproof dish, and heat gently. Remove from the heat, pour in the batter, smooth it lightly, and bake for about 10 minutes until light brown in colour. Cut out spoonfuls of the nockerl, and arrange on a warmed serving plate. Serve immediately, sprinkled with icing sugar.

SERVES FOUR TO SIX

Gâteaux, Trifles and Charlottes

A chapter of glorious gâteaux, lusciously decorated with whipped cream or lavishly filled with chocolate concoctions. These are the perfect desserts to present on any special dinner party occasion.

GATEAUX

A splendid gâteau always looks impressive and it is not necessarily a difficult dessert to prepare. The base may be a sponge cake, pastry or meringue, either plain or flavoured.

FREEZING

For best results, freeze the unfilled gâteau, separating the layers with sheets of freezer film. These do not have to be thawed before being filled and decorated, provided the finished gâteau is set aside for some time before it is served.

COATING THE SIDE OF A GATEAU

Gâteaux are often covered completely in cream, with chopped nuts, grated chocolate or vermicelli used to decorate the sides. To coat the sides, the layers must first be sandwiched together. The coating ingredient should be spread out on a sheet of greaseproof paper. Spread the side of the gâteau thinly with cream, or a similar covering. Using both hands to support the gâteau on its side, roll it in the chosen coating.

TRIFLES

The classic British sherry trifle transforms plain sponge cake into a luscious sweet by flavouring it with a fruit preserve and adding a creamy custard. A good trifle of this type has a plain, pleasing flavour that complements a rich main course. By adding fresh fruits and by varying the custard topping a wide variety of interest-

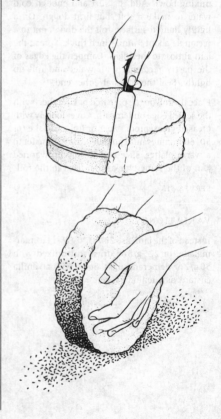

ing trifles may be created. A selection of recipes is included in this chapter.

A good trifle is well balanced, with the right proportion of custard topping to complement the sponge base and enough fruit or other ingredients to add a contrasting flavour. If the proportions of sponge and custard topping are not balanced the trifle will be disappointing.

The choice of cake used for the trifle base plays an important role in determining the quality of the dessert. Home-made fatless sponge cake or plain Madeira-type cake is by far the best. Creamed sponge cakes of the Victoria sandwich type, with equal quantities of fat and flour, may also be used but they have a distinct flavour which can dominate the fruit and custard. Bought trifle sponges are popular but they do not give as good a flavour or texture as home-made cake. Ratafia biscuits and almond macaroons are also classic ingredients to include in the base. Flavoured cake may be used to make a completely different trifle. For example, chocolate or orange sponge cake may be used.

Traditional trifle made with egg custard topping is not set firm like that made with a custard made from a powder mix. Thin egg custard soaks into the sponge base and sets slightly on chilling; however, for a thicker, creamy topping use egg yolks and cornflour to make a boiled custard. Chocolate-flavoured custard may be made by melting grated chocolate in the custard.

A trifle should be chilled for a few hours so that the flavours have time to mingle; then it should be removed from the refrigerator about 30 minutes before serving so that it is not too cold. Some fruit trifles benefit from being prepared a day ahead, allowing time for the fruit juices to soak into the sponge. Leave the final decoration until the last minute.

CHARLOTTES

Chilled charlottes are moulded desserts consisting of a light mixture set in a casing of sponge fingers. A custard-based mixture, mousse or jellied dessert usually forms the centre of a charlotte and this may be poured over a thin layer of fruit set with jelly.

Charlotte moulds are deeper than cake tins; however a straight-sided cake tin that does not have a loose bottom may be used instead.

Charlotte mixtures should be lightly set, not rubbery. The charlotte must not be unmoulded too long before serving or it may lose its shape. Tying a wide ribbon around the charlotte helps to support the sponge casing as well as being a splendid way of decorating a rather special dessert.

Charlottes do not freeze well as the mixture tends to soften during freezing and the unmoulded dessert will not hold its shape. However, rich charlottes filled with creamy mousses may be served iced, or part frozen.

The term 'charlotte' is also used to describe a hot fruit pudding which traditionally consists of pieces of buttered bread baked around a stewed fruit filling – usually apples. A recipe for Apple Charlotte is included on page 766.

STORING FRESH CREAM DESSERTS

Gâteaux, trifles and charlottes are all highly perishable desserts, often containing fresh cream, and they should be eaten freshly prepared or chilled until ready to serve. Store a gâteau in a large lidded plastic container and cover a trifle before placing it in the refrigerator. Never leave these desserts to stand in a warm room for any length of time.

MOUSSELINE CAKE

fat for greasing
caster sugar for dusting
50 g/2 oz plain flour
50 g/2 oz cornflour
4 eggs, separated
100 g/4 oz caster sugar
vanilla essence or grated rind of ½ lemon

DECORATION
125 ml/4 fl oz double cream
100 g/4 oz strawberries
100 g/4 oz icing sugar
5-10 ml/1-2 tsp orange-flavoured liqueur

Base line and grease two 18 cm/7 inch sandwich cake tins. Dust with caster sugar, tapping out the excess. Set the oven at 190°C/375°F/gas 5. Sift the flour and cornflour together into a bowl and set aside.

In a large heatproof bowl, whisk the egg yolks with the sugar until thick, creamy and pale, adding the essence or grated lemon rind. Whisk the egg whites in a clean, grease-free bowl until they form soft peaks, then add to the yolk mixture.

Set the bowl of mixture over gently simmering water and whisk until the volume is greatly increased and the mixture is thick enough to hold the mark of a trail for 2-3 seconds. Remove the bowl from the heat and continue whisking until the mixture is cold.

Fold the sifted flours into the cold cake mixture. Divide between the prepared sandwich tins and bake for 20-25 minutes until well risen and browned. Leave in the tins for 1-2 minutes, then turn out on to wire racks to cool.

To decorate the cake, whip the cream in a bowl. Put one third of the cream into a piping bag fitted with a star nozzle. Set aside 4 of the best strawberries. Chop the rest and add to the remaining cream. Mix lightly, then spread over one layer of the cake. Add the top layer.

In a small bowl, mix the icing sugar with enough of the liqueur to form a glacé icing. Warm the icing by placing the bowl in a basin of hot water, if necessary.

Pipe whirls of whipped cream around the top edge of the cake. Carefully spoon the liqueur icing over the top of the cake to form an even coating. Cut the reserved strawberries in half or in slices and decorate the top of the cake. Serve as soon as possible.

SERVES SIX

VARIATIONS

Ring the changes with different fresh or well-drained canned fruit. Raspberries, pineapple, peaches or nectarines are good. Flavour the cream with a complementary liqueur. The exotic combination of kiwi fruit and cream flavoured with advocaat is delicious.

✷ FREEZER TIP

The cooked, cooled cakes may be frozen. Wrap them in foil or pack them in a freezer bag, placing a sheet of foil between them. Unwrap the cakes and leave at room temperature until softened before filling and decorating as above.

APRICOT GATEAU

fat for greasing
75 g/3 oz plain flour
pinch of salt
50 g/2 oz margarine
3 eggs
75 g/3 oz caster sugar

FILLING AND TOPPING
30 ml/2 tbsp sherry
22-24 sponge fingers
1 (540 g/18 oz) can unsweetened apricot
    halves in natural juice
1 (142 g/5 oz) packet lemon jelly
30 ml/2 tbsp smooth apricot jam
600 ml/1 pint double cream
25 g/1 oz caster sugar
angelica (see method)

Line and grease a 15 cm/6 inch round cake tin. Set the oven at 180°C/350°F/gas 4.

Sift the flour and salt into a bowl and put in a warm place. Melt the margarine in a saucepan without letting it get hot. Set aside.

Whisk the eggs lightly in a heatproof bowl. Add the sugar and place the bowl over a saucepan of hot water. Whisk for 10-15 minutes until thick. Take care that the bottom of the bowl does not touch the water. Remove from the heat and continue whisking until at blood-heat. The melted margarine should be at the same temperature.

Sift half the flour over the eggs, then pour in half the melted margarine in a thin stream. Fold in gently. Repeat, using the remaining flour and fat. Spoon gently into the prepared tin and bake for 30-40 minutes. Cool the cake on a wire rack.

To assemble the gâteau, place the sponge on a serving plate and sprinkle the sherry over. Trim the sponge fingers to a length of about 7.5 cm/3 inches. The base of each sponge finger should be level, so that it will stand straight. Drain the apricots, reserving 125 ml/4 fl oz juice.

Heat the reserved apricot juice, add the lemon jelly and stir until dissolved. Pour into a shallow bowl and leave to cool but not set. Heat the apricot jam in the saucepan.

Brush the sugar-free side of each trimmed sponge finger with apricot jam to a depth of 2.5 cm/1 inch. Dip one long side of each finger into the liquid jelly and attach to the sponge cake. The sponge fingers should touch each other, with the jam-coated sides facing inwards and the jelly sealing each to its neighbour. They should extend above the cake to form a shell. When all the sponge fingers are in place, tie a 2 cm/¾ inch wide ribbon around the finished cake, if liked, to hold the fingers in position. Place in a cool place until set.

Reserve 6 apricot halves for decoration and chop the rest. Put the cream in a bowl and whip until just stiff; stir in the sugar. Spoon 45 ml/3 tbsp of the cream into a piping bag fitted with a small star nozzle. Keep in the refrigerator until required. Stir the chopped apricots and the rest of the liquid jelly into the remaining cream. Chill until on the point of setting, then spoon on top of the cake, filling the cavity formed by the wall of sponge fingers.

Return the gâteau to the refrigerator for 1 hour until set, then arrange the reserved apricot halves on top. Pipe the reserved cream on top of the gâteau in a decorative border. Alternatively, the cream may be piped between the fruit. Decorate with angelica.

SERVES EIGHT TO TEN

 MICROWAVE TIP

If the jelly sets while you are working, simply warm it for a few seconds in the microwave on High.

DEVIL'S FOOD CAKE

In America, it is often the custom to serve a cake as a dessert. Devil's Food Cake is an excellent choice to follow a simple main course.

fat for greasing
plain flour for dusting
100 g/4 oz butter
350 g/12 oz granulated sugar
5 ml/1 tsp vanilla essence
3 eggs, separated
250 g/9 oz plain flour
50 g/2 oz cocoa
7.5 ml/1½ tsp bicarbonate of soda
5 ml/1 tsp salt

FROSTING
100 g/4 oz soft light brown sugar
60 ml/4 tbsp golden syrup
1 egg white
pinch of cream of tartar
pinch of salt
5 ml/1 tsp vanilla essence

Grease and lightly flour three 20 cm/8 inch sandwich tins. Tap out excess flour. Set the oven at 180°C/350°F/gas 4.

In a mixing bowl, cream the butter with 225 g/8 oz of the sugar until light, then add the vanilla essence. Beat in the egg yolks, one at a time, alternately with 275 ml/9 fl oz cold water. Beat well after each addition. Beat in the flour, cocoa, soda and salt.

In a clean, grease-free bowl, whisk the egg whites to soft peaks, add the remaining sugar and continue whisking until stiff peaks form. Fold the egg whites into the chocolate mixture lightly but thoroughly.

Gently pour one third of the mixture into each prepared tin. Bake for 30–35 minutes until each layer is firm in the centre and has shrunk

from the sides of the tin. Cool lightly, then transfer to wire racks. Set aside until cold.

Meanwhile make the frosting. Combine all the ingredients except the vanilla essence in the top of a double saucepan. Set the pan over boiling water and cook, beating constantly with an electric whisk or rotary whisk until the mixture thickens and stands in peaks.

Remove the pan from the heat and add the vanilla essence. Continue to beat until the mixture is thick and forms swirls. Use the icing immediately to fill and cover the cake.

SERVES EIGHT

BLACK FOREST GATEAU

fat for greasing
150 g/5 oz butter or margarine
150 g/5 oz caster sugar
3 eggs, beaten
few drops of vanilla essence
100 g/4 oz self-raising flour or plain flour
    and 5 ml/1 tsp baking powder
25 g/1 oz cocoa
pinch of salt

FILLING AND TOPPING
250 ml/8 fl oz double cream
125 ml/4 fl oz single cream
1 (540 g/18 oz) can Morello cherries
kirsch (see method)
25 g/1 oz plain chocolate, grated

Line and grease a 20 cm/8 inch cake tin. Set the oven at 180°C/350°F/gas 4.

In a mixing bowl, cream the butter or margarine with the sugar until light and fluffy. Add the eggs gradually, beating well after each addition. Stir in the vanilla essence.

Sift the flour, cocoa, salt and baking powder, if used, into a bowl. Stir into the creamed mixture, lightly but thoroughly, until evenly mixed.

Spoon into the tin and bake for 40 minutes. Cool on a wire rack. When quite cold, carefully cut the cake into three layers, brushing all loose crumbs off the cut sides.

Make the filling. Combine the creams in a bowl and whip until stiff. Place half the whipped cream in another bowl.

Drain the cherries, reserving the juice. Set aside 11 whole cherries and halve and stone the remainder. Gently fold the halved cherries into one of the bowls of cream. Set aside. Strain the reserved cherry juice into a measuring jug and add kirsch to taste.

Prick the cake layers and sprinkle with the cherry juice and kirsch until well saturated. Sandwich the layers together with the whipped cream and cherries. When assembled, cover with the remaining plain cream and use the whole cherries to decorate the top. Sprinkle the grated chocolate over the cream.

SERVES TEN TO TWELVE

MALAKOFF GATEAU

150 g/5 oz butter
4 egg yolks
200 g/7 oz caster sugar
200 g/7 oz ground almonds
250 ml/8 fl oz double cream
30–32 sponge fingers

DECORATION
250 ml/8 fl oz double cream
100 g/4 oz caster sugar
1 (410 g/14 oz) can apricot halves, drained

Line a 1 kg/2¼ lb loaf tin with foil. In a mixing bowl, beat the butter until light and creamy. Stir in the egg yolks one at a time, then add the sugar and ground almonds. Bind with the double cream.

Arrange a layer of sponge fingers along the base of the prepared tin. Spread a layer of filling over them. Repeat the layers until all the ingredients have been used, finishing with a layer of sponge fingers. Cover with foil and place heavy weights evenly on top. Chill for 2–3 hours until firm.

Shortly before serving, combine the cream and sugar in a bowl and whip until stiff. Carefully turn the gâteau out on a serving dish. Remove the foil and decorate with the cream and apricot halves. Serve lightly chilled.

SERVES EIGHT TO TEN

 MRS BEETON'S TIP

If no weights are available, use large cans of fruit.

AUSTRIAN HAZELNUT LAYER

fat for greasing
200 g/7 oz hazelnuts
5 eggs, separated
150 g/5 oz caster sugar
grated rind of ½ lemon
flour for dusting

FILLING
250 ml/8 fl oz double cream
vanilla essence

DECORATION
whole hazelnuts
grated chocolate

Grease and flour two 25 cm/10 inch springform or loose-bottomed cake tins. Set the oven at 180°C/350°F/gas 4.

Spread the hazelnuts out on a baking sheet and roast for 10 minutes or until the skins start to split. While still warm, rub them in a rough cloth to remove the skins. Grind the nuts in a nut mill or process briefly in a blender.

Combine the egg yolks and sugar in a bowl and beat until light and creamy. Mix in the ground nuts and lemon rind. Whisk the egg whites in a clean, grease-free bowl, until stiff but not dry. Fold the egg whites quickly and gently into the nut mixture. Divide between the prepared tins and bake for 1 hour. Test that the cakes are cooked (see Mrs Beeton's Tip), then cool the

 MRS BEETON'S TIP

When the cakes are ready, a warmed skewer pushed into the centre of each layer should come out dry. The sides of the cake should have begun to shrink slightly from the edges of the tin.

layers on wire racks, removing the sides and bases of the tins after a few minutes.

To make the filling, whip the cream with a few drops of vanilla essence until stiff. When the cake layers are cold, sandwich them together with some of the cream, and cover the top with the remainder. Decorate with a few whole hazelnuts and a sprinkling of grated chocolate.

SERVES TWELVE

COFFEE GATEAU

fat for greasing
20 ml/4 tsp instant coffee
150 g/5 oz butter
150 g/5 oz caster sugar
3 eggs, beaten
150 g/5 oz self-raising flour

COFFEE BUTTERCREAM
30 ml/2 tbsp instant coffee
150 g/5 oz butter
450 g/1 lb icing sugar

DECORATION
50-75 g/2-3 oz walnuts, chopped
10-12 walnut halves

Line and grease two 20 cm/8 inch sandwich tins. Set the oven at 160°C/325°F/gas 3. In a cup, mix the instant coffee with 20 ml/4 tsp boiling water. Set aside to cool.

In a mixing bowl, cream the butter with the sugar until light and fluffy. Beat in the cooled coffee. Add the eggs gradually, beating well after each addition. If the mixture shows signs of curdling, add a little of the flour.

Sift the flour and fold it into the creamed mixture, using a metal spoon. Divide between the tins and bake for 35-40 minutes or until well risen, firm and golden brown. Leave in the tins for 2–3 minutes, then cool on a wire rack. Make the buttercream. In a cup, mix the instant coffee with 30 ml/2 tbsp boiling water and leave to cool. Cream the butter with half the icing sugar in a bowl. Beat in the cooled coffee, then beat in the rest of the icing sugar.

Using about a quarter of the buttercream, sandwich the cake layers together. Spread about half the remaining buttercream on the sides of the cake, then roll in the chopped walnuts. Spread most of the remaining buttercream on top of the cake and mark with a fork in a wavy design. Spoon any remaining buttercream into a piping bag fitted with a small star nozzle and pipe 10–12 rosettes on top of the cake. Decorate each rosette with a walnut half.

SERVES EIGHT TO TWELVE

CHOCOLATE ROULADE

This cake is best baked the day before it is to be served.

oil and butter for greasing
150 g/5 oz plain dessert chocolate, in squares
4 eggs, separated
100 g/4 oz caster sugar
15 g/½ oz icing sugar, plus extra for dusting
about 175 ml/6 fl oz double cream
few drops of vanilla essence

Brush a 42 × 30 cm/17 × 12 inch Swiss roll tin with oil. Line with a piece of greaseproof paper, letting the paper overlap the edge a little. Cut out a second sheet of greaseproof paper to the same size, to cover the cooked roulade, and have ready a damp clean tea-towel with which to cover the paper-topped roulade. Set the oven at 190°C/375°F/gas 5.

Heat a saucepan of water. Place the chocolate in a heatproof bowl. When the water boils, remove the pan from the heat and set the bowl over it. Leave to melt, stirring occasionally.

Combine the egg yolks and caster sugar in a bowl and beat briskly until the mixture is pale and creamy. Add 45 ml/3 tbsp hot water to the melted chocolate and beat until well blended. Stir the chocolate into the egg yolk mixture, then whisk thoroughly.

In a clean, grease-free bowl, whisk the egg whites until fairly stiff. Using a metal spoon, fold them carefully into the chocolate mixture. Tip into the prepared Swiss roll tin and bake for 20 minutes until the roulade is firm.

Butter the remaining sheet of greaseproof paper. Remove the tin from the oven and immediately cover the cake with the buttered paper and the damp tea-towel. Leave to stand for several hours or overnight.

Next day, remove the cloth. Turn the paper buttered side up, sprinkle with icing sugar and replace sugared side down. Grip the paper and tin and invert both together so that the roulade is upside-down. Lay it down on the paper and remove the tin. Peel off the lining paper.

In a bowl, whip the cream until very stiff, stir in the vanilla essence and spread evenly over the surface of the roulade. Roll the roulade up from one long side, using the paper as a guide. Place on a serving plate, with the join underneath, dust with extra icing sugar and chill for several hours before serving.

SERVES SIX

 MRS BEETON'S TIP

Do not worry too much if cracks appear in the roulade during rolling. The mixture does not include any flour so that the baked roulade is rich and sweet with a fragile texture. Dusting with icing sugar disguises the cracks.

GLAZED ALMOND RING

Lightened by reducing the proportion of ground almonds to eggs, then cooked in a ring tin, this plain cake makes an impressive pudding when served with a salad of fresh oranges. Alternatively, serve the cake savarin-style by filling the middle with a mixed fruit salad.

6 eggs, separated
100 g/4 oz caster sugar
grated rind of 1 lemon
½ tsp oil of bitter almonds or natural
   almond essence
75 g/3 oz plain flour
50 g/2 oz ground almonds
50 g/2 oz butter, melted
225 g/8 oz orange marmalade
15 ml/1 tbsp brandy
150 ml/¼ pint double cream
Mrs Beeton's Orange Salad (page 809)

Set the oven at 180°C/350°F/gas 4. Grease and flour a 23 cm/9 inch ring tin.

Cream the egg yolks in a large bowl with the sugar, lemon rind and almond oil or essence until pale and thick. Gently stir in the flour and almonds, then stir in the butter.

In a clean, grease-free bowl, whisk the egg whites until stiff. Stir in about a third, or slightly less, of the whites to soften the almond mixture. Use a clean metal spoon to fold in the remaining whites. Turn the mixture into the tin and bake for 45–50 minutes, until risen, golden and firm to the touch. Turn out on a wire rack.

While the cake is cooling, heat the marmalade, then sieve it and return it to the saucepan. When the cake is removed from the oven, boil the marmalade for 30 seconds, stir in the brandy and remove from the heat at once. Use a spoon and brush to glaze the cake all over with the marmalade. Leave to cool.

Whip the cream until thick, then place it in a piping bag fitted with a large star nozzle. Pipe cream around the top of the cake and serve. Arrange a little of the orange salad and its juices on individual plates with slices of the cake.

SERVES TEN TO TWELVE

MRS BEETON'S TIPSY CAKE

1 (15 cm/6 inch) sponge cake
30 ml/2 tbsp redcurrant jelly
75 ml/3 fl oz brandy
50 g/2 oz whole blanched almonds
375 ml/13 fl oz milk
125 ml/4 fl oz single cream
8 egg yolks
75 g/3 oz caster sugar
extra redcurrant jelly to decorate

Put the cake in a glass bowl or dish 16 cm/6½ inches in diameter and slightly deeper than the cake. Spread the cake thinly with jelly, then pour over as much brandy as the cake can absorb. Cut the almonds lengthways into spikes and stick them all over the top of the cake.

Mix the milk and cream in a bowl. In a second, heatproof, bowl beat the yolks until liquid, and pour the milk and cream over them. Stir in the sugar. Transfer the mixture to the top of a double saucepan and cook over gently simmering water for about 20 minutes or until the custard thickens, stirring all the time. Let the custard cool slightly, then pour it over and around the cake. Cover with dampened grease-proof paper. When cold, refrigerate the tipsy cake for about 1 hour. Decorate with small spoonfuls of redcurrant jelly and serve.

SERVES FOUR TO SIX

SACHER TORTE

Invented by Franz Sacher, this is one of the most delectable (and calorific) cakes imaginable. Serve it solo, or with whipped cream. The icing owes its gloss to glycerine, which is available from chemists.

butter for greasing
175 g/6 oz butter
175 g/6 oz icing sugar
6 eggs, separated
175 g/6 oz plain chocolate, in squares
2-3 drops of vanilla essence
150 g/5 oz plain flour, sifted
**about 125 ml/4 fl oz apricot jam, warmed
    and sieved, for filling and glazing**

ICING
150 g/5 oz plain chocolate, in squares
125 g/4½ oz icing sugar, sifted
12.5 ml/2½ tsp glycerine

Line and grease a 20 cm/8 inch loose-bottomed cake tin. Set the oven at 180°C/350°F/gas 4.

In a mixing bowl, beat the butter until creamy. Add 100 g/4 oz of the icing sugar, beating until light and fluffy. Add the egg yolks, one at a time, beating after each addition.

Melt the chocolate with 30 ml/2 tbsp water in a heatproof bowl over hot water. Stir into the cake mixture with the vanilla essence.

In a clean, grease-free bowl, whisk the egg whites to soft peaks. Beat in the remaining icing sugar and continue beating until stiff but not dry. Fold into the chocolate mixture alternately with the sifted flour, adding about 15 ml/1 tbsp of each of a time.

Spoon the mixture into the prepared cake tin and set the tin on a baking sheet. With the back of a spoon, make a slight depression in the centre of the cake to ensure even rising. Bake for 1-1¼ hours or until a skewer inserted in the centre of the cake comes out clean.

Leave the cake in the tin for a few minutes, then turn out on to a wire rack. Cool to room temperature.

Split the cake in half and brush the cut sides with warmed apricot jam. Sandwich the layers together again and glaze the top and sides of the cake with apricot jam. Set aside.

Make the icing. Melt the chocolate with 75 ml/5 tbsp water in a heatproof bowl over hot water. Stir in the icing sugar and whisk in the glycerine, preferably using a balloon whisk.

Pour the icing over the cake, letting it run down the sides. If necessary, use a metal spatula, warmed in hot water, to smooth the surface. Avoid touching the icing too much at this stage, or the gloss will be lost. Serve when the icing has set.

SERVES TWELVE

 MRS BEETON'S TIP

Do not refrigerate this cake after baking; chilling would spoil the glossy appearance of the icing.

HAZELNUT MERINGUE GATEAU

75 g/3 oz hazelnuts
3 egg whites
150 g/5 oz caster sugar
2–3 drops of vinegar
2–3 drops of vanilla essence

FILLING AND TOPPING
125 ml/4 fl oz double cream
5–10 ml/1–2 tsp caster sugar

Reserve a few hazelnuts for decorating the gâteau. Bake the rest in a preheated 180°C/ 350°F/gas 4 oven for 10 minutes. Rub off the skins. Chop the nuts very finely or process briefly in a blender or food processor. Set aside. Do not turn off the oven.

Line two baking sheets with greaseproof paper or non-stick baking parchment. Draw a 15 cm/6 inch circle on each and very lightly oil the greaseproof paper, if used.

Combine the egg whites and caster sugar in a heatproof bowl. Set over a saucepan of gently simmering water and whisk until the meringue is very thick and holds its shape. Add the vinegar, vanilla essence and chopped nuts.

Spread the meringue inside the marked circles or place it in a piping bag with a 1 cm/½ inch plain nozzle. Starting from the middle of one circle, pipe round and round to form a coiled, flat round 15 cm/6 inches in diameter. Pipe a similar round on the other sheet. Bake for 35–40 minutes, until each layer is crisp and lightly browned. Leave to cool.

Whip the cream in a bowl until it stands in stiff peaks, then stir in caster sugar to taste. Place one of the meringue rounds on a serving plate and spread with most of the cream. Put the second meringue round on top and decorate with the rest of the cream and hazelnuts.

SERVES FOUR TO SIX

STRAWBERRY MERINGUE TORTE

4 egg whites
pinch of salt
100 g/4 oz granulated sugar
100 g/4 oz caster sugar

FILLING
450 g/1 lb fresh strawberries, hulled
juice of 1 lemon
30 ml/2 tbsp caster sugar
125 ml/4 fl oz double cream or whipped cream flavoured with brandy or kirsch

Line a baking sheet with greaseproof paper or non-stick baking parchment. Draw a 15 cm/6 inch circle on the paper and very lightly oil the greaseproof paper if used. Set the oven at 110°C/225°F/gas ¼.

Combine the egg whites, salt and sugars in a heatproof bowl. Set over a saucepan of gently simmering water and whisk until the mixture is very thick and holds its shape.

Spread some of the meringue all over the circle to form the base of a meringue case. Put the rest of the mixture into a piping bag fitted with a large star nozzle. Pipe three quarters of the mixture around the edge of the ring to make a 5 cm/2 inch rim or border. Use the remaining mixture to pipe small meringue shapes. Bake the case for 3–4 hours; the small shells for 1½–2 hours. Leave to cool.

Make the filling. Put the strawberries in a bowl and sprinkle with the lemon juice and caster sugar. Chill in the refrigerator until the meringue case is cool. Reserve a few choice berries for decoration. Drain and halve the rest and put them into the meringue case. In a bowl, whip the cream (or use the liqueur-flavoured cream) and cover the fruit. Decorate with the meringues and strawberries. Serve at once.

SERVES FOUR

RASPBERRY VACHERIN

3 egg whites
pinch of salt
150g/5oz caster sugar

FILLING AND TOPPING
350g/12oz fresh raspberries
300ml/½ pint double cream
5ml/1tsp caster sugar
kirsch
a few angelica leaves

Line two baking sheets with greaseproof paper or non-stick baking parchment. Draw a 15cm/6 inch circle on each and very lightly oil the greaseproof paper, if used. Set the oven at 110°C/225°F/gas ¼.

Combine the egg whites, salt and sugar in a heatproof bowl. Set over a saucepan of gently simmering water and whisk until the meringue mixture is very thick and holds its shape.

Put the meringue mixture into a piping bag fitted with a 1cm/½ inch plain nozzle. Starting from the middle on one circle, pipe round and round until the 15cm/6 inch circle is completely filled. Pipe a similar round on the other piece of paper. Use any remaining mixture to pipe small meringues on the paper around the circles. Bake for 1-1½ hours, then leave to cool.

Make the filling. Rinse the raspberries, patting them dry with absorbent kitchen paper. Reserve a few choice berries for decoration and set the rest aside in a bowl. Whip the cream in a bowl to firm peaks, then stir in the caster sugar and kirsch to taste.

Place one of the meringue rounds on a serving plate, spread with some of the cream (see Mrs Beeton's Tip) and arrange half the raspberries on it in a layer. Put the second meringue on top of the raspberries and arrange the reserved raspberries in the centre. Put the remaining cream into a piping bag fitted with a star or shell nozzle and pipe rosettes or a decorative edge of cream around the berries. Decorate the sides of the vacherin with the tiny meringues and angelica leaves.

Serve the vacherin in slices, like a cake, using a flat cake slice to transfer the slices to individual plates.

SERVES FOUR TO SIX

VARIATIONS

Grape Vacherin Use small seedless grapes instead of the raspberries. A mixture of black and green grapes looks attractive.

Mango Vacherin Peel a large ripe mango, then cut the flesh off the stone in slices. Dice the fruit before arranging on the cream. Decorate with another sliced mango or omit the fruit decoration.

Strawberry and Orange Vacherin Substitute strawberries for the raspberries and use orange liqueur, such as Grand Marnier or Cointreau instead of the kirsch.

 MRS BEETON'S TIP

When filling the vacherin, do not make the cream layer too thick or it will ooze out when the vacherin is cut, making it messy to serve and eat.

PAVLOVA

3 egg whites
150 g/5 oz caster sugar
2.5 ml/½ tsp vinegar
2.5 ml/½ tsp vanilla essence
10 ml/2 tsp cornflour
glacé cherries and angelica to decorate

FILLING
250 ml/8 fl oz double cream
caster sugar (see method)
2 peaches, skinned and sliced

Line a baking sheet with greaseproof paper or non-stick baking parchment. Draw a 20 cm/8 inch circle on the paper and very lightly grease the greaseproof paper, if used. Set the oven at 150°C/300°F/gas 2.

In a large bowl, whisk the egg whites until very stiff. Continue whisking, gradually adding the sugar until the mixture stands in stiff peaks. Beat in the vinegar, vanilla and cornflour.

Spread the meringue over the circle, piling it up at the edges to form a rim, or pipe the circle and rim from a piping bag fitted with a large star nozzle.

Bake for about 1 hour or until the pavlova is crisp on the outside and has the texture of marshmallow inside. It should be pale coffee in colour. Leave to cool, then carefully remove the paper. Put the pavlova on a large serving plate.

Make the filling by whipping the cream in a bowl with caster sugar to taste. Add the sliced peaches and pile into the cold pavlova shell. Decorate with glacé cherries and angelica and serve as soon as possible.

SERVES FOUR

SAVOY CAKE WITH GINGER CREAM

This light sponge may be used as a base for making fruit and cream gâteaux or for trifles. Originally, the ginger cream was set in a mould to be served on its own as a rich dessert. Combined, the cake and cream make an irresistible dessert duo.

6 eggs, separated
15 ml/1 tbsp orange flower water or rose water
grated rind of 1 lemon
175 g/6 oz caster sugar
175 g/6 oz plain flour

GINGER CREAM
15 ml/1 tbsp gelatine
4 egg yolks
600 ml/1 pint double cream
75 g/3 oz preserved stem ginger, finely sliced
15 ml/1 tbsp syrup from preserved ginger
icing sugar for dredging

Set the oven at 180°C/350°F/gas 4. Grease and flour a 20 cm/8 inch round deep cake tin.

Cream the egg yolks with the orange flower water or rose water, lemon rind and sugar until pale and thick. In a clean, grease-free bowl, whisk the egg whites until stiff, then fold them into the yolks.

Sift the flour over the mixture and fold it in gently. Turn the mixture into the prepared tin and bake for about 45 minutes, until the cake is risen, browned and firm. Turn the cake out on to a wire rack to cool.

To make the ginger cream, sprinkle the gelatine over 30 ml/2 tbsp cold water in a heatproof basin and set aside for 15 minutes, until spongy. Place over a saucepan of hot water and stir until dissolved completely.

Beat the yolks in a heatproof bowl. Stir in the cream, ginger and syrup. Place over a saucepan of hot water and stir until the mixture has thickened sufficiently to thinly coat the back of a spoon.

Stir a little of the cream into the gelatine, then pour it into the main batch of mixture and stir well. Leave to cool, stirring often. Chill well.

To serve, dredge the top of the cake thickly with icing sugar. Serve each slice of cake topped with a generous spoonful of ginger cream; offer the remaining ginger cream separately.

SERVES TEN

SAVARIN

oil for greasing
75 ml/5 tbsp milk
10 ml/2 tsp dried yeast
150 g/5 oz strong white flour
1.25 ml/¼ tsp salt
10 ml/2 tsp sugar
75 g/3 oz butter
3 eggs, beaten

RUM SYRUP
75 g/3 oz lump sugar
30 ml/2 tbsp rum
15 ml/1 tbsp lemon juice

APRICOT GLAZE
45 ml/3 tbsp apricot jam
5 ml/1 tsp lemon juice

Oil a 20 cm/8 inch savarin mould (ring tin). Set the oven at 200°C/400°F/gas 6.

Warm the milk in a saucepan until tepid. Remove from the heat and sprinkle on the dried yeast. Stir in 15 ml/1 tbsp of the flour and leave in a warm place for 20 minutes.

Sift the rest of the flour and the salt into a mixing bowl. Stir in the sugar, then rub in the butter. Add the yeast liquid to the mixture, then

add the eggs. Beat well until smooth; the batter should be quite elastic. Pour the mixture into the prepared tin. Cover with a large, lightly oiled polythene bag, and leave in a warm place until the mixture has almost reached the top of the tin.

Bake for about 40 minutes or until the savarin is golden brown and firm to the touch. Check after 30 minutes and cover the savarin loosely with foil if it is becoming too dark on top.

Meanwhile make the rum syrup. Put the sugar in a saucepan with 125 ml/4 fl oz water. Heat, stirring, until the sugar has dissolved, then boil the mixture steadily for 6–8 minutes, without stirring, until it forms a syrup. Stir in the rum and lemon juice.

Turn the warm savarin on to a serving dish, prick it all over with a fine skewer and spoon the hot rum syrup over it. Use as much of the syrup as the savarin will absorb. Set the savarin aside until cold.

Make the glaze by sieving the apricot jam into a small saucepan. Add the lemon juice with 30 ml/2 tbsp water and bring to the boil, stirring constantly. When the mixture is smooth and shiny, use a pastry brush to glaze the savarin.

SERVES SIX TO EIGHT

RUM BABAS

oil for greasing
75 ml/5 tbsp milk
10 ml/2 tsp dried yeast
150 g/5 oz strong white flour
1.25 ml/¼ tsp salt
10 ml/2 tsp caster sugar
75 g/3 oz butter
3 eggs, beaten
50 g/2 oz currants

RUM SYRUP
75 g/3 oz lump sugar
30 ml/2 tbsp rum
15 ml/1 tbsp lemon juice

Oil 12 baba tins. Set the oven at 200°C/400°F/gas 6. Warm the milk until tepid. Sprinkle on the dried yeast. Stir in 15 ml/1 tbsp of the flour and leave in a warm place for 20 minutes.

Sift the rest of the flour, the salt and the sugar into a mixing bowl. Rub in the butter. Add the yeast liquid to the mixture, then add the eggs. Beat until well mixed, then work in the currants. Half fill the prepared tins with mixture. Cover with oiled polythene, and leave in a warm place until the tins are two-thirds full. Bake for 10–15 minutes or until the babas are golden brown and spongy to the touch.

Heat the lump sugar in a saucepan with 125 ml/4 fl oz water. Stir until the sugar has dissolved, then boil the mixture steadily for 6–8 minutes, without stirring, until it forms a syrup. Stir in the rum and lemon juice.

Remove the babas from the tins, prick all over with a fine skewer and transfer to individual dishes. Spoon hot rum syrup over each baba. Serve cold, with cream.

SERVES TWELVE

INDIVIDUAL APRICOT TRIFLES

6 small rounds of sponge cake, about 2 cm/¾ inch thick and 6 cm/2¼ inches across
15 ml/1 tbsp sweet sherry
175 ml/6 fl oz orange juice
6 fresh apricots, halved and stoned
25 g/1 oz granulated sugar

DECORATION
125 ml/4 fl oz double cream
6 pistachio nuts

Place the sponge cake rounds in individual dishes. In a jug, mix the sherry with 30 ml/2 tbsp of the orange juice, and pour it over the sponge cakes. Place 2 apricot halves in each dish, on top of the sponge cake. Set aside.

Put the remaining orange juice in a saucepan with the sugar and heat gently until all the sugar has dissolved. Bring to the boil and boil steadily for 10 minutes until the mixture forms a thick syrup. Glaze the apricots with the syrup. Leave to cool.

In a bowl, whip the cream until thick. Blanch, skin, dry and chop the pistachios. Pipe the cream on to the trifles, surrounding the glazed apricots, and decorate with the pistachios. Chill before serving.

SERVES SIX

VARIATION

Peach halves or pineapple rings may be used instead of apricots. This recipe also works well with drained canned fruit.

INDIAN TRIFLE

The original idea was to set the rice mixture in a dish, then cut out a star shape from the middle and fill the space with custard. This simpler version is equally decorative and avoids having leftover rice.

45 ml/3 tbsp rice flour
600 ml/1 pint milk
grated rind of 1 lemon
50 g/2 oz sugar
25 g/1 oz blanched almonds
about 50 g/2 oz candied peel and crystallized fruit, roughly chopped

CUSTARD
25 g/1 oz cornflour
25 g/1 oz caster sugar
4 egg yolks
5 ml/1 tsp vanilla essence
600 ml/1 pint milk

Mix the rice flour to a cream with a little of the milk and the lemon rind. Heat the remaining milk until hot, pour some on to the rice, then return the mixture to the saucepan. Bring to the boil, stirring constantly, then simmer the rice gently for 5 minutes. Stir in the sugar. Cool the rice slightly before pouring it into a glass dish. Cover the surface with dampened greaseproof paper and set aside.

For the custard, blend the cornflour, caster sugar, egg yolks and vanilla to a smooth cream with a little of the milk. Heat the remaining milk until hot. Pour some of the milk on the egg mixture, stirring, then replace the mixture in the saucepan with the rest of the milk. Bring to the boil, stirring constantly, then simmer for 3 minutes.

Pour the custard over the rice. Sprinkle with the almonds, candied peel and fruit and set aside to cool. The fruit and nut topping prevents a skin forming on the custard. Chill before serving.

SERVES SIX TO EIGHT

GOOSEBERRY TRIFLE

When in season, add a washed head of elderflower to the gooseberries during cooking, then remove the head before turning the fruit into the dish. Alternatively, add a little bought elderflower cordial to the fruit.

450 g/1 lb gooseberries
100 g/4 oz sugar
300 ml/½ pint double cream
30 ml/2 tbsp icing sugar
30 ml/2 tbsp sherry
crystallized ginger to decorate (optional)

CUSTARD
25 g/1 oz cornflour
25 g/1 oz caster sugar
4 egg yolks
5 ml/1 tsp vanilla essence
600 ml/1 pint milk

Top and tail the gooseberries, then place them in a saucepan with the sugar. Heat, stirring often, until the juice begins to run from the fruit and the sugar dissolves. Continue to cook for 15-20 minutes, until the gooseberries are soft. Cool slightly before transferring to a trifle dish.

For the custard, blend the cornflour, caster sugar, egg yolks and vanilla to a smooth cream with a little of the milk. Heat the remaining milk until hot. Pour some of the milk on the egg mixture, stirring, then replace the mixture in the saucepan with the rest of the milk. Bring to the boil, stirring constantly, and simmer for 3 minutes. Pour the custard over the gooseberries. Cover the surface with dampened greaseproof paper and allow to cool.

Pour the cream into a basin. Add the icing sugar and sherry, then whip until the mixture stands in soft peaks. Spread the cream over the trifle and chill. Decorate with pieces of crystallized ginger if liked.

SERVES SIX

MRS BEETON'S TRIFLE

Plain whisked or creamed sponge cake, individual buns, or Madeira cake are ideal for this trifle. Originally, Mrs Beeton made her custard by using 8 eggs to thicken 600 ml/1 pint milk, cooking it slowly over hot water. Using cornflour and egg yolks is more practical and it gives a creamier, less 'eggy' result.

4 slices of plain cake or individual cakes
6 almond macaroons
12 ratafias
175 ml/6 fl oz sherry
30–45 ml/2–3 tbsp brandy
60–90 ml/4–6 tbsp raspberry or strawberry
  jam
grated rind of ½ lemon
25 g/1 oz flaked almonds
300 ml/½ pint double cream
30 ml/2 tbsp icing sugar
candied and crystallized fruit and peel to
  decorate

CUSTARD
25 g/1 oz cornflour
25 g/1 oz caster sugar
4 egg yolks
5 ml/1 tsp vanilla essence
600 ml/1 pint milk

Place the sponge cakes in a glass dish. Add the macaroons and ratafias, pressing them down gently. Pour about 50 ml/2 fl oz of the sherry into a basin and set it aside, then pour the rest over the biscuits and cake. Sprinkle with the brandy. Warm the jam in a small saucepan, then pour it evenly over the trifle base, spreading it lightly. Top with the lemon rind and almonds.

For the custard, blend the cornflour, caster sugar, egg yolks and vanilla to a smooth cream with a little of the milk. Heat the remaining milk until hot. Pour some of the milk on the egg mixture, stirring, then replace the mixture in the saucepan with the rest of the milk. Bring to the boil, stirring constantly, and simmer for 3 minutes. Pour the custard over the trifle base and cover the surface with a piece of dampened greaseproof paper. Set aside to cool.

Add the cream and icing sugar to the reserved sherry and whip until the mixture stands in soft peaks. Swirl the cream over the top of the trifle and chill. Decorate with pieces of candied and crystallized fruit and peel before serving.

SERVES SIX

WINE TRIFLES

grated rind and juice of ½ lemon
3 eggs
100 g/4 oz caster sugar
5 ml/1 tsp cornflour
375 ml/13 fl oz sweet white wine
6 individual sponge cakes or trifle sponges

Put the lemon rind and juice into a heatproof bowl. Add the eggs, sugar, and cornflour and stir the mixture well. Gradually whisk in the sweet white wine.

Place the bowl over a saucepan of hot water and heat very gently, whisking all the time until light and fluffy. The mixture must not be allowed to boil; it may be prepared in the top of a double saucepan and will take about 20 minutes to thicken.

Remove the bowl from the heat and leave to cool slightly. Place the sponge cakes in six individual dishes. Just before serving, pour over the sauce.

SERVES SIX

APPLE TRIFLE

1 kg/2¼ lb cooking apples
grated rind and juice of ½ lemon
150 g/5 oz granulated sugar
6 trifle sponges
350 ml/12 fl oz milk
2 eggs, plus 1 yolk
15 ml/1 tbsp caster sugar
few drops of vanilla essence

DECORATION
175 ml/6 fl oz double cream
25 g/1 oz flaked almonds, browned

Peel, quarter and core the apples. Put them into a saucepan with the lemon rind and juice and granulated sugar. Add 30 ml/2 tbsp water and cover the pan. Simmer the apple mixture gently until the fruit is reduced to a pulp. Purée in a blender or food processor and allow the mixture to cool slightly.

Slice the sponges and place in a large glass dish. Spread with the apple purée and set aside.

In a saucepan, bring the milk to just below boiling point. Put the eggs and caster sugar into a bowl, mix well, then stir in the scalded milk and vanilla essence. Strain the custard mixture into a heavy-bottomed saucepan or a heatproof bowl placed over a saucepan of simmering water. Alternatively, use a double saucepan, but make sure the water does not touch the upper pan.

Cook the custard over very gentle heat for 15-25 minutes, stirring all the time with a wooden spoon, until the custard thickens to the consistency of single cream. Stir well around the sides as well as the base of the pan or bowl to prevent the formation of lumps, especially if using a double saucepan. Do not allow the custard to boil.

As soon as the custard thickens, pour it carefully over the apple purée in the dish (see Mrs Beeton's Tip). Cover the surface of the custard with dampened greaseproof paper to prevent the formation of a skin. Cool.

In a bowl, whip the cream until stiff. Spread it on the cold custard and decorate with the almonds. Serve chilled.

SERVES SIX

VARIATION

Gooseberry Trifle Use 1 kg/2¼ lb gooseberries, topped and tailed, instead of apples.

 MRS BEETON'S TIP

When adding the hot custard to the glass dish, pour it over a metal spoon whose bowl rests in the dish. This will reduce the possibility of the hot liquid causing the dish to crack.

APRICOT TRIFLE

6 slices of Swiss roll filled with jam
2 almond macaroons
1 (540 g/18¼ oz) can apricot halves
30 ml/2 tbsp sherry
500 ml/17 fl oz milk
3 eggs, plus 2 yolks
25 g/1 oz caster sugar
few drops of vanilla essence

DECORATION
150 ml/¼ pint double cream
25 g/1 oz blanched almonds

Cut the Swiss roll into cubes and break the macaroons into chunks. Arrange them on the base of a glass dish.

Drain the apricots, reserving 125 ml/4 fl oz of the juice in a measuring jug and adding the sherry. Pour the mixture over the cake in the dish. Reserve half the apricot halves, cutting the remainder into chunks and adding them to the dish.

In a saucepan, bring the milk to just below boiling point. Put the eggs and sugar into a bowl, mix well, then stir in the scalded milk. Strain the custard mixture into a heavy-bottomed saucepan or a heatproof bowl placed over a saucepan of simmering water. Alternatively, use a double saucepan, but make sure the water does not touch the upper pan.

Cook the custard over very gentle heat for 15–25 minutes, stirring all the time with a wooden spoon, until the custard thickens to the consistency of single cream. Stir well around the sides as well as the base of the pan or bowl to prevent the formation of lumps. especially if using a double saucepan.

As soon as the custard thickens, pour it carefully over the apricots in the dish (see Mrs Beeton's Tip, page 665). Cover the surface of the custard with dampened greaseproof paper

to prevent the formation of a skin and set aside for 30 minutes to cool and set.

In a bowl, whip the cream until stiff. Spread it on the cold custard and decorate with the reserved apricots and the almonds. Serve the trifle chilled.

SERVES SIX

VARIATIONS

Peach Trifle Use peach slices instead of apricots and add 15 ml/1 tbsp lemon juice to the syrup.

Pineapple Trifle Use pineapple cubes instead of apricots.

 MRS BEETON'S TIP

For a firmly set custard, use 25 g/1 oz cornflour mixed with a little cold milk. Add 3 egg yolks to the cornflour mixture and mix in the 25 g/1 oz sugar. Heat the milk, pour some of it on the cornflour mixture, then return the whole batch to the saucepan and bring to the boil, stirring all the time. Simmer for 3 minutes, stirring.

PEAR AND CHOCOLATE TRIFLE

6 individual sponge cakes or trifle sponges
6 canned pear halves

SAUCE
25 g/1 oz butter
25 g/1 oz cocoa
25 g/1 oz plain flour
500 ml/17 fl oz milk
25 g/1 oz sugar
10 ml/2 tsp gelatine

DECORATION
150 ml/¼ pint double cream
angelica

Place the sponges in six individual dishes. Drain the canned pears well on absorbent kitchen paper, then place a pear half, rounded side uppermost, on each sponge cake.

To make the sauce, melt the butter in a saucepan, add the cocoa and flour and cook for 2 minutes. Stir in the milk gradually, add the sugar and bring the mixture to the boil, stirring all the time. Lower the heat and simmer for 2 minutes, then remove from the heat.

Place 30 ml/2 tbsp water in a small heatproof bowl. Sprinkle the gelatine on to the liquid. Set aside for 15 minutes until the gelatine is spongy. Stand the bowl over a saucepan of hot water and stir the gelatine until it has dissolved completely. Stir it into the sauce. Leave to cool to a coating consistency.

Pour the chocolate sauce over the pears and allow some to run into the dish. Cool. In a bowl, whip the cream until stiff, and use with the angelica to decorate the trifles.

SERVES SIX

MRS BEETON'S CHARLOTTE RUSSE

45 ml/3 tbsp icing sugar, sifted
24 sponge fingers
15 ml/1 tbsp gelatine
500 ml/17 fl oz single cream
45 ml/3 tbsp any sweet liqueur
1 (15 cm/6 inch) round sponge cake, 1 cm/
¼ inch thick

In a small bowl, mix 30 ml/2 tbsp of the icing sugar with a little water to make a thin glacé icing. Cut 4 sponge fingers in half, and dip the rounded ends in the icing. Line a 15 cm/6 inch soufflé dish with the halved fingers, placing them like a star, with the sugared sides uppermost and the iced ends meeting in the centre. Dip one end of each of the remaining biscuits in the icing; use to line the sides of the dish, with the sugared sides outward and the iced ends at the base. Trim the biscuits to the height of the soufflé dish.

Place 45 ml/3 tbsp water in a small heatproof bowl and sprinkle the gelatine on to the liquid. Set aside for 15 minutes until the gelatine is spongy. Stand the bowl over a saucepan of hot water and stir the gelatine until it has dissolved completely.

Combine the cream, liqueur and remaining icing sugar in a bowl. Add the gelatine and whisk until frothy. Stand the mixture in a cool place until it begins to thicken, then pour carefully into the charlotte. Cover the flavoured cream with the sponge cake, making sure it is set enough to support the cake. Chill for 8–12 hours, until firm.

Loosen the biscuits from the sides of the dish with a knife, carefully turn the charlotte out on to a plate and serve.

SERVES SIX

CHARLOTTE RUSSE WITH COINTREAU

250 ml/8 fl oz Clear Lemon Jelly (page 686)
20 sponge fingers
4 egg yolks or 1 whole egg and 2 yolks
50 g/2 oz caster sugar
250 ml/8 fl oz milk
thinly pared rind and juice of 1 lemon
15 ml/1 tbsp Cointreau
10 ml/2 tsp gelatine
150 ml/¼ pint double cream
150 ml/¼ pint single cream

Pour enough jelly into the base of an 18 cm/7 inch soufflé dish or charlotte mould to give a depth of 5 mm/¼ inch. Refrigerate until set. Place the remaining jelly in a heatproof bowl over hot water so that it remains liquid.

Trim one end of each sponge finger so that they will stand upright. Dip the long side of one of the sponge fingers in the liquid jelly and stand in the mould, with the cut end resting on the layer of jelly, and the sugared side outwards. Repeat with a second sponge finger, sticking it to its neighbour with the aid of the jelly coating. Repeat until the mould is lined, then chill for about 2½ hours until set.

Meanwhile make the bavarois filling. In a bowl, beat the eggs and sugar together until fluffy and pale. Warm the milk in a saucepan with the lemon rind; do not let it boil. Remove from the heat and slowly strain the flavoured milk into the egg mixture, then return the custard to the clean pan or to a double saucepan or heatproof bowl placed over hot water. Cook over very low heat until the custard thickens.

Strain the thickened custard in a bowl, stir in the lemon juice and Cointreau. Cool.

Place 15 ml/1 tbsp water in a small bowl and sprinkle the gelatine on to the liquid. Set aside for 15 minutes until the gelatine is spongy.

Stand the bowl over a saucepan of hot water and stir the gelatine until it has dissolved completely. Cool until tepid and add to the custard. Leave in a cool place until the mixture thickens at the edges, stirring from time to time to prevent the formation of a skin.

Combine the creams in a bowl and whip lightly. Fold into the custard mixture, and set aside in a cool place until on the point of setting. Pour carefully into the charlotte shell, taking care not to disturb the sponge fingers.

Chill the charlotte until the bavarois filling is completely set, then loosen the biscuits from the sides of the dish with a knife, carefully turn the charlotte out on to a plate and serve.

SERVES SIX

CHARLOTTE ST JOSE

250 ml/8 fl oz Clear Lemon Jelly (page 686)
glacé pineapple
20 sponge fingers
1 (127 g/4½ oz) tablet pineapple jelly
1 (376 g/13 oz) can crushed pineapple
30 ml/2 tbsp custard powder
250 ml/8 fl oz milk
250 ml/8 fl oz double cream

Line a 1.25 litre/2¼ pint charlotte mould with a thin layer of the clear lemon jelly and leave to set. Decorate the jelly (see page 672) with pieces of glacé pineapple, dipping them in liquid lemon jelly before setting into place. Spoon over a very thin layer of jelly to hold them firmly, then refrigerate until set.

Trim one end of each sponge finger and use to line the sides of the mould, placing the trimmed end of each on to the jelly on the base. Chill the lined mould while preparing the pineapple jelly cream filling.

Chop the pineapple jelly tablet roughly. Heat 100 ml/3½ fl oz water in a saucepan, add the jelly and stir until dissolved. Drain the crushed pineapple, stirring the juice into the jelly mixture in the pan, and reserving the fruit. Set the jelly mixture aside to cool.

Meanwhile, in a bowl, blend the custard powder with a little of the milk. Put the rest of the milk into a saucepan and bring to the boil. Pour it slowly on to the blended custard powder, stirring all the time until the custard thickens. Cool the custard slightly, then stir into the jelly mixture. Cool again until beginning to set, then fold in the reserved crushed pineapple.

In a clean bowl, whip 125 ml/4 fl oz of the cream until it leaves a trail, then fold into the setting mixture. Spoon into the prepared mould and refrigerate for 2–3 hours until set.

Trim the sponge fingers level with the top of the mould and turn out on to a serving dish. Put the remaining cream into a bowl and whip until stiff. Use to decorate the charlotte.

SERVES EIGHT

 MRS BEETON'S TIP

A traditional charlotte mould is made of metal. By chilling the mould first, the setting time for the first layer of jelly and decoration can be greatly reduced. The small amount of jelly sets almost immediately when poured into a well-chilled metal mould.

DEAN'S CREAM

This is a very old recipe for a dessert that was one of the forerunners of the standard modern trifle.

6 individual sponge cakes
raspberry jam
apricot jam
100 g/4 oz ratafias
250 ml/8 fl oz sherry
75 ml/5 tbsp brandy
500 ml/17 fl oz double cream
50 g/2 oz caster sugar

DECORATION
angelica
glacé cherries
crystallized pineapple

Cut the sponge cakes in half lengthways, and spread half with raspberry jam and half with apricot jam. Arrange them in a deep glass dish, jam sides upwards.

Break the ratafias into pieces and sprinkle on top of the sponge cakes. Pour the sherry over the cakes and leave to soak for about 30 minutes.

Put the brandy, cream, and sugar into a bowl and whisk until very thick. Pile into the dish and decorate with angelica, cherries, and crystallized pineapple. Chill well before serving.

SERVES EIGHT

Fruit Desserts and Jellies

*A colourful bowl of fresh fruit is the simplest of desserts. The introduction to this chapter
provides a guide to some of the many exotic fruits that are available.
In the recipes you will find these, and more familiar fruits used in a variety of
desserts and jellies, some simple, some stunning.*

A wide variety of fruit is now available thoughout the country all year round, including many exotics that were unheard of in Mrs Beeton's day. Fruit salads may be as simple or as exciting as you please, offering just two or three fresh fruits, a combination of exotic fresh fruits, or some familiar fresh fruits with exotic canned fruits. A fruit salad always looks good, expecially when served in a container made from the shell of one of the component fruits. For example, Pineapple and Kirsch Salad (page 675), served in pineapple half-shells, looks spectacular, as would the Red Fruit Salad (page 676), served in a hollowed-out watermelon.

The diet-conscious may prefer an unsweetened fruit salad, or a little honey may be used in place of the traditional syrup. Serve cream, yogurt or fromage frais with fruit salad and offer some plain biscuits to complete the dessert.

EXOTIC FRUITS

New fruits appear on the supermarket shelves regularly. Some sell well and soon become familiar, others are only seen once or twice. The following is a brief guide to some of the unusual fruits that are available.

Apple Bananas These are very small bananas with thin skins. Their flesh is quite dry but they taste similar to a banana with a hint of apple. They are grown in Kenya and Malaysia. Their size and good flavour make apple bananas ideal dessert fruit, for topping with vanilla ice cream or serving flamed with brandy.

Carambola The carambola is known as star fruit because of its ridged shape. The slices resemble stars. The pale yellow, waxy-looking skin may be left on unless the fruit is particularly tough. The flesh has a very delicate flavour, making the fruit ideal for decorating a wide variety of desserts, including cheesecakes, trifles and gâteaux.

Figs Purple-skinned figs should be just soft when ripe. They have a deep red-coloured flesh with lots of small pale seeds. When the skin is removed thinly, the flesh will be found to have a sweet flavour. Whole figs may be quartered and served with a small scoop of orange sorbet or good ice cream to make a tempting dessert. Figs are also exceedingly good with creamy goat's cheese.

Guava An oval, pale yellow-skinned fruit, pear or plum-shaped. The guava has a slightly scented, tangy flesh with lots of small seeds in the middle. The peel should be removed before the fruit is sliced. It is best lightly poached in syrup, after which the slices may be added to cool fruit salads or used in a variety of desserts.

Kiwi Fruit A green fruit with a brown, slightly furry skin that is quite thin. When cut across, the small oval fruit has a pale core, surrounded by small dark seeds and bright green flesh. The fruit should be peeled before being sliced. It is often used for decorating desserts or for adding to fruit salads.

Kumquats These look like tiny oranges. They are citrus fruit with a slightly bitter, orange flavour. They may be poached and eaten whole but they do contain pips. If sliced, the pips may be removed before the fruit is cooked. Kumquats may be eaten raw but they are quite sharp; their skin resembles fine orange peel.

Mango The mango is oval and about the size of a medium potato. The skin is red when the fruit is fully ripe, by which time the mango should feel slightly soft. There is a large, thin, oval stone in the centre of the juicy orange flesh. The mango has a flavour reminiscent of peaches but it is slightly more scented and a little tangy. The fruit should be peeled and the flesh cut off the stone in long wedges or slices.

Papaya An oval fruit with a deep yellow skin which is slightly green before the fruit ripens. Cut open, the papaya has seeds in the middle and sweet apricot-coloured flesh. It is very good in fruit salads.

Passion Fruit Small, round, dimpled fruit with a hard, purple skin. When cut in half the passion fruit reveals a soft, orange-coloured, juicy flesh with small, dark, edible seeds. The flesh is scooped out with a teaspoon, and may then be sieved and used to flavour desserts or sweet sauces.

 MRS BEETON'S TIP

A wide variety of fruit is available canned, either in syrup or in natural juice. Peaches, pears, pineapple, mandarins, fruit salad and many other familiar fruits have long held an established place in the store cupboard. However, in addition, many exotic fruit are now available canned, including carambola, kiwi fruit, mango, cherry apples (miniature apples), guava, green figs and papaya.

Persimmon A small, round, orange-coloured fruit with a large stalk end. The skin is thin but tough. The soft flesh is evenly coloured and it has a slightly bitter flavour.

STEWED FRUIT

Stewed fruit may be served hot or cold. A common mistake is to overcook stewed fruit until it is reduced to a pulp. Perfectly stewed fruit should consist of large pieces of tender fruit in a small amount of syrup.

The fruit should be washed, dried and prepared according to its type.

Apples Peel, core and quarter or cut into thick slices.

Blackberries Pick over, wash and drain.

Blackcurrants String both redcurrants and blackcurrants.

Gooseberries Top and tail.

Peaches Place in a bowl, cover with boiling water and leave for 1 minute, then skin. Halve and remove stones.

Pears Peel, core and halve, quarter or slice.

Plums Leave whole or halve and stone.

Rhubarb Trim and slice into 2.5-5 cm/1-2 inch lengths. If rhubarb is old, then peel it thinly to remove any tough strings.

Fruits that discolour should be sprinkled with lemon juice or kept in brine as they are prepared. Drain and thoroughly rinse fruit soaked in brine. Prepare a syrup, allowing 50-175 g/2-6 oz sugar to 150 ml/¼ pint water, depending on the fruit and on personal taste. This quantity is sufficient for 450 g/1 lb fruit. Sharp fruits, such as blackcurrants or rhubarb, may require extra sugar. Dissolve the sugar in the water over low heat, then bring the syrup to the boil. Reduce the heat before adding the fruit, then cover the pan and allow the liquid to simmer very gently so that the fruit yields its syrup to come about one-third of the way up the fruit, although this depends on the size of the pan. Cook the fruit until tender but not mushy, turning large pieces occasionally so that they cook evenly.

Medium or dry cider, or fruit juice, may be used to make the syrup instead of water. Honey may be added instead of sugar, in which case extra liquid should be used. The cooking syrup may be flavoured with a strip of lemon or orange rind, or with whole spices such as cloves or cinnamon.

Use a large spoon to transfer the fruit to a heatproof serving dish or individual dishes and coat with the cooking syrup. Alternatively, leave the fruit to cool in the covered pan and lightly chill it before serving.

MICROWAVE STEWED FRUIT

Most types of fruit cook well in the microwave. Use a large lidded dish or mixing bowl with a plate as a cover. Prepare the syrup first, allowing about 2–3 minutes on High for 150 ml/ ¼ pint of liquid. The more sugar, the longer the cooking time. Stir the syrup well so that the sugar has dissolved before the fruit is added. Make sure that the fruit is well coated with syrup and cover the dish. Cook the fruit on High, stirring once or twice during cooking. The following is a guide to cooking times for 450 g/1 lb fruit:

apples – 4–6 minutes
blackcurrants – 8–10 minutes
blackberries – 3–5 minutes
gooseberries – 5–7 minutes
peaches (4) – 4–5 minutes
pears – 6–8 minutes
plums – 3–5 minutes
rhubarb – 6–8 minutes

The exact cooking times depend on the size and ripeness of the fruit. Allow the fruit to stand for 2 minutes before serving.

JELLIES

Home-made fruit jelly makes a refreshing, healthy dessert. The recipes in this chapter range from sparkling jellies flavoured with wine to creamy milk jellies. An indication of the size of mould to use is given in each recipe. Always check the size of the mould before pouring the jelly into it. The mould should be full but not overflowing; if it is only half full the turned out jelly will not look attractive.

Allow plenty of time for a jelly to set. Stand the mould on a small baking sheet. When cool place the jelly in the refrigerator. If the jelly is strongly scented of fruit cover the mould with cling film to prevent the flavour of the jelly from tainting other foods in the refrigerator. The jelly may be set in a cool place other than the refrigerator but this usually takes longer. Cover the mould to prevent any dust or dirt from falling on to the jelly.

A small amount of jelly may be set quickly by placing the mould in the freezer. Check that the mould is freezerproof before doing this. A larger volume of jelly may be placed in the freezer for 10 minutes to speed up the chilling process before transferring it to the refrigerator to set completely. Never place hot jellies in the refrigerator or freezer.

COATING A MOULD WITH JELLY

Pour in just enough jelly to cover the base and sides of the mould. Rotate the mould in your hands until it has a thin, even coating of jelly, then place it in the refrigerator to set completely. For speed, the jelly may be placed in the freezer to set. Keep the remaining jelly in a warm place so that it does not set.

If canned fruit is being added for decoration, drain this thoroughly before putting it into the mould. Cut pieces of fruit to fit the shape of the mould and make a decorative pattern on top of the set jelly. It is a good idea to dip each piece of fruit in the remaining liquid jelly before arranging it in the mould. When the pattern is complete, spoon a little more liquid jelly over it, taking care not to disturb the arrangement of the fruit.

Allow the lined mould to set before adding the filling. When the filling is added, it should come to the top of the mould so that when the jelly or jellied dessert is turned out, the shape is perfect. If a creamed filling is used which does not fill the mould completely, allow it to set lightly, then spoon liquid jelly on top to fill the mould.

GREEN FRUIT SALAD

A fruit salad, fresh, crisp and flavoursome, is the perfect ending for a meal. Using shades of a single colour can be most effective. Here the theme is green and white, but golden or red colours can look equally attractive (see Red Fruit Salad, page 676). There is no need to stick to the selection or the proportions of fruit in the recipe; simply remember that you will need a total of about 1 kg/2¼lb. The fruit is traditionally served in syrup, as here, but fresh fruit juices, sometimes sparked with alcohol, are equally popular today.

175 g/6 oz green-fleshed melon, scooped into balls
175 g/6 oz seedless green grapes
2 Granny Smith apples
2 kiwi fruit, peeled and sliced
2 greengages, halved and stoned
2 passion fruit
mint sprigs to decorate

SYRUP
175 g/6 oz sugar
30 ml/2 tbsp lemon juice

Make the syrup. Put the sugar in a saucepan with 450 ml/¾ pint water. Heat gently, stirring until the sugar has dissolved, then bring to the

boil and boil rapidly until the syrup has been reduced by about half. Add the lemon juice, allow to cool, then pour the syrup into a glass serving bowl.

When the syrup is quite cold, add the fruit. Leave the skin on the apples and either slice them or cut them into chunks. Cut the passion fruit in half and scoop out the pulp, straining it to remove the seeds, if preferred. Serve well chilled, decorated with mint.

SERVES FOUR TO SIX

PLUMS WITH PORT

1 kg/2¼ lb firm plums
100–150 g/4–5 oz soft light brown sugar
150 ml/¼ pint port

Set the oven at 150°C/300°F/gas 2. Cut the plums neatly in half and remove the stones.

Put the plums into a baking dish or casserole, sprinkle with the sugar (the amount required will depend on the sweetness of the plums) and pour the port on top.

Cover the dish securely with a lid or foil and bake for 45–60 minutes or until the plums are tender. Serve hot, or lightly chilled.

SERVES SIX

 MICROWAVE TIP

Cook in a covered dish for 10–12 minutes on High, stirring gently once or twice during the cooking time.

DRIED FRUIT COMPOTE

100 g/4 oz dried apricots
100 g/4 oz prunes
100 g/4 oz dried figs
50 g/2 oz dried apple rings
30 ml/2 tbsp liquid honey
2.5 cm/1 inch cinnamon stick
2 cloves
pared rind and juice of ¼ lemon
50 g/2 oz raisins
50 g/2 oz flaked almonds, toasted

Combine the apricots, prunes and figs in a bowl. Add water to cover and leave to soak. Put the apples in separate bowl with water to cover and leave both bowls to soak overnight.

Next day, place the honey in a saucepan with 600 ml/1 pint water. Add the cinnamon stick, cloves and lemon rind. Bring to the boil. Stir in the lemon juice.

Drain both bowls of soaked fruit. Add the mixed fruit to the pan, cover and simmer for 10 minutes. Stir in the drained apples and simmer for 10 minutes more, then add the raisins and simmer for 2–3 minutes. Discard the cinnamon, cloves and lemon rind.

Spoon the compote into a serving dish and sprinkle with the almonds. Serve warm or cold.

SERVES SIX

 MICROWAVE TIP

There is no need to presoak the dried fruit. Make the honey syrup in a large bowl, using 450 ml/¾ pint water. Microwave on High for about 4 minutes, then stir in all the dried fruit with the cinnamon, cloves and lemon rind. Cover and cook on High for 15–20 minutes or until all the fruit is soft. Stir several times during cooking, each time pressing the fruit down into the syrup.

ORANGE AND GRAPEFRUIT SALAD

Ortaniques would make a delicious addition to this salad. These juicy citrus fruits are a cross between a tangerine and an orange. Their thin skins make them very easy to peel and segment.

4 oranges
2 pink grapefruit

SYRUP
225 g/8 oz sugar
30 ml/2 tbsp orange liqueur

Using a vegetable peeler, remove the rind from 1 orange, taking care not to include any of the bitter pith. Cut the rind into strips with a sharp knife. Bring a small saucepan of water to the boil, add the orange strips and cook for 1 minute, then drain and set aside on absorbent kitchen paper.

Peel the remaining oranges and remove all the pith. Using a sharp knife, carefully cut between the segment membranes to remove the flesh. Work over a bowl to catch any juice, and squeeze out all the juice from the remaining pulp. Segment the grapefruit in the same way.

Make the syrup. Put the sugar in a pan with 200 ml/7 fl oz water. Heat gently, stirring until the sugar has dissolved, then bring to the boil and boil rapidly, without stirring, until the syrup turns golden. Remove from the heat and carefully add the fruit juice and liqueur. Set aside to cool.

Arrange the citrus segments in concentric circles in a shallow serving dish or large quiche dish. Pour the caramel syrup over the top and chill thoroughly before serving.

SERVES SIX

MRS BEETON'S ORANGE SALAD

5 oranges
50 g/2 oz caster sugar (or to taste)
2.5 ml/½ tsp ground mixed spice
100 g/4 oz muscatel raisins
60 ml/4 tbsp brandy

Peel four oranges, removing all pith. Slice them, discarding the pips. Mix the sugar and spice in a bowl. Layer the orange slices in a serving dish, sprinkling each layer with the sugar mixture and raisins.

Squeeze the juice from the remaining orange and sprinkle it over the salad. Pour the brandy over, cover and leave to macerate for 24 hours before serving.

SERVES FOUR

PINEAPPLE AND KIRSCH SALAD

2 small pineapples
100 g/4 oz black grapes
1 banana
1 pear
15 ml/1 tbsp lemon juice
30–45 ml/2–3 tbsp kirsch
sugar

Cut the pineapples in half lengthways. Cut out the core from each, then scoop out the flesh, using first a knife, then a spoon, but taking care to keep the pineapple shells intact. Discard the core, and working over a bowl, chop the flesh.

Add the pineapple flesh to the bowl. Halve the grapes and remove the pips. Add to the pineapple mixture. Peel and slice the banana; peel, core, and slice the pear. Put the lemon juice in a shallow bowl, add the pear and banana slices

and toss both fruits before adding to the pineapple and grapes. Mix all the fruit together, pour the kirsch over and sweeten to taste with the sugar. Pile the fruit back into the pineapple shells and chill until required.

SERVES FOUR

TROPICAL FRUIT SALAD

This fruit salad utilizes both fresh and canned fruits.

1 small pineapple
1 mango
1 (312 g/11 oz) can lychees, drained
3 bananas, sliced
1 (425 g/15 oz) can guava halves, drained
250 ml/8 fl oz tropical fruit juice

Peel the pineapple, removing the eyes. Cut in half or quarters lengthways and cut out the hard core. Cut the fruit into neat chunks and place in a serving dish.

Peel and slice the mango, discarding the stone. Add the mango flesh to the bowl with the lychees, bananas and guavas. Pour over the tropical fruit juice and chill.

SERVES EIGHT

VARIATION

Orange juice, spiked with a little rum, may be used instead of tropical fruit juice. Alternatively, try ginger ale.

RED FRUIT SALAD

Choose small strawberries, if possible, for this dessert, since they are juicier when left whole. Do not strip the redcurrants from the stalks.

225 g/8 oz redcurrants
6 red plums, stoned and quartered
225 g/8 oz strawberries, hulled
225 g/8 oz raspberries, hulled
100 g/4 oz slice watermelon, seeded and
   cubed

TO SERVE
Greek yogurt or clotted cream
caster sugar

Using a pair of kitchen scissors, neatly snip the redcurrants into small bunches.

Combine the plums, strawberries, raspberries and watermelon on a large platter. Arrange the redcurrants around or over the salad.

Serve as soon as possible, with yogurt or cream. Offer a bowl of caster sugar.

SERVES SIX

FROSTED APPLES

oil for greasing
6 cooking apples (about 800 g/1¾ lb)
30 ml/2 tbsp lemon juice
100 g/4 oz granulated sugar
15 ml/1 tbsp fine-cut marmalade
2.5 cm/1 inch cinnamon stick
2 cloves
2 egg whites
100 g/4 oz caster sugar, plus extra for dusting

DECORATION
125 ml/4 fl oz double cream
glacé cherries
angelica

Line a large baking sheet with greaseproof paper or non-stick baking parchment. Oil the lining paper. Set the oven at 180°C/350°F/gas 4. Wash, core and peel the apples, leaving them whole. Reserve the peelings. Brush the apples all over with the lemon juice to preserve the colour.

Combine the granulated sugar, marmalade, cinnamon stick, cloves and apple peelings in a large saucepan. Stir in 250 ml/8 fl oz water. Heat gently, stirring occasionally, until the sugar and marmalade have melted, then boil for 2–3 minutes without stirring to make a thin syrup.

Place the apples in a baking dish and strain the syrup over them. Cover with a lid or foil and bake for about 30 minutes or until the apples are just tender. Lower the oven temperature to 120°C/250°F/gas ¼.

Using a slotted spoon, carefully remove the apples from the syrup, dry well on absorbent kitchen paper, then place on the prepared baking sheet. Whisk the egg whites in a clean, grease-free bowl until they form stiff peaks, then gradually whisk in the caster sugar, a teaspoon at a time (see Mrs Beeton's Tip).

Coat each apple completely with the meringue, and dust lightly with caster sugar. Return to the oven and bake for about 1½ hours or until the meringue is firm and very lightly coloured. Remove from the oven and leave to cool.

In a bowl, whip the cream until it just holds its shape. Pile a spoonful on top of each apple and decorate with small pieces of cherry and angelica. Serve the apples on a bed of whipped cream in individual bowls, or with the cold baking syrup poured over them.

SERVES SIX

 MRS BEETON'S TIP

If using an electric whisk to make the meringue, whisk in all the sugar. If whisking by hand, however, whisk in only half the sugar and fold in the rest.

DANISH APPLE CAKE

1 kg/2¼ lb cooking apples
150 g/5 oz dried white breadcrumbs
75 g/3 oz sugar
100–125 g/4–4½ oz butter

DECORATION
300 ml/½ pint whipping cream
red jam, melted

Set the oven at 180°C/350°F/gas 4. Place the apples on a baking sheet and bake for 1 hour. When cool enough to handle, remove the peel and core from each apple; purée the fruit in a blender or food processor or rub through a sieve into a bowl.

In a separate bowl, mix the breadcrumbs with the sugar. Melt the butter in a frying pan, add the crumb mixture, and fry until golden.

Place alternate layers of crumbs and apple purée in a glass dish, starting and finishing with crumbs.

Whip the cream in a bowl and put into a piping bag fitted with a large star nozzle. Decorate the top of the apple cake with cream rosettes and drizzle a little red jam over the top. Chill lightly before serving.

SERVES FOUR TO SIX

TOFFEE-TOPPED GRAPE CREAM

fat for greasing
225 g/8 oz seedless grapes
250 ml/8 fl oz double cream
30 ml/2 tbsp brandy
45–60 ml/3–4 tbsp demerara sugar

Grease an ovenproof dish suitable for using under the grill. Halve the grapes, and put them into the prepared dish.

In a bowl, whip the cream until it holds its shape, then spread it over the grapes. Chill in a refrigerator for at least 8 hours.

Just before serving, sprinkle the cream topping with the brandy and sugar, put under a preheated moderately hot grill, and grill for 3–4 minutes until the sugar melts and bubbles.

Serve at once with sponge fingers or Wine Biscuits (page 801)

SERVES FOUR

ORANGES IN CARAMEL SAUCE

6 oranges
200 g/7 oz sugar
50–125 ml/2–4 fl oz chilled orange juice

Using a vegetable peeler, remove the rind from 1 orange, taking care not to include any of the bitter pith. Cut the rind into strips with a sharp knife. Bring a small saucepan of water to the boil, add the orange strips and cook for 1 minute, then drain and set aside on absorbent kitchen paper.

Carefully peel the remaining oranges, leaving them whole. Remove the pith from all the oranges and place the fruit in a heatproof bowl.

Put the sugar in a saucepan with 125 ml/4 fl oz water. Heat gently, stirring until the sugar has dissolved, then bring to the boil and boil rapidly, without stirring, until the syrup turns a golden caramel colour. Remove from the heat and carefully add the orange juice. Replace over the heat and stir until just blended, then add the reserved orange rind.

Pour the caramel sauce over the oranges and chill for at least 3 hours before serving.

SERVES SIX

 FREEZER TIP

Cool the oranges quickly in the sauce, place in a rigid container, cover and freeze for up to 12 months. Remember to allow a little headspace in the top of the container, as the syrup will expand upon freezing. Thaw, covered, in the refrigerator for about 6 hours.

BANANAS IN RUM

45 ml/3 tbsp soft light brown sugar
2.5 ml/½ tsp ground cinnamon
4 large bananas
25 g/1 oz butter
45–60 ml/3–4 tbsp rum
150 ml/¼ pint double cream to serve

Mix the sugar and cinnamon in a shallow dish. Cut the bananas in half lengthways and dredge them in the sugar and cinnamon mixture.

Melt the butter in a frying pan and fry the bananas, flat side down, for 1–2 minutes or until lightly browned underneath. Turn them over carefully, sprinkle with any remaining sugar and cinnamon and continue frying.

When the bananas are soft but not mushy, pour the rum over them. Tilt the pan and baste the bananas, then ignite the rum; baste again. Scrape any caramelized sugar from the base of the pan and stir it into the rum sauce. Shake the pan gently until the flames die down.

Arrange the bananas on warmed plates, pour the rum sauce over and serve with cream.

SERVES FOUR

BANANA BONANZA

4 bananas (about 450 g/1 lb)
15 ml/1 tbsp lemon juice
30 ml/2 tbsp soft dark brown sugar
150 ml/¼ pint soured cream
30 ml/2 tbsp top-of-the-milk
grated chocolate to decorate

Mash the bananas with the lemon juice in a bowl. Stir in the sugar, soured cream and top-of-the-milk. Serve decorated with grated chocolate.

SERVES FOUR

BANANA SNOW

6 bananas (about 675 g/1½ lb)
50 g/2 oz sugar
15 ml/1 tbsp lemon juice
125 ml/4 fl oz double cream
300 ml/½ pint plain yogurt
3 egg whites
25 g/1 oz flaked almonds, toasted

Mash the bananas in a bowl with the sugar and lemon juice, or purée in a blender or food processor. Tip into a bowl. Whip the cream in a bowl until it just holds its shape, then fold it into the banana purée with the yogurt.

In a clean, grease-free bowl, whisk the egg whites until they form stiff peaks, then fold into the banana mixture. Pile into one large or six dishes. Sprinkle with the almonds.

SERVES SIX

SUMMER PUDDING

This delectable dessert started life with the cumbersome name of Hydropathic Pudding. It was originally invented for spa patients who were forbidden rich creams and pastries. Vary the fruit filling if you wish – blackberries or bilberries make very good additions – but keep the total quantity of fruit at about 1 kg/2¼ lb.

150 g/5 oz caster sugar
225 g/8 oz blackcurrants or redcurrants,
  stalks removed
225 g/8 oz ripe red plums, halved and stoned
1 strip of lemon rind
225 g/8 oz strawberries, hulled
225 g/8 oz raspberries, hulled
8-10 slices of day-old white bread, crusts
  removed

Put the sugar into a saucepan with 60 ml/4 tbsp water. Heat gently, stirring, until the sugar has

dissolved. Add the black- or redcurrants, plums and lemon rind and poach until tender.

Add the strawberries and raspberries to the saucepan and cook for 2 minutes. Remove from the heat and, using a slotted spoon, remove the lemon rind.

Cut a circle from 1 slice of bread to fit the base of a 1.25 litre/2¼ pint pudding basin. Line the base and sides of the basin with bread, leaving no spaces. Pour in the stewed fruit, reserving about 45-60 ml/3-4 tbsp of the juice in a jug. Top the stewed fruit filling with more bread slices. Cover with a plate or saucer that exactly fits inside the basin. Put a weight on top to press the pudding down firmly. Leave in a cool place for 5-8 hours, preferably overnight.

Turn out carefully on to a plate or shallow dish to serve. If there are any places on the bread shell where the juice from the fruit filling has not penetrated, drizzle a little of the reserved fruit juice over. Serve with whipped cream or plain yogurt.

SERVES SIX

 FREEZER TIP

After the pudding has been weighted, pack the basin in a polythene bag, seal and freeze for up to 3 months. Thaw overnight in the refrigerator. Alternatively, line the basin completely with cling film before making the pudding. Thicker microwave cooking film is stronger than ordinary film, or use a double layer. Leave plenty of film overhanging the rim of the basin. Freeze the weighted pudding, then use the film to remove it from the basin. Pack and label before storing.

CHERRY COMPOTE

675 g/1½ lb red cherries
grated rind and juice of 1 orange
100 ml/3½ fl oz red wine
45 ml/3 tbsp redcurrant jelly
15 ml/1 tbsp caster sugar
pinch of ground cinnamon

Set the oven at 160°C/325°F/gas 3. Stone the cherries and put them into a shallow ovenproof dish.

Add the orange rind and juice to the cherries with all the remaining ingredients. Cover securely with a lid or foil and bake for about 30 minutes. Leave to cool, and chill before serving.

SERVES SIX

CHERRIES JUBILEE

This famous dish was created for Queen Victora's Diamond Jubilee. It is often finished at the table, with the cherries and sauce kept warm in a chafing dish and the kirsch ignited and added at the last moment.

50 g/2 oz sugar
450 g/1 lb dark red cherries, stoned
10 ml/2 tsp arrowroot
60 ml/4 tbsp kirsch

Put the sugar in a heavy-bottomed saucepan. Add 250 ml/8 fl oz water. Heat gently, stirring, until the sugar has dissolved, then boil steadily without stirring for 3–4 minutes to make a syrup. Lower the heat, add the cherries, and poach gently until tender. Using a slotted spoon, remove the cherries from the pan and set them aside on a plate to cool.

In a cup, mix the arrowroot with about 30 ml/ 2 tbsp of the syrup to a thin paste. Stir back into the pan. Bring to the boil, stirring constantly, until the mixture thickens. Remove from the heat.

Pile the cherries in a heatproof serving bowl. Pour the sauce over them. Heat the kirsch in a small saucepan or ladle. Ignite it, pour it over the cherries and serve at once.

SERVES FOUR

PEARS IN WINE

100 g/4 oz sugar
30 ml/2 tbsp redcurrant jelly
1.5 cm/¾ inch cinnamon stick
4 large ripe cooking pears (about 450 g/1 lb)
250 ml/8 fl oz red wine
25 g/1 oz flaked almonds

Combine the sugar, redcurrant jelly, and cinnamon stick in a saucepan wide enough to hold all the pears upright so that they fit snugly and will not fall over. Add 250 ml/8 fl oz water and heat gently, stirring, until the sugar and jelly have dissolved.

Peel the pears, leaving the stalks in place. Carefully remove as much of the core as possible without breaking the fruit. Stand the pears upright in the pan, cover, and simmer gently for 15 minutes.

Add the wine and cook, uncovered, for 15 minutes more. Remove the pears carefully with a slotted spoon, arrange them on a serving dish.

Remove the cinnamon stick from the pan and add the almonds. Boil the liquid remaining in the pan rapidly until it is reduced to a thin syrup. Pour the syrup over the pears and serve warm. This dessert can also be served cold. Pour the hot syrup over the pears, leave to cool, then chill before serving.

SERVES FOUR

STUFFED PEACHES IN BRANDY

100 g/4 oz sugar
150 ml/¼ pint medium-dry or slightly sweet
  white wine
30 ml/2 tbsp brandy
6 large ripe peaches
125 ml/4 fl oz double cream
50 g/2 oz cut mixed peel
25 g/1 oz blanched almonds, chopped

Put 250 ml/8 fl oz water into a saucepan and add the sugar, wine and brandy. Place over low heat, stirring, until the sugar dissolves. Skin the peaches (see Microwave Tip), then poach them gently in the brandy syrup for 15 minutes. Leave in the syrup to cool completely.

Whip the cream in a bowl until it just holds its shape. Fold in the mixed peel and almonds. With a slotted spoon, remove the peaches from the cold syrup. Cut them in half and remove the stones. Put about 15 ml/1 tbsp of the cream mixture in the hollow of 6 halves, then sandwich the peaches together again. Arrange in a shallow serving dish, and pour the syrup over the fruit. Chill until ready to serve.

SERVES SIX

 MICROWAVE TIP

Prick the peach skins, then put the fruit in a shallow dish. Cover and microwave on High for 1–1½ minutes. Allow to stand for 5 minutes. The skins will slip off easily.

GOOSEBERRY FOOL

When elderflowers are available, try adding 2 heads, well washed and tied in muslin, to the gooseberries while poaching. Discard the muslin bags when the gooseberries are cooked.

575 g/1¼ lb gooseberries, topped and tailed
150 g/5 oz caster sugar
300 ml/½ pint whipping cream

Put the gooseberries in a heavy-bottomed saucepan. Stir in the sugar. Cover the pan and cook the gooseberries over gentle heat for 10–15 minutes until the skins are just beginning to crack. Leave to cool.

Purée the fruit in a blender or food processor, or rub through a sieve into a clean bowl.

In a separate bowl, whip the cream until it holds its shape. Fold the cream gently into the gooseberry purée. Spoon into a serving dish or six individual glasses. Chill before serving.

SERVES SIX

VARIATIONS

If a fruit is suitable for puréeing, it will make a creamy fool. Try rhubarb, apricots, red- or blackcurrants, raspberries or blackberries. Sieve purée if necessary.

 MICROWAVE TIP

Combine the gooseberries and sugar in a deep 1.2 litre/2 pint dish. Cover lightly and cook for 6 minutes on High. Proceed as in the above recipe.

RHUBARB AND BANANA FOOL

450 g/1 lb young rhubarb
75 g/3 oz soft light brown sugar
piece of pared lemon rind
6 bananas
caster sugar (see method)
250 ml/8 fl oz cold Cornflour Custard Sauce
   (page 496) or lightly whipped double
   cream
ratafias to decorate

Remove any strings from the rhubarb and cut the stalks into 2.5 cm/1 inch lengths. Put into the top of a double saucepan and stir in the brown sugar and lemon rind. Set the pan over simmering water and cook for 10–15 minutes until the rhubarb is soft. Remove the lemon rind.

Meanwhile peel the bananas and purée in a blender or food processor. Add the rhubarb and process briefly until mixed. Alternatively, mash the bananas in a bowl and stir in the cooked rhubarb. Taste the mixture and add caster sugar, if necessary.

Fold the custard or cream into the fruit purée and turn into a serving bowl. Decorate with ratafias.

SERVES SIX TO EIGHT

 MRS BEETON'S TIP

If time permits, cook the rhubarb very slowly overnight. Layer the fruit in a casserole, add the sugar and lemon rind. Do not add any liquid. Cover and bake at 110°C/225°F/gas ¼.

REDCURRANT AND RASPBERRY FOOL

225 g/8 oz redcurrants
225 g/8 oz raspberries
75–100 g/3–4 oz caster sugar
15 ml/1 tbsp cornflour
extra caster sugar for topping
25 g/1 oz flaked almonds to decorate

Put the redcurrants and raspberries in a saucepan. Add 375 ml/13 fl oz water and simmer gently for about 20 minutes or until very tender. Purée in a blender or food processor, then sieve the mixture to remove any seeds. Return the mixture to the clean pan.

Stir in caster sugar to taste. Put the cornflour into a cup and stir in about 30 ml/2 tbsp of the purée. Bring the remaining purée to the boil.

Stir the cornflour mixture into the purée and bring back to the boil, stirring all the time until the fool thickens. Remove from the heat and spoon into six individual serving dishes. Sprinkle the surface of each fool with a little extra caster sugar to prevent the formation of a skin. Cool, then chill thoroughly.

Top with the flaked almonds just before serving. Serve with whipped cream, Greek yogurt or fromage frais.

SERVES SIX

BLACKCURRANT JELLY

**250 ml/8 fl oz blackcurrant syrup, bought or
home-made**
45 ml/3 tbsp sugar
20 ml/4 tsp gelatine

Heat the syrup and sugar in a saucepan, stirring
until the sugar has dissolved. Set aside to cool.

Place 125 ml/4 fl oz water in a small bowl and
sprinkle the gelatine on to the liquid. Set aside
for 15 minutes until the gelatine is spongy.
Stand the bowl over a saucepan of hot water
and stir the gelatine until it has dissolved
completely. Stir in a further 125 ml/4 fl oz cold
water, then add the dissolved gelatine to the
cooled syrup.

Pour the blackcurrant jelly into wetted individual moulds or a 600 ml/1 pint mould and
chill until set.

SERVES FOUR

FRESH LEMON JELLY

pared rind and juice of 4 lemons
20 ml/4 tsp gelatine
100–175 g/4–6 oz caster sugar

Put the lemon rind into a saucepan. Add
175 ml/6 fl oz water and simmer for 5 minutes.
Set aside until cool.

Place 75 ml/3 fl oz water in a small bowl and
sprinkle the gelatine on to the liquid. Set aside
for 15 minutes until the gelatine is spongy.
Stand the bowl over a saucepan of hot water
and stir the gelatine until it has dissolved
completely. Stir a further 75 ml/3 fl oz water
into the dissolved gelatine. Remove the lemon
rind from the cool liquid and add the liquid to
the gelatine mixture with the lemon juice and
sugar to taste. Stir until the sugar has dissolved,
heating gently if necessary.

Pour the mixture into four individual wetted
moulds or a 750 ml/1¼ pint mould and leave for
about 1 hour to set.

SERVES FOUR

VARIATIONS

Fresh Orange Jelly   Use 2 oranges instead of
lemons and only 50 g/2 oz caster sugar.

LEMON SMOOTHIE

pared rind and juice of 3 large lemons
750 ml/1¼ pints milk
200 g/7 oz sugar
25 g/1 oz gelatine

Combine the lemon rind, milk and sugar in a
saucepan. Heat until the sugar has dissolved.
Set aside to cool.

Place 60 ml/4 tbsp water in a small bowl and
sprinkle the gelatine on to the liquid. Set aside
for 15 minutes until the gelatine is spongy.
Stand the bowl over a saucepan of hot water
and stir the gelatine until it has dissolved
completely.

Stir the gelatine mixture into the cooled milk
mixture. Stir in the lemon juice and strain into
a wetted 1.1 litre/2 pint mould. Chill until set.

SERVES SIX

ORANGE JELLY BASKETS

100 g/4 oz sugar
6 oranges
2 lemons
40 g/1½ oz gelatine

DECORATION
6 angelica strips
125 ml/4 fl oz double cream

Put 500 ml/17 fl oz water into a saucepan. Add the sugar. Pare the rind from three of the oranges. Add the rind to the pan and bring slowly to the boil. Leave to infuse for 10 minutes, keeping the pan covered.

Squeeze the juice from all the oranges and lemons; make up to 500 ml/17 fl oz with water if necessary. Reserve the unpeeled orange halves for the baskets.

Place 30 ml/2 tbsp of the mixed citrus juice in a small bowl and sprinkle the gelatine on to the liquid. Set aside for 15 minutes until the gelatine is spongy. Stand the bowl over a saucepan of hot water and stir the gelatine until it has dissolved completely. Stir the remaining citrus juice and dissolved gelatine into the sugar syrup.

Remove any pulp from the 6 reserved orange halves and put the orange skins into patty tins to keep them rigid. Strain the jelly into the orange shells; chill for about 2 hours until set.

Make handles from the angelica, keeping them in place by pushing the ends into the set jelly. Whip the cream in a bowl until stiff, then spoon into a piping bag. Decorate the baskets with the cream.

SERVES SIX

SHAPED APPLE JELLY

1 kg/2¼ lb cooking apples
175 g/6 oz sugar
2 cloves
grated rind and juice of 2 small lemons
40 g/1½ oz gelatine

Wash the apples and cut them into pieces. Put them into a saucepan with the sugar, cloves, lemon rind and juice. Add 500 ml/17 fl oz water. Cover, and cook until the apples are soft.

Place 60 ml/4 tbsp water in a small bowl and sprinkle the gelatine on to the liquid. Set aside for 15 minutes until the gelatine is spongy. Stand the bowl over a saucepan of hot water and stir the gelatine until it has dissolved completely.

Rub the cooked apples through a sieve into a bowl and stir in the dissolved gelatine. Pour into a wetted 1.1 litre/2 pint mould and chill until set.

SERVES SIX

VARIATION

Gooseberry Jelly Use 1 kg/2¼ lb prepared gooseberries instead of apples, and omit the cloves.

BLACK MAMBA

500 ml/17 fl oz strong black coffee
50 g/2 oz sugar
20 ml/4 tsp gelatine
15 ml/1 tbsp rum or liqueur
whipped cream to decorate

Set aside 30 ml/2 tbsp coffee in a small bowl. Put the remaining coffee into a saucepan with the sugar and heat, stirring, until the sugar has dissolved. Set aside to cool.

Sprinkle the gelatine on to the coffee in the small bowl. Set aside for 15 minutes until the gelatine is spongy. Stand the bowl over a saucepan of hot water and stir until the gelatine has dissolved. Add to the coffee syrup with the rum or liqueur. Strain the mixture into a wetted 750 ml/1¼ pint mould and chill until set. When ready to serve the jelly, turn out and decorate with whipped cream.

SERVES FOUR

 MRS BEETON'S TIP

To turn out, or unmould, a jelly, run the tip of a knife around the top of the mould. Dip the mould into hot water for a few seconds, remove and dry it. Wet a serving plate and place upside down on top of the mould. Hold plate and mould together firmly and turn both over. Check that the mould is correctly positioned on the plate, sliding it into place if necessary. Shake gently and carefully lift off the mould.

MILK JELLY

500 ml/17 fl oz milk
30 ml/2 tbsp sugar
grated rind of 1 lemon
20 ml/4 tsp gelatine

Put the milk, sugar and lemon rind into a saucepan. Heat, stirring, until the sugar has dissolved. Set aside to cool. Place 60 ml/4 tbsp water in a small bowl and sprinkle the gelatine on to the liquid. Set aside for 15 minutes until the gelatine is spongy. Stand the bowl over a saucepan of hot water and stir the gelatine until it has dissolved. Stir the gelatine mixture into the cooled milk, then strain into a bowl. Stir the mixture from time to time until it is the consistency of thick cream.

Pour the milk jelly into a wetted 750 ml/1¼ pint mould and chill until set.

SERVES FOUR

VARIATIONS

The jelly may be flavoured with vanilla, coffee or other essence, if liked. If coffee essence is used, substitute orange rind for the lemon. Omit the rind if peppermint flavouring is used.

 MRS BEETON'S TIP

Do not be tempted to dissolve the gelatine in milk. It will curdle.

PORT WINE JELLY

25 ml/5 tsp gelatine
50 g/2 oz sugar
30 ml/2 tbsp redcurrant jelly
250 ml/8 fl oz port
few drops of red food colouring

Place 30 ml/2 tbsp water in a small bowl and sprinkle the gelatine on to the liquid. Set aside for 15 minutes until the gelatine is spongy. Stand the bowl over a saucepan of hot water and stir the gelatine until it has dissolved.

Combine the sugar and redcurrant jelly in a pan. Add 400 ml/14 fl oz water and heat gently, stirring, until all the sugar has dissolved.

Add the gelatine liquid to the syrup and stir in the port and colouring. Pour through a strainer lined with a single thickness of scalded fine cotton or muslin into a wetted 900 ml/1½ pint mould. Chill until set.

SERVES SIX

CLEAR LEMON JELLY

It takes time to make a perfect clear jelly, but the effort is well worthwhile. To create jewel-like clarity, the mixture must be filtered through a foam of coagulated egg whites and crushed egg shells.

4 lemons
150 g/5 oz sugar
4 cloves
2.5 cm/1 inch cinnamon stick
40 g/1½ oz gelatine
whites and shells of 2 eggs

Before you begin, scald a large saucepan, a measuring jug, a bowl, a whisk and a 1.1 litre/2 pint jelly mould in boiling water, as the merest trace of grease may cause cloudiness in the finished jelly.

Pare the rind from three of the lemons; squeeze the juice from all of them into the measuring jug. Make up to 250 ml/8 fl oz with water, if necessary.

Combine the rind, lemon juice, sugar, cloves, cinnamon stick and gelatine in the large pan. Add 750 ml/1¼ pints water.

Put the egg whites into the bowl; wash the shells in cold water, dry with absorbent kitchen paper and crush finely.

Add the egg whites and crushed shells to the mixture in the pan and heat, whisking constantly until a good head of foam is produced.

The mixture should be hot but not boiling. When the foam begins to form a crust, remove the whisk, but continue to heat the liquid until the crust has risen to the top of the pan. Do not allow the liquid to boil. Lower the heat and simmer for 5 minutes.

Remove the pan from the heat, cover and let the contents settle in a warm place for 5-10 minutes. Scald a jelly bag in boiling water and place it on a stand (see Mrs Beeton's Tip). Scald two large bowls, placing one of them under the jelly bag.

Strain the settled, clear jelly through the hot jelly bag into the bowl. When all the jelly has passed through the bag, replace the bowl of jelly with the second scalded bowl and strain the jelly again, pouring it very carefully through the foam crust which covers the bottom of the bag and acts as a filter.

If the jelly is not clear when looked at in a spoon or glass, the filtering must be carried out again, but avoid doing this too many times, as repeated filtering will cool the jelly and cause some of it to stick to the cloth.

Rinse the jelly mould in cold water. When the jelly is clear, pour it into the wetted mould and chill until set.

SERVES SIX

> **MRS BEETON'S TIP**
>
> If you do not have a jelly bag and stand, improvise by tying the four corners of a perfectly clean, scalded cloth, to the legs of an upturned stool. Alternatively, line a large, scalded, metal sieve with muslin.

CANDIED FRUIT CREAM JELLY

4 lemons
150 g/5 oz sugar
65 g/2¼ oz gelatine
whites and shells of 2 eggs
125 ml/4 fl oz port
few drops of red food colouring (optional)
250 ml/8 fl oz double cream
2 strips of angelica, each measuring
   5 × 1 cm/2 × ½ inch, chopped
50–75 g/2–3 oz glacé fruit (cherries, preserved
   ginger, glacé pineapple), chopped

Before you begin, scald a large saucepan, measuring jug, bowl, whisk and ring jelly mould in boiling water, as the merest trace of grease may cause cloudiness in the finished jelly.

Pare the rind from two of the lemons; squeeze the juice from all of them into the measuring jug. Make up to 125 ml/4 fl oz with water, if necessary.

Combine the rind, lemon juice and sugar in the large pan. Add 40 g/1½ oz of the gelatine and 625 ml/21 fl oz water.

Put the egg whites into the bowl; wash the shells in cold water, dry with absorbent kitchen paper and crush finely.

Add the egg whites and crushed shells to the mixture in the pan and heat, whisking constantly until a good head of foam is produced. The mixture should be hot but not boiling. When the foam begins to form a crust, remove the whisk, but continue to heat the liquid until the crust has risen to the top of the saucepan. Do not allow the liquid to boil.

Pour in the port without disturbing the foam crust. Boil the liquid again until it reaches the top of the pan. Remove the saucepan from the heat, cover and let the contents settle in a warm place for 5 minutes. Meanwhile scald a jelly

bag in boiling water and place it on a stand (see Mrs Beeton's Tip, opposite). Scald two large bowls, placing one of them under the jelly bag.

Strain the settled, clear jelly through the hot jelly bag into the bowl. When all the jelly has passed through the bag, replace the bowl of jelly with the second scalded bowl and strain the jelly again, pouring it very carefully through the foam crust which covers the bottom of the bag and acts as a filter. Repeat, if necessary, until the jelly is clear.

A few drops of food colouring may be added to the jelly at this stage to give a rich colour. Measure 500 ml/17 fl oz of the jelly and set aside. Pour the remaining jelly into a shallow dish and chill until set.

Rinse the jelly mould in cold water. Pour in the liquid port jelly. Leave to set.

Place 30 ml/2 tbsp water in a small bowl and sprinkle the remaining gelatine on to the liquid. Set aside for 15 minutes until the gelatine is spongy. Stand the bowl over a saucepan of hot water and stir the gelatine until it has dissolved completely.

In a bowl, whip the cream until just stiff; stir in the dissolved gelatine, angelica and glacé fruits.

Pour the cream mixture into the mould, on top of the layer of port wine jelly, then chill the dessert until set. Turn out on to a serving dish. Serve, surrounded by cubes of the reserved jelly, if liked.

SERVES FOUR TO SIX

CLARET JELLY

4 lemons
150 g/5 oz sugar
40 g/1½ oz gelatine
whites and shells of 2 eggs
125 ml/4 fl oz claret
few drops of red food colouring

Before you begin, scald a large saucepan, measuring jug, a bowl, a whisk and 900 ml/1½ pint jelly mould in boiling water, as the merest trace of grease may cause cloudiness in the finished jelly.

Pare the rind from two of the lemons; squeeze the juice from all of them into the measuring jug. Make up to 125 ml/4 fl oz with water, if necessary.

Combine the rind, lemon juice, sugar and gelatine in the large pan. Add 625 ml/21 fl oz water.

Put the egg whites into the bowl; wash the shells in cold water, dry with absorbent kitchen paper and crush finely.

Add the egg whites and crushed shells to the mixture in the pan and heat, whisking constantly until a good head of foam is produced. The mixture should be hot but not boiling. When the foam begins to form a crust, remove the whisk, but continue to heat the liquid until the crust has risen to the top of the saucepan. Do not allow the liquid to boil.

Pour in the claret without disturbing the foam crust. Boil the liquid again until it reaches the top of the pan. Remove the saucepan from the heat, cover and let the contents settle in a warm place for 5 minutes. Meanwhile scald a jelly bag in boiling water and place it on a stand (see Mrs Beeton's Tip, page 686). Scald two large bowls; place one under the jelly bag.

Strain the settled, clear jelly through the hot jelly bag into the bowl. When all the jelly has

passed through the bag, replace the bowl of jelly with the second scalded bowl and strain the jelly again, pouring it very carefully through the foam crust which covers the bottom of the bag and acts as a filter.

If the jelly is not clear when looked at in a spoon or glass, the filtering must be carried out again, but avoid doing this too many times, as repeated filtering will cool the jelly and cause some of it to stick to the cloth.

When the jelly is clear, add the colouring. Rinse the jelly mould in cold water. Pour the jelly into the wetted mould and chill until set.

SERVES SIX

FRUIT CHARTREUSE

4 lemons
150 g/5 oz sugar
4 cloves
2.5 cm/1 inch cinnamon stick
40 g/1½ oz gelatine
whites and shells of 2 eggs
30 ml/2 tbsp sherry
100 g/4 oz black grapes, seeded
100 g/4 oz green grapes, seeded
100 g/4 oz tangerine segments

Before you begin, scald a large saucepan, measuring jug, a bowl, a whisk and a 1.1 litre/2 pint ring mould in boiling water, as the merest trace of grease may cause cloudiness in the finished jelly.

Pare the rind from three of the lemons and squeeze the juice from all of them into the measuring jug. Make up to 250 ml/8 fl oz with water, if necessary.

Combine the rind, lemon juice, sugar, cloves, cinnamon stick and gelatine in the large pan. Add 750 ml/1¼ pints water.

Put the egg whites into the bowl; wash the shells in cold water, dry with absorbent kitchen paper and crush finely.

Add the egg whites and crushed shells to the mixture in the pan and heat, whisking constantly until a good head of foam is produced. The mixture should be hot but not boiling. When the foam begins to form a crust, remove the whisk, but continue to heat the liquid until the crust has risen to the top of the pan. Do not allow the liquid to boil. Lower the heat and simmer for 5 minutes.

Remove the saucepan from the heat, cover and let the contents settle in a warm place for 5-10 minutes. Stir in the sherry.

Scald a jelly bag in boiling water and place it on a stand (see Mrs Beeton's Tip, page 686). Scald two large bowls, placing one of them under the jelly bag. Strain the settled, clear jelly through the hot jelly bag into the bowl. When all the jelly has passed through the bag, replace the bowl of jelly with the second scalded bowl and strain the jelly again, pouring it very carefully through the foam crust which covers the bottom of the bag and acts as a filter.

Rinse the ring mould in cold water. Pour enough of the jelly into the wetted mould to cover the base. Chill in the refrigerator until set. Arrange black grapes on the surface, pour on just enough jelly to cover, then leave to set. Add another layer of jelly, leave to set, then arrange a design of green grapes on top. Repeat the process, this time adding a layer of tangerine segments.

Continue adding layers of jelly and fruit until the mould is full, finishing with a layer of jelly. Chill until set, then turn out and decorate with whipped cream or chopped jelly.

SERVES SIX TO EIGHT

BANANA FROTH

The addition of whisked egg whites increases the volume of the jelly while boosting the nutritional value.

20 ml/4 tsp gelatine
100 g/4 oz caster sugar
75 ml/5 tbsp lemon juice
3 egg whites
3 bananas

Place 45 ml/3 tbsp water in a large bowl and sprinkle the gelatine on to the liquid. Set aside for 15 minutes until the gelatine is spongy. Stand the bowl over a saucepan of hot water and stir the gelatine until it has dissolved completely. Add 375 ml/13 fl oz boiling water and the sugar and stir until it has dissolved. Add the lemon juice. Chill the mixture.

When the mixture is beginning to set, remove it from the refrigerator and whisk until frothy. In a clean, grease-free bowl, whisk the egg whites until just stiff; fold them into the jelly.

Slice the bananas and arrange them on the base of a glass serving dish. Pile the whipped jelly mixture on top and chill until firm.

SERVES FOUR TO SIX

BANANA CHARTREUSE

A commercial jelly may be used as the basis of this dessert, but the flavour will be better if a fruit juice jelly is used. When filling the mould, keep the unused jelly at warm room temperature so that it does not set prematurely.

150g/5oz caster sugar
90ml/6tbsp lemon juice
350ml/12floz orange juice
juice of 4 oranges
30ml/2tbsp gelatine
5 bananas
angelica
milk (see method)
250ml/8floz double cream

Put 250ml/8floz water in a saucepan. Add 100g/4oz of the sugar and heat gently, stirring, until the sugar has dissolved.

Set aside 15ml/1tbsp lemon juice in a cup. Add the rest of the lemon juice to the pan with the orange juice. Dissolve 20ml/4tsp of the gelatine in a little of the hot liquid in a small bowl. Cool, then stir into the remaining liquid in the pan.

Rinse a 750ml/1¼ pint mould and line with some of the jelly (see page 802). Chill for 10–20 minutes until set. Slice a banana thinly and arrange overlapping slices in a design on the set jelly. Cut the angelica into leaf shapes and arrange over the bananas. Carefully spoon over just enough of the remaining jelly to cover the decoration. Chill again. When all the jelly in the mould is set, add enough extra jelly to give a total depth of about 10cm/4 inches.

Mash the remaining 4 bananas or process briefly in a blender or food processor. Pour the banana purée into a measuring jug and make up to 250ml/8floz with milk. In a bowl, whip the cream to soft peaks; fold in the banana mixture.

Place 60ml/4tbsp water in a small bowl and sprinkle the remaining gelatine on to the liquid. Set aside for 15 minutes until the gelatine is spongy. Stand the bowl over a saucepan of hot water and stir the gelatine until it has dissolved completely. Remove from the heat and stir in the remaining sugar, with the reserved lemon juice. Set aside.

When the gelatine mixture is cool, but not set, stir it into the banana cream. Pour into the prepared mould and chill until set. Turn out on to a wetted serving plate.

SERVES FOUR

VARIATIONS

250ml/8floz of any fruit purée may be used instead of bananas and milk. Apricots, strawberries and raspberries are particularly suitable.

Iced Specialities

Delicate ice creams, smooth sorbets, refreshing water ices and bombes are all included in this chapter. There are also many recipes for desserts based on ice creams, including Baked Alaska and impressive Knickerbocker Glory.

With the increased ownership of home freezers there has been a tremendous growth in the variety of commercial ice creams that are available. The very best bought ice cream can be very good but, in general, the home-made product is superior. That is if the ice cream is smooth, well flavoured and frozen but not too hard. To achieve an excellent result, follow these guidelines:

- The mixture should be a little sweeter than if it is merely to be served chilled, as the sweetness is lost slightly when the ice cream is frozen.
- The mixture should have a good flavour as this tends to taste slightly weaker when the ice cream is frozen.
- During freezing the ice cream should be beaten, whisked or churned regularly. For the very best results the mixture should be churned continuously until frozen but this is only possible if you own an ice cream maker. When working by hand, the mixture should be whisked when it is first beginning to freeze. It should be whisked at least twice more to remove all ice particles before it is allowed to freeze completely.

Ices that have been thoroughly frozen may be very hard. They should be allowed to stand in the refrigerator for up to 15 minutes before they are served. This will not only serve to soften them, but will also allow the flavours to be fully appreciated.

Lastly remember that home-made ices do not keep as well as commercial products. Most will keep for 2-3 weeks; some for 6-8 weeks.

ICE CREAM MAKERS

There are a number of different ice cream making machines available. The most basic model is a small container with a battery-operated paddle in the middle. The ice cream mixture is placed in the container, the paddle switched on and the appliance put into the freezer. The constant churning of the mixture produces a smooth ice cream but the freezing process takes as long as for a similar mixture whisked by hand.

A more sophisticated ice cream maker is one which allows the ice cream mixture to be churned in a free-standing machine rather than in the freezer. The container of ice cream mixture is placed in an outer, insulated box which holds ice. Once the lid is fitted, the mixture is churned and frozen in about 30–45 minutes.

The most expensive and elaborate ice cream maker combines a small freezing unit in a work-top appliance. These are very large but they produce ice cream extremely quickly.

FREEZING TIMES

It is difficult to estimate the length of time necessary to freeze a mixture. This depends on the freezer as well as on the size and shape of the container. The rule is to make iced desserts at least a day ahead of when they are required to avoid having a part-frozen disaster. Normally, freezing compartments in refrigerators will not freeze an ice cream as quickly as a separate freezer or the freezing compartment of a fridge-freezer.

The recipes usually suggest that the fast-freeze setting, or the lowest setting on the freezer, be used to freeze the ice cream. The quicker the ice cream freezes, the fewer ice crystals are formed. Always check the manufacturer's instructions for using the fast-freeze setting and re-set the freezer to normal setting when the ice cream has frozen.

MEASURING ICE CREAM

When a recipe calls for ready-made ice cream, the amount is expressed in volume form, such as 250 ml/8 fl oz, unless the amount relates directly to a recipe quantity. This corresponds to the method of measuring pack or container sizes for bought ice cream. To measure bought ice cream, compare the pack size with the recipe; to measure home-made ice cream add the volume of liquid to the weight of sugar. Alternatively, pack the ice cream into a chilled measuring jug.

LEMON WATER ICE

Water ices are simple desserts made from fruit or flavoured syrup or a combination of fruit purée and sugar syrup. They are usually beaten halfway through the freezing process, but may be frozen without stirring, in which case they are called granités. When hot syrup is used as the basis for a water ice, it must be allowed to cool before freezing.

6 lemons
2 oranges

SYRUP
350 g/12 oz caster sugar
5 ml/1 tsp liquid glucose

Turn the freezing compartment or freezer to the coldest setting about 1 hour before making the water ice.

Make the syrup. Put the sugar in a heavy-bottomed saucepan with 250 ml/8 fl oz water. Dissolve the sugar over a gentle heat, stirring occasionally. Bring to the boil and boil steadily, without stirring, for about 10 minutes or to a temperature of 110°C/225°F. Remove any scum from the surface.

Strain the syrup into a large bowl and stir in the liquid glucose. Pare the rind very thinly from the lemons and oranges and add to the bowl of syrup. Cover and cool.

Squeeze the fruit and add the juice to the cold syrup mixture. Strain through a nylon sieve into a suitable container for freezing.

Cover the container closely and freeze until half-frozen (when ice crystals appear around the edge of the mixture). Beat the mixture thoroughly, scraping off any crystals. Replace the cover and freeze until solid. Return the freezer to the normal setting.

Transfer the water ice to the refrigerator about 15 minutes before serving, to allow it to soften and 'ripen'. Serve in scoops in individual dishes or glasses.

SERVES SIX

 MRS BEETON'S TIP

If an ice or ice cream is to be made by hand, rather than in a sorbetière or ice cream churn, it is helpful to freeze it in a container which allows for it to be beaten. If there is room in your freezer or freezing compartment, use a deep bowl or box which can be securely closed. A rigid plastic bowl is ideal, since the finished ice or ice cream can be stored in the same container. If your freezing compartment is shallow, or if you wish to freeze the mixture particularly quickly, use a shallow container such as an ice tray, and tip the contents into a chilled bowl for beating.

RASPBERRY WATER ICE

450 g/1 lb ripe raspberries
juice of 2 lemons

SYRUP
225 g/8 oz caster sugar
3.75 ml/¾ tsp liquid glucose

Turn the freezing compartment or freezer to the coldest setting about 1 hour before making the water ice.

Make the syrup. Put the sugar in a heavy-bottomed saucepan with 175 ml/6 fl oz water. Dissolve the sugar over gentle heat, without stirring. Bring the mixture to the boil and boil gently for about 10 minutes or until the mixture registers 110°C/225°F on a sugar thermometer. Remove the scum as it rises in the pan.

Strain the syrup into a large bowl and stir in the liquid glucose. Cover and cool.

Purée the raspberries in a blender or food processor, or rub through a sieve into a bowl. Strain, if necessary, to remove any seeds. Stir in the lemon juice. Stir the mixture into the syrup, then pour into a suitable container for freezing.

Cover the container closely and freeze until half-frozen (when ice crystals appear around the edge of the mixture). Beat the mixture thoroughly, scraping off any crystals. Replace the cover and freeze until solid. Return the freezer to the normal setting.

Transfer the water ice to the refrigerator about 15 minutes before serving, to allow it to soften and 'ripen'. Serve in scoops in individual dishes or glasses.

SERVES SIX

MANDARIN WATER ICE

50 g/2 oz lump sugar
6 mandarins
225 g/8 oz caster sugar
3.75 ml/¾ tsp liquid glucose
2 lemons
2 oranges

Turn the freezing compartment or freezer to the coldest setting about 1 hour before making the water ice.

Rub the sugar lumps over the rind of the mandarins to extract some of the zest. Put the sugar lumps in a heavy-bottomed saucepan with the caster sugar and 300 ml/½ pint water.

Dissolve the sugar over gentle heat, without stirring. Bring the mixture to the boil and boil gently for about 10 minutes or until the mixture registers 110°C/225°F on a sugar thermometer. Remove the scum as it rises in the pan.

Strain the syrup into a large bowl and stir in the liquid glucose. Pare the rind very thinly from 1 lemon and 1 orange and add to the bowl of syrup. Cover and cool.

Squeeze all the fruit and add the juice to the cold syrup mixture. Strain through a nylon sieve into a suitable container. Cover the container closely and freeze until half-frozen (when ice crystals appear around the edge of the mixture). Beat the mixture thoroughly, scraping off any crystals. Replace the cover and freeze until solid. Return the freezer to the normal setting.

Transfer the water ice to the refrigerator about 15 minutes before serving, to allow it to soften and 'ripen'. Serve in scoops in individual dishes or glasses.

SERVES SIX TO EIGHT

BLACKCURRANT WATER ICE

450g/1lb blackcurrants
100g/4oz caster sugar
45ml/3tbsp white rum
mint sprigs to decorate

Turn the freezing compartment or freezer to the coldest setting about 1 hour before making the water ice.

Prepare the fruit and put into a heavy-bottomed saucepan. Add the sugar with 350ml/12fl oz water. Simmer until the fruit is soft.

Purée the blackcurrant mixture in a blender or food processor or rub through a sieve into a clean bowl. Strain if necessary; the mixture should be smooth. Cool.

Pour the blackcurrant mixture into a suitable container for freezing. Cover the container closely and freeze until half-frozen (when ice crystals appear around the edge of the mixture). Beat the mixture thoroughly, scraping off any crystals. Stir in the rum. Replace the cover and freeze until firm. The mixture will not freeze hard. Return the freezer to the normal setting.

Transfer the water ice to the refrigerator about 15 minutes before serving, to allow it to 'ripen'. Serve in scoops in individual dishes or glasses. Decorate with mint.

SERVES SIX TO EIGHT

LEMON SORBET

Traditionally, sorbets were eaten between the entrée and roast courses at a formal dinner, to cleanse the palate.

10ml/2tsp gelatine
150g/5oz caster sugar
2.5ml/½tsp grated lemon rind
250ml/8fl oz lemon juice
2 egg whites

Turn the freezing compartment or freezer to the coldest setting about 1 hour before making the sorbet.

Place 30ml/2tbsp water in a small bowl and sprinkle the gelatine on to the liquid. Set aside for 15 minutes until the gelatine is spongy. Stand the bowl over a pan of hot water; stir the gelatine until it has dissolved.

Put the sugar in a heavy-bottomed saucepan with 200ml/7fl oz water. Dissolve the sugar over gentle heat, without stirring. Bring the mixture to the boil and boil gently for about 10 minutes. Stir the dissolved gelatine into the syrup, with the lemon rind and juice. Cover and cool.

Pour the cool syrup mixture into a suitable container for freezing. Cover the container closely and freeze until half-frozen.

In a clean, grease-free bowl, whisk the egg whites until stiff. Beat the sorbet mixture until smooth, scraping off any ice crystals. Fold in the egg whites, replace the cover on the bowl and freeze. The mixture should be firm enough to scoop; it will not freeze hard. Return the freezer to the normal setting.

Serve straight from the freezer, in dishes, glasses or lemon shells.

SERVES SIX TO EIGHT

PINEAPPLE SORBET

200 g/7 oz lump sugar
250 ml/8 fl oz pineapple juice
2 egg whites

Turn the freezing compartment or freezer to the coldest setting about 1 hour before making the sorbet.

Put the sugar in a heavy-bottomed saucepan with 500 ml/17 fl oz water. Dissolve the sugar over gentle heat, without stirring. Bring the mixture to the boil and boil gently for about 10 minutes or until the mixtures registers 110°C/225°F on a sugar thermometer. Remove the scum as it rises in the pan. Strain into a bowl, cover and leave to cool.

Add the pineapple juice to the syrup and pour into a suitable container for freezing. Cover the container closely and freeze until half-frozen.

In a clean, grease-free bowl, whisk the egg whites until stiff. Beat the sorbet mixture until smooth, scraping off any ice crystals. Fold in the egg whites, replace the cover on the bowl and freeze. The mixture should be firm enough to scoop; it will not freeze hard. Return the freezer to the normal setting.

Serve straight from the freezer, either in individual dishes or glasses, or in scoops in a decorative bowl.

SERVES SIX

VANILLA ICE CREAM

30 ml/2 tbsp custard powder
500 ml/17 fl oz milk
100 g/4 oz caster sugar
125 ml/4 fl oz double cream
5 ml/1 tsp vanilla essence

Turn the freezing compartment or freezer to the coldest setting about 1 hour before making the ice cream.

In a bowl, mix the custard powder to a cream with a little of the milk. Bring the remaining milk to the boil in a saucepan, then pour it into the bowl, stirring constantly.

Return the custard mixture to the clean pan and simmer, stirring all the time, until thickened. Stir in the sugar, cover closely with dampened greaseproof paper and set aside to cool.

In a large bowl, whip the cream to soft peaks. Add the cold custard and vanilla essence. Spoon into a suitable container for freezing. Cover the container closely and freeze until half-frozen (when ice crystals appear around the edge of the mixture). Beat the mixture until smooth, scraping off any crystals. Replace the cover and freeze until firm. Return the freezer to the normal setting.

Transfer the ice cream to the refrigerator about 15 minutes before serving, to allow it to soften and 'ripen'. Serve in scoops in individual dishes or in a large decorative bowl.

SERVES SIX

RICH VANILLA ICE CREAM

500 ml/17 fl oz milk
3 eggs
175 g/6 oz caster sugar
250 ml/8 fl oz double cream
5 ml/1 tsp vanilla essence

Turn the freezing compartment or freezer to the coldest setting about 1 hour before making the ice cream.

In a saucepan, bring the milk to just below boiling point. Put the eggs into a bowl with 100 g/4 oz of the sugar. Mix well, then stir in the scalded milk. Strain the custard mixture into a heavy-bottomed saucepan or a heatproof bowl placed over a saucepan of simmering water. Alternatively, use a double saucepan, but make sure the water does not touch the upper pan.

Cook the custard over very gentle heat for 15–25 minutes, stirring all the time with a wooden spoon, until the custard coats the back of the spoon. Strain into a bowl, cover closely with damp greaseproof paper and cool.

In a large bowl, whip the cream to soft peaks. Add the cold custard, vanilla essence and remaining sugar. Stir lightly. Spoon into a suitable container for freezing.

Cover the container closely and freeze until half-frozen (when ice crystals appear around the edge of the mixture). Beat the mixture until smooth, scraping off any crystals. Replace the cover and freeze until firm. Return the freezer to the normal setting.

Transfer the ice cream to the refrigerator about 15 minutes before serving, and allow it to soften and 'ripen'. Serve in scoops in individual dishes or in a large decorative bowl.

SERVES SIX TO EIGHT

BROWN BREAD ICE CREAM

150 g/5 oz fresh brown breadcrumbs
3 egg whites
100 g/4 oz caster sugar
350 ml/12 fl oz double cream

Turn the freezing compartment or freezer to the coldest setting about 1 hour before making the ice cream.

Set the oven at 120°C/250°F/gas ½. Spread the breadcrumbs on a baking sheet and bake in the oven until golden brown, stirring occasionally. Set aside until cool.

In a clean, grease-free bowl, whisk the egg whites until stiff. Gradually whisk in the caster sugar. In a second bowl, whip the cream to soft peaks.

Fold the breadcrumbs and whipped cream into the whisked egg whites; spoon into a 1.1 litre/2 pint pudding basin. Cover and freeze until firm. Return the freezer to the normal setting.

Invert the ice cream on a serving plate while still frozen. Allow it to soften and 'ripen' in the refrigerator for about 15 minutes before serving.

SERVES SIX TO EIGHT

TEA ICE CREAM

250 ml/8 fl oz hot strong tea
175 g/6 oz caster sugar
30 ml/2 tbsp custard powder
500 ml/17 fl oz milk
75 ml/3 fl oz single cream

Turn the freezing compartment or freezer to the coldest setting about 1 hour before making the ice cream.

Strain the tea into a bowl, stir in 50 g/2 oz of the caster sugar and leave to cool.

In a bowl, mix the custard powder to a cream with a little of the milk. Bring the remaining milk to the boil in a saucepan, then pour it into the bowl, stirring constantly.

Return the custard mixture to the clean pan and simmer, stirring all the time, until thickened. Stir in the remaining sugar and pour the mixture into a large bowl. Cover closely with dampened greaseproof paper and set aside to cool completely.

Stir the custard and gradually add the cold tea and cream. Pour into a suitable container for freezing. Cover the container closely and freeze until half-frozen (when ice crystals appear around the edge of the mixture). Beat the mixture until smooth, scraping off any crystals. Replace the cover and freeze until firm. Return the freezer to the normal setting.

Transfer the ice cream to the refrigerator about 15 minutes before serving, to allow it to soften and 'ripen'. Serve in scoops in individual dishes or in a large decorative bowl, with sponge fingers.

SERVES SIX

WALNUT ICE CREAM

750 ml/1¼ pints milk
4 eggs, plus 1 yolk
150 g/5 oz caster sugar
100 g/4 oz walnuts
10 ml/2 tsp orange flower water
5 ml/1 tsp vanilla essence

Turn the freezing compartment or freezer to the coldest setting about 1 hour before making the ice cream.

In a saucepan, bring the milk to just below boiling point. Put the eggs and egg yolk into a bowl with the sugar. Mix well, then stir in the scalded milk. Strain the custard mixture into a heavy-bottomed saucepan or a heatproof bowl placed over a saucepan of simmering water.

Cook the custard over very gentle heat for 15-25 minutes, stirring all the time with a wooden spoon, until the custard coats the back of the spoon. Strain into a bowl, cover with dampened greaseproof paper; cool.

Chop and pound the nuts on a board or in a food processor, gradually adding the orange flower water to prevent them oiling.

Stir the vanilla essence into the cold custard. Spoon into a suitable container for freezing. Cover the container closely and freeze until half-frozen (when ice crystals appear around the edge of the mixture). Beat the mixture until smooth, scraping off any crystals. Stir in the walnuts, replace the cover and freeze until firm. Return the freezer to the normal setting.

Transfer the ice cream to the refrigerator about 15 minutes before serving, to allow it to soften and 'ripen'. Serve in scoops in individual dishes or in a large bowl.

SERVES SIX

BLACKCURRANT ICE CREAM

15 ml/1 tbsp custard powder
250 ml/8 fl oz milk
75 g/3 oz caster sugar
200 g/7 oz ripe blackcurrants
grated rind and juice of 1 lemon
red food colouring
125 ml/4 fl oz double cream

Turn the freezing compartment or freezer to the coldest setting about 1 hour before making the ice cream.

In a bowl, mix the custard powder to a cream with a little of the milk. Bring the remaining milk to the boil in a saucepan, then pour it into the bowl, stirring constantly.

Return the custard mixture to the clean pan and simmer, stirring all the time, until thickened. Stir in 50 g/2 oz of the sugar, cover closely with dampened greaseproof paper and cool.

Meanwhile put the blackcurrants into a saucepan with the remaining sugar. Add 125 ml/4 fl oz water, the lemon rind and juice and a few drops of red food colouring. Simmer until the fruit is tender. Purée the fruit mixture in a blender or food processor or rub through a nylon sieve into a clean bowl. Set aside to cool.

When both mixtures are cool, combine them in a suitable container for freezing. Cover the container closely and freeze until half-frozen.

Whip the cream in a bowl. Beat the ice cream mixture until smooth, scraping off any ice crystals, then fold in the whipped cream. Replace the cover on the container and freeze until firm. Return the freezer to the normal setting.

Transfer the ice cream to the refrigerator about 15 minutes before serving, to allow it to soften and 'ripen'. Serve in scoops in individual dishes or in a decorative bowl.

SERVES SIX

APRICOT ICE CREAM

15 ml/1 tbsp custard powder
250 ml/8 fl oz milk
150 g/5 oz caster sugar
300 g/11 oz fresh apricots, halved and stoned
grated rind and juice of 1 lemon
yellow food colouring
125 ml/4 fl oz double cream

Turn the freezing compartment or freezer to the coldest setting about 1 hour before making the ice cream.

In a bowl, mix the custard powder to a cream with a little of the milk. Bring the remaining milk to the boil in a saucepan, then pour it into the bowl, stirring constantly.

Return the custard mixture to the clean saucepan and simmer, stirring all the time, until thickened. Stir in 50 g/2 oz of the sugar, cover closely with dampened greaseproof paper and set aside to cool.

Meanwhile put the apricots into a saucepan with the remaining sugar. Add 125 ml/4 fl oz water, the lemon rind and juice and a few drops of yellow food colouring. Simmer until the fruit is tender. Purée the fruit mixture. Cool.

When both mixtures are cool, combine them in a suitable container for freezing. Cover the container closely and freeze until half-frozen.

Whip the cream in a bowl. Beat the ice cream mixture until smooth, scraping off any ice crystals, then fold in the whipped cream. Replace the cover on the container and freeze until firm. Return the freezer to the normal setting.

Transfer the ice cream to the refrigerator about 15 minutes before serving, to allow it to soften and 'ripen'. Serve in scoops in individual dishes or in a large bowl.

SERVES SIX

BURNT ALMOND ICE CREAM

50 g/2 oz shredded almonds
12 egg yolks
175 g/6 oz caster sugar
1.1 litres/2 pints single cream
50 g/2 oz lump sugar
15 ml/1 tbsp kirsch

Turn the freezing compartment or freezer to the coldest setting about 1 hour before making the ice cream.

Spread the shredded almonds out on a baking sheet and toast under a preheated grill until brown (see Mrs Beeton's Tip).

Combine the egg yolks and caster sugar in a deep bowl and beat together until very thick. Put 1 litre/1¾ pints of the cream in a saucepan and bring slowly to the boil. Pour the cream over the yolks and sugar, stirring well. Return the mixture to the clean pan. Cook, stirring constantly, until the custard thickens. Do not allow it to boil. Pour the thickened custard into a large heatproof bowl and keep hot over a saucepan of simmering water.

Put the lump sugar into a small heavy-bottomed saucepan. Add a few drops of water and heat gently until melted, then boil until the syrup is a deep golden colour. Remove from the heat, carefully add the remaining cream and beat gently. Stir this caramel mixture into the hot custard. Cover closely with dampened greaseproof paper and set aside to cool.

> **MRS BEETON'S TIP**
>
> Shake the baking sheet frequently when cooking the almonds so that they brown evenly. Watch them closely; almonds scorch very quickly if left unattended.

When the custard is quite cold, stir in the almonds and kirsch. Spoon into a suitable container for freezing. Cover the container closely and freeze until half-frozen (when ice crystals appear around the edge of the mixture). Beat the mixture until smooth, scraping off any crystals. Replace the cover and freeze until firm. Return the freezer to the normal setting.

Transfer the ice cream to the refrigerator about 15 minutes before serving, to allow it to soften and 'ripen'. Serve in scoops in individual dishes or in a large decorative bowl.

SERVES EIGHT TO TEN

VARIATIONS

Burnt Almond Ice Cream with Orange   Add the grated rind of 1 orange to the egg yolks and caster sugar when making the ice cream. If you like, the ice cream may be served with a salad of fresh oranges. Simply remove all peel and pith from the oranges, then slice the fruit removing the pips. Place the slices in a bowl and sprinkle with sweet sherry or orange liqueur.

Chocolate Chip and Burnt Almond Ice Cream   Add 100 g/4 oz plain or milk chocolate chips to the cold custard with the almonds and kirsch.

CARAMEL ICE CREAM

750 ml/1¼ pints milk
3 eggs, plus 12 egg yolks
175 g/6 oz caster sugar
50 g/2 oz lump sugar
100 ml/3½ fl oz single cream

Turn the freezing compartment or freezer to the coldest setting about 1 hour before making the ice cream.

Heat the milk in a heavy-bottomed saucepan until just below boiling point. Beat the eggs and egg yolks with the caster sugar in a large bowl until thick and white, then add the hot milk, stirring well. Return the mixture to the clean pan and cook over gentle heat, stirring constantly, until the custard thickens. Do not allow it to boil. Pour the thickened custard into a large heatproof bowl and keep it hot over a saucepan of simmering water.

Put the lump sugar into a small heavy-bottomed pan. Add a few drops of water and heat gently until dissolved, then boil until the syrup is a deep golden colour. Remove from the heat, carefully add the cream and beat gently. Return the pan to the heat. As soon as the mixture starts to rise in the pan, stir it into the hot custard. Cover closely with dampened greaseproof paper and cool.

Spoon the cold mixture into a suitable container for freezing. Cover the container closely and freeze until half-frozen (when ice crystals appear around the edge of the mixture). Beat the mixture until smooth, scraping off any crystals. Replace the cover and freeze until firm. Return the freezer to the normal setting.

Transfer the ice cream to the refrigerator about 15 minutes before serving, to allow it to soften and 'ripen'. Serve in scoops in individual dishes or in a large bowl.

SERVES EIGHT TO TEN

RICH CHOCOLATE ICE CREAM

4 egg yolks
50 g/2 oz caster sugar
250 ml/8 fl oz single cream
100 g/4 oz plain chocolate, in squares
125 ml/4 fl oz double cream
5 ml/1 tsp vanilla essence

Turn the freezing compartment or freezer to the coldest setting about 1 hour before making the ice cream.

Combine the egg yolks and caster sugar in a deep bowl and beat together until very thick. Put the single cream in a saucepan and bring slowly to the boil. Pour the cream over the yolks and sugar, stirring well. Return the mixture to the clean pan. Cook, stirring, until the custard thickens. Do not allow it to boil. Pour the thickened custard into a heatproof bowl and keep hot over a pan of simmering water.

Put the chocolate in a heatproof bowl and add 65 ml/2½ fl oz water. Bring a saucepan of water to the boil, remove it from the heat, and set the bowl over the hot water until the chocolate has melted. Stir, then add the chocolate mixture to the hot custard; mix lightly. Cover closely with dampened greaseproof paper and cool.

In a bowl, whip the double cream until thick. Fold it into the cool chocolate custard, with the vanilla essence. Spoon into a suitable container for freezing. Cover the container closely and freeze until half-frozen (when ice crystals appear around the edge of the mixture). Beat the mixture until smooth. Replace the cover and freeze until firm. Return the freezer to the normal setting.

Transfer the ice cream to the refrigerator about 15 minutes before serving, to allow it to soften and 'ripen'.

SERVES SIX

COFFEE ICE CREAM

45 ml/3 tbsp instant coffee powder
300 ml/½ pint double cream
75 g/3 oz caster sugar

Turn the freezing compartment or freezer to the coldest setting about 1 hour before making the ice cream.

Pour 60 ml/4 tbsp boiling water into a cup, add the instant coffee and stir until dissolved. Set aside until cool.

Whip the cream in a bowl until stiff. Stir in the sugar and fold in the dissolved coffee. Spoon into a suitable container for freezing. Cover the container closely and freeze until half frozen (when ice crystals appear around the edge of the mixture). Beat the mixture until smooth, scraping off any crystals. Replace the cover and freeze until firm. Return the freezer to the normal setting.

Transfer the ice cream to the refrigerator about 15 minutes before serving, to allow it to soften and 'ripen'. Serve in individual dishes or in a large bowl.

SERVES FOUR

MOCHA ICE CREAM

50 g/2 oz caster sugar
30 ml/2 tbsp instant coffee powder
150 g/5 oz plain chocolate, in squares
3 egg yolks
250 ml/8 fl oz double cream

Turn the freezing compartment or freezer to the coldest setting about 1 hour before making the ice cream.

Mix the sugar and coffee powder in a saucepan. Add 30 ml/2 tbsp water and bring to the boil. Boil for 1 minute, then remove from the heat and add the chocolate. When the chocolate has melted, stir lightly, then set the pan aside.

When the chocolate mixture is cool, stir in the egg yolks. In a bowl, whip the cream to soft peaks. Fold in the chocolate mixture.

Spoon into a suitable container for freezing. Cover the container closely with foil; freeze until half-frozen (when ice crystals appear around the edge of the mixture). Tip the mixture into a bowl and beat until smooth, scraping off any crystals. Freeze until firm. Return the freezer to the normal setting.

Transfer the ice cream to the refrigerator about 15 minutes before serving, to allow it to soften and 'ripen'. Serve in scoops in individual dishes or in a large bowl.

SERVES FOUR

 MRS BEETON'S TIP

An ice cream scoop is a useful piece of equipment. Dip it into tepid water before use, and dip again after each scoop.

WHITE MAGIC

15–30 ml/1–2 tbsp freshly roasted coffee
  beans
500 ml/17 fl oz milk
2 eggs, plus 8 egg yolks
100 g/4 oz caster sugar
125 ml/4 fl oz double cream

Turn the freezing compartment or freezer to the coldest setting about 1 hour before making the ice cream.

Combine the coffee beans and milk in the top of a double saucepan. Bring to just below boiling point. Place the pan over hot water and leave to infuse for 1 hour.

Strain the milk into a clean pan, discarding the coffee beans. Heat the flavoured milk until just below boiling point. Beat the eggs, egg yolks and sugar in a large bowl until thick and white, then add the hot milk, stirring well. Return the mixture to the clean pan and cook the custard over very gentle heat, stirring constantly, until it thickens. Do not allow it to boil. Cover the coffee-flavoured custard closely with dampened greaseproof paper and cool.

In a large bowl, whip the cream to soft peaks. Add the cold coffee custard. Spoon into a suitable container for freezing. Cover the container closely and freeze until half-frozen (when ice crystals appear around the edge of the mixture). Beat the mixture until smooth. Freeze until firm. Return the freezer to the normal setting.

Transfer the ice cream to the refrigerator about 15 minutes before serving, to allow it to soften and 'ripen'. Serve in scoops in individual dishes or in a large bowl.

SERVES EIGHT TO TEN

GINGER ICE CREAM

125 ml/4 fl oz milk
3 egg yolks
75 g/3 oz caster sugar
75 g/3 oz preserved ginger in syrup
60 ml/4 tbsp ginger syrup (from the jar of
  preserved ginger)
10 ml/2 tsp ground ginger
250 ml/8 fl oz double cream

Turn the freezing compartment or freezer to the coldest setting about 1 hour before making the ice cream.

In a saucepan, bring the milk to just below boiling point. Put the egg yolks into a bowl with 25 g/1 oz of the sugar. Mix well, then stir in the scalded milk. Return the mixture to the clean pan and cook gently, stirring constantly, until the custard coats the back of a wooden spoon. Do not allow it to boil. Cover the custard closely with dampened greaseproof paper and set aside to cool.

Dice the preserved ginger. Heat the ginger syrup in a small saucepan and stir in the ground ginger until dissolved.

In a large bowl, whip the cream until stiff. Add the custard, diced ginger, syrup mixture and remaining sugar. Mix lightly. Spoon into a suitable container for freezing. Cover the container closely and freeze until half-frozen (when ice crystals appear around the edge of the mixture). Beat the mixture until smooth, scraping off any crystals. Replace the cover and freeze until firm. Return the freezer to the normal setting.

Transfer the ice cream to the refrigerator about 15 minutes before serving, to allow it to soften and 'ripen'. Serve in scoops in individual dishes or in a large decorative bowl.

SERVES SIX

LEMON ICE CREAM

8 egg yolks
200g/7oz caster sugar
juice of 2 lemons
250ml/8fl oz double cream

Turn the freezing compartment or freezer to the coldest setting about 1 hour before making the ice cream.

In a bowl, beat the egg yolks until very thick. Add the caster sugar and beat again. Stir in the lemon juice.

Whip the cream to soft peaks in a deep bowl, then add carefully to the egg and sugar mixture. Spoon into a suitable container for freezing. Cover the container closely and freeze until half-frozen (when ice crystals appear around the edge of the mixture). Beat the mixture until smooth, scraping off any crystals. Replace the cover and freeze until firm. Return the freezer to the normal setting.

Transfer the ice cream to the refrigerator about 15 minutes before serving, to allow it to soften and 'ripen'. Serve in scoops in individual dishes or in a large decorative bowl.

SERVES SIX

STRAWBERRY LICK

400g/14oz ripe strawberries, hulled
15ml/1tbsp granulated sugar
125ml/4fl oz milk
250ml/8fl oz double cream
2 egg yolks
150g/5oz caster sugar
5ml/1tsp lemon juice
red food colouring

Turn the freezing compartment or freezer to the coldest setting about 1 hour before making the ice cream. Rub the strawberries through a nylon sieve into a bowl. Stir in the granulated sugar and set aside.

Combine the milk and cream in a saucepan and bring to just below boiling point. Beat the egg yolks with the caster sugar until thick and creamy, and stir in the milk and cream.

Return the custard mixture to the clean pan and simmer, stirring all the time, until thickened. Pour into a large bowl and stir in the strawberry purée and lemon juice. Tint pale pink with the food colouring.

Spoon the mixture into a suitable container for freezing. Cover the container closely and freeze until half-frozen (when ice crystals appear around the edge of the mixture). Beat the mixture until smooth, scraping off any crystals. Replace the cover and freeze until firm. Return the freezer to the normal setting.

Transfer the ice cream to the refrigerator about 15 minutes before serving, to allow it to soften and 'ripen'. Serve in scoops in individual dishes or a large bowl.

SERVES SIX

BOMBE CZARINE

A bombe is a moulded ice cream dessert. It usually consists of an outer shell of one flavour, with an inner core made from either a contrasting ice cream or a mousse mixture. There may be several layers, or the bombe may be made from a single flavour of ice cream, perhaps with the addition of crushed biscuits, praline or crumbled meringue.

1 quantity Vanilla Ice Cream (page 829)

FILLING
125 ml/4 fl oz double cream
25 g/1 oz icing sugar, sifted
2 egg whites
5 ml/1 tsp kummel or liqueur of own choice

Turn the freezing compartment or freezer to the coldest setting about 1 hour before making the bombe. Chill 2 bowls; a 1.4 litre/2½ pint pudding basin or bombe mould, and a smaller 600 ml/1 pint bowl.

Make the vanilla ice cream and freeze until half-frozen (when ice crystals appear around the edge of the mixture). Beat the mixture until smooth, scraping off any crystals.

Spoon a layer of the vanilla ice cream into the chilled mould. Centre the smaller bowl inside the mould, with its rim on a level with the top of the mould. Fill the space between the outer mould and the inner bowl with vanilla ice cream. Cover the mould and freeze until firm. Reserve any remaining ice cream in the freezer.

Meanwhile prepare the filling. In a bowl, whip the cream with half the sugar. Put the egg whites in a second, grease-free bowl and whisk until stiff. Fold in the remaining sugar. Carefully mix the cream and egg whites and add the liqueur. Chill lightly.

When the vanilla ice cream is firm, remove the bowl from the centre of the mould (filling it with warm water if necessary to dislodge it).

Fill the centre of the ice cream mould with the liqueur mixture, covering it with any remaining ice cream.

Put on the lid on the bombe mould or cover the basin with foil. Freeze until firm. Return the freezer to the normal setting. To turn out, dip the mould or basin in cold water, and invert on to a chilled serving dish. Transfer to the refrigerator 15 minutes before serving, to allow the ice cream to soften and 'ripen'.

SERVES SIX TO EIGHT

VARIATIONS

Bombe Zamora Use coffee ice cream instead of vanilla to line the mould, and flavour the filling with curaçao.

Bombe Nesselrode As above, but add 60 ml/4 tbsp chestnut purée to the filling, which should be flavoured with kirsch instead of kummel or other liqueur.

BOMBE DIPLOMATE

1 quantity Vanilla Ice Cream (page 829)

FILLING
50 g/2 oz crystallized fruit, chopped
30 ml/2 tbsp maraschino liqueur
125 ml/4 fl oz double cream
25 g/1 oz icing sugar, sifted
2 egg whites

Turn the freezing compartment or freezer to the coldest setting about 1 hour before making the bombe. Chill two bowls; a 1.4 litre/2½ pint pudding basin or bombe mould, and a smaller 600 ml/1 pint bowl.

Make the vanilla ice cream and freeze until half-frozen (when ice crystals appear around the edge of the mixture). Beat the mixture until smooth.

Spoon a layer of the vanilla ice cream into the chilled mould. Centre the smaller bowl inside the mould, with its rim on a level with the top of the mould. Fill the space between the outer mould and the inner bowl with vanilla ice cream. Cover and freeze until firm.

Meanwhile prepare the filling. Put the chopped crystallized fruit into a shallow dish. Pour the liqueur over and set aside for 30 minutes to macerate.

In a bowl, whip the cream with half the sugar. Put the egg whites in a second, grease-free bowl and whisk until stiff. Fold in the remaining sugar. Carefully mix the cream and egg whites together, and add the crystallized fruit, with the liqueur used for soaking. Chill lightly.

When the vanilla ice cream is firm, remove the bowl from the centre of the mould (filling it with warm water if necessary to dislodge it). Fill the centre of the ice cream mould with the maraschino and fruit mixture, covering it with any remaining ice cream.

Put the lid on the bombe mould or cover the basin with foil. Freeze until firm. Return the freezer to the normal setting. To turn out, dip the mould or basin in cold water, and invert on to a chilled serving dish. Transfer to the refrigerator 15 minutes before serving to allow the ice cream to soften and 'ripen'.

SERVES SIX TO EIGHT

BOMBE TORTONI

This is absurdly easy to make, yet it makes an impressive finale for a dinner party.

300 ml/½ pint double cream
150 ml/¼ pint single cream
50 g/2 oz icing sugar, sifted
2.5 ml/½ tsp vanilla essence
2 egg whites
100 g/4 oz hazelnut biscuits or ratafias, crushed
30 ml/2 tbsp sherry

Turn the freezing compartment or freezer to the coldest setting about 1 hour before making the bombe. Lightly oil a 1.25 litre/2½ pint bombe mould or pudding basin.

Combine the creams in a large bowl and whip until thick, adding half the icing sugar. Add the vanilla essence.

In a clean, grease-free bowl, whisk the egg whites until stiff. Fold in the remaining icing sugar.

Lightly fold the meringue mixture into the whipped cream. Stir in the hazelnut biscuits and sherry. Spoon the mixture into the prepared mould.

Put the lid on the bombe mould or cover the basin with foil. Freeze until firm, then return the freezer to the normal setting. To turn out, dip the mould or basin in cold water, and invert on to a chilled serving dish. Transfer to the refrigerator 15 minutes before serving to allow the ice cream to soften and 'ripen'.

SERVES SIX TO EIGHT

VARIATIONS

Try crushed ginger biscuits with coffee liqueur instead of sherry, or crumbled meringue with cherry brandy.

NEAPOLITAN ICE

250 ml/8 fl oz milk
1 egg, plus 4 egg yolks
150 g/5 oz caster sugar
250 ml/8 fl oz double cream
125 ml/4 fl oz strawberry or raspberry purée
red food colouring (optional)
1.25 ml/¼ tsp almond or ratafia essence
green food colouring
10 ml/2 tsp vanilla essence

Turn the freezing compartment or freezer to the coldest setting about 1 hour before making the ice cream.

Heat the milk in a heavy-bottomed saucepan until just below boiling point. Beat the egg and egg yolks with 50 g/2 oz of the caster sugar in a bowl until thick and white, then add the hot milk, stirring well. Return the mixture to the clean pan and cook over gentle heat, stirring constantly, until the custard thickens. Do not allow it to boil. Pour the thickened custard into a large bowl. Cover with dampened grease-proof paper and allow to cool.

In a separate bowl, whip the cream to soft peaks. Fold it into the cold custard. Divide the mixture equally between three bowls. To one bowl add the fruit purée, with 25 g/1 oz of the remaining sugar and a few drops of red food colouring if necessary. Add the almond or ratafia essence to the second bowl and tint it a bright but not vivid green. Stir in half the remaining sugar. To the third bowl add the vanilla essence and the rest of the sugar.

Pour the contents of each bowl into a separate ice tray. Cover and freeze until almost firm, then pack in layers in a suitable square or oblong mould. Cover and freeze until solid. Return the freezer to the normal setting. To serve, cut the block of ice cream in slices.

SERVES SIX

COTTAGE YOGURT ICE CREAM

This is a good choice for slimmers. Serve it with fresh strawberries or raspberries.

225 g/8 oz plain cottage cheese
125 ml/4 fl oz thick plain yogurt
30 ml/2 tbsp liquid honey

Turn the freezing compartment or freezer to the coldest setting about 1 hour before making the ice cream.

Sieve the cheese into a bowl. Gently stir in the yogurt and honey. Spoon into a suitable container for freezing, allowing at least 2.5 cm/1 inch headspace (see Mrs Beeton's Tip, page 692). Leave to stand for 30 minutes.

Cover the container closely and freeze until ice crystals appear around the edge of the mixture. Beat the mixture until smooth, scraping off any crystals. Replace the cover and freeze until firm. Return the freezer to the normal setting.

If left in the freezer, the ice cream will get progressively harder. To obtain the right consistency it will need to be thawed for 2–4 hours at room temperature, then returned to the freezer for about 30 minutes.

SERVES FOUR

JAPANESE PLOMBIERE

A plombière is an ice cream mixture containing almonds or chestnuts. It may be frozen in a decorative mould but is more often scooped into balls and piled up to form a pyramid. It is often served with a sauce poured over the top.

50 g/2 oz apricot jam
few drops of lemon juice
8 egg yolks
100 g/4 oz caster sugar
500 ml/17 fl oz single cream
2.5 ml/½ tsp vanilla essence
100 g/4 oz ground almonds
250 ml/8 fl oz double cream
100 g/4 oz almond macaroons, crushed
12 ratafias to decorate

Turn the freezing compartment or freezer to the coldest setting about 1 hour before making the ice cream.

Make an apricot marmalade by boiling the apricot jam in a small saucepan with a few drops of lemon juice until thick. Keep a little aside for decoration and sieve the rest into a bowl.

Combine the egg yolks and caster sugar in a deep bowl and beat together until very thick. Put the single cream in a saucepan and bring slowly to the boil. Pour the cream over the yolks and sugar, stirring well. Return the mixture to the clean pan. Cook, stirring constantly, until the custard thickens. Do not allow it to boil. Pour the thickened custard into a large bowl and stir in the sieved apricot marmalade, the vanilla essence and the ground almonds. Cover closely with dampened greaseproof paper and cool.

In a bowl, whip the double cream to the same consistency as the custard. Fold it into the custard, with the crushed macaroons. Spoon the mixture into a suitable container for freez-

ing (a bowl that is deep enough to allow the ice cream to be scooped is ideal). Freeze the mixture until firm.

To serve, scoop into balls, arranging these as a pyramid on a chilled plate. Drizzle the reserved apricot marmalade over the top and decorate with the ratafias.

SERVES SIX TO EIGHT

 MICROWAVE TIP

The apricot marmalade may be prepared in a small bowl in the microwave. It will only require about 30 seconds on High. Reheat it, if necessary, before pouring it over the ice cream pyramid.

VANILLA PLOMBIERE

1 quantity Vanilla Ice Cream (page 695)
125 ml/4 fl oz double cream
50 g/2 oz flaked almonds

Make the ice cream and freeze it until firm in a suitable container.

In a bowl, whip the cream to soft peaks. Beat the ice cream until smooth, scraping off any ice crystals, then fold in the whipped cream and almonds. Spoon into a suitable container, cover and freeze the ice cream until firm.

If the ice cream has been made in a mould or basin, turn it out on to a chilled plate and transfer it to the refrigerator about 15 minutes before serving, to allow it to soften and 'ripen'. If a plastic box or bowl has been used, scoop the ice cream into balls and form these into a pyramid on a dish.

SERVES SIX

NESSELRODE PUDDING

24 chestnuts
250 ml/8 fl oz milk
4 egg yolks
150 g/5 oz caster sugar
250 ml/8 fl oz double cream
vanilla essence
50 g/2 oz glacé cherries

Turn the freezing compartment or freezer to the coldest setting about 1 hour before making the pudding.

Using a sharp knife, make a small slit in the rounded side of the shell of each chestnut. Bring a saucepan of water to the boil, add the chestnuts and boil for 5 minutes. Drain. Peel the chestnuts while still very hot. Return them to the clean pan and add 125 ml/4 fl oz of the milk. Simmer gently until the chestnuts are tender, then rub them through a fine sieve into a bowl.

Put the egg yolks in a bowl and beat lightly. Pour the rest of the milk into a saucepan and bring to just below boiling point. Pour the milk on to the egg yolks, stirring well. Return the mixture to the clean pan and simmer, stirring constantly, until the custard thickens. Do not let it boil.

Remove the custard from the heat and stir in the chestnut purée and the sugar. Leave until cool.

In a bowl, whip half the cream to soft peaks. Add to the chestnut mixture with a few drops of vanilla essence. Pour into a a suitable bowl for freezing, cover and freeze until half-frozen (when ice crystals appear around the edge of the mixture).

Meanwhile rinse the cherries, pat dry on absorbent kitchen paper, and chop finely. In a bowl, whip the remaining cream until stiff.

Beat the ice cream mixture until smooth, scraping off the crystals. Stir in the chopped cherries

and fold in the whipped cream. Return to the freezer until almost set, stirring the mixture frequently. Press into a 750 ml/1¼ pint mould, cover, and return to the freezer until firm. Return the freezer to the normal setting.

Transfer the pudding to the refrigerator about 15 minutes before serving, to allow it to soften and 'ripen'.

SERVES SIX

OMELETTE SOUFFLE EN SURPRISE

Not an omelette, but a liqueur-soaked cake whose hot soufflé topping hides a layer of ice cream.

15 ml/1 tbsp Grand Marnier or liqueur of
**   own choice**
1 egg, separated, plus 2 whites
50 g/2 oz caster sugar
vanilla essence
1 quantity Vanilla Ice Cream (page 695)
icing sugar for dredging
glacé cherries and angelica to decorate

CAKE
fat for greasing
2 eggs
50 g/2 oz caster sugar
few drops of vanilla essence
50 g/2 oz plain flour, sifted
30 ml/2 tbsp melted butter, cooled

Make the cake several hours before you intend to serve the dessert. Line and grease a 20 cm/ 8 inch sandwich cake tin. Set the oven at 180°C/350°F/gas 4.

Combine the eggs, sugar and vanilla essence in a heatproof bowl. Place over a saucepan of simmering water and whisk until the mixture is thick, pale lemon in colour, and has doubled in bulk. This will take 6-8 minutes. Remove the bowl from the heat and continue to beat until cooled and very thick.

Working swiftly and lightly, fold in the flour, then the butter. Spoon into the prepared tin and bake for 25-30 minutes or until cooked through and firm to the touch. Cool on a wire rack.

Set the oven at 230°C/450°F/gas 8. Place the cold cake on a metal or flameproof dish and drizzle the liqueur over the surface. Set aside to allow the liqueur to soak in.

In a bowl, whisk the egg yolk and sugar until thick. Put all the egg whites in a clean, grease-free bowl and whisk until very stiff. Fold them into the yolk mixture with a few drops of vanilla essence.

Spoon the vanilla-flavoured soufflé mixture into a piping bag fitted with a large rose nozzle. Pile the ice cream on to the cake, leaving a 1 cm/½ inch clear border all around. Quickly pipe the soufflé mixture over the cake, making sure that both the ice cream and the cake are completely covered. Dredge with icing sugar.

Immediately put the dessert into the oven and bake for 3 minutes. Decorate with glacé cherries and angelica and serve at once.

SERVES SIX TO EIGHT

PEACH MELBA

Escoffier's original recipe, created for Dame Nellie Melba, consisted of fresh peaches poached in vanilla syrup and arranged in the centre of a bowl of vanilla ice cream. Cold Melba Sauce was poured over the peaches and the bowl containing the dessert was presented on a dish of crushed ice. The version that follows is the one that is more often served today.

500 ml/17 fl oz Vanilla Ice Cream (page 695)
6 canned peach halves
125 ml/4 fl oz double cream

MELBA SAUCE
575 g/1¼ lb fresh raspberries
150 g/5 oz icing sugar

Make the Melba Sauce. Put the raspberries in a sieve over a heatproof bowl. Using a wooden spoon, crush them against the sides of the sieve to extract as much of the juice as possible. Stir the sugar into the purée and place the bowl over a saucepan of simmering water. Stir for 2-3 minutes to dissolve the sugar. Cool the sauce, then chill until required.

Place a scoop or slice of ice cream in each of six sundae dishes. Cover each portion with a peach half. Coat with the Melba Sauce.

In a bowl, whip the cream until stiff. Spoon into a piping bag and pipe a large rose on top of each portion. Serve at once.

SERVES SIX

SPUMA GELATO PAOLO

30 ml/2 tbsp gelatine
250 g/9 oz caster sugar
100 ml/3½ fl oz Marsala
30 ml/2 tbsp brandy or orange liqueur
1 whole egg, plus 3 yolks
finely grated rind of ¼ lemon
90 ml/6 tbsp lemon juice
300 ml/½ pint double cream
3 drops of orange essence
150 g/5 oz peeled orange segments

Turn the freezing compartment or freezer to the coldest setting about 1 hour before making the ice cream. In a bowl, mix the gelatine with 150 g/5 oz of the caster sugar to form jelly crystals. Stir in 150 ml/¼ pint boiling water and stir until the crystals have dissolved. Cool.

Warm the Marsala and brandy gently in a small saucepan. Combine the egg and egg yolks in a large heatproof bowl. Whisk for at least 8 minutes until light and fluffy, then place over a pan of simmering water.

Add the warmed Marsala mixture and lemon rind to the bowl and stir in 60 ml/4 tbsp lemon juice. Cook the custard mixture, whisking constantly, until it is thick enough to coat a spoon. Stir in the cooled gelatine mixture.

Whip the cream to soft peaks. Fold in the remaining sugar, then fold into the Marsala custard. Add the orange essence with the remaining lemon juice. Spoon into a wetted 1 litre/1¾ pint mould and freeze for at least 4 hours. Return the freezer to the normal setting.

To serve, unmould on to a plate and thaw at room temperature for 15 minutes. Decorate with orange segments.

SERVES SIX

CHOCOLATE FREEZER PUDDING

fat for greasing
100 g/4 oz butter
100 g/4 oz drinking chocolate powder
100 g/4 oz ground almonds
100 g/4 oz caster sugar
1 egg, beaten
100 g/4 oz Petit Beurre biscuits
whipped cream to decorate

Grease a 20 cm/8 inch square baking tin. In a mixing bowl, cream the butter and chocolate powder together. Work in the ground almonds.

Put the sugar into a heavy-bottomed saucepan. Add 30 ml/2 tbsp water and heat gently until the sugar has melted. Set aside to cool.

Gradually add the syrup to the ground almond mixture, working it in well. Add the egg in the same way and beat the mixture until light and creamy.

Break the biscuits into small pieces and fold into the pudding mixture. Spoon into the prepared tin, pressing the mixture down well. Cover and freeze until firm.

To serve the pudding, thaw at room temperature for 45 minutes, then turn out on a serving dish. Decorate with whipped cream.

SERVES TEN TO TWELVE

STRAWBERRY ICE CREAM LAYER GATEAU

1 litre/1¾ pints Strawberry Lick (page 703)
1 litre/1¾ pints Lemon Ice Cream (page 703)
125 g/4½ oz digestive biscuits, crushed
50 g/2 oz chopped mixed nuts
75 g/3 oz butter
25 g/1 oz soft light brown sugar
250 g/9 oz strawberry jam
60 ml/4 tbsp kirsch
100 g/4 oz whole strawberries
icing sugar (see method)
200 ml/7 fl oz double cream

Line an 18 cm/7 inch loose-bottomed deep cake tin with non-stick baking parchment. Soften both ice creams. Put 25 g/1 oz of the biscuit crumbs aside in a small bowl with half the nuts.

Melt the butter in a saucepan, stir in the remaining crumbs and nuts and add the brown sugar. Press the mixture into the lined cake tin and chill until firm.

Sieve the jam into a bowl and stir in 15 ml/1 tbsp of the kirsch. In another bowl, mix the whole strawberries with 15 ml/1 tbsp of the remaining kirsch, adding a little icing sugar if liked. Chill for at least 1 hour.

Cover the chilled biscuit crumb base with half the strawberry ice cream. Spread the top with a third of the jam. Sprinkle with a third of the reserved crumb and nut mixture. Freeze until

the ice cream is firm. Repeat the process with half the lemon ice cream. Continue in this fashion, creating alternate layers of ice cream, jam, crumbs and nuts, until all the ingredients have been used, ending with a layer of lemon ice cream. Freeze each successive layer of ice cream before adding the next.

In a bowl, whip the cream with the remaining kirsch until stiff, adding icing sugar to taste. Remove the chilled gâteau from the cake tin and peel off the lining paper. Transfer the gâteau to a suitable plate and cover the top with whipped cream. Decorate with the liqueur-soaked strawberries and chill until ready to serve.

SERVES EIGHT TO TEN

POIRES BELLE-HELENE

4 firm pears
250 ml/8 fl oz Vanilla Ice Cream (page 695)

CHOCOLATE SAUCE
200 g/7 oz plain chocolate, in squares
350 g/12 oz sugar
salt
2.5 ml/½ tsp vanilla essence

Make the sauce. Put the chocolate into a saucepan with the sugar, salt and vanilla essence. Add 250 ml/8 fl oz water and heat gently, stirring, until the chocolate and sugar have melted and the mixture is smooth.

Peel the pears, cut them in half and remove the cores. Place a scoop or slice of ice cream in each of four dishes. Top with the pear halves and mask with the hot chocolate sauce.

SERVES FOUR

 MRS BEETON'S TIP

Crush the digestive biscuits by working briefly in a food processor. Alternatively, put them in a strong polythene or paper bag and use a rolling pin the reduce them to crumbs.

BAKED ALASKA

For this popular dessert to be a success it must be assembled and cooked at the last minute. Make sure that the ice cream is as hard as possible, that the ice cream and sponge are completely coated in meringue, and that the oven has reached the recommended temperature. Watch the Baked Alaska closely as it cooks, and remove it from the oven as soon as the swirls of meringue are golden brown.

2 egg whites
150 g/5 oz caster sugar
1 quantity Vanilla Ice Cream (page 695)

CAKE
fat for greasing
2 eggs
50 g/2 oz caster sugar
few drops of vanilla essence
50 g/2 oz plain flour, sifted
30 ml/2 tbsp melted butter, cooled

Make the cake several hours before you intend to serve the dessert. Line and grease a 20 cm/ 8 inch sandwich cake tin. Set the oven at 180°C/350°F/gas 4.

Combine the eggs, sugar and vanilla essence in a heatproof bowl. Place over a saucepan of simmering water and whisk until the mixture is thick, pale lemon in colour, and has doubled in bulk. This will take 6–8 minutes. Remove the bowl from the heat and continue to beat until cooled and very thick.

Working swiftly and lightly, fold in the flour, then the butter. Spoon into the prepared tin and bake for 25–30 minutes or until cooked through and firm to the touch. Cool the cake on a wire rack.

When almost ready to serve the Baked Alaska, set the oven at 230°C/450°F/gas 8. Put the egg whites in a clean, grease-free bowl and whisk until very stiff, gradually whisking in half the sugar. Fold in the remaining sugar.

Place the cold cake on an ovenproof plate and pile the ice cream on to it, leaving a 1 cm/$\frac{1}{2}$ inch clear border all around. Cover quickly with the meringue, making sure that both the ice cream and the cake are completely covered. Draw the meringue into swirls, using the blade of a knife or a palette knife.

Immediately put the Alaska into the oven and bake for 3–4 minutes until the meringue is just beginning to brown. Serve at once.

SERVES SIX TO EIGHT

VARIATIONS

The dessert may be made with a slab of sponge cake and a family brick of bought ice cream. Fresh or drained canned fruit may be laid on the sponge base before the ice cream and meringue is added.

 MRS BEETON'S TIP

Wash and dry half an egg shell, pop a sugar cube into it, and soak the sugar cube liberally in brandy. Just before serving the dessert, set the egg shell firmly on the top of the meringue and ignite the brandy for a spectacular effect.

KNICKERBOCKER GLORY

1 (142 oz/5 oz) tablet orange jelly
1 (142 g/5 oz) tablet strawberry jelly
1 (227 g/8 oz) can peaches, drained and
   chopped
1 (227 g/8 oz) can pineapple slices, drained
   and chopped
1 quantity Vanilla Ice Cream (page 695)
50 g/2 oz chopped mixed nuts
150 ml/¼ pint double cream
5 ml/1 tsp caster sugar
6 maraschino cherries to decorate

MELBA SAUCE
450 g/1 lb fresh raspberries
75 g/3 oz icing sugar

Make up both jellies in separate bowls, following packet directions. Leave to set.

Make the sauce. Put the raspberries in a sieve over a heatproof bowl. Using a wooden spoon, crush them against the sides of the sieve to extract as much of the juice as possible. Stir the sugar into the purée and place the bowl over a pan of simmering water. Cool the sauce, then chill until required.

Mix the chopped peaches and pineapple together in a bowl. Chop the set jellies. Put some chopped fruit in each of six tall sundae glasses. Cover with orange jelly, add a scoop of ice cream, then coat with the raspberry sauce. Repeat the process using the strawberry jelly. Sprinkle with nuts.

In a bowl, whip the cream and caster sugar until stiff. Put into a piping bag and pipe a generous swirl of whipped cream on top of each sundae. Decorate each portion with a maraschino cherry.

SERVES SIX

MERINGUE GLACE CHANTILLY

250 ml/8 fl oz Vanilla Ice Cream (page 695)
8 small meringue shells
125 ml/4 fl oz double cream
caster sugar (see method)
4 maraschino cherries to decorate

Place a scoop or slice of ice cream in each of four small oval dishes. Set a meringue shell on either side of the ice cream.

In a bowl, whip the cream until stiff. Sweeten to taste, then spoon into a piping bag. Pipe a large rose of the cream on top of the ice cream. Decorate with the cherries.

SERVES FOUR

COUPE JACQUES

50 g/2 oz seedless grapes
1 banana
1 peach
50 g/2 oz raspberries
30 ml/2 tbsp kirsch
250 ml/8 fl oz Lemon Water Ice (page 692) or
   Vanilla Ice Cream (page 695)
250 ml/8 fl oz Strawberry Lick (page 693)
125 ml/4 fl oz double cream
caster sugar (see method)

Chop all the fruit and mix it together in a bowl. Add the kirsch and macerate the fruit for 4 hours.

Place one portion of each ice in each of six sundae dishes. Cover with the macerated fruit. Whip the cream to soft peaks; sweeten to taste. Decorate with the cream.

SERVES SIX

Cake-making Methods and Techniques

This section explains all-important basic methods and techniques, from preparing tins to understanding some common faults when making cakes. Finally, classic recipes highlight the different types of cake mixtures.

PREPARING TINS FOR BAKING

There is nothing quite as frustrating as battling unsuccessfully to release a beautifully cooked cake in one piece from an ill-prepared tin. Difficulties with turning cakes out of tins can often be avoided if the tin is properly prepared in the first instance. Each recipe offers guidance on the size and shape of tin required and the method by which it should be prepared before the mixture is turned into it. Good cake tins are those to which the cooked mixture is not supposed to stick but this is little consolation when there is a fair chance that the tin you intend to use is quite likely to end up with the cake firmly stuck to it. So, if you have doubts about whether a particular tin is going to release the cake easily, do plan ahead and at least line the bottom of the tin. There are four main ways to prepare tins:

1. Bun tins, patty tins and baking sheets should be greased. In some instances the sheets should be dusted with flour after greasing.
2. For rubbed-in cakes each tin should be greased and the base should be lined. The lining paper should be greased before the mixture is placed in the tin.
3. For creamed mixtures it is best to line the base of each tin and in some cases, where the cake requires lengthy cooking, the sides of the tin should also be lined. The lining

paper should be greased. The same preparation applies to cakes made by the melted method, for example gingerbread.
4. For whisked sponge cakes each tin should be greased and dusted with a little flour. If the tin is one to which the cake may stick on the base, then a circle of paper should be used to line the base of the tin. The floured sides of the tin provide a surface to which very light sponge mixtures may adhere as they rise during cooking.

Non-stick Tins Many non-stick tins do not have to be lined before they are used. The manufacturer's instructions should be followed carefully when preparing this type of tin.

FAT FOR GREASING

The most convenient fat for greasing is oil. A special 'oil well' gadget is designed to hold a small amount of oil with a suitable brush ready for greasing tins. Alternatively, a few drops of oil can be tipped into the tin and brushed evenly over its surface. Lard or other white cooking fat is suitable for greasing tins but butter and margarine are not recommended. If butter or margarine is used it should be clarified first to remove all excess moisture and salt which it contains.

The purpose of greasing is obvious – to prevent the cake from sticking to the tin or to the lining paper. The process of lining tins is made easy if the tin itself is lightly greased first.

The lining paper clings to the greased surface, allowing it to be pushed neatly up against the sides. Where the lining paper overlaps slightly, the under-piece should be lightly greased so that the top piece clings to it and stays in place.

CHOICE OF LINING PAPER

Greaseproof paper is the most common form of lining which is used when preparing tins. However, non-stick baking parchment is available and this can be used instead. Follow the manufacturer's instructions when using this product as, in many cases, it does not require greasing before the cake mixture is placed on it. Heavy, re-usable non-stick baking paper is also available and this is particularly useful if you want to make a semi-permanent lining for a frequently used tin. The tin should of course be washed and the paper wiped clean between uses. Again, the manufacturer's instructions should be followed for using this type of paper.

For making small cakes, paper cake cases can be used, either by standing them on a baking sheet or placing them in patty tins. If the cases are fairly flimsy, it is best to place them in tins for support. It is also possible to purchase large fluted paper cases that can be used to line full-sized cake tins. This is particularly useful if the cake is to be frozen once it is cooked.

For making rich fruit cakes, the tins are best lined with a double thickness of greaseproof paper. To protect the outside of the cake, near the sides and base of the tin, a thick piece of brown paper or newspaper can be tied securely around the outside of the tin, or a piece can be placed on a baking sheet underneath the tin. This is really only necessary when large cakes are baked for several hours and there may be a danger of the outside crust becoming dry.

LINING A SQUARE OR RECTANGULAR TIN

1. Place the tin flat on a single or double thickness of lining paper and draw all around the outside of the bottom. Cut out the shape, cutting slightly inside the pencil mark to allow for the thickness of the tin.

2. Measure a strip of paper for the sides of the tin as for lining a round tin. Make sure that there is enough to go all the way around the inside of the tin and that the strip is wide enough for a 2.5 cm/1 inch fold all around the bottom as well as allowing at least 2.5 cm/1 inch to stand above the rim of the tin.

3. Lightly grease the tin and place one square of paper in the base if a double thickness is used; grease this lightly. Make a 2.5 cm/1 inch fold all along one side of the strip of paper.

4. Carefully lift the strip of paper into the sides of the tin. Have a pair of scissors ready to snip and fit the corners of the paper into the tin. The overlap in the strip of paper should be positioned on one side of the tin, not at a corner.

5. Press the paper against the sides of the tin and into the first corner. Snip into the corner of the strip of paper sitting in the base of the tin.

6. Overlap the paper in the base of the tin in the first corner, to make a neat squared lining. Continue to press the paper smoothly against the side of the tin up to the next corner, then cut and fit the paper as before. Fit the paper into all four corners in this way.

7. Place the square of lining paper in the base of the tin and brush all the inside evenly with a little oil.

LINING A ROUND TIN

1. Place the tin on a single or double piece of lining paper and draw around the outside edge of the bottom in pencil. Remove the tin and cut out the circle of paper, cutting slightly inside the drawn circle to allow for the thickness of the tin and to ensure that the paper will fit neatly inside the base of the tin.

2. Cut out a strip of paper which is long enough to go around the outside of the tin and overlap by 5 cm/2 inches. The paper should be at least 5 cm/2 inches wider than the depth of the tin, to allow for 2.5 cm/1 inch to sit neatly in the bottom of the tin and at least 2.5 cm/1 inch to stand above the rim of the tin.

3. Make a 2.5 cm/1 inch fold all along one side of the strip of paper. Open out the fold and snip diagonally from the edge in as far as the foldline at 1–2.5 cm/½–1 inch intervals all along the length of the paper.

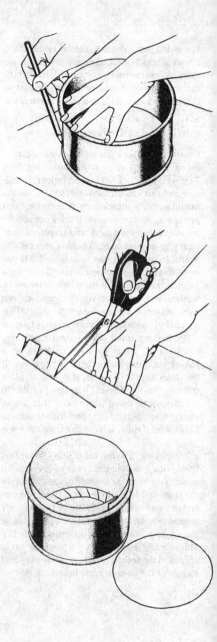

4. Very lightly grease the inside of the tin. If you are using a double thickness of paper, then place one circle in the base of the tin and grease it very lightly. If you are using a single thickness, then put the lining paper around the sides first. Carefully lower the strip of paper into the tin, placing the snipped folded edge downwards. The fold in the base of the strip should tuck neatly all around the inside of the bottom of the tin and the pieces of snipped paper should be overlapped. Place the circle of lining paper in the base of the tin.

5. Lightly grease the lining paper all over, making sure that it is pressed well into the shape of the tin.

LINING A SWISS ROLL TIN

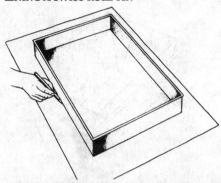

1. Stand the tin on a sheet of greaseproof paper and draw all around the outside of the bottom. Remove the tin.

3. Cut from each outer corner of the paper into the corner of the drawn shape of the tin.

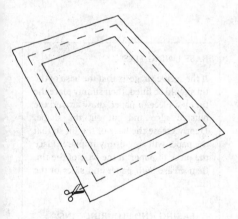

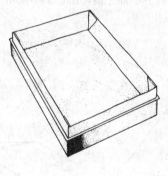

2. Cut out the shape, about 5 cm/2 inches outside of the drawn shape. This is to allow enough paper to line the sides of the tin and to stand about 2.5 cm/1 inch above the rim of the tin. The paper should not stand more than 2.5 cm/1 inch above the rim as this may impair the process of browning.

4. Lightly grease the inside of the tin. Turn the paper over so that the pencil mark is facing downwards, into the tin. Press the paper into the tin, overlapping it at the corners to make a neatly squared lining.

5. The paper will stay in place at the corners if it is greased between the overlap. Grease the lining paper evenly.

LINING A LOAF TIN

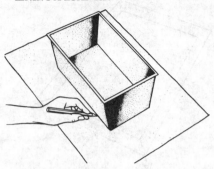

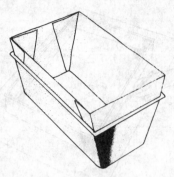

1. Cut a piece of paper large enough to cover the bottom of the tin, to come up both sides and the ends and to stand at least 2.5 cm/1 inch above the tin.

2. Stand the tin in the middle of the paper and draw all around the outside of the bottom.

5. Press the paper neatly into the tin, overlapping the cut corners to make neat squares. Grease lightly between the overlap so that the paper clings together.

6. Grease the lining paper well.

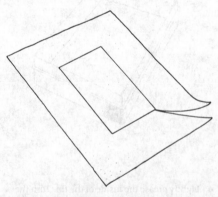

3. Cut in from each outer corner of the piece of paper to the corner of the drawn shape.

4. Lightly grease the tin, then turn the paper over so that the pencil marks are downwards; lift the paper into the tin.

BASE LINING TINS

If the recipe suggests that the base of the tin should be lined, then simply place the tin on a piece of paper, draw around the outside edge and cut out the shape. Lightly grease the base of the tin so that the paper will stay firmly in place. Place the piece of paper in the base of the tin, then grease both paper and sides of the tin.

GREASING AND FLOURING TINS

Lightly grease the inside of the tin. Place a spoonful of flour in the tin. Hold the tin at an angle and turn it around and around, tapping the sides as you turn the tin, so that the flour evenly coats the inside. Tip out any excess flour. A little cocoa may be added to the flour for a chocolate cake.

BASIC METHODS OF MIXING CAKES

CREAMED METHOD

For this method, the fat and sugar are creamed together until they are very soft, pale in colour and light. If a brown sugar is used the mixture will not become very pale in colour but it should turn paler than it was when you started.

The fat should be warmed to room temperature if necessary so that it creams easily. Butter or margarine are the most common fats to use. Soft margarine can be creamed straight from the refrigerator.

When the creaming stage is complete the eggs are added. They should be beaten first so that they can be added gradually. The eggs should be lightly beaten in and a little of the measured flour sprinkled in if the mixture looks as though it may curdle.

When the eggs are incorporated the flour is folded in. It is important that this process is carried out correctly. A large metal spoon should be used and the mixture must not be beaten. The flour is folded in – it is sprinkled over the mixture and the spoon is used to lift the mixture and to cut the flour through it. Rather than stirring, a figure of eight motion is used. The aim is to incorporate the flour with the creamed ingredients without knocking out all the air that was beaten in during the first stage.

Dried fruit or other flavouring ingredients are folded in with the flour or immediately afterwards. Sometimes a little extra liquid is added to soften the mixture.

RUBBED-IN METHOD

The flour is sifted into a bowl and the fat is rubbed into it in the same way as for making short crust pastry.

For this method the fat should be chilled and all the other ingredients should be kept cool. When rubbing fat into flour it is important to use just the tips of the fingers. Lift the mixture up and lightly rub it together, letting it fall back into the bowl. By lifting the mixture and rubbing it lightly you are incorporating air. This keeps it light.

Once the fat is incorporated the sugar and other dry ingredients are added and stirred in. The liquid is added last to bind the ingredients.

WHISKED METHOD

The whisked method is used for making very light sponges. The eggs should be allowed to warm to room temperature. They are combined with the sugar in a bowl which is placed over a saucepan of barely simmering water. The water must not be boiling. An electric whisk can be used. It is hard work if an ordinary hand whisk of the balloon or spiral type is used. Whisking can take a very long time with these simple utensils.

The eggs and sugar are whisked together until they are very thick, very pale and quite creamy. A common mistake with this method is to consider that the mixture is whisked sufficiently as soon as it is slightly thickened. The mixture should be thick enough to hold the trail of the whisk for at least 30 seconds. Once it is whisked sufficiently, remove the bowl from the pan of water and continue whisking for a further 5 minutes, until the mixture has cooled.

At this stage the other ingredients are folded in. Flour and a small amount of fat can be added. The fat is usually butter which is melted before it is dribbled slowly over the whisked mixture and folded in. The folding in process is vital to the success of whisked mixtures – a figure of eight motion should be used as for creamed mixtures and the whisked mixture should be gently lifted over the flour. On no account should the mixture be stirred or whisked as the air will be knocked out by the rapid movement. This type of cake relies on the air content to rise; if the air is knocked out the cake will not rise.

MELTED METHOD

For this type of mixture the fat and sugar are melted together, usually with some form of flavouring. Treacle or syrup is often used, either in place of the sugar or with it.

Once all the fat is melted the mixture should be allowed to cool very slightly before the beaten eggs are added. Do not overheat the melted ingredients, use low heat and stir the mixture frequently. Any crystals of sugar on the sides of the saucepan may be brushed down into the mixture with a pastry brush.

Lastly, the dry ingredients are beaten in. The majority of melted mixtures should be quite soft when all the ingredients are mixed and some may have the consistency of a thick batter.

ONE-STAGE METHOD

This is a modern method of cake mixing, popularized by margarine manufacturers to promote soft margarine in the early days of its availability. As well as the development of soft margarine which requires less creaming than hard fats, the growth in the ownership of electric food mixers has also helped to make this method an easy and convenient alternative to the creaming method.

All the ingredients are placed in a bowl and are beaten together until thoroughly combined, pale and creamy. A little extra raising agent is usually added to ensure a good rise and all the ingredients should be at room temperature, the best fat to use being soft margarine.

BAKING CAKES AND TURNING THEM OUT

For good results it is important that the oven has an even heat distribution, that it heats correctly to the temperature selected and holds that temperature steadily. The oven should stand evenly; most cookers, whether built in or free standing, have adjustable feet to compensate for any uneven floors. If the oven is not level, the cake mixture will rise unevenly, giving a lopsided result.

One of the most difficult areas of cake making is deciding exactly when the cake is cooked. Firstly, follow the timing given in the recipe as a guide, checking the cake at the first suggested time.

Open the oven door carefully – if you can see that the cake still looks raw, then shut the door quickly. Do not bang it and cause the oven to jerk as the cake is cooking.

The appearance of the cooked cake will vary slightly according to its type. Most cakes will be well risen, the exception being very rich fruit cakes which are not intended to rise during cooking. Sponge cakes should have risen to the top of the tin; about doubled in volume. The cake should be evenly browned, not too light and not too dark. The cake should have shrunk away from the sides of the tin very slightly and when pressed lightly it should feel springy on top and the cake should bounce back. If the surface feels at all wet and if the impression of a finger-print remains on top, then the sponge cake is not cooked.

Fruit cakes should not feel spongy, they should be firm and quite well browned. For deep cakes and fruit cakes the skewer test is a good way of determining whether the cake is cooked through.

The Skewer Test   Take a clean metal skewer and insert it into the middle of the cake. Leave it for a few seconds, then take it out. If the cake is cooked the skewer should not have any mixture adhering to it. The skewer will be slightly greasy and there may be sticky marks on it, particularly if the cake contains a lot of fruit. However, there should not be crumbs or any wet mixture sticking to it. Instead of a skewer, the blade of a slim knife can be inserted into the middle of the cake.

Protecting the Top of a Cake   Some cakes that require fairly long cooking may begin to look slightly too dark on top before the middle is cooked. This may be due to the type of mixture, in which case the recipe should warn you to check the cake during cooking, or it may be due to the oven. To prevent the surface of the cake from burning while the middle of the cake cooks through, a piece of foil should be placed loosely over the top the cake, shiny side up. This will prevent the upper crust from burning.

RELEASING CAKES FROM TINS AND COOLING

It is important that the tin is well prepared because this stage can be disastrous if the cake is stuck to the base of the tin.

Some fruit cakes should be allowed to cool in the tin for a while before being turned out and the recipe will suggest this if necessary. If this is the case, drape a clean tea-towel over the top of the tin to absorb steam and to prevent the cake from being exposed to dust or dirt.

To turn a cake out of a tin which is not fully lined, first slide a round-bladed knife gently around the inside of the tin, between it and the cake. Place a wire rack over the top of the tin and use an oven glove to hold both rack and tin firmly. Then invert the tin on to the rack and place it on the work surface. Lift the tin off the cake and remove any lining paper. To turn the cake back up the right way, place a second rack on it and invert it yet again.

If the tin has a loose bottom, then prepare some form of stand on which to place the cake in its tin, allowing the side to fall down, away from the cake. A suitable storage jar or large upturned basin is ideal. Carefully lower the side of the tin off the cake, then lift the cake and its base to a wire rack. Slide the cake from the base of the tin on to the rack and remove any lining paper. Alternatively, simply invert the cake and tin on to the rack as before and lift off the sides and base of the tin.

Certain cakes may require special treatment, for example Swiss roll. Light sponge cakes mark very easily and they can be turned on to a wire rack covered with a clean tea-towel, or on to a piece of greaseproof paper which is sprinkled with caster sugar.

The cake should be allowed to cool completely before it is stored or wrapped, unless the recipe states otherwise.

STORING AND FREEZING

The keeping quality of cakes depends on the individual mixtures. Some cakes, particularly fruit cakes, improve with keeping. Light fruit cakes often taste better a few days after they are baked and very rich fruit cakes should be allowed to mature for at least a month in order to let all the individual flavours mingle.

Fatless sponge cakes do not keep well and they quickly become very dry. Ideally they should be eaten on the same day or at least the day after they are baked.

Victoria sandwich type cakes keep quite well in an airtight container and they can be stored for about a week, although the time depends on the flavouring ingredients and any filling, covering or decoration which is added. Cakes covered in soft icings do not keep as well as plain cakes.

Most cakes should be stored in an airtight container in a cool, dry place. Fruit cakes which are to be kept for long periods are best stored with the lining paper from cooking left on. The underside is usually pierced all over and sprinkled with a little brandy or rum, then the cake is wrapped in two or three layers of greaseproof paper. To introduce the liquor, the base lining paper should be peeled back and then replaced. The cake can be stored in a clean cardboard cake box or wrapped in foil. Foil must not be placed directly on the cake as it reacts with the fruit acids and may disintegrate in places, causing the surface of the cake to be dusted with foil particles. Rich cakes of this type should not be stored in plastic containers as they may sweat. It is important to keep a rich cake in a cool, dry place and to check it occasionally during storage.

Extra brandy or rum can be used to 'feed' the cake occasionally if it is stored for a long period but it is important not to overdo the liquor feeding as the cake can become soggy.

FREEZING CAKES

Most cakes that are not decorated freeze well. There is no point in freezing a rich fruit cake as it will improve on keeping as described left. Light fruit cakes can be frozen successfully; also cakes made by the creamed or melted methods. Fatless sponges, or those with little fat added, made by the whisked method freeze particularly well and they also thaw quickly at room temperature. Cakes covered with royal icing, glacé icing or the softer moulding icings should not be frozen as the icing will not thaw successfully.

Packing Plain Cakes   The cake should be allowed to cool completely before it is packed for freezing. When it is completely cold, pack the cake in a polythene bag, extracting all the air from the bag, and close it tightly. Label the cake with its type and date, then place it safely in the freezer, where it will not be crushed or damaged by other items.

Layers of cake should be separated by placing double thicknesses of greaseproof paper or special interleaving freezer film between them. The layers can then be packed together in one bag and frozen.

Undecorated cakes which are sandwiched together with a filling such as jam can be frozen as one plain cake, but it is best to freeze them unfilled, ready to be sandwiched together when thawed.

Freezing Decorated Cakes   Cakes which are filled and covered with fresh cream, buttercream or frosting can be frozen successfully. Although the cake can be frozen with its filling and this type of icing, no decorations should be added before freezing. Decorated cakes should not be frozen for long periods and it is best to keep them for just two to four weeks. It is sometimes useful to be able to make a decorated cake in advance of an occasion and freeze it, provided that the icing is of an appropriate type.

The technique to use when packing these cakes is to open freeze them. The decorated cake should be placed on freezer film or foil on a baking sheet and frozen uncovered until it is firm. Remember that the icing will not freeze hard and that it can be easily damaged during storage, particularly if there are any piped decorations. Once the cake is frozen it can be packed loosely in a polythene bag (it is best to support the cake on a piece of card first) or, better still, it can be placed in a large rigid container. Place a little crumpled absorbent kitchen paper around the side of the cake to prevent it from slipping against the sides of the container when moved.

The cake should be unpacked and transferred to a serving plate before being allowed to thaw in the refrigerator, preferably overnight or for several hours.

Packing Individual Slices It can be useful to have slices of cake in the freezer, to be removed one piece at a time as required. Either plain or decorated cakes can be packed in this way.

The cake should be cut into slices or wedges. A piece of interleaving film should be placed carefully between each slice and the cake re-shaped. Plain cakes can be packed as before or decorated cakes should be open frozen.

The required number of slices can be removed as they are wanted – this is particularly useful for lunch boxes or hasty family teas. A piece of plain cake can be packed still frozen in a lunch box first thing in the morning and it will have thawed in time for the midday break.

Freezing Small Cakes Small cakes cooked in paper cases can be packed neatly in rigid containers or polythene bags for freezing. Tray cakes can be cut into squares or portions and frozen in rigid containers, or interleaved with freezer film and packed in bags. They can be removed and thawed a few at a time, as required.

HINTS FOR SUCCESSFUL CAKE MAKING

- Check that all the ingredients and equipment are ready before you begin to mix the cake.
- Weigh and measure correctly, and prepare the tins as suggested in the recipe.
- Follow the recipe carefully, heating the oven when necessary.
- For cakes made by the creamed method make sure that the fat is soft before beginning to beat it with the sugar – this makes the task much easier. Have the other ingredients at room temperature.
- When making a cake by the melting method do not overheat the ingredients. Melt them over low heat until the fat is just melted. Do not let it become too hot. Leave the melted ingredients to cool slightly, if necessary, before adding any eggs.
- Do not open the oven door when the cake is cooking until you think it is ready for checking. Opening the door in the early stages of cooking introduces colder air and can cause the cake to sink.
- Test the cake to check if it is cooked before fully removing it from the oven. Use a pair of oven gloves and slide the shelf out slightly. Check the colour and texture of the cake, and use a skewer to test if the middle is cooked if necessary.
- Allow the cake to stand for a few minutes in the tin and there is less chance of it breaking around the edges as it is being turned out. A rich cake should be allowed to cool in the tin until warm; a very rich cake is best left to cool completely in the tin.

SOME COMMON FAULTS AND THEIR LIKELY CAUSES

CAKE SUNK IN THE CENTRE

1. Too much raising agent used.
2. The fat and sugar were beaten for too long or the fat was too soft (almost runny when creamed).
3. The mixture was too soft before baking – this could be due to too little flour or too much liquid.
4. The oven door was opened too early or the cake removed from the oven before the mixture had time to set.
5. The cake was removed from the oven before it was fully cooked, in which case it would have sunk on cooling slightly.

CAKE RISEN TO A PEAK AND CRACKED ON TOP

1. Fat and sugar not creamed enough.
2. Oven too hot or uneven heat distribution in oven and cake cooked too near to the top of the oven, or in too hot an area of the oven.
3. The tin was too small for the amount of mixture.

UNEVENLY RISEN CAKE

1. The mixture was not levelled out before baking.
2. The oven was not prepared before the cake was put in – this does depend on the type of oven and the time it takes to heat up.
3. The oven was not level. This could be because the floor of the kitchen is uneven. Most appliances have adjustable feet to compensate for this.
4. The cake was placed on a far corner or to one side of the shelf.
5. Too much raising agent used.

A VERY DRY CAKE

1. Not enough liquid added to the mixture.
2. The cake was baked for too long.
3. Far too much raising agent used.

THE CAKE HAS A COARSE, OPEN TEXTURE

1. If the mixture is a rubbed-in type, then the fat was not rubbed in enough. Alternatively, the fat may have been of poor quality.
2. The fat and sugar were not creamed together for long enough.
3. The oven temperature was too high.
4. Too much raising agent used.

FRUIT SUNK TO THE BOTTOM OF THE CAKE

1. The mixture was too soft and would not support the fruit.
2. Cherries are the most common offender in this example. If the cherries are added to a light fruit cake they must be washed and dried first, then dusted with a little of the measured flour. If they are left coated in syrup they will sink. The dusting of flour helps them to adhere to the surrounding mixture and this prevents them from sinking.

THE CAKE HAS A SUGARY CRUST

1. Fat and sugar not creamed together long enough.
2. Too much sugar used.
3. The sugar was too coarse.

RECIPES FOR BASIC CAKES

The proportions of ingredients and the essential techniques that are used in the preparation of basic cakes apply equally to the most complicated gâteaux. Once the balance of fat to flour, eggs to sugar, dry ingredients to moisture and the use of raising agents are understood, cake-making becomes a simple and highly satisfying pursuit.

PLAIN CAKE

fat for greasing
200 g/7 oz self-raising flour or 200 g/7 oz
   plain flour and 10 ml/2 tsp baking powder
1.25 ml/¼ tsp salt
75 g/3 oz margarine or blended white
   cooking fat, diced
75 g/3 oz sugar
2 small eggs
about 125 ml/4 fl oz milk

Line and grease a 15 cm/6 inch cake tin. Set the oven at 180°C/350°F/gas 4.

Mix the flour and salt together in a mixing bowl. Rub in the margarine or cooking fat until the mixture resembles fine breadcrumbs. Add the baking powder, if used, and the sugar.

In a bowl, beat the eggs with some of the milk and stir into the flour mixture. Add a little more milk if necessary to give a consistency which just drops off the end of a wooden spoon.

Spoon the mixture into the prepared tin and bake for 1-1½ hours or until cooked through. Cool on a wire rack.

MAKES ONE 15 CM/6 INCH CAKE

ONE-STAGE FRUIT CAKE

fat for greasing
225 g/8 oz self-raising flour
5 ml/1 tsp mixed spice (optional)
100 g/4 oz soft margarine
100 g/4 oz glacé cherries, chopped
100 g/4 oz currants
75 g/3 oz sultanas
25 g/1 oz cut mixed peel
100 g/4 oz soft light brown sugar
2 eggs
75 ml/3 fl oz milk

Line and grease an 18 cm/7 inch round cake tin. Set the oven at 180°C/350°F/gas 4. Mix the flour and spice, if used.

Put all the ingredients in a bowl, stir, then beat until smooth, allowing 2-3 minutes by hand or 1-1½ minutes with an electric mixer. Spoon the mixture into the prepared tin and bake for 2 hours. Cool on a wire rack.

MAKES ONE 18 CM/7 INCH CAKE

 MRS BEETON'S TIP

The cherries will be easy to chop if you use a pair of kitchen scissors whose blades have been dipped in boiling water.

VICTORIA SANDWICH CAKE

The original Victoria Sandwich was oblong, filled with jam or marmalade and cut into fingers or sandwiches. Now, the basic mixture is used with many different flavourings and fillings and is served as a single, round cake. For a softer-centred cake bake the mixture in a 20 cm/8 inch round cake tin, then split and fill. All loose crumbs must be brushed off before filling. Keep the filling fairly firm – if it is too moist, it will seep into the cake.

fat for greasing
150 g/5 oz butter or margarine
150 g/5 oz caster sugar
3 eggs, beaten
150 g/5 oz self-raising flour or plain flour
  and 5 ml/1 tsp baking powder
pinch of salt
raspberry or other jam for filling
caster sugar for dredging

Line and grease two 18 cm/7 inch sandwich tins. Set the oven at 180°C/350°F/gas 4.

In a mixing bowl cream the butter or margarine with the sugar until light and fluffy. Add the eggs gradually, beating well after each addition. Sift the flour, salt and baking powder, if used, into a bowl. Stir into the creamed mixture, lightly but thoroughly, until evenly mixed.

Divide between the tins and bake for 25–30 minutes. Cool on a wire rack, then sandwich together with jam. Sprinkle the top with caster sugar or spread with Glacé Icing (page 771).

MAKES ONE 18 CM/7 INCH CAKE

ONE-STAGE VICTORIA SANDWICH

fat for greasing
150 g/5 oz self-raising flour
pinch of salt
150 g/5 oz soft margarine
150 g/5 oz caster sugar
3 eggs

Line and grease two 18 cm/7 inch sandwich tins. Set the oven at 180°C/350°F/gas 4.

Put all the ingredients in a mixing bowl and stir. Beat until smooth, allowing 2-3 minutes by hand or 1-1½ minutes with an electric mixer.

Divide the mixture evenly between the tins; level each surface. Bake for 25-30 minutes. Cool on a wire rack, then fill and top as desired.

MAKES ONE 18 CM/7 INCH CAKE

 MRS BEETON'S TIP

A wholemeal Victoria sandwich cake can be made by substituting self-raising wholemeal flour for white flour. If self-raising wholemeal flour is not available, then use the plain type and add 10 ml/2 tsp baking powder. Soften the mixture with 30 ml/2 tbsp of milk or orange juice after the flour is added. The resulting cake tends to have a closer, heavier texture.

FLAVOURINGS AND FILLINGS FOR VICTORIA SANDWICH CAKES

The basic mixture for Victoria Sandwich Cake can be adapted to make a variety of cakes. For example, sweet spices or citrus rinds can be added to the mixture. Alternatively flavourings such as vanilla essence or almond essence can be added in small quantities to alter the result slightly.

There is a wide variety of commercial preserves and sweet spreads available and many of these are ideal for filling the sandwich cake. The following ideas can be used with the traditional recipe or the one-stage recipe.

Chocolate Sandwich Cake Substitute 60 ml/4 tbsp of cocoa for an equal quantity of the flour. Sift the cocoa with the flour and continue as in the main recipe. Sandwich the cooled cakes together with chocolate spread and sift a little icing sugar over the top of the chocolate cake.

Cinnamon and Apple Sandwich Cake Add 10 ml/2 tsp of ground cinnamon to the flour. Continue as in the main recipe. Peel, core and slice a large cooking apple, then cook it with a little sugar until it is reduced to a pulp. Press the pulp through a sieve, return it to the saucepan and add 10 ml/2 tsp of cornflour blended with 30 ml/2 tbsp of milk. Bring to the boil, stirring, and cook until thickened. Sweeten the purée to taste, then leave it to cool. Gradually fold in 50 ml/2 fl oz of whipped double cream, then use this apple cream to sandwich the cooled cakes together.

Coffee Sandwich Cake Dissolve 30 ml/2 tbsp of instant coffee in 30 ml/2 tbsp boiling water and leave to cool. Fold this into the mixture last. Whip 150 ml/¼ pint double cream with 5 ml/1 tsp of instant coffee dissolved in 15 ml/1 tbsp of boiling water and 30 ml/2 tbsp of icing sugar. Sandwich the cooled cakes with this coffee cream.

Ginger Sandwich Cake The combination of ground ginger and lemon rind makes a delicious cake. Add the grated rind of 1 lemon to the fat and sugar. Sift 15 ml/1 tbsp of ground ginger with the flour. Prepare and bake the cake as in the main recipe. When cool, sandwich the layers with ginger marmalade.

Harlequin Sandwich Cake Make the cake mixture as in the main recipe, then put half in one sandwich tin. Add pink food colouring to the second portion of mixture, making it a fairly strong colour. Put the second portion in the other sandwich tin and bake the cake. When cool, cut both cakes into rings: cut a 5 cm/2 inch circle from the middle of each cake, then cut a 10 cm/4 inch circle around it. Either use plain pastry cutters or cut out circles of paper and use a pointed knife to cut around them. You should have three rings of each cake. Carefully put the rings of cake together alternating the colours to make two layers. Sandwich the layers together with raspberry jam. Spread warmed raspberry jam over the top of the cake and sift icing sugar over it. Alternatively, fill the cake with whipped cream and swirl more whipped cream over the top. When slices are cut the pattern will show.

Lemon Sandwich Cake Add the grated rind of 1 large lemon to the fat and sugar. Continue as in the main recipe, then sandwich the cooled cakes together with lemon curd.

Mocha Sandwich Cake Substitute 30 ml/2 tbsp of cocoa for an equal quantity of flour and sift it with the flour. Prepare the mixture as in the main recipe. Dissolve 10 ml/2 tsp of instant coffee in 15 ml/1 tbsp of boiling water and add it to the mixture. Sandwich the cooled cakes together with chocolate spread.

Orange Sandwich Cake Add the grated rind of 1 large orange to the fat and sugar, then continue as in the main recipe. Sandwich the cooled cakes together with orange marmalade.

SMALL RICH CAKES

fat for greasing (optional)
100 g/4 oz self-raising flour
pinch of salt
100 g/4 oz butter or margarine
100 g/4 oz caster sugar
2 eggs, beaten

Grease 12–14 bun tins or support an equivalent number of paper cases in dry bun tins. Set the oven at 180°C/350°F/gas 4. Mix the flour and salt in a bowl.

In a mixing bowl, cream the butter or margarine with the sugar until light and fluffy. Beat in the eggs, then lightly stir in the flour and salt.

Divide the mixture evenly between the prepared paper cases or bun tins, and bake for 15–20 minutes until golden brown. Cool on a wire rack.

MAKES TWELVE TO FOURTEEN

VARIATIONS

Cherry Cakes   Add 50 g/2 oz chopped glacé cherries with the flour.

Chocolate Cakes   Add 30 ml/2 tbsp cocoa with the flour and add 15 ml/1 tbsp milk.

Coconut Cakes   Add 50 g/2 oz desiccated coconut with the flour and 15–30 ml/1–2 tbsp milk with the eggs.

Coffee Cakes   Dissolve 10 ml/2 tsp instant coffee in 5 ml/1 tsp boiling water. Add with the eggs.

Queen Cakes   Add 100 g/4 oz currants with the flour.

RICH CAKE

fat for greasing
200 g/7 oz plain flour
1.25 ml/¼ tsp salt
2.5 ml/½ tsp baking powder
150 g/5 oz butter or margarine
150 g/5 oz caster sugar
4 eggs, beaten
15 ml/1 tbsp milk (optional)

Line and grease a 15 cm/6 inch cake tin. Set the oven at 180°C/350°F/gas 4.

Sift the flour, salt and baking powder into a bowl. Place the butter or margarine in a mixing bowl and beat until very soft. Add the sugar and cream together until light and fluffy. Add the beaten eggs gradually, beating well after each addition. If the mixture shows signs of curdling, add a little flour.

Fold in the dry ingredients lightly but thoroughly, adding the milk if too stiff.

Spoon into the prepared tin, smooth the surface and make a slight hollow in the centre. Bake for 30 minutes, then reduce the oven temperature to 160°C/325°F/gas 3 and bake for 50 minutes more until firm to the touch. Cool on a wire rack.

MAKES ONE 15 CM/6 INCH CAKE

VARIATIONS

Cornflour Cake   Use a mixture of equal parts cornflour and plain flour.

Ground Rice Cake   Use a mixture of 150 g/5 oz plain flour and 50 g/2 oz ground rice.

Lemon or Orange Cake   Add the grated rind of 2 lemons or oranges and use fruit juice instead of milk.

SPONGE CAKE

fat for greasing
flour for dusting
3 eggs
75 g/3 oz caster sugar
75 g/3 oz plain flour
pinch of salt
pinch of baking powder

Grease an 18 cm/7 inch round cake tin or two 15 cm/6 inch sandwich tins. Dust with sifted flour, tapping out the excess. Set the oven at 180°C/350°F/gas 4.

Whisk the eggs and sugar together in a bowl over a saucepan of hot water, taking care that the base of the bowl does not touch the water. Continue whisking for 10–15 minutes until the mixture is thick and creamy. Remove the bowl from the pan. Whisk until cold.

Sift the flour, salt and baking powder into a bowl. Add to the creamed mixture, using a metal spoon. Do this lightly, so that the air incorporated during whisking is not lost. Pour the mixture into the prepared tin or tins.

Bake a single 18 cm/7 inch cake for 40 minutes; two 15 cm/6 inch cakes for 25 minutes. Leave the sponge in the tins for a few minutes, then cool on a wire rack. Fill and top as desired.

MAKES ONE 18 CM/7 INCH CAKE OR TWO 15 CM/6 INCH LAYERS

 MRS BEETON'S TIP

If an electric mixer is used there is no need to place the bowl over hot water. Whisk at high speed for about 5 minutes until thick. Fold in the flour by hand.

FLAVOURINGS AND FILLINGS FOR SPONGE CAKES

Both the Sponge Cake and the Genoese Sponge cake are light in texture, with a delicate flavour, and this should be reflected in the choice of flavouring ingredients or fillings that are added. Jams and other sweet preserves can be used to fill the cakes or whipped cream is ideal for this type of cake. Fresh fruit perfectly complements the lightness of these sponges.

The following suggestions can be used for both the recipes.

Chocolate Cream Sponge Make plain sponge cakes or substitute 15 ml/1 tbsp of cocoa for an equal quantity of flour, sifting it in with the flour to flavour the cakes. For the filling, melt 100 g/4 oz of milk chocolate with 50 g/2 oz of butter in a basin over hot water. Stir well and leave to cool but do not allow to set. Carefully fold in 150 ml/¼ pint of whipped double cream, then use this chocolate cream to sandwich the cakes together.

Lemon Cream Sponge Add the grated rind of 1 lemon to the eggs and sugar, then continue as in the main recipe. Whip 150 ml/¼ pint of double cream and fold in 60–90 ml/4–6 tbsp of lemon curd, to taste. Use this to sandwich the cakes together.

Peaches and Cream Cake Make the cakes as in the main recipe. Finely chop peeled and stoned fresh peaches or drained canned peaches and mix them with whipped cream or soft cheese. Sweeten with icing sugar and use this to sandwich the cakes together.

Strawberry Cream Cake Make the cakes as in the main recipe and leave to cool. Hull and halve 225 g/8 oz of strawberries. Whip 150 ml/¼ pint of double cream with icing sugar to taste, then fold in the halved strawberries. Sandwich the cooled cakes together with the strawberry cream.

GENOESE SPONGE OR PASTRY

For an 18 cm/7 inch square or 25 × 15 cm/10 × 6 inch oblong cake, use 75 g/3 oz flour, pinch of salt, 50 g/2 oz clarified butter or margarine, 3 eggs and 75 g/3 oz caster sugar.

fat for greasing
100 g/4 oz plain flour
2.5 ml/½ tsp salt
75 g/3 oz clarified butter (see page 424) or
  margarine
4 eggs
100 g/4 oz caster sugar

Line and grease a 30 × 20 cm/12 × 8 inch Swiss roll tin. Set the oven at 180°C/350°F/gas 4.

Sift the flour and salt into a bowl and put in a warm place. Melt the clarified butter or margarine without letting it get hot.

Whisk the eggs lightly in a mixing bowl. Add the sugar and place the bowl over a saucepan of hot water. Whisk for 10–15 minutes until thick. Take care that the base of the bowl does not touch the water. Remove from the heat and continue whisking until at blood-heat. The melted butter should be at the same temperature.

Sift half the flour over the eggs, then pour in half the melted butter or margarine in a thin stream. Fold in gently. Repeat, using the remaining flour and fat. Spoon gently into the prepared tin and bake for 30–40 minutes. Cool on a wire rack.

MAKES ONE 30 × 20 CM/12 × 8 INCH CAKE

 MICROWAVE TIP

Melt the clarified butter or margarine in a bowl on High for 45–60 seconds.

GINGERBREAD

fat for greasing
200 g/7 oz plain flour
1.25 ml/¼ tsp salt
10–15 ml/2–3 tsp ground ginger
2.5 ml/½ tsp bicarbonate soda
75 g/3 oz lard
50 g/2 oz soft light brown sugar
50 g/2 oz golden syrup
50 g/2 oz black treacle
1 egg
milk (see method)

Line and grease a 15 cm/6 inch square tin. Set the oven at 160°C/325°F/gas 3.

Sift the flour, salt, ginger and bicarbonate of soda into a mxing bowl. Warm the lard, sugar, syrup and treacle in a saucepan until the fat has melted. Do not let the mixture become hot.

In a measuring jug, beat the egg lightly and add enough milk to make up to 125 ml/4 fl oz. Add the melted mixture to the dry ingredients with the beaten egg and milk mixture. Stir thoroughly; the mixture should run easily off the spoon.

Pour into the prepared tin and bake for 1¼–1½ hours until firm to the touch. Cool the gingerbread on a wire rack.

MAKES ONE 15 CM/6 INCH SQUARE CAKE

Large Plain Cakes and Fruit Cakes

An array of simple cakes for every day. Ideal for storing in cake tin or freezer, these are tempting enough to be a treat but not too rich for frequent baking.

PLAIN CHOCOLATE LOAF

Serve this simple loaf sliced, with a chocolate and hazelnut spread for those who like to gild the lily.

fat for greasing
175 g/6 oz plain flour
50 g/2 oz cocoa
10 ml/2 tsp baking powder
2.5 ml/½ tsp bicarbonate of soda
1.25 ml/¼ tsp salt
150 g/5 oz sugar
2 eggs, beaten
75 g/3 oz butter or margarine, melted
250 ml/8 fl oz milk

Line and grease a 23 × 13 × 7.5 cm/9 × 5 × 3 inch loaf tin. Set the oven at 180°C/350°F/gas 4. Sift the flour, cocoa, baking powder, bicarbonate of soda and salt into a mixing bowl. Stir in the sugar.

In a second bowl beat the eggs with the melted butter or margarine and milk. Pour the milk mixture into the dry ingredients and stir lightly but thoroughly.

Spoon into the prepared tin and bake for 40–50 minutes until cooked through and firm to the touch. Cool on a wire rack.

MAKES ONE 23 × 13 × 7.5 CM/9 × 5 × 3 INCH LOAF

A VARIETY OF CHOCOLATE LOAF CAKES

The recipe for Plain Chocolate Loaf can be used as a basis for making deliciously different chocolate cakes.

Chocolate Layer Loaf The simplest way to enrich the loaf cake is to cut it horizontally into three layers and sandwich them together with chocolate and hazelnut spread. If you like, coat the top of the cake with melted chocolate softened with a knob of butter, and top with toasted hazelnuts.

Chocolate Orange Split Add the grated rind of 1 orange to the dry ingredients, then continue as in the main recipe. Beat 225 g/8 oz curd cheese with enough orange juice to make it soft and creamy, then add icing sugar to taste. Stir in 50 g/2 oz of finely grated plain chocolate. Split the loaf vertically along its length into four slices. Sandwich the slices together with the cheese mixture and spread a thin layer over the top of the loaf. Sprinkle the top with extra grated chocolate.

Chocolate Walnut Loaf Add 100 g/4 oz of finely chopped walnuts to the dry ingredients, then continue as in the main recipe. Melt 50 g/2 oz of plain chocolate with 25 g/1 oz butter and stir in about 50 g/2 oz of chopped walnuts. Top the loaf with this mixture.

PLAIN ALMOND CAKE

fat for greasing
100 g/4 oz butter or margarine
100 g/4 oz caster sugar
275 g/10 oz plain flour
10 ml/2 tsp baking powder
3 eggs
200 ml/7 fl oz milk
2.5 ml/½ tsp almond essence
50 g/2 oz flaked almonds

Line and grease a 15 cm/6 inch round cake tin.
Set the oven at 160°C/325°F/gas 3.

In a mixing bowl, cream the butter or margarine with the sugar until light and fluffy. Into another bowl, sift the flour and baking powder. In a measuring jug, beat the eggs with the milk.

Add the dry ingredients to the creamed mixture in 3 parts, alternately with the egg and milk mixture. Beat well after each addition. Lightly stir in the almond essence and the flaked almonds.

Spoon lightly into the prepared tin and bake for 1¼-1½ hours until cooked through and firm to the touch. Cool on a wire rack.

MAKES ONE 15 CM/6 INCH CAKE

 MICROWAVE TIP

If the butter or margarine is too hard to cream readily, soften it in the mixing bowl on High for 15-30 seconds.

WEEKEND WALNUT LOAF

fat for greasing
275 g/10 oz plain flour
50 g/2 oz cornflour
5 ml/1 tsp salt
150 g/5 oz caster sugar
50 g/2 oz walnuts, chopped
225 g/8 oz dates, stoned and chopped
30 ml/2 tbsp oil
1 large egg
10 ml/2 tsp bicarbonate of soda

Line and grease a 23 × 13 × 7.5 cm/9 × 5 × 3 inch loaf tin. Set the oven at 180°C/350°F/gas 4.

Sift the flour, cornflour and salt into a mixing bowl. Add the sugar, walnuts and dates. In a second bowl, whisk together the oil and egg. Add to the flour, fruit and nuts and mix well. Pour 250 ml/8 fl oz boiling water into a measuring jug, add the bicarbonate of soda and stir until dissolved. Add to the mixing bowl and mix well. Beat to a soft consistency.

Pour into the prepared loaf tin and bake for about 1 hour until cooked through and firm to the touch. Leave to cool slightly before inverting on a wire rack to cool completely.

MAKES ONE 23 × 13 × 7.5 CM/9 × 5 × 3 INCH LOAF

 MRS BEETON'S TIP

Use a light unflavoured oil, such as corn oil, for the best results. Never use olive oil; its flavour is too strong.

DATE AND WALNUT CAKE

fat for greasing
200 g/7 oz self-raising flour or 200 g/7 oz
   plain flour and 10 ml/2 tsp baking powder
pinch of grated nutmeg
75 g/3 oz margarine
75 g/3 oz dates, stoned and chopped
25 g/1 oz walnuts, chopped
75 g/3 oz soft light brown sugar
2 small eggs
about 125 ml/4 fl oz milk

Line and grease a 15 cm/6 inch tin. Set the oven at 180°C/350°F/gas 4.

Mix the flour and nutmeg in a mixing bowl, and rub in the margarine until the mixture resembles fine breadcrumbs. Add the dates and walnuts with the sugar and baking powder, if used.

In a bowl, beat the eggs with the milk and stir into the dry ingredients. Mix well.

Spoon the mixture into the cake tin and bake for 1¼-1½ hours or until cooked through and firm to the touch. Cool on a wire rack.

MAKES ONE 15 CM/6 INCH CAKE

 MICROWAVE TIP

Dried dates in a compact slab are often difficult to chop. Soften them by heating for 30-40 seconds on Defrost and the job will be made much easier.

BANANA AND WALNUT CAKE

fat for greasing
200 g/7 oz plain flour
1.25 ml/¼ tsp baking powder
3.75 ml/¾ tsp bicarbonate of soda
pinch of salt
100 g/4 oz butter
150 g/5 oz caster sugar
3 large bananas, mashed
2 eggs, beaten
45 ml/3 tbsp soured milk
50 g/2 oz walnuts, finely chopped

Line and grease either a 20 cm/8 inch ring tin, or two 23 cm/9 inch sandwich tins. Set the oven at 180°C/350°F/gas 4. Sift the flour, baking powder, bicarbonate of soda and salt into a bowl.

In a mixing bowl, cream the butter and sugar until light and creamy. Mix in the mashed banana at once, blending well. Add the eggs, one at a time, beating well after each addition. Add the dry ingredients, one-third at a time, alternately with the soured milk, beating well after each addition.

Stir in the walnuts and spoon into the prepared tin. Bake the ring cake for about 40 minutes; the sandwich cakes for about 30 minutes. Cool on a wire rack.

MAKES ONE 20 CM/8 INCH RING CAKE OR TWO 23 CM/9 INCH LAYERS

 MRS BEETON'S TIP

Mash the bananas with a fork or purée in a blender or food processor.

GOLDEN GINGERBREAD

fat for greasing
200 g/7 oz plain flour
1.25 ml/¼ tsp salt
10–15 ml/2–3 tsp ground ginger
2.5 ml/½ tsp bicarbonate of soda
grated rind of 1 orange
75 g/3 oz butter or margarine
50 g/2 oz golden granulated sugar
100 g/4 oz golden syrup
1 egg
milk (see method)

Line and grease a 15 cm/6 inch square tin. Set the oven at 160°C/325°F/gas 3.

Sift the flour, salt, ginger and bicarbonate of soda into a mixing bowl. Stir in the orange rind. Warm the butter or margarine with the sugar and syrup in a saucepan until the fat has melted but the mixture is not hot.

In a measuring jug, beat the egg lightly and add enough milk to make up to 125 ml/4 fl oz. Add the melted mixture to the dry ingredients with the beaten egg and milk mixture. Stir thoroughly; the mixture should run easily off the spoon.

Pour into the prepared tin and bake for 1¼–1½ hours until firm. Cool on a wire rack.

MAKES ONE 15 CM/6 INCH SQUARE CAKE

 MRS BEETON'S TIP

The easiest way to measure the ingredients for melting is to weigh the empty saucepan, then add the butter or margarine until the scale registers an additional 75 g/3 oz. Add the sugar to increase the weight by a further 50 g/2 oz, then, using a spoon dipped in boiling water, ladle in syrup until the scale registers a further 100 g/4 oz.

GINGERBREAD WITH PINEAPPLE

fat for greasing
200 g/7 oz plain flour
1.25 ml/¼ tsp salt
10–15 ml/2–3 tsp ground ginger
2.5 ml/½ tsp bicarbonate of soda
50 g/2 oz crystallized ginger, chopped
50 g/2 oz crystallized pineapple, chopped
75 g/3 oz butter or margarine
50 g/2 oz soft light brown sugar
50 g/2 oz golden syrup
50 g/2 oz black treacle
1 egg
milk (see method)

Line and grease a 15 cm/6 inch square tin. Set the oven at 160°C/325°F/gas 3.

Sift the flour, salt, ground ginger and bicarbonate of soda into a mixing bowl. Stir in the crystallized fruit. Warm the butter or margarine with the sugar, syrup and treacle in a saucepan until the fat has melted. Do not allow the mixture to become hot.

In a measuring jug, beat the egg lightly and add enough milk to make up to 125 ml/4 fl oz. Add the melted mixture to the dry ingredients with the beaten egg and milk mixture. Stir thoroughly; the mixture should run easily off the spoon.

Pour into the prepared tin and bake for 1¼–1½ hours until firm to the touch. Cool on a wire rack.

MAKES ONE 15 CM/6 INCH SQUARE CAKE

OATMEAL GINGERBREAD

fat for greasing
100 g/4 oz plain flour
1.25 ml/¼ tsp salt
15 ml/1 tbsp ground ginger
5 ml/1 tsp bicarbonate of soda
100 g/4 oz fine oatmeal
50 g/2 oz butter or margarine
50 g/2 oz soft light brown sugar
20 ml/4 tsp black treacle
1 egg
75 ml/5 tbsp milk or soured milk

Line and grease a 18 cm/7 inch square tin. Set the oven at 180°C/350°F/gas 4. Sift the flour, salt, ginger and bicarbonate of soda into a mixing bowl. Add the oatmeal.

Heat the butter or margarine with the sugar and treacle gently in a saucepan until the fat has melted.

In a bowl, beat the egg and milk together. Add the melted mixture to the dry ingredients with the beaten egg and milk mixture. Stir well. Pour into the prepared tin and bake for 1-1¼ hours until cooked through and firm to the touch. Cool on a wire rack.

MAKES ONE 18 CM/7 INCH CAKE

✳ **FREEZER TIP**

Cut the cake into squares and wrap individually in foil before freezing for a ready supply of lunchbox or after-school treats.

RICH GINGERBREAD

fat for greasing
225 g/8 oz plain flour
1.25 ml/¼ tsp salt
10 ml/2 tsp ground ginger
2.5-5 ml/½-1 tsp ground cinnamon or grated nutmeg
5 ml/1 tsp bicarbonate of soda
100 g/4 oz butter
100 g/4 oz soft light brown sugar
100 g/4 oz golden syrup
1 egg
45 ml/3 tbsp plain yogurt
30 ml/2 tbsp ginger preserve

Line and grease a 20 cm/8 inch square tin. Set the oven at 160°C/325°F/gas 3.

Sift the flour, salt, spices and bicarbonate of soda into a mixing bowl. Heat the butter, sugar and syrup gently in a saucepan until the butter has melted.

In a bowl, beat the egg and yogurt together. Add to the dry ingredients, with the melted mixture, to give a soft, dropping consistency. Stir in the preserve.

Spoon into the prepared tin and bake for 50-60 minutes until cooked through and firm to the touch. Cool on a wire rack.

MAKES ONE 23 CM/9 INCH CAKE

APPLE AND GINGER CAKE

fat for greasing
175 g/6 oz plain flour
1.25 ml/¼ tsp salt
2.5 ml/½ tsp bicarbonate of soda
5 ml/1 tsp baking powder
5 ml/1 tsp ground ginger
100 g/4 oz crystallized ginger, chopped
100 g/4 oz butter or margarine
150 g/5 oz caster sugar
2 eggs, beaten
250 ml/8 fl oz sieved apple purée

Line and grease a 18 cm/7 inch square tin. Set the oven at 180°C/350°F/gas 4. Sift the flour, salt, bicarbonate of soda, baking powder and ground ginger into a bowl. Stir in the crystallized ginger and mix well. Set aside.

Place the butter or margarine in a mixing bowl and beat until very soft. Add the sugar and cream together until light and fluffy. Add the beaten eggs gradually, beating well after each addition. If the mixture shows signs of curdling, add a little of the flour mixture. Stir in the apple purée. Fold in the dry ingredients lightly but thoroughly. Spoon into the prepared tin, smooth the surface and make a slight hollow in the centre.

Bake for 30 minutes, then reduce the oven temperature to 160°C/325°F/gas 3 and bake for 15 minutes more until firm to the touch. Cool on a wire rack.

MAKES ONE 18 CM/7 INCH CAKE

YEAST CAKE

fat for greasing
50 g/2 oz butter
2 eggs
125 ml/4 fl oz milk
275 g/10 oz plain flour
100 g/4 oz soft light brown sugar
25 g/1 oz fresh yeast
150 g/5 oz currants
50 g/2 oz cut mixed peel

Line and grease a 15-18 cm/6-7 inch cake tin. Melt the butter in a saucepan and leave to cool. Add the eggs and milk and whisk until frothy. Combine the flour and sugar in a large bowl. In a cup, cream the yeast with a little warm water and set aside until frothy.

Make a hollow in the flour mixture and pour in the yeast. Add the butter and egg mixture, and mix well. Knead on a clean work surface to a smooth, soft dough, then return to the clean mixing bowl. Cover with a damp cloth, and place in a warm, draught-free place. Leave to rise for about 1½ hours or until the dough has doubled in bulk.

Add the dried fruit and peel, and knead until it is well distributed. Form the dough into a round and place in the prepared cake tin. Leave to rise for 30 minutes.

Set the oven at 200°C/400°F/gas 6. Bake the cake for 30 minutes, then reduce the oven temperature to 160°C/325°F/gas 3 and bake for a further 1 hour or until the cake sounds hollow when rapped on the base. Cool on a wire rack.

MAKES ONE 15-18 CM/6-7 INCH CAKE

 MRS BEETON'S TIP

Excessive heat kills yeast so take care that the water mixed with the yeast is merely at blood temperature.

Ribbon Bavarois (page 590)

Knickerbocker Glory (page 713) **and Neapolitan Ice** (page 706)

Port Wine Jelly (page 685) **and Red Fruit Salad** (page 676)

Apricot and Almond Pudding (page 569) **with a jug of Apricot Sauce** (page 501) **and Washington Ripple** (page 569) **and Vanilla Custard** (page 498)

Lemon Rice (page 581)

Dundee Cake (page 753)

English Madeleines (page 761) **and Butterfly Cakes** (page 760)

Melting Moments (page 795) **and Piped Almond Rings** (page 797)

Irish Soda Bread (page 839) **and Texas Cornbread** (page 839)

Gooseberry Jam (page 888) **Peach Jam** (page 887) **in the stand, and
Plum and Apple Jam** (page 884) **in the dish**

Mincemeat and Lemon Curd (both on page 898), **and**
Spiced Apple Butter (page 897)

Clockwise from top: Creamy Fudge (page 870), **Peanut Brittle** (page 868),
Buttered Brazils (page 871), **and Butterscotch** (page 868);
Centre: Mint Humbugs (page 875)

Apple, Apricot and Pear Fritters (page 445)

Basic White Bread (page 812) **and Wheatmeal Bread** (page 819)

Hot Cross Buns (page 834) **and Chelsea Buns** (page 833)

Bara Brith (page 829) **and Cherry Bread** (page 831)

BOILED FRUIT CAKE

fat for greasing
100 g/4 oz mixed dried fruit
50 g/2 oz margarine
25 g/1 oz soft light brown sugar
grated rind of 1 orange
200 g/7 oz plain flour
2.5 ml/½ tsp mixed spice
2.5 ml/½ tsp bicarbonate of soda

Line and grease a 15 cm/6 inch tin. Set the oven at 180°C/350°F/gas 4.

Combine the dried fruit, margarine, sugar and orange rind in a saucepan. Add 200 ml/7 fl oz water. Bring to the boil, reduce the heat and simmer for 5 minutes. Leave to cool until tepid.

Sift the flour, spice and bicarbonate of soda into the fruit mixture and mix well. Spoon into the prepared tin. Cover with greased paper or foil and bake for 1½–2 hours or until cooked through and firm to the touch. Cool the cake on a wire rack.

MAKES ONE 15 CM/6 INCH CAKE

 MICROWAVE TIP

Combine the dried fruit, margarine, sugar, water and orange rind in a mixing bowl. Cover lightly and microwave on High for 5 minutes, stirring twice. Leave to cool until tepid, then proceed as in the recipe above.

ONE-STAGE CHERRY CAKE

fat for greasing
225 g/8 oz glacé cherries
175 g/6 oz soft margarine
175 g/6 oz caster sugar
3 eggs
225 g/8 oz plain flour
12.5 ml/2½ tsp baking powder
50 g/2 oz ground almonds (optional)

Line and grease an 18 cm/7 inch round cake tin. Set the oven at 160°C/325°F/gas 3. Wash, dry and halve the cherries.

Put all the ingredients in a bowl and beat for 2–3 minutes until well mixed. Spoon the mixture into the prepared tin and bake for 1½–1¾ hours or until cooked through and firm to the touch. Cool on a wire rack.

MAKES ONE 18 CM/7 INCH CAKE

 MRS BEETON'S TIP

Instead of using plain flour, self-raising flour can be substituted and the quantity of baking powder reduced to 2.5 ml/½ tsp.

It is important to wash the syrup coating off glacé cherries before adding them to cake mixtures. Place them in a sieve, rinse them under hot water; drain well. Then dry the fruit on absorbent kitchen paper. Lastly, when the method is not a one-stage one, toss the cherries in some of the measured flour.

CHERRY CAKE

fat for greasing
200g/7oz plain flour
1.25ml/¼tsp salt
2.5ml/½tsp baking powder
100g/4oz glacé cherries, washed, dried and
    quartered
150g/5oz butter or margarine
150g/5oz caster sugar
4 eggs, beaten
15ml/1tbsp milk (optional)

Line and grease a 15cm/6 inch cake tin. Set the oven at 180°C/350°F/gas 4. Sift the flour, salt and baking powder into a bowl. Add the cherries and mix well. Set aside.

Place the butter or margarine in a mixing bowl and beat until very soft. Add the sugar and cream together until light and fluffy. Add the beaten eggs gradually, beating well after each addition. If the mixture shows signs of curdling, add a little of the flour mixture.

Fold in the dry ingredients lightly but thoroughly, adding the milk if too stiff.

Spoon into the prepared tin, level the surface and make a slight hollow in the centre. Bake for 30 minutes, then reduce the oven temperature to 160°C/325°F/gas 3 and bake for 50 minutes more until cooked through and firm to the touch. Cool on a wire rack.

MAKES ONE 15CM/6INCH CAKE

FESTIVAL FRUIT CAKE

fat for greasing
225g/8oz plain flour
1.25ml/¼tsp salt
2.5ml/½tsp baking powder
50g/2oz currants
50g/2oz sultanas
50g/2oz glacé cherries, washed, dried and
    chopped
50g/2oz cut mixed peel
150g/5oz butter or margarine
150g/5oz caster sugar
2 eggs, beaten
15ml/1tbsp milk (optional)

Line and grease an 18cm/7 inch cake tin. Set the oven at 180°C/350°F/gas 4. Sift the flour, salt and baking powder into a bowl. Stir in the dried fruit and mixed peel and mix well. Set aside.

Place the butter or margarine in a mixing bowl and beat until very soft. Add the sugar and cream together until light and fluffy. Add the beaten eggs gradually, beating well after each addition. If the mixture shows signs of curdling, add a little of the flour mixture.

Fold in the dry ingredients lightly but thoroughly, adding the milk if too stiff.

Spoon into the prepared tin, smooth the surface and make a slight hollow in the centre. Bake for 30 minutes, then reduce the oven temperature to 160°C/325°F/gas 3 and bake for 40 minutes more until firm to the touch. Cool on a wire rack.

MAKES ONE 18CM/7INCH CAKE

 MRS BEETON'S TIP

When adding the cherries to the flour, be sure to mix them in thoroughly. If the cherries are coated in flour they will not sink to the bottom of the cake.

COUNTESS SPICE CAKE

fat for greasing
100 g/4 oz plain flour
100 g/4 oz cornflour
2.5 ml/½ tsp ground ginger
3.75 ml/¾ tsp grated nutmeg
3.75 ml/¾ tsp ground cinnamon
1.25 ml/¼ tsp salt
75 g/3 oz margarine
10 ml/2 tsp baking powder
75 g/3 oz sugar
2 small eggs
about 125 ml/4 fl oz milk
50 g/2 oz currants
50 g/2 oz seedless raisins

Line and grease a 15 cm/6 inch tin. Set the oven at 180°C/350°F/gas 4.

Mix the flour, cornflour, spices and salt in a mixing bowl. Rub in the margarine until the mixture resembles fine breadcrumbs. Add the baking powder and the sugar.

In a bowl, beat the eggs with 50 ml/2 fl oz of the milk and stir into the flour mixture. Add more milk, if necessary, to give a consistency which just drops off the end of a wooden spoon. Stir in the currants and raisins.

Spoon the mixture into the prepared cake tin and bake for 1-1½ hours or until cooked through. Cool on a wire rack.

MAKES ONE 15 CM/6 INCH CAKE

MIXED FRUIT LOAF

fat for greasing
200 g/7 oz self-raising flour
pinch of salt
100 g/4 oz margarine
100 g/4 oz caster sugar
grated rind of 1 orange
225 g/8 oz mixed dried fruit, for example
    25 g/1 oz glacé cherries, 25 g/1 oz cut mixed
    peel, 75 g/3 oz sultanas, 75 g/3 oz seedless
    raisins
1 egg
milk (see method)

Line and grease a 23 × 13 × 7.5 cm/9 × 5 × 3 inch loaf tin. Set the oven at 180°C/350°F/gas 4.

Mix the flour and salt in a mixing bowl and rub in the margarine until the mixture resembles fine breadcrumbs. Stir in the sugar and orange rind. Wash and dry the cherries, if used, cut into 4-6 pieces each, depending on size, and add with the remaining fruit.

In a measuring jug, beat the egg lightly and add enough milk to make up to 125 ml/4 fl oz. Add to the flour mixture, stir in, then mix well. Spoon into the prepared tin and bake for about 1 hour or until firm to the touch. Cool the cake on a wire rack.

MAKES ONE 23 × 13 × 7.5 CM/9 × 5 × 3 INCH LOAF

 MICROWAVE TIP

The dried fruit may be cleaned and plumped in a single operation in the microwave. Place the fruit in a bowl with cold water to cover. Heat on High until the water boils, allow to stand until cool enough to handle, then drain the fruit, removing any stalks.

LUNCH CAKE

It is always useful to have a cake ready to slice for lunchboxes. If making this with children in view you may wish to reduce the amount of spice.

fat for greasing
225 g/8 oz plain flour
1.25 ml/¼ tsp salt
10 ml/2 tsp mixed spice
2.5 ml/½ tsp ground cloves
5 ml/1 tsp ground cinnamon
5 ml/1 tsp cream of tartar
2.5 ml/½ tsp bicarbonate of soda
75 g/3 oz margarine
100 g/4 oz sugar
75 g/3 oz currants
50 g/2 oz seedless raisins
25 g/1 oz cut mixed peel
2 eggs
60 ml/2 fl oz milk

Line and grease a 15 cm/6 inch round cake tin. Set the oven at 180°C/350°F/gas 4.

Sift the flour, salt, spices, cream of tartar and bicarbonate of soda into a mixing bowl. Rub in the margarine until the mixture resembles fine breadcrumbs. Add the sugar, dried fruit and mixed peel.

In a bowl beat the eggs lightly with the milk. Make a hollow in the dry ingredients and pour in the milk mixture. Stir, then beat lightly to a soft consistency. Spoon into the prepared tin and bake for 1¼ hours or until cooked through and firm to the touch. Cool on a wire rack.

MAKES ONE 15 CM/6 INCH CAKE

VINEGAR CAKE

fat for greasing
200 g/7 oz plain flour
1.25 ml/¼ tsp salt
75 g/3 oz margarine
75 g/3 oz soft dark brown sugar
50 g/2 oz currants
50 g/2 oz sultanas
25 g/1 oz cut mixed peel
175 ml/6 fl oz milk
5 ml/1 tsp bicarbonate of soda
15 ml/1 tbsp malt vinegar

Line and grease a 15 cm/6 inch round tin. Set the oven at 180°C/350°F/gas 4.

Mix the flour and salt in a mixing bowl and rub in the margarine until the mixture resembles fine breadcrumbs. Stir in the sugar, dried fruit and peel.

Warm half the milk in a small saucepan. Stir in the bicarbonate of soda until dissolved. Add this with the remaining milk and the vinegar to the dry ingredients and mix thoroughly.

Bake for 1 hour, then reduce the oven temperature to 160°C/325°F/gas 3 and bake for a further 30-40 minutes, or until cooked through and firm to the touch. Cool on a wire rack.

MAKES ONE 15 CM/6 INCH CAKE

Special Cakes

*A special cake is an essential feature of any celebration, whether the occasion is a birthday tea,
an informal gathering of friends or a grand wedding. Alongside seasonal cakes, this chapter includes
exciting recipes that are just that bit different.*

CHRISTMAS CAKE

fat for greasing
200 g/7 oz plain flour
1.25 ml/¼ tsp salt
5–10 ml/1–2 tsp mixed spice
200 g/7 oz butter
200 g/7 oz caster sugar
6 eggs, beaten
30–60 ml/2–4 tbsp brandy or sherry
100 g/4 oz glacé cherries, chopped
50 g/2 oz preserved ginger, chopped
50 g/2 oz walnuts, chopped
200 g/7 oz currants
200 g/7 oz sultanas
150 g/5 oz seedless raisins
75 g/3 oz cut mixed peel

COATING AND ICING
Almond Paste (page 766)
Royal Icing (page 774)

Line and grease a 20 cm/8 inch round cake tin.
Use doubled greaseproof paper and tie a strip of
brown paper around the outside. Set the oven at
160°C/325°F/gas 3.

Sift the flour, salt and spice into a bowl. In a
mixing bowl, cream the butter and sugar
together until light and fluffy. Gradually beat in
the eggs and the brandy or sherry, adding a
little flour if the mixture starts to curdle. Add
the cherries, ginger and walnuts. Stir in the
dried fruit, peel and flour mixture. Spoon into
the prepared tin and make a slight hollow in
the centre.

Bake for 45 minutes, then reduce the oven
temperature to 150°C/300°F/gas 2 and bake for
a further hour. Reduce the temperature still
further to 140°C/275°F/gas 1, and continue
cooking for 45–60 minutes until cooked
through and firm to the touch. Cool in the tin.
Cover the cake with almond paste and decorate
with royal icing.

MAKES ONE 20 CM/8 INCH CAKE

 MRS BEETON'S TIP

The quickest way to complete the decoration on a Christmas cake is to apply the
royal icing in rough peaks, then add bought
decorations. For a change, why not bake
the cake mixture in a shaped tin, for example in the shape of a star or a bell? Shaped
tins can be hired from kitchen shops and
cake decorating suppliers.

To decide on the quantity of mixture
which will fill an unusually-shaped tin,
pour water into the tin until it is full to the
brim. Measure the quantity of water as you
are pouring it into the tin. Do the same with
a 20 cm/8 inch round tin. Compare the
volumes and adjust the weight of ingredients accordingly.

TWELFTH NIGHT CAKE

The tradition of the Twelfth Night Cake goes back to the days of the early Christian Church and beyond. In the Middle Ages, whoever found the bean in his cake became the 'Lord of Misrule' or 'King' for the festivities of Twelfth Night, with the finder of the pea as his 'Queen'. Finding the bean was thought to bring luck. The tradition survived until near the end of the nineteenth century.

fat for greasing
150 g/5 oz margarine
75 g/3 oz soft dark brown sugar
3 eggs
300 g/11 oz plain flour
60 ml/4 tbsp milk
5 ml/1 tsp bicarbonate of soda
30 ml/2 tbsp golden syrup
2.5 ml/½ tsp mixed spice
2.5 ml/½ tsp ground cinnamon
pinch of salt
50 g/2 oz currants
100 g/4 oz sultanas
100 g/4 oz cut mixed peel
1 dried bean (see above)
1 large dried whole pea (see above)

Line and grease a 15 cm/6 inch round cake tin. Set the oven at 180°C/350°F/gas 4.

In a mixing bowl, cream the margarine and sugar until light and fluffy. Beat in the eggs, one at a time, adding a little flour with each. Warm the milk, add the bicarbonate of soda and stir until dissolved. Add the syrup.

Mix the spices and salt with the remaining flour in a bowl. Add this to the creamed mixture alternately with the flavoured milk. Lightly stir in the dried fruit and peel. Spoon half the cake mixture into the prepared tin, lay the bean and pea in the centre, then cover with the rest of the cake mixture. Bake for about 2 hours. Cool on a wire rack.

MAKES ONE 15 CM/6 INCH CAKE

SIMNEL CAKE

fat for greasing
200 g/7 oz plain flour
2.5 ml/½ tsp baking powder
1.25 ml/¼ tsp salt
150 g/5 oz butter
150 g/5 oz caster sugar
4 eggs
100 g/4 oz glacé cherries, halved
150 g/5 oz currants
150 g/5 oz sultanas
100 g/4 oz seedless raisins
50 g/2 oz cut mixed peel
50 g/2 oz ground almonds
grated rind of 1 lemon

DECORATION
double quantity Almond Paste (page 766) or
    450 ml/1 lb marzipan
30 ml/2 tbsp smooth apricot jam (see
    method)
1 egg, beaten
White Glacé Icing (page 771) using 50 g/2 oz
    icing sugar
Easter decorations

Line and grease a 18 cm/7 inch cake tin. Set the oven at 180°C/350°F/gas 4.

Sift the flour, baking powder and salt into a bowl. In a mixing bowl, cream the butter and sugar together well and beat in the eggs, adding a little of the flour mixture if necessary. Fold the flour mixture, cherries, dried fruit, peel and ground almonds into the creamed mixture. Add the lemon rind and mix well.

Spoon half the mixture into the prepared tin. Cut off one third of the almond paste and roll it to a pancake about 1 cm/½ inch thick and slightly smaller than the circumference of the tin. Place it gently on top of the cake mixture and spoon the remaining cake mixture on top.

Bake for 1 hour, then reduce the oven temperature to 160°C/325°F/gas 3 and bake for 1½ hours more. Cool in the tin, then turn out on a wire rack.

Warm, then sieve the apricot jam. When the cake is cold, divide the remaining almond paste in half. Roll one half to a round of a slightly smaller diameter than the top of the cake. Brush the top of the cake with apricot jam and press the almond paste lightly on to it. Trim the edge neatly.

Make 11 small balls with the remaining paste and place them around the edge of the cake. Brush the balls with the beaten egg and brown under the grill. Pour the glacé icing into the centre of the cake and decorate with chickens and Easter eggs.

MAKES ONE 18CM/7INCH CAKE

PINEAPPLE UPSIDE-DOWN CAKE

Serve this delicious cake with cream as a dessert, or cold for afternoon tea.

1 (227g/8oz) can pineapple rings
100g/4oz butter
275g/10oz soft dark brown sugar
8 maraschino or glacé cherries
450g/1lb self-raising flour
5ml/1tsp ground cinnamon
5ml/1tsp ground nutmeg
2 eggs
250ml/8floz milk

Drain the pineapple rings, reserving the syrup. Melt 50g/2oz of the butter in a 20cm/8 inch square baking tin. Add 100g/4oz of the sugar and 15ml/1tbsp pineapple syrup and mix well. Arrange the pineapple rings in an even pattern on the base of the tin, and place a cherry in the centre of each ring. Set the oven at 180°C/350°F/gas 4.

Sift the flour, cinnamon and nutmeg into a mixing bowl. In a second bowl, beat the eggs with the remaining brown sugar. Melt the remaining butter in a saucepan and add to the eggs and sugar with the milk; stir into the spiced flour and mix well.

Pour this mixture carefully over the fruit in the baking tin without disturbing it. Bake for 45–50 minutes. Remove the tin from the oven and at once turn upside-down on to a plate; allow the caramel to run over the cake before removing the baking tin.

MAKES ONE 20CM/8INCH CAKE

VARIATIONS

Apricot Upside-down Cake Substitute canned apricot halves for the pineapple, placing them rounded-side down in the tin. Arrange the cherries between the apricots.

Plum Upside-down Cake Arrange halved and stoned fresh plums in the bottom of the tin instead of pineapple. Use orange juice instead of the pineapple syrup and place the plums cut side down. Omit the cherries.

Pear Upside-down Cake Use canned pears instead of the pineapple. If you like, substitute ground ginger for the nutmeg.

SWISS ROLL

fat for greasing
3 eggs
75 g/3 oz caster sugar
75 g/3 oz plain flour
2.5 ml/½ tsp baking powder
pinch of salt
about 60 ml/4 tbsp jam for filling
caster sugar for dusting

Line and grease a 30 × 20 cm/12 × 8 inch Swiss roll tin. Set the oven at 220°C/425°F/gas 7.

Combine the eggs and sugar in a heatproof bowl. Set the bowl over a pan of hot water, taking care that the bottom of the bowl does not touch the water. Whisk for 10-15 minutes until thick and creamy, then remove from the pan. Continue whisking until the mixture is cold.

Sift the flour, baking powder and salt into a bowl, then lightly fold into the egg mixture. Pour into the prepared tin and bake for 10 minutes. Meanwhile warm the jam in a small saucepan.

When the cake is cooked, turn it on to a large sheet of greaseproof paper dusted with caster sugar. Peel off the lining paper. Trim off any crisp edges. Spread the cake with the warmed jam and roll up tightly from one long side. Dredge with caster sugar and place on a wire rack, with the join underneath, to cool.

MAKES ONE 30 CM/12 INCH SWISS ROLL

A VARIETY OF ROLLED CAKES

The classic Swiss Roll is quick and easy to make once you have mastered the technique of rolling the hot cake. The basic recipe for the light, rolled sponge can be used as a base for making cakes that are just that little bit different. The following variations suggest suitable combinations of flavouring ingredients, fillings and coatings.

Chocolate Ice Roll   Make the Chocolate Roll following the recipe on the right. Leave the rolled cake to cool completely. Using a shallow spoon, scoop flat portions of ice cream and place them on a baking sheet lined with cling film. Replace them in the freezer so that they are firmly frozen. Just before the cake is to be served, unroll it and fill with the ice cream, pressing it down lightly with a palette knife. Quickly re-roll the cake and sprinkle with icing sugar. Serve at once, with whipped cream.

Chocolate Rum Roll   Make this luscious, rich, rolled cake for special occasions. Prepare the Chocolate Roll, following the recipe on the right, and allow it to cool. Soak 50 g/2 oz of seedless raisins in 60 ml/4 tbsp of rum for 30 minutes. Drain the raisins and add the rum to 150 ml/¼ pint of double cream. Add 15 ml/1 tbsp of icing sugar to the cream and lightly whip it. Fold in the raisins and 30 ml/2 tbsp of chopped maraschino cherries. Spread this cream over the unrolled cake and re-roll.

Easter Almond Roll   Make the Swiss Roll following the recipe on the left. Leave to cool completely. Roll out 350 g/12 oz marzipan or almond paste into an oblong the same width as the length of the roll, and long enough to wrap around the roll. Brush the outside of the Swiss Roll with warmed apricot jam and place it on the rolled out marzipan or almond paste. Wrap the paste around the roll, trimming off excess and making sure that the join is underneath. Decorate the top of the roll with miniature chocolate Easter eggs.

Ginger Cream Roll   Make the plain Swiss Roll following the recipe on the left. Roll up with a sheet of greaseproof paper in the hot cake instead of jam, then leave it to cool completely. Remove the paper. Whip 300 ml/½ pint of double cream with 45 ml/3 tbsp of ginger wine. Mix 30 ml/2 tbsp of finely chopped crystallized ginger into half the cream and spread this over the unrolled cake, then re-roll it. Cover the outside with a thin layer of the remaining cream and pipe rosettes of cream along the top. Decorate the roll with crystallized ginger.

Raspberry Meringue Roll   Make a plain Swiss Roll as left, rolling it up with a sheet of greaseproof paper instead of spreading it with jam. Remove the paper when the roll is cold. Whip 150 ml/¼ pint of double cream with 30 ml/2 tbsp of icing sugar, then fold in 175 g/6 oz of raspberries. Spread this over the unrolled cake and roll it up again.

Whisk 2 egg whites until stiff, then whisk in 100 g/4 oz caster sugar. Continue whisking until the mixture is smooth, stiff and glossy. Swirl or pipe this meringue all over the roll. Brown the meringue under a moderately hot grill. Decorate with a few raspberries.

St Clement's Roll   Make a Swiss Roll as left, adding the grated rind of 1 orange to the eggs and sugar. Instead of jam, use lemon curd to fill the cake.

Walnut and Orange Roll   Make a Swiss Roll following the recipe on the left and adding the grated rind of 1 orange to the eggs and sugar. Roll the cake with a sheet of greaseproof paper instead of adding the jam, then leave it to cool. Remove the paper.

Finely chop 100 g/4 oz of fresh walnuts. Beat 15-30 ml/1-2 tbsp of honey, to taste, into 100 g/4 oz of soft cheese. Stir in the nuts and spread this mixture over the cake before re-rolling it.

CHOCOLATE ROLL

fat for greasing
3 eggs
75 g/3 oz caster sugar
65 g/2½ oz plain flour
30 ml/2 tbsp cocoa
2.5 ml/½ tsp baking powder
pinch of salt
Chocolate Buttercream (page 769) for filling
caster sugar for dusting

Line and grease a 30 × 20 cm/12 × 8 inch Swiss roll tin. Set the oven at 220°C/425°F/gas 7.

Combine the eggs and sugar in a heatproof bowl. Set the bowl over a pan of hot water, taking care that the bottom of the bowl does not touch the water. Whisk for 10-15 minutes until thick and creamy, then remove from the pan and continue whisking until cold.

Sift the flour, cocoa, baking powder and salt into a bowl, then lightly fold into the egg mixture. Pour into the prepared tin and bake for 10 minutes.

When the cake is cooked, turn it on to a large sheet of greaseproof paper dusted with caster sugar. Peel off the lining paper. Trim off any crisp edges. Place a second piece of greaseproof paper on top of the cake and roll up tightly from one long side, with the paper inside. Cool completely on a wire rack.

When cold, unroll carefully, remove the paper, spread with the buttercream and roll up again. Dust the roll with caster sugar.

MAKES ONE 30 CM/12 INCH SWISS ROLL

ALMOND MACAROON CAKE

fat for greasing
150 g/5 oz self-raising flour
pinch of salt
150 g/5 oz butter or margarine
150 g/5 oz caster sugar
3 eggs
100 g/4 oz ground almonds
grated rind of 1 lemon
25 g/1 oz blanched split almonds to decorate

MACAROON
1 egg white
50 g/2 oz ground almonds
75 g/3 oz caster sugar
5 ml/1 tsp ground rice
few drops of almond essence

Line and grease a 15 cm/6 inch loose-bottomed cake tin. Set the oven at 180°C/350°F/gas 4. Start by making the macaroon mixture; whisk the egg white in a bowl until frothy, then add the rest of the ingredients, beating well.

Make the cake mixture. Mix the flour and salt in a bowl. In a mixing bowl, cream the butter or margarine and sugar. Add the eggs, one at a time with a spoonful of flour. Stir in, then beat well. Fold in the remaining flour, the ground almonds, and the lemon rind.

Spread a 2 cm/¾ inch layer of the cake mixture on the base of the prepared tin. Divide the macaroon mixture into two equal portions; put half in the centre of the cake mixture. Add the rest of the mixture and spread the rest of the macaroon mixture on top. Cover with the blanched split almonds.

Bake for 1¼ hours, covering the top with grease-proof paper as soon as it is pale brown. Cool on a wire rack.

MAKES ONE 15 CM/6 INCH CAKE

GRANDMOTHER'S CAKE

200 g/7 oz mixed dried fruit
60 ml/4 tbsp milk or brandy
fat for greasing
100 g/4 oz butter or margarine
100 g/4 oz soft light brown sugar
30 ml/2 tbsp golden syrup
150 g/5 oz plain flour
2.5 ml/½ tsp salt
5 ml/1 tsp baking powder
5 ml/1 tsp mixed spice
75 g/3 oz glacé cherries
50 g/2 oz mixed peel or coarse-cut
   marmalade
3 eggs, beaten
milk (see method)

Soak the dried fruit in a bowl with the milk or brandy for 2 hours before making the cake.

Line and grease a 15 cm/6 inch cake tin. Set the oven at 180°C/350°F/gas 4. In a large mixing bowl, cream the butter or margarine with the sugar until light and fluffy. Beat in the syrup.

In a second bowl, sift the flour, salt, baking powder and spice. Mix 25–50 g/1–2 oz of the flour mixture with the plumped-up dried fruit, cherries and mixed peel, if used.

Stir the beaten eggs and the flour mixture alternately into the creamed mixture, beating well between each addition. Lightly fold in the floured fruit mixture with the marmalade, if used. Stir in just enough milk to make a soft dropping consistency.

Spoon the mixture into the prepared tin and bake for 25 minutes, then reduce the oven temperature to 150°C/300°F/gas 2 and bake for a further 2–2½ hours. Cool on a wire rack, then coat with almond paste and decorate with royal icing, if liked.

MAKES ONE 15 CM/6 INCH CAKE

BATTENBURG CAKE

fat for greasing
100 g/4 oz self-raising flour
pinch of salt
100 g/4 oz butter or margarine
100 g/4 oz caster sugar
2 eggs
pink food colouring
Apricot Glaze (page 766)
200 g/7 oz Almond Paste (page 766)

Line and grease a 23 × 18 cm/9 × 7 inch Battenburg tin, which has a metal divider down the centre; or use a 23 × 18 cm/9 × 7 inch tin and cut double greaseproof paper to separate the mixture into 2 parts. Set the oven at 190°C/375°F/gas 5. Mix the flour and salt in a bowl.

In a mixing bowl, cream the butter or margarine and sugar together until light and fluffy. Add the eggs, one at a time, with a little flour. Stir in, then beat well. Stir in the remaining flour lightly but thoroughly.

Place half the mixture in one half of the tin. Tint the remaining mixture pink, and place it in the other half of the tin. Smooth both mixtures away from the centre towards the outside of the tin.

Bake for 25-30 minutes. Leave the cakes in the tin for a few minutes, then transfer them to a wire rack and peel off the paper. Leave to cool completely.

To finish the Battenburg, cut each slab of cake lengthways into 3 strips. Trim off any crisp edges and rounded surfaces so that all 6 strips are neat and of the same size. Arrange 3 strips with 1 pink strip in the middle. Where the cakes touch, brush with the glaze and press together lightly. Make up the other layer in the same way, using 2 pink with 1 plain strip in the middle. Brush glaze over the top of the base layer and place the second layer on top.

Roll out the almond paste thinly into a rectangle the same length as the strips and wide enough to wrap around them. Brush it with glaze and place the cake in the centre. Wrap the paste around the cake and press the edges together lightly. Turn so that the join is underneath; trim the ends. Mark the top of the paste with the back of a knife to make a criss-cross pattern.

MAKES ONE 23 × 18 CM/9 × 7 INCH CAKE

✳ MICROWAVE TIP

Almond paste that has hardened will become soft and malleable again if heated in the microwave for a few seconds on High.

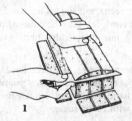

1

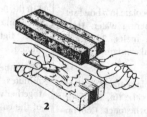

2

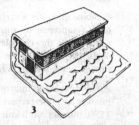

3

MARBLE CAKE

fat for greasing
175 g/6 oz butter or margarine
175 g/6 oz caster sugar
3 eggs, beaten
few drops of vanilla essence
225 g/8 oz self-raising flour
pinch of salt
30 ml/2 tbsp milk
30 ml/2 tbsp strong black coffee
50 g/2 oz chocolate, broken into chunks
Chocolate Buttercream (page 769)
15 ml/1 tbsp grated chocolate

Line and grease a 20 cm/8 inch round cake tin.
Set the oven at 180°C/350°F/gas 4.

In a mixing bowl cream the butter or margarine
with the sugar until light and fluffy. Add the
eggs gradually, beating well after each addition. Stir in the vanilla.

Sift the flour and salt into a bowl. Stir into the
creamed mixture, lightly but thoroughly, until
evenly mixed. Place half the mixture in a
second bowl and beat in the milk.

Combine the coffee and chocolate in a bowl set
over a saucepan of simmering water. Heat
gently until the chocolate melts. Stir thoroughly, then add to the cake mixture in the
mixing bowl, beating well.

Put alternate spoonfuls of plain and chocolate
mixture into the prepared cake tin. Bake for
45-60 minutes, until firm to the touch. Cool on
a wire rack. Top with the buttercream and
grated chocolate.

MAKES ONE 20 CM/8 INCH CAKE

VARIATION

Three-tone Marble Cake This is popular
with children. Divide the cake mixture into
three equal parts, leaving one plain, flavouring
one with chocolate and tinting the third pink
with food colouring. Combine and bake as
suggested left.

CHOCOLATE LAYER CAKE

fat for greasing
150 g/5 oz butter or margarine
150 g/5 oz caster sugar
3 eggs, beaten
few drops of vanilla essence
100 g/4 oz self-raising flour or plain flour
   and 5 ml/1 tsp baking powder
25 g/1 oz cocoa
pinch of salt
Chocolate Buttercream (page 769) for filling
caster sugar for dredging

Line and grease two 18 cm/7 inch sandwich
tins. Set the oven at 180°C/350°F/gas 4.

In a mixing bowl cream the butter or margarine
with the sugar until light and fluffy. Add the
eggs gradually, beating well after each addition
and adding a little of the flour if the mixture
shows signs of curdling. Stir in the vanilla
essence.

Sift the flour, cocoa, salt and baking powder, if
used, into a bowl. Stir into the creamed mixture, lightly but thoroughly, until evenly
mixed.

Divide between the tins and bake for 25-30
minutes. Cool on a wire rack, then sandwich
together with the buttercream. Spinkle the top
of the cake with caster sugar.

MAKES ONE 18 CM/7 INCH CAKE

INGREDIENTS FOR RICH FRUIT CAKE

ROUND	15 cm/6 inch	18 cm/7 inch	20 cm/8 inch	23 cm/9 inch	25 cm/10 inch	28 cm/11 inch	30 cm/12 inch	33 cm/13 inch
SQUARE	13 cm/5 inch	15 cm/6 inch	18 cm/7 inch	20 cm/8 inch	23 cm/9 inch	25 cm/10 inch	28 cm/11 inch	30 cm/12 inch
Currants	225 g/8 oz	275 g/10 oz	400 g/14 oz	500 g/18 oz	575 g/1¼ lb	675 g/1½ lb	900 g/2 lb	1.25 kg/2½ lb
Raisins	100 g/4 oz	150 g/5 oz	200 g/7 oz	250 g/9 oz	300 g/11 oz	375 g/13 oz	450 g/1 lb	575 g/1¼ lb
Sultanas	100 g/4 oz	150 g/5 oz	200 g/7 oz	250 g/9 oz	300 g/11 oz	375 g/13 oz	450 g/1 lb	575 g/1¼ lb
Butter, softened	100 g/4 oz	150 g/5 oz	200 g/7 oz	250 g/9 oz	300 g/11 oz	375 g/13 oz	450 g/1 lb	575 g/1¼ lb
Moist dark brown sugar	100 g/4 oz	150 g/5 oz	200 g/7 oz	250 g/9 oz	300 g/11 oz	375 g/13 oz	450 g/1 lb	575 g/1¼ lb
Lemon, grated rind of	½	½	1	1	1½	1½	2	2
Almonds, shelled	25 g/1 oz	25 g/1 oz	40 g/1½ oz	65 g/2½ oz	75 g/3 oz	90 g/3½ oz	100 g/4 oz	100 g/4 oz
Citrus peel, chopped	25 g/1 oz	25 g/1 oz	40 g/1½ oz	65 g/2½ oz	75 g/3 oz	90 g/3½ oz	100 g/4 oz	100 g/4 oz
Glacé cherries	50 g/2 oz	50 g/2 oz	75 g/3 oz	90 g/3½ oz	100 g/4 oz	150 g/5 oz	175 g/6 oz	175 g/6 oz
Plain flour	100 g/4 oz	150 g/5 oz	200 g/7 oz	250 g/9 oz	300 g/11 oz	375 g/13 oz	450 g/1 lb	575 g/1¼ lb
Ground mixed spice	1.25 ml/¼ tsp	2.5 ml/½ tsp	2.5 ml/½ tsp	5 ml/1 tsp	5 ml/1 tsp	7.5 ml/1½ tsp	7.5 ml/1½ tsp	10 ml/2 tsp
Eggs, beaten	2	2	3	4	5	6	8	10
Black treacle	10 ml/2 tsp	10 ml/2 tsp	15 ml/1 tbsp	15 ml/1 tbsp	22.5 ml/4½ tsp	22.5 ml/4½ tsp	30 ml/2 tbsp	30 ml/2 tbsp
PORTION GUIDE:								
round	20	30	40	58	70	85	100	120
square	15	25	38	55	75	90	115	135

This chart provides an alternative to the recipe for the wedding cake on the next page. It also gives quantities for cakes of different sizes and a guide to portions.

Set the oven at 150°C/300°F/gas 2. Line and grease the appropriate tin. Mix the currants, raisins and sultanas. Cream the butter and sugar with the lemon rind until very soft. Beat in the almonds and the citrus peel. Wash and dry the cherries, then roughly chop them and toss them with a little of the measured flour. Sift the remaining flour with the spice and toss a little with the mixed dried fruit. Beat the eggs and treacle into the creamed mixture, adding a spoonful of the flour occasionally to prevent the mixture curdling. Fold in the remaining flour. Lastly fold in the fruit and the cherries.

Turn the mixture into the tin and smooth the top with the back of a wetted metal spoon, hollowing out the centre slightly. The cooking time depends on the size of the cake. The small cakes will take about 1½–2 hours, the cakes of between 20–23 cm/8–9 inches about 4–5 hours and the larger cakes about 7–8 hours. Insert a clean metal skewer into the centre of the cake to test if it is cooked: it should come out clean when the cake is ready. If there is any sticky mixture on the skewer the cake is not cooked.

Leave the cake to cool in the tin for at least an hour, then transfer it to a wire rack to cool completely. Do not remove the lining paper. Wrap the cake, still in the lining paper, in fresh greaseproof paper and store it in an airtight tin.

THREE TIERED WEDDING CAKE

If possible, prepare the three tiers together, using a very large bowl. Cream the butter and sugar, and mix in the other ingredients by hand. Few ovens are large enough to bake all the tiers simultaneously; leave the cake(s) awaiting baking in a cool place overnight if necessary.

Make the cakes at least two months before covering and icing them with almond paste and royal icing to allow time for the cakes to mature. When cool, the outside of each tier may be pricked with a skewer and sprinkled with brandy. To store, wrap in clean greaseproof paper and place in an airtight container or wrap in foil or a large polythene bag outside the complete covering of greaseproof paper. Keep in a cool, dry place. If the top tier of a wedding cake is to be kept for some time, fresh almond paste and royal icing should be applied when it is used.

SMALL TIER
fat for greasing
100 g/4 oz currants
100 g/4 oz sultanas
100 g/4 oz seedless raisins
50 g/2 oz glacé cherries, chopped
25 g/1 oz blanched whole almonds, chopped
25 g/1 oz cut mixed peel
grated rind of 1 small orange
30 ml/2 tbsp brandy
100 g/4 oz plain flour
1.25 ml/¼ tsp salt
2.5 ml/½ tsp mixed spice
1.25 ml/¼ tsp grated nutmeg
100 g/4 oz butter
100 g/4 oz soft dark brown sugar
2 large eggs, beaten
15 ml/1 tbsp treacle
25 g/1 oz ground almonds

Line and grease a 15 cm/6 inch round or 13 cm/5 inch square cake tin. Use doubled greaseproof paper and tie a strip of doubled brown paper around the outside of the tin. Set the oven at 140°C/275°F/gas 1. Place the dried fruit in a bowl, removing any stalks. Add the cherries, almonds, peel, orange rind and brandy and stir well. Cover and set aside. Sift the flour, salt and spices into a large bowl. In a large mixing bowl, cream the butter and sugar until pale and fluffy. Add the beaten eggs, a quarter at a time, with a little of the flour, beating thoroughly after each addition. Add the treacle with the rest of the flour, the ground almonds and the fruit in brandy. Stir until evenly mixed. Spoon the mixture into the prepared tin and make a slight hollow in the centre. Bake for 2¼–3 hours, until firm to the touch. Cover with ungreased greaseproof paper after 1½ hours to prevent overbrowning. Cool in the tin. Leave for 24 hours before turning out.

MIDDLE TIER
225 g/8 oz currants
200 g/7 oz sultanas
200 g/7 oz seedless raisins
100 g/4 oz glacé cherries
50 g/2 oz blanched whole almonds
50 g/2 oz cut mixed peel
grated rind of 1 large orange
45 ml/3 tbsp brandy
200 g/7 oz plain flour
2.5 ml/½ tsp salt
5 ml/1 tsp mixed spice
5 ml/1 tsp grated nutmeg
30 ml/2 tbsp treacle
200 g/7 oz butter
200 g/7 oz soft dark brown sugar
4 large eggs
50 g/2 oz ground almonds

Make as for the small tier. Bake in a prepared 20 cm/8 inch round tin or 18 cm/7 inch square tin, in an oven preheated to 140°C/275°F/gas 1 for 4–4½ hours. Cover the top with ungreased greaseproof paper when the cake is sufficiently brown. Cool.

LARGE TIER
575 g/1¼ lb currants
450 g/1 lb sultanas
450 g/1 lb seedless raisins
225 g/8 oz glacé cherries
100 g/4 oz blanched whole almonds
100 g/4 oz cut mixed peel
grated rind of 2 large oranges
125 ml/4 fl oz brandy
450 g/1 lb plain flour
5 ml/1 tsp salt
10 ml/2 tsp mixed spice
10 ml/2 tsp grated nutmeg
75 ml/5 tbsp treacle
450 g/1 lb butter
450 g/1 lb soft dark brown sugar
10 large eggs
100 g/4 oz ground almonds

Line and grease a 28 cm/11 inch round or
25 cm/10 inch square cake tin. Use doubled
greaseproof paper and tie at least three bands of
brown paper around the outside of the tin.
Make the cake as for the small tier. Bake in an
oven preheated to 140°C/275°F/gas 1 for about
5½ hours. After 2 hours cover the top with
doubled greaseproof paper, and gently give the
tin a quarter turn. Turn again after each 30
minutes to avoid overbrowning. Cool.

MRS BEETON'S
BRIDE CAKE

900 g/2 lb plain flour
7.5 ml/1½ tsp baking powder
7.5 ml/1½ tsp grated nutmeg
7.5 ml/1½ tsp ground mace
2.5 ml/½ tsp ground cloves
350 g/12 oz ground almonds
900 g/2 lb currants
350 g/12 oz good-quality candied citron and
   orange peel, chopped
675 g/1½ lb butter
575 g/1¼ lb caster sugar
11 eggs (size 3)
75 ml/3 fl oz brandy
75 ml/3 fl oz port or medium sherry

Line and grease a 30 cm/12 inch round tin. Set
the oven at 150°C/300°F/gas 2. Sift the flour,
baking powder and spices together, then stir in
the ground almonds. In a separate bowl, mix
the currants with the candied peel.

Cream the butter and sugar until the mixture is
pale and soft. Beat the eggs together, then
gradually beat them into the creamed mixture,
adding spoonfuls of the flour mixture between
each addition to prevent the mixture from
curdling. Continue alternating additions of egg
and flour until both are fully incorporated.

Mix in the currants and candied peel, brandy
and port or sherry. Turn the mixture into the
prepared tin and bake for about 4½ hours, or
until the cake is cooked through. Test by
inserting a skewer into the middle of the cake –
if it comes out free of mixture the cake is
cooked.

Leave the cake to cool in the tin for 1-2 hours,
then turn it out on a wire rack to cool completely. Leave the greaseproof paper on the
cake, wrap it in a clean covering of paper and
store in an airtight container for at least a
month. Ice and decorate in the usual way.

Traditional British Cakes

This short chapter celebrates traditional British cake-making, with recipes that are both seasonal and regional, ranging from Classic Madeira Cake and Dundee Cake to Westmorland Parkin and Black Bun.

BLACK BUN

A rich cake, encased in pastry, from the Highlands of Scotland, served either on Twelfth Night (traditionally) or at Hogmanay to celebrate the new year.

400 g/14 oz plain flour
100 g/4 oz blanched whole almonds, roughly
   chopped
675 g/1½ lb muscatel raisins, seeded
675 g/1½ lb currants
100 g/4 oz cut mixed peel
200 g/7 oz caster sugar
30 ml/2 tbsp ground ginger
30 ml/2 tbsp ground cinnamon
30 ml/2 tbsp mixed spice
2.5 ml/½ tsp freshly ground black pepper
10 ml/2 tsp bicarbonate of soda
5 ml/1 tsp cream of tartar
350 ml/12 fl oz milk
15 ml/1 tbsp brandy

PASTRY
450 g/1 lb plain flour
225 g/8 oz butter
5 ml/1 tsp baking powder
flour for rolling out
beaten egg for glazing

Sift the flour into a large bowl. Add the almonds, dried fruit, peel, sugar and spices and mix well. Stir in the bicarbonate of soda and the cream of tartar, then moisten with the milk and brandy. Set the oven at 200°C/400°F/gas 6.

Make the pastry. Put the flour into a mixing bowl. Rub in the butter until the mixture resembles fine breadcrumbs, then add the baking powder. Stir in enough water (about 125 ml/4 fl oz) to form a stiff dough. Leave the dough to rest for a few minutes, then roll out on a lightly floured surface to a thickness of about 5 mm/¼ inch. Using three-quarters of the pastry, line a 23 cm/9 inch round cake tin (about 10 cm/4 inches deep), leaving a border around the edges for overlap. Roll out the remaining pastry for the lid.

Fill the pastry-lined tin with the cake mixture, and turn the edges of the pastry over it. Moisten the edges with water, put on the lid and seal. Decorate the pastry with any trimmings, prick with a fork all over the top and brush with egg.

Bake for 1 hour, then lower the oven temperature to 160°C/325°F/gas 3, cover the top of the bun loosely with paper or foil and continue baking for 2 hours more.

Leave the bun to cool in the tin for 20 minutes, then remove it from the tin and cool completely. Keep for 1 month in an airtight tin before using.

MAKES ONE 23 CM/9 INCH CAKE

CLASSIC MADEIRA CAKE

fat for greasing
150 g/5 oz butter or margarine
150 g/5 oz caster sugar
4 eggs, beaten
200 g/7 oz plain flour
10 ml/2 tsp baking powder
pinch of salt
grated rind of 1 lemon
caster sugar for dredging
1 thin slice of candied or glacé citron peel

Line and grease a 15 cm/6 inch round cake tin. Set the oven at 180°C/350°F/gas 4.

In a mixing bowl, cream the butter or margarine with the sugar until light and fluffy. Gradually add the eggs, beating well after each addition. Sift the flour, baking powder and salt together into a second bowl, then fold into the creamed mixture. Stir in the lemon rind and mix well. Spoon into the prepared tin. Dredge the top with caster sugar.

Bake for 20 minutes, then lay the slice of peel on top. Bake for a further 45–50 minutes or until cooked through and firm to the touch. Cool on a wire rack.

MAKES ONE 15 CM/6 INCH CAKE

 MRS BEETON'S TIP

If you do not have a sugar dredger, place a small amount of sugar in a tea strainer and pass it over the top of the cake.

DUNDEE CAKE

fat for greasing
200 g/7 oz plain flour
2.5 ml/½ tsp baking powder
1.25 ml/¼ tsp salt
150 g/5 oz butter
150 g/5 oz caster sugar
4 eggs, beaten
100 g/4 oz glacé cherries, quartered
150 g/5 oz currants
150 g/5 oz sultanas
100 g/4 oz seedless raisins
50 g/2 oz cut mixed peel
50 g/2 oz ground almonds
grated rind of 1 lemon
50 g/2 oz blanched split almonds

Line and grease an 18 cm/7 inch round cake tin. Set the oven at 180°C/350°F/gas 4. Sift the flour, baking powder and salt into a bowl. In a mixing bowl, cream the butter and sugar together well, and beat in the eggs. Fold the flour mixture, cherries, dried fruit, peel and ground almonds into the creamed mixture. Add the lemon rind and mix well.

Spoon into the prepared tin and make a slight hollow in the centre. Bake for 20 minutes, by which time the hollow should have filled in. Arrange the split almonds on top.

Return the cake to the oven, bake for a further 40–50 minutes, then reduce the temperature to 160°C/325°F/gas 3 and bake for 1 hour more. Cool on a wire rack.

MAKES ONE 18 CM/7 INCH CAKE

WESTMORLAND PARKIN

This makes a dense, dark parkin with excellent keeping qualities.

fat for greasing
200 g/7 oz butter or clarified dripping (page 424)
450 g/1 lb black treacle
450 g/1 lb fine oatmeal
200 g/7 oz plain flour
5 ml/1 tsp ground ginger
2.5 ml/½ tsp salt
10 ml/2 tsp baking powder
200 g/7 oz demerara sugar
100 ml/3½ fl oz milk
5 ml/1 tsp bicarbonate of soda

Line and grease two 20 cm/8 inch square tins. Set the oven at 160°C/325°F/gas 3.

Heat the butter or dripping and treacle gently in a saucepan, stirring until the fat has melted. Mix all the dry ingredients, except the bicarbonate of soda, in a mixing bowl and make a well in the centre.

Warm the milk in a saucepan over low heat to hand-hot. Stir in the bicarbonate of soda until dissolved. Pour into the dry ingredients and mix well. Stir in the melted butter and treacle.

Spoon the mixture into the prepared tins and bake for about 1¼ hours or until cooked through and firm to the touch. Cool in the tins, then cut into squares.

MAKES TWO 20 CM/8 INCH CAKES (ABOUT 32 SQUARES)

 MRS BEETON'S TIP

A lighter cake may be made by substituting liquid honey for half the treacle.

OLD ENGLISH CIDER CAKE

fat for greasing
225 g/8 oz plain flour
7.5 ml/1½ tsp grated nutmeg
1.25 ml/¼ tsp ground cinnamon
5 ml/1 tsp baking powder
pinch of salt
100 g/4 oz butter or margarine
100 g/4 oz caster sugar
2 eggs
125 ml/4 fl oz dry still cider

Line and lightly grease a shallow 20 cm/8 inch square cake tin. Set the oven at 180°C/350°F/gas 4.

Sift the flour into a bowl with the spices, baking powder and salt. Cream the butter or margarine with the sugar until light and fluffy, then beat in the eggs. Beat half the flour mixture into the creamed mixture. Beat in half the cider. Repeat, using the remaining flour and cider.

Spoon the mixture into the prepared tin and bake for 50–55 minutes until the cake is cooked through and firm to the touch. Cool the cake on a wire rack.

MAKES ONE 20 CM/8 INCH CAKE

 MRS BEETON'S TIP

A nutmeg grater is an invaluable accessory, but is difficult to clean. A child's toothbrush, kept specifically for the purpose, is ideal.

PATTERDALE PEPPER CAKE

Store this traditional British cake for at least a week before cutting.

fat for greasing
450 g/1 lb self-raising flour
15 ml/1 tbsp ground ginger
1.25 ml/¼ tsp ground cloves
2.5 ml/½ tsp freshly ground black pepper
100 g/4 oz butter
200 g/7 oz caster sugar
100 g/4 oz seedless raisins
100 g/4 oz currants
25 g/1 oz cut mixed peel
200 g/7 oz golden syrup, warmed
2 large eggs, lightly beaten
125 ml/4 fl oz skimmed milk

Line and grease a deep 18 cm/7 inch square cake tin or a somewhat shallower 20 cm/8 inch cake tin.

Set the oven at 160°C/325°F/gas 3. Sift the flour, spices and black pepper into a mixing bowl. Rub in the butter until the mixture resembles fine breadcrumbs. Stir in the sugar, and add the fruit and peel. Make a well in the flour mixture, pour in the syrup, eggs and milk, and beat lightly.

Spoon the mixture into the prepared tin and bake for 2½ hours or until cooked through and firm to the touch. Cool on a wire rack.

MAKES ONE 18 CM/7 INCH CAKE

 MICROWAVE TIP

Warming the syrup will make it easier to measure. If you are using syrup in a glass jar, remove the lid and heat the jar on High for 1 minute. Do not attempt this if the syrup is in a tin.

BOODLES CAKE

fat for greasing
200 g/7 oz self-raising flour or 200 g/7 oz
  plain flour and 10 ml/2 tsp baking powder
2.5 ml/½ tsp mixed spice
75 g/3 oz margarine
75–100 g/3–4 oz sugar
75 g/3 oz sultanas
75 g/3 oz seedless raisins
50 g/2 oz currants
2 small eggs
about 125 ml/4 fl oz milk

Line and grease a 15 cm/6 inch cake tin. Set the oven at 180°C/350°F/gas 4.

Mix the flour and spice in a mixing bowl and rub in the margarine until the mixture resembles fine breadcrumbs. Add the sugar, dried fruit and baking powder, if used.

In a bowl, beat the eggs with the milk and add to the dry ingredients and fruit. Stir well.

Spoon the mixture into the prepared tin and bake for 45 minutes, then lower the oven temperature to 160°C/325°F/gas 3 and bake for a further 30 minutes until cooked through and firm to the touch. Cool on a wire rack.

MAKES ONE 15 CM/6 INCH CAKE

DRIPPING CAKE

Perhaps not the healthiest of cakes, but certainly economical. Dripping may be clarified in the same way as butter (see information on butter, page 424).

fat for greasing
200 g/7 oz self-raising flour
pinch of salt
1.25 ml/¼ tsp mixed spice
100 g/4 oz clarified beef dripping
75 g/3 oz sugar
75 g/3 oz seedless raisins
50 g/2 oz currants
1 egg
100 ml/3½ fl oz milk

Line and grease a 15 cm/6 inch round cake tin. Set the oven at 180°C/350°F/gas 4.

Mix the flour, salt and spice in a mixing bowl. Rub in the dripping until the mixture resembles breadcrumbs. Add the sugar and dried fruit.

In a bowl, beat the egg with the milk and add to the dry ingredients. Stir well, then beat until smooth. Spoon into the prepared tin and bake for 1 hour 10 minutes or until cooked through and firm to the touch. Cover the top with greaseproof paper after 1 hour if the cake is already brown enough.

MAKES ONE 15 CM/6 INCH CAKE

 MRS BEETON'S TIP

Use clarified dripping which does not have too strong a flavour. If it has been kept in the refrigerator, allow it to come to room temperature.

SHEARING CAKE

In Welsh this simple cake is known as 'Cacen Gneifio' and traditionally it was prepared to serve with tea for all the farm workers who gathered to help on days when the sheep were sheared and dipped.

butter for greasing
400 g/14 oz plain flour
pinch of salt
10 ml/2 tsp baking powder
200 g/7 oz butter
225 g/8 oz soft light brown sugar
grated rind of ½ lemon
20 ml/4 tsp caraway seeds
5 ml/1 tsp grated nutmeg or to taste
2 eggs
200 ml/7 fl oz milk

Line and grease a 20 cm/8 inch round cake tin. Set the oven at 180°C/350°F/gas 4.

Sift the flour, salt and baking powder into a mixing bowl. Rub in the butter until the mixture resembles breadcrumbs, then stir in the sugar, lemon rind and spices.

In a second bowl, beat the eggs lightly with the milk, then stir the liquid gradually into the dry ingredients.

Spoon the mixture into the prepared tin and bake for 1½ hours or until cooked through and firm to the touch, covering the surface with a piece of greased paper or foil if it browns too quickly. Cool for 10 minutes in the tin, then invert on a wire rack to cool completely.

MAKES ONE 20CM/8 INCH CAKE

 FREEZER TIP

Wrap in foil or freeze in a sealed polythene bag. Thaw the cake, still wrapped, for 3-4 hours at room temperature.

SEED CAKE

fat for greasing
200 g/7 oz plain flour
1.25 ml/¼ tsp salt
2.5 ml/½ tsp baking powder
15 ml/1 tbsp caraway seeds
150 g/5 oz butter or margarine
150 g/5 oz caster sugar
4 eggs, beaten
15 ml/1 tbsp milk (optional)

Line and grease a 15 cm/6 inch cake tin. Set the oven at 180°C/350°F/gas 4. Sift the flour, salt and baking powder into a bowl. Stir in the caraway seeds and mix well. Set aside.

Place the butter or margarine in a mixing bowl and beat until very soft. Add the sugar and cream together until light and fluffy. Add the beaten eggs gradually, beating well after each addition. If the mixture shows signs of curdling, add a little of the flour mixture.

Fold in the dry ingredients lightly but thoroughly, adding the milk if too stiff.

Spoon into the prepared tin, smooth the surface and make a slight hollow in the centre. Bake for 30 minutes, then reduce the oven temperature to 160°C/325°F/gas 3 and bake for a further 50 minutes until firm to the touch. Cool the cake on a wire rack.

MAKES ONE 15 CM/6 INCH CAKE

GUY FAWKES GINGERBREAD

Make this gingerbread at least a week before eating and store in an airtight tin. It is best eaten sliced and spread lightly with butter. An excellent treat for November 5th!

fat for greasing
200 g/7 oz plain flour
1.25 ml/¼ tsp salt
15 ml/1 tsp ground ginger
50 g/2 oz soft light brown sugar
50 g/2 oz butter or margarine
100 g/4 oz black treacle
75 ml/5 tbsp milk
5 ml/1 tsp bicarbonate of soda
1 egg, beaten

Line and grease an 18 cm/7 inch square tin or a 23 × 13 × 7.5 cm/9 × 5 × 3 inch loaf tin. Set the oven at 180°C/350°F/gas 4.

Sift the flour, salt and ginger into a mixing bowl. Add the sugar. Heat the butter or margarine, treacle, and most of the milk gently in a saucepan until the fat has melted.

In a second saucepan, warm the remaining milk and stir in the bicarbonate of soda until dissolved. Pour the melted mixture into the dry ingredients. Add the beaten egg with the milk and soda mixture and beat well.

Pour into the prepared tin and bake for 20 minutes. Reduce the oven temperature to 150°C/300°F/gas 2 and bake for a further 30–40 minutes until cooked through and firm to the touch.

MAKES ONE 18 CM/7 INCH SQUARE CAKE OR ONE 23 × 13 × 7.5 CM/9 × 5 × 3 INCH LOAF

Small Cakes

From Basic Buns and tray bakes to English Madeleines and Coconut Pyramids, this section illustrates that small cakes can be simple or special. Whether you intend to batch bake for the freezer or prepare a treat for tea, small cakes are quick to make and easy to serve.

BASIC BUNS

These small buns may be baked in paper cases or greased patty tins if preferred, in which case the consistency should be softer than when the buns are put on a baking sheet. The mixture should drop off the spoon with a slight shake, so increase the egg and milk mixture to about 150 ml/¼ pint. If baked in patty tins, the mixture will make 14 to 16 buns.

fat for greasing
200 g/7 oz self-raising flour
1.25 ml/¼ tsp salt
75 g/3 oz margarine
75 g/3 oz sugar
1 egg
milk (see method)
Glacé Icing (page 771), to decorate
  (optional)

Thoroughly grease two baking sheets. Set the oven at 200°C/400°F/gas 6.

Sift the flour and salt into a mixing bowl. Rub in the margarine until the mixture resembles fine breadcrumbs. Stir in the sugar. Put the egg into a measuring jug and add enough milk to make up to 125 ml/4 fl oz. Add the liquid to the dry ingredients and mix with a fork to a sticky stiff mixture that will support the fork.

Divide the mixture into 12-14 portions. Form into rocky heaps on the prepared baking sheets, allowing about 2 cm/¾ inch between each for spreading. Bake for 15-20 minutes or until each bun is firm to the touch on the base. Cool on a wire rack, then coat with glacé icing, if liked.

MAKES TWELVE TO FOURTEEN

VARIATIONS

Chocolate Buns Add 50 g/2 oz cocoa to the flour and 5 ml/1 tsp vanilla essence with the milk.

Chocolate Chip Buns Add 100 g/4 oz of chocolate chips with the sugar.

Coconut Buns Add 75 g/3 oz desiccated coconut with the flour and an extra 10 ml/2 tsp milk.

Fruit Buns Add 75 g/3 oz mixed dried fruit with the sugar.

Seed Buns Add 15 ml/1 tbsp caraway seeds with the sugar.

Spice Buns Add 5 ml/1 tsp mixed spice or 2.5 ml/½ tsp ground cinnamon and 2.5 ml/½ tsp grated nutmeg with the flour.

Walnut Orange Buns Add the grated rind of 1 orange to the flour. Stir in 100 g/4 oz finely chopped walnuts with the sugar.

 MRS BEETON'S TIP

Plain flour may be used for the buns, in which case add 10 ml/2 tsp baking powder with the sugar.

RASPBERRY BUNS

fat for greasing
200 g/7 oz self-raising flour
1.25 ml/¼ tsp salt
75 g/3 oz margarine
75 g/3 oz sugar
1 egg
milk (see method)
60-75 ml/4-5 tbsp raspberry jam
beaten egg for brushing
caster sugar for spinkling

Thoroughly grease two baking sheets. Set the oven at 200°C/400°F/gas 6.

Sift the flour and salt into a mixing bowl. Rub in the margarine until the mixture resembles fine breadcrumbs. Stir in the sugar. Put the egg into a measuring jug and add enough milk to make up to 125 ml/4 fl oz. Add the liquid to the dry ingredients and mix with a fork to a sticky stiff mixture that will support the fork.

Divide the mixture into 12-14 portions. Form into 12-14 balls with lightly floured hands. Make a deep dent in the centre of each and drop 5 ml/1 tsp raspberry jam inside. Close the bun mixture over the jam. Brush with egg and sprinkle with sugar, then arrange on the prepared sheets, allowing about 2 cm/¾ inch between each for spreading. Bake for 15-20 minutes or until each bun is firm to the touch on the base. Cool on a wire rack.

MAKES TWELVE TO FOURTEEN

GINGER BUNS

fat for greasing (optional)
150 g/5 oz self-raising flour
pinch of salt
5 ml/1 tsp ground ginger
1.25 ml/¼ tsp ground cinnamon
75 g/3 oz butter or margarine
50 g/2 oz soft light brown sugar
25 g/1 oz blanched almonds, chopped
1 egg
20 ml/4 tsp black treacle
20 ml/4 tsp golden syrup
30 ml/2 tbsp milk

Grease 18-20 bun tins or arrange an equivalent number of paper cake cases on baking sheets. Set the oven at 190°C/375°F/gas 5.

Sift the flour, salt and spices into a mixing bowl. Rub in the butter or margarine until the mixture resembles fine breadcrumbs. Stir in the sugar and almonds.

Put the egg into a jug and add the treacle, syrup and milk. Mix well. Add the liquid to the dry ingredients and beat until smooth.

Divide the mixture between the prepared bun tins or paper cases. Bake for 15-20 minutes or until well risen and cooked through. Cool on a wire rack.

MAKES EIGHTEEN TO TWENTY

 MICROWAVE TIP

The jug in which the egg, treacle, syrup and milk were mixed will be easy to clean if filled with water and heated in the microwave on High for 2-3 minutes. Take care when pouring the water away; it will be very hot. The steam generated in the microwave oven will have the added effect of loosening any grease on the walls, so give the cabinet a quick wipe at the same time.

HONEY BUNS

fat for greasing (optional)
200 g/7 oz self-raising flour
pinch of salt
75 g/3 oz butter or margarine
25 g/1 oz caster sugar
1 egg
30 ml/2 tbsp liquid honey
30 ml/2 tbsp milk

Grease 18-20 bun tins or arrange an equivalent number of paper cake cases on baking sheets. Set the oven at 190°C/375°F/gas 5.

Sift the flour and salt into a mixing bowl. Rub in the butter or margarine until the mixture resembles fine breadcrumbs. Stir in the sugar.

Put the egg into a jug and add the honey and milk. Mix well. Add the liquid to the dry ingredients and beat until smooth.

Divide the mixture between the prepared bun tins or paper cases. Bake for 15-20 minutes or until well risen and cooked through. Cool on a wire rack.

MAKES EIGHTEEN TO TWENTY

BUTTERFLY CAKES

fat for greasing
100 g/4 oz self-raising flour
pinch of salt
100 g/4 oz butter or margarine
100 g/4 oz caster sugar
2 eggs, beaten

DECORATION
150 ml/¼ pint double cream
5 ml/1 tsp caster sugar
1.25 ml/¼ tsp vanilla essence
icing sugar for dusting

Grease 12-14 bun tins. Set the oven at 180°C/350°F/gas 4. Mix the flour and salt in a bowl.

In a mixing bowl, cream the butter or margarine with the sugar until light and fluffy. Beat in the eggs, then lightly stir in the flour and salt. Divide the mixture evenly between the prepared bun tins, and bake for 15-20 minutes until golden brown. Cool on a wire rack.

In a bowl, whip the cream with the caster sugar and vanilla essence until stiff. Transfer to a piping bag fitted with a large star nozzle.

When the cakes are cold, cut a round off the top of each. Cut each round in half to create two 'butterfly wings'. Pipe a star of cream on each cake, then add the 'wings', placing them cut side down, and slightly apart. Dust with icing sugar.

MAKES TWELVE TO FOURTEEN

ENGLISH MADELEINES

fat for greasing
100 g/4 oz self-raising flour
pinch of salt
100 g/4 oz butter or margarine
100 g/4 oz caster sugar
2 eggs, beaten

DECORATION
45 ml/3 tbsp smooth apricot jam
25 g/1 oz desiccated coconut
glacé cherries, halved
20 angelica leaves

Thoroughly grease 10 dariole moulds. Set the oven at 180°C/350°F/gas 4. Mix the flour and salt in a bowl.

In a mixing bowl, cream the butter or margarine with the sugar until light and fluffy. Beat in the eggs, then lightly stir in the flour and salt. Divide the mixture evenly between the prepared moulds and bake for 15-20 minutes until golden brown. Cool on a wire rack.

Trim off the rounded ends of the cakes, if necessary, and stand upright. Warm the jam in a small saucepan, then brush the cakes all over. Toss in the coconut. Decorate the top of each madeleine with a glacé cherry or angelica leaves or both.

MAKES TEN

APRICOT BASKETS

fat for greasing
100 g/4 oz self-raising flour
pinch of salt
100 g/4 oz butter or margarine
100 g/4 oz caster sugar
2 eggs, beaten

DECORATION
1 (425 g/15 oz) can apricot halves in syrup
¼ (142 g/5 oz) packet lemon jelly cubes
1 (15 cm/6 inch) stick of angelica
150 ml/¼ pint double cream
5 ml/1 tsp caster sugar

Grease 12-14 bun tins. Set the oven at 180°C/350°F/gas 4. Mix the flour and salt in a bowl.

In a mixing bowl, cream the butter or margarine with the sugar until light and fluffy. Beat in the eggs, then lightly stir in the flour and salt. Divide the mixture evenly between the prepared bun tins, and bake for 15-20 minutes until golden brown. Cool on a wire rack.

While the cakes are cooling, drain the apricots, reserving 125 ml/4 fl oz of the syrup in a small saucepan. Bring the syrup to the boil, then add the jelly cubes and stir until dissolved. Set aside to cool.

Soften the angelica by placing it in a bowl of very hot water for 3-4 minutes. Pat dry on absorbent kitchen paper. Cut it into 12-14 strips 5 mm/¼ inch wide. In a bowl, whip the cream with the sugar until stiff.

When the cakes are cold and the jelly is just on the point of setting, place half an apricot, rounded side uppermost, on the top of each cake. Coat each apricot with jelly. Using a piping bag fitted with a small star nozzle, pipe stars of cream around the apricots. Arch the strips of angelica over the cakes to form handles, pushing them in to the sides of the cakes.

MAKES TWELVE TO FOURTEEN

CHOCOLATE SPICE SQUARES

The combination of chocolate and cinnamon makes these delicious tray-bake cakes just that bit different. If you want to make them extra special, top them with melted chocolate.

fat for greasing
225 g/8 oz margarine
225 g/8 oz soft light brown sugar
4 eggs
225 g/8 oz self-raising flour
30 ml/2 tbsp cocoa
10 ml/2 tsp cinnamon

Base-line and grease a roasting tin, measuring about 30 × 25 cm/12 × 10 inches. Set the oven at 180°C/350°F/gas 4.

Cream the margarine and sugar together until soft and light. Beat in the eggs. Sift the flour with the cocoa and the cinnamon, then fold these dry ingredients into the mixture.

Turn the mixture into the prepared tin and smooth it out evenly. Bake for about 1 hour, until the mixture is evenly risen and firm to the touch. Leave to cool in the tin for 15 minutes, then cut the cake into 5 cm/2 inch squares and transfer them to a wire rack to cool completely.

MAKES 30

✳ FREEZER TIP

The squares of cake freeze very well and individual portions can be removed as required – ideal for lunch boxes. Pack the pieces of cake in a large rigid container leaving a very small space between each square. Alternatively, open freeze the squares on a baking sheet lined with freezer film. When solid, stack the squares in polythene bags and seal.

A VARIETY OF TRAY BAKES

By baking a large quantity of cake mixture in a roasting tin or large baking tin, then cutting it into squares, you can make a good batch of individual cakes very speedily. It is a good idea to set aside a roasting tin specifically for baking cakes. Use the mixture for the Chocolate Spice Squares as a base and try some of the ideas given here.

Fruit 'n' Nut Squares Omit the cocoa from the mixture. Instead, fold in 225 g/8 oz of chopped nuts – walnuts, hazelnuts or mixed nuts – and 100 g/4 oz of mixed dried fruit.

Almond Squares Omit the cocoa from the Chocolate Spice Squares. Add a few drops of almond essence to the fat and sugar. Fold in 225 g/8 oz of ground almonds with the flour. Sprinkle 100 g/4 oz of flaked almonds over the mixture once it is smoothed in the tin.

Coconut Squares The chocolate can be omitted if liked, or it can be left in the mixture as its flavour is complementary to the coconut. Add 225 g/8 oz of desiccated coconut after the flour is folded in. Soften the mixture with 60 ml/4 tbsp of milk or orange juice. The cooked squares can be spread with apricot or raspberry jam and sprinkled with desiccated or long-thread coconut.

Marbled Squares Prepare the mixture, omitting the cocoa. Divide it into two portions and flavour one half with cocoa. Add a little grated orange rind and juice to the second portion. Drop small spoonfuls of the mixture into the prepared tin and drag the point of a knife through just once. Do not over-swirl the two flavours or they will blend into one during cooking. Top the cooked cakes with melted chocolate.

Marmalade Squares Make up the cake mixture, creaming 60 ml/4 tbsp of marmalade with the fat and sugar and omitting the cocoa. Glaze the cakes with warmed marmalade.

BUTTERSCOTCH BROWNIES

Rich, gooey and delightfully chewy, these are bound to prove popular.

fat for greasing
75 g/3 oz butter
175 g/6 oz soft light brown sugar
1 egg, beaten
5 ml/1 tsp vanilla essence
75 g/3 oz plain flour
5 ml/1 tsp baking powder
1.25 ml/¼ tsp salt
50 g/2 oz dates, chopped
50 g/2 oz blanched almonds, chopped

Line and grease an 18 cm/7 inch square tin. Set the oven at 160°C/325°F/gas 3.

Combine the butter and sugar in a large heavy-bottomed saucepan and heat gently until all the sugar has dissolved, stirring occasionally. Remove from the heat, cool slightly, then blend in the egg and vanilla essence.

Sift the flour, baking powder and salt into a bowl. Add the dates and mix to coat in flour. Stir the flour mixture into the pan with the almonds and mix well.

Spoon the mixture into the prepared tin and bake for 20-30 minutes. Cool in the tin. When cold, cut into squares.

MAKES TWENTY

ROCK CAKES

fat for greasing
200 g/7 oz self-raising flour
1.25 g/¼ tsp salt
1.25 g/¼ tsp grated nutmeg
75 g/3 oz margarine
75 g/3 oz sugar
75 g/3 oz mixed dried fruit (currants,
    sultanas, mixed peel, glacé cherries)
1 egg
milk (see method)

Thoroughly grease two baking sheets. Set the oven at 200°C/400°F/gas 6.

Sift the flour and salt into a mixing bowl. Add the nutmeg. Rub in the margarine until the mixture resembles fine breadcrumbs. Stir in the sugar and dried fruit.

Put the egg into a measuring jug and add enough milk to make up to 125 ml/4 fl oz. Add the liquid to the dry ingredients and mix with a fork to a sticky stiff mixture that will support the fork.

Divide the mixture into 12-14 portions. Form into rocky heaps on the prepared baking sheets, allowing about 2 cm/¾ inch between each for spreading. Bake for 15-20 minutes or until each bun is firm to the touch on the base. Cool on a wire rack.

MAKES TWELVE TO FOURTEEN

VARIATION

Coconut Cakes Omit the dried fruit. Stir in 50 g/2 oz desiccated coconut instead. Bake as above.

SWISS SHORTCAKES

150g/5oz butter
50g/2oz caster sugar
150g/5oz plain flour
few drops of vanilla essence

DECORATION
glacé cherries
angelica, cut into diamonds
smooth red jam

Place 16 paper cases in dry bun tins. Set the oven at 180°C/350°F/gas 4.

In a mixing bowl, cream the butter and sugar until light and fluffy. Work in the flour and vanilla essence, then spoon the mixture into a piping bag fitted with a large star nozzle. Pipe the mixture in whorls into the paper cases.

Bake for 15–20 minutes. Cool on a wire rack. Decorate the shortcakes with glacé cherries and angelica diamonds kept in place with a tiny dab of jam.

MAKES SIXTEEN

 MRS BEETON'S TIP

Make mini-shortcakes for a child's birthday party. Fit a small star nozzle on the piping bag and pipe the mixture into paper sweet cases instead of cupcake cases. Bake for about 10 minutes.

COCONUT PYRAMIDS

fat for greasing
2 eggs, separated
150g/5oz caster sugar
150g/5oz desiccated coconut

Grease a baking sheet and cover with rice paper. Set the oven at 140°C/275°F/gas 1. In a clean dry bowl, whisk the egg whites until stiff, then fold in the sugar and coconut, using a metal spoon. Divide the mixture into 12 portions and place in heaps on the rice paper. Using a fork, form into pyramid shapes. Bake for 45–60 minutes until pale brown in colour. Cool on the baking sheet.

MAKES TWELVE

WHOLEMEAL ALMOND SHORTCAKES

fat for greasing
75g/3oz butter
40g/1½oz soft dark brown sugar
100g/4oz wholemeal flour
1.25ml/¼ tsp salt
25g/1oz ground almonds

Grease a 15cm/6 inch sandwich tin. Set the oven at 160°C/325°F/gas 3.

Cream the butter and sugar in a mixing bowl until light and fluffy. Mix the flour and salt in a second bowl, then add to the creamed mixture with the ground almonds, working the mixture with the hands until the dough is smooth. Press into the prepared sandwich tin and bake for 50 minutes. Cut into 8 wedges while still warm. Cool in the sandwich tin.

MAKES EIGHT

ICED PETITS FOURS

fat for greasing
75 g/3 oz plain flour
2.5 ml/½ tsp salt
50 g/2 oz clarified butter (see page 424) or
  margarine
3 eggs
75 g/3 oz caster sugar

FILLING
jam, lemon curd or Buttercream (page 769)
  using 50 g/2 oz butter

ICING AND DECORATION
Glacé Icing (page 775)
food colouring (optional)
crystallized violets
silver balls
glacé fruits
angelica
chopped nuts

Line and grease a 25 × 15 cm/10 × 6 inch rectangular cake tin. Set the oven at 180°C/350°F/
gas 4.

Sift the flour and salt into a bowl and put in a
warm place. Melt the clarified butter or margarine without letting it get hot. Set aside.

Whisk the eggs lightly in a mixing bowl. Add
the sugar and place the bowl over a saucepan of
hot water. Whisk for 10-15 minutes until
thick. Take care that the bottom of the bowl
does not touch the water. Remove from the heat
and continue whisking until at blood-heat. The
melted butter or margarine should be at the
same temperature.

Sift half the flour over the eggs, then pour in
half the melted butter or margarine in a thin
stream. Fold in gently. Repeat, using the
remaining flour and fat. Spoon gently into the
prepared tin and bake for 30–40 minutes. Cool
on a wire rack.

Cut the cold cake in half horizontally, spread
with the chosen filling and sandwich together
again. Cut the cake into small rounds, triangles
or squares and place on a wire rack set over a
large dish. Brush off any loose crumbs.

Make up the icing to a coating consistency
which will flow easily. Tint part of it with food
colouring, if wished. Using a small spoon, coat
the tops and sides of the cakes with the icing or,
if preferred, pour it over the cakes, making sure
that the sides are coated evenly all over. Decorate the tops of the cakes and leave to set. The
cakes may be served in paper cases, if liked.

MAKES 18 TO 24

 MRS BEETON'S TIP

For perfect petits fours it is important that
all loose crumbs are brushed away so that
they do not spoil the appearance of the
icing. The cake is easier to cut, and produces fewer crumbs, if it is chilled in the
freezer for about an hour. It should be firm
but not thoroughly frozen. Use a very
sharp, serrated knife to cut the petits fours
shapes cleanly and chill them again briefly
before coating them with the icing. Any
cake trimmings can be used to make trifle,
or frozen for later use.

Fillings and Toppings for Cakes

Even a simple cake can be made extra special by adding a little icing, a golden glaze or a nutty topping.
This chapter includes recipes to complement formal cakes as well as plain ones.
In addition, a quick-reference chart provides a guide to selecting the right consistency of royal icing.

GLAZES AND COATINGS

Glazes are used to give a shiny coating to food. Pastry, cakes and biscuits may be glazed with egg white, egg wash, sugar syrup or warmed jam such as apricot glaze, and then covered with crumbs, ground nuts, coconut, marzipan, almond paste or praline. Fruit flans or tartlets are often coated with a sweet liquid thickened with arrowroot.

APRICOT GLAZE

Brush this glaze over a cake before applying the marzipan. Any yellow jam or marmalade may be used.

225 g/8 oz apricot jam

Warm the jam with 30 ml/2 tbsp water in a small saucepan over a low heat until the jam has melted. Sieve the mixture and return the glaze to the clean pan. Bring slowly to the boil. Allow to cool slightly before use.

SUFFICIENT TO COAT THE TOP AND SIDES OF ONE 20 CM/8 INCH CAKE

ALMOND PASTE

This recipe makes a pale, creamy yellow–coloured paste that can be used to cover and decorate cakes, as well as for a base coat before applying icing.

225 g/8 oz ground almonds
100 g/4 oz caster sugar
100 g/4 oz icing sugar
5 ml/1 tsp lemon juice
few drops of almond essence
1 egg, beaten

Using a coarse sieve, sift the almonds, caster sugar and icing sugar into a mixing bowl. Add the lemon juice, almond essence and sufficient egg to bind the ingredients together. Knead lightly with the fingertips until smooth.

Wrap in cling film and overwrap in foil or a plastic bag to prevent the paste drying out. Store in a cool place until required.

MAKES ABOUT 450 G/1 LB

 MRS BEETON'S TIP

Don't knead the paste too much: this can draw the oils from the almonds and make the paste greasy. It will then be unsuitable as a base for icing.

ALMOND PASTE AND MARZIPAN

Either almond paste or marzipan may be used to cover a Battenburg cake, to fill a simnel cake or as a base for royal icing on a Christmas or wedding cake. Both almond paste and marzipan provide a flat, even surface over which icing will flow in a smooth glossy sheet, and as a bonus, will prevent crumbs from the cake spoiling the appearance of the icing. Marzipan resembles almond paste, but is smoother and more malleable. It is easier to use than almond paste when making moulded decorations or petits fours. For use and quantities required for individual cakes see overleaf.

MARZIPAN

1 egg
1 egg white
200 g/7 oz icing sugar, sifted
200 g/7 oz ground almonds
5 ml/1 tsp lemon juice
few drops of almond essence

Whisk the egg, egg white and icing sugar in a heatproof bowl over hot water until thick and creamy. Add the ground almonds with the lemon juice and almond essence and mix well. Work in more lemon juice, if necessary. When cool enough to handle, knead lightly until smooth. Use as for almond paste.

MAKES ABOUT 400G/14OZ

GLAZE FOR SWEET FLANS

This slightly thickened glaze is useful for coating fruit as a decoration for light gâteaux. It can also be used with fresh fruit to top a plain cheesecake.

5 ml/1 tsp arrowroot
150 ml/¼ pint fruit syrup from canned or
   bottled fruit or 150 ml/¼ pint water and
   25 g/1 oz sugar
1-3 drops of food colouring
lemon juice (see method)

In a bowl, mix the arrowroot to a paste with a little of the cold fruit syrup or water. Pour the remaining syrup into a saucepan and bring to the boil. If using water, add the sugar and bring to the boil, stirring constantly until all the sugar has dissolved. Pour on to the arrowroot mixture, stir well, then return to the pan. Bring to the boil, stirring constantly. Add the appropriate food colouring, then stir in lemon juice to taste. Use at once.

SUFFICIENT TO GLAZE ONE 18CM/7INCH
FRUIT FLAN OR TWELVE TO SIXTEEN
TARTLETS

 MICROWAVE TIP

Mix the arrowroot with a little of the syrup in a medium bowl. Add the remaining syrup and cook on High for 1 minute. Stir, then cook for 1 minute more or until the glaze clears. Add food colouring and lemon juice.

ALMOND PASTE/MARZIPAN

Quick guide to quantities required to cover fruit cakes

Round	Quantity
15 cm/6 inches	350 g/12 oz
18 cm/7 inches	500 g/18 oz
20 cm/8 inches	575 g/1¼ lb
23 cm/9 inches	800 g/1¾ lb
25 cm/10 inches	900 g/2 lb
28 cm/11 inches	1 kg/2¼ lb
30 cm/12 inches	1.25 kg/2¾ lb

Square	Quantity
15 cm/6 inches	500 g/18 oz
18 cm/7 inches	575 g/1¼ lb
20 cm/8 inches	800 g/1¾ lb
23 cm/9 inches	900 g/2 lb
25 cm/10 inches	1 kg/2¼ lb
28 cm/11 inches	1.1 kg/2½ lb
30 cm/12 inches	1.4 kg/3 lb

COOKED ALMOND PASTE

This makes a smoother and more malleable paste than the uncooked mixture. Use it for moulding decorations and for covering wedding cakes.

450 g/1 lb granulated sugar
1.25 ml/¼ tsp cream of tartar
300 g/11 oz ground almonds
2 egg whites
5 ml/1 tsp almond essence
50 g/2 oz icing sugar

Place the sugar with 150 ml/¼ pint water in a saucepan over moderate heat. Stir occasionally until all the sugar has dissolved, then bring the syrup to the boil.

In a cup, dissolve the cream of tartar in 5 ml/1 tsp water and stir it into the syrup. Boil, without stirring, until the syrup registers 115°C/240°F on a sugar thermometer, the soft ball stage (see Mrs Beeton's Tip).

Remove the pan from the heat and immediately stir in the ground almonds followed by the unbeaten egg whites and almond essence. Return the pan to low heat and cook, stirring constantly, for 2 minutes. Set the pan aside until the mixture is cool enough to handle.

Sift the icing sugar on to a clean work surface, place the almond paste in the centre and knead with the fingertips until the sugar is absorbed. If the almond paste is sticky, leave to cool for longer and then add a little more icing sugar, if necessary. Cover lightly until cold, then wrap and store in a cool place, as for uncooked almond paste.

MAKES ABOUT 900 G/2 LB

 MRS BEETON'S TIP

If you do not have a sugar thermometer, drop about 2.5 ml/½ tsp syrup into a bowl of iced water. If you can mould the syrup between your fingers to make a soft ball, the syrup is ready.

BUTTERCREAMS AND FUDGE ICINGS

These are soft icings made with butter and icing sugar, which may be used for filling or covering lighter cakes and gâteaux. On drying, an outer crust forms, but the icing remains soft underneath. The iced cake should be stored away from heat or direct sunlight.

Use unsalted butter if possible and flavour the icing as required. Soften the butter before using or try using a butter mixture that spreads easily even when chilled – these usually contain vegetable oil and therefore little or no extra liquid will be required when mixing the icing.

When adding food colouring to butter-based icings, do not expect clear colours. Avoid adding blue, as the yellow in the butter will turn it green! If a clear colour is essential, use white vegetable fat instead of butter.

All these icings may be spread with a palette knife or piped using a savoy nozzle.

 **FREEZER TIP**

Buttercream can be frozen successfully, unless the recipe contains egg, in which case it may curdle. When piping with buttercream it is necessary to make slightly more than required; however any leftovers can be frozen for future use as a filling for cakes. The prepared buttercream can be flavoured before or after freezing. Pack the buttercream in a rigid container, then leave it to thaw in the refrigerator or in a cool place; beat it thoroughly before use.

RICH BUTTERCREAM

This buttercream is enriched by the addition of an egg yolk. Use only very fresh eggs and make sure that all utensils used to prepare the buttercream are perfectly clean.

1 egg yolk
200 g/7 oz icing sugar, sifted
100 g/4 oz butter, softened
flavouring

Beat the egg yolk in a mixing bowl, adding the sugar gradually until the mixture is smooth. Beat in the butter, a little at a time with the flavouring.

SUFFICIENT TO FILL AND COAT THE TOP OF ONE 20 CM/8 INCH CAKE

BUTTERCREAM

100 g/4 oz butter, softened
15 ml/1 tbsp milk or fruit juice
225 g/8 oz icing sugar, sifted

In a mixing bowl, cream the butter with the milk or juice and gradually work in the icing sugar. Beat the icing until light and fluffy. Alternatively, work all the ingredients in a food processor, removing the plunger for the final mixing to allow air to enter the buttercream mixture.

SUFFICIENT TO FILL AND COAT THE TOP OF ONE 20 CM/8 INCH CAKE

CHOCOLATE FUDGE ICING

100 g/4 oz plain chocolate, broken into
  pieces
50 g/2 oz butter, cut up
1 egg, beaten
175 g/6 oz icing sugar, sifted

Combine the chocolate and butter in a heat-proof bowl. Set over hot water until the chocolate has melted. Beat in the egg, then remove the bowl from the heat and stir in half the icing sugar. Beat in the remaining sugar and continue beating until the icing is smooth and cold. Use immediately.

SUFFICIENT TO FILL AND COAT THE TOP OF
ONE 20 CM/8 INCH CAKE

VARIATIONS

Chocolate Walnut Fudge Icing   Add 50 g/2 oz of finely chopped walnuts to the icing just before spreading it on the cake.

Chocolate Rum Fudge Icing   Add 30 ml/2 tbsp of rum to the icing with the egg and continue as in the main recipe.

Chocolate Orange Fudge Icing   Add the grated rind of 1 orange to the chocolate and butter. Continue as in the main recipe. This icing is excellent on a Victoria Sandwich Cake which has the grated rind of 1 orange added to the mixture.

 MICROWAVE TIP

Melt the chocolate with the butter in a small bowl on Medium for 1–2 minutes.

DARK FUDGE ICING

75 g/3 oz butter
75 g/3 oz soft dark brown sugar
30 ml/2 tbsp milk
225 g/8 oz icing sugar, sifted

Combine the butter, brown sugar and milk in a saucepan. Place over moderate heat, stirring occasionally until the sugar has melted. Remove the pan from the heat, add the icing sugar and beat until cool. Use immediately.

SUFFICIENT TO COAT THE TOP AND SIDES
OF ONE 20 CM/8 INCH CAKE

VARIATIONS

Dark Honey Fudge Icing   Use 15 ml/1 tbsp of honey instead of 25 g/1 oz of the sugar in the main recipe.

Coffee Fudge Icing   Add 5 ml/1 tsp of instant coffee to the butter, sugar and milk mixture. Continue as in the main recipe.

Dark Nut Fudge Icing   Stir in 30 ml/2 tbsp of smooth peanut butter before adding the icing sugar. This icing can be used to sandwich plain biscuits in pairs or it can be used as a topping for chocolate brownies or small plain cakes.

Dark Ginger Fudge Icing   Add a pinch of ground ginger to the butter, sugar and milk mixture. Beat in 30 ml/2 tbsp of finely chopped preserved stem ginger or crystallized ginger. This icing makes an unusual topping for gingerbread.

 MICROWAVE TIP

Melt the butter and sugar in a bowl with the milk on Medium for 1–2 minutes.

GLACE ICING

Glacé icing is mainly used as a covering for small cakes, sponge cakes or other light cakes. It is quick and easy to make and therefore ideal for simple, informal cakes. It gives a smooth, slightly crisp coating that complements piped buttercream edges. This icing can also be used to coat plain biscuits. Basically a mixture of icing sugar and water, it may also contain flavourings and colourings or extra ingredients as in Chocolate Glacé Icing right.

The consistency of the icing is all important; it should be stiff enough to coat the back of a wooden spoon thickly, otherwise it will run off the surface of the cake and drip down the sides.

Glacé icing should be used immediately. If left to stand, even for a short while, the surface should be covered completely with damp greaseproof paper or cling film. Any crystallized icing on the surface should be scraped off before use. Because the icing sets so quickly, any additional decorations must be put on as soon as the cake is iced, or the surface will crack.

The choice of decorations to use with glacé icing is important. Do not use decorations liable to melt, run or be damaged by damp. Crystallized flower petals, chocolate decorations and small sweets which will shed colour should not be used.

GLACE ICING

This simple basic icing is quickly prepared and is ideal for topping a plain sponge cake or a batch of small cakes. Make the icing just before it is to be used and keep any extra decorations to the minimum.

100 g/4 oz icing sugar, sifted
food colouring, optional

Place the icing sugar in a bowl. Using a wooden spoon gradually stir in sufficient water (about 15 ml/1 tbsp) to create icing whose consistency will thickly coat the back of the spoon. Take care not to add too much liquid or the icing will be too runny. At first the icing will seem quite stiff, but it slackens rapidly as the icing sugar absorbs the water. Stir in 1–2 drops of food colouring, if required.

SUFFICIENT TO COVER THE TOP OF ONE
18 CM/7 INCH CAKE

VARIATIONS

Lemon or Orange Glacé Icing Use 15 ml/1 tbsp strained lemon or orange juice instead of the water.

Chocolate Glacé Icing Combine 50 g/2 oz plain chocolate, a knob of butter and 15 ml/1 tbsp water in a heatproof bowl. Set over hot water until the chocolate and butter melt. Stir the mixture, gradually adding 100 g/4 oz icing sugar. Stir in a little more water if required. This icing sets particularly quickly; use at once.

Coffee Glacé Icing Dissolve 5 ml/1 tsp instant coffee in 15 ml/1 tbsp warm water and add instead of the water in the main recipe.

Liqueur-flavoured Glacé Icing Replace half the water with the liqueur of your choice.

FROSTINGS

Frosting is usually spread thickly all over a cake, covering the sides as well as the top. When set, it is crisper than glacé icing, because the sugar is heated or boiled when making it. It should have a soft, spreading consistency when applied. Have the cake ready before starting to make the frosting.

AMERICAN FROSTING

225 g/8 oz granulated sugar
pinch of cream of tartar
1 egg white
2.5 ml/½ tsp vanilla essence or a few drops of lemon juice

Combine the sugar and cream of tartar in a small saucepan. Add 60 ml/4 tbsp water. Place over low heat, stirring occasionally until the sugar has melted. Heat, without stirring, until the syrup registers 115°C/240°F, the soft ball stage, on a sugar thermometer (see Mrs Beeton's Tip page 768). Remove from the heat.

In a large grease-free bowl, whisk the egg white until stiff. Pour on the syrup in a thin stream, whisking continuously. Add the flavouring and continue to whisk until the frosting is thick and glossy and stands in peaks.

Quickly spread over the cake. As the frosting cools, it may be swirled with a knife.

SUFFICIENT TO COVER THE TOP AND SIDES OF ONE 18 CM/7 INCH CAKE

 MRS BEETON'S TIP

Make sure that both bowl and whisk are free from grease, otherwise the frosting will not whisk up well.

QUICK AMERICAN FROSTING

175 g/6 oz caster sugar
1 egg white
pinch of cream of tartar
pinch of salt

Heat a mixing bowl over a large saucepan of simmering water. Remove the bowl and place all the ingredients in it. Add 30 ml/2 tbsp water and whisk with a rotary or electric whisk until the ingredients are well mixed.

Remove the pan of simmering water from the heat, place the bowl over the water, and whisk until the frosting forms soft peaks. Use immediately.

SUFFICIENT TO COVER THE TOP AND SIDES OF ONE 18 CM/7 INCH CAKE

CARAMEL FROSTING

350 g/12 oz soft light brown sugar
1.25 ml/¼ tsp cream of tartar
2 egg whites
pinch of salt
5 ml/1 tsp vanilla essence

Heat a mixing bowl over a large saucepan of boiling water. Remove the bowl and add all the ingredients except the vanilla essence. Add 150 ml/¼ pint water and whisk with a rotary or electric whisk until well mixed.

Place the bowl over the water and continue to whisk until the frosting forms soft peaks. Remove the bowl from the water, add the essence and whisk the frosting for about 2 minutes more, until it reaches a spreading consistency. Use immediately.

SUFFICIENT TO FILL AND COVER THE TOP AND SIDES OF ONE 18 CM/7 INCH CAKE

TRADITIONAL FONDANT

Not to be confused with moulding icings or sugar paste icing. Traditional fondant is poured over the cake. It sets to a dry, shiny finish that remains soft inside. It is widely used by commercial confectioners for petits fours and is also used as a filling for chocolates or to make sweets. Some specialist shops sell fondant icing in powdered form. This is a boon because small quantities may be made up by adding water or stock syrup. To use fondant, dilute with stock syrup. You will need a sugar thermometer to make fondant.

450 g/1 lb caster or lump sugar
20 ml/4 tsp liquid glucose

Put the sugar in a heavy-bottomed saucepan which is absolutely free from grease. Add 150 ml/¼ pint water and heat gently until the sugar has completely dissolved. Stir very occasionally and use a wet pastry brush to wipe away any crystals that form on the sides of the pan. When the sugar has dissolved add the liquid glucose and boil to 115°C/240°F, the soft ball stage (see Mrs Beeton's Tip page 768), without stirring. Keep the sides of the pan clean by brushing with the wet brush when necessary. Remove from the heat and allow the bubbles in the mixture to subside.

Pour the mixture slowly into the middle of a wetted marble slab and allow to cool a little. Work the sides to the middle with a sugar scraper or palette knife to make a smaller mass.

With a wooden spatula in one hand and the scraper in the other, make a figure of eight with the spatula, keeping the mixture together with the scraper. Work until the whole mass is completely white.

Break off small amounts and knead well, then knead together to form a ball.

Store in a screw-topped jar, or wrap closely in several layers of polythene. When required, dilute with stock syrup (below).

MAKES ABOUT 450 G/1 LB FONDANT

STOCK SYRUP

Use this syrup when diluting fondant. It may also be kneaded into commercially made almond paste to make the paste more pliable.

150 g/5 oz granulated sugar

Put the sugar in a saucepan and add 150 ml/¼ pint water. Heat, stirring occasionally, until the sugar has dissolved; boil without stirring for 3 minutes. Use a spoon to remove any scum that rises to the surface.

Allow the syrup to cool, then strain into a screw-topped jar; close the jar tightly. If not required immediately, store in a cool place (not the refrigerator) for up to 2 months.

MAKES ABOUT 200 ML/7 FL OZ

 MRS BEETON'S TIP

To give the fondant a hint of flavour use vanilla sugar instead of ordinary caster sugar or lump sugar. Vanilla sugar is made by placing a vanilla pod in a jar of caster sugar. The sugar should be left for a few weeks, shaking the jar occasionally, until it has absorbed the flavour of the vanilla.

ROYAL ICING

Royal icing is used for special celebration cakes, especially for wedding cakes, because the icing has sufficient strength when it sets hard to hold the tiers. The icing cannot be applied directly to the cake because it would drag the crumbs and discolour badly, so rich fruit cakes are usually covered with a layer of almond paste or marzipan before the royal icing is applied.

Traditionalists believe that royal icing can only be made successfully with egg whites and hard beating, but dried egg white or albumen powder is fast gaining in popularity because the icing can be made in a food mixer or with an electric whisk. Whichever method you choose, the secret of successful royal icing work, be it flat icing or piping, depends upon making the icing to the correct consistency. This is discussed further on the opposite page.

ROYAL ICING QUANTITIES

Quick guide to quantities required to cover cakes (sufficient for 3 coats)

ROUND	ROYAL ICING
15 cm/6 inch	575 g/1¼ lb
18 cm/7 inch	675 g/1½ lb
20 cm/8 inch	800 g/1¾ lb
23 cm/9 inch	900 g/2 lb
25 cm/10 inch	1 kg/2¼ lb
28 cm/11 inch	1.25 kg/2¾ lb
30 cm/12 inch	1.4 kg/3 lb

SQUARE	ROYAL ICING
15 cm/6 inch	675 g/1½ lb
18 cm/7 inch	800 g/1¾ lb
20 cm/8 inch	900 g/2 lb
23 cm/9 inch	1 kg/2¼ lb
25 cm/10 inch	1.25 kg/2¾ lb
28 cm/11 inch	1.4 kg/3 lb
30 cm/12 inch	1.5 kg/3¼ lb

ROYAL ICING (USING EGG WHITE)

It is vital to ensure that the bowl is clean and free from grease. Use a wooden spoon kept solely for the purpose and do not be tempted to skimp on the beating – insufficient beating will produce an off-white icing with a heavy, sticky texture.

2 egg whites
450 g/1 lb icing sugar, sifted

Place the egg whites in a bowl and break them up with a fork. Gradually beat in about two-thirds of the icing sugar with a wooden spoon, and continue beating for about 15 minutes until the icing is pure white and forms soft peaks. Add the remaining icing sugar, if necessary, to attain this texture. Cover the bowl with cling film and place a dampened tea-towel on top. Place the bowl inside a polythene bag if storing overnight or for longer.

Before use, lightly beat the icing to burst any air bubbles that have risen to the surface. Adjust the consistency for flat icing or piping.

SUFFICIENT TO COAT THE TOP AND SIDES OF ONE 20 CM/8 INCH CAKE

 MRS BEETON'S TIP

If the icing is to be used for a single cake, glycerine may be added to prevent it from becoming too brittle when dry. Add 2.5 ml/½ tsp glycerine during the final beating. Do not, however, use glycerine for a tiered cake where the icing must be hard in order to hold the tiers.

**QUICK GUIDE TO CONSISTENCY OF ROYAL ICING FOR
DIFFERENT APPLICATIONS**

Once the required consistency has been achieved, cover the icing with a damp cloth,
even during use.

CONSISTENCY	DESCRIPTION	USE
Thin Icing	Just finds its own level when gently tapped	Run-outs and flooding
Soft Peak (1)	Forms a soft peak when the spoon is lifted out but readily falls over	Embroidery work. Very fine no 00 writing nozzles
Soft Peak (2)	Forms a soft peak but only tip bends over	Flat icing
Medium Peak	Firmer peak that holds its shape	Most piping except patterns using the larger nozzles
Firm Peak	Stiffer peak but still soft enough to push through a nozzle without excessive pressure	Petals for flowers, large shell and similar nozzles

ROYAL ICING (USING DRIED EGG WHITE)

**15 ml/1 tbsp dried egg white (albumen
powder)**
450 g/1 lb icing sugar

Place 60 ml/4 tbsp warm water in a bowl. Add
the dried egg white, mix thoroughly and leave
for 10–15 minutes. Whisk with a fork and
strain the mixture into a mixing bowl.

 MRS BEETON'S TIP

Be careful not to beat the icing for too long
or it may break when piped.

Gradually beat in about two-thirds of the icing
sugar and continue beating for 5 minutes in a
food mixer or with a hand-held electric whisk
until the icing is pure white, light and stands in
soft peaks. Add extra icing sugar, if necessary.

Cover and use as for the royal icing (using fresh
egg white) except that fewer air bubbles will be
present.

SUFFICIENT TO COAT THE TOP AND SIDES
OF ONE 20 CM/8 INCH CAKE

VARIATION

Albumen Substitute May be used in place
of albumen powder. Sift it into the bowl. Beat
for 5 minutes as above.

SUGAR PASTE

Since the introduction of this versatile and easy-to-use icing from the humid regions of Australia and South Africa, where royal icing does not dry well, cake decorating in this country has been revolutionized. Sugar paste, also known as decorating icing or mallow paste, resembles commercially made marzipan in its properties, texture and application (although not in colour or flavour). Sometimes it is referred to as fondant icing but it must not be confused with a traditional, pouring fondant. It is rolled out and moulded over the cake. In many cases this makes a base layer of marzipan unnecessary. It is, therefore, widely used on sponge cakes and because it can be easily coloured, makes wonderful novelty cakes and plaques.

There are several recipes for sugar paste: try them all and find the one which suits you best.

If well wrapped in polythene the paste will keep for several weeks in a cupboard. Do not store it in the refrigerator as it would lose its elasticity and become difficult to work.

Sugar paste is malleable and may be moulded into shapes and petals for flowers. When worked into very thin pieces, it will dry hard and brittle and can be used for plaques and Garrett frills.

As a general rule, it is best not to freeze a whole cake covered in this icing, especially if different colours have been used. This is because the icing becomes wet and the colours may run into each other. If only a small area of the cake has sugar paste icing, as in a novelty cake covered in buttercream with moulded icing features, the cake can be frozen. When required, it must be taken out of the freezer, all wrappings removed and left at room temperature for 4–5 hours to allow the icing to dry off.

SUGAR PASTE

675 g/1½ lb icing sugar, sifted
2 medium egg whites
30 ml/2 tbsp warmed liquid glucose
5 ml/1 tsp glycerine

Place the icing sugar in a clean, grease-free bowl. Add the remaining ingredients and work together with either a clean wooden spoon or the fingertips. Place the rough mixture on a clean surface dusted with icing sugar and knead hard for several minutes until smooth, pliable and not sticky, adding a little extra icing sugar if necessary. Wrap the sugar paste in polythene and leave to rest for 24 hours before using.

SUFFICIENT TO COVER THE TOP AND SIDES OF ONE 20 CM/8 INCH CAKE

SUGAR PASTE QUANTITIES

Quick guide to quantities required to cover cakes

ROUND	SUGAR PASTE
15 cm/6 inch	450 g/1 lb
18 cm/7 inch	575 g/1¼ lb
20 cm/8 inch	675 g/1½ lb
23 cm/9 inch	800 g/1¾ lb
25 cm/10 inch	900 g/2 lb
28 cm/11 inch	1 kg/2¼ lb
30 cm/12 inch	1.1 kg/2½ lb

SQUARE	SUGAR PASTE
15 cm/6 inch	575 g/1¼ lb
18 cm/7 inch	675 g/1½ lb
20 cm/8 inch	800 g/1¾ lb
23 cm/9 inch	900 g/2 lb
25 cm/10 inch	1 kg/2¼ lb
28 cm/11 inch	1.1 kg/2½ lb
30 cm/12 inch	1.4 kg/3 lb

CREAM FILLINGS

Fresh cream is still a prime favourite as a filling for gâteaux and afternoon tea cakes. Double cream has the best flavour and may be whipped and piped in much the same way as royal icing. Once whipped, it may be frozen on the decorated gâteaux and will not lose its shape when thawed. To reduce the risk of over-whipping, which might cause the cream to separate in hot weather, add 15 ml/1 tbsp milk to each 150 ml/ $\frac{1}{4}$ pint cream or replace up to one-third of the double cream with single cream. There is no need to add sugar to whipped cream.

TO WHIP THE CREAM

Choose a cool area of the kitchen in which to work and chill the bowl and whisk before use, by placing them in the refrigerator or freezer for a few minutes. A small wire balloon whisk is the best utensil, but for large quantities a hand-held electric whisk may be used with care.

Stand the bowl on a wet cloth or a non-slip surface, add the cream and tip the bowl. While whipping, incorporate as much air as possible. If using an electric whisk, start on high and reduce speed to low as the cream begins to thicken. Be very careful not to overwhip. Stop whipping as soon as the cream will stand in soft peaks and has doubled in volume.

The cream will continue to thicken slightly on standing and when piped, so stop whipping just before you think the cream is ready. It should be smooth and shiny in appearance. Overwhipped cream will 'frill' at the edges when piped.

For best results, use the whipped cream immediately, or cover the bowl and store in the refrigerator until required, giving it a gentle stir before use.

If the finished gâteau is to stand in a warm room for any length of time, whip in 5 ml/1 tsp gelatine, dissolved in 10 ml/2 tsp warm water and cooled.

FLAVOURINGS

Add any flavouring to cream when it has been whipped to soft peaks. Lemon or orange juice, liqueur or sherry may be used and should be added gradually during the final whipping. Once the cream has been whipped, finely chopped nuts, glacé fruits or grated citrus rind may be added.

REDUCING THE FAT CONTENT

For a low-fat whipped cream, replace up to one third with low or full-fat plain yogurt. This will not only make the cream less rich, but will prevent overwhipping and keep the cream smooth and shiny.

FREEZING

Cakes decorated with cream should be frozen and stored in a large domed plastic box. Alternatively, open freeze and then cocoon carefully in a dome of foil. Label well to avoid other items being inadvertently placed on top.

To thaw, remove the wrappings and thaw the cakes in a cool place, refrigerator or microwave (following the manufacturer's directions).

Small quantities of leftover cream may be whipped with a little caster sugar and piped in small stars on non-stick baking parchment for freezing. They may then be lifted off and placed, still frozen, on desserts and gâteaux for instant decoration.

CUSTARD FILLINGS

Confectioners' Custard, sometimes called Crème Pâtissière, makes an excellent filling for cakes. Thickened with eggs, flour or cornflour, the custard sets to a thick cream when cold. Mock Cream is a simple filling based on milk thickened with cornflour and enriched with butter, while Quick Diplomat Cream is richer still, with double cream used as its base.

Unless using a double saucepan, it is easier to make these custards with yolks rather than whole eggs as the whites cook more quickly and lumps of cooked egg white may spoil the texture.

Vanilla sugar may be used instead of caster sugar in the recipes that follow. The vanilla pod or essence should then be omitted.

To prevent the formation of a skin on the cooked custard, press a dampened piece of greaseproof paper lightly on the surface. Do not use plasticized cling film for this purpose when the custard is hot.

 MRS BEETON'S TIP

These light fillings, thickened with eggs, go very well with light sponge cakes and gâteaux that are filled or decorated with fresh fruit. They can also be used to decorate cheesecakes. This type of filling should not be frozen as it tends to curdle.

CONFECTIONERS' CUSTARD

300 ml/½ pint milk
1 vanilla pod or a few drops of vanilla essence
2 egg yolks
50 g/2 oz caster sugar
25 g/1 oz plain flour

Place the milk and vanilla pod, if used, in a small saucepan and bring to the boil over low heat. Remove from the heat and leave to one side, adding the vanilla essence, if used.

Whisk the egg yolks with the sugar in a bowl until thick and creamy, then add the flour. Remove the vanilla pod and very gradually add the milk to the egg mixture, beating constantly until all has been incorporated. Pour the mixture back into the pan and stir over low heat for 1–2 minutes to cook the flour. The custard should thickly coat the back of the wooden spoon and be smooth and shiny.

Pour the custard into a clean bowl, cover and leave to cool. Beat well, then cover again and chill until required.

MAKES ABOUT 300 ML/½ PINT

VARIATIONS

Chocolate Custard Stir 25 g/1 oz grated chocolate into the custard while still hot.

Crème St Honoré Whisk 2 egg whites with 10 ml/2 tsp of caster sugar until stiff. Fold into cold custard. Use for choux pastry or as an alternative cream for gâteaux.

Crème Frangipane Omit the vanilla flavouring. Add 40 g/1½ oz finely chopped butter to final cooking. When cold, fold in 75 g/3 oz crushed almond macaroons or 50 g/2 oz ground almonds and a few drops of almond essence.

CONFECTIONERS' CUSTARD WITH BRANDY

25 g/1 oz cornflour
300 ml/½ pint milk
3 egg yolks
40 g/1½ oz caster sugar
2.5 ml/½ tsp brandy, rum or liqueur

In a bowl mix the cornflour with a little milk, then beat in the egg yolks and sugar. Heat the remaining milk in a saucepan until tepid and pour slowly on to the cornflour mixture, stirring constantly. Pour the mixture back into the pan and stir over low heat, without boiling, until the custard thickens and thickly coats the back of the wooden spoon. Remove from the heat, stir in the brandy, rum or liqueur and pour into a clean bowl. Cover and cool, then beat well. Cover again and chill until required.

MAKES ABOUT 300 ML/½ PINT

MOCK CREAM

10 ml/2 tsp cornflour
150 ml/¼ pint milk
50 g/2 oz butter, softened
50 g/2 oz icing or caster sugar
few drops of vanilla or almond essence

Mix the cornflour with a little milk in a small saucepan. Gradually stir in the remaining milk and cook over low heat, stirring constantly until the mixture thickens. Cover and leave until tepid.

Cream the butter and sugar together in a bowl until light and fluffy. Gradually add the custard mixture to the butter, beating well between each addition. Beat in the essence, cover the bowl and chill.

SUFFICIENT FOR TWO LAYERS IN ONE
18 CM/7 INCH CAKE

QUICK DIPLOMAT CREAM

15 ml/1 tbsp custard powder
10 ml/2 tsp caster sugar
150 ml/¼ pint milk
150 ml/¼ pint double cream
few drops of vanilla essence

Mix the custard powder and sugar with a little milk in a small saucepan. Gradually stir in the remaining milk and stir over low heat for 1 minute until thick. Transfer the mixture to a bowl, cover and leave to cool. Beat well then cover again and chill.

In a clean bowl, whip the cream with the vanilla essence until thick. Beat the custard until smooth and lightly fold in the cream until well blended. Chill until required.

MAKES ABOUT 300 ML/½ PINT

VARIATIONS

Orange or Lemon Fold in 5 ml/1 tsp finely grated orange or lemon rind.

Chocolate Stir 50 g/2 oz grated chocolate into the hot custard.

Liqueur Replace the essence with brandy or liqueur.

TOPPINGS

These simple toppings may be prepared in advance and used to decorate and finish a cake or gâteau quickly. Most toppings can be stored in a screw-topped jar or in a cardboard box for several months. A wide variety of simple decorations are available from grocers, supermarkets and sweet shops. The choice includes chocolate vermicelli and buttons, crystallized flowers and fruits, dragees, liquorice sweets, sugar strands and sugared almonds.

COCONUT

Coconut has an interesting texture and makes a good topping on plain cakes. Choose good-quality desiccated coconut with large strands and use plain or colour as follows: Place about 50 g/2 oz coconut in a screw-topped jar, leaving at least 2.5 cm/1 inch space at the top. Add a few drops of food colouring (liquid colours are best), screw on the lid and shake the jar vigorously for a few minutes until the coconut is evenly coloured. Use the same day or spread the coconut out on a piece of greaseproof paper and leave in a warm place to dry before storing in a dry screw-topped jar.

Toasted coconut is prepared in the same way as Toasted Nuts (method below).

COLOURED SUGAR CRYSTALS

Use either granulated sugar or roughly crushed sugar lumps and colour and dry in the same way as the coloured coconut above.

TOASTED NUTS

Whole flaked or chopped nuts may be lightly toasted to improve both colour and flavour. Almonds and hazelnuts are the most commonly used varieties.

To toast nuts, remove the rack from the grill pan and line the pan with a piece of foil. Spread the nuts over the foil. Heat the grill and toast the nuts under a medium heat, stirring occasionally until evenly browned. This will only take a few seconds. Lift out the foil carefully and leave the nuts to cool. This method may also be used to remove the skins from hazelnuts. Roast them under the grill, then rub the skins off while still hot.

Toasted nuts are best used on the same day; alternatively, store when cold in a screw-topped jar for a few days.

PRALINE

This is a fine powder of crushed nuts and caramel used to flavour creams and fillings. Crushed roughly, it may be used as a cake decoration.

oil for greasing
100 g/4 oz caster sugar
100 g/4 oz blanched almonds, toasted

Brush a baking sheet with oil. Place the sugar in a small, heavy-bottomed saucepan with 15 ml/1 tbsp water. Heat slowly until the sugar dissolves, stirring occasionally. Continue cooking until the sugar turns from pale golden in colour to deep golden. Stir in the toasted blanched almonds. Quickly pour the mixture on to the prepared baking sheet and leave until cold.

Crush the caramel to a fine powder with a rolling pin or pestle and mortar. Alternatively, break it up roughly and crush in a blender. Store the powder in a dry screw-topped jar for up to 3 months.

MAKES ABOUT 225 G/8 OZ

CHOCOLATE AND ITS USES

Dark and bitter, smooth and milky or pale and creamy – there are many types of chocolate available now and they can be put to a wide variety of uses.

Chocolate is a blend of cocoa solids and cocoa butter to which varying quantities of vegetable fats, milk and sugar have been added. The quantity of added fat determines the hardness or softness of the chocolate.

A block of chocolate can be finely or coarsely grated, chopped, slivered and curled for decorating or coating the sides and tops of cakes.

Melted chocolate is malleable; it dries to a smooth, glossy film. It flavours and provides texture, as well as setting quality, to icings and fillings. Melted chocolate has many other uses: it can be poured over cakes, or fruits or marzipan and nuts can be dipped in it. Chocolate leaves are made by coating real leaves. Chocolate curls, known as caraque, are a widely used decoration. Melted chocolate can also be set in a thin sheet, then cut into shapes, for example squares, triangles or shapes using cutters. The melted chocolate can also be piped.

Milk and Plain Chocolate Milk chocolate has added milk products and is paler and softer in texture than plain chocolate which is darker and more brittle. The quantity of added sugar determines the sweetness. Milk chocolate contains more sugar than plain chocolate which is available as bitter, semi-sweet or plain. The quality of the product varies widely, particularly with plain chocolate.

Chocolate-flavoured Cake Covering This is not true chocolate. In this product the cocoa butter is replaced by other fats which make it more malleable. The resulting flavour is poor and the texture waxy. It is useful for inexpensive, everyday cakes but it should not be applied when a good result is required.

White Chocolate This is made from cocoa butter, sugar and milk and does not contain any of the cocoa solids or non-fat parts of the cocoabean. Quality varies, with some bars of white chocolate having a poor, very sweet flavour. This is best bought from a good cake decorating supplier.

Carob This is manufactured from the pulp of the carob or locust bean to resemble chocolate in appearance. It is naturally sweeter than cocoa so less sugar is added; also, it is caffeine-free. It is available in powder form for cooking and in block form for eating uncooked. Carob can be used instead of chocolate for some of the following decorations but it is waxy in consistency and does not have such a glossy appearance as chocolate.

STORING CHOCOLATE DECORATIONS

Store chocolate decorations in a cool, dry atmosphere for the shortest possible time, and no longer than seven to ten days. Chocolate will sweat if it is kept in a warm room. On very hot days keep the chocolate in the refrigerator but bring it to room temperature before melting it.

CHOCOLATE ICINGS AND DECORATIONS

Use a hard, plain dessert chocolate for the best flavour and texture. Do not be disappointed by the appearance of chocolate decorations: they will not have the same high gloss as commercial chocolates. Chocolate icing made with added ingredients may be glossy. Avoid handling the chocolate decorations once set as fingermarks will readily show and the surface will become dull.

CHOPPING CHOCOLATE

Break the chocolate into pieces and place it on a chopping board. Use a sharp knife with a long blade and hold the tip of the knife on to the board with one hand. Pivot the blade, bringing it up and down with the other hand. Scrape the chocolate back to the centre of the board and continue until the pieces are even and quite small.

GRATING CHOCOLATE

Place the grater on a piece of greaseproof paper on a large plate or chopping board. Rub the block of chocolate on the coarse side of the grater. Use long, even strokes and keep your hands as cool as possible.

CHOCOLATE SLIVERS

Hold your hands under cold running water, then dry them. Hold the chocolate in the palm of the hand and shave off thin pieces of chocolate with a potato peeler, letting them fall on to a chilled plate or a sheet of greaseproof paper or parchment.

MELTED CHOCOLATE

Break up or roughly chop the chocolate and place it in a bowl that fits over a saucepan. Place about 5 cm/2 inches of water in the pan and bring it to the boil, then remove the pan from the heat and stand the bowl over it. Leave for a few minutes, then stir the chocolate until it has melted and is smooth and glossy. If you leave the pan on the heat, the chocolate will overheat and white streaks may appear in it when it sets again.

DIPPING FOOD IN CHOCOLATE

Biscuits, choux buns, nuts, marzipan shapes, real leaves and fruits such as maraschino cherries, grapes, raisins, dates and slices of banana can all be dipped in melted chocolate. They can be part-dipped or fully dipped according to the effect required. Special dipping forks have two long prongs that are bent at the ends to stop the food falling off when dipped. Alternatively, use a corn-on-the-cob fork, cocktail stick or two fine skewers, one on either side of the food. For larger pieces of food such as choux buns, or hard foods such as almonds, it is best to use your fingers to dip the ingredients.

Melt the chocolate following the instructions left. For dipping food the consistency should be thick enough to coat the back of a spoon. If the chocolate is too thin, remove the bowl from the pan and leave it to cool slightly, until the chocolate thickens. Keep the chocolate warm (over the saucepan of water), while you are working. If the chocolate becomes too thick, remove the bowl, reheat the water, then replace the bowl. Stir the chocolate occasionally as you are dipping the food; this gives you a glossy finish.

You will need a good depth of melted chocolate to dip food successfully; it should be at least 5 cm/2 inches deep. (When the chocolate becomes too shallow for successful dipping, do not discard it; stir the excess into buttercreams or similar icings to avoid wastage.)

Line a baking sheet or wire rack with a sheet of waxed paper or non-stick baking parchment. Have ready all the food to be dipped and start with firm items, such as nuts and marzipan. Finish with soft foods, such as fruits. Plunge the food into the chocolate to the depth required, then quickly withdraw it at the same angle at which it was plunged. Do not rotate part-dipped food in the chocolate or the top line of chocolate will be uneven. Gently shake the food to allow the excess chocolate to fall back into the bowl, then place it on the prepared sheet or rack to dry.

TO DIP LEAVES

Select clean, undamaged leaves, such as rose leaves. Thoroughly wash the leaves, rubbing them to remove any dust, dirt or sap. Dry well and brush the underside of each leaf over the surface of the chocolate. Dry the leaves chocolate side uppermost, then carefully peel away the leaf, leaving the impression of the leaf on the chocolate.

PIPING CHOCOLATE

When adding chocolate decoration to the top of a cake, melted chocolate is difficult to pipe because it begins to set in the nozzle. Mixing a little icing sugar with it will make it more malleable; however this is not suitable for piping shapes that have to set hard.

25 g/1 oz icing sugar, sifted
100 g/4 oz chocolate, melted

Stir the icing sugar into the melted chocolate with a few drops of water to make a mixture of a thick piping consistency that drops from the spoon.

 MRS BEETON'S TIP

If using piping chocolate in large quantities to pipe shells around a cake, use stock syrup (page 773) instead of icing sugar to soften the chocolate.

PIPING WITH CHOCOLATE

The chocolate should be of a thin flowing consistency. Very little pressure is required to pipe with chocolate as it should flow slowly out of the bag without any encouragement.

TO DRIZZLE CHOCOLATE OVER CAKES AND BISCUITS

Place 15 ml/1 tbsp of melted chocolate in a small paper icing bag. Snip off the end and quickly move the bag backwards and forwards over the cake or biscuit. Finish by lowering the bag and quickly withdrawing it.

TO PIPE MOTIFS AND SHAPES

Trace a design on to thick white card and cover it with waxed paper, taping both securely on to a board. Alternatively, work freehand on to the waxed paper.

Place 30–45 ml/2–3 tbsp melted chocolate in an icing bag made of baking parchment (or purchased from cake decorating suppliers) and snip off the end. Start with a fine hole until you have checked the size of the piping. It is a good idea to practise piping beads and buttons on the paper first. Pipe the shapes, making sure that all the lines of piping are joined somewhere in the design. Shapes may be filled in using a different coloured chocolate, such as milk chocolate or white chocolate with plain chocolate. Leave the shapes to dry hard.

TO PIPE CHOCOLATE SHELLS AROUND A CAKE

Prepare piping chocolate (left). Use a strong bag made from double non-stick baking parchment and fitted with a small star nozzle. Pipe a shell pattern quickly around the cake. This method can also be used to pipe around homemade Easter eggs.

TO MAKE CURLS, FRILLS AND SHAPES

Melted chocolate can be used to make a variety of different decorations without the need for piping. Here are a few examples: the key to success is to make sure that you use good quality chocolate and to leave the decorations to set firmly before using them.

CHOCOLATE CURLS OR SCROLLS (CARAQUE)

Whether you are making curls or frills the chocolate is prepared in the same way: pour melted chocolate over a clean, dry surface, such as a marble slab or a clean smooth area of work surface. Spread the chocolate backwards and forwards with a large palette knife until it is smooth, fairly thin and even. Leave to dry until almost set; do not allow the chocolate to set hard.

Hold a long, thin-bladed knife at an acute angle to the chocolate. Hold the top of the knife with the other hand and pull the knife towards you with a gentle sawing action, scraping off a thin layer of chocolate which curls into a roll.

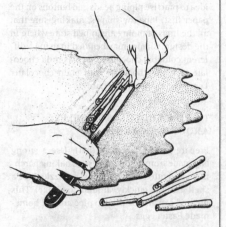

CHOCOLATE FRILLS

Starting at the edge of the chocolate, hold the tip of a small palette knife at an angle of 45 degrees or lower to the surface, and push the palette knife away from you. A thin layer of chocolate will frill as you push. Place the frills on waxed paper as you make them.

TO CUT CHOCOLATE SHAPES

Spread the melted chocolate on to waxed paper or non-stick baking parchment paper. Use petits fours cutters or small biscuit cutters, to stamp shapes out of the chocolate, cutting them as close together as possible. Leave to set hard before peeling away the paper. The excess chocolate can be finely chopped for decorations or melted for use in making more shapes.

TO CUT SQUARES, TRIANGLES OR WEDGES

Prepare a precise pattern, drawing a large square and dividing it up into smaller squares or triangles. Alternatively, draw a circle and divide it into equal wedges. In either case extend the dividing lines beyond the square or circle outline so that when the pattern has been covered in chocolate, the ends of the lines will still be visible. Place the paper pattern under non-stick baking parchment.

Spread the melted chocolate over the marked shape and leave to set but not harden. Use a long-bladed knife and cut the chocolate into extend the dividing lines beyond the square or circle outline so that when the pattern has been covered in chocolate, the ends of the lines will still be visible. Place the paper pattern under non-stick baking parchment.

Sweet Biscuits

Home-made biscuits are quite inexpensive in their use of ingredients and they taste particularly good. The recipes in this chapter will ensure that the biscuit jar is always brimming over with variety, from buttery Shortbread to favourite Flapjacks.

The ingredients used for making biscuits are much the same as those for making cakes and the same applies to some of the basic methods that are involved.

RUBBED-IN BISCUITS

This is a simple method of making biscuit dough. The flour is sifted into a bowl and the fat is rubbed in. The proportion of fat to flour in biscuit mixtures of this type is smaller than in rubbed-in cake mixtures.

Once the fat has been incorporated other flavouring ingredients are added and liquid is used to bind the dough. The method is much the same as for making short crust pastry.

All the ingredients should be cool and the fat should be chilled. When rubbing the fat into the flour, lift the ingredients and rub them lightly between your fingertips. Add the liquid carefully because the dough must not be too sticky or it will be difficult to roll.

This type of dough can be sweetened with sugar or it can be seasoned with salt. Various flavouring ingredients can be added, including spices, dried fruit, nuts or seeds.

CREAMED BISCUITS

The fat and sugar are creamed together until they are pale and soft, then the dry ingredients are worked in to make a biscuit dough. An egg yolk may be added to enrich the dough or other liquid may be used to moisten and bind particular combinations of ingredients.

Biscuits made by this method tend to be richer than those made by the rubbed-in method and this technique is used mainly for sweet biscuits. Before it is suitable for rolling, the dough should be chilled until it is firm.

This basic method is also used to make mixtures which are pushed through biscuit presses or they may be piped into shapes using large nozzles. The mixture is not chilled before shaping but it is chilled after shaping and before cooking.

MELTED METHOD

Some delicate biscuits are made by the melted method. The fat and sugar or other ingredients are gently heated until they are melted, then the flour is added with selected flavourings. The mixture is very moist but not too runny.

Small amounts of mixture are cooked well apart on baking sheets. As it begins to heat, the mixture melts and spreads out to make very thin biscuits. As the cooking progresses the biscuits set.

A good baking sheet that does not stick is essential for this type of mixture and the knack of sliding the cooked biscuits off the sheet is made easier with practice. Non-stick baking parchment can be a useful aid when cooking this type of biscuit.

NO-COOK MIXTURES

Simple biscuits and cookies can be made without the necessity for cooking. A melted mixture is combined with other ingredients such as breakfast cereals, nuts and dried fruits. The mixture is set in the refrigerator, then cut into individual pieces.

REFRIGERATOR BISCUITS

These avoid the necessity for rolling out the dough. The dough is usually prepared by the creamed method, then it is shaped into a long roll, wrapped in foil and thoroughly chilled. When the dough is really firm it is cut into slices and these are placed on a prepared baking sheet and cooked.

The uncooked dough can be kept in the refrigerator for several days or up to a couple of weeks, depending on the ingredients used. A large quantity of dough can be prepared and slices cut off for baking as and when required.

ROLLING, CUTTING OR SHAPING

ROLLING

The rules that apply to pastry cookery should be remembered when rolling out biscuits. The dough should be chilled or allowed to rest before it is rolled. The work surface must be absolutely clean and dry and it should be dusted with a little flour. In some cases the recipe may suggest that cornflour or icing sugar is used instead.

When rolling the dough work in one direction only, pushing the pin away from you. Keep the dough evenly thick, gently pressing the edges together if they begin to crack slightly. Lift the dough lightly occasionally, if necessary, and turn it round slightly to keep it dusted with flour underneath. This prevents it from sticking to the work surface. Do not turn the dough over.

Once the dough is rolled to the required thickness cut out the biscuits and transfer them to prepared baking sheets. Carefully stack the trimmings and re-roll them, pressing them together gently.

USING CUTTERS

Metal cutters tend to be better than the plastic ones but both types are adequate. Have a little mound of flour on the work surface, keeping it well away from the dough, otherwise it will get in the way when it comes to rolling out the trimmings. Dip the cutter first in the flour, then stamp out the shape in the dough. Do not twist the cutter as you press it into the dough. Cut all the shapes as near to each other as possible and keep stamping the cutter in the flour to prevent the dough from sticking to it. Use a palette knife or other round-bladed knife to slide underneath each of the biscuit shapes, leaving the trimmings in place on the work surface.

PIPING AND USING A BISCUIT PRESS

The consistency of the biscuit mixture must be just right for this method. It must be soft enough to pipe but if it is too warm, then it will become oily as it is pushed out on to the baking sheet.

Always place the shapes slightly apart on the baking sheet to allow for them to spread during cooking. When piping fingers, use a knife to cut a neat finish to the dough when the required length has been piped on to the baking sheet. When piping circles, one way to obtain a neat finish is to pipe the mixture up into a small star when the circle is completed.

Before cooking, the majority of shapes of this type should be chilled. When piping sponge fingers the opposite is true and the essence of success is in speed. The sponge mixture will run if it is allowed to stand and it should be piped quickly, pulling the nozzle end of the bag up sharply at the end of each biscuit.

SHAPING WITH SPOONS

Soft biscuit mixtures can be dropped off spoons on to baking sheets. You will need two spoons: scoop up a small amount of mixture with one spoon, then use a second spoon to push it off cleanly on to the baking sheet.

ROLLING BALLS

One of the easiest ways to shape biscuit dough and ideal for those doughs which are prepared by the creamed method. Take a small lump of mixture about the size of a walnut and roll it into a ball between the palms of your hands. Place the balls slightly apart on prepared baking sheets, then flatten them with a fork. Press down once or twice with the prongs of the fork to make a pattern of lines or a criss-cross design. Chill the biscuits before baking them.

SHAPING A ROLL FOR SLICING

Press the dough together and roughly shape it into a roll. Wrap it in foil, then carefully shape it into an even roll, neatening the ends by patting them flat. The dough is easier to shape when it is within the confines of the wrapping. When the roll is well chilled check its shape again, rolling it and patting it gently.

PRESSING INTO TINS

Some biscuits, such as shortbread, are formed into a shape by pressing the mixture into a tin. The mixture must be unchilled and the tin should be greased. Place the dough in it and gradually press it out to fill the tin, making sure it is the same thickness all over. Use the back of your fingers and knuckles for this. Smooth the surface with your fingertips or a moistened palette knife. Mark the edges with a fork if you like and cut the dough into portions. It should be well chilled before cooking.

COOKING, COOLING AND STORING

The cooking time is crucial for many types of biscuit and a few extra minutes can be long enough to turn golden to black!

Once the biscuits are cooked leave them on the baking sheet for a few minutes unless the recipe states otherwise. Use a palette knife to slide each biscuit off the sheet and on to a wire rack to cool.

Very delicate mixtures may have to set slightly before they can be lifted off the baking sheet. Biscuits such as brandy snaps may be shaped after cooking, over a greased rolling pin or wooden spoon handle. Alternatively, they may be formed into cups in greased patty tins. They should be left to cool completely before they are moved.

Once the biscuits are completely cool they can be stored in an airtight container – a tin, plastic container or bag which is firmly closed. Most biscuits keep very well in a cool dry place. Decorated biscuits do not keep well and those with soft creamy fillings should be eaten within a few hours of filling, although the unfilled biscuits can be stored successfully.

FREEZING

Biscuits freeze well, either cooked or as uncooked dough. The cooked biscuits should be stored in an airtight, rigid freezer container to protect them from being crushed.

Uncooked dough can be stored in a neat lightly kneaded lump, ready to be rolled out. Alternatively, it can be stored in a roll, as for refrigerator biscuits. The roll can be cut into slices and these can be re-shaped, interleaved with film, before freezing. This enables you to remove a few slices at a time for cooking. It is best to thaw the dough partially but it should not be allowed to thaw completely before cooking as it tends to become sticky.

RUBBED-IN BISCUITS

This simple method may be used for making a wide variety of biscuits.

fat for greasing
200 g/7 oz plain flour
1.25 ml/¼ tsp salt
75-100 g/3-4 oz butter or margarine
50 g/2 oz caster sugar
5 ml/1 tsp baking powder
1 egg yolk
flour for rolling out

Grease two baking sheets. Set the oven at 180°C/350°F/gas 4.

In a mixing bowl, mix the flour and salt. Rub in the butter or margarine until the mixture resembles fine breadcrumbs, then stir in the sugar and baking powder. Bind to a stiff paste with the egg yolk.

Knead well and roll out to a thickness of just under 1 cm/½ inch on a lightly floured surface. Cut into rounds with a 5 cm/2 inch cutter. Re-roll and re-cut any trimmings.

Place the biscuits on the prepared baking sheets, pricking the top of each in several places. Bake for 12-15 minutes or until firm and pale golden brown. Leave to stand for a few minutes, then cool on a wire rack.

MAKES 20 TO 26

VARIATIONS

Plain Mocha Biscuits Add 50 g/2 oz powdered drinking chocolate with the flour and 10 ml/2 tsp instant coffee dissolved in 7.5 ml/1½ tsp boiling water with the eggs.

Plain Cinnamon or Spice Biscuits Add 5 ml/1 tsp ground cinnamon or mixed spice to the flour. When cold, sandwich the biscuits together in pairs with jam, and dredge with icing sugar.

Plain Coconut Biscuits Use 150 g/5 oz flour and 50 g/2 oz desiccated coconut. As soon as the biscuits are cooked, brush with warm Apricot Glaze (page 766) and sprinkle with coconut.

SIMPLE BISCUITS

The mixture for these plain biscuits is simply rolled into balls, which are then flattened slightly on the baking sheet.

fat for greasing
100 g/4 oz butter
100 g/4 oz soft light brown sugar
1 egg, beaten
grated rind of 1 lemon
225 g/8 oz self-raising flour

Grease two or more baking sheets. Set the oven at 160°C/325°F/gas 3. Cream the butter and sugar together until soft and creamy. Beat in the egg and lemon rind, then stir in the flour to make a soft dough.

Roll small pieces of dough into balls about the size of walnuts. Wet your hands under cold running water to prevent the mixture from sticking to them. Place the balls well apart on the baking sheets and flatten them slightly with a fork.

Bake for 20-25 minutes, until the biscuits are spread, risen and brown. Leave the biscuits on the baking sheets for a minute or so, then transfer them to a wire rack to cool.

MAKES 25 TO 30

REFRIGERATOR BISCUITS

The dough for refrigerator biscuits is prepared, shaped and wrapped in foil. Then it is chilled until firm and sliced into biscuits. The uncooked dough can be stored in the refrigerator for one to two weeks.

fat for greasing
150 g/5 oz butter
100 g/4 oz caster sugar
5 ml/1 tsp vanilla essence
1 small egg, beaten
225 g/8 oz plain flour

Thoroughly grease two or more baking sheets. Cream the butter with the sugar and vanilla until very pale and soft. Beat in the egg, then stir in the flour to make a soft dough.

Press the mixture together with a spatula, then turn it out on to a sheet of foil. Roughly shape the dough into a roll, then wrap the foil over it. Roll the wrapped dough until it forms a smooth, evenly thick roll measuring about 3.75-5 cm/1½-2 inches in diameter. Open the foil and pat the ends of the roll neatly into shape, then re-wrap the dough and chill it for about 1 hour or until quite firm.

The dough can be stored until the biscuits are to be cooked. Set the oven at 180°C/350°F/gas 4. Cut the dough into slices about 5 mm/¼ inch thick, or slightly less, and place them on the prepared baking sheets. Set the biscuits apart to allow room for spreading.

Bake the biscuits for 12-15 minutes, until golden, then leave them on the sheets for about a minute before transferring them to a wire rack.

MAKES ABOUT 50

VARIATION

Pinwheel Biscuits   Divide the dough in half and flavour one portion to taste – add cocoa, coffee essence, orange rind or finely chopped nuts. Cut both types of dough in half. Roll out a portion of plain dough into an oblong measuring about 25 × 35 cm/12 × 14 inches. Roll out a portion of flavoured dough the same size. Lift the flavoured dough on the rolling pin and place it over the plain dough. Roll up the sheets of dough together like a Swiss Roll. Press firmly into shape, wrap and chill. Repeat with the remaining portions of dough. Slice and bake the biscuits as in the main recipe.

CREAMED BISCUITS

fat for greasing
200 g/7 oz plain flour
1.25 ml/¼ tsp salt
100-150 g/4-5 oz butter or margarine
100-150 g/4-5 oz caster sugar
1 egg yolk
flour for rolling
caster sugar for dredging (optional)

Thoroughly grease two or three baking sheets. Set the oven at 180°C/350°F/gas 4. Mix the flour and salt in a bowl.

In a mixing bowl, beat the butter or margarine until soft, add the sugar and continue to beat until light and fluffy. Beat in the egg yolk. Fold in the flour, first using a knife and then the fingers.

Knead the dough lightly on a floured surface, then roll out to a thickness of 5 mm/¼ inch. Cut into rounds with a 6 cm/2½ inch cutter. Re-roll and re-cut any trimmings.

Place the biscuits on the prepared baking sheets, pricking the top of each in several places. Bake for 12-15 minutes, until golden. Leave to stand for 5 minutes, then cool on a wire rack. Dredge with caster sugar, if liked.

MAKES 26 TO 30

SHORTBREAD

Shortbread should be handled as lightly – and as little – as possible; if the dough is worked too much, it will toughen. Wooden moulds, carved with an appropriate motif, such as a thistle, are sometimes used for this Scottish speciality but it is easier to shape the dough by hand.

fat for greasing
100 g/4 oz plain flour
1.25 ml/¼ tsp salt
50 g/2 oz rice flour, ground rice or semolina
50 g/2 oz caster sugar
100 g/4 oz butter

Invert a baking sheet, then grease the surface now uppermost. Set the oven at 180°C/350°F/ gas 4.

Mix all the ingredients in a mixing bowl. Rub in the butter until the mixture binds together to a dough. Shape into a large round about 1 cm/ ½ inch thick. Pinch up the edges to decorate. Place on the prepared baking sheet, and prick with a fork. Bake for 40-45 minutes. Cut into wedges while still warm.

MAKES EIGHT WEDGES

VARIATIONS

Shortbread Biscuits   Roll out the dough on a lightly floured surface to a thickness of just under 1 cm/½ inch. Cut into rounds with a 5-6 cm/2-2½ inch cutter. Place on 1-2 greased baking sheets, allowing room for spreading. Prick the surface of each biscuit in several places with a fork. Bake for 15-20 minutes. Leave to stand for a few minutes, then cool on a wire rack.

Original Scotch Shortbread   Omit the salt and rice flour, and use 225 g/8 oz plain flour. Reduce the sugar to 25 g/1 oz. Add 10 ml/2 tsp caraway seeds. Top the shortbread round with strips of candied peel.

SOYA FLOUR SHORTBREAD

fat for greasing
flour for dusting
125 g/4½ oz plain flour
25 g/1 oz soya flour
100 g/4 oz butter
50 g/2 oz caster sugar

Grease and flour a baking sheet and the inside of a 15 cm/6 inch flan ring. Set the oven at 140-150°C/275-300°F/gas 1-2. Mix the plain and soya flours in a mixing bowl. Rub in the butter until the mixture resembles fine bread-crumbs. Mix in the sugar, and knead the dough until it forms a single mass. Place the ring on the prepared baking sheet, and press the short-bread dough into it in an even layer. Prick the centre of the dough deeply with a fork.

Bake for 45-50 minutes or until very lightly coloured. Leave for 5 minutes. Mark into six wedges and leave to cool completely. When cold, remove the flan ring and cut into sections as marked.

MAKES SIX WEDGES

 MRS BEETON'S TIP

Soya flour has a high protein content. It is also high in fat, which is why a cool oven is always recommended for baking: a higher oven temperature would cause the short-bread to overbrown.

WHOLEMEAL ORANGE SHORTBREAD

Zesty orange rind contrasts well with the wholemeal flour in this recipe, adding a lively note of flavour to complement the wholemeal texture.

fat for greasing
175 g/6 oz butter
75 g/3 oz caster sugar
grated rind of 1 orange
225 g/8 oz wholemeal flour
caster sugar for sprinkling

Base-line and grease a 20 cm/8 inch round sandwich cake tin. Set the oven at 150°C/300°F/gas 2.

Cream the butter and sugar together until very soft, pale and fluffy. It is important that the creamed mixture is very light. Beat in the orange rind, then work in the flour to make a soft dough.

Lightly knead the dough together in the bowl, then press it into the prepared tin. Prick the shortbread all over with a fork and mark the edges with the fork. Chill the shortbread for at least 15 minutes, preferably for 30 minutes.

Bake the shortbread for 40-50 minutes, until firm and lightly browned on top. Cut into wedges at once but do not remove from the tin. Sprinkle with caster sugar while hot. Leave the shortbread in the tin until it is firm enough to lift out. This will take about 15 minutes. Carefully remove the first wedge by easing the point of a knife all round it; the remaining wedges are easily lifted out of the tin.

Cool on a wire rack and store in an airtight container once cooled.

MAKES EIGHT WEDGES

CINNAMON BARS

fat for greasing
175 g/6 oz plain flour
5 ml/1 tsp ground cinnamon
50 g/2 oz caster sugar
100 g/4 oz butter
25 g/1 oz flaked almonds
15 ml/1 tbsp granulated sugar

Grease a 30 × 20 cm/12 × 8 inch Swiss roll tin. Set the oven at 180°C/350°F/gas 4.

Sift the flour and 2.5 ml/½ tsp of the cinnamon into a mixing bowl and add the caster sugar. Rub in the butter until the mixture resembles firm breadcrumbs and work into a soft dough. Press the mixture into the prepared tin. Flatten and level the surface, then sprinkle with the flaked almonds, granulated sugar and remaining cinnamon.

Bake for 15-20 minutes until golden brown. Cut into bars or fingers while still warm.

MAKES ABOUT TWENTY

 MRS BEETON'S TIP

For a look that children will love, substitute coloured sugar granules (sometimes called coffee sugar) for the granulated sugar in the topping. Omit the cinnamon.

JUMBLES

fat for greasing
50 g/2 oz plain flour
pinch of salt
50 g/2 oz caster sugar
40 g/1½ oz butter or margarine
10 ml/2 tsp beaten egg
flour for rolling out

Grease two baking sheets. Set the oven at 160°C/325°F/gas 3.

Mix the flour, salt and sugar in a mixing bowl, then lightly rub in the butter or margarine until the mixture resembles coarse breadcrumbs. Stir in the egg and mix to a soft dough. Roll out with the hands on a floured surface to a long sausage shape about 2 cm/½ inch thick. Divide into 20 pieces and roll each into a 7.5 cm/3 inch long sausage.

Form each piece into an 'S' shape and place well apart on the prepared baking sheets. Bake for 12–15 minutes. Leave the Jumbles to stand for a few minutes, then cool on a wire rack.

MAKES 28 TO 30

 MRS BEETON'S TIP

The remaining beaten egg may be used to glaze the Jumbles if liked.

DOVER BISCUITS

fat for greasing
200 g/7 oz plain flour
1.25 ml/¼ tsp salt
2.5 ml/½ tsp ground cinnamon
50 g/2 oz currants
100–150 g/4–5 oz butter or margarine
100–150 g/4–5 oz caster sugar
1 egg, separated
flour for rolling out
caster sugar for topping

Thoroughly grease two or three baking sheets. Set the oven at 180°C/350°F/gas 4. Mix the flour, salt and cinnamon in a bowl, then add the currants and stir to coat thoroughly.

In a mixing bowl, beat the butter or margarine until soft, add the sugar and continue to beat until light and fluffy. Beat in the egg yolk, reserving the white. Fold in the flour mixture, first using a knife and then the fingers.

Knead the biscuit dough lightly on a floured surface, then roll out to a thickness of 5 mm/¼ inch. Cut into rounds with a 6 cm/2½ inch cutter. Re-roll and re-cut any trimmings.

Place the biscuits on the prepared baking sheets, pricking the top of each in several places. Bake for 10 minutes, then remove from the oven and add the topping: brush the biscuits with beaten egg white and sprinkle with caster sugar. Return to the oven and bake for a further 5 minutes. Leave to stand for 5 minutes, then cool on a wire rack.

MAKES 26 TO 30

SMILES

Children love these cheerful-looking biscuits and enjoy adding the smiles to the basic shapes.

fat for greasing
200g/7oz plain flour
1.25ml/¼ tsp salt
grated rind of 1 orange
100g/4oz butter or margarine
100g/4oz caster sugar
1 egg yolk
flour for rolling out

TOPPING
12-15 jellied orange and lemon slices

Throughly grease two large baking sheets. Set the oven at 180°C/350°F/gas 4. Mix the flour, salt and orange rind in a bowl.

In a mixing bowl, beat the butter or margarine until soft, add the sugar and continue to beat until light and fluffy. Beat in the egg yolk. Fold in the flour mixture, first using a knife and then the fingers.

Knead the biscuit dough lightly on a floured surface, then roll out to a thickness of 5mm/ ¼ inch. Cut the dough into rounds with a 7.5cm/3 inch cutter. Re-roll and re-cut any trimmings.

Place the biscuits on the prepared baking sheets. Using a sharp knife dipped in hot water, trim the orange and lemon slices to emphasize the smile shapes. Press one smile on to each biscuit. Use the jelly slice trimmings to make 'eyes', if liked.

Bake for 12-15 minutes. Leave to stand for 5 minutes, then cool on a wire rack.

MAKES TWELVE TO FIFTEEN

JIM-JAMS

fat for greasing
150g/5oz plain flour
50g/2oz ground almonds
1.25ml/¼ tsp salt
100g/4oz butter or margarine
100g/4oz caster sugar
1 egg yolk
flour for rolling
strawberry jam for filling
sifted icing sugar for dredging

Thoroughly grease two or three baking sheets. Set the oven at 180°C/350°F/gas 4. Mix the flour, ground almonds and salt in a bowl.

In a mixing bowl, beat the butter or margarine until soft, add the sugar and continue to beat until light and fluffy. Beat in the egg yolk. Fold in the flour mixture, first using a knife and then the fingers.

Knead the biscuit dough lightly on a floured surface, then roll out to a thickness of 5mm/ ¼ inch. Cut the dough into rounds with a 6cm/ 2½ inch cutter. Re-roll and re-cut trimmings.

Place the biscuits on the prepared baking sheets, pricking the top of each in several places. Bake for 12-15 minutes, until golden. Leave to stand for 5 minutes, then cool on a wire rack.

When quite cold, sandwich the biscuits together in pairs with strawberry jam and dredge with icing sugar, if liked.

MAKES 26 TO 30

COCONUT CIRCLES

fat for greasing
100 g/4 oz butter or margarine
100 g/4 oz caster sugar
1 egg, separated
150 g/5 oz self-raising flour or 150 g/5 oz
    plain flour and 5 ml/1 tsp baking powder
pinch of salt
50 g/2 oz desiccated coconut
flour for rolling out
desiccated coconut for dusting

Grease two or three baking sheets. Set the oven at 160°C/325°F/gas 3.

Cream the butter or margarine with the sugar in a mixing bowl until light and fluffy. Beat in the egg yolk, then beat in the flour, salt, and coconut, adding a little of the egg white if necessary, to bind together.

Roll out the dough to a thickness of 5 mm/¼ inch on a floured board and cut into rounds with a 5–6 cm/2–2½ inch cutter. Prick the biscuits and brush with lightly beaten egg white. Sprinkle with coconut. Place on the prepared baking sheets and bake for 15–20 minutes. Leave to stand for a few minutes, then cool on a wire rack.

MAKES TWENTY EIGHT TO THIRTY

 MICROWAVE TIP

If biscuits become soft on keeping, firm them in batches of 6–8 in the microwave for 10–20 seconds on High. Allow them to stand for 1–2 minutes.

AFTER DINNER BISCUITS

fat for greasing
100 g/4 oz butter
200 g/7 oz plain flour
100 g/4 oz caster sugar
3 eggs
2.5 ml/½ tsp of any of the following
    flavourings: ground ginger, ground
    cinnamon, grated lemon rind or a few
    drops of lemon essence

Lightly grease two or three baking sheets. Set the oven at 160°C/325°F/gas 3.

Cream the butter in a mixing bowl. Add the flour gradually, beating well after each addition. Beat in the sugar, eggs, and flavouring.

Place tablespoons of the mixture, well apart, on the prepared baking sheets; flatten the biscuits slightly, and bake for about 15 minutes. Cool on the baking sheets.

MAKES 30 TO 36

CRUNCHIES

fat for greasing
100 g/4 oz margarine
125 g/4½ oz rolled oats
75 g/3 oz demerara sugar

Grease a 28 × 18 cm/11 × 7 inch baking tin. Set the oven at 190°C/375°F/gas 5.

Melt the margarine in a large saucepan and stir in the oats and the sugar. Press into the prepared tin and bake for 15–20 minutes. Cut into squares or strips while warm, and leave in the tin until cool.

MAKES ABOUT TWENTY

GINGER SQUARES

fat for greasing
200g/7oz plain flour
1.25ml/¼tsp salt
10ml/2tsp ground ginger
75g/3oz butter or margarine
50g/2oz sugar
75g/3oz golden syrup
2 eggs, beaten
flour for rolling out

Grease a large baking sheet. Set the oven at 180°C/350°F/gas 4. Sift the flour, salt, and ginger into a bowl.

In a mixing bowl, cream the butter or margarine with the sugar and syrup. Add the dry ingredients and work enough beaten egg into the mixture to make a stiff dough.

Roll out the dough to a thickness of 5mm/ ¼ inch. Cut into squares using a plain 6cm/ 2½ inch or 7.5cm/3 inch cutter. Place on the prepared baking sheet and bake for about 15-20 minutes. Leave to stand for a few minutes, then transfer the ginger squares to a wire rack.

MAKES ABOUT SIXTEEN

 MRS BEETON'S TIP

If liked, the biscuits may be decorated before being baked with small pieces of crystallized ginger.

MELTING MOMENTS

fat for greasing
100g/4oz margarine or half margarine and
    half blended white vegetable fat
75g/3oz caster sugar
30ml/2tbsp beaten egg
125g/4½oz self-raising flour
pinch of salt
rolled oats for coating
4-5 glacé cherries, quartered

Grease two baking sheets. Set the oven at 180°C/350°F/gas 4.

In a mixing bowl, cream the margarine or mixed fats and sugar until pale and fluffy. Add the egg with a little flour and beat again. Stir in the remaining flour with the salt, mix well, then shape the mixture into 16-20 balls with the hands.

Place the rolled oats on a sheet of greaseproof paper and toss the balls in them to coat them evenly all over. Space the balls on the prepared baking sheets. Place a small piece of glacé cherry in the centre of each.

Bake for about 20 minutes until pale golden brown. Leave to stand for a few minutes on the baking sheets, then cool on a wire rack.

MAKES SIXTEEN TO TWENTY

VARIATION

Custard Treats   Substitute 40g/1½oz of the flour with custard powder for a deliciously creamy biscuit with a rich buttery colour. Omit the rolled oats coating.

DIGESTIVE BISCUITS

fat for greasing
75 g/3 oz wholemeal flour
25 g/1 oz plain white flour
25 g/1 oz fine or medium oatmeal
2.5 ml/½ tsp baking powder
1.25 ml/¼ tsp salt
15 ml/1 tbsp soft light brown sugar
50 g/2 oz butter or margarine
30 ml/2 tbsp milk
flour for rolling out

Grease a baking sheet. Set the oven at 180°C/350°F/gas 4. Mix all the dry ingredients in a mixing bowl, sifting the sugar if it is lumpy. Rub in the butter or margarine until the mixture binds together and mix to a pliable dough with the milk.

Knead the biscuit dough lightly on a floured board and roll out to a thickness of of just under 5 mm/¼ inch. Cut into rounds with a 6 cm/2½ inch round cutter, place on the prepared baking sheet and prick with a fork. Bake for 15 minutes or until golden brown. Leave to stand for a few minutes, then cool on a wire rack.

MAKES ABOUT TWELVE

GINGER SNAPS

fat for greasing
200 g/7 oz self-raising flour
pinch of salt
5 ml/1 tsp ground ginger
100 g/4 oz soft light brown sugar
75 g/3 oz margarine
100 g/4 oz golden syrup
1 egg, beaten

Thoroughly grease several baking sheets. Set the oven at 160°C/325°F/gas 3. Sift together the flour, salt and ginger. Stir in the sugar.

Melt the margarine with the syrup in a large heavy-bottomed saucepan. When the fat has melted, add the dry ingredients and beaten egg alternately and beat until smooth and thick.

Using 2 teaspoons, place rounds of the mixture on to the prepared baking sheets, allowing plenty of room for spreading. Bake for 15 minutes. Leave to stand for a few minutes, then cool on a wire rack.

MAKES ABOUT 56

 MRS BEETON'S TIP

If the biscuit mixture has to stand before baking – perhaps because a shortage of baking sheets makes it necessary to batch-bake – it will thicken. When this happens, simply shape the biscuit mixture into small balls and bake as above.

PIPED ALMOND RINGS

fat for greasing
175 g/6 oz butter
100 g/4 oz caster sugar
1 egg, beaten
225 g/8 oz self-raising flour
50 g/2 oz ground almonds
1-2 drops of vanilla essence
about 10 ml/2 tsp milk

Thoroughly grease two baking sheets. In a mixing bowl, cream the butter and sugar until light and fluffy. Add the beaten egg, beating thoroughly and adding a little of the flour if the mixture begins to curdle. Blend in the remaining flour and ground almonds gradually. Add the vanilla essence and enough milk to give a piping consistency. Leave the mixture to stand for about 20 minutes in a cool place.

Set the oven at 200°C/400°F/gas 6. Put the biscuit mixture into a piping bag fitted with a medium star nozzle, and pipe small rings on to the prepared baking sheets. Bake for 10 minutes or until golden. Leave to stand for a few minutes, then cool on a wire rack.

MAKES ABOUT 24

FLAPJACKS

fat for greasing
50 g/2 oz margarine
50 g/2 oz soft light brown sugar
30 ml/2 tbsp golden syrup
100 g/4 oz rolled oats

Grease a 28 × 18 cm/11 × 7 inch baking tin. Set the oven at 160°C/325°F/gas 3. Melt the margarine in a large saucepan. Add the sugar and syrup, and warm gently. Do not boil. Remove from the heat and stir in the oats.

Press into the prepared tin, then bake for 25 minutes or until firm. Cut into fingers while still warm and leave in the tin to cool.

MAKES ABOUT TWENTY

VARIATIONS

Sultana Flapjacks Add 50 g/2 oz sultanas to the basic mixture, stirring them in with the oats.

Sesame Flapjacks Sesame seeds contribute their own, distinctive flavour to this traditional recipe. Press the flapjack mixture into the tin, then sprinkle a layer of sesame seeds over the top and press them down well with the back of a spoon. Do not use roasted sesame seeds.

Honey Flapjacks Use clear honey instead of golden syrup; continue as in the main recipe.

SPONGE FINGERS

Speed is the secret ingredient of successful sponge fingers. Do not allow the mixture to stand before baking or it will collapse, resulting in solid rather than spongy biscuits.

fat for greasing
caster sugar for dusting
3 eggs, separated
100g/4oz caster sugar
100g/4oz plain flour
pinch of salt

Grease 18 sponge finger tins and dust with caster sugar. Set the oven at 160°C/325°F/gas 3. In a bowl, beat the egg yolks with the sugar until pale and thick. Sift the flour with the salt into a second bowl. Fold half the flour into the egg mixture very lightly.

In a clean, dry bowl, whisk the egg whites until stiff. Fold very lightly into the yolk mixture with the rest of the flour. Half fill the prepared tins and bake for 12 minutes. Leave to cool slightly before removing from the tins and cooling completely on a wire rack.

MAKES EIGHTEEN

ALMOND MACAROONS

fat for greasing
2 egg whites
150g/5oz caster sugar
100g/4oz ground almonds
10ml/2tsp ground rice
split almonds or halved glacé cherries

Grease two baking sheets and cover with rice paper. Set the oven at 160°C/325°F/gas 3.

In a clean dry bowl, whisk the egg whites until frothy but not stiff enough to form peaks. Stir in the sugar, ground almonds, and ground rice. Beat with a wooden spoon until thick and white.

Put small spoonfuls of the mixture 5cm/2 inches apart on the prepared baking sheets or pipe them on. Place a split almond or halved glacé cherry on each macaroon and bake for 20 minutes or until pale fawn in colour. Cool slightly on the baking sheets, then finish cooling on wire racks.

MAKES SIXTEEN TO TWENTY

VARIATION

Ratafias Ratafias are used in trifles, to decorate desserts, and as petits fours. Follow the recipe above, but reduce the size of the biscuits so that when cooked they are only 2cm/¾ inch in diameter. Omit the split almond or glacé cherry topping.

MERINGUES

This basic meringue mixture may be used for a wide variety of dishes, from the individual meringues of various sizes to shells, cases and toppings. Provided the cooked meringues are dried out thoroughly, they will keep for 2 weeks in an airtight tin.

4 egg whites
pinch of salt
200 g/7 oz caster sugar, plus extra for dusting
1.25 ml/¼ tsp baking powder (optional)
whipped cream, to fill (optional)

Line a baking sheet with oiled greaseproof paper or with non-stick baking parchment. Set the oven at 110°C/225°F/gas ¼.

Combine the egg whites and salt in a mixing bowl and whisk until the whites are very stiff and standing in points. They must be completely dry. Gradually add half the caster sugar, 15 ml/1 tbsp at a time, whisking well after each addition until the meringue is stiff. If the sugar is not thoroughly blended in it will form droplets of syrup which may brown, spoiling the appearance and texture of the meringues, and making them difficult to remove from the paper when cooked.

When half the sugar has been whisked in, sprinkle the rest over the surface of the mixture and, using a metal spoon, fold it in very lightly with the baking powder, if used. Put the meringue mixture into a piping bag fitted with a large nozzle and pipe into rounds on the paper. Alternatively, shape the mixture using two wet tablespoons. Take up a spoonful of the mixture and smooth it with a palette knife, bringing it up into a ridge in the centre. Slide it out with the other spoon on to the prepared baking sheet, with the ridge on top.

Dust the meringues lightly with caster sugar, then dry off in the oven for 3-4 hours, until they are firm and crisp but still white. If the meringues begin to brown, prop the oven door open a little. When they are crisp on the outside, lift the meringues carefully off the sheet, using a palette knife. Turn them on to their sides and return to the oven until the bases are dry. Cool on a wire rack and, if liked, sandwich them together with whipped cream. Filled meringues should be served within 1 hour or they will soften.

MAKES 24 TO 30 MEDIUM MERINGUES

VARIATIONS

Meringue Fingers Pipe the meringue mixture into fingers instead of shaping rounds. Dip one end of each meringue in melted chocolate when cool, then leave to set on waxed paper. Alternatively, sandwich the fingers together with whipped cream and coat the top of each with melted chocolate.

Meringue Petits Fours Make half the quantity of mixture. Pipe very small meringues and dry out as in the main recipe, for about 2-3 hours. Set the meringues on small circles of almond paste, attaching them with warmed apricot jam. Alternatively, sandwich them in pairs with whipped cream.

 MRS BEETON'S TIP

It is vital that the egg whites have been separated with great care. The fat in even a trace of egg yolk would prevent the whites from whisking properly. For the same reason, the bowl and whisk must be dry and absolutely clean and grease-free.

FLORENTINES

oil for greasing
25 g/1 oz glacé cherries, chopped
100 g/4 oz cut mixed peel, finely chopped
50 g/2 oz flaked almonds
100 g/4 oz chopped almonds
25 g/1 oz sultanas
100 g/4 oz butter or margarine
100 g/4 oz caster sugar
30 ml/2 tbsp double cream
100 g/4 oz plain or couverture chocolate

Line three or four baking sheets with oiled greaseproof paper. Set the oven at 180°C/ 350°F/gas 4.

In a bowl, mix the cherries and mixed peel with the flaked and chopped almonds and the sultanas. Melt the butter or margarine in a small saucepan, add the sugar and boil for 1 minute. Remove from the heat and stir in the fruit and nuts. Whip the cream in a separate bowl, then fold it in.

Place small spoonfuls of the mixture on to the prepared baking sheets, leaving room for spreading. Bake for 8-10 minutes. After the biscuits have been cooking for about 5 minutes, neaten the edges by drawing them together with a plain biscuit cutter. Leave the cooked biscuits on the baking sheets to firm up slightly before transferring to a wire rack to cool completely.

To finish, melt the chocolate in a bowl over hot water and use to coat the flat underside of each biscuit. Mark into wavy lines with a fork as the chocolate cools.

MAKES 20 TO 24

BRANDY SNAPS

These traditional treats make a popular addition to a buffet table or may be served as a tempting dessert. Fill them at the last moment with fresh whipped cream or Confectioners' Custard (page 778).

fat for greasing
50 g/2 oz plain flour
5 ml/1 tsp ground ginger
50 g/2 oz margarine
50 g/2 oz soft dark brown sugar
30 ml/2 tbsp golden syrup
10 ml/2 tsp grated lemon rind
5 ml/1 tsp lemon juice

Grease two or three 25 × 20 cm/10 × 8 inch baking sheets. Also grease the handles of several wooden spoons, standing them upside down in a jar until required. Set the oven at 180°C/350°F/gas 4.

Sift the flour and ginger into a bowl. Melt the margarine in a saucepan. Add the sugar and syrup and warm gently, but do not allow to become hot. Remove from the heat and add the sifted ingredients with the lemon rind and juice. Mix well.

Put spoonfuls of the mixture on to the prepared baking sheets, spacing well apart to allow for spreading. Do not put more than 6 spoonfuls on a baking sheet. Bake for 8-10 minutes.

Remove from the oven and leave to cool for a few seconds until the edges begin to firm. Lift one of the biscuits with a palette knife and roll loosely around the greased handle of one of the wooden spoons. Allow to cool before removing the spoon handle. Repeat with the remaining biscuits. Alternatively, make brandy snap cups by moulding the mixture in greased patty tins or over oranges.

MAKES FOURTEEN TO EIGHTEEN

WINE BISCUITS

225 g/8 oz plain flour
1.25 ml/¼ tsp salt
1.25 ml/¼ tsp ground cloves
5 ml/1 tsp ground cinnamon
2.5 ml/½ tsp ground ginger
2.5 ml/½ tsp bicarbonate of soda
100 g/4 oz butter
150 g/5 oz caster sugar
50 g/2 oz ground almonds
30 ml/2 tbsp beaten egg
30 ml/2 tbsp white wine
fat for greasing
flour for rolling out
halved almonds (optional)

Sift the flour, salt, spices and bicarbonate of soda into a mixing bowl. Rub in the butter until the mixture resembles fine breadcrumbs and add the sugar and ground almonds. In a bowl, mix the egg with the wine. Add to the dry ingredients and mix to a stiff dough. Leave to stand for several hours or overnight.

Grease three or four baking sheets. Set the oven at 220°C/425°F/gas 7. Roll out the dough on a lightly floured surface to a thickness of 3 mm/⅛ inch. Cut into rounds with a 5 cm/2 inch cutter and put these, well apart, on the prepared baking sheets. Place half an almond on each biscuit, if liked. Bake for 10 minutes. Cool slightly on the baking sheets, then complete cooling on wire racks.

MAKES ABOUT 60

BOURBON BISCUITS

fat for greasing
50 g/2 oz butter or margarine
50 g/2 oz caster sugar
15 ml/1 tbsp golden syrup
100 g/4 oz plain flour
15 g/½ oz cocoa
2.5 ml/½ tsp bicarbonate of soda
flour for rolling out

FILLING
50 g/2 oz butter or margarine
75 g/3 oz icing sugar, sifted
15 ml/1 tbsp cocoa
5 ml/1 tsp coffee essence or 2.5 ml/½ tsp
  instant coffee dissolved in 5 ml/1 tsp
  boiling water and cooled

Line and grease a baking sheet. Set the oven at 160°C/325°F/gas 3.

In a mixing bowl, cream the butter or margarine with the sugar very thoroughly; beat in the syrup. Sift the flour, cocoa and bicarbonate of soda into a second bowl, mix well, then work into the creamed mixture to make a stiff dough. Knead well, and roll out on a lightly floured surface into an oblong strip about 23 × 13 cm/9 × 5 inches and 5 mm/¼ inch thick. Cut in half to form two rectangles about 6 cm/2½ inches wide. Place on the prepared baking sheet and bake for 15–20 minutes. Cut into equal-sized fingers while still warm. Cool on wire rack.

Prepare the filling. In a bowl, beat the butter or margarine until soft, then add the sugar, cocoa, and coffee. Beat until smooth. Sandwich the cooled fingers in pairs with the filling.

MAKES FOURTEEN TO SIXTEEN

NUT CLUSTERS

50 g/2 oz soft margarine
50 g/2 oz sugar
30 ml/2 tbsp beaten egg
2.5 ml/½ tsp vanilla essence
50 g/2 oz plain flour
pinch of salt
1.25 ml/¼ tsp bicarbonate of soda
50 g/2 oz seedless raisins
50 g/2 oz salted peanuts

Set the oven at 190°C/375°F/gas 5. In a mixing bowl beat the margarine and sugar until light and fluffy. Beat in the egg and vanilla essence.

Sift the flour, salt and bicarbonate of soda into a second bowl and beat them into the creamed mixture in three portions, mixing well after each addition. Stir in the raisins and nuts. Place small portions on two ungreased baking sheets and bake for 9 minutes. Cool on the baking sheets.

MAKES 20 TO 24

PRINCESS PAIRS

fat for greasing
100 g/4 oz butter or margarine
25 g/1 oz caster sugar
pinch of salt
100 g/4 oz self-raising flour
grated rind of 1 orange

FILLING
Orange Buttercream (page 903), using
  25 g/1 oz butter

Grease two baking sheets. Set the oven at 180°C/350°F/gas 4. In a mixing bowl, cream the butter or margarine with the sugar. Work in the salt, flour and half the orange rind. Put the mixture in a piping bag fitted with a large star nozzle, and pipe 9 cm/3½ inch lengths on to the prepared baking sheets, making 20 biscuits. Bake for 15 minutes. Cool on the baking sheets. When cool, sandwich together in pairs with the butter-cream flavoured with the remaining orange rind.

MAKES TEN

RING O' ROSES

fat for greasing
100 g/4 oz margarine
50 g/2 oz caster sugar
1 egg yolk
100 g/4 oz plain flour
flour for rolling out

ALMOND TOPPING
1 egg white
75 g/3 oz caster sugar
50 g/2 oz ground almonds

DECORATION
60 ml/4 tbsp red jam or jelly

Grease a baking sheet. Set the oven at 180°C/350°F/gas 4. In a mixing bowl, cream the margarine and sugar thoroughly. Work in the egg yolk and then the flour to form a dough. On a lightly floured surface, knead well, then roll out to a thickness of 5 mm/¼ inch. Cut into 4 cm/1½ inch rounds. Place on the prepared baking sheet.

Make the almond topping. In a bowl, whisk the egg white until frothy, then stir in the caster sugar and the ground almonds. Using a piping bag fitted with a plain nozzle, pipe a circle of the almond mixture around the edge of each biscuit. Bake for 15 minutes, then cool on the baking sheet. When cold, fill the centres of the biscuits with jam or jelly.

MAKES TWELVE

ANZACS

These Australian specialities became popular during World War One, when they were often sent to the Anzacs – soldiers of the Australian and New Zealand Army Corps.

fat for greasing
75 g/3 oz rolled oats
100 g/4 oz plain flour
150 g/5 oz sugar
50 g/2 oz desiccated coconut
100 g/4 oz butter
15 ml/1 tbsp golden syrup
7.5 ml/1½ tsp bicarbonate of soda

Grease two baking sheets. Set the oven at 160°C/325°F/gas 3. Mix the rolled oats, flour, sugar and coconut in a bowl. In a saucepan, melt the buter and syrup gently. Meanwhile put 30 ml/2 tbsp boiling water in a small bowl, add the bicarbonate of soda and stir until dissolved. Add to the melted mixture and stir into the dry ingredients.

Spoon scant tablespoons of the mixture on to the prepared baking sheets, leaving plenty of space between them. Bake for 20 minutes. Cool on the baking sheets.

MAKES ABOUT 36

GERMAN SPICE BISCUITS

fat for greasing
100 g/4 oz plain flour
50 g/2 oz caster sugar
1.25 ml/¼ tsp mixed spice
75 g/3 oz margarine
flour for rolling out

Grease a baking sheet. Set the oven at 160°C/325°F/gas 3.

Mix the flour, sugar and spice in a mixing bowl. Rub in the margarine until the mixture binds together and forms a pliable dough.

Roll out on a floured board to a thickness of 5 mm/¼ inch and cut into rounds with a 6 cm/2½ inch round cutter. Place on the prepared baking sheet. Bake for about 20 minutes until very pale gold in colour. Leave to stand for a few minutes, then cool on a wire rack.

MAKES ABOUT TWELVE

 MRS BEETON'S TIP

A glass makes a good biscuit cutter. Dip it in flour before use to prevent the dough from sticking to the rim.

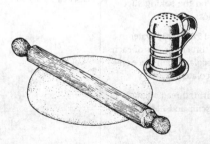

CHOCOLATE-TIPPED CINNAMON STARS

fat for greasing
350 g/12 oz plain flour
5 ml/1 tsp bicarbonate of soda
10 ml/2 tsp ground cinnamon
2.5 ml/½ tsp ground ginger
150 g/5 oz butter
100 g/4 oz sugar
100 g/4 oz honey
1 egg yolk
30 ml/2 tbsp milk
flour for rolling out
150 g/5 oz plain chocolate, broken into
    squares, to decorate.

Thoroughly grease three or four baking sheets. Set the oven at 180°C/350°F/gas 4. Mix the flour, bicarbonate of soda and spices in a bowl.

In a mixing bowl, beat the butter until soft, add the sugar and continue to beat until light and fluffy. Beat in the honey and egg yolk, then the milk. Fold in the flour mixture.

Knead the biscuit dough lightly on a floured surface, then roll out to a thickness of 3 mm/ ⅛ inch. Cut into stars with a 5 cm/2 inch star-shaped biscuit cutter. Using a straw, make a small hole in each star. The hole should be on a point, but not too near the edge. Transfer the biscuits to the prepared baking sheets.

Bake for about 8 minutes, until golden brown. Cool for a few minutes on the baking sheets, then transfer to wire racks.

Melt the chocolate with 15 ml/1 tbsp water in a saucepan over low heat. Brush the tips of each star generously with chocolate, then place on a wire rack until the chocolate has set.

When the chocolate is firm, thread a length of ribbon through each biscuit and hang on the Christmas tree.

MAKES ABOUT 60

CHOCOLATE CHIP COOKIES

America's contribution to the biscuit barrel.

fat for greasing
150 g/5 oz plain flour
1.25 ml/¼ tsp salt
2.5 ml/½ tsp bicarbonate of soda
100 g/4 oz butter or margarine
50 g/2 oz caster sugar
50 g/2 oz soft light brown sugar
1 egg, beaten
2.5 ml/½ tsp vanilla essence
75 g/3 oz chocolate chips

Thoroughly grease two or three baking sheets. Set the oven at 180°C/350°F/gas 4. Mix the flour, salt and bicarbonate of soda in a bowl.

Beat the butter or margarine until soft, add the sugars and continue to beat until light and fluffy. Beat in the egg and vanilla essence. Stir in the flour and chocolate chips.

Using a teaspoon, scoop up a little of the dough. Use a second teaspoon to transfer the dough to one of the prepared baking sheets. Repeat with the remaining dough, making the heaps about 5 cm/2 inches apart.

Bake the biscuits for 10–12 minutes, until golden. Leave to stand for 5 minutes, then cool on a wire rack.

MAKES 26 TO 30

Savoury Biscuits

Here you will find recipes that Mrs Beeton considered to be the most wholesome of the class of 'unfermented breads'. Crisp and light or deliciously savoury, their value today is as accompaniments for cheese or as mouthwatering cocktail snacks.

CHEESE BUTTERFLIES

fat for greasing
100 g/4 oz plain flour
pinch of mustard powder
pinch of salt
pinch of cayenne pepper
75 g/3 oz butter
75 g/3 oz grated Parmesan cheese
1 egg yolk
flour for rolling out

TOPPING
100 g/4 oz cream cheese
few drops of anchovy essence
few drops of red food colouring

Grease two baking sheets. Set the oven at 200°C/400°F/gas 6.

Sift the flour, mustard, salt and cayenne into a bowl. In a mixing bowl, cream the butter until soft and white, then add the flour mixture with the Parmesan. Stir in the egg yolk and enough cold water to form a stiff dough.

Roll out on a lightly floured surface to a thickness of about 3 mm/⅛ inch and cut into rounds about 6 cm/2½ inches in diameter. Cut half the rounds across the centre to make 'wings'.

With a palette knife, lift both the whole rounds and the 'wings' on to the prepared baking sheets and bake for 10 minutes. Cool on the baking sheets.

Meanwhile make the topping. Put the cream cheese in a bowl and cream until soft with a fork, adding the anchovy essence for flavour and just enough of the red food colouring to tint the mixture a pale pink. Transfer the topping to a piping bag fitted with a shell nozzle.

When the biscuits are quite cold, pipe a line of cheese across the centre of each full round and press the straight edges of two half-rounds into the cheese to make them stand up like wings.

MAKES TWELVE TO EIGHTEEN

VARIATIONS

Use the basic recipe for the biscuits to make a variety of different-flavoured cocktail snacks. This is achieved by varying the flavour of the cream cheese which is piped on to the biscuits.

Parmesan and Pine Nut   Add a little grated Parmesan cheese to the cream cheese and omit the anchovy essence and colouring. Sprinkle toasted pine nuts down the middle of the cheese when the 'wings' are in place.

Tomato and Olive   Leave out the anchovy essence and colouring, then flavour the cream cheese with a little tomato purée and add a little lemon juice, to taste. Top with a few pieces of black olive when the 'wings' are in place.

CHEESE STRAWS

fat for greasing
100 g/4 oz plain flour
pinch of mustard powder
pinch of salt
pinch of cayenne pepper
75 g/3 oz butter
75 g/3 oz grated Parmesan cheese
1 egg yolk
flour for rolling out

Grease four baking sheets. Set the oven at 200°C/400°F/gas 6.

Sift the flour, mustard, salt and cayenne into a bowl. In a mixing bowl, cream the butter until soft and white, then add the flour mixture with the cheese. Stir in the egg yolk and enough cold water to form a stiff dough.

Roll out on a lightly floured surface to a thickness of about 5 mm/¼ inch and cut into fingers, each measuring about 10 × 1 cm/4 inches × ½ inch. From the pastry trimmings make several rings, each about 4 cm/1½ inches in diameter.

With a palette knife, transfer both rings and straws to the prepared baking sheets and bake for 8-10 minutes or until lightly browned and crisp. Cool on the baking sheets.

To serve, fit a few straws through each ring and lay the bundles in the centre of a plate with any remaining straws criss-crossed around them.

MAKES 48 TO 60

 MRS BEETON'S TIP

For a decorative effect, the straws may be twisted, corkscrew-fashion.

HOT PEPPER CHEESES

When freshly cooked, these savouries are inclined to crumble and break easily. For this reason it is best to allow them to cool completely, then reheat gently until warm.

fat for greasing
200 g/7 oz plain flour
200 g/7 oz butter
200 g/7 oz Lancashire cheese, grated
few drops of hot pepper sauce
1.25 ml/¼ tsp salt
flour for rolling out

Grease four baking sheets. Sift the flour into a mixing bowl. Rub in the butter until the mixture resembles fine breadcrumbs. Add the cheese and seasonings. Work the mixture thoroughly by hand to make a smooth dough. Use a few drops of water if necessary, but the dough will be shorter and richer without it. Chill for 30 minutes.

Meanwhile, set the oven at 180°C/350°F/gas 4. Roll out the dough on a floured surface to a thickness of 5 mm/¼ inch. Cut into rounds or shapes.

With a palette knife, transfer the shapes to the prepared baking sheets and bake for 10-12 minutes or until lightly browned and crisp. Cool on the baking sheets.

MAKES 40 TO 50

 MRS BEETON'S TIP

When cutting out the cheese dough it is best to stick to regular shapes such as rounds, crescents, squares or stars. The mixture is so short that any thin projections on the biscuits are likely to break off.

CHEESE MERINGUES

2 egg whites
50g/2oz finely grated Parmesan cheese
pinch of salt
pinch of cayenne pepper
oil for deep frying
grated Parmesan cheese and cayenne pepper
  for sprinkling

In a clean dry bowl, whisk the egg whites until stiff peaks form. Lightly fold in the cheese and seasonings.

Heat the oil to 180-190°C/350-375°F or until a cube of bread added to the oil browns in 30 seconds. Using a rounded spoon, gently lower puffs of the mixture into the hot oil or fat (see Mrs Beeton's Tip). Fry the puffs until golden brown, then carefully remove with a slotted spoon and drain thoroughly on absorbent kitchen paper. Serve warm, sprinkled with Parmesan and cayenne.

MAKES FOURTEEN TO SIXTEEN

 MRS BEETON'S TIP

If preferred, the cheese meringue mixture may be put into a piping bag with a large nozzle. Squeeze out the meringue into the hot oil, cutting off small lengths with a sharp knife. Proceed as in the recipe above.

CRISP CRACKERS

These plain crackers are the ideal accompaniment for cheese. If you use very small cutters to cut the dough, the crackers can be used as a base for making little canapés – top them with piped smooth pâté or cream cheese, olives and parsley.

fat for greasing
225g/8oz plain flour
2.5ml/½ tsp salt
about 125ml/4floz milk
1 egg yolk, beaten

Grease two baking sheets. Set the oven at 180°C/350°F/gas 4. Sift the flour and salt into a bowl, then make a well in the middle and add about half the milk. Add the egg yolk to the milk and gradually work in the flour to make a firm dough, adding more milk as necessary.

Turn the dough out on to a lightly floured surface and knead it briefly until it is perfectly smooth. Divide the piece of dough in half and wrap one piece in cling film to prevent it from drying out while you roll out the other piece.

Roll out the dough very thinly and use a 7.5cm/3 inch round cutter to stamp out crackers. Gather up the trimmings and re-roll them. Place the crackers on the prepared baking sheets and bake them for 12-18 minutes, until they are golden. Transfer the crackers to a wire rack to cool.

MAKES ABOUT 24

CARAWAY CRACKERS

Originally, these simple biscuits were sweetened with 50 g/2 oz caster sugar but the flavour of the caraway seeds makes such an excellent savoury cracker that the sugar is omitted in this recipe. However, if you particularly like the flavour of caraway you may like to try the old recipe and add the sugar to the flour. If you are making the savoury crackers try using brown flour instead of white.

fat for greasing
50 g/2 oz butter
225 g/8 oz plain flour
30 ml/2 tbsp caraway seeds
good pinch of salt
1 egg, beaten
milk for glazing

Grease two baking sheets. Set the oven at 180°C/350°F/gas 4. Place the butter in a small bowl and beat it until it is very soft. Gradually beat in the flour, caraway seeds and salt until the ingredients are thoroughly mixed.

Add the beaten egg and mix well to make a firm dough. Knead the dough briefly on a floured surface, then roll it out thinly and cut out 5 cm/2 inch circles.

Place the crackers on the baking sheets and brush them with a little milk, then bake them for about 12–15 minutes. Transfer the crackers to a wire rack to cool.

MAKES ABOUT 30

OATCAKES

fat for greasing
25 g/1 oz bacon fat or dripping
225 g/8 oz medium oatmeal
1.25 ml/¼ tsp salt
1.25 ml/¼ tsp bicarbonate soda
fine oatmeal for rolling out

Grease two baking sheets. Set the oven at 160°C/325°F/gas 3.

Melt the bacon fat or dripping in a large saucepan. Remove from the heat and stir in the dry ingredients, then add 60–75 ml/4–5 tbsp boiling water to make a stiff dough.

When cool enough to handle, knead the dough thoroughly and cut it in half. Roll out one portion of dough on a surface dusted with fine oatmeal, to a thickness of 5 mm/¼ inch and about 18 cm/7 inch in diameter. Cut into eight wedges and transfer to the prepared baking sheets. Repeat with the remaining dough. Bake for 20–30 minutes. Cool on a wire rack.

MAKES ABOUT SIXTEEN

RUSKS

This is an old Suffolk recipe for simple, dry biscuits which are made from a yeasted bread dough. The original recipe used fresh yeast but this version takes advantage of easy-blend yeast. The sugar may be omitted if preferred.

fat for greasing
225 g/8 oz strong plain flour
15 g/½ oz easy-blend dried yeast
25 g/1 oz sugar
2.5 ml/½ tsp salt
25 g/1 oz butter
75 ml/3 fl oz milk
1 egg, beaten
flour for kneading

Grease a large baking sheet. Set the oven at 220°C/425°F/gas 7.

Place the flour, yeast, sugar and salt in a mixing bowl. Stir the ingredients together, then make a well in the middle. In a small saucepan, heat the butter and milk together very gently until the butter has melted, then remove the pan from the heat and leave to cool until warm.

Pour the milk mixture into the well in the dry ingredients, add the beaten egg and stir well. Gradually stir in the flour mixture to make a firm dough. Turn the dough out on to a lightly floured surface and knead thoroughly until smooth and elastic. The dough should be kneaded for about 10 minutes.

Place the dough in a clean, lightly floured bowl and cover it with a clean cloth. Set the dough to rise in a warm place until it has doubled in bulk. This may take up to 1½ hours.

Lightly knead the dough again, then divide it into six portions. Shape each portion of dough into an oblong roll measuring about 13 cm/5 inches in length. Place the rolls on the baking sheet and bake them for about 15-20 minutes, or until they are evenly golden.

Remove the rolls from the oven and reduce the temperature to 180°C/350°F/gas 4. Using a clean tea-towel to protect your hand, split each roll in half lengthways to make a slim rusk. Return them to the baking sheet, cut side uppermost, and cook for a further 30-40 minutes, or until they are crisp and lightly browned on the cut side. The rusks are ready when they are quite dry.

Leave the rusks to cool on a wire rack, then transfer them to an airtight container.

MAKES TWELVE

SIMPLE CRISPIES

fat for greasing
225 g/8 oz plain flour
good pinch of salt
150 ml/¼ pint milk
25 g/1 oz butter

Grease two baking sheets. Set the oven at 190°C/375°F/gas 5. Sift the flour and salt into a bowl, then make a well in the middle.

Heat the milk and butter in a small saucepan until the butter has dissolved, then pour the mixture into the well in the flour. Gradually work the flour into the milk to make a stiff dough. Knead the dough briefly until it is smooth, then roll it out thinly and cut out 7.5 cm/3 inch crackers.

Place the crackers on the baking sheets and bake them for 6-10 minutes, or until they are golden. Transfer the crackers to a wire rack to cool.

MAKES ABOUT 30

ANCHOVY APPETIZERS

fat for greasing
75 g/3 oz plain flour
40 g/1½ oz butter or margarine
1 egg yolk
few drops of anchovy essence
flour for rolling out

ANCHOVY CREAM
1 (50 g/2 oz) can anchovy fillets, drained
1 egg, hard-boiled (yolk only)
25 g/1 oz butter
pinch of cayenne pepper
45 ml/3 tbsp double cream
few drops of red food colouring

Grease two baking sheets. Set the oven at 200°C/400°F/gas 6.

Sift the flour into a mixing bowl and rub in the butter or margarine until the mixture resembles fine breadcrumbs. Add the egg yolk, anchovy essence and enough water to mix to a stiff dough. Roll out thinly on a lightly floured surface and cut into rounds about 2.5-4 cm/1-1½ inches in diameter.

Place on the prepared baking sheets and bake for about 12 minutes until crisp. Cool for a few minutes on the baking sheets, then transfer to wire racks to cool completely.

Make the anchovy cream. Put the anchovies in a bowl and pound with the yolk of the hard-boiled egg and the butter until smooth, adding a little cayenne for seasoning. In a second bowl, whip the cream until fairly stiff, then fold it into the anchovy mixture. Add the colouring until the mixture is pale pink. Transfer it to a piping bag fitted with a star nozzle and pipe rosettes of anchovy cream on to the biscuits.

MAKES TWELVE

CHESHIRE CHIPS

fat for greasing
50 g/2 oz plain flour
50 g/2 oz butter
50 g/2 oz Cheshire cheese, grated
50 g/2 oz fresh white breadcrumbs
1.25 ml/¼ tsp cayenne pepper
1.25 ml/¼ tsp salt
flour for rolling out

Grease four baking sheets. Sift the flour into a mixing bowl. Rub in the butter until the mixture resembles fine breadcrumbs. Add the cheese, breadcrumbs and seasonings. Work the mixture thoroughly by hand to make a smooth dough. Chill for 30 minutes.

Meanwhile, set the oven at 180°C/350°F/gas 4. Roll out the dough on a floured surface to a thickness of 5 mm/¼ inch. Cut into thin chips, each measuring about 3 mm × 5 cm/⅛ inch × 2 inches.

With a palette knife, transfer the chips to the prepared baking sheets and bake for 7-10 minutes or until lightly browned and crisp. Cool on the baking sheets.

MAKES 48 TO 60

Yeasted Breads

The aroma of freshly baked bread is unmistakable and appetizing, and the results are worth the effort. This chapter offers an excellent selection of recipes, from plain white or wholemeal loaves to specialist International breads.

The choice of ingredients for making yeast mixtures is important. Strong flour is used because of its high gluten content. Gluten is the strengthening agent which forms the elastic dough during kneading, to trap the bubbles of gas given off by the yeast during proving. This makes the dough rise and gives the light result.

YEAST

There are various options and all work well.

Fresh yeast Available from bakers who cook on the premises, small bread shops, hot bread shops or the hot bread counters at larger supermarkets.

Fresh yeast should be pale, firm and slightly crumbly in texture. It should smell fresh. Yeast that is very broken, dark, soft or sour-smelling is old and should not be used. Wrapped in polythene, fresh yeast will keep for several days in the refrigerator or it may be frozen. Freeze 25 g/1 oz portions ready for use.

Cream fresh yeast with a little sugar and lukewarm liquid to make a paste. Add a little extra liquid, then place the mixture in a warm place until it becomes frothy. This process gives the yeast a good start so that it is very active when mixed with the other ingredients. It is also a very good way of checking that the yeast is fresh and working.

There has been some controversy over whether the yeast should be creamed with sugar or just with water. The addition of sugar was thought to give an unacceptably strong 'yeasty' flavour to the finished baking but as long as the quantities in recipes are followed,

and the liquid is not left too long, the results using sugar are better than without.

Other methods of starting the yeast include sponging it – mixing it to a paste, then adding all the liquid and enough flour to make a batter. This is left to rise and bubble before mixing the ingredients to a dough.

Sometimes the yeast liquid may be poured into a well in the dry ingredients and allowed to ferment, usually sprinkled with a little flour.

Dried yeasts There are two types, so always read the manufacturer's instructions and follow them carefully.

The first is a granular product that is sprinkled over warm liquid and left to dissolve, then ferment until frothy before being stirred and mixed with the remaining ingredients. Usually the granules contain enough food for the yeast to work without having to add extra sugar.

The second, newer and now more popular type is a finer-grained dried yeast which should be added to the dry ingredients. Slightly hotter liquid is used to mix the dough and only one rising, or proving, is necessary.

TECHNIQUES

Kneading The kneading is important as it mixes the yeast evenly with the other ingredients and it develops the gluten in the flour to make the dough elastic. Once the dough is toughened, it traps the bubbles of gas produced by the yeast and rises.

Proving This is the process of rising. The dough must be left in a warm place until it has doubled in bulk. It must be covered to keep in moisture and prevent a skin forming on the dough (polythene, cling film or a damp cloth may be used). The covering is removed after proving, before baking. The warmer the place, the faster the rising but if the dough becomes hot the yeast will be killed. Dough may be left overnight in the refrigerator to rise slowly, or in a cool place for many hours. In a warm room dough will rise in a couple of hours.

Except when using fast-action dried yeast (the type combined with dry ingredients), most doughs are proved twice.

Knocking Back   After the first proving, the dough is very lightly kneaded to knock out the gas, then it is shaped and allowed to prove for a second time. The second kneading is known as knocking back.

STORING

Breads should be stored in a clean airtight container. If kept in a polythene bag, they should be placed in a cool place (but not the refrigerator which tends to promote staling) to prevent them from sweating.

FREEZING

Yeasted goods freeze well, they should be cooked and cooled, then packed and frozen promptly. Most breads freeze well for up to 2 months. Loaves should be left to thaw for several hours at room temperature; rolls and small items thaw within a couple of hours at room temperature.

BASIC WHITE BREAD

fat for greasing
800 g/1¾ lb strong white flour
10 ml/2 tsp salt
25 g/1 oz lard
25 g/1 oz fresh yeast or 15 ml/1 tbsp dried
  yeast
2.5 ml/½ tsp sugar
flour for kneading
beaten egg or milk for glazing

Grease two 23 × 13 × 7.5 cm/9 × 5 × 3 inch loaf tins. Sift the flour and salt into a large bowl. Rub in the lard. Measure 500 ml/17 fl oz luke-warm water.

Blend the fresh yeast to a thin paste with the sugar and a little of the warm water. Set aside in a warm place until frothy – about 5 minutes. Alternatively, sprinkle dried yeast over all the warm water and set aside. When frothy, stir well.

Add the yeast liquid and remaining water to the flour mixture and mix to a soft dough. Turn on to a floured surface and knead for about 8 minutes or until the dough is smooth, elastic and no longer sticky. Return to the bowl and cover with cling film. Leave in a warm place until the dough has doubled in bulk – this will take up to 2 hours, or longer.

Knead the dough again until firm. Cut into two equal portions and form each into a loaf shape. Place the dough into the prepared loaf tins and brush the surface with beaten egg or milk. Place the tins in a large, lightly oiled polythene bag. Leave in a warm place for about 45 minutes or until the dough has doubled in bulk. Set the oven at 230°C/450°F/gas 8.

Bake for 35–40 minutes, until the loaves are crisp and golden brown, and sound hollow when tapped on the bottom.

MAKES TWO 800G/1¾LB LOAVES

SHAPING YEAST DOUGH

Yeast doughs of all types may be shaped in many ways to make attractive breads. The following ideas may be used for making two loaves from the Basic White Bread dough recipe.

Twist Divide the dough in half and roll each piece into a strip. Pinch the two ends of the strips together on a greased baking sheet, then twist the strips together, tucking the ends under neatly and pinching them in place.

Ring Make a long, fairly slim twist, then shape it in a ring on a greased baking sheet.

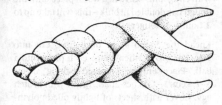

Plait Divide the dough for one loaf into three equal portions and roll them into long strips. Pinch the ends of the strips together on a greased baking sheet, then plait the strips neatly. Fold the ends under at the end of the plait, pinching them underneath to secure the plait.

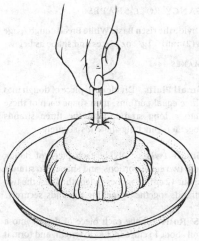

Cottage Loaf Shape two-thirds of the dough into a round loaf and place on a greased baking sheet. Shape the remaining dough into a ball. Make an indentation in the middle of the round loaf, then dampen the dough in the middle and place the ball on top. Make a deep indentation with your fingers or a wooden spoon handle down through the ball of dough and the round base. Before baking, score several slits down the side of the base of the loaf.

TOPPINGS FOR BREADS

Before baking, the risen dough may be glazed with beaten egg or milk for a golden crust. Brushing with water makes a crisp crust. Then the dough may be sprinkled with any of the following:

- Poppy seeds – dark or white.
- Sesame seeds – black or white, for flavour as well as texture and appearance.
- Cracked wheat – good on wholemeal loaves.
- Caraway, fennel or cumin seeds – when used generously these all contribute flavour.

FANCY ROLL SHAPES

Divide the risen Basic White Bread dough (page 812) into 50 g/2 oz pieces and shape as below:

MAKES 24

Small Plaits Divide each piece of dough into three equal portions; then shape each of these into a long strand. Plait the three strands together, pinching the ends securely.

Small Twists Divide each piece of dough into two equal portions, and shape into strands about 12 cm/4½ inches in length. Twist the two strands together, pinching the ends securely.

'S' Rolls Shape each piece of dough into a roll about 15 cm/6 inches in length, and form it into an 'S' shape.

Cottage Rolls Cut two-thirds off each piece of dough and shape into a ball. Shape the remaining third in the same way. Place the small ball on top of the larger one and push a hole through the centre of both with one finger, dusted with flour, to join the two pieces firmly together.

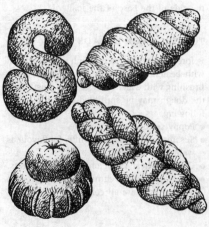

DINNER ROLLS

fat for greasing
800 g/1¾ lb strong white flour
10 ml/2 tsp sugar
400 ml/14 fl oz milk
25 g/1 oz fresh yeast or 15 ml/1 tbsp dried yeast
10 ml/2 tsp salt
50 g/2 oz butter or margarine
1 egg
flour for kneading
beaten egg for glazing

Grease two baking sheets. Sift about 75 g/3 oz of the flour and all the sugar into a large bowl. Warm the milk until lukewarm, then blend in the fresh yeast or stir in the dried yeast. Pour the yeast liquid into the flour and sugar and beat well. Leave the bowl in a warm place for 20 minutes.

Sift the remaining flour and the salt into a bowl. Rub in the butter or margarine. Beat the egg into the yeast mixture and stir in the flour mixture. Mix to a soft dough. Turn on to a lightly floured surface and knead for about 5 minutes or until the dough is smooth and no longer sticky. Return to the bowl and cover with cling film. Leave in a warm place until the dough has doubled in bulk – this will take up to 2 hours, or longer.

Knead the dough again until firm. Cut into 50 g/2 oz pieces, then shape each piece into a ball. Place on the prepared baking sheets 5–7.5 cm/2–3 inches apart. Brush with beaten egg. Cover with sheets of lightly oiled polythene. Leave in a warm place for about 20 minutes or until the rolls have doubled in bulk. Set the oven at 220°C/425°F/gas 7.

Bake for 12–15 minutes until the rolls are golden brown.

MAKES 24

ENRICHED BREAD

fat for greasing
900 g/2 lb strong white flour
10 ml/2 tsp sugar
400 ml/14 fl oz milk
25 g/1 oz fresh yeast or 15 ml/1 tbsp dried
  yeast
10 ml/2 tsp salt
100 g/4 oz butter or margarine
2 eggs
flour for kneading
milk for glazing

Grease two 23 × 13 × 7.5 cm/9 × 5 × 3 inch loaf tins. Sift about 75 g/3 oz of the flour and all the sugar into a large bowl. Warm the milk until lukewarm, then blend in the fresh yeast or stir in the dried yeast. Pour the yeast liquid into the flour and sugar and beat well. Leave the bowl in a warm place for 20 minutes.

Sift the remaining flour and the salt into a bowl. Rub in the butter or margarine. Beat the eggs into the yeast mixture and stir in the flour mixture. Mix to a soft dough. Turn on to a lightly floured surface and knead for about 6 minutes or until the dough is smooth and no longer sticky. Return to the bowl and cover with cling film. Leave in a warm place until the dough has doubled in bulk – this will take up to 2 hours, or longer.

Knead the dough again until firm. Cut into two equal portions and form each into a loaf shape. Place the dough in the prepared loaf tins. Place the tins in a large, lightly oiled polythene bag. Leave in a warm place for about 30 minutes or until the dough has doubled in bulk. Set the oven at 220°C/425°F/gas 7.

Brush the surface of the dough with milk. Bake for 35-40 minutes until the loaves sound hollow when tapped on the bottom.

MAKES TWO 800 G/1¾ LB LOAVES

VARIATIONS

Bread Plait Make as for Enriched Bread. Cut the risen dough into two equal portions. Cut one of these into three equal pieces. Roll each piece into a strand 25-30 cm/10-12 inches long and plait the strands together. Repeat, using the second portion. Place the plaits on a greased baking sheet. Cover, leave to rise and bake the plait as for Enriched Bread.

Cheese Bread Plait Make as for Bread Plait but add 200 g/7 oz grated Cheddar cheese to the dry ingredients.

Caraway Bread Make as for Enriched Bread but add 10 ml/2 tsp dried sage, 5 ml/1 tsp grated nutmeg and 15 ml/1 tbsp caraway seeds to the dry ingredients.

Fruit Bread Make as for Enriched Bread but add 200 g/7 oz sultanas, currants or raisins to the dough when kneading for the second time.

Nut Bread Make as for Enriched Bread but add 200 g/7 oz chopped nuts, such as walnuts or peanuts, to the dough when kneading for the second time.

Poppy Seed Bread Make as for Enriched Bread but sprinkle poppy seeds thickly over the dough before baking.

Bridge Rolls Make as for Enriched Bread but cut the risen dough into 50 g/2 oz pieces. Roll each piece into a finger shape about 10 cm/4 inches long. Place on a greased baking sheet so that the rolls almost touch each other. Dust the surface of the rolls with flour. Cover and leave to rise for about 20 minutes or until the rolls have joined together. Bake as for Enriched Bread but reduce the baking time to 12-15 minutes.

MAKES ABOUT 28

FRENCH BREAD

Apart from the obvious difference in shape, French bread differs from the common British loaf in the type of flour which is used to make the dough. French bread is made from softer flour, or flour which has a lower gluten content; therefore, strong white flour, which has a high gluten content, is not suitable for this recipe.

flour for dusting and kneading
350 g/12 oz plain white flour
50 g/2 oz cornflour
5 ml/1 tsp salt
15 g/½ oz fresh yeast or 10 ml/2 tsp dried
  yeast
2.5 ml/½ tsp sugar
beaten egg for glazing

Flour a baking sheet thoroughly. Sift the flours and salt into a large bowl. Measure 250 ml/8 fl oz lukewarm water.

Blend the fresh yeast to a thin paste with the sugar and a little of the warm water. Set aside in a warm place until frothy – about 5 minutes. Alternatively, sprinkle dried yeast over all the warm water and set aside until frothy, then stir well.

Stir the yeast liquid and remaining water into the flours and mix to a firm dough. Turn on to a floured surface and knead for about 4 minutes or until the dough is smooth and no longer sticky. Return to the bowl and cover with cling film. Leave in a warm place until the dough has doubled in bulk – this will take up to 2 hours, or longer.

Cut the dough into two or four equal portions. On a floured surface, roll out one piece to an oval 40 cm/16 inches or 20 cm/8 inches in length. The smaller size is used if the dough is divided into quarters. Roll up like a Swiss roll and place on the prepared baking sheet. With a sharp knife, slash the top surface at intervals.

Brush the surface with beaten egg. Repeat with the other piece of dough. Leave both, *uncovered*, in a warm place until doubled in bulk.

Meanwhile, place a pan of boiling water in the bottom of the oven. (This is to provide steam to make the French bread expand fully before using dry heat to form the typical crisp crust.) Set the oven at 220°C/425°F/gas 7. Bake for 15 minutes, remove the pan of water, then continue baking for 15–20 minutes until the sticks are very crisp and well browned.

MAKES TWO LONG OR FOUR SHORT FRENCH STICKS

 MRS BEETON'S TIP

The dough is left uncovered to rise for the second time, so that the surface dries out and a very crisp crust is obtained after the loaf has been 'blown up' by steam heat in the oven. This can be done only when the volume of dough is as small as it is here, otherwise the bread splits open on baking.

RICE BREAD

This unusual bread is moist with a close, slightly elastic, texture. It is delicious thickly sliced when warm or cut into thin slices when cold.

100 g/4 oz long-grain rice (not the easy-cook
  type)
450 ml/¾ pint milk
25 g/1 oz fresh yeast or 15 ml/1 tbsp dried
  yeast
2.5 ml/½ tsp sugar
450 g/1 lb strong plain flour
10 ml/2 tsp salt
beaten egg to glaze (optional)

Add the rice to a small saucepan of boiling water. Bring back to the boil, then drain. Put the rice back in the pan and add the milk. Bring to the boil, stirring occasionally, then reduce the heat and partially cover the pan. Simmer for 15 minutes.

Blend the fresh yeast to a thin paste with the sugar and 50 ml/2 fl oz lukewarm water. Set aside in a warm place until frothy – about 5 minutes. Alternatively, sprinkle dried yeast over the water and set aside until frothy, then stir well.

Mix the flour and salt in a bowl. Make a well in the middle and pour in the rice with the cooking milk. Mix in the flour, using a wooden spoon and a cutting action. When the rice and milk are evenly distributed and have cooled slightly, pour in the yeast liquid and mix to a soft dough. The flour should have cooled the rice sufficiently to avoid killing the yeast but the dough should still feel hot.

Turn out on a well-floured surface and knead until smooth and elastic, sprinkling with a little flour to prevent the dough sticking. Place in a bowl, cover and leave in a warm place until doubled in bulk. Meanwhile, grease a baking sheet.

Turn the dough out, knead briefly and divide it in half. Shape two long oval loaves and place them on the baking sheet. Cover loosely with oiled polythene and leave in a warm place until well risen and spread into slightly flattened loaves. Meanwhile, set the oven at 220°C/425°F/gas 7. Brush the risen loaves with beaten egg and bake for 35-45 minutes, until well browned and firm. The loaves should sound hollow when tapped on the bottom. Cool on a wire rack.

MAKES TWO LOAVES

INDIAN CORN (MAIZE) FLOUR BREAD

fat for greasing
25 g/1 oz fresh yeast or 15 ml/1 tbsp dried yeast
5 ml/1 tsp sugar
450 g/1 lb strong white flour
25 g/1 oz butter
225 g/8 oz maize flour
7.5 ml/1½ tsp salt
flour for kneading

Grease two baking sheets. Measure 450 ml/¾ pint lukewarm water. Blend the fresh yeast with the sugar and a little of the lukewarm water. Set aside until frothy. For dried yeast, sprinkle the yeast over all the water, then leave until frothy.

Sift the flour and salt into a bowl. Rub in the butter, then stir in the maize flour. Make a well in the middle and add the yeast liquid. Pour in the remaining water and stir well. Gradually work in the dry ingredients to a firm dough.

Turn out the dough on a lightly floured surface and knead thoroughly until smooth and elastic – about 10 minutes. Place the dough in a clean, lightly floured bowl. Cover with cling film and leave in a warm place until doubled in bulk. This will take about 2 hours.

Knead the dough lightly, then cut it in half and shape each portion into a round loaf. Place on the baking sheets, cover loosely with oiled polythene or cling film and leave in a warm place until doubled in bulk again.

Meanwhile, set the oven at 220°C/425°F/gas 7. When the bread is risen, use a sharp knife to make three slashes across the top of each loaf. Brush with water and bake for about 45 minutes, until golden brown and crisp. The loaf should sound hollow when tapped on the base. Cool on a wire rack.

MAKES TWO LOAVES

MALTED BROWN BREAD

fat for greasing
800 g/1¾ lb wholemeal flour
15 ml/1 tbsp salt
25 g/1 oz fresh yeast or 15 ml/1 tbsp dried
  yeast
2.5 ml/½ tsp sugar
30 ml/2 tbsp malt extract
flour for kneading

Grease two 23 × 13 × 7.5 cm/9 × 5 × 3 inch loaf
tins. Mix the flour and salt in a large bowl.
Measure 500 ml/17 fl oz lukewarm water.

Blend the fresh yeast to a thin paste with the
sugar and a little of the warm water. Set aside in
a warm place until frothy – about 5 minutes.
Alternatively, sprinkle the dried yeast over all
the warm water and set aside until frothy.

Stir the malt extract into the yeast liquid and
remaining water. Add to the flour and mix to a
soft dough. Turn on to a lightly floured surface
and knead for about 4 minutes or until the
dough is smooth, elastic and no longer sticky.
Return to the bowl and cover with cling film.
Leave in a warm place until the dough has
doubled in bulk – this takes 2 hours, or longer.

Knead the dough again until firm. Cut into two
equal portions and form each into a loaf shape.
Place the dough in the prepared loaf tins. Place
the tins in a large, lightly oiled polythene bag.
Leave in a warm place for about 45 minutes or
until the dough has doubled in bulk. Set the
oven at 230°C/450°F/gas 8.

Bake for 35–45 minutes, until the loaves are
golden brown and crisp, and sound hollow
when tapped on the bottom.

MAKES TWO 800 G/1¾ LB LOAVES

SCOTTISH BROWN BREAD

fat for greasing
575 g/1¼ lb wholemeal flour
200 g/7 oz fine or medium oatmeal
15 ml/1 tbsp salt
25 g/1 oz fresh yeast or 15 ml/1 tbsp dried
  yeast
2.5 ml/½ tsp sugar
5 ml/1 tsp bicarbonate of soda
flour for kneading

Grease two 23 × 13 × 7.5 cm/9 × 5 × 3 inch loaf
tins. Mix the flour, oatmeal and salt in a large
bowl. Measure 500 ml/17 fl oz lukewarm
water.

Blend the fresh yeast to a thin paste with the
sugar and a little of the warm water. Set aside in
a warm place until frothy – about 5 minutes.
Alternatively, sprinkle dried yeast over all the
warm water and set aside until frothy, then stir.

Add the bicarbonate of soda to the yeast liquid
and remaining water, then stir this into the
flour mixture to form a soft dough. Turn on to a
lightly floured surface and knead for about 4
minutes or until the dough is smooth and no
longer sticky. Return to the bowl and cover
with cling film. Leave in a warm place until the
dough has doubled in bulk – this will take up to
2 hours, or longer.

Knead the dough again until firm. Cut into two
equal portions and form each into a loaf shape.
Place the dough in the prepared loaf tins. Place
the tins in a large, lightly oiled polythene bag.
Leave in a warm place for about 45 minutes or
until the dough has doubled in bulk. Set the
oven at 230°C/450°F/gas 8.

Bake for 20 minutes, then reduce the oven
temperature to 190°C/375°F/gas 5. Continue
baking for 25–35 minutes, until the loaves are
crisp and golden brown, and sound hollow
when tapped on the bottom.

MAKES TWO 800 G/1¾ LB LOAVES

GRANT LOAF

fat for greasing
800 g/1¾ lb wholemeal flour
15 ml/1 tbsp salt
25 g/1 oz fresh yeast or 15 ml/1 tbsp dried
   yeast
2.5 ml/½ tsp sugar

Grease three 20 × 10 × 6 cm/8 × 4 × 2½ inch loaf tins. Mix the flour and salt in a large bowl. Have ready 700 ml/scant 1¼ pints lukewarm water.

Blend the fresh yeast to a thin paste with the sugar and a little of the warm water. Set aside in a warm place until frothy – about 5 minutes. Alternatively, sprinkle dried yeast over all the warm water and set aside until frothy, then stir well.

Pour the yeast liquid and remaining water into the flour and stir until the flour is evenly wetted. The resulting dough should be wet and slippery. Spoon it into the prepared loaf tins. Place the tins in a large, lightly oiled polythene bag. Leave in a warm place until the dough has risen by a third. Set the oven at 190°C/375°F/ gas 5.

Bake for 50-60 minutes, until the loaves are golden brown and crisp, and sound hollow when tapped on the bottom.

MAKES THREE 400 G/14 OZ LOAVES

WHEATMEAL BREAD

fat for greasing
400 g/14 oz wholemeal flour
400 g/14 oz strong white flour
10 ml/2 tsp salt
25 g/1 oz lard
25 g/1 oz fresh yeast or 15 ml/1 tbsp dried
   yeast
2.5 ml/½ tsp sugar
flour for kneading
salted water

Grease two 23 × 13 × 7.5 cm/9 × 5 × 3 inch loaf tins. Mix the flours and salt in a large bowl. Rub in the lard. Measure 450 ml/¾ pint lukewarm water.

Blend the fresh yeast to a thin paste with the sugar and a little of the warm water. Set aside in a warm place until frothy. Alternatively, sprinkle dried yeast over all the warm water and set aside until frothy, then stir well.

Add the yeast liquid and remaining water to the flour mixture and mix to a soft dough. Turn on to a floured surface and knead for about 4 minutes or until the dough is smooth and elastic. Replace in the bowl, cover and leave in a warm place until doubled in bulk.

Cut the dough into two equal portions and form each into a loaf shape. Place the dough in the prepared loaf tins, then brush the surface with salted water. Place the tins in a large, lightly oiled polythene bag. Leave the tins in a warm place for about 50 minutes or until the dough has doubled in bulk. Set the oven at 230°C/ 450°F/gas 8.

Bake for 30-40 minutes, until the loaves are golden brown and crisp, and sound hollow when tapped lightly on the bottom.

MAKES TWO 800 G/1¾ LB LOAVES

RYE COBS

fat for greasing
900 g/2 lb strong white flour
25 g/1 oz fresh yeast or 15 ml/1 tbsp dried
   yeast
2.5 ml/½ tsp sugar
450 g/1 lb coarse rye flour
500 ml/17 fl oz skimmed milk
20 ml/4 tsp salt
60 ml/4 tbsp molasses
60 ml/4 tbsp cooking oil
flour for kneading

Grease a baking sheet or four 15 cm/6 inch sandwich tins. Sift the white flour into a large bowl. Measure 250 ml/8 fl oz lukewarm water.

Blend the fresh yeast to a thin paste with the sugar and a little of the warm water. Set aside in a warm place until frothy – about 5 minutes. Alternatively, sprinkle dried yeast over all the warm water and set aside until frothy, then stir well.

Mix the rye flour into the white flour. Add the yeast liquid, remaining water, skimmed milk, salt, molasses and oil, then knead to a soft dough. Cover the bowl with cling film. Leave in a warm place until the dough has doubled in bulk – this will take at least 2 hours, or longer. (Rye bread is slow to rise).

When risen, shape into four loaves. Place on the prepared baking sheet or press into the sandwich tins. Place in a large, lightly oiled polythene bag. Leave to rise for 30–45 minutes. Set the oven at 190°C/375°F/gas 5.

Sprinkle the dough with warm water. Bake for about 40 minutes, until the loaves sound hollow when tapped on the bottom.

MAKES FOUR LOAVES

GRANARY BREAD

fat for greasing
800 g/1¾ lb granary flour or meal
10 ml/2 tsp salt
10 ml/2 tsp molasses
25 g/1 oz fresh yeast or 15 ml/1 tbsp dried
   yeast
10 ml/2 tsp corn oil
flour for kneading
15 ml/1 tbsp cracked wheat

Grease two 23 × 13 × 7.5 cm/9 × 5 × 3 inch loaf tins. Mix the flour and salt in a large bowl. Measure 500 ml/17 fl oz lukewarm water. Stir in the molasses.

Blend the fresh yeast to a thin paste with a little of the warm water and molasses. Set aside in a warm place until frothy – about 5 minutes. Alternatively, sprinkle dried yeast over all the warm water and molasses and set aside until frothy, then stir well. Add the yeast liquid, remaining liquid and the oil to the flour and mix to a soft dough. Turn on to a floured surface and knead for about 4 minutes or until the dough is smooth, elastic and no longer sticky. Return to the bowl and cover with cling film. Leave in a warm place until doubled in bulk – this will take about 2 hours, or longer.

Knead the dough again until firm. Cut into two equal portions and form each into a loaf shape. Place the dough in the prepared loaf tins, brush the surface with salted water and sprinkle with the cracked wheat. Place the tins in a large, lightly oiled polythene bag. Leave in a warm place for about 45 minutes or until the dough has doubled in bulk. Set the oven at 230°C/450°F/gas 8.

Bake for 30–40 minutes, until the loaves are browned and crisp, and sound hollow when tapped on the bottom.

MAKES TWO 800 G/1¾ LB LOAVES

SAFFRON BREAD

fat for greasing
400 g/14 oz strong white flour
5 ml/1 tsp salt
125 ml/4 fl oz milk
75 g/3 oz butter
large pinch of powdered saffron
75 g/3 oz caster sugar
1 egg
25 g/1 oz fresh yeast or 15 ml/1 tbsp dried yeast
50 g/2 oz ground almonds
flour for kneading
50 g/2 oz chopped mixed peel
50 g/2 oz currants
50 g/2 oz raisins
beaten egg for glazing
10 ml/2 tsp granulated sugar
4 blanched almonds, roughly chopped

Grease a 23 × 13 × 7.5 cm/9 × 5 × 3 inch loaf tin. Sift the flour and salt together. Measure 100 ml/3½ fl oz lukewarm water. Warm the milk and butter together until the butter has melted. Transfer to a bowl, add the saffron and leave to stand for 10 minutes. Beat in the caster sugar, reserving 2.5 ml/½ tsp if using fresh yeast, and add the egg.

Blend the fresh yeast to a thin paste with the reserved sugar and a little of the warm water. Set aside in a warm place until frothy – about 5 minutes. Alternatively, sprinkle dried yeast over all the warm water and set aside until frothy, then stir well.

Add the yeast liquid and remaining water to the milk and saffron mixture and stir in a third of the flour. Leave in a warm place for 20 minutes.

Work in the rest of the flour and ground almonds to form a very soft dough. Turn on to a well floured surface and knead for about 5 minutes or until the dough is smooth. Return to the bowl and cover with cling film. Leave in a warm place until the dough has doubled in bulk – this will take at least 2 hours, or longer.

Work in the dried fruit and form the dough into a loaf shape. Place the dough in the prepared loaf tin. Brush the top with beaten egg. Sprinkle on the granulated sugar and almonds. Place the tin in a large, lightly oiled polythene bag. Leave in a warm place for about 45 minutes or until the dough has doubled in bulk. Set the oven at 220°C/425°F/gas 7.

Bake for 10 minutes, then reduce the oven temperature to 190°C/375°F/gas 5. Continue baking for a further 30 minutes, until golden brown.

MAKES ONE 800 G/1¾ LB LOAF

VARIATION

Kulich Make as for Saffron Bread. After working the fruit into the dough, divide into two equal pieces. Well grease two 450–500 g/1 lb circular empty cans. For example, large fruit or coffee cans may be used. They should be washed and dried before use. Shape the pieces of dough to fit the tins and put the dough in them. Place the tins in a large, lightly oiled polythene bag. Leave in a warm place for about 35 minutes or until the dough has reached the top of the tins. Set the oven at 220°C/425°F/gas 7. Bake for 35–40 minutes, until golden brown. When cold, ice with Glacé Icing (page 771).

MAKES TWO 400 G/14 OZ KULICH

NAAN

fat for greasing
25 g/1 oz fresh yeast or 15 ml/1 tbsp dried
  yeast
5 ml/1 tsp sugar
450 g/1 lb strong white flour
5 ml/1 tsp salt
150 ml/¼ pint plain yogurt
flour for kneading
50 g/2 oz butter, melted

Grease four baking sheets. Sift the flour and salt
into a bowl. Measure 150 ml/¼ pint lukewarm
water. Blend the fresh yeast with the sugar and
a little lukewarm water, then stir in the remaining water; set aside until frothy. Alternatively,
sprinkle dried yeast over all the warm water
and set aside until frothy, then stir well.

Make a well in the centre of the dry ingredients
and pour in the yogurt with the yeast liquid.
Gradually mix in the dry ingredients to make a
firm dough. Knead the dough on a lightly
floured surface until smooth and elastic – about
10 minutes. Place the dough in a clean bowl,
cover with cling film and leave in a warm place
until doubled in bulk.

Set the oven at 250°C/475°F/gas 9. Heat the
prepared baking sheets in the oven. Knead
about a third of the dough again, then divide it
into three. Stretch each portion of dough into a
large, thin oblong, about 20 cm/8 inches long.
Slap the thin breads on the sheets and brush the
breads with melted butter.

Bake for 5–7 minutes, until bubbling and well
browned. Shape a second batch of naan while
the first breads are baking, then place them
straight on to the hot sheets. Transfer to a wire
rack when cooled.

MAKES NINE

PRINCESS ROLLS

fat for greasing
400 g/14 oz strong white flour
250 ml/8 fl oz milk
15 g/½ oz fresh yeast or 10 ml/2 tsp dried
  yeast
15 ml/1 tbsp caster sugar
50 g/2 oz margarine
5 ml/1 tsp salt
flour for kneading
about 150 g/5 oz butter

Grease a baking sheet. Sift the flour into a large
bowl. Warm the milk until lukewarm. Blend
the fresh yeast to a thin paste with 2.5 ml/½ tsp
of the sugar and half of the warm milk. Set
aside in a warm place until frothy. Alternatively, sprinkle dried yeast over the warm milk
and set aside until frothy.

Add the margarine, remaining sugar and salt to
the remaining milk, and heat until the fat has
melted. Leave until lukewarm. Stir with the
yeast liquid into the flour and mix to a soft
dough. Turn on to a lightly floured surface and
knead until smooth. Return the dough to the
bowl and cover with cling film. Leave in a
warm place until doubled in bulk.

Lightly knead the dough again. Roll out on a
floured surface to 8 mm/⅓ inch thickness. Cut
into rounds, using a plain 7.5 cm/3 inch cutter.
Place a small piece of butter on one half of each
round. Fold over the other half and pinch the
edges firmly together. Place the rolls on the
prepared baking sheet. Put the sheet in a large,
lightly oiled polythene bag. Leave in a warm
place for about 30 minutes or until the rolls
have almost doubled in size. Set the oven at
220°C/425°F/gas 7. Bake for 10–15 minutes,
until golden brown.

MAKES EIGHTEEN

BAGELS

These ring buns are poached in water before baking. The result is a close-textured, moist bread with a deep-golden-coloured crust which is quite thick but not hard. It is worth making a large batch and freezing them: the bagels may be frozen after poaching but before baking, then they should be baked after thawing. Alternatively, they may be fully cooked before cooling and freezing.

fat for greasing
400 g/14 oz strong-white flour
5 ml/1 tsp salt
30 ml/2 tbsp sugar
50 g/2 oz margarine
15 g/½ oz fresh yeast or 10 ml/2 tsp dried
  yeast
1 egg, separated
flour for kneading
poppy seeds

Grease a baking sheet. Sift the flour into a large bowl. Measure 250 ml/8 fl oz lukewarm water. Put the salt, sugar (reserving 2.5 ml/½ tsp if using fresh yeast), the margarine and half the water in a saucepan and warm gently until the fat has melted. Leave until lukewarm.

Blend the fresh yeast to a thin paste with the reserved sugar and the remaining warm water. Set aside in a warm place until frothy – about 5 minutes. Alternatively, sprinkle dried yeast over the warm water and set aside until frothy, then stir well.

Whisk the egg white lightly, then add to the flour with the cooled margarine mixture and the yeast liquid. Mix to a soft dough. Cover the bowl with cling film. Leave in a warm place until the dough has almost doubled in bulk – this will take up to 2 hours, or longer.

Knead the dough again until firm. Cut into 25 g/1 oz pieces. Roll each piece into a sausage shape 15-20 cm/6-8 inches in length; then form this into a ring, pinching the ends

securely together. Place the rings on a floured surface and leave for 10 minutes or until they begin to rise.

Heat a saucepan of water deep enough to float the bagels, to just under boiling point. Drop in the bagels, a few at a time. Cook them on one side for 2 minutes, then turn them over and cook on the other side for about 2 minutes or until they are light and have risen slightly. Place on the prepared baking sheet. Set the oven at 190°C/375°F/gas 5.

Beat the egg yolk, brush it over the top surface of the bagels and sprinkle with poppy seeds. Bake for 20-30 minutes, until golden brown and crisp.

MAKES 28

 MRS BEETON'S TIP

For a luxurious, weekend breakfast, serve warm bagels with smoked salmon and soured cream. If you favour sweet preserves to savoury food for breakfast, offer an excellent black cherry conserve and soured cream with the bagels.

CROISSANTS

Rich, flaky French croissants make the perfect break-fast, especially when home-made.

fat for greasing
400 g/14 oz strong white flour
5 ml/1 tbsp salt
75 g/3 oz lard
25 g/1 oz fresh yeast or 15 ml/1 tbsp dried
   yeast
2.5 ml/½ tsp sugar
1 egg, beaten
flour for kneading
100 g/4 oz unsalted butter
beaten egg for glazing

Grease the baking sheet. Sift the flour and salt into a large bowl. Rub in 25 g/1 oz of the lard. Measure 200 ml/7 fl oz lukewarm water.

Blend the fresh yeast to a thin paste with the sugar and a little of the warm water. Set aside in a warm place until frothy – about 5 minutes. Alternatively, sprinkle the dried yeast over all the warm water and set aside until frothy, then stir well.

Stir the egg, yeast liquid and remaining water into the flour and mix to a soft dough. Turn on to a lightly floured surface and knead for about 8 minutes or until the dough is smooth and no longer sticky. Return the dough to the bowl and cover with cling film. Leave at room temperature for 15 minutes.

Meanwhile, roughly chop the remaining lard and the butter together until well mixed; then chill. On a lightly floured surface, roll out the dough carefully into an oblong 50 × 20 cm/ 30 × 8 inches. Divide the chilled fat into three. Dot one-third over the top two-thirds of the dough, leaving a small border. Fold the dough into three by bringing the bottom third up and the top third down. Seal the edges by pressing with the rolling pin. Give the dough a quarter turn and repeat the rolling and folding twice,

using the other two portions of fat. Place the dough in a large, lightly oiled polythene bag. Leave in a cool place for 15 minutes.

Repeat the rolling and folding three more times. Rest the dough in the polythene bag in a cool place for 15 minutes. Roll out to an oblong 34 × 23 cm/14 × 9 inches and then cut it into six 13 cm/5 inch squares. Cut each square into triangles. Brush the surface of the dough with beaten egg and roll each triangle loosely, towards the point, finishing with the tip underneath. Curve into a crescent shape. Place on the prepared baking sheet and brush with beaten egg. Place the baking sheet in the polythene bag again. Leave at room temperature for about 1 hour or until the dough is light and puffy. Set the oven at 220°C/425°F/gas 7.

Bake for 15–20 minutes, until golden brown and crisp. Cool on a wire rack.

MAKES TWELVE

 MRS BEETON'S TIP

The difficulty many cooks experience with croissants is combining the need for warmth, to set the yeast into action, with the process of cooling the dough so that the fat does not melt as it is being rolled into the dough. In the first stages, before the rolling process, the warmth is vital to ensure the dough rises. Thereafter, it is better to allow more time for the dough to rise and to keep it cool than to speed up the process and cause the fat to melt.

BRIOCHES

fat for greasing
400 g/14 oz strong white flour
5 ml/1 tsp salt
50 g/2 oz butter
15 g/½ oz fresh yeast or 10 ml/2 tsp dried
  yeast
2.5 ml/½ tsp sugar
2 eggs
flour for kneading
beaten egg for glazing

Grease 22 × 7.5 cm/3 inch brioche or deep bun tins. Sift the flour and salt into a large bowl. Rub in the butter. Blend the fresh yeast with the sugar and 40 ml/8 tsp lukewarm water. Set aside in a warm place until frothy. Alternatively, sprinkle dried yeast over the warm water and set aside until frothy.

Beat the eggs into the yeast liquid and stir into the flour to form a soft dough. Turn on to a floured surface and knead for about 5 minutes or until the dough is smooth and no longer sticky. Return to the bowl and cover with cling film. Leave in a warm place for about 45 minutes or until doubled in bulk.

Knead the dough again until firm. Cut into 22 equal pieces. Cut off one-quarter of each piece used. Form the larger piece into a ball and place in a prepared tin. Firmly press a hole in the centre and place the remaining quarter as a knob in the centre. Place the tins on a baking sheet and cover with a large, lightly oiled polythene bag. Leave in a warm place for about 30 minutes or until the dough is light and puffy. Set the oven at 230°C/450°F/gas 8. Brush with beaten egg. Bake for 15–20 minutes, until golden brown.

MAKES TWELVE

SALLY LUNN

Sally Lunn was a cake seller in Bath during the 18th century and her cake, or bun, became very famous.

fat for greasing
400 g/14 oz strong white flour
5 ml/1 tsp salt
50 g/2 oz butter
150 ml/¼ pint milk
15 g/½ oz fresh yeast or 10 ml/2 tsp dried
  yeast
2.5 ml/½ tsp sugar
1 egg
15 ml/1 tbsp caster sugar for glazing

Grease two 15 cm/6 inch round cake tins. Sift the flour and salt into a large bowl. Rub in the butter. Warm the milk until lukewarm.

Blend the fresh yeast to a thin paste with the sugar and warm milk. Set aside in a warm place until frothy – about 5 minutes. Alternatively, sprinkle dried yeast over the warm milk and set aside until frothy, then stir well.

Beat the egg into the yeast liquid and stir into the flour mixture to form a very soft dough. Beat well. Pour the mixture into the prepared cake tins.

Place the tins in a large, lightly oiled polythene bag. Leave in a warm place until the dough has doubled in bulk – this will take up to 2 hours, or longer. Set the oven at 220°C/425°F/gas 7.

Bake for 20–25 minutes, until golden brown. To make the glaze, boil together 15 ml/1 tbsp water and the sugar until syrupy. Brush the hot glaze over the top of the Sally Lunns.

To serve, split each Sally Lunn crossways, into three rounds and toast each piece on both sides. Butter thickly or fill with clotted cream, re-form the cake, and cut into slices or wedges.

MAKES TWO 15 CM/6 INCH SALLY LUNNS

CHALLAH

fat for greasing
800 g/1¾ lb strong white flour
10 ml/2 tsp sugar
25 g/1 oz fresh yeast or 15 ml/1 tbsp dried
  yeast
10 ml/2 tsp salt
100 g/4 oz butter or margarine
2 eggs
flour for kneading
beaten egg for glazing

Grease two baking sheets. Sift about 75 g/3 oz of the flour and all the sugar into a large bowl. Measure 400 ml/14 fl oz lukewarm water. Blend the fresh yeast into the water or stir in the dried yeast. Pour the yeast liquid into the flour and sugar and beat well. Leave the bowl in a warm place for 20 minutes.

Sift the remaining flour and the salt into a bowl. Rub in the butter or margarine. Beat the eggs into the yeast mixture and stir in the flour mixture. Mix to a soft dough. Turn on to a lightly floured surface and knead for about 6 minutes or until the dough is smooth and no

longer sticky. Return to the bowl and cover with cling film. Leave in a warm place until the dough has doubled in bulk – this will take up to 2 hours, or longer.

Knead the dough again until firm. Cut into two equal portions. Cut one of these into two equal pieces and roll these into long strands 30–35 cm/12–14 inches in length. Arrange the two strands in a cross on a flat surface. Take the two opposite ends of the bottom strand and cross them over the top strand in the centre. Repeat this, using the other strand. Cross each strand alternately, building up the plait vertically, until all the dough is used up. Gather the short ends together and pinch firmly. Lay the challah on its side and place on the prepared baking sheet. Brush with beaten egg. Repeat, using the second portion. Cover with lightly oiled polythene. Leave in a warm place for about 30 minutes or until the dough has doubled in bulk. Set the oven at 220°C/425°F/gas 7.

Bake for 35–40 minutes, until the loaves are golden brown and sound hollow when tapped on the bottom.

MAKES TWO 800 G/1¾ LOAVES

Sweet Yeast Doughs

Yeasted tea breads and buns are the perfect weekend treat, and they are sure to be superior if you make them at home. This chapter includes instructions for making Danish pastries too – they are ideal candidates for batch baking and freezing.

Sweet yeast doughs differ from plain breads in that they are enriched as well as sweetened. All the information on flour, yeast and the techniques used for bread making applies to the recipes in this chapter.

UNDERSTANDING RICH DOUGHS

Even more so than when making plain breads, patience plays a vital role when handling rich yeasted mixtures. Although a little sugar is used to speed up the initial action of yeast, when it is added to doughs in quantity, it tends to have the opposite effect, so sweet doughs usually take longer to rise.

The addition of extra fat and eggs to enrich the dough also tends to slow down the action of the yeast. Therefore it is important to allow plenty of time for sweet breads to rise. As well, some of the very rich mixtures (for example, Danish pastries) are best left in a cool place to rise over a long period so that their high butter content does not melt.

ADAPTING BASIC RECIPES

Sweet yeast doughs may be used as the basis for making many exciting breads. Ready-to-eat dried fruits such as apricots, apples and peaches, as well as raisins, sultanas and dates, are all ideal for kneading into sweet breads. Nuts may be added too – chopped walnuts, hazel nuts, Brazils or pistachios make loaves or buns quite different. With imagination, sweet doughs can be swirled with rich fillings – grated chocolate, ground almonds and icing sugar combine well; cinnamon, brown sugar, chopped walnuts and butter may be used; or chopped candied citron peel mixed with honey and chopped almonds makes a tempting combination. Roll out the dough, spread the filling in the middle, then roll it up and place it in a tin. Or flatten small pieces of dough and fill them, then shape them into buns.

Place shaped round buns in a square tin, slightly apart, so that they rise together into a bubbly loaf. Drizzle with melted butter and sprinkle with sugar for a golden glaze when the loaf is baked.

STORING AND FREEZING

Allow the breads to cool on a wire rack before storing them in airtight containers. When cool, most sweet breads freeze well. However, remember not to add any icing or glaze before freezing; apply this after the bread has thawed.

If sweet breads do become stale they may be toasted and served hot and buttered. Stale bun loaves make good bread and butter pudding. Soak other sweet breads in eggs and milk, then bake them slowly before topping with jam and meringue and browning (rather like Queen of Puddings).

DANISH PASTRIES

200 g/7 oz plain flour
pinch of salt
25 g/1 oz lard
15 g/½ oz fresh yeast or 10 ml/2 tsp dried
yeast
2.5 ml/½ tsp caster sugar
1 egg, beaten
flour for dusting
125 g/4½ oz butter, chilled

Sift the flour and salt into a bowl. Rub in the lard.

Blend the fresh yeast to a thin paste with the sugar and 75 ml/3 fl oz lukewarm water. Set aside in a warm place until frothy – about 5 minutes. Sprinkle dried yeast over the warm water and set aside until frothy, then stir well. Add the beaten egg.

Pour the yeast liquid into the flour mixture and mix to a soft dough. Turn on to a floured surface and knead lightly until smooth. Return the dough to the bowl and cover with cling film. Leave in a cool place for 10 minutes.

Shape the butter into a long rectangle about 1 cm/½ inch thick. Roll out the dough to about 25 cm/10 inches square. Place the butter down the centre. Fold the sides of the dough over the middle to overlap about 1 cm/½ inch only. Roll the dough into a strip 40 × 15 cm/16 × 6 inches. Fold it evenly into three. Place the dough in a large, lightly oiled polythene bag. Leave for 10 minutes. Roll and fold the dough in the same way twice more, letting it rest for 10 minutes each time. The dough is now ready for making the pastry shapes. Each batch of dough makes 16 pastries. Choose two shapes, using half the dough for each.

Windmills   Roll out half the dough to about 40 × 20 cm/16 × 8 inches. Cut into eight 10 cm/4 inch squares; place the squares on a baking sheet. Put a little Almond Paste (page 900) in the centre of each square (about 50 g/2 oz in all). Brush the paste lightly with beaten egg. Make a cut from the corners of each square towards the middle. Fold the corners of each triangular piece towards the centre, then press the points into the almond paste firmly. Brush with beaten egg. Cover the pastries with oiled polythene and leave in a warm place for about 10–15 minutes until puffy. (It is important not to have the temperature too warm or the butter will run out.) Set the oven at 220°C/425°F/gas 7 and bake the pastries for about 10 minutes. When cool, place a little raspberry jam in the centre of each pastry.
MAKES EIGHT

Fruit Snails   Cream together 50 g/2 oz butter, 50 g/2 oz caster sugar and 10 ml/2 tsp ground cinnamon. Roll out half the dough into a 40 × 15 cm/16 × 6 inch rectangle. Spread with the spiced butter and scatter 25 g/1 oz sultanas over it. Roll up from the short side to make a fat roll. Cut it into eight slices and place on a baking sheet. Flatten slightly. Prove and bake as above. Decorate with white Glacé Icing (page 771) when cold.
MAKES EIGHT

Cockscombs   Roll out half the dough and cut it into squares as for windmills. Spread the middle of each square with a little bought chocolate hazelnut spread and top with a thin sausage shape of Almond Paste (page 766). Fold each square in half and pinch the edges together to seal in the filling. Make four or five cuts into the pastries, then place on a baking sheet, curving them slightly to open the slits. Prove and bake as for windmills. Brush with Apricot Glaze (page 766) when cool.
MAKES EIGHT

BUN LOAF

fat for greasing
400 g/14 oz strong white flour
5 ml/1 tsp sugar • 125 ml/4 fl oz milk
25 g/1 oz fresh yeast or 15 ml/1 tbsp dried
  yeast
5 ml/1 tsp salt
7.5 ml/1½ tsp ground mixed spice
2.5 ml/½ tsp ground cinnamon
2.5 ml/½ tsp grated nutmeg
50 g/2 oz butter • 50 g/2 oz caster sugar
100 g/4 oz currants
50 g/2 oz chopped mixed peel
1 egg • flour for kneading

GLAZE
30 ml/2 tbsp milk • 40 g/1½ oz caster sugar

Grease a 23 × 13 × 7.5 cm/9 × 5 × 3 inch loaf
tin. Sift about 75 g/3 oz of the flour and the
5 ml/1 tsp sugar into a large bowl. Warm the
milk and 75 ml/3 fl oz water until lukewarm.
Blend in the fresh yeast or sprinkle on the dried
yeast. Beat the yeast liquid into the flour and
sugar. Leave in a warm place for 20 minutes.

Sift the rest of the flour, the salt and spices into
a bowl. Rub in the butter. Add the caster sugar
and dried fruit. Beat the egg into the yeast
mixture and add the flour, fat and fruit mixture.
Mix to a soft dough. Turn on to a lightly floured
surface and knead for about 5 minutes until
smooth. Return to the bowl and cover. Leave in
a warm place until doubled in bulk – this will
take up to 2 hours, or longer.

Knead the dough again until firm. Shape into a
loaf and place in the prepared loaf tin. Place the
tin in a large, lightly oiled polythene bag. Leave
for about 45 minutes until the dough has
doubled. Set the oven at 220°C/425°F/gas 7.
Bake for 30-40 minutes. For the glaze, boil the
milk, sugar and 30 ml/2 tbsp water for 6
minutes. Brush the loaf with the glaze.

MAKES TWELVE SLICES

BARA BRITH

fat for greasing
450 g/1 lb strong plain flour
75 g/3 oz lard or butter
50 g/2 oz chopped mixed peel
150 g/5 oz seedless raisins
50 g/2 oz currants
75 g/3 oz soft light brown sugar
5 ml/1 tsp ground mixed spice
pinch of salt
25 g/1 oz fresh yeast
5 ml/1 tsp sugar
250 ml/8 fl oz lukewarm milk
1 egg, beaten
flour for kneading
honey for glazing

Grease a 20 × 13 × 7.5 cm/8 × 5 × 3 inch loaf
tin. Sift the flour into a bowl and rub in the lard
or butter. Stir in the peel, raisins, currants,
brown sugar, mixed spice and salt. Blend the
fresh yeast to a thin paste with the sugar and
milk. Set aside in a warm place until frothy –
about 5 minutes.

Make a well in the centre of the dry ingredients
and add the yeast mixture and the beaten egg.
Mix to a soft dough, then cover the bowl with
cling film. Leave in a warm place until the
dough has doubled in bulk – this will take about
2 hours, or longer.

Turn out the dough on to a floured board and
knead well. Place in the prepared loaf tin,
pressing it well into the corners. Place the tin in
a large, lightly oiled polythene bag. Leave for a
further 30 minutes to rise. Set the oven at
200°C/400°F/gas 6.

Bake for 15 minutes, then lower the oven
temperature to 160°C/325°F/gas 3. Continue
baking for about 1¼ hours. Turn out on to a wire
rack and brush the top with clear honey.

MAKES TWELVE SLICES

SWEET ALMOND BREAD

A layer of almond paste is baked into this bread.

fat for greasing
200 g/7 oz strong white flour
5 ml/1 tsp sugar
100 ml/3½ fl oz milk
15 g/½ oz fresh yeast or 10 ml/2 tsp dried
  yeast
2.5 ml/½ tsp salt
25 g/1 oz butter or margarine
1 egg
flour for kneading
milk for glazing
sifted icing sugar for dredging

ALMOND PASTE
75 g/3 oz icing sugar, sifted
75 g/3 oz ground almonds
5 ml/1 tsp lemon juice
few drops of almond essence
beaten egg white

Grease a baking sheet. Sift about 50 g/2 oz of the flour and the sugar into a bowl. Warm the milk until lukewarm. Blend in the fresh yeast or sprinkle on the dried yeast. Pour the yeast liquid into the flour and sugar, then beat well. Leave the bowl in a warm place for 20 minutes.

Sift the remaining flour and salt into a bowl. Rub in the butter or margarine. Beat the egg into the yeast mixture and stir in the flour and fat mixture. Mix to a soft dough. Turn on to a lightly floured surface and knead for about 5 minutes or until the dough is smooth and no longer sticky. Return to the bowl and cover with cling film. Leave in a warm place until the dough has doubled in bulk – this will take about 40 minutes, or longer.

To make the almond paste, mix the icing sugar, ground almonds, lemon juice and almond essence with enough egg white to bind the mixture together.

Roll out the dough on a lightly floured surface to a 25 cm/10 inch round.

Break the almond paste in lumps and sprinkle them on to half the dough round. Fold the uncovered half of the dough over to cover the paste. Press the edges of dough firmly together. Brush the surface with milk. Place on the prepared baking sheet and cover with oiled polythene. Leave for about 30 minutes to rise. Set the oven at 220°C/425°F/gas 7.

Bake for 10 minutes, then lower the oven temperature to 190°C/375°F/gas 5. Continue baking for 15–25 minutes, until golden brown. When cold, dredge the bread with a little sifted icing sugar.

MAKES ONE 400 G/14 OZ LOAF

CHERRY BREAD

fat for greasing
200 g/7 oz strong white flour
5 ml/1 tsp sugar
100 ml/3½ fl oz milk
15 g/½ oz fresh yeast or 10 ml/2 tsp dried
  yeast
2.5 ml/½ tsp salt
25 g/1 oz butter or margarine
1 egg
flour for kneading
75 g/3 oz glacé cherries
milk for glazing

Grease a 15 cm/6 inch cake tin. Sift about 50 g/2 oz of the flour and the sugar into a bowl. Warm the milk until lukewarm. Blend in the fresh yeast or sprinkle on the dried yeast. Pour the yeast liquid into the flour and sugar, then beat well. Leave in a warm place for 20 minutes.

Sift the remaining flour and salt into a bowl. Rub in the butter or margarine. Beat the egg into the yeast mixture and stir in the flour and fat mixture. Mix to a soft dough. Turn on to a lightly floured surface and knead for about 5 minutes or until the dough is smooth and no longer sticky. Return to the bowl and cover with cling film. Leave in a warm place until doubled in bulk – about 40 minutes, or longer.

Chop the cherries roughly and knead them into the risen dough until well distributed. Press the dough into the prepared cake tin and brush the surface with a little milk. Place the tin in a large, lightly oiled polythene bag. Leave in a warm place for about 30 minutes or until the dough reaches just above the edge of the tin. Set the oven at 220°C/425°F/gas 7.

Bake for 10 minutes, then lower the oven temperature to 190°C/375°F/gas 5. Continue baking for 15-25 minutes, until golden brown.

MAKES ONE 400 G/14 OZ LOAF

WHOLEMEAL FRUIT BREAD

fat for greasing
400 g/14 oz wholemeal flour
7.5 ml/1½ tsp salt
15 g/½ oz lard
15 g/½ oz fresh yeast or 10 ml/2 tsp dried
  yeast
2.5 ml/½ tsp sugar
flour for kneading
100 g/4 oz stoned prunes
grated rind of 1 orange
25 g/1 oz caster sugar

Grease a 23 × 13 × 7.5 cm/9 × 5 × 3 inch loaf tin. Mix the flour and salt in a large bowl. Rub in the lard. Measure 250 ml/8 fl oz lukewarm water. Blend the fresh yeast to a thin paste with the sugar and a little of the water. Set aside in a warm place until frothy – about 5 minutes. Alternatively, sprinkle dried yeast over all the warm water and set aside until frothy.

Add the yeast liquid and remaining water to the flour mixture and mix to a soft dough. Turn on to a floured surface and knead for about 4 minutes or until the dough is smooth and elastic and no longer sticky. Return to the bowl and cover with cling film. Leave in a warm place until the dough has doubled in bulk – this will take up to 2 hours, or longer.

Meanwhile, chop the prunes roughly. Knead the dough again until firm, incorporating the prunes, orange rind and caster sugar. Place the dough in the prepared loaf tin. Place the tin in a large, lightly oiled polythene bag. Leave in a warm place for about 1 hour or until the dough has doubled in bulk. Set the oven at 230°C/450°F/gas 8.

Bake for 30-40 minutes, until the loaf is golden brown and crisp, and sounds hollow when tapped on the bottom.

MAKES ONE 800 G/1¾ LB LOAF

PLAIN BUNS

These may be varied by adding a few currants, some
chopped candied peel or mixed peel, or caraway
seeds.

fat for greasing
25 g/1 oz fresh yeast or 15 ml/1 tbsp dried
   yeast
75 g/3 oz plus 5 ml/1 tsp caster sugar
300 ml/½ pint lukewarm milk
450 g/1 lb strong plain flour
5 ml/1 tsp salt
50 g/2 oz butter, melted

Grease a baking sheet. Blend the fresh yeast
with the 5 ml/1 tsp caster sugar and a little of
the lukewarm milk. Set aside until frothy. For
dried yeast, sprinkle the yeast over all the milk,
then leave until frothy.

Sift the flour and salt into a bowl, then stir in
the remaining sugar. Make a well in the middle
and pour in the yeast liquid with the remaining
milk. Stir in the melted butter and gradually
mix in the dry ingredients to a firm dough.

Turn out the dough on a lightly floured surface
and knead thoroughly until smooth and elastic
– about 10 minutes. Place the dough in a clean,
lightly floured bowl. Cover with cling film and
leave in a warm place until doubled in bulk.
This will take 2 hours or longer, depending on
the warmth of the room.

Knead the dough lightly, then cut it into 12
equal pieces and quickly knead them into egg
shapes. Arrange in neat rows on the baking
sheet, cover loosely with oiled polythene or
cling film and leave until doubled in bulk.

Meanwhile, set the oven at 220°C/425°F/gas 7.
Brush the risen buns with a little milk and bake
for 15–20 minutes, until risen and golden. Cool
on a wire rack.

MAKES TWELVE

CORNISH SPLITS

fat for greasing
400 g/14 oz strong white flour
50 g/2 oz sugar
125 ml/4 fl oz milk
15 g/½ oz fresh yeast or 10 ml/2 tsp dried
   yeast
5 ml/1 tsp salt
50 g/2 oz butter
flour for kneading

Grease a baking sheet. Sift about 75 g/3 oz of
the flour and 5 ml/1 tsp of the sugar into a large
bowl. Warm the milk and 125 ml/4 fl oz water
until lukewarm. Blend in the fresh yeast or
sprinkle on the dried yeast. Pour the yeast
liquid into the flour and sugar, then beat well.
Leave the bowl in a warm place for 20 minutes.

Sift the rest of the flour and sugar and the salt
together in a bowl. Rub in the butter. Stir into
the yeast mixture and mix to form a soft dough.
Turn on to a lightly floured surface and knead
for about 6 minutes or until the dough is
smooth and no longer sticky. Return to the
bowl and cover with cling film. Leave in a
warm place until the dough has doubled in bulk
– this will take up to 2 hours, or longer.

Knead the dough again until firm. Divide into
50 g/2 oz pieces and form each into a round
bun. Place the buns on the prepared baking
sheet. Place the sheet in a large, lightly oiled
polythene bag. Leave in a warm place for about
30 minutes or until the buns have doubled in
size. Set the oven at 220°C/425°F/gas 7.

Bake for 15–20 minutes, until golden brown.
Serve cold, split the buns and spread with
cream and jam.

MAKES FOURTEEN

CHELSEA BUNS

fat for greasing
400 g/14 oz strong white flour
5 ml/1 tsp sugar
200 ml/7 fl oz milk
25 g/1 oz fresh yeast or 15 ml/1 tbsp dried
   yeast
5 ml/1 tsp salt
50 g/2 oz butter plus 15 ml/1 tbsp
1 egg
flour for kneading
150 g/5 oz currants
50 g/2 oz chopped mixed peel
100 g/4 oz soft light brown sugar
honey for glazing

Grease a baking sheet. Sift about 75 g/3 oz of the flour and the sugar into a large bowl. Warm the milk until lukewarm. Blend in the fresh yeast or sprinkle on the dried yeast. Pour the yeast liquid into the flour and sugar, then beat well. Leave the bowl in a warm place for 20 minutes.

Sift the remaining flour and the salt into a bowl. Rub in the 50 g/2 oz butter. Beat the egg into the yeast mixture and add the flour and fat mixture. Mix to a soft dough. Turn on to a lightly floured surface and knead for about 6 minutes or until the dough is smooth and no longer sticky. Return to the bowl and cover with cling film. Leave in a warm place until the dough has doubled in bulk.

On a floured surface, roll out the dough to a 50 cm/20 inch square. Melt the remaining butter and brush it all over the surface of the dough. Sprinkle with the dried fruit and sugar. Roll up the dough like a Swiss roll. Cut the roll into 16 equal pieces. Place the buns, about 2.5 cm/1 inch apart, on the prepared baking sheet with the cut side uppermost. Place the baking sheet in a large, lightly oiled polythene bag. Leave in a warm place for about 30 minutes or until the buns have joined together

and are light and puffy. Set the oven at 220°C/425°F/gas 7.

Bake for 15–20 minutes, until golden brown. While still hot, brush with honey.

MAKES SIXTEEN

VARIATIONS

Use this classic recipe as a basis for making rolled buns with different fillings. Try chopped ready-to-eat dried apricots with chopped walnuts and a little honey; chopped dates with orange marmalade and some grated cooking apple; or chocolate chips with chopped hazelnuts and chopped mixed peel.

 MRS BEETON'S TIP

Chelsea buns should be arranged in a square shape on the baking sheet so that they join together when risen and cooked. A square deep cake tin may be used instead of a baking sheet.

HOT CROSS BUNS

flour for dusting
400 g/14 oz strong white flour
5 ml/1 tsp sugar
125 ml/4 fl oz milk
25 g/1 oz fresh yeast or 15 ml/1 tbsp dried
  yeast
5 ml/1 tsp salt
7.5 ml/1½ tsp ground mixed spice
2.5 ml/½ tsp ground cinnamon
2.5 ml/½ tsp grated nutmeg
50 g/2 oz butter
50 g/2 oz caster sugar
100 g/4 oz currants
50 g/2 oz chopped mixed peel
1 egg
flour for kneading

GLAZE
30 ml/2 tbsp milk
40 g/1½ oz caster sugar

Sift about 75 g/3 oz of the flour and the
5 ml/1 tsp sugar into a large bowl. Warm the
milk and 75 ml/3 fl oz water until lukewarm.
Blend in the fresh yeast or sprinkle on the dried
yeast. Pour the yeast liquid into the flour and
sugar, then beat well. Leave the bowl in a warm
place for 20 minutes.

Sift the rest of the flour, the salt and spices into
a bowl. Rub in the butter. Add the caster sugar
and dried fruit. Beat the egg into the frothy
yeast mixture and add the flour, fat and fruit
mixture. Mix to a soft dough. Turn on to a
lightly floured surface and knead for about 5
minutes. Return to the bowl and cover with
cling film. Leave in a warm place until the
dough has almost doubled in bulk.

Knead the dough again until firm. Cut into 12
equal pieces and shape each into a round bun.

Place on a floured baking sheet. With a sharp
knife slash a cross on the top of each bun, or
make crosses with pastry trimmings. Cover
with oiled polythene. Leave for about 35
minutes, until the dough has doubled in bulk.
Set the oven at 220°C/425°F/gas 7. Bake for
15-20 minutes, until golden. Boil the milk,
sugar and 30 ml/2 tbsp water for 6 minutes.
Brush over the hot buns.

MAKES TWELVE

LARDY CAKE

fat for greasing
¼ quantity risen Basic White Bread dough,
  about 350 g/12 oz (page 812)
flour for rolling out
125 g/4½ oz lard
100 g/4 oz caster sugar
100 g/4 oz sultanas or currants
5 ml/1 tsp ground mixed spice
10 ml/2 tsp caster sugar for glazing

Grease a 20 cm/8 inch square cake tin. Roll out
the dough on a floured surface to a strip 2 cm/¾
inch thick. Place a third of the lard in small pats
over the dough. Sprinkle one-third of the sugar,
dried fruit and spice over. Fold the dough into
three, bringing the bottom third up and the top
third down. Repeat the rolling twice more.

Roll out to fit the tin. Score diamond shapes in
the surface of the dough with a sharp knife.
Place the tin in a large, lightly oiled polythene
bag. Leave in a warm place for about 45
minutes or until risen by half. Set the oven at
200°C/400°F/gas 6.

Bake for 40 minutes, until golden. To make the
glaze, boil the sugar and 15 ml/1 tbsp water in a
saucepan until syrupy, then brush over the
warm cake.

MAKES EIGHTEEN TO TWENTY SLICES

REVEL BUNS

These take a day to prove.

fat for greasing
large pinch of powdered saffron
125 ml/4 fl oz milk
20 g/¾ oz fresh yeast
100 g/4 oz caster sugar
450 g/1 lb plain flour
2.5 ml/½ tsp ground cinnamon
pinch of salt
100 g/4 oz butter
150 ml/¼ pint double cream
2 eggs, beaten
100 g/4 oz currants
beaten egg for glazing

Put the saffron in a heatproof jug. Warm the milk until steaming and pour it over the saffron. Leave to infuse for 30 minutes.

Strain 60 ml/4 tbsp of the milk and leave until lukewarm. Blend the yeast to a thin paste with 2.5 ml/½ tsp of the sugar and the strained warm milk. Set aside in a warm place until frothy – about 5 minutes.

Sift the flour with the cinnamon and salt into a bowl. Rub in the butter. Strain the remaining saffron-flavoured milk and cream into the dry ingredients, with the eggs and yeast mixture. Mix thoroughly, then add the currants. Knead well. Cover and prove in the refrigerator overnight.

Next day, grease a baking sheet. Shape the mixture into 12 buns. Place on the prepared baking sheet and leave to rise for 20–30 minutes. Set the oven at 190°C/375°F/gas 5. Brush the tops with beaten egg and sprinkle with the remaining sugar. Bake for about 15 minutes. Serve warm or cold with butter.

MAKES TWELVE

BATH BUNS

fat for greasing
400 g/14 oz strong white flour
5 ml/1 tsp sugar
125 ml/4 fl oz milk
25 g/1 oz fresh yeast or 15 ml/1 tbsp dried
  yeast
5 ml/1 tsp salt
50 g/2 oz butter
50 g/2 oz caster sugar
150 g/5 oz sultanas
50 g/2 oz chopped mixed peel
2 eggs • beaten egg for glazing
50 g/2 oz sugar lumps, coarsely crushed

Grease a baking sheet. Sift about 75 g/3 oz of the flour and the 5 ml/1 tsp sugar into a large bowl. Warm the milk and 75 ml/3 fl oz water until lukewarm. Blend in the fresh yeast or sprinkle on the dried yeast. Pour the yeast liquid into the flour and sugar, then beat well. Leave the bowl in a warm place for 20 minutes.

Sift the rest of the flour and the salt into a bowl. Rub in the butter. Add the caster sugar and dried fruit. Beat the eggs into the yeast mixture and add the flour, fat and fruit mixture. Mix to a very soft dough. Use your hand to beat the dough for 3 minutes. Cover the bowl with cling film. Leave in a warm place until the dough has almost doubled in bulk – this will take about 45 minutes, or longer.

Beat the dough again for 1 minute. Place 15 ml/1 tbsp spoonfuls of the mixture on the baking sheet, leaving plenty of space between them. Place the baking sheet in a large, lightly oiled polythene bag. Leave in a warm place for about 20 minutes or until the buns have almost doubled in size. Set the oven at 220°C/425°F/gas 7.

Glaze each bun with egg and sugar. Bake for 15–20 minutes, until golden brown.

MAKES TWELVE

CHRISTMAS STOLLEN

This is the classic German Christmas bread.

butter for greasing
1 kg/2¼ lb plain flour
75 g/3 oz fresh yeast
200 ml/7 fl oz lukewarm milk
350 g/12 oz butter
grated rind and juice of 1 lemon
250 g/9 oz caster sugar
2 egg yolks
5 ml/1 tsp salt
500 g/18 oz seedless raisins
225 g/8 oz sultanas
150 g/5 oz blanched slivered almonds
100 g/4 oz chopped mixed peel
flour for dusting
100 g/4 oz unsalted butter
icing sugar for dusting

Butter a baking sheet. Sift the flour into a bowl. Blend the yeast with the warm milk and 50 g/2 oz of the flour. Set aside until frothy.

Meanwhile, melt the butter. Cool slightly, then blend into the remaining flour with the lemon juice. Add the milk and yeast liquid together with the lemon rind, sugar, egg yolks and salt. Beat well together. Knead the dough until it is very firm and elastic, and leaves the sides of the bowl. Cover with cling film. Leave in a warm place until the dough has doubled in bulk. This will take about 2 hours.

Meanwhile, mix the dried fruit with the nuts and mixed peel. Knead the dough again, pull the sides to the centre, turn it over and cover once more. Leave to rise for a further 30 minutes. When the dough has doubled in bulk again, turn it on to a floured surface and knead in the fruit and nut mixture.

Divide the dough in half and roll each half into a pointed oval shape. Lay each on the prepared baking sheet. Place a rolling pin along the length of each piece of the dough in the centre. Roll half the dough lightly from the centre outwards. Brush the thinner rolled half with a little water and fold the other half over it, leaving a margin of about 5 cm/2 inches all around which allows the dough to rise. Press well together; the water will bind it. Cover the stollen and leave to rise in a warm place until doubled in bulk again. Set the oven at 190°C/375°F/gas 5.

Melt 50 g/2 oz of the unsalted butter and brush it over the stollen. Bake for about 1 hour, until golden. When baked, melt the remaining unsalted butter, brush it over the stollen, then sprinkle with sifted icing sugar. Keep for a day before cutting.

The stollen will remain fresh for many weeks if well wrapped in foil or greaseproof paper and stored in an airtight tin.

MAKES TWO LOAVES, ABOUT 24 SLICES EACH

Breads
Without Yeast

*A short section of doughs that rely on alternative raising agents, including Irish Soda Bread,
Mrs Beeton's excellent Quick Currant Buns and sour dough bread.*

SOUR DOUGH RYE BREAD

*Prepare the starter paste four days before proceeding
with the bread recipe.*

fat for greasing
500 g/18 oz rye flour
200 g/7 oz strong white flour
10 ml/2 tsp salt
15 ml/1 tbsp sugar
15 ml/1 tbsp oil

STARTER PASTE
100 g/4 oz strong white flour
50 g/2 oz sugar
175 ml/6 fl oz milk

To make the starter paste, sift the flour and
sugar into a bowl. Warm the milk until hand-
hot, then stir into the flour. Beat to a smooth
paste. Place the starter paste in a screw-topped
jar and leave in a warm place *for 4 days.*

Grease two 23 × 13 × 7.5 cm/9 × 5 × 3 inch loaf
tins. Put the flours, salt and sugar in a large
bowl. Add the starter paste, 375 ml/13 fl oz
warm water and the oil, then mix to a slack
dough. Beat with a wooden spoon for 3
minutes. Place the dough in the prepared loaf
tins. Cover with a large, lightly oiled polythene
bag. Leave at room temperature for about 24
hours or until the dough reaches the top of the
tins. Set the oven at 230°C/450°F/gas 8.

Bake for 10 minutes, then lower the oven
temperature to 190°C/375°F/gas 5. Continue to
bake for 30–35 minutes, until the loaves are
well browned and sound hollow when tapped
on the bottom.

MAKES TWO 800 G/1¾ LB LOAVES

 MRS BEETON'S TIP

To reduce the second rising of the dough to
2 hours, 15 g/½ oz fresh yeast or 10 ml/2 tsp
dried yeast can be added when mixing the
dough. The fresh yeast should be blended
into the warm water or the dried yeast
sprinkled over the water.

BASIC QUICK BREAD

fat for greasing
400 g/14 oz self-raising flour or a mixture of
    white and brown self-raising flours or
    400 g/14 oz plain flour and 20 ml/4 tsp
    baking powder
5 ml/1 tsp salt
50 g/2 oz margarine or lard
250 ml/8 fl oz milk or water or a mixture,
    as preferred
flour for kneading

Grease a baking sheet. Set the oven at 200°C/
400°F/gas 6. Sift the flour, baking powder (if
used) and salt into a large bowl. Rub in the
margarine or lard. Mix in enough liquid to
make a soft dough.

Turn the dough on to a floured surface and
knead lightly for 1 minute. Shape the dough
into two rounds and place them on the prepared baking sheet. Make a cross in the top of
each with the back of a knife.

Bake for 30–40 minutes. Cool on a wire rack.

MAKES TWO BUN LOAVES

VARIATIONS

Wholemeal Quick Bread Substitute
400 g/14 oz wholemeal flour for the plain flour
in the basic recipe. Note that the wholemeal
flour will give a closer-textured loaf.

Nut Bread Make Wholemeal Quick Bread.
Add 75 g/3 oz chopped nuts and 50 g/2 oz sugar
to the dry ingredients, and add 1 beaten egg to
the liquid.

Apricot and Walnut Loaf Make the Basic
Quick Bread, but use butter as the fat. Add
100 g/4 oz dried and soaked chopped apricots
and 50 g/2 oz chopped walnuts to the dry ingredients, and add 1 beaten egg to the liquid.

BASIC SOURED MILK QUICK BREAD

fat for greasing
400 g/14 oz plain flour
5 ml/1 tsp salt
10 ml/2 tsp bicarbonate of soda
10 ml/2 tsp cream of tartar
about 250 ml/8 fl oz soured milk or
    buttermilk

Grease a baking sheet. Set the oven at 220°C/
425°F/gas 7. Sift the flour, salt, bicarbonate of
soda and cream of tartar into a large bowl. Mix
to a light spongy dough with the milk.

Divide the dough into two equal pieces and
form each into a round cake. Slash a cross on
the top of each loaf with a sharp knife. Place on
the prepared baking sheet.

Bake for about 30 minutes, until golden brown.
Cool on a wire rack.

MAKES TWO LOAVES

 MRS BEETON'S TIP

The keeping quality of this bread will be
improved if 50 g/2 oz lard is rubbed into the
sifted flour.

IRISH SODA BREAD

fat for greasing
575 g/1¼ lb plain flour
5 ml/1 tsp bicarbonate of soda
5 ml/1 tsp salt
5 ml/1 tsp cream of tartar (if using fresh
  milk)
300 ml/½ pint buttermilk or soured milk or
  fresh milk
flour for dusting

Grease a baking sheet. Set the oven at 190-200°C/375-400°F/gas 5-6. Mix all the dry ingredients in a bowl, then make a well in the centre. Add enough milk to make a fairly slack dough, pouring it in almost all at once, not spoonful by spoonful. Mix with a wooden spoon, lightly and quickly.

With floured hands, place the mixture on a lightly floured surface and flatten the dough into a round about 2.5 cm/1 inch thick. Turn on to the prepared baking sheet. Make a large cross in the surface with a floured knife to make it heat through evenly.

Bake for about 40 minutes. Pierce the centre with a thin skewer to test for readiness; it should come out clean. Wrap the loaf in a clean tea-towel to keep it soft until required.

MAKES ONE 750 G/1¾ LB LOAF

TEXAS CORNBREAD

This golden bread makes an ideal accompaniment to soups, stews and casseroles.

fat for greasing
125 g/4½ oz bacon fat or beef dripping
125 g/4½ oz cornmeal (polenta)
50 g/2 oz plain flour
5 ml/1 tsp salt
5 ml/1 tsp baking powder
2.5 ml/½ tsp bicarbonate of soda
200 ml/7 fl oz buttermilk or fresh milk with
  a squeeze of lemon juice
2 eggs, beaten

Grease a 20 cm/8 inch cake tin. Set the oven at 230°C/450°F/gas 8. Melt the bacon fat or dripping, then leave to cool slightly.

Mix the cornmeal, flour, salt, baking powder and bicarbonate of soda in a bowl. Add the buttermilk or soured milk, eggs and melted fat or dripping. Mix well. Turn into the prepared cake tin.

Bake for 30 minutes. The bread should be firm to the touch when done. Serve warm.

MAKES ONE 225 G/8 OZ CORNBREAD

QUICK CURRANT BUNS

fat for greasing
450 g/1 lb plain flour
2.5 ml/½ tsp cream of tartar
2.5 ml/½ tsp bicarbonate of soda
50 g/2 oz butter
50 g/2 oz caster sugar
100 g/4 oz currants
10 ml/2 tsp caraway seeds (optional)
1 egg
300 ml/½ pint milk
flour for kneading
milk to glaze

Grease a baking sheet. Set the oven at 200°C/400°F/gas 6. Sift the flour, cream of tartar and bicarbonate of soda into a bowl. Rub in the butter, then stir in the sugar, currants and caraway seeds, if used. Make a well in the middle of the dry mixture.

Beat the egg with the milk, pour this into the dry ingredients and mix to form a soft dough. Turn the dough out on a floured surface and knead it briefly into a smooth ball. Cut the dough into 12 equal portions. Shape each piece of dough into a neat bun and place them slightly apart on the baking sheet.

Brush the buns with a little milk, then bake them for 20 minutes, until risen, well browned and cooked through. Cool on a wire rack. Serve split and buttered.

MAKES 24

MIXED GRAIN SODA BREAD ROLLS

fat for greasing
225 g/8 oz wholemeal flour
225 g/8 oz plain flour
5 ml/1 tsp bicarbonate of soda
5 ml/1 tsp cream of tartar
5 ml/1 tsp salt
60 ml/4 tbsp rolled oats
60 ml/4 tbsp sunflower seeds
60 ml/4 tbsp sesame seeds
60 ml/4 tbsp cracked wheat
300 ml/½ pint milk plus extra for glazing
flour for kneading

Grease a baking sheet. Set the oven at 200°C/400°F/gas 6. Mix both types of flour in a bowl. Stir in the bicarbonate of soda, cream of tartar, salt, oats, sunflower seeds, sesame seeds and cracked wheat. Mix in the milk to make a soft dough. Turn the dough out on a lightly floured surface and knead very briefly into a smooth ball.

Divide the dough into 12 equal portions and quickly knead each portion into a round roll. Place the rolls well apart on the baking sheet. Use a sharp knife to cut a cross in the top of each roll. Brush with a little milk, then bake for about 30 minutes, until well risen, golden brown and cooked through. Cool on a wire rack.

MAKES TWELVE

Muffins, Crumpets and Teabreads

This is a chapter of recipes to ensure that every winter table is laden with delicious traditional tea-time goods – and they do not have to be fresh from the stove as they are all ideal for batch cooking and freezing.

AMERICAN MUFFINS

Unlike English muffins, American muffins are quick breads. They are light, savoury or sweet buns made with a slightly more puffed, richer dough than scones. They are very popular breakfast breads.

butter for greasing
200 g/7 oz plain flour
15 ml/1 tbsp baking powder
2.5 ml/½ tsp salt
50 g/2 oz granulated sugar
50 g/2 oz butter
1 egg
200 ml/7 fl oz milk

Butter twelve 6 cm/2½ inch muffin tins or deep bun tins. Set the oven at 200°C/400°F/gas 6. Sift the dry ingredients into a bowl.

Melt the butter. Mix with the egg and milk in a separate bowl. Pour the liquid mixture over the dry ingredients. Stir only enough to dampen the flour; the mixture should be lumpy. Spoon into the prepared muffin tins, as lightly as possible, filling them only two-thirds full.

Bake for about 15 minutes, until well risen and browned. The cooked muffins should be cracked across the middle. Cool in the tins for 2–3 minutes, then turn out on to a wire rack to finish cooling.

MAKES TWELVE

VARIATIONS

Blueberry Muffins Reserve 50 g/2 oz of the flour. Sprinkle lightly over 225 g/8 oz firm blueberries. Stir into the mixture last.

Jam Muffins Before baking, top each muffin with 5 ml/1 tsp sharp-flavoured jam.

Walnut Muffins Increase the sugar to 100 g/4 oz. Add 75 g/3 oz chopped walnuts before adding the liquids. After filling the muffin tins, sprinkle with a mixture of sugar, cinnamon, and extra finely chopped walnuts.

Raisin Muffins Add about 50 g/2 oz seedless raisins before adding the liquids.

Orange Apricot Muffins Add 50 g/2 oz chopped ready-to-eat dried apricots and 15 ml/1 tbsp grated orange rind before adding the liquids.

Wholemeal Muffins Substitute 100 g/4 oz wholemeal flour for 100 g/4 oz of the plain flour. Do not sift the wholemeal flour, but add it after sifting the plain flour.

 MRS BEETON'S TIP

American muffin tins should not be confused with ordinary patty tins. Muffin tins are slightly larger and far deeper than patty tins to allow room for the muffin batter to rise during cooking.

ENGLISH MUFFINS

The correct way to serve muffins is to split each one open around the edges almost to the centre. Toast slowly on both sides so that the heat penetrates to the centre, then pull the muffin halves apart, butter thickly, put together again and serve at once.

400 g/14 oz strong white flour
5 ml/1 tsp salt
25 g/1 oz butter or margarine
225 ml/7½ fl oz milk
10 ml/2 tsp dried yeast
1 egg
fat for frying

Sift the flour and salt into a large bowl. Rub in the butter or margarine. Place the milk in a saucepan and warm gently. It should be just hand-hot. Pour the milk into a small bowl, sprinkle the dried yeast on top and leave for 10–15 minutes until frothy. Beat in the egg.

Add the yeast liquid to the flour to make a very soft dough. Beat the dough by hand or with a wooden spoon for about 5 minutes until smooth and shiny. Cover the bowl with a large lightly oiled polythene bag and leave in a warm place for 1–2 hours or until doubled in bulk. Beat again lightly.

Roll out on a well floured surface to a thickness of about 1 cm/½ inch. Using a plain 7.5 cm/3 inch cutter, cut the dough into rounds. Place the rounds on a floured baking sheet, cover with polythene and leave to rise for about 45 minutes or until light and puffy.

Heat a griddle or heavy-bottomed frying pan, then grease it. Cook the muffins on both sides for about 8 minutes until golden.

MAKES TWENTY

CRUMPETS

200 g/7 oz strong white flour
2.5 ml/½ tsp salt
2.5 ml/½ tsp sugar
100 ml/3½ fl oz milk
10 ml/2 tsp dried yeast
pinch of bicarbonate of soda
fat for frying

Sift the flour, salt and sugar into a large bowl. Place the milk in a saucepan, add 125 ml/4 fl oz water and warm gently. The mixture should be just hand-hot. Pour the mixture into a small bowl, sprinkle the dried yeast on top and leave for 10–15 minutes or until frothy.

Add the yeast liquid to the flour and beat to a smooth batter. Cover the bowl with a large lightly oiled polythene bag and leave in a warm place for about 45 minutes or until the batter has doubled in bulk.

Dissolve the bicarbonate of soda in 15 ml/1 tbsp warm water; beat into the batter. Cover and leave to rise again for 20 minutes.

Heat a griddle or heavy-bottomed frying pan over medium heat, then grease it when hot. Grease metal crumpet rings, poaching rings or large plain biscuit cutters about 7.5 cm/3 inches in diameter. Place the rings on the hot griddle, pour a spoonful of batter into each to cover the base thinly and cook until the top is set and the bubbles have burst.

Remove the rings and turn the crumpets over. Cook the other side for 2–3 minutes only, until firm but barely coloured. Cool the crumpets on a wire rack. Serve toasted, with butter.

MAKES TEN TO TWELVE

AMERICAN COFFEE BREAD

This bread, made with walnuts, derives its name from the fact that it is served at coffee time.

fat for greasing
200 g/7 oz plain flour
100 g/4 oz soft light brown sugar
10 ml/2 tsp baking powder
5 ml/1 tsp salt
30 ml/2 tbsp butter
1 egg, beaten
200 ml/7 fl oz milk
75 g/3 oz walnuts, chopped

Grease a 23 × 13 × 7.5 cm/9 × 5 × 3 inch loaf tin. Set the oven at 180°C/350°F/gas 4.

Sift the dry ingredients into a large bowl. Melt the butter, add to the flour mixture with the egg, milk and walnuts. Beat thoroughly. Spread the mixture in the prepared loaf tin, then level the top.

Bake for about 1 hour, until risen, firm and browned. Cool on a wire rack.

MAKES ABOUT TWELVE SLICES

VARIATIONS

Orange Nut Coffee Bread Reduce the milk to 100 ml/3½ fl oz. Instead of sugar, use 250 g/9 oz orange marmalade.

Banana Nut Coffee Bread Reduce the milk to 100 ml/3½ fl oz; add 3 ripe medium bananas, well mashed.

HONEY GINGERBREAD

fat for greasing
225 g/8 oz plain flour
1.25 ml/¼ tsp salt
10 ml/2 tsp ground ginger
2.5–5 ml/½–1 tsp ground cinnamon or grated nutmeg
5 ml/1 tsp bicarbonate of soda
100 g/4 oz butter
100 g/4 oz soft light brown sugar
100 g/4 oz honey
1 egg
45 ml/3 tbsp plain yogurt

Line and grease a 20 cm/8 inch square tin. Set the oven at 160°C/325°F/gas 3.

Sift the flour, salt, spices and bicarbonate of soda into a mixing bowl. Heat the butter, sugar and honey in a saucepan until all the butter has melted.

In a bowl, beat the egg and yogurt together. Add to the dry ingredients, with the melted mixture, to give a soft, dropping consistency.

Spoon into the prepared tin and bake for 50–60 minutes until cooked through and firm to the touch. Cool on a wire rack.

MAKES ABOUT SIXTEEN SQUARES

ALMOND BREAD

fat for greasing
250 g/9 oz plain flour, plus extra for dusting
   and for shaping dough
20 ml/4 tsp baking powder
pinch of salt
2 eggs
100 g/4 oz granulated sugar
90 ml/6 tbsp oil
few drops of almond or vanilla essence
75 g/3 oz blanched almonds, roughly
   chopped
50 g/2 oz caster sugar

Grease and flour a baking sheet. Set the oven at 180°C/350°F/gas 4.

Sift the flour, baking powder and salt together. Beat the eggs and granulated sugar lightly together in a large bowl. Add the oil, flavouring, flour mixture and almonds, and mix to form a dough. With floured hands, form into a long roll about 7.5 ml/3 inches wide. Place on the prepared baking sheet.

Bake for about 30-40 minutes, until lightly browned. Lower the oven temperature to 150°C/300°F/gas 2. Leave the bread on a wire rack until nearly cold, then cut slantways into slices about 1 cm/½ inch thick. Sprinkle lightly with caster sugar and place them on a baking sheet. Return to the oven for about 50-60 minutes until dry and lightly browned.

MAKES ABOUT TWELVE SLICES

BANANA BREAD

The riper the bananas used for this popular teabread the more flavoursome will be the result.

fat for greasing
300 g/11 oz plain flour
pinch of salt
5 ml/1 tsp bicarbonate of soda
75 g/3 oz margarine
100 g/4 oz granulated sugar
3 eggs, beaten
3 ripe bananas
15 ml/1 tbsp lemon juice

Grease a 23 × 13 × 7.5 cm/9 × 5 × 3 inch loaf tin. Set the oven at 190°C/375°F/gas 5. Sift the flour, salt and bicarbonate of soda together.

Cream the margarine and sugar in a bowl. Beat in the eggs. Mash the bananas with the lemon juice. Add to the creamed mixture, then work in the dry ingredients. Put the mixture into the prepared loaf tin.

Bake for 50-60 minutes, until golden brown. Cool on a wire rack.

MAKES ABOUT TWELVE SLICES

BANANA AND WALNUT BREAD

fat for greasing
3 ripe bananas
50 g/2 oz walnuts, chopped
200 g/7 oz self-raising flour
5 ml/1 tsp baking powder
1.25 ml/¼ tsp bicarbonate of soda
125 g/4½ oz caster sugar
75 g/3 oz soft margarine
grated rind of ½ lemon
2 eggs
50 g/2 oz seedless raisins

Grease a 23 × 13 × 7.5 cm/9 × 5 × 3 inch loaf tin. Set the oven at 180°C/350°F/gas 4. Mash the bananas.

Mix all the ingredients in a large bowl. Beat for about 3 minutes by hand using a wooden spoon, or for 2 minutes in an electric mixer, until smooth. Put the mixture into the prepared loaf tin.

Bake for 1 hour 10 minutes, or until firm to the touch. Cool on a wire rack.

MAKES ABOUT TWELVE SLICES

APPLE LOAF

fat for greasing
200 g/7 oz plain flour
pinch of salt
5 ml/1 tsp baking powder
2.5 ml/½ tsp ground mixed spice
100 g/4 oz butter or margarine
150 g/5 oz caster sugar
50 g/2 oz currants
100 g/4 oz seedless raisins
200 g/7 oz cooking apples
5 ml/1 tsp lemon juice
2 eggs
about 25 ml/1 fl oz milk
50 g/2 oz icing sugar, sifted
1 tart red-skinned eating apple

Grease a 23 × 13 × 7.5 cm/9 × 5 × 3 inch loaf tin. Set the oven at 190°C/375°F/gas 5. Sift the flour, salt, baking powder and mixed spice into a large bowl. Rub in the butter or margarine. Add the sugar and dried fruit.

Peel and core the cooking apples, slice thinly, then toss in the lemon juice. Add to the dry mixture. Stir in the eggs and enough milk to make a soft dropping consistency. Put the mixture into the prepared loaf tin.

Bake for about 50–60 minutes, until the loaf is golden brown and a skewer pushed into the centre comes out clean. Cool on a wire rack.

Add enough cold water to the icing sugar to make a brushing consistency. Core the eating apple, cut it into thin segments, and arrange these in a decorative pattern on the loaf. Immediately brush the apple with the icing sugar glaze to prevent discoloration. Leave the glaze to set before serving.

MAKES ABOUT TWELVE SLICES

FATLESS FRUIT LOAF

fat for greasing
300 g/11 oz mixed dried fruit
150 g/5 oz dark Barbados sugar
200 ml/7 fl oz strong hot tea
1 egg, beaten
300 g/11 oz self-raising flour

Put the fruit and sugar in a large bowl. Pour the hot tea over them. Cover and leave overnight.

Next day, line and grease a 20 × 13 × 7.5 cm/ 8 × 5 × 3 inch loaf tin. Set the oven at 180°C/ 350°F/gas 4. Stir the egg into the tea mixture. Stir in the flour and mix well. Put the mixture into the prepared loaf tin.

Bake for 1½ hours. Cool on a wire rack. When cold, wrap in foil and store in a tin.

MAKES ABOUT TWELVE SLICES

 MRS BEETON'S TIP

Vary the flavour of this fruit loaf by using different varieties of tea. As well as the lightly flavoured types, such as Earl Grey, try some of the stronger fruit teas and spiced teas.

DATE OR RAISIN BREAD

fat for greasing
200 g/7 oz plain flour
15 ml/1 tbsp baking powder
5 ml/1 tsp salt
large pinch of bicarbonate of soda
100 g/4 oz dates or seedless raisins
50 g/2 oz walnuts or almonds, whole or
  chopped
25 g/1 oz lard
50 g/2 oz black treacle
50 g/2 oz dark Barbados sugar
150 ml/¼ pint milk

Grease a 20 × 13 × 7.5 cm/8 × 5 × 3 inch loaf tin. Set the oven at 180°C/350°F/gas 4. Sift the flour, baking powder, salt and bicarbonate of soda into a large bowl. Chop the fruit and nuts finely if necessary, and add them to the dry ingredients.

Warm the lard, treacle, sugar and milk together in a saucepan. The sugar should dissolve, but do not overheat it. Add the liquid to the dry ingredients, then mix to a stiff batter. Pour into the prepared loaf tin.

Bake for 1½ hours. Cool on a wire rack. When cold, wrap in foil and store for 24 hours before cutting.

MAKES ABOUT TWELVE SLICES

MALT BREAD

fat for greasing
400 g/14 oz self-raising flour
10 ml/2 tsp bicarbonate of soda
100 g/4 oz sultanas or seedless raisins
250 ml/8 fl oz milk
60 ml/4 tbsp golden syrup
60 ml/4 tbsp malt extract
2 eggs

Grease a 23 × 13 × 7.5 cm/9 × 5 × 3 inch loaf tin. Set the oven at 190°C/375°F/gas 5. Sift the flour and bicarbonate of soda into a large bowl. Add the dried fruit. Warm the milk, syrup and malt extract in a saucepan. Beat in the eggs. Stir the mixture into the flour. Put into the prepared loaf tin.

Bake for 40–50 minutes, until a skewer pushed into the bread comes out clean. Cool on a wire rack.

MAKES TWELVE SLICES

 FREEZER TIP

Freeze teabreads and loaf cakes cut into slices. Separate the slices with freezer film, then re-shape the loaf and pack it in a polythene bag. Individual slices may be removed as required.

COCONUT BREAD

fat for greasing
100 g/4 oz butter
150 g/5 oz granulated sugar
150 g/5 oz seedless raisins, chopped
50 g/2 oz chopped mixed peel
250 g/9 oz desiccated coconut
5 ml/1 tsp vanilla essence
1 egg
175 ml/6 fl oz milk
400 g/14 oz self-raising flour
pinch of salt
flour for kneading

Grease a 23 × 13 × 7.5 cm/9 × 5 × 3 inch loaf tin. Set the oven at 190°C/375°F/gas 5.

Cream the butter and sugar in a bowl. Add the raisins, then the rest of the ingredients. Mix well. Turn on to a floured surface and knead until smooth. Put the mixture into the prepared loaf tin.

Bake for 50–60 minutes, until golden brown. Cool on a wire rack.

MAKES ABOUT TWELVE SLICES

 MRS BEETON'S TIP

This teabread is delicious served sliced and thinly topped with chocolate spread instead of butter.

SWEET DATE BREAD

Buy blocks of compressed, stoned dates sold specifically for cooking or look for packets of ready chopped dates, usually rolled in caster sugar.

fat for greasing
400 g/14 oz plain flour
pinch of salt
20 ml/4 tsp bicarbonate of soda
150 g/5 oz soft dark brown sugar
125 g/4½ oz sultanas or seedless raisins
75 g/3 oz walnuts, chopped
50 g/2 oz margarine
400 g/14 oz stoned dates, finely chopped
2 eggs
5 ml/1 tsp vanilla essence

Grease a 23 × 13 × 7.5 cm/9 × 5 × 3 inch loaf tin. Set the oven at 190°C/375°F/gas 5. Sift the flour, salt and bicarbonate of soda into a large bowl. Add the sugar and sultanas or raisins, then the walnuts.

Add the margarine to the dates and pour on 250 ml/8 fl oz boiling water. Add the date mixture, eggs and vanilla essence to the dry ingredients and mix thoroughly. Put the mixture into the prepared loaf tin.

Bake for 40–50 minutes, until the loaf is golden brown and a skewer pushed into the bread comes out clean. Cool on a wire rack.

MAKES ABOUT TWELVE SLICES

DATE AND CHEESE BREAD

Use a mild cheese such as Lancashire, Caerphilly, Wensleydale or mild Cheddar to enrich this bread rather than to give it a strong flavour.

fat for greasing
flour for dusting
200 g/7 oz stoned dates
1 egg
100 g/4 oz mild cheese, grated
175 g/6 oz plain flour
5 ml/1 tsp bicarbonate of soda
1.25 ml/¼ tsp salt
50 g/2 oz granulated sugar
50 g/2 oz soft light brown sugar

Grease and flour a 23 × 13 × 7.5 cm/9 × 5 × 3 inch loaf tin. Set the oven at 160°C/325°F/gas 3. Place the dates in a bowl and pour 125 ml/4 fl oz boiling water on to them. Allow to stand for 5 minutes.

Mix in the egg, then add the cheese. Sift the flour, bicarbonate of soda and salt into the date mixture. Add both sugars and mix thoroughly. Put the mixture into the prepared loaf tin.

Bake for about 50 minutes, until the loaf is springy to the touch and a skewer pushed into the centre comes out clean. Cool on a wire rack.

MAKES ABOUT TWELVE SLICES

HONEY BREAD

fat for greasing
100 g/4 oz margarine
100 g/4 oz caster sugar
2 eggs, beaten
90 ml/6 tbsp liquid honey
250 g/9 oz self-raising flour or 250 g/9 oz
   plain flour and 15 ml/1 tbsp baking
   powder
5 ml/1 tsp salt
about 125 ml/4 fl oz milk

Grease a 20 × 13 × 7.5 cm/8 × 5 × 3 inch loaf tin. Set the oven at 180°C/350°F/gas 4.

Cream the margarine and sugar in a bowl until pale and fluffy. Beat in the eggs and honey. Add the dry ingredients alternately with the milk until a soft dropping consistency is obtained. (Add the milk carefully as the full amount may not be needed.) Put the mixture into the prepared loaf tin.

Bake for 1¼ hours. Cool on a wire rack. When cold, wrap in foil and keep for 24 hours before serving. Serve sliced and buttered.

MAKES ABOUT TWELVE SLICES

 MRS BEETON'S TIP

Warm the jar of honey by standing it in a dish of hot water for 5 minutes. This makes it more runny and easier to measure accurately.

ORANGE BREAD

This loaf is best left overnight before eating.

fat for greasing
50 g/2 oz lard
200 g/7 oz granulated sugar
2 eggs, beaten
400 g/14 oz plain flour
10 ml/2 tsp baking powder
10 ml/2 tsp bicarbonate of soda
pinch of salt
250 ml/8 fl oz orange juice
15 ml/1 tbsp grated orange rind
100 g/4 oz chopped mixed nuts

Grease a 23 × 13 × 7.5 cm/9 × 5 × 3 inch loaf tin. Set the oven at 190°C/375°F/gas 5.

Melt the lard; add it to the sugar in a bowl. Beat in the eggs. Sift the flour, baking powder, bicarbonate of soda and salt. Add the flour mixture alternately with the orange juice to the lard and sugar. Stir in the orange rind and nuts. Put the mixture into the prepared loaf tin.

Bake for 50–60 minutes, until the loaf is springy to the touch. Cool on a wire rack.

MAKES ABOUT TWELVE SLICES

 MRS BEETON'S TIP

Mixtures with bicarbonate of soda should be baked as soon as they are mixed. The bicarbonate of soda begins to work when it is moistened, and becomes more vigorous as a raising agent when heated.

NORTH RIDING BREAD

This rich, dark fruit bread is better if kept in a tin for a week before use.

fat for greasing
400g/14oz plain flour
2.5ml/½tsp salt
15ml/1tbsp baking powder
2.5ml/½tsp grated nutmeg
100g/4oz lard
150g/5oz demerara sugar
150g/5oz currants
150g/5oz seedless raisins
75g/3oz chopped mixed peel
15ml/1tbsp black treacle
2.5ml/½tsp almond essence
250ml/8floz milk

Grease a 23 × 13 × 7.5 cm/9 × 5 × 3 inch loaf tin. Set the oven at 190°C/375°F/gas 5.

Sift the flour, salt, baking powder and nutmeg into a large bowl. Rub in the lard. Add the sugar and dried fruit. Stir the treacle and almond essence into the milk and mix into the dry ingredients to give a soft dough. Put the mixture into the prepared loaf tin.

Bake for 45–50 minutes, until a skewer pushed into the bread comes out clean. Cool on a wire rack, then store in a tin.

MAKES ABOUT TWELVE SLICES

SODA CAKE

This plain loaf cake of Mrs Beeton's day is similar to a teabread. Serve it thickly sliced and buttered.

225g/8oz plain flour
50g/2oz butter or margarine
100g/4oz currants
100g/4oz moist brown sugar
2 eggs, beaten
2.5ml/½tsp bicarbonate of soda
75ml/3floz milk

Base-line and grease a 900g/2lb loaf tin. Set the oven at 190°C/375°F/gas 5.

Sift the flour into a bowl, then rub in the butter. Stir in the currants and sugar and make a well in the middle of the mixture. Pour in the eggs. Stir the bicarbonate of soda into the milk, then pour the mixture over the eggs and mix lightly. Gradually work in the dry ingredients and beat the mixture well.

Spoon the mixture into the prepared tin, then level the surface. Bake for 45 minutes. Cover the top of the cake loosely with a piece of foil, keeping the oven door open for the shortest possible time. Continue to cook for a further 15 minutes, or until as skewer inserted into the centre of the loaf comes out clean. Cool on a wire rack.

MAKES ONE 900G/2LB LOAF

TEA BRACK

'Brac' is a Celtic word for bread. The dried fruits in this teabread are soaked overnight in tea to flavour and plump them up.

fat for greasing
500 g/18 oz sultanas
500 g/18 oz seedless raisins
500 g/18 oz soft light brown sugar
750 ml/1¼ pints black tea
3 eggs, beaten
500 g/17 oz plain flour
5 ml/1 tsp baking powder
15 ml/1 tbsp ground mixed spice (optional)
honey for glazing

Soak the dried fruit and sugar in the tea overnight.

Next day, grease three 20 × 10 × 7.5 cm/ 8 × 4 × 3 inch loaf tins. Set the oven at 150°C/ 300°F/gas 2.

Add the eggs to the tea mixture, alternately with the flour in three equal parts. Stir in the baking powder and spice, if used. Turn the mixture into the prepared loaf tins.

Bake for 1½ hours, or until the loaves sound hollow when tapped underneath. Leave to cool. Melt the honey and brush it on the cooled loaves to glaze them.

MAKES THREE LOAVES

MOGGY

fat for greasing
350 g/12 oz plain flour
pinch of salt
7.5 ml/1½ tsp baking powder
75 g/3 oz margarine
75 g/3 oz lard
100 g/4 oz caster sugar
100 g/4 oz golden syrup
about 50 ml/2 fl oz milk

Grease a baking sheet. Set the oven at 180°C/ 350°F/gas 4. Sift the flour, salt and baking powder in a bowl. Rub in the margarine and lard, then mix in the sugar. Mix the syrup with the dry ingredients, adding enough milk to make the mixture into a stiff dough. Shape into a round or oval flat bun about 2.5 cm/1 inch thick. Place on the prepared baking sheet.

Bake for 25–35 minutes, until firm and light brown. Serve warm or cold, cut in wedges or slices, and thickly buttered.

MAKES ONE 675 G/1½ LB BUN

LINCOLNSHIRE PLUM BREAD

Prunes give a delightfully rich taste to this bread.

fat for greasing
100 g/4 oz prunes
100 g/4 oz butter
100 g/4 oz soft light brown sugar
2.5 ml/½ tsp ground mixed spice
2.5 ml/½ tsp ground cinnamon
2.5 ml/½ tsp gravy browning (optional)
2 eggs, lightly beaten
15 ml/1 tbsp brandy
100 g/4 oz sultanas
100 g/4 oz currants
175 g/6 oz self-raising flour
pinch of salt

Soak the prunes overnight in cold water. Next day, grease and line a 23 × 13 × 7.5 cm/ 9 × 5 × 3 inch loaf tin. Set the oven at 140°C/ 275°F/gas 1. Drain the prunes well and pat dry. Remove the stones and chop the prunes finely.

Cream the butter and sugar in a bowl until light and fluffy. Beat in the spices and gravy browning, if used. Mix the eggs with the brandy, then beat into the creamed mixture. Toss the chopped prunes and other dried fruit in a little of the flour. Mix the rest of the flour with the salt. Fold it into the creamed mixture, then fold in all the dried fruit. Turn the mixture into the prepared tin and level the top.

Bake for 3 hours. Cool in the tin. When cold, turn out and store in an airtight tin.

MAKES ABOUT TWELVE SLICES

LAVENHAM BUNS

fat for greasing
325 g/11½ oz plain flour
100 g/4 oz ground rice
10 ml/2 tsp baking powder
100 g/4 oz butter
75 g/3 oz caster sugar
2 eggs, beaten
milk
75 g/3 oz currants or 35 g/1¼ oz caraway seeds
flour for rolling out

Grease a baking sheet. Set the oven at 180°C/ 350°F/gas 4. Sift the flour, ground rice and baking powder into a bowl. Rub in the butter and stir in the sugar. Add the beaten egg to bind the dry ingredients to a firm dough. Stir in a very little milk, if required. Mix in the dried fruit or caraway seeds.

On a lightly floured surface, pat or roll out the dough to 2.5 cm/1 inch thick. Cut out in 7.5 cm/3 inch rounds. Place on the prepared baking sheet.

Bake for 20-30 minutes, until firm and lightly browned. Serve hot with butter.

MAKES TWELVE TO SIXTEEN

Scones

From basic scones and their many variations to deliciously different Pumpkin Scones:
a few ideas for some of the easiest and quickest of traditional baked goods.

PLAIN SCONES

fat for greasing
225 g/8 oz self-raising flour
2.5 ml/½ tsp salt
25-50 g/1-2 oz butter or margarine
125-150 ml/4-5 fl oz milk
flour for kneading
milk or beaten egg for glazing (optional)

Grease a baking sheet. Set the oven at 220°C/
425°F/gas 7. Sift the flour and salt into a large
bowl. Rub in the butter or margarine, then mix
to a soft dough with the milk, using a round-
bladed knife. Knead very lightly on a floured
surface until smooth.

Roll or pat out the dough to about 1 cm/½ inch
thick and cut into rounds, using a 6 cm/2½ inch
cutter. (Alternatively, divide into two equal
portions and roll each piece into a round
1-2 cm/½-¾ inch thick. Mark each round into
six wedges.) Re-roll the trimmings and re-cut.

Place the scones on the prepared baking sheet.
Brush the tops with milk or beaten egg, if liked.
Bake for 10-12 minutes. Cool on a wire rack.

MAKES TWELVE

OTHER RAISING AGENTS

Scones can be made using plain flour with
raising agents: for 225 g/8 oz plain flour, use
5 ml/1 tsp bicarbonate of soda and 10 ml/2 tsp
cream of tartar. Or use 20 ml/4 tsp baking
powder as the raising agent.

SCRAP CAKES

These take their name from the original recipe which
used flare, flead or leaf, the skin tissue left after
melting down pig fat for making lard. The soft fat
was cut from the inside of belly pork of fatty animals,
then rendered to make lard. The leftovers were
chopped and mixed with flour, currants, sugar and
spice to make scone-like cakes.

fat for greasing
350 g/12 oz self-raising flour
100 g/4 oz lard
50 g/2 oz soft light brown sugar
5 ml/1 tsp ground allspice
100 g/4 oz currants
25 g/1 oz chopped mixed peel

Grease a baking sheet. Set the oven at 220°C/
425°F/gas 7. Place the flour in a bowl. Rub in
the lard, then stir in the sugar, spice, currants
and peel. Mix in about 175 ml/6 fl oz cold water
to bind the ingredients into a soft dough.

Turn the dough out on a floured surface, knead
it lightly into a ball, then roll it out to about
1 cm/½ inch thick and cut out 6 cm/2½ inch
rounds. Place the scrap cakes on the greased
baking sheet and brush their tops with milk.

Bake for 10-12 minutes, until risen and lightly
browned. Cool on a wire rack. Serve split and
buttered.

MAKES ABOUT TWENTY

A VARIETY OF SCONE DOUGHS

The following are all variations on Plain Scones (previous page).

Cheese Scones Add 75 g/3 oz grated cheese to the dry ingredients before mixing in the milk. Cut into finger shapes or squares.

Savoury Herb Scones Add 50 g/2 oz diced cooked ham, 30 ml/2 tbsp grated Parmesan cheese and 5 ml/1 tsp dried mixed herbs to the dry ingredients before mixing in the milk.

Cheese Whirls Add 75 g/3 oz grated cheese to the dry ingredients. Roll out the dough into a rectangle. Sprinkle with another 50 g/2 oz grated cheese, then roll up the dough like a Swiss roll. Cut into 1 cm/½ inch slices and lay them flat on greased baking sheets. Brush with milk or egg and bake as in the basic recipe.

Fruit Scones Add 50 g/2 oz caster sugar and 50 g/2 oz currants, sultanas or other dried fruit to the basic recipe.

Griddle Scones Add 50 g/2 oz sultanas to the basic recipe. Roll out to 1 cm/½ inch thick, then cut into 6 cm/2½ inch rounds. Cook on a moderately hot, lightly floured griddle or heavy frying pan for 3 minutes or until the scones are golden brown underneath and the edges are dry. Turn over and cook for about another 2 minutes until golden brown on both sides. Cool in a linen tea-towel or similar cloth.

Inverary Muffins Use only 75 ml/3 fl oz buttermilk or soured milk to make the dough, and add 25 g/1 oz caster sugar and 1 egg. Roll out 1 cm/½ inch thick, and cut into 7.5 cm/3 inch rounds. Cook on a griddle or heavy frying pan in the same way as Griddle Scones but for slightly longer.

Nut Scones Add 50 g/2 oz chopped nuts to the basic recipe.

Syrup or Treacle Scones Add 20 ml/4 tsp soft light brown sugar, 2.5 ml/½ tsp ground cinnamon or ginger, 2.5 ml/½ tsp mixed spice and 15 ml/1 tbsp warmed golden syrup or black treacle to the basic recipe. Add the syrup or treacle with the milk.

Potato Scones Use 100 g/4 oz flour and 100 g/4 oz sieved cooked mashed potato. Reduce the milk to 65 ml/2½ fl oz.

Rich Scones Add 25 g/1 oz sugar to the mixed dry ingredients for the basic recipe. Instead of mixing with milk alone, use 1 beaten egg with enough milk to make 125 ml/4 fl oz.

Wholemeal Scones Use half wholemeal flour and half plain white flour to make the scone dough.

Scones Made with Oil Use 45 ml/3 tbsp olive oil or corn oil instead of the fat in the basic recipe. Reduce the milk to 75 ml/3 fl oz and add 1 egg.

 MRS BEETON'S TIP

Soured milk or buttermilk used instead of milk makes delicious scones. They are best made with the plain flour plus 5 ml/1 tsp bicarbonate of soda and 5 ml/1 tsp cream of tartar.

Scones may be used to make cobblers, both savoury and sweet. For a savoury cobbler, overlap savoury scones on a meat sauce or vegetables in sauce, or on a casserole. For sweet cobblers (see pages 634–637).

SWEET BROWN SCONES

These scones are delicious filled with full-fat soft cheese or butter and spread with honey.

fat for greasing
225 g/8 oz wholemeal or brown flour
2.5 ml/½ tsp salt
2.5 ml/½ tsp baking powder
50 g/2 oz margarine
50 g/2 oz soft light brown sugar
50 g/2 oz seedless raisins
1 egg, plus milk to give 125–150 ml/4–5 fl oz
flour for rolling out

Grease a baking sheet. Set the oven at 220°C/425°F/gas 7. Mix the flour, salt and baking powder in a large bowl. Rub in the margarine, then stir in the sugar and dried fruit. Beat the egg and milk together. Reserve a little for brushing the tops of the scones and add the rest to the dry ingredients. Mix to a soft dough. Knead lightly.

Roll out the dough on a floured surface to just over 1 cm/½ inch thick. Cut into rounds, using a 6 cm/2½ inch cutter. Re-roll the trimmings and re-cut. Place the scones on the prepared baking sheet. Brush the tops with the reserved egg and milk mixture.

Bake for 10–15 minutes. Serve warm or cold, split and buttered.

MAKES TEN TO TWELVE

VARIATION

Bran Scones Use 175 g/6 oz self-raising flour, 2.5 ml/½ tsp salt, 5 ml/1 tsp baking powder, 25 g/1 oz soft light brown sugar, 50 g/2 oz currants or sultanas, instead of the quantities given above. Add 25 g/1 oz bran when mixing the dry ingredients.

PUMPKIN SCONES

For these delicious scones, use leftover steamed or baked pumpkin cooked without liquid.

fat for greasing
300 g/11 oz well-drained cooked pumpkin
25 g/1 oz softened butter
15 ml/1 tbsp caster sugar
15 ml/1 tbsp golden syrup or honey
1 egg, beaten
250 g/9 oz self-raising flour
pinch of salt
2.5 ml/½ tsp ground cinnamon
1.25 ml/¼ tsp grated nutmeg

Grease a baking sheet. Set the oven at 230°C/450°F/gas 8. Mash the pumpkin.

Mix the butter with the sugar and syrup or honey in a bowl. Mix the egg with the pumpkin. Add to the butter and sugar, mixing thoroughly. Sift the flour, salt and spices into a bowl, then fold into the pumpkin mixture, to make a soft but not sticky scone dough.

Knead the dough lightly and pat it out to 2 cm/¾ inch thick. Cut into rounds with a 5 cm/2 inch cutter. Put the scones on the prepared baking sheet. Bake for 12–15 minutes, until golden brown.

MAKES TWELVE

Pizza and Dough Bakes

Pizza is now a familiar food but there are many versions which are far removed from this tasty snack of Italian origins. In this chapter there is a basic, traditional-style recipe as well as alternatives that are one step removed from authenticity.

ITALIAN-STYLE PIZZA

This should be thin and crisp with a slightly bubbly dough base and a moist topping.

fat for greasing
25 g/1 oz fresh yeast or 15 ml/1 tbsp dried
  yeast
5 ml/1 tsp sugar
450 g/1 lb strong white flour
5 ml/1 tsp salt
30 ml/2 tbsp olive oil
flour for rolling out

TOPPING
60 ml/4 tbsp olive oil
2 garlic cloves, crushed
1 large onion, chopped
15 ml/1 tbsp dried oregano or marjoram
1 (397 g/14 oz) can chopped tomatoes
30 ml/2 tbsp tomato purée
salt and pepper
375 g/12 oz mozzarella cheese, sliced

Grease four large baking sheets. Measure 300 ml/½ pint lukewarm water. Blend the fresh yeast with the sugar and a little lukewarm water. Set aside until frothy. For dried yeast, sprinkle the yeast over all the water, then leave until frothy.

Sift the flour and salt into a bowl, make a well in the middle and add the yeast liquid, any remaining water and oil. Mix the flour into the liquid to make a firm dough.

Turn out the dough on to a lightly floured surface and knead thoroughly until smooth and elastic – about 10 minutes. Place the dough in a clean, lightly floured bowl. Cover with cling film and leave in a warm place until doubled in bulk. This will take about 2 hours.

To make the topping, heat the oil in a saucepan and cook the garlic and onion until soft but not browned – about 15 minutes. Stir in the oregano, tomatoes and tomato purée. Bring to the boil, reduce the heat and simmer for 15 minutes. Remove the pan from the heat and add salt and pepper to taste.

Set the oven at 240°C/475°F/gas 9. Knead the dough again, then divide it into four. Roll out each portion into a 25–30 cm/10–12 inch circle. Place a piece of dough on each prepared baking sheet. Top with the tomato mixture and mozzarella, then leave in a warm place for about 5 minutes, or until the dough bases begin to rise slightly.

Bake for about 15 minutes, or until the topping is well browned and the dough is crisp and bubbly. Serve freshly baked.

MAKES FOUR

CALZONE

A type of pizza pasty, calzone is a pizza which is folded in half to enclose its filling. Often filled with a meat sauce (bolognese) and mozzarella, the filling may be varied according to taste.

fat for greasing
25 g/1 oz fresh yeast or 15 ml/1 tbsp dried
   yeast
5 ml/1 tsp sugar
450 g/1 lb strong white flour
5 ml/1 tsp salt
30 ml/2 tbsp olive oil
flour for rolling out

FILLING
225 g/8 oz minced beef
salt and pepper
2.5 ml/$\frac{1}{2}$ tsp chilli powder
1 quantity tomato pizza topping (opposite)
50 g/2 oz mushrooms, sliced
225 g/8 oz mozzarella cheese, sliced

Grease two baking sheets. Using the yeast, sugar, flour, salt and olive oil, with water as required, make the dough following the recipe for Italian-style Pizza (opposite) and leave it to rise.

Meanwhile make the filling. Dry-fry the mince in a heavy-bottomed saucepan over medium heat until well browned. If the meat is very lean you may have to add a little olive oil. Add salt, pepper and the chilli powder. Stir in the tomato topping and bring to the boil. Cover, lower the heat and simmer the mixture very gently for about 30 minutes. Set aside to cool. Stir in the mushrooms when the meat has cooled, just before the filling is to be used.

Set the oven at 220°C/425°F/gas 7. Knead the dough again, then divide it into quarters. Roll out one portion into a 23 cm/9 inch circle. Place it on a prepared baking sheet. Top one side with about a quarter of the meat mixture and a quarter of the mozzarella. Fold over the other half of the dough and pinch the edges together firmly to seal in the filling.

Repeat with the remaining portions of dough and filling. Use the second baking sheet to fill the second calzone, then slide it on to the first sheet next to the first calzone. To shape the last calzone, sprinkle a little flour over the calzone on the baking sheet, then lift the final portion of dough on to the sheet, allowing one half to drape over the filled calzone while filling the opposite side. Otherwise the large calzone can be difficult to lift once filled.

Leave the filled dough to rise in a warm place for about 5 minutes. Bake for 30–40 minutes, or until the dough is golden, risen and cooked. Leave to stand on the baking sheets for a few minutes, then transfer to individual plates.

MAKES FOUR

FILLING IDEAS

Courgette and Two Cheeses Make the tomato pizza topping (opposite). Top the calzone first with the tomato mixture, then add courgette slices (allow 1 small courgette for each calzone) and mozzarella cheese. Sprinkle with grated Parmesan cheese and finish as in the main recipe.

Ham and Olive Calzone Spread half the prepared dough with ricotta cheese, then top with a slice of ham. Add a couple of onion slices and 4 halved, pitted black olives.

Salami Calzone Make the tomato pizza topping (opposite). Top the calzone first with the tomato mixture, then add 4 slices of salami, overlapping them to fit half the dough, and mozzarella cheese. Finish as in the main recipe.

SCONE PIZZA

fat for greasing
225 g/8 oz self-raising flour
10 ml/2 tsp baking powder
salt and pepper
50 g/2 oz margarine
5 ml/1 tsp dried marjoram
2.5 ml/½ tsp dried thyme
150 ml/¼ pint milk

TOPPING
1 (200 g/7 oz) can tuna in oil
1 onion, chopped
1 garlic clove (optional)
15 ml/1 tbsp roughly chopped capers
30 ml/2 tbsp chopped parsley
4 large tomatoes, peeled and sliced
100 g/4 oz Cheddar cheese, grated

Grease a large baking sheet. Set the oven at 220°C/425°F/gas 7. Sift the flour, baking powder and salt into a bowl, then rub in the margarine. Stir in the herbs and milk to make a soft dough. Knead the dough lightly.

Roll out the dough on a lightly floured surface into a 30 cm/12 inch circle. Lift the dough on to the prepared baking sheet and turn the edge over, pinching it neatly.

Drain the oil from the tuna into a small saucepan and heat it gently. Add the onion and garlic (if used) and cook for about 10 minutes, until the onion is just beginning to soften. Off the heat, add the capers, parsley and flaked tuna. Spread this topping over the scone base, cover with tomato slices, then sprinkle with the cheese.

Bake for 20-25 minutes, until the topping is bubbling hot and golden and the base is risen, browned around the edges and cooked through. Serve cut into wedges.

SERVES FOUR TO SIX

DEEP-PAN PIZZA

This is a thick-based, American-style pizza, cooked in a shallow tin or flan tin and having a generous proportion of topping ingredients. Pepperoni sausage is a spicy uncooked sausage, available from delicatessens and large supermarkets.

fat for greasing
15 g/½ oz fresh yeast or 10 ml/2 tsp dried yeast
5 ml/1 tsp sugar
225 g/8 oz strong white flour
2.5 ml/½ tsp salt
15 ml/1 tbsp olive oil
flour for rolling out

FILLING
30 ml/2 tbsp olive oil
1 large onion, chopped
1 green pepper, seeded and chopped
1 garlic clove, crushed
salt and pepper
30 ml/2 tbsp tomato purée
100 g/4 oz mushrooms, sliced
100 g/4 oz pepperoni sausage, cut into chunks
100 g/4 oz sweetcorn kernels
75 g/3 oz Cheddar cheese, grated

Grease a 25 cm/10 inch loose-bottomed flan tin or sandwich tin. Make the dough following the recipe for Italian-style Pizza (page 856) and leave it to rise.

Roll out the dough on a lightly floured surface large enough to line the prepared tin. Press it into the tin, pinching it around the upper edges to keep in place. Cover with cling film and set aside. Set the oven at 220°C/425°F/gas 7.

To make the filling, heat the oil in a small saucepan and cook the onion, pepper and garlic until beginning to soften – about 10 minutes. Stir in salt, pepper and the tomato purée, then remove the pan from the heat and mix in the mushrooms. Spread this mixture over the dough. Top with the pepperoni sausage and sweetcorn, then sprinkle with the grated cheese.

Bake for about 40 minutes, until the dough and topping is golden brown and bubbling. Serve cut into wedges.

SERVES FOUR

PIZZA TOPPERS

Any of the following topping ingredients may be used for an Italian-style Pizza, Deep-pan Pizza or Scone Pizza. They may also be varied according to taste.

Spicy Prawn Pizza   Seed and finely chop 1 green chilli, then cook it with 1 chopped onion in some olive oil. Add 4 diced peeled tomatoes and 225 g/8 oz peeled cooked prawns (thawed and drained if frozen). Spread over the pizza and top with plenty of sliced mozzarella cheese (more if making 4 Italian-style bases than on a single pizza).

Quickie Sardine Pizza   This one is best on a scone base: arrange canned sardines like the spokes of a wheel on a scone base. Sprinkle with plenty of chopped spring onion, then arrange chopped peeled tomato between the sardines. Sprinkle with plenty of salt, pepper and grated cheese.

Anchovy and Olives   Chop 1 (50 g/2 oz) can anchovy fillets with their oil. Divide between 4 Italian-style bases, sprinkling them over the tomato topping. Add the mozzarella, then top with 50 g/2 oz stoned black olives, either left whole or halved, as preferred. Sprinkle with 30 ml/2 tbsp chopped capers before baking.

Ham and Egg Pizza   Make the 4 Italian-style Pizzas or the dough for 1 Deep-pan Pizza. Spread the tomato topping for Italian-style

Pizzas over the chosen bases. Top with 225 g/8 oz roughly chopped cooked ham and 225 g/8 oz sliced mozzarella cheese. Make a slight nest in the middle of each Italian Pizza or 4 in the Deep-pan Pizza and crack 4 eggs into the nests. Bake as in the main recipes.

Salami and Whole Flat Mushroom   Top the chosen base with tomato purée and cooked chopped onion. Add slices of salami. Remove the stalks from small to medium flat mushrooms, allowing 4 each for individual pizzas, 8–12 for a large pizza. Chop the stalks and sprinkle them over the bases, then arrange the mushrooms on top. Sprinkle the mushrooms with salt and pepper, then top each with a thin slice of mozzarella cheese before baking.

Spicy Sausage Topping   Place 450 g/1 lb good quality pork sausagemeat in a bowl. Add 1 small grated onion, 2 crushed garlic cloves, 1.25–5 ml/$\frac{1}{4}$–1 tsp chilli powder, 15 ml/1 tbsp ground coriander and 15 ml/1 tbsp paprika. Mix the ingredients really well, with a spoon at first, then wash your hands and knead the sausage mixture. Dot small lumps of the mixture over the chosen pizza, between any mozzarella topping or over any grated cheese so that the meat cooks and browns.

Courgette Pizza   Make the tomato topping for the Italian-style Pizza. Spread the tomato mixture over the chosen base, then add a good layer of sliced courgettes and sprinkle them with lots of fresh basil leaves. Drizzle a little olive oil over the top and dust the courgettes with grated Parmesan cheese. Dot with a few pieces of mozzarella but leave at least half the courgettes uncovered so they brown slightly during baking.

EMPANADAS

fat for greasing
15 g/½ oz fresh yeast or 10 ml/2 tsp dried
    yeast
5 ml/1 tsp sugar
225 g/8 oz strong white flour
2.5 ml/½ tsp salt • 15 ml/1 tbsp olive oil
flour for rolling out

FILLING
30 ml/2 tbsp oil
1 small onion, chopped
1 green chilli, seeded and chopped
1 garlic clove, crushed
225 g/8 oz minced beef
15 ml/1 tbsp ground cumin
25 g/1 oz raisins
2 tomatoes, peeled and chopped
salt and pepper

Grease a baking sheet. Make the dough following the recipe for Italian-style Pizza (page 856)
and leave it to rise.

To make the filling, heat the oil in a frying pan
and gently cook the onion, chilli and garlic for
about 15 minutes, until the onion has softened.
Remove the pan from the heat, then add the
mince, cumin, raisins and tomatoes. Add salt
and pepper to taste and stir well.

Set the oven at 200°C/400°F/gas 6. Knead the
dough again and divide it into quarters. On a
lightly floured surface, roll out one portion into
a 15-18 cm/6-7 inch round. Mound a quarter
of the meat mixture on one half, leaving a
space around the edge of the dough. Dampen
the dough edge, then fold the dough to make a
semi-circular pasty. Pinch the edges of the
dough to seal in the filling, then place on the
baking sheet. Make three more empanadas.
Cover with cling film and leave for 5 minutes,
so that the dough begins to rise. Bake for 30-40
minutes, until golden brown.

MAKES FOUR

ONION TRAY BAKE

This German-style bake is delicious hot or cold.

fat for greasing
25 g/1 oz fresh yeast or 15 ml/1 tbsp dried
    yeast
5 ml/1 tsp sugar
450 g/1 lb strong white flour
5 ml/1 tsp salt
30 ml/2 tbsp olive oil
flour for rolling out

TOPPING
25 g/1 oz butter
450 g/1 lb onions, thinly sliced
15 ml/1 tbsp caraway seeds
salt and pepper
225 g/8 oz quark or curd cheese

Grease a 33 × 23 cm/13 × 9 inch oblong baking
tin. Make the dough following the recipe for
Italian-style Pizza (page 856) and leave it to
rise.

To make the topping, melt the butter in a large
frying pan and cook the onions and caraway
seeds, stirring often, for about 10 minutes,
until the onions have softened slightly. Add
salt and pepper to taste, then set aside.

Set the oven at 220°C/425°F/gas 7. On a lightly
floured surface, knead the dough again, then
roll out to fit the tin. Press the dough into the
tin, then spread the quark or curd cheese over
it. Top with the onions, spreading them in an
even layer and pressing down lightly. Leave the
dough in a warm place for about 15 minutes,
until beginning to rise.

Bake for about 30 minutes, until golden brown.
Allow the bake to stand for 5-10 minutes
before serving, cut into oblong portions. Alternatively, the tray bake may be left until just
warm or served cold.

SERVES EIGHT

PLUM SLICE

Firm, tart plums perfectly complement the sweet yeast dough base in this classic, Eastern European style bake. Quartered apples, dipped in lemon juice to prevent them from discolouring, halved apricots or a mixture of these fruits may be used instead of plums. Plum slice may be served as a dessert or as a coffee-time treat.

fat for greasing
450 g/1 lb strong white flour
5 ml/1 tsp salt
50 g/2 oz butter
50 g/2 oz sugar
25 g/1 oz fresh yeast or 15 ml/1 tbsp dried yeast
150 ml/¼ pint milk
soured cream to serve

TOPPING
900 g/2 lb plums, halved and stoned
Apricot Glaze (page 766)

Grease a 33 × 23 cm/13 × 9 baking tin or line a roasting tin with foil and grease that. Sift the flour and salt into a bowl. Rub in the butter and stir in the sugar, reserving 5 ml/1 tsp if using fresh yeast. Measure 150 ml/¼ pint lukewarm water in a jug.

Blend the fresh yeast with the reserved sugar and a little lukewarm water, then stir in the remaining water and set aside until frothy. For dried yeast, sprinkle it over all the water, then set aside until frothy.

Heat the milk until just lukewarm. Make a well in the centre of the dry ingredients and pour in the milk with the yeast liquid. Gradually mix in the dry ingredients to make a firm dough.

Knead the dough on a lightly floured surface until smooth and elastic – about 10 minutes.

Place the dough in a clean bowl, cover with cling film and leave in a warm place until doubled in bulk. This will take up to 2 hours.

Set the oven at 220°C/425°F/gas 7. On a lightly floured surface, knead the dough again, then roll out and press it into the prepared tin. Press the dough up around the edge slightly.

Arrange the plum halves on top of the dough, placing them cut sides down and pressing them in slightly. Leave in a warm place for 30 minutes, until risen.

Bake for about 30 minutes, or until the dough is browned around the edges and cooked. Allow to cool slightly, then brush apricot glaze all over the plums. Serve hot, warm or cold with soured cream.

SERVES EIGHT TO TEN

 MRS BEETON'S TIP

Select firm plums for best results. The quickest method of stoning plums is to slit them all around in as far as the stone lengthways, then twist the two halves of fruit. This frees one half, leaving the stone in the second half. Use a sharp pointed knife to cut out the stone from the second half.

Candied Fruit
and Confectionery

*Home-candied fruit, hand-made sweets and filled chocolates make highly acceptable gifts
and are the ultimate dinner-party sweetmeat. This comprehensive chapter includes
instructions for making all these, some simple, others more difficult, to suit your ability and
the time you want to spend on creating confectionery.*

With good basic equipment, plenty of time, patience and enthusiasm, skills such as working with sugar or tempering chocolate can readily be mastered.

EQUIPMENT

A stainless steel or other high-quality saucepan and sugar thermometer are the first items you need. A marble board and large palette knife are best for working boiled sugar syrup, although a plain white (fairly heavy) enamelled tray may be used instead. Some work surfaces withstand the heat of the boiled sugar; others do not. Marble gives the best results.

Chocolate Work Depending on the type of chocolates you hope to make, you may need moulds and/or a dipping fork (a fine, two-pronged fork). To pipe detail on the set chocolates you will need small greaseproof paper icing bags and a small, plain piping nozzle (from suppliers of cake decorating materials).

SIMPLE TESTS FOR SUGAR BOILING

A sugar thermometer takes the guesswork out of sweet-making, but syrup can be boiled without stirring and the temperature gauged approximately by using the following tests:

Thread Stage (105°C/220°F) Test by dipping a spoon in the syrup and then pressing another spoon on to the back of it and pulling away. If a thread forms, the syrup is ready.

Blow Stage (110°C/225°F) Test by dipping the top of a metal skewer in the syrup, draining it over the saucepan and then blowing through the hole. A small bubble should form which floats in the air for a second.

Soft Ball Stage (115°C/235°F) Test by dropping about 2.5 ml/½ tsp of the syrup into a bowl of iced water. You should be able to mould the syrup between your fingers to make a soft ball.

Hard Ball Stage (120°C/250°F) Test as for soft ball, but boil for 2–3 minutes longer. A larger, harder ball should be formed.

Small Crack Stage (140°C/275°F) Test by adding a few drops of the mixture to a bowl of iced water. The mixture should become brittle; a thin piece should snap.

Large Crack Stage (155°C/310°F) Test as for small crack, but boil for 2–3 minutes longer. The syrup will be very brittle and will not stick to the teeth when bitten.

CANDIED AND CRYSTALLIZED FRUIT

Shop-bought candied fruit is a succulent and expensive luxury but it can be made at home without great skill or special equipment. The main requirement is patience as the process takes about 15 minutes a day for 10–14 days. Any attempt to increase the strength of the syrup too quickly will result in tough, hardened, and shrivelled fruit. Sugar alone can be used for syrup making but the fruit's texture is better if part of the sugar is replaced by glucose. Powdered glucose weighs the same as sugar, but if using liquid glucose, increase the weight by one-fifth.

Use well-flavoured fruits, fresh or canned, for example apricots, pineapple or large, juicy plums. Very soft fruits, such as raspberries, tend to disintegrate. Fresh fruit should be firm yet ripe. Good quality canned fruit can be used; it lacks some of the full fresh flavour, but the canning process gives a good texture for candying. Canned fruit does not require cooking and the process is quicker than for fresh fruit.

Processed fruit should be packed in waxed-paper lined cardboard boxes. Interleave layers of fruit with waxed paper. Store in a cool, *dry* place; well processed fruit will keep for several months in these conditions.

FRESH FRUIT

Day 1 Prepare the fruit according to type, discarding stones and cores or peel. Prick small perfect crab-apples, apricots, fleshy plums or greengages several times to the centre with a stainless fork.

Cover the prepared fruit with boiling water and simmer gently until just tender, 10–15 minutes for firm fruits, only 3–4 minutes for tender fruits. Overcooking at this stage makes the fruit squashy, while undercooking makes it dark and tough.

For each 450g/1lb fruit, make a syrup from 250ml/8fl oz poaching water, 50g/2oz sugar and 100g/4oz glucose. Alternatively, use 150g/5oz preserving sugar instead of sugar and glucose. Stir until the sugar has dissolved, then bring to the boil.

Drain the fruit and place it in a small bowl, then pour the boiling syrup over it. If there is not enough syrup to cover it, make up some more, using the same proportions. Cover with a plate to keep the fruit under the syrup and leave for 24 hours.

Day 2 Drain the syrup into a saucepan. Add 50g/2oz sugar for each original 250ml/8fl oz water. Bring to the boil, then pour the syrup over the fruit. Cover and leave as before.

Days 3–7 Repeat Day 2.

Day 8 Drain the syrup into a saucepan. Add 75g/3oz sugar for every original 250ml/8fl oz water, heat and stir until dissolved. Add the drained fruit and boil for 3–4 minutes, then pour the fruit and syrup back into the bowl. This boiling makes the fruit plump. Leave for 48 hours.

Day 10 Repeat Day 8. When cooled, the resulting syrup should be of the consistency of fairly thick honey. If the syrup is still thin, repeat Day 8 again. Leave for 4 days.

Day 14 The fruit will keep in this heavy syrup for 2–3 weeks or for 2 months in a covered jar in the refrigerator. To complete the process, remove the fruit from the syrup. *Do not pierce the fruit.* Place it on a wire rack over a plate and allow to drain for a few minutes.

Put the rack into a very cool oven (not higher than 50°C/122°F). Use an oven thermometer to check the temperature and wedge the door ajar to prevent the temperature from increasing.

Candied fruit caramelizes easily and the flavour is then spoilt. Drying should take 3–6 hours if the heat is continuous; it may take 2–3 days if using residual heat on several occasions. Do not allow the metal rack to touch the hot sides of the oven as this will cause the wire to become too hot. Turn the fruit gently with a fork, until it is no longer sticky to handle.

Pack in cardboard boxes with waxed paper lining each box and separating the layers. Store in a dry, cool place and do not keep for many months as the succulence will be lost.

Candied fruit should have a dry surface. If it remains sticky, the final sugar concentration in the fruit is probably too low. Humid storage conditions should be avoided.

 MRS BEETON'S TIP

If you are candying several fruits at the same time, use separate syrups. Use surplus syrup for fruit salads, stewed fruit or sweetening puddings.

CANNED FRUIT

Try pineapple rings or cubes, plums, peaches or halved apricots. Keep the sizes as uniform as possible. These quantities are for about 450 g/1 lb drained fruit.

Day 1 Put the drained fruit into a large bowl. Measure the syrup into a saucepan and make it up to 250 ml/8 fl oz with water if necessary. Add 200 ml/7 oz preserving sugar or 100 g/4 oz sugar and 100 g/4 oz glucose. Heat gently and stir until the sugar has dissolved. Bring to the boil, the pour the syrup over the fruit. If there is not enough syrup to cover the fruit, prepare some more by using 225 g/8 oz sugar to 200 ml/7 fl oz water. Keep the fruit under the syrup with a plate. Leave for 24 hours.

Day 2 Drain the fruit, dissolve 50 g/2 oz sugar in the syrup, bring to the boil and pour over the fruit. Leave for 24 hours.

Days 3–4 Repeat Day 2.

Day 5 Pour the syrup into a saucepan. Add 75 g/3 oz sugar, warm the syrup to dissolve the sugar, then add the fruit. Boil for 3–4 minutes. Replace in the bowl. Leave for 48 hours.

Day 7 Repeat Day 5 and let the fruit boil until a little syrup cooked on a plate has the consistency of thick honey. Leave to soak for 3–4 days. If the syrup seems thin, add a further 75 g/3 oz sugar, dissolve it and boil the syrup with the fruit for a further few minutes. Leave to soak for 3–4 days.

Day 11 Finish the fruit as when candying fresh fruit (Day 14).

CANDIED ANGELICA

Pick bright, tender stalks in April, cut off the root ends and leaves. Make a brine with 15 g/½ oz salt in 2 litres/3½ pints water; bring it to the boil. Soak the stalks in brine for 10 minutes. Rinse in cold water. Put in a pan of fresh boiling water and boil for 5–7 minutes. Drain. Scrape to remove the outer skin. Continue as for candying fresh fruit from Day 1.

CANDIED PEEL

Use oranges, lemons or grapefruit. Scrub the fruit thoroughly. Halve and remove the pulp carefully to avoid damaging the peel. Boil the peel for 1 hour. Give grapefruit peel, which is bitter, several changes of water. Drain, and continue as for candying fresh fruit from Day 1. It is customary to pour some glacé syrup into half peels to set.

CRYSTALLIZING FRUIT

Have some granulated sugar on a sheet of polythene, greaseproof paper or foil. Lift a piece of fruit on a fork, dip it quickly into *boiling* water, drain briefly, then roll it in the sugar until evenly coated.

MAKING A GLACE FINISH

This gives a smooth, shiny finish. Over gentle heat, dissolve 450 g/1 lb granulated sugar in 150 ml/¼ pint water, then boil. Dip each fruit into boiling water for 20 seconds, then drain. Pour a little boiling syrup into a warm cup, quickly dip the fruit and place it on a wire rack. When all the fruit has been dipped, place the rack in a temperature not exceeding 50°C/122°F, and turn the fruit often to ensure even drying.

When the syrup in the small cup becomes cloudy, it must be discarded and replaced from the saucepan, which must be kept hot (but not boiling) and closely covered.

QUICK CANDIED PEEL

Soak grapefruit or lemon peel overnight to extract some of the bitterness. Cut the peel into long strips, 5 mm/¼ inch wide. Put in a saucepan, cover with cold water and bring slowly to the boil. Drain, add fresh water and bring to the boil again. Drain, and repeat 3 more times. Weigh the cooled peel and place with an equal quantity of sugar in a pan. Just cover with boiling water, and boil gently until the peel is tender and clear. Cool, strain from the syrup, and toss the peel in caster or granulated sugar on greaseproof paper. Spread out on a wire rack to dry for several hours. Roll again in sugar if at all sticky. When quite dry, store in covered jars. Use within 3–4 months.

PULLING SUGAR

In some sweet recipes the boiled sugar mixture is pulled while still warm and pliable to give it a satiny, shiny look. The technique is similar to that employed when making barley sugar. When the syrup has reached the correct temperature, pour it on to an oiled, heat-resistant surface. Allow it to settle for a few minutes until a skin has formed, then using two oiled palette knives, turn the mixture sides to the centre until it cools enough to handle. Oil your hands as a protective measure, then carefully pull the syrup into a sausage shape, working quickly. Fold in the ends, twist and pull again. Repeat the pulling until the candy has a shiny surface. When it is beginning to harden, shape it into a long rope as thick as is needed, and cut quickly into small pieces with oiled scissors. If all the mixture cannot be pulled at once, leave it on an oiled baking sheet in a warm place to keep it soft.

Several colours can be introduced by dividing the hot syrup into different portions before cooling, and introducing a few drops of food colouring to each. Pull these separately, then lay them together for the final pulling and shaping. One portion may be left unpulled and clear and added at the final shaping stage.

SIMPLE TOFFEE

oil for greasing
400 g/14 oz lump sugar
pinch of cream of tartar

Grease a 15 cm/6 inch square baking tin. Put the sugar into a saucepan, add 125 ml/4 fl oz water and heat gently, stirring until all the sugar has dissolved. Bring to the boil, add the cream of tartar and boil, without stirring, until the syrup registers 140°C/275°F on a sugar thermometer, the small crack stage (page 862).

When ready, pour the syrup into the prepared tin, leave to cool, then score the surface deeply with a knife, marking it into squares. When set, break into squares as marked, wrap in waxed paper and store in an airtight tin.

MAKES ABOUT 400G/14OZ

VARIATIONS

Nut Toffee   Add 75 g/3 oz flaked or chopped blanched almonds, or chopped walnuts with the sugar and water.

Ginger Toffee   Add 2.5 ml/½ tsp ground ginger with the water.

Vanilla Toffee   Add 2.5 ml/½ tsp vanilla essence with the cream of tartar.

BARLEY SUGAR

oil for greasing
30 ml/2 tbsp pearl barley
450 g/1 lb lump sugar
juice of ¼ lemon
pinch of cream of tartar

Put the barley in a saucepan with 300 ml/½ pint cold water. Bring to the boil, drain and rinse the barley under cold water. Return it to the clean pan and add 1 litre/1¾ pints cold water. Bring to the boil, lower the heat and simmer, covered, for about 1¾ hours.

Strain the mixture into a measuring jug. Make up to 500 ml/18 fl oz with cold water. Put the sugar in a heavy-bottomed saucepan with the barley water. Stir over low heat for 3–4 minutes until the sugar has dissolved. Increase the heat and boil, without stirring, until the syrup registers 115°C/235°F on a sugar thermometer, the soft ball stage (page 862).

Add the lemon juice and continue boiling until the syrup reaches 155°C/310°F, the large crack stage (page 862).

Pour the mixture on to a lightly oiled slab or large flat laminated board. Allow to cool for a few minutes, then fold the sides of the centre, using an oiled palette knife. Cut into strips with oiled scissors, and twist each strip. When cold and set, store in an airtight jar.

MAKES ABOUT 375G/13OZ

EVERTON TOFFEE

oil for greasing
200 g/7 oz granulated sugar
75 g/3 oz soft light brown sugar
pinch of cream of tartar
10 ml/2 tsp lemon juice
50 g/2 oz butter

Grease a 20 cm/8 inch square baking tin. Combine the sugars in a saucepan, add 175 ml/6 fl oz water and heat gently, stirring, until all the sugar has dissolved. Bring to the boil, add the cream of tartar and boil without stirring until the syrup registers 140°C/274°F on a sugar thermometer, the small crack stage (page 862). Add the lemon juice and butter and continue boiling, without stirring until the syrup reaches 155°C/310°F, the large crack stage (page 862).

Pour the mixture immediately into the prepared tin. When beginning to set score the surface deeply with a knife, marking it into squares. When set, break into squares as marked, wrap in waxed paper and store in an airtight tin.

MAKES ABOUT 350G/12OZ

RUSSIAN TOFFEE

oil for greasing
400g/14oz sugar
200g/7oz redcurrant jelly
100g/4oz butter
125ml/4fl oz single cream
pinch of cream of tartar
2.5ml/½tsp vanilla essence

Grease a 20 cm/8 inch square baking tin. Combine the sugar, redcurrant jelly, butter and cream in a saucepan. Heat gently, stirring, until all the sugar has dissolved. Add the cream of tartar and bring to the boil, stirring frequently. Boil, without stirring, until the mixture registers 120°C/250°F on a sugar thermometer, the hard ball stage (page 862).

Pour immediately into the prepared tin and score the surface deeply with a knife, marking it into squares. When set, separate into squares as marked, wrap in waxed paper and store in an airtight tin.

MAKES ABOUT 675G/1½LB

TREACLE TOFFEE

oil for greasing
100g/4oz butter
100g/4oz black treacle
150g/5oz soft dark brown sugar
pinch of cream of tartar

Grease a 15 cm/6 inch square baking tin. Combine the butter, treacle and sugar in a heavy-bottomed saucepan and add 30ml/2tbsp water. Heat gently, stirring, until all the sugar has dissolved.

Add the cream of tartar, bring to the boil and boil, without stirring, until the mixture registers 120°C/250°F on a sugar thermometer, the hard ball stage (page 862).

Pour immediately into the prepared tin and score the surface deeply with a knife, marking it into squares. When set, break into squares as marked, wrap in waxed paper and store in an airtight tin.

MAKES ABOUT 300G/11OZ

 MRS BEETON'S TIP

When buying a sugar thermometer, look for one with a movable clip that fits on the side of the saucepan. Test it after purchase by putting it in a saucepan of cold water and heating slowly to boiling point. Check that it reads 100°C/220°F. Allow it to cool in the water. Always warm the thermometer in a jug of warm water before using it to test boiling syrup, returning it to the jug of water after use.

PEANUT BRITTLE

oil for greasing
300 g/11 oz unsalted peanuts
350 g/12 oz granulated sugar
150 g/5 oz soft light brown sugar
150 g/5 oz golden syrup
50 g/2 oz butter
1.25 ml/¼ tsp bicarbonate of soda

Grease a 20 cm/8 inch square baking tin. Spread out the nuts on a baking sheet and warm them very gently in a 150°C/300°F/gas 2 oven. Meanwhile combine the sugars, golden syrup and 125 ml/4 fl oz water in a heavy-bottomed saucepan and heat gently, stirring, until all the sugar has dissolved.

Add the butter, bring to the boil and boil gently, without stirring, until the syrup registers 155°C/310°F on a sugar thermometer, the large crack stage (page 862). Stir in the bicarbonate of soda and the warmed nuts.

Pour the mixture into the prepared tin. When almost set, score the surface deeply with a knife, marking it into bars. When set, break as marked, wrap in waxed paper and store in an airtight tin.

MAKES ABOUT 1 KG/2¼ LB

 MRS BEETON'S TIP

Use a strong, heavy-bottomed saucepan for sweet-making, to prevent mixture sticking and burning. Syrups and sugar-based mixtures tend to rise very quickly during cooking, so make sure you use a large enough pan.

BUTTERSCOTCH

oil for greasing
100 g/4 oz caster sugar
100 g/4 oz butter
75 ml/3 fl oz liquid glucose
125 ml/4 fl oz single cream

Grease an 18 cm/7 inch square baking tin. Combine all the ingredients in a large heavy-bottomed saucepan. Heat very gently, stirring, until all the sugar has dissolved. Bring to the boil and boil, without stirring, until the mixture registers 140°C/275°F on a sugar thermometer, the small crack stage (page 862).

Pour the mixture immediately into the prepared tin. When beginning to set, score the surface deeply with a knife, marking it into squares. When set, break into squares as marked, wrap in waxed paper and store in an airtight tin.

MAKES ABOUT 225 G/8 OZ

 MRS BEETON'S TIP

For a special gift, overwrap each piece of butterscotch in brightly coloured cellophane paper, twist the end and pack in a decorative box or tin.

CREAM CARAMELS

oil for greasing
200 g/7 oz sugar
200 g/7 oz golden syrup
125 ml/4 fl oz evaporated milk
2.5 ml/½ tsp vanilla essence

Grease a 20 cm/8 inch square baking tin. Combine all the ingredients except the vanilla essence in a heavy-bottomed saucepan. Heat gently, stirring, until the sugar has dissolved. Bring to the boil and boil, without stirring, until the mixture registers 120°C/250°F on a sugar thermometer, the hard ball stage (page 862).

Stir in the vanilla essence and pour the mixture into the prepared tin. When the caramel is cold, score the surface deeply with a knife, marking it into squares. When set, cut into squares as marked, wrap in waxed paper and store in an airtight tin.

MAKES ABOUT 400 G/14 OZ

VARIATIONS

Walnut Caramels Chop 100 g/4 oz walnuts and add to the caramel mixture with the vanilla essence.

Fruit and Nut Caramels Add 50 g/2 oz chopped hazelnuts and 50 g/2 oz raisins to the caramel mixture with the vanilla essence.

CHOCOLATE CARAMELS

oil for greasing
150 g/5 oz caster sugar
15 ml/1 tbsp drinking chocolate powder
75 ml/5 tbsp milk
15 ml/1 tbsp liquid glucose
100 g/4 oz butter
75 ml/5 tbsp single cream
2.5 ml/½ tsp vanilla essence

Grease an 18 cm/7 inch square baking tin. Combine the sugar, chocolate powder, milk and glucose in a heavy-bottomed saucepan. Add one third of the butter and heat gently, stirring until all the sugar has dissolved.

Bring the mixture rapidly to the boil, stirring to prevent burning, and boil until the mixture registers 110°C/225°F on a sugar thermometer, the blow stage (page 862).

Stir in half the remaining butter and boil for 5 minutes more or until the mixture registers 112°C/230°F. Remove the pan from the heat and quickly stir in the remaining butter, with the cream and vanilla essence.

Return the pan to the heat. Stirring constantly, boil the mixture until it registers 115°C/235°F, the soft ball stage (page 862). Pour into the prepared tin. When beginning to set, score the surface deeply with a knife, marking it into squares. When set, cut into squares as marked.

MAKES ABOUT 300 G/11 OZ

 MRS BEETON'S TIP

Grated chocolate may be used instead of the drinking chocolate powder, if preferred. You will need about 75 g/3 oz.

CREAMY FUDGE

oil for greasing
400 g/14 oz sugar
125 ml/4 fl oz milk
50 g/2 oz butter
2.5 ml/½ tsp vanilla essence

Grease an 18 cm/7 inch square baking tin. Combine all the ingredients except the vanilla essence in a large saucepan. Heat gently until the sugar has dissolved, then bring to the boil.

Boil, stirring constantly, until the mixture registers 115°C/235°F on a sugar thermometer, the soft ball stage (page 862). Remove the pan from the heat and stir in the vanilla essence. Cool for 2 minutes, then beat the mixture until it becomes thick and creamy.

Pour into the prepared tin. When nearly set, score the surface of the fudge deeply with a knife, marking it into squares. When set, cut into squares as marked and store in an airtight tin lined with waxed paper.

MAKES ABOUT 450 G/1 LB

 **MRS BEETON'S TIP**

Fudge crystallizes if the sugar is not dissolved properly and if crystals are allowed to form on the sides of the saucepan. To prevent this happening, either grease the saucepan lightly with a little of the butter used in the recipe or cover the saucepan with a lid as soon as the mixture comes to the boil. The steam will wash down the sides of the pan. Remove the lid after 2–3 minutes and boil without stirring until the soft ball stage is reached. The crystals may also be brushed down from the sides of the pan into the mixture, using a clean brush dipped in cold water.

CHOCOLATE FUDGE

oil for greasing
400 g/14 oz sugar
50 g/2 oz golden syrup
50 g/2 oz butter
25 g/1 oz cocoa
75 ml/5 tbsp milk
45 ml/3 tbsp single cream

Grease a 15 cm/6 inch square cake tin. Combine all the ingredients in a heavy-bottomed saucepan and heat gently until all the sugar has dissolved. Bring to the boil.

Boil, stirring constantly, until the mixture registers 115°C/235F on a sugar thermometer, the soft ball stage (page 862). Cool for 5 minutes, then beat the fudge until creamy and matt in appearance.

Pour the fudge into the prepared tin. Leave until cold before cutting into squares. Store in an airtight tin lined with waxed paper.

MAKES ABOUT 450 G/1 LB

VARIATION

Chocolate Nut Fudge Stir in 100 g/4 oz chopped walnuts or almonds during the final beating.

 MRS BEETON'S TIP

It is important to observe the short cooling time before beating fudge, but the mixture must not overcool or it will be difficult to pour it into the prepared tin.

BUTTERED ALMONDS, WALNUTS OR BRAZILS

Brown, buttery and practically irresistible, buttered nuts make a most acceptable gift. Set each one in an individual fluted paper case and pack in a pretty box or tin.

oil for greasing
50 g/2 oz blanched almonds, halved walnuts
  or whole Brazil nuts
200 g/7 oz demerara sugar
10 ml/2 tsp liquid glucose
pinch of cream of tartar
50 g/2 oz butter

Spread out the nuts on an oiled baking sheet and warm them very gently in a 150°C/300°F/gas 2 oven. Put the sugar into a saucepan, add 90 ml/6 tbsp water and heat gently, stirring, until the sugar has dissolved.

Bring the mixture to the boil. Add the glucose, cream of tartar and butter. When the butter has dissolved, boil the mixture until it registers 140°C/275°F on a sugar thermometer, the small crack stage (page 862).

Using a teaspoon, pour a little toffee over each nut; it should set very quickly. When cold, remove all the nuts from the baking sheet, wrap separately in waxed paper, and store in an airtight container.

MAKES ABOUT 50 ALMONDS, 20 WALNUTS OR 15 BRAZILS

ALMOND ROCK

oil for greasing
400 g/14 oz lump sugar
75 ml/5 tbsp liquid glucose
100 g/4 oz blanched almonds
few drops of almond essence

Grease a Swiss roll tin. Put the sugar in a heavy-bottomed saucepan, add 250 ml/8 fl oz water and heat gently, stirring until the sugar has dissolved.

Add the glucose, bring to the boil and boil until the mixture registers 140°C/275°F on a sugar thermometer, the small crack stage (page 862). Remove the pan from the heat.

Stir in the almonds, with essence to taste. Return the pan to the heat and boil for 2–3 minutes until golden brown. Pour on to the prepared baking tin and leave to set. Break into pieces, wrap in waxed paper and store in an airtight tin.

MAKES ABOUT 450 G/1 LB

 MRS BEETON'S TIP

Liquid glucose is a thick colourless liquid made up of glucose and maltose; not to be confused with powdered glucose (chemically pure glucose). When added to sugar syrups, it prevents crystallization. It is available from cake decorating shops and some chemists and will keep indefinitely if stored in a screw-topped jar in a cool place (not the refrigerator). Acids, such as cream of tartar, also inhibit crystallization but do not necessarily prevent the process.

SNOWBALLS

Soft sugar sweets that melt in the mouth, snowballs hide a chocolate coating beneath a layer of coconut.

25 g/1 oz gelatine
400 g/14 oz sugar
5 ml/1 tsp vanilla essence
plain chocolate for coating
desiccated coconut for coating

Place 125 ml/4 fl oz water in a small bowl and sprinkle the gelatine on to the liquid. Set aside for 15 minutes until the gelatine is spongy. Stand the bowl over a saucepan of hot water and stir the gelatine until it has dissolved.

Put the sugar in a pan, add 175 ml/6 fl oz water and heat gently, stirring, until the sugar has dissolved. Bring the syrup to the boil and boil for 5 minutes.

Add the dissolved gelatine to the syrup and boil for 10 minutes more. Remove the pan from the heat, stir in the vanilla essence, then whisk until the mixture is stiff enough to roll into small balls.

As soon as the mixture is cool enough to handle, roll it into 30-35 small balls. Melt the chocolate in a heatproof bowl over a pan of hot water (see Mrs Beeton's Tip). Spread out the coconut thickly on a baking sheet.

When the chocolate is ready, drop in one of the soft toffee balls. Make sure it is completely covered with chocolate, then lift it out on a

fork. Tap the fork on the side of the bowl to remove surplus chocolate then transfer the ball to the coconut-coated baking sheet. Shake the sheet gently to coat the snowball. Repeat until all the balls have been coated in chocolate and coconut, transferring the finished snowballs to a baking sheet covered in waxed paper. Leave to set for 1 hour, then arrange in paper sweet cases.

MAKES 30 TO 35

PEPPERMINT CREAMS

Children love making these simple sweets. The only problem is that they are seldom prepared to let them dry out for 12 hours before eating!

400 g/14 oz icing sugar, plus extra for
    dusting
2 egg whites
10 ml/2 tsp peppermint essence

Sift the icing sugar into a bowl. Work in the egg white and peppermint essence and mix to a moderately firm paste.

Knead well, then roll out on a board lightly dusted with icing sugar to a thickness of about 5 mm/¼ inch. Cut into small rounds.

Arrange the peppermint creams on baking sheets covered with greaseproof paper and leave to dry for 12 hours, turning each sweet once. Store in an airtight container lined with waxed paper.

MAKES ABOUT 48

🥣 **MRS BEETON'S TIP**

During melting, be very careful that no steam or condensation gets on to the chocolate, as the slighest drop of moisture will thicken it and make it useless for dipping the snowballs.

TURKISH DELIGHT

25 g/1 oz gelatine
400 g/14 oz sugar
1.25 ml/¼ tsp citric acid
2.5 ml/½ tsp vanilla essence
10 ml/2 tsp triple-strength rose water
few drops of pink food colouring (optional)
50 g/2 oz icing sugar
25 g/1 oz cornflour

Place 250 ml/8 fl oz water in a large saucepan and sprinkle the gelatine on to the liquid. Set aside for 15 minutes until the gelatine is spongy. Add the sugar and citric acid, place the pan over gentle heat, and stir constantly until dissolved. Bring the mixture to the boil and boil for 20 minutes without stirring. Remove from the heat and allow to stand for 10 minutes.

Stir in the vanilla essence, rose water and colouring if used. Pour into a wetted 15 cm/6 inch square baking tin. Leave uncovered in a cool place for 24 hours.

Sift the icing sugar and cornflour together on to a sheet of greaseproof paper. Turn the Turkish delight on to the paper and cut into squares, using a sharp knife dipped in the icing sugar mixture. Toss well in the mixture, so that all sides are coated. Pack in airtight containers lined with waxed paper and dusted with the remaining icing sugar and cornflour.

MAKES ABOUT 500 G/18 OZ

VARIATION

Turkish Delight with Nuts Add 50 g/2 oz skinned and coarsely chopped pistachios, almonds or walnuts to the mixture when adding the vanilla essence.

COCONUT ICE

To achieve the traditional pink and white effect, make two separate batches of coconut ice, colouring the second batch pale pink and pouring it on to the set white mixture.

oil for greasing
300 g/11 oz sugar
2.5 ml/½ tsp liquid glucose
100 g/4 oz desiccated coconut
few drops of pink food colouring

Thoroughly grease a 15 cm/6 inch square baking tin. Put the sugar into a saucepan, add 125 ml/4 fl oz water and heat gently, stirring until all the sugar has dissolved.

Add the glucose, bring to the boil and boil until the mixture registers 115°C/235°F on a sugar thermometer, the soft ball stage (page 862). Remove the pan from the heat and add the coconut. Stir as little as possible, but shake the pan to mix the syrup and coconut.

Pour the mixture quickly into the prepared tin and leave to set. Do not scrape any mixture left in the pan into the tin, as it will be sugary. Top with a layer of pink coconut ice as suggested in the introduction, if liked.

MAKES ABOUT 400 G/14 OZ OF EACH
COLOUR

 MRS BEETON'S TIP

It is advisable to make two separate quantities of coconut ice, rather than to add colouring to half the first mixture, as the extra stirring will make the mixture grainy. Add the pink food colouring to the second batch just before it reaches soft ball stage.

NOUGAT

50 g/2 oz blanched almonds, chopped
225 g/8 oz icing sugar
5 ml/1 tsp liquid glucose
50 g/2 oz honey
1 egg white
25 g/1 oz glacé cherries, chopped

Line the sides and base of a 15 × 10 cm/6 × 4 inch baking tin with rice paper. Spread out the almonds on a baking sheet and brown them lightly under a preheated grill. Watch them carefully; they will soon scorch if left. Whisk the egg white in a heatproof bowl until stiff.

Combine the sugar, glucose, honey and 30 ml/2 tbsp water in a small saucepan. Stir over very low heat until melted; boil until the mixture registers 140°C/275°F on a sugar thermometer, the small crack stage. This takes only a few minutes. Remove from the heat. Whisking all the time, trickle the syrup into the egg white and continue whisking until the mixture is very glossy and beginning to stiffen.

Stir in the almonds and cherries. Turn the mixture into the prepared tin and press it down well. Cover with a single layer of rice paper. Place a light, even weight on top and leave until quite cold. Cut into oblong pieces or squares and wrap in waxed paper. Store in an airtight container.

MAKES ABOUT 200 G/7 OZ

MARSHMALLOWS

400 g/14 oz sugar
15 ml/1 tbsp golden syrup
30 ml/2 tbsp gelatine
2 egg whites
2.5 ml/½ tsp vanilla or lemon essence
pink food colouring (optional)
50 g/2 oz icing sugar
25 g/1 oz cornflour

Line a 20 cm/8 inch baking tin with grease-proof paper and brush with oil. Combine the sugar and golden syrup in a saucepan, add 125 ml/4 fl oz water and heat gently, stirring, until the sugar has dissolved. Bring to the boil and boil until the mixture registers 120°C/250°F on a sugar thermometer, the hard ball stage (page 862).

Meanwhile, place 125 ml/4 fl oz water in a small bowl and sprinkle the gelatine on to the liquid. Set aside for 15 minutes until the gelatine is spongy. Stand the bowl over a saucepan of hot water and stir the gelatine until it has dissolved completely.

When the syrup is ready, remove the pan from the heat and stir in the dissolved gelatine. Whisk the egg whites in a large, grease-free bowl until stiff. Pour on the syrup in a steady stream, whisking constantly. Add the flavouring and colouring, if used. Continue to whisk the mixture until it is thick and foamy. Pour into the prepared tin and leave for 24 hours.

Remove from the tin and cut into squares. Mix the icing sugar and cornflour together in a bowl and roll each piece of marshmallow thoroughly in the mixture. Leave in a single layer on a dry baking sheet at room temperature for 24 hours, then pack the marshmallows and store in boxes lines with waxed paper.

MAKES 40 TO 44

MINT HUMBUGS

oil for greasing
400g/14oz sugar
75 ml/5 tbsp liquid glucose
2.5 ml/½ tsp cream of tartar
2.5 ml/½ tsp oil of peppermint or to taste
few drops of green food colouring

Combine the sugar and glucose in a saucepan. Add 250 ml/8 fl oz water and heat gently, stirring until all the sugar has dissolved. Add the cream of tartar, bring to the boil and boil until the mixture registers 140°C/275°F on a sugar thermometer, the small crack stage (page 862).

Remove the pan from the heat and add peppermint oil to taste. Pour on to a lightly oiled slab or large plate. Divide into 2 portions, adding green colouring to one portion.

Allow the mixture to cool until workable, then pull each portion separately as described on page 1049. Using oiled scissors cut into 1 cm/½ inch pieces, turning the rope at each cut. When cold and hard, wrap the humbugs individually in waxed paper and store in an airtight tin.

MAKES ABOUT 375G/13OZ

 MRS BEETON'S TIP

An old-fashioned spill or cone, brought up to date by using modern textured paper in a bold design, is an attractive way of presenting sweets like these. If the sweets are to be a present for a child, use the cartoon section of a Sunday newspaper, backing it with thin card or construction paper for extra strength.

FRUIT DROPS

If you like the idea of stocking your pantry with a supply of these sweets, for the family, as gifts and donations to bazaars, it may be worthwhile investing in a set of old-fashioned metal sweet rings, if you can find them. Otherwise, make the mixture in a baking tin and break into squares.

fat for greasing
200g/7oz sugar
10 ml/2 tsp liquid glucose
pinch of cream of tartar
flavourings and colourings

If using sweet rings, grease them thoroughly and place on a greased baking sheet. Alternatively, grease a 15 cm/6 inch square baking tin.

Combine the sugar and glucose in a saucepan, add 50 ml/2 fl oz water and heat gently, stirring until the sugar has dissolved. Add the cream of tartar, bring to the boil and boil until the mixture registers 120°C/250°F on a sugar thermometer, the hard ball stage (page 862). Remove from the heat and allow to cool for 5 minutes.

Add the flavouring and colouring. Stir the syrup with a wooden spoon, pressing a little syrup against the sides of the pan to give it a grainy appearance.

Pour the syrup at once into the rings or in a 1 cm/½ inch layer in the prepared baking tin. Mark at once into squares and break into pieces when cold.

MAKES ABOUT 200G/7OZ

FLAVOURINGS AND COLOURINGS

Marry lemon flavouring with pale yellow or green colouring; raspberry or strawberry flavouring with pale pink colouring; pineapple flavouring with yellow colouring and orange or tangerine flavouring with orange colouring.

FRIANDISES

oil for greasing
8 cherries
8 grapes
8 small strawberries
8 cherries
1 satsuma, in segments
8 Brazil nuts
200 g/7 oz granulated sugar

Prepare the fruit, leaving the stems on the cherries, grapes, strawberries and cherries. Remove any pith from the satsuma segments. Generously grease a large baking sheet and have ready two oiled forks.

Put the sugar in a heavy-bottomed saucepan and add 175 ml/6 fl oz water. Heat gently, stirring until the sugar has dissolved. Increase the heat and boil the syrup until it turns a pale gold in colour. Immediately remove the pan from the heat and dip the bottom of the pan in cold water to prevent the syrup from darkening any further.

Spear a fruit or nut on a fork, dip it in the hot caramel syrup, then allow the excess caramel to drip back into the pan. Use the second fork to ease the fruit or nut on to the baking sheet. Continue until all the fruits and nuts have been glazed, warming the syrup gently if it becomes too thick to use.

When the coating on all the fruits and nuts has hardened, lift them carefully off the baking sheet. Serve in paper sweet cases.

MAKES ABOUT 48

RUM TRUFFLES

50 g/2 oz nibbed almonds
150 g/5 oz plain chocolate, in squares
150 g/5 oz ground almonds
30 ml/2 tbsp double cream
75 g/3 oz caster sugar
15 ml/1 tbsp rum
grated chocolate or chocolate vermicelli for
  coating

Spread out the almonds on a baking sheet and toast them lightly under a preheated grill. Bring a saucepan of water to the boil.

Put the chocolate in a heatproof bowl that will fit over the pan of water. When the water boils, remove the pan from the heat, set the bowl over the water and leave until the chocolate has melted.

Remove the bowl from the pan and stir in the toasted almonds, ground almonds, cream, sugar and rum. Mix to a stiff paste.

Roll the paste into small balls and toss at once in grated chocolate or chocolate vermicelli. Serve in sweet paper cases.

MAKES ABOUT FIFTEEN

GANACHE TRUFFLES

Ganache is a rich chocolate cream, made by melting chocolate with cream, then allowing it to set. The chocolate cream may be whipped before it is firm to make a rich topping for cakes; for truffles the mixture is chilled until it is firm enough to be shaped and coated.

350 g/12 oz plain chocolate
300 ml/½ pint double cream
5 ml/1 tsp vanilla essence
15 ml/1 tbsp icing sugar
cocoa for coating

Break the chocolate into squares and place them in a small saucepan. Add the cream and heat gently, stirring often, until the chocolate melts. Remove from the heat and stir in the vanilla, then allow to cool, stirring occasionally.

Chill the mixture until it is firm enough to shape. Place the cocoa in a small basin. Use two teaspoons to shape small balls of mixture and drop them in the cocoa one at a time. Turn the truffles in the cocoa to coat them completely, then place them on a plate or baking sheet and chill again until firm.

MAKES ABOUT 25

FONDANT SWEETS

The recipe for Traditional Fondant (page 911) is in the chapter on Fillings and Toppings for Cakes. A fondant mat is a very useful piece of equipment for sweet making. It consists of a sheet of plastic about 2 cm/¾ inch deep, with fancy shapes inset, into which the liquid fondant, jelly or chocolate is poured. When set, sweets can be removed by bending back the sheet.

Peppermint Softies Dust a fondant mat with cornflour. Soften 300 ml/11 oz fondant in a bowl over hot water. Do not overheat it. Add a few drops of peppermint essence and enough stock syrup to make a cream with the consistency of thick pouring cream. Pour into the prepared mat and set overnight. Makes about 300 g/11 oz.

Walnut Fondants Colour 100 g/4 oz fondant pale green and flavour with pineapple essence. Set out 36 walnut halves. Divide the fondant into 18 equal portions and roll them into balls. Flatten into pieces about the same diameter as the walnuts. Sandwich one piece of fondant between two walnut halves, pressing firmly. Allow the sweets to harden in a dry, warm place. Serve in paper sweet cases. Makes 18.

Fondant Fruits or Nuts Any firm fruit that will not discolour may be used. Clean and dry the fruit, removing any stones or pips. Divide oranges or mandarins into segments. To coat 18-20 small fruits or 36-40 nuts, you will need about 200 g/7 oz fondant. Warm the fondant in a bowl over hot water, stirring it until it has the appearance of thick cream. Add some stock syrup if necessary. Dip the fruits or nuts individually in the fondant and place on a plate to dry. Cherries and grapes can be held by the stem, but other fruits and nuts must be immersed and lifted out with a fork. Use within two days.

HAND-MADE CHOCOLATES

Many of the sweets in this chapter are suitable for coating with chocolate, but the process takes time and patience. Couverture chocolate, available from supermarkets or delicatessens, should ideally be used, but must be tempered first (see below).

Alternatively, use a super-fatted commercial dipping or coating chocolate. The flavour may not be quite so good as that of couverture, but the product is much easier to use: simply break it into small pieces and melt in a bowl over a saucepan of hot water.

Tempering Couverture Chocolate   Break the chocolate into pieces and put it in a bowl over a saucepan of hot water. Stirring frequently, heat to about 50°C/120°F, then allow the chocolate to cool again until it thickens (at about 28°C/82°F). Heat again to about 31°C/88°F; thin enough to use but thick enough to set quickly.

CENTRES FOR COATING

The technique for dipping in chocolate is described on page 782.

Marzipan   Colour and flavour marzipan, cut into attractive shapes and dip in melted chocolate.

Fondant   Colour, flavour, cut into shapes and allow to dry, then dip in melted chocolate.

Ginger or Pineapple   Cut preserved ginger or glacé pineapple into small pieces, then dip in melted chocolate.

Nuts   Dip blanched almonds, Brazil nuts or walnuts in melted chocolate.

Caramels, Toffee or Nougat   Cut into squares or rectangles; dip in melted chocolate.

Coconut Ice   Dip completely in melted chocolate or just half dip each piece.

Sweet Preserves

*There are a few areas of culinary craft more satisfying than making sweet preserves – a line
of pots full of glistening jam, jelly or marmalade is reward in itself for the effort involved.
You only have to sample the excellent flavour of your produce to understand why preserving
is an annual treat as much as a task.*

The majority of sweet preserves may be roughly grouped into two categories: those that set and those that are runny. Jams, jellies and marmalades are all set preserves, whereas conserves have a syrupy texture. Mincemeat is a combination of ingredients preserved by combining uncooked dried fruits, sugar and alcohol. It is thick rather than set. A third category comprises butters and cheeses which are thickened by cooking. Finally, this chapter includes fruit curd. Although this is not strictly speaking a preserve, it is used in the same way as jams and is regarded as a related product.

ACHIEVING A SET

Three ingredients are essential for a good set – pectin, sugar and acid. When these are correctly balanced the mixture will set.

Pectin   Naturally present in some fruit, this is the glue-like ingredient found in the cell walls of the fruit. It is extracted by cooking, assisted by the presence of acid.

Sugar   Sugar is added in proportion, depending on the pectin content of the fruit, then dissolved and boiled down to the right concentration for producing a set.

Acid   Some fruits contain acid, others with a low acid content require the addition of lemon juice for making a good preserve. Not only does this promote pectin extraction but it also helps to give the preserve a good colour and sparkle.

INGREDIENTS

Fruit   Fruit contains the maximum amount of pectin before it ripens; however in this state its flavour is not at its best. For a good preserve, the ideal is to use some fruit which is not quite ripe along with ripe fruit for flavour. Overripe fruit is not suitable for set preserves, although it may be used for butters and cheeses.

It is important to know or to check the pectin content of the fruit. Fruits with a low pectin content may be combined with others which have a high pectin content, thus ensuring that the preserve sets well.

Acid   If the fruit does not have a good acid content, then this should be added in the form of lemon juice. It should be added in the initial stages of cooking to assist in pectin extraction.

Sugar   Sugar should be measured carefully: too much will cause the jam to be syrupy, not set; too little and the jam will require long boiling to give a set at all, making it dark and overcooked.

Any sugar can be used; however special preserving sugar gives the best results as the large crystals dissolve slowly and evenly, producing less scum and giving a sparkling preserve. This said, granulated sugar is probably the more frequently used type and it is perfectly acceptable.

The practice of warming the sugar before adding it to the cooked fruit helps to make it dissolve evenly and quickly.

Special sugar with pectin and acid added in the correct proportions for setting should be used according to the manufacturer's instructions. The boiling time is usually significantly shorter than with traditional ingredients. This type of sugar is very useful with low-pectin fruits or with exotic fruits.

Pectin   Bottled pectin is also available for use with fruits that do not contain a good natural supply. Again, this should be used exactly according to the manufacturer's instructions.

Alternatively, fruit with a good pectin content such as apples, redcurrants and gooseberries may be cooked to a purée and used to set preserves made with fruit which does not have enough pectin. The purée is known as *pectin stock*. The whole, washed fruit (trimmed of bad parts, stalks and leaves) should be cooked to a pulp with water, then strained through muslin. Pectin stock may be combined with fruit such as strawberries, cherries or rhubarb to make a set preserve.

EQUIPMENT

Cooking Pan   Do not use aluminium, copper, uncoated iron or zinc pans as these metals react with the fruit, adding unwanted deposits to the preserve and, in some cases, spoiling both colour and flavour.

A stainless steel pan is best. Alternatively, a heavy, well-coated (unchipped) enamel pan may be used. Good-quality non-stick pans are also suitable.

Although a covered pan is used for long cooking of fruit which needs tenderizing (particularly citrus fruit for marmalade), for boiling with sugar a wide, open pan is best. The wider the pan, the larger the surface area of preserve and the more efficient will be the process of evaporating unwanted liquid to achieve a set. Whatever the shape of pan, it is essential that it is large enough to hold both cooked fruit and

sugar without being more than half to two-thirds full, so that the preserve does not boil over when it is brought to a full rolling boil.

Knife   Use a stainless steel knife for cutting fruit. A carbon steel implement reacts with the fruit causing discoloration.

Sugar Thermometer   This is invaluable for checking the temperature of the preserve.

Saucer   For testing for set (not essential).

Jelly Bag and Stand   For making jellies and jelly marmalades you need a jelly bag and stand to strain the cooked fruit. You also need a large bowl to collect the juice. If you do not have a stand you can improvise by tying the four corners of the jelly bag to the legs of an upturned traditional kitchen stool by means of elastic. Instead of a jelly bag a large, double-thick piece of muslin may be used.

Jars   Use sturdy, heatproof jars that are thoroughly cleaned, rinsed in hot water and dried. Unless they are exceedingly dirty or have food deposits, there is no need to sterilize jars. However they must be washed in very hot soapy water (use rubber gloves to withstand the heat), then rinsed in hot or boiling water. Turn the jars upside down on folded clean tea-towels placed on a baking sheet or in a roasting tin, then put in a warm oven about 15 minutes before use.

Alternatively, wash the jars in a dishwasher just before use and leave them undisturbed to avoid contamination. They will be hot and perfectly clean.

Jam Funnel   A wide metal funnel which fits into jars and makes filling them far easier.

Small Jug   For ladling the preserve into the jars.

Covers and Lids   The surface of the preserve should be covered with discs or waxed paper. Airtight lids should be plastic-coated as bare metal will react with fruit acids in the jam and corrode. Cellophane discs may be used with elastic bands; they are not ideal for long-term storage but are useful under lids which may not be well coated in plastic.

Labels It is important to label each pot with the type of preserve and date.

PREPARATION TECHNIQUES

All fruit should be trimmed of bad parts, stalks and leaves. Then it should be prepared according to type – peeled, cored, stoned, cut up and so on. All these trimmings including any pips, should be tied in a piece of scalded muslin and cooked with the fruit, as they contain valuable pectin.

Make sure you have enough clean and warm jars, covers and labels.

COOKING TECHNIQUES

Cooking the Fruit The prepared fruit should be cooked with acid and a little water if necessary. Soft fruits and others that yield a good volume of juice need only a little water to prevent them from drying out in the first stages of heating. The fruit must be initially cooked until it is thoroughly softened, preferably in a covered pan to prevent excessive evaporation. It is at this stage that the pectin is extracted. Undercooking not only results in tough pieces of fruit in the preserve but also in insufficient pectin for a good set.

Adding Sugar When the fruit is thoroughly cooked the sugar may be added. If possible warm the sugar first, then add it to the fruit. Keep the heat low and stir until the sugar has dissolved completely. This is important – if the preserve boils before all the sugar has dissolved, this may encourage the sugar to crystallize.

Boiling until Set Once the sugar has dissolved, the preserve should be brought to a full,

or rolling, boil. This must be maintained until setting point is reached. This rapid boiling concentrates the sugar to the level needed to balance with the pectin.

Skimming At the end of cooking any scum which has collected on the surface of the preserve should be removed with a metal spoon. Sometimes a small knob of butter is added to disperse this scum or any remaining scum which cannot be removed.

Removing Stones If fruit is not stoned before cooking, the stones may be removed with a slotted spoon or small sieve as the preserve boils.

TESTING FOR SETTING

It is important to turn the heat off or take the pan off the heat when testing for setting. If the preserve continues to cook it may boil beyond the setting point, then it will not set.

Flake Test The least reliable. Lift a mixing spoon out of the preserve and allow the mixture to drip off it. When setting point is reached the preserve does not drip off cleanly but tends to fall off, leaving small drips of flakes building up on the edge of the spoon.

Saucer Test A reliable method: have a cold saucer ready in the refrigerator, spoon a little preserve on it and set it aside in a cool place for a few minutes. Push the sample of preserve with your finger; it should have formed a distinct skin which wrinkles. If the sample does not have a skin, the preserve will not set.

Temperature Test The best test: when the correct sugar concentration is reached the boiling preserve should achieve a temperature of 105°C/220°F. Do not let the temperature go any higher.

POTTING

Before potting, warm the jars and spread clean tea-towels or paper on the surface where the jars will stand. Have ready a tea-towel to hold or steady the jars (an oven glove is too bulky) and a dry tea-towel or absorbent kitchen paper for wiping up any bad spills on the jars. Never wipe the sides of very hot jars with a damp dish cloth.

Most preserves should be put into jars as soon as they are cooked. The jars should be full but not overfilled. There should be just a small space below the rim of the jar to prevent the preserve from touching the lid. Cover the surface of the hot preserve immediately with a disc of waxed paper, wax-side down, then put on lids at once.

Preserves with pieces of fruit or rind which tend to float should be left to stand for 15 minutes after cooking and before potting. This allows the preserve to set just enough to hold the fruit or rind in position. The preserve should be stirred and potted, covered with waxed discs, then *left to cool completely* before covering with lids.

STORING

Store preserves in a cool, dark cupboard. They will keep from 6 to 12 months or longer in the right conditions. Since most modern homes have central heating, preserves tend to dry out during storage by slow evaporation. This can be averted if the rims of lids are sealed with heavy freezer tape.

BASIC FRUIT JAMS

To make a fruit jam you should know the pectin content. Fruits which have a good pectin content require an equal weight of sugar. Fruit with an excellent pectin content – currants, gooseberries or apples – can take up to 1.25/$1\frac{1}{4}$ times their weight in sugar. Fruit with medium or poor pectin content will only set 0.75/$\frac{3}{4}$ their weight in sugar. If the pectin content is poor, add pectin stock (page 880), plenty of lemon juice or commercial pectin.

PECTIN TEST

Place a little methylated spirits in a clean, old jar. Add a spoonful of the thoroughly cooked fruit pulp (before sugar is added) and gently swirl the mixture. Allow the pulp to settle. If it forms a large lump, the fruit has a good pectin content. If there are a few lumps, then the fruit has a moderate pectin content. If the pulp is separated in lots of small lumps, it has little pectin and more should be added for a good set. These lumps are known as clots. Discard jar and contents after testing.

YIELD

Although it is possible to estimate the yield of most jams and many marmalades, jellies rely on the volume of juice which is extracted from the fruit for the weight of sugar which has to be added. In the recipes that follow, it has therefore not always been possible to estimate yields accurately.

APRICOT JAM

Using dried fruit and flaked almonds from the pantry, this delectable jam can be made at any time of year.

575 g/1¼ lb dried apricots
2 lemons
1.5 kg/3¼ lb sugar
50 g/2 oz flaked almonds

Wash the apricots and cut up each fruit in two or three pieces. Put them into a large bowl, cover with 1.5 litres/2¾ pints water and leave to soak for 24 hours.

Transfer the fruit and soaking liquid to a preserving pan. Squeeze the juice from the lemons. Chop one shell and tie it in scalded muslin. Add the juice and muslin bag to the apricots. Bring to the boil, lower the heat and simmer for about 30 minutes or until tender, stirring occasionally. Remove the muslin bag, squeezing it to extract all juice.

Stir in the sugar and almonds. Stir over low heat until the sugar is dissolved, then bring to the boil. Boil rapidly until setting point is reached. Remove from the heat, skim, pot, cover and label.

MAKES ABOUT 2 KG/4½ LB

APPLE AND GINGER JAM

1.5 kg/3¼ lb apples
25 g/1 oz fresh root ginger, bruised
30 ml/2 tbsp lemon juice
100 g/4 oz crystallized ginger, chopped
1.5 kg/3¼ lb sugar

Peel, core and cut up the apples, putting the peel and cores in a square of muslin with the bruised ginger. Tie the muslin to make a bag. Put the apples, muslin bag and 600 ml/1 pint water in a preserving pan with the lemon juice. Cook slowly until the fruit is pulpy.

Remove the muslin bag, squeezing it into the preserving pan. Add the crystallized ginger and sugar and stir over low heat until all the sugar has dissolved. Bring to the boil and boil rapidly until setting point is reached. Remove from the heat, skim, pot, cover and label.

MAKES ABOUT 2.5 KG/5½ LB

 MRS BEETON'S TIP

Central heating poses special problems when it comes to keeping jam in good condition. It is a good idea to use modern twist-topped jam jars which can create an airtight seal when closed immediately after potting. Seal the tops in place with freezer tape to ensure an airtight result.

Preserving Equipment

PLUM AND APPLE JAM

675 g/1½ lb apples
675 g/1½ lb plums
1.5 kg/3½ lb sugar

Peel, core and slice the apples. Tie the trimmings in a piece of muslin. Wash the plums and put them into a preserving pan with the apples and the muslin bag. Add 450 ml/¾ pint water. Bring to the boil, then cook over gentle heat until the apples are pulpy and the skins of the plums are soft.

Add the sugar, stir over low heat until dissolved, then bring to the boil. Boil rapidly until setting point is reached. Use a slotted spoon to remove the plum stones as they rise to the surface (see Mrs Beeton's Tip). Remove from the heat, skim, pot, cover and label.

MAKES ABOUT 2.5 KG/5½ LB

> **MRS BEETON'S TIP**
>
> A stone basket, clipped to the side of the preserving pan, may be used to hold the stones while allowing the juice to drip back into the pan. A metal sieve, hooked over one side of the pan and supported by the handle on the other, performs equally well.

Testing for Setting: Saucer Test

BLACKBERRY AND APPLE JAM

450 g/1 lb sour apples
1 kg/2¼ lb blackberries
1.5 kg/3¼ lb sugar

Peel, core and slice the apples. Tie the trimmings in muslin. Put the apples and muslin bag in a saucepan, add 150 ml/¼ pint water and bring to the boil. Lower the heat and simmer the fruit until it forms a pulp.

Meanwhile, pick over the blackberries, wash them gently but thoroughly and put them in a second pan. Add 150 ml/¼ pint water, bring to the boil, then lower the heat and cook until tender.

Combine the fruits, with their cooking liquid, in a preserving pan. Add the sugar and stir over low heat until dissolved. Bring to the boil and boil rapidly until setting point is reached. Remove from the heat, skim, pot, cover and label.

MAKES ABOUT 2.5 KG/5½ LB

VARIATION

Seedless Blackberry and Apple Jam Make the apple purée and cook the blackberries as described in paragraphs 1 and 2 above, then rub through a fine nylon sieve set over a bowl to remove the seeds. Mix all the fruit together and weigh the mixture. Weigh out an equal quantity of sugar. Transfer the fruit to a preserving pan and simmer until thick. Add the sugar and stir over low heat until dissolved, then bring to the boil and boil rapidly until setting point is reached. Pot as suggested above.

MORELLO CHERRY JAM

Cherries are poor in pectin and need a little help if they are to set properly. In the recipe below, commercially produced pectin is used.

1 kg/2¼ lb Morello cherries, stoned
45 ml/3 tbsp lemon juice
1.4 kg/3 lb sugar
1 (227 ml/8 fl oz) bottle pectin

Wash the cherries and put them in a preserving pan with the lemon juice. Add 200 ml/7 fl oz water. Bring to the boil, lower the heat, cover and simmer for 15 minutes.

Remove the lid, add the sugar and stir over low heat until dissolved. Bring to the boil and boil rapidly for 3 minutes. Remove from the heat again, skim if necessary and stir in the pectin thoroughly.

Cool for 15 minutes, pot and cover with waxed paper discs. Put on lids and label when cold.

MAKES ABOUT 2.25 KG/5 LB

 MRS BEETON'S TIP

If you make a lot of jam, it is worth investing in a good quality preserving pan. Stainless steel pans are best. Avoid iron, zinc, copper and brass pans as the fruit will react with the metal. Cooking in copper can enhance the colour of jams such as green gooseberry but the use of such pans is no longer recommended.

MARROW AND GINGER JAM

1.5 kg/3¼ lb marrow, peeled and cut up
2 lemons
100 g/4 oz crystallized ginger, cut up
1.5 kg/3¼ lb sugar

Put the marrow in a metal colander set over a saucepan of boiling water, cover the marrow with the pan lid and steam for 10-20 minutes or until tender. Drain thoroughly and mash to a pulp.

Meanwhile, grate the rind from the lemons, squeeze out the juice and place both in a small saucepan. Chop the remaining lemon shells and tie them in muslin. Add the muslin bag to the lemon mixture and pour in just enough water to cover. Bring to the boil, lower the heat and cover the pan. Simmer for 30 minutes. Squeeze the bag and boil the liquid, without the lid on the pan, until reduced to the original volume of lemon juice.

Combine the marrow, ginger and lemon liquid in a preserving pan. Bring to the boil, add the sugar, and stir over low heat until dissolved. Boil until setting point is reached.

Remove from the heat, skim, pot, cover and label.

MAKES ABOUT 2.5 KG/5½ LB

 MRS BEETON'S TIP

This jam will not produce a definite set; it is potted when it reaches the desired volume and consistency.

MULBERRY AND APPLE JAM

1 kg/2¼ lb mulberries
450 g/1 lb apples
1.5 kg/3¼ lb sugar

Pick over the mulberries, wash them gently but thoroughly and put them in a saucepan with 125 ml/4 fl oz water. Bring to the boil, lower the heat and simmer until soft. Rub through a fine nylon sieve into a bowl.

Peel, core and slice the apples. Tie all trimmings in muslin. Put the apple slices in a preserving pan, add the muslin bag and 125 ml/4 fl oz water, then bring to the boil. Lower the heat and simmer the fruit until soft. Squeeze and discard the muslin.

Stir in the sieved mulberries and the sugar and stir over low heat until the sugar has dissolved. Bring to the boil. Boil rapidly until setting point is reached. Remove from the heat, skim, pot, cover and label.

MAKES 2.5 KG/5½ LB

RASPBERRY CONSERVE

This conserve does not set firmly but it has a wonderful fresh flavour.

1.25 g/2¾ lb raspberries
1.5 kg/3¼ lb sugar

Put the sugar in a heatproof bowl and warm in a preheated 150°C/300°F/gas 2 oven.

Meanwhile wash the raspberries lightly but thoroughly and drain them very well.

Put them in a preserving pan without any additional water, bring them gently to the boil, then boil rapidly for 5 minutes.

Draw the preserving pan off the heat and add the warmed sugar. Return the pan to the heat and stir well until all the sugar has dissolved. Bring to the boil and boil rapidly for 1 minute.

Remove from the heat, skim quickly, pot at once and label.

MAKES ABOUT 2.5 KG/5½ LB

QUINCE JAM

This jam has a delicious flavour but is rather solid, almost like a fruit cheese.

1.5 kg/3¼ lb quinces, peeled, cored and cut up (see Mrs Beeton's Tip)
juice of 1 large lemon
1.5 kg/3¼ lb sugar

Combine the quinces and lemon juice in a preserving pan. Add 250 ml/8 fl oz water, bring to the boil, then lower the heat and simmer until soft.

Add the sugar, stirring over low heat until dissolved. Bring to the boil and boil quickly until setting point is reached. Remove from the heat, skim, pot, cover and label.

MAKES ABOUT 2.5 KG/5½ LB

 MRS BEETON'S TIP

If the quinces are very hard, they may be grated or minced coarsely, in which case the amount of water used should be doubled.

WHOLE STRAWBERRY JAM

1.5 kg/3¼ lb strawberries, hulled
juice of 1 lemon
1.5 kg/3¼ lb sugar

Combine the strawberries and lemon juice in a preserving pan. Heat gently for 10 minutes, stirring all the time, to reduce the volume. Add the sugar, stirring over low heat until it has dissolved.

Bring to the boil and boil rapidly until setting point is reached. Remove from the heat and skim. Leave the jam undisturbed to cool for about 20 minutes or until a skin forms on the surface and the fruit sinks. Stir gently to distribute the strawberries. Pot and top with waxed paper discs. Cover and label when cold. Do not use twist-topped jars; the jam will have cooled down too much before potting.

MAKES ABOUT 2.5 KG/5½ LB

 MICROWAVE TIP

Small amounts of strawberry jam can be successfully made in the microwave. The jam will have very good colour and flavour but will only be lightly set. Put 450 g/1 lb hulled strawberries in a large deep mixing bowl; the mixture rises considerably during cooking. Add 450 g/1 lb sugar and mix lightly. Cover and allow to stand overnight. Next day uncover and cook on High until setting point is reached, stirring occasionally and checking for setting every 10 minutes. Remove from the microwave, using oven gloves to protect your hands. Leave to stand, then pot as suggested above. Makes about 675 g/1½ lb.

PEACH JAM

1.8 kg/4 lb small firm peaches, peeled and
    quartered (see Mrs Beeton's Tip)
5 ml/1 tsp tartaric acid
1.5 kg/3¼ lb sugar

Combine the fruit, with the stones, and tartaric acid in a preserving pan. Add 300 ml/½ pint water, bring to the boil, lower the heat and simmer until the fruit is tender.

Add the sugar and stir over gentle heat until dissolved. Bring to the boil and boil rapidly, removing the stones as they rise to the surface (see Mrs Beeton's Tip, page 884). Test for set after about 10 minutes of rapid boiling.

When ready, remove from the heat skim, pot, cover and label.

MAKES ABOUT 2.5 KG/5½ LB

 MRS BEETON'S TIP

To peel peaches, place them in a heatproof bowl, pour on boiling water to cover and leave for 30 seconds. Drain, cut a small cross in the top of each fruit and peel away the skin. Do this just before using the peaches, as they will discolour if allowed to stand.

GOOSEBERRY JAM

1.25 kg/2¾ lb gooseberries, topped and tailed
1.5 kg/3¼ lb sugar

Put the gooseberries in a preserving pan. Add 500 ml/17 fl oz water and bring to the boil. Lower the heat and simmer for 20–30 minutes, until the fruit is soft.

Add the sugar, stirring over gentle heat until dissolved. Bring to the boil and boil rapidly until setting point is reached. Test for set after about 10 minutes of rapid boiling. Remove from the heat, skim, pot, cover and label.

MAKES ABOUT 2.5 KG/5½ LB

 MICROWAVE TIP

Jam jars may be scalded in the microwave. Half fill perfectly clean jars (without metal trims) with water, place in the microwave and bring the water to the boil on High. Watch the jars closely, turning off the power as soon as the water boils. Carefully remove the jars from the microwave, protecting your hand with an oven glove or tea-towel. pour away the water, invert the jars on a sheet of absorbent kitchen paper and leave to dry. Fill with jam while still hot.

GREENGAGE JAM

1.5 kg/3¼ lb greengages
1.5 kg/3¼ lb sugar

Remove the stalks, wash the greengages and put them into a preserving pan. Add 125 ml/4 fl oz water (see Mrs Beeton's Tip). Cook slowly for 5–20 minutes, until the fruit is broken down.

Add the sugar and stir over gentle heat until dissolved. Bring to the boil and boil rapidly, removing the stones as they rise to the surface (see Mrs Beeton's Tip, page 884). Test for set after about 10 minutes of rapid boiling.

When ready, remove from the heat, skim, pot, cover and label.

MAKES ABOUT 1.5 KG/3¼ LB

 MRS BEETON'S TIP

Ripe or very juicy fruit will need very little water and only a short cooking time; firmer varieties may take as long as 20 minutes to break down and will require up to 250 ml/8 fl oz water.

DAMSON JAM

1.25 kg/2¾ lb damsons, stalks removed
1.5 kg/3¼ lb sugar
2.5 ml/½ tsp ground cloves
2.5 ml/½ tsp grated nutmeg

Put the damsons in a preserving pan with 500 ml/17 fl oz water. Place over gentle heat and cook for about 15 minutes, until the damsons are well broken down.

Add the sugar and spices and stir over gentle heat until dissolved. Bring to the boil and boil rapidly, removing the stones as they rise to the surface (see Mrs Beeton's Tip, page 884). Test for set after about 10 minutes of rapid boiling. When ready, remove from the heat, skim, pot, cover and label.

MAKES ABOUT 2.5 KG/5½ LB

RHUBARB AND ORANGE JAM

Mrs Beeton noted that this jam is made 'to resemble Scotch marmalade'. Opinion may vary as to the truth of the comparison but the preserve is certainly worth trying. Lemon is added to give the jam a good set; alternatively omit the lemon and use commercial pectin or preserving sugar with pectin.

6 oranges
1 lemon
900 g/2 lb rhubarb, sliced
900 g/2 lb sugar

Wash, dry and peel the oranges, removing all the pith. Cut the peel from three oranges into fine strips and place them in a large saucepan. Roughly chop the orange flesh, discarding the pips, and add it to the peel.

Squeeze the lemon and add the juice to the pan. Finely chop the lemon shells, tie them in scalded muslin and add to the pan with the rhubarb. Add 300 ml/½ pint water and heat gently, stirring often until the juice runs from the rhubarb.

Bring to the boil, lower the heat and simmer, covered, for about 1¼ hours, or until the orange peel is tender. Remove the muslin bag, squeezing it over the pan. Add the sugar and heat gently, stirring, until it has dissolved completely.

Bring the jam to the boil and boil rapidly until setting point is reached. Remove from the heat, skim, pot, cover and label.

MAKES ABOUT 2.25 KG/5 LB

CARROT PRESERVE

Mrs Beeton's carrot jam was intended to imitate apricot preserve. Sampled in ignorance, the association between carrots and this smooth, pleasant-tasting preserve is not immediately apparent. Adding the whole of the lemon, instead of the rind alone, gives the cooked pulp a better consistency.

2 large lemons
900 g/2 lb carrots, sliced
5 ml/1 tsp oil of bitter almonds or natural
  almond flavouring
25 g/1 oz blanched almonds, chopped
675 g/1½ lb sugar
60 ml/4 tbsp brandy

Wash, dry and grate the lemons. Squeeze out the juice and reserve with the rind. Finely chop the shells and place them in a small saucepan. Pour in just enough water to cover the lemon. Bring to the boil, cover tightly, lower the heat and simmer for about 1 hour or until the pulp is soft. Strain the cooking liquid through a fine sieve into a jug; set aside.

Cook the carrots in a saucepan of boiling water until tender, then drain and mash. Place the mashed carrots in a preserving pan. Add the grated lemon rind and juice, strained cooking liquid, almond oil or flavouring and nuts. Add the sugar and heat gently, stirring all the time until the sugar has dissolved completely.

Bring to the boil and boil rapidly until setting point is reached. Remove from the heat and skim. Stir in the brandy, pot, cover and label.

MAKES ABOUT 1.4 KG/3 LB

RAISIN PRESERVE

The fruit may be boiled down for about 1½ hours, or longer, to make a very sweet, dark fruit cheese. This lighter recipe, pepped up with rum, is ideal for winter preserving sessions. The preserve is good with pancakes or scones.

450 g/1 lb raisins
50 g/2 oz candied citron peel, chopped
10 ml/2 tsp ground cinnamon
1.25 ml/¼ tsp ground cloves
225 g/8 oz sugar
75 ml/3 fl oz rum

Mix the raisins and citron peel in a large bowl. Add 150 ml/¼ pint water, the cinnamon, cloves and sugar. Mix well, then cover the bowl and leave to stand for 24 hours, stirring occasionally.

Tip the raisin mixture into a saucepan, scraping in all the juices from the bowl. Heat gently, stirring, until any remaining sugar has dissolved. Bring to the boil, lower the heat and cover the pan, then simmer steadily for 30 minutes. Mash the raisins with a potato masher to crush some of them. Stir in the rum, cover the pan again, then cook for a further 5 minutes. Stir well and pot, pressing the fruit down. Cover at once.

MAKES ABOUT 900 G/2 LB

PUMPKIN PRESERVE

Originally, Mrs Beeton advised cutting the pumpkin into 'pieces about the size of a five-shilling piece'. This recipe may also be used for marrow and, of course, it may be doubled, trebled or increased according to the weight of pumpkin flesh you have to preserve. Do not do more than double the ginger or it will be overpowering.

450 g/1 lb pumpkin flesh
450 g/1 lb sugar
2.5 cm/1 inch fresh root ginger, sliced
grated rind of 1 lemon
150 ml/¼ pint lemon juice

The pumpkin should be weighed after peeling and discarding the seeds. Cut the flesh into 2.5 cm/1 inch cubes. Layer them in a large bowl, sprinkling each layer with sugar, ginger slices and grated lemon rind. Pour the lemon juice over, cover the bowl and leave to stand for 2–3 days, stirring occasionally.

Turn the pumpkin into a large preserving pan, scraping in all the juices from the bowl. Add 100 ml/3½ fl oz water. Bring to the boil, stirring, then lower the heat and simmer for 30–40 minutes, until the pumpkin is tender but not reduced to a pulp. Stir occasionally.

Spoon the pumpkin and juices into a bowl, cover and leave in a cold place for 1 week, stirring every day. Strain the syrup into a saucepan, adding the ginger slices from the strainer. Pack the pumpkin into jars. Bring the syrup mixture to the boil and boil until reduced by half. Pour the boiling syrup over the pumpkin, cover and label.

MAKES ABOUT 1.4 KG/3 LB

MINT JELLY

1 kg/2¼ lb green apples
1 small bunch of mint
500 ml/17 fl oz distilled vinegar
sugar (see method)
20 ml/4 tsp finely chopped mint
green food colouring (optional)

Wash the apples, cut into quarters and put in a preserving pan with the small bunch of mint. Add 500 ml/17 fl oz water, bring to the boil, lower the heat and simmer until the apples are soft and pulpy. Add the vinegar, bring to the boil and boil for 5 minutes.

Strain through a scalded jelly bag and leave to drip for several hours or overnight (see page 880). Measure the juice and return it to the clean pan. Add 800 g/1¼ lb sugar for every 1 litre/1¾ pints of juice.

Heat gently, stirring until the sugar has dissolved, then boil rapidly until close to setting point. Stir in the chopped mint, with colouring, if used, and boil steadily until setting point is reached. Remove from the heat, pot and cover immediately.

 PRESSURE COOKER TIP

Combine the apples and 500 ml/17 fl oz water in the pressure cooker. Bring to 10 lb pressure and cook for 5 minutes. Reduce the pressure slowly. Stir in the vinegar and boil in the open pressure cooker for 5 minutes. Mash the apples until well pulped, then strain as above and return to the clean cooker. Stir in sugar in the proportions above and add the bunch of mint, tied with string. Continue boiling until close to setting point. Remove mint bouquet and add chopped mint, with colouring, if used. Pot as above.

ORANGE SHRED
AND APPLE JELLY

1 kg/2¼ lb crab-apples or windfalls
2 oranges
sugar (see method)

Wash the apples and cut into chunks, discarding any bruised or damaged portions. Place in a preserving pan with just enough water to cover. Bring to the boil, lower the heat and simmer for about 1 hour or until the fruit is tender. Strain through a scalded jelly bag, leaving it to drip for 1 hour.

Meanwhile wash the oranges. Squeeze and strain the juice, retaining the empty orange shells. Remove and discard the pith form each shell, then cut them in half. Put the quarters of peel into a small saucepan, add 100 ml/3½ fl oz water and cook over gentle heat for 1 hour or until tender.

Strain the water used for cooking the orange peel into a large measuring jug. Add the apple extract and the orange juice. Weigh out 800 g/1¾ lb sugar for every litre/1¾ pints of liquid.

Dry the cooked peel in a clean cloth and cut into fine shreds. Set aside.

Combine the liquid and sugar in the clean preserving pan. Heat gently until the sugar has dissolved, then bring to the boil and boil fast until setting point is reached. Remove from the heat and skim quickly. Add the reserved shreds of peel; do not stir.

Leave to cool slightly until a skin forms on the surface of the jelly, then pot and top with waxed paper discs. Cover and label when cold.

CLEAR SHRED ORANGE MARMALADE

1.5 kg/3½ lb Seville or bitter oranges
2 lemons
1 sweet orange
sugar (see method)

Wash the oranges and lemons. Squeeze the fruit and strain the juice into a large bowl. Reserve the fruit shells, pulp and pips.

Scrape all the pith from the shells and put it in a large bowl with the pulp and pips. Add 2 litres/ 3½ pints water and set aside. Shred the orange and lemon peel finely and add it to the bowl of juice. Stir in 2 litres/3½ pints water. Leave both mixtures to soak for 24 hours if liked.

Line a strainer with muslin and strain the liquid containing the pips into a preserving pan. Bring up the sides of the muslin and tie to make a bag containing the pith, pips and pulp. Add the bag to the pan, with the contents of the second bowl.

Bring the liquid to simmering point and simmer for 1½ hours or until the peel is tender. Remove from the heat. Squeeze the muslin bag between two plates over the pan to extract as much of the pectin-rich juice as possible (see Mrs Beeton's Tip).

Measure the liquid, return it to the pan and add 800 g/1¾ lb sugar for every litre/1¾ pints of juice. Heat gently until the sugar has dissolved, then bring to the boil and boil fast until setting point is reached. Remove from the heat and skim quickly.

Leave to cool slightly until a skin forms on the surface of the marmalade, then pot and top with waxed paper discs. Cover and label when cold.

MAKES ABOUT 4 KG/9 LB

VARIATIONS

Lemon Shred Marmalade Wash and peel 675 g/1½ lb lemons. Shred the peel finely, removing some of the pith if thick. Cut up the fruit, reserving the pips, pith and coarse tissue. Put the fruit and shredded peel in a large bowl with 1 litre/1¾ pints water. Put the pips, pith and coarse tissue from the lemons in a second bowl and add 1 litre/1¾ pints water. Proceed as in the recipe above, boiling the marmalade rapidly in the final stages for about 20 minutes until setting point is reached.

Orange Marmalade Made with Honey Follow the main recipe, substituting honey for the sugar. Allow 450 g/1 lb honey for every 600 ml/1 pint of juice.

 MRS BEETON'S TIP

If a very clear jelly is required, do not squeeze the muslin bag; instead tie it to the handle and allow the liquid to drip slowly back into the pan.

DARK COARSE-CUT MARMALADE

1.5 kg/3¼ lb Seville oranges
2 lemons
3 kg/6½ lb sugar
15 ml/1 tbsp black treacle

Wash the oranges and lemons. Squeeze the fruit and strain the juice into a preserving pan. Reserve the fruit shells, pulp and pips. Slice the peel into medium-thick shreds, then add it to the pan.

Scrape all the pith from the shells and tie it loosely in a muslin bag with the pulp and pips. Add to the preserving pan with 4 litres/8 pints water. Bring the liquid to simmering point and simmer for 1½–2 hours or until the peel is tender and the liquid has reduced by at least one third. Remove from the heat. Squeeze the muslin bag gently over the pan.

Add the sugar and treacle. Return to a low heat and stir until the sugar has dissolved, then bring to the boil and boil fast until setting point is reached. Remove from the heat and skim quickly.

Leave to cool slightly until a skin forms on the surface of the marmalade, then stir, pot, and top with waxed paper discs. Cover and label when cold.

MAKES ABOUT 5 KG/11 LB

 MRS BEETON'S TIP

The quickest method of preparing fruit for marmalade is to opt for a chunky style preserve, then simply wash and chop the whole fruit, discarding pips as you work.

FIVE FRUIT MARMALADE

1 kg/2¼ lb fruit (1 orange, 1 grapefruit,
  1 lemon, 1 large apple, 1 pear)
1.5 kg/3¼ lb sugar

Wash the citrus fruit, peel it and shred the peel finely. Scrape off the pith and chop the flesh roughly. Put the pips and pith in a bowl with 500 ml/17 fl oz water. Put the peel and chopped flesh in a second, larger bowl with 1.5 litres/2¾ pints water. Leave both mixtures to soak for 24 hours if liked.

Line a strainer with muslin and strain the liquid containing the pips into a preserving pan. Bring up the sides of the muslin and tie to make a bag containing the pith and pips. Add the bag to the pan, with the contents of the second bowl. Peel and dice the apple and pear and add to the pan.

Bring the liquid to the boil, lower the heat and simmer for 1¼ hours or until the volume is reduced by one-third. Remove from the heat. Squeeze the muslin bag over the pan to extract as much of the pectin-rich juice as possible.

Return the pan to the heat, add the sugar and stir over low heat until dissolved. Bring to the boil and boil rapidly for about 30 minutes or until setting point is reached. Remove from the heat and skim quickly.

Leave to cool slightly until a skin forms on the surface of the marmalade, then stir, pot and top with waxed paper discs. Cover and label when cold.

MAKES ABOUT 2.5 KG/5½ LB

THREE FRUIT MARMALADE

One of the most popular forms of home-made marmalade, this combines the flavours of grapefruit, lemon and orange.

1 grapefruit
2 lemons
1 sweet orange
1.5 kg/3¼ lb sugar

Wash the citrus fruit, peel it and shred the peel finely or coarsely as preferred. Scrape off the pith if very thick and chop the flesh roughly. Tie the pips and any pith or coarse tissue in a muslin bag. Put the peel, chopped flesh and muslin bag in a large bowl, add 2 litres/3½ pints water and soak for 24 hours.

Next day, transfer the contents of the bowl to a preserving pan. Bring the liquid to the boil, lower the heat and simmer for 1½ hours or until the peel is tender and the contents of the pan are reduced by one third. Remove from the heat. Squeeze the muslin bag over the pan to extract as much of the juice as possible.

Return the pan to the heat, add the sugar and stir over low heat until dissolved. Bring to the boil rapidly until setting point is reached. Remove from the heat and skim quickly.

Leave to cool slightly until a skin forms on the surface of the marmalade, then stir, pot and top with waxed paper discs. Cover and label when cold.

MAKES ABOUT 2.5 KG/5½ LB

GRAPEFRUIT MARMALADE

1 kg/2¼ lb grapefruit
3 lemons
2 kg/4½ lb sugar

Wash the fruit and cut it in half. Squeeze it and strain the juice into a large bowl. Reserve the fruit shells, pulp and pips.

Scrape any thick pith from the shells and tie it in a muslin bag with the pips. Shred the peel finely and add it to the bowl of juice, with the muslin bag. Add 2 litres/3½ pints water and leave overnight to soften and bring out the flavour.

Next day, transfer the contents of the bowl to a preserving pan. Bring the liquid to the boil, lower the heat and simmer for 2 hours or until the peel is tender. Remove from the heat. Squeeze the muslin bag over the pan to extract all the juice.

Return the pan to the heat, add the sugar and stir until it has dissolved. Bring to the boil and boil fast until setting point is reached. Remove from the heat and skim quickly. Leave to cool slightly until a skin forms on the surface of the marmalade, then stir, pot and top with waxed paper discs. Cover and label when cold.

MAKES ABOUT 3.5 KG/8 LB

 PRESSURE COOKER TIP

To adapt the recipe above, reduce the quantity of water to 1.1 litres/2 pints. Combine the juice, peel, water and muslin bag in the base of the cooker, bring to 15 lb pressure and cook for 8 minutes. Reduce the pressure quickly and remove the muslin bag. Return the open cooker to heat, add sugar and finish as above.

GRAPEFRUIT AND PINEAPPLE MARMALADE

450g/1lb grapefruit
1 small pineapple
juice of 1 lemon
1.5 kg/3¼ lb sugar

Wash the grapefruit, peel it and shred the peel finely. Scrape off the pith and cut up the flesh, putting the pips, coarse tissue and a little of the pith to one side. Measure the total volume of fruit and peel; it should equal 750 ml/1¼ pints. Put the flesh and peel in a bowl with 1 litre/1¾ pints water. Combine the pips, coarse tissue and pith in a second bowl and add 500 ml/ 17 fl oz water. Leave both mixtures to soak for 24 hours.

Next day, line a strainer with muslin and strain the liquid containing the pips into a preserving pan. Bring up the sides of the muslin and tie to make a bag containing the pith and pips. Add the bag to the pan, with the contents of the second bowl.

Cut the pineapple into slices, removing the skin, eyes and hard core; chop the flesh into small pieces. Measure the pineapple with the lemon juice; there should be 250 ml/8 fl oz. Add the mixture to the preserving pan.

Bring the liquid to the boil, lower the heat and simmer until the volume is reduced by one-third. Remove from the heat; squeeze out the muslin bag. Return the pan to the heat, add the sugar and stir over low heat until dissolved. Bring to the boil and boil rapidly for about 30 minutes or until setting point is reached. Remove from the heat and skim quickly.

Leave to cool slightly until a skin forms on the surface of the marmalade, then stir, pot and top with waxed paper discs. Cover and label when cold.

MAKES ABOUT 2.5 KG/5¼ LB

TANGERINE MARMALADE

Tangerine marmalade does not set readily without the addition of extra pectin.

1 kg/2¼ lb tangerines, mandarins or
**   clementines**
juice of 3 lemons
2 kg/4½ lb sugar
1 (227 g/8 oz) bottle pectin

Wash the fruit and put it into a preserving pan. Add 1 litre/1¾ pints water. Bring to the boil, lower the heat and simmer covered, for 40 minutes. When cool enough to handle, remove the peel and cut up the fruit, removing the pips and coarse tissue. Return the pips and tissue to the liquid and boil hard for 5 minutes.

Meanwhile shred half the peel; discard the rest. Strain the liquid, discarding the pips and tissue, and return to the preserving pan with the fruit, shredded peel, lemon juice and sugar.

Stir over gentle heat until the sugar has dissolved, then bring to a full rolling boil. Boil hard for 3 minutes. Remove from the heat, stir in the pectin thoroughly, then return to the heat and boil for 1 minute.

Remove from the heat and skim quickly, if necessary. Leave to cool slightly until a skin forms on the surface of the marmalade, then stir, pot and top with waxed paper discs. Cover and label when cold.

MAKES ABOUT 3 KG/6¼ LB

KUMQUAT CONSERVE

575 g/1¼ lb kumquats
1 lemon
400 g/14 oz sugar

Slice the kimquats in half and remove the pips, setting them aside. Peel the lemon, then roughly chop the flesh, setting aside the pips and any coarse tissue or pith. Tie all the trimmings in a muslin bag and put the kumquats and lemon flesh in a large saucepan. Add the muslin bag and pour in 400 ml/14 fl oz water.

Bring to the boil, lower the heat, cover the pan and simmer for 30 minutes or until the kumquats feel tender when pierced with a skewer. Squeeze out the muslin bag over the pan.

Stir the sugar into the pan, trying not to break up the fruit. Cook gently, stirring until all the sugar has dissolved, then boil until setting point is reached.

Remove from the heat and skim quickly, if necessary. Leave to cool slightly until a skin forms on the surface of the conserve, then stir, pot and top with waxed paper discs. Cover and label when cold.

MAKES ABOUT 800 G/1¾ LB

 MRS BEETON'S TIP

Kumquats are closely related to citrus fruits; the name actually means 'gold orange'. Unlike oranges, however, they have thin edible rind and may be eaten whole. When buying kumquats, look for firm fruits with a rich aromatic smell.

PINEAPPLE CONSERVE

One large or two medium pineapples should yield enough fruit for this conserve. Cut the pineapples into slices, removing the skin, eyes and hard core, then chop into small cubes.

4 lemons
450 g/1 lb fresh pineapple cubes
450 g/1 lb sugar

Cut the lemons in half and squeeze the juice into a bowl. Cut the lemon shells into quarters and tie them in a muslin bag with the pips and pulp.

Put the pineapple cubes into a preserving pan with 60 ml/4 tbsp of the lemon juice. Add the muslin bag and 150 ml/¼ pint water. Bring the liquid to the boil, lower the heat and simmer until the pineapple cubes are tender. Remove and discard the muslin bag and use a slotted spoon to transfer the pineapple to a bowl.

Add the sugar to the preserving pan and stir over low heat until dissolved. Return the pineapple cubes to the syrup. Cook until the cubes are clear and the syrup is thick. Remove from the heat and skim quickly. Leave to cool for 5 minutes, then pot, cover and label.

MAKES ABOUT 900 G/2 LB

 MRS BEETON'S TIP

It isn't always easy to tell whether a pineapple is ripe or not. A delicious aroma is a good guide, as is a dull solid sound when the side of the fruit is tapped with a finger. Good quality pineapples generally have small, compact crowns. Green fruit are not ripe.

SPICED APPLE BUTTER

3 kg/6½ lb crab-apples or windfalls
1 litre/1¾ pints cider
sugar (see method)
5 ml/1 tsp ground cloves
5 ml/1 tsp ground cinnamon

Wash the apples and cut into chunks, discarding any bruised or damaged portions. Place the preserving pan with the cider and add 1 litre/1¾ pints water. Bring to the boil, lower the heat and simmer for about 1 hour or until the fruit is tender. Sieve into a bowl.

Weigh the pulp, return it to the clean pan and simmer until it thickens. Add three-quarters of the pulp weight in sugar, with the ground spices. Stir over gentle heat until the sugar has dissolved, then boil steadily, stirring frequently, until no free liquid runs out when a small sample is cooled on a plate. Pot, cover at once, then label.

MAKES ABOUT 3.25 KG/7 LB

DAMSON CHEESE

Fruit cheeses contain a high proportion of sugar and are thus more concentrated and stiffer than other preserves. Carefully made and stored, cheeses will keep for up to two years; flavour improves with keeping.

2.75 kg/6 lb damsons
sugar (see method)
glycerine for jars

Remove the stalks and wash the fruit. Put into a heavy-bottomed saucepan or flameproof casserole (see Mrs Beeton's Tip). Add 250 ml/8 fl oz water and bring to the boil. Cover the pan, lower the heat and simmer gently for 2-3 hours or until the fruit is very tender. Drain, reserving the juice.

Have ready small clean jars without shoulders. Using perfectly clean absorbent kitchen paper, smear the inside of each jar with glycerine.

Sieve the fruit and weigh the pulp; there should be about 2.25 kg/5 lb. Put it into a preserving pan with a little of the drained juice and boil gently until very thick. Add 400 g/14 oz sugar per 450 g/1 lb fruit pulp and continue cooking, stirring all the time, until the mixture leaves the sides of the pan clean, and a spoon drawn across the base of the pan leaves a clean line.

Spoon the cheese into the prepared jars, knocking them several times on the table top while filling to force out any air holes. Cover while still hot, cool, then label.

Store for several weeks, then use like jam. For a traditional stiff cheese, store for at least a year, then turn out, slice and serve with gingerbread, butter and Cheshire or Lancashire cheese.

MAKES ABOUT 3.25 KG/7 LB

 MRS BEETON'S TIP

The fruit may be baked in a traditional ovenproof earthenware jar, if preferred. It will require 2-3 hours in a preheated 110°C/225°F/gas ¼ oven.

MINCEMEAT

200 g/7 oz cut mixed peel
200 g/7 oz seedless raisins
25 g/1 oz preserved stem ginger
200 g/7 oz cooking apples
200 g/7 oz shredded suet
200 g/7 oz sultanas
200 g/7 oz currants
200 g/7 oz soft light brown sugar
50 g/2 oz chopped blanched almonds
generous pinch each of mixed spice, ground
    ginger and ground cinnamon
grated rind and juice of 2 lemons and 1
    orange
150 ml/¼ pint brandy, sherry or rum

Mince or finely chop the peel, raisins and ginger. Peel, core and grate the apples. Combine all the ingredients in a very large bowl, cover and leave to stand for two days in a cool place, stirring occasionally (see Mrs Beeton's Tip). Pot, cover and label. Store in a cool, dry place.

MAKES ABOUT 1.8 KG/4 LB

VARIATIONS

Use a vegetarian 'suet' if you prefer a mincemeat free from animal products. If an alcohol-free mincemeat is desired, use apple juice instead of brandy and store the jars in the refrigerator if not using at once. Alternatively, freeze for up to 6 months.

 MRS BEETON'S TIP

Observing the standing and stirring time helps to stop the mincemeat from fermenting later.

LEMON CURD

Lemon curd is not a true preserve but it keeps for a while in the refrigerator. Use very fresh eggs bought from a reputable source.

2 lemons
225 g/8 oz lump or granulated sugar
75 g/3 oz butter, cut up
3 eggs

Wash, dry and grate the lemons. Squeeze out the juice and put it with the sugar in the top of a double saucepan or heatproof bowl set over boiling water. Stir occasionally until the sugar has dissolved. Remove from the heat and stir in the butter. Leave to cool.

Beat the eggs lightly in a bowl. Pour the cooled lemon mixture over them, mix well, then strain the mixture back into the pan or bowl. Place over gentle heat, stirring frequently until the mixture thickens enough to coat the back of a wooden spoon lightly. Pour into warmed clean jars. Cover with waxed paper discs. Put on lids and label when cold. Leave for 24 hours to thicken; store in the refrigerator. Use within 2-3 weeks.

MAKES ABOUT 450 G/1 LB

VARIATION

Orange Curd Substitute 2 oranges and add the juice of 1 lemon. Use only 50 g/2 oz butter, melting it in the double saucepan or bowl before adding the rind, juices and sugar.

LEMON MINCEMEAT

2 large lemons
900 g/2 lb cooking apples, peeled, cored and
    minced
225 g/8 oz shredded suet
450 g/1 lb currants
225 g/8 oz sugar
75 g/3 oz candied citron and lemon or
    orange peel, chopped
10 ml/2 tsp ground mixed spice

Wash, dry and pare the lemons thinly, avoiding the pith. Place the rind in a small saucepan
with water to cover. Bring to the boil, lower the
heat and simmer for 15 minutes, or until the
rind is tender. Drain and chop the rind. Squeeze
the lemons and put the juice in a mixing bowl.

Add the apples to the bowl with the lemon rind,
suet, currants, sugar, candied peel and spice.
Stir well, cover tightly and leave for 1 week,
stirring occasionally.

The mincemeat will be ready to use at the end
of the week; however, it may be potted or put in
containers, covered tightly and stored in a cool
place for a further 2-3 weeks. It will also freeze
well.

MAKES ABOUT 2.25 KG/5 LB

EXCELLENT MINCEMEAT

3 large cooking apples, cored
3 large lemons
450 g/1 lb raisins
450 g/1 lb currants
450 g/1 lb suet
900 g/2 lb soft light brown sugar
25 g/1 oz candied orange peel, chopped
25 g/1 oz candied citron or lemon peel,
    chopped
30 ml/2 tbsp orange marmalade
250 ml/8 fl oz brandy

Set the oven at 200°C/400°F/gas 6. Place the
apples in an ovenproof dish, cover tightly and
bake for 50-60 minutes, until thoroughly
tender. Leave to cool.

Wash, dry and grate the lemons. Squeeze out
the juice and reserve with the rind. Chop the
shells, place them in a small saucepan and add
cold water to cover. Bring to the boil, lower the
heat and cover the pan. Simmer for about 1
hour, or until the shells are soft enough to chop
very finely. Drain, cool and chop.

Scoop the apple flesh from the skins. Place it in
a large bowl. Stir in the reserved lemon rind
and juice with all the remaining ingredients.
Cover the bowl and leave for 2 days, stirring
occasionally. Pot, pressing the mincemeat
down well. Cover tightly and store for at least 2
weeks before using.

MAKES ABOUT 4 KG/9 LB

Bottled Fruits
and Syrups

Preserve the best of the summer fruits ready for very special, particularly easy, winter desserts. As well as bottled fruits, this chapter includes wonderful fruit syrups to serve with waffles, ice cream and sponge puddings. Both bottled fruits and syrups also make very acceptable gifts.

Here is a selection of preserves that may be served for the sweet course of a meal. Fruit syrups to serve with hot and cold puddings are also included.

BOTTLED FRUIT

Bottled fruits are excellent served very simply with cream or they may be served with pancakes, as a filling for a gâteau, with meringues and whipped cream or in a sponge flan. They are the superior convenience foods.

For success and food safety, it is vital to follow the timings and instructions exactly when bottling fruit. The cooking method and the timings given ensure that any bacteria present are killed. When the jars are sealed, following the instructions in this chapter, all outside moulds and other micro-organisms that could spoil the food are kept out while the fruit is stored.

Before storing bottled fruit always check that each jar is sealed. Should you discover a reject jar within a day of the fruit being processed, transfer the fruit to a covered container, chill it and use it within two days, as you would fresh poached fruit. If you discover that the seal on bottled fruit is gone some time after it has been stored, discard the contents in case they have been contaminated with organisms that may cause food poisoning.

Similarly, if you find that fruit is fermenting or that it looks or tastes strange, discard it for safety's sake.

FRUIT SYRUPS

Capture the flavour of summer fruits in syrups that may be used for flavouring desserts. The syrups may be used to sweeten and flavour mousses, jellies, trifles or many other desserts. For the simplest of desserts, spoon a little home-made fruit syrup over good vanilla ice cream.

PREPARATION AND PROCESSING OF BOTTLED FRUIT

Bottled fruit is preserved by heating. The fruit and liquid in the jar are heated to high enough temperature, and for sufficient time, to kill micro-organisms (bacteria, yeasts and moulds). The jar must be sealed while the contents are at the high temperature to prevent any new micro-organisms from entering.

EQUIPMENT

Preserving Jars Special preserving jars must be used for bottled fruit. They are manufactured to withstand high temperatures and to form an airtight seal when the contents are processed correctly. The jars must be in good condition; any that are chipped, cracked or damaged in any way will not seal properly even if they do withstand the temperature during processing.

There are two types of preserving jars: screw band jars or clip jars. Screw bands, made of metal or plastic, usually have a built-in rubber (or plastic) ring which provides the seal. New screw bands or sealing rings may be purchased and they should be replaced after each use. Screw bands should be loosened by a quarter turn before processing to allow for expansion when the jars are heated.

Clip jars have metal clips and separate rubber rings to seal the lids. The rubber rings should be replaced each time they are used, otherwise they will not seal the jar properly. Old, unused rubber rings should not be used as they tend to perish during prolonged storage. The metal clips expand slightly as they are heated so these jars are sealed before processing.

Saucepan and Stand The fruit may be processed in the oven or in a saucepan. The saucepan must be deep enough to submerge the jars or bottles in water. The bottles must be placed on a stand in the base of the saucepan. Slats of wood may be placed in the bottom of the saucepan or a thick pad of newspaper may be used as a stand for the jars.

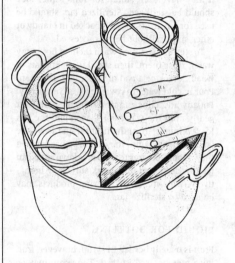

Oven Method If the fruit is processed in the oven, the jars are placed on a pad of paper in a roasting tin.

Tongs, Thermometer, Oven Glove and Wooden Board Special preserving tongs are best for lifting the hot jars out of a saucepan; they are also useful for lifting jars processed in the oven. A thermometer should be used to check the temperature of the water when processing. An oven glove is essential for holding the jars and a clean, dry wooden board must be used as a stand for hot jars. Hot jars that are placed on a cold or damp surface will crack.

PREPARING THE JARS

The jars must be spotlessly clean. They should be washed in hot, soapy water, rinsed in hot or boiling water and allowed to drain upside down on clean tea-towels. The jars should be left upside down to drain until they are filled.

If the jars are particularly dirty (for example if they have been stored for some time) they should be sterilized. Sterilized jars should be used for any fruits that are packed in brandy or other spirit without being processed.

To sterilize jars, first wash them in hot soapy water, rinse them, then stand them on slats of wood, a rack or a pad of paper in a deep pan. Pour in cold water to cover the jars completely. Put any lids, clips and rings into the pan. Heat gently until the water boils, then boil the jars for 5 minutes. Turn the heat off and leave the jars submerged until they are to be used, when they should be drained upside down on clean tea-towels spread on a work surface. Alternatively, wine-making sterilizing products may be used to sterilize jars.

LIQUID FOR BOTTLING

Fruit is usually bottled in syrup; however, fruit juice may be used instead. The syrup may be combined with brandy or other spirits or liqueurs, or it may be flavoured with spices, such as cinnamon sticks or cloves. Strips of orange or lemon rind may also be used to flavour the syrup.

Syrup There is no rule about the quantity of sugar used in a syrup for bottling. Heavy syrups tend to make the fruit rise in the jar which spoils the appearance of the preserve (only a problem if the bottled fruit is prepared for a competition or exhibition). Brown sugar may be used if preferred but the fruit will take on the dark colour. Honey may also be used to sweeten the bottling liquid. The following is a guide to quantities of sugar to add to 1 litre/1¾ pints of water when making syrup.

light syrup	200 g/7 oz (for apples)
medium syrup	400–575 g/14 oz–1¼ lb (for all fruit)
heavy syrup	800 g/1¾ lb (for peaches)

Dissolve the sugar in the water, bring to the boil and boil for 2 minutes. Remove from the heat and cover the pan to prevent any extra water from evaporating.

PREPARING THE FRUIT

Only bottle perfectly fresh, prime-quality fruit. Wash, dry and trim the fruit, then cut it into even-sized pieces if necessary. Avoid over-handling the fruit. Soft fruits, in particular, should be handled as little as possible to avoid bruising or spoiling them. Scald a wooden spoon and use its handle to ease the fruit into position when packing the jars. The fruit should be closely packed but not squashed. Apples may be solid packed, leaving little air space or room for syrup.

Apples Peel, core and cut into 5 mm/¼ inch thick slices or rings. Put into brine until all the apples are prepared to prevent discoloration. Drain and rinse well, then dry before packing. For solid packs, blanch apples in boiling water for 2 minutes, drain and pack.

Apricots Ripe, not soft, apricots may be bottled whole or halved with stones removed. Crack some stones and add a few kernels to jars of halved fruit.

Blackberries Select large, fully ripe fruit.

Cherries Select plump fruit with small stones. Morello cherries are best. Remove stalks. Stone fruit if liked, reserving all juice to add to syrup.

Currants (black, red or white) Select large, ripe fruit. String and pack. Redcurrants and whitecurrants have large seeds and are best mixed with raspberries.

Damsons Remove stalks. Wipe to remove bloom. Pack whole.

Gooseberries Select green, hard and unripe fruit. Top and tail, then cut off a small slice at each end if preserving in syrup to prevent skins from shrivelling. Use a stainless steel knife to cut the fruit.

Loganberries Select firm, deep red fruit. Remove stalks and discard any fruit attacked by maggots.

Mulberries Bottle freshly picked fruit that is not overripe.

Peaches or Nectarines A free-stone variety is best so that the stone may be removed easily. Pour freshly boiling water over fruit, or plunge the fruit into a pan of boiling water, and leave for 30–60 seconds. Drain and skin. Halve the peaches and remove their stones. Work quickly as peaches discolour on standing.

Pears (cooking) Firm cooking pears should be prepared as for dessert pears, then poached in medium syrup until tender. Use the cooking syrup for packing the fruit.

Pears (dessert) Select fruit that is just ripe, for example Conference or William's. Peel, halve and scoop out cores with any loose fibrous flesh. Submerge prepared fruit in acidulated water (water with lemon juice added) or lemon juice until ready to pack. Drain or rinse before packing if the flavour of the lemon juice is not required.

Pineapple Trim, peel and core. Remove all the eyes and cut the fruit into rings or cubes.

Plums Select Victoria plums that are fully grown, firm and just turning pink. Select purple varieties that are still bright red. Yellow plums should be firm and lemon-yellow in colour. Trim and wipe to remove bloom. Free-stone varieties may be halved and stoned, others should be left whole as the flesh easily becomes mushy.

Raspberries Fruit must not be overripe. Pack freshly picked raspberries.

Rhubarb Select tender young rhubarb. Cut it into short lengths and pack. For a tight pack (not quite a solid pack), soak the prepared rhubarb in medium syrup for 8–12 hours. The rhubarb shrinks during soaking. When hard water is used for bottling rhubarb, a harmless white deposit collects on the top of the liquid. Use boiled or softened water to avoid this.

Strawberries Hull the fruit. Soak prepared strawberries in syrup as for rhubarb.

PROCESSING METHODS

Follow these instructions very closely. When packing different fruits together, follow the highest temperature and longest processing time suggested for the types of fruit used.

QUICK DEEP PAN METHOD

1 Prepare the syrup or botting liquid and the fruit. Pack the fruit into prepared jars and heat the syrup or bottling liquid to 60°C/140°F.

2 Have ready a saucepan deep enough to submerge the jars. Place a rack, wooden slats or a thick pad of newspaper in the bottom of the pan, then half fill it with water. Heat the water to 38°C/100°F.

3 Check the temperature of the syrup or packing liquid, making sure it is still 60°C/140°F, then pour it into the jars. Dislodge any air bubbles from between the pieces of fruit by gently shaking the jars. The jars should be just overflowing with liquid.

4 Dip rubber rings (if used) in boiling water and put them on the jars. Fix the lids with metal clips. Put on screw bands, tighten them, then undo them by a quarter turn to allow room for each jar to expand as it is heated.

5 Stand the jars in the saucepan and make sure that they are submerged in the water. The jars must not touch each other or the side of the pan.
6 Cover the pan and bring to 90°C/194°F in 20–25 minutes. Simmer for time indicated in chart below. Using wooden tongs, transfer jars to a wooden surface. Tighten screw bands, if used. Clips should hold properly without attention. Leave for 24 hours.
7 Test the seal on each jar by removing the screw bands or clips and lifting the jars by their lids. If the lids stay firm they are properly sealed. Label and store.

PROCESSING TIMES FOR QUICK DEEP PAN METHOD

The following times are for jars with a maximum capacity of 1 litre/1¾ pints:

2 minutes	apple rings, blackberries, currants, gooseberries (for cooked puddings), loganberries, mulberries, raspberries, rhubarb (for cooked puddings), damsons and strawberries
10 minutes	apricots, cherries, gooseberries (for cold desserts), whole plums, greengages, rhubarb (for cold desserts) and solid packs of soft fruit (excluding strawberries)
20 minutes	solid pack apples, nectarines, peaches, pineapples, halved plums and solid pack strawberries
40 minutes	whole tomatoes, pears
50 minutes	tomatoes (in own juice)

MODERATE OVEN METHOD

The traditional oven method processes the fruit in the oven before adding the syrup; however, the fruit tends to shrink when processed without the syrup. The following method heats the fruit in the syrup to keep shrinkage to the minimum.

1 Set the oven at 150°C/300°F/gas 2. Fill warmed jars with the prepared fruit.
2 Pour in boiling syrup or the chosen liquid to within 2 cm/¾ inch of the top of each jar.
3 Dip rubber rings (if used) and lids in boiling water and fit them on the jars. Do not fit clips and screw bands.
4 Line a roasting tin with three or four layers of newspaper. Stand the jars 5 cm/2 inches apart on the paper.
5 Put the jars in the middle of the oven and process for the times given in the table opposite.
6 Prepare a clean, dry wooden surface on which to stand the jars. Immediately check that the necks of the jars are clean, wiping them with absorbent kitchen paper, and fit the screw bands or clips. **Do not wipe the jars with a damp cloth or they will crack**.
7 Leave for 24 hours before testing the seal by removing the screw bands or clips and lifting the jars by their lids. If the lids stay firm they are properly sealed. Label and store.

PROCESSING TIMES FOR MODERATE OVEN METHOD

Note 4 (350 ml/12 fl oz) jars require the same processing time as 2 (700 ml/1 pint 3½ fl oz) jars.

30–40 minutes (up to 2 kg/ 4½ lb) *or* 50–60 minutes (2–4.5 kg/ 4½–10 lb)	apple rings, blackberries, currants, gooseberries (for cooked puddings), loganberries, mulberries, raspberries and rhubarb
40–50 minutes (up to 2 kg/ 4½ lb) *or* 55–70 minutes (2–4.5 kg/ 4½–10 lb)	apricots, cherries, damsons, gooseberries (for cold desserts), whole plums and rhubarb (for cold desserts)
50–60 minutes (up to 2 kg/ 4½ lb) *or* 65–80 minutes (2–4.5 kg/ 4½–10 lb)	solid pack apples, nectarines, peaches, pineapple and halved plums
60–70 minutes (up to 2 kg/ 4½ lb) *or* 75–90 minutes (2–4.5 kg/ 4½–10 lb)	pears

STORING BOTTLED FRUIT

Store the sealed jars or bottles in a cool, dark, dry cupboard.

APRICOTS IN BRANDY

1.8 kg/4 lb apricots
225 g/8 oz sugar
250 ml/8 fl oz brandy

You will need three (450 g/1 lb) preserving jars. Sterilize the jars (see page 902) and drain thoroughly, then warm in an oven set at 120°C/250°F/gas ½. Wash and drain the apricots and prick them with a darning needle. Pour 300 ml/½ pint water into a large heavy-bottomed saucepan or preserving pan. Add 100 g/4 oz of the sugar; heat gently, stirring, until dissolved.

Add enough of the apricots to cover the base of the pan in a single layer. Bring the syrup back to the boil and remove the riper fruit at once. Firmer fruit should be boiled for 2 minutes, but do not let it become too soft. As the fruit is ready, transfer it to the warmed jars, using a slotted spoon.

Add the remaining sugar to the syrup in the pan, lower the temperature and stir until the sugar has dissolved. Boil the syrup, without stirring, until it registers 105°C/220°F on a sugar thermometer, the thread stage (see page 862). Remove the syrup from the heat.

Measure out 250 ml/8 fl oz of the syrup. Stir in the brandy, then pour the mixture over the apricots, covering them completely.

Process the jars following the instructions and timings given for apricots, either by the Quick Deep Pan Method or by the Moderate Oven Method. When cold, test the seals, label the jars and store for at least 1 month in a cool place before opening.

MAKES ABOUT 1.4 KG/3 LB

FRUIT SYRUPS

Fruit syrups may be made from overripe fruit which is not worth freezing or bottling. The juice is extracted from the fruit, then it is sweetened and processed so that it may be stored until required.

EXTRACTING THE JUICE

Cold Method   This method yields the best-flavoured juice. Place the fruit in a large china or earthenware bowl and crush it with a wooden spoon. Cover the bowl and leave the fruit for 4–5 days, crushing it daily. During this standing time, the pectin which is naturally present in the fruit breaks down and the juice is released. The process may be speeded up, or tough fruits such as blackcurrants may be encouraged to soften, by adding a pectin-decomposing enzyme which may be purchased from a wine-making supplier.

Hot Method   Place the fruit in a bowl over simmering water. Crush the fruit. Add 600 ml/1 pint water for each 1 kg/2¼ lb blackcurrants or 100 ml/3½ fl oz for each 1 kg/2¼ lb blackberries. Other soft fruits do not need water. Heat the fruit gently until the juice flows easily, which will take about 1 hour for 3 kg/6½ lb fruit. Check that the water in the saucepan does not boil dry.

Straining the Juice   Strain the juice through a scalded jelly bag into a large bowl. For a clear result strain the juice twice. Achieving a clear result is not essential when making syrups, so the juice may be strained through a sieve lined with scalded muslin.

 MRS BEETON'S TIP

Steam juice extractors may be purchased to ease the hot method and for processing large quantities of fruit, including apples.

SWEETENING AND PROCESSING THE JUICE

Measure the juice, pour it into a bowl and stir in 600 g/1 lb 5 oz sugar for each 1 litre/1¾ pints. Stir until the sugar dissolves – you may have to stand the bowl over a pan of simmering water.

Have ready thoroughly cleaned strong bottles with screw tops. Boil the tops for 5 minutes. Pour the syrup into the bottles, leaving 2 cm/¾ inch headspace at the top of each. Tighten the caps, then loosen them by a quarter turn. Stand the bottles on a thick pad of newspaper in a deep saucepan and pour in cold water to come up to the top of the bottles. Wedge pieces of cardboard or crumpled foil between the bottles to hold them upright.

Heat the water to 77°C/170°F and keep it at that temperature for 30 minutes. If the water is brought to 88°C/190°F it must be maintained for 20 minutes.

Have ready a clean, dry wooden board. Transfer the bottles to it and tighten their caps immediately. Allow to cool, label and store in a cool, dark, dry cupboard.

 FREEZER TIP

Instead of bottling the syrup, pour it into suitable freezer containers and freeze when cold. Freezing is the easiest, and safest, storage method.

BLACKBERRY OR BLACKCURRANT SYRUP

Blackberry or blackcurrant syrups may be used to flavour mousses, ice cream, jelly or jellied desserts. This recipe produces a concentrated syrup which may be trickled in small quantities over ice cream or dessert pancakes.

blackberries or blackcurrants
1 kg/2¼ lb crushed sugar or preserving sugar
    and 15 ml/1 tbsp water for each 1 kg/2¼ lb
    of fruit
125 ml/4 fl oz brandy for each 1 litre/1¾ pints
    of syrup

Put the fruit, sugar and water (if used) in a large heatproof bowl. Cover with foil or a plate. Stand the bowl over a saucepan of simmering water and cook the fruit gently until the juice flows freely.

Strain the juice through a scalded jelly bag or sieve lined with scalded muslin. Measure it and pour it into a preserving pan.

Bring the juice to the boil, then lower the heat and simmer it for 20 minutes. Skim the syrup and leave to cool.

Add the brandy, then bottle the syrup, leaving 2 cm/¾ inch headspace.

Put lids on the bottles and process the syrup following the instructions opposite. Tighten the lids at once, then cool, label and store the syrup.

APRICOT SYRUP

Apricot syrup makes an unusual dessert sauce to go with pancakes, waffles or fruit fritters as well as with ice cream. Whip a little of the syrup with double cream and use to fill profiteroles or meringues.

sound ripe apricots
800 g/1¾ lb lump sugar, crushed, for each
    1 litre/1¾ pints of juice

Stone and halve the apricots, then put them in a large heatproof bowl. Crack half the stones and stir the kernels into the fruit.

Stand the bowl over a saucepan of water and simmer until the fruit is quite soft and the juice flows freely. Crush the fruit occasionally.

Strain the liquid through a scalded jelly bag or sieve lined with scalded muslin. Measure the juice and weigh out the sugar. Place the sugar in a saucepan and add the juice. Heat, stirring, until the sugar dissolves, then bring to the boil. Lower the heat and simmer for 10 minutes.

Skim the syrup and pour it into warmed clean, dry bottles. Leave 2 cm/¾ inch headspace and process the syrup following the instructions opposite. Tighten the caps, label and store.

VARIATIONS

Substitute cherries, greengages, peaches, plums or rhubarb for apricots.

FIG SYRUP

A rich syrup to complement tangy fruit desserts: trickle a little over fresh orange segments and serve them as a topping for waffles or use the syrup with fresh orange juice to flavour home-made ice cream.

3 lemons
1 kg/2¼ lb sound, ripe, fresh figs
800 g/1¾ lb lump sugar, crushed, for each
1 litre/1¾ pints of liquid

Use a potato peeler to pare the lemon rind thinly. Squeeze out and strain the lemon juice.

Slice the figs and put them in a bowl with 2.25 litres/4 pints water. Add the lemon rind and juice. Stand the bowl over a saucepan of simmering water and cook gently for 3 hours. Check to ensure the pan does not boil dry.

Strain the fruit through a scalded jelly bag or fine sieve lined with scalded muslin. Measure the juice carefully.

Pour the juice into a large saucepan and add the sugar. Stir until the sugar has dissolved, then bring to the boil, lower the heat and simmer for 10 minutes.

Skim the syrup and set aside until quite cold. Bottle, leaving 2 cm/½ inch headspace, and process as described on page 902.

CRANBERRY SYRUP

Cranberry syrup has an excellent, rich and fruity flavour with a good bright colour. Use it to pep up bought vanilla ice cream or add it to chilled custard to make an unusual fool. It also tastes good with pancakes, waffles or steamed sponge puddings.

sound ripe cranberries
800 g/1¾ lb lump sugar, crushed for each
1 litre/1¾ pints of juice

Place the fruit in a heatproof bowl and crush it with a wooden spoon. Stand the bowl over a saucepan of simmering water. Cook gently for 2 hours. Check that the saucepan does not boil dry, adding more boiling water as necessary.

Strain the liquid through a scalded jelly bag or sieve lined with scalded muslin. Measure carefully, pour into a saucepan and add sugar in the proportion given above.

Bring to the boil, lower the heat and cook for 15 minutes. Skim, then leave until cold.

Pour the syrup into thoroughly clean bottles, leaving 2 cm/½ inch headspace. Process following the instructions on page 902.

VARIATIONS

Use gooseberries, raspberries or strawberries.

Pickles

A selection of pickles is a prerequisite of a good pantry to complement cold meats, cheeses and home-made crackers. The selection of recipes in this chapter also includes interesting preserves to complement spiced dishes.

Vinegar is the main preserving agent used in pickles, sometimes with sugar. Since vinegar is a strong preservative, preparing pickles is comparatively easy with none of the pitfalls involved in achieving a good jam or marmalade.

PREPARING PICKLES

Vegetables should be prepared according to type, then salted for several hours or overnight. Sprinkle salt over every layer of vegetables. This extracts excess liquid and any bitter juices or very strong flavours. The salt should be rinsed off before pickling and the ingredients dried with absorbent kitchen paper. Brine solution may be used instead of salting vegetables.

Packing in Jars Thoroughly clean and dry jars must be well filled without squashing the vegetables or other ingredients. Unless the jars have been stored in dirty conditions (for example in a shed or outhouse) it is not necessary to sterilize them: a very hot wash and rinse with very hot or boiling water is adequate. If, however, the jars have been neglected for a long period and have become mouldy or very dirty, follow the instructions on page 902 for sterilizing them.

Vinegar White or distilled vinegar, cider vinegar or white wine vinegar gives pickles the best colour. Dark vinegars discolour the vegetables or fruit. The vinegar may be spiced, flavoured or sweetened as required.

Spiced vinegar may be used hot, immediately after straining, or cold. Opinions differ as to the best method but as a rule cold vinegar is always safest and should always be used for eggs and fruit whose texture may suffer from having boiling vinegar poured over them.

Pour the vinegar into the jars, shaking them gently to free any trapped air bubbles. Check the vinegar level about 24 hours after bottling the pickles, and add extra to cover the pickles if necessary.

Maturing Leave the pickles to mature for 1–3 weeks before using. Pickled eggs (hard-boiled eggs which are simply shelled and packed in jars promptly after cooking) should be left for a week; onions and other vegetables for at least 2–3 weeks.

STORING PICKLES

Cover with airtight lids, making sure that the lids do not have any exposed metal which will react with the vinegar. Label and store in a cool, dark cupboard.

Pickled eggs and fruit keep for up to 3 months. Properly stored, most vegetables keep for 6–9 months. Red cabbage should be eaten within 3 months as it tends to soften and become limp with prolonged storage.

PICKLED ONIONS

This is a recipe for onions without tears. Soaking the unskinned onions in brine makes them easy to peel.

450 g/1 lb salt
1.4 kg/3 lb pickling onions
2.25 litres/4 pints cold Spiced Vinegar (page 925)
5 ml/1 tsp mustard seeds (optional)

Dissolve half the salt in 2 litres/3½ pints of water in a large bowl. Add the onions. Set a plate inside the bowl to keep the onions submerged, weighting the plate with a jar filled with water. Do not use a can as the salt water would corrode it. Leave for 24 hours.

Drain and skin the onions and return them to the clean bowl. Make up a fresh solution of brine, using the rest of the salt and a further 2 litres/3½ pints water. Pour it over the onions, weight as before and leave for a further 24 hours.

Drain the onions, rinse them thoroughly to remove excess salt, and drain again. Pack into wide-mouthed jars. Cover with cold spiced vinegar, adding a few mustard seeds to each jar, if liked. Cover with vinegar-proof lids. Label and store in a cool, dark place. Keep for at least 1 month before using.

MAKES ABOUT 1.4 KG/3 LB

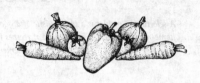

PICKLED RED CABBAGE

Do not make too much of this pickle at one time, as it will lose its crispness if stored for longer than two or three months.

1 firm red cabbage
100–150 g/4–5 oz salt
2–3 onions, very thinly sliced
soft dark brown sugar (see method)
600–900 ml/1–1½ pints Spiced Vinegar (page 925)

Remove any discoloured outer leaves from the cabbage, cut it into quarters and then into shreds. Layer the shreds in a large bowl, sprinkling each layer with salt. Cover the bowl and leave overnight. Next day, rinse the cabbage, drain it very thoroughly in a colander, pressing out all the surplus liquid.

Pack a 7.5 cm/3 inch layer of cabbage in a large glass jar. Cover with a layer of onion and sprinkle with 5 ml/1 tsp brown sugar. Repeat the layers until the jar is full, using additional jars if necessary. Fill the jar or jars with spiced vinegar. Cover with vinegar-proof lids. Label and store in a cool, dark place. Keep for at least 1 week before using.

MAKES ABOUT 1.4 KG/3 LB

PICKLED HORSERADISH

Fresh horseradish is best for cooking, but it can be hard to come by and available only in the autumn. It can be useful to keep a few jars of pickled horseradish in the larder.

**horseradish roots
vinegar
salt**

Wash the roots in hot water, peel off the skin, then either grate or mince them. Pack loosely in small clean jars.

Horseradish does not need to be soaked in brine, but 5 ml/1 tsp salt should be added to each 250 ml/8 fl oz vinegar used for filling the jars. Pour the salted vinegar over the horseradish to cover, close the jars with vinegar-proof lids and store in a cool, dark place.

PICKLED BEETROOT

**1.4 kg/3 lb beetroot
600–750 ml/1–1¼ pints Spiced Vinegar (page 925)
15–20 g/½–¾ oz salt**

Set the oven at 180°C/350°F/gas 4. Wash the beetroot thoroughly but gently, taking care not to break the skin. Place in a roasting tin and bake for 45-60 minutes or until tender. Cool, then skin and cube. Pour the spiced vinegar into a saucepan, add the salt and bring to the boil.

Meanwhile, pack the beetroot cubes into wide-mouthed jars. Cover with boiling vinegar and put on vinegar-proof covers. Seal, label and store in a cool, dark place for 3 months before eating.

MAKES ABOUT 1.4 KG/3 LB

MIXED PICKLE

When garden and greenhouse are bursting with new young vegetables, it is a good idea to pickle some of the surplus. For this versatile recipe any of the following can be used: small cucumbers, cauliflower, baby onions, small French beans. Only the onions need to be peeled; everything else should merely be cut into suitably sized pieces.

**1 kg/2¼ lb prepared mixed vegetables
50 g/2 oz cooking salt
600–750 ml/1–1¼ pints Spiced Vinegar (page 925)**

Put all the vegetables in a large bowl, sprinkle with the salt, cover and leave for 24 houts.

Rinse, drain thoroughly, then pack into jars. Cover with cold spiced vinegar and seal with vinegar-proof covers. Store in a cool, dark place for at least 1 month before using.

MAKES ABOUT 1 KG/2¼ LB

 MRS BEETON'S TIP

A variety of covers are vinegar-proof and thus suitable for pickles and chutneys. The most obvious choice are the twist-top or screw-on plastic-coated lids used commercially. Press-on plastic covers are also suitable. Alternatively, cut a circle of clean card or paper to the size of the top of the jar. Set it in place and cover with a piece of linen dipped in melted paraffin wax. Tie the linen firmly in place.

BREAD AND BUTTER PICKLES

1.5 kg/3¼ lb large cucumbers
1.5 kg/3¼ lb small onions, thinly sliced
75 g/3 oz cooking salt
375 ml/13 fl oz white wine vinegar or
    distilled vinegar
300 g/11 oz soft light brown sugar
2.5 ml/½ tsp turmeric
2.5 ml/½ tsp ground cloves
15 ml/1 tbsp mustard seeds
2.5 ml/½ tsp celery seeds

Wash the cucumbers but do not peel them. Slice thinly. Layer with the onions and salt in a large bowl (see Mrs Beeton's Tip). Cover with a plate weighted down with a jar filled with water. Leave for 3 hours.

Rinse the vegetables thoroughly, drain and place in a large saucepan. Add the vinegar and bring to the boil. Lower the heat and simmer for 10–12 minutes or until the cucumber slices begin to soften.

Add the remaining ingredients, stirring over low heat until the sugar has dissolved. Bring to the boil, then remove from the heat. Turn the contents of the pan carefully into a large heat-proof bowl. Leave until cold. Spoon into clean jars, seal with vinegar-proof covers, label and store in a cool dark place.

MAKES ABOUT 3.25 KG/7 LB

 MRS BEETON'S TIP

To make the pickle especially crisp and crunchy, cover the final layer of cucumber with about 600 ml/1 pint crushed ice before leaving the salted mixture to stand.

PICCALILLI

This colourful pickle is made from a variety of vegetables. In addition to the selection below, chopped peppers (green, yellow and red), young broad beans, shallots or marrow may be used. The prepared mixed vegetables should weigh about 1 kg/2¼ lb.

450 g/1 lb green tomatoes, diced
½ small firm cauliflower, broken into florets
1 small cucumber, peeled, seeded and cubed
2 onions, roughly chopped
100 g/4 oz firm white cabbage, shredded
50 g/2 oz cooking salt
750 ml/1¼ pints vinegar
12 chillies
225 g/8 oz sugar
25 g/1 oz mustard powder
15 g/½ oz turmeric
30 ml/2 tbsp cornflour

Combine all the vegetables in a large bowl, sprinkle with the salt, cover and leave to stand for 24 hours. Rinse thoroughly, then drain well.

Heat the vinegar in a saucepan with the chillies. Boil for 2 minutes, leave to stand for 30 minutes, then strain the vinegar into a jug and allow to cool.

Combine the sugar, mustard, turmeric and cornflour in a large bowl. Mix to a paste with a little of the cooled vinegar. Bring the rest of the vinegar back to the boil in a saucepan, pour over the blended mixture, return to the pan; boil for 3 minutes.

Remove from the heat, stir in the drained vegetables, pack into clean jars and seal at once with vinegar-proof covers.

MAKES ABOUT 1 KG/2¼ LB

PICKLED GHERKINS

Small cucumbers known as dills or gherkins require longer processing than most vegetables.

25 (7.5 cm/3 inch) dill cucumbers
100 g/4 oz cooking salt
600 ml/1 pint Spiced Vinegar (page 925)
4–6 garlic cloves, peeled
4–6 dill sprigs

Select dill cucumbers/gherkins of the same size. Put them in a saucepan and cover with a solution of brine made in the proportion of 225 g/8 oz salt to 2 litres/3½ pints water.

Bring the liquid to just below boiling point, lower the temperature and simmer for 10 minutes. Drain and leave until cold, then pack into clean jars and cover with spiced vinegar. Add 1 garlic clove and 1 dill sprig to each jar. Seal with vinegar-proof cover, label and store in a cool, dark place.

MAKES ABOUT 1.4 KG/3 LB

PICKLED PEARS

10 ml/2 tsp whole cloves
10 ml/2 tsp allspice berries
5 ml/1 tsp crushed cinnamon stick
small piece of root ginger, bruised
225 g/8 oz sugar
300 ml/½ pint vinegar
1 kg/2¼ lb cooking pears

Crush the spices together and tie in a piece of muslin. Combine the sugar and vinegar in a saucepan. Add the muslin bag and heat until the sugar has dissolved.

Peel and core the pears, cut into eighths and simmer gently in the sweetened spiced vinegar until tender but not overcooked or broken. Lift out and pack in warm clean jars. Remove the muslin bag, pressing it to extract liquid.

Continue to boil the vinegar until it thickens slightly, then pour it over the pears to fill each jar. Leave until cold, then seal securely with vinegar-proof covers. Label and store in a cool, dry place for 2–3 months before use.

MAKES ABOUT 1.25 KG/2¾ LB

PICKLED NASTURTIUM SEEDS

Pickled nasturtium seeds are a good substitute for capers.

nasturtium seeds
brine in the proportion 100 g/4 oz salt to 1
  litre/1¾ pints water
Spiced Vinegar (page 925)
tarragon leaves (optional)

Gather the seeds while still green on a dry day. Steep them in a bowl of brine for 24 hours.

Set the oven at 150°C/300°F/gas 2. Drain the nasturtium seeds, rinse and drain again. Pack in small clean jars (see Mrs Beeton's Tip), place on a baking sheet and warm in the oven for 10 minutes.

Meanwhile boil enough spiced vinegar to cover the seeds. Fill the jars with vinegar, adding a few leaves of tarragon to each, if liked. Store in the refrigerator.

 MRS BEETON'S TIP

It is important to use small jars so that the contents can be used at once when opened.

SPICED PEACH PICKLE

2 kg/4½ lb peaches, peeled (see Mrs Beeton's
  Tip, page 887)
20 g/¾ oz whole cloves
20 g/¾ oz allspice berries
1 cinnamon stick, broken in short lengths
1 kg/2¼ lb sugar
1 litre/1¾ pints distilled vinegar

Cut the peaches in half. Remove the stones,
crack a few of them and put the kernels in a
small saucepan. Add water to cover, bring to
the boil and blanch for 3 minutes. Drain.

Tie the spices in muslin and place with the
sugar and vinegar in a preserving pan or heavy-
bottomed saucepan. Heat gently to dissolve the
sugar, then bring to the boil. Lower the heat,
stir in the peaches, and simmer until the fruit is
just tender, but not overcooked or broken.

Using a slotted spoon, transfer the peach halves
to warm clean jars, adding a few of the
blanched kernels to each. Continue to boil the
liquid in the pan until it thickens, then remove
the bag of spices and pour the liquid into the
jars. Put on vinegar-proof covers while hot.
When cold, label and store in a cool dark place
for at least a week.

MAKES ABOUT 3.25 KG/7 LB

 MRS BEETON'S TIP

Cinnamon is the dried bark of an evergreen
tree belonging to the laurel family. Its
sweet aromatic flavour is much valued in
cakes, puddings, beef and lamb dishes,
where the ground form is generally used.
Stick cinnamon is used in pickling, making mulled drinks, in stewed fruits and to
flavour sugar in the same way as a vanilla
pod might be used.

PICKLED WALNUTS

*One of the most delicious pickles and an integral part
of the Boxing Day cold table. Use green walnuts
whose shells have not begun to form. Prick well with
a stainless steel fork; if the shell can be felt – and it
begins forming opposite the stalk, about 5 mm/¼
inch from the end – do not use the walnut.*

soft green walnuts
brine in the proportion 100 g/4 oz salt to 1
  litre/1¾ pints water
Spiced Vinegar (page 925)

Place the pricked walnuts in a large bowl, cover
with brine and leave to soak for about 6 days.
Drain, cover with a fresh solution of brine and
leave to soak for 7 days more. Drain again and
spread in a single layer on greaseproof paper.
Cover loosely with more paper, then leave,
preferably in sunshine for 1–2 days or until
blackened.

Pack into warm clean jars. Bring the spiced
vinegar to the boil and fill the jars. When cold,
put on vinegar-proof covers. Store in a cool
dark place for at least 1 month before using.

 MRS BEETON'S TIP

Always wear gloves when handling walnuts to avoid staining your hands.

PICKLED LEMONS

6 thick-skinned lemons
salt
750 ml–1 litre/1¼–1¾ pints vinegar
6–8 whole peppercorns
2.5 cm/1 inch fresh root ginger, bruised
75–175 g/3–6 oz mustard seed
12 garlic cloves, sliced

Slit the lemons lengthways into quarters, but do not cut right through. Rub dry salt sparingly into the cuts. Put the lemons in a shallow dish, cover and leave in a cool place for 5 days or until all the salt has dissolved, turning the lemons occasionally in the liquor that forms.

Drain the lemons, reserving the liquor in a saucepan. Pack 2 lemons into each of 3 warm clean jars. Add the vinegar to the lemon liquor, with the peppercorns and ginger. Bring to the boil, skim well, then set aside to cool.

Add 25–50 g/1–2 oz mustard seeds and 4 sliced garlic cloves to each jar. Fill with the vinegar mixture, seal with vinegar-proof covers, label and store in a cool place.

MAKES THREE JARS

VARIATION

Mrs Beeton's Pickled Lemons Wash and dry whole lemons, then place in brine or sprinkle generously with salt and leave for 6 days, turning often. Drain and cook in boiling water for 15 minutes. Drain and pack in jars. Spice the vinegar with 15 g/½ oz each of cloves and white peppercorns, 25 g/1 oz bruised root ginger, 25 g/1 oz mustard seeds, 7 g/¼ oz each of blades of mace and dried red chillies, 30 ml/2 tbsp grated horseradish and 4 halved garlic cloves instead of ingredients above. Finish as in the main recipe.

PICKLED MELON OR PUMPKIN

2 large melons (honeydew or cantaloup) or
  2 pumpkins
750 ml/1¼ pints white vinegar
675 g/1½ lb sugar
5 ml/1 tsp celery salt
2 long cinnamon sticks
15 ml/1 tbsp white mustard seeds
6 whole cloves
25 g/1 oz fresh root ginger, grated

Halve the melons or pumpkins and discard their seeds. Cut into wedges. Peel the wedges, then cut the flesh into small cubes. Put the cubes in a large bowl. Bring the vinegar and sugar to the boil in a saucepan, stir well and pour over the fruit. Cover and leave for 24 hours in a cool place.

Drain the melon or pumpkin cubes, reserving all the liquor and transferring it to a saucepan. Bring the liquor to the boil and add the celery salt, cinnamon, mustard seeds, cloves and ginger. Stir in the fruit cubes, lower the heat and simmer steadily for 3 hours, then pack the fruit into warm clean jars, pour on the hot vinegar and cover with vinegar-proof lids.

MAKES ABOUT 1.4 KG/3 LB

Chutneys, Ketchups and Relishes

Chutneys, long-cooked and rich in colour are ideal for sandwiches or serving with a ploughman's lunch. Ketchups are full-flavoured preserves and relishes are ideal for adding zest to plain meats or poultry. This chapter also includes mild relishes suitable for serving with burgers or sausages; just right for summer barbecues.

PREPARING INGREDIENTS

As usual, the way in which ingredients are prepared depends on type. They should be chopped or even minced so that they eventually cook down to a thick pulp.

Peel, cores and pips should be removed. Tomatoes are best peeled but this is not necessary if they are minced or very finely chopped.

Spices Ground or whole spices may be added; usually a combination of both is used. Whole spices should be tied in a small piece of scalded muslin so that they may be removed after cooking and before potting. Cinnamon sticks are usually easy to spot in the cooked preserve, so these do not have to be tied in muslin.

Sugar Brown sugar gives chutneys a good flavour and rich colour. For lighter fruit chutneys, granulated sugar may be preferred.

COOKING CHUTNEYS

Long slow cooking is the secret of success. A stainless steel pan is ideal (the information on saucepans to use for making sweet preserves, page 1064, is also relevant to chutneys) and it must be large enough to hold all the ingredients and allow room for them to simmer steadily.

Stir the mixture occasionally until the sugar dissolves, then bring the chutney to the boil and lower the heat so that it simmers. Cover the pan and cook for the time recommended in the recipe or until the chutney has darkened and become thick and pulpy. Stir the mixture occasionally during cooking to prevent it sticking to the bottom of the pan.

If the chutney is too liquid at the end of the recommended cooking time, or when all the ingredients are well reduced, allow it to boil, without a lid on the pan, until some of the excess liquid has evaporated. Stir frequently to prevent the mixture burning on the pan.

POTTING

Have thoroughly clean, hot jars ready on a large sheet of paper or folded tea-towel. You also need a tea-towel to hold or steady the jars, a jam funnel and a small jug. The jars must have airtight lids which will not react with the metal and you should have sufficient waxed paper discs to top each preserve.

Pot the chutney as soon as it is cooked, cover with waxed paper and put on airtight lids at once. Seal the lids in place with freezer tape. If for any reason the chutney is allowed to stand before potting, lids should not be put on the jars until preserve is cold.

RED TOMATO CHUTNEY

3 kg/6½ lb ripe red tomatoes
450 g/1 lb sugar
20 g/¾ oz salt
pinch of paprika
pinch of cayenne pepper
300 ml/½ pint Spiced Vinegar, made with
  white vinegar (page 925)

Peel the tomatoes (see Mrs Beeton's Tip). Immediately cut them up, removing the hard cores, and put them in a large saucepan. Add a very little water and bring slowly to the boil. Lower the heat and simmer until thick.

STORING

Store as for other preserves, in a cool, dark cupboard. Most chutneys will keep well for up to a year.

Add the remaining ingredients, stirring well. Continue cooking over low heat until the mixture is thick. Test the consistency by spooning a little of the chutney on to a cold plate.

When ready, pour the chutney into warm clean jars and cover with vinegar-proof lids. When cool, wipe the jars, label and store in a cool dry place.

 MRS BEETON'S TIP

Make chutney in stainless steel pans if possible. Keep a long-handled heat-resistant plastic spoon for stirring pickles and chutneys.

MAKES ABOUT 3 KG/6½ LB

 MRS BEETON'S TIP

If this chutney is to have a good red colour, it is essential to use white sugar and white vinegar. To achieve the correct texture, the tomatoes should be processed in one continuous action from peeling to potting.

To peel tomatoes, place in a bowl and cover with freshly boiling water. Leave for 30-60 seconds, then drain and slit the skins which will rub off easily.

APPLE CHUTNEY

3 kg/6½ lb apples
2 litres/3½ pints vinegar
1.5 kg/3¼ lb sugar
25 g/1 oz salt
10 ml/2 tsp ground allspice
300-400 g/11-14 oz preserved ginger, chopped
1 kg/2¼ lb sultanas, chopped

Peel and core the apples; chop them into small pieces. Combine the vinegar, sugar, salt and allspice in a saucepan or preserving pan. Bring to the boil, add the apples, lower the heat and simmer for 10 minutes.

Add the ginger and sultanas to the pan and simmer the mixture until fairly thick. Pour into warm clean jars and cover with vinegar-proof lids. When cool, wipe the jars, label and store in a cool dry place.

MAKES ABOUT 5 KG/11 LB

GREEN TOMATO CHUTNEY

450 g/1 lb cooking apples
450 g/1 lb onions, chopped
2 kg/4 lb green tomatoes, roughly chopped
450 g/1 lb sultanas
15 g/½ oz salt
1.25 ml/¼ tsp cayenne pepper
15 ml/1 tbsp mustard seeds
1 cm/½ inch fresh root ginger, bruised
750 ml/1¼ pints malt vinegar
450 g/1 lb demerara sugar

Peel, core and chop the apples. Put them in a large saucepan or preserving pan with the onions, tomatoes and sultanas. Stir in the salt and cayenne. Tie the mustard seeds and root ginger in a muslin bag and add to the pan with just enough of the vinegar to cover. Bring to simmering point and simmer for 20 minutes.

Meanwhile combine the remaining vinegar and the sugar in a second pan, stirring constantly over gentle heat until the sugar has dissolved. Add the vinegar mixture to the large saucepan or preserving pan and boil steadily until the chutney reaches the desired consistency. Remove the spice bag.

Pour the chutney into warm clean jars and cover with vinegar-proof lids. When cool, wipe the jars, label and store in a cool dry place.

MAKES ABOUT 3 KG/6½ LB

 MRS BEETON'S TIP

When filling jars, stand them on a sheet of paper to catch any drips.

YELLOW PEACH CHUTNEY

2 kg/4½ lb yellow peaches, peeled (see Mrs Beeton's Tip, page 887) and stoned
2 large onions
2 green peppers, seeded
225 g/8 oz sugar
15 ml/1 tbsp cornflour
5 ml/1 tsp salt
5 ml/1 tsp turmeric
15 ml/1 tbsp curry powder
15 ml/1 tbsp coriander seeds
7.5 ml/1½ tsp allspice berries
750 ml/1¼ pints vinegar

Mince the peaches, onions and green peppers together. In a bowl, combine the sugar, cornflour, salt, turmeric and curry powder; set aside.

Tie the coriander seeds and allspice in a muslin bag. Put the vinegar into a large saucepan or preserving pan, add the muslin bag and simmer over gentle heat for 4–5 minutes.

Remove the pan from the heat, add the sugar and spice mixture and bring to the boil, stirring frequently. Add the minced peach mixture and simmer until the chutney is thick. Remove the spice bag.

Pour into warm clean jars and cover with vinegar-proof lids. When cool, wipe the jars, label and store in a cool dry place.

MAKES ABOUT 2.5 KG/5½ LB

BANANA CHUTNEY

30 small bananas
1 small onion, sliced
25–50 g/1–2 oz chillies, chopped (see Mrs
  Beeton's Tip)
1.5 litres/2¾ pints white vinegar
225 g/8 oz seedless raisins
50 g/2 oz salt
50 g/2 oz ground ginger
450 g/1 lb soft light brown sugar

Slice the bananas into a large saucepan. Add
the remaining ingredients, bring to the boil and
cook over moderate heat for 2 hours, stirring
occasionally. When the chutney reaches the
desired consistency, pour into warm clean jars
and cover with vinegar-proof lids. When cool,
wipe the jars, label and store in a cool dry place.

MAKES ABOUT 3 KG/6¼ LB

 MRS BEETON'S TIP

Leave the seeds in the chillies if you like a
fiery chutney. For a milder result, remove
them. Always take great care when working with chillies not to touch your lips or
eyes; a strong reaction may occur on delicate skin. Wash your hands very carefully
after chopping the chillies.

KIWI FRUIT CHUTNEY

12 kiwi fruit, peeled and chopped
2 lemons, peeled and roughly chopped
3 onions, grated
1 large banana
150 g/5 oz sultanas or raisins
100 g/4 oz preserved ginger
10 ml/2 tsp salt
5 ml/1 tsp ground ginger
225 g/8 oz brown sugar
2.5 ml/½ tsp pepper
250–300 ml/8 fl oz–½ pint vinegar

Combine the kiwi fruit, lemons and onions in a
large saucepan. Slice the banana into the pan
and stir in all the remaining ingredients, using
just enough vinegar to cover.

Bring to simmering point and simmer gently
for 1½ hours, then mash with a potato masher.
Continue cooking until fairly thick, then pour
into warm clean jars and cover with vinegar-
proof lids. When cool, wipe the jars, label and
store in a cool dry place.

MAKES ABOUT 1 KG/2¼ LB

 MRS BEETON'S TIP

Although kiwi fruit is now associated with
New Zealand, it originated in China and
was for many years known as the Chinese
gooseberry. An excellent source of vitamin
C, the fruit is ready to eat when it is slightly
soft to the touch. Firmer kiwi fruit – often
cheaper than when fully ripe – can be used
for this chutney.

GOOSEBERRY CHUTNEY

450 g/1 lb soft light brown sugar
1.5 litres/2¾ pints vinegar
450 g/1 lb onions, finely chopped
675 g/1½ lb seedless raisins
50 g/2 oz mustard seeds, gently bruised
50 g/2 oz ground allspice
50 g/2 oz salt
2 kg/4½ lb gooseberries, topped and tailed

Put the sugar in a large saucepan or preserving pan with half the vinegar. Heat gently, stirring, until the sugar dissolves, then bring to the boil and boil for a few minutes until syrupy. Add the onions, raisins, spices and salt.

Bring the remaining vinegar to the boil in a second pan, add the gooseberries, lower the heat and simmer until tender. Stir the mixture into the large saucepan or preserving pan, cooking until the mixture thickens to the desired consistency. Pour into warm clean jars and cover with vinegar-proof lids. When cool, wipe the jars, label and store in a cool dry place.

MAKES ABOUT 3 KG/6½ LB

 MRS BEETON'S TIP

Allspice is a berry grown in the Caribbean area. Its name derives from the flavour, which suggests a blend of cinnamon, nutmeg and cloves. It is added whole to pickles, chutneys, stews and marinades, while the ground form is used in all foods, especially cakes and puddings.

BLATJANG

Blatjang is a sweet, spicy apricot chutney from South Africa. It is particularly good with baked ham.

450 g/1 lb dried apricots, roughly chopped,
    soaked overnight in cold water to cover
3-4 large onions, sliced
450 g/1 lb seedless raisins, minced
450 g/1 lb soft light brown sugar
5 ml/1 tsp cayenne pepper
5 ml/1 tsp ground ginger
10 ml/2 tsp pickling spice
2 garlic cloves, crushed
1 litre/1¾ pints vinegar
50 g/2 oz ground almonds
25 g/1 oz salt

Transfer the apricots, with their soaking liquid, to a saucepan. Cook over moderate heat until soft. Put the onions in a second saucepan, add water to cover, and cook until soft.

Put the apricots and onions, with the liquid in which both were cooked, in a large saucepan or preserving pan. Add all the remaining ingredients and simmer over low until the mixture is smooth and firm (see Mrs Beeton's Tip). Pour into warm clean jars and cover with vinegar-proof lids. When cool, wipe the jars, label and store in a cool dry place.

MAKES ABOUT 1.5 KG/3¼ LB

 MRS BEETON'S TIP

To test the chutney, spoon a little on to a cold plate. As soon as the chutney is cool, tilt the plate. The chutney should not flow.

MANGO CHUTNEY

5 slightly under-ripe mangoes, peeled,
  stoned and sliced
25 g/1 oz salt
450 ml/¾ pint Spiced Vinegar (page 925)
5 ml/1 tsp cayenne pepper
25 g/1 oz fresh root ginger, bruised
25 g/1 oz whole black peppercorns
450 g/1 lb demerara sugar

Put the mango slices in a bowl. Sprinkle with
the salt, cover and leave overnight. Next day,
drain and rinse the fruit, drain it again and put
it in a large saucepan or preserving pan. Add
the vinegar and cayenne. Tie the ginger and
peppercorns in a muslin bag and add the bag to
the pan.

Bring the mixture to the boil, lower the heat
and simmer for 15–20 minutes or until the
mangoes are soft. Remove the spice bag and
stir the sugar into the pan. Heat gently until the
sugar has dissolved, then bring to the boil and
boil rapidly until the chutney thickens, stirring
all the time. Pour into warm, clean jars and
cover with vinegar-proof lids. When cool, wipe
the jars, label and store in a cool dry place.

MAKES ABOUT 1.5 KG/3¼ LB

 PRESSURE COOKER TIP

Reduce the quantity of vinegar to
375 ml/13 fl oz. Put the mangoes in the
cooker and add 250 ml/8 fl oz of the vinegar
with the cayenne and spice bag. Bring to
the boil, cover and cook for 5 minutes at
15 lb High pressure. Reduce pressure
quickly, remove the spice bag and stir in
the sugar and remaining vinegar. Continue
cooking in the open pan.

FRESH CORIANDER CHUTNEY

*Unlike the other recipes in this section, this chutney
must be served within a short time of being made. If
stored in an airtight jar in the refrigerator, it will
keep for up to 5 days. Serve it as an accompaniment
to an Indian meal.*

2 onions, finely chopped or grated
1 garlic clove, crushed
1 tomato, peeled and chopped
1 green chilli, chopped (see Mrs Beeton's
  Tip, page 1107)
1 cm/½ inch fresh root ginger, peeled and
  grated
15 ml/1 tbsp chopped fresh coriander leaves
45 ml/3 tbsp Tomato Ketchup (page 925)
30 ml/2 tbsp vinegar
2.5 ml/½ tsp salt
1.25 ml/¼ tsp black peppercorns

Combine all the ingredients in a bowl. Mix
well. Serve at once or store in the refrigerator as
suggested above.

SERVES FOUR TO FIVE

VARIATION

For a smooth chutney, substitute 150 ml/¼ pint
water for the vinegar and process in a blender
or food processor.

 MRS BEETON'S TIP

Fresh coriander, sometimes known as Chinese parsley, is widely used in the East.
Most countries use only the leaves but the
roots can be used in curry pastes, while the
stalks are sometimes used for flavouring in
Indian lentil and bean dishes.

WALNUT KETCHUP

Walnuts for pickling or ketchup must be picked before the shell has hardened (see page 1102). In England, this usually means that picking must take place before the first week in July.

400 g/14 oz onions, chopped
2 litres/3½ pints vinegar
200 g/7 oz salt
25 g/1 oz whole peppercorns
15 g/½ oz whole allspice berries
2.5 ml/½ tsp whole cloves
1.25 ml/¼ tsp ground nutmeg
about 10 green walnuts

Combine all the ingredients except the walnuts in a large saucepan or preserving pan. Bring to the boil. Meanwhile, wearing gloves to protect your hands from staining, cut up the walnuts, crush them and put them in a large heatproof bowl. Pour over the boiling mixture and leave for 14 days in a cool place, stirring daily.

Strain the liquid into a clean saucepan, discarding the solids in the strainer. Bring the liquid to the boil, lower the heat and simmer for about 1 hour. Bottle as for Tomato Ketchup (right).

MAKES ABOUT 1.5 LITRES/2¾ PINTS

 MRS BEETON'S TIP

The choice of which vinegar to use in sauce-making is literally a matter of personal taste. Where keeping the true colour of the prime ingredient is important, as when making tomato ketchup, distilled white vinegar is generally used, but for other sauces malt vinegar is often preferred. Cider vinegar is particularly good with spicy fruit sauces.

TOMATO KETCHUP

Use white sugar and white vinegar to maintain the colour in this excellent ketchup.

3 kg/6½ lb ripe tomatoes, cut in quarters
30 ml/2 tbsp salt
600 ml/1 pint white vinegar
225 g/8 oz sugar
2.5 ml/½ tsp each of ground cloves,
   cinnamon, allspice and cayenne pepper

Put the tomatoes in a preserving pan with the salt and vinegar. Simmer until they are soft and pulpy. Rub the mixture through a fine nylon sieve or coarse muslin, then return it to the clean pan.

Stir in the sugar, place over gentle heat, and simmer the mixture until it starts to thicken. Add spices to taste, a little at a time, stirring after each addition.

Heat sufficient clean bottles to hold the ketchup; prepare vinegar-proof seals. When the ketchup reaches the desired consistency, fill the hot bottles, leaving a headspace. The ketchup will thicken on cooling, so do not reduce it too much. Seal the bottles immediately. Alternatively, allow the ketchup to cool slightly, then fill the bottles (leaving a headspace) and sterilize at 88°C/190°F for 30 minutes. Seal immediately. Label when cold.

MAKES ABOUT 1.5 LITRES/2¾ PINTS

 MRS BEETON'S TIP

Bottles of ketchup for keeping should be wrapped in foil. This helps to keep the colour bright.

MUSHROOM KETCHUP

Taken directly from Mrs Beeton's first edition recipe this ketchup must be sterilized when bottled to ensure that it keeps safely. However, a more practical, and safer, alternative is to freeze the ketchup in small quantities. The exact yield depends on the mushrooms.

600 ml/8 pints open mushrooms
100 g/4 oz salt

FLAVOURING INGREDIENTS (SEE METHOD)
cayenne pepper • allspice
blades of mace • brandy

The mushrooms should be clean and dry. Layer then in a large bowl, sprinkling each layer with salt. Cover and leave in a cool place for 4 hours. Break the mushrooms into small pieces using your fingers, not a knife. Press them down well in the bowl and cover closely. Leave the mushrooms to stand for 3 days, mashing them at least twice a day to extract their liquor and stirring well.

Measure the volume of mushrooms and liquor at the end of the salting process, then pour both into a large heatproof bowl. To every 1.1 litres/ 2 pints, add 7 g/¼ oz of cayenne pepper, 15 g/ ½ oz each of ground allspice and ginger, and 2 blades of mace, pounded to a powder. Stir well, then stand the bowl over a saucepan of boiling water and boil for 30 minutes stirring occasionally. Pour the mushrooms into one or more clean jugs, cover and leave to cool overnight.

Pour off the ketchup carefully, leaving all the sediment behind. Do not squeeze the mushrooms. Add a little brandy (a few drops to every 600 ml/1 pint), then decant the ketchup into suitable bottles. Cover, sterilize at 88°C/190°F for 30 minutes and seal immediately. Cool, then check the seal before storing the ketchup to ensure the bottles are airtight.

BROWN SAUCE

1.5 kg/2¼ lb tomatoes, chopped
100 g/4 oz onions, chopped
225 g/8 oz soft light brown sugar
225 g/8 oz raisins
75–100 g/3–4 oz salt
25 g/1 oz ground ginger
1.25 ml/¼ tsp cayenne pepper
1 litre/1¾ pints malt vinegar

Combine all the ingredients in a large saucepan or preserving pan. Heat gently, stirring until the sugar has dissolved, then raise the heat slightly and cook until the tomatoes and onions are soft.

Rub the the mixture through a nylon or stainless steel sieve, then return it to the clean pan. Place over gentle heat and simmer until the sauce reaches the desired consistency. Bottle as for Tomato Ketchup (opposite). Label when cold.

MAKES ABOUT 2 LITRES/3½ PINTS

WORCESTERSHIRE SAUCE

4 shallots, finely chopped or minced
1 litre/1¾ pints good malt vinegar
90 ml/6 tbsp Walnut Ketchup (opposite)
75 ml/5 tbsp anchovy essence
60 ml/4 tbsp soy sauce
2.5 ml/½ tsp cayenne pepper
salt

Combine all the ingredients in a perfectly clean bottle. Seal it tightly. Shake several times daily for about 14 days, then strain the sauce into small bottles, leaving a headspace in each. Seal tightly, label and store in a cool, dry place.

MAKES ABOUT 1.25 LITRES/2¼ PINTS

EPICUREAN SAUCE

Mrs Beeton recommended this sauce for steaks, chops and fish. She also advised adding a dash of it to gravy, stew or meat hash.

150 ml/¼ pint Walnut Ketchup (page 922) or 1 (250 g/9 oz) jar pickled walnuts, mashed with their liquid
150 ml/¼ pint mushroom ketchup
30 ml/2 tbsp soy sauce
30 ml/2 tbsp port
15 ml/1 tbsp white pepper
2 shallots, finely chopped
15 ml/1 tbsp cayenne pepper
15 ml/1 tbsp ground cloves
450 ml/¾ pint malt vinegar (see method)

Combine all the ingredients in a large, perfectly clean bottle, reducing the quantity of vinegar to 300 ml/½ pint if using pickled walnuts. Seal it tightly. Shake several times daily for about 14 days, then strain the sauce into small bottles, leaving a headspace in each. Seal tightly, label and store in a cool, dry place.

MAKES ABOUT 600 ML/1 PINT

FRUIT SAUCE

450 g/1 lb cooking apples
1 lemon, peeled and roughly chopped
450 g/1 lb onions, roughly chopped
450 g/1 lb tomatoes, roughly chopped
25 g/1 oz salt
225 g/8 oz sultanas
75 g/3 oz sugar
25 g/1 oz mixed spice
1 litre/1¾ pints cider vinegar
25 g/1 oz cornflour

Combine all the ingredients except the corn-flour in a large saucepan or preserving pan. Bring to the boil, lower the heat and simmer until the fruit and vegetables are cooked.

In a cup, blend the cornflour to a paste with a little cold water.

Sieve the cooked mixture, return it to the pan and stir in the cornflour paste. Bring to the boil and boil for 5 minutes. Bottle as for Tomato Ketchup (page 922). Label when cold.

MAKES ABOUT 2 LITRES/3½ PINTS

LEAMINGTON SAUCE

As with Walnut Ketchup (page 1110), this sauce is made from walnuts picked early in the season, before the shells have hardened. No quantities are given for ingredients other than the walnuts, since proportions depend on the amount of juice released by the nuts.

2 kg/4½ lb green walnuts
salt • Spiced Vinegar (page 925)
soy sauce
cayenne pepper
shallots, finely chopped
garlic cloves, crushed
port

Pound the walnuts to a pulp, using a mortar and pestle. Alternatively, grind them in a food processor.

Spread out the walnut pulp in shallow dishes, sprinkle with salt and set aside for 2–3 days, stirring frequently.

Strain the walnut pulp through a sieve into a bowl, pressing the walnuts against the side of the sieve with a spoon to extract all the juice.

Measure the juice. To each 600 ml/1 pint, add 900 ml/1½ pints spiced vinegar, 300 ml/½ pint soy sauce, 15 ml/1 tbsp cayenne pepper, 4 finely chopped shallots, 2 crushed garlic cloves and 150 ml/¼ pint port. Mix well.

Pour the sauce into perfectly clean, small bottles, leaving a headspace in each. Seal tightly, label and store in a cool, dry place.

CRANBERRY KETCHUP

1 kg/2¼ lb cranberries
2 onions, finely chopped
5 ml/1 tsp mustard seeds
1 cinnamon stick
1 cm/½ inch fresh root ginger, bruised
2.5 ml/½ tsp peppercorns
2 bay leaves
15 ml/1 tbsp salt
250 ml/8 fl oz white vinegar
450 g/1 lb white sugar

Put the cranberries and onions in a large saucepan or preserving pan. Add 250 ml/8 fl oz water and simmer for 20-30 minutes or until very soft.

Rub the cranberry mixture through a fine nylon sieve, then return the purée to the clean pan. Tie the spices in a muslin bag.

Stir the salt and vinegar into the cranberry purée, add the spice bag and simmer the mixture for 10-15 minutes, stirring occasionally.

Stir in the sugar, place over gentle heat, and simmer the mixture until it starts to thicken. Stir frequently to prevent the sauce from sticking to the base of the pan.

Heat sufficient clean bottles to hold the ketchup; prepare vinegar-proof seals. When the mixture reaches the desired consistency, discard the spice bag and fill the bottles as for Tomato Ketchup (page 922). Store in a cool, dry place for at least two weeks before using.

MAKES 1-1.25 LITRES/1½-2¼ PINTS

SPICED VINEGAR

7 g/¼ oz each of the following spices: cloves,
    allspice berries, cinnamon sticks (broken
    into short lengths), fresh root ginger,
    bruised
1 litre/1¾ pints white or malt vinegar

Fold the spices in a clean cloth. Using a rolling pin, beat lightly to release all the flavour. Combine the spices and vinegar in a large jug, mix well, then pour the liquid into a 1.1 litre/2 pint bottle. Seal the bottle tightly.

Shake the bottle daily for 1 month, then store in a cool dry place for at least 1 month more before straining out the spices and returning the vinegar to the clean bottle.

MAKES 1 LITRE/1¾ PINTS

RASPBERRY VINEGAR

raspberries
white wine vinegar
caster sugar

Clean the fruit thoroughly and measure it by volume. Put it in a bowl and add an equal quantity each of vinegar and water. Leave to stand overnight.

Next day, strain the liquid through a fine sieve or jelly bag and measure it again. To each 300 ml/½ pint liquid add 200 ml/7 fl oz caster sugar. Pour the mixture into a saucepan, bring to the boil and boil for 10 minutes. Pour the hot liquid into heated clean bottles and seal at once. Label when cold.

HORSERADISH VINEGAR

600 ml/1 pint white vinegar
50 g/2 oz grated horseradish
15 g/½ oz chopped shallot
2.5 ml/½ tsp salt
pinch of cayenne pepper
25 g/1 oz sugar

Bring the vinegar to the boil in a saucepan. Combine all the remaining ingredients in a heatproof bowl. When the vinegar boils, pour it into the bowl. Cover and set aside to cool.

Bottle the mixture and store for 10 days. It may then be used unstrained as horseradish sauce. To store the vinegar for longer than 10 days, strain it into a clean pan, bring to the boil and pour into heated bottles. Seal securely.

MAKES ABOUT 600ML/1 PINT

CRANBERRY VINEGAR

2 kg/4½ lb sound ripe cranberries
2.5 litres/4½ pints white wine vinegar
800 g/1¾ lb sugar for every 1 litre/1¾ pints of
    liquid

Put the fruit in a large, preferably earthenware, bowl. Add the vinegar, cover with a clean cloth and leave to stand in a cool place for 10 days, stirring daily. Strain the liquid through a fine sieve or jelly bag, measure its volume and pour it into a pan.

Stir in the sugar, bring to the boil and boil steadily for 10 minutes or until the mixture is syrupy when a small quantity is tested by cooling on a plate. Skim, bottle and seal at once. Label when cold.

MAKES ABOUT 3.5 LITRES/6 PINTS

VARIATION

Mulberry Vinegar   Make as above, using 1 kg/2¼ lb ripe mulberries, 1.75 litres/3 pints vinegar and sugar in the proportion suggested. Leave for 1 week before straining.

STONE FRUIT VINEGAR

Any good quality ripe fruit with stones may be used for this vinegar. Choose from apricots, cherries, damsons, greeengages, peaches or plums. Measure by volume as suggested below.

3 litres/5¼ pints fruits with stones
1 litre/1¾ pints white vinegar
800 g/1¾ lb sugar

Halve the fruit, leaving the stones in place, and put it in a large bowl. Add the vinegar, cover with a clean cloth and leave to stand in a cool place for 6 days. Stir the mixture and press down the fruit with a wooden spoon once a day. Finally press the fruit again and strain the liquid through a fine sieve or jelly bag into a saucepan.

Stir in the sugar, bring to the boil and boil steadily for 15 minutes, or until the mixture is syrupy when a small quantity is tested by cooling on a plate. Skim, bottle and seal at once. Label when cold.

MAKES ABOUT 2.8 LITRES/5 PINTS

VARIATION

Brandied Fruit Vinegar   Allow the vinegar syrup to cool in the pan, measure its volume, then add 200 ml/7 fl oz brandy for every litre/1¾ pints. Stir, bottle and seal.

CAMP VINEGAR

This is an extremely hot, garlic-flavoured sauce which should be used sparingly as it is similar to a chilli sauce in intensity.

8 garlic cloves, sliced
15 ml/1 tbsp cayenne pepper
10 ml/2 tsp soy sauce
10 ml/2 tsp Walnut Ketchup (page 922) or
   1 pickled walnut, chopped
600 ml/1 pint malt vinegar
red food colouring

Combine the garlic, cayenne, soy sauce, walnut ketchup and vinegar in a perfectly clean bottle. Add just enough food colouring to give a good, rich colour. Seal the bottle tightly. Shake daily for 1 month,, then strain through muslin into a measuring jug. Pour into small bottles, leaving a headspace in each. Seal tightly, label and store in a cool, dry place.

MAKES ABOUT 600ML/1 PINT

CUCUMBER VINEGAR

Use this peppery vinegar in salad dressings or sauces. On standing, the seasoning ingredients tend to separate, so give the jar a good shake.

5 large cucumbers or 10 ridge cucumbers
2 onions, sliced
15 ml/1 tbsp salt
30 ml/2 tbsp pepper
1.25 ml/¼ tsp cayenne pepper
1.1–1.4 litres/2–2½ pints malt vinegar

Peel the cucumbers. Slice them thinly and pack them into a large bowl. Add the sliced onions between the layers of cucumber and sprinkle with salt, pepper and cayenne. Pour in the vinegar to cover the cucumber completely. Cover and set aside in a cool place for 4–5 days.

Transfer the contents of the jar to a large saucepan. Bring to the boil and boil for 5 minutes, then remove from the heat. When the vinegar mixture is cold, strain it through muslin into a large jug. Pour into small bottles. Cover tightly with vinegar-proof seals.

MAKES ABOUT 1.25 LITRES/2¼ PINTS

CHEROKEE SAUCE

A potent sauce for pepping up gravies and savoury mixtures, such as meat loaves, stews and sauces.

15 ml/1 tbsp cayenne pepper
5 garlic cloves, crushed
30 ml/2 tbsp soy sauce
15 ml/1 tbsp Walnut Ketchup (page 922) or
   1 pickled walnut, crushed
600 ml/1 pint malt vinegar

Combine all the ingredients in a saucepan. Bring to the boil, lower the heat and simmer very gently for 30 minutes.

Heat sufficient clean bottles to hold the sauce; prepare vinegar-proof lids. Fill the hot bottles with the sauce and cover. Label when cold.

MAKES ABOUT 450ML/¾ PINT

TOMATO RELISH

900 g/2 lb ripe tomatoes, peeled and roughly
    chopped
450 g/1 lb cooking apples, peeled, cored and
    roughly chopped
900 g/2 lb onions, chopped
2 garlic cloves, crushed
2 green chillies, seeded and chopped (see
    Mrs Beeton's Tip, page 919)
50 g/2 oz fresh root ginger, grated
15 ml/1 tbsp paprika
15 ml/1 tbsp ground coriander
pinch of cayenne pepper
15 ml/1 tbsp salt
300 ml/½ pint white vinegar
2 bay leaves
175 g/6 oz sugar

Place all the ingredients in a large saucepan
and stir the mixture over low heat until the
sugar dissolves. Bring to the boil, then lower
the heat and cover the pan. Simmer the relish
for 20 minutes.

Uncover the pan and stir the relish, then
continue to cook at a steady simmer for 30–40
minutes more. Stir the relish occasionally to
prevent it from sticking to the pan. When
cooked the fruit and onions should be pulpy
and the relish should be thick.

Remove and discard the bay leaves, then pot
the relish and top with waxed discs. Cover at
once with airtight lids. Label and store for at
least 3 weeks before eating.

MAKES ABOUT 1.8KG/4LB

SWEETCORN RELISH

2 green peppers, seeded and diced
2 large carrots, dicd
2 large onions, chopped
6 celery sticks, diced
salt
2 garlic cloves, crushed
30 ml/2 tbsp mustard powder
5 ml/1 tsp turmeric
15 ml/1 tbsp cornflour
600 ml/1 pint white vinegar
100 g/4 oz sugar
900 g/2 lb frozen sweetcorn, thawed

Place the peppers, carrots, chopped onion and
celery in a bowl, sprinkling each layer with a
little salt. Sprinkle more salt on top of the
vegetables, cover the bowl and leave them to
stand overnight.

Next day, drain, rinse, drain again and dry the
vegetables, then place them in a large saucepan
with the garlic. In a cup, blend the mustard,
turmeric and cornflour to a paste with a little of
the vinegar. Pour the rest of the vinegar into the
pan and bring the vegetable mixture to the boil.

Lower the heat and cover the pan, then simmer
the mixture for 5 minutes. Add the sweetcorn
and cook, covered, for a further 5 minutes. Stir
in the sugar and cook gently, stirring, until it
has dissolved.

Spoon a little of the hot liquid into the mustard
mixture, then stir the thin paste into the relish.
Add 5 ml/1 tsp salt and stir well. Bring to the
boil, stirring all the time, then lower the heat
and simmer steadily for 5 minutes without a lid
on the pan. Pot and cover at once, then label
and store for at least a week. The relish will
keep for 6–9 months.

MAKES ABOUT 2.25KG/5LB

CITRUS RELISH

2 oranges
2 lemons
4 limes
1 cinnamon stick
15 ml/1 tbsp salt
900 g/2 lb onions, chopped
2 garlic cloves, crushed
300 ml/½ pint vinegar
175 g/6 oz sugar

Cut all the citrus fruit into quarters, then roughly chop each piece, discarding the pips as you work. Place the prepared fruit in a bowl, adding the cinnamon stick halfway through. Sprinkle with the salt, cover and leave for 24 hours.

Turn the fruit mixture into a large saucepan, scraping in all the juices. Stir in the onions, garlic and vinegar. Bring to the boil, then lower the heat and cover the pan. Simmer the mixture for 1 hour, stirring occasionally, or until the fruit is tender.

Discard the cinnamon stick, then stir in the sugar and cook over low heat until the sugar has dissolved, stirring all the time. Raise the heat and simmer the relish for a further 15 minutes without a lid on the pan.

Pot and cover the relish, then label and leave for about 3 weeks for the flavour to mature.

MAKES ABOUT 1.4 KG/3 LB

CRANBERRY RELISH

450 g/1 lb cranberries
450 g/1 lb cooking apples, peeled, cored and
  chopped
450 g/1 lb onions, chopped
450 g/1 lb sugar
1 cinnamon stick
6 cloves
10 allspice berries, coarsely crushed
6 juniper berries, coarsely crushed
2 blades of mace
pared rind of 1 orange
600 ml/1 pint white vinegar

Combine the cranberries, apples and onions in a large saucepan. Add the sugar. Tie all the spices and orange rind together in a square of scalded muslin and add them to the pan.

Pour in the vinegar and heat the mixture gently, stirring until the sugar has dissolved. Bring to the boil, then lower the heat and cover the pan. Cook the relish gently for 1 hour, stirring occasionally to prevent it from sticking to the base of the pan.

Remove the spices, then pot and cover the relish. Leave it to mature for at least 2 weeks before using. It keeps well for up to a year.

MAKES ABOUT 1.4 KG/3 LB

Beverages

From making the perfect pot of British tea to shaking up a classy cocktail, this is a chapter
that blends nostalgia with contemporary inspiration.

Most large supermarkets offer an astonishing array of teas, coffees, and drink mixes. Packaged beverages, whether in jars, cans, sachets or packets, come complete with instructions. As these are well researched and tested, it is sensible to follow the manufacturer's advice when trying for the first time a milk drink, an instant drink mix or a savoury soup-in-a cup type of beverage.

There is a wide range of different teas and coffees on offer, each with its own strength and flavour. Many teas are scented with fruit, spices, flowers or herbs, while herb teas are infusions of the herb without any tea leaves. Decaffeinated coffee, both instant and fresh, is also readily available. The best way to discover the nature of the many blends of tea and coffee is to experiment with small packets or sample tins, or by mixing small amounts from specialist shops.

MAKING GOOD TEA

- Use fresh water. Warm the pot by pouring some boiling water into it, swirling it around, and then pouring it away.
- The tradition is to allow 5 ml/1 tsp loose tea per person plus 5 ml/1 tsp per pot; however, if the tea is strong and the pot small (literally allowing 1 generous cup per person), this may be too much. Experiment to find the quantity that produces the perfect brew for you.
- Pour freshly boiling water on the tea and cover the tea pot. Use a tea-cosy to keep the beverage piping hot.

- Leave the tea to brew: small-leafed varieties should be left for 3 minutes; large leaf tea for 6 minutes. When ready, the tea leaves should have sunk to the bottom of the pot.
- Use a tea strainer when pouring tea.
- Although some teas are best enjoyed black, always offer cold milk or lemon: the latter with delicate, weak teas and scented types.

Iced Tea Make a weak, delicate brew, such as Earl Grey, strain it into a clean jug, then allow to cool. Serve sweetened to taste, with mint, thin lemon slices and ice cubes.

MAKING GOOD COFFEE

There are various ways of making coffee, from the simple jug method to sophisticated machines that include a water heater, filter, coffee holder and jug. Most automatic coffee makers give some indication of the quantity of coffee to use for the number of cups; otherwise allow about 30–45 ml/2–3 tbsp per 600 ml/1 pint of water.

Filter Method Use a filter paper in a strainer placed over a suitable jug. Use fine ground coffee and pour boiling water from the kettle directly on to it. Top up the water as necessary.

Percolator Method A coffee percolator may be an automatic electrical appliance or it may be a relatively simple pot heated on the hob. Water is placed in the pot and the coffee (medium ground) is placed in a perforated container above. The water rises through a pipe as it heats, then flows through the coffee and back into the pot.

Cafetiere A jug with a built-in fine strainer which works on a plunger basis: the coffee (medium ground) and water are combined in the jug and allowed to brew for 3–5 minutes, then the plunger is depressed and the coffee may be poured. This is one of the simplest and most satisfactory methods, giving hot but not overheated coffee.

Espresso Coffee This is very fine ground strong coffee through which boiling water has been forced at pressure. The resultant beverage is strong and very dark. Espresso coffee may be used as an essence or diluted with hot milk.

Cappuccino Espresso coffee topped up with milk which is heated by steam, causing it to froth. Cocoa or grated bitter chocolate may be sprinkled over the frothy coffee.

Traditional Jug Method Water, just off the boil, is poured on to medium or ground coffee in a pre-warmed jug. The coffee should be allowed to stand for about 3 minutes. Any floating grounds should then be skimmed from the surface. The coffee is then poured into cups through a fine strainer, leaving the grounds in the jug.

Turkish Coffee Very fine ground coffee is boiled with water and varying amounts of sugar in a small pan. When the coffee is poured out, most of the grounds remain in the pan; however the powdery coffee also collects at the bottom of each small cup. The grounds are not drunk.

Irish Coffee Sweetened black coffee laced with whiskey, served in a glass cup. Single cream is poured over the back of a teaspoon to float on the surface of the coffee. The coffee must be sweetened and laced with alcohol to support the cream. The coffee is drunk through the cream. There are many variations on this theme, all of them popular. For example, liqueurs flavoured with coconut or fruit may be added to the coffee, before the cream.

Iced Coffee An excellent summer drink. Strong black coffee is thoroughly chilled. Iced coffee is usually served in tall glasses, topped up with chilled milk and sweetened to taste. Ice cubes are usually added. Alternatively, scoops of ice cream make a luscious addition to glasses of iced coffee. Whipped cream may be swirled on the surface of the drink or single cream swirled into it.

Coffee Essence This is very strong coffee, made by using about 100 g/4 oz fine grounds to each 600 ml/1 pint water. When cool, it is strained for use as a flavouring in cooking. Coffee essence may be frozen in ice cube trays.

DAIRY DRINKS

Hot Milk Drinks Cocoa is unsweetened, drinking chocolate is sweetened and there is a wide variety of malted and flavoured powders which should be used according to the manufacturer's instructions. If in doubt, the best method of making a mug of flavoured hot milk drink is to dissolve about 30 ml/2 tbsp powder in a little boiling water, then to pour in boiling milk, stirring vigorously.

Milk Shakes Fresh chilled milk, flavoured and shaken or whipped to a froth. Concentrated fruit syrups may be used to flavour the milk or an essence of coffee or chocolate may be added. Instant coffee or cocoa powder dissolved in a little boiling water makes an excellent flavouring.

Yogurt Drinks Combined with fruit juice or purée and flavoured syrups, natural yogurt makes a refreshing drink.

SAVOURY HOT DRINKS

In addition to soups and bouillons, there are several beef or yeast extracts which can be mixed with boiling water to make warming hot drinks. A dash of lemon juice may be added, if liked.

HOME-MADE DRINKS

From nostalgic images of lemonade on the lawn to heady sips of sloe gin, this section provides all the information needed to conjure up the right drink for the occasion.

Home brewing is a separate subject, requiring attention beyond the scope of this book. These recipes are for refreshing drinks that may be prepared and chilled for several days or frozen for a few months. A couple of heart-warming recipes of different types are also included, including a beef tea, and several restorative drinks such as mulled ale and mulled wine. Festive occasions will be enlivened by the wine cups and punches, and there's a fruit punch for drivers and others who prefer not to indulge in alcohol.

STORING HOME-MADE DRINKS

Most alcohol-free drinks should be used within 3-5 days of being made. In summer, make a double quantity of lemonade or other soft drink to keep covered in the refrigerator – it will be appreciated by those drivers avoiding alcohol as well as youngsters. Or simply serve a cold drink instead of tea.

Concentrated fruit drinks will not keep for long periods unless they are correctly bottled and processed as for bottled fruit. This time-consuming task can be avoided by freezing the drink instead. Freeze in ice-cube trays until firm, then transfer to bags. When added to mineral water, a few cubes of the drink will thaw quickly.

Savoury beverages, such as beef tea, may be reduced to a concentrate before freezing; when required, they can be quickly thawed by adding the required volume of hot water and heating gently. Remember to note the extent to which the drink was reduced on the pack label – this way you know how much water to add when reheating it.

Some of the alcoholic drinks in this chapter, such as the Orange Brandy, improve with keeping. Store them in a cool, dark place, following the instructions given in individual recipes.

SERVING DRINKS

If you have gone to the trouble of preparing a special drink, it is certainly worth the effort of adding a few finishing touches when serving it. Chilling glasses in the refrigerator for 30 minutes before serving a cold drink is a professional touch; always remember to add ice to cold drinks. Here are some additional suggestions:

- Add sprigs of mint or lemon balm to iced teas or fruit drinks.
- Cut thin slices of lemon, orange or lime to decorate fruit drinks.
- In summer, strawberries and wafer-thin slices of cucumber combine well in light fruit drinks.
- Make a light alcoholic punch by combining equal quantities of dry white wine and diluted Elderflower Cordial (page 934) or Lemonade (opposite).
- To frost the rims of glasses, dip them first in a little water or lemon juice, then in sugar. Add pink or green food colouring to the water for a pretty effect.

LEMONADE

A jug of refreshing iced lemonade is the perfect cooler for a hot summer's day.

1.8 kg/4 lb sugar
grated rind of 2 lemons
1 litre/1¾ pints lemon juice

Put the sugar in a saucepan with 1 litre/1¾ pints water. Heat gently, stirring until all the sugar has dissolved, then stir in the lemon rind. Boil for 5 minutes without further stirring. Cool.

Stir in the lemon juice, strain into clean jugs or bottles and store in the refrigerator. Dilute with iced water to serve.

MAKES ABOUT 3 LITRES/5¼ PINTS

GINGER BEER

As anyone who has ever experienced the explosion caused by unwisely stored ginger beer will know, fermentation causes strong pressure inside bottles. It is therefore important to use sturdy, properly sterilized beer bottles with clip-on bottle seals or screw tops. Store in a cardboard box in a cool dark place, preferably on a concrete floor.

25 g/1 oz fresh root ginger, bruised
thinly pared rind and juice of 2 lemons
450 g/1 lb sugar
7.5 ml/1½ tsp cream of tartar
1 sachet dried beer yeast

Combine the ginger, lemon rind, sugar and cream of tartar in a suitable white brewing bucket with lid. Add 5 litres/8½ pints hot water. Stir gently until the sugar has dissolved, then leave to cool.

Add the lemon juice to the cooled liquid and sprinkle the yeast over the surface. Cover and leave in a warm place for 48 hours, skimming off the yeast head after 24 hours. When fermentation has finished, skim the surface again before bottling.

Thoroughly wash sufficient beer bottles to hold the ginger beer, and sterilize them in Campden solution (see Mrs Beeton's Tip) or by using another suitable wine-making product. Siphon the ginger beer into the bottles, being careful not to disturb the deposit in the bottom of the container. Seal the bottles tightly and leave in a warm place for 3 days. Use at once or store in a cool dark place until required, checking the bottles frequently.

MAKES ABOUT 5 LITRES/8¼ PINTS

 MRS BEETON'S TIP

Use proper beer bottles as mineral bottles may not be strong enough to withstand the pressures. Wash them thoroughly inside and out, then sterilize them and the closures in a solution of 2 crushed Campden tablets and 2.5 ml/½ tsp citric acid in 500 ml/17 fl oz water.

SPARKLING MINT TEA

20 ml/4 tsp tea leaves
75 g/3 oz caster sugar
12 mint leaves
300 ml/½ pint soda water or sparkling
    mineral water
ice cubes
4 lemon slices

Put the tea leaves into a large heatproof jug and
add 600 ml/1 pint boiling water. Infuse for 3–7
minutes. Strain into a clean jug and stir in the
sugar and 4 mint leaves. Allow to cool. The tea
may be covered and kept in the refrigerator for
up to 2 days. Alternatively, it may be frozen in
ice cube trays.

Stir in the soda or sparking mineral water and
pour into 4 tall glasses. Add ice cubes, 1 lemon
slice and 2 mint leaves to each glass. Stir, then
serve at once.

SERVES FOUR

SLOE GIN

450 g/1 lb ripe sloes
225 g/8 oz caster sugar
1 litre/1¾ pints dry gin

Remove stalks and leaves from the sloes, then
wash and prick them all over. Put them in a jar
which can be fitted with an airtight seal.

In a large jug or bowl, dissolve the sugar in the
gin and pour it on to the sloes. Cover the jar and
store it in a cool dark place for 3 months, giving
it a gentle shake every few days to extract and
distribute the fruit flavour. Strain, bottle and
store for 3 months more before serving.

MAKES ABOUT 1.25 LITRES/2¼ PINTS

ELDERFLOWER CORDIAL

*Diluted with plenty of iced water, this makes a
refreshing drink. Small quantities may also be used
to flavour stewed fruit such as gooseberries.*

900 g/2 lb caster sugar
30 g/1¼ oz citric acid
1 lemon
10 elderflower heads, washed and drained

Put the sugar in a large heatproof bowl. Add
600 ml/1 pint boiling water and stir until all the
sugar has dissolved. Stir in the citric acid.

Grate the lemon and add the rind to the bowl,
then slice the fruit. Add the lemon slices to the
bowl with the elderflower heads. Cover and
allow to stand for 12 hours or overnight. Strain
through muslin, bottle and store for 1 month
before serving.

MAKES ABOUT 600ML/1 PINT

BEEF TEA

*Beef tea freezes very well and thaws quickly if frozen
in ice cube trays.*

400 g/14 oz shin, flank or skirt of beef
salt and pepper

Set the oven at 140°C/275°F/gas 1. Trim off all
visible fat from the meat; cut it into 2.5 cm/1
inch cubes, then put it in a casserole. Add
500 ml/17 fl oz water and 2.5 ml/½ tsp salt.
Cover and cook for 4 hours.

Strain the liquid through a fine sieve lined with
scalded muslin into a clean bowl. Allow to
cool, then chill the beef tea and skim off any
fat. Reheat, without boiling, add salt and pepper to taste and serve as a light soup or
beverage.

SERVES TWO

ORANGE SQUASH

Campden tablets, available from chemists and shops specializing in wine-making equipment, consist of sodium metabisulphite. They are used for killing off wild yeasts in fruit when making wine. Adding a Campden tablet to this squash prevents the orange juice from fermenting.

grated rind of 3 oranges
450 g/1 lb sugar
¼ lemon, cut in wedges
300 ml/½ pint fresh orange juice
1 Campden tablet

Combine the orange rind, sugar and lemon wedges in a saucepan. Add 450 ml/½ pint water and heat gently, stirring to dissolve the sugar, until boiling. Leave over low heat for 30 minutes, then set aside until cold.

Add the orange juice, stir and strain into a clean jug. Squeeze, then discard the lemon wedges in the strainer. Crush the Campden tablet in a mug and add a little boiling water. Stir until dissolved, then add to the squash. Stir well before pouring into a bottle. Cover and store in the refrigerator for up to 3 weeks.

To serve, dilute to taste with water, soda water or mineral water.

MAKES ABOUT 1 LITRE/1¾ PINTS

ALCOHOL-FREE PUNCH

300 g/11 oz caster sugar
150 ml/¼ pint strong black tea
250 ml/8 fl oz lemon juice
350 ml/12 fl oz orange juice
1 litre/1¾ pints white grape juice
1 (227 g/8 oz) can crushed pineapple
2 litres/3½ pints ginger ale
ice cubes
1 (170 g/6 oz) bottle maraschino cherries, drained
2 lemons, sliced
2 oranges, sliced

Put the sugar in a large saucepan with 3.5 litres/6 pints water. Stir over gentle heat until the sugar has dissolved, then boil for 6 minutes. Stir in the tea and set aside until cool. Pour into one or two large jugs or bowls; cover and chill.

When quite cold, add the fruit juices and crushed pineapple. Just before serving, pour in the ginger ale and add the ice cubes. Add the maraschino cherries, stir once and serve with the citrus slices floating on top.

SERVES ABOUT 48

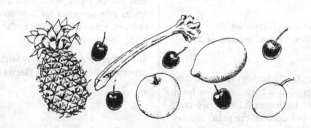

BARLEY WATER

This makes a nutritious drink, which keeps well in the refrigerator. If the lemon juice is omitted, it may be stirred into milk.

25 g/1 oz pearl barley
grated rind of 1 lemon
125 ml/4 fl oz lemon juice
sugar to taste

Put the pearl barley in a saucepan with water to cover. Bring to the boil and boil for 2 minutes, then strain into a clean pan. Stir in the lemon rind, juice and 1.1 litres/2 pints water. Heat gently, stirring occasionally, until boiling. Reduce the heat, cover the pan and cook gently for 45 minutes. Leave, covered, until cold.

Strain, sweeten to taste, then store in a covered container in the refrigerator for up to 1 week. Alternatively, freeze in ice-cube trays or small containers.

MAKES ABOUT 1.2 LITRES/2¼ PINTS

WELSH NECTAR

With a flavour reminiscent of grape juice, Welsh Nectar is a pleasant alcohol-free drink. Those who find it rather sweet may prefer to dilute it with soda water or carbonated spring water.

2 lemons
225 g/8 oz sugar lumps, crushed
225 g/8 oz seedless raisins, minced or finely chopped

Pare the lemons thinly, taking care to avoid the pith. Put the peel in a large heatproof bowl. Add the sugar. Pour over 2.25 litres/4 pints boiling water. Stir until all the sugar has dissolved. Cover and leave to stand until cool.

Squeeze the lemons; strain the juice into the bowl. Stir in the raisins. Pour into a large jar, close tightly and set aside for 4–5 days, stirring several times a day.

Strain the mixture through a jelly bag into clean bottles. Cover and refrigerate. Use within 2 weeks.

MAKES ABOUT 2 LITRES/3½ PINTS

 MRS BEETON'S TIP

If you do not have a jelly bag, but possess a filter coffee maker, use the jug, cone and filter paper to strain the nectar.

MULLED WINE

This traditional Christmas drink used to be heated by means of a red-hot mulling poker. Today the mixture is more likely to be made on top of the stove, but it remains a welcome warmer on a cold winter's night.

100 g/4 oz caster sugar
4 cinnamon sticks
4 cloves
1 nutmeg
2 oranges, thinly sliced
1 bottle red wine

Boil 600 ml/1 pint water with the sugar and spices in a saucepan for 5 minutes. Add the oranges, remove the pan from the heat and set aside for 15 minutes.

Stir in the wine. Heat slowly without boiling. Serve very hot, in heated glasses.

SERVES EIGHT TO TEN

STRAWBERRIES IN WINE

Strawberries, macerated in sherry or Madeira, make a delicious addition to punches and wine cups. With its rich strawberry-flavoured syrup, the fruit is also ideal as a last-minute dessert sauce, while the filled jars make attractive presents.

900 g/2 lb strawberries
100 g/4 oz caster sugar
dry sherry or Madeira (see method)

The fruit should be in perfect condition; clean, dry and hulled. Place the strawberries in sterilized wide-necked jars, sprinkling the sugar over the layers. The jars should be filled, but not overflowing.

Pour sherry or Madeira into the jars to fill them completely, covering the fruit. Tap the jars on the work surface to release any air bubbles. Cover tightly and set aside for 2–3 days, then top up with more liquor if necessary. Leave for at least 2 weeks before using; preferably 1 month.

MAKES ABOUT 900G/2LB

CIDER CUP

65 ml/2½ fl oz brandy
a few thin strips of cucumber peel
a few thin strips of lemon rind
10 ml/2 tsp lemon juice
10 ml/2 tsp caster sugar
1 litre/1¾ pints cider, chilled
500 ml/17 fl oz soda water, chilled

Combine the brandy, cucumber peel, lemon rind and juice in a large jug. Stir in the sugar. Just before serving, add the chilled cider and soda water.

SERVES TEN TO TWELVE

FRUIT CLARET CUP

This is a good basic fruit cup. The proportions of claret and soda water may be altered to suit personal taste.

cracked ice
50 ml/2 fl oz brandy
30 ml/2 tbsp caster sugar
30 ml/2 tbsp maraschino liqueur
6 maraschino cherries
30 ml/2 tbsp lemon juice
1 lemon, sliced and quartered
1 orange, sliced and quartered
6 thin slices of fresh pineapple, quartered
1 litre/1¾ pints claret
175 ml/6 fl oz soda water

Put some cracked ice into a large jug. Add the brandy, sugar, maraschino liqueur and cherries. Strain in the lemon juice and add the fresh fruit. Stir in the claret.

Just before serving, add the soda water and stir once.

SERVES TWELVE

VARIATIONS

Curaçao and Claret Cup Substitute curaçao for the brandy. Increase the quantity of maraschino to 40 ml/1½ fl oz. Omit the lemon and pineapple. When serving the cup, add 1 sliced red apple.

Claret and Lemonade Cooler Pour the claret on to cracked ice in a large bowl or jug. Strain in 450 ml/¾ pint lemon juice. Add 1 litre/1¾ pints lemonade or soda water just before serving.

CLARET CUP

Claret is the generic name for a wide range of red wines from the Bordeaux region in south western France. For this popular punch, try a Cabernet Sauvignon.

8 ice cubes or the equivalent quantity of
    crushed ice
1 bottle of claret (about 750 ml/1¼ pints)
75 ml/3 fl oz maraschino liqueur
50 g/2 oz icing sugar
500 ml/17 fl oz soda water
1 orange, sliced
2-3 borage sprigs

Put the ice in a large jug. Stir in the claret, maraschino and icing sugar. Just before serving, add the soda water and decorate with orange slices and borage sprigs.

SERVES FOUR TO SIX

CHAMPAGNE CUP

12 ice cubes or the equivalent quantity of
    crushed ice
1.1 litres/2 pints champagne
75 ml/3 fl oz curaçao
25 g/1 oz icing sugar
600 ml/1 pint soda water
10 cm/4 in strip of cucumber peel

Put the ice in a large jug. Stir in the champagne, curaçao and icing sugar. Add the soda water and decorate with the cucumber peel. Serve the champagne cup at once.

SERVES EIGHT TO TEN

SANGRIA

50 g/2 oz sugar
1 orange, sliced
1 lime or lemon, sliced
1 bottle of red wine (about 750 ml/1¼ pints)
12 ice cubes

Put the sugar in a small saucepan with 50 ml/2 fl oz water. Stir over gentle heat until the sugar has dissolved.

Put the citrus slices in a large heatproof bowl, pour over the hot syrup and set aside until cool. Add the wine and ice cubes. Stir well. Pour the sangria into a tall jug and serve at once, spooning 2-3 slices of fruit into each glass.

SERVES EIGHT

VARIATION

Party Sangria For a party, use double the amount of red wine. To the citrus slices add 5 fresh peaches, skinned and thinly sliced. Pour the hot syrup over the fruit, as above, and stir in the wine when cool. Add 50 ml/2 fl oz brandy, if liked. Just before serving, stir in about 20 ice cubes and 600 ml/1 pint soda water. 1 green apple, thinly sliced, may be added for extra colour.

NEGUS

Mrs Beeton's Negus had more water and it was originally a drink served at children's parties. Sherry or sweet white wine were sometimes used.

100 g/4 oz sugar lumps
1 lemon
600 ml/1 pint port
grated nutmeg

Rub a few of the sugar lumps over the lemon to absorb the oil. Put all the sugar lumps in a large heatproof jug.

Squeeze the lemon and strain the juice into the jug. Pour in the port. Stir the mixture, crushing the sugar lumps. Add 600 ml/1 pint boiling water, with grated nutmeg to taste. Stir well to dissolve all the sugar, cover the jug and set aside to cool slightly before serving.

SERVES SIX TO EIGHT

RUM AND BRANDY TODDY

This recipe yields a magnificent, warming drink!

225 g/8 oz sugar lumps
2 large lemons
600 ml/1 pint rum
600 ml/1 pint brandy
5 ml/1 tsp grated nutmeg

Rub a few of the sugar lumps over the lemon to absorb the oil. Put them in a heatproof bowl with the remaining sugar lumps. Squeeze the lemons and strain the juice into the bowl, then crush the sugar with a wooden spoon.

Pour 1.1 litres/2 pints boiling water into the bowl, stir well, then add the remaining ingredients. Mix thoroughly. Serve at once.

SERVES EIGHT TO TEN

HOME-MADE NOYEAU

This nut-flavoured liqueur can be used to flavour puddings and cakes.

150 ml/¼ pint milk
100 g/4 oz whole unblanched almonds
15 ml/1 tbsp liquid honey
225 g/8 oz caster sugar
grated rind of 1 lemon
1 (700 ml/24 fl oz) bottle Irish whiskey
150 ml/¼ pint single cream

Combine the milk, almonds and honey in a saucepan. Bring to the boil, remove from the heat, cover and leave to stand until quite cold.

Strain the milk into a jug. Grind the almonds in a nut mill or food processor, or pound in a mortar with a pestle.

Transfer the ground almonds to a bowl and stir in the sugar. Add the lemon rind and whiskey, then stir in the cold milk and honey mixture. Add the cream. Pour into a large jar, close tightly and store for 10 days, shaking daily.

Pour the mixture through a filter paper into a large jug. Fill small bottles, corking them tightly. Store in a cool, dry place.

MAKES ABOUT 900ML/1½ PINTS

WHISKEY CORDIAL

450 g/1 lb ripe white currants
grated rind of 2 lemons
100 g/4 oz root ginger, grated
1.1 litres/2 pints whiskey
450 g/1 lb sugar lumps, crushed

Strip the currants from the stalks and put them in a large jug. Add the lemon rind, ginger and whisky. Cover the jug closely and set it aside for 24 hours.

Strain through a fine sieve into a clean jug, stir in the sugar lumps and leave to stand for 12 hours more, stirring occasionally to dissolve the sugar lumps. Pour into clean bottles, cork tightly and store in a cool dry place.

MAKES ABOUT 1.25 LITRES/2¼ PINTS

GINGER BEER SHANDY

A time-honoured British drink for hot, sunny days.

900 ml/1½ pints chilled lager
500 ml/17 fl oz chilled Ginger Beer (see page 933)

Combine the ingredients in a large jug. Mix lightly, pour into tall glasses and serve at once, while the ginger beer is still effervescing.

SERVES FOUR

VARIATION

Lemonade Shandy   Substitute lemonade for the ginger beer.

ORANGE BRANDY

For the best flavour, use Seville oranges.

175 g/6 oz sugar lumps
2 oranges
1 (680 ml/23 fl oz) bottle of brandy

Rub a few of the sugar lumps over the oranges to absorb the oil. Put them in a large bowl with the remaining sugar lumps.

Pare the orange peel in thin strips, taking care to avoid the pith, and add to the bowl. Squeeze the oranges and strain the juice into the bowl. Crush the sugar cubes with a spoon. Stir in the brandy. Pour into a large jar, close tightly and set aside for 3 days, stirring several times a day.

When all the sugar has dissolved, strain the mixture into clean bottles. Cork tightly and store in a cool, dry place. The flavour will improve on keeping, and the brandy should ideally be stored for 1 year before being opened.

MAKES ABOUT 1 LITRE/1¾ PINTS

MULLED ALE

1 litre/1¾ pints ale
15-30 ml/1-2 tbsp caster sugar
generous pinch of ground cloves
pinch of grated nutmeg
generous pinch of ground ginger
100 ml/3½ fl oz rum or brandy

Combine the ale, 15 ml/1 tbsp caster sugar and the spices in a large saucepan. Bring to just below boiling point. Remove from the heat and stir in the rum or brandy, with more sugar if required. Ladle into heated glasses and serve at once.

SERVES EIGHT TO TEN

COCKTAILS

The popularity of the cocktail waxes and wanes, and whether you elect to surprise your guests with a Sidecar or Screwdriver depends very much on the state of your liquor cabinet, the sophistication of your bar equipment and whether anyone is expecting to drive home. Many cocktails taste deceptively innocent, but are in fact highly alcoholic. There are hundreds of different cocktails; a few of the more popular varieties are listed below:

Americano 1 part each of Campari and sweet vermouth, stirred in a tall glass and topped up with soda. Add a slice of orange.

Black Velvet 1 part each of dry champagne and bitter stout (usually Guiness). Pour simultaneously into a tall jug. Serve in tall glasses or tankards.

Bloody Mary 1 part vodka to 2 parts tomato juice. Serve on crushed ice and stir in Worcestershire sauce, lemon juice, salt and pepper to taste. Tabasco may also be added if liked.

Bronx 3 parts gin to 1 part each of dry vermouth, sweet vermouth and orange juice, shaken, then strained into tall glasses.

Bucks Fizz 1 part orange juice to 2 parts chilled champagne. Serve in tall glasses; do not add ice.

Champagne Cocktail Put 1 sugar lump into a champagne flute. Soak in Angostura bitters. Add about 5 ml/1 tsp brandy and top up with chilled champagne.

Daiquiri 3 parts white rum to 1 part fresh lime or lemon juice. Add 1.25 ml/¼ tsp caster sugar, shake, then strain into cocktail glasses.

Dry Martini 2 parts dry gin to 1 part dry vermouth, stirred in a mixing glass, then strained over cracked ice in a cocktail glass. Serve with a twist of lemon rind.

Horse's Neck Pare the rind of a lemon in a long spiral; hook it over the rim of a tumbler so that it curls over. Anchor the end inside the glass with 2 ice cubes. Add 40 ml/1½ fl oz brandy and fill with ginger ale. Add a few drops of Angostura bitters, if liked.

Kir 1 part Crème de Cassis to 6 parts chilled white burgundy. Pour the wine over the Cassis in a balloon glass. Ice is optional.

Manhattan 2 parts bourbon to 1 part sweet vermouth. Stir in a mixing glass with a few drops of Angostura bitters, if liked. Serve over cracked ice and top with a maraschino cherry.

Negroni 1 part each of dry gin, sweet vermouth and Campari. Pour over ice cubes in a tall glass and top up with soda water if liked. Add a slice of orange.

Old Fashioned Put 1 sugar lump into a tall glass. Soak in Angostura bitters. Add enough water to dissolve the sugar (about 10 ml/2 tsp). Pour over 75 ml/3 fl oz rye or bourbon. Decorate with a maraschino cherry and an orange slice.

Pink Gin Shake a few drops of Angostura bitters into a wine or cocktail glass. Roll the bitters around the glass. Pour away, if liked. Add 40 ml/1½ fl oz gin to the glass with ice cubes, if liked.

Screwdriver 2 parts orange juice to 1 part vodka. Stir in a wine or cocktail glass. Add ice cubes and decorate with a slice of orange.

Sidecar 2 parts brandy to 1 part each of Cointreau and lemon juice. Shake with cracked ice, then strain into a cocktail glass.

Vodkatini 2 parts vodka to 1 part dry vermouth, stirred together in a mixing glass, then strained into a cocktail glass. Serve with ice and a twist of lemon rind.

Whisky Mac 1 part each of whisky and ginger wine, stirred together in a wine or cocktail glass. Do not add ice.

Cooking for One

This brief chapter shows that cooking and eating alone does not have to be dull, nor should it mean relying on convenience foods. If you cook for yourself it can be easy to slip into the habit of opting for a ready-made bought dish or a quick snack instead of preparing a proper meal. On an occasional basis this is unlikely to be a dietary disaster, although it will tax the food budget, but it is not a good idea to eat this way frequently.

BUYING AND STORING FOOD

A certain amount of freezer space, as in a fridge freezer, is a valuable asset since it means that larger portions may be purchased and the surplus frozen.

Selecting your own vegetables at supermarkets means you can buy as little as you need, but meat and poultry are often packed in portions for two. An independent butcher will sell you as little as you want of any cut – if you happen to fancy four pork spare ribs or one lamb cutlet and two sausages, most will happily oblige. A good fishmonger is also worth finding. Some will not only provide individual portions but offer advice on cooking at the same time.

Buying cans and packets is not as significant a problem. If you have sufficient storage space, it is still worth buying larger, more economical, packs of dry foods. Remember to check the best-before date on the packet. Single portion cans, of fish or meat, for instance, can be expensive. The food will keep in a clean, covered container for 24 hours in the refrigerator, so with a little imagination one large tin can be made into two meals.

CREATIVE COOKING

Cooking double portions of meat dishes, such as sauces or stews, makes sense if you don't mind eating the same style of dish twice. Vary the result by changing accompaniments or adding finishing touches. For example, the unbiquitous meat sauce can be served with baked potatoes, pasta or rice; or it can be topped with a thick layer of breadcrumbs and cheese and grilled until golden before being served with a salad.

Adapting recipes intended to serve four is not necessarily difficult, but there are a few possible pitfalls. Dividing the quantities of main ingredients is fairly straightforward, but quartering a clove of garlic can pose problems. Look for products like minced garlic or garlic salt, which allow tiny amounts to be used. When in season, pickling onions are more convenient than halved or quartered onions, and using a little instant mashed potato as a quick thickening agent for sauces or soups is simpler than messing about with beurre manié, whatever the purists may say.

Another knack to master is that of adjusting cooking methods to suit your facilities. For example food braised in the oven can usually be cooked on the hob. Even the succulent browning effect typical of roasting can be duplicated by cooking on the hob in a heavy-bottomed pan with a tight-fitting lid. A heavy pan with a coated cast-iron base and a lid that fits snugly is a boon. Getting to know your appliances – learning to adjust the heat on an electric ring or gas burner to give a low setting – is also important.

Lastly, with practice and imagination, it is surprising how easy it is to adapt many recipes which incorporate several stages and many pans for one-pot cooking. When attempting to combine stages and ingredients, remember to work out individual cooking times, so you will have a good idea of when to add ingredients to the cooking pot.

HADDOCK WITH ORANGE

fat for greasing
1 portion haddock fillet (about 175 g/6 oz)
30 ml/2 tbsp orange juice
salt and pepper
pinch of grated nutmeg
2.5 ml/½ tsp grated orange rind
knob of butter

Set the oven at 180°C/350°F/gas 4. Lay the haddock fillet in a lightly greased shallow ovenproof dish. Sprinkle with the orange juice and season lightly with salt, pepper and nutmeg. Add the orange rind. Dot with the butter, cover with foil and bake for about 20 minutes.

Alternatively, steam the fish in a suitable dish or between two plates over a saucepan of simmering water for about 20 minutes. Serve the fish with the cooking juices spooned over. A baked potato, some cooked rice or pasta, and a salad of tomatoes with chopped onion are excellent accompaniments.

SERVES ONE

 MICROWAVE TIP

Prepare as suggested above, putting the haddock in a covered shallow dish. Cook on High for about 3 minutes, depending on the thickness of the fish.

CREAMY GRILLED COD

1 cod steak
salt and pepper
5 ml/1 tsp French mustard
30 ml/2 tbsp Greek yogurt
15 ml/1 tbsp olive oil
1.25 ml/¼ tsp dried mixed herbs
30 ml/2 tbsp soft cheese with herbs and garlic

GARNISH
watercress sprigs
10 ml/2 tsp French dressing (optional)

Trim the fish of skin, if liked, then place on the rack of a grill pan. In a small bowl, mix the salt and pepper, mustard, yogurt, oil and herbs. Use a teaspoon to spread a little of this mixture over the top of the fish. Heat the grill on medium.

Cook the fish steak until lightly browned on one side, spreading a second spoonful of the yogurt mixture over it after 1 minute. Turn the fish carefully using a fish slice, then spread with half the remaining yogurt mixture. Continue cooking, topping with the rest of the yogurt after about 5 minutes, until cooked through and lightly browned. This should take about 15 minutes in all, depending on the thickness of the fish.

Serve at once, topped with the soft cheese. Garnish with watercress, and spoon a little French dressing over the garnish.

SERVES ONE

 MICROWAVE TIP

Place the fish and topping mixture in a suitable dish. Cover and cook on High for about 5 minutes, turning once. Top with the soft cheese and serve as above.

MARINATED MACKEREL

1 mackerel
parsley sprig to garnish

MARINADE
30 ml/2 tbsp olive oil
5 ml/1 tsp lemon juice
fresh thyme sprig
½ bay leaf
1 parsley stalk, broken into short lengths
salt and pepper

Rinse the fish inside and out and pat dry on absorbent kitchen paper. Make 3 diagonal slashes in the flesh on both sides of the fish.

Mix all the ingredients for the marinade in a shallow dish just large enough to hold the fish. Add the mackerel, turning to coat it evenly in the marinade. Cover the dish and marinate the fish for 1 hour.

Drain the fish, reserving the marinade, and place on a rack over a grill pan. Grill under moderate heat for 5–7 minutes each side, turning once and basting frequently with the reserved marinade. Serve very hot, garnished with the parsley sprig.

SERVES ONE

BRAISED LAMB CHOP WITH BARLEY

15 ml/1 tbsp oil
1 lamb chop, trimmed
¼ onion, finely chopped
½ bay leaf
salt and pepper
125 ml/4 fl oz lamb or vegetable stock
45 ml/3 tbsp pearl barley, washed
75 g/3 oz frozen peas

Heat the oil in a small heavy-bottomed saucepan. Brown the chop quickly on both sides, then add the onion, bay leaf and salt and pepper to taste. Pour in the stock, bring to the boil, and lower the heat. Cover tightly and simmer for 15 minutes. Stir in the barley and simmer for 30 minutes more.

Add the frozen peas to the pan, bring the liquid to the boil, then lower the heat and simmer, covered for 5–7 minutes or until the peas are tender. Serve in a warmed soup bowl, with garlic croûtons (see Mrs Beeton's Tip), if liked.

SERVES ONE

 MRS BEETON'S TIP

To make garlic croûtons, remove the crusts from 2 slices of bread. Cut the bread into cubes. Heat 30 ml/2 tbsp oil in a small frying pan, add 1 crushed garlic clove and fry over gentle heat for 3–4 minutes. Remove the garlic with a slotted spoon. Add the bread cubes to the garlic-flavoured oil and fry until crisp. Drain and serve.

PRAWNS IN ONION AND TOMATO SAUCE

15 ml/1 tbsp olive oil
1 small onion, finely chopped
1 small garlic clove, crushed
2 tomatoes, peeled and chopped
5 ml/1 tsp chopped parsley
salt and pepper
pinch of dried tarragon
150 g/5 oz peeled cooked prawns
50 g/2 oz cheese, grated

Heat the oil in a frying pan, add the onion and garlic and fry for 7–10 minutes or until soft. Stir in the tomatoes and parsley, with salt and pepper to taste. Add the tarragon, cover the pan and cook gently for 15 minutes.

Stir in the prawns and heat through gently. Spoon into a flameproof dish and sprinkle the cheese over the top. Grill until golden brown. Serve at once, with crusty bread. Alternatively, omit the cheese and use as a filling for a baked jacket potato (see page 358) or serve on rice or noodles.

SERVES ONE

CHICKEN AND HAM CHARLOTTE

1 large slice of bread
butter
50 g/2 oz cooked chicken, finely chopped
1 slice of cooked ham, finely chopped
150 ml/¼ pint milk or chicken stock
1 egg yolk, beaten
salt and pepper

Set the oven at 160°C/325°F/gas 3. Remove the crusts, then butter the bread. Put one piece, buttered side up, on the base of an individual ovenproof dish. Cover with the chopped chicken and ham.

Place the second piece of bread, again buttered side up, on top of the chicken. Warm the milk or chicken stock in a small saucepan, remove from the heat and beat in the egg yolk. Add plenty of salt and pepper.

Pour the egg mixture into the dish, put the dish in a small roasting tin, and add enough boiling water to come halfway up the sides of the dish. Bake for 45 minutes.

SERVES ONE

CHICKEN IN A JACKET

1 (75 g/3 oz) chicken breast, trimmed
15 ml/1 tbsp corn oil
freshly ground black pepper
15 ml/1 tbsp fine cut orange marmalade
5 ml/1 tsp sesame seeds
7.5 ml/1½ tsp natural wheat bran

GARNISH
thin slices of fresh orange
watercress sprigs

Wipe the chicken breast and dry it well on absorbent kitchen paper. Brush with oil on both sides, and sprinkle lightly with pepper. Grill under very gentle heat for 15–20 minutes, basting twice with oil. Turn, then grill for a further 15 minutes, basting twice.

Remove the chicken from the heat and spread the top with marmalade. Sprinkle with the sesame seeds and bran. Return to the grill and cook very gently for 4–5 minutes, taking care that the coating does not burn. Serve hot, garnished with orange slices and watercress sprigs.

SERVES ONE

GRILLED PORK CHOP WITH APPLE

1 pork loin chop, trimmed
5 ml/1 tsp oil
ground pepper
dried sage
dried marjoram
caster sugar
salt
1 sharp eating apple
30 ml/2 tbsp apple sauce

Put the chop on an oiled grill rack. Brush with half the oil and sprinkle with pepper, sage, marjoram and a pinch of caster sugar. Cook under a hot grill until lightly browned.

Using a spoon and fork, carefully turn the chop over. Brush the second side with oil and sprinkle with pepper, herbs and sugar as before. Brown quickly, then lower the heat and cook for 15–20 minutes until cooked through. Sprinkle lightly with salt and keep hot.

Peel and core the apple. Cut 4 thick slices and put them on the grill rack. Brush with the fat in the grill pan and grill lightly until golden brown on both sides.

Put the chop on a heated plate, spoon the apple sauce next to it and fan the apple slices on the other side. Serve at once.

SERVES ONE

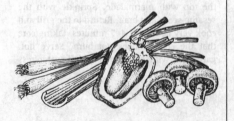

CHICKEN IN FOIL

butter for greasing
1 boneless chicken breast
½ small carrot, sliced
1 small onion, sliced
50 g/2 oz mushrooms, sliced
30 ml/2 tbsp white wine
salt and pepper
1 bay leaf

Set the oven at 180°C/350°F/gas 4. Butter a square of foil large enough to wrap the chicken breast. Put the chicken on the foil, top with the carrot, onion and mushroom slices and carefully pour the wine over. Sprinkle with salt and pepper, tuck a bay leaf among the vegetables and close the foil to make a loose parcel.

Put the foil parcel in a baking tin and bake for 45 minutes. Open the parcel carefully to avoid losing any of the juices. Make sure that the chicken is cooked, then transfer it, still in the foil parcel, to a serving plate.

SERVES ONE

ONE-POT STIR FRY

30 ml/2 tbsp oil
1 carrot, halved and thinly sliced
1 thick slice of bread, cut into 2.5 cm/1 inch squares
2 small courgettes, sliced
2 spring onions, chopped
50 g/2 oz mushrooms, sliced
50 g/2 oz sliced garlic sausage, cut in strips
2 tomatoes, roughly chopped
salt and pepper

Heat the oil in a frying pan or wok. Stir fry the carrot for 3 minutes, then add the bread and continue stir frying for about 5 minutes, or until the chunks are lightly browned in parts.

Add the courgettes, spring onions and mushrooms and continue to stir fry for 3 minutes. Tip in the garlic sausage and cook for a further minute before adding the tomatoes. Once the tomatoes have been added, toss the mixture for just a few seconds as the bread will soon become soft. Add salt and pepper to taste. Serve piping hot.

SERVES ONE

SAVOURY SAUSAGE TOASTS

2 rindless streaky bacon rashers
4 chipolata sausages
4 tomato slices
4 apple slices
15 ml/1 tbsp melted butter
2 slices of bread, toasted

Roll up the bacon rashers and secure with wooden cocktail sticks. Grill the sausages and bacon rolls under moderate heat for about 5 minutes, turning once. Add the tomato and apples slices, brush with butter and cook for 5 minutes.

Brush any remaining butter over the toast, then top with apple, tomato, chipolatas and bacon rolls.

SERVES ONE

KIDNEYS ON CROUTES

2 lamb's kidneys
15 ml/1 tbsp butter
1 shallot, finely chopped
5 ml/1 tsp plain flour
15 ml/1 tbsp sherry or Madeira
60 ml/4 tbsp thin gravy
salt and pepper
Worcestershire sauce (see method)
oil for frying
2 slices of bread, crusts removed
15 ml/1 tbsp chopped parsley

Skin and core the kidneys; slice as thinly as possible. Melt the butter in a frying pan, add the shallot and fry for 2-3 minutes. Add the sliced kidneys and toss gently over moderate heat for 4-5 minutes.

Using a slotted spoon, transfer the kidneys to a small bowl and keep hot. Sprinkle the flour into the fat remaining in the pan, stir and cook for 1 minute. Gradually add the sherry or Madeira and the thin gravy. Cook, stirring, until the mixture boils and thickens. Add salt, pepper and Worcestershire sauce to taste.

Add the kidneys to the sauce and warm through gently. Meanwhile heat the oil in a large frying pan. Add the slices of bread and fry quickly until golden on both sides. Remove from the heat, drain on absorbent kitchen paper and place on a hot plate. Top with the kidney mixture, sprinkle with parsley.

SERVES ONE

 MRS BEETON'S TIP

If frying the bread is unacceptable – either because it takes too long or for dietary reasons – simply serve the kidney mixture on toast.

BACON OLIVES

50 g/2 oz cooked ham, finely chopped
30 ml/2 tbsp fresh white breadcrumbs
2.5 ml/½ tsp finely chopped onion
2.5 ml/½ tsp finely chopped parsley
pinch of dried mixed herbs
pinch of grated nutmeg
salt and pepper
beaten egg or milk (see method)
4 rindless streaky bacon rashers

Combine the ham, breadcrumbs, onion, herbs and nutmeg in a bowl. Add salt and pepper to taste. Gradually stir in enough beaten egg or milk to bind the mixture. Set aside for 30 minutes.

Set the oven at 190°C/375°F/gas 5. Divide the ham mixture into four portions. Form each portion into a cork shape, roll in a bacon rasher and secure with string. Put on a baking sheet and bake for 30 minutes.

Serve at once, with wholemeal bread, pasta or brown rice and lightly cooked beans or carrots. Alternatively, serve on toast, with a single portion of Waldorf Salad (page 378).

SERVE ONE

 MRS BEETON'S TIP

If you want to avoid heating the oven, bind the stuffing mixture with milk instead of egg and spread it over the bacon instead of forming the cork shape. Roll up and thread on a metal skewer. Cook under a medium-hot grill until the bacon rolls are cooked through and golden outside. Turn occasionally during cooking.

DEVILLED CHICKEN LIVERS

15 ml/1 tbsp butter
225 g/8 oz chicken livers, trimmed and cut in half
2 spring onions, chopped
1 garlic clove, crushed
15 ml/1 tbsp tomato purée
5 ml/1 tsp French mustard
dash of Worcestershire sauce
pinch of chilli powder

Melt the butter in a saucepan. Add the chicken livers, spring onions and garlic and fry lightly for about 10 minutes over moderate heat, stirring all the time. The livers should be browned and just cooked.

Stir in the remaining ingredients and cook for 1-2 minutes more. Serve on toast, as a filling for a baked potato or with rice.

SERVES ONE

Menu Planning

The success of any snack or meal, both in aesthetic and dietary terms, hinges upon the combination of food or dishes which comprise it. A few important guideline summarize the approach to planning menus for every day as well as for special occasions.

The key points to consider when planning a menu, apart from the likes and dislikes or dietary restrictions of the diners, are the flavours, textures, colour and weight of the meal. A well-planned menu balances all these elements. Additional, practical, aspects to consider are your ability and confidence as a cook; the budget for one meal or for a weekly – or monthly – run of meals; and the cooking facilities available.

When planning a menu, it is usual to consider the main course of the meal first, then to fit the starter, fish course or dessert around it. This does not always have to be the rule – if you have a particularly splendid starter or dessert which you want to serve at a dinner party, or even for a family meal, there is absolutely no reason why you should not work the rest of the meal around it. If, for example, you wanted to serve a chocolate fondue as the finale of a dinner party, it would be logical to keep the preceding courses light. Equally, traditional steamed sponge pudding with custard is a real family treat but is not suitable for serving after a very filling main course, so a light salad and grilled fish would be the better option.

FLAVOURS AND TEXTURES

As well as considering the accompaniments for the main dish, remember that a strongly flavoured starter will put a lightly seasoned main course in the shade, just as a very spicy main course will ruin the palate for a delicate dessert. Balance strong flavours and aim to accentuate more subtle dishes.

Texture is a less obvious but equally important characteristic of food. A meal that consists solely of soft food is dull, and three courses of dry or crunchy dishes can be a disaster, leaving everyone gasping for water. Balance soft and smooth mixtures with crunchy textures; combine moist dishes with dry ones. Offer crisp salads with zesty dressings to counteract rich fried foods; serve plain, crunchy, lightly cooked vegetables to balance heavily sauced casseroles and stews.

COLOUR AND WEIGHT

The importance of colour in a dish and on a menu does not simply refer to the piece of parsley dropped on to a grey sauce. The ingredients used in individual dishes, the quality of cooking juices and sauces and the choice of accompaniments are all factors in achieving a menu that looks appealing. Some cooked foods inevitably look uninteresting; this is when the choice of accompaniments is vital. Remember that flavour and texture must also be considered.

The overall weight of the meal is important. Light dishes should balance richer foods. A filling dish should always be flanked by delicate courses.

FOOD VALUE

The chapter on Nutrition and Diet outlines the importance of eating a balanced diet. Dinner parties and special meals are occasions for breaking or bending the rules and indulging in favourite foods. When planning everyday meals or snacks, however, it is very important to consider food value alongside the flavour, texture and appearance of the dishes. Applying rigid guidelines to every meal is not practical but considering the overall food value of the day's diet is prudent. Taking a sensible, overall view of food eaten over a period of a few days, or within a week, is also a reasonable way of ensuring that snacks and meals provide a balanced diet. From breakfast through to supper, whether considering the main meal of the day or an in-between meal snack, variety is one of the keys to success, both in the range of foods eaten and the cooking or serving methods used.

CATERING FOR SPECIAL DIETS

Be aware of any dietary restrictions for social or medical reasons, planning them into the menu for all diners as far as possible. In some cases, for example when catering for vegartarians as well as meat eaters, it is quite possible to provide one menu to suit everyone. Contemporary vegetarian dishes are acceptable to all, not simply to those who avoid animal products; it is far trickier to plan a vegan menu to suit all tastes. Limitations imposed for health reasons may be more difficult to accommodate; if in doubt, check details with the prospective guest or consult an official source of information for guidance.

If the whole menu cannot be adapted to suit everyone, plan the meal around one or two of the key dishes. It is usually quite easy to serve a first course to suit all diets. Either the main dish or vegetable accompaniments should be selected for their versatility: if the main dish is unsuitable for certain diners, then the vegetable accompaniments should make equally interesting main dishes on their own. For example, ratatouille, a mixed vegetable gratin or stir-fried vegetables with noodles are all suitable for serving with plain meat dishes but they are equally good vegetarian dishes when served with appropriate accompaniments.

Adopt this approach whenever you plan meals and snacks but pay special attention to the food value of restricted diets if you cater for them on a regular basis. Make up for nutrients lost in banned foods by including compensatory alternatives.

PARTIES

The choice of party food depends on the number of guests and the budget – these factors influence the style of food, choice of ingredients, balance of hot and cold dishes and the number of courses. Whether you are planning a formal meal or cocktail-style buffet with snacks and nibbles, remember the following points as they are crucial to the success – or failure – of the menu.

● Time available for food preparation.
● Refrigerator space for storing ingredients and/or dishes which require chilling.
● Kitchen facilities, particularly oven and hob space.
● Freezer space and suitability of dishes for preparing in advance.
● Availability of crockery and cutlery for serving.
● The time available for last-minute work, finishing dishes, garnishing and so on.
● Your own ability as cook – opt for a menu which you will tackle with confidence.
● Ease of serving and eating the food: the only thing worse than a host or hostess who is overstretched by last-minute cooking between courses at a formal dinner party is the poor guest who is struggling with a knife and fork while standing and balancing a plate, glass and napkin, at the same time chatting politely to other guests.

COOKING IN QUANTITY

Forward planning is all-important when cooking for a crowd, from considering the likes and dislikes of guests, planning the menu, checking the serving arrangements and crockery through to clearing up afterwards. It is vital to select a menu which is manageable kitchenwise and to batch cook ahead, if possible, to avoid running out of oven space, cooking utensils or equipment for one massive cooking session.

The following are all practical choices for buffets for large numbers up to fifty (or more), for informal parties or occasions such as weddings. The dishes selected may either be cooked ahead and frozen or they are a sensible choice for same-day cooking. Remember that you can hire large cooking pans for potatoes or rice that require last minute cooking. When batch baking these recipes, double the quantities; this is practical and speedy. The recipes suggested all feature in this book or a guide to proportions is included here. Consult the Index for page numbers.

Fresh Salmon Mousse Take one quantity to serve 10 as part of a buffet. Make the day before, or add a little extra gelatine if freezing ahead.

Smoked Mackerel Pâté One quantity to serve 12 as part of a buffet. Freeze ahead.

Galantine of Chicken Bone, stuff and freeze well ahead. Thaw thoroughly, cook, dress and chill the day before. Allow 12–15 portions per galantine, depending on other buffet dishes.

Chicken Mayonnaise Allow 1 small boneless chicken breast per person, skinned. Roast, covered, cool and chill the day before. The chicken may be diced before chilling. Coat with mayonnaise thinned with a little cream or yogurt and dress with chopped parsley, chives and tarragon. For a well-dressed dish, allow

600 ml/1 pint mayonnaise and 300 ml/½ pint plain yogurt or cream for 25 chicken breasts. Browned flaked almonds or grated lemon rind may be sprinkled over instead of the herbs.

Baked Ham Order a whole cooked ham, preferably on the bone, from a good butcher, delicatessen or large supermarket. The rind may be removed and the fat coated with brown sugar, then browned in a hot oven before serving the ham.

Carbonnade of Beef Cook in double-quantity batches, with slightly less liquid; each batch to serve 12. Cool and freeze well ahead, packing in small quantities that thaw quickly. Thoroughly reheat in the oven just before serving the carbonnade.

New Potatoes Scrub and boil small new potatoes, then drain and toss in butter with chives or mint. They should be scrubbed the day before, boiled early on the day of the party until only just cooked, then drained and tossed in butter. Cool quickly and reheat well in their butter before serving. Allow 1.8–2.25 kg/4–5 lb for 16–20 portions; 5.5–6.75 kg/12–15 lb for 50 portions.

For a delicious salad, cook the potatoes completely, then toss them in an oil and vinegar dressing, adding lots of snipped chives and chopped parsley, cover and cool.

Cooked Rice Allow 50 g/2 oz per person as a side dish, 75 g/3 oz per person as part of a main dish (for example, risotto) on a buffet. Cook with twice the volume of water. If serving hot, cook ahead, cool and chill promptly. Reheat thoroughly to a high temperature in covered serving dishes and serve promptly: do not reheat more than once and do not allow to stand, lukewarm, on the buffet for long periods. Rice salads should be kept chilled until served.

Quiche Make, chill and freeze quiches in advance, allowing 10–12 portions from a

20-23 cm/8-9 inch round quiche, depending on other buffet food. Thaw and reheat just before serving.

Salad Green salad is practical and a refreshing accompaniment to most buffet food; however, it is seldom eaten in any quantity. Select a crisp lettuce and shred or cut all ingredients finely. A salad of 1 large lettuce, with cucumber, spring onions and green pepper will yield up to 30 portions as part of a buffet. Serve dressing separately.

Meringues Make ahead – when thoroughly dried, meringues keep well in airtight containers in a cool place for at least a couple of weeks. Pile them high in a dish and serve with a bowl each of whipped cream and strawberries for a 'do-it-yourself' dessert. Allow 600 ml/1 pint cream, whipped to serve 15-20 and 75 g/3 oz strawberries per portion.

Brownies These make a good dessert for freezing ahead. Thaw on the day of serving, stack them up and serve with a bowl of whipped cream.

Mousseline Cake Another good dessert to bake ahead and freeze.

Sachertorte Make ahead and freeze, assemble and coat the day before. Serve with whipped cream.

ADAPTING RECIPES

There are a number of important factors to bear in mind when catering in quantity. If you are planning to scale up a favourite recipe, you must first look at it carefully to see if it contains any strong flavourings. These do not need to be scaled up in the same proportions as the meat or vegetable content of the recipe, as a small amount of flavouring will penetrate quite large quantities of food. Spices, garlic, strong herbs, and proprietary sauces all need to be handled with care.

The liquid content of the dish also needs to be looked at carefully. A fish dish with sauce, for example, will not need as much sauce when produced in quantity. Stews and casseroles, too, may not need the same proportion of liquid.

Apart from the logical reasons for these differences when increasing quantities, there is also a psychological factor. When dishes are prepared for four or six people, the cook wishes the food not only to be sufficient but to look sufficient, and very often enough food is made for five or seven. Unless this factor is taken into account when scaling up, the resultant recipe for fifty would actually feed sixty or more.

APPROXIMATE QUANTITIES OF BASIC FOODS PER PERSON

Bread
French bread 2 slices (with dinner; more may be eaten with salad); 3-4 slices (served with just wine and cheese)
Rolls 2

Butter 25 g/1 oz

Cheese 100 g/4 oz (served at wine and cheese party); 50 g/2 oz (served as last course of dinner)

Pâté 50 g/2 oz (as first-course dish)

Soup 150 ml/¼ pint

Meat
On the bone 150-225 g/5-8 oz (main course: depending on whether used in casserole with vegetables or on its own)
Off the bone 100-150 g/4-5 oz (main course: depending on whether used in casserole with vegetables or on its own)

Chicken
On the bone 150-225 g/5-8 oz (main course: depending on whether used in casserole with vegetables or on its own)
Off the bone 100-150 g/4-5 oz (main course: depending on whether used in casserole with vegetables or on its own)

Fish *Fillet or steak* 100–150 g/4–5 oz (depending on whether main or subsidiary course)

Vegetables 100 g/4 oz (served with one other vegetable and potatoes as accompaniment to main course)

Rice 25–50 g/1–2 oz (uncooked)

Pasta 50–100 g/2–4 oz (depending on whether main course or subsidiary)

Gravy/sauces 75–100 ml/3–3½ fl oz (served with main dish)

Salad dressings 15–20 ml/3–4 tsp (smaller quantity for French dressing, larger for mayonnaise)

Desserts
Ice cream 50–75 ml/2–3 fl oz (depending on richness, whether an accompaniment, etc)
Fruit 150 g/5 oz (for fruit salad)
Pouring cream 75 ml/3 fl oz

Tea 5 ml/1 tsp tea leaves per person; 125 ml/4 fl oz milk for 4 people

Coffee 125 ml/4 fl oz per person; 125 ml/4 fl oz cream for 4 people

For finger buffets and cocktail canapés, check by making a mental picture of one of each of all the items you are planning to serve set out together on a plate. This will give you an idea of the quantity allowed for each person.

OUTDOOR EATING AND PACKED LUNCHES

The days of the Great British Picnic, when teams of servants set up groaning tables in field and forest, may have passed, but eating out of doors can still be a significant social occasion, with several families or friends gathering for an outdoor party or a sophisticated meal at a sporting event or an alfresco theatrical performance.

Food which can be cooked ahead and eaten cold, salads that travel well without becoming limp and crusty bread are all ideal. Make sure the food arrives in prime condition by using chiller bags for perishable foods. Sturdy plastic containers which seal well are ideal for salads and desserts as well as savouries such as stuffed vine leaves or an array of cooked cold meats.

When ease of preparation takes priority over economy, shop for salami, cooked ham, pork pie, cooked continental sausages, smoked chicken or turkey and smoked mackerel, trout or salmon. Opt for thinly sliced rye breads and a variety of rolls, then make a good mixed salad and take a jar of dressing to toss into it at the last minute.

Finger foods, selected for their portability, are always acceptable. Tiny pizzas, individual filo pastries, quiches or pasties, spiced chicken drumsticks, crudités with a selection of dips, pinwheel sandwiches, filled bridge rolls or prawns will all prove popular.

PACKED LUNCHES

These are far more down-to-earth than picnics. They may be a regular meal, in which case special attention should be paid to food value.

Sandwiches are practical and easy, and do not have to be boring. Keep the fat content low, particularly in an adult's daily lunch box, by doing away with lashings of butter: it is not essential and once you are accustomed to sandwiches without butter or margarine, they are fine. Low-fat spreads and soft cheeses are worth considering but they are not necessary.

Combine salad ingredients such as cucumber, lettuce, tomatoes and spring onions with cold cooked poultry, meat or cheese. Peanut butter provides food value as well as flavour; it goes well with lettuce and cucumber. Easy-to-eat pasties and pies can be included from time to time but pastry products contribute a significant amount of fat, so should be used sparingly. Mixed salads are excellent and easy to eat – with a chunk of bread or a roll they can be satisfying and nutritious.

Small vacuum flasks are ideal for soup or hot drinks and can equally well be used for cold drinks in summer. Milk drinks, hot or cold, are nutritious for young children who may be less eager to eat all the packed lunch provided. Fresh fruit is the simplest and most nutritious sweet. Bananas, apples and pears are the most practical choices; oranges, peaches and other refreshing fruit are suitable but can be messy to eat. Dried fruit, boxed in individual portions, is another option, and it is also possible to buy individual cans of fruit with ring-pull tops, as occasional treats. Yogurt may also be offered. Small insulated containers are available, which will keep yogurt cartons cool. Don't forget to pack a teaspoon.

It is best to avoid crisps, sweet biscuits or chunks of sweet cake as regular lunch-box features. Semi-sweet biscuits, scones and tea-breads are all easy to pack and are not too sugar-rich.

Remember that food which is packed early in the morning should be kept as cool as possible until it is eaten. Insulated lunch boxes and small chiller bags are ideal for this purpose.

BARBECUES

Make sure that you have sufficient charcoal and enough grilling space for the food to be cooked. Light the barbecue at least 30 minutes before you plan to cook: depending on the size barbecue, you may need to light it up to 1 hour ahead. The barbecue is ready for cooking when the coals have stopped flaming. When cooking for a crowd, part-cook chicken in the oven and finish it on the barbecue.

Plan your menu around the barbecuing: have nibbles and drinks for guests while the food is cooking. Dips and crudités are ideal starters. Serve salads, baked potatoes or crusty bread as accompaniments. Have relishes and chutneys with plain grilled foods. Desserts should be simple and fruit may be grilled on the barbecue.

Pay special attention to safety at all times, from lighting up to over-imbibing and risking an accident. Always ensure children are supervised and pets restrained.

VEGETARIAN ALTERNATIVES

Combining a part-vegetarian menu with fish, poultry or meat dishes requires planning. Include a side dish which is ideal as a vegetarian main course, then plan the meat main dish. For example, vegetables or ratatouille with a gratin topping, a vegetable curry or chilli may be served on their own or as accompaniments for grilled fish, poultry or meat. Remember to cook a slightly larger quantity to allow for main dish servings as well as asides. Baked potatoes, rice or pasta are also versatile and a salad offers a palate-refreshing accompaniment for both options.

Everyday packed lunches seldom cause problems but the person who is entertaining may be concerned about providing suitable, interesting vegetarian picnic and barbecue food. Apart from salads, tempting vegetable or bean pasties, pastes and spreads, made from beans and pulses, and quiches with vegetable and dairy fillings are ideal. Vegetables can be delicious grilled on the barbecue, either threaded on skewers to make kebabs or marinated and grilled whole. Aubergines, peppers, courgettes, small whole onions and tomatoes are typical examples. Vegetable or lentil burgers and Haloumi cheese also grill well. Remember to set aside a distinct area or separate grill to avoid any contact between poultry or meat and vegetarian food.

The most important point when entertaining vegetarians is to avoid offering miserable plain vegetables or a completely separate dish which is not served to other diners.

MENUS AND PREPARATION PLANS

Having a complete meal perfectly cooked and served with the minimum of fuss requires either experience or careful planning, or in some cases both. Here are a few examples of typical menus, with a guide to the order in which to prepare the food. The aim of this section is not to provide a detailed schedule which must be slavishly followed, but rather to provide a blueprint to help you plan – and cook – with confidence.

Preparing or cooking vegetables in advance and keeping them fresh in iced water, or covered for reheating, is useful for special occasions but not recommended for everyday cooking when it is important to conserve the nutrients.

=== SUNDAY ROAST ===
Roast Beef
Yorkshire Pudding
Roast and Boiled Potatoes
Boiled Fresh Vegetables
Gravy

Apple Tart
Custard

The day before

- Make the pastry for the tart, wrap it in polythene and chill it.
- Note the weight of the beef and determine the cooking time, following the guidelines in the chapter on Meat. Make a note of what time it will need to go into the oven.

Sunday morning

- Prepare the meat for the oven and set it to roast on time.
- Lay the table
- Prepare the potatoes and other vegetables. Unless they are very large leave the peeled potatoes for roasting whole. Add them to the roast about 30 minutes after it has started cooking; baste them with a little fat.
- Finish making the apple tart.
- About 1 hour before the meat is cooked, make the batter for the Yorkshire pudding. Transfer a little fat from the beef to the cooking tin for the pudding and place it in the oven to heat 35 minutes before the meat is cooked. Pour the batter into the tin after 5 minutes heating time, when the fat should be very hot.
- Place the tart in the oven at the same time as the Yorkshire pudding.
- Warm serving plates and vegetable dishes. Make sure carving knife is sharp.
- Put the potatoes for boiling on to cook 20 minutes before the meat is cooked. Prepare the saucepans and water for other vegetables, adding each according to its cooking time: green vegetables which are best cooked very briefly should be added to boiling water while the gravy is being prepared.
- Set plates and serving dishes to heat. Get out the ingredients for the custard. The custard can be made at this stage, covered with dampened greaseproof paper and stood in a bain marie to keep hot.
- When the meat and roast potatoes are cooked remove them from the oven as quickly as possible. Transfer them to serving dishes, leave to rest or keep hot. Tent meat under foil if leaving to rest. Do not cover roast potatoes.
- Use the meat juices to make gravy, straining the cooking water from the potatoes to use as well as, or in place of stock.
- By the time the gravy has simmered, the Yorkshire pudding should be cooked. Strain any remaining vegetables and serve the main course, or carve the meat first, then serve.
- The apple tart should be cooked about the same time as the Yorkshire pudding but it may be left in the oven, with heat turned off.
- If you have not already done so, make the custard after the main course is finished.

NO-FUSS
===INFORMAL SUPPER===

Tsatsiki or Hummus
Crudités
Pitta Bread

Quiche Lorraine
Baked Jacket Potatoes
Green Salad

Cheese and Biscuits and/or
Bananas in Rum

The day before or early in the day
- Prepare the hummus, if serving, or buy good quality alternative, place in a serving dish, cover and chill.
- Prepare the pastry case and bake blind. Prepare all other filling ingredients ready to go into the quiche; cover and chill. The quiche may be cooked in advance and reheated just before serving but it is best freshly cooked.

2 hours before serving
- Lay the table.
- Scrub the potatoes, prepare the salad ingredients and wash, peel or scrub the vegetables for the crudités.
- Make the tsatsiki, if serving. Place in a serving dish, cover and chill.

1½ hours before serving
- Set the potatoes to cook, setting the oven at the temperature for cooking the quiche.
- Cut the crudités and arrange them on a dish, cover and keep cool.
- Make a dressing for the salad.
- Mix the salad ingredients in a bowl. Do not add the dressing. Cover and set aside in a cool place.
- Have the ingredients ready for the bananas and prepare a pan for cooking them.
- Prepare the cheese and biscuits, keeping both covered at room temperature.

45 minutes before serving
- Sprinkle the prepared ingredients into the pastry case for the quiche. Beat the eggs and milk and pour in, then set the quiche to cook.
- Warm serving plates and have a napkin-lined basket ready for the potatoes.
- Set the pitta bread to heat in the oven for 5 minutes.
- Serve the pitta, tsatsiki or hummus and crudités.

Serving the quiche
- Transfer the potatoes to the basket and the quiche to a serving platter or place on a table mat on the table.
- Toss the salad with dressing.

After the main course
- Serve cheese and biscuits before the dessert if preferred.
- Put dessert plates to warm for the bananas.
- Cook the bananas just before they are served.

===FORMAL DINNER PARTY===

Vichysoisse or Asparagus Soup
Hot Bread Rolls

Coquilles St Jacques Mornay

Coq au Vin
New Potatoes
Glazed Carrots
French Beans

Port Wine Jelly
Red Fruit Salad
or
Gâteau de Pithiviers
Whipped Cream

Cheese and Biscuits

The day before
- Make and chill the chosen soup.
- Prepare the ingredients for the coq au vin, setting the chicken to marinate.

- Make the port wine jelly, if serving.
- Prepare the gâteau de Pithiviers, if serving. Chill it uncooked – it will benefit from being cooked on the same day as serving.

Early on the day
- Prepare the red fruit salad, if serving, cover and chill.
- Bake the gâteau de Pithiviers, if serving.
- Prepare the coquilles St Jacques mornay up to the final stage of baking.
- Prepare the vegetables: scrub the potatoes, peel or scrub and slice the carrots, then leave covered with iced water. Trim and wash the beans.
- Lay the table; set out all crockery.

2½ hours before serving
- Complete the preparation on the coq au vin, ready to go into the oven.
- Prepare the beurre mainé for thickening, cover and set aside.
- Whip the cream for dessert, cover and chill in a serving dish.
- Ladle the vichysoisse into serving bowls and chill. Alternatively, place the asparagus soup into a pan ready to heat.
- Drain the carrots and place them in the cooking pan with the glazing ingredients; cover and set aside ready to cook at the last minute.

1½ hours before serving.
- Place the coq au vin in the oven.
- Prepare the croûtes of bread for garnishing the coq au vin.
- Place the bread rolls on a baking tray ready to heat.
- Cook the potatoes until only just tender, drain and set in a pan with butter, cover.
- Prepare a pan with water for cooking the beans.
- Turn out the jelly if serving, then chill.
- Prepare the cheese board and biscuits, cover and set aside at room temperature.

20 minutes before serving
- Warm serving plates and dishes.
- Finish the coq au vin, replacing the chicken in the thickened sauce in the ovenproof dish. Cover tightly and replace in the oven: this saves having to thicken the sauce between courses.
- If serving the asparagus soup, heat it gently.
- Put the coquilles St Jacques to bake at the same temperature as the coq au vin – remembering they have to reheat completely and noting that they are being cooked at a lower temperature than when prepared according to the recipe.
- Heat the bread rolls and serve the soup course.

After the soup
- Set the buttered potatoes over low to medium heat.
- Set the carrots to cook and the water to boil for the beans.
- Serve the coquilles St Jacques.

After the fish course
- Add the beans to the cooking water and boil rapidly.
- Transfer the potatoes to a serving dish.
- Increase the heat under the carrots, if necessary, to glaze them, then transfer to a serving dish.
- Drain and serve the beans.
- Garnish the coq au vin with the croûtes and serve.

After the main course
- Serve the fruit salad, port wine jelly or gâteau.
- Take the cheese and biscuits to the table.
- Set the water to boil for coffee, or prepare the coffee machine.

Nutrition and Diet

A basic understanding of nutrition leads to an awareness of the food we eat in relation to its use by the body and, consequently, to an appreciation of the importance of eating a balanced diet.

Food is the essential fuel for life, maintaining the body as well as building and repairing it. Foods are made up of a combination of different nutrients and, as the body digests the food, these nutrients are released and utilized. General guidelines are provided regarding the nutritional needs of the population; however, individual requirements vary. Factors that influence any one person's dietary needs include gender, age, build, lifestyle and health.

BALANCED DIET

A balanced diet provides all the essential nutrients and sufficient energy to meet an individual's needs and to maintain a healthy body weight without causing obesity. In young people, the diet must also include sufficient nutrients to sustain growth. Nutritional requirements relating to pregnancy, lactation, illness and special conditions should be provided by a doctor and/or dietician.

A balanced diet should include a wide selection of different types of foods, prepared and cooked in a variety of ways. Fresh foods and 'whole' foods are important in providing a balanced variety of nutrients. Raw and lightly cooked fruit and vegetables are also essential.

In general terms, the carbohydrate and vegetable content of the diet should dominate the protein and fat. A diet that lacks carbohydrate, fruit and vegetables is likely to have too high a fat content and to be lacking in fibre. Fibre, from vegetable and cereal sources, is also a vital ingredient for a balanced diet.

BASIC GUIDE TO NUTRIENTS

PROTEIN

Used by the body for growth and repair, protein foods are composed of amino acids, in various amounts and combinations according to the food. There are eight specific amino acids which are an essential part of an adult's diet as they cannot be manufactured by the body from other foods; an additional one is necessary for young children, to sustain their rapid growth. In addition, nine other amino acids are widely available in protein foods, although a high intake of these is not vital as the human body can manufacture them if they are not adequately supplied by the diet.

The quality of any one protein food is determined by the number and proportion of amino acids it contains. Animal foods have a higher biological value than vegetable foods because they provide all the essential amino acids. Generally, no single vegetable food provides all the essential amino acids and they are not present in the proportions best suited to the human body. There are, however, important exceptions to this rule; certain non-animal foods are excellent sources of protein, notably soya beans, some types of nut and mycoprotein (quorn). Other beans and pulses, nuts and cereals are also excellent sources of good-quality protein. Since the amino acid content of vegetable foods varies, by mixing different foods and eating them in sufficient amounts, the necessary types and quantities of amino acids may be obtained.

As amino acids are not stored in a digestible form in the body, a regular supply is essential. This is most easily obtained from a mixture of animal and vegetable sources; if fish, poultry and meat are not eaten, then it is vital that a broad selection of vegetable sources and dairy foods are included to provide sufficient quantities of amino acids.

CARBOHYDRATES

These are the energy-giving foods and may be divided into two main categories: starches and sugars. Starch is obtained from vegetables, cereals, some nuts and under-ripe bananas; sugar is found in fruit (including ripe bananas), honey, molasses and cane sugar.

Carbohydrates in the form of starch, known as complex carbohydrates, should form a significant proportion of the diet. For example, they should be eaten in larger quantities than protein foods, such as meat, poultry and fish. The sugar content of the diet should be limited.

If the diet is deficient in carbohydrates, the body will break down other foods to supply energy, eventually including proteins which have a more valuable role to play.

FIBRE

At one time referred to as roughage, fibre is a complex carbohydrate which is not totally digested and absorbed by the body; however, it is vital as a carrier of moisture and waste products through the digestive system.

Fibre is obtained from cereals and vegetables. Good sources are wholegrain rice, oats, wholemeal flour and its products. Sources of vegetable fibre include beans and pulses, some types of fruit, as well as vegetables.

Raw and lightly cooked foods (where appropriate) generally provide more fibre than well-cooked foods; similarly more refined foods offer less fibre than wholefoods and unrefined ingredients.

FATS

Fat and oils provide energy as well as being important sources of certain vitamins and fatty acids. They may be loosely divided into saturated fats and unsaturated fats. Unsaturated fats may be further grouped into polyunsaturated and monounsaturated, depending on their chemical compositions. Although the majority of fatty foods contain both saturated and unsaturated fats, as a general rule animal sources have a higher proportion of saturated fats and vegetable sources are richer in unsaturates.

The recommended fat intake is calculated as a percentage of the total energy value of the diet. The energy value (in calories or joules) of fat eaten should be no more than 35% of the total energy intake with the major proportion of fat in the diet being the unsaturated type.

It is important to remember that young children (under five years of age) should not follow low-fat diets. Although their meals should not contain high proportions of fatty foods (fried foods, chips, high-fat snacks), their fat intake should not be limited by the use of skimmed milk, low-fat cheese and low-fat spreads.

VITAMINS

Although each of the vitamins has specific functions within the body, they also play vital roles in regulating metabolism, helping to repair tissues and assisting in the conversion of carbohydrates and fats into energy. Vitamin deficiency results in general poor health as well as certain specific illnesses.

Vitamins fall into two groups; fat-soluble and water-soluble. Fat-soluble vitamins include A, D, E and K; water-soluble vitamins include C and B-group vitamins. Fat-soluble vitamins can be stored by the body, whereas any excess of the water-soluble type is passed out. This means that a regular supply of water-soluble vitamins is essential and that an excess is unlikely to be harmful. Conversely, the fat-soluble vitamins which are stored in the body should not be consumed to excess as this can result in a condition known as hypervitaminosis. It is important to remember that an excess can be dangerous when taking vitamin supplements, or when eating a very high proportion of foods which are particularly rich in any one (or more) of the fat-soluble vitamins.

Vitamin A Found in fish liver oils, liver, kidney, dairy produce and eggs, vitamin A is important to prevent night blindness. It also contributes to the general health of the eyes and to the condition of the skin. Carotene, found in carrots and yellow or dark green vegetables such as peppers and spinach, can be converted into vitamin A in the body.

If the diet is excessively rich in vitamin A, or supplements are taken for a prolonged period, it is possible for stores to build up to toxic levels in the human liver.

B-group Vitamins This is a large group of water-soluble vitamins, linked because of their importance and use in the body. They play vital roles in promoting chemical reactions, in the release of energy from food and in the efficient functioning of the nervous system. They are essential for general good health and deficiency diseases occur comparatively quickly if these vitamins are missing from the diet.

Thiamin (vitamin B1), riboflavin (vitamin B2), vitamin B12, vitamin B6 (pyridoxine), nicotinic acid, folate, pantothenic acid and biotin are all included in this group (or complex) and each has its own particular characteristics.

In general, meat, offal, dairy produce, and cereals are good sources of B-group vitamins. Some of these vitamins are destroyed by prolonged cooking, notably thiamin, and long exposure to sunlight destroys riboflavin which is found in milk. Refined flour and bread are fortified with thiamin to meet natural levels in comparable wholemeal products. Breakfast cereals are also enriched with, or naturally rich in, B-group vitamins.

Vitamin C or Ascorbic Acid A water-soluble vitamin, this cannot be stored in the body, therefore a regular supply is essential. The main function of this vitamin is to maintain healthy connective tissue (the cell-structure within the body) and healthy blood. It also plays an important role in the healing of wounds. A deficiency can lead to susceptibility to infections.

Vitamin C is found in fresh and frozen vegetables, notably peppers and green vegetables, and in fruit, particularly blackcurrants and citrus fruit. Many fruit juices and drinks are fortified with vitamin C. Potatoes are also a valuable supply; although they are not a rich source, when eaten regularly and in quantity they make an important contribution to a healthy diet.

Vitamin C is the most easily destroyed of all vitamins and may be affected by light, heat, staleness, exposure to air and overcooking. The vitamin is also destroyed by alkaline substances, such as bicarbonate of soda.

Note Raw, fresh fruit and vegetables and lightly-cooked vegetables are an important source of vitamins, particularly C. Vegetables should be freshly prepared and cut up as little as possible before cooking. They should not be soaked in water. Cook them lightly and quickly in the minimum of liquid and use the cooking liquid, whenever suitable, in sauces and soups to benefit from any vitamins lost in seepage.

Vitamin D Essential in promoting calcium absorption, a deficiency will result in an inadequate supply of calcium being made available for building and repairing bones and teeth. A diet which is too rich in vitamin D can result in excessive calcium absorption and storage which can be damaging, so supplements should only be taken on medical advice.

Vitamin D is manufactured by the body from the action of sunlight on the skin – this is the primary source for most adults. The vitamin is naturally present in cod liver oil and oily fish such as herrings, mackerel, salmon and sardines. Eggs contain vitamin D, and it can also be manufactured from vegetable sources. Some foods, such as margarine, are fortified with vitamin D.

Vitamin E This vitamin is found in small amounts in most foods and the better sources include vegetable oils, eggs and cereals (especially wheatgerm).

Its role in the body is not clearly established, although unsubstantiated claims are made about its contribution to fertility and its role in improving circulation.

Vitamin K Widely found in vegetables and cereals, this vitamin can be manufactured in the body. Vitamin K contributes towards normal blood clotting. Deficiency is rare, due to a ready supply being available in a mixed diet.

A broad mixed diet, including plenty of raw and lightly cooked fruit and vegetables as well as animal and dairy foods, is likely to provide an adequate supply of vitamins. The value of fresh foods, dairy produce, bread and cereals is obvious. Deficiency can occur in restricted diets where meat and poultry are not eaten and corresponding levels of vitamins are not taken from dairy products or cereals. Those following a vegan diet are most vulnerable, and a diet free of animal products is not recommended.

MINERALS

Minerals and trace elements are essential for a healthy body as they play important roles in metabolic processes relating to to the nervous system, glands, muscle control and the supply of water. They are only required in minute quantities and a well balanced diet containing plenty of fresh and whole foods should provide an adequate supply. Mineral supplements should only be taken on medical advice as overdoses can upset metabolism.

Iron An essential constituent of red blood cells and important in muscles, iron can be stored in the body. The diet must maintain the store as, if it becomes depleted, anaemia can result. An adequate supply of iron is especially important during menstruation and pregnancy, as both use up the iron supply.

Found in meat, offal and green vegetables, such as spinach, and eggs, the iron in meat and offal is the most readily absorbed; it is less easily utilized from vegetable sources. The availability of vitamin C is important to promote iron absorption; other factors, such as the presence of tannin, can impair absorption.

Calcium Important in building and maintaining healthy teeth and bones, as well as for normal blood clotting, muscle function and a healthy nervous system, calcium is obtained from milk, cheese, bread, fortified flour and vegetables. The calcium found in milk and dairy produce is likely to be more easily absorbed than that in green vegetables or whole grains (although the system can adjust to utilizing the mineral from less ready sources) and an adequate supply of vitamin D is necessary for efficient calcium absorption.

Phosphorus Along with calcium, this is valuable for bones and teeth. It is widely distributed in food and deficiency is unknown in man.

Potassium, Chlorine and Sodium These play an important role in the balance of body fluids and they are essential for muscle and nerve function. Sodium and chlorine are added to food in the form of salt; sodium is found naturally in meat and milk, and it is added to bread, cereal products and manufactured foods. Potassium is found naturally in meat, vegetables and milk.

Trace Elements These are required by the body in very small amounts and include iodine, fluorine, magnesium, zinc, manganese, cobalt, selenium, molybdenum and chromium. An adequate supply of trace elements is almost always found in the diet and deficiency is extremely rare. Unprescribed supplements should be avoided as they can be detrimental to health.

SPECIFIC NEEDS

Most people have particular dietary needs at some time during their life, if only as babies or young children.

BABIES

Breast milk is the ideal food for young babies as it provides all the nutrients they require for the first few months of life. Even if this method of feeding is not continued in the long term, it is a very good idea to breast-feed a baby for the first few days, as valuable antibodies are passed from the mother to help the baby fight infection in the early months.

Bottle-fed babies should be given one of the manufactured milk formulas. These should be prepared exactly according to the manufacturer's instructions or according to the health visitor's or doctor's advice.

Regular checks on the baby's progress are important and any problems should be brought to professional attention immediately.

The weaning process varies from infant to infant; however, between the ages of four to six months a baby should be ready to try a little solid food. By eighteen months, the infant should be able to cope with a mixed diet based on adult foods, following general guidelines for balanced eating. Milk is still an important supplement during this time of rapid growth.

TODDLERS AND YOUNG CHILDREN

Fads and eating difficulties are common in young children, who are too busy discovering the world around them to concentrate for the length of time necessary to learn about meals. Since toddlers and young children are quickly satisfied, it is important that they are introduced to good eating habits and that their meals are nutritious; sweet or fatty snacks are to be avoided and bread, milk, vegetables, fruit, cheese and other valuable foods should be introduced. New foods should be presented in small amounts along with familiar ingredients. Milk is still an important source of nutrients, particularly for difficult eaters.

Providing a meal-time routine and making the process of eating a pleasure is all-important. Children should not be encouraged to play with food, but they should look foward to eating it. Small, frequent yet regular meals, are ideal: in theory, these occasions should be relaxed, free of distractions from the business of eating, and traumatic scenes relating to food rejection should be avoided.

SCHOOL CHILDREN

Fast-growing and active children need a highly nutritious diet, so the substitution of sweets, fatty snacks, sweet drinks and sticky cakes for meals should be avoided. These types of foods should be rare treats.

Breakfasts and packed lunches need special attention. The first meal of the day should be nutritious and provide sufficient energy to keep the child on the move until lunchtime: bread, cereals and milk, eggs and fruit are all practical and useful foods. Raw vegetables, semi-sweet biscuits and crackers are practical mid-morning snack foods but they should not spoil the appetite for lunch. Packed lunches, if eaten, should contain a variety of foods – bread, salad vegetables, some form of protein and a piece of fruit. If a packed lunch is the norm, tea and an early supper are important meals.

As a general guide, every meal should provide growing children with a good balance of valuable nutrients, and additional milk drinks (whole or semi-skimmed) are excellent sources of the calcium which is so important for strong teeth and bones, as well as other nutrients. Sweet foods and confectionery should be avoided as they cause tooth decay and can lead to obesity; similarly, fatty cooking methods and high-fat foods should not be a regular feature in the diet. The importance of fibre, raw fruit and vegetables must be stressed.

ADOLESCENTS AND TEENAGERS

This group also requires a highly nutritious, energy-packed diet, but unfortunately, young people are particularly prone to food fads and fashions and it can be difficult to get a teenager to eat a balanced diet. While it is essential to provide all the necessary nutrients, it is important to avoid obesity in this group. Reduced-calorie diets are not recommended, but over-eating must be controlled and the types of food eaten should be carefully monitored.

During this period of rapid growth and development, adopting an active lifestyle and participating in regular exercise is of equal importance as eating well. Young people in this age group should be encouraged to take an interest in nutrition, food and the relationship between a balanced diet, health and fitness.

Parents should try to pass on an understanding of food shopping, meal planning and food preparation, together with an appreciation of the positive benefits of a good diet. This is particularly important for young people who are about to embark on their first experience of living alone and catering for themselves.

PREGNANCY AND LACTATION

A woman should pay special attention to diet during pregnancy as she will need to provide sufficient nutrients and energy for her own needs as well as those of the growing baby. The nutritional requirements continue after birth and during lactation, when the mother is feeding the new baby. The doctor or clinic should provide dietary advice, recommending supplements as necessary.

The mother's responsibility is to ensure that her diet is varied, with emphasis on foods rich in minerals, vitamins and energy. Sweets, chocolates and foods which satisfy without offering nutritional benefit should be avoided in favour of fruit, vegetables, dairy produce, bread and protein foods.

ELDERLY PEOPLE

Problems relating to nutrition and the elderly are often linked to social factors. The cost and effort of eating well can deter some elderly people from shopping for a variety of foods and therefore from cooking fresh ingredients. Although many elderly people are extremely active, others may have physical difficulty in shopping or spending long periods standing to prepare meals; in this case help should be sought with planning a practical diet. Equally, dental problems restrict some elderly people from eating well and these can, and should, be overcome by visiting a dentist.

Hot, solid meals are important, particularly in winter. Some elderly people get through the day by eating lots of snacks and this can be detrimental to health; cakes, biscuits and favourite puddings may be pleasant and comforting but they do not constitute a balanced diet. The appetite is often reduced, particularly as the person becomes less active, so meals that are small must contain a high proportion of valuable nutrients. Wholemeal bread, dairy products and cereals with milk are all practical snacks.

The pleasure often disappears from eating when meals are lonely occasions and the palate is not as efficient as it once was. Special centres and meal services exist and these should be used, not only by those who are prevented from cooking for themselves by physical limitations, but also by all who need the company and contact that such services offer.

SPECIAL DIETS

Individuals and whole sections of the population follow special diets for different reasons: religion, medical and health-related conditions, cultural and personal factors can all influence the choice of food. Many diets are self-imposed, others are dictated by society and some are prescribed by a dietician or doctor. The following brief notes indicate some typical dietary restrictons. Remember that some diets are influenced by food fashions while others have genuine social or medical backgrounds.

DAIRY-FREE

Young children under three years old are sometimes unable to digest the protein found in cows' milk; however, they tend to grow out of this. Adults may react adversely to lactose, the carbohydrate found in milk. This means that all milk products have to be avoided, including butter, cheese, cream, yogurt, dishes containing milk and milk drinks.

Soya milk is a useful alternative as it is a non-dairy product. It may be used for cooking as well as for adding to drinks.

DIABETIC

Insulin, a hormone produced by the pancreas, plays a vital role in sugar absorption. If the pancreas fails to produce insulin, or slows down production to inadequate levels, the condition known as diabetes results.

The control of the condition varies according to the individual case; however, attention to diet is always an important factor. Sugar, in all its forms, is avoided or used in small, carefully controlled amounts. In some cases the overall carbohydrate intake may be controlled, as starch is also converted into sugar during digestion.

As well as direct carbohydrate control, other factors affecting carbohydrate metabolism must be taken into account and, for general good health, a balanced diet is essential.

GLUTEN-FREE

People suffering from coeliac disease react adversely to gluten, a protein found in wheat. This means that all wheat products such as flour, bread, traditional pastry, biscuits, sauces thickened with wheat flour and so on, have to be avoided.

The gluten in wheat flour is the substance which gives it its strength and makes it ideal for yeast-risen bread doughs. For those on a gluten-free diet, alternatives are available for most wheat-based products: cornflour and rice flour are typical thickening agents which may be used in place of wheat flour. Rice crackers and cakes may be used instead of savoury wheat crackers and specially manufactured breads, biscuits and cakes can also be found.

LOW-FAT

Under normal circumstances the value of a rational approach to fat in the diet must be emphasized. In the right proportions, fat is important in the diet and extremely low-fat or fat-free diets are not generally recommended. If, for medical reasons, a low-fat diet is imposed or suggested, then the doctor's or dietician's advice should be followed. Full-fat dairy produce, fatty meat, margarine, butter and high-fat convenience foods are typical examples of food to avoid; frying, particularly deep-frying, and other cooking methods which employ fat should also be avoided.

LOW-SALT

This is another example of a diet which should not be taken to extremes as a certain amount of salt is essential in a normal diet. By eating a balanced diet, with plenty of fresh foods or a watchful choice of ready-prepared items, and by avoiding the use of large amounts of salt either in cooking or at the table, a sensible salt intake can be maintained. Careful, light seasoning should provide a good flavour without being harmful; sprinkling extra salt over cooked seasoned food, with a few rare exceptions, should be avoided. Remember, many convenience foods and snacks have a high salt content, so eating them frequently in large quantities is not advisable.

REDUCED-CALORIE

In order to lose excess weight, a person's calorie intake must be reduced, ideally in combination with a sensible exercise programme. A very low calorie diet should be avoided as this can result in the breakdown of muscle for energy as well as nutrient deficiency.

Often, unless the problem is simply one of eating far too much food for the body's requirements, the cause of obesity is a diet too rich in sugary and/or fatty foods. The first steps should be to cut out sweetened foods and to significantly reduce the amount of fat consumed, substituting plenty of vegetables and sufficient carbohydrate, along with fibre. Foods should be baked, steamed or grilled; frying, especially deep-frying, should be avoided.

The doctor should be consulted before embarking on a major weight-loss programme or prolonged diet. As well as dietary guidelines, he/she will provide a general health check and advice on increasing the exercise level to improve the body's energy consumption and reduce excess fat stores.

SEMI-VEGETARIAN

Sometimes referred to as demi-vegetarian, this dietary option involves avoiding meat. Fish, and sometimes poultry, are eaten, as are dairy products.

VEGETARIAN

Fish, poultry and all types of meat are avoided in any form; however, dairy products may be eaten. By ensuring that the diet is mixed, including a variety of vegetables and pulses as well as dairy produce, the vegetarian diet can provide all the essential nutrients. There are two factors of which to be aware: firstly, by eating large amounts of dairy produce to replace meat, fish and poultry the fat content can be high; secondly, nutrient deficiency can result if dairy foods are avoided to reduce the fat content without substituting high-value vegetable foods. The importance of variety and balance must be stressed.

VEGAN

The vegan diet excludes all animal products, including dairy foods, and it is often related to other food restrictions. Following a diet which limits nutrient intake to this extent is not recommended. Ensuring that the body receives essential vitamins and minerals in sufficient quantities and in a form which is available is difficult, resulting in the necessity for consuming a large bulk of vegetable foods. This type of diet should never be imposed on children or young people.

Home Safety

A great number of accidents occur in and around the home every year: this chapter points to some of the causes and notes the pitfalls to avoid.

In addition to the many hazardous jobs carried out in the home, the average house will contain many dangerous pieces of equipment and substances. Since home is the place where we all relax, where children play and the elderly spend the majority of their time, being aware of the potential dangers makes good sense.

GENERAL HOME SAFETY

Here are a few general points to observe in order to avoid minor accidents, the possibility of serious injury or the danger of fire.

Flooring Avoid slippery flooring or loose rugs or matting on slippery surfaces. This applies particularly to hall, kitchen, bathroom and any other area that is frequently used.

Lighting Hall, stairs, bathroom, kitchen and any other work area or area through which people walk must be well lit. Awkward steps, either inside or outside, or landings which may be the cause of a fall should be lit with a spotlight.

Storage Untidy or overfilled cupboards are dangerous, as items can be difficult to find or reach and can fall out unexpectedly. Heavy items or others that are used frequently should always be stored in places where they are easy to reach.

Ladders and Steps These should be in good condition, sturdy and easy to lift and handle. Steps and ladders must be used on a level surface; never climb on chairs or furniture instead of using steps. Steps of an appropriate size should be stored in places where they are used frequently and ladders should be kept where they are readily available to the owner but locked away from outside intruders.

Electricity Never overload the electric circuits in the house. An adapter to take several plugs may be useful for serving television and video but do not link several adapters and do not plug several appliances into one socket.

Old or faulty wiring in the house or on appliances must be changed as it can easily cause a fire.

Extension leads are handy for short-term use but they are not designed for permanent installations. They must be fully unwound before use, particularly if you are using a highly rated appliance, as the leads can overheat when coiled or curled.

Do not leave flexes trailing across the floor for someone to trip over, and plugs should not be left lying about with pins uppermost in case someone treads on them and injures their foot.

Tidiness and Overcrowding General tidiness is vital to safety. Papers, magazines and objects lying around on the floor are a hazard, particularly toys and pins or needles. Items left stacked on stairs are especially dangerous.

Rooms and hallways which are overcrowded with furniture are dangerous as it is easy to trip, or to bump against a corner when walking through or moving around. When something is being carried, for example a sharp object or a pot of hot liquid, the accident can be more serious than a fall or bump.

Dangerous or Poisonous Substances If there are children in the house, all cleaning agents, medicines, decorating materials such as paints and strippers and any other substances that are dangerous when ingested or rubbed into sensitive skin must be kept out of reach. Household cleaning products have childproof closures but these are not always effective, so it is also a good idea to keep toddlers away from the cupboard under the sink where most cleaners are stored, and to keep sprays and other fluids in higher cupboards.

BATHROOM SAFETY

- The floor must not be slippery. Some finishes, for example ceramic floor tiles, are especially slippery, therefore dangerous, when wet. Bath mats must have a non-slip backing.
- Baths and showers for use by the elderly or children should have grips and a non-slip base, or a non-slip mat should be placed in the base. Showers are available with integral seats for the elderly.
- Never leave young children unattended in the bath – not even for a minute to answer the telephone or open the door. They can easily drown.
- Always test the water temperature before bathing a baby and run cold water first.
- Always supervise older children who are bathing.
- Water conducts electricity, therefore freestanding electrical appliances must not be used in the bathroom. There should not be a socket or switch in the bathroom; pull switches must be used for lights and fixed heating appliances. Special shaver sockets are the only type of power point for bathroom use.
- Never use an extension lead in a bathroom.
- Never bath after drinking alcohol and do not have a very hot bath when very tired – you

may doze off and slip under the water and possibly drown.
- The medicine cabinet must be out of reach of children.
- Razors and blades must be kept out of the reach of children.
- Heavy glass bottles or cosmetic jars and drinking glasses slip easily through wet hands, so keep them away from washbasin and bath.
- All areas must be kept clean.

KITCHEN SAFETY

- Water and electricity must be separated. Sockets should not be positioned near the sink and appliances should not be used when hands are wet.
- Flooring should be non-slip and broken flooring or loose matting which can slide around must not be used in the kitchen.
- If possible, the cooker should be away from the door to avoid any danger of the door being opened when someone is handling a large saucepan or container of hot food.
- Always leave enough space on the work surface to rest heavy or hot pots and pans.
- Knives and other sharp objects should be kept out of the reach of children.
- A stable, reasonably large area of work surface must be available when working in the kitchen. Preparing food in crowded conditions or on a rickety surface can be dangerous.
- All pan handles should be pushed backwards when in use on the cooker.
- Flexes must not trail from work-top appliances as they can easily be pulled down by children or caught by anyone walking by.
- Never leave food to grill or fry unattended.
- Plastic bags should be kept where children cannot reach them.
- Have a fire extinguisher and fire blanket in the kitchen.

- Keep strong, thick oven gloves close to the oven and use them.
- Practise high standards of personal and household hygiene in the kitchen, where food safety is important.

BEDROOM SAFETY

- Electric blankets should conform to the current national standard and should be used only according to the manufacturer's instructions. They should not be used when the bed is occupied unless they are designed for the purpose. Electric blankets must be cleaned and serviced regularly, and replaced when old.
- Babies and young children should not have pillows.
- Cots and bedding for young children must be safe and secure, with narrowly spaced railings on cots and cribs to prevent a child squeezing its head through the bars and becoming trapped.
- Items surrounding a cot must be secure and out of reach of the standing child.
- Windows should shut securely in a household with children, and lock if necessary, to avoid the danger of a child falling out.
- There should be some opening windows on upper floors to allow escape in the event of fire.

SAFETY AND CLOTHING

- Long dressing-gowns can be dangerous on stairs, particularly if you are carrying a tea tray.
- Long nightwear should be flame-resistant, particularly for children.
- Flapping sleeves can catch in door handles or on furniture.
- Long-sleeved items, dressing-gowns and loose clothing are not suitable garments to wear when you are doing jobs in the kitchen

or, indeed, anywhere else; take extra care when making tea in a dressing-gown.
- Ill-fitting and worn slippers or house shoes are dangerous.
- Open shoes or slippers are not suitable for heavy work, such as home repairs or decorating, moving furniture, gardening or mowing the lawn.
- Eye or face masks, gloves and appropriate protective clothing should always be worn when sanding, using noxious substances or dangerous appliances, such as a chain saw.

FIRES AND HEATERS

- A fire guard should always be used with an unattended open fire.
- A child must not be left alone with any fire or infra-red heater without a large, closed, fixed guard in position.
- Open fires must be made safe last thing at night or before going out.

OUTDOOR SAFETY

- Pathways and steps should be well lit.
- Garages, sheds and other outhouses should be tidy and reasonably clean.
- Gardening and garage products and tools must be kept safely out of the reach of children.
- Great care must be taken when using sharp tools and with bean poles or sticks which can easily cause injuries – particularly to eyes.
- Garden pools, no matter how small, are potential death traps for young children. Children should not be allowed to play unsupervised in a garden with a pool as they can fall into the water and drown quickly before an adult has noticed the accident or has had time to rescue them.
- If children are allowed to play unsupervised in a garden, the fences and walls should be safe and secure. Gates should have a high catch to prevent young children wandering.

FIRE IN THE HOME

Here are some important points to remember.
● Get everyone out of the house as quickly as possible and dial 999 – in a neighbouring house if necessary.
● Take a towel to wrap around your face if you have to walk through smoke. If possible wet the towel, but do not waste time.
● If you are trapped on a first floor, with flames and thick smoke on the stairs, them jump out of a window and make children jump too.
● Crouch down or crawl if you are going through a smoke-filled area, as the smoke and hot air rises and it will be less dense near the floor.
● Do not attempt to put out a fire or to deal with smouldering furniture: the fumes are highly toxic and they kill in minutes.

CHIP PAN OR GRILL PAN ON FIRE

● Turn off the heat source if you can but do not lean across a flaming pan to do so.
● Do **not** pour water on the pan.
● Cover with a fire blanket or thick pad of fabric, a door mat is ideal, or put a large lid or sturdy plate straight down on top of the pan. Take care to avoid burning your hands and arms.
● Push the object down over the flames in a direction away from you.
● Turn off the heat source if you could not do so before.
● Leave the pan covered. If you could only lightly smother the flames, place another thick object on top of the pan. A baking tray, tin or other object will cut off the supply of air which keeps the fat burning.

FLOOD

Burst pipes caused by freezing and problems of malfunctioning valves or worn washers can result in flooding. Even minor 'floods' can be damaging and dangerous, so always adopt a 'better safe than sorry' attitude.
● Turn off the water at the main pipe – usually found in the kitchen.
● Turn off the electricity supply at the main switch; water conducts electricity and it can easily seep into sockets and connections.
● Turn on all the taps in sinks and bath, and flush the toilets to drain as much water out of the system as possible.
● If the flooding is severe or if it comes from the main outside your house, call the local water authority. Remember, too, that the Fire Brigade are used to dealing with flooding emergencies.

EMERGENCY SERVICES

In cases of emergency, dial 999 and an operator will ask which service you require; the functions of the various services are outlined below. State the service, the address or location, the problem and your name. Emergency calls are free – just dial.

Police For emergencies related to traffic accidents, offences such as burglary or violence and public disorder. Also remember that the Police can provide advice in an emergency if you do not know whom else to call for help.

Distinguish between an emergency call and a complaint or query and address the latter to the local Police station (number in telephone directory).

Ambulance In case of accidents causing injury, sudden or severe illness or other health or maternity problems requiring urgent hospital attention.

Fire Brigade In case of house fire, garden or country fires which are out of control, fire hazard in accident cases, severe flooding and any danger from chemical spillage or other serious problem with hazardous substances.

First Aid

Read this chapter for future reference as the information it contains can save life.

First aid is the help given to a victim of injury or severe and sudden ill health. It is important to recognize life-threatening situations, when professional help is essential as fast as possible. This chapter deals first with such emergencies, then with other, equally important, aspects of first aid which allow nominally more time for coping with the situation but still require prompt attention.

FIRST-AID KIT

Every home and car should have a first-aid kit; these can be purchased fully stocked, but it is just as easy to make up your own. Keep all the items together in a clearly marked box, or neatly arranged in a cupboard. They should be easily accessible, but away from the reach of young children. Replace items as they are used or become out-of-date and discard opened packets of dressings which are no longer sterile.

The kit should contain medicines for dealing with everyday minor illnesses, creams and antiseptics for minor accidents and a variety of sterile dressings and bandages. Useful equipment includes such items as a small pair of scissors, safety pins, a pair of tweezers and some tissues; a concise, clear, illustrated first-aid handbook should be ready at hand. The exact selection of ointments and medicines is up to you; think about the likely reasons for needing minor first aid – burns and scalds, bites, cuts, foreign bodies in the eye, stomach upsets, toothache, headache, sore throats, earache and so on – then select products to deal with these common problems.

SUGGESTED CONTENTS

- Antiseptic solution and cream
- Cream for stings and bites
- Surgical spirit
- Iodine
- Cream or lotion for skin irritations (for example, calamine lotion)
- Toothache tincture or oil of cloves
- Eye bath and eye-cleansing solution
- Aspirin for adults
- Similar product to above for children: take current advice from a chemist as opinions change and new products are often available.
- Product for easing upset stomachs
- Thermometer
- A good selection of plasters
- Sterile dressings and bandages
- Safety pins
- Cotton wool
- Tissues
- Sling
- Scissors
- Tweezers
- First aid manual

The above is only a guide and there may be other items for your household situation.

LIFE-THREATENING EMERGENCIES

Dial 999 for an ambulance. In rural areas, where the nearest ambulance station is many miles away, the local doctor may be able to get to the patient more speedily. **In rural areas, keep the emergency number for the doctor near the telephone.**

EMERGENCY PROCEDURE

Check Airways Make sure that the person's mouth is not obstructed. Turn the head to one side and remove false teeth, if appropriate. Use fingers to clear out any food or vomit.

Check for Breathing Look for signs of movement in the chest and listen for the sound of breathing. If necessary, hold your ear to the person's chest to listen for breathing, or lean close to their face to feel any air movement.

Check Pulse for Circulation Checking the pulse tells you whether the heart has stopped beating. Practise this on yourself, a friend or relative. Hold your first two or three fingers to the neck, placing them in the hollow between the voice box and adjoining muscle; alternatively, turn the hand palm-up and feel the wrist on the thumb side. The neck is the more reliable area if you are familiar with the position. Do not use your thumb to feel the pulse as you may confuse your own pulse with that of the patient. If you cannot feel a pulse then the heart has stopped beating and heart compression must be applied immediately.

Coping with the Unconscious Patient
Once you have checked the breathing and pulse, the patient should be put into the recovery position (see page 1266) and treated for shock; then professional help should be sought immediately.

If there are any people within hearing distance, ask them to telephone for help while you deal with the patient.

THE KISS OF LIFE

If the patient has stopped breathing, give the kiss of life as follows:
1 Turn the person face upwards if possible. Turn the head backwards so that the chin is pointing up.
2 Clear the airways.

3 Tilt the head back again, pressing down on the forehead so that the chin points up – this ensures the tongue does not slip to the back of the throat to block the air passage.

4 Pinch the nose between thumb and forefinger of one hand.
5 Take a deep breath, then place your mouth over that of the patient to seal it completely; blow out steadily. The patient's chest should rise – this shows that the air you breathe in is reaching the lungs. If not, the air passage is blocked, possibly the head is in the wrong position or you are not sealing the patient's mouth with yours.

6 If the patient's mouth is inaccessible for above, but you can keep it closed, then breathe in through the nose. *continued* ▶

7 Give another breath, then remove your mouth for a moment before continuing to breathe into the patient.

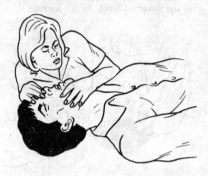

8 Check for a pulse after applying breath four or five times. If the heart is beating, continue giving the kiss of life and do not give up until help arrives.

9 If there is no pulse, heart compression (see opposite) should be applied alternately with the kiss of life. If there is help available, apply both similtaneously.

Note Continue giving the kiss of life even if the patient does not immediately respond. It is sensible and not unusual to continue for period of twenty to thirty minutes.

BABIES

Since the face is very small, you should cover the nose and mouth of the infant completely.

ALTERNATIVE ARTIFICIAL RESPIRATION

If the kiss of life may not be applied due to facial injury, the following method should be adopted. It is less easy to apply and more exhausting but should be kept up as it can save life. This method is not suitable for patients with back, arm or neck injuries unless it is the only, vital method of respiration.

1 Lay the patient on the stomach, with arms above the head. Turn the head on one side, resting on the hands.

2 Hold the head and slide the chin up, neck back, to allow free access for air.

3 Adopt a semi-kneeling position above the patient's head, looking down his or her back. Lean on one knee by the patient's head and place the other foot near the patient's elbow.

4 Spread out your hands just below the shoulder blades, with thumbs towards the spine, then rock forward, keeping your elbows straight. Exert firm but not heavy pressure for about two seconds – this should make the patient breathe out.

5 Rock backwards, sliding your hands up the patient's upper arms to the elbows, then pull the arms straight backwards for about three seconds – this should make the patient breathe in.

6 Lower the arms, slide your hands back to their original position and continue the process. You may have to continue for some time, trying to ensure the patient breathes in and out about twelve times a minute.

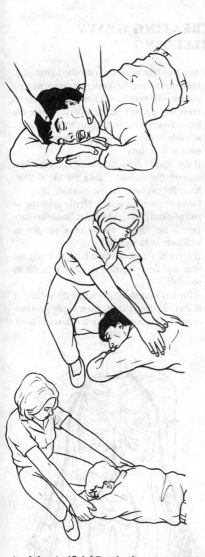

Applying Artificial Respiration

HEART COMPRESSION

Also referred to as chest or heart massage, this must be applied if there is no pulse and the heart has stopped beating. It is essential to get the heart beating again so that blood is pumped to the brain.

The kiss of life should be given at the same time – if there are two of you, then take a task each and swop over occasionally. If you are alone, then alternate the treatment every few minutes to provide air and to try to stimulate the heart.

1 Lay the person face upwards, head back and chin up (as for the kiss of life). Kneel over the patient above the chest.
2 Find the breast bone, located down the middle of the chest. Move your hand along to the bottom of the breast bone, where you can feel the lower ribs meeting it, then move your hand back by 2.5-3 cm/1-1½ inches upwards from the end of the bone.
3 Place the heel of your hand on the bone. Cover with the heel of your other hand, interlocking your fingers to avoid digging them into the chest.
4 Keeping your elbows straight, lean down firmly on both hands to compress the chest by about 3 cm/1½ inches. Release the pressure at once.
5 Repeat this pumping process at a rate of eighty times a minute – that is more than one pump per second.
6 Check for breathing and give the kiss of life if necessary, applying two breaths between every fifteen heart compressions.
7 Check the pulse every three minutes and stop the heart compression once it returns. Keep giving the kiss of life and checking the pulse.

Note When the patient begins to breathe, move the body into the recovery position (see below): this prevents the air passage from being blocked by the tongue or other obstructions, such as vomit.

CHILD HEART MASSAGE

The process is lighter and faster – about one hundred compressions per minute. On a baby, the process is yet lighter and faster and two fingers should be used instead of the heel of the hand.

THE RECOVERY POSITION

An unconscious patient who is breathing and with pulse should be placed in the recovery position. However, if there is any sign or likelihood of back or neck injury the patient must **not** be moved.

1 Kneel next to the patient.
2 Remove spectacles and any jewellery. Lay the patient on his back.
3 Tilt the head back and chin up. Cross the arm farthest away from you over the front of the body. Tuck the arm nearest you under the patient.
4 Roll the patient towards you so that the body moves on to its side. Use your knees to support the patient, and support the head as the body rolls.
5 The arms should support the body on its side. The arm which is facing towards the front should be bent and supporting the chest off the ground.
6 Bend the legs so that they support the patient on one side, with the chest slightly raised off the floor. The head should be to one side to allow easy breathing. Make sure that the chin is jutting out and that the neck is arched with head up, not resting on the chest.

TREATING HEAVY BLEEDING

Heavy bleeding must be controlled promptly.
● Make the patient lie down, but do not move a patient who may have a back or neck injury. Press down firmly on the wound to ease the blood flow. Do not waste time trying to find a suitable cloth or dressing, just use your hand even if it is dirty.
● If the wound is in an arm or leg, raise and support the limb to reduce the blood flow. Keep the pressure on the wound.
● Cover the wound with a sterile dressing or pad of clean cloth and wrap it firmly in place (use a tie, tights, sleeve of a jumper or whatever is to hand).
● If there is a gaping wound, try to bring the skin and flesh together to close it as far as possible.
● If there is something pucturing the wound or if there is debris in it, then apply pressure around the wound to ease the flow of blood.

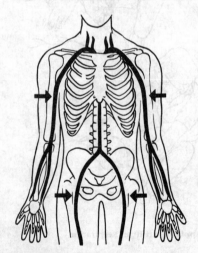

Arteries: if blood is spurting from a wound, one of the arteries has been cut and immediate, direct pressure must be applied.

- When a wound is bandaged tightly, the flow of blood will be stopped or limited and it is vital to get immediate professional help as the blood supply should not be cut off for more than about fifteen minutes.
- Apply more pressure and dressings if the bleeding continues. Do not remove the first pad or dressing, simply add to it.
- If blood is spurting from the arm or leg, apply pressure to the main arteries to ease the blood flow.

Note If the blood is spurting from the body, one of the main arteries (see left) has been cut and prompt action is vital: immediate direct pressure must be applied by hand, with or without any cloth or dressing.

TREATING SHOCK

When a person is injured, the body goes into a state of shock, a weak condition which can result in collapse. As a general rule, in case of accident all patients should be treated for shock.

1 Put the patient in the recovery position or lay the person down, with feet up and head to one side.
2 Cover with a blanket, clothing or whatever is available to retain body heat.
3 Loosen tight clothing – tight belts or waist-bands, neck ties or collars.
4 Call professional help.
5 Do not give anything to drink. If the patient is thirsty, you can moisten the lips with water.

CHOKING

In case of choking, or if there is some severe problem with breathing, give the person four firm thumps between the shoulder blades with the flat of the hand. If this does not release the blockage, get the patient to bend over so that the head is lower than the chest and apply a further four thumps.

CHOKING BABIES

Lay a baby or infant face-down on your lap, head and arms towards your feet, then slap between the shoulder blades four times.

PATIENTS NOT IN IMMEDIATE DANGER

If the patient is breathing, the heart is beating, they are conscious and not bleeding profusely, then you will probably have to cope with their state of fright and panic. Professional help should still be sought promptly but, if possible, ask someone else to telephone while you deal with the patient.

CONSCIOUS PATIENTS

1 Calm and reassure the patient. Treat bleeding at once.
2 If there is no risk of back or neck injury, then make them lie down, adopting the recovery position if there is likelihood of fainting or falling unconscious.
3 Treat for shock: keep warm and dry, loosen tight clothing and do not give anything to drink.

BROKEN LIMBS

If there is any chance of damage to the neck or back, do not move the patient. In the case of severe fracture, it is best not to attempt to move the limb but to deal with bleeding, treat for shock and call professional help as soon as possible.

COMMON ACCIDENTS AND SUDDEN ILLNESS

Even minor accidents should be dealt with promptly and efficiently to avoid any possible risk of infection. The following are all situations in which first aid should be given.

ASTHMA ATTACK

This is indicated by difficulty in breathing and gasping for air. The person should sit down on an upright chair. If they are lying down, they should be helped into an upright position, leaning against pillows if in bed.

In a bad attack, face the person towards the back of the chair, legs astride the seat, and lift the arms to rest on the top of the chair back, so lifting as much body weight as possible off the chest.

Help the sufferer to find their inhaler or other medication and calm them. If the attack does not subside, call a doctor or ambulance. If the patient begins to turn blue from lack of breath, dial 999 and be prepared to give the kiss of life. If the heart stops, then heart massage should be applied.

BITES AND STINGS

Insect Bites The treatment depends on the severity but the majority of insect bites received in Britain are not dangerous. Cleaning the infected area with antiseptic, then drying it and applying a suitable cream is sufficient. The bite should not be scratched or the skin broken.

Wasp and Bee Stings These stings are not dangerous unless the person is known to be allergic to them or someone is attacked by a swarm. Use tweezers to remove the sting which is left in the skin, then clean the area with antiseptic. Place the area under cold water to reduce swelling or apply a cold compress of ice cubes in a clean dressing. If someone develops a severe reaction to a sting, call the doctor.

If the person has been stung by a swarm, call an ambulance and treat for shock.

Snake Bites The adder is the only poisonous snake in Britain, so any snake bites are unlikely to be highly dangerous. Do not try to suck the poison out of the wound, but make the person rest, loosen clothing and support a bitten limb. Wash the bite with antiseptic, keep the patient warm and either take them to hospital, call a doctor or call an ambulance.

Dog Bites Treatment depends on the severity of the attack. If the skin is not broken, the bite is unlikely to cause a problem and the person should simply be calmed. If the skin is broken, clean the wound and take the person to the doctor or hospital.

BURNS AND SCALDS

Burns may result from contact with fire or a heat source, boiling water or steam, electric shock or certain chemicals. Friction (for example by having a rope pulled through the hands) and contact with ice-cold metal can also burn the skin.

In cases of minor burns, give the following treatment.

- Loosen or remove tight clothing, shoes, jewellery or watch.
- Submerge the area in cold water or place under slow-running cold water. Do not place under fast-flowing cold water as this can further damage the skin and flesh.
- If you cannot get the burn under water, then douse the area well with cold water.
- Apply a sterile lint dressing and bandage it loosely in place. Do not cover with a fluffy dressing as this will stick to the wound.
- Do not burst any blisters.
- Do not rub creams, oils or ointment into the skin.

• Burns which cover an area larger than a medium-sized coin should be given medical attention.

Severe Burns In case of severe burns to large areas of the body, call an ambulance. Loosen tight clothing and treat for shock, keeping the patient warm and allowing sips of water.

Note If a small burn does not heal quickly, consult a doctor as the area can become infected.

CUTS AND ABRASIONS

Wash your hands and then wash the area under cool, slow-running water. Use antiseptic and cotton wool to clean the area gently, removing any dirt and debris. If there are any larger pieces of debris (such as gravel, splinters or glass) which can be easily removed with tweezers, do so. If the debris is embedded and your efforts are likely to push it further into the wound, then take the patient to the doctor or hospital. Otherwise, when the wound is thoroughly cleaned, apply a sterile dressing.

Change the dressing if it is obviously soiled or about twenty-four hours after it was applied. If the wound is not beginning to heal but shows signs of oozing pus, a doctor should be consulted as there is a risk of infection.

Larger cuts should be taken to the hospital or doctor immediately as stitches may be required to close the area and promote healing.

ELECTRIC SHOCK

Do not touch the person if he or she is still grasping the source of electricity.

• Turn off the power supply.
• If you cannot turn the supply off, use a dry, poor conductor to push the electric source away from the patient. If you touch the person, the electric current will pass on to you. A wooden broom handle, heavy plastic object, wooden chair leg or coffee table are all

suitable – metal conducts electricity and should not be used.

• If the patient is conscious, deal with the burns and treat for shock, then call an ambulance.
• If the patient is unconscious, check breathing and pulse, giving the kiss of life and/or heart massage as necessary. Call an ambulance.

High-voltage Shock If the accident occurs with high-voltage outdoor cables, such as on a railway line, do not approach the person; call the emergency services **at once**. The power supply must be switched off before anyone can approach the patient. If there is no one in authority to see that the supply is switched off, call the Police as well as the ambulance; the fire service may also be called in to help.

EYE INJURY

Professional attention is vital to avoid any possibility of permanent damage. Take the person to hospital or the doctor, or call an ambulance, depending on the severity of the injury and the quickest solution.

If the person has something in the eye, this may be washed out with plenty of clean cool water. Pour plenty of cold water over the affected eye, holding the head over the sink or wash basin.

If the object does not come out with washing, wash hands thoroughly before inspecting the eye; hold the top and lower part gently apart while the head is tilted back. Ask the person to look up, down and around so that you can see any foreign body. Most particles can be removed by gently touching them with the corner of a clean tissue or dressing.

The eye should be washed out with a suitable eye-cleansing solution and it should feel normal, if tired, within a few hours. If there is any prolonged discomfort, for example overnight, then visit the hospital or doctor.

FAINTING

People may faint due to tiredness or after very long periods of standing up. Hot and airless rooms can lead to faintness, as can distress or anxiety.

If a person indicates that they feel faint, dizzy and that everything is beginning to look slightly grey, they are about to faint. Make them sit down on a chair and lower the head between the knees. If a chair is not available, make the person lie down with the head on the floor and feet and legs raised on cushions, a low stool, a pile of books or any suitable object. Loosen tight clothing, belts and collar or tie. If the person has already fainted, then lower the head and raise the legs as above, loosening tight clothing.

Allow plenty of room around the person; ask onlookers to stand aside and increase the ventilation.

The person should come round quickly, but they should remain lying down or keep the head between the knees for a few minutes to recover. Then make the patient more comfortable, preferably lying down, and keep them warm. Once they are fully conscious again, provide a drink of water or a hot drink. The cause of fainting may be lack of food, in which case a sweetened drink can help.

Do not:
- try to lift or move a person who is fainting or about to faint
- pour any liquid into the person's mouth if they are about to faint or have fainted
- give any alcohol
- allow the person to walk away alone immediately they regain consciousness. Make sure they rest briefly and that they have company.

Note If the person does not regain consciousness within seconds, then hold their hand, speak to them clearly, encouraging them to come out of the faint. If this does not work rapidly, check the breathing and pulse: be prepared to apply the kiss of life and heart massage, if necessary. Call an ambulance or medical help.

FIT, EPILEPTIC

During an epileptic fit, the sufferer loses consciousness, becomes rigid, then the muscles will relax and contract causing the body and limbs to jerk and twitch. Following this the patient remains still for about ten minutes. The whole process takes about fifteen minutes in all. During the fit, the person may become temporarily incontinent.

Do not try to restrain the patient; however, do try to avoid injury by removing furniture and by preventing the person from falling. Loosen tight clothing and, once the limbs have stopped jerking, move the person into the recovery position (see page 1266).

Towards the end of an epileptic fit, when the body begins to stop moving and starts to become rigid, there is a danger that the person may bite his or her tongue. It may be possible to place something between the teeth to prevent this (a handkerchief folded into a pad, for example); however, do not try to stuff something into the mouth which may consequently block air access.

There should be no cause for alarm if the person is a known sufferer and recovers quickly. If the person lapses into a second or series of fits, call an ambulance. If the person (adult or child) is suffering a first fit, then consult the doctor.

The patient may have medicine which should be taken and they may need help with this on recovering from the fit. Establish whether they have the necessary medicines or whether a doctor should be summoned for help before leaving the patient.

HEART ATTACK

A sudden heart attack without any warning and with dramatic symptoms is not common. If it does occur, the patient suffers severe pain down the left arm and up the chest, or towards the jaw. This is accompanied by dizziness or loss of consciousness and a grey pallor.

- Call an ambulance or doctor – whichever is quicker.
- Support the conscious patient in a sitting position to ease breathing and keep them calm. Keep them warm but loosen any tight clothing, belts and collars.
- If the patient is unconscious, check the breathing and pulse. Give the kiss of life, if necessary, and heart massage. However, **do not apply heart massage if there is any sign of pulse**.

NOSE BLEED

If this is associated with injury, for example in case of accident or fall, then call an ambulance. Keep the patient warm and treat for any other injury.

The majority of nose bleeds are harmless. The person should press the soft part at the side of the nostril to prevent the blood flowing and promote clotting. At the same time, they should breathe through the mouth and avoid coughing, sniffing or talking.

The bleeding should stop within ten minutes but the treatment may have to be continued for up to thirty minutes, with the patient resting, lying down if possible. If the bleeding continues for longer, then take the patient to the doctor or hospital.

Children often panic if they have a nose bleed, so it is important to calm them down and make them rest. Make sure they are breathing calmly through the mouth.

Do not blow the nose for several hours after a nose bleed. If nose bleeds are frequent, consult the doctor.

POISON

If a person has swallowed or eaten a poisonous or dangerous substance, either call an ambulance or take them to the hospital or doctor immediately, depending on which is quickest and most practical.

Do not try to make the patient sick, as this can increase the internal damage in some cases. If the person is vomitting, keep some of the vomit as it may be helpful in identifying the poison.

- Keep the person as calm and warm as possible, making sure tight clothing is loosened for easy breathing.
- If the person is unconscious, check breathing and pulse, applying the kiss of life or heart massage if necessary.
- Place in the recovery position (see page 1266) once breathing has been established and the heart is beating.

Note   If acid has been swallowed, make the patient drink milk but do not make them vomit.

FIRST AID COURSES

These are available in most areas, run by local branches of national organizations and local authorities. They usually include practical instruction, which is invaluable in emergencies, and guidance on dealing with a broad range of situations as well as on current techniques. The benefits of attending such a course cannot be over emphasized, especially to adults in a family household.

Health Care

An appreciation of everyday factors which contribute to good health and a common-sense approach to medical conditions or illness, as well as to the medical profession, are important aspects of household general knowledge.

Thankfully, today, professional support is likely to arrive in minutes rather than hours in the case of accident or serious illness, and broader access to comprehensive professional health care has eliminated the need for crude or dangerous home treatment. However, thoughts on hygiene, diet and the life-saving importance of understanding first aid are just as relevant to the contemporary reader as to those of the last century.

This chapter covers basic information on professional medical care, with useful background notes on various common ailments and conditions. In addition, there are a few reminders on caring for a patient at home, such as an elderly relative, a child or someone convalescing after illness or an operation.

DIET AND EXERCISE

An informed view of diet and exercise is important for a fit and healthy life. A balanced diet provides all the nourishment the body needs and light but regular exercise is equally important.

STRESS AND RELAXATION

The latter part of the twentieth century has witnessed a marked change in the demands we make on our bodies. In many cases the burden of essential physical activity has been reduced; however, the actual pace of life has increased, as well as individual expectations and goals. Stress has become a common problem; relaxation the essential antidote. Establishing a balance between the demands of everyday living and time off to unwind is vital in achieving overall well-being of mind and body.

THE DOCTOR

Medical Card This must be kept safe as it shows your National Health Service number and proves that you are entitled to NHS treatment. It shows the address of your local family practitioner committee as well as the name of your existing doctor. This card should be shown when registering with a new doctor or changing doctors.

Family Practitioner Committee This is your link with the local health authority. The address is shown on your health card, or it may be obtained from the local library or through the telephone directory. Contact the FPC if you lose your medical card.

The FPC can provide a list of doctors, dentists, opticians and pharmacists in your area, and provide information on health services which are available, including family planning and maternity clinics. If you have special needs or a problem finding a doctor or other health care, then contact the FPC for help.

CHOOSING A DOCTOR

It is essential to register with a local general practitioner when you move to an area – do not wait until you are ill. If you live in a larger town with a choice of health centres or surgeries, make some enquiries about the various options before making your choice. The district family practitioner committee provides lists of local doctors – as usual, the local library is the first stop for information.

Before registering with a doctor, find out about the way in which the practice is run. For example, are patients seen by an appointment system or does the practice operate an open surgery where the patients simply queue?

The location of the surgery is important. You should be able to visit the doctor easily from home and the doctor should be able to get to you in time to cope with an emergency.

The best approach is to visit the surgeries of local doctors and ask the receptionist for information. Many practices provide leaflets detailing the way in which they are run and listing the doctors.

When you have made a decision, take your medical card to the surgery and explain that you would like to register. Remember the doctor is not obliged to accept you.

Once you have been accepted, your medical records will be transferred from your previous doctor through the family practitioner committee system. This may take some time.

Many surgeries like to do a health check for new patients and continue to do so at regular intervals.

YOU AND YOUR DOCTOR

You should expect your doctor to treat you with respect, professionalism and patience and you should adopt a similar courteous and patient attitude towards him or her. Developing a good relationship with your doctor is important, but in practice this will depend on your general health or family situation. If you have young children, then you probably have frequent and justified cause for seeing the doctor; if you happen to be young, active and healthy you may not see your doctor from one year to the next.

YOU AND THE RECEPTIONIST

The receptionist has to ensure that as many patients as possible see the doctor, at the same time allowing for home visits, keeping to the surgery hours and making sure that inevitable urgent problems are fitted into the appointment system, if there is one. Most receptionists are also responsible for organizing records, sorting out repeat prescription requests and taking messages and telephone calls, so they tend to be busy.

Doctors' receptionists do not have a reputation for providing a warm welcome, but they should not be rude or difficult with patients. The receptionist should not ask for your reason for wanting an appointment, but it is often helpful to give this information in advance. In cases where special arrangements or preparations are required, such as for immunizations or procedures which require a nurse, you should make sure the receptionist knows the purpose of your visit. However, you should never be pressurized to give any information about your reasons for seeing the doctor and you should never be dissuaded from making the appointment.

If you do have serious difficulties in dealing with the receptionist but generally have a good relationship with your doctor, it may be worth bringing the problem to the doctor's attention.

CHANGING DOCTORS

You are entitled to change to another doctor without having to give reasons. This may simply be a change of doctors within one practice, which is usually a case of asking to see one of the other doctors, then asking for the change to be made.

If you want to change from one practice to another, you will have to take your medical card to the surgery and ask to be taken on the list. If the new doctor agrees to accept you, the information will be filled in on your medical card and returned to the family practitioner committee. Your records will be transferred through the system.

Remember that, just as you are entitled to change doctors, the doctor is free to ask to have you removed from the practice's list.

VISITING THE DOCTOR

The following pointers will help towards a successful relationship with your doctor.

- If the doctor is likely to want to examine you, wear clothing that is easy to remove and put back on again. This saves valuable time.
- Explain your problem simply and clearly, giving the doctor as much relevant detail as possible. It's a good idea to write a few brief notes beforehand so that you remember exactly what you wanted to say.
- If you do not understand any of the doctor's questions or comments, then ask for an explanation so that you can give accurate information or follow the advice properly.
- Take note of the doctor's advice and follow it. Do take any course of treatment which is suggested. Do not leave the surgery and dismiss the medical or social care which has been given.

HOME VISITS

These are intended for emergencies which occur outside surgery hours – that is, when the problem cannot wait until the following surgery time – or for those who are too ill to attend surgery or unable to do so for some other reason. Home visits are not intended for your convenience, they should only be requested when they are essential.

If you need a home visit, then ring the surgery as early as possible in the morning, certainly before 10am.

In an emergency, if you do have to call the doctor out of surgery hours, explain the problem as clearly as you can over the telephone as this will help the doctor decide whether a visit is necessary.

THE DOCTOR'S PARTNERS IN PROVIDING CARE

The doctor has a back-up team of professionals who fulfil specific roles. The district nurse visits patients at home to perform routine medical tasks, such as changing dressings, giving injections and so on. Many practices employ nurses who are available in the surgery to attend to visiting patients and the practice nurse will perform the same duties as the district nurse for those who are able to visit the surgery. In addition, the nurse is able to ease the load on the doctor by checking blood pressure, giving some routine health checks and injections.

The midwife provides ante- and post-natal care to a doctor's patients as well as, occasionally, delivering babies in the home. The latter depends on the attitude and professional judgement of the doctor.

Health visitors provide important back-up before and after childbirth and with any other social aspects related to medical care.

Home helps are also linked to the back-up provided by a doctor. For example, they work with elderly people providing the support needed for independence. Their contribution is also of value in maintaining the comfort and good health of many people.

THE DENTIST

It is important to find a local dentist in whom you have confidence and to visit the surgery for regular check-ups. Children should be introduced to the dentist at an early age by the example of their parents. Dental practice has changed a good deal since the days when teeth were pulled out with pliers in the market square on a Friday morning. If you make regular visits to your dentist, you will find that today's treatments are quick and relatively painless.

A list of dentists who offer NHS treatment is available from the family practitioner committee. A dentist is not obliged to accept you as a patient and some dentists provide only private care. The FPA or the dentist's receptionist will be able to provide details of concessions and other aspects of treatment relating to the NHS.

GENERAL DENTAL CARE

Most dentists offer leaflets and advice on how to take care of your teeth. Your diet and dental hygiene are both important.

- Avoid eating large or regular amounts of sugary foods.
- Avoid frequent and large quantities of acidic drinks.
- Clean your teeth at least twice a day, brushing between and behind the teeth and around the gum area.
- Use a toothbrush as recommended by your dentist – this should not be too harsh.
- A balanced diet is vital to the development and continued maintenance of teeth.

THE CHIROPODIST

The chiropodist specializes in foot care. The doctor may refer patients to the chiropodist, for example elderly or diabetic patients, and treatment may be available on the National Health Service. However, you do not have to be referred to the chiropodist by a doctor and many people have regular, private, appointments.

If you do have a problem with your feet and are not registered with a chiropodist, then it is sensible to consult your doctor first for advice.

GENERAL FOOT CARE

The choice of footwear and hygiene are two main aspects of foot care.

Children and young people with growing or developing feet should wear shoes which provide support as well as room for growth and do not restrict or bend the feet or toes. Children should have their feet measured at a reputable shoe shop before buying shoes. Tight shoes and restrictive styles cause permanent damage to the feet.

Although most women have some frivolous shoes for special occasions, daily footwear for adults should be comfortable and suitable for their lifestyle. Similarly, footwear for sport must be suitable for the activity, providing support and cushioning as appropriate.

Slippers or equivalent shoes for use in the home should be warm and, preferably, washable if worn without socks or stockings.

Feet should be thoroughly washed and dried every day. Using a proprietary foot cream helps to keep the skin and nails in good condition; many also promote good circulation. Regularly massaging cream into the feet is also good for the circulation – equally important for men as as women.

Nails should be cut or filed straight across, not down at the sides. Rough skin should be removed using a pumice-stone or suitable cream. Foot powders, antiperspirants and other products are all helpful in the prevention of foot odour and for comfort; however, these should complement a rigid hygiene routine, not replace it.

THE OPTICIAN

An ophthalmic optician is someone who is qualified to give sight tests as well as to provide spectacles; a dispensing optician is not qualified to test the eyes but is able to supply and fit 'optical appliances' (the official term for spectacles).

You should visit an optician regularly even if you do not wear spectacles as sight does change with age and health. When you have had an eye test you will be given a prescription for spectacles if you need them. You are free to take this prescription to any dispensing optician to buy new spectacles. The optician will provide details about NHS treatment and concessions – it is a good idea to ask when you make a first appointment or before you begin to select frames for spectacles, as there is a range available for a fixed charge through the NHS.

You may decide to investigate the possibility of wearing contact lenses instead of glasses. You should be examined specifically for this purpose and your eyes should be examined following fitting to ensure that you are adapting to wearing lenses.

SUPPORT GROUPS AND OTHER ORGANIZATIONS

As well as standard health and welfare care, your doctor will be aware of local groups and national organizations dealing with your problem, condition, long-term or terminal illness or disability, offering moral support and technical assistance as appropriate.

PRIVATE HEALTH CARE

There is a large network of professionals offering private health care; some working for the NHS as well. Your NHS doctor can refer you to a private practitioner if you wish, for example for consultation on a problem or for specific treatment. You may also opt for the private medical system for your choice of general practitioner.

The most popular form of private medical care is through a personal insurance policy. There are a number of large organizations specializing in this field and many large companies offer free membership to a private health scheme as an employment bonus.

In addition to on-going health care, there is the option for occasional use of private facilities for a particular purpose, such as birth control or dental treatment.

HOSPITALS

You may have to visit a hospital as an out-patient on a one-off occasion for tests or a consultation, or for a series of visits while undergoing treatment. Alternatively, you may have to be admitted for a period of time.

No-one enjoys going to hospital but there are ways of easing the process. You are going to be dealing with an organization of considerable size, so fitting in with the way in which it works makes for smoother progress through the system.

Find out as much detail as possible about your visit and the treatment you will be having in advance. If you are going to stay in hospital, pack sensible nightwear that is fairly cool and comfortable – most hospitals are well heated. Pack a practical dressing gown and slippers, a toilet bag and towel, a small bedside clock (but not one with a loud tick) and something to read or do while lying in bed. On the formal side, make sure you take any regular medication with you and any letters of introduction from your doctor.

Do not take valuable jewellery, watches, clothes or lots of money. Ask a relative or friend to come in with you and take your clothes away when you are admitted. Keep a small amount of change for using the telephone, buying a newspaper and so on.

While you are in hospital, try to maintain a positive outlook and friendly approach to fellow patients and to staff. Being miserable, negative and grumpy will not help your condition and will make life unpleasant for everyone else. On the other hand, being the life and soul of the party when other people are trying to rest is equally undesirable, so try to strike a happy medium.

Make sure friends and relatives are aware of visiting arrangements and adhere to them.

When the time comes to go home, make arrangements for someone to bring your clothes and organize your journey home, remembering that you may not feel fit enough to cope with public transport. Make sure that there is someone at home to welcome you, with some essential food supplies in store, the heating turned on and so on. Before leaving, make sure you are clear about any after-care, such as how to cope with a wound while it is healing.

CARING FOR A PATIENT AT HOME

If you have to take care of a sick member of your family, put the patient in a single bed (if possible) with a firm mattress. Place the bed so that you can walk all round it. Ideally the bed should be by a window, so that the patient can look out. Make sure that the light is good enough to read by. The less furniture there is in a sick-room the better: a minimum of two chairs to put the bedclothes and pillows on when you make the bed, and a bedside table for books, drinks, a lamp, etc. It takes two people to make a bed easily; the aim is to leave the bed flat, clean, and unwrinkled. A sick person usually needs four pillows behind him to be able to sit up enough to eat and drink, and where there is difficulty in breathing he will need a back rest so that he can sit upright, or a bed-table on which he can lean forwards. A foot-rest will keep him from sliding down the bed.

The areas of skin that need attention in the bedridden are over the heels, elbows, shoulders and hips, knees, buttocks, and the lower part of the back. The position of the patient must be changed at least every two hours to prevent the pressure falling on the same area of skin all the time; the skin must be kept dry and clean and must never be irritated by wrinkles in the lower sheet. If redness develops in the places mentioned above, skilled attention is necessary. In some cases bedclothes must be kept away from the legs and feet; if you cannot get a bed cradle, use a pillow at each side of the legs to raise the bedclothes.

Do not use an electric blanket or pad in a sick-bed. Never fill a hot-water-bottle with boiling water, and always use a cover on it.

Wash the patient's face and hands two or three times a day, as it is refreshing, and make sure that toe nails as well as finger nails are properly cut. Attend to the hair regularly; this is good for morale.

The doctor will tell you whether a special diet is needed. Always make sure that the sick person has enough to drink within easy reach, for in most short, acute illnesses solid food is not nearly as important as water. The patient must never become dehydrated, especially when the bowels are upset. One can often get children to drink by making up flavoured drinks with soda water; in very difficult cases try giving plain or flavoured ice to suck. When patients improve they become hungry, and common sense suggests nourishing soups, boiled or grilled fish, scrambled eggs, chicken, bread and butter – no fried food.

Old people and children easily become bored and lonely, and need to be kept occupied. People get better much more quickly if they are contented.

PRIVATE NURSING HOMES

Rest homes are establishments providing a caring environment and assistance for people who are convalescing, but they do not necessarily offer professional nursing or medical support except through local doctors. Private nursing homes provide in-house nursing facilities and medical back-up. However, the standards vary enormously. Selecting a nursing home is difficult, particularly if the stay is expected to be long term. Your doctor will be able to provide a list of local nursing homes and may well be able to provide guidance on current information available from charitable, private and health authority sources. Find out as much as you can about the options available before making a decision and visit a few homes (if there are that many available) to assess the differences. The following points will be helpful in choosing a suitable nursing home.

- Nursing homes must be registered with the local authorities – check this first.
- Find out about fees: what the fee covers, any extras, the source of payment should the stay be extended beyond the period originally planned, and so on.
- Find out about the staffing in the home, the facilities offered and any links it has with other organizations.
- Take a thorough look around the home; ask to see typical residents' rooms and public rooms, dining facilities, gardens, etc.
- When you are visiting take note of the general standards of cleanliness and neatness – look at floors, walls, curtains and furnishings.
- Be aware of the occupants – are they bright and cheerful or asleep and bored? Are they suitably occupied and aware of you as a visitor when you walk through public areas?
- Be aware of needs for privacy and safety factors such as alarm buttons near beds.

- If shared rooms are the norm, then find out who the person sharing will be.
- Check arrangements for medical as well as social care – can the occupants remain registered with their existing doctors or do they have to re-register with the home's doctor?
- Can the occupants take some items of their own furniture, have private televisions, radios or pets?
- What about the staff? Are there plenty of them around, neat and clean in appearance, cheerful and friendly in their attitude to the residents?
- Think about the general atmosphere. The home should be clean and fresh, pleasant and homely, active and alive.

It is difficult to assess all these things in one go but it becomes easier once you can compare several different places. However, miserable surroundings, general poor standards of housekeeping and unpleasant smells, such as a prevailing odour of boiled cabbage or stale urine, are fairly obvious to the visitor.

HOSPICES

The hospice movement is growing rapidly in more than forty countries, but there are still many people who have only a hazy notion of what a hospice is. Primarily, hospices exist to offer specialized care to patients with severe and progressive diseases such as advanced cancer or AIDS. They also provide respite care for patients who are not yet in the final stages of their disease, but who would benefit from a short stay in such a caring environment – or whose relatives would benefit from a break from the often exhausting task of caring for someone who is seriously ill.

The aim of all hospices is to improve the quality of life. The control of pain and other symptoms is a priority, as is the provision of a calm, supportive and dignified environment for both patients and their families. Many hospices have day centres, which provide an opportunity for patients being cared for at home to receive clinical assessment, nursing care and support through creative and leisure activities.

Admission is normally arranged by the patient's own doctor or hospital, and care is usually free of charge. Charitable hospice organizations share with the NHS the principle of free access, based only on the criteria of medical, social and emotional need.

ALTERNATIVE MEDICINE

The various health-care practices which do not fit directly into the current medical system of doctors, hospitals and related teams are covered by the term alternative medicine. There is a broad range of techniques and beliefs, many of which are respected by some doctors. But unfortunately, as thinking develops on the use of methods other than those traditionally observed in Western medicine, the whole subject and practice area is open to exploitation by individuals who have little experience and no qualifications.

The alternative approach to health care undoubtedly has a valuable role in society, with the emphasis on encouraging the body to activate its own natural defences to illness and less reliance on non-essential medication. However, it is important to remember that natural and alternative medicines and methods can be potent and, therefore, potentially dangerous in the wrong hands. Without a thorough knowledge of the medical history of a case, they can offer more problems than solutions.

Before embarking on any course of alternative treatment, it is a good idea to consult your doctor. The informed person will offer a balanced opinion and point out any aspects to be wary of. When finding a practitioner, do not simply extract a name from a telephone directory. Ask about relevant experience and qualifications and check up on affiliation to, or membership of, any organizations. Do not take a long line of letters after the name of a practitioner as a sign of experience or competence without investigating what they stand for and their credibility.

In summary, do not try alternative medicine in ignorance of the disadvantages or possible dangers: if you feel it is relevant and helpful to your condition, then find out about the various organizations, their reputation and standing.

IMMUNIZATION

The doctor and health visitor will advise on immunization related to babies and children. You can expect a baby to receive a series of injections or oral immunization during the first year of life, then at intervals during early childhood, including protection against diseases such as diphtheria, tetanus, polio and measles. Up-to-date information is related to on-going research and to the individual needs of the child.

In adulthood, tetanus is an important form of immunization to maintain, with a booster following accidents such as cuts or animal bites.

Immunization is also necessary before foreign travel. The exact programme depends on the countries to be visited and the time of year. In some cases immunization is compulsory, in others it is optional but highly recommended. Your doctor will offer up-to-date advice. Be sure to arrange an appointment to discuss immunization about three months ahead of travel when visiting countries in Africa, India and the Orient. Some immunization is given over a period of weeks or months and the course must be completed by a certain period ahead of exposure to the disease.

Travel companies and British Airways also provide advice, the latter offering an immunization service.

Immunization against common illness, such as influenza, may also be offered to groups of the population who are at risk of complications, for example the elderly or very young.

HEALTH AND TRAVEL

Consult your doctor well in advance of foreign travel to discuss the necessary immunization requirements. These change according to the time of year and current conditions, so the doctor may have to check with a specialist body: this relates to protection against malaria as well as to other diseases.

Apart from the importance of immunization against disease (see above), always pack a small first-aid kit when travelling, either in this country or abroad. The kit should include plasters and antiseptic cream, along with a suitable cooling lotion for sunburn if appropriate. Take tablets or medicine to ease diarrhoea – it makes sense to take both a mild type and a more potent type, depending on where you are travelling and for how long. The chemist or your doctor will offer sensible advice.

Changes in diet often cause diarrhoea, as indeed can the sub-conscious anxiety of foreign travel. Adopt a sensible approach to eating and drinking when holidaying abroad.

- Do not drink tap water, instead buy sealed bottles of mineral water.
- Avoid eating food which is obviously prepared in unhygienic conditions.
- Avoid buying meats, cheeses, seafood and similar items which are obviously stale, displayed in the sun and attracting flies. Do not confuse simplicity with disregard for maintaining the quality of the food.
- Pay particular attention to the diet of infants

and toddlers: it is worthwhile taking a supply of suitable canned food for the first few days until they are accustomed to the local food or you find a source of familiar items.
- Sunburn can be extremely painful and is very bad for the skin and, more seriously, sunstroke or over-exposure to the sun is extremely dangerous. Do not stay in the sun for long periods or during the middle of the day, particularly at the beginning of a holiday. Gradually acclimatize yourself and use a protective cream, lotion or oil suitable for your skin type, remembering to re-apply it regularly. When visiting very hot countries it is also worth checking locally on arrival for any sun creams which are particularly suitable for the climate. Do not allow children to spend long periods in the sun; keep them shaded, in the cool during the hottest time of the day and make them wear a sun hat.

IN CASE OF ILLNESS

Make sure you find out about the medical care and customs of the country you are visiting and always take out suitable health insurance before departure. Find out about health cover within Europe before travelling (ask the travel company, doctor or local health authority). Up-to-date information on foreign travel is available in a leaflet produced by the relevant government department. This is regularly revised and may be found in post offices, chemists or at the doctor's surgery.

At your resort, make sure you know where to go should an emergency arise, then relax.

In case of mild sickness and diarrhoea, make sure the person is kept as cool as possible and drinks plenty of bottled water. The patient should refrain from eating until the attack has subsided, and then avoid eating fruit and salad ingredients. Plain, fresh bread is always excellent sustenance the day after an attack of sickness. If sickness does not subside within twenty-four hours, then contact a local doctor.

Social Customs

This chapter serves as an introduction to contemporary social customs, from feeling at ease when entertaining to being aware of the etiquette surrounding sad occasions, such as funerals.

In a society which has abandoned rigid rules about etiquette, customs still hold a place of importance and play a vital role. Their existence facilitates the organization of formal functions and ceremonies. They are also invaluable in easing the stressful procedures related to events such as death.

ENGAGEMENT

Engagements are not as formal as they once were. However, the couple may wish to make a formal announcement through a local or national newspaper and/or hold a celebration party.

Unless the couple are under eighteen, there is no legal obligation for parental consent, and the traditional interview between prospective husband and the bride's father is no longer an essential feature of the occasion. In some families, the bride's father may expect to 'interview' the young man, even if only on an informal basis. More commonly, the couple may prefer to announce their engagement jointly to each set of parents, at the same time seeking their blessing.

Press announcements are traditionally paid for by the bride's family. The wording is usually simple: *'The engagement is announced between (John) son of (parents' name and address) and (Anne) daughter of (parents' name and address).'*

It is customary for the man to give his betrothed a ring (traditionally a diamond ring) which is worn on the third finger of the left hand. The man may be given a gift by his fiancée to mark the engagement. Nowadays,

however, some couples dispense with the engagement ring.

Cards may be sent and gifts may be given to a couple on their engagement, but this is not essential. Any gifts should be acknowledged promptly.

Once a couple are engaged it is usual for both sets of parents to meet, although this may be postponed until the date for the wedding is set. If the parents do not meet soon after the engagement, then letters may be exchanged.

BROKEN ENGAGEMENT

This is a private affair. If the engagement was announced in the press, then a simple statement that the wedding will not now take place may be sent to the paper. If the engagement is broken off after the wedding plans have been made, these should be cancelled promptly and cards simply stating that the wedding will not be taking place should be sent to cancel invitations. Any gifts should be returned. The engagement ring should be returned, unless the man particularly wants the woman to keep the ring and she agrees.

Family and friends should be supportive, but they should not dwell on the subject of the broken engagement.

MARRIAGE

Organizing a wedding can be a daunting prospect, eased by the contemporary trend towards sharing out the responsibility and cost between the families and couple (where appropriate). Indeed, many couples who are established in their careers may wish to take on the main part of organizing and paying for the wedding.

The couple usually decides where and when to marry – traditionally this is in the bride's home parish – and they decide whether the wedding is to be a grand occasion or a simple affair for close family and friends. The ceremony may take place in church or in a registry office. A registry office wedding may be followed by a church blessing, often attended only by the bride and groom, attendants and immediate family.

The wedding is followed by a reception or wedding breakfast. This may be held at an hotel, in a hall or other suitable venue, or at the bride's parents' home. There are several options and a daytime reception may be followed by an evening party, often an opportunity for inviting friends or colleagues who were not present at the wedding.

There are various customs relating to the organization of different aspects of the celebration and the roles adopted during the day. The traditional procedure is outlined here; however, it may be varied according to the wishes of the couple and their families.

The Bride's Parents   organize and pay for the reception, the bride's dress, the wedding cake, cars to the church, flowers for the church and reception, and the photographer. They send out the invitations and receive replies.

The bride's father leads her up the aisle on his left arm, taking her to the groom. He then steps back to take his place next to the bride's mother.

The Groom   pays for the ceremony and wedding ring(s). He buys presents and flowers for the bridesmaids and buttonholes and sprays for the other attendants. He also pays for the car which takes him and the best man to the church and the bride and himself to the reception.

The groom awaits his bride at a church wedding, standing before the altar on the right side of the aisle, his best man on his right.

The Best Man and Ushers   pay for their own clothes. Ushers greet guests at the church, give them the order of service and hymn books, then show them to their seats. The best man looks after the ring and ensures that the groom is at the church or registry office in good time. The best man and ushers ensure that the wedding party and guests all have transport from ceremony to the reception. The best man acts as a master of ceremonies at the reception.

The Bridesmaids and Attendants   may pay for their own clothes, or sometimes the bride or bride's mother may pay. Where there are a number of attendants, there may be a chief bridesmaid; if there are any young children, either bridesmaids or page boys, it may be the chief bridesmaid's job to look after them. A married or older bridesmaid is usually referred to as a matron of honour. The chief bridesmaid or matron of honour takes the bride's flowers during the ceremony.

The bridesmaids greet the bride and her father at the door of the church, then follow them in procession down the aisle.

RECEPTION AND SPEECHES

The bride and groom usually receive the guests, along with best man, bridesmaids and both sets of parents. A welcoming drink is usually provided, followed by the food. This may be a formal 'sit-down' meal, a buffet, or finger food which is handed around.

It is customary for the best man to act as the master of ceremonies when the time comes for the speeches. The bride's father makes the first speech and toasts the bride and groom. The groom follows with a speech of thanks to the bride's parents and good wishes and proposes a toast to the bridesmaids. The best man thanks the groom on behalf of the bridesmaids. He toasts the parents and reads greetings from absent friends. In a suitable gathering, the best man's speech may offer a light-hearted view of the matrimonial match.

The Bride   Although it is traditional for the bride to remain blissfully silent throughout the reception, she may feel inclined to make a speech, often to thank her parents and other friends or relatives who have helped in her preparations. Although her parents may have paid for her wedding dress, she will usually buy her own going-away outfit and may well pay for all her trousseau. The bride changes towards the end of the reception, before leaving for the honeymoon. Following a daytime reception, some brides change into evening wear before an evening party.

The Wedding Cake   is cut by the bride and groom after the speeches. Everyone's attention should be drawn to this ceremony. The bottom tier of the cake is removed and cut up, then handed around.

Cake is sent in special boxes to relatives, friends and colleagues who could not be at the wedding. It is the custom to keep the top tier for the christening of the first child. But, since many couples do not plan to have a family for some time, this tier may be used for another special occasion, such as the first wedding anniversary.

WEDDING PRESENTS

The couple may draw up a list of suitable presents which should contain a broad range of items, with a selection of small and inexpensive ideas as well as many moderately priced gifts. Often, providing an idea of colours, styles and ranges of goods is an excellent way of compiling a guide to useful gifts.

Usually, the bride's mother will take charge of the list and give a copy to those who ask for it, or provide suggestions. It is important that items are crossed off as they are chosen, to avoid duplications.

Today many couples choose to place their list at a particular shop or department store. Guests can visit or telephone the store and choose their gift, which will then be deleted from the list. Some stores will also wrap and deliver the present.

However, it is worth remembering that many people do not favour lists.

WEDDING ANNIVERSARIES

Although some couples mark each wedding anniversary with some form of celebration (see the list below for the names of anniversaries from one to sixty years), it is customary for relatives and friends to acknowledge silver, ruby and golden wedding anniversaries (twenty-five, forty and fifty years) with greetings and gifts. The couple, their children or close relatives may organize a celebration with a cake.

1 year – Paper	13 years – Lace
2 years – Cotton	14 years – Ivory
3 years – Leather	15 years – Crystal
4 years – Linen	20 years – China
5 years – Wood	25 years – Silver
6 years – Iron	30 years – Pearl
7 years – Wool	35 years – Jade
8 years – Bronze	40 years – Ruby
9 years – Pottery	45 years – Sapphire
10 years – Tin	50 years – Gold
11 years – Steel	55 years – Emerald
12 years – Silk	60 years – Diamond

BIRTHS AND CHRISTENINGS

Immediate family and close friends should be told of the birth promptly, usually by the father. The parents may then send out announcement cards which generally include details such as the baby's name, date and time of birth, and birth weight. Sometimes, a birth is also announced in a local or national paper. Congratulation cards may be sent, and close friends and relatives often send flowers to the mother or give small gifts to the baby.

CHRISTENING

This may take place during a regular church service or separately. Godparents are selected as guardians of the child's Christian upbringing. There may be two godfathers for a boy, and one godmother; or two godmothers for a girl, with one godfather. The gift from godparents to child should be something which will last, and traditionally it is of silver.

Although a christening and the role of godparents is, strictly speaking, a religious one, social custom makes the commitment a special one. Godparents should remember their godchild's birthday and they usually give Christmas presents. They should take an interest in the child and often the special relationship will continue into later life.

Celebration Christening celebrations are not usually formal occasions and they can range from tea and cake after the ceremony to a party for family and friends.

VISITING MOTHER AND BABY

Always check with the partner to find out whether mother and child are ready to receive visitors and the best time to call. Unless you are a close friend or relative, or invited to stay for a specific length of time, keep visits brief. Some parents, particularly with a first baby, may feel pressurized and tired when first coping with a baby awake at night and needing much attention during the day. Never pick up a baby unless invited to do so.

FUNERALS AND MOURNING

Relatives and close friends have to be informed of a death promptly, preferably in person or by telephone. Warn the person that the news is sad and make sure that the elderly or anyone who is likely to be shocked and distraught has a companion to look after them.

An announcement may be placed in the local or national paper and this is one of the tasks handled by the funeral director. The announcement may include information about the funeral and the wishes of the deceased with regard to floral tributes or, alternatively, donations. Requests for a private, or family only, funeral and for donations rather than floral tributes should be announced promptly.

If flowers are sent, they should be delivered to the funeral director or to the house on the morning of the funeral (unless there is an announcement to the contrary). A card or note accompanying the flowers should have a message addressed to the deceased.

Letters of Sympathy Letters or cards may be sent to the next of kin or chief mourners as soon as possible after the death. These should be acknowledged in due course.

FUNERAL SERVICE

The chief mourners usually assemble beforehand at the house and the family sit in the front pews, traditionally on the right of the aisle for the service. There are few rules and guidance is usually offered by the clergy.

Today, it is not obligatory to wear black to a funeral; however, dark clothing is usually the best choice. If the coffin is already at the church or crematorium, the mourners may wait outside until the next of kin and chief mourners take their place. In some families, the women may prefer not to attend the graveside.

ENTERTAINING

Entertaining should be enjoyable, but it inevitably involves a certain amount of planning and work.

INFORMAL ENTERTAINING

Spending a day with friends or inviting friends to an informal meal does not involve formal invitations but the host and hostess should plan the event well and make sure the guests know about what time to arrive. If the invitation is a very loose one, just inviting people to turn up at some point during the day, then it should be clear whether guests are expected to leave after tea or whether they are invited for the evening as well.

The important point to remember about this type of entertaining is that the better organized you are, the more relaxed you will be; and the more relaxed you are, the more welcome and at ease your guests will feel.

FORMAL DINNER PARTIES

These may be organized by telephone, a few weeks ahead of the proposed date, and the arrangements should be confirmed a day or two beforehand. The menu should be planned well in advance, making allowance for any special diets and usually offering a choice of desserts.

Guests usually spend a while relaxing before being seated for the meal. Canapés or other nibbles should be prepared along with a selection of pre-dinner drinks. The host and hostess should introduce guests who do not know each other and open some suitable topic of conversation. Coffee may be served at the table or in the lounge.

LARGE PARTIES

Written invitations are sent about a month ahead. The invitation should indicate the type of gathering and suitable dress, if appropriate. At home, drinks, sherry, lunch, buffet or supper are all terms which indicate the type of event. Combined with the time of day, this will indicate the likely refreshment and when the guests are expected to leave.

GUESTS TO STAY

If guests are made aware of plans and/or routines which affect their stay, they can relax and enjoy themselves without fear of embarrasing mistakes. For example, always tell people roughly when you intend to get up in the morning and approximately when you have breakfast; guests who are already bathed and dressed and trying to help in a strange kitchen at the crack of dawn while the hostess flies around in a dressing-gown, will feel awkward.

Provide clean towels, drinking water and tissues in the guest room. Fresh flowers are a nice touch, as are magazines or a book or two for anyone who is staying for more than a night.

An early morning drink of tea, coffee or fruit juice always goes down well. You may take a tray to close friends or relatives or, more usually, have everything prepared downstairs for those who are up first, so that they can relax while everyone gathers for breakfast. It is a good idea to show friends where the tea, kettle, milk and other essentials are kept so that they can make an early morning drink if they wish.

Exactly how you prepare for guests who stay depends on how well you know them and on the household routine. If you do find yourself in a formal situation, with guests who do not know you well, it is especially important to plan ahead and keep them well informed as to what is expected of them.

BEING A STAYING GUEST

The ideal guest is one who fits into the household routine. If in doubt, ask your host or hostess about any plans they have and what the normal routine is in the morning.

Although taking a gift is not essential on every occasion, some flowers, confectionery, wine or similar are often appreciated, but do not be too lavish.

When you are staying with friends, try to be sensitive about helping and mixing with family and other guests. For example, find out whether the host or hostess is relaxed about having you in the kitchen, helping or chatting, or whether your interest in a tour around the garden is welcome or likely to break up a peaceful after-breakfast interlude reading the papers.

FRIENDS, ACQUAINTANCES AND COMMUNITY CUSTOMS

Meeting people, making friends and becoming part of a community or social group is important but not always easy. During school years or at institutions such as colleges, a ready social framework exists to support individuals; once a young person begins work, particularly if this involves moving to a new area, this framework can disappear completely – and very suddenly. Similarly, when an individual, a couple or family move from one area to another, they may not know anyone and will have to integrate with a new, often quite different, community. This can be particularly difficult for people who live alone.

WORK-RELATED SOCIAL GROUPS

Many large organizations have social clubs or their employees may arrange various out-of-work activities. In smaller companies, people of the same age or interests may develop a friendship but this can be limited to young single people, particularly in large towns and cities.

SPECIAL INTEREST CLUBS AND CLASSES

Joining clubs or attending classes can be good ways of meeting people and, in turn, making friends. This depends on the type of classes; for example, few people attend car-maintenance classes with a view to making friends, whereas individuals joining a squash club usually expect to meet others who share their interest in the sport.

The most important point to remember about getting involved with clubs and classes is that you must have a genuine interest in the subject and be prepared to spend your spare time participating in the specific activity. As a consequence, you are likely to get to know people with similar interests and the acquaintanceship may develop into a broader friendship.

NEIGHBOURS

Links with neighbours vary enormously according to area, age and lifestyle. In many large towns and cities the people living next door can be totally anonymous, whereas in small communities neighbours can be life-long friends.

As a general rule, it is a good idea to get to know immediate neighbours and to develop a pleasant relationship with them. It is customary for existing residents to introduce themselves to newcomers. The idea of offering neighbours tea on the day they move in, when cups and kettle are not unpacked, is still an excellent way of creating an opportunity for an introduction which may, or may not, develop.

Although neighbours can become friends, keeping a certain distance in the relationship can be important; time should be allowed for a genuine link to be formed once both parties get to know each other. In places where many long-established friendships exist between neighbours, being accepted into the community may be slightly difficult.

COMMUNITY GROUPS AND CHURCH GROUPS

Belonging to a group related to some aspect of everyday life is a common way of meeting people. Many groups of this type actively welcome new members.

COMMITTEES

Committees are the basis for most forms of public life. The members are usually voted on by the organization and the committee has a chairperson (someone to oversee the proceedings) who is usually an experienced committee member. Other members of the committee fulfil different roles in running the organization. Being on a committee means sharing the work involved and accepting the decisions which are reached by the group. An agenda, or order or business, is prepared and circulated before each meeting and all members should be prepared to make relevant contributions.

Being offered a position on a committee is a vote of confidence in your opinion and judgement: meet the honour by working hard to fulfil your role in the organization.

STYLES OF ADDRESS

When speaking to royalty, the address 'Your Majesty' or 'Your Royal Highness' should not be used more than once and, indeed, may be omitted altogether in favour of the simpler 'Ma'am' (pronounced to rhyme with Pam) for the Queen and 'Madam' or 'Sir' for other members of the Royal Family.

The Queen   Letters to the Queen should be addressed to the Private Secretary to Her Majesty the Queen. Begin the letter 'Dear Sir', and ask him, for instance, 'to submit for Her Majesty's approval/consideration...'. Never refer to the Queen as 'she', but always as 'Her Majesty'. Close the letter 'Your faithfully'. If you do wish to write to the Queen direct, the opening style is 'Madam, With my humble duty'. Use 'Your Majesty' and 'Your Majesty's' instead of 'you' and 'your', and close the letter 'I have the honour to be/remain, Madam, Your Majesty's most humble and obedient servant'.

Other Royalty   Letters to other members of the Royal Family should be addressed to their Equerry, Private Secretary or Lady-in-Waiting. Begin '(Dear) Sir' or '(Dear) Madam'. Refer to the member of the Royal Family first as 'His/Her Royal Highness' and subsequently as 'Prince/Princess ...' or 'The Duke/Duchess of ...' as appropriate. End the letter 'Yours faithfully'. When writing direct, open the letter 'Sir' or 'Madam', use 'Your Royal Highness' instead of 'you', and end 'I have the honour to be, Sir/Madam, Your Royal Highness's most humble and obedient servant'.

When writing to royalty or people of title, the envelope should bear their most important title.

Titled Persons   When addressing a person of title, either verbally or in writing, the form of address varies according to whether the communication is formal or social. Thus, when writing formally to a Duke, the style of address is 'My Lord Duke', and the formal verbal address is 'Your Grace'; but socially, the written form of address is 'Dear Duke', and the verbal form simply 'Duke'. A Duchess is written to formally as 'Madam' or 'Dear Madam', and spoken to as 'Your Grace', but socially she is addressed in writing as 'Dear Duchess'.

A Marquis, Earl, Viscount or Baron is addressed formally as 'My Lord' and socially as 'Lord ...' both verbally and in writing.

The wife of a Peer is addressed formally in writing as '(Dear) Madam' and verbally as 'Madam'; socially she is addressed as 'Lady (surname)'. Style of address for a Peeress in her own right is the same as that for a wife of a Peer, although she may choose to be known as 'Baroness (surname)' rather than 'Lady (surname)'. A Baroness in her own right and the wife of a Baron are also addressed in the same way.

A Baronet or Knight is written to formally '(Dear) Sir', and addressed socially as 'Sir (Christian name)'. The surname should be added if the acquaintance is only slight. Formal and social verbal address is 'Sir (Christian name)'. His wife is written to formally '(Dear) Madam', but for all other purposes the style of address is 'Lady (surname)'.

An Archbishop, like a Duke, is addressed formally as 'Your Grace', and socially as 'Archbishop'. Bishops, Deans and Archdeacons are addressed simply using these titles. Vicars and Rectors are addressed formally as 'The Reverend (Christian name + surname), Vicar/Rector of ...', and socially as 'Mr ...' or 'Father ...' according to his preference. Wives of all clergymen are addressed simply as 'Mrs ...', unless they have a title in their own right.

The formal style of address for a Lord Mayor is 'My Lord Mayor', and his wife is 'My Lady Mayoress'; socially the style is 'Lord Mayor' and 'Lady Mayoress'. A mayor is formally addressed 'Mr Mayor'; a woman mayor may prefer to be addressed 'Madam Mayor'. Socially the style is 'Dear (Mr/Madam) Mayor'.

ROYAL AND OTHER FORMAL OCCASIONS

An invitation to Buckingham Palace itself, or to one of the official buildings, used for royal or government functions, will include suitable instructions.

Ladies normally wear gloves when shaking hands with the Queen, as a courtesy and no longer as a bounden duty. The gloves should be thin and light but do not need to be white as once was the custom. They are worn for the Queen's comfort since she can get hot and painful hands from too much handshaking. Never grasp her hand firmly for the same reason, merely lay your hand in hers while making a 'bob' curtsey. For men, gloves are optional, but preferred. Again, the handshake should be very light and be accompanied by a slight bow.

When royalty is present at a private function, formalities are more relaxed. If you are to be presented, you will be warned and briefed in advance.

At other formal occasions, banquets, receptions, and so on, be prepared to meet a reception committee. Your name and that of your escort, if you have one, will be taken by an attendant or toastmaster who will announce your arrival. You then shake hands with those who are there to receive you before proceeding to join the party. If the occasion is a formal dinner, it is incorrect to smoke before the loyal toast is drunk.

INDEX

997